2002

Better Homes and Gardens®

ANNUAL
Recipes
2002

Spring Garlic Pesto
Perciatelli, page 94

Better Homes and Gardens® Family Food Collection™
Des Moines, Iowa

The Mount Everest of Spice Cake,
page 179

The large, extended family of *Better Homes and Gardens®* magazine celebrated a milestone this year: 2002 marked the 100th anniversary of our parent company, Meredith Corporation. Founded in 1902 in Des Moines, Iowa, by E.T. Meredith, this company was built on a mission of service to American farmers and their families. As our country grew and changed, E.T. recognized a need to serve a broader audience, so in 1922, he created a new magazine, *Fruit, Garden & Home*, designed for passionate homeowners with young families. As the magazine's focus galvanized around the home, a "better" title was chosen. Today, the resulting *Better Homes and Gardens* magazine is still very much grounded in E.T.'s original vision.

One constant in our magazine throughout the past 80 years has been our family-friendly kitchen-tested recipes. Our food section has always provided practical and delicious recipes for home-cooked meals and special occasions. We continue that tradition in our magazine and in our recipe annual, with bigger pictures and bolder flavors that today's families love.

Also, celebrating all those years of creative recipes is the newly released 12th edition of our *Better Homes and Gardens® New Cook Book*, the plaid cookbook our grandmothers, our mothers, and we grew up with. As a bonus, our food editors selected a few of their favorites from the hundreds of recipes in the *New Cook Book* to feature in *Better Homes and Gardens® Annual Recipes 2002*.

So you'll find all of our anniversary year's magazine recipes, plus best-loved classics in *Better Homes and Gardens Annual Recipes 2002*. This cookbook celebrates the best of what we do—delicious recipes, all thoroughly tested and tasted by the Better Homes and Gardens® Test Kitchen you've come to know and trust.

Better Homes and Gardens magazine, the *New Cook Book*, and this recipe annual still underscore what our founder E.T. knew instinctually: That our homes and gardens are much more than an address or a hobby. They are expressions of who we are, what we believe, and what we dare dream to do tomorrow.

Here's to another 100 years of bringing that truth to life.

Karol

Karol De Wulf Nickell
Editor in Chief
Better Homes and Gardens® magazine

Better Homes and Gardens.

ANNUAL
Recipes
2002

Editor	Julia Martinusen
Assistant Art Director	Stephanie Hunter
Test Kitchen Product Supervisor	Maryellyn Krantz
Contributing Copy Editors	Gretchen Kauffman, Spectrum Communication Services

BETTER HOMES AND GARDENS® FAMILY FOOD COLLECTION™

Executive Editor	Joy Taylor
Art Director	Nick Crow
Food Editors	David Feder, Sandra Mosley, Lois White
Associate Art Director	Shawn Roorda
Test Kitchen Director	Lynn Blanchard
Administrative Assistants	Sandy Kinter, Maria McCleese

VICE PRESIDENT, PUBLISHING DIRECTOR
WILLIAM R. REED

Group Publisher	Maureen Ruth
Consumer Product Marketing Director	Ben Jones
Senior Marketing Manager	Steve Swanson
Marketing Manager	Karrie Nelson
Business Manager	Jie Lin
Production Director	Douglas M. Johnston
Books Production Managers	Pam Kvitne, Marjorie J. Schenkelberg
Assistant to Publisher	Cheryl Eckert

BETTER HOMES AND GARDENS® MAGAZINE

Editor in Chief	Karol DeWulf Nickell
Executive Editor	John Riha
Managing Editor	Lamont D. Olson
Creative Director	Bradford W. S. Hong
Art Director	Michael D. Belknap
Food and Entertaining Editor	Nancy Wall Hopkins
Nutrition Editor	Jeanne Ambrose
Associate Editors	Richard Swearinger, Stephen J. Exel
Editorial Assistants	Karen Pollock, Anna Anderson

MEREDITH PUBLISHING GROUP

President	Stephen M. Lacy
President, Magazine Group	Jerry Kaplan
Corporate Solutions	Michael Brownstein
Creative Services	Ellen de Lathouder
Manufacturing	Bruce Heston
Consumer Marketing	Karla Jeffries
Finance and Administration	Max Runciman

EDITORIAL OFFICE

For more information about Better Homes and Gardens publications, log onto www.bhg.com
If you have comments or questions about the editorial material in this book, write to: Editor, *Better Homes and Gardens® Annual Recipes 2002*, Family Food Collection™, Meredith Corporation, 1716 Locust Street, Des Moines, IA 50309-3023. Send e-mail to spoon@mdp.com, or call 800/678-2872, option 2.

CORPORATION

CHAIRMAN AND CHIEF EXECUTIVE OFFICER
WILLIAM T. KERR

CHAIRMAN OF THE EXECUTIVE COMMITTEE
E. T. MEREDITH III

Better Homes and Gardens® Annual Recipes 2002 is published by Family Food Collection™, Publishing Group of Meredith Corporation, 1716 Locust Street, Des Moines, IA 50309-3023.

We're celebrating
with our best book ever!

Cover photograph:
Best-Ever Chocolate
Cake, page 235

*As always, our seal assures
you that every recipe in
Better Homes and
Gardens® Annual Recipes
2002 has been tested in the
Better Homes and Gardens®
Test Kitchen. This means
that each recipe is practical
and reliable, and meets our
high standards of taste
appeal. We guarantee your
satisfaction with the book
for as long as you own it.*

In celebration of our 100th birthday at Meredith Corporation, we've really put the frosting on the cake for the 2002 edition of our *Better Homes and Gardens® Annual Recipes* book.

More recipes, bigger photographs! You still get absolutely every single recipe that we published in *Better Homes and Gardens®* magazine during 2002, whether it ran in one of our main feature stories or in one of our page stories—more than 400 recipes in all! You'll also notice that the photographs are bigger and appear alongside their corresponding recipes.

Prizewinning recipes: The top winners from our monthly Prize Tested Recipe contest are featured together in one big section beginning on page 260. And, for the first time ever, you have all of the Honor Roll winners too—outstanding recipes from our contest that have never before been published!

New Cook Book classics: As a bonus, this edition is peppered with classic recipes from the brand new 12th edition of the *Better Homes and Gardens® New Cook Book*. These special recipes are marked with a plaid symbol. The Best-Ever Chocolate Cake splashed on the cover, our birthday cake, comes from our 12th edition. It's the result of hours of testing after searching our recipe files to make sure that our chocolate cake is the best ever—truly deserving of its name.

Low-fat recipes and nutrition information: The low-fat symbol marks those recipes that have 3 or fewer grams of fat per every hundred calories to help you plan balanced family meals. Every recipe has complete nutrition information, and if you're interested in how we calculate that, turn to page 335.

Quick recipes and emergency substitutions: If you're short on time, look for the "30" symbols by quick recipes, which indicate you can prepare the recipes in 30 minutes or less. And if you can't find something on your shelves when you're in the middle of cooking, our handy Emergency Substitutions chart is on page 336.

Menu ideas: Throughout our month-by-month story section, you'll find deliciously flexible menus to suit the season and your lifestyle. For special-occasion menus you can serve any time of the year, plus low-fat menus, turn to page 310.

contents

Zesty Ravioli Salad,
page 56

Mango Whip,
page 112

Valentine Granita,
page 30

Mustard-Rosemary Grilled Lamb,
page 278

Nutty Cucumber Sandwich,
page 139

J a n

Nibbles 'n' Bits

P l u s . . .

uary

The new year spurs vows to eat better, even as we turn to cozy gatherings, made fun with indoor games and tasty morsels.

Pick a little, talk a little, pick a little, talk a little. That's what'll happen when a roomful

nibbles n bits

of friends says hello to a table filled with amazing appetizers.

Bloody Mary Swizzlers

PHOTOGRAPHS: COLLEEN DUFFLEY. FOOD STYLIST: WES MARTIN. PROP STYLIST: NANCY HOPKINS. STORY AND RECIPES BY JEANNE AMBROSE WITH STEPHEN EXEL.

low fat Caesar Salad Cracker Cups

Roasting the beets and baking the cracker cups in advance will save time on party day.

Prep: 30 minutes

Bake: 10 minutes for cracker cups; 45 minutes for beets

¾ cup all-purpose flour	1 clove garlic, minced
¼ cup whole wheat flour	⅓ cup buttermilk
1 tsp. sugar	Nonstick cooking spray
¼ tsp. baking soda	4 cups chopped romaine
⅛ tsp. coarse salt or salt	lettuce
⅛ tsp. freshly ground black pepper	2 to 3 Tbsp. bottled Caesar salad dressing
1 Tbsp. butter (no substitutes)	1 hard-cooked egg, chopped
¼ cup finely shredded Parmesan cheese	1 recipe Roasted Beets
	Shaved Parmesan cheese

1. Preheat oven to 375° F. In a medium bowl stir together all-purpose flour, whole wheat flour, sugar, baking soda, salt, and pepper. Using a pastry blender, cut in butter until mixture resembles coarse crumbs. Stir in shredded Parmesan cheese and garlic. Make a well in center of flour mixture. Add buttermilk. Using a fork, stir until mixture can be shaped into a ball.

2. Turn dough out onto a lightly floured surface. Knead for 8 to 10 strokes or until dough is almost smooth. Divide dough in half. Roll each portion into a 12x9-inch rectangle. Use a pastry wheel or knife to cut rectangles into 3-inch squares. Use a fork to prick squares several times. Coat the bottom side of a mini muffin pan with cooking spray. Lay dough squares over muffin cup bottoms, making sure edges of squares don't overlap. Place inverted muffin pan on a shallow baking pan.

3. Bake about 10 minutes or until golden brown. Remove cracker cups from muffin pan; cool on a wire rack. (Cracker cups may be made up to 3 days ahead. Store in an airtight container at room temperature. Or, freeze the baked cracker cups in a freezer container for up to 3 months.)

4. In a medium bowl toss romaine with salad dressing. To serve, sprinkle some chopped egg in the bottom of each cracker cup. Fill with romaine mixture and top with Roasted Beets and shaved Parmesan cheese. Makes 24 appetizers.

Roasted Beets: Preheat oven to 375° F. Scrub one medium beet (or 12 baby beets); trim off stem and root ends. Peel the medium beet and cut into ¾-inch pieces or halve the baby beets. Place beets in an 8x8x2-inch baking pan. In a small bowl combine 1 tablespoon olive oil, 1½ teaspoons balsamic vinegar, 1 small clove minced garlic, ⅛ teaspoon salt, and ⅛ teaspoon freshly ground black pepper. Drizzle over beets; toss to coat. Cover pan with foil; roast for 35 minutes. Uncover; roast for 10 minutes more or until tender. Cool to room temperature.

Nutrition facts per appetizer: 49 cal., 2 g total fat (1 g sat. fat), 11 mg chol., 80 mg sodium, 5 g carbo., 1 g fiber, and 2 g pro. Daily Values: 6% vit. A, 4% vit. C, 2% calcium, and 2% iron.

---

30 low fat Bloody Mary Swizzlers

Vodka-flavored veggies will remind you of the classic cocktail.

Prep: 30 minutes **Marinate:** Overnight

24 cherry tomatoes	3 or 4 stalks celery with tops removed, bias-sliced into ¾- to 1-inch pieces (24 pieces total)
1 cup lemon-flavored vodka	
24 almond-stuffed green olives or vermouth-marinated green olives	24 cocktail picks or skewers
	Celery salt

1. Using a plastic or wooden pick or a sharp skewer, pierce the skins of the tomatoes in several places. Place tomatoes in a self-sealing, food-safe plastic bag; add vodka. Seal bag. Turn bag to coat tomatoes. Marinate in refrigerator overnight.

2. Drain tomatoes; discard vodka. Skewer an olive, a piece of celery, and a cherry tomato on each pick. Sprinkle lightly with celery salt. Transfer to serving platter. Makes 24 skewers.

Nutrition facts per skewer: 21 cal., 1 g total fat (0 g sat. fat), 0 mg chol., 92 mg sodium, 1 g carbo., 0 g fiber, and 0 g pro. Daily Values: 2% vit. A, 6% vit. C, 1% calcium, and 1% iron.

Caesar Salad Cracker Cups

30 Thai Spinach Dip

This stir-together treat delivers big peanut flavor with a hit of heat. The dip takes just minutes to prepare.

Prep: 15 minutes **Chill:** 2 hours

1 cup chopped fresh spinach	¼ cup peanut butter
1 8-oz. carton dairy sour cream	1 Tbsp. honey
1 8-oz. carton plain fat-free yogurt	1 Tbsp. soy sauce
¼ cup snipped fresh mint	1 to 2 tsp. crushed red pepper
¼ cup finely chopped peanuts	Peeled baby carrots or other vegetables for dipping

1. In a medium bowl combine the spinach, sour cream, and yogurt. Stir in mint, peanuts, peanut butter, honey, soy sauce, and crushed red pepper.

2. Cover and chill for 2 to 24 hours. Serve with baby carrots or other vegetable dippers. Makes about 2½ cups.

Nutrition facts per 1 tablespoon dip: 34 cal., 3 g total fat (1 g sat. fat), 3 mg chol., 41 mg sodium, 2 g carbo., 0 g fiber, and 1 g pro. Daily Values: 2% vit. A, 1% vit. C, 2% calcium, and 1% iron.

Horseradish-Radish Sandwiches

WARMING WINTER PARTY MENU

Pork and Chicken Barbecue Bites (recipe, page 18)

Filled-Up Phyllo Logs (recipe, page 17)

Thai Spinach Dip (recipe, left)

Assorted vegetables and crackers

Bloody Mary Swizzlers (recipe, page 11)

Horseradish-Radish Sandwiches

Take a shortcut by placing the herbed cheese mixture into a plastic sandwich bag, snipping a small hole in one corner, then piping the mixture onto the puff pastry circles.

Prep: 45 minutes **Bake:** 10 minutes

1⅓ cups herbed goat cheese (chèvre) or two 5-oz. containers semisoft cheese with garlic and herbs	1 17¼-oz. pkg. frozen puff pastry (2 sheets), thawed
6 to 8 tsp. hot-style prepared horseradish	1 Tbsp. milk
	Coarse salt (optional)
2 Tbsp. finely chopped green onion	1 large English cucumber, very thinly sliced
	10 radishes, very thinly sliced

1. In a medium bowl combine goat cheese, horseradish, and green onion. Cover and chill until ready to use.

2. Preheat oven to 375° F. Unfold one of the puff pastry sheets on a lightly floured surface. With the tines of a fork, generously prick pastry. Use a 2-inch round cutter to cut pastry into circles. Transfer circles to an ungreased baking sheet. Brush pastry lightly with milk. Sprinkle with salt, if desired. Bake for 10 to 12 minutes or until golden brown. Cool on wire rack. Repeat with remaining puff pastry.

3. To assemble, use a knife to split the baked pastries horizontally. Spread about 1 teaspoon of the cheese mixture onto the cut side of each bottom pastry. Top with several cucumber slices and radish slices. Spread the cut side of each top pastry with about 1 teaspoon of the cheese mixture. Place on top of radish slices. Makes 32 appetizers.

Nutrition facts per appetizer: 94 cal., 7 g total fat (1 g sat. fat), 4 mg chol., 94 mg sodium, 6 g carbo., 0 g fiber, and 2 g pro. Daily Values: 2% vit. A, 1% vit. C, 2% calcium, and 1% iron.

No
excuses.
Pick up the
phone,
invite the
friends,
and
party on.

Thai Spinach Dip

Good and thick, this dip really grabs onto
the nearest veggie. Your guests will want
to latch ahold, too. It's full of mint and
packed with peanut power.

When the gang is engrossed in a cornball game of Parcheesi, bring on those crunchy cones stuffed with a sassy relish.

Keep them small and you can have another, and another, and another.

Deviled Eggs
with Spicy Crab

Corn-Relish Crisps

Shape each cilantro-flecked crisp into a mini taco shell by draping a warm crisp over a rolling pin. Or, keep crisps flat by cooling on a flat surface.

Prep: 30 minutes **Bake:** 6 minutes per batch

¾ cup all-purpose flour	Pointed rolled sugar
2 Tbsp. snipped fresh	ice-cream cones or
cilantro	metal cone shapes
1 Tbsp. sugar	¾ cup crème fraîche or
½ tsp. salt	dairy sour cream
¼ tsp. ground red pepper	4 tsp. snipped fresh chives
½ cup butter, softened	½ cup purchased corn relish
3 egg whites	

1. Preheat oven to 375° F. In a small bowl stir together the flour, cilantro, sugar, salt, and ground red pepper; set aside. In a medium mixing bowl beat butter with an electric mixer on medium to high speed until fluffy. Beat in egg whites until combined. Beat in flour mixture until combined.

2. Line a baking sheet with parchment paper. For each shell, drop one heaping teaspoon of batter onto the prepared sheet. Using the back of a spoon, spread batter into a 3-inch circle. Repeat with the remaining batter, baking only five or six crisps at a time.

3. Bake 6 to 7 minutes or until bubbly and golden brown on edges. Remove from oven. Allow to cool 15 seconds. Working quickly, roll each warm crisp around pointed ice-cream cone or metal cone. Allow to cool; remove from cones and set aside. Or, transfer flat crisps to a wire rack to cool.

4. To serve, in a small mixing bowl combine crème fraîche and chives. Spoon 1 to 2 teaspoons of the crème fraîche mixture into each shell. Top with 1 teaspoon corn relish. Arrange on a serving platter. Makes 24 appetizers.

Make-ahead directions: Bake, shape, and cool crisps as directed. Arrange in a single layer in a freezer container and freeze for up to 1 month. To serve, thaw crisps for 15 minutes.

Nutrition facts per appetizer: 76 cal., 6 g total fat (4 g sat. fat), 17 mg chol., 107 mg sodium, 4 g carbo., 0 g fiber, and 1 g pro. Daily Values: 4% vit. A, 1% vit. C, 1% calcium, and 1% iron.

30 Deviled Eggs with Spicy Crab

Crab and chutney atop deviled eggs make a favorite appetizer doubly delightful.

Start to finish: 25 minutes

8 hard-cooked eggs	¼ tsp. salt
¼ cup mayonnaise or	¼ tsp. ground red pepper
salad dressing	1 to 2 Tbsp. mango
1 Tbsp. finely chopped	chutney
green onion	3 Tbsp. mayonnaise or
1 to 2 tsp. flavored	salad dressing
mustard, such as	½ tsp. curry powder
Dijon-style mustard	½ cup cooked crabmeat
or horseradish mustard	(about 2¾ oz.)

1. Halve the hard-cooked eggs lengthwise and remove yolks. Place egg yolks, the ¼ cup mayonnaise, the green onion, mustard, and ⅛ teaspoon each of the salt and red pepper in a quart-size, self-sealing, food-safe plastic bag. Seal bag; squeeze to mash the egg yolks and combine the ingredients. Snip one corner of the bag; pipe mixture into egg halves.

2. Cut up any large pieces of mango chutney. In a bowl combine the chutney, the remaining 3 tablespoons mayonnaise, curry powder, and remaining salt and red pepper. Gently fold in crabmeat. Top each deviled egg with a spoonful of crab mixture. Cover and chill up to 2 hours. Makes 16 appetizers.

Nutrition facts per appetizer: 91 cal., 8 g total fat (1 g sat. fat), 113 mg chol., 119 mg sodium, 1 g carbo., 0 g fiber, and 4 g pro. Daily Values: 4% vit. A, 1% vit. C, 2% calcium, and 2% iron.

Filled-Up Phyllo Logs

Roll 'em up. Move 'em out. Spread a mushroom-onion filling or a spinach-bean combo onto buttery phyllo, then roll. They're fit to be tied.

Call them tapas, hors d'oeuvres, or appetizers. Or call them a darn good substitute for dinner tonight.

¼	cup thinly sliced green onion	⅛	tsp. pepper
2	cloves garlic, minced	24	Medjool dates (about 16 oz. unpitted)

1. Preheat oven to 350° F. In a medium bowl stir together the bacon or prosciutto, green onion, and garlic. Add Cambazola or blue cheese, cream cheese, mustard, and pepper to bacon mixture. Stir to combine.

2. Using a knife, make a lengthwise slit in each date. Spread each date open slightly. Remove pits. Fill each date with a rounded teaspoon of the bacon mixture. Place dates, filling side up, on a baking sheet. Bake for 5 to 8 minutes or until heated through. Serve warm. Makes 24 appetizers.

Make-ahead directions: Stuff dates, cover, and chill up to 24 hours. Just before serving, uncover and bake as directed.

Nutrition facts per appetizer: 77 cal., 2 g total fat (1 g sat. fat), 6 mg chol., 55 mg sodium, 14 g carbo., 1 g fiber, and 1 g pro. Daily Values: 2% vit. A, 2% calcium, and 2% iron.

Bacon 'n' Cheese
Stuffed Dates

ples 'n' Bits

...urant and Bar in
...ks.

...tes

...er or margarine,

...armesan cheese

...ional)

...and Mushroom-
...y brush a sheet of
...th another sheet
...(Keep remaining phyllo covered with plastic wrap to prevent drying.) Using a sharp knife or rotary blade, cut the stacked phyllo in half lengthwise and then crosswise to make four equal rectangles.

2. Spread about 2 tablespoons of the bean filling in a ¾-inch-wide strip on a long side and to within 1 inch of short ends of each rectangle. Tightly roll the phyllo dough into a thin log, starting with the filled side. Brush seam side with butter. Place log, seam side down, on a baking sheet; brush with butter and sprinkle with shredded Parmesan cheese.

3. Repeat with remaining bean filling and four more phyllo sheets. Fill remaining six sheets of phyllo with the mushroom-onion filling, following the same procedure, except use 4 teaspoons filling per log and sprinkle logs with pepper.

4. Bake about 18 minutes or until logs are golden brown. Cool on wire racks. Tie ends with chive strands, if desired. Serve warm or cool. Makes 24 logs.

Spinach-White Bean Filling: Thaw and thoroughly drain one 10-ounce package frozen chopped spinach; finely chop. Set aside. Drain one 15-ounce can white beans (cannellini); rinse and drain. In a food processor bowl or blender container combine beans, 1 tablespoon water, and 3 cloves minced garlic. Cover and process or blend until smooth. Transfer bean mixture to a medium bowl. Add spinach; mix well.

Nutrition facts per bean-filled log: 92 cal., 5 g total fat (3 g sat. fat), 11 mg chol., 211 mg sodium, 11 g carbo., 3 g fiber, and 4 g pro. Daily Values: 40% vit. A, 5% vit. C, 5% calcium, and 6% iron.

Mushroom-Onion Filling: In a large skillet heat 1 tablespoon cooking oil until hot. Cook 2 cups finely diced fresh crimini and/or shiitake mushrooms, 1 finely chopped large onion, and 1 clove minced garlic over medium-high heat for 5 to 7 minutes or until liquid has evaporated. Stir occasionally.

Nutrition facts per mushroom-filled log: 84 cal., 6 g total fat (3 g sat. fat), 11 mg chol., 113 mg sodium, 7 g carbo., 1 g fiber, and 1 g pro. Daily Values: 3% vit. A, 1% vit. C, 1% calcium, and 2% iron.

Hot Ribeye Bites

30 low fat Hot Ribeye Bites

Make sure the pickled peppers you use are a mild variety or your guests will really feel the burn.

Prep: 15 minutes **Broil:** 12 minutes

¼ cup jalapeño pepper jelly	24 pickled baby banana
2 Tbsp. Kansas City steak seasoning or steak seasoning	chili peppers, jalapeño peppers, or other mild baby chili peppers
2 boneless beef ribeye steaks, cut 1 inch thick (about 1¼ lb.)	

1. For glaze, in a small saucepan stir together pepper jelly and steak seasoning. Cook and stir for 1 to 2 minutes over low heat or until jelly is melted. Set aside.

2. Preheat broiler. Place steaks on the unheated rack of a broiler pan. Broil steaks 3 to 4 inches from the heat to desired doneness, turning the steaks once. Allow 12 to 14 minutes for medium rare (center of meat is 145° F) or 15 to 18 minutes for medium doneness (center of meat is 160° F). Brush steaks with glaze during the last 5 minutes and turn again to glaze other side.

3. Cut steak into 1-inch cubes. Top each cube with a pickled pepper. Makes about 24 appetizers.

Nutrition facts per appetizer: 47 cal., 1 g total fat (1 g sat. fat), 11 mg chol., 179 mg sodium, 3 g carbo., 0 g fiber, and 5 g pro. Daily Values: 4% vit. C, 1% calcium, and 3% iron.

Pork and Chicken BBQ Sticks

An indoor grill makes speedy work of these meaty treats, but an oven broiler also offers a quick option.

Prep: 20 minutes **Chill:** 15 minutes **Grill:** 5 minutes

12 oz. pork tenderloin	Salt
12 oz. skinless, boneless chicken thighs	Pepper
16 6-inch wooden skewers	1 recipe Chipotle Barbecue Sauce

1. Trim fat from pork. Cut pork into 1-inch cubes. Cut chicken into 1-inch pieces. Thread three pork pieces onto eight of the skewers, leaving ¼ inch between pieces. Thread three chicken pieces on each of the remaining eight skewers, leaving ¼ inch between pieces. Place skewers on a tray.

2. Sprinkle salt and pepper evenly over pork and chicken. Cover with plastic wrap; refrigerate 15 minutes to 2 hours.

3. Lightly grease the rack of an indoor electric grill or lightly coat with nonstick cooking spray. Preheat grill. Place the pork kabobs on the grill rack. (Keep chicken kabobs covered and refrigerated). If using a covered grill, close lid. Grill until meat is slightly pink in center and juices run clear, brushing generously with Chipotle Barbecue Sauce halfway through cooking. (For a covered grill, allow 5 to 7 minutes, giving kabobs a quarter turn once halfway through grilling. For an uncovered grill, allow 12 to 15 minutes, turning kabobs occasionally to cook evenly.) Remove from grill and keep warm.

4. Place chicken kabobs on the grill rack. If using a covered grill, close lid. Grill until chicken is tender and no longer pink, brushing generously with the remaining sauce halfway through cooking. (For a covered grill, allow 3 to 5 minutes, giving kabobs a quarter turn once halfway through grilling. For an uncovered grill, allow 10 to 12 minutes, turning occasionally to cook evenly.) Makes 16 appetizers.

Broiler method: Arrange all of the kabobs on the rack of an unheated broiler pan. Broil 4 to 5 inches from the heat for 8 to 10 minutes or until pork and chicken are done, turning occasionally. Brush generously with sauce the last 5 minutes.

Chipotle Barbecue Sauce: In a small saucepan combine ½ cup bottled barbecue sauce, 1 tablespoon chopped canned chipotle peppers in adobo sauce, 1 tablespoon honey, and 2 cloves minced garlic. Bring to boiling; reduce heat. Boil gently, uncovered, about 5 minutes or until slightly thickened. Set aside to cool slightly. Makes about ½ cup.

Nutrition facts per appetizer: 63 cal., 2 g total fat (0 g sat. fat), 31 mg chol., 116 mg sodium, 2 g carbo., 0 g fiber, and 9 g pro. Daily Values: 2% vit. A, 2% vit. C, 1% calcium, and 3% iron.

Pork and Chicken BBQ Sticks

You can't get too stuck up about having a party. Thread juicy chunks of meat onto skewers and slather with a spicy sauce. What can we say—when you're hot, you're hot!

Lemony Oven Fries

OK, everybody on the floor in front of the tube.
Pull up a pile of crispy fries with frizzled lemon
and munch away while the movie plays.

Soy-Glazed Squash

Lemony Oven Fries

Wow! Adding a zap of lemon to frozen french fries before baking makes for a surprising burst of fresh flavor.

Prep: 10 minutes   **Bake:** 30 minutes

⅓ cup olive oil	1 20-oz. pkg. frozen
1 large lemon, thinly sliced	french-fried shoestring
¼ cup fresh Italian flat-leaf	potatoes (about 5 cups)
parsley sprigs	Coarse sea salt
	Lemon wedges

1. In a large skillet heat olive oil over medium heat. Carefully add lemon slices. Cook for 3 to 5 minutes or until lemon begins to brown. Use tongs to turn lemon slices. Add the parsley to the oil. Cook for 20 to 30 seconds more or until parsley is crisp. Remove lemon slices and parsley with slotted spoon; drain on paper towels. Reserve the lemon-flavored oil (you should have about 3 tablespoons).

2. In a large bowl toss frozen shoestring potatoes with the reserved oil until well coated. Place potatoes in a 15x10x1-inch baking pan. Bake according to package directions or until the potatoes are browned and crisp, stirring occasionally.

3. To serve, toss lemon and parsley with the hot potatoes. Sprinkle generously with sea salt. Squeeze lemon wedges over fries. Serve immediately. Makes about 5 cups.

Nutrition facts per ½-cup serving: 126 cal., 7 g total fat (1 g sat. fat), 0 mg chol., 72 mg sodium, 14 g carbo., 1 g fiber, and 2 g pro. Daily Values: 2% vit. A, 20% vit. C, 1% calcium, and 1% iron.

Soy-Glazed Squash

The tan rind of bell-shaped butternut squash is easy to remove with a vegetable peeler.

Prep: 25 minutes   **Roast:** 20 minutes

1½ lb. butternut squash, peeled, seeded, and cut into ¾-inch cubes	½ cup blood orange juice or orange juice
1 tsp. finely shredded blood orange peel or orange peel	2 scallions or green onions, finely chopped
	3 Tbsp. soy sauce
	1 Tbsp. brown sugar
	2 tsp. chili oil

1. Preheat oven to 425° F. Place squash cubes in a lightly greased 13x9x2-inch baking pan. In a bowl combine orange peel, orange juice, scallions or green onions, soy sauce, brown sugar, and chili oil. Drizzle over squash, tossing to coat. Roast, uncovered, 20 to 25 minutes or until squash is tender, stirring twice.

2. Stir cubes again before serving. Place a toothpick in each squash cube. Serve warm. Makes about 48 appetizers.

Nutrition facts per appetizer: 10 cal., 0 g total fat (0 g sat. fat), 0 mg chol., 58 mg sodium, 2 g carbo., 0 g fiber, and 0 g pro. Daily Values: 11% vit. A, 5% vit. C, 1% calcium, and 1% iron.

Pull together a few tasty tidbits and a few close friends and bask in the camaraderie.

▼ Baby Broccoli

These bitsy buds (below) are a cross between broccoli and gai lan (far right). The slender stalks cook quickly. We love sautéing these babies in olive oil and garlic for 5 minutes or so, then adding a generous splash of chicken broth before covering and cooking for a few minutes more.

▲ Broccoli Raab

Until recently, broccoli raab (above) was pretty scarce outside of Italian neighborhoods. Now you'll spot it in most supermarkets. Be sure to cook broccoli raab to help tame its radishlike bite. Try it chopped and stirred into your favorite spicy sausage soup or creamy risotto.

▲ Broccoli Romanesco

With its chartreuse color and pinecone-shaped flowerets (above), this is the most exotic-looking of the broccoli family. But it tastes more like cauliflower. Show it off by steaming it until crisp tender, or serve it raw with a bit of garlic-mayo or a yogurt-herb dip.

Eat Your Broccoli

Broccoli in all its glorious, green form is a nutritional powerhouse packed with vitamin C, heart-protecting beta-carotene, and plant chemicals that may keep breast cancer at bay. That's why it's good to "stalk" up on this winter-friendly vegetable. As you can see from the photographs, you have a lot to choose from when scouting for broccoli at the supermarket. Just look for firm stalks with deep green or purplish green heads that are tightly packed. Heads that are light green or those that have tiny yellow flowers are past their prime, so avoid them. To store fresh broccoli, keep it in a plastic bag in the refrigerator for up to 4 days. You can also blanch or steam broccoli slightly and freeze it for up to a year. If broccoli stems seem tough, use a sharp knife to peel away the tough outer skin to use the more tender center portion of the stems.

◀ Gai Lan

Look for this green (left), also called Chinese broccoli, in Asian food stores. To cook, separate leaves from stalks. Cook stalks in boiling water until tender. Add leaves; cook until wilted. Stir-fry cooked greens in peanut oil; add ginger, chili peppers, and/or hoisin sauce.

▲ Broccoli

You can't miss this familiar green (above) in the produce aisles because it's there nearly year-round. For a change, finely chop raw broccoli, mix with shredded carrot, and sprinkle with an herbed salt. Use the crunchy mix to fill a sandwich of whole-grain bread slathered with cream cheese.

PHOTOGRAPHS: COLLEEN DUFFLEY. STORY: BEV BENNETT.

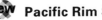 Pacific Rim Stir-Fry

Prep: 25 minutes **Cook:** 15 minutes

3	oz. rice sticks, rice noodles, or thin vermicelli, broken
12	oz. skinless, boneless chicken thighs or breast halves
½	cup chicken broth
2	Tbsp. soy sauce
2	tsp. cornstarch
½	tsp. crushed red pepper
½	tsp. ground turmeric
1	Tbsp. cooking oil
2	medium carrots, cut into short strips or thinly sliced (1 cup)
2	cups broccoli flowerets
1	red or green sweet pepper, cut into 1-inch strips (½ cup)
2	Tbsp. snipped fresh basil
¼	cup cashew halves or peanuts

1. In a saucepan cook rice sticks or noodles in boiling water for 3 minutes. (Or, cook vermicelli according to package directions.) Drain; keep warm.

2. Meanwhile, cut chicken into thin, bite-size strips. For sauce, combine broth, soy sauce, cornstarch, crushed red pepper, and turmeric; set aside.

3. Add oil to wok or skillet. Preheat over medium-high heat (add more oil if necessary during cooking). Cook and stir carrots in hot oil for 1 minute. Add broccoli; cook and stir 2 minutes. Add sweet pepper; cook and stir 1½ to 2 minutes more or until crisp-tender. Remove.

4. Add chicken; cook and stir 2 to 3 minutes or until no longer pink. Push from center. Stir sauce; add to center. Cook and stir until bubbly. Return vegetables; add basil. Cook and stir 2 minutes or until heated through. Serve over rice sticks; sprinkle with nuts. Makes 4 servings.

Nutrition facts per serving: 313 cal., 13 g total fat (2 g sat. fat), 70 mg chol., 703 mg sodium, 30 g carbo., 3 g fiber, and 22 g pro. Daily Values: 201% vit. A, 146% vit. C, 5% calcium, 13% iron.

Oat Cuisine

Nutty-tasting oat groats— whole oat kernels with the hulls removed—go beyond the basic breakfast oatmeal. In fact, they're main-dish delicious, as this recipe (right) shows. "People, especially those at risk for heart disease, should consider eating oats regularly," says Dr. David Katz, Yale School of Medicine. A small Yale study led by Katz showed that oatmeal consumed immediately after a fat-laden milk shake kept participants' arteries from narrowing, which happens to some people after eating foods high in saturated fats.

"A bowl of oatmeal showed the same ability to keep blood vessels open as 800 IU of vitamin E. It looks like oats may be comfort food for our blood vessels," Katz says.

Whole grains, such as oats, wheat, and brown rice, are so nutritionally powerful that the USDA urges you to use them for half of the suggested six daily servings of grain-based products.

Oats are packed with soluble fiber, which helps remove cholesterol and reduces blood pressure. For diabetics, fiber may slow digestion—preventing steep rises in blood sugar levels. Fiber also gives the body long-lasting energy and helps keep you feeling full longer.

THE MIGHTY OAT

Take your pick from the oat family. Look in natural foods stores if you don't see them on your grocer's shelves.

- Groats: Whole oat kernels with hulls removed; wild rice texture, nutty taste.
- Steel-cut oats: Groats that are thinly sliced; hearty, chewy consistency.
- Rolled oats: Groats that are steamed and rolled flat.
- Quick-cooking: Sliced rolled oats.
- Instant oats: Precooked and dried rolled oats.

---

30 low fat

Seared Peppers, Black Beans, and Groats
Start to finish: 25 minutes

2	cups water
¾	cup oat groats
¼	tsp. salt
1	Tbsp. olive oil or cooking oil
1	large sweet green pepper, cut into strips
1½	tsp. Cajun seasoning
1	15-oz. can black beans, rinsed and drained
1	cup cherry tomatoes, halved
¼	cup sliced green onion
2	Tbsp. crumbled kasseri or farmer cheese

1. In a saucepan bring water, groats, and salt to boiling; reduce heat. Cover and simmer about 15 minutes or until the groats are tender. Drain excess liquid.

2. Meanwhile, in a large nonstick skillet heat oil. Add pepper strips. Cook and stir over medium-high heat for 4 minutes or until peppers begin to brown. Add Cajun seasoning; cook and stir for 30 seconds. Reduce heat to medium. Add beans. Cook and stir for 2 minutes more or until heated through. Stir in tomatoes. Remove from heat.

3. To serve, place groats in bowl. Top with sweet pepper mixture, green onions, and cheese. Makes 3 servings.

Nutrition facts per serving: 343 cal., 10 g total fat (3 g sat. fat), 7 mg chol., 718 mg sodium, 53 g carbo., 13 g fiber, and 18 g pro. Daily Values: 14% vit. A, 85% vit. C, 13% calcium, and 24% iron.

Treat yourself to your heart's desire this month with delectable desserts and heart-healthy soups and sides.

F e b
Desserts

P l u s . . .

r u a r y

Desserts

As the curtain rises on dinner's finale, the spotlight is on a company-friendly sweet soufflé, a jewel-like granita, or pixie-size chocolate pies. Encore!

Strawberry Soufflé

Jam Roly-Polys

Strawberry Soufflé

low fat

Plan ahead so you can prepare this airy dessert with minimal fuss at dinnertime. Before sitting down to dine, prepare the soufflé dishes, separate the egg whites, blend the strawberries, and preheat the oven. After dinner, just whip the egg whites, fold in the strawberries, and bake.

Prep: 20 minutes   **Bake:** 15 minutes

5 egg whites	¼ to ⅓ cup sugar
Margarine or butter	4 tsp. cornstarch
Sugar	½ cup sugar
2 cups sliced fresh strawberries	Strawberry or chocolate syrup

1. Let egg whites stand at room temperature for 30 minutes. Using margarine or butter, grease six 1-cup soufflé dishes or 10-ounce custard cups. Sprinkle with sugar, shaking out any excess sugar. Place on a shallow baking pan or baking sheet.

2. Meanwhile, in a medium bowl combine strawberries and the ¼ to ⅓ cup sugar. Let stand 15 minutes until strawberries become juicy. In a blender container or food processor bowl combine strawberry mixture and cornstarch. Cover and blend or process until smooth. Set aside.

3. Preheat oven to 350° F. In a large mixing bowl beat egg whites until soft peaks form (tips curl). Gradually add the ½ cup sugar, beating for 2 to 3 minutes or until stiff glossy peaks form (see photo below).

4. With a rubber spatula, push beaten egg whites to the side of the bowl. Pour strawberry mixture into bottom of the bowl. Carefully stir a little of the beaten egg whites into strawberry mixture. Then gently fold the two mixtures together (there should be a few white streaks remaining). Divide mixture evenly among prepared dishes.

5. Bake for 15 to 18 minutes or until a knife inserted near the center comes out clean. Serve immediately with strawberry or chocolate syrup. Makes 6 individual soufflés.

Nutrition facts per soufflé: 248 cal., 2 g total fat (1 g sat. fat), 4 mg chol., 70 mg sodium, 57 g carbo., 1 g fiber, and 3 g pro. Daily Values: 1% vit. A, 45% vit. C, 1% calcium, and 1% iron.

Jam Roly-Polys

We chose apricot and raspberry jam because we love them together, but feel free to substitute other fruit preserves.

Prep: 25 minutes   **Bake:** 20 minutes

1 cup all-purpose flour	2 Tbsp. apricot or peach preserves or jam
1½ tsp. baking powder	
¼ tsp. salt	2 Tbsp. seedless raspberry or strawberry jam
3 Tbsp. shortening	
⅓ cup milk	1 recipe Lemon-Sour Cream Sauce

1. Preheat oven to 375° F. In a medium bowl stir together the flour, baking powder, and salt. Cut in the shortening until mixture resembles coarse crumbs. Make a well in the center. Add milk all at once. Using a fork, stir just until moistened. Turn dough out onto a lightly floured surface. Quickly knead dough 10 to 12 strokes or until nearly smooth.

2. Roll dough to a 12x8-inch rectangle. Spread apricot or peach preserves lengthwise over half of the dough, leaving a ½-inch border around the edges. Spread raspberry or strawberry jam lengthwise over remaining half of dough, leaving a ½-inch border around edges. Roll the two long sides, scroll fashion, to meet in the center. Where the rolls come together, brush with water and lightly squeeze together.

3. Line a baking sheet with foil; grease the foil. Transfer the roll to the baking sheet. Bake for 20 minutes or until golden. Cool for 10 minutes on the baking sheet. Cut roll into 1-inch-thick slices. Place two warm slices in each shallow bowl and pass Lemon-Sour Cream Sauce. Makes 5 servings.

Lemon-Sour Cream Sauce: In a small saucepan combine ⅔ cup lemon curd and ⅓ cup dairy sour cream. Heat over low heat just until warm (do not boil).

Nutrition facts per serving: 374 cal., 13 g total fat (5 g sat. fat), 39 mg chol., 288 mg sodium, 63 g carbo., 5 g fiber, and 4 g pro. Daily Values: 3% vit. A, 3% vit. C, 12% calcium, and 8% iron.

Egg whites are considered stiff when they form peaks that stand up straight and form a curl as you lift the beaters.

Caramel-Bourbon
Upside-Down Cake

VALENTINE'S DAY MENU

Mixed greens and fruit salad

Garlicky Steak and Asparagus (recipe, page 47)

Baked potatoes and sour cream

Valentine Granita (recipe, below) or

Chocolate-Cherry Cheesecake (recipe, page 34)

Cabernet or Merlot wine

Caramel-Bourbon Upside-Down Cake

As a shortcut, use the pre-peeled, pre-cored, fresh pineapple that's now available in many grocery stores.

Prep: 30 minutes **Bake:** 20 minutes **Cool:** 35 minutes

¼ cup butter or margarine	¼ cup toasted slivered
½ cup packed brown sugar	almonds, pine nuts, or
¼ cup bourbon or	chopped macadamia
orange juice	nuts
1 cup chopped fresh	1 cup all-purpose flour
pineapple, well drained,	½ cup cornmeal
or one 8-oz. can	2 Tbsp. granulated sugar
pineapple chunks or	1½ tsp. baking powder
tidbits, drained	¼ tsp. salt
½ cup snipped dried	⅛ tsp. ground nutmeg
apricots	2 eggs, beaten
¼ cup golden raisins	½ cup milk
	2 Tbsp. cooking oil

1. Preheat oven to 400° F. Melt the butter or margarine in a 9x9x2-inch baking pan in the oven about 5 minutes. Stir in brown sugar and bourbon or orange juice. Spoon pineapple, apricots, raisins, and nuts into the pan. Stir together to mix, then spread out to form an even layer. Set pan aside.

2. In a medium mixing bowl stir together flour, cornmeal, granulated sugar, baking powder, salt, and nutmeg. Make a well in the center of the flour mixture. Set aside.

3. In another bowl combine the eggs, milk, and oil. Add all at once to flour mixture. Stir just until moistened. Carefully spoon batter in mounds over fruit mixture in pan; spread evenly.

4. Bake about 20 minutes or until a wooden toothpick inserted near center comes out clean. Cool on a wire rack for 5 minutes. Loosen sides; invert onto a plate. Spoon on any topping that falls off. Serve warm. Makes 8 servings.

Test Kitchen Tip: To reheat, place on a microwave-safe plate. Microwave on 100 percent power (high) for 20 seconds.

Nutrition facts per serving: 327 cal., 11 g total fat (3 g sat. fat), 62 mg chol., 210 mg sodium, 50 g carbo., 3 g fiber, and 6 g pro. Daily Values: 17% vit. A, 6% vit. C, 11% calcium, and 14% iron.

low fat Valentine Granita

A granita is an Italian ice, similar to sorbet, only icier. This raspberry-mango combination flies the color of the day.

Prep: 20 minutes **Freeze:** 9 hours **Stand:** 5 minutes

1 cup water	1 medium fresh mango,
½ cup sugar	peeled, seeded, and
1 12-oz. pkg. frozen lightly	chopped
sweetened red	Fresh red raspberries
raspberries	(optional)

1. In a medium saucepan combine water and sugar. Cook over medium heat just until mixture boils, stirring to dissolve sugar. Remove from heat and add the frozen raspberries and mango. Pour into a blender container or food processor bowl. Cover and blend or process until smooth. Strain through a fine mesh sieve (should have about 2 cups sieved fruit mixture).

2. Pour sieved mixture into a 13x9x2-inch baking pan or freezer container. Cover and freeze for 1 to 2 hours or until mixture is nearly frozen. Stir well, scraping frozen mixture from sides of pan or container (see photo, below). Spread mixture to evenly cover bottom of pan or container. Cover and freeze at least 8 hours or overnight.

3. To serve, let stand at room temperature for 5 to 10 minutes. Use an ice cream scoop to spoon into four demitasse cups or dessert dishes. If desired, garnish with fresh berries. Makes 4 servings.

Nutrition facts per serving: 214 cal., 0 g total fat (0 g sat. fat), 0 mg chol., 4 mg sodium, 56 g carbo., 2 g fiber, and 0 g pro. Daily Values: 41% vit. A, 48% vit. C, 2% calcium, and 3% iron.

Stir the granita when it is still slushy. If you wait too long, it may freeze solid.

Valentine Granita

Alchemy! Conjure Tiffany rubies for your loved one from a bag of frozen berries. Perform your Valentine magic by sweetening raspberries with sugar, adding a mango, blending, then freezing to gem-like beauty.

Lavender Crème Brûlée

The flowery whisper of lavender
accompanies each tender spoonful
of this delicate custard.

Pear Ginger Flan

Lavender Crème Brûlée

Caramelizing sugar in a pan means you don't have to place cold dishes under a hot broiler, which can cause them to shatter.

Prep: 20 minutes **Bake:** 30 minutes **Chill:** 1 hour

2	cups half-and-half or light cream	5	egg yolks, slightly beaten
2	to 3 tsp. dried lavender flowers or 1 Tbsp. snipped fresh basil	⅓	cup sugar
		1	tsp. vanilla
		⅛	tsp. salt
		1	recipe Caramelized Sugar

1. Preheat oven to 325° F. In a heavy small saucepan heat half-and-half or light cream and lavender or basil over medium-low heat just until bubbly. Remove from heat. Strain through a fine mesh sieve; discard lavender or basil. Set cream aside.

2. Meanwhile, in a medium bowl combine egg yolks, sugar, vanilla, and salt. Beat with a wire whisk or rotary beater just until combined. Slowly whisk the hot half-and-half or light cream into the egg mixture.

3. Place eight 4-ounce ramekins or six 6-ounce custard cups in a 13x9x2-inch baking pan. Place baking pan on the oven rack. Pour custard mixture evenly into the dishes or cups. Pour boiling water into baking pan around dishes, reaching halfway up the sides of dishes (about 1 inch deep).

4. Bake the custards for 30 to 35 minutes or until a knife inserted near the center of each custard comes out clean. Remove custards from baking pan; cool on wire rack. Cover and chill at least 1 hour or up to 8 hours.

5. Before serving, remove custards from refrigerator; let stand at room temperature for 20 minutes. Meanwhile, prepare Caramelized Sugar. Quickly drizzle the caramelized sugar over custards in desired pattern. If sugar starts to harden, return skillet to heat, stirring until melted. Makes 8 servings.

Caramelized Sugar: Place ⅓ cup sugar in a heavy skillet. Heat sugar over medium-high heat until it begins to melt. Do not stir. Once the sugar starts to melt, reduce heat to low and cook about 5 minutes more or until all of the sugar is melted and golden, stirring as needed with a wooden spoon.

Nutrition facts per serving: 178 cal., 10 g total fat (5 g sat. fat), 155 mg chol., 65 mg sodium, 19 g carbo., 0 g fiber, and 4 g pro. Daily Values: 9% vit. A, 1% vit. C, 8% calcium, and 2% iron.

Pear Ginger Flan

To make sure all the flans are done, check one in the middle and one that's in the back of the oven.

Prep: 45 minutes **Bake:** 50 minutes **Chill:** 4 hours

3	cups chopped, peeled pears	3	eggs, beaten
½	cup sugar	1½	cups half-and-half or light cream
⅓	cup water	⅓	cup sugar
2	Tbsp. shredded fresh ginger	1	recipe Cheese Crisps

1. In a heavy medium saucepan combine pears, the ½ cup sugar, the ⅓ cup water, and ginger. Bring to boiling; reduce heat. Cover and cook until pears are tender. Drain, reserving liquid. Discard pears and ginger. Return liquid to saucepan. Cook over medium-high heat about 10 minutes or until liquid is syrupy and reduced to ¼ cup. Quickly pour the syrup into four 6-ounce custard cups.

2. Preheat oven to 325° F. Place custard cups in a 2-quart square baking dish. Combine eggs, half-and-half or cream, and the ⅓ cup sugar. Pour over syrup in cups. Place baking dish on oven rack. Pour boiling water into dish around cups, reaching halfway up sides of cups (about 1 inch deep). Bake for 40 to 45 minutes or until a knife inserted near centers comes out clean. Remove cups from baking dish. Cool slightly on wire rack. Cover and chill for 4 to 24 hours.

3. To serve, unmold the flans onto dessert plates, scraping any remaining syrup in cups onto flans. Serve with cooled Cheese Crisps. Makes 4 servings.

Cheese Crisps: In a small bowl combine 2 tablespoons shredded white cheddar cheese and 2 tablespoons finely shredded Parmesan cheese. Using 1 tablespoon cheese mixture for each, place the shredded cheese on a nonstick baking sheet. Spread into 2-inch circles, spacing the circles about 2 inches apart. Bake in a 325° F oven for 10 to 12 minutes or just until the cheese begins to brown. Allow to cool on the baking sheet for 30 seconds, and then remove. Cool on a wire rack.

Nutrition facts per serving: 356 cal., 16 g total fat (9 g sat. fat), 200 mg chol., 129 mg sodium, 44 g carbo., 0 g fiber, and 9 g pro. Daily Values: 14% vit. A, 1% vit. C, 16% calcium, and 4% iron.

30 low fat Caramel Clementines

Clementines, tangerines, and Dancy tangerines are all types of Mandarin oranges that you can use interchangeably.

Prep: 10 minutes **Cook:** 20 minutes

6	clementines or other tangerine variety	2	Tbsp. Southern Comfort, orange liqueur, or orange juice
1	14½-oz. can apricot nectar (1¾ cups)		Pomegranate seeds (optional)
½	cup sugar		
	Dash ground red pepper (optional)		

1. Peel clementines and remove any of the fibrous strands of pith on the fruit. In a medium saucepan place clementines, apricot nectar, sugar, and, if desired, ground red pepper. Bring to boiling; reduce heat. Cover and simmer for 5 minutes. Using a slotted spoon, transfer fruit to six individual serving bowls.

2. Continue to gently boil apricot nectar mixture about 15 minutes or until thick and syrupy. Remove from heat. Stir Southern Comfort, orange liqueur, or juice into syrupy mixture. Spoon over fruit. If desired, sprinkle each serving with pomegranate seeds. Serve warm. Makes 6 servings.

Nutrition facts per serving: 151 cal., 0 g total fat (0 g sat. fat), 0 mg chol., 3 mg sodium, 36 g carbo., 2 g fiber, and 1 g pro. Daily Values: 35% vit. A, 44% vit. C, 2% calcium, and 2% iron.

Caramel Clementines

Chocolate-Cherry Cheesecake

To crush the cookies for the crust, put them into a resealable plastic bag, then press with a rolling pin.

Prep: 30 minutes **Bake:** 25 minutes
Cool: 2 hours **Chill:** 4 hours

½	cup dried cherries	⅓	cup sugar
¼	cup chocolate liqueur	1	Tbsp. all-purpose flour
1	8-oz. pkg. cream cheese, softened	1	egg
1	4½-oz. round Brie cheese, rind removed and cut up	1	egg yolk
		2	Tbsp. milk
		1	recipe Almond Crust

1. Preheat oven to 375° F. In a small bowl combine dried cherries and chocolate liqueur. Set aside.

2. For filling, in a large mixing bowl beat cream cheese, Brie, sugar, and flour with an electric mixer on medium speed until combined. Add egg and yolk all at once, beating on low speed just until combined. Stir in milk and undrained cherries.

3. Pour filling into Almond Crust-lined pan. Place on a shallow baking pan in the oven. Bake about 25 minutes or until center appears nearly set when gently shaken.

4. Cool in pan on a wire rack for 15 minutes. Loosen the crust from side of pan; cool 30 minutes more. Remove the side of the pan; cool cheesecake completely. Cover and chill at least 4 hours before serving. Makes 8 servings.

Almond Crust: In a medium bowl combine 1 cup crushed shortbread cookies (about 13 cookies) and ½ cup ground almonds. Stir in 3 tablespoons melted butter. Press the crumb mixture onto the bottom and about 2 inches up the side of a 7-inch springform pan or about 1 inch up the side of an 8-inch springform pan (use a measuring cup to press crumbs onto pan). Set pan aside.

Nutrition facts per serving: 400 cal., 27 g total fat (13 g sat. fat), 115 mg chol., 294 mg sodium, 28 g carbo., 2 g fiber, and 10 g pro. Daily Values: 16% vit. A, 9% calcium, and 8% iron.

Chocolate-Cherry Cheesecake

Serve this when you need a grand
finale. Dried cherries, chocolate
liqueur, and a little Brie offer taste
surprises that incite oohs and ahs.

Chocolate Tartlettes

Creamy, smooth mousse, made from
semisweet and milk chocolates,
nestles in rich tart pastries. Two bites
and one's gone.

Chocolate Tartlettes

If you're running a little behind, skip the petite tart shells and spoon the mousse onto shortbread cookies.

Prep: 35 minutes **Bake:** 20 minutes **Chill:** 1 hour

⅔ cup whipping cream
3 oz. semisweet or bittersweet chocolate, chopped
3 oz. milk chocolate, chopped

1 recipe Cream Cheese Tart Shells
Unsweetened cocoa powder (optional)

1. Preheat oven to 325° F. For filling, in a small saucepan bring the cream just to simmering over medium heat. Remove from heat. Add semisweet or bittersweet chocolate and milk chocolate; let stand for 2 minutes. Using a wooden spoon, stir until smooth and melted. Transfer to a medium bowl; cover and chill for 1 hour.

2. Beat chilled chocolate mixture with an electric mixer on medium speed until soft peaks form. Spoon into Cream Cheese Tart Shells. Cover and chill about 2 hours or until serving time.

3. If desired, just before serving, sprinkle tartlettes lightly with unsweetened cocoa powder. Makes 24 servings.

Cream Cheese Tart Shells: For pastry, in a medium mixing bowl combine ½ cup softened butter and one 3-ounce package softened cream cheese; beat until combined. Stir in ⅔ cup all-purpose flour. Press a slightly rounded teaspoon of pastry evenly onto the bottom and up the side of 24 ungreased 1¾-inch muffin cups. Bake for 20 to 25 minutes or until pastry is golden. Cool in pans for 5 minutes. Remove from pans. Carefully transfer to wire racks; cool completely.

Nutrition facts per serving: 139 cal., 11 g total fat (6 g sat. fat), 29 mg chol., 59 mg sodium, 8 g carbo., 0 g fiber, and 2 g pro. Daily Values: 7% vit. A, 2% calcium, and 3% iron.

WHAT TO DRINK?

■ After-dinner coffee, decaf or regular, becomes infinitely more compelling when you make it a bit stronger than usual and serve it in tiny demitasse cups.
■ Or, pour hot chocolate, again a little stronger, dusted with cocoa powder or powdered sugar.
■ Use petite glasses to serve liqueurs or sweet wines, such as moscato or vin santo.

---

low fat Winter Fruit Soup

No tricky timings to worrry about. Just cut up the fruit, cook a little while, and serve.

Prep: 20 minutes **Cook:** 12 minutes **Stand:** 1 hour

1 cup pinot gris wine or white grape juice
1 cup water
½ cup sugar
¼ cup dried cranberries
1 3-inch piece vanilla bean, split, or 1 tsp. vanilla
¼ to ½ tsp. ground white pepper (optional)

2 cups cut-up mixed fruit, such as fresh orange sections, halved kumquats, tangerine sections, and/or cored sliced pears
4 scoops lemon sorbet (optional)

1. In a small saucepan combine wine or juice, water, sugar, dried cranberries, vanilla bean (if using), and, if desired, white pepper. Cook and stir over medium heat until sugar dissolves and mixture comes to a boil. Remove from heat. If using, add vanilla. Cover and let stand 1 hour. Remove vanilla bean. Scrape seeds from vanilla bean pod and stir into soup mixture.

2. To serve, warm soup slightly. Divide fruit among four bowls. Divide warmed soup among bowls. If desired, add a small scoop of sorbet to each serving. Makes 4 servings.

Nutrition facts per serving: 228 cal., 0 g total fat (0 g sat. fat), 0 mg chol., 7 mg sodium, 48 g carbo., 3 g fiber, and 1 g pro. Daily Values: 2% vit. A, 43% vit. C, 3% calcium, and 3% iron.

Winter Fruit Soup

Sweetheart Shakes and
Chocolate Shortbread Bites

For a big-hearted end to Valentine's
dinner, give loved ones a chocolate
embrace with these rich, smooth
shakes and not-too-sweet cookies.

30 Sweetheart Shakes

Crème fraîche adds a creamy smoothness and tang.

Start to finish: 10 minutes

½ cup purchased crème fraîche or dairy sour cream

¼ cup dark, bittersweet, or triple chocolate-flavored syrup or ice-cream topping

1½ pints chocolate ice cream, softened

Ground cinnamon (optional)

1. Place crème fraîche or sour cream and chocolate syrup or ice-cream topping in a blender container. Cover and blend until smooth, stopping blender and scraping down sides as necessary.

2. Add ice cream and blend until smooth, scraping down sides. Divide among four small glasses. If desired, sprinkle with cinnamon. Serve immediately. Makes 4 servings.

Nutrition facts per serving: 337 cal., 20 g total fat (12 g sat. fat), 60 mg chol., 106 mg sodium, 40 g carbo., 2 g fiber, and 5 g pro. Daily Values: 8% vit. A, 2% vit. C, 14% calcium, and 7% iron.

30 Chocolate Shortbread Bites

Savor these with a great pot of coffee.

Prep: 15 minutes **Bake:** 12 minutes

1 cup all-purpose flour

⅓ cup packed brown sugar

¼ cup unsweetened cocoa powder

1 tsp. instant coffee crystals or ½ tsp. instant espresso coffee powder

½ tsp. ground cinnamon

½ cup butter

1 recipe Chocolate Glaze (optional)

1. Preheat oven to 325° F. In a medium bowl combine flour, brown sugar, cocoa powder, coffee powder, and cinnamon. Using a pastry blender, cut in butter until mixture resembles fine crumbs. With hands, knead dough until it forms a smooth ball.

2. On a lightly floured surface, roll dough ¼ inch thick (about 9x8-inch rectangle). Use various sizes of heart-shaped cookie cutters to cut out dough. Place 1 inch apart on an ungreased cookie sheet. Reroll as necessary.

3. Bake for 12 to 15 minutes or until edges are set and tops appear dry. Transfer cookies to a wire rack and let cool. If desired, dip one corner of each cookie into Chocolate Glaze. Transfer to a waxed-paper-lined cookie sheet. Let stand until chocolate sets. Makes about eighty 1-inch cookies.

Chocolate Glaze: In a small saucepan combine ½ cup semisweet chocolate pieces and 1 teaspoon shortening. Cook and stir over low heat until melted. Cool.

Nutrition facts per cookie: 21 cal., 1 g total fat (1 g sat. fat), 3 mg chol., 13 mg sodium, 2 g carbo., 0 g fiber, and 0 g pro. Daily Values: 1% iron.

Vanilla-Fudge Marble Cake

Prep: 25 minutes **Bake:** 50 minutes **Cool:** 15 minutes

¾ cup butter, softened

2 eggs

2¾ cups all-purpose flour

1½ tsp. baking powder

½ tsp. baking soda

½ tsp. salt

1½ cups sugar

2 tsp. vanilla

1¼ cups buttermilk or sour milk

⅔ cup chocolate-flavored syrup

1 recipe Semisweet Chocolate Icing

1. Allow butter and eggs to stand at room temperature for 30 minutes. Meanwhile, grease and lightly flour a 10-inch fluted tube pan. In a medium bowl stir together flour, baking powder, baking soda, and salt. Set aside.

2. Preheat oven to 350° F. In large mixing bowl beat butter with an electric mixer on low to medium speed about 30 seconds. Add sugar and vanilla; beat until fluffy. Add eggs, 1 at a time, beating on low to medium speed, for 1 minute after each addition and scraping bowl frequently. Alternately add flour mixture and buttermilk to butter mixture, beating on low speed after each addition just until combined. Reserve 2 cups batter. Pour remaining batter into the prepared pan.

3. In a small mixing bowl combine chocolate syrup and reserved 2 cups batter. Beat on low speed until combined. Pour chocolate batter over vanilla batter in pan. Do not mix.

4. Bake about 50 minutes or until wooden toothpick inserted near center comes out clean. Cool for 15 minutes on a wire rack. Remove from pan; cool completely on rack. Drizzle with Semisweet Chocolate Icing. Makes 12 servings.

Semisweet Chocolate Icing: In a small saucepan heat ½ cup semisweet chocolate pieces, 2 tablespoons butter, 1 tablespoon light-colored corn syrup, and ¼ teaspoon vanilla over low heat, stirring until chocolate is melted and mixture is smooth. Use immediately.

Nutrition facts per serving: 416 cal., 18 g total fat (10 g sat. fat), 75 mg chol., 400 mg sodium, 59 g carbo., 2 g fiber, and 5 g pro. Daily Values: 12% vit. A, 7% calcium, and 9% iron.

PHOTOGRAPHS: (TOP LEFT) © 2001 STOCKFOOD IMAGES. (TOP MIDDLE AND RIGHT) © 2001 GETTYONE IMAGES. (BOTTOM RIGHT) COLLEEN DUFFLEY. STORY: BEV BENNETT.

There's Something About Dairy

Adding some light dairy products to a smart diet was first seen as a way to lower blood pressure. Then researchers recognized a bounty of extra benefits as they developed and tested a diet plan for hypertension.

Rewards of the DASH (Dietary Approaches to Stop Hypertension) plan—based on a diet rich in low-fat dairy foods, whole grains, fruits, and vegetables—included the expected drop in blood pressure. As a bonus, the plan also improved levels of cholesterol and homocysteine—possible risk factors for heart disease and stroke. The DASH diet may also help people to stay lean, according to University of Tennessee (UT) studies.

Researchers, supported by the National Heart, Lung, and Blood Institute (NHLBI) of the National Institutes of Health, have been looking at the diet and its impact on health. But they still have questions about where all the DASH benefits come from.

"Dairy means increased protein, riboflavin, and calcium, so it's hard to key out which nutrients did the job. Any of those dairy components may have contributed to the blood-pressure effect," says Eva Obarzanek, Ph.D., research nutritionist with the NHLBI.

"The svelte factor may be linked to the calcium in dairy products," says UT's Michael Zemel, Ph.D. "Lack of calcium triggers the production of calcium-preserving hormones. Unfortunately, these hormones prevent your body from breaking down fat, plus they stimulate the production of more fat," Zemel says. "Non-dairy sources of calcium, such as white beans and broccoli, also may fight fat, but factors in dairy products besides calcium markedly enhance this effect. We have not yet identified the factors," he says.

DINE AND "DASH"

For a brochure detailing the DASH diet—with sample menus—call the National Heart, Lung, and Blood Institute (NHLBI) of the National Institutes of Health, 301/592-8573. The information also is available at the NHLBI Internet site at www.nhlbi.nih.gov/hbp/prevent/h_eating/h_eating.htm

The heart-healthy DASH eating plan includes the following recommendations:

Grains	7 to 8 servings / day
Vegetables	4 to 5 servings / day
Fruits	4 to 5 servings / day
Low-fat or fat-free dairy	2 to 3 servings / day
Meat/fish/poultry	2 or less servings / day
Nuts, seeds, dry beans	4 to 5 servings / week
Fats and oils	2 to 3 servings / day
Sweets	5 servings / week

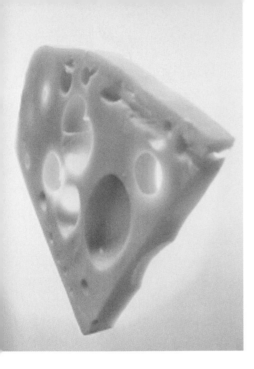

 30 low fat

Salmon Confetti Chowder

Start to finish: 25 minutes

2	cups frozen pepper stir-fry vegetables (yellow, green, and red peppers and onion)	2	cups refrigerated diced potatoes with onions
2	Tbsp. minced seeded jalapeño pepper	1	15-oz. can salmon, drained and flaked
1	Tbsp. butter or margarine	¼	cup snipped watercress
2	Tbsp. all-purpose flour	½	tsp. finely shredded lemon peel
2	cups fat-free milk	½	tsp. salt
1	cup fat-free half-and-half	½	tsp. ground black pepper

1. In a large saucepan cook stir-fry vegetables and jalapeño pepper in hot butter or margarine for 3 to 5 minutes or until tender. Stir in flour. Stir in milk and half-and-half. Cook and stir until slightly thickened. Cook and stir 2 minutes more.

2. Stir in diced potatoes, salmon, watercress, shredded lemon peel, salt, and black pepper. Cook and stir until chowder is heated through. Makes 4 servings.

Nutrition facts per serving: 349 cal., 10 g total fat (2 g sat. fat), 61 mg chol., 1,174 mg sodium, 33 g carbo., 3 g fiber, and 29 g pro. Daily Values: 11% vit. A, 25% vit. C, 42% calcium, and 8% iron.

30 low fat

Curried Sweet Potato Chowder

Start to finish: 30 minutes

2	tsp. butter or margarine
1⅓	cups ½-inch cubes peeled sweet potatoes
⅓	cup minced shallot (1 large)
½	tsp. curry powder
1	Tbsp. all-purpose flour
1½	cups fat-free milk
1	cup frozen baby peas
½	cup fat-free half-and-half
4	tsp. curried pumpkin seeds or pumpkin seeds
	Crackers (optional)

1. In a saucepan melt butter. Add sweet potatoes and shallot. Cook and stir over medium heat for 2 minutes. Add curry powder; cook and stir for 30 seconds. Stir in flour. Gradually stir in milk until smooth. Add peas and half-and-half; season with salt and pepper to taste. Cover and simmer about 15 minutes or until potatoes are tender.

2. Spoon the soup into four bowls. Sprinkle each serving with pumpkin seeds. If desired, serve with crackers. Makes 4 servings.

Nutrition facts per serving: 173 cal., 3 g total fat (0 g sat. fat), 2 mg chol., 293 mg sodium, 28 g carbo., 4 g fiber, and 8 g pro. Daily Values: 174% vit. A, 22% vit. C, 16% calcium, and 9% iron.

Curried Sweet Potato Chowder

The dairy-vegetable duo offers plenty of heart-healthy benefits in these 30-minute scrumptious chowders.

Bringing Out the Best in Beans

Soak 'em if you've got 'em. That's the secret to unlocking the soul-bracing, velvety richness hidden within dry beans.

There's no problem that water can't solve, and you'll give the H_2O a head start if you begin by presoaking your beans. You can soak them overnight in cold water, but boiling and soaking lets you proceed more quickly with your recipe. And, the boiling/soaking method has the added benefit of making the beans more digestible, say some cooking experts.

Once the soaked beans are in the pot and cooking is underway, keep an open ear. What you want to hear is silence, because the beans need to cook slowly to retain their shape and texture. If the lid is rattling or the water is boiling, they're cooking too fast and you run the danger of the beans sticking to the bottom of the pan and burning (something you really want to avoid).

The Beans and Greens recipe (opposite) calls for great northern beans, but the kind of beans you'll find on your supermarket shelf depends on where you live. That's why this recipe lets you use nearly any variety of dry bean. Keep in mind though, the darker the bean, the stronger the flavor. Begin testing for doneness after an hour of cooking. As long as you've presoaked them, the beans shouldn't have to cook more than 90 minutes.

When it comes to serving, it's strictly up to you and your family how much of the cooking liquid to serve with the beans. In the South, beans get ladled up with lots of the broth and served with a square of corn bread.

Beans and Greens

Prep: 10 minutes **Stand:** 1 hour **Cook:** 1¼ hours

½ lb. dry great northern beans, navy beans, pinto beans, or kidney beans (1 cup plus 2 Tbsp.)	4 slices bacon
	1 medium onion, chopped (½ cup)
6½ cups cold water	1 clove garlic, minced
1 14-oz. can reduced-sodium chicken broth	¼ tsp. crushed red pepper (optional)
1 bay leaf	4 cups torn fresh mustard greens or spinach
1 tsp. dried thyme, crushed	2 cups chopped tomato (optional)
¼ tsp. salt	
¼ tsp. ground black pepper	

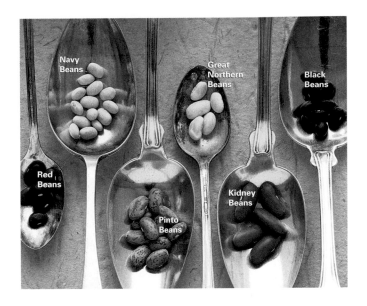

1. Rinse beans. In a large saucepan combine beans and 4 cups of the cold water. Bring to boiling; reduce heat. Simmer 2 minutes. Remove from heat. Cover; let stand 1 hour.

2. Drain and rinse beans. Return beans to the saucepan and add the 2½ cups fresh cold water, the chicken broth, bay leaf, thyme, salt, and black pepper. Bring to boiling; reduce heat. Cover and simmer about 1¼ hours or until beans are tender, stirring occasionally (see photo, below). (Add more water if needed to prevent the beans from sticking or burning.)

3. Meanwhile, in a skillet cook bacon over medium heat until crisp. Drain on paper towels, reserving 1 tablespoon drippings in skillet. Add onion, garlic, and, if desired, crushed red pepper. Cook and stir over medium heat until onion is tender.

4. Add greens and, if desired, tomato to skillet. Cover and cook for 1 to 2 minutes.

5. Drain beans; if desired, reserve liquid. Discard bay leaf. Return beans to saucepan. Add onion mixture, tossing gently to combine. Season with additional salt and black pepper. Spoon into serving bowl. Crumble bacon over top. If desired, pass reserved liquid. Makes 6 servings.

Nutrition facts per serving: 176 cal., 3 g total fat (1 g sat. fat), 4 mg chol., 355 mg sodium, 27 g carbo., 9 g fiber, and 12 g pro. Daily Values: 19% vit. A, 30% vit. C, 10% calcium, and 13% iron.

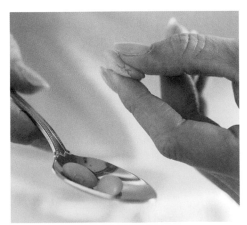

How do you know if beans are done? Pinch one, or try biting one (after cooling it under cold water). Either way, if you feel a hard core, cook an additional 10 to 15 minutes and try again.

A GUIDE TO BEANS

Red beans. Like the more familiar kidney bean, reds have a robust, full-bodied flavor, and soft texture. They hold their shape and firmness when cooked.

Navy beans. The name reflects the fact that it's been served to United States Navy sailors for more than 100 years. The bean has a mild flavor with powdery texture (and yes, it's still on ships' menus, says a Navy spokesperson).

Pinto beans. This relative of the kidney bean has a rich flavor. ("Pinto" is the Spanish word that means painted.)

Great northern beans. Popular in the Midwest, this medium-sized, white oval bean has a mild flavor with powdery texture. Navy beans are the best substitute.

Light red and dark red kidney beans. Kidney beans are noted for their robust, full-bodied flavor and soft texture. Lights and darks can be used interchangeably.

Black beans. The black's earthy sweet flavor comes with a hint of mushroom. These are also called Turtle beans.

March

BusyLivesEasyMeals

Plus...

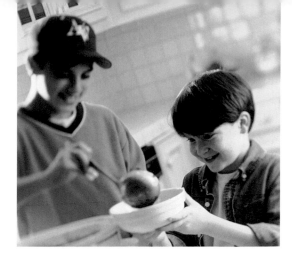

Hot, hearty, and comforting—those are the foods we share at home while we wait for the lion to turn into a lamb.

BusyLives**EasyMeals**

Psst. Want the secret to quick meal prep?
Smart kitchen appliances. These cooking
workhorses are easier than ever to use.
And, we've created convenient,
great-tasting recipes to prove it.

Garlicky Steak
and Asparagus

30 Garlicky Steak and Asparagus

One steak, a handful of fresh asparagus, and less than five minutes on the grill are all it takes to whip up this feast for two.

Prep: 15 minutes **Grill:** 3 minutes

1	12- to 14-oz. boneless beef top loin (strip) steak, cut about ¾ inch thick
1	or 2 large cloves garlic, coarsely chopped
½	tsp. cracked or coarsely ground black pepper
¼	tsp. salt
8	to 10 thin asparagus spears, trimmed (6 oz.)
2	tsp. garlic-flavored olive oil or olive oil
½	cup beef broth
1	Tbsp. dry white wine
¼	tsp. Dijon-style mustard

Indoor grill method:

1. Rub steak on both sides with a mixture of garlic, pepper, and salt. Place asparagus in shallow dish; drizzle with the oil.

2. For sauce, in medium skillet stir together broth and wine. Cook over high heat for 4 to 5 minutes or until mixture is reduced to ¼ cup. Whisk in mustard; keep warm.

3. Preheat an indoor electric grill. Place steak on grill rack. If using a covered grill, close lid. Grill until steak is desired doneness. (For a covered grill, allow 3 to 4 minutes for medium rare or 5 to 7 minutes for medium. For an uncovered grill, allow 6 to 8 minutes for medium rare or 8 to 10 minutes for medium, turning steak once.) If space allows, add asparagus to covered grill the last 2 to 3 minutes of grilling. Or, for uncovered grill, add asparagus for the last 4 to 5 minutes. Cook the asparagus just until crisp-tender.*

4. Spoon sauce onto plate. If desired, cut steak in half crosswise; stack atop sauce. Top with asparagus. Makes 2 servings.

Conventional method: Prepare steak and asparagus as in Step 1. Place steak on unheated rack of a broiler pan. Broil 3 to 4 inches from heat for 8 to 10 minutes for medium rare or 10 to 12 minutes for medium, turning once and adding asparagus the last 2 minutes of broiling. Serve as above.

*Note: For smaller grills, you can grill the asparagus after the steak. Grill for 2 to 5 minutes or until crisp tender.

Nutrition facts per serving: 458 cal., 32 g total fat (11 g sat. fat), 110 mg chol., 549 mg sodium, 3 g carbo., 1 g fiber, and 37 g pro. Daily Values: 2% vit. A, 37% vit. C, 3% calcium, and 19% iron.

Deluxe Chicken and Roasted Pepper Sandwich
recipe on page 48

INDOOR GRILL

Portable, table-top indoor grills may be covered or uncovered. Below are some of the differences you may find.

COVERED INDOOR GRILL

Covered grills typically have a hinged lid, and foods are cooked with the lid closed. Therefore, foods are heated from the top and bottom, and cook more quickly than they would on an uncovered grill. Boneless cuts of meat work best on these grills because you can cover them tightly.

From our Test Kitchen expert, Marilyn Cornelius: "I didn't think I would like this appliance when we first got one in the Test Kitchen, but I found out how easy and quick it was for grilling and I fell in love with it."

UNCOVERED INDOOR GRILL

Just as it sounds, the uncovered grill is open. Foods are heated from the bottom only, so tend to cook slower than on a covered grill. You'll find interchangeable grill and griddle plates on some models; others feature extras such as heat indicators that light up when the grill reaches the ideal cooking temperature. You can use these timings for stove-top grills as well.

From our Test Kitchen expert, Colleen Weeden: "Once the grill is preheated, you can grill just about anything small. I love using my indoor grill to toast bread for sandwiches—no messing with lighting coals and setting up the grill."

Quick Grilled Herbed Ratatouille and Polenta

This dish is a whole meal when spooned over grilled polenta slices. For a meatier supper, grill smoked sausages along with the vegetables.

Prep: 25 minutes **Grill:** 17 minutes

½	of a small eggplant (about 6 oz.)	½	tsp. salt
1	small zucchini (about 4 oz.)	½	tsp. cracked black pepper
1	small fennel bulb (about 6 oz.)	1	16-oz. tube plain refrigerated cooked polenta, cut into 12 slices
¼	cup olive oil		
2	tsp. snipped fresh rosemary	1	14½-oz. can diced tomatoes with garlic and onion

Indoor grill method:

1. If desired, peel eggplant. Slice eggplant, zucchini, and fennel crosswise into ¼-inch-thick slices (see photo, below). In a small bowl combine oil, rosemary, salt, and pepper. Brush vegetables with about half of the oil mixture, reserving remaining oil mixture.

2. Preheat an uncovered indoor electric grill. Arrange half of the vegetables on grill rack. Grill for 6 to 8 minutes or until crisp-tender and grill marks appear, turning once. Remove from grill rack; set aside. Repeat with remaining vegetables.

3. Brush polenta with reserved oil mixture. Place polenta on grill rack. Grill for 5 to 10 minutes or until heated through and lightly browned, turning once.

4. Meanwhile, in saucepan heat undrained tomatoes until boiling. Add grilled vegetables. Simmer, uncovered, 5 minutes or until desired consistency, stirring occasionally.

5. To serve, place polenta slices in four shallow bowls; spoon the vegetable mixture over polenta. Makes 4 servings.

Conventional method: Prepare vegetables and oil mixture as in Step 1. Preheat a grill pan or skillet over medium-high heat. Cook half of the vegetables as in Step 2; repeat with remaining vegetables. Use the grill pan to grill polenta slices as in Step 3. Continue as in Step 4. Serve as above.

Nutrition facts per serving: 275 cal., 14 g total fat (2 g sat. fat), 0 mg chol., 1,247 mg sodium, 33 g carbo., 13 g fiber, and 6 g pro. Daily Values: 3% vit. A, 23% vit. C, 4% calcium, and 9% iron.

For fennel, carefully cut about 1 inch above the bulb. Discard the stalks, saving some of the feathery leaves for a garnish.

Deluxe Chicken and Roasted Pepper Sandwich

This recipe works well on either a covered or uncovered indoor grill since the chicken cooks quickly and remains juicy. Pictured on page 47.

Prep: 15 minutes **Marinate:** 15 minutes **Grill:** 4 minutes

¼	cup olive oil	¼	cup semisoft cheese with herbs or semisoft goat cheese (chèvre)
4	tsp. red wine vinegar		
1	Tbsp. snipped fresh thyme	1	cup roasted red sweet peppers (about one 7-oz. jar), cut into strips
½	tsp. salt		
¼	tsp. crushed red pepper		
4	skinless, boneless chicken breast halves (about 1¼ lb.)	½	cup fresh basil, watercress, or baby spinach leaves
4	1-inch-thick bias-cut slices Italian bread		

Indoor grill method:

1. For marinade, whisk together oil, vinegar, thyme, salt, and crushed red pepper. Reserve 2 tablespoons; set aside.

2. Place chicken between two sheets of plastic wrap; pound lightly with a meat mallet to about ½-inch thickness (see photo, page 81). Place in a plastic bag; add remaining marinade. Seal bag; marinate at room temperature about 15 minutes or in the refrigerator for up to 1 hour.

3. Lightly grease the rack of an indoor electric grill or lightly coat with nonstick cooking spray. Preheat grill. Brush cut sides of bread with reserved marinade. Place bread, cut sides down, on grill rack. If using a covered grill, close the lid. Grill until lightly toasted. (For a covered grill, allow 1 to 2 minutes. For an uncovered grill, allow 2 to 4 minutes, turning once halfway through grilling.) Remove bread from grill; set aside.

4. Drain chicken, discarding marinade. Place chicken on grill rack. If using a covered grill, close the lid. Grill until chicken is tender and no longer pink. (For covered grill, allow 3 to 4 minutes. For an uncovered grill, allow 8 to 10 minutes, turning once halfway through grilling.) Remove from grill; spread or sprinkle with semisoft cheese.

5. To serve, place one chicken breast on each bread slice. Top with roasted pepper strips and basil. Makes 4 servings.

Conventional method: Prepare marinade and chicken as in Steps 1 and 2. Toast bread slices in a skillet or grill pan or on a griddle over medium heat for 2 to 4 minutes, turning once. Remove bread from pan or griddle. Place chicken in the skillet, grill pan, or on the griddle. Cook over medium heat for 8 to 10 minutes or until tender and no longer pink, turning once. Remove from pan; spread or sprinkle with cheese. Serve as above.

Nutrition facts per serving: 418 cal., 20 g total fat (5 g sat. fat), 82 mg chol., 629 mg sodium, 21 g carbo., 2 g fiber, and 37 g pro. Daily Values: 5% vit. A, 177% vit. C, 5% calcium, and 14% iron.

Quick Grilled Herbed Ratatouille and Polenta

Wow! Look at those gorgeous grill marks. Who knew you could grill polenta on an indoor grill? We just had to try, and think you'll love the hearty result. Our Mediterranean mélange starts with purchased polenta, which we sliced and grilled with zucchini, fennel, and eggplant.

Beef and Red Bean Chili

Hey, no blaming this chili if you're late for piano lessons or soccer practice. It's ready when you walk through the door. Laced with chipotle peppers for smoky kicks, we like it served with a handful of soup crackers.

Beef and Red Bean Chili

Chipotle (smoked jalapeño peppers) in adobo sauce is doubly delicious. The jalapeño provides a direct hit of heat, while the adobo sauce is a slow burn. Together, they leave a warm glow.

Prep: 1¼ hours **Cook:** 5 or 10 hours

1	cup dry red beans or kidney beans	1	or 2 chipotle chili peppers in adobo sauce, finely chopped, plus 2 tsp. adobo sauce
1	Tbsp. olive oil	2	tsp. dried oregano, crushed
2	lb. boneless beef chuck, cut into 1-inch cubes	1	tsp. ground cumin
1	large onion, coarsely chopped	½	tsp. salt
1	15-oz. can tomato sauce	1	medium red sweet pepper, chopped
1	14½-oz. can diced tomatoes with mild chilies	¼	cup snipped fresh cilantro
1	14-oz. can beef broth		

Crockery cooker method:

1. Rinse beans; place in large saucepan. Add water to cover. Bring to boiling; reduce heat. Simmer, uncovered, for 10 minutes. Remove from heat. Cover and let stand 1 hour.

2. In a skillet heat oil over medium-high heat. Cook half of the beef and all of the onion until mixture is lightly browned. Transfer to a 3½- or 4-quart crockery cooker. Repeat with remaining beef. Add tomato sauce, undrained tomatoes, broth, chipotle peppers and adobo sauce, oregano, cumin, and salt. Stir until combined. Drain and rinse beans. Stir into cooker.

3. Cover and cook on low-heat setting for 10 to 12 hours or high-heat setting for 5 to 6 hours or until meat and beans are tender (see photo, page 43). Serve with red sweet pepper and cilantro. Makes 6 servings.

Conventional method: Prepare beans as in Step 1, except use a 4- to 5-quart Dutch oven. Drain and rinse beans; set aside. Brown beef and onion as in Step 2, except use Dutch oven. Return all meat to pan. Stir in the tomato sauce, undrained tomatoes, broth, chipotle peppers and adobo sauce, oregano, cumin, salt, and beans. Bring to boiling; reduce heat. Cover and simmer for 1½ to 2 hours or until meat and beans are tender (see photo, page 43). Serve as above.

Nutrition facts per serving: 516 cal., 26 g total fat (9 g sat. fat), 98 mg chol., 1,162 mg sodium, 32 g carbo., 8 g fiber, and 38 g pro. Daily Values: 34% vit. A, 91% vit. C, 7% calcium, and 34% iron.

Tangy Barbecue Beef
recipe on page 52

CROCKERY COOKERS

Today, most crockery cookers are continuous slow cookers—they cook foods slowly and continuously at a low wattage via heating coils that wrap around the sides and remain on during cooking. Continuous cookers have fixed settings: low (200° F) or high (300 F). Our recipes are designed for continuous cookers and will not work in intermittent cookers. (Intermittent cookers have dials indicating the temperature in degrees and heat with coils below the food that cycle on and off.) Crockery cookers range in size from 1 to 6 quarts. Be sure your crockery cooker is the right size for the recommendation in the recipe so the food will cook properly. For best results, fill the crockery cooker at least half full, but no more than two-thirds full. For most recipes, you do not need to stir. Lifting the lid to stir can lower the cooker temperature and prolong the cooking time.

From our Test Kitchen expert, Judy Comstock: "The crockery cookers with removable liners are my favorite. They're so easy to clean."

Tangy Barbecue Beef

Freeze any remaining beef in a tightly covered freezer container for up to three months. Pictured on page 51.

Prep: 25 minutes **Cook:** 10 hours **Stand:** 15 minutes

2	Tbsp. chili powder	½	cup beer or ginger ale
1	tsp. celery seed	8	large sandwich buns or
½	tsp. salt		Portuguese rolls, split
½	tsp. ground black pepper		and toasted
1	3-lb. fresh beef brisket,		Bottled hot pepper sauce
	trimmed of fat		(optional)
2	onions, thinly sliced		Mango slices
1	cup bottled		
	smoke-flavored		
	barbecue sauce		

Crockery cooker method:

1. In a small bowl combine chili powder, celery seed, salt, and pepper. Rub the spice mixture onto all sides of the brisket. Scatter half of the sliced onions in the bottom of a 3½- to 6-quart crockery cooker. Place the brisket on the onions, cutting the meat to fit the cooker, if necessary. Scatter remaining onions on top of the brisket. In small bowl stir together barbecue sauce and beer or ginger ale. Pour over brisket and onions.

2. Cover and cook on low-heat setting for 10 to 12 hours or until meat is fork-tender. Transfer meat to cutting board; let stand 15 minutes. Halve meat crosswise. Using 2 forks, pull meat into shreds. Return meat to sauce mixture in cooker. Heat sauce through using the high-heat setting.

3. To serve, use a slotted spoon to fill buns with beef mixture. If desired, season with bottled hot pepper sauce. Top with mango. Makes 8 servings.

Conventional method: Preheat oven to 325° F. Combine the seasoning mixture and rub onto brisket as in Step 1. Place meat in a shallow roasting pan. Top with all the sliced onions; pour a mixture of barbecue sauce and beer over meat. Cover and roast about 3 hours or until meat is fork tender. Remove meat; let stand 15 minutes. Halve meat crosswise and shred. Pour sauce into saucepan; add meat. Heat through. Serve as above.

Nutrition facts per serving: 442 cal., 11 g total fat (3 g sat. fat), 98 mg chol., 971 mg sodium, 41 g carbo., 3 g fiber, and 41 g pro. Daily Values: 36% vit. A, 16% vit. C, 9% calcium, and 28% iron.

Spicy Lamb Shanks

Infused with orange and aromatic spices, this dish is the perfect warming supper for chilly March days.

Prep: 25 minutes **Cook:** 8 hours

2	large oranges	4	large cloves garlic,
1¼	cups beef broth		thinly sliced
1½	tsp. ground cardamom	4	lb. lamb foreshanks
1	tsp. ground cumin		(3 or 4)
½	tsp. salt	2	3-inch cinnamon sticks
½	tsp. ground turmeric	2	Tbsp. water
½	tsp. pepper	4	tsp. cornstarch
5	carrots, cut into	⅓	cup pitted kalamata or
	2-inch lengths		other black olives,
1½	cups boiling onions,		halved, if desired
	peeled*	1	Tbsp. snipped fresh
			cilantro

Spicy Lamb Shanks

Entertaining after work? Then this Moroccan-inspired potage is for you. It's simple, savory, and luxe in the looks department. Better still, it cooks to fork-tender, melt-in-your-mouth perfection while you're at the office. Your guests will love the heady flavor bursts from fresh oranges, lots of garlic, cumin, turmeric, cardamom, and kalamata olives.

Crockery cooker method:

1. Using a vegetable peeler, remove orange part of peel from an orange. Cut into thin strips (about ¼ cup); set aside. Squeeze juice from oranges to make about ⅔ cup. Stir together juice, broth, cardamom, cumin, salt, turmeric, and pepper. Set aside.

2. Place carrots, onions, and garlic in 5- to 6-quart crockery cooker. Top with lamb shanks, cinnamon sticks, and orange peel. Pour orange juice mixture over all. Cover and cook on low-heat setting for 8 to 9 hours or until lamb pulls easily from bone.

3. To serve, use a slotted spoon to transfer lamb shanks and vegetables to serving dish. Skim fat from cooking liquid. Remove and discard cinnamon sticks. Measure 1½ cups juices; transfer to small saucepan. Combine water and cornstarch; add to juices. Cook and stir over medium heat until thickened and bubbly. Cook and stir 2 minutes more. Spoon sauce over lamb. Sprinkle with olives and cilantro. Makes 4 to 6 servings.

Conventional method: Prepare orange peel and orange juice mixture as in Step 1. Place lamb shanks in bottom of 5- to 6-quart Dutch oven. Top with cinnamon sticks and orange peel. Pour the orange juice mixture over all. Bring to boiling; reduce heat. Cover and simmer for 1 hour. Top with carrots, onions, and garlic. Cover and simmer for 30 minutes to 1 hour longer or until meat and vegetables are tender. Continue as in Step 3, except prepare and thicken the sauce using a Dutch oven. Serve as directed.

*Test Kitchen Tip: To make it easier to peel boiling onions, place the onions in a saucepan with water. Bring to boiling and cook for 30 seconds. When cool enough to handle, slice off the root ends of onions and squeeze the onions from their peels.

Nutrition facts per serving: 461 cal., 21 g total fat (8 g sat. fat), 150 mg chol., 760 mg sodium, 22 g carbo., 6 g fiber, and 44 g pro. Daily Values: 538% vit. A, 38% vit. C, 9% calcium, and 24% iron.

PRESSURE COOKERS

In these pots, food cooks on the stove top in a sealed environment, trapping steam and building up pressure so liquids become about 38° F hotter than boiling, or 250° F. The higher temperature translates to faster cooking. In a pressure cooker, foods actually cook three to ten times faster than ordinary cooking methods. Follow the manufacturer's directions when filling and opening the pan. You don't want the release of steam to burn you. The best kinds of foods to cook in a pressure cooker are those that cook well in moist heat at a fairly high temperature without losing quality: pot roasts, vegetables, chicken, and stews. From our Test Kitchen expert, Jennifer Kalinowski: "I was always afraid of pressure cookers, because of the steam. But, after using one, I discovered how safe and easy they are to use. Our recipes are flavorful and cook in minutes."

Sicilian Artichokes

Jamaican Pork Stew

It's 5:30 p.m., you've had one tough day, and you're tired of takeout. How about Jamaican Pork Stew? Isn't it amazing what a little pressure (à la pressure cooker) can do—this spicy one-dish dinner cooks in eight minutes and trades the typical potatoes and carrots for sweet potatoes and plantains.

Jamaican Pork Stew

Until recently, plantains and yuca were produce items found only in Latino markets and American border towns. With the interest in foods of Central and South America, these starches are now in practically every well-stocked supermarket.

Prep: 40 minutes **Cook:** 6 minutes (at pressure)

1	small yuca or white potato (about 12 oz.), peeled	1	to 1½ tsp. Jamaican jerk seasoning
2	Tbsp. olive oil	½	tsp. salt
1½	lb. boneless pork loin, cut into 1-inch cubes	2	large sweet potatoes (about 24 oz. total), peeled and cut into ½- to 1-inch cubes
1	plantain, peeled and cut into ¾-inch-thick slices	1¼	cups chicken broth
1	large onion, sliced	½	cup dried apricots, halved
3	cloves garlic, minced		

Pressure cooker method:

1. Halve yuca lengthwise; discard fibrous center. Cut into 1-inch pieces; set aside.

2. Remove rack from a 6-quart pressure cooker. Heat oil in pressure cooker. Cook and stir pork, plantain, and onion, half at a time, in hot oil over medium-high heat until lightly browned. Return all pork mixture to pan. Add garlic, jerk seasoning, and the ½ teaspoon salt. Cook and stir for 30 seconds. Add yuca, sweet potatoes, broth, and apricots to cooker.

3. Cover and lock lid in place. Bring up to pressure over high heat. Reduce heat just enough to maintain pressure. Cook 6 minutes. Quick-release pressure. Carefully remove lid. Season to taste with salt and pepper. Makes 6 servings.

Conventional method: Prepare yuca as in Step 1. Heat oil in Dutch oven; cook and stir pork, plantain, and onion, half at a time, in hot oil over medium-high heat until lightly browned. Return all of the pork mixture to pan. Add garlic, jerk seasoning, and ½ teaspoon salt; cook and stir for 30 seconds. Add only 1 cup broth. Bring to boiling; reduce heat. Cover and simmer for 30 minutes. Stir in yuca, sweet potatoes, and apricots. Return to boiling; reduce heat. Cover and simmer for 20 to 30 minutes or until meat is tender.

Nutrition facts per serving: 480 cal., 11 g total fat (3 g sat. fat), 62 mg chol., 566 mg sodium, 65 g carbo., 6 g fiber, and 31 g pro. Daily Values: 434% vit. A, 91% vit. C, 6% calcium, and 14% iron.

Sicilian Artichokes

This is a classic Sicilian Lenten dish both because it is meatless and because artichokes are in season during this time of year.

Prep: 45 minutes **Cook:** 8 minutes (at pressure)

3	cups onion and/or garlic croutons	1	Tbsp. snipped fresh oregano or 1 tsp. dried oregano, crushed
½	cup finely chopped red or yellow sweet pepper	1	Tbsp. balsamic vinegar
½	cup shredded mozzarella cheese (2 oz.)	¼	tsp. salt
¼	cup finely shredded Parmesan cheese	¼	tsp. freshly ground black pepper
4	anchovy fillets, rinsed, patted dry, and finely chopped (optional)	¼	to ⅓ cup chicken broth
		4	large artichokes (about 10 oz. each)
2	Tbsp. olive oil	2	Tbsp. lemon juice
		1	cup water

Pressure cooker method:

1. For filling, in a large bowl coarsely crush croutons. Add sweet pepper, mozzarella and Parmesan cheeses, and, if desired, anchovies. In small bowl combine oil, oregano, vinegar, salt, and pepper; drizzle over crouton mixture. Stir in enough broth for desired moistness. Set aside.

2. Wash artichokes; trim stems and remove loose outer leaves. Cut off 1 inch from top of each artichoke; snip off leaf tips with kitchen scissors. Brush edges with some of the lemon juice. Thump artichokes, point sides down, on countertop and centers will open to expose yellow center leaves and chokes. Pull outer leaves away from center leaves. Scoop out inner yellow leaves and fuzzy centers. Brush insides with remaining lemon juice. Spoon filling into artichokes, packing lightly.

3. Pour water into a 6-quart pressure cooker. (Recipe works best in a stainless steel pressure cooker. Artichokes tend to discolor with aluminum.) Place artichokes, stuffing sides up, on rack in pressure cooker.

4. Cover and lock lid in place. Bring up to pressure over high heat (allow about 10 minutes). Adjust heat for moderate cooking. Cook 8 minutes. Quick-release pressure. Carefully remove lid. Pass additional oil for drizzling. Makes 4 servings.

Conventional method: Prepare artichokes as through Step 2. Place artichokes, stuffing sides up, in a 4- to 5-quart stainless steel or enamel-coated Dutch oven. Add 1½ cups water to pan. Bring to boiling; reduce heat. Cover and simmer for 25 to 30 minutes or until leaf pulls out easily. Carefully remove with tongs. Serve as above.

Nutrition facts per serving: 418 cal., 16 g total fat (4 g sat. fat), 14 mg chol., 1,089 mg sodium, 55 g carbo., 19 g fiber, and 24 g pro. Daily Values: 24% vit. A, 113% vit. C, 29% calcium, and 19% iron.

DEEP FRYERS

What's not to like? Today's deep fryers are easy to use and, better yet, easy to clean. Tightly sealing covers eliminate the messy spatters and reduce the odors of regular frying. Many models even have extra-large viewing windows, so you can watch foods fry without opening the cover.

From our Test Kitchen expert, Jill Moberly: "I never liked frying until I tried the newer fryers. Once your oil is preheated, you simply add the food, shut the lid, and you're frying. I also love not having to use a thermometer to monitor the heat."

new Egg Rolls

Prep: 25 minutes **Cook:** 2 minutes per batch

8 egg roll skins	1⅓ cups bottled sweet-and-sour sauce or ½ cup prepared Chinese-style hot mustard
1 recipe Pork Filling	
Cooking oil for deep frying	

Deep fryer method:

1. For each egg roll, place an egg roll skin on a flat surface with a corner pointing toward you. Spoon about ¼ cup of the Pork Filling across and just below center of egg roll skin. Fold bottom corner over filling, tucking it under on the other side. Fold the side corners over filling, forming an envelope shape. Roll egg roll toward remaining corner. Moisten top corner with water; press firmly to seal.

2. Heat oil in electric deep-fryer according to manufacturer's directions. Fry egg rolls, a few at a time, for 2 to 3 minutes or until golden brown. Remove with slotted spoon; drain on paper towels. Keep warm in 300° F oven while frying remaining egg rolls. Serve with sweet-and-sour sauce or hot mustard. Makes 8 egg rolls.

Conventional method: Prepare egg rolls as in Step 1. For frying, use heavy 3-quart saucepan filled with about 2 inches cooking oil. Attach a deep-fat frying thermometer to side of saucepan. Heat oil over medium heat to 365° F. Fry egg rolls as in Step 2. Serve as above.

Pork Filling: In skillet cook ½ pound ground pork, 1 teaspoon grated fresh ginger, and 1 clove minced garlic for 2 to 3 minutes or until meat is brown; drain fat. Add ½ cup finely chopped bok choy or cabbage, ½ cup chopped water chestnuts, ½ cup shredded carrot, and ¼ cup finely chopped onion. Cook and stir for 2 minutes. In a small bowl combine 2 tablespoons soy sauce, 2 teaspoons cornstarch, ½ teaspoon sugar, and ¼ teaspoon salt; add to skillet. Cook and stir for 1 minute more. Cool slightly.

Nutrition facts per egg roll: 240 cal., 3 g total fat (1 g sat. fat), 16 mg chol., 794 mg sodium, 44 g carbo., 1 g fiber, and 9 g pro. Daily Values: 46% vit. A, 17% vit. C, 8% calcium, and 10% iron.

Zesty Ravioli Salad

Any flavor ravioli tastes great. Your choice. We especially like the ones with multiple cheeses.

Prep: 25 minutes **Cook:** 2 minutes per batch

1 9-oz. pkg. refrigerated ravioli (any flavor)	1 cup halved or quartered cherry tomatoes
1 cup seasoned fine dry bread crumbs	¼ cup torn fresh basil
¼ cup whole milk, half-and-half, or light cream	¼ cup bottled balsamic vinaigrette or Italian vinaigrette
1 egg, slightly beaten	Finely shredded Parmesan cheese
Cooking oil for deep frying	
6 cups torn mixed salad greens	

Deep fryer method:

1. In a large saucepan cook ravioli in salted boiling water for 3 minutes; drain well. Place bread crumbs in a shallow dish. In another shallow dish stir together milk and egg until combined. Dip ravioli into egg mixture, then into bread crumb mixture. Cover and chill while oil heats.

2. Heat oil in electric deep-fryer according to manufacturer's directions. Fry ravioli, half at a time, about 2 minutes or until golden. Remove with slotted spoon; drain on paper towels. Keep warm in 300° F oven.

3. Meanwhile, for salad, in a large bowl combine greens, tomatoes, and basil. Add vinaigrette; toss to coat. Divide among serving plates. Top with ravioli. Sprinkle with Parmesan cheese. Pass additional vinaigrette. Makes 4 main-dish servings.

Conventional method: Prepare ravioli as in Step 1. For frying, use heavy 3-quart saucepan filled with about 2 inches cooking oil. Attach deep-fat frying thermometer to side of pan. Heat oil over medium heat to 365° F. Carefully add ravioli to oil, 4 or 5 at a time (do not add too many at once or oil temperature will drop). Fry about 2 minutes or until golden. Remove with a slotted spoon; drain on paper towels and keep warm. Continue as in Step 3.

Nutrition facts per serving: 520 cal., 28 g total fat (6 g sat. fat), 118 mg chol., 1,215 mg sodium, 49 g carbo., 2 g fiber, and 19 g pro. Daily Values: 17% vit. A, 22% vit. C, 17% calcium, and 18% iron.

Zesty Ravioli Salad

Sometimes you crave that delicious deep-fried flavor. Zesty Ravioli Salad provides it with quick help from convenient new fryers—they're a cinch to use, cleanup is simple, and there's no lingering "just-fried" smell. Pass the dressing, please.

30 Oriental Cashew Asparagus
Prep: 20 minutes **Cook:** 6 minutes

1 lb. asparagus spears	1 Tbsp. butter or
1½ cups quartered fresh	margarine
button mushrooms	1 tsp. cornstarch
1 medium red onion,	¼ tsp. ground black pepper
cut into thin wedges	2 Tbsp. teriyaki sauce
¼ cup chopped red	1 Tbsp. water
sweet pepper	2 Tbsp. cashew halves

Tabletop steamer method:

1. Snap off and discard woody bases from asparagus (see photo, page 63). If desired, scrape off scales. Bias-slice asparagus into 1-inch pieces (you should have 3 cups).

2. Place asparagus in bottom of steamer basket. Steam the asparagus according to manufacturer's directions for 2 minutes. Carefully add mushrooms, onion, and sweet pepper. Steam for 2 to 5 minutes more or until vegetables are crisp-tender.

3. Meanwhile, in a medium saucepan melt butter or margarine; stir in cornstarch and black pepper. Add the teriyaki sauce and water. Cook and stir until thickened and bubbly. Add vegetables to saucepan; toss gently to coat. Top with cashews. Makes 4 servings.

Conventional method: Prepare asparagus as in Step 1. In a medium saucepan bring 1 cup water to boiling; reduce heat. Place asparagus in a steamer basket. Place steamer basket in saucepan. Cover and steam asparagus, and then mushrooms, onion, and sweet pepper as in Step 2. Remove basket; discard liquid. In the same saucepan melt butter or margarine. Continue as in step 3. Serve as above.

Nutrition facts per serving: 105 cal., 6 g total fat (2 g sat. fat), 8 mg chol., 381 mg sodium, 11 g carbo., 3 g fiber, and 5 g pro. Daily Values: 23% vit. A, 46% vit. C, 3% calcium, and 9% iron.

30 Lime-Steamed Salmon
Prep: 15 minutes **Cook:** 12 minutes

2 limes	⅛ tsp. pepper
1 1-lb. salmon fillet (about	2 Tbsp. toasted sesame oil
1 inch thick), skinned	2 cups trimmed small
and cut into 3 pieces	green beans (about 8 oz.)
1 Tbsp. grated fresh ginger	or one 9-oz. pkg. frozen
⅛ tsp. salt	French-cut green beans

Tabletop steamer method:

1. Shred 2 teaspoons of peel from limes; set aside. Thinly slice limes; place slices in bottom of steamer basket. Rinse fish; pat dry. Place fish in a single layer on top of lime slices. Stir reserved lime peel, ginger, salt, and pepper into oil; brush onto fish.

2. Place the fresh or frozen beans in the upper section of steamer container. Steam the fish and beans according to manufacturer's directions for 12 to 15 minutes or until fish flakes easily when tested with a fork and beans are crisp-tender. Arrange beans in serving dish; top with fish. Makes 3 servings.

Conventional method: Prepare limes, fish, and oil mixture as in Step 1. In a medium saucepan cover and cook fresh or frozen green beans in a small amount of boiling salted water about 15 minutes for fresh beans (5 to 6 minutes for frozen beans). Drain. Meanwhile, in a very large skillet bring 4 cups water to boiling; reduce heat. Place lime slices and fish in a steamer basket. Brush fish with oil mixture. Place steamer basket in skillet. Cover and steam about 10 minutes or until fish flakes easily when tested with a fork. Serve as above.

Nutrition facts per serving: 293 cal., 14 g total fat (2 g sat. fat), 78 mg chol., 204 mg sodium, 11 g carbo., 4 g fiber, and 32 g pro. Daily Values: 13% vit. A, 42% vit. C, 6% calcium, and 12% iron.

Lime-Steamed Salmon

Our Test Kitchen experts loved using a table-top steamer. Sure, they knew it could cook perfect rice, but they were blown away by the moist salmon and crisp-tender beans.

Flex Your Mussels

Don't be shy; show your mussels. Steamed fresh mussels, that is. Fresh mussels are becoming more available throughout the country and are especially popular in soups, appetizers, and pastas. If you buy fresh mussels, scrub them well and remove the beards that are visable between the shells. Then try them in this simple appetizer and favorite seafood soup.

Mussels Steamed in Wine
Use any leftovers as a delicious stir-in for marinated salads, pastas, or fish stews.

Prep: 1 hour **Cook:** 6 minutes

- 1 lb. live mussels
- 4 qt. cold water
- ⅓ cup salt
- 1 medium onion, finely chopped (about ½ cup)
- 3 cloves garlic, minced
- 2 Tbsp. olive oil
- ½ cup dry white wine, chicken broth, or vegetable broth
- ½ cup water
- 2 bay leaves
- ¼ tsp. salt
- 2 Tbsp. snipped fresh parsley
  Freshly cracked black pepper
  Lemon wedges (optional)

1. Discard mussels with broken shells. Pull off "beards." Using a stiff brush, scrub mussels under cold running water.

2. In a Dutch oven combine 4 quarts cold water and the ⅓ cup salt; add mussels. Soak for 15 minutes. Drain and rinse. Soak, drain, and rinse twice more in unsalted water.

3. In the same Dutch oven cook onion and garlic in hot olive oil over medium heat for 3 to 4 minutes or just until tender. Carefully add wine, water, bay leaves, and the ¼ teaspoon salt. Bring to boiling. Place the mussels in a steamer basket. Set basket in Dutch oven. Cover and steam for 3 to 5 minutes or until shells open.

PHOTOGRAPHS: COLLEEN DUFFLEY. FOOD STYLIST: BROOKE LEONARD. STORY: KEN HAEDRICH.

 new **low fat**

Quick Cioppino

This version of San Francisco's delicious fish stew is very easy to make.

Start to finish: 50 minutes

6	oz. fresh or frozen cod fillets
6	oz. fresh or frozen peeled and deveined shrimp
8	oz. live mussels
4	qt. cold water
⅓	cup salt
1	medium green sweet pepper, cut into thin bite-size strips
1	cup chopped onion (1 large)
2	cloves garlic, minced
1	Tbsp. olive oil or cooking oil
2	14½-ounce cans Italian-style stewed tomatoes, undrained
½	cup water
3	Tbsp. snipped fresh basil

1. Thaw cod and shrimp, if frozen. Discard mussels with broken shells. Pull off "beards." Using a stiff brush, scrub mussels under cold running water.

2. In a Dutch oven combine the 4 quarts cold water and the ⅓ cup salt; add mussels. Soak for 15 minutes. Drain and rinse. Soak, drain, and rinse twice more in unsalted water.

3. Rinse cod and shrimp; pat dry. Cut cod into 1-inch pieces.

4. In the same Dutch oven cook sweet pepper, onion, and garlic in hot oil until tender. Stir in undrained tomatoes and the ½ cup water. Bring to boiling. Stir in cod, shrimp, and mussels. Return to boiling; reduce heat. Cover and simmer for 3 to 4 minutes or until cod flakes easily when tested with a fork, shrimp turn opaque, and mussel shells open. Discard any unopened mussel shells. Stir in basil. Makes 4 main-dish servings.

Nutrition facts per serving: 268 cal., 7 g total fat (1 g sat. fat), 99 mg chol., 684 mg sodium, 22 g carbo., 3 g fiber, and 26 g pro. Daily Values: 8% vit. A, 51% vit. C, 11% calcium, and 24% iron.

4. Lift steamer basket from Dutch oven, reserving steaming liquid. Discard any unopened mussels and the bay leaves. Divide the mussels among four large, shallow soup bowls. Pour the steaming liquid over each portion. Sprinkle with parsley and pepper. If desired, serve with lemon wedges. Makes 4 appetizer servings.

Mussels with Tomato: Prepare recipe as directed, except add 1 ripe tomato, seeded and finely chopped, along with the wine.)

Nutrition facts per serving: 114 cal., 7 g total fat (1 g sat. fat), 8 mg chol., 231 mg sodium, 4 g carbo., 1 g fiber, and 4 g pro. Daily Values: 3% vit. A, 10% vit. C, 2% calcium, and 9% iron.

Mediterranean

Prince Edward

Green Lip

BETWEEN THE SHELLS

- Mussels are available year-round. They may come from either coast, Europe, or New Zealand (Green Lip).
- Allow ¼ to ½ pound mussels per person to serve as an appetizer, ½ to 1 pound as a main course.
- Buy mussels only from reputable, licensed seafood dealers.
- When you purchase mussels, they should be alive, with shells slightly agape. To check, tap the mussel hard with your fingertip. If the shell closes, even slightly, that means the mussel is alive, fresh, and okay to cook.
- Store live mussels in the refrigerator, uncovered, for up to two days.
- Before cooking, soak mussels in salt water for 15 minutes, then rinse twice.

TEN IDEAS FOR SERVING UP THE SPEARS

■ Dress up a melted cheese-and-bacon sandwich by adding stalks of blanched or roasted asparagus.

■ Toss cooked asparagus pieces with cooked pasta, grated Parmesan, olive oil, and lemon juice.

■ Wrap cooked spears in prosciutto for a simple hors d'oeuvre.

■ Roll thin fish fillets around spears of blanched asparagus, then bake.

■ Marinate uncooked asparagus in balsamic vinegar, then grill.

■ Toss cooked, chopped asparagus into cooked risotto or wild rice.

■ Add asparagus and fresh herbs, such as tarragon, to soup broths.

■ Fold cooked asparagus and smoked salmon into an omelet.

■ Roast asparagus drizzled with orange juice, olive oil, and orange peel in a 450° F oven.

■ Puree cooked stalks with a small amount of water, lemon juice, and olive oil for an asparagus sauce.

Asparagus

The appearance of thin, young asparagus spears in the market is a surefire sign of spring. While available year-round, asparagus is at its peak in March and April. But don't just grab any bunch in the produce aisle. Check out how it's stocked. Ideally, asparagus should be standing upright in a container filled with a couple of inches of water.

To store asparagus at home, wrap the stalk bottoms in a damp paper towel, then wrap that in foil. The shoots will stay crisp and tender in the fridge for two to four days before they start to lose their flavor.

When cooked to crisp-tender, asparagus has a distinctive, pleasantly pungent flavor. And, cooking asparagus is a snap, really. To know exactly where the tender, edible part begins, hold the stalk at the bottom and just below the tip. Bend the spear several times until you find the place that is most flexible; snap it off there. Then, tidy up the end with a knife.

Lay the stalks in a skillet filled with about ½ inch of boiling water and cook 3 to 4 minutes (depending on the thickness of the stalks) or until the stalks turn bright green. Don't overcook; asparagus will become woody and fibrous, with an assertive odor and a wilted appearance. To serve asparagus cold, place cooked, drained asparagus in a colander under cold water or place in an ice bath.

To ensure you get tender and flavorful stalks, follow these guidelines for selecting fresh asparagus spears at your market:

■ Tightly closed tips.

■ Deep green and/or purplish color (not sage or grayish green).

■ Taut skin. You don't want to see any wrinkling along the stalk, which is a sure sign of age.

■ Firm stalks. Here's an easy test: Hold a stalk from the bottom and it should stand up straight—even if it's pencil thin.

One last word on the finished product: According to today's etiquette experts, it's okay to eat asparagus with your fingers as long as the stalks are firm and not dripping with a sauce or melted butter. Otherwise, use a knife and fork.

Asparagus with Almond Sauce
Start to finish: 15 minutes

1	lb. asparagus spears or one 10-oz. pkg. frozen asparagus spears
1	Tbsp. butter or margarine
2	Tbsp. sliced almonds
1¼	tsp. cornstarch
½	cup water
2	tsp. lemon juice
½	tsp. instant chicken bouillon granules
Dash pepper	

1. Snap off and discard woody bases from fresh asparagus. If desired, scrape off scales. Cover and cook fresh asparagus in a small amount of boiling lightly salted water for 3 to 5 minutes or until crisp-tender. (Or, cook frozen asparagus according to package directions.) Drain well; transfer asparagus to a serving platter.

2. Meanwhile, for sauce, in a small saucepan melt butter or margarine; add almonds. Cook and stir over medium-low heat for 3 to 5 minutes or until golden. Stir in cornstarch. Stir in water, lemon juice, bouillon granules, and pepper. Cook and stir until thickened and bubbly. Cook and stir for 2 minutes more. Spoon over asparagus. Makes 4 servings.

Nutrition facts per serving: 73 cal., 6 g total fat (2 g sat. fat), 8 mg chol., 179 mg sodium, 3 g carbo., 1 g fiber, and 3 g pro. Daily Values: 4% vit. A, 26% vit. C, 2% calcium, and 4% iron.

Measuring Up

Two types of measuring cups—liquid and dry measures—are essential in the kitchen. The main difference between the two? A liquid measure filled to capacity leaves room to move the cup without spilling the liquid. A dry measure is designed to be filled, then leveled to get a precise reading. Leveling with a knife blade works best.

A trip up the housewares aisle of major department stores or specialty kitchen shops is an easy way to buy measuring tools. The sturdy glass or plastic liquid measures you'll find are hard to beat. Most liquid measures require that you check the amount at eye level.

For dry ingredients, pick a set of ¼-, ⅓-, ½-, and 1-cup measures. If they nest, you'll save on storage space. With measuring spoons, you'll want to have more than one set (in ⅛ teaspoon to 1 tablespoon increments) so you don't have to wash spoons in mid-recipe. Leave spoons attached to the ring they come on, so they won't get lost in action.

Pack solid vegetable shortening or butter into dry measures to eliminate air spaces. Level the top with a knife blade.

Measuring spoons should be dry when used. Scoop your ingredient to overflowing, then level with a table knife. Narrow spoons that fit easily into spice jars are a wise choice.

Measure flour by gently spooning it into your cup. Don't pack down the flour. Slide a knife blade over the rim to level, letting excess fall back into the bag.

Place the liquid measuring cup on a level surface; bend down to read at eye level while pouring to the correct mark. Select glass cups for easier reading; a 2-cup measure is standard, and a 4-cup measure is helpful to have on hand.

All Hail the
Mighty Kale

It's time to step outside of your comfort zone and venture into the green unknown. We're talking about eating kale, collards, turnip greens, and mustard greens. These veggies are nutritionally supercharged and bursting with plant chemicals that medical studies indicate we should consume to prevent cancer, heart disease, and even vision problems.

Ruffly bluish-green kale leads the leafy group in phyto-chemicals—the substances that give plants color, flavor, and health-boosting abilities. Researchers are constantly uncovering more health benefits of these plant chemicals. For instance, the hefty load of lutein in kale is linked to a reduced risk of eye problems. Other components of kale make it a cancer-fighting vegetable, especially against cancers of the colon, stomach, lung, and breast. Kale also is high in vitamin A, has almost as much calcium as milk, and contains a burst of potassium.

Before cooking greens, wash them well. Soil likes to hide amid their ruffles. Remove tough stems, and cook leaves in a bit of boiling broth or salted water until tender—two to four minutes—before using in a recipe. Serve cooked greens in soups, tossed with garlic-flavored olive oil and a splash of vinegar, or in these recipes (right).

30 Dino Kale Sauté
Prep: 5 minutes **Cook:** 3 minutes

- 12 oz. dinosaur kale or regular kale, cut or torn into 1- to 2-inch pieces (about 12 cups)
- 2 Tbsp. olive oil
- ¼ cup soft sourdough or French bread crumbs
- ⅛ tsp. pepper
- 1 tsp. white wine Worcestershire sauce
- Lemon wedges (optional)

1. Rinse kale thoroughly under cold running water. Drain well; set aside.

2. In a small skillet heat 2 teaspoons of the oil over medium heat. Cook and stir bread crumbs in hot oil for 1 to 2 minutes or until browned. Sprinkle with pepper; set aside.

3. In a large nonstick skillet heat the remaining 4 teaspoons oil. Add kale. Cover and cook for 1 minute. Uncover. Cook and stir for 1 minute more or just until wilted.

4. Transfer kale to a serving dish. Drizzle with Worcestershire sauce. Sprinkle with browned bread crumbs. If desired, squeeze lemon wedges over all. Makes 4 side-dish servings.

Nutrition facts per serving: 89 cal., 5 g total fat (1 g sat. fat), 0 mg chol., 53 mg sodium, 9 g carbo., 4 g fiber, 3 g pro. Daily Values: 96% vit. A, 94% vit. C, 8% calcium, 8% iron.

Mustard greens are more tender than kale, so they can be used raw in salads. They have a zesty mustard bite. The leaves mellow with simmering. Or you can steam them, sauté them, or stir-fry them.

 new **low fat**

Lamb and Orzo Soup

Prep: 15 minutes **Cook:** 1½ hours

2½ lb. lamb shanks
4 cups water
4 cups chicken or vegetable broth
2 bay leaves
1 Tbsp. snipped fresh oregano
    or 1 tsp. dried oregano, crushed
1½ tsp. snipped fresh marjoram or
    ½ tsp. dried marjoram, crushed
¼ tsp. pepper
2 medium carrots, cut into short thin
    strips (1 cup)
1 cup sliced celery (2 stalks)
¾ cup dried orzo (rosamarina) pasta
3 cups torn fresh kale, mustard
    greens, turnip greens, collard
    greens, or spinach
    Finely shredded Parmesan cheese
    (optional)

1. In a large Dutch oven combine lamb shanks, water, broth, bay leaves, oregano, marjoram, and pepper. Bring to boiling; reduce heat. Cover and simmer for 1¼ to 1½ hours or until meat is tender.

2. Remove shanks from Dutch oven. When cool enough to handle, cut meat off bones; coarsely chop meat. Discard bones. Strain broth through a large sieve or colander lined with double thickness of 100-percent-cotton cheesecloth; discard bay leaves and herbs. Skim fat; return broth to Dutch oven.

3. Stir chopped meat, carrots, celery, and orzo into Dutch oven. Return to boiling; reduce heat. Cover and simmer about 15 minutes or until vegetables and orzo are tender. Stir in kale or spinach. Cook for 1 to 2 minutes more or just until kale is cooked. If desired, serve with Parmesan cheese. Makes 6 servings.

Nutrition facts per serving: 258 cal., 6 g total fat (2 g sat. fat), 82 mg chol., 635 mg sodium, 17 g carbo., 2 g fiber, 33 g pro. Daily Values: 163% vit. A, 71% vit. C, 8% calcium, and 22% iron.

Turnip greens, as you probably guessed, are simply the tops of turnips. Young greens are tender enough to eat raw in salads. Mature greens should be cooked like other leafy greens. Six ounces of cooked turnip greens contain 220 mg of calcium. By comparison, an 8-ounce glass of milk has 300 mg.

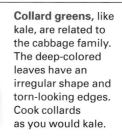

Collard greens, like kale, are related to the cabbage family. The deep-colored leaves have an irregular shape and torn-looking edges. Cook collards as you would kale.

Kale is often used as a garnish because of its frilly edges and varying colors of white, green, or purple. But it's a garnish you should eat because it's loaded with nutrients—phytochemicals, lutein, vitamin A, calcium, and potassium.

Hash Browns

Most folks have an opinion on how they like their hash-brown potatoes—divided between those who like a crispy jumble of chopped golden nuggets and those who prefer long delicate shreds fried into an orderly, soul-fortifying cake.

We'll teach you both methods. But whichever camp you belong to, the secret to perfect hash browns is patience. Let hash browns cook for the full time called for in the recipe before turning, so they'll develop a nice brown crust (peek after about 4 minutes to make sure they don't burn). Then, if making the shredded style, turn carefully—using two spatulas or a spatula and a fork—to keep the potatoes together. Turn chopped potatoes the same way, keeping them together as much as you can.

We've discovered that plain russet potatoes work the best for creating incredible shredded hash browns. You can also use whites or Yukon golds, if that's what you have on hand. For the chopped style, any potato works well.

PHOTOGRAPHS: COLLEEN DUFFLEY. FOOD STYLIST: BROOKE LEONARD. STORY: RICHARD SWEARINGER.

Chopped Hash Browns

Russet potatoes (the brown ones) have a slightly drier, crumblier texture; the whites and reds are firmer and smoother in texture (see bottom photo, page 68).

Prep: 15 minutes **Cook:** 25 minutes

¼ tsp. salt	¼ tsp. salt
4 to 5 small russet, white, or red potatoes (1 lb.)	⅛ tsp. coarsely ground black pepper (optional)
¼ cup finely chopped onion	3 Tbsp. butter, cooking oil, or margarine
1 small jalapeño or banana pepper, seeded and cut into thin strips (optional)	

1. Fill a medium saucepan one-third full of water; add ¼ teaspoon salt. Coarsely chop unpeeled potatoes by slicing lengthwise into strips, then cutting crosswise (see middle photo, lower left). Place potatoes in the saucepan. Bring water to boiling over high heat; reduce heat. Cook, uncovered, for 5 minutes. Drain well.

2. In a medium bowl combine potatoes, onion, jalapeño pepper strips (if desired), the remaining ¼ teaspoon salt, and, if desired, black pepper.

3. In a large nonstick skillet melt butter. Add potato mixture; cook over medium heat about 20 minutes or until potatoes are soft and browned, turning occasionally. Makes 4 servings.

Nutrition facts per serving: 159 cal., 8 g total fat (8 g sat. fat), 21 mg chol., 280 mg sodium, 19 g carbo., 3 g fiber, and 3 g pro. Daily Values: 6% vit. A, 27% vit. C, 2% calcium, and 5% iron.

30 Shredded Hash Browns

Prep: 10 minutes **Cook:** 13 minutes

3 to 4 small russet or white potatoes (about ¾ lb.)	¼ tsp. salt
	⅛ tsp. coarsely ground black pepper
¼ cup finely chopped onion	2 Tbsp. butter, cooking oil, or margarine
1 small jalapeño, banana, or Anaheim pepper, seeded and chopped (optional)	

1. Peel potatoes and coarsely shred using the coarsest side of the grater (see photo, bottom left)—you should have about 2 cups. Rinse shredded potatoes in a colander; drain well and pat dry. In a medium bowl combine shredded potatoes, onion, jalapeño pepper (if desired), salt, and black pepper.

2. In a large nonstick skillet heat butter over medium heat. Carefully add potatoes, pressing into an even pancake-like round (7 to 8 inches in diameter). Using a spatula, press potato mixture firmly. Cover and cook over medium heat about 8 minutes or until golden brown. Check occasionally; reduce heat, if necessary, to prevent overbrowning.

3. Turn the hash browns using two spatulas or a spatula and fork. (If you're not sure you can turn the potatoes in a single flip, cut into quarters and turn by sections. See photo, bottom middle.) Cook, uncovered, for 5 to 7 minutes more or until golden brown and crisp. Remove from skillet; serve in wedges. Makes 2 or 3 servings.

Nutrition facts per serving: 168 cal., 9 g total fat (1 g sat. fat), 0 mg chol., 197 mg sodium, 19 g carbo., 2 g fiber, and 3 g pro. Daily Values: 27% vit. C, 1% calcium, and 5% iron.

Pineapple
Short & Sweet

We all love the king of pineapples, crowned with a plume of vibrant greenery. But the king has some short and chubby cousins that are well worth the slicing. See if you can find these fresh gems in your supermarket. As for regular pineapples, look for fresh-looking fruits that are plump, slightly soft to the touch, and heavy for their size. You can refrigerate an uncut pineapple for 1 to 2 days. Peeled pineapples will hold for a few days longer. Eat them plain or try one in our colorful salad.

Golden pineapple: This big guy looks like the standard fresh pineapple, but take a bite of its succulent flesh and you'll notice the difference. The fruit is sweeter and more brilliant in color than the common variety. Golden is ready to eat when you buy it, so there's no waiting for it to ripen. The core is edible, but is a tad tougher than the baby varieties.

PHOTOGRAPHS: COLLEEN DUFFLEY, PETER KRUMHARDT. STORY: NANCY S. HUGHES.

South African baby pineapple: Topping off at 4 inches tall, this cutie is super sweet. It's dense with rich-textured fruit and low in acid. When purchasing, look for a golden color and use the sniff test; when ripe, these are very aromatic. South African baby pineapples are available year-round in major markets. Can't find them? Ask your produce manager to order some.

 low fat

Fruit Salad with Cranberry Dressing
Prep: 25 minutes **Chill:** 2 hours

- 2   cups cranberries
- ⅓   cup water
- 1   cup sugar
- ¼   cup orange juice
     Bibb lettuce leaves
- 2   large seedless oranges, peeled and sectioned
- ½   of a large pineapple, peeled, cored, sliced, and cut into wedges
- 2   large ripe pears, cored and sliced into wedges*
- 2   kiwifruit and/or golden kiwifruit, peeled and sliced lengthwise into wedges

Baby Hawaiian pineapple: This one hails from the islands of *aloha* and stands about an inch taller than the South African baby pineapple. A mini version of the flavorful Sugar Loaf, the baby Hawaiian has a mild sweetness with a slightly crunchy but edible core. The fruit is low in acid. Like the South African variety, it can be found all year at most major markets.

QUICK PINEAPPLE TIPS

■ Lop off the top and bottom of the pineapple. Slice remaining fruit into thin wedges. Nibble around the rind. Or, cut off the top and scoop out fruit.

■ Use the hollow shell to serve pineapple salsa or exotic tropical drinks.

1. For dressing, in a medium saucepan combine cranberries and water. Bring to boiling; reduce heat. Cover and simmer for 4 to 5 minutes or just until berries begin to pop.

2. Remove saucepan from heat; stir in sugar and orange juice. When cool, press mixture through a sieve. Discard cranberry skins. Cover and refrigerate about 2 hours or until well chilled. (The dressing will thicken slightly as it chills.)

3. To serve, line six small bowls with lettuce leaves. Arrange fruit on lettuce. Drizzle with dressing. Makes 6 servings.

***Test Kitchen Tip:** To prevent pears from darkening, brush the cut edges with lemon juice.

Nutrition facts per serving: 231 cal., 1 g total fat (0 g sat. fat), 0 mg chol., 4 mg sodium, 58 g carbo., 5 g fiber, and 2 g pro. Daily Values: 11% vit. A, 113% vit. C, 5% calcium, and 5% iron.

Let April showers
mushroom
into fresh ideas
for family
chicken dinners.

April

Spring Chicken

Plus . . .

Good Ol' Buttermilk
Fried Chicken

SpringChicken

That giddy grin is
contagious. One sure
way to catch it is by
crunching into the
ultimate finger food:
fried chicken. Or, find
bliss by munching
on tandoori, kabobs,
or scallopini.

PHOTOGRAPHS: ALEXANDRA GRABLEWSKI. FOOD STYLIST: ANN DISRUDE. PROP STYLIST: BARBARA FRITZ. STORY: JEANNE AMBROSE.

Good Ol' Buttermilk Fried Chicken

An electric skillet works wonders for fried chicken, but be careful when adding the chicken because the oil can splatter. A Dutch oven or large pot produces crispy chicken too.

Prep: 25 minutes **Marinate:** 30 minutes **Cook:** 20 minutes

3 lb. small meaty chicken pieces (drumsticks, thighs, and/or breast halves)	2 tsp. paprika
	½ tsp. pepper
	2 eggs, beaten
	4 cups cooking oil
1½ tsp. salt	1 recipe Vinegar Splash or malt vinegar
1½ cups buttermilk	
1¼ cups all-purpose flour	

1. If desired, remove skin from chicken. Place chicken pieces into a self-sealing plastic bag set in a large bowl. Sprinkle chicken with ½ teaspoon of the salt. Pour buttermilk over chicken. Seal bag. Marinate in the refrigerator for 30 minutes or overnight, turning bag occasionally to coat chicken.

2. Drain chicken, reserving ½ cup of the buttermilk. In a shallow dish combine flour, paprika, the remaining 1 teaspoon salt, and pepper. In another shallow dish combine the eggs and the reserved buttermilk. Coat chicken with the flour mixture, then dip into egg mixture, then dip into flour mixture again. Place chicken pieces on a tray; set aside while oil heats.

3. In a 12-inch electric skillet heat ½ inch of oil (about 3 cups) to 350° F (about 10 to 15 minutes). Using tongs, carefully add chicken to the skillet. Reduce temperature setting to 325° F. Cook, uncovered, for 10 minutes. Turn chicken and cook for 10 to 12 minutes more or until coating is golden, chicken is no longer pink, and an instant-read thermometer registers 170° F for breasts or 180° F for thighs and drumsticks. Drain on paper towels. Transfer chicken to a serving platter. Sprinkle with Vinegar Splash or malt vinegar. Makes 6 servings.

Vinegar Splash: In a small bowl whisk together ½ cup cider vinegar, 1 tablespoon snipped fresh cilantro, and several dashes bottled hot pepper sauce.

Dutch-oven method: In a Dutch oven heat 1½ inches of oil (about 6½ cups) over medium heat to 350° F. Using tongs, carefully add a few pieces of chicken to Dutch oven. (Oil temperature will drop; maintain at 325° F.) Cook for 12 to 15 minutes or until coating is golden, chicken is no longer pink, and an instant-read thermometer registers 170° F for breasts or 180° F for thighs and drumsticks, turning once. Drain on paper towels. Keep warm in a 300° F oven while cooking remaining.

Nutrition facts per serving: 390 cal., 18 g total fat (3 g sat. fat), 169 mg chol., 625 mg sodium, 22 g carbo., 1 g fiber, and 34 g pro. Daily Values: 13% vit. A, 6% vit. C, 7% calcium, and 15% iron.

Ravioli Chicken Soup

30 low fat Ravioli Chicken Soup

Just a pinch of saffron goes a long way in adding flavor and more intense color to food. The aromatic spice is a tad expensive, so feel free to leave it out. This soup is terrific with or without it.

Start to finish: 25 minutes

Nonstick cooking spray	¼ tsp. saffron threads, slightly crushed (optional)
12 oz. skinless, boneless chicken breast halves, cut into ½ inch cubes	
	1 9-oz. pkg. vegetable ravioli or herb chicken tortellini
6 cups reduced-sodium chicken broth	
½ cup sliced leek or chopped onion	½ cup fresh baby spinach leaves or shredded fresh spinach
1 Tbsp. finely chopped fresh ginger	

1. Lightly coat a large saucepan with cooking spray. Heat saucepan over medium-high heat. Add chicken; cook and stir for 3 minutes. Carefully add broth, leek or onion, ginger, and, if desired, saffron.

2. Bring to boiling. Add ravioli or tortellini. Return to boiling; reduce heat. Simmer, uncovered, for 5 to 9 minutes or until ravioli is tender, stirring occasionally. Remove from heat. To serve, ladle into four small bowls. Top with spinach. Makes 4 main-dish servings.

Nutrition facts per serving: 222 cal., 3 g total fat (0 g sat. fat), 59 mg chol., 1,221 mg sodium, 21 g carbo., 3 g fiber, and 29 g pro. Daily Values: 18% vit. A, 9% vit. C, 6% calcium, and 13% iron.

Chicken and
Sausage Kabobs

Chicken and Sausage Kabobs

Go ahead and make your own skewers from apple tree sticks. Twigs from oak, maple, or hickory trees will work too. Just be sure those trees have not been sprayed with pesticides or other chemicals.

Prep: 25 minutes **Marinate:** 2 hours **Grill:** 12 minutes

4	medium skinless, boneless chicken breast halves (about 1 lb. total)
2	Tbsp. finely chopped green onion
2	Tbsp. olive oil
1	Tbsp. snipped fresh Italian flat-leaf parsley
1	Tbsp. snipped fresh oregano
1	Tbsp. lime juice

1	clove garlic, minced
8	oz. apple-flavored smoked chicken sausage or other smoked sausage, halved lengthwise and cut into ¾-inch pieces
1	recipe Herbed Dipping Sauce
	Grilled lime wedges

1. Cut chicken into ½-inch-thick strips. Place in a bowl. For marinade, combine green onion, olive oil, parsley, oregano, lime juice, and garlic. Pour marinade over chicken; stir to coat. Cover and marinate in the refrigerator for 2 to 8 hours.

2. Drain chicken, discarding marinade. Thread strips of chicken and sausage onto six long skewers.

3. For a charcoal grill, place the kabobs on the rack of an uncovered grill directly over medium coals. Grill for 12 to 14 minutes or until chicken is no longer pink, turning to brown evenly. (For a gas grill, preheat grill. Reduce heat to medium. Place kabobs on grill rack over heat. Cover and grill as directed.) Remove kabobs from grill. Serve with Herbed Dipping Sauce and lime wedges. Makes 6 servings.

Herbed Dipping Sauce: In a bowl combine ¼ cup dairy sour cream, ¼ cup mayonnaise or salad dressing, 2 tablespoons finely chopped green onion and/or chives, 1 tablespoon snipped fresh Italian flat-leaf parsley, 1 tablespoon snipped fresh oregano, 1 tablespoon lime juice, and 1 clove minced garlic.

Nutrition facts per serving: 262 cal., 18 g total fat (4 g sat. fat), 61 mg chol., 347 mg sodium, 1 g carbo., 0 g fiber, and 23 g pro. Daily Values: 3% vit. A, 8% vit. C, 3% calcium, and 5% iron.

CHICKEN TIPS

■ When you can't even wait that long, start with deli-roasted chicken or precooked, seasoned chicken pieces. Use them in main-dish salads, in pastas, or on pizza.

■ Check chicken doneness with a meat thermometer. The internal temperature of a whole bird or drumsticks and thighs should reach 180° F; breasts, 170° F; and ground chicken, 165° F.

■ Visit the National Chicken Council Web site: www.EatChicken.com for more tips and information.

Provençal Herb-Rubbed Roaster

Prepare this bird for the oven the night before you plan to serve it. The next day, just pile the potatoes around the chicken and pop the whole dish into the oven.

Prep: 20 minutes **Marinate:** 2 hours
Roast: 1¼ hours **Stand:** 10 minutes

1	3- to 4-lb. whole broiler-fryer chicken
¼	cup olive oil
2	Tbsp. herbes de Provence
1	tsp. smoked salt or salt
1	tsp. crushed red pepper

¾	tsp. coarsely ground black pepper
1½	lb. tiny yellow and purple potatoes and/or fingerling potatoes, halved

1. Remove neck and giblets from chicken. Skewer neck skin to back; tie legs with 100-percent-cotton string. Twist wings under back. Brush chicken with 2 tablespoons of the olive oil.

2. In a small bowl stir together herbes de Provence, salt, crushed red pepper, and black pepper. Rub 2 tablespoons of the herb mixture onto the bird. Cover the remaining herb mixture; set aside. Place chicken in a large self-sealing plastic bag. Seal bag. Marinate in the refrigerator for 2 to 24 hours.

3. Preheat oven to 375° F. Remove chicken from bag. Place chicken, breast side up, on a rack in a shallow roasting pan. Insert a meat thermometer into center of an inside thigh muscle. Do not allow thermometer bulb to touch bone.

4. In a large bowl combine the remaining 2 tablespoons oil and remaining herb mixture. Add potatoes; toss to combine. Arrange potatoes around chicken. Roast chicken, uncovered, for 1¼ to 1¾ hours or until drumsticks move easily in their sockets and meat thermometer registers 180° F. Remove chicken from oven; cover. Let stand 10 minutes before carving.

5. To serve, place chicken and potatoes on a large serving platter. Makes 6 servings.

Nutrition facts per serving: 543 cal., 35 g total fat (9 g sat. fat), 134 mg chol., 492 mg sodium, 18 g carbo., 3 g fiber, and 37 g pro. Daily Values: 6% vit. A, 31% vit. C, 5% calcium, and 16% iron.

Provençal Herb-Rubbed Roaster

Imagine a cozy bistro on a busy Paris street.
Then feast on a piece of this golden bird with
its herb-heavy perfume and you're there…in
your dreams, that is.

Mushroom-Smothered Chicken

The chunky sauce is over the top in more ways than one. It's one of those little extras that goes to flavorful extremes. We're talking onions, garlic, and mushrooms enhanced with white wine and herbs. And, of course, the chicken soaks up all that good stuff.

Mushroom-Smothered Chicken

The mushroom sauce is swooning material as is, but a splash of cream sends it over the top. There's plenty of sauce to ladle over the chicken on a toasted baguette. We also love it with hot cooked potato gnocchi.

Prep: 20 minutes **Cook:** 30 minutes

¼ cup all-purpose flour	2 cloves garlic, minced
½ tsp. salt	¾ cup dry white wine or
¼ tsp. pepper	chicken broth
2½ to 3 lb. meaty chicken	¾ cup chicken broth
pieces (breast halves,	2 Tbsp. snipped fresh basil
thighs, and drumsticks),	or 1 tsp. dried basil,
skinned	crushed
2 Tbsp. olive oil or	1 Tbsp. snipped fresh
cooking oil	thyme or 1 tsp. dried
6 cups halved fresh	thyme, crushed
mushrooms, such as	2 Tbsp. whipping cream
morel, chanterelle,	(optional)
shiitake, and/or button	Toasted baguette slices
2 large onions, chopped	(optional)
(2 cups)	

1. In a plastic bag combine flour, salt, and pepper. Add chicken pieces, a few at a time, shaking to coat. In a 12-inch skillet brown chicken in hot oil over medium-high heat for 8 minutes, turning occasionally. Remove from skillet; set aside.

2. Add mushrooms, onions, and garlic to skillet. Cook for 4 minutes, stirring occasionally and scraping up any browned bits. Return chicken to pan. Add wine, broth, basil, and thyme. Bring to boiling; reduce heat. Cover and simmer for 25 to 30 minutes or until chicken is no longer pink and an instant-read thermometer registers 170° F for breasts or 180° F for thighs and drumsticks. Remove chicken; cover and keep warm.

3. Increase heat to medium and gently boil sauce, uncovered, for 5 minutes. If desired, stir in whipping cream. If desired, serve chicken and sauce over toasted baguette slices. Season to taste with salt and pepper. Makes 6 servings.

Nutrition facts per serving: 293 cal., 13 g total fat (3 g sat. fat), 77 mg chol., 368 mg sodium, 12 g carbo., 2 g fiber, and 30 g pro. Daily Values: 1% vit. A, 7% vit. C, 4% calcium, and 12% iron.

SPRING CHICKEN MENU

Leaf lettuce and strawberry salad with

red wine vinaigrette

Mushroom-Smothered Chicken (recipe, above)

Steamed sugar snap peas

Toasted baguette slices

Pear Ginger Flan (recipe, page 33)

Tandoori Chicken Burger

low fat Tandoori Chicken Burger

Feel free to separate the onions from the cucumbers before piling them onto your burgers. That way, those who aren't fond of onions can share with those who are.

Prep: 30 minutes **Grill:** 14 minutes

¼ cup fine dry bread	2 Tbsp. plain yogurt
crumbs	4 seeded hamburger buns
2 tsp. garam masala or	or kaiser rolls, split
curry powder	and toasted
¼ tsp. salt	1 recipe Minty Cucumbers
¼ tsp. ground red pepper	Kale or lettuce
1 lb. uncooked ground	
chicken*	

1. In a large mixing bowl combine bread crumbs, garam masala or curry powder, salt, and ground red pepper. Add ground chicken and yogurt; mix well. Shape chicken mixture into four ¾-inch-thick patties.

2. For a charcoal grill, place patties on the rack of an uncovered grill directly over medium coals. Grill for 14 to 18 minutes or until no longer pink (165° F), turning once halfway through grilling. (For a gas grill, preheat grill. Reduce heat to medium. Place patties on grill rack over heat. Cover and grill as above.) Remove from grill. Serve burgers on toasted buns with Minty Cucumbers and kale or lettuce. Makes 4 servings.

Minty Cucumbers: Combine 1 cup thinly sliced cucumber, ½ cup thinly sliced red onion, ¼ cup snipped fresh mint, 1 tablespoon balsamic vinaigrette, and ¼ teaspoon salt.

***Test Kitchen Tip:** If you ask your butcher to prepare ground chicken for you, be sure to request it coarsely ground.

Nutrition facts per serving: 383 cal., 13 g total fat (1 g sat. fat), 0 mg chol., 841 mg sodium, 37 g carbo., 2 g fiber, and 27 g pro. Daily Values: 2% vit. A, 10% vit. C, 12% calcium, and 25% iron.

Coconut Chicken Salad

After simmering in mellow coconut milk, this chicken is ready for an onion and chili pepper perk up.

Spring Chicken
Scallopini

30 Spring Chicken Scallopini

A buttery white wine sauce and a little heap of herbs dress up the chicken and add incredibly fresh flavor. Best of all, it's fast and flashy.

Start to finish: 25 minutes

4 medium skinless, boneless chicken breast halves (about 1 lb. total)	½ cup mixed snipped fresh herbs (such as oregano, thyme, lemon thyme, and/or mint)
¼ cup all-purpose flour	
¼ tsp. salt	¼ tsp. coarsely ground black pepper
¼ cup butter	
½ cup dry white wine (such as Sauvignon Blanc) and/or chicken broth	⅛ tsp. salt
	Steamed asparagus* (optional)
¼ cup sliced green onions	

1. Place each chicken piece between two pieces of waxed paper or plastic wrap. Pound lightly with the flat side of a meat mallet, working from the center to the edges until pieces are an even ¼-inch thickness (see photo, below). Remove the plastic wrap. In a shallow dish combine flour and the ¼ teaspoon salt. Coat chicken pieces with flour mixture.

2. In a 12-inch skillet heat 2 tablespoons of the butter over medium heat. Add chicken; cook for 6 to 8 minutes or until chicken is tender and no longer pink, turning once. Remove chicken from skillet. Transfer chicken to a serving platter; cover and keep warm.

3. Add white wine and/or broth and green onions to the skillet. Cook and stir for 1 minute, scraping up any browned bits in skillet, if necessary. Cook 1 minute more or until reduced to ⅓ cup. Remove from heat. Whisk in remaining 2 tablespoons butter until melted. Stir in 2 tablespoons of the snipped fresh herbs, the pepper, and the ⅛ teaspoon salt. (If using chicken broth, omit the ⅛ teaspoon salt.)

4. If desired, serve chicken with steamed asparagus. Drizzle wine sauce over all. Pile remaining fresh herbs onto each serving. Makes 4 servings.

*Test Kitchen Tip: To steam asparagus spears, snap off and discard woody bases from asparagus. Steam for 4 to 6 minutes or until tender.

Nutrition facts per serving: 320 cal., 14 g total fat (8 g sat. fat), 115 mg chol., 422 mg sodium, 7 g carbo., 0 g fiber, and 34 g pro. Daily Values: 12% vit. A, 8% vit. C, 4% calcium, and 8% iron.

30 Coconut Chicken Salad

To give the Indian flat bread a sculptured look, use a pair of kitchen tongs to carefully hold bread a few inches above the open flame of a gas burner. As the bread heats up, it softens and curls. Or let it stay flat and serve it at room temperature.

Prep: 10 minutes **Cook:** 12 minutes **Chill:** 1 hour

12 oz. skinless, boneless chicken breast halves and/or thighs	2 red chili peppers, seeded and finely chopped, (optional)
1 14-oz. can unsweetened light coconut milk	1 cup shredded lettuce
¼ tsp. salt	½ cup coconut chips, toasted
⅛ tsp. ground black pepper	Indian flat bread (pappadam or naan) or 3-inch rounds Armenian cracker bead
¼ cup thinly sliced red onion or Vidalia onion	
2 Tbsp. lime juice	

1. In a large skillet place chicken, coconut milk, the ¼ teaspoon salt, and the ⅛ teaspoon black pepper. Bring to boiling; reduce heat. Cover and simmer for 12 to 14 minutes or until chicken is no longer pink and an instant-read thermometer registers 170° F for breasts or 180° F for thighs. Drain well; discard milk mixture. Cool chicken slightly; cut into bite-size pieces.

2. In a medium bowl combine chicken pieces, onion, lime juice, and chili peppers. Cover and chill in the refrigerator for 1 hour. Just before serving, gently stir shredded lettuce and half of the toasted coconut chips into the chicken mixture. Season to taste with additional salt and black pepper. Sprinkle with remaining coconut chips. Serve with Indian flat bread (pappadam or naan). Makes 4 servings.

Nutrition facts per serving: 201 cal., 10 g total fat (7 g sat. fat), 49 mg chol., 294 mg sodium, 7 g carbo., 1 g fiber, and 20 g pro. Daily Values: 8% vit. A, 17% vit. C, 2% calcium, and 10% iron.

Use a meat mallet to lightly pound chicken to ¼ inch thickness.

Guava-Glazed Chicken

The technique may be unfamiliar, but removing the backbone and flattening the chicken shortens the cooking time for a whole bird. Great on the grill, this chicken also can be oven-roasted.

Prep: 20 minutes **Cook:** 15 minutes **Grill:** 50 minutes

1 3- to 4-lb. whole broiler-fryer chicken	1 recipe Guava Sauce
½ tsp. salt	Sliced fresh guava (optional)
¼ tsp. pepper	Green onion (optional)

1. Remove the neck and giblets from chicken. Place the chicken, breast side down, on a cutting board. Use kitchen shears to make a lengthwise cut down one side of the backbone, starting from the tail end. Repeat the lengthwise cut on the opposite side of the backbone. Remove and discard backbone.

2. Turn chicken cut side down. Flatten chicken with your hands. (Try to make it as flat as possible.) Use kitchen shears to remove the wing tips. Sprinkle the salt and pepper over chicken.

3. For direct grilling, place chicken, cut side up, on the rack of an uncovered grill directly over medium coals. Grill for 25 minutes. Turn, using tongs. Grill for 20 minutes more. To glaze, brush with some Guava Sauce. Grill 5 minutes more or until an instant-read thermometer inserted in the thigh portion registers 180° F. (For indirect grilling, arrange medium-hot coals around a drip pan. Test for medium heat above the pan. Place chicken, cut side up, on grill rack over drip pan. Cover and grill for 45 minutes. Turn; brush with some of the sauce. Grill 5 minutes more or until an instant-read thermometer inserted in the thigh portion registers 180° F.)

4. Bring remaining sauce to boiling; pass with chicken. If desired, serve with sliced guava and onions. Makes 6 servings.

Guava Sauce: In a small saucepan combine 1 cup guava, mango, peach, or apricot nectar; ¼ cup bottled hoisin sauce; 2 cloves minced garlic; and, if desired, several dashes bottled hot pepper sauce. Bring to boiling; reduce heat. Boil gently, uncovered, about 15 minutes or until thickened and sauce is reduced to about ¾ cup.

Oven-roasting method: Prepare the chicken and sauce as through Step 2. Place chicken on a rack in a shallow baking pan. Roast, uncovered, in a 425° F oven for 35 minutes. To glaze, brush chicken with some of the sauce. Roast for 5 to 10 minutes more or until an instant-read thermometer inserted in the thigh portion registers 180° F.

Nutrition facts per serving: 272 cal., 12 g total fat (3 g sat. fat), 79 mg chol., 478 mg sodium, 13 g carbo., 0 g fiber, and 25 g pro. Daily Values: 12% vit. C, 2% calcium, and 7% iron.

low fat Chicken Cobbler

To really show off this all-in-one dish, cut a 16x2½-inch strip of parchment paper and wrap it around each dish. Tie it in place with 100-percent-cotton string before baking (see photo, below).

Prep: 15 minutes **Bake:** 45 minutes

6 skinless, boneless chicken thighs (3 oz. each)	2 Tbsp. butter
Salt	⅓ cup all-purpose flour
Pepper	½ tsp. snipped fresh tarragon or ¼ tsp. dried tarragon, crushed
1 cup shelled fresh peas or frozen peas	2 cups chicken broth
½ cup chopped Vidalia, Maui, or other sweet onion	1 recipe Carrot Cobbler Topping

1. Preheat oven to 400° F. Arrange chicken in a 13x9x2-inch baking pan. Season with salt and pepper. Bake about 20 minutes or until chicken is no longer pink and juices run clear; set aside.

2. Meanwhile, if using fresh peas, cook peas in a small amount of boiling salted water for 2 minutes; drain.

3. For sauce, in a saucepan cook and stir onion in hot butter over medium heat about 5 minutes or until onion is tender. Stir in flour and tarragon. Add broth all at once. Cook and stir until thickened and bubbly. Stir in peas. Cover; keep warm while preparing cobbler topping.

4. Place a baked chicken thigh in each of six individual ungreased 10-ounce ramekins, custard cups, or baking dishes. Pour warm sauce over the chicken. Dollop Carrot Cobbler Topping over sauce. Place dishes in a 15x10x1-inch baking pan. Bake about 25 minutes or until topping is golden brown and a wooden toothpick inserted in the center of topping comes out clean. Makes 6 servings.

Carrot Cobbler Topping: In a medium mixing bowl stir together 2 cups all-purpose flour, 1 cup coarsely shredded carrot, 2 tablespoons sugar, 1 tablespoon baking powder, and ½ teaspoon salt. Stir in 1⅓ cups milk and 2 tablespoons melted butter until all is moistened.

Nutrition facts per serving: 425 cal., 13 g total fat (7 g sat. fat), 85 mg chol., 943 mg sodium, 48 g carbo., 4 g fiber, and 28 g pro. Daily Values: 115% vit. A, 11% vit. C, 22% calcium, and 19% iron.

Fill each ramekin before wrapping in parchment paper.

Chicken Cobbler

Guava-Glazed Chicken

A glossy, sweet-hot tropical nectar gets slathered over this grilled temptation. We're trying a new technique here too. It involves snipping out the backbone of a chicken, then flattening the whole thing before plopping it in one piece onto the barbecue. It's a faster method of cooking an entire bird.

PHOTOGRAPHS: COLLEEN DUFFLEY. FOOD STYLIST: BROOKE LEONARD. STORY: KEN HAEDRICH.

Less is often more. Take granola, for instance. If you keep it simple, kids will launch into it. Start padding it with grits, groats, and other UFOs and they'll quickly depart for Planet Apathy. The aroma of granola baking is tantalizing, but wait until you taste these recipes. Out of this world!

 Nuts About Granola

Prep: 15 minutes **Bake:** 40 minutes

2	cups regular rolled oats	½ cup coconut (optional)
1	cup coarsely chopped walnuts or pecans	¼ cup toasted wheat germ
½	cup shelled sunflower seeds	½ cup honey or maple-flavored syrup
		2 Tbsp. cooking oil

1. Preheat oven to 300° F. In a large bowl mix oats, nuts, sunflower seeds, coconut (if desired), and wheat germ. Stir together honey and cooking oil; stir into oat mixture.

2. Spread oat mixture evenly in a 15x10x1-inch baking pan. Bake, uncovered, for 30 to 35 minutes or until lightly browned, stirring after 20 minutes.

3. Spread on a large piece of foil to cool. Break into clumps. Store in an airtight container for up to 1 week or in freezer for 2 months. Makes 6 cups (12 servings).

Nutrition facts per ½ cup serving: 234 cal., 12 g total fat (1 g sat. fat), 0 mg chol., 1 mg sodium, 27 g carbo., 4 g fiber, and 7 g pro. Daily Values: 5% calcium, and 9% iron.

Down to Earth Granola

Prep: 15 minutes **Bake:** 40 minutes

4	cups regular rolled oats	¼ cup cooking oil
1½	cups sliced almonds	¼ cup honey
½	cup packed light brown sugar	1 tsp. vanilla
½	tsp. salt	1½ cups raisins or dried cranberries
½	tsp. ground cinnamon	

1. Preheat oven to 300° F. In a bowl mix oats, almonds, brown sugar, salt, and cinnamon. In a saucepan warm oil and honey. Whisk or stir in vanilla. Carefully pour liquid over oat mixture. Stir gently with a wooden spoon; finish mixing by hand.

2. Spread evenly in a 15x10x1-inch baking pan. Bake for 40 minutes or until lightly browned, stirring every 10 minutes. Cool in pan on a wire rack. Stir in raisins or dried cranberries. Store in an airtight container for up to 1 week or in freezer for 3 months. Makes 8 cups (24 servings).

Nutrition facts per ⅓ cup serving: 186 cal., 8 g total fat (1 g sat. fat), 0 mg chol., 52 mg sodium, 27 g carbo., 3 g fiber, and 4 g pro. Daily Values: 1% vit. C, 4% calcium, and 7% iron.

Wholly granola!

Just What Is It?

1

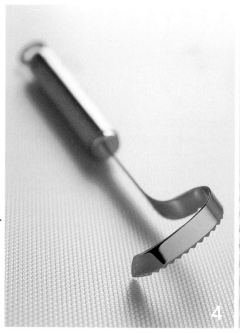

4

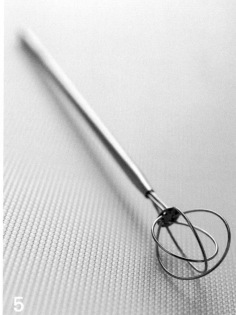

5

6

The kitchen gadget aisle can hold a curious selection of tools that defy description. What can all these do-hickeys and thingama-jigs accomplish? We took a closer look and turned up some useful options. See if you can guess what each one does before you read the description—a point for each correct guess. The prize? An opportunity to try your gadgets by making a delicious salmon dish for dinner. You can use your fish scaler, your utility cutter, your grater, and your citrus reamer. And while you're at it, use your cocktail whisk to make a drink for quenching your thirst while cooking.

7

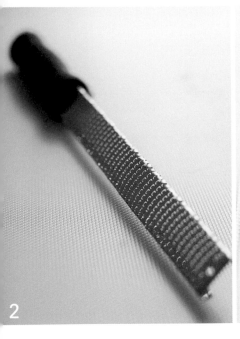

2

3

1. The blade on this **chocolate shaver** adjusts to different widths; use it for cutting chocolate into chunks or delicate swirls.

2. Yes, the **microplane grater** had its origins in the wood shop. However, this kitchen version finely shreds citrus peel perfectly and does wonders shaving hard cheeses.

3. The pleats in this **citrus reamer** gently pull the fruit away from the skin to make peeling your favorite citrus decidedly easier.

4. This simply designed **fish scaler** cleans your catch without digging into the fish's flesh.

5. A wandlike **cocktail whisk** whips up any libation served in an extra-tall glass—it's cute to boot.

6. The retractable blade on this **utility cutter** is a safety feature we like. We also like the way this tool minces herbs and slices through pizza and pastry dough with ease.

7. A **tenderizing roller** rolls along on chicken, beef, or pork.

8. Sleek and stylish, this **wired cheese slicer** performs elegantly on soft and semisoft cheeses.

8

PHOTOGRAPHS: COLLEEN DUFFLEY. STORY: STEPHEN EXEL.

new Salmon-Veggie Bake

Use your utility cutter to slice the vegetables and snip the herbs.

Prep: 30 minutes **Bake:** 30 minutes

1 lb. fresh or frozen salmon, orange roughy, cod, flounder, or sea bass fillets, about ¾ inch thick
2 cups thinly sliced carrots
2 cups sliced fresh mushrooms
½ cup sliced green onions
2 tsp. grated orange peel
2 tsp. snipped fresh oregano or ½ tsp. dried oregano, crushed
4 cloves garlic, halved
¼ tsp. salt
¼ tsp. pepper
4 tsp. olive oil
Salt
Pepper
2 medium oranges, thinly sliced
Fresh oregano sprigs (optional)

1. Thaw fish, if frozen. Use a fish scaler to remove any scales. Rinse fish; pat dry. Cut into four serving-size pieces.

2. In a small saucepan cover and cook carrots in a small amount of boiling water for 2 minutes. Drain and set aside.

3. Tear off four 24-inch pieces of 18-inch-wide heavy foil. Fold each in half to make four 18x12-inch rectangles.

4. In a large bowl combine carrots, mushrooms, green onions, orange peel, oregano, garlic, the ¼ teaspoon salt, and ¼ teaspoon pepper; toss gently.

5. Divide vegetables among foil. Add fish. Drizzle with oil; sprinkle with salt and pepper. Top with orange slices and, if desired, oregano sprigs. Bring together two opposite edges of foil; seal with a double fold. Fold remaining ends to enclose food, allowing space for steam. Place in a single layer on a baking pan.

6. Bake in a 350° oven about 30 minutes or until carrots are tender and fish flakes easily with a fork. Open packets slowly to allow steam to escape. Makes 4 servings.

Nutrition facts per serving: 252 cal., 10 g total fat (1 g sat. fat), 59 mg chol., 393 mg sodium, 18 g carbo., 4 g fiber, and 26 g pro. Daily Values: 314% vit. A, 73% vit. C, 8% calcium, and 10% iron.

The Power of
Mushrooms

Lovers of mushrooms know the magic these earthy delights bring to just about any dish. Now, scientists are learning that mushrooms may deserve a spot on the list of cancer-fighting foods.

Cancer researchers are beginning to uncover the potential of mushrooms, including the common white button. Components of button mushrooms may help prevent breast cancer by reducing the activity of an enzyme that makes estrogen, according to a study in the *Journal of Nutrition*. "Estrogen promotes breast cancer cell growth in 60 percent of breast cancer patients," says lead researcher Shiuan Chen, Ph.D., of the City of Hope's Beckman Research Institute in California. Other mushrooms provide similar effects.

Additional anticancer properties of mushrooms may come from their ability to inhibit tumor growth by boosting the immune system. Plant chemicals called beta-glucans—found heavily in maitake and shiitake mushrooms—are believed to activate immune cells that fight infection.

Mushrooms are rich in potassium and selenium, known for its antioxidant properties and tested recently for its ability to combat prostate cancer and cardiovascular disease. They are also rich in riboflavin, niacin, and pantothenic acid, which promote healthy skin and help regulate the nervous system.

Dried mushrooms have a more intense flavor than fresh mushrooms, making them a terrific seasoning. Before using dried mushrooms, soak them in warm water until they're soft.

30 Dancing Mushrooms

This dish is a major hit as an appetizer, but it can also be the start of so much more. Toss it with cooked spring peas, serve over pasta, or pile it on a burger.

Prep: 15 minutes **Cook:** 12 minutes

- 3 cloves garlic, minced
- 3 shallots, peeled and cut into thin wedges
- 2 Tbsp. olive oil or cooking oil
- 1¼ lb. fresh mushrooms (such as maitake, oyster, white button, or shiitake), broken into clusters or sliced (about 8 cups)
- ¼ cup snipped mixed fresh herbs (such as tarragon, rosemary, basil, oregano, and/or parsley)
- ¼ tsp. coarse salt or salt
- ¼ tsp. cracked black pepper

1. In a large skillet cook the garlic and shallots in hot oil over medium-high heat for 2 minutes.

2. Add maitake mushrooms. Cook, stirring occasionally, for 10 to 12 minutes or until tender. If using oyster or button mushrooms, add them during the last 6 to 8 minutes. Add shiitakes during last 4 minutes. Stir in herbs, salt, and pepper. Makes 6 to 8 servings.

Nutrition facts per serving: 74 cal., 5 g total fat (1 g sat. fat), 0 mg chol., 86 mg sodium, 6 g carbo., 1 g fiber, and 3 g pro. Daily Values: 3% vit. A, 5% vit. C, 1% calcium, and 6% iron.

Shiitake (shee-TAH-kay)
These have a rich, earthy taste with a hint of smokiness. Let them strut in more intensely flavored dishes.

Maitake (my-TAH-kay)
A meaty texture with a woodsy taste makes these a good match for pasta, smoked meats, or risotto.

Enoki (eh-NO-key)
Heat tends to wilt and toughen these tiny mild mushrooms. Best to serve them raw on salads.

Oyster
With their mild flavor, these do best in subtle soups or sautés.

Portobello
These are the big humdingers that make good meat substitutes. Great on the grill or sautéed.

White button
You'll have no trouble finding this common variety. Slice them for nibbling raw, or toss them in sauces or soups.

shiitake
oyster
maitake
portobello
enoki
white button

May

4 Chefs Great Pasta Happy Families

Toss around a few fun ideas this month— great pasta dishes and some fresh looks for spring greens and fruits. It's time to play!

By day, they're the superstars of America's culinary universe, but at night, they're just dads who face the challenge of creating dinners their families will love.

4 chefs great pasta happy families

Orecchiette with
Pancetta and Broccoli Rabe

Orecchiette with Pancetta and Broccoli Rabe

To prepare broccoli rabe, Chef Michael Chiarello trims away any wilted leaves and the woody ends of stems. In case you were wondering, pancetta is unsmoked Italian bacon.

Start to finish: 35 minutes

4 oz. pancetta, coarsely chopped	⅓ cup reduced-sodium chicken broth
6 oz. dried orecchiette pasta (1¾ cups) or small shell pasta	¼ cup pitted Greek black olives or ripe olives, or 2 Tbsp. drained capers or caper berries
2 tsp. olive oil	
4 cloves garlic, minced	¼ cup finely shredded Parmesan cheese
¼ tsp. crushed red pepper	
3 cups cut-up broccoli rabe or broccoli (see page 22)	

1. In a large skillet cook the pancetta over medium heat about 10 minutes or until browned and crisp. Drain on paper towels, reserving 1 tablespoon drippings in skillet. Set aside.

2. Cook pasta according to package directions. Drain; return to pan. Toss with olive oil; cover and keep warm.

3. In the same skillet heat the reserved drippings over medium heat. Add garlic and crushed red pepper; cook and stir for 30 seconds. Add broccoli rabe or broccoli and broth. Bring to boiling; reduce heat. Cover and simmer about 3 minutes or until broccoli rabe is tender. Stir in pancetta and olives or capers; heat through.

4. Add broccoli rabe mixture to pasta in saucepan. Add half of the Parmesan cheese and toss to combine. Transfer to a serving dish. Sprinkle with remaining cheese. Makes 6 servings.

Nutrition facts per serving: 211 cal., 9 g total fat (3 g sat. fat), 11 mg chol., 244 mg sodium, 25 g carbo., 2 g fiber, and 8 g pro. Daily Values: 14% vit. A, 59% vit. C, 7% calcium, and 7% iron.

"A good bowl of pasta is like getting a hug from the inside."

—Michael Chiarello

CHEFS' SPECIALTIES

For more great recipes from our featured chefs, try these cookbooks available at book stores everywhere.

Michael Chiarello's **The Tra Vigne Cookbook: Seasons in the California Wine Country** is a behind-the-scenes look at recipes from his Napa Valley restaurant. Lush photos and a contemporary design show off such seasonal dishes as Roasted Asparagus, Pumpkin Polenta, and Italian Holiday Cookies. The 215-page hardcover book is from Chronicle Books.

Pino Luongo's **Simply Tuscan** shares the cooking of the author's native land and helps to satisfy America's appetite for all things Tuscan. Recipes include Upside-Down Warm Apple Tart, Trout Roasted Porchetta-Style, and Carrot and Apple Puree. The 292-page hardcover book is from Random House.

Todd English became a star in the culinary world with his distinctive style of layering flavors and textures. **The Olives Dessert Table** is not a cookbook for those fearful of fat or short on time. Desserts such as Mango Tarte Tatin with Pastry Cream and Chocolate Pastry or Blue Cheese Danish with Port-Poached Pears combine familiar and comfortable flavors in unique and unexpected ways. The 256-page hardcover book is from Simon and Schuster.

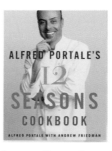

Alfred Portale's **12 Seasons Cookbook** takes the home cook on a journey through the year in food. Using the best of seasonal ingredients, he includes recipes for Lamb Chops and Truffled Mashed Potatoes, Grilled Soft-Shell Crabs with Asparagus, and Coconut Panna Cotta. The 400-page hardcover book is from Random House.

PERFECT PASTA MENU

Asparagus Finger Salad

(recipe, page 107)

Pork and Porcini Bolognese

(recipe, right)

Anytime Breadsticks (recipe, page 105)

Keen Nectarine (recipe, page 113)

Spring Garlic Pesto Perciatelli

This is a milder version of regular pesto. Spring garlic is garlic that has been picked when the plant is young and the flavor is mild. Look for it from February through the end of spring.

Start to finish: 35 minutes

15	cloves garlic or 6 oz. spring garlic	⅛	tsp. freshly ground black pepper
⅓	cup fresh basil leaves	1	Tbsp. olive oil
¾	cup olive oil	1	lb. dried perciatelli or spaghetti
⅓	cup pine nuts, toasted	¼	cup freshly grated pecorino Romano or Parmesan cheese
4	tsp. finely shredded pecorino Romano (a hard sheep's milk cheese) or Parmesan cheese		Small basil leaves
¾	tsp. sea salt or salt		Basil flowers

1. Bring a 4-quart Dutch oven or large pot of salted water to boiling. If using spring garlic, trim off the green part of garlic. Add garlic to the water and cook for 8 minutes. Remove garlic with a slotted spoon and immerse in a bowl of ice water. Add the ⅓ cup basil leaves to the boiling water and cook for 5 seconds; remove basil with a slotted spoon and drain well on paper towels. Peel garlic when cool enough to handle. Don't drain water; it is needed for cooking pasta.

2. For pesto, in a blender container or food processor bowl combine the garlic, briefly cooked basil, and the ¾ cup olive oil; cover and blend or process just until combined. Add 2 tablespoons of the pine nuts, 4 teaspoons cheese, salt, and pepper. Cover; blend or process mixture until nearly smooth.

3. Meanwhile, add the 1 tablespoon olive oil to the boiling water in which garlic and basil were cooked. Add pasta and cook according to package directions. Drain and return to pot. Toss pasta with the pesto mixture. Transfer to a serving bowl. Sprinkle with the remaining pine nuts, the ¼ cup cheese, small basil leaves, and basil flowers. Makes 6 to 8 servings.

Nutrition facts per serving: 461 cal., 27 g total fat (4 g sat. fat), 3 mg chol., 193 mg sodium, 46 g carbo., 2 g fiber, and 10 g pro. Daily Values: 6% vit. A, 5% vit. C, 7% calcium, and 15% iron.

Pork and Porcini Bolognese

You can substitute dried fettuccine for the refrigerated pasta.

Start to finish: 45 minutes

8	cups water	¾	cup beef broth
2¼	tsp. sea salt or salt	½	cup purchased chunky marinara sauce
1	oz. dried porcini mushrooms	1	Tbsp. snipped fresh parsley
1	bunch escarole, core removed, or 8 cups fresh spinach	1	Tbsp. olive oil
12	oz. bulk pork sausage	¼	tsp. freshly ground black pepper
½	cup chopped onion	2	9-oz. pkg. refrigerated tagliatelle or fettuccine
6	cloves garlic, minced	⅓	cup shaved Parmesan cheese
1	Tbsp. snipped fresh sage		
⅓	cup dry white wine		

1. In a 4-quart Dutch oven or large pot bring the 8 cups water and 2 teaspoons of the salt to boiling. Place mushrooms in a small bowl; add 1 cup of the boiling water. Let stand for 15 minutes.

2. Meanwhile, add escarole or spinach to the remaining boiling water. Return water to boiling; immediately drain escarole or spinach in a colander and rinse with cold water. Drain well, pressing out extra liquid. Chop greens and set aside. Drain mushrooms, reserving 2 tablespoons of the liquid. Chop mushrooms; set mushrooms and liquid aside.

3. In a large skillet cook sausage, onion, garlic, and sage until meat is brown, stirring to break up sausage. Drain off fat. Stir in white wine and reserved mushroom liquid. Bring to boiling; reduce heat. Boil gently, uncovered, about 7 minutes or until most of the liquid is evaporated. Add broth, marinara sauce, parsley, oil, pepper, and remaining ¼ teaspoon salt. Bring to boiling; reduce heat. Simmer, uncovered, for 2 minutes.

4. Meanwhile, cook pasta in the Dutch oven or pot according to package directions using fresh water. Drain pasta, reserving ¼ cup pasta water. Add pasta water, mushrooms, and cooked escarole or spinach to pork mixture. Heat through; spoon over cooked pasta. Toss before serving. Top with Parmesan cheese. Makes 6 servings.

Nutrition facts per serving: 540 cal., 23 g total fat (9 g sat. fat), 128 mg chol., 688 mg sodium, 56 g carbo., 5 g fiber, and 21 g pro. Daily Values: 31% vit. A, 16% vit. C, 14% calcium, and 18% iron.

Spring Garlic Pesto
Perciatelli

MICHAEL CHIARELLO

"Try this" is high on the list of favorite phrases for Michael Chiarello (key-a-rello). It's a constant refrain from the father of Margaux, 17, Felicia, 14, and Giana, 10. He views every meal as an opportunity to broaden the girls' taste buds and pass on values he learned growing up in his extended Italian-American family in Turlock, California. His enthusiasm for Italian cuisine is secondary to his real mission: Teaching people that the surest route to great food is through their heritage. "If you're not from a family rich in tradition, start your own," he says. Besides Italian, Chiarello is known for using seasonal foods on his PBS cooking series *Michael Chiarello's Napa*. The theme continues at NapaStyle, a company that includes his TV shows, Web site, and specialty foods. His cookbooks include *Casual Cooking* (2002), *Napa Stories* (2001), *The Tra Vigne Cookbook* (1999), *Flavored Vinegars* (1996), and *Flavored Oils* (1995).

Pork and Porcini
Bolognese

Pappardelle alla
Pepolino

PINO LUONGO

Great pasta is only half of the recipe for a successful dinnertime at the home of Pino Luongo. The author and restaurateur works hard to create a great atmosphere—an attitude he grew up with during his boyhood in Tuscany.

Pasta sets the mood when 48-year-old Luongo sits down with his wife, Jessie, and children Marcoantonio, 13, Jacobella, 12, and Lorenzo, 6.

"Pasta is a dish that's meant to be shared," he says. "It's the smell of the sauce, the cheese, the big bowl in the middle of the table, of everyone serving themselves. In Italy, we all learn to cook pasta dishes—everybody takes pride in shopping for food, and in buying only the best ingredients."

Pino has turned his firsthand knowledge of Italian cooking into a line of specialty foods and three books: *Simply Tuscan* (2000), *Fish Talking* (1994), and *A Tuscan in the Kitchen* (1988).

"Cooking pasta isn't about ego, it's about sharing."

—Pino Luongo

Fettuccine with Baby
Artichokes and Shrimp

Fettuccine with Baby Artichokes and Shrimp

Fresh baby artichokes are available mid-March through May.

Prep: 30 minutes **Cook:** 20 minutes

8 oz. dried fettuccine or spaghetti	1 cup Shrimp Broth or chicken broth
8 baby artichokes or one 9-oz. pkg. frozen artichoke hearts, thawed and halved lengthwise	1 Tbsp. butter
	1 tsp. finely shredded lemon peel
4 cloves garlic, minced	½ tsp. salt
3 Tbsp. olive oil	½ tsp. ground nutmeg
1 lb. shrimp in shells, peeled and deveined (reserve shells for broth)	1 Tbsp. snipped fresh Italian flat-leaf parsley
	4 slices Italian country bread or other hearty bread, toasted
½ cup dry white wine	Lemon halves or wedges
2 plum tomatoes, finely chopped	

1. In a large saucepan cook the pasta according to package directions; drain well and set aside.

2. Meanwhile, if using baby artichokes, cut off the bases of artichokes. Snap off outer leaves until pale green petals are reached. Cut off top third of an artichoke; trim the artichoke stem. Quarter the artichoke lengthwise and remove fuzzy "choke," if necessary. Repeat with remaining artichokes.

3. In a large skillet cook garlic in 2 tablespoons of the hot olive oil for 30 seconds; remove from skillet. Add artichokes to skillet and cook for 1 minute. Add shrimp and wine to skillet. Cook and stir for 2 minutes. Stir in tomatoes, Shrimp Broth, butter, lemon peel, salt, nutmeg, and cooked pasta; heat through. Stir in the parsley; drizzle with remaining olive oil.

4. To serve, place bread slices in four shallow soup bowls. With a slotted spoon, divide pasta mixture among bowls. Add additional Shrimp Broth as desired. Squeeze lemon halves over pasta mixture. Makes 4 servings.

Shrimp Broth: In a large saucepan combine 3 cups water, the reserved shells from the 1 pound of shrimp, 4 sprigs fresh Italian flat-leaf parsley, 1 slice lemon, and ¼ teaspoon pepper. Bring to boiling over high heat; reduce heat. Simmer, uncovered, for 10 minutes. Strain broth.

Nutrition facts per serving: 564 cal., 17 g total fat (4 g sat. fat), 137 mg chol., 477 mg sodium, 66 g carbo., 6 g fiber, and 30 g pro. Daily Values: 10% vit. A, 21% vit. C, 12% calcium, and 28% iron.

Pappardelle alla Pepolino

To turn this recipe into a main dish, add cooked shrimp or cooked tuna just before heating through.

Start to finish: 40 minutes

12 oz. dried pappardelle, mafalda, or fettuccine	¼ tsp. crushed red pepper
	1 recipe Roasted Tomatoes
1 clove garlic, minced	¼ tsp. freshly ground black pepper
2 Tbsp. olive oil	
1 8-oz. can tomato sauce	¼ cup coarsely shaved pecorino Romano or Parmesan cheese*
1 Tbsp. snipped fresh thyme	

1. In a large saucepan cook pasta according to package directions; drain and set aside.

2. In the same pan cook garlic in hot olive oil for 30 seconds. Stir in tomato sauce, half of the thyme, and the crushed red pepper. Bring to boiling; reduce heat. Simmer, uncovered, for 2 minutes.

3. Add pasta, Roasted Tomatoes, remaining thyme, and black pepper. Heat through. Season to taste with additional salt and black pepper. Transfer to a serving dish. Sprinkle with cheese. Makes 8 side-dish or 4 main-dish servings.

Roasted Tomatoes: Preheat oven to 450° F. Line a 15x10x1-inch baking pan with foil. Halve 8 plum tomatoes; place, cut sides up, on the prepared pan. Drizzle with 1 tablespoon olive oil; sprinkle with salt and black pepper. Roast, uncovered, for 20 to 25 minutes or until bottoms of tomatoes are dark brown. Remove from pan; carefully halve each piece.

***Test Kitchen Tip:** To shave cheese into strips, draw a vegetable peeler across the block of cheese.

Nutrition facts per side-dish serving: 234 cal., 7 g total fat (1 g sat. fat), 2 mg chol., 248 mg sodium, 36 g carbo., 2 g fiber, and 7 g pro. Daily Values: 7% vit. A, 19% vit. C, 4% calcium, and 10% iron.

30 Quick Tomato Sauce

Pino Luongo stirs up this sauce when fresh tomatoes are not at their best. He uses canned tomatoes imported from Italy.

Start to finish: 20 minutes

1. In a food processor bowl or blender container puree one 28-ounce can whole tomatoes. Cover and blend or process until smooth. Add 3 tablespoons snipped fresh basil; blend or process until mixed.

2. In a medium saucepan, cook 2 minced cloves garlic in 2 tablespoons hot olive oil over medium heat until garlic is just lightly browned. Remove garlic. Add pureed tomatoes, ¼ teaspoon salt, and ¼ teaspoon freshly ground black pepper. Bring to boiling; reduce heat. Simmer, uncovered, for 10 minutes. Remove from heat. Serve over cooked pasta. Makes 3 cups, enough for 4 to 6 servings.

Nutrition facts per ¾ cup sauce: 98 cal., 7 g total fat (1 g sat. fat), 0 mg chol., 439 mg sodium, 9 g carbo., 2 g fiber, and 2 g pro.

30 low fat

White Beans, Spiral Pasta, and Lobster

This dish works well with any firm-fleshed white fish or, if you prefer, substitute peeled cooked shrimp.

Start to finish: 30 minutes

8	oz. dried cavatappi, fusilli, or rotini (corkscrew) pasta	12	oz. cooked lobster* or 12 oz. fresh or frozen cod fillets, cooked and cut into 1-inch pieces
1	15- to 19-oz. can cannellini (white kidney) beans, rinsed and drained	¼	cup snipped fresh Italian flat-leaf parsley
½	cup chicken broth	½	to 1 tsp. cracked black pepper
3	cloves garlic, thinly sliced	½	tsp. salt
1	Tbsp. olive oil		Fresh Italian flat-leaf parsley sprigs (optional)
6	plum tomatoes, coarsely chopped (about 2 cups)		Olive oil (optional)

1. In a large saucepan cook the pasta according to package directions; drain well and set aside.

2. In a blender container or food processor bowl combine ¾ cup of the drained beans and the chicken broth; cover and blend or process until smooth. Add to the pan used for cooking the pasta; bring to boiling. Return pasta to pan.

3. Meanwhile, in a large skillet cook garlic in 1 tablespoon hot olive oil for 1 minute. Add tomatoes; cook for 1 minute. Add the remaining beans, cooked lobster or cod, snipped parsley, pepper, and salt. Heat through.

4. Add the tomato mixture to hot pasta; toss to coat. Top with parsley sprigs and additional olive oil. Serve immediately. Makes 4 servings.

*Test Kitchen Tip: If cooked lobster is not available, cook 3 lobster tails; remove meat from shells and cut up. To broil lobster, use a large knife to cut through top shell, cutting just to bottom shell; press lobster open. Place, cut side up, on broiler pan. If desired, brush with melted butter. Broil 4 to 5 inches from heat for 12 to 15 minutes or until meat is opaque.

Nutrition facts per serving: 450 cal., 7 g total fat (1 g sat. fat), 77 mg chol., 786 mg sodium, 65 g carbo., 7 g fiber, and 37 g pro. Daily Values: 16% vit. A, 41% vit. C, 10% calcium, and 26% iron.

Free-Form Basil Lasagna

If you have no pasta machine and you're a very patient person, you can roll the homemade lasagna with a rolling pin on a lightly floured surface. Or, use dried noodles (see below).

Prep: 1 hour **Roast:** 50 minutes **Bake:** 30 minutes

1	cup unbleached all-purpose flour or all-purpose flour	½	cup finely shredded Parmesan cheese
⅛	tsp. salt	½	cup snipped fresh basil or ¼ cup snipped fresh oregano or sage
1	egg		
2	Tbsp. water	⅛	tsp. freshly ground black pepper
1	tsp. olive oil		
8	oz. fresh mozzarella cheese, cubed	1	recipe Roasted Tomato Sauce or 2¼ cups purchased meatless spaghetti sauce
6	oz. fontina cheese, shredded		
½	cup ricotta cheese		Fresh sage sprigs (optional)

1. For pasta*, in a medium bowl combine flour and salt. Beat together egg, water, and olive oil. Pour into flour mixture; stir until combined. Knead on a lightly floured surface until smooth and elastic (8 to 10 minutes). Cover; let rest for 10 minutes. For filling, stir together cheeses, desired herb, and pepper.

2. Preheat oven to 350° F. Divide dough into 5 pieces. Roll out in a pasta machine according to manufacturer's directions. Sheets should be 15x4½ inches. Trim each sheet to a 12x4-inch rectangle. Spread about ⅔ cup filling over each rectangle, leaving a 1-inch border along long sides. Fold the two long sides over edges of filling, then roll up from a short side to enclose filling. Place in individual au gratin dishes or shallow casseroles. Top each with about ½ cup Roasted Tomato Sauce, covering pasta. Bake, uncovered, about 30 minutes or until sauce is bubbly. If desired, garnish with sage sprigs. Makes 5 servings.

Roasted Tomato Sauce: Preheat oven to 375° F. In a large roasting pan toss together 1½ pounds tomatoes, cored and halved; 1 medium onion, sliced; ⅓ cup water or chicken broth; ¼ cup fresh basil leaves; 2 tablespoons cooking oil; 1 teaspoon kosher salt; and ¼ to ½ teaspoon freshly ground black pepper. Bake 50 minutes or until skins are slightly charred. Cool slightly. With a slotted spoon, remove tomatoes; coarsely chop. In a medium bowl combine tomatoes and juices and herbs from pan. Cover; chill until ready to use. Makes 2¼ cups.

*Test Kitchen Tip: You can use 10 dried lasagna noodles instead of fresh pasta. Cook noodles according to package directions; drain well and cool. Spread about ⅓ cup filling onto each noodle; roll up from a short side and place two rolls, seam sides down, in each au gratin dish. Cover with sauce, being careful to cover edges so they won't dry out. Bake as above.

Nutrition facts per serving: 540 cal., 34 g total fat (17 g sat. fat), 139 mg chol., 1,046 mg sodium, 29 g carbo., 3 g fiber, and 29 g pro. Daily Values: 41% vit. A, 37% vit. C, 60% calcium, and 13% iron.

White Beans, Spiral Pasta, and Lobster

"It's wonderful cooking pasta for kids; it's something they'll always remember."

—Todd English

TODD ENGLISH

The aroma of olive oil, garlic, and onions sizzling in a pan for pasta sauce is one of chef Todd English's favorite memories of growing up—an experience he tries to re-create for his kids Oliver, 11, Isabelle, 8, and Simon, 6.

He believes simplicity is crucial to success in pasta cooking with— or without—children in mind.

"Try not to be too fussy—the pasta should be as important as the sauce; it should never be too heavy." he says.

The 41-year-old father developed his philosophy on his long and wandering route from captain of his Connecticut high school baseball team through the prestigious Culinary Institute of America, to head a company that now operates 16 restaurants in seven states.

His practical approach has served him well as host of *Cooking In with Todd English* on PBS and as author of three books: *The Olives Dessert Table* (2000), *The Figs Table* (1998), and *The Olives Table* (1997).

Free-Form Basil Lasagna

Fusilli with Prosciutto
and Fava Beans

"Pasta is the consummate comfort food. It's easy, it's versatile, it's satisfying."

—Alfred Portale

Chicken Soup
with Ham and Orzo

ALFRED PORTALE

Pasta topped with a favorite little something is the key to Alfred Portale's success in getting daughters Olympia, 13, and Victoria, 10, to enjoy dinner.

"I pair it with foods they like," says the 46-year-old chef of Gotham Bar and Grill restaurant in New York City. Though Portale (por-TAL-ee) uses his restaurant magic at home, cooking for family is different from being a chef. "With my children," he says, "I'm trying to expand their horizons. I talk about how to taste, about texture and flavor, and when one is eating too fast, I try to teach her to slow down and savor it." Portale trained first as a jewelry designer, then enrolled at the Culinary Institute of America, graduating first in his class. After stints in other restaurants, he became chef at Gotham in 1984. He offers up lessons from his two decades in the kitchen in his two books: *The 12 Seasons Cookbook* (2000) and The *Gotham Bar and Grill Cookbook* (1997).

Chicken Soup with Ham and Orzo

low fat

Chef Portale suggests drizzling each portion with a little extra-virgin olive oil.

Start to finish: 35 minutes

7 cups White Chicken Stock or four 14-oz. cans reduced-sodium chicken broth	4 cups lightly packed, thinly sliced Swiss chard
2 bone-in chicken breast halves (1 lb.)	4 plum tomatoes, seeded and chopped
1 cup dried orzo (rosamarina) pasta (small, rice-shaped pasta)	2 oz. cooked ham, cut into ½-inch cubes
¾ lb. asparagus spears	Coarse salt Freshly ground black pepper Snipped fresh chives Snipped fresh Italian flat-leaf parsley

1. In a 4-quart Dutch oven combine White Chicken Stock or broth and chicken. Bring to boiling; reduce heat. Cover and simmer about 20 minutes or until chicken is no longer pink. Remove chicken from broth; cool slightly. Discard skin and bones. Shred chicken into bite-size pieces.

2. Return broth to boiling; add orzo. Return to boiling; reduce heat. Cook, uncovered, for 7 minutes. Meanwhile, wash asparagus; break off woody bases where spears snap easily (see photo, page 63). Cut the asparagus diagonally into 1½-inch pieces. Add asparagus to broth in Dutch oven. Cook for 3 minutes more.

3. Stir Swiss chard, tomatoes, ham, and shredded cooked chicken into broth in Dutch oven. Heat through. Season to taste with salt and pepper.

4. To serve, top individual portions with snipped chives and parsley. Makes 6 servings.

White Chicken Stock: In a very large pot combine 6 pounds chicken bones, cut up (substitute wings if bones or carcasses are unavailable), and 4 quarts cold water (water should cover chicken by about 2 inches). Bring to boiling. Skim any foam that rises to the surface. Add 1 large onion, chopped; 1 small carrot, coarsely chopped; 1 small stalk celery; 1 bulb garlic, halved crosswise; 2 sprigs fresh thyme; 2 sprigs fresh Italian flat-leaf parsley; 1 bay leaf; and 1 teaspoon whole pepper. Reduce heat. Simmer, uncovered, about 6 hours. Strain the stock through a sieve into a large bowl. Cool completely. Cover and refrigerate. Skim off and discard fat on the surface. Makes 15 cups.

Nutrition facts per serving: 286 cal., 8 g total fat (2 g sat. fat), 44 mg chol., 1,115 mg sodium, 26 g carbo., 2 g fiber, and 25 g pro. Daily Values: 25% vit. A, 32% vit. C, 4% calcium, and 6% iron.

30 Fusilli with Prosciutto and Fava Beans

You can prepare Herbed Garlic Butter up to a week in advance and freeze it until you're ready to use it.

Start to finish: 25 minutes

12 oz. dried fusilli or bow-tie pasta	¼ cup coarsely shredded pecorino Toscano cheese or grated Parmesan cheese
1 recipe Herbed Garlic Butter	
1 19-oz. can fava or cannellini (white kidney) beans, rinsed and drained	1½ cups loosely packed torn arugula or watercress
2 cups grape tomatoes or halved cherry tomatoes	3 Tbsp. snipped fresh chives Coarse salt
4 oz. thinly sliced prosciutto, torn into bite-size pieces	Freshly ground white pepper Coarsely shredded pecorino Toscano cheese or grated Parmesan cheese

1. In a 4-quart Dutch oven cook pasta in 3 quarts of lightly salted boiling water according to package directions. Just before draining pasta, remove ½ cup of the pasta cooking water and set aside. Drain pasta; return to warm pan.

2. Immediately add Herbed Garlic Butter to pasta along with beans, tomatoes, prosciutto, and the ¼ cup cheese. Gradually add ⅓ to ½ cup of the reserved cooking liquid while tossing constantly over low heat, as the butter and cheese melt to form a sauce. Add the arugula and chives; toss again. Season to taste with salt and pepper. Serve immediately. Top with additional coarsely shredded cheese. Makes 8 servings.

Herbed Garlic Butter: In a small bowl combine ⅓ cup softened butter, 4 cloves minced garlic, 2 teaspoons snipped fresh thyme, 1 teaspoon lemon juice, and ¼ teaspoon freshly ground black pepper; stir until smooth. Wrap tightly and refrigerate until ready to use.

Nutrition facts per serving: 331 cal., 12 g total fat (6 g sat. fat), 74 mg chol., 722 mg sodium, 41 g carbo., 8 g fiber, and 15 g pro. Daily Values: 15% vit. A, 22% vit. C, 8% calcium, and 11% iron.

SPRING GARDEN MENU

Mesclun with Pears and Blue Cheese
(recipe, page 108)

Fusilli with Prosciutto and Fava Beans
(recipe, above)

Crusty Italian Bread

Rhubarb Crisp (recipe, page 115)

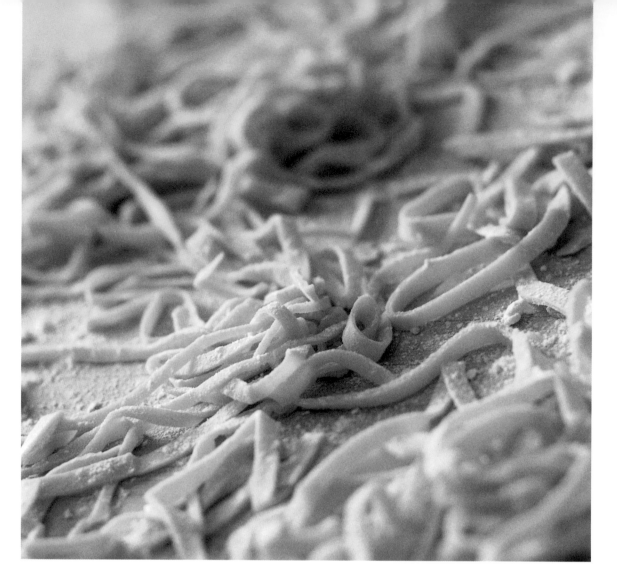

Handmade
Pasta

This is one of those recipes where joy

is as much in the mixing, kneading, and rolling as it is in the delight you and your family share when you finally sit down to eat it.

Your hands, not your brain, are in charge on this job. "Pasta is a feel, not a recipe," says chef Michael Chiarello, who bases his recipe on one he helped his

mother and aunts make countless times as a child in the California farm belt. His mother taught him to appreciate the pairing of pasta and fresh vegetables.

These noodles—enriched by egg yolks—taste great with extra virgin olive oil, a shower of herbs, Parmesan cheese, and a quick tomato sauce. "Make a vinaigrette with shallots, garlic, parsley, lemon juice, basil oil, salt, and pepper, and toss in whatever's in season: zucchini, roasted peppers, or vine-ripe tomatoes," Michael says.

Little additions with big impact are the foundation of Chiarello's pasta dishes. His shelves are packed with foods he has either made or holds close to his heart—cans of Italian tuna, homemade pickled vegetables, home-canned tomato sauce, and his favorite red peppers.

Michael's Family Handmade Pasta

Start to finish: 1 hour

2½ cups all-purpose flour
1 tsp. gray or kosher salt
6 egg yolks
1½ Tbsp. olive oil
4 to 6 Tbsp. water

1. On a work surface, heap flour and make a large well in the center. Sprinkle flour with salt, and place egg yolks and oil in the well. With your fingertips, mix yolk mixture into flour. Sprinkle with water, and mix with hands until it forms a ball.

2. Knead 10 minutes or until dough feels smooth (it will still appear slightly lumpy). Flatten into a disk, wrap, and refrigerate for 20 minutes.

3. On a lightly floured surface, roll dough to 1/16-inch-thick circle. Dust top lightly with flour. Roll up from one edge.

4. Cut crosswise into 1/4-inch-wide strips. Unroll and separate strips.

5. Allow to dry (about 5 minutes).

6. To cook, drop pasta into a large pot containing a large amount of boiling salted water. Cook 5 to 8 minutes or until tender. Makes 4 to 6 servings.

Nutrition facts per serving: 289 cal., 10 g total fat (2 g sat. fat), 213 mg chol., 330 mg sodium, 40 g carbo., 1 g fiber, and 8 g pro.

Making Michael's Pasta

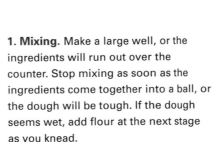

1. Mixing. Make a large well, or the ingredients will run out over the counter. Stop mixing as soon as the ingredients come together into a ball, or the dough will be tough. If the dough seems wet, add flour at the next stage as you knead.

2. Kneading. Push dough down with the heels of your hands, give it a quarter turn, fold, and do it again—for about 10 minutes. "This is the meditative side of cooking," says Michael.

3. Rolling. Patience is the key to successful rolling—steady work will get the dough to about the thickness of a penny. To help the dough relax and soften, roll each time in a different direction. If the dough shrinks back when you roll, cover with plastic wrap and let rest about 10 minutes. To prevent noodles from getting too thin on the edges, ease up on the pin as you reach the edge of the dough.

4. Slicing. After you roll up the dough, use a sharp, thin knife to cut noodles.

5. Drying. Allow the noodles to dry slightly before cooking. Part of their charm is their irregularity. "I could make them perfect," says Michael. "But what would I have gained? You want people to be able to see you took the time to make pasta."

Anytime Breadsticks

Come on, baby, do the twist. Refrigerated breadstick dough turns into rustic bakery-fresh snacks for anytime of day. Start with a 10-ounce package of refrigerated breadstick dough and choose from the flavor options to the left. Depending on the flavor, the sticks make great dinnertime serve-alongs, especially with pasta, salads, and soups. Or serve them as an after-school or picnic snack. Fill and roll, grab and go!

Parmesan-Prosciutto

Spread dough with Dijon-style mustard. Layer with thinly sliced, snipped prosciutto and grated Parmesan cheese or sliced Swiss cheese.

Pile-on-Pesto

Slather dough with a generous amount of prepared pesto sauce. Add a few pine nuts, if you like.

Herbal Blend

Brush dough with olive oil. Heap on a handful each of coarsely chopped thyme and parsley. Drizzle top with additional olive oil. Sprinkle with coarse salt.

Trail Mix

Coat dough with honey; sprinkle with cinnamon. Press raisin-nut trail mix lightly into dough. (Some mix will fall out when you twist.) Brush top with melted butter.

Cheese-Stuffed

Brush dough with your favorite Italian salad dressing. Add fresh Parmesan cheese or spread with Boursin cheese. Spoon additional dressing on top.

Olive-Rosemary

Press pitted, chopped kalamata olives into dough. Twist to enclose olives. (Expect some olives to spill out.) Scatter top with snipped fresh rosemary.

Start with a 10-ounce package of refrigerated breadstick dough. Preheat oven according to the breadstick dough package directions. Separate dough into strips. Flavor each one as you please (suggestions, left).

Twist the breadstick dough around the fillings. Don't worry if the breadsticks aren't perfect or if some of the filling falls out.

Place breadsticks on a baking sheet. Brush with olive oil or melted butter. Sprinkle with salt or fresh or dried herbs. Bake as package directs.

PHOTOGRAPHS: COLLEEN DUFFLEY. FOOD STYLIST: BROOKE LEONARD. STORY: STEPHEN EXEL.

Don't Forget Folate

PHOTOGRAPHS: COLLEEN DUFFLEY. FOOD STYLIST: BROOKE LEONARD. STORY: BEV BENNETT.

It's a no brainer. Get enough

of the vitamin B folate and you may prevent some of the forgetfulness that occurs with aging. Folate and its manmade version, folic acid, play a key role in brain function.

Forget where you put your cell phone again? Chow down on a handful of folate-rich peanuts. Actually it's not as simple as all that, but "keeping folate levels high is extremely important to memory," says scientist Martha Morris, Ph.D., of Tufts University in Boston.

Folate and other B vitamins also assist the body in lowering levels of homocysteine, an amino acid that increases the risk of heart disease. In fact, this finding appears to be closely related to claims of a poor memory.

In a report published in the *American Journal of Clinical Nutrition*, Morris and her colleagues found a link between poor recall and high homocysteine.

Further digging provided evidence that high levels of folate seemed to offer some protection against memory loss.

Remember this

So if you find yourself at a party fumbling for the name of that person you just met, maybe you need to alter your diet a bit.

Black beans and other dried beans and peas are full of folate. So are deep-green leafy vegetables, asparagus, strawberries, artichokes, and citrus fruits (see chart, opposite). Enriched grain products, including bread, flour, rice, breakfast cereal, and pasta, have been fortified with folic acid since 1998. That requirement—set by the U.S. Food and Drug Administration—came about when it was determined that adequate folate taken by women in their child-bearing years reduced the risk of certain birth defects affecting the brain and spinal cord.

Your daily dose

The recommended daily intake of folate is 400 micrograms (mcg). Pregnant women should take in 800 mcg. Most people get adequate folate in their diets, Morris says, but pregnant women may be advised to take a vitamin supplement with folic acid.

A serving of most breakfast cereals, for instance, provides about 25 percent of the daily folate requirement for the average person in the country. Check the nutrition label on the package to find the exact amount of folate.

The latest folate buzz also has researchers looking at the nutrient's impact on Parkinson's disease and Alzheimer's disease. Trials will be launched by the National Institute on Aging this year to see if a regimen of folate and other B vitamins slows the rate of progression of Alzheimer's disease. Studies on mice have shown that a group that got less folic acid had higher levels of homocysteine in their bodies and were more susceptible to Parkinson's-like abnormalities.

Folate also reduces your risk of colon cancer. Several studies have shown that high levels of folate in the body lower the risk of colon cancer. Folic acid commonly found in vitamin supplements appears to offer the same protection.

FINDING FOLATE

Here are some of your best folate choices:

FOOD	SERVING SIZE	FOLATE AMOUNT (MICROGRAMS)
Breakfast cereal	½ cup to 1½ cups	100 - 400 mcg
Lentils	½ cup cooked	179 mcg
Black beans	½ cup cooked	178 mcg
Artichoke	1 medium boiled	153 mcg
Asparagus	½ cup cooked	131 mcg
Turnip greens	½ cup boiled, chopped	85 mcg
Orange juice, fresh	1 cup	75 mcg
Kidney beans	½ cup cooked	65 mcg

30 Asparagus Finger Salad

Aparagus is a good source of folate to enjoy as a snack or side dish.

Prep: 15 minutes **Cook:** 2 minutes

8 oz. fresh asparagus spears	2 tsp. finely shredded lemon peel
4 large butterhead lettuce or romaine lettuce leaves	1 recipe Tarragon Dipping Sauce
1 small carrot, halved lengthwise	

1. Snap off and discard woody bases from asparagus (see photo, page 63). If desired, scrape off scales. Cover and cook asparagus in a small amount of boiling water for 2 to 4 minutes or until crisp-tender. Transfer asparagus to a bowl filled with ice water. Set aside.

2. To serve, cut center vein from each lettuce leaf, keeping each leaf in one piece. Place lettuce leaves on a serving plate. Pat asparagus dry with paper towels. Cut each carrot half into four equal lengthwise strips.

3. Divide asparagus and carrot strips evenly across the middle of the lettuce. Sprinkle each serving with finely shredded lemon peel. Wrap lettuce around asparagus and carrots. Place each asparagus salad upright in a small cup. Serve or drizzle with Tarragon Dipping Sauce. Makes 4 servings.

Tarragon Dipping Sauce: In a small bowl combine ⅓ cup light dairy sour cream, 1 tablespoon fresh snipped chives, 2 teaspoons lemon juice, 1 teaspoon fresh snipped tarragon, ⅛ teaspoon salt, and ⅛ teaspoon freshly ground black pepper. Cover and chill until serving time.

Nutrition facts per serving: 49 cal., 3 g total fat (2 g sat. fat), 8 mg chol., 93 mg sodium, 5 g carbo., 2 g fiber, and 2 g pro. Daily Values: 96% vit. A, 19% vit. C, 4% calcium, and 3% iron.

 new 30

Mesclun with Pears and Blue Cheese

In a real rush? Substitute your favorite balsamic vinaigrette for the dressing.
Start to finish: 25 minutes

10	cups mesclun and/or baby greens
3	medium red and/or green pears, cored and thinly sliced
1	recipe Pear-Ginger Vinaigrette
½	cup broken walnuts, toasted, or
1	recipe Candied Nuts
½	cup crumbled blue cheese

In a large salad bowl combine mesclun and pear slices. Toss gently to combine. Pour Pear-Ginger Vinaigrette over salad; toss gently to coat. Divide the salad evenly among eight salad plates. Sprinkle with nuts and blue cheese. Makes 8 servings.

Pear-Ginger Vinaigrette: In a screwtop jar combine ¼ cup pear nectar, 2 tablespoons walnut oil or salad oil, 2 tablespoons white wine vinegar, 1 teaspoon Dijon-style mustard, ⅛ teaspoon ground ginger, and ⅛ teaspoon pepper. Cover and shake well to mix.

Candied Nuts: Line a baking sheet with foil; butter foil. In a 10-inch heavy skillet combine 1½ cups raw or roasted cashews, peanuts, almonds, and pecan or walnut halves; ½ cup sugar; 2 tablespoons butter; and ½ teaspoon vanilla. Cook over medium-high heat, shaking skillet occasionally, until sugar begins to melt. Do not stir. Reduce heat to low. Continue cooking until sugar is golden brown, stirring occasionally. Remove from heat. Pour nut mixture onto the prepared baking sheet. Cool completely. Break into clusters. Store nuts, tightly covered, in the refrigerator for up to 3 weeks. Makes 1½ cups.

Nutrition facts per serving with walnuts: 152 cal., 11 g total fat (2 g sat. fat), 5 mg chol., 110 mg sodium, 13 g carbo., 3 g fiber, and 4 g pro. Daily Values: 6% vit. A, 10% vit. C, 7% calcium, and 4% iron.

Micro Greens

Little lettuces mimic their mature family members in flavor—but in a sweetly mild manner. Add them to just about anything for a bite of freshness. You can look for these baby greens on their own or buy a mixture of greens called mesclun, which may be sold in a package or loose. The greens in mesclun may vary, but can include arugula, dandelion, frissée, greens, mâche, mizuna, oak leaf lettuce, radicchio, sorrel, and tatsoi. For mesclun or any green, look for crisp leaves with no signs of wilting. Before serving, wash leaves in cold water, drain in a colander, and pat dry with paper towels. Store in a plastic bag lined with paper towels for up to 5 days.

Red Mustard Greens　　**Micro Red Mustard Greens**

You'll see micro greens in trendy restaurants and upscale food markets. They're just basic greens snipped while the leaves are still tiny. Typically, you'll find them packaged as a mix of miniatures. Don't see them in the store? Beg your produce manager to order some. They're available year-round. Or grow your own. Call Johnny's Seeds for guidance, 207/437-4301, or check the Web site: www.johnnyseeds.com and do a search for "greens."

Tatsoi　　**Micro Tatsoi**

Mizuna　　**Micro Mizuna**

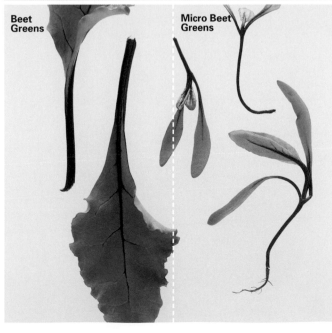

Beet Greens　　**Micro Beet Greens**

Red Mustard Greens

The teeny version is tangy and tender. Its horseradish-like bite gives sandwiches some snap.

Tatsoi

These small spoon-shaped leaves will remind you of Swiss chard with a little zip.

Mizuna

A jaggedy shape and a sharp-but-mellow taste make this bitsy green a dressy topper for just about anything.

Beet Greens

Its purplish-red veins and stem add great color. These mild-mannered fellas have a very subtle beet flavor. They're delicately delicious floating on a light soup.

Apple mint
Lightly scented
with apple.

Pineapple mint
Fragrant multicolor leaves
of green and cream.

Peppermint
Widely available;
a bit more
pungent and
peppery than
spearmint.

Lime mint
Very aromatic with
a full flavor.

Spearmint
A mild-tasting
variety, commonly
found in super-
markets and
garden shops.

Ginger mint
A mingling
of two
warm flavors.

A Touch of Mint

Mint can do much more than dress up a julep or a lamb chop. This flavorful, internationally popular herb is a tasty player with a variety of foods.

Mint's pronounced effect shows up immediately in dishes, making it a worthwhile last-minute stir-in. Smelling and tasting are the best ways to judge how much mint to use. Start with a small amount, then add more as needed. If a recipe calls for dried mint, substitute three times the amount of fresh.

When adding snipped fresh mint to hot mixtures, stir it in just before serving; its flavor lessens during long cooking. Try it a number of ways:

■ Steep it: Add ½ cup of fresh mint leaves when you make a pot of tea.

■ Soak it: Combine slightly crushed fresh mint leaves in a saucepan with 2 parts water and 1 part sugar; bring to boiling. Stir to dissolve sugar. Cool; spoon over ice cream or fresh fruit.

■ Roll it: Stir together equal amounts of tahini paste and mayonnaise. Spread on top of a flour tortilla; layer with deli roast beef, mint leaves, and mesclun salad mix. Roll up and serve.

■ Whip it: Combine snipped fresh mint and cooked fresh asparagus in a blender. Add enough of the vegetable cooking water to blend until smooth. Chill for a refreshing summer soup.

■ Toss it: Stir a generous amount of snipped fresh mint into cooked couscous with grilled chicken and vegetables. Drizzle with olive oil.

To store fresh mint, rinse it well and place the stems in a vase of water; don't immerse the leaves. The sprigs will stay fresh for 2 to 3 days at room temperature. For longer storage, place a plastic bag over the leaves and refrigerate for up to a week, changing the water every two days.

Spearmint is the variety you'll find most often in the grocery store. However, the common garden types (pictured) can be used interchangeably in recipes.

AROMATIC GARDENING

When planting your garden, consider tucking in a few mint plants. This perennial is easy to grow, but it spreads quickly and can overtake a garden. Use a permanent barrier to separate it from other plants, or grow it in big pots. The flavor of mint is strongest just before it begins to flower. Pick mint early in the morning because the sun draws out some of the plant's essential oils.

new Tabbouleh

There is no need to cook the bulgur for this salad—the mint-lemon dressing softens it while the salad chills.

Prep: 25 minutes   **Chill:** 4 hours

¾ cup bulgur	2 Tbsp. thinly sliced green
1 small cucumber, peeled, seeded, and chopped	onion
3 Tbsp. snipped fresh parsley	1 recipe Mint-Lemon Vinaigrette
2 Tbsp. snipped fresh mint or 2 tsp. dried mint, crushed	½ cup chopped, seeded tomato (1 small)

1. Place bulgur in a colander; rinse with cold water and drain. In a medium bowl combine bulgur, cucumber, parsley, mint, and green onion. Pour Mint-Lemon Vinaigrette over bulgur mixture. Toss gently to coat. Cover and chill for 4 to 24 hours.

2. Before serving, bring tabbouleh to room temperature. Just before serving, stir in tomato. Makes 4 to 6 servings.

Mint-Lemon Vinaigrette: In a screw-top jar combine ¼ cup olive oil or salad oil, 3 tablespoons lemon juice, 2 tablespoons water, ¼ teaspoon salt, and ⅛ teaspoon pepper. Cover and shake well to mix. Makes ½ cup.

Nutrition facts per serving: 228 cal., 14 g total fat (2 g sat. fat), 0 mg chol., 156 mg sodium, 24 g carbo., 6 g fiber, and 4 g pro. Daily Values: 8% vit. A, 31% vit. C, 3% calcium, and 9% iron.

Luscious, Fast
Fruit Desserts

With a little dressing up, you can turn fresh fruit into light, showstopper desserts that use just four ingredients or less. These three easy ideas take advantage of what's in favor for summer—mangoes, peaches, cherries, and nectarines. They're perfect for a refreshing ending to a spicy backyard cookout because you just cut 'em up, add a little of this and a little of that, and bring 'em out on a tray.

Mango Whip

Seed and peel two mangoes or peaches. Cut into wedges. Divide fruit between two chilled dessert bowls. In a mixing bowl beat together $\frac{1}{4}$ cup softened light cream cheese and 2 tablespoons white grape or orange juice. Spoon over mangoes. Top with chopped pistachios.

Cherry Dream

Mound ¼ cup prepared vanilla custard, vanilla pudding, or tapioca pudding into a chilled dessert bowl. Spoon about ½ cup pitted, halved dark sweet cherries over custard. Drizzle with a cherry liqueur, such as kirsch.

Keen Nectarine

Scoop ⅓ cup vanilla or peach-flavored frozen yogurt (or vanilla or peach-flavored ice cream) into a chilled dessert bowl. Add half of a pitted ripe nectarine or peach. Sprinkle with crumbled amaretti cookies or gingersnaps.

Tomato-Rhubarb
Chutney

Ready for
Rhubarb

Rhubarb is nature's little sweet-tart vegetable. It has a not-so-demure flavor that sends some fans into a swoon, while others just pucker up to its sassy taste. Hothouse rhubarb (found almost year-round in grocery stores) has pink to pale red stalks. The more assertively flavored field-grown rhubarb sports ruby red stalks and is available from late winter to early summer. The leaves of both varieties are highly toxic and should never be eaten.

When purchasing rhubarb, look for stalks that are crisp and brightly hued. Refrigerate it tightly wrapped in plastic, and use within three days of purchase.

Rhubarb is also known as "pieplant," because of its most obvious association. Try it in our pie, crisp, and bold chutney.

 Rhubarb Pie

Serve with ice cream, of course.

Prep: 30 minutes **Bake:** 45 minutes

¾ cup sugar
⅓ cup all-purpose flour
½ tsp. ground cinnamon
6 cups fresh or frozen unsweetened sliced rhubarb, thawed
1 15-oz. package folded refrigerated unbaked piecrust (2 crusts)

1. Preheat oven to 375° F. For filling, in a large bowl stir together sugar, flour, and cinnamon; stir in undrained rhubarb.

2. Line a 9-inch pie plate with pastry; trim. Transfer filling to pastry. Trim bottom pastry to edge of plate. Cut slits in remaining pastry; place on filling and seal. Crimp edge as desired. If desired, brush with milk; sprinkle with sugar.

3. Cover edge of plate with foil. Bake for 25 minutes; remove foil. Bake for 20 to 30 minutes more or until filling is bubbly in center and pastry is golden. Cool on a wire rack. Makes 8 servings.

Nutrition facts per serving: 365 cal., 13 g total fat (5 g sat. fat), 12 mg chol., 129 mg sodium, 58 g carbo., 24 g fiber, and 4 g pro. Daily Values: 5% vit. A, 10% vit. C, 10% calcium, 10% iron.

 Rhubarb Crisp

Prep: 30 minutes **Bake:** 30 minutes

5 cups fresh or frozen unsweetened sliced rhubarb, thawed
¾ cup granulated sugar
½ cup regular rolled oats
½ cup packed brown sugar
⅓ cup all-purpose flour
¼ tsp. ground nutmeg, ginger, or cinnamon
¼ cup butter
¼ cup chopped nuts or coconut
Vanilla ice cream (optional)

1. Preheat oven to 375° F. Place rhubarb in a 2-quart square baking dish. Stir in the granulated sugar.

2. For topping, in a medium bowl combine oats, brown sugar, flour, and nutmeg. Cut in butter until mixture resembles coarse crumbs. Stir in the nuts. Sprinkle topping over filling.

3. Bake 30 to 35 minutes (40 minutes for thawed rhubarb) or until rhubarb is tender and topping is golden. Serve warm. If desired, serve with vanilla ice cream. Makes 6 servings.

Microwave Directions: Prepare filling as in Step 1. Microwave filling, covered with vented plastic wrap, on 100 percent power (high) for 4 to 6 minutes or until rhubarb is tender, stirring twice. Prepare topping as in Step 2. Sprinkle over filling. Cook, uncovered, on high 2 to 4 minutes or until topping is heated through, giving the dish a half-turn once.

Nutrition facts per serving: 360 cal., 13 g total fat (6 g sat. fat), 22 mg chol., 92 mg sodium, 61 g carbo., 4 g fiber, and 4 g pro. Daily Values: 8% vit. A, 12% vit. C, 12% calcium, 8% iron.

low fat **Tomato-Rhubarb Chutney**

Serve this chutney with grilled beef or chicken, spread it on a cold pork sandwich, or top a round of Brie cheese and serve with crackers for a party snack (pictured opposite).

Prep: 20 minutes **Cook:** 40 minutes

3 medium tomatoes, cored, seeded, and chopped (about 1½ cups)
⅓ cup chopped onion
⅓ cup coarsely chopped red sweet pepper
⅓ cup dried cherries, cranberries, or raisins
⅓ cup white vinegar
¼ cup granulated sugar
¼ cup packed brown sugar
¼ cup water
1 Tbsp. lime or lemon juice
2 cloves garlic, minced
1 tsp. grated fresh ginger or ¼ tsp. ground ginger
¼ tsp. salt
1 cup fresh rhubarb cut into ½-inch pieces or 1 cup frozen cut rhubarb, thawed and drained

1. In a saucepan combine tomatoes, onion, sweet pepper, dried cherries, vinegar, sugars, water, lime juice, garlic, ginger, and salt. Bring to boiling; reduce heat. Cover and simmer for 25 minutes, stirring occasionally. Stir in rhubarb.

2. Cover and simmer for 10 minutes. Uncover. Simmer about 5 minutes more for fresh rhubarb (15 minutes more for frozen rhubarb) or until thickened. Cool. To store, cover and refrigerate up to 1 week or freeze up to 3 months. Makes about 2¾ cups.

Nutrition facts per 2 tablespoons chutney: 30 cal., 0 g total fat (0 g sat. fat), 0 mg chol., 29 mg sodium, 8 g carbo., 0 g fiber, and 0 g pro. Daily Values: 11% vit. C, 1% calcium, and 1% iron.

Cookies
and Ice Cream

Gather the family round to try a fondue-inspired dessert that combines the best of fudge and hot cocoa—a dip for dunking or a sauce for spooning. Then pair it with ice cream, fruit, and cookies. You can make everything from scratch or take the supermarket shortcut and buy readymade. Either way, it's a taste of summer, any time of year.

30 No-Drip Chocolate Dip

Prep: 5 minutes **Cook:** 10 minutes

- 8 oz. unsweetened chocolate, chopped
- 1 14-oz. can (1¼ cups) sweetened condensed milk
- 2 Tbsp. light-colored corn syrup
- ½ cup milk
- 1 tsp. vanilla
- ½ tsp. ground cinnamon

Milk

1. In a medium saucepan melt chocolate over low heat, stirring constantly.

2. Stir in the sweetened condensed milk and corn syrup until combined. Gradually stir in the ½ cup milk until combined. Stir in vanilla and cinnamon. Serve warm, stirring in additional milk, as necessary until of dipping consistency. Makes 2 cups.

Nutrition facts per 1 tablespoon: 83 cal., 5 g total fat (3 g sat. fat), 4 mg chol., 20 mg sodium, 10 g carbo., 1 g fiber, and 2 g pro. Daily Values: 1% vit. A, 1% vit. C, 5% calcium, and 3% iron.

Shortbread

Prep: 15 minutes **Bake:** 20 minutes

- 1¼ cups all-purpose flour
- 3 Tbsp. granulated sugar
- ½ cup butter

1. Preheat oven to 325° F. In a small mixing bowl combine flour and sugar; cut in butter until mixture resembles fine crumbs and starts to cling. Form mixture into a ball; knead until smooth.

2. On a lightly floured surface roll dough into an 8x6-inch rectangle about ½ inch thick. Using a knife, cut into twenty-four ½-inch strips. Place 1 inch apart on an ungreased cookie sheet.

3. Bake for 20 to 25 minutes or until bottoms just starts to brown. Transfer to a wire rack; cool. Makes 24 cookies.

Spiced Shortbread: Prepare as above, except substitute brown sugar for the granulated sugar and stir ½ teaspoon ground cinnamon, ¼ teaspoon ground ginger, and ⅛ teaspoon ground cloves into the flour mixture.

Nutrition facts per cookie: 98 cal., 6 g total fat (4 g sat. fat), 16 mg chol., 62 mg sodium, 10 g carbo., 0 g fiber, and 1 g pro. Daily Values: 5% vit. A and 3% iron.

Vanilla Ice Cream

Prep: 5 minutes **Freeze:** per directions
Ripen: 4 hours

- 4 cups half-and-half, light cream, or milk
- 1½ cups sugar
- 1 Tbsp. vanilla
- 2 cups whipping cream

1. In a large bowl combine half-and-half, sugar, and vanilla. Stir until sugar dissolves. Stir in whipping cream.

2. Freeze ice cream mixture in a 4- or 5-quart ice cream freezer according to the manufacturer's directions. Ripen for 4 hours. Makes 2 quarts (15 servings).

Strawberry or Peach Ice Cream: Prepare as above, except in a blender container place 4 cups fresh strawberries; frozen unsweetened strawberries, thawed; or cut-up, peeled peaches. Cover and blend until nearly smooth (you should have 2 cups). Stir fruit into cream mixture before freezing.

Nutrition facts per serving: 253 cal., 18 g total fat (11 g sat. fat), 63 mg chol., 36 mg sodium, 22 g carbo., 0 g fiber, and 2 g pro. Daily Values: 14% vit. A, 1% vit. C, and 8% calcium.

June

A Cherry Jubilee

Plus . . .

School's out and summer's on. Pick the perfect picnic spot and pack your basket high.

A cherry
jubilee

A baby blue sky that goes on and on and on. Comfy soft blankets on the grass. A plump drippy sandwich nearly too big to bite. You know what it all means: an old-fashioned outdoor summer feast.

PHOTOGRAPHS: COLLEEN DUFFLEY. FOOD STYLIST: WILLIAM SMITH. PROPS: NICK HAMBLEN, CAROLYN BARTEL. STORY: NANCY WALL HOPKINS AND JEANNE AMBROSE.

Hit-the-Spot
Lemon Water

Cheery Cherry-Lemon Cake

Tote the frosting separately in a cooler until you're ready to serve this lemony cake flecked with chopped cherries. Then just plop a big spoonful of the fluffy stuff onto each serving of cake and add a jaunty cherry.

Prep: 40 minutes **Bake:** 30 minutes

1½ cups coarsely chopped pitted sweet cherries	1¼ cups milk
2½ cups all-purpose flour	2 tsp. finely shredded lemon peel
2½ tsp. baking powder	1 recipe Cream Cheese Frosting
½ tsp. salt	Sweet cherries with stems (optional)
¾ cup butter, softened	Fresh mint leaves (optional)
1¾ cups sugar	
1½ tsp. vanilla	
3 eggs	

1. Preheat oven to 375° F. Grease a 13x9x2-inch baking pan; set aside. Pat the coarsely chopped cherries as dry as possible with paper towels to prevent bleeding. In a medium bowl combine flour, baking powder, and salt; set aside.

2. In a large mixing bowl beat butter with an electric mixer on medium to high speed for 30 seconds. Add sugar and vanilla; beat until combined. Add eggs, one at a time, beating for 1 minute after each. Add dry mixture and milk alternately to beaten mixture, beating on low speed after each addition just until combined. Stir lemon peel into batter. Pour batter into the prepared pan. Sprinkle the chopped cherries evenly over top of batter. (The cherries will sink during baking.)

3. Bake for 30 to 35 minutes or until a wooden toothpick inserted near center comes out clean. Place cake in pan on a wire rack; cool thoroughly.

4. To serve, cut cake into 12 pieces. Top each piece with a generous dollop of Cream Cheese Frosting. If desired, add a cherry and mint leaf. Makes 12 large servings.

Cream Cheese Frosting: In a large bowl combine one 8-ounce package cream cheese, softened; ⅔ cup butter, softened; 2 teaspoons finely shredded lemon peel; and 2 tablespoons lemon juice. Beat with an electric mixer on medium speed until light and fluffy. Gradually add 3 cups sifted powdered sugar, beating well. Gradually beat in about 1½ cups more sifted powdered sugar to reach a spooning consistency.

Nutrition facts per serving: 676 cal., 32 g total fat (20 g sat. fat), 138 mg chol., 498 mg sodium, 94 g carbo., 1 g fiber, and 8 g pro. Daily Values: 26% vit. A, 8% vit. C, 12% calcium, and 10% iron.

30 low fat Hit-the-Spot Lemon Water

You'll be amazed at the subtle flavors that pop out when you soak lemons and fresh herbs in water for a few hours. It's pure, thirst-quenching goodness—no sugar needed.

Prep: 15 minutes **Chill:** 1 hour

4 lemons, sliced	6 to 8 cups water
1½ cups firmly packed fresh mint or basil leaves	6 to 8 cups ice cubes
	Fresh mint or basil sprigs

1. Place lemon slices in a large pitcher. Carefully rub the 1½ cups mint or basil leaves between the palms of your hands to slightly bruise the leaves. Add to the pitcher with lemon. Pour in water. Cover and chill for 1 to 8 hours.

2. Strain lemon-water mixture. Discard herbs. Divide lemon slices and additional fresh mint or basil leaves equally among six to eight pint-sized canning jars (or plastic water bottles). For each serving, add 1 cup of ice cubes; fill with the lemon water. Add lids when transporting the jars. Makes 6 to 8 servings.

Nutrition facts per serving: 11 cal., 0 g total fat (0 g sat. fat), 0 mg chol., 8 mg sodium, 4 g carbo., 1 g fiber, and 0 g pro. Daily Values: 34% vit. C, 1% calcium, and 1% iron.

30 Potato Gnocchi Salad

Look for small fresh gnocchi in sealed plastic pouches.

Prep: 25 minutes **Cook:** 5 minutes **Chill:** 4 hours

2	cups sugar snap peas (8 oz.), ends trimmed and halved crosswise	½	of a 4-oz. pkg. (½ cup) crumbled garlic-and-herb feta cheese
8	oz. potato gnocchi or tiny new potatoes, quartered	¼	cup thin wedges red onion
		1	recipe Herb Vinaigrette

1. In a large saucepan cook peas in lightly salted boiling water for 1 minute. Remove with slotted spoon; rinse and drain.

2. Add gnocchi to the boiling water in saucepan; cook according to package directions or until tender but firm. (Or, add potatoes to boiling water; cook, covered, for 10 minutes or until just tender.) Drain and rinse with cold water; drain again.

3. In a large bowl toss together sugar snap peas, gnocchi or potatoes, feta cheese, and onion. Cover and chill 4 to 24 hours.

4. Before serving, shake Herb Vinaigrette; pour over salad. Toss lightly to coat. Makes 8 servings.

Herb Vinaigrette: In a screw-top jar combine 3 tablespoons olive oil, 3 tablespoons lemon juice, 1 tablespoon snipped fresh dill, 1 tablespoon snipped fresh chives, ¼ teaspoon salt, and ⅛ teaspoon pepper. Cover; chill. Makes ½ cup.

Nutrition facts per serving: 114 cal., 7 g total fat (2 g sat. fat), 6 mg chol., 282 mg sodium, 12 g carbo., 1 g fiber, and 3 g pro. Daily Values: 1% vit. A, 19% vit. C, 4% calcium, and 2% iron.

30 Cantaloupe and Tomato Salad

Carry the dressing and other ingredients in separate containers and keep them in the cooler. Toss everything together just before it's time to summon picnickers to the table.

Prep: 25 minutes

¼	cup olive oil	1	medium cantaloupe, halved, seeded, peeled, and cut into thin wedges
2	Tbsp. balsamic vinegar		
1	green onion, finely chopped	2	cups red and/or yellow pear or cherry tomatoes, halved or quartered
¼	tsp. salt		
¼	tsp. pepper	4	oz. crumbled goat cheese with garlic and herbs
2	cups lightly packed watercress		

1. For dressing, in a screw-top jar combine olive oil, balsamic vinegar, green onion, salt, and pepper. Cover and shake well.

2. In a large bowl carefully toss together watercress, cantaloupe wedges, and tomatoes. Sprinkle with goat cheese. Drizzle with dressing. Toss gently to coat. Makes 8 servings.

Nutrition facts per serving: 149 cal., 11 g total fat (4 g sat. fat), 11 mg chol., 160 mg sodium, 9 g carbo., 1 g fiber, and 4 g pro. Daily Values: 62% vit. A, 70% vit. C, 6% calcium, and 4% iron.

PICNIC MENU

Salmon Picnic Sandwiches (recipe, page 125)

Gingered Salt with Cukes and Radishes (recipe, page 125)

Potato Gnocchi Salad (recipe, left)

Cantaloupe and Tomato Salad (recipe, left)

Peachy Baked White Beans (recipe, below)

Cheery Cherry Lemon Cake (recipe, page 121)

Hit-the-Spot Lemon Water (recipe, page 121)

Peachy Baked White Beans

Tote these summertime baked beans to the feast in an insulated carrier to keep them hot.

Prep: 20 minutes **Stand:** 1 hour **Cook:** 1 hour **Bake:** 1½ hours

1	lb. dry white beans, such as great northern, cannellini, or navy beans (about 2⅓ cups)	1	cup peach nectar or apple juice
		¼	cup packed brown sugar
1	to 1½ lb. meaty smoked pork hocks	2	Tbsp. snipped fresh sage or 2 tsp. dried sage, crushed
3	medium peaches, pitted and cut into wedges (about 3 cups)	½	tsp. salt
		½	tsp. pepper
1	cup chopped onion (1 large)	1	or 2 medium peaches, pitted and sliced
			Fresh sage sprig (optional)

1. Rinse beans. In a large Dutch oven or pot combine beans and 8 cups water. Bring to boiling; reduce heat. Simmer for 2 minutes. Remove from heat. Cover and let stand for 1 hour. (Or, place beans in water in Dutch oven. Cover and let soak in a cool place overnight.)

2. Drain and rinse beans. Return beans to Dutch oven. Add pork hocks. Stir in 8 cups water. Bring to boiling; reduce heat. Cover; simmer for 1 to 1½ hours or until beans are tender, stirring occasionally. Remove hocks; set aside. Drain beans. When cool enough to handle, cut meat from bones; coarsely chop meat.

3. Preheat oven to 300° F. In a 2½- to 3-quart casserole combine beans, meat, the 3 cups peach wedges, and onion. Stir in peach nectar, brown sugar, sage, salt, and pepper.

4. Bake, covered, for 1 hour. Uncover and bake about 15 minutes more or until desired consistency, stirring occasionally. Before serving, top with remaining peach slices and fresh sage sprig, if desired. Makes 10 to 12 servings.

Nutrition facts per serving: 229 cal., 2 g total fat (1 g sat. fat), 6 mg chol., 139 mg sodium, 43 g carbo., 10 g fiber, and 12 g pro. Daily Values: 6% vit. A, 11% vit. C, 8% calcium, and 12% iron.

Potato Gnocchi Salad

Cantaloupe and Tomato Salad

Peachy Baked White Beans

This over-the-top alfresco feast is worth a little extra fuss. Roomy baskets and tubs make charming carryalls for plates, napkins, and other essentials. And fresh cherries go everywhere. Turn them into fanciful table weights—with the help of some wooden clothespins—to keep your tablecloth from flapping skyward in the breeze. Just bunch up the dangling tablecloth at each corner and tie it with a ribbon. Then use clothespins to clip a couple of cherries by their stems to the ribbon or cloth.

Bright beams

of sunshine bursting from a sleepy morning sky are all the incentive you need to kick off your picnicking hoopla. Food is the focus here, but the setting—and the setup—adds the fun. Get a little hype going by hand-delivering a delicious invitation, in this case on a jar of jaunty red Just Cherries or preserves like the ones pictured at right. Try our recipe on *page 126*, or pick up some cherry preserves at the store. On picnic day, tote it all to the park—or just step outside your back door. Take along your favorite flea-market finds—an old chair or two, chunky go-anywhere dishes, and reliable Mason jars. And remember to toss in big, cushy pillows and blankets.

Just Cherries
recipe on page 126

Gingered Salt with
Cukes and Radishes

Salmon Picnic Sandwiches

Avoid last-minute scurrying by putting together these two-fisted sandwiches in advance.

Prep: 30 minutes **Cook:** 10 minutes
Chill: 1 hour

1	lb. fresh or frozen skinless salmon fillets, cut 1 inch thick
1	cup Chardonnay, other dry white wine, or chicken broth
1	medium Vidalia or other sweet onion, cut into thin wedges (½ cup)
½	tsp. coarse-grain sea salt or kosher salt

½ tsp. cracked black pepper
2 sprigs fresh oregano
1 8- to 12-oz. loaf ciabatta or baguette-style French bread
Olive oil
1 recipe Olive-and-Onion Relish
Lemon wedges (optional)

1. Thaw fish, if frozen. Rinse fish. In a large skillet or fish poacher combine wine or broth, onion, salt, pepper, and oregano. Bring to boiling; add salmon. Reduce heat and simmer, covered, for 10 to 12 minutes or until fish flakes easily when tested with a fork.

2. Use a slotted spatula to transfer salmon and onion to a large bowl. Discard cooking liquid. Cover and refrigerate about 1 hour or until chilled.

3. Cut bread into quarters; slice in half horizontally. Drizzle cut sides lightly with olive oil. Cut salmon into 4 equal pieces. Place a piece of salmon on bread bottoms. Top with Olive-and-Onion Relish and bread tops. Wrap securely in plastic wrap. Refrigerate for up to 4 hours. Before serving, squeeze lemon over salmon and relish, if desired. Makes 4 sandwiches.

Olive-and-Onion Relish: In a small bowl combine reserved onion wedges (from poaching liquid); ½ cup pitted green olives, halved; ½ cup pitted kalamata olives, halved; 2 tablespoons snipped fresh Italilan flat-leaf parsley; and 2 teaspoons snipped fresh oregano.

Nutrition facts per sandwich: 398 cal., 17 g total fat (2 g sat. fat), 70 mg chol., 1,269 mg sodium, 32 g carbo., 3 g fiber, and 29 g pro. Daily Values: 7% vit. A, 6% vit. C, 7% calcium, and 15% iron.

Salmon Picnic Sandwiches

Herb-poached salmon sandwiches are tastier when made with a freshly baked crusty bread.

30 low fat Gingered Salt with Cukes and Radishes

Candied ginger, which you can buy in major markets or specialty stores, adds a spicy snap to this dipping salt.

Prep: 10 minutes **Stand:** 24 hours

½ cup coarse sea salt or kosher salt
2 to 3 Tbsp. chopped crystallized ginger
Radishes

Baby cucumbers, halved lengthwise, or medium cucumbers, halved crosswise and cut lengthwise into wedges, peeled, if desired

1. In a screw-top jar combine salt and ginger. Screw on the lid. Shake well to combine. Let stand for 24 hours or up to 1 month.

2. To serve, pass salt with radishes and cucumbers. Makes ⅔ cup salt (48 servings).

Nutrition facts per ½ teaspoon salt: 12 cal., 0 g total fat (0 g sat. fat), 0 mg chol., 804 mg sodium, 3 g carbo., 1 g fiber, and 1 g pro. Daily Values: 3% vit. A, 10% vit. C, 1% calcium, and 1% iron.

low fat Just Cherries

These lemongrass-infused cherries are refreshingly tart, so they're perfect to pair with sweeter companions, such as chocolate or vanilla ice cream. Pictured on page 24.

Prep: 45 minutes **Cook:** 35 minutes

2½	lb. fresh tart red cherries or two 1-lb. pkg. frozen unsweetened pitted tart red cherries	4	large stalks fresh lemongrass, trimmed and cut into 2-inch pieces, or 4 tsp. finely shredded lemon peel
1	cup sugar	1½	tsp. vanilla
½	cup water		

1. If using fresh cherries, rinse and drain cherries; remove stems and pits. Measure 6 cups. In a large saucepan combine cherries, sugar, water, and lemongrass or lemon peel. Bring to boiling; reduce heat. Simmer, uncovered, for 35 minutes. Remove from heat. Stir in vanilla.

2. Ladle the fruit mixture into clean half-pint jars or storage containers. Cover and store for up to 3 weeks in the refrigerator. About 1 week before serving, remove lemongrass, if using. Makes 4 half-pint jars.

Nutrition facts per ¼-cup serving: 79 cal., 0 g total fat (0 g sat. fat), 0 mg chol., 2 mg sodium, 20 g carbo., 1 g fiber, and 1 g pro. Daily Values: 16% vit. A, 11% vit. C, 1% calcium, and 1% iron.

30 Carrots with Dried Fruit Confetti

Cut the get-ready time to nearly nothing by buying carrot sticks.

Prep: 15 minutes **Chill:** 1 hour

12	small carrots with tops or 6 medium carrots (1 lb.)	2	to 3 tsp. milk
1	8-oz. tub flavored cream cheese, such as honey-nut or apple-cinnamon	1½	cups dried blueberries, dried cranberries, and/or golden raisins

1. Peel carrots. If using small carrots, serve whole. Cut medium carrots into sticks about 3 inches long and ½ inch wide. Pat dry with paper towels.

2. In a medium bowl combine cream cheese and milk, stirring until smooth; spread onto half of each carrot.

3. Sprinkle dried blueberries onto the cream cheese mixture. Cover and chill for 1 to 4 hours. Makes 12 snack servings.

Nutrition facts per serving: 139 cal., 5 g total fat (3 g sat. fat), 18 mg chol., 76 mg sodium, 21 g carbo., 2 g fiber, and 1 g pro. Daily Values: 192% vit. A, 6% vit. C, 4% calcium, and 3% iron.

30 Lumpy PB&J Roosters

Thick slices of firm bread work best to support the lollipop sticks. Pile finished sandwiches on a "nest" of shoestring potatoes (which come in a variety of kid-pleasing flavors).

Prep: 25 minutes **Chill:** 1 hour

1	10-oz. jar raspberry or strawberry spreadable fruit	½	cup chopped strawberries, bananas, and/or pineapple
¼	cup chopped peanuts	6	4- to 5-inch lollipop sticks
¼	cup shredded coconut		
3	Tbsp. orange juice	6	dried currants or miniature semisweet chocolate pieces or 3 raisins, snipped in half
12	slices firm-textured white or whole wheat sandwich bread		
¾	cup peanut butter		

1. In a small bowl combine spreadable fruit, chopped peanuts, coconut, and orange juice. Set aside.

2. Cut 12 shapes from bread slices using 3- to 4-inch rooster or other shaped cutters. (Reserve bread you've cut away for another use.)

3. Spread 1 tablespoon of the peanut butter onto one side of each shape, making sure that shapes will match up when placed together. Sprinkle chopped fruit over peanut butter on 6 of the shapes. Top each fruit-covered shape with matching top, peanut butter side down. Press shapes together, forming a sandwich. Insert a lollipop stick into the filling of sandwich. Press slightly to secure stick. Repeat with remaining shapes and sticks.

4. Spread a small amount of peanut butter onto bottom of a currant. Place a currant "eye" on each rooster sandwich. Wrap and chill for up to 1 hour. Serve with spreadable fruit mixture as a dipping sauce. Makes 6 sandwiches.

Nutrition facts per sandwich: 486 cal., 24 g total fat (5 g sat. fat), 0 mg chol., 421 mg sodium, 64 g carbo., 3 g fiber, and 14 g pro. Daily Values: 18% vit. C, 6% calcium, and 13% iron.

KIDS' PICNIC

Lumpy PB&J Roosters (recipe, above)

Carrots with Dried Fruit Confetti (recipe, left)

Turtle Pretzels (recipe, page 129)

Wild Blueberry Pies (recipe, page 129)

Just Cherries with ice cream (recipe, left)

Lemonade or fruit punch

Lumpy PB&J Roosters,
Carrots with Dried
Fruit Confetti

Allow wide open spaces for play.

All the whooping and hollering and zigzagging between the trees will stir up kids' appetites. Bring a favorite red wagon, hula hoops, and a net for chasing butterflies. Even the grown-ups might join in on a giddy game of "Ring Around the Rosey." And when appetites are ready, give the small-fry their very own lunch baskets and a kid-size dining nook far enough from the adults to encourage general silliness and goofy gobbling.

Wild Blueberry Pies

Take your pick from the farmer's market or a tromp in the woods and fields. You can fill these flowery pies with either a blueberry or raspberry fillng.

Wild Blueberry Pies

Prepare the pastry first and have the cutouts ready before making either fruit filling so the filling doesn't get too juicy.

Prep: 30 minutes **Bake:** 18 minutes

2	cups all-purpose flour	1	recipe Wild Blueberry
½	tsp. salt		Filling or Raspberry
½	tsp. ground cardamom		Filling
⅔	cup shortening	1	beaten egg
6	to 7 Tbsp. cold water		Coarse sugar or sugar

1. Line a large baking sheet with foil; set aside. In a medium mixing bowl stir together flour, salt, and cardamom. Using a pastry blender, cut in shortening until pieces are pea-size.

2. Sprinkle 1 tablespoon of the water over part of the mixture; gently toss with a fork. Push moistened dough to side of bowl. Repeat, using 1 tablespoon water at a time, until dough is moistened. Divide dough in half. Form into 2 balls.

3. On a lightly floured surface flatten 1 ball of dough; roll into a 16x8-inch rectangle. Use a 3¾- to 4-inch scalloped or round cutter to cut 8 circles. Stack cutouts between pieces of waxed paper. Repeat with remaining dough to make 16 cutouts.

4. Preheat oven to 375° F. Prepare Wild Blueberry Filling or Raspberry Filling. Place 8 pastry cutouts 2 inches apart on the prepared baking sheet. Spoon about 2 tablespoons filling onto each cutout. Moisten edges with water. Top with remaining cutouts. Seal edges with tines of a fork. Prick tops of pies two or three times to allow steam to escape. Brush with beaten egg; sprinkle with sugar.

5. Bake for 18 to 20 minutes or until golden brown. Remove from pan; cool on a wire rack. Makes 8 pies.

Wild Blueberry Filling: In a medium bowl stir together 2 to 3 tablespoons sugar, 1 tablespoon all-purpose flour, and ½ teaspoon finely shredded lemon peel. Stir in 1½ cups fresh or frozen wild or cultivated blueberries. (If berries are frozen, do not thaw before using.)

Raspberry Filling: In a mixing bowl stir together 3 to 4 tablespoons sugar, 4 teaspoons all-purpose flour, and ½ teaspoon finely shredded lemon peel. Stir in 1½ cups raspberries.

Nutrition facts per serving: 305 cal., 17 g total fat (4 g sat. fat), 27 mg chol., 156 mg sodium, 33 g carbo., 2 g fiber, and 4 g pro. Daily Values: 1% vit. A, 7% vit. C, 2% calcium, and 11% iron.

Use scalloped or round cutters to make these individual mini pies. Pressing the tines of a fork onto the edges will seal in the filling.

Turtle Pretzels

Turtle Pretzels

Enjoy these pretzels the same day they're prepared because the pretzels may soften on standing.

Prep: 45 minutes **Chill:** 20 minutes

	Butter	1	tsp. shortening
1	14-oz. pkg. vanilla		Chopped pecans, snipped
	caramels (about 48)		dried cranberries or
1	Tbsp. water		dried blueberries, or
15	to 20 large pretzel twists		miniature candy-coated
	(4 inches wide and		semisweet chocolate
	½ inch thick)		pieces
4	oz. semisweet chocolate,		
	chopped		

1. Lightly butter a large cookie sheet; set aside. In a small saucepan combine unwrapped caramels and 1 tablespoon water. Cook and stir over low heat until caramels are just melted and smooth. Remove from heat.

2. Dip top portions of pretzels into caramel mixture, tilting pan as necessary to help coat each pretzel and letting excess caramel drip off. Arrange on prepared cookie sheet. (If caramel mixture is running off pretzels, wait a few minutes to let it cool and thicken slightly.) Cool until caramel is set.

3. Place chocolate and shortening in another small saucepan. Cook and stir over low heat until chocolate is just melted and smooth. Cool slightly. Spoon melted chocolate mixture into a small plastic bag; snip a small hole in one corner. Squeeze chocolate onto pretzels, forming decorative lines. Sprinkle with nuts, dried fruit, or chocolate pieces. Chill pretzels in refrigerator about 20 minutes or until chocolate is firm. Transfer to waxed paper or cellophane bags. Makes 15 to 20 pretzels.

Nutrition facts per serving: 283 cal., 10 g total fat (3 g sat. fat), 4 mg chol., 503 mg sodium, 46 g carbo., 2 g fiber, and 5 g pro. Daily Values: 6% calcium and 5% iron.

Steak on the Grill

Grab your tongs and get ready to put some fire into your backyard cooking career.

1. Pick the right cut. The route to a great steak begins at the meat counter. The six best-for-grilling cuts are shown opposite. Buy steaks that measure ³⁄₄ to 1¹⁄₂ inches thick—any thinner and the inside may overcook. The most tender and flavorful steaks are those with the most marbling—tiny white flecks and veins of fat within the meat. The grades reflect the amount of marbling. Select-grade meat has less fat, choice has more, and prime has the most.

2. Read before you cook. Your grill owner's manual has all the information you need to be the best backyard chef on your block. And the best chefs keep it clean. Scrub the grill with a wire brush when it's still hot after grilling.

3. Season. Shake your favorite seasoning blend or pepper onto the steaks, then brush or rub with olive oil or cooking oil to lessen sticking and help create steak-house-style grill marks.

4. Keep the fire moderate. A steady, medium temperature is the key to success. If using charcoal, put in enough coals to make one layer on the bottom. After you light the coals, let them burn until covered with gray ash. About 5 minutes before adding the meat, preheat the cooking grill over the coals. The coals will stay at the right cooking temperature for 45 minutes. For gas grills, adjust controls to the manufacturer's recommendation.

5. Follow the chart. Cook steaks for the minimum time suggested on our charts, turning them once halfway through cooking. If they stick, leave them on for another minute, then gently lift until they release from the grill.

To check doneness, cut into one of the steaks for a peek (that's the steak you'll give yourself) or use an instant-read thermometer inserted horizontally into the meat. The USDA doesn't recommend serving steaks that are less than medium rare, and well-done steaks are usually drier and less tender. A steak is rare at 140° F and well-done at 170° F.

For steaks thicker than 1¹⁄₂ inches, remove from the grill when a thermometer registers 5° F under the desired doneness. Cover loosely with foil and the steak will cook to the proper degree of doneness. If thinner steaks are not quite done, pop them back over the coals for 2 or 3 more minutes.

Once you take meat off the grill, cover it with foil and let it stand for 5 to 10 minutes.

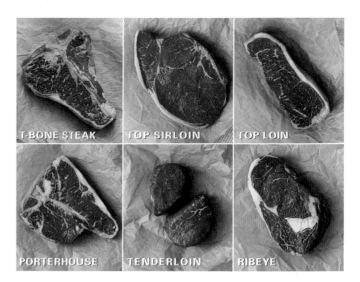

T-BONE STEAK TOP SIRLOIN TOP LOIN

PORTERHOUSE TENDERLOIN RIBEYE

Roasted Garlic Steak

Prep: 15 minutes **Grill:** 30 minutes

1 or 2 whole garlic bulb(s)	2 Tbsp. olive oil or cooking oil
3 to 4 tsp. snipped fresh basil or 1 tsp. dried basil, crushed	1½ lb. boneless beef ribeye steaks or sirloin steak, cut 1 inch thick
1 Tbsp. snipped fresh rosemary or 1 tsp. dried rosemary, crushed	1 to 2 tsp. cracked pepper
	½ tsp. salt

1. With a sharp knife, cut off the top ½ inch from garlic bulb(s) to expose the ends of the individual cloves. Leaving garlic bulb(s) whole, remove any loose, papery outer layers.

2. Fold a 20x18-inch piece of heavy foil in half crosswise. Trim into a 10-inch square. Place garlic bulb(s), cut sides up, in center of foil square. Sprinkle garlic with basil and rosemary; drizzle with oil. Bring up opposite edges of foil; seal with a double fold. Fold remaining edges together to completely enclose garlic, leaving space for steam to build.

3. For a charcoal grill, grill garlic on the rack of an uncovered grill directly over medium coals about 30 minutes or until garlic feels soft when packet is squeezed, turning occasionally.

4. Meanwhile, trim fat from steaks. Sprinkle the pepper and salt evenly onto both sides of steaks; rub in. Add steaks to grill. Grill to desired doneness, turning once halfway through grilling. For ribeye steaks, allow 11 to 15 minutes for medium rare (145° F) and 14 to 18 minutes for medium (160° F). For sirloin steak, allow 14 to 18 minutes for medium rare (145° F) and 18 to 22 minutes for medium (160° F). (For a gas grill, preheat grill. Reduce heat to medium. Place garlic, then steaks on grill rack over heat. Cover and grill as above.)

5. To serve, cut steaks into 6 serving-size pieces. Remove garlic from foil, reserving the oil mixture. Squeeze garlic pulp onto steaks; mash pulp slightly and spread onto steaks. Drizzle with the reserved oil mixture. Makes 6 servings.

Nutrition facts per serving: 189 cal., 9 g total fat (2 g sat. fat), 52 mg chol., 139 mg sodium, 4 g carbo., 0 g fiber, and 22 g pro. Daily Values: 1% vit. A, 6% vit. C, 3% calcium, and 14% iron.

CHOOSING MEAT

■ The **T-bone** and the **porterhouse** are very similar. They're both made up of two other cuts—a top loin and a tenderloin—with the t-shape bone in the middle. (The porterhouse has a larger tenderloin).

■ **Top sirloin** is firmer and slightly lower in fat than the other four steak cuts.

■ The **top loin**, also called a New York or Kansas City strip, among other names, is tender and among the leanest.

■ As the name implies, **tenderloin** is often singled out as a very tender cut. It also has the mildest taste of the steaks shown here. It tastes best if not cooked beyond medium.

■ A **ribeye** is a very flavorful steak, almost like eating grilled roast beef. This is a good cut for those who prefer well-done.

HOW LONG WILL IT TAKE?

These timings produce steaks that are medium rare at an internal temperature of 145° F. The actual grilling times will vary according to the air temperature and wind. Cover thicker steaks with the grill lid to cook evenly.

CUT	THICKNESS	TIME
Ribeye	¾ inch	6 to 8 minutes
	1 inch	11 to 14 minutes
	1½ inches	17 to 22 minutes *(covered)*
T-bone, Top loin, Porterhouse	¾ inch	10 to 12 minutes
	1 inch	14 to 18 minutes
	1½ inches	20 to 24 minutes *(covered)*
Top sirloin	¾ inch	13 to 16 minutes
	1 inch	17 to 21 minutes
	1½ inches	22 to 26 minutes *(covered)*
Tenderloin	1 inch	13 to 15 minutes
	1½ inches	14 to 16 minutes *(covered)*

Cocktail Cool

Grab a jigger and a shaker for the latest libations from the cocktail circuit. Whether you're sipping to the beat of lounge music CDs or hitting the hammock with glass in hand, relax and say cheers!

Basil Martini
Fill a shaker with ice, add a dash of vermouth, shake, and strain. Add 2 jiggers basil-infused vodka (for infusion tips, see opposite). Shake vigorously; strain. Note: 1 jigger equals approximately 1½ fluid ounces.

Mojito Sparkler
Samba, anyone? Crush 6 fresh mint leaves in the bottom of a glass. Pour in 1½ to 2 jiggers gold rum, 2 teaspoons extra-fine granulated sugar, and 1 teaspoon lime juice. Add ice, stir, and top with soda.

Mai Tai Me
Fill a shaker with ice. Add 1 jigger each of dark rum and orange liqueur, ⅓ cup pineapple juice, 2 tablespoons grenadine syrup, a dash of lime juice, and sugar. Shake and serve. Umbrella required.

Dandy Shandy
This British tradition is just smashing, mate. Top a good dark stout or porter (or nonalcoholic beer) with an equal amount of ginger ale or ginger beer.

Ultra Alexander
Dessert in a glass. In a shaker filled with ice, add 1⅓ jiggers brandy, ⅓ jigger crème de cacao, and 1 tablespoon each of whipping cream and chocolate syrup. Shake, strain, and serve. Sprinkle with chocolate shavings.

Clove Julep
Spice up the Derby classic. Crush 5 fresh mint sprigs along with 3 teaspoons of extra-fine granulated sugar in the bottom of a glass. Add ice and clove-infused vodka. Stir and serve.

INFUSION MIXOLOGY

Infused vodkas, or vodkas that have had a flavoring agent added, are popular on restaurant bar menus. Infusing subtle flavor is easy. Start with a half-pint bottle of vodka. For basil-infused vodka, gently crush six basil leaves and immerse in the bottle. Try mint as an alternative. For clove-infused vodka, place eight whole cloves in a piece of cheesecloth; tie into a bundle. Gently crush some of the cloves. Insert the bundle into the vodka. Peppercorns or anise seed lend their flavors nicely too. Or, insert slices of fresh gingerroot, cucumber, or citrus peel. Store the infused vodka in the freezer for at least four days. Strain and discard the solids before serving.

PHOTOGRAPHS: COLLEEN DUFFLEY. FOOD STYLIST: BROOKE LEONARD. RESEARCH: BEV BENNETT.

Take 5 at the very least

Eat five servings a day of fruits and vegetables. How hard can that be? It's not. And we're here to show you how easy it is.

"In fact, five is just the starting point," says Lorelei DiSogra, R.D., director of the 5 a Day for Better Health program at the National Cancer Institute. "Women should be eating closer to seven. And men should be eating nine."

Research shows that the more fruits and vegetables you eat, the lower your risk of developing chronic diseases, including cancer, heart disease, diabetes, and macular degeneration. "The brighter the color of what you eat, the better," DiSogra says. "The natural plant chemicals that make cherries a vivid red and blueberries so blue also take on double-duty as disease fighters."

The best colors to pick when you're purchasing produce? Red, orange, yellow, green, and bluc-purple. So go ahead and color your world, using the easy ideas opposite.

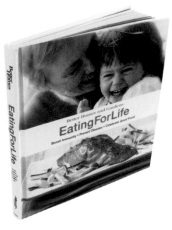

new 30 low fat

Snow Peas and Tomatoes

Look for tiny tomatoes available in a rainbow of colors and shapes.

Start to finish: 10 minutes

6	cups fresh pea pods (1 lb.)
1	large shallot, sliced
2	tsp. peanut oil
¼	tsp. toasted sesame oil
1	Tbsp. teriyaki sauce
¼	cup grape, cherry, and/or pear-shape red and/or yellow tomatoes
2	tsp. sesame seed, toasted

1. Remove strings and tips from the pea pods; set aside. In a 12-inch skillet cook shallot in hot peanut oil and sesame oil over medium heat until tender. Stir in pea pods and teriyaki sauce. Cook and stir for 2 to 3 minutes or until the pea pods are crisp-tender.

2. Add tomatoes; cook for 1 minute more. Sprinkle with sesame seed. Makes 6 servings.

Nutrition facts per serving: 115 cal., 3 g total fat (2 g sat. fat), 8 mg chol., 53 mg sodium, 17 g carbo., 4 g fiber, and 4 g pro. Daily Values: 2% vit. A, 47% vit. C, 6% calcium, and 10% iron.

5 FROM YOUR KITCHEN

1. Sneak more fruit into peanut butter and jelly sandwiches by making your own easy blender jam. Blend well-drained canned apricots, peaches, or pineapple until smooth, then slather onto whole wheat bread.

2. Pile grilled veggies onto one side of a flour tortilla. Sprinkle with shredded cheese. Fold over and heat in a skillet until both sides are golden brown, turning once. Serve with salsa.

3. Blend blueberries or strawberries into milk. Try ½ cup berries with ¾ cup milk. Sweeten with a little honey.

4. Cook chopped mushrooms and onion in olive oil. Add a handful or two of fresh baby spinach and toss together. Stuff the mixture into pockets cut in chicken breast halves and bake. Or pile it onto baked potatoes.

5. Build a stack of mini pancakes, piling chopped fresh strawberries or peaches between each layer. Add fresh blueberries to a favorite pancake syrup, and spoon on top.

5 TO BOOKMARK

Better Homes and Gardens® Eating for Life, Kristi Fuller, R.D., Editor (2001). Big flavors with little effort is a recurring theme in this book. Each recipe includes a tidbit explaining its health benefits.

The Color Code, by James A. Joseph, Ph.D.; Daniel A. Nadeau, M.D.; and Anne Underwood (2002). Two nutrition pros at Tufts University teamed up with *Newsweek* reporter Underwood to provide an easy-to-read rainbow of reasons to eat colorful plant foods. The book is packed with good information and includes recipes.

5 a Day, by Dr. Elizabeth Pivonka and Barbara Berry (2002). Think it's tough to to meet your fruit and veggie quota? This book's recipe for a mango, banana, grapefruit-juice shake alone has 3½ servings. We tested a few recipes in the Better Homes and Gardens® Test Kitchen. Good stuff.

www.aboutproduce.com. This great site serves anyone who wants to eat "in season." An A-to-Z produce guide pinpoints availability dates, gives health information, features a nutrition dictionary, and offers a recipe search engine.

www.5aday.com or www.5aday.gov Both sites have great information and some fun interactive tools. The first is sponsored by the Produce for Better Health Foundation; the second by the National Cancer Institute. They spread the word about the 5 a Day for Better Health program.

July

Big Easy

Plus...

Summer brings with it warm weather that insists we enjoy the outdoors, be it snoozing in the hammock, grilling on the deck, or dining alfresco.

Nutty Cucumber
Sandwich

big easy

I just can't wait to play in the kitchen. But I also want to
get out of it. So my cohorts at our magazine challenged
me, "Give us some recipes that'll let you do both. Keep
them fresh, simple, and quick. Tell us what makes them
great." As a food editor, I couldn't say no, so here goes!

—Stephen Exel

PHOTOGRAPHS: JOYCE OUDKERK POOL. FOOD STYLIST: POUKÉ. PROP STYLIST: CAROL HACKER. STORY: STEPHEN EXEL.

Stuffed Caprese

This is one of those ideas you get when you play around in the kitchen—a delicious spin on the classic Italian mozzarella salad—insalata caprese.

30 Stuffed Caprese

Go beyond red tomatoes, if you can. Yellow tomatoes will be sweeter; green a little more tart.

Prep: 25 minutes **Chill:** up to 2 hours

4	small tomatoes (3 to 4 oz. each)	3	oz. fresh mozzarella or fresh buffalo mozzarella, drained and cut into small chunks (about ½ cup)
¼	tsp. sea salt or salt		
⅛	tsp. pepper		
3	Tbsp. olive oil		
3	Tbsp. white wine vinegar	¼	cup slivered red onion
½	tsp. sugar	¼	cup snipped fresh basil

1. Cut a ¼-inch slice from the stem end of each tomato. Using a spoon, carefully scoop out core, seeds, and pulp, leaving up to a ½-inch-thick shell. Discard pulp. Sprinkle tomato shells with salt and pepper. Stand tomato shells on a plate; set aside.

2. For dressing, in a screw-top jar combine olive oil, vinegar, and sugar. Cover; shake well. Reserve 1½ tablespoons of dressing. Spoon remaining dressing into tomato shells.

3. In a bowl combine mozzarella, red onion, basil, and reserved dressing; toss to mix. Spoon cheese mixture into shells. Cover; refrigerate until ready to serve or up to 2 hours.

4. To serve, place stuffed tomatoes on plates. Sprinkle with additional salt and pepper. Makes 4 servings.

Nutrition facts per serving: 177 cal., 15 g total fat (4 g sat. fat), 16 mg chol., 187 mg sodium, 6 g carbo., 1 g fiber, and 5 g pro. Daily Values: 29% vit. C, 12% calcium, and 4% iron.

30 low fat Nutty Cucumber Sandwich

Select chèvre that has been rolled in cracked black pepper to add another flavor dimension to this sandwich.

Start to finish: 15 minutes

½	cup fresh snow pea pods, trimmed	⅓	cup seasoned roasted soy nuts (such as ranch or garlic)
½	medium cucumber		
8	thin slices rye bread	1	medium tomato, thinly sliced
3	to 4 oz. soft goat cheese (chèvre)		Salt

1. In a saucepan cook pea pods in lightly salted boiling water for 2 minutes. Drain; rinse with cold water. Drain again. Place pea pods in a small bowl; chill.

2. Use a vegetable peeler to remove a few lengthwise strips of peel from cucumber. Thinly slice cucumber.

3. Spread one side of each bread slice with goat cheese. Sprinkle 4 bread slices with soy nuts, gently pressing nuts into the cheese. Top with cucumber slices, tomato slices, and pea pods. Sprinkle with salt. Top with remaining bread slices. Makes 4 sandwiches.

Nutrition facts per serving: 276 cal., 9 g total fat (4 g sat. fat), 10 mg chol., 540 mg sodium, 36 g carbo., 6 g fiber, and 14 g pro. Daily Values: 24% vit. C, 10% calcium, and 17% iron.

Small tomatoes are the best size to choose for this salad. Take care not to break the shell when scooping; the curved bowl of a soup spoon is a helpful tool.

Grilled Halibut with Blueberry-Pepper Jam

A drizzle of olive oil just before serving keeps the sage-crouton topping moist. If some topping tumbles off, so be it, because that's just the way crunchy crust crumbles.

Prep: 25 minutes **Grill:** 12 minutes

4	5- to 6-oz. fresh or frozen halibut steaks or fillets or sea bass or salmon fillets, cut 1 inch thick	1	tsp. finely shredded orange peel
1	cup garlic croutons, coarsely crushed	¼	tsp. pepper
		2	Tbsp. orange juice
¼	cup snipped fresh sage	1	Tbsp. olive oil
		1	recipe Blueberry-Pepper Jam

1. Thaw fish, if frozen. Rinse fish; pat dry.

2. For topping, in a small bowl combine crushed croutons, sage, orange peel, and pepper. Stir in orange juice and olive oil until lightly moistened; set aside.

3. Lightly grease the rack of a grill. For a charcoal grill, cook fish, skin side up if using fillets, on the rack of the grill, uncovered, directly over medium coals for 5 minutes. Turn fish; top evenly with crouton topping, pressing onto fish. Grill for 7 to 10 minutes more or until fish flakes easily when tested with a fork. (For a gas grill, preheat grill. Reduce heat to medium. Place fish on greased grill rack over heat. Cover and cook as above.)

4. To serve, place fish on a serving platter. Drizzle fish with additional olive oil. If desired, garnish with additional sage leaves. Serve with Blueberry-Pepper Jam. Makes 4 servings.

Blueberry-Pepper Jam: In a bowl place ¾ cup fresh blueberries; mash with a potato masher or fork. Stir in ¾ cup blueberries, 1 teaspoon snipped fresh sage, and ½ teaspoon freshly ground black pepper. Cover; chill until ready to serve.

Nutrition facts per serving: 222 cal., 7 g total fat (1 g sat. fat), 45 mg chol., 101 mg sodium, 8 g carbo., 1 g fiber, and 30 g pro. Daily Values: 16% vit. C, 9% calcium, and 8% iron.

Soy-Lime Scallops with Leeks

When purchasing fresh sea scallops, look for color between pale beige and pink, a sweet smell, and a moist sheen.

Prep: 10 minutes **Marinate:** 30 minutes **Grill:** 8 minutes

1	lb. fresh or frozen sea scallops	¼	cup soy sauce
1	small leek or 4 baby leeks	¼	cup rice vinegar
		1	medium lime, halved
8	medium green or red scallions		Black sesame seed (optional)
		¼	cup butter, melted*

1. Thaw scallops, if frozen. Rinse scallops; pat dry with paper towels. Set aside.

2. Trim root end and green tops of leek and scallions. Rinse leek thoroughly to remove any grit. Cut the small leek lengthwise into quarters; insert a wooden toothpick crosswise through each leek quarter to hold layers together when grilling. Or, trim the baby leeks.

3. Place scallops, leeks, and scallions in a plastic bag set in a shallow bowl. For marinade, in a small bowl whisk together soy sauce and rice vinegar; add to bag. Seal bag; turn to coat scallops and vegetables. Marinate in refrigerator for 30 minutes.

4. Remove scallops, leeks, and scallions from the bag. Discard the marinade. For a charcoal grill, place scallops, leeks, scallions, and lime halves, cut side down, on the rack of an uncovered grill directly over medium coals. Grill for 8 to 10 minutes or until scallops are opaque, turning scallops and vegetables occasionally. Remove scallions before they over-brown. (For a gas grill, preheat grill. Reduce heat to medium. Place scallops, leeks, scallions, and lime halves on rack over heat. Grill as above.)

5. To serve, transfer leeks and scallions to four serving plates. Top with scallops. Using grilling tongs, remove limes from grill; squeeze over scallops. Sprinkle with black sesame seed. Serve with melted butter. Makes 4 servings.

*Test Kitchen Tip: Melt butter in heat-resistant bowl or ramekin on grill alongside scallops and leeks.

Nutrition facts per serving: 229 cal., 13 g total fat (8 g sat. fat), 70 mg chol., 467 mg sodium, 8 g carbo., 1 g fiber, and 20 g pro. Daily Values: 24% vit. C, 6% calcium, and 6% iron.

Grilled Halibut with Blueberry-Pepper Jam

Is it really jam? Call it that if you like. It's a simple mash of summer berries combined with just-picked sage. Then, there's more sage in the halibut's crusty crouton topper. The end result is the union of sweet and savory, simple and sublime.

Soy-Lime Scallops with Leeks

Marinated sea scallops get a big burst of flavor from a good, healthy squeeze of grilled lime. Grilling caramelizes the sugars in citrus fruits, making them sweeter. Try this little trick with oranges and lemons as well.

Chilled Thai Tenderloin and Pasta with Tons of Basil, Curried Green and Yellow Bean Salad

These two recipes pack loads of Far Eastern flavor, and they come out-of-doors right when you want them. One more thing: When I say "tons of basil," I mean it. If you love the flavor of an herb (most are so plentiful in summer), pile it on. Let the recipe be a starting point, not an end.

Chilled Thai Tenderloin and Pasta with Tons of Basil

This recipe can be made two days in advance of a party. Tying the tenderloin butcher-style helps keep its shape during cooking. Just follow the tying directions below.

Prep: 30 minutes **Grill:** 1 hour **Chill:** 8 hours

1	3-lb. center-cut beef tenderloin	2	lb. angel hair pasta, cooked according to package directions
	Pepper		
½	cup purchased Thai peanut sauce	1½	cups purchased Thai peanut sauce
3	cups packed purple or green basil sprigs (do not remove leaves from stems)	2	cups sliced fennel strips
		1	cup slivered fresh purple or green basil
		2	Tbsp. olive oil

1. Butcher-wrap the beef tenderloin (see instructions, below). Season with pepper. Spread the ½ cup peanut sauce onto the beef until coated. Tuck basil sprigs under string, covering as much of the beef as possible.

2. For a charcoal grill, arrange preheated coals around a drip pan. Test for medium-high heat above pan. Place beef on grill rack over drip pan. Cover; grill to desired doneness. Allow 1 to 1¼ hours for medium rare (135° F) or 1¼ to 1½ hours for medium (150° F). (For a gas grill, preheat grill. Reduce heat to medium. Adjust for indirect cooking. Grill as above, except place beef on rack in a roasting pan.)

3. Remove beef from grill; cover with foil and let stand for 40 minutes. (The temperature of the meat should rise 10° F during cooking.) Wrap beef tightly in plastic wrap; cover and store in refrigerator at least 8 hours or up to 2 days until ready to serve.

4. In a very large bowl toss cooked angel hair pasta with the 1½ cups peanut sauce and fennel. Add slivered basil. Cover and chill until ready to serve.

5. To serve, toss pasta mixture with olive oil; arrange on a serving platter. Cut string from tenderloin; remove basil sprigs and discard. Slice tenderloin into ¼-inch-thick slices. To serve, arrange sliced tenderloin beside pasta. Makes 10 servings.

Nutrition facts per serving: 670 cal., 19 g total fat (5 g sat. fat), 62 mg chol., 828 mg sodium, 83 g carbo., 7 g fiber, and 37 g pro. Daily Values: 9% vit. C, 6% calcium, and 33% iron.

Curried Green and Yellow Bean Salad

The snap of curry complements the crunch of chilled beans in this salad and the flavors of Chilled Thai Tenderloin.

Prep: 25 minutes **Cook:** 10 minutes **Chill:** 2 hours

12	oz. green beans, trimmed	1½	tsp. sugar
12	oz. yellow wax beans, trimmed	1	tsp. grated fresh ginger
2	Tbsp. white wine vinegar	1	tsp. curry powder
2	Tbsp. olive oil	½	tsp. ground turmeric
		¼	tsp. salt
		¼	tsp. pepper

1. In a saucepan cook beans, covered, in a small amount of boiling salted water for 10 minutes or until crisp-tender. Drain and immerse in a bowl half-filled with ice water. Drain again. Return beans to bowl. Cover and refrigerate until serving.

2. Meanwhile, for salad dressing, in a screw-top jar combine vinegar, olive oil, sugar, ginger, curry powder, turmeric, salt, and pepper. Cover; shake well. Refrigerate until serving time.

3. To serve, pour salad dressing over beans. Toss gently to coat. Makes 8 to 10 servings.

Nutrition facts per serving: 60 cal., 4 g total fat (0 g sat. fat), 0 mg chol., 78 mg sodium, 7 g carbo., 3 g fiber, and 2 g pro. Daily Values: 17% vit. C, 3% calcium, and 5% iron.

BUTCHER-WRAP A TENDERLOIN

1. Slide an 8-foot-long, 100-percent-cotton string under meat about 2 inches from end. Pull to top. Make a knot, keeping one end short.

2. Pull long end toward other end. About 2 inches from first tie, loop string under, bring up and around. Insert long end under top string to secure; pull to tighten. Repeat, making a loop every 2 inches to the end.

3. Bring the string lengthwise around the underside of the roast and back to the starting point at the top side of the tenderloin, twisting the string around each loop as you go. Knot it around the initial loop. Cut the string.

30 **low fat** **Smooth and Chunky Melon Soup**

Soy milk, an increasingly popular alternative to milk, is now available at most grocery stores.

Prep: 15 minutes **Chill:** 3 hours

6 cups cubed cantaloupe	2 cups cubed cantaloupe and/or honeydew melon (optional)
1½ cups mango nectar	
1 tsp. freshly ground dried whole green or black peppercorns	1 recipe Peppered Yogurt (optional)
1½ cups vanilla-enriched soy-based beverage (soy milk) or 1½ cups plain yogurt	1 recipe Prosciutto Gremolata (optional)
	Yellow sweet pepper spears (optional)

1. Place 3 cups of the cantaloupe, half of the mango nectar, and ½ teaspoon of the pepper in a blender container or food processor bowl. Cover and blend or process until cantaloupe is smooth. Transfer to a large bowl with a spout. Repeat with remaining 3 cups cantaloupe, nectar, and pepper.

2. Stir soy milk into the cantaloupe mixture in bowl. Cover and refrigerate until serving time, up to 3 hours.

3. To serve, pour soup into eight soup bowls. Top with cantaloupe cubes. If desired, garnish with Peppered Yogurt and/or Prosciutto Gremolata. Makes 8 servings.

Peppered Yogurt: In a small bowl stir ½ teaspoon freshly cracked whole dried green or black peppercorns into ½ cup plain yogurt. Cover; store in the refrigerator. Makes ½ cup.

Prosciutto Gremolata: In a bowl combine 2 ounces chopped prosciutto, 1½ teaspoons snipped fresh parsley, and 1 teaspoon finely shredded lemon peel. Makes about ½ cup.

Nutrition facts per serving: 99 cal., 1 g total fat (0 g sat. fat), 38 mg sodium, 21 g carbo., 1 g fiber, and 2 g pro. Daily Values: 94% vit. C, 7% calcium, and 4% iron.

30 **low fat** **Mad Mad Martian Juice**

Chill this herbal concoction in the refrigerator for at least one hour before serving to let the flavors blend.

Prep: 15 minutes **Chill:** 1 hour

½ cup snipped fresh mint or basil or ¼ cup snipped fresh tarragon	1½ cups water
	2 cups ice cubes
1 recipe Simple Syrup	Lavender sprigs (optional)
	Lemon wedges (optional)

1. In a blender container combine herb, Simple Syrup, and water. Cover; blend until nearly smooth.

2. With blender running, gradually add ice cubes through hole in lid, blending until slushy. To serve, pour into three or four glasses. If desired, garnish with lavender sprigs and/or lemon wedges. Makes 3 or 4 servings.

Simple Syrup: In a small saucepan combine ¼ cup sugar and ¼ cup water. Bring just to boiling, stirring to dissolve sugar. Cool; cover and chill for at least 1 hour before using. Makes about ⅓ cup.

Nutrition facts per serving: 65 cal., 0 g total fat (0 g sat. fat), 0 mg chol., 8 mg sodium, 16 g carbo., 0 g fiber, and 0 g pro. Daily Values: 15% vit. C, 2% calcium, and 14% iron.

Smooth and Chunky Melon Soup

Mad Mad Martian Juice

This alternative to fruit juice is so cool. Loaded with garden-fresh mint, basil, or tarragon, it's deceptively easy to prepare. A make-ahead simple syrup adds a touch of sweet.

Afternoon Coffee Vodka Cooler

This thirst-quenching cocktail perks you up with coffee for a boost, ice to chill, and espresso-infused vodka to give it punch. It's perfect for a post-biking afternoon pick-me-up or as a Sunday brunch eye-opener.

30 Fill-the-Grill Nectarine Toss

If your mother begged you to eat fresh fruit, here's your answer: Have it with a big bowl of ice cream.

Prep: 15 minutes **Grill:** 8 minutes

6 medium nectarines, halved and pitted	3 cups vanilla ice cream Coarsely chopped chocolate chunks
2 Tbsp. olive oil	
Ground cinnamon or nutmeg (optional)	

1. Brush nectarines with olive oil. Sprinkle with cinnamon. Place a grill wok or grill basket on the rack of an uncovered grill directly over medium coals; heat for 5 minutes. Place nectarine halves in the wok or basket. Grill for 8 to 10 minutes or until heated through, turning gently halfway through cooking time. (For gas grill, preheat grill. Reduce heat to medium. Place grill wok or basket on grill rack over heat. Cover; grill as above.)

2. To serve, scoop ice cream into a serving bowl. Top with grilled nectarines. Sprinkle with chocolate. Makes 6 servings.

Nutrition facts per serving: 312 cal., 19 g total fat (9 g sat. fat), 46 mg chol., 46 mg sodium, 36 g carbo., 2 g fiber, and 4 g pro. Daily Values: 13% vit. C, 10% calcium, and 1% iron.

Fill-the-Grill
Nectarine Toss

30 Afternoon Coffee Vodka Cooler

Prepare the Coffee Bean Vodka (see instructions, right) at least four days in advance. Save some of the morning coffee—the stronger the better—to make these afternoon refreshers.

Prep: 5 minutes

Ice cubes	1 Tbsp. whipping cream, half-and-half, or light cream
½ cup cold brewed coffee	
2 Tbsp. Coffee Bean Vodka	
	1 tsp. extra-fine or regular granulated sugar

1. To serve, fill a short glass with ice cubes. Add coffee, Coffee Bean Vodka, whipping cream, and sugar to glass. Stir gently. Makes 1 cooler.

Espresso Martini: Fill a martini shaker with ice. Add 2 tablespoons Coffee Bean Vodka. Shake vigorously. Strain vodka into a well-chilled martini glass. Add ½ cup cold brewed coffee; stir gently. Add a splash of cream or cream-based liqueur if you like. Makes 1 martini.

Nutrition facts per serving: 143 cal., 6 g total fat (3 g sat. fat), 21 mg chol., 8 mg sodium, 5 g carbo., 0 g fiber, and 0 g pro. Daily Values: 1% calcium.

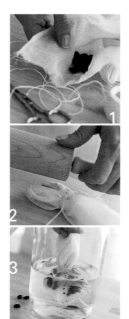

HOW TO MAKE COFFEE BEAN VODKA

1. Place 16 whole espresso or coffee beans on a piece of 100-percent-cotton cheesecloth and tie into a bundle with clean 100-percent-cotton string.

2. Gently crush a few beans by tapping the tied coffee bean bundle lightly with a rolling pin.

3. Pour a 750-milliliter bottle of vodka into a plastic freezer container; add bean bundle. Cover; store in the freezer for at least four days or up to two weeks. To chill longer, remove the coffee bean bundle.

You Say Tomato

PHOTOGRAPHS: COLLEEN DUFFLEY. STORY: BEV BENNETT.

30 **Go-with-Anything Tomato Sauté**

Prep: 12 minutes **Cook:** 3 minutes

2½ cups whole red grape and yellow teardrop tomatoes and/or cherry tomatoes
   Nonstick olive oil cooking spray
¼ cup finely chopped shallots
1 clove garlic, minced
1 tsp. snipped fresh lemon-thyme or thyme
¼ tsp. salt
¼ tsp. pepper
1 cup fresh mozzarella cut into ½-inch cubes (4 oz.)

1. Halve about 1½ cups of the tomatoes; set aside. Lightly coat a 10-inch nonstick skillet with olive oil cooking spray. Add shallots, garlic, and thyme. Cook and stir over medium heat for 2 to 3 minutes or until shallots are tender.

2. Add remaining tomatoes, salt, and pepper. Cook and stir for 1 to 2 minutes more or until tomatoes are just warmed. Remove from heat. Stir in mozzarella cubes. Makes 4 side-dish servings.

Nutrition facts per serving: 107 cal., 5 g total fat (3 g sat. fat), 16 mg chol., 289 mg sodium, 9 g carbo., 1 g fiber, and 8 g pro. Daily Values: 14% vit. A, 43% vit. C, 19% calcium, and 5% iron.

A spell-binding blush may be the tomato's seductive lure, but its wholesome nutrition is the best reason to keep coming back for more. An average-size tomato supplies about 40 percent of the vitamin C, 20 percent of the vitamin A, and 10 percent of the potassium you should get in a day.

Red tomato varieties are rich in lycopene too. This plant chemical, which puts the red color in tomatoes, also acts as a powerful antioxidant in the body. A Harvard study of men who consumed a tomato-rich diet (at least 10 servings a week) showed that they may have reduced their risk of prostate cancer by 45 percent. Researchers also are looking at lycopene's role in protecting against other cancers, as well as heart disease. Since the body absorbs lycopene more easily from heat-processed tomatoes, cooked tomato dishes and canned tomato products will give you a boost of the antioxidant—two to four times more than fresh tomatoes.

With all this going for tomatoes, is it any wonder the French originally called them the fruit of love? To savor the of the end-of-summer tomato harvest, cook up a quick sauté (right)—terrific over pasta or wilted greens—or stir together a great gazpacho (right) that's a meal in itself.

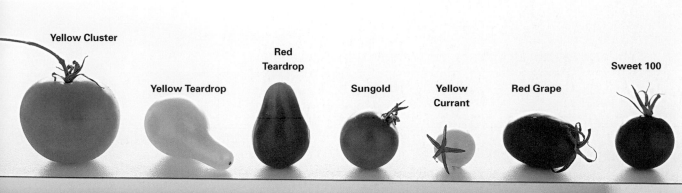

Yellow Cluster

Yellow Teardrop

Red Teardrop

Sungold

Yellow Currant

Red Grape

Sweet 100

HOT LITTLE TOMATOES

You'll see this sweetie linked on the vine with other little ones. Bite through its slightly thick skin, and this mild tomato bursts.

Stunning color and a voluptuous shape make this babe irresistible. The yellow teardrop is meaty with a mild flavor.

Just like the yellow teardrop, the pear shape is alluring. It tastes like a vine-ripened tomato with an extra hint of sweetness.

Popular in home gardens, this hybrid has a rich orange color and a sweet-as-candy taste.

This itsy-bitsy cutie is among the tiniest of tomatoes. Its flavor has a bit of a tomato tang.

Loaded with vitamin C, this sugary, grape-size version of the cherry tomato was first cultivated in China.

Some people pop this super-sweet, 1-inch wonder into their mouths like candy. There's a yellow variety too.

30 low fat **Red and Green Gazpacho**
Prep: 30 minutes **Chill:** 1 hour

3 cups chopped red and/or partially green tomatoes (3 large)
½ cup chopped tomatillo (2 medium)
1 16-oz. can tomato juice (2 cups)
½ cup chopped cucumber
1 large jalapeño pepper, seeded and finely chopped
¼ cup finely chopped green onion

1 clove garlic, minced
¼ tsp. bottled hot green pepper sauce
1 Tbsp. olive oil
1 Tbsp. lime juice
¼ cup finely snipped cilantro
6 oz. peeled, cooked medium shrimp (12 to 15)
Fat-free dairy sour cream (optional)
Green onion curl (optional)

1. In a bowl combine tomatoes, tomatillo, tomato juice, cucumber, jalapeño pepper, green onion, garlic, pepper sauce, olive oil, lime juice, and cilantro. Cover; chill at least 1 hour.

2. To serve, reserve 6 shrimp. Coarsely chop remaining shrimp. Stir chopped shrimp into gazpacho. Spoon gazpacho into six chilled soup bowls. Top each serving with a dollop of sour cream, a whole shrimp, and a green onion curl, if desired. Makes 6 side-dish servings.

Nutrition facts per serving: 90 cal., 3 g total fat (0 g sat. fat), 55 mg chol., 371 mg sodium, 10 g carbo., 2 g fiber, and 8 g pro. Daily Values: 27% vit. A, 64% vit. C, 3% calcium, and 11% iron.

Summer Ripe

Aug

u s t

Ah!!! August.
Hot days of garden
trading, farmer's
market strolling,
and relishing
summer's most
colorful gems.

Open yourself to the charms of your favorite garden bedfellows: gleaming plump tomatoes, sweet peppers (crisp, spicy, oh-so-amenable), and onions, the strongmen of the vegetable kingdom. This trio of vegetables peaks in August, so cook 'em up quick.

Stand-Up
Tomato Salad

summer ripe

PHOTOGRAPHS: (RIGHT) COLLEEN DUFFLEY; (ALL OTHERS) JOYCE OUDKERK POOL. FOOD STYLIST: POUKÉ. PROP STYLIST: CAROL HACKER. STORY: RICHARD SWEARINGER.

Tomato
Bread Pudding

30 low fat Stand-Up Tomato Salad

The tequila dressing echos of a margarita, but, if you prefer, you may substitute your favorite vinaigrette.

Prep: 30 minutes **Chill:** 2 hours

3 small yellow, orange, ripe green, and/or red tomatoes (about 12 oz. total), cored	1 cup peeled jicama, peeled kohlrabi, yellow summer squash, and/or zucchini, coarsely shredded (about 6 oz.)
1 recipe Margarita Dressing	6 large shrimp, peeled, deveined, and cooked

1. Cut each tomato horizontally into 6 slices. Keeping slices together, place in a 2-quart square baking dish. Pour Margarita Dressing over slices. Cover and chill for 2 to 4 hours.

2. Remove tomatoes from dish, reserving dressing. Place a tomato slice on each of six individual salad plates. Top with about 1 tablespoon of the shredded vegetables. Repeat layers, ending with a tomato slice. Top each salad with a cooked shrimp. Drizzle with reserved dressing. Makes 6 servings.

Margarita Dressing: In a screw-top jar combine 2 tablespoons lime juice, 2 tablespoons tequila, 1 tablespoon salad oil, 2 teaspoons snipped fresh marjoram, ¼ tcaspoon salt, and ¼ tcaspoon pepper. Cover and shake well to mix.

Nutrition facts per serving: 75 cal., 3 g total fat (0 g sat. fat), 28 mg chol., 138 mg sodium, 5 g carbo., 0 g fiber, and 5 g pro. Daily Values: 1% vit. A, 22% vit. C, 2% calcium, and 6% iron.

TOMATOES

Tasty heirloom tomatoes are now more available than ever, as are many newer varieties, making the tomato picking fun. Choosing: Look for shiny, smooth skins and a plump shape. The skin of the tomato should just give slightly to thumb pressure.
Keeping: To ripen tomatoes, put them on the counter in a brown bag to speed the process. After ripening, they'll keep on the counter about seven days. Cold renders tomatoes tasteless, so don't store them in the refrigerator.

Tomato Bread Pudding

For the best results, seek out crusty, firm-textured bread.

Prep: 25 minutes **Bake:** 15 minutes

4 oz. French bread, Italian bread, or Italian Country bread, torn into 1-inch chunks	3 Tbsp. snipped fresh dill or 1 tsp. dried dillweed
2 cloves garlic, minced	¼ tsp. pepper
2 Tbsp. olive oil	¼ cup reduced-sodium chicken broth
2 lb. tomatoes, cored, seeded, and coarsely chopped (about 4 cups)	Finely shredded Parmesan cheese (optional)
	Sprigs of fresh dill (optional)

1. Preheat oven to 350° F. Place bread pieces in a large shallow baking pan. Bake about 15 minutes or until golden brown, stirring once.

2. In a large skillet cook garlic in hot olive oil over medium heat for 30 seconds. Add tomatoes, dill, and pepper. Cook, uncovered, over medium heat for 2 minutes, stirring occasionally. Add broth; bring to boiling. Remove from heat.

3. To serve, place toasted bread pieces in a serving bowl. Pour tomato mixture over bread; toss gently to mix. If desired, top with Parmesan cheese and sprigs of fresh dill. Serve immediately. Makes 4 to 6 servings.

Nutrition facts per serving: 189 cal., 8 g total fat (1 g sat. fat), 0 mg chol., 232 mg sodium, 26 g carbo., 3 g fiber, and 5 g pro. Daily Values: 28% vit. A, 73% vit. C, 4% calcium, and 10% iron.

One of the joys of summer eating is a side dish loaded with tomatoes. Their blend of sweet and sour brings a brightness to the table that elevates dinner into a feast.

Yellow Pepper Soup with Yogurt and Cucumbers

Fennel and cardamom add a spicy niceness to warm or chilled soup. Crush the fennel seed with the back of a spoon.

Prep: 25 minutes **Cook:** 20 minutes

1	8-oz. carton plain or low-fat yogurt (do not use nonfat)	¾	tsp. ground cardamom
1	tsp. fennel seed, crushed	2	Tbsp. olive oil
4	to 7 medium yellow sweet peppers (1½ lb.), seeded and coarsely chopped (about 5 cups)	1	14-oz. can reduced-sodium chicken broth
2	medium shallots, chopped (¼ cup)	1	cup water
		2	Tbsp. cider vinegar
			Plain or low-fat yogurt
		¼	cup coarsely chopped cucumber
			Fennel seed

1. In a bowl stir together the yogurt and fennel seed. Cover; let stand at room temperature for 30 minutes.

2. Meanwhile, in a large saucepan cook sweet peppers, shallots, and cardamom in hot oil about 15 minutes or until peppers are just beginning to soften, stirring occasionally. Add chicken broth, water, and vinegar. Bring to boiling; reduce heat. Simmer, covered, for 5 minutes more.

3. Remove from heat; cool slightly. In a blender container or food processor bowl blend or process half at a time until smooth. Return all to saucepan; cook and stir until warm.

4. Serve warm or chilled. Ladle soup into four bowls. Top with yogurt, cucumber, and fennel seed. Makes 4 servings.

Nutrition facts per serving: 154 cal., 9 g total fat (2 g sat. fat), 8 mg chol., 306 mg sodium, 15 g carbo., 2 g fiber, and 5 g pro. Daily Values: 10% vit. A, 365% vit. C, 10% calcium, and 6% iron.

PEPPERS

The mild member of the pepper family comes in many colors. All sweet peppers start out green, then ripen into red, orange, yellow, purple, and even chocolate brown. The riper peppers are sweeter than the greens, but differ only slightly in flavor. Choosing: Look for well-shaped peppers with deep color, glossy sheen, relatively heavy weight for their size, and firm sides. Don't buy peppers with very thin walls, those that are are wilted or wrinkly, or those that have cuts or punctures or soft, watery spots on the sides (which would indicate the pepper has started to go bad).
Keeping: Refrigerate unwashed peppers in a plastic bag for up to five days.

Grilled Pickled Peppers

Serve with an assortment of pickles, olives, chips, and raw vegetables or with grilled sausages or other meats.

Prep: 20 minutes **Cool:** 1 hour **Chill:** overnight

4	medium orange, red, and/or yellow sweet peppers	2	whole cloves
1	Tbsp. olive oil	½	cup red wine vinegar
1	tsp. mustard seeds, toasted*	5	sprigs fresh thyme
		¼	tsp. salt
		¼	tsp. ground black pepper

1. Halve the sweet peppers; remove the stems, seeds, and membranes. Brush pepper halves with olive oil. Place pepper halves on the rack of an uncovered grill directly over medium coals. Grill about 10 minutes or until crisp-tender and peppers have grill marks, turning once. Remove from grill and cool. Cut into chunks.

2. While peppers cool, place the toasted mustard seeds and cloves on a small square of double thickness 100-percent-cotton cheesecloth. Bring up corners to make a bundle; tie with 100-percent-cotton string. Place the spice bag in a small stainless steel saucepan with the vinegar and thyme sprigs. Bring to boiling; remove from heat. Cool completely.

3. In a medium glass bowl stir together peppers, vinegar mixture, salt, and black pepper; cover and chill overnight. To serve, remove spice bag. Makes 3 cups.

*Test Kitchen Tip: To toast mustard seeds, place seeds in a small skillet. Heat over medium-high heat for 2 to 3 minutes or until toasted, shaking the skillet occasionally. Watch carefully as the seeds may "pop" in skillet, jumping out when hot.

Nutrition facts per ¼ cup serving: 42 cal., 2 g total fat (0 g sat. fat), 0 mg chol., 67 mg sodium, 5 g carbo., 1 g fiber, and 1 g pro. Daily Values: 4% vit. A, 202% vit. C, 1% calcium, and 3% iron.

Sweet peppers can be a puzzle. How do you make the most of their sweet, slightly spicy flavor beyond chopping for pasta and salads? The solution is the gentle application of heat.

Yellow Pepper Soup with
Yogurt and Cucumbers

Grilled Pickled Peppers

Dinner—with all its fussing, and
steaming, and stirring—can wait.
Hang out on the porch and enjoy the
quiet wonder of a simple appetizer
such as Grilled Pickled Peppers, marinated in spices and herbs.

peppers

Square Summer Pie

The filling of peppers, potatoes, mustard, and artichoke hearts was created to bake in the cool of the morning. When the heat of the day lifts and your appetite stirs, you can pull it out to serve at the right "thank heavens" moment.

peppers

Square Summer Pie

Prep: 50 minutes **Bake:** 40 minutes **Cool:** 10 minutes

4	medium red or orange sweet peppers, seeded
1	medium baking potato
8	cloves garlic, sliced
2	Tbsp. cooking oil
1	9-oz. pkg. frozen artichoke hearts

1	cup shredded Swiss cheese (4 oz.)
1	Tbsp. coarse-grain brown mustard
½	tsp. salt
1	recipe Pastry for Lattice-Top Pie
	Milk

1. Cut peppers into 1-inch pieces. Peel and slice potatoes ¼ inch thick. In a 12-inch skillet cook peppers, potato slices, and garlic in hot oil over medium heat for 5 minutes, stirring occasionally. Thaw, drain, and chop artichoke hearts; stir into pepper mixture. Cook, covered, about 4 minutes more or until crisp-tender, stirring occasionally.

2. Transfer vegetable mixture to a large bowl; add cheese, mustard, and salt. Toss gently to coat; spoon into pan lined with Pastry for Lattice-Top Pie.

3. Move oven rack to lowest position in oven. Preheat oven to 450° F. Roll out remaining pastry into an 11-inch square. Cut into 1-inch-wide strips. Arrange strips on filling in a free-form lattice pattern. Press ends into crust edges. Brush with milk. Cover edges with foil. Bake for 20 minutes. Remove foil; bake about 20 minutes more or until crust is brown. Cool in pan on a wire rack 10 minutes; remove sides of pan. Makes 8 servings.

Pastry for Lattice-Top Pie: In a bowl stir together 2 cups all-purpose flour and ½ teaspoon salt. Using a pastry blender, cut in ⅔ cup shortening until pieces are pea-size. Sprinkle 1 tablespoon cold water over part; gently toss with a fork. Push dough to side. Repeat, using 5 to 6 more tablespoons cold water, until all is moistened. Divide in half; form each half into a ball. (If making ahead, wrap in plastic wrap; seal. Refrigerate up to 24 hours. Bring to room temperature before rolling out.)

On a lightly floured surface slightly flatten one ball. Roll from center to edges to form an 11-inch square. To transfer pastry, roll around rolling pin. Unroll pastry into a 9-inch square tart pan or a 2-quart square baking dish, being careful not to stretch. If necessary, trim edge even with top edge of pan.

Nutrition facts per serving: 392 cal., 25 g total fat (7 g sat. fat), 13 mg chol., 377 mg sodium, 33 g carbo., 4 g fiber, and 9 g pro. Daily Values: 68% vit. A, 170% vit. C, 17% calcium, and 11% iron.

The lattice looks better if you arrange it casually rather than in rigid lines. If the dough does not come up to the rim in a deeper pan, tuck the edges of the strips under the edge of the bottom crust.

GARDEN-STYLE SUPPER

Onion Dip with dippers (recipe, page 160)

Stand-Up Tomato Salad (recipe, page 153)

Square Summer Pie (recipe, left)

Keen Nectarine (recipe, page 112)

Sparkling water

new 30 low fat Peppers Stuffed with Cinnamon Bulgur

For your sweet pepper "bowls," choose from a variety of colors—green, red, yellow, and orange.

Start to finish: 30 minutes

1¾	cups water
½	cup shredded carrot
¼	cup chopped onion
1	tsp. instant chicken bouillon granules
⅛	tsp. salt
3	inches stick cinnamon or dash ground cinnamon
¾	cup bulgur
⅓	cup dried cranberries or raisins

2	large or 4 small green, red, yellow, or orange sweet peppers
¾	cup shredded Muenster, brick, or mozzarella cheese (3 oz.)
½	cup water
2	Tbsp. sliced almonds or chopped pecans, toasted

1. In a large skillet stir together the 1¾ cups water, carrot, onion, bouillon granules, salt, and cinnamon. Bring to boiling; reduce heat. Simmer, covered, for 5 minutes.

2. Stir in bulgur and cranberries. Remove from heat. Cover and let stand for 5 minutes. If using stick cinnamon, remove from the bulgur mixture. Drain off excess liquid.

3. Meanwhile, halve sweet peppers lengthwise; remove the seeds and membranes.

4. Stir cheese into bulgur mixture; spoon into sweet pepper halves. Place sweet pepper halves in skillet. Add the ½ cup water. Bring to boiling; reduce heat. Simmer, covered, for 5 to 10 minutes or until peppers are crisp-tender and bulgur mixture is heated through. Sprinkle with nuts. Makes 4 servings.

Nutrition facts per serving: 253 cal., 9 g total fat (4 g sat. fat), 20 mg chol., 496 mg sodium, 36 g carbo., 8 g fiber, and 10 g pro. Daily Values: 83% vit. A, 92% vit. C, 19% calcium, and 8% iron.

ONIONS

Spring onions are usually sweeter and milder than fall and winter onions. Both work well in these recipes, although summer onions tend to take a little longer to brown.

Choosing: White onions have a pungent, sharp aroma and flavor. Reds are about as sharp as yellows, but the color fades during cooking. Look for dry outer skins free of spots or blemishes. Onions should be heavy for their size with no scent (scent indicates internal breakdown or bruising).

Keeping: Onions keep about 10 days in a well-ventilated, cool, dry place—not in the refrigerator. You can freeze chopped onion, tightly wrapped, for up to three months.

Glazed Onions

Onion Gratin with Country Ham

Tangles of tender onions, chunks of smoky ham, and eddies of melted cheese share a creamy sauce—a little on the rich side, but what could you possibly leave out?

Glazed Onions

Sauté pearl onions and walnuts, then splash with fig vinegar.
Prep: 25 minutes **Cook:** 13 minutes

¼ cup broken walnuts
1½ lb. pearl onions, peeled (see photo, below)
1 Tbsp. cooking oil
¼ tsp. salt
⅛ tsp. pepper
2 Tbsp. dried currants, raisins, or chopped dried figs
3 Tbsp. black fig vinegar*, or red wine vinegar with ½ tsp. sugar stirred in
1 Tbsp. snipped fresh savory or oregano
1 recipe Sherry Whipped Cream (optional)
Black fig vinegar*

1. In a large skillet cook walnuts over medium-high heat for 4 to 5 minutes or until toasted, stirring occasionally. Remove from skillet; set aside.

2. In the same skillet cook onions in hot oil over medium-low heat for 12 to 15 minutes until golden brown and tender, stirring occasionally. Sprinkle with salt and pepper. Stir in walnuts, currants, and the 3 tablespoons vinegar. Cook and stir about 1 minute until vinegar has evaporated and onions are glazed.

3. Transfer onions to a serving bowl. Sprinkle with savory or oregano. If desired, spoon Sherry Whipped Cream onto onions. Pass additional fig vinegar. Makes 5 to 6 servings.

Sherry Whipped Cream: Place 2 tablespoons heavy whipping cream (not ultra-pasteurized) and 1 tablespoon dry sherry in a screw-top jar. Cover; shake until cream thickens slightly.

***Test Kitchen Tip:** Find fig vinegar in specialty food stores or order it at www.cuisineperel.com or from Gourmet Country, 800/665-9123.

Nutrition facts per serving: 142 cal., 7 g total fat (1 g sat. fat), 0 mg chol., 123 mg sodium, 18 g carbo., 4 g fiber, and 3 g pro. Daily Values: 15% vit. C, 4% calcium, and 4% iron.

VEGETABLE MATH

Vegetable sizes and yields vary with growing conditions—peppers especially have a wide range of size and weight. Your best bet is to buy by weight rather than size when possible, but use these guidelines to eliminate some of the guesswork. The "What you get" column is what you have after seeding, trimming, and cutting.

Vegetable	What you buy	What you get
Onions	1 medium (5 oz.)	½ cup chopped
Peppers	1 medium (3 oz.)	¾ cup chopped or 1 cup strips
Tomatoes	1 medium (5 oz.)	½ cup chopped

Onion Gratin with Country Ham

We used country-style ham in this recipe for its full flavor and bold saltiness. You can buy 6-ounce steaks from many grocery stores or sliced ham at your store's deli counter, but regular smoked ham works very well as a substitute.

Prep: 30 minutes **Bake:** 1¼ hours **Stand:** 10 minutes

¼ cup butter
¼ cup all-purpose flour
1 tsp. salt
½ tsp. pepper
2 cups milk
2 lb. large onions, peeled
1 15-oz. can cannellini beans or great northern beans, rinsed and drained
6 oz. cooked, country-style ham or smoked ham, cut into bite-size strips
½ cup smoked provolone or plain provolone cheese, shredded (about 2 oz.)

1. Preheat oven to 350° F. In a large saucepan melt butter over medium heat. Stir in flour, salt, and pepper. Cook and stir for 2 to 3 minutes until light brown. Add milk all at once. Cook and stir over medium heat until thickened and bubbly.

2. Slice onions ½ inch thick; separate into rings. Stir onions, beans, and ham into saucepan. Transfer to a 1½-quart oval or 2-quart rectangular baking dish; place on a baking sheet.

3. Bake, covered, for 1 hour. Uncover and sprinkle with cheese. Bake, uncovered, about 15 minutes more or until onions are tender and top is golden. Let stand for 10 minutes before serving. Makes 6 to 8 servings.

Nutrition facts per serving: 309 cal., 15 g total fat (8 g sat. fat), 54 mg chol., 1,318 mg sodium, 30 g carbo., 6 g fiber, and 19 g pro. Daily Values: 11% vit. A, 14% vit. C, 22% calcium, and 10% iron.

To peel small onions, bring a small saucepan of water to boiling. Cook onions for 30 seconds. Drain and cool. Cut a thin slice off of the root end and squeeze from other end to remove peel.

Onion Dip

Cornmeal-Crusted Onion Rings

Use a saucepan that's taller than it is wide to minimize the oil spattering.

Prep: 30 minutes **Cook:** 3 minutes per batch

3 Tbsp. honey	½ cup cornmeal
1 tsp. snipped fresh rosemary	¼ cup finely chopped peanuts or pecans
1 48-oz. bottle cooking oil for deep-fat frying	½ tsp. salt
½ cup buttermilk	¼ tsp. pepper
1 egg, beaten	1 lb. white onions (3 medium)
1 cup all-purpose flour	

1. In a small saucepan heat honey and rosemary over very low heat about 3 minutes or until heated through. Set aside.

2. Preheat oven to 300° F. Line a baking sheet with waxed paper; set aside. In a heavy, deep, 3-quart saucepan or deep-fat fryer, heat oil to 365° F.

3. In a medium bowl combine buttermilk and egg. In a shallow dish combine flour, cornmeal, peanuts or pecans, salt, and pepper.

4. Cut 1 onion in half crosswise; set aside half. Cut remaining onions into ½-inch-thick slices; separate into rings.

5. Working in batches, dip onion rings into egg mixture, letting excess drip into bowl. Toss rings into flour mixture until well-coated; gently shake off excess. Place onion rings on prepared baking sheet. Repeat process with remaining onions, egg, and flour mixtures.

6. With long-handled tongs, carefully add onion rings, a few at a time, to hot oil. Fry about 3 minutes, turning rings a few times, until onions are golden brown and cooked through. Drain on paper towels. Transfer to another baking sheet; keep warm in oven. Repeat with remaining onion rings.

7. To serve, place reserved onion half, cut side down, on a plate. Insert a fork into the top so the fork is upright. Stack onion rings on fork handle. Arrange remaining rings on plate around onion. Drizzle with rosemary-honey mixture. Sprinkle with additional salt, if desired. Makes 6 servings.

Nutrition facts per serving: 385 cal., 23 g total fat (3 g sat. fat), 36 mg chol., 229 mg sodium, 41 g carbo., 3 g fiber, and 6 g pro. Daily Values: 2% vit. A, 9% vit. C, 5% calcium, and 10% iron.

Onion Dip

Splurge on a big bag of thick, sea-salt-sprinkled potato chips to serve with this recipe.

Prep: 15 minutes **Cook:** 21 minutes

1⅓ lb. medium onions (4), halved and coarsely chopped (2 cups)	2 Tbsp. finely chopped red onion
½ tsp. salt	Potato chips or Armenian cracker bread (lahvosh), broken into serving-size pieces
2 Tbsp. cooking oil	
2 tsp. snipped fresh sage	
⅓ cup dairy sour cream	
2 Tbsp. grated Parmesan cheese	

1. In a large skillet cook the coarsely chopped onions and salt in hot oil, uncovered, over medium-low heat about 20 minutes or until very soft and lightly browned, stirring occasionally.

2. Stir in sage. Cook for 1 minute more. Remove from heat; stir in sour cream and Parmesan cheese. Transfer to a serving bowl. Sprinkle with red onion. Serve with chips or cracker bread. Makes about 1 cup (8 servings).

Nutrition facts per 2 tablespoons dip: 69 cal., 6 g total fat (2 g sat. fat), 5 mg chol., 174 mg sodium, 4 g carbo., 1 g fiber, and 1 g pro. Daily Values: 2% vit. A, 4% vit. C, 4% calcium, and 1% iron.

The gentler side of onions comes out in the cooking—but even when their pungency has been tamed, they retain a little bite to remind you of their wild past.

Cornmeal-Crusted Onion Rings

Just a few chopped peanuts add a crunchy element to the batter of Cornmeal-Crusted Onion Rings. Out of the fryer, they receive a drizzle of honey kissed with rosemary.

Market-Fresh Corn Favorites

Nothing says summer quite like the crunch of sweet, fresh corn right off the cob. Take corn from the market to the table in the same day for the very best flavor. First, you remove the husks and scrub with a stiff brush to remove the silks. Then, for these delightfully corny classics, you scrape uncooked corn kernels from the cob. Or, for good ol' corn on the cob, plunge the ears into boiling lightly salted water for 5 to 7 minutes or until juicy and tender. Serve with a dollop of butter.

Summer Bounty Salad

For this no-cook salad, combine fresh uncooked corn kernels, slivered red onion, shredded basil leaves, and finely chopped sweet peppers. Toss with balsamic vinegar, olive oil, salt, and pepper. Cover; chill up to 2 hours before serving.

PHOTOGRAPHS: COLLEEN DUFFLEY. FOOD STYLIST: BROOKE LEONARD. STORY: MARGE PERRY.

Fresh Corn Fritters
Mix 2 cups fresh uncooked corn kernels with one 8½-ounce package corn muffin mix, snipped fresh sage, 1 egg, and ¼ cup milk. Drop batter by tablespoons into deep hot oil (365° F). Fry 2 to 3 minutes or until golden brown, turning once. Drain well; serve warm.

Sassy Garden Relish
Stir together 2 cups fresh uncooked corn kernels, ¾ cup chopped sweet peppers, ½ cup chopped cucumber, ¼ cup sliced green onions, 2 tablespoons snipped fresh cilantro, and 1 chopped, seeded habañero pepper. Add vinegar, sugar, salt, and bottled hot pepper sauce to taste. Cover; chill for up to 2 days.

picnic
eggs

Postponing summer's itchy chores in favor of an afternoon enjoying the cool breezes off a lake doesn't mean that you have to do your basking on an empty stomach.

Bring sandwiches, of course, but add a plate of deviled eggs. They're everything you want in a hot-weather food: cool, easy, and the right size to sustain you between lunch and dinner.

Follow our recipe and you'll learn a couple of things. The first is a little food science: Too much heat causes a chemical reaction that makes yolks turn gray-green. If you follow our boiling method below, your eggs won't overcook.

The second lesson is to trust your taste buds. You know what your family loves, so use the kind of mustard they prefer and adjust the balance of mustards, salt, and pepper to suit yourselves.

Deviled Eggs

Prep: 20 minutes   **Cook:** 15 minutes

7 Hard-Cooked Eggs
¼ cup mayonnaise or salad dressing
1 to 2 tsp. Dijon-style mustard, balsamic herb mustard, honey mustard, or other favorite mustard
½ tsp. dry mustard
Salt
Pepper
Several leaves Italian flat-leaf parsley or paprika (optional)

1. Cut 6 eggs in half lengthwise; gently remove yolks; set whites aside. Coarsely chop the remaining egg.

2. In a self-sealing plastic bag combine egg yolks, chopped egg, mayonnaise, mustard, and dry mustard. Seal bag; gently squeeze to combine ingredients. Season to taste with salt and pepper.

3. Snip one corner of the bag (see top photo, right). Squeeze bag, pushing egg yolk mixture through hole into egg white halves (see bottom photo, right). Top with fresh parsley or paprika. Cover and chill for up to 12 hours. Makes 12 halves.

Nutrition facts per egg half: 72 cal., 6 g total fat (1 g sat. fat), 109 mg chol., 63 mg sodium, 0 g carbo., 0 g fiber, and 3 g pro. Daily Values: 3% vit. A, 1% calcium, and 2% iron.

THE HARD-BOILED BASICS

Hard-Cooked Eggs: Place the eggs in a single layer in a large saucepan. Add enough cold water to cover 1 inch above the eggs. Bring to a full rolling boil over high heat. Reduce the heat so the water is just below simmering, then cover and cook for 15 minutes. Remove the eggs from the pan, place them in a colander, and run cold water over them until they're cool enough to handle. To peel, gently tap each egg on the counter. Roll the egg between the palms of your hands. Peel off the eggshell. Cover and refrigerate the eggs until they're thoroughly chilled, about 1 hour.

Italian-Style Deviled Eggs: Prepare Deviled Eggs as directed left, except omit mayonnaise and mustards. Stir ¼ cup bottled creamy Italian salad dressing and 2 tablespoons grated Parmesan cheese into mashed yolks; mix well.

Greek-Style Deviled Eggs: Prepare Deviled Eggs as directed left, except fold 2 tablespoons feta cheese, 1 tablespoon finely chopped pitted kalamata olives or other pitted ripe olives, and 2 teaspoons snipped fresh oregano into yolk mixture. If desired, season with black pepper.

Mexican-Style Deviled Eggs: Prepare Deviled Eggs as directed left, except except omit mayonnaise and mustards. Fold 3 tablespoons dairy sour cream, 1 tablespoon salsa, and ½ teaspoon ground cumin into yolk mixture. Top with snipped fresh cilantro.

Indian-Style Deviled Eggs: Prepare Deviled Eggs as directed at left, except except omit mayonnaise and mustards. Fold 3 tablespoons plain low-fat yogurt, 1 tablespoon chopped chutney, and ½ teaspoon curry powder into yolk mixture. Sprinkle with chopped peanuts.

counting beans

PHOTOGRAPHS: SCOTT LITTLE. RECIPES: DARI CARRÉ. STORY: BEV BENNETT.

30 **low fat** **White Beans and Spinach Ragout**
Start to finish: 15 minutes

2 slices bacon, cut into 1-inch pieces
1 medium onion, halved and thinly sliced
1 14½-oz. can diced tomatoes
1 15-oz. can cannellini or navy beans, rinsed and drained
4 cups torn fresh spinach
4 tsp. bottled balsamic or red wine vinaigrette

1. In a large skillet cook bacon pieces until crisp. Remove with slotted spoon, reserving 1 tablespoon drippings in skillet. Drain bacon on paper towels.

2. Add onion to skillet; cook about 3 minutes or until just tender. Drain tomatoes, reserving ⅓ cup liquid. Stir tomatoes, reserved liquid, and beans into onion. Cook and stir over medium heat about 2 minutes or until heated through.

3. Stir in 3 cups spinach; cover and cook until just wilted, about 30 seconds. Stir in bacon and remaining spinach. Spoon into four bowls. Drizzle each serving with 1 teaspoon vinaigrette. Makes 4 servings.

Nutrition facts per serving: 131 cal., 3 g total fat (1 g sat. fat), 3 mg chol., 508 mg sodium, 23 g carbo., 9 g fiber, and 9 g pro. Daily Values: 20% vit. A, 27% vit. C, 7% calcium, 18% iron.

With their coats of many colors, dry beans are more than pretty packages. The skins—in tints of sienna, earthy black, and red—may deliver a potent nutritional boost.

It turns out that beans contain eight flavonoids, plant substances that act as nature's dyes and give many fruits and vegetables their colors. Scientists say those plant chemicals act as antioxidants to provide some protection against certain cancers and heart disease.

"You really have to go for the color," said George Hosfield, Ph.D., geneticist at the U.S. Department of Agriculture's Agricultural Research Service at Michigan State University.

More research may develop beans with more flavonoids and a more powerful antioxidant effect. Meanwhile, Hosfield suggests that you reuse the cooking liquid from beans in soups. When you soak or cook beans, flavonoids leach into the liquids but aren't destroyed.

BEAN BOOSTERS

■ To perk up a humble bean dish, add a handful of intensely flavored ingredients, such as Parmesan cheese, bacon, or prosciutto.

■ Use canned beans to cut cooking time to minutes. Rinse beans first to trim sodium levels. Rinsing also freshens the taste of canned beans.

■ Combine tomatoes, which are high in vitamin C, with plant sources of iron, such as beans. Your body will absorb more of the iron.

30 **low fat** **Red Beans and Orzo**
Start to finish: 30 minutes

1	14½-oz. can chicken broth (about 1¾ cups)	1	oz. prosciutto or cooked ham, cut into thin strips (⅓ cup)
1½	cups water		
1⅓	cups orzo (rosamarina)	2	Tbsp. snipped fresh Italian flat-leaf parsley
¼	cup finely chopped onion		
1	tsp. herbes de Provence or dried Italian seasoning, crushed	⅓	cup finely shredded Parmesan cheese
1	15-oz. can red beans or pinto beans, rinsed and drained		

1. In a medium saucepan bring chicken broth and water to boiling. Stir in orzo, onion, and herbes de Provence. Reduce heat. Simmer, uncovered, for 12 to 15 minutes or until orzo is just tender and most of the liquid is absorbed, stirring often.

2. Stir in beans, prosciutto or ham, and parsley; heat through. Spoon into four bowls. Top each serving with Parmesan cheese. Makes 4 servings.

Nutrition facts per serving: 363 cal., 6 g total fat (2 g sat. fat), 7 mg chol., 800 mg sodium, 59 g carbo., 7 g fiber, and 22 g pro. Daily Values: 3% vit. A, 5% vit. C, 17% calcium, and 19% iron.

PUMPING IRON

The flavonoid factors are highest in red, black, and deep-colored beans. But all beans, including cream-colored navy beans and garbanzo beans, contain some iron, folate, zinc, and a bit of calcium.

■ Iron: Beans supply anywhere from 1 to 4 milligrams of iron in every half-cup serving. That's an amount similar to what you'd get in a serving of beef. Your body does a better job of taking in iron from animal sources, but you can compensate by mixing a little meat in with the beans.

■ Folate: You probably know that women of childbearing age should eat foods rich in folate to help prevent neural-tube defects in their babies. You also need folate as you age to reduce your blood levels of homocysteine, a substance that puts you at greater risk for heart disease.

■ Zinc: Some people have trouble getting enough zinc, which is essential for your body's growth, insulin function, and immune system. Beans are an excellent source of zinc.

■ Calcium: Don't trade in your glass of milk or calcium-fortified orange juice for beans. However, every bit helps, and a half-cup serving of beans supplies 4 to 8 percent of the calcium you should have every day.

The Art of
Choosing Fruit

Just like us older folk, kids absolutely adore fresh fruit when it is at the top of its game—juicy, plump, and almost as sweet as candy. Consider this quest for the best fruit to be reason enough to hustle your children into the produce section for a quick, easy, and delicious lesson in the art of choosing fruits. After all, peachy peaches, perfect plums, fat sun-kissed berries, and deluxe ripe melons don't just show up on the family table. They're chosen.

Need more reasons? Fresh fruit is an essential part of a healthy kid's diet, a good source of vitamins and fiber. And it's a thrill to handle, like playing with big, brilliant jewels. Read on for a fruit-by-fruit guide and ideas for tossing together a yummy salad.

FRUITY FUN...

Follow these simple tips to select fruits whose beauty is more than skin deep.

■ **Look**
A bright hue, a rosy blush, pretty skin that's blemish free, and a plump shape—these are generally key for ripe fruits. No bruises, bumps, cracks, mold, or oozing, please.

■ **Sniff**
Delicious fruits are fragrant and sweetly aromatic. Avoid fruits that have a stale, odd odor. An overly strong smell indicates overripeness.

■ **Poke; Push; Lift**
Skip fruits that are hard and overly firm—this is an indication of underripeness. Overly soft fruits indicate overripeness. Most fruits should feel heavy for their size and be well-shaped for their variety.

■ **Taste**
Sweet, moist, and juicy. Bottom line: Ripe fruit should taste FRESH.

Fruit Salad Bowl Turnover

Start to finish: 30 minutes

4 cups sliced fresh peaches, nectarines, plums, and/or apricots

1 to 2 cups assorted fresh berries, such as blueberries, blackberries, raspberries, and/or halved strawberries

1 to 2 cups 1-inch chunks honeydew or cantaloupe melon

1 to 2 Tbsp. fresh lemon juice

1 to 2 Tbsp. sugar (optional)

3 small cantaloupes, halved (optional)

1. Refrigerate a large glass serving bowl for 20 to 30 minutes. Add desired fruit to the bowl. Toss gently until fruits are just mixed. Sprinkle with the lemon juice. Sprinkle with sugar to taste; toss gently until sugar is dissolved. To serve, spoon mixed fruits into cantaloupe halves, if desired. Makes 6 to 8 servings.

Nutrition facts per serving: 73 cal., 0 g total fat (0 g sat. fat), 0 mg chol., 4 mg sodium, 19 g carbo., 3 g fiber, and 1 g pro. Daily Values: 13% vit. A, 32% vit. C, 1% calcium, and 1% iron.

BEST OF SEASON

A street-smart fruit detective uses his or her sight, smell, touch, and taste to spot superior goods. Your kids can too.

- **Apricots**

Look for plump, firm apricots with a pretty red blush. Avoid fruit that is pale yellow or green-yellow, very firm, very soft, or bruised. Availability: late May to mid-August.

- **Blueberries, Strawberries, Raspberries, Blackberries**

Look for blueberries with a rounded shape and a tiny star-shaped cap. They should be firm, plump, and sweet. Strawberries should be plump with bright green caps and a healthy red color. Size does not indicate quality; the largest strawberries aren't necessarily the most flavorful. Raspberries grow in various shades of yellow, red, and black, and contain many tiny, edible seeds. Blackberries should have an inviting color, ranging from purplish black to black. Beware of excess juices in the bottom of the containers—this is a sign of spoilage. Sniff for mold too. Availability: all summer long, depending on the region.

- **Melons**

Pick a juicy, heavyweight contender. Cantaloupes should have tightly-netted skin; honeydews should be smooth and unblemished. Poke and whiff the belly-button, or blossom, end; it should give a little and smell melony. Melons will soften but not sweeten further when left to sit at room temperature. Availability: nearly year-round.

- **Peaches and Nectarines**

Watch out for greenish ones; they won't ripen. A rosy blush is nice, but not an indicator of ripeness. Use finger pressure; ripe peaches feel slightly soft, yielding. Ditto on nectarines. Availability: peak from June through September.

- **Plums**

A plump shape, vibrant coloring, smooth skin, and moderately yielding flesh are good signs. Stay away from soft, leaky ones. The bloom (light gray cast) on the skin is natural and doesn't affect quality. Avoid exceptionally hard or soft fruits. Availability: June through September.

With cooler days comes a longing for the comfortable and the familiar. September calls family favorites to the dinner table, with some clever back-to-school twists.

Sept

Big Flavor

Plus...

ember

strategies for
Big Flavor

Spirited cooking starts with don't-be-shy flavor. One big idea can add robust taste and simple sophistication to dinnertime. Here are our eight clever ideas, with quick notes on terms and techniques. Let the lesson begin!

Steamed Salmon and
Swiss Chard Stack

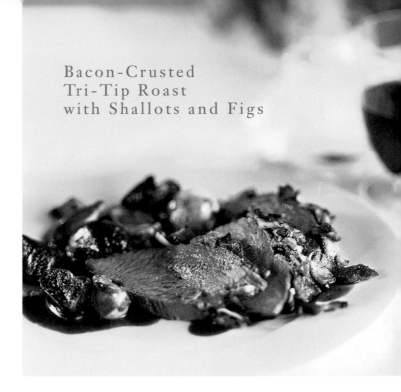

*Bacon-Crusted
Tri-Tip Roast
with Shallots and Figs*

Steamed Salmon and Swiss Chard Stack

Lemon, both oil and fresh, rules in these fanciful phyllo stacks.

Prep: 30 minutes **Bake:** 12 minutes **Cook:** 8 minutes

1 lb. fresh or frozen skinless, boneless salmon fillets, cut ½ to ¾ inch thick	½ tsp. kosher salt
5 sheets frozen phyllo dough (18x14-inch rectangles)	2 Tbsp. snipped fresh parsley
	Pepper
4 Tbsp. lemon-infused olive oil, or other flavored oils, such as garlic- or rosemary-infused olive oil	2 medium lemons, very thinly sliced and seeded
	4 cups torn fresh Swiss chard or spinach leaves
	¼ cup thin red onion slivers

1. Thaw salmon and phyllo dough, if frozen. Preheat oven to 350° F. Unroll phyllo dough. Carefully transfer a sheet to a large cutting board. (Keep remaining phyllo covered with plastic wrap.) Set aside 1 tablespoon lemon oil. Brush phyllo sheet with some of the remaining 3 tablespoons oil. Top with a second phyllo sheet; brush with oil. Sprinkle with half of the salt and parsley. Repeat layers. Place remaining phyllo sheet atop phyllo stack. Brush with oil.

2. Trim edges to make a 16x12-inch rectangle (discard trimmings). Cut stack lengthwise into thirds. Cut each third into four squares, making twelve 4x4-inch squares. Place phyllo stacks on an ungreased 15x10-inch baking sheet. Bake for 12 to 14 minutes or until golden. Cool on baking sheet. Set aside.

3. Rinse salmon. Cut salmon into 8 pieces; set aside. Fill a 12-inch skillet with water to a depth of 1 inch. Bring water to boiling; reduce heat. Place salmon pieces in the bottom of a double-tiered bamboo steamer or steamer basket. Sprinkle with pepper; top with one of the sliced lemons. Layer remaining sliced lemon and Swiss chard in top basket of bamboo steamer or on top of salmon in steamer basket. Place over simmering water. Cover and steam for 8 to 12 minutes or until salmon flakes easily with a fork.

4. To serve, place one stack of phyllo on each of four individual serving plates. Divide half of the salmon, lemon, and chard among phyllo stacks. Top each with another phyllo stack and remaining salmon, lemon, and chard. Crumble remaining phyllo stacks over individual servings. Drizzle with the reserved 1 tablespoon oil. Sprinkle with onion. Makes 4 servings.

Nutrition facts per serving: 401 cal., 25 g total fat (4 g sat. fat), 70 mg chol., 489 mg sodium, 20 g carbo., 4 g fiber, and 27 g pro. Daily Values: 30% vit. A, 92% vit. C, 7% calcium, and 14% iron.

 ## Bacon-Crusted Tri-Tip Roast with Shallots and Figs

We took a spin on the classic wrapped filet by crusting a roast with two cured meats—bacon and prosciutto.

Prep: 30 minutes **Roast:** 35 minutes **Stand:** 30 + 10 minutes

1 lb. fresh or dried Turkish, Mission, or Calimyrna figs, halved	4 oz. chopped prosciutto
	1 Tbsp. Dijon-style mustard
1 1½- to 2-lb. boneless beef bottom sirloin roast (tri-tip)	2 cloves garlic, slivered
	1 lb. shallots or small white onions, skinned, ends trimmed
4 oz. chopped bacon (about 4 slices)	Dry red wine

1. If using dried figs, in a bowl combine figs and enough boiling water to cover; let stand 30 minutes or until plump.

2. Preheat oven to 425° F. Place roast, fat side up, on a rack in a roasting pan. Insert thermometer. Combine bacon, prosciutto, mustard, and garlic; divide in half. Press half onto roast.

3. Drain figs. Halve large shallots. In a large bowl toss together figs, shallots, and remaining bacon mixture; scatter in pan.

4. Roast for 35 to 45 minutes or until thermometer registers 140° F for medium-rare doneness and bacon crust is crisp.

5. Transfer roast, figs, and shallots to a platter. Cover with foil; let stand 10 minutes. (The temperature should rise 5° to 10° F.)

6. Meanwhile, remove any drippings from pan; skim fat. Measure juices; add wine to equal 1½ cups total. Return to pan. Bring to boiling, scraping up any brown bits from pan. Simmer, uncovered, for 5 to 10 minutes or until the wine is reduced by half; serve with roast. Makes 6 to 8 servings.

Nutrition facts per serving: 421 cal., 14 g total fat (5 g sat. fat), 75 mg chol., 734 mg sodium, 27 g carbo., 3 g fiber, and 35 g pro. Daily Values: 18% vit. A, 12% vit. C, 7% calcium, and 22% iron.

Spaghetti and Porcini Meatballs with Cabernet-Tomato Sauce

Porcini mushrooms and a bold Cabernet make this dish sassy enough for company, but still hearty enough for the family.

Stand: 30 minutes **Prep:** 30 minutes **Cook:** 38 minutes

3	Tbsp. olive oil	2	Tbsp. snipped fresh
1	recipe Porcini Meatballs		parsley
4	cups chopped, peeled	2	Tbsp. snipped fresh
	plum tomatoes (10 to		thyme
	12 tomatoes)	1	tsp. sugar
1	cup plus 1 to 2 Tbsp.	¼	tsp. pepper
	Cabernet Sauvignon or		Hot cooked spaghetti
	dry red wine		or fettuccine
¼	cup finely chopped		Salt
	onion		Pepper

1. In a large skillet heat olive oil over medium-high heat. Add Porcini Meatballs; cook about 8 minutes or until brown, turning occasionally. Drain on paper towels. Drain off fat.

2. Add tomatoes, 1 cup of the wine, onion, parsley, thyme, sugar, pepper, and the reserved ½ cup mushrooms (from the meatball recipe) to the hot skillet; stir well. Bring to boiling; reduce heat. Add meatballs. Simmer, uncovered, about 30 minutes or until sauce is the desired consistency, gently stirring to keep meatballs moistened.

3. Just before serving, add 1 to 2 tablespoons wine. Serve sauce and meatballs over spaghetti or fettuccine. Season to taste with salt and pepper. Makes 6 servings.

Porcini Meatballs: Rinse 2½ ounces dried porcini mushrooms*. In a medium bowl combine dried mushrooms and enough boiling water to cover. Let stand for 30 minutes. Drain. Rinse mushrooms under running water. Drain well, squeezing out excess liquid. Set aside ½ cup of the mushrooms for the sauce (see recipe, above). Finely chop remaining mushrooms.

In a large bowl combine 1 beaten egg, finely chopped mushrooms, ¾ cup onion, ¼ cup fine dry bread crumbs, 1 tablespoon Cabernet Sauvignon, 2 cloves minced garlic, 2 teaspoons snipped fresh thyme, and ½ teaspoon salt. Add 1 pound ground beef; mix well. Shape into 18 meatballs.

*Test Kitchen Tip: September and October are the short peak season months for fresh porcini mushrooms. If you find fresh mushrooms, substitute 10 ounces of fresh for the 2½ ounces of dried. You can order fresh or dried porcini from Melissa's at 800/588-0151 or www.melissas.com.

Nutrition facts per serving: 549 cal., 19 g total fat (5 g sat. fat), 83 mg chol., 374 mg sodium, 64 g carbo., 5 g fiber, and 26 g pro. Daily Values: 18% vit. A, 48% vit. C, 5% calcium, and 26% iron.

Mediterranean Parsnips.

30 low fat Mediterranean Parsnips

Open a jar of your favorite condiment to zip up plain vegetables, pasta, or salads. Capers, olives, caramelized onions, and flavored mustards are just a few off-the-shelf ideas.

Prep: 20 minutes **Cook:** 7 minutes

3½	lb. parsnips	1	cup pitted kalamata
3	Tbsp. olive oil		olives, drained and
¼	tsp. salt		coarsely chopped
¼	tsp. pepper	½	cup capers, drained
			(3½-oz. jar)

1. Peel and slice the parsnips lengthwise into ¼-inch-thick slices. In a large saucepan cook parsnips, covered, in a small amount of boiling lightly salted water for 7 to 9 minutes or until tender; drain.

2. Gently toss parsnips with oil, salt, and pepper; transfer to a serving dish. Top with olives and capers. Makes 8 servings.

Honey-Mustard Parsnips: Prepare parsnips as above, except omit olive oil. Toss parsnips with ¼ cup raspberry mustard; drizzle with 2 tablespoons honey.

Caramelized Onion Parsnips: Prepare parsnips as above, except omit olives and capers. Top parsnips with 1 cup of caramelized onions from a jar.

Nutrition facts per serving of Mediterranean Parsnips: 234 cal., 8 g total fat (1 g sat. fat), 0 mg chol., 535 mg sodium, 41 g carbo., 9 g fiber, and 3 g pro. Daily Values: 44% vit. C, 8% calcium, and 7% iron.

Spaghetti and Porcini Meatballs with Cabernet-Tomato Sauce

Let the rich aroma and wild berry flavor of Cabernet Sauvignon woo you into trying this twist on tradition. When added just before serving, wine gives sauce a vigor that jumps off the plate. However, it's also nice to introduce the flavor by splashing in a little during cooking.

Big Green Salad with Two-Pepper Dressing

We love using whole fresh herbs, stems and all, as an elemental recipe ingredient, instead of the obligatory chopped-up sprinkle. So we recharged the dinner salad with sprigs of mint and cilantro, and tossed it with a sweet-hot pepper dressing. Sliced daikon adds crunch to this crisp, cool dinner partner.

30 **Big Green Salad with Two-Pepper Dressing**

You can make Two-Pepper Dressing ahead; just bring it back to room temperature before you toss together the salad.

Start to finish: 30 minutes

4 cups torn butterhead lettuce (2 medium heads)	¾ cup fresh cilantro sprigs
1 cup fresh mint sprigs	1 cup daikon, peeled and cut into 1-inch strips
1 cup fresh watercress sprigs	1 recipe Two-Pepper Dressing

1. Rinse lettuce, mint, watercress, and cilantro in cold water; pat dry. In a salad bowl toss together greens and daikon. Slowly add Two-Pepper Dressing; toss to coat. Makes 6 servings.

Two-Pepper Dressing: In a screw-top jar combine ½ cup finely chopped green sweet pepper; ⅓ cup rice vinegar; 3 tablespoons salad oil; 1 fresh anaheim or jalapeño chili pepper, seeded and finely chopped*; 1 clove garlic, minced; ½ teaspoon sugar; ¼ teaspoon salt; and ¼ teaspoon ground black pepper. Cover and shake well. Refrigerate until ready to use.

***Test Kitchen Tip:** Because chili peppers contain volatile oils that can burn your skin and eyes, wear plastic or rubber gloves when working with them. If you do touch the peppers, wash your hands well with soap and water.

Nutrition facts per serving: 86 cal., 7 g total fat (1 g sat. fat), 0 mg chol., 112 mg sodium, 4 g carbo., 1 g fiber, and 1 g pro. Daily Values: 26% vit. A, 57% vit. C, 5% calcium, and 17% iron.

Brined Skillet-Roasted
Brussels Sprouts

HARVEST DINNER

Big Green Salad with Two-Pepper Dressing (recipe, left)

Bacon-Crusted Tri-Tip Roast with Shallots and Figs
(recipe, page 173)

Steamed green beans

The Mount Everest of Spice Cake (recipe, page 179)

Dry red wine or sparkling water

Brined Skillet-Roasted Brussels Sprouts

Brining acts as a preservative, but it also enhances flavor. Use intensely flavored kosher and sea salts to bring out the taste.

Prep: 20 minutes **Stand:** 1 hour **Roast:** 25 minutes

1½ lb. brussels sprouts	1 tsp. mustard seeds
8 cups cold water	¼ tsp. sea salt
½ cup kosher salt	¼ tsp. cracked black pepper
¼ cup olive oil	

1. Trim stems and remove any wilted outer leaves from brussels sprouts; wash. Halve any large brussels sprouts; set aside. In a very large mixing bowl or deep container stir together the cold water and the kosher salt until salt is completely dissolved. Add brussels sprouts to salt mixture, making sure the sprouts are covered (hold sprouts down with a plate if necessary to keep them submerged). Let stand for 1 hour.

2. Preheat oven to 350° F. Drain brussels sprouts; do not rinse. In a large cast-iron skillet or roasting pan toss sprouts with olive oil to coat. Roast, uncovered, for 25 to 30 minutes or until tender, stirring once.

3. Meanwhile, in a skillet heat mustard seeds over medium heat about 5 minutes or until seeds are lightly toasted, shaking skillet occasionally. Remove seeds from skillet; crush slightly. Add crushed seeds, sea salt, and pepper to roasted sprouts; toss well. Makes 6 servings.

Nutrition facts per serving: 131 cal., 10 g total fat (1 g sat. fat), 0 mg chol., 415 mg sodium, 10 g carbo., 5 g fiber, and 4 g pro. Daily Values: 18% vit. A, 121% vit. C, 5% calcium, and 9% iron.

Buttery Sage and
Acorn Squash Tart

The Mount Everest
of Spice Cake

Tossing one more spice into
the mix piles up flavor. We
took our favorite spice cake
recipe from the newly
released 12th edition of the
*Better Homes and Gardens®
New Cook Book* and topped
it with a mile-high meringue
laced with ginger. It's a
showstopper that'll earn an
avalanche of compliments.

Buttery Sage and Acorn Squash Tart

Browning butter to drizzle atop this quichelike appetizer tart gives every bite a toasty, mellow richness.

Prep: 60 minutes **Bake:** 40 minutes **Cool:** 20 minutes

½ cup plus 1 Tbsp. unsalted butter, softened	¼ tsp. salt
3 eggs	1 recipe Butter-Pepper Pastry
2 cups mashed, cooked acorn squash	¼ cup broken black walnuts or broken walnuts
½ cup milk	
¼ cup honey	½ tsp. pepper
1 Tbsp. snipped fresh sage	

1. Preheat oven to 350° F. For filling, in a large bowl beat ¼ cup butter with an electric mixer on medium-high speed for 30 seconds. Add eggs, one at a time, beating until combined. Stir in squash, milk, honey, sage, and salt.

2. Spoon filling into Butter-Pepper Pastry, smoothing top (tart will be very full). Place on foil-lined baking sheet. Bake about 40 minutes or until a knife inserted near center comes out clean. Cool for 20 minutes on a wire rack. Remove pan sides; place on platter.

3. Meanwhile, in a small saucepan melt ¼ cup plus 1 tablespoon butter; set aside 1 tablespoon. Heat remaining butter about 15 minutes until butter turns a delicate brown.

4. In a small bowl combine walnuts, the 1 tablespoon reserved melted butter, and pepper; toss to coat. Sprinkle over tart. Cut tart into wedges; spoon browned butter over each serving. Makes 10 to 12 appetizer servings.

Butter-Pepper Pastry: Preheat oven to 450° F. In a bowl combine 1 cup all-purpose flour, ½ teaspoon salt, and ½ teaspoon pepper. Cut in ⅓ cup cold unsalted butter until pieces are pea-size. Sprinkle 1 tablespoon cold water over part of the mixture; toss with a fork. Push to the side. Repeat with 2 to 3 tablespoons more cold water, using 1 tablespoon water at a time, until dough is moistened. Form into a ball. If necessary, cover with plastic wrap; refrigerate for 30 to 60 minutes or until easy to handle.

On a lightly floured surface roll pastry into a 12-inch circle. Ease into an ungreased 10-inch tart pan with a removable bottom. Press pastry into fluted sides of pan; trim edges. Generously prick the bottom of the pastry. Line pastry with a double thickness of foil. Place tart pan on a foil-lined baking sheet. Bake for 10 minutes. Remove foil from pastry; bake for 6 to 8 minutes more or until golden. Cool on a wire rack.

Nutrition facts per serving: 285 cal., 21 g total fat (12 g sat. fat), 112 mg chol., 203 mg sodium, 21 g carbo., 2 g fiber, and 5 g pro. Daily Values: 45% vit. A, 7% vit. C, 4% calcium, and 6% iron.

The Mount Everest of Spice Cake

To prepare the meringue, use pasteurized egg whites from pasteurized (not regular) eggs. Or use powdered dried egg whites.

Prep: 45 minutes **Bake:** 30 minutes **Cool:** 2 hours

1¼ cups buttermilk	¼ tsp. ground nutmeg
2 eggs	¼ tsp. ground cloves
¼ cup butter	¼ cup shortening
2 cups all-purpose flour	1½ cups sugar
1½ tsp. baking powder	½ tsp. vanilla
1½ tsp. baking soda	1 18-oz. jar apricot or peach preserves
1 tsp. ground cinnamon	
¼ tsp. ground ginger	1 recipe Ginger Meringue*

1. Allow buttermilk, eggs, and butter to stand at room temperature for 30 minutes. Meanwhile, grease and lightly flour two 8x1½-inch round baking pans; set aside. In a bowl stir together flour, baking powder, baking soda, cinnamon, ginger, nutmeg, and cloves; set aside.

2. Preheat oven to 350° F. In a bowl beat butter and shortening for 30 seconds. Add sugar and vanilla, beat on medium speed until combined, scraping side of bowl occasionally. Add eggs, one at a time, beating for 30 seconds after each addition. Alternately add flour mixture and buttermilk, beating on low speed just until combined. Spread batter in prepared pans.

3. Bake for 30 to 35 minutes or until a wooden toothpick inserted in centers comes out clean. Cool cakes in pans on wire racks for 10 minutes. Carefully remove. Cool on wire racks.

4. To assemble, using a serrated knife, carefully split each cake layer horizontally in half. Place bottom layer of cake on serving plate. Spread with about ½ cup apricot preserves. Top with second cake layer, ½ cup preserves, third layer, remaining preserves, and fourth layer. Top with Ginger Meringue; lightly brown meringue peaks with a small kitchen torch. Serve at once or cover and chill for up to 4 hours. (Chilling firms the meringue and makes cake easier to cut.) Makes 8 to 10 servings.

Ginger Meringue: Allow 6 pasteurized egg whites from pasteurized eggs in shell to stand at room temperature for 30 minutes. (Or combine 3 tablespoons dried egg whites and ½ cup plus 1 tablespoon warm water; stir about 2 minutes or until powder is completely dissolved.) In a large, non-aluminum mixing bowl combine egg whites, ½ teaspoon cream of tartar, and ½ teaspoon ground ginger or ¼ teaspoon ground nutmeg. Beat with an electric mixer on medium speed about 5 minutes or until soft peaks form (tips curl). Gradually add ¾ cup sugar (½ cup for powdered egg whites), 1 tablespoon at a time, beating on high speed about 5 minutes more or until mixture forms soft, glossy peaks (tips stand straight), and sugar is dissolved.

*Test Kitchen Tip: As an alternative to the meringue, you can stir a little ground ginger into 2 cups sweetened whipped cream. Top cake with whipped cream and chill up to 1 hour.

Nutrition facts per serving: 651 cal., 14 g total fat (6 g sat. fat), 71 mg chol., 334 mg sodium, 123 g carbo., 2 g fiber, and 9 g pro. Daily Values: 7% vit. A, 10% vit. C, 12% calcium, and 11% iron.

Harvest Lamb

Harvest Leg of Lamb

There's much to be said for cooking a lamb roast for a crowd—not the least of which is the vision of you deftly carving slice after juicy slice for an appreciative audience.

Cooking big roasts is not an everyday feat anymore. But with long, slow cooking, there's lots of time to check on the process. That kind of leisurely pace makes creating a crown roast or leg of lamb for a weekend crowd very doable.

For both of these roasts, you rub herbs and seasonings on the outside to let the flavor penetrate into the meat. Be sure to use a meat thermometer so you can cook the meat to the exact degree of doneness you want. (We recommend medium rare.) And make sure the thermometer is not touching fat or bone.

new low fat Roast Rack of Lamb

The classic crown shape is made by sewing together two rib roasts. The little paper crowns on each bone are optional.

Prep: 20 minutes **Roast:** 45 minutes **Stand:** 15 minutes

2 1- to 1½-lb. lamb rib roasts (6 to 8 ribs each), with or without backbone	½ tsp. salt
	¾ cup soft bread crumbs
3 Tbsp. Dijon-style mustard	1 Tbsp. butter or margarine, melted
3 Tbsp. lemon juice	Bottled chutney (optional)
1 Tbsp. snipped fresh rosemary or thyme	

1. Preheat oven to 325° F. Trim fat from meat. Stir together mustard, lemon juice, rosemary, and salt. Rub onto meat. Toss together crumbs and butter. Sprinkle onto meat.

2. Place meat on a rack in a shallow roasting pan. Insert a meat thermometer into center of meat, without touching fat or bone. Roast, uncovered, until desired doneness. For medium rare, roast for ¾ to 1 hour or until thermometer registers 140° F. For medium, roast for 1 to 1½ hours or until meat thermometer registers 155° F. Cover with foil; let stand 15 minutes. (The temperature of the meat will rise 5° to 10° F during standing.) Serve warm with chutney, if desired. Makes 6 servings.

Nutrition facts per serving: 299 cal., 9 g total fat (3 g sat. fat), 50 mg chol., 332 mg sodium, 41 g carbo., 3 g fiber, and 16 g pro. Daily Values: 11% vit. A, 16% vit. C, 5% calcium, and 12% iron.

Harvest Leg of Lamb

Prep: 30 minutes **Marinate:** 12 hours
Roast: 1¾ hours **Stand:** 15 minutes

1 5- to 7-lb. whole lamb leg roast (bone in)	2 Tbsp. olive oil or cooking oil
6 cloves garlic, cut into thin slices	1 Tbsp. dried Italian seasoning or dried oregano, crushed
2 to 3 Tbsp. lemon juice	1 tsp. pepper
3 Tbsp. snipped fresh parsley	

1. Trim fat from meat. With a knife, cut ½-inch-wide slits into roast at 1-inch intervals (approximately 36 holes) inserting a thin slice of garlic in each. Brush with lemon juice. Stir together parsley, oil, Italian seasoning or oregano, and pepper; pat onto meat. Wrap in plastic wrap; chill overnight.

2. Preheat oven to 325° F. Place meat, fat side up, on a rack in a shallow roasting pan. Insert a meat thermometer. Roast, uncovered, until desired doneness. For medium rare, roast for 1¾ to 2¼ hours or until thermometer registers 140° F. For medium, roast for 2 to 2½ hours or until meat thermometer registers 155° F. Cover with foil; let stand 15 minutes. (The temperature of the meat will rise 5° to 10° F during standing.)

3. To carve, cut away large, round side. The opposite side will also come off in a single piece. Cut off the 2 smaller pieces on either side of bone. Slice meat. Makes 12 to 16 servings.

Nutrition facts per serving: 187 cal., 8 g total fat (3 g sat. fat), 79 mg chol., 68 mg sodium, 2 g carbo., 0 g fiber, and 25 g pro. Daily Values: 2% vit. A, 6% vit. C, 2% calcium, and 15% iron.

Make the slits in the meat as you go; don't try to save time by making all the slits first—they close up too quickly. It's fine if some of the garlic cloves stick out slightly.

To spread the herbs evenly, sprinkle them onto meat first, then pat them down so they don't fall off.

Octo

Cooking Together

Fall weekends lure us into the kitchen to cook and share our favorite comfort foods.

ber

COOKING TOGETHER

If sharing time in the kitchen keeps us all connected, then fall is the time to start. Fall weekends lend themselves to lazy brunches, a hearty stew suppers, and quick-to-fix pasta dinners.

Harvest Vegetable Stew

Harvest Vegetable Stew

A combination of hearty fall vegetables makes this meatless stew so satisfying, you can eat it as a main dish.

Prep: 25 minutes **Cook:** 30 minutes

5 cups water	2 cups shredded cabbage
3 beef bouillon cubes or 3 tsp. instant beef bouillon granules	4 oz. fresh green beans, trimmed and cut in half (1 cup)
2 medium Yukon gold potatoes, peeled and cut into 1-inch pieces (8 oz.)	1 small zucchini, chopped (1 cup)
3 plum tomatoes, chopped, or one 14½-oz. can diced tomatoes	1 15-oz. can red kidney beans, rinsed and drained
2 stalks celery, chopped (1 cup)	8 to 10 fresh oregano sprigs, tied in a bunch with kitchen string
1 small green sweet pepper, chopped (½ cup)	¼ cup catsup
1 small onion, chopped (⅓ cup)	¼ tsp. pepper
	Dash bottled hot pepper sauce
	Salt
	Pepper

1. In a Dutch oven combine water and bouillon cubes or granules; bring to boiling. Add potatoes, undrained tomatoes, celery, green pepper, and onion. Return to boiling; reduce heat. Simmer, uncovered, for 15 minutes.

2. Add remaining ingredients. Simmer, uncovered, about 15 minutes more or until vegetables are tender. Remove and discard oregano. Season to taste with salt and pepper. Makes 8 to 10 servings.

Nutrition facts per serving: 93 cal., 0 g total fat (0 g sat. fat), 0 mg chol., 702 mg sodium, 19 g carbo., 6 g dietary fiber, and 4 g pro. Daily Values: 9% vit. A, 41% vit. C, 4% calcium, and 8% iron.

STEW SUPPER

Harvest Vegetable Stew (recipe, above)

Dad's Rolls (recipe, page 190)

Hedy's Oatmeal Cookies (recipe, page 191)

Milk

THE FAMILY THAT COOKS TOGETHER...

Spending time in the kitchen together is a major part of the recipe for staying connnected, at least that's what one North Carolina family has found. The Leiters of Raleigh have found that cooking together is more than

Neil

a creative outlet for family members who pursue writing, music, glassblowing, flower arranging, and acting. For them, time together in the kitchen is time to catch up and to show that they care. "It's not that we especially like to cook together," says son Neil, a junior at Indiana University, "so much as it is that we like to cook for each other."

Cole

That's not always easy to do. Family schedules are tight. Neil has college. His sister Hedy, a high school senior, rows competitively, teaches fitness, and bakes for neighbors. Younger brother Cole, a sixth grader, plays baseball and is apprenticed to a glassblower. Mom Carrie Knowles

Carrie, Hedy and Jeff

writes and speaks on Alzheimer's nationally, often discussing her mother's battle with the disease. Dad Jeff is a sociology professor, who is involved in local politics.

Yet, making time to cook for each other is important. For Hedy, baking is a passion and dessert is her daily gift to her family. "I'm the kind of person who would rather give presents than get them," says Hedy. "It's the way I've always been."

Another key to finding time to cook together is finding foods that are quick to prepare or easy to put together, then leave to bake or simmer.

"Cooking can't take too long because we always have something else to do," says Neil.

For Jeff and Carrie, cooking meals with their kids lets them watch the lessons that they have tried to teach take hold.

"I get the sense that here are three people who are going to be able to

Jeff

take care of themselves in the kitchen," Jeff says.

College Chicken and Pasta

Beet and Blue Cheese Salad

Serve this salad as a starter or for a light lunch or outdoor dinner.

Prep: 20 minutes **Cook:** 40 minutes

6 medium beets (2 lb.)	5 cups torn mixed greens,
¼ cup balsamic vinegar	such as baby spinach
3 Tbsp. olive oil	leaves, bibb lettuce, or
2 tsp. Dijon-style mustard	mesclun mix
¼ tsp. salt	½ cup hazelnuts (filberts),
¼ tsp. pepper	toasted and coarsely
1 15-oz. can chickpeas	chopped*
(garbanzo beans), rinsed	6 oz. blue cheese, cut into
and drained	5 or 6 wedges
4 to 5 small green onions,	
sliced	

1. Cut stems off beets, but leave roots; wash. Do not peel. Cook whole beets, covered, in boiling salted water for 40 to 50 minutes or until crisp-tender.

2. Meanwhile, for dressing, in a screw-top jar combine vinegar, olive oil, mustard, salt, and pepper. Cover; shake well. Set dressing aside.

3. Drain, cool, peel, and cut beets into wedges. Rinse beets until water runs almost clear. In a medium bowl combine beets, chickpeas, and green onions. Pour dressing over beet mixture; toss gently to coat. Cover and chill until serving time.

4. Arrange greens on six salad plates; spoon beet mixture onto greens. Sprinkle with hazelnuts. Serve with wedges of blue cheese. Makes 6 servings.

***Test Kitchen Tip:** To toast hazelnuts, spread them in a single layer on a shallow baking pan. Bake in a 350° F oven for 8 to 10 minutes or until golden, watching carefully and stirring once or twice so they don't overbrown. To remove skin from toasted nuts, roll warm nuts vigorously in a towel.

Nutrition facts per serving: 414 cal., 28 g total fat (8 g sat. fat), 26 mg chol., 957 mg sodium, 28 g carbo., 8 g dietary fiber, and 16 g pro. Daily Values: 47% vit. A, 24% vit. C, 28% calcium, and 18% iron.

DINNER ON THE QUICK

College Chicken and Pasta (recipe, right)

Beet and Blue Cheese Salad (recipe, above)

Pear-Peach Crisp (recipe, page 193)

Dry red wine or grape juice

30 College Chicken and Pasta

Start to finish: 30 minutes

1½ tsp. coarsely ground	3 medium tomatoes,
pepper blend	chopped (1 lb.)
¾ tsp. salt	1 Tbsp. tomato paste
1 clove garlic, minced	2 to 3 tsp. grated fresh
4 medium skinless,	ginger
boneless chicken breast	8 oz. dried spaghetti
halves	¼ cup Homemade Pesto or
2 large onions, sliced	purchased pesto
2 Tbsp. olive oil	Parmesan cheese (optional)

1. Combine 1 teaspoon of the pepper blend, ½ teaspoon of the salt, and the garlic. Rub onto chicken. In a 12-inch skillet cook chicken and onions in hot oil over medium heat about 15 minutes or until onions are tender and chicken is no longer pink and registers 170° F on an instant-read thermometer, turning chicken once and stirring onions occasionally.

2. Remove chicken from skillet; slice crosswise into strips. Return to pan; add tomatoes, tomato paste, ginger, remaining pepper blend, and remaining ¼ teaspoon salt. Heat through.

3. Meanwhile, in a large saucepan cook spaghetti according to package directions; drain. Return spaghetti to pan; stir in pesto. Serve chicken and sauce over pesto-coated spaghetti. If desired, top with Parmesan cheese. Makes 6 servings.

Homemade Pesto: In a blender container combine 2 cups firmly packed, fresh basil leaves; ½ cup chopped walnuts or pine nuts; ½ cup grated Parmesan cheese; ¼ cup olive oil; 4 cloves peeled garlic; ¼ teaspoon salt; and a dash pepper. Cover and blend until nearly smooth, stopping and scraping sides as necessary.

Nutrition facts per serving: 373 cal., 12 g total fat (2 g sat. fat), 56 mg chol., 444 mg sodium, 38 g carbo., 3 g dietary fiber, and 29 g pro. Daily Values: 11% vit. A, 28% vit. C, 6% calcium, and 14% iron.

Beet and Blue Cheese Salad

You can't *beet* this playful fall medley to kick off your dinner. Scarlet beets splash color into a tumble of fresh greens. The piquant flavor of blue cheese (or another favorite cheese) just cries for crusty bread.

Shortcut
Nutty Fruit
Cinnamon
Rolls

Zucchini Quiche

"Cooking can't take
too long, because
we always have
something else to do."

—Neil Leiter

low fat Shortcut Nutty Fruit Cinnamon Rolls

Shape these rolls the night before, then cover with plastic wrap and refrigerate overnight to bake them fresh for brunch.

Prep: 40 minutes **Rise:** 30 minutes **Prep:** 20 minutes

5¾ to 6¼ cups bread flour or all-purpose flour	2 tsp. salt
2 pkg. active dry yeast	1 cup packed brown sugar
2¼ cups warm water (105° to 115° F)	5 Tbsp. butter, softened
1 Tbsp. packed brown sugar	1 cup chopped walnuts or pecans
¼ cup butter, softened	1 cup raisins or other dried fruit, such as apricots or cherries
2 Tbsp. ground cinnamon	1 recipe Almond Icing

1. In a large mixing bowl stir together ½ cup of the bread flour, yeast, ½ cup of the warm water, and 1 tablespoon brown sugar. Let stand about 15 minutes or until surface is bubbly.

2. Add 1¾ cups of the warm water, 1 cup of the bread flour, ¼ cup butter, 1 tablespoon cinnamon, and salt. Beat with a wooden spoon until smooth. Stir in as much of the remaining flour as you can. Turn out onto a lightly floured surface and knead in enough of the remaining flour to make a moderately soft dough that is smooth and elastic (3 to 5 minutes). (Or, to prepare dough in a stand mixer with a dough hook, beat on low speed until smooth. Add 4 cups of the flour, 1 cup at a time, beating with a dough hook on low speed about 5 minutes or until a moderately soft dough that is not sticky forms, adding additional flour, if necessary.) Let dough rise in bowl in a warm place for 15 minutes.

3. Preheat oven to 400° F. Meanwhile, for filling, in a bowl combine the 1 cup brown sugar, the 5 tablespoons softened butter, and 1 tablespoon cinnamon. Stir in nuts and fruit (if using dried apricots, cut into small pieces).

4. On a lightly floured surface, roll the dough into a 20x12-inch rectangle. Sprinkle with the filling, then carefully roll up into a spiral, starting from one of the long sides. Slice into 20 equal pieces. Place rolls in a greased 15x10x1-inch baking pan or two 9x9x2 baking pans.

5. Bake about 20 minutes or until tops are golden brown. Cool slightly; remove rolls from pans. Drizzle with Almond Icing. Serve warm. Makes 20 rolls.

Almond Icing: In a medium bowl stir together 1 cup sifted powdered sugar, 1 tablespoon light cream or half-and-half, 1 teaspoon vanilla, and ½ teaspoon almond extract. If necessary, stir in additional powered sugar until of drizzling consistency.

Nutrition facts per roll: 322 cal., 10 g total fat (4 g sat. fat), 15 mg chol., 296 mg sodium, 53 g carbo., 2 g dietary fiber, and 6 g pro. Daily Values: 4% vit. A, 1% vit. C, 4% calcium, and 15% iron.

Zucchini Quiche

The quickie for this quiche? There's no crust to roll and shape.

Prep: 20 minutes **Bake:** 40 minutes **Stand:** 10 minutes

4 eggs	¼ cup cooking oil
3 cups finely shredded zucchini	4 green onions, cut diagonally into 1-inch pieces
1 cup packaged biscuit mix	2 Tbsp. snipped fresh dill or 1½ tsp. dried dillweed
½ cup grated Parmesan cheese	1 recipe Dill-Tomato Topper (optional)
2 oz. Gruyère cheese or Swiss cheese, shredded	

1. Preheat oven to 350° F. In a large bowl beat eggs; stir in remaining ingredients except Dill-Tomato Topper. Pour into a greased 9-inch quiche dish.

2. Bake, uncovered, for 40 to 45 minutes or until a knife inserted near the center comes out clean.

3. Let stand for 10 minutes. If desired, top with Dill-Tomato Topper. Makes 6 servings.

Dill-Tomato Topper: In a medium mixing bowl stir together 2 large tomatoes, chopped; 1½ teaspoons snipped fresh dill; and a dash salt.

Nutrition facts per serving: 313 cal., 21 g total fat (7 g sat. fat), 158 mg chol., 527 mg sodium, 18 g carbo., 2 g dietary fiber, and 13 g pro. Daily Values: 18% vit. A, 25% vit. C, 27% calcium, and 10% iron.

Hedy's Black Walnut Cake

If you're not a fan of black walnut's distinctive flavor, of course you can use regular walnuts.

Prep: 25 minutes **Bake:** 65 minutes **Cool:** 1 hour

1½	cups chopped black walnuts or English walnuts, toasted	½	tsp. vanilla
2	Tbsp. all-purpose flour	2⅔	cups all-purpose flour
1¾	cups granulated sugar	¾	cup carob powder* or unsweetened cocoa powder
1½	cups butter, melted	½	tsp. baking powder
1	cup packed dark brown sugar	¼	tsp. salt
5	eggs	1	cup milk
2	Tbsp. rum or milk	1	recipe Rum Glaze (optional)

1. Preheat oven to 325° F. Grease and flour a 10-inch square tube pan or a 10-inch fluted tube pan; set aside. In a small bowl stir together nuts and the 2 tablespoons flour; set aside.

2. In a large mixing bowl stir together granulated sugar, melted butter, and brown sugar until combined. Using a wooden spoon, beat in eggs, one at a time. Stir in 2 tablespoons rum or milk and vanilla.

3. In a medium bowl stir together the 2⅔ cups flour, carob or cocoa powder, baking powder, and salt. Stir flour mixture into egg mixture. Gradually stir in milk. Fold in nut mixture.

4. Pour batter into the prepared pan. Bake about 65 minutes or until a toothpick inserted near the center comes out clean. Let cool in pan on a wire rack for 10 minutes. Remove from pan. Let stand for 1 hour. If desired, drizzle with Rum Glaze. Cool completely. Makes 12 servings.

Rum Glaze: In a small bowl combine 1⅓ cups sifted powdered sugar; 2 tablespoons butter, melted; and 1 tablespoon rum or milk. Stir in 1 tablespoon whipping cream or milk. If necessary, add additional cream or milk, 1 teaspoon at a time, until glaze reaches drizzling consistency.

*Test Kitchen Tip: Carob powder has a sweet, mildly chocolaty flavor and is available at health food stores and the health-food aisles of some supermarkets.

Nutrition facts per serving: 540 cal., 29 g total fat (14 g sat. fat), 122 mg chol., 286 mg sodium, 66 g carbo., 3 g dietary fiber, and 8 g pro. Daily Values: 19% vit. A, 1% vit. C, 8% calcium, and 11% iron.

low fat Dad's Rolls

To make these rolls extra crusty, put a baking pan of water in the oven along with the rolls to create steam.

Prep: 40 minutes **Rise:** 60 minutes **Bake:** 25 minutes

1	Tbsp. active dry yeast	5¼	to 5¾ cups all-purpose flour
2	cups warm water (105° to 115° F)		Olive oil
1	Tbsp. sugar		Yellow cornmeal
1¼	tsp. salt		Coarse salt (optional)

1. In a large mixing bowl dissolve yeast in the warm water. Stir in sugar and salt. With a wooden spoon, stir in as much of the flour as you can. Turn out onto a lightly floured surface and knead in enough of the remaining flour to make a moderately stiff dough that is smooth and elastic (6 to 8 minutes). (Or, to prepare dough in a stand mixer with a dough hook, add flour to yeast mixture, 1 cup at a time, beating with the dough hook on low speed until a moderately stiff, smooth dough forms.)

2. Lightly coat a large bowl with olive oil. Shape dough into a ball; place in oiled bowl. Turn dough once; cover with a clean kitchen towel. Let rise in a warm place until double in size (45 to 60 minutes).

3. Punch dough down. Turn dough out onto a lightly floured board or surface. Cover; let rest for 10 minutes.

4. Grease a very large baking sheet or two smaller baking sheets; sprinkle heavily with cornmeal. Shape dough into 14 round rolls. Place rolls on prepared baking sheet. Let rise for 5 minutes.

5. Preheat oven to 400° F. Slash roll tops in 2 or 3 places with a sharp knife. Brush rolls with water. If desired, sprinkle with coarse salt. Place an empty baking pan on the bottom rack of an unheated oven. Pour boiling water into the pan to a depth of 1 inch. Place rolls on second rack. Bake for 25 to 30 minutes or until crusty and golden brown. Remove from pan; cool slightly on a wire rack. Serve warm. Makes 14 rolls.

Nutrition facts per roll: 182 cal., 1 g total fat (0 g sat. fat), 0 mg chol., 417 mg sodium, 37 g carbo., 1 g dietary fiber, and 5 g pro. Daily Values: 1% calcium and 13% iron.

"It's not that we like to cook together as much as we like to cook for each other."

—Neil Leiter

Dad's Rolls

Hedy's Oatmeal Cookies

Choose any dried fruit, such as raisins, currants, cranberries, cherries, or snipped apricots, for this old-fashioned favorite.

Prep: 20 minutes **Bake:** 9 minutes per batch

½	cup butter, softened	¼	cup pure maple syrup or maple-flavored syrup
½	cup packed dark brown sugar	1	tsp. vanilla
¼	cup granulated sugar	1½	cups all-purpose flour
1	tsp. baking soda	2	cups quick-cooking rolled oats
½	tsp. salt	1	cup dried blueberries
1	egg		

1. Preheat oven to 350° F. In a large mixing bowl beat butter with an electric mixer on medium to high speed for 30 seconds. Add brown and granulated sugars, baking soda, and salt. Beat until combined, scraping sides of bowl occasionally. Beat in egg, maple syrup, and vanilla until combined. Beat in as much of the flour as you can with the mixer. Stir in remaining flour with a wooden spoon. Stir in the rolled oats and blueberries.

2. Using a small cookie scoop (about 1¼ inches in diameter) or a spoon, drop dough 2 inches apart onto an ungreased cookie sheet. Bake for 9 to 11 minutes or until edges are golden brown. Let stand for 1 minute on the cookie sheet. Remove and cool on a wire rack. Makes about 48 cookies.

Nutrition facts per cookie: 80 cal., 2 g total fat (1 g sat. fat), 10 mg chol., 74 mg sodium, 13 g carbo., 1 g dietary fiber, and 1 g pro. Daily Values: 2% vit. A, 1% calcium, and 2% iron.

Hedy's Oatmeal Cookies
and Hedy's Black Walnut Cake

Lemon-and-Spice Applesauce

Is it a dessert or a side dish? We'll let you decide. You can rest asured that Grandma would approve of the gentle twist of lemon and sprinkling of spice in her applesauce.

low fat Lemon-and-Spice Applesauce

Lightly mashing the apples keeps the applesauce chunky.

Prep: 45 minutes **Cook:** 40 minutes

4¾	to 5½ lb. cooking apples, such as Granny Smith or Golden Delicious (15 cups), peeled, cored, and sliced
2½	cups water
1	to 1½ cups packed brown sugar
3	Tbsp. finely shredded lemon peel
¾	cup lemon juice
1½	tsp. apple pie spice or 2 tsp. ground cinnamon
1	Tbsp. vanilla

1. In a 6-quart heavy kettle or Dutch oven combine apples, water, brown sugar, lemon peel, lemon juice, and apple pie spice or cinnamon. Bring to boiling; reduce heat. Simmer, covered, for 40 minutes or until the apples are very soft, stirring occasionally.

2. Remove from heat. Stir in vanilla. Mash mixture lightly with the back of a large wooden spoon. Serve warm or cover and chill before serving. Makes about 8½ cups (16 servings).

Nutrition facts per serving: 127 cal., 0 g total fat (0 g sat. fat), 0 mg chol., 7 mg sodium, 33 g carbo., 3 g dietary fiber, and 0 g pro. Daily Values: 1% vit. A, 17% vit. C, 2% calcium, and 3% iron.

Pear-Peach Crisp

Farmer's market fans: try this luscious way to use the bumper crop of the week. For fall, the crisp also works well with apples.

Prep: 25 minutes **Bake:** 55 minutes

6	cups peeled, sliced pears (about 6 medium)
2	cups peeled, pitted, and sliced fresh peaches (2 to 3 medium) or 2 cups frozen, unsweetened peach slices, thawed
½	cup raisins
3	Tbsp. packed brown sugar
¾	tsp. ground ginger
1½	cups quick-cooking rolled oats
½	cup Grape Nuts® cereal
½	cup chopped walnuts or pecans
¼	cup granulated sugar
¼	cup packed brown sugar
½	cup butter, melted
1	cup orange juice or apple juice
	Vanilla ice cream (optional)

1. Preheat oven to 350° F. In a large bowl toss together sliced pears and peaches, raisins, the 3 tablespoons brown sugar, and ½ teaspoon of the ginger. Spread in the bottom of a 3-quart rectangular baking dish.

2. For topping, in a small bowl combine oats, cereal, nuts, the granulated sugar, ¼ cup brown sugar, and ¼ teaspoon of the ginger. Stir in the butter. Spoon over the fruit. Pour orange or apple juice evenly over the topping.

3. Bake, uncovered, about 55 minutes or until topping is golden and filling is bubbly. Transfer to a wire rack. Cool slightly. Serve warm with ice cream, if desired. Makes 12 servings.

Nutrition facts per serving: 303 cal., 13 g total fat (6 g sat. fat), 22 mg chol., 116 mg sodium, 47 g carbo., 5 g dietary fiber, and 4 g pro. Daily Values: 12% vit. A, 26% vit. C, 4% calcium, and 10% iron.

Pear-Peach Crisp

"I always cook from what really looks wonderful. It's more fun to get pushed to do different things."

—Carrie Knowles

Celebration Roasts

As entertaining season revs up, chances are a favorite roast will be making its appearance at your dinner table. If you're investing time and money in one of these special cuts of meat, you'll want to be sure of two things: It's as handsome as can be, and it's as tasty as it is handsome.

No one can deny the convenience of cooking a roast—the oven does most of the work—but here's some savory advice: Don't wing it. Follow the roasting guidelines on page 197 using an oven-safe meat thermometer and you'll achieve spectacular results every time.

To go with that perfect roast, the produce aisle now offers a few new sidekicks for creating an exciting, mouth-watering presentation. That means you can set aside the traditional carrots, onions, and potatoes for their more exotic cousins.

Pork Rib Crown Roast
There's no denying it: This roast is a WOW. Pork roasts are leaner these days, so don't overcook them. Place your roast in a 325° F oven until the juices run clear and the center is pink and juicy. Before serving, fill the center with a favorite cooked bread stuffing sprinkled with red and green apples, then surround it with a barely-simmered compote of dried fruits (try apricots, plums, figs, and raisins) and fresh sage.

Beef Tenderloin Roast

Watch your cooking times with this roast. You'll be cooking at a higher temperature (425° F) than with other roasts. A tenderloin is oh-so-grown-up and elegant, so why not pull out all the stops with equally elegant baby vegetables (here, braised baby cauliflower and pearl carrots with dill) and a classic French sauce, such as peppercorn or bordelaise.

Beef Ribeye Roast

Trim the roast of some, but not all, of its fat, and roast the meat fat side up. As the beef cooks, the fat melts and adds its flavor. The naturally robust nature of this cut finds a happy match with such aromatic root vegetables as sweet potatoes and turnips, most of the onion family members (including garlic), wild mushrooms, and starchy squashes—all of which sweeten up as they caramelize in the roasting pan.

Celebration Roasts

Veal Rib Roast
"Velvety" best describes the texture of a well-prepared veal roast. If you need to special order this roast from the butcher, ask for the chine bone (or backbone) to be removed. Toss on a mass of fresh herbs, such as thyme or basil, or rub the roast with garlic and olive oil.

Boneless Pork Double Top Loin Roast
A double top loin is simply two top loins tied together. Ask the butcher to do this for you. Cooking two loins together yields a tender, succulent roast, especially if you rub first with olive oil, dry mustard, and fresh herbs. Match with roasted fruits that have firm enough flesh to stand up to long cooking, such as apples and slightly under-ripe pears like the russet-hued Seckel pear shown.

Leg of Lamb

Be sure to remove the "fell," or thin outer skin, from the roast before cooking. Lamb benefits from pungent herb or spice rubs. Try caraway, marjoram, oregano, paprika, curry powder, or a mix of several of them. Or liven the mint-lamb relationship by using a fresh mint rub. A Mediterranean medley of steamed baby artichokes, tiny hard-cooked quail eggs, and fresh lemon make an appealing accompaniment.

ROASTING BASICS

■ Preheat oven to the desired temperature. Use meat taken directly from the refrigerator. Place the roast, fat side up, on a rack in a shallow roasting pan. Season as desired.

■ Insert an oven-safe thermometer into the thickest portion of the roast, not resting on fat or bone. Do not add water. Do not cover.

■ Roast the meat according to the Roasting Chart below, until the thermometer registers the Final Roasting Temperature. For accuracy, double-check the temperature with an instant-read thermometer.

■ As a general rule of thumb, add vegetables and fruits to the roasting pan approximately 30 to 45 minutes before the end of the roasting time.

■ Remove the roast from the oven; cover with foil. Let stand for 10 to 15 minutes until the temperature reaches the desired doneness.

■ Figure on four servings per pound of boneless meat.

ROASTING CHART

CUT	OVEN TEMPERATURE	WEIGHT	APPROXIMATE ROASTING TIME	FINAL ROASTING TEMPERATURE	FINAL DONENESS AND TEMPERATURE
Pork rib crown roast	325° F	6 to 8 pounds	2 ½ to 3 ¼ hours	155°	160° medium
Boneless pork double top loin roast	325° F	3 to 4 pounds	1 ½ to 2 ¼ hours	155°	160° medium
		4 to 5 pounds	2 to 2 ½ hours	155°	160° medium
Beef ribeye roast	350° F	3 to 4 pounds	1 ½ to 1 ¾ hours	135°	145° medium rare
			1 ¾ to 2 hours	150°	160° medium
		4 to 6 pounds	1 ¾ to 2 hours	135°	145° medium rare
			2 to 2 ½ hours	150°	160° medium
Beef tenderloin roast	425° F	2 to 3 pounds	35 to 40 minutes	135°	145° medium rare
			45 to 50 minutes	150°	160° medium
		4 to 5 pounds	50 to 60 minutes	135°	145° medium rare
			60 to 70 minutes	150°	160° medium
Leg of lamb (whole leg with bone)	325° F	5 to 7 pounds	1 ¾ to 2 ¼ hours	140°	145° medium rare
			2 ¼ to 2 ¾ hours	155°	160° medium
		7 to 8 pounds	2 ¼ to 2 ¾ hours	140°	145° medium rare
			2 ½ to 3 hours	155°	160° medium
Veal rib roast	325° F	4 to 5 pounds	1 ½ to 2 ¼ hours	155°	160° medium

For information about roasting meat cuts not listed here, please contact the National Cattleman's Beef Association at www.beef.org or www.veal.org; the National Pork Board at www.otherwhitemeat.com; or the American Lamb Council at www.lambchef.com.

Better Breakfast Lo

Before bakery-fresh artisanal bread became the rising star of discerning palates, the good old American homemade white loaf was king. That bread was easy on the baker. There was no need to make a starter three weeks ahead. The loaf yielded big, soft slices. And best of all, the bread was versatile: every bit as good served warm with soup as it was toasted for breakfast.

Our Rosemary-Raisin Bread is in the tradition of classic homemade loaves, only—we think—a little better. It has milk and butter for an extra-tender, tasty slice. An egg yolk leaves a creamy tint and acts as a natural preservative. The unlikely duet of raisins and rosemary strikes a savory-sweet chord that works as well with omelets as it does for French toast. Try it toasted and slathered with honey butter or topped with cream cheese and smoked salmon. It's also wonderful for scooping up the last of the scrambled eggs.

PHOTOGRAPHS: COLLEEN DUFFLEY. FOOD STYLIST: BROOKE LEONARD. TEXT: KEN HAEDRICH.

low fat Rosemary-Raisin Bread

We were inspired to create this rosemary-raisin loaf by Sue and Julie Campoy, the mother and daughter team who own Julienne, a beautiful brasserie in San Marino, California. We feasted on a fabulous breakfast and sampled their rosemary-raisin bread. See if you agree.

Prep: 30 minutes **Rise:** 75 minutes **Bake:** 40 minutes

6	to 6½ cups all-purpose flour	1	egg yolk
2	pkg. active dry yeast	1½	cups golden or dark raisins
2½	cups milk	4	tsp. dried rosemary, crushed
3	Tbsp. sugar		
2	Tbsp. butter	1	egg yolk, beaten
2	tsp. salt	1	Tbsp. milk

1. In a very large mixing bowl stir together 3 cups of the flour and the yeast; set aside. In a medium saucepan heat and stir the 2½ cups milk, the sugar, butter, and salt until warm (120° to 130° F) and butter is almost melted. Add warm milk mixture to flour mixture. Add 1 egg yolk; stir until combined.

2. Beat with an electric mixer on low speed for 30 seconds, scraping the side of the bowl constantly. Beat mixture on high speed for 3 minutes more. Sprinkle raisins and rosemary onto flour mixture (see photo 1). Using a wooden spoon, stir in as much of the remaining flour as you can (see photo 2).

3. Turn dough out onto a lightly floured surface. Knead in enough of the remaining flour to make a moderately stiff dough that is smooth and elastic (see photo 3), about 6 to 8 minutes total. Shape dough into a ball. Place dough in a lightly greased bowl; turn once to grease the surface. Cover and let rise in a warm place until double in size (about 45 to 60 minutes).

4. Punch dough down (see photo 4). Turn out onto a lightly floured surface. Divide dough in half. Cover and let rest for 10 minutes. Lightly grease two 8x4x2-inch or 9x5x3-inch loaf pans. Shape each half of the dough into a loaf. Place in prepared pans. Cover and let rise in a warm place until nearly double in size (30 to 40 minutes).

5. Meanwhile, preheat oven to 375° F. For the glaze, combine the remaining egg yolk and milk; brush lightly onto tops of risen dough. Using a serrated knife, make a long shallow cut down the length of dough in each pan.

6. Bake about 40 minutes or until the loaf is golden brown and crusty. The bread should sound hollow when tapped. Cover loosely with foil during the last 10 minutes of baking to prevent overbrowning, if necessary. Loosen bread and remove from pans immediately. Cool on wire racks. Makes 2 loaves (32 slices).

Nutrition facts per slice: 135 cal., 2 g total fat (1 g sat. fat), 13 mg chol., 166 mg sodium, 26 g carbo., 1 g dietary fiber, and 4 g pro. Daily Values: 2% vit. A, 1% vit. C, 3% calcium, and 8% iron.

Purely Persimmon

The apple of the orient is what some old-timers call this soft-textured winter fruit, although we think it looks more like a tomato in color and in shape. Ripe persimmons have a shiny, brilliant orange skin and red-orange meat. The flavor has a spicy sweetness, although people who've bitten into an unripe persimmon know that it can have an astringent, puckery quality. When cooking with persimmons, you usually mash and strain them to use the pulp, as we've done for the coffee cake and pudding recipe opposite. So pull out your strainer and rediscover an old favorite.

Persimmon-Walnut Coffee Cake

Prep: 45 minutes **Bake:** 1 hour

4	fresh, very ripe Hachiya persimmons* (about 1¾ lb.) or 1 cup applesauce
⅓	cup packed light brown sugar
1	Tbsp. all-purpose flour
2	cups all-purpose flour
2	tsp. baking powder
½	tsp. baking soda
½	tsp. salt
½	cup butter, softened
1	cup granulated sugar
1	tsp. vanilla
2	eggs
1	8-oz. carton dairy sour cream
1	recipe Walnut Streusel

1. Preheat oven to 350° F. Grease and flour a 9-inch springform pan; set aside.

2. Press persimmons into pulp (see below). (You should have 1 cup persimmon pulp.) In a small bowl stir together brown sugar and 1 tablespoon flour; stir in persimmon pulp or applesauce. Set aside.

3. In a medium bowl stir together the 2 cups flour, baking powder, baking soda, and salt; set aside. In a large bowl beat butter with an electric mixer on medium to high speed for 30 seconds. Beat in granulated sugar and vanilla. Add eggs, one at a time, beating after each addition. Add flour mixture and sour cream alternately to beaten mixture, beating just until combined after each addition. (The batter will be stiff.)

4. Spread half of the batter into prepared pan, building up a 1-inch rim of batter around edges of pan. Spoon persimmon mixture into center of pan. Carefully spoon remaining batter in small mounds, covering persimmon mixture. Sprinkle Walnut Streusel over batter.

5. Bake about 1 hour or until toothpick inserted into cake near center comes out clean. (The filling will sink as coffee cake bakes.) Cool in pan on a wire rack for 10 minutes. Loosen and remove sides. Cool completely on wire rack. Makes 12 servings.

Walnut Streusel: In a medium bowl stir together ½ cup all-purpose flour, ½ cup granulated sugar, and ½ teaspoon cinnamon. Cut in ¼ cup butter until mixture resembles coarse crumbs. Stir in ½ cup chopped walnuts; set aside.

*Test Kitchen Tip: Store ripe persimmons in the refrigerator. Let persimmons stand at room temperature about an hour before using. Peel persimmons or scrape pulp from peel with a metal spoon. Press persimmons through a coarse single-mesh strainer until you have pulp.

Nutrition facts per serving: 410 cal., 20 g total fat (11 g sat. fat), 77 mg chol., 364 mg sodium, 53 g carbo., 1 g dietary fiber, and 5 g pro. Daily Values: 10% vit. C, 9% calcium, and 10% iron.

THE VARIETIES

Fuyu: The smaller, tomato-shaped Fuyu persimmon is firm when ripe. Because its flesh is firm, it can be rinsed and eaten out-of-hand or may be peeled and sliced for salads.

Hachiya: This variety is the most widely available in the United States and is also called the Japanese persimmon or Kaki. Let the heart-shaped Hachiya ripen until very soft, when it has a smooth, creamy texture. It's great to use in baked goods.

new Persimmon Pudding

Serve this warm, bready baked pudding in squares and top it with a spoonful of whipped cream.

Prep: 20 minutes **Bake:** 35 minutes

4	fresh, very ripe Hachiya persimmons (about 1¾ lb.)
2	tsp. butter, melted
1	cup all-purpose flour
1	tsp. baking powder
	Dash ground cinnamon
½	cup light cream or half-and-half
½	cup buttermilk or sour milk**
½	tsp. baking soda
1	egg
1	cup sugar
½	tsp. finely shredded orange peel
2	Tbsp. butter, melted
	Whipped cream (optional)

1. Grease an 8x8x2-inch baking pan with the 2 teaspoons of butter. Set aside. Press persimmons* into pulp (see below left). (You should have 1 cup pulp.)

2. In a small bowl stir together flour, baking powder, and cinnamon; set aside. In another small bowl combine light cream, buttermilk, and baking soda; set aside.

3. In a medium bowl beat egg; stir in persimmon pulp, sugar, and orange peel. Add flour mixture and buttermilk mixture alternately to persimmon mixture, stirring well after each addition. Stir in 2 tablespoons melted butter. Pour into prepared pan.

4. Bake in a 325° F. oven for 35 minutes. Serve warm with whipped cream, if desired. Makes 6 to 8 servings.

**Test Kitchen Tip: To make ½ cup sour milk, place 1½ teaspoons lemon juice or vinegar in a glass measuring cup. Add enough milk to make ½ cup liquid; stir. Let the mixture stand for 5 minutes before using.

Nutrition per serving: 336 cal., 9 g total fat (5 g sat. fat), 58 mg chol., 268 mg sodium, 61 g carbo., 1 g dietary fiber, and 5 g pro. Daily Values: 23% vit. A, 43% vit. C, 10% calcium, and 11% iron.

PHOTOGRAPHS: COLLEEN DUFFLEY. FOOD STYLIST: BROOKE LEONARD. STORY: KEN HAEDRICH.

DO THE PUMPKIN MASH

Not all pumpkins are created equal. Cooking pumpkins weigh, on average, from 4 to 7 pounds. When you see them in the market, they're often called "sugar" or "pie" pumpkins. From a 4- to 4½-pound pie pumpkin, you will get about 3½ cups cooked pumpkin puree. Cut a pumpkin into large pieces. Remove seeds and strings. Arrange pieces in a single layer, skin side up, in a large shallow baking pan. Cover with foil. Bake in a 375° F oven for 1 to 1½ hours or until tender. Cool. Remove pulp, discarding peel. Place pulp, half at a time, in a food processor bowl. Cover and process until smooth, scraping sides as needed. Line a strainer with a double layer of 100-percent-cotton cheesecloth. Transfer to a strainer; press to remove liquid. Use in recipes calling for cooked pumpkin puree.

It's a pretty safe bet that no vegetable tickles our kids' collective fancy like the pumpkin. Is it any wonder? While kids tend to view most vegetables as something you simply eat—oftentimes with less than relish—the colorful pumpkin is blessed with multiple personalities. In fact, it's literally a seasonal smorgasbord of edible and decorative possibilities.

Of course, a carved pumpkin is the candle-lit symbol of every child's favorite spooky day. But you can use one for a centerpiece and toast the seeds to make a snack. Furthermore, the pumpkin doesn't even take its role as a veggie all that seriously: about the only thing that stands between it and some delicious desserts is a little sugar and spice.

Pumpkin

Pumpkin Chocolate Cheesecake Bars

These bars are special when they're made with your own homemade pumpkin puree. But canned pumpkin also works beautifully for this recipe, and no one is likely to be the wiser.

Prep: 1½ hours **Bake:** 55 minutes

2	8-oz. pkg. cream cheese, softened	¼	tsp. salt
1¾	cups sugar	6	oz. semisweet chocolate, cut up
3	large eggs	2	Tbsp. butter
1	cup cooked and pureed pumpkin (see left) or canned pumpkin	1	recipe Graham Cracker Crust
½	tsp. pumpkin pie spice	1¼	cups dairy sour cream
½	tsp. vanilla	¼	cup sugar
			Grated fresh nutmeg

1. Preheat oven to 325° F. For filling, in a large bowl combine cream cheese and 1¾ cups sugar; beat with an electic mixer on medium speed until mixed. Add eggs, one at a time, beating on low speed after each addition until just combined. Stir in the cooked or canned pumpkin, pumpkin pie spice, vanilla, and salt. Pour 1¼ cups of the filling into a medium bowl. Set both bowls of filling aside.

2. In a small saucepan melt chocolate and butter over very low heat, stirring frequently until smooth. Stir melted chocolate into the 1¼ cups reserved filling. Carefully spread the chocolate filling evenly over Graham Cracker Crust. Bake for 15 minutes. Remove from oven. Carefully pour remaining pumpkin filling over baked chocolate layer, spreading evenly.

3. Bake for 40 to 45 minutes or until mixture is slightly puffed around edges and just set in center. Remove from oven; cool for 30 minutes. Meanwhile, combine sour cream and ¼ cup sugar. Cover; let stand at room temperature while bars cool.

4. Gently spread the sour cream layer onto bars. Cool. Refrigerate for several hours or overnight before cutting. Sprinkle with nutmeg just before serving. To serve, loosen the edges by moving a knife around the pan. Keep any remaining bars refrigerated. Makes 24 servings.

Graham Cracker Crust: Lightly grease a 13x9x2-inch baking pan. In a large mixing bowl stir together 1¼ cups graham cracker crumbs and ¼ cup sugar. Add ⅓ cup melted butter; mix thoroughly. Press evenly onto the bottom of the prepared pan; set aside.

Nutrition facts per serving: 256 cal., 16 g total fat (9 g sat. fat), 62 mg chol., 155 mg sodium, 27 g carbo., 1 g fiber, and 3 g pro. Daily Values: 15% vit. A, 1% vit. C, 3% calcium, and 5% iron.

MORE FUN IDEAS

Just one pumpkin will never do. You'll need several to sample all the fun ways you and your kids can make the most with pumpkins. For instance:

■ Create a centerpiece: A hollowed pumpkin is a fitting place to tuck a small pot of mums or an arrangement of fresh or dried flowers. For fresh flowers, you can ease a glass of water inside to secretly house the blossoms. A bit of sand in the pumpkin helps stabilize dried flowers.

■ Toast the seeds: First, separate the seeds from the pulp and gently rinse them to remove pulp and any strings. Drain seeds well. Place them in a bowl and toss with about a tablespoon of oil. Spread seeds onto a waxed-paper-lined 15x10x1-inch baking pan. Let stand for 24 to 48 hours or until seeds are dry. Remove the waxed paper from the baking pan. Toast seeds in a 325° F oven for 40 minutes, stirring once or twice. Season to taste with salt.

You say Vanilla

Whoever coined the phrase "plain vanilla" obviously didn't know beans—vanilla beans, that is. The fruit of a tropical orchid, vanilla beans have an exotic aroma and a heavenly range of flavor notes.

For everyday cooking, vanilla extract is just fine. But when you want to pin a badge of vanilla authenticity on your cooking, use beans. Half a bean has about as much flavor as one teaspoon of vanilla extract. To use, cut as much of the bean (or seed pod, really) as you'll need, then slit it lengthwise. Scrape the seeds from the pod, and add both to your dish. Save the remainder for a future use. Store the whole beans in an airtight jar in a cool, dry place. Look for vanilla beans that are 5 to 7 inches long, a sure sign they've grown to full ripeness. Stay away from partial or cut beans, a sign the bean might have been moldy. The bean should glisten and be leathery but supple—never dry or brittle.

Creamy Desserts
Using between ½ to a whole bean, scrape the seeds into the milk when making your favorite custard, crème brûlée, or rice pudding. Cook the custard mixture to bring out the flavor of the seeds, then remove the seeds before cooling.

PHOTOGRAPHS: COLLEEN DUFFLEY. FOOD STYLIST: BROOKE LEONARD. STORY: KEN HAEDRICH.

Hot Chocolate

Scrape the seeds from ¼ of a vanilla bean into a single serving of hot chocolate. Whip the seeds from an additional ¼ of a bean into some whipping cream to use as a topper for the hot chocolate. For fun, serve a vanilla bean as a stir stick.

Hot Cereals

Add ½ of a bean, split and seeded, to the water or milk when cooking four servings of oatmeal. Remove the bean before serving. You can also use vanilla to flavor cream of wheat, grits, cornmeal mush, and rice during cooking.

N o v

Keeping the Feast

P l u s . . .

The harvest is in with pumpkins, squash, pears, and apples, so now it's time to plan the traditional feast, with a few new twists.

e m b e r

Keeping the FEAST

Three incredible cooks dish up heaping portions of nostalgia with their cherished Thanksgiving recipes. Follow their lead and tuck away your own memories.

Cranberry-Stuffed Pork Loin

30 low fat Cranberry-Stuffed Pork Loin

Ask your butcher to butterfly the pork loin for you, or do it your-self, using the directions below.

Prep: 30 minutes **Roast:** 1¼ to 1½ hours **Stand:** 15 minutes

1 4½- to 5-lb. boneless pork center loin roast (single loin)	¾ cup dried cranberries
	1 tsp. garlic salt
Salt	1 tsp. pepper
Pepper	¾ cup dry white wine or apple juice
1 cup Roasted Garlic and Sweet Onion Jam (see recipe, page 211)	Chicken broth
	3 Tbsp. all-purpose flour

1. Preheat the oven to 325° F. To butterfly the roast, turn the roast fat side down. Make a single lengthwise cut down the center of the loin, cutting to within ½ inch of the other side. Spread open like a book. Place knife in the "V" of the first cut. Make another cut—knife should be parallel to the table—to the right of the "V" to within ½ inch of the end (do not cut all the way through roast). Repeat the parallel cut to the left of the "V." Spread open the sections. Cover with plastic wrap. Working from center to edges, pound with flat side of meat mallet to ¾- to 1-inch thickness. Remove plastic wrap.

2. Sprinkle meat with salt and pepper; spread with ⅔ cup Roasted Garlic and Sweet Onion Jam. Sprinkle cranberries onto jam. Starting at a long side, roll meat up. Tie snugly at 3-inch intervals with 100-percent-cotton string. Place the rolled pork loin roast on a rack in a shallow roasting pan. Sprinkle with garlic salt and pepper. Insert a meat thermometer into center of roast. Roast, uncovered, for 1¼ to 1½ hours or until ther-mometer (or instant-read thermometer) registers 155° F, spreading with remaining jam the last 15 minutes of roasting.

3. Remove roast from pan. Cover with foil; let stand for 15 minutes before carving. (The temperature of the meat will rise 5° F during standing.)

4. Meanwhile, for gravy, carefully pour wine into roasting pan, stirring to scrape up browned bits from bottom of pan. Strain and measure pan juices. Add chicken broth, if necessary, to equal 1½ cups total. In a saucepan stir ¾ cup chicken broth into flour until smooth; stir in the wine mixture. Cook and stir until thickened and bubbly; cook and stir for 1 minute more.

5. To carve, cut string. Using a carving knife, cut roast into 1-inch-thick slices. Serve with gravy. Makes 10 to 12 servings.

Nutrition facts per serving: 404 cal., 11 g total fat (4 g sat. fat), 128 mg chol., 399 mg sodium, 24 g carbo., 1 g fiber, and 46 g pro. Daily Values: 7% vit. C, 6% calcium, and 12% iron.

ROOTED IN THE HEARTLAND

Judith Fertig (in photo, left, in 1962) and her family, with their Midwestern roots, celebrate the holidays with heartland foods inspired by the past. Her Pesto Rolls (page 216) evolved from a cloverleaf roll recipe passed on from her great-grandmother. Cloverleaf rolls often appear on the holiday table, although Judith, a Kansas City food writer and cookbook author, adds her own updates.

Her grown son and daughter always joke that their mother never serves the same dish twice. "Our family has a collective sense of humor, so we usually laugh down memory lane through Thanksgiving dinner," Judith says.

Because her children are not turkey fans, Judith created a Thanksgiving feast focusing on Cranberry-Stuffed Pork Loin, slathered with a garlic-onion jam. (If your family, like most, insists on turkey, you can use the jam on that too.) Judith also serves acorn squash, a hearty stuffing of freshly baked herb bread, and a make-ahead mashed potato casserole.

Making slight adjustments to traditional recipes has become part of the holiday dinner ritual at the Fertig home. The main ingredients may not change from year to year, but the flavors almost always do. "What matters most to me at Thanksgiving is celebrating the abundance we enjoy with the people I love," she says.

Holding memories and recipes close to the heart is a trait Judith inherited. Her great-grandmother's recipe collection was just the beginning. Her grandmother maintained the tradition, using a fountain pen to include recipes in a "house-hold book"—now a torn and tattered family keepsake.

"Then my mother collected recipes and family photos and compiled a book for my sister and me, which I treasure," Judith says. That spiral notebook is called *The Family Heirloom Cookbook* (a page is shown below). Judith has started putting together a similar feast journal for her two children, now 26 and 21 years old. "I think the kids will appreciate it more when they have their own households," she says.

Judith also includes family anecdotes in the cookbooks she writes. Her latest books are *Prairie Home Cooking* and *Prairie Home Breads*.

Roast Turkey with Roasted Garlic and Sweet Onion Jam

When slowly roasted alongside the big bird, onions and garlic take on a sweet and mellow caramel flavor that's right in step with the garlic-onion jam that's brushed onto the turkey at the end of roasting. Another helping, please?

Roast Turkey with Roasted Garlic and Sweet Onion Jam

If you don't have time to make the jam yourself, grab a jar in a specialty food market. We like Stonewall Kitchen's version.

Prep: 15 minutes **Roast:** 2¾ hours **Stand:** 15 minutes

1 10- to 12-lb. turkey	1 recipe Roasted Garlic
Salt	and Sweet Onion Jam
Cooking oil	(see right) or 1 cup
6 medium red and/or	purchased roasted
white onions, peeled and	onion jam
cut into wedges	Chicken broth (optional)
10 to 12 cloves unpeeled	¼ cup dry white wine or
garlic	apple juice
	3 Tbsp. all-purpose flour

1. Preheat oven to 325° F. Remove turkey neck from body cavity and giblets from neck cavity. Rinse inside and outside of turkey; pat dry with paper towels. If desired, season body cavity with salt. Pull the neck skin to the back; fasten with a skewer.

2. Tuck the ends of the drumsticks under the band of skin across the tail. If there is no band of skin, tie the drumsticks securely to the tail. Twist wing tips under the back.

3. Place turkey, breast side up, on a rack in a shallow roasting pan. Brush with cooking oil. Insert a meat thermometer into the center of an inside thigh muscle. The thermometer should not touch bone. Cover turkey loosely with foil. Place turkey in oven. Roast for 1 hour.

4. In a bowl toss onion wedges and unpeeled garlic cloves with 2 tablespoons cooking oil. Spoon the onion mixture around the turkey; roast for 1¼ hours more.

5. Remove foil from turkey. (The thermometer should register 160° F.) Cut band of skin or string between drumsticks so that thighs cook evenly. Carefully spread Roasted Garlic and Sweet Onion Jam onto turkey. Roast for 30 to 45 minutes more or until the thermometer registers 180° F. (The juices should run clear and drumsticks should move easily in their sockets.)

6. Remove turkey from oven. Transfer turkey, garlic, and onions to a platter. Cover and let stand for 15 to 20 minutes.

7. Meanwhile, pour pan drippings into a large measuring cup. Skim fat from drippings and strain remaining broth. Add chicken broth, if necessary, to equal 1¾ cups. In a medium saucepan, combine wine and flour. Stir in strained pan juices. Cook and stir until thickened and bubbly; cook and stir for 1 minute more. Serve with turkey. Makes 12 to 14 servings.

Nutrition facts per serving: 590 cal., 27 g total fat (7 g sat. fat), 202 mg chol., 199 mg sodium, 19 g carbo., 1 g fiber, and 62 g pro. Daily Values: 8% vit. C, 8% calcium, and 25% iron.

low fat Roasted Garlic and Sweet Onion Jam

Prep: 15 minutes **Roast:** 45 minutes **Cook:** 30 minutes

1 bulb garlic	½ cup finely chopped
1 Tbsp. olive oil	Granny Smith apple
1 large sweet onion, peeled	½ cup sugar
and finely chopped (1 cup)	½ cup balsamic vinegar

1. Preheat the oven to 350° F. Slice about ¼ inch off the pointed end of the garlic bulb so the individual cloves show. Place the bulb in a small baking dish, cut side up, and drizzle with olive oil. Cover and roast for 45 to 60 minutes or until the garlic cloves have softened. Cool.

2. Gently squeeze the garlic cloves and juices into a saucepan. Stir in the onion, apple, sugar, and balsamic vinegar. Bring to boiling over medium-high heat, stirring occasionally. Reduce heat; simmer about 30 minutes or until the onion and apple have softened and turned transparent and the mixture has thickened, stirring occasionally. Makes about 1 cup.

Nutrition facts per tablespoon: 46 cal., 1 g total fat (0 g sat. fat), 0 mg chol., 1 mg sodium, 10 g carbo., 1 g fiber, and 0 g pro. Daily Values: 2% vit. C and 1% calcium.

TURKEY ROASTING TIMES

To prepare a whole bird for roasting, follow the steps in the recipe, left. Then refer to the timings below as a guide. Because birds vary in size and shape, the timings can also vary. These timings are for unstuffed birds. For stuffed birds, add 15 to 45 minutes per pound. Always verify the doneness with a thermometer to see that the meat reaches 180° F for whole birds and 170° F for turkey parts.

TURKEY	WEIGHT	OVEN TEMP.	ROASTING TIME
Whole	8 to 12 lb.	325° F	2¾ to 3 hours
(unstuffed)	12 to 14 lb.	325° F	3 to 3¾ hours
	14 to 18 lb.	325° F	3¾ to 4¼ hours
	18 to 20 lb.	325° F	4¼ to 4½ hours
	20 to 24 lb.	325° F	4½ to 5 hours
Boneless, whole	2½ to 4 lb.	325° F	2 to 2½ hours
	4 to 6 lb.	325° F	2½ to 3½ hours
Breast, whole	4 to 6 lb.	325° F	1½ to 2¼ hours
	6 to 8 lb.	325° F	2¼ to 3¼ hours
Drumstick	1 to 1½ lb.	325° F	1¼ to 1¾ hours

Artisanal Bread Stuffing

For this recipe, "artisanal" simply refers to any homemade or bakery-fresh loaf, typically with a burst of flavor from added ingredients, such as herbs, olives, or cheese.

Prep: 30 minutes **Bake:** 1 hour

12	cups 1-inch cubes artisanal bread, such as rosemary, olive, or sun-dried tomato (about a 1¼-lb. loaf)	6	Tbsp. butter
½	cup pine nuts	1½	cups sliced, pitted kalamata olives
4½	cups coarsely chopped fennel (reserve leafy tops for another use)	3	Tbsp. snipped fresh thyme or 1 Tbsp. dried thyme, crushed
1½	cups chopped onion	¾	tsp. pepper
		2¼	cups chicken broth
			Nonstick cooking spray

1. Preheat oven to 350° F. In a large roasting pan toast bread and pine nuts for 15 to 20 minutes or until bread is crisp and pine nuts are light brown, tossing once. Set aside.

2. Meanwhile, in a large skillet cook fennel and onion in butter over medium-high heat about 10 minutes or until tender, stirring occasionally.

3. Stir olives, thyme, and pepper into onion mixture; transfer to an extra-large bowl. Add bread cubes and pine nuts; toss to combine. Add chicken broth, stirring until moistened. Lightly coat a 3-quart casserole with cooking spray; spoon in bread mixture. Cover and bake for 45 minutes.

4. Remove cover; bake about 15 minutes more or until stuffing is heated through. Serve warm. Makes 10 to 12 servings.

Nutrition facts per serving: 319 cal., 16 g total fat (6 g sat. fat), 20 mg chol., 818 mg sodium, 38 g carbo., 5 g fiber, and 8 g pro. Daily Values: 7% vit. A, 12% vit. C, 7% calcium, and 14% iron.

Mashed Baked Potatoes with Garden Confetti

Crowned with autumn colors, this rustic version of an American classic can be made a day ahead.

Prep: 30 minutes **Bake:** 40 minutes + 1¼ hours

5	lb. red potatoes (about 15 medium potatoes), baked*	1½	cups half-and-half, light cream, or fat-free evaporated milk
1	8-oz. pkg. cream cheese or reduced-fat cream cheese (Neufchâtel), cut up and softened	1	tsp. salt
		1	tsp. cracked black pepper
			Nonstick cooking spray
		1	recipe Garden Confetti
		2	Tbsp. butter, melted

1. Preheat oven to 325° F. While the potatoes are still hot, transfer half of the potatoes to a very large bowl. (Cut large potatoes in half for easier mashing.) Using a potato masher or an electric mixer, mash potatoes (with their skins still on) until slightly lumpy; transfer to another bowl. Use the same bowl to mash the remaining potatoes. Return all potatoes to the bowl.

2. Add cream cheese, half-and-half, salt, and pepper to potatoes; beat until combined. Coat a 3-quart casserole with cooking spray; spoon potato mixture into casserole. Top with Garden Confetti; drizzle with melted butter. Bake, uncovered, about 1¼ hours or until heated through. Makes 10 to 12 servings.

Garden Confetti: In a large skillet melt 2 tablespoons butter over medium heat. Add 2 medium carrots, shredded; 1 stalk celery, finely chopped; and 1 medium onion, thinly sliced. Cook and stir for 4 to 5 minutes or until vegetables are tender.

*Test Kitchen Tip: To bake potatoes, scrub potatoes thoroughly with a brush; pat dry. Prick potatoes with a fork. Bake in a 425° F oven for 40 to 60 minutes or until tender.

Make-ahead directions: Prepare as above, except after drizzling with melted butter, cover and refrigerate overnight. Bake, covered, in the 325° F oven for 1 hour. Uncover and bake for 1 to 1¼ hours more or until heated through.

Nutrition facts per serving: 304 cal., 17 g total fat (11 g sat. fat), 51 mg chol., 386 mg sodium, 33 g carbo., 3 g fiber, and 7 g pro. Daily Values: 75% vit. A, 42% vit. C, 9% calcium, and 16% iron.

"What matters most to me at Thanksgiving is celebrating the abundance we enjoy with the people I love."

—Judith Fertig

Mashed Baked Potatoes
with Garden Confetti and
Artisanal Bread Stuffing

Pumpkin Rolls with
Maple Streusel Filling and
Caramelized Acorn Squash

Pumpkin Rolls with Maple Streusel Filling

There's a sweet surprise inside these pumpkin-flavored rolls: a crumbly combo of hickory nuts, apricots, and brown sugar.

Prep: 1 hour **Chill:** overnight
Rise: 40 minutes **Bake:** 12 minutes

4½	to 5 cups all-purpose flour	¼	cup sugar
1	pkg. active dry yeast	¾	tsp. salt
½	cup milk	1	egg
½	cup water	½	cup canned pumpkin
¼	cup butter	1	recipe Maple Streusel Filling

1. In a large mixing bowl stir together 1½ cups of the flour and yeast; set aside.

2. In a medium saucepan heat and stir milk, water, butter, sugar, and salt just until warm (120° to 130° F) and butter almost melts.

3. Add milk mixture to dry mixture; add egg. Beat with an electric mixer on low to medium speed for 30 seconds, scraping side of bowl constantly. Beat on high speed for 3 minutes. Stir in canned pumpkin. Using a wooden spoon, stir in as much of the remaining flour as you can.

4. Turn dough out onto a lightly floured surface. Knead in enough of the remaining flour to make a moderately stiff dough that is smooth and elastic (6 to 8 minutes total). Shape dough into a ball. Place in a lightly greased large bowl; turn once to grease surface. Cover with plastic wrap; refrigerate overnight.

5. Punch dough down. Turn dough out onto a lightly floured surface. Divide dough in half. Cover; let rest for 10 minutes.

6. Meanwhile, lightly grease 2 baking sheets. Divide each half of dough into 8 pieces. On a lightly floured surface flatten each piece into a 3½-inch round. For each roll, place the round of dough in the palm of your hand. Place 1 generous tablespoon of Maple Streusel Filling in the center of each round. Shape dough into a ball by pulling the edges of dough up and over streusel, pinching edges of dough to seal. Place rolls, smooth side up, on prepared baking sheets. Cover; let rise in a warm place until nearly double in size (30 to 40 minutes).

7. Preheat oven to 375° F. Bake rolls for 12 to 14 minutes or until golden brown. Immediately remove rolls from baking sheets. Cool on wire racks. Makes 16 rolls.

Maple Streusel Filling: In a medium mixing bowl stir together ⅔ cup chopped hickory nuts or hazelnuts (filberts), ⅓ cup maple granulated sugar or packed brown sugar, ⅓ cup all-purpose flour, and ¼ cup snipped dried apricots. Stir in ⅓ cup melted butter until combined.

Make-ahead directions: Follow the same instructions for storing and reheating Pesto Rolls (recipe, page 216).

Nutrition facts per roll: 274 cal., 11 g total fat (5 g sat. fat), 33 mg chol., 191 mg sodium, 38 g carbo., 2 g fiber, and 6 g pro. Daily Values: 43% vit. A, 1% vit. C, 3% calcium, and 13% iron.

Caramelized Acorn Squash

Prep: 25 minutes **Bake:** 40 minutes **Chill:** overnight

4	1- to 1½-lb. acorn squash	1	tsp. ground cinnamon
½	cup sugar	½	tsp. ground nutmeg
½	cup butter	½	tsp. salt
½	cup apple cider		

1. Preheat oven to 350° F. Carefully cut each squash into 4 rings; discard seeds and remove fibrous material. Line 2 shallow baking pans with parchment paper or foil. Arrange rings in a single layer on pans. Cover with foil; bake for 40 to 45 minutes or until squash is tender. Cool; place in a container, cover, and refrigerate overnight. (Let squash to come to room temperature before finishing recipe.)

2. Before serving, heat sugar in a 12-inch nonstick skillet over medium-high heat until it starts to melt, shaking occasionally. Do not stir. Reduce heat; cook and stir 3 minutes or until sugar is melted and medium caramel in color.

3. Whisk in the butter until completely melted. Whisk in cider, cinnamon, nutmeg, and salt. (The mixture will bubble up and sizzle before it reaches sauce consistency.)

4. Transfer a few rings to the skillet; turn to coat with caramel mixture. Warm rings in caramel for 3 minutes; transfer to an ovenproof platter. Keep warm in a 300° F oven. Repeat with remaining squash rings. Pour sauce over squash rings. Makes 10 to 12 servings.

Nutrition facts per serving: 185 cal., 10 g total fat (6 g sat. fat), 26 mg chol., 220 mg sodium, 26 g carbo., 2 g fiber, and 1 g pro. Daily Values: 16% vit. A, 22% vit. C, 5% calcium, and 6% iron.

THANKSGIVING DINNER

Cranberry-Raspberry Spinach Salad (recipe, page 220)

Roast Turkey with Roasted Garlic and

Sweet Onion Jam (recipes, page 211)

Artisanal Bread Stuffing (recipe, page 212)

Mashed Baked Potatoes with Garden Confetti
(recipe, page 212)

Caramelized Acorn Squash (recipe, above)

Pumpkin Rolls with Maple Streusel Filling
(recipe, left)

Caramel-Pecan Pumpkin Pie (recipe, page 224)

Wine, coffee, or tea

new low fat Dill Batter Bread

If time is a little precious, remember this speedy yeast bread. It rises just once and requires no kneading or shaping.

Prep: 20 minutes **Rise:** 50 minutes **Bake:** 25 minutes

2 cups all-purpose flour	1 Tbsp. butter or margarine
1 pkg. active dry yeast	
½ cup water	1 tsp. dried minced onion
½ cup cream-style cottage cheese	1 tsp. salt
1 Tbsp. sugar	1 egg
1 Tbsp. dillseed or caraway seed	½ cup toasted wheat germ

1. Grease a 9x1½-inch round baking pan or a 1-quart casserole; set aside. In a large mixing bowl combine 1 cup of the flour and the yeast; set aside.

2. In a medium saucepan heat and stir water, cottage cheese, sugar, dillseed, butter, dried onion, and salt just until warm (120° to 130° F) and butter almost melts.

3. Add cottage cheese mixture to flour mixture; add egg. Beat with an electric mixer on low to medium speed for 30 seconds, scraping side of bowl constantly. Beat on high speed for 3 minutes. Using a wooden spoon, stir in the wheat germ and the remaining flour (the batter will be stiff).

4. Spoon batter into the prepared pan or casserole, spreading to edges. Cover and let rise in a warm place until double in size (50 to 60 minutes).

5. Preheat oven to 375° F. Bake for 25 to 30 minutes or until golden. Immediately remove from pan or casserole. Serve warm, or cool on a wire rack. Makes 1 loaf (8 servings).

Nutrition facts per slice: 185 cal., 4 g total fat (2 g sat. fat), 33 mg chol., 369 mg sodium, 30 g carbo., 2 g fiber, and 8 g pro. Daily Values: 3% vit. A, 1% vit. C, 3% calcium, and 13% iron.

Pesto Rolls

You can make these flavorful rolls a day ahead and store them in an airtight container. Or prepare them several weeks in advance and keep in freezer containers.

Prep: 35 minutes **Chill:** overnight
Rise: 40 minutes **Bake:** 12 minutes

4½ to 5 cups all-purpose flour	⅓ cup sugar
2 pkg. active dry yeast	1 tsp. salt
¾ cup milk	1 egg
½ cup water	½ cup basil pesto
⅓ cup butter	½ cup finely shredded Parmesan cheese

1. In a large mixing bowl stir together 1¾ cups of the flour and yeast; set aside.

2. In a medium saucepan heat and stir milk, water, butter, sugar, and salt just until warm (120° to 130° F) and butter almost melts.

3. Add milk mixture to dry mixture; add egg. Beat with an electric mixer on low to medium speed for 30 seconds, scraping side of bowl constantly. Beat on high speed for 3 minutes. Stir in pesto. Using a wooden spoon, stir in as much of the remaining flour as you can.

4. Turn dough out onto a lightly floured surface. Knead in enough of the remaining flour to make a moderately stiff dough that is smooth and elastic (6 to 8 minutes total). Shape dough into a ball. Place in a lightly greased large bowl; turn once to grease surface. Cover with plastic wrap; refrigerate overnight.

5. Punch dough down. Turn dough out onto a lightly floured surface. Divide dough in half. Cover; let rest for 10 minutes. Meanwhile, lightly grease eighteen 2½-inch muffin cups.

6. Divide each half of dough into 9 equal portions. Divide each portion into 3 pieces. Shape each piece into a ball, pulling edges under to make a smooth top. Place 3 balls in each muffin cup, smooth sides up. Sprinkle with Parmesan cheese. Cover and let rise in a warm place until nearly double in size (about 30 minutes).

7. Preheat oven to 375° F. Bake for 12 to 14 minutes or until rolls are golden brown. Immediately remove rolls from pans. Serve warm, or cool on wire racks. Makes 18 rolls.

Make-ahead directions: To reheat rolls from room temperature, wrap in foil and warm in a 375° F oven about 7 minutes or until heated through. To reheat frozen rolls, wrap and warm in a 375° F oven about 20 minutes or until warm.

Nutrition facts per roll: 217 cal., 8 g total fat (4 g sat. fat), 26 mg chol., 258 mg sodium, 29 g carbo., 1 g fiber, and 6 g pro. Daily Values: 5% vit. A, 6% calcium, and 10% iron.

Pesto Rolls

Bits of green basil fleck these flavorful buns and shreds of pungent Parmesan crown the tops. The rolls are delicious with roast turkey, but remember them next time you serve minestrone, lasagna, or just plain spaghetti and meatballs.

Vegetable-Topped Mussels with Chardonnay Cream

Start Thanksgiving dinner off in an unexpected way, with a fresh mussel appetizer served in the shell and floating in a creamy garden of vegetables and herbs.

Vegetable-Topped Mussels
with Chardonnay Cream

You can store the bread mixture and sauce separately overnight in the refrigerator. Or steam the mussels in the wine mixture; cover and refrigerate overnight, then reheat just before serving.

Prep: 1 hour **Cook:** 30 minutes **Bake:** 15 minutes

½	cup chopped zucchini	1	sprig fresh thyme
½	cup chopped fresh mushrooms	1	clove garlic, minced
⅓	cup chopped red or yellow sweet pepper	20	green-lip mussels (about 2 lb.), cleaned*
¼	cup chopped leek	½	tsp. curry powder
2	tsp. olive oil		Dash ground red pepper
1	cup Chardonnay wine	1	recipe Herbed Bread Crumbs
1	Tbsp. finely chopped shallot	½	cup whipping cream
1	bay leaf		Toasted baguette slices

1. In a 4-quart Dutch oven cook zucchini, mushrooms, sweet pepper, and leek in hot olive oil over medium heat for 2 to 3 minutes or until vegetables are crisp tender. Remove from pan.

2. Add wine, shallot, bay leaf, thyme, and garlic to pan. Bring to boiling. Add mussels; return to boiling. Reduce heat. Cook, covered, for 5 to 9 minutes or until mussels open.

3. Remove mussels, discarding any unopened shells; set aside. Strain remaining liquid; return to pan. Bring to boiling. Stir in curry powder and red pepper. Simmer, uncovered, about 10 minutes or until mixture is reduced by half (about ⅔ cup).

4. Meanwhile, pull apart mussel shells. Using a sharp knife, cut mussel loose, but do not remove from bottom shell. Discard empty shells. Place remaining mussel shells on a 15x10x1-inch baking pan. Spoon about 1 teaspoon of the vegetables over each mussel; top with about 2 teaspoons of the Herbed Bread Crumbs. Reserve remaining vegetables.

5. When curry liquid has been reduced, add cream; simmer, uncovered, for 5 minutes more. Stir in remaining vegetables.

6. Preheat oven to 425° F. Just before serving, bake mussels for 15 minutes or until heated through and bread crumbs are golden brown. Spoon some of the hot vegetable-cream mixture into ten shallow soup plates. Top each serving with 2 mussels. Serve with toasted baguette slices. Makes 10 appetizer servings.

Herbed Bread Crumbs: In a bowl combine 1 cup coarse bread crumbs, 4 teaspoons olive oil, 2 teaspoons snipped fresh thyme, and 2 teaspoons snipped fresh parsley. Season to taste.

*Test Kitchen Tip: To clean mussels, scrub under cold running water. Remove beards. In an 8-quart Dutch oven combine 4 quarts cold water and ⅓ cup salt; add mussels. Soak for 15 minutes; drain and rinse. Discard water. Repeat soaking in salt water, draining, and rinsing twice.

Nutrition facts per serving: 346 cal., 13 g total fat (5 g sat. fat), 46 mg chol., 806 mg sodium, 29 g carbo., 2 g fiber, and 23 g pro. Daily Values: 28% vit. A, 24% vit. C, 12% calcium, and 26% iron.

A TOAST TO THE FAMILY

Jamie Davies (at right with her sister in 1943) believes in holding true to tradition, especially on Thanksgiving Day. As they've done for years, her three sons (below) and their families gather at her Calistoga, California, home—a majestic Victorian—where they grew up. "We celebrate Thanksgiving here because of the great memories," says Jamie, who purchased Schramsberg Vineyards in 1965 with her late husband, Jack. The Napa Valley winery is known for its sparkling wines.

Now the family includes grandchildren who take part in the pre-dinner hustle and bustle along with their parents. "Everyone gets an assignment. The prepping becomes a family experience," Jamie says. Someone picks the wine. Another chooses the china. Someone else mashes the potatoes.

The celebration begins with seafood, such as a mussel appetizer, followed by a salad of winter greens. Then there's the roast turkey with corn bread stuffing, plus mashed potatoes. Jamie might tweak the flavors and presentation of the remaining side dishes, but the basics are always there.

Dessert also reflects the season, typically featuring pumpkin and mincemeat. The pumpkin could flavor a crème brûlée and the mincemeat just might show up in a tart or turnover, or the two flavors might be melded.

Keeping the family's recipes neatly organized is second nature to Jamie, whose organizational skills are evident to those who know her. She oversees 60 vineyards that cover 200 acres and stretch across four counties. In fact, she has so many recipes that she keeps them categorized in file folders. Some come from the Napa Valley cooking class she founded with friends about 30 years ago.

Her photos, such as the holiday table setting (right), are just as cherished. She keeps them in photo albums, but pulls a few out every so often to display on her kitchen walls. "The photo walls are another way to share our family memories," Jamie says.

THANKSGIVING WITH A TWIST

Vegetable-Topped Mussels with
Chardonnay Cream (recipe, page 219)

Sparkling Kumquat Salad (recipe, left)

Cranberry-Stuffed Pork Loin (recipe, page 209)

Steamed pea pods

Pesto Rolls (recipe, page 216)

Chocolate-Pear Spice Cake (recipe, page 223)

Sparkling wine, coffee, or tea

Sparkling Kumquat Salad

Jamie uses a sparkling wine from Schramsberg Vineyards, which we recommend. You can use another wine or even an alcohol-free version for the vinaigrette.

Start to finish: 30 minutes

⅓	cup walnut pieces, toasted	12	cups torn mixed salad greens
⅓	cup pomegranate seeds	1	fennel bulb, thinly sliced
2	Tbsp. snipped fresh fennel leafy tops	½	cup kumquats, seeds removed and thinly sliced
1	recipe Sparkling Vinaigrette	¼	tsp. salt
		⅛	tsp. pepper

1. In a small mixing bowl combine walnut pieces, pomegranate seeds, fennel tops, and 1 tablespoon of the Sparkling Vinaigrette; set aside.

2. In a large bowl combine salad greens, sliced fennel, kumquats, salt, and pepper. Drizzle with remaining Sparkling Vinaigrette. Toss gently to coat. Sprinkle with the walnut mixture. Makes 10 servings.

Sparkling Vinaigrette: In a blender container or small food processor bowl combine ½ cup coarsely chopped and seeded kumquats, ½ cup chilled sparkling white wine or chilled alcohol-free sparkling white grape beverage, ¼ cup walnut oil, 1 quartered shallot, ¼ teaspoon salt, ⅛ teaspoon pepper, and ⅛ teaspoon ground coriander or ground cardamom. Cover and blend or process until nearly smooth.

Nutrition facts per serving: 130 cal., 8 g total fat (1 g sat. fat), 0 mg chol., 139 mg sodium, 12 g carbo., 4 g fiber, and 2 g pro. Daily Values: 16% vit. A, 33% vit. C, 6% calcium, and 5% iron.

 ## Cranberry-Raspberry Spinach Salad
Prep: 35 minutes **Chill:** 1 hour

1	10-oz. pkg. fresh spinach, stems removed and torn (8 cups)	¼	cup sunflower seeds
½	cup broken walnuts	3	green onions, thinly sliced
⅓	cup dried cranberries	1	recipe Cranberry-Raspberry Vinaigrette

1. In a large bowl combine spinach, walnuts, cranberries, sunflower seeds, and green onions. Drizzle with some of the Cranberry-Raspberry Vinaigrette; toss gently to coat. Pass remaining dressing. Makes 6 servings.

Cranberry-Raspberry Vinaigrette: In a blender container or a food processor bowl place one 10-ounce package frozen red raspberries in syrup, thawed. Cover and blend or process until smooth; strain through a sieve to remove seeds. Discard seeds. In a medium saucepan combine ¼ cup sugar and 2 teaspoons cornstarch. Stir in strained raspberries, ½ cup cranberry-raspberry juice cocktail, ¼ cup red wine vinegar, ¼ teaspoon celery seed, ¼ teaspoon ground cinnamon, and ⅛ teaspoon ground cloves. Cook and stir over medium heat until thickened and bubbly; cook and stir for 2 minutes more. Transfer to a non-metal container. Cover and chill for at least 1 hour.

Nutrition facts per serving: 195 cal., 10 g total fat (1 g sat. fat), 0 mg chol., 48 mg sodium, 25 g carbo., 4 g fiber, and 4 g pro. Daily Values: 64% vit. A, 32% vit. C, 7% calcium, and 14% iron.

"I may tweak the traditional Thanksgiving dinner, but the basic flavors are always there."

—Jamie Davies

Sparkling Kumquat Salad

A little bit of bubbly adds its effervesence to this spritely toss of greens and colorful winter fruits. The glisten from such juicy gems as amber kumquats and ruby pomegranate seeds makes it sparkle even more.

Chocolate-Pear Spice Cake

You can't just tell 'em it's a pear cake. You have to show 'em, with a paper-thin slice of roasted Bosc pear. It's so easy and so elegant, you'll wonder why you didn't think of it before.

Chocolate-Pear Spice Cake

You'll get a pretty good idea of how this dessert is going to taste by breathing in its spicy aroma while it bakes.

Prep: 35 minutes **Bake:** 1 hour
Stand: 45 minutes **Cool:** 10 minutes

2 cups all-purpose flour	1 Tbsp. finely shredded orange peel
1 Tbsp. ground cinnamon	
2 tsp. baking soda	1 small Bosc pear, peeled, cored, and thinly sliced
1 tsp. ground nutmeg	
½ tsp. baking powder	2 oz. bittersweet and/or milk chocolate, coarsely chopped
½ tsp. salt	
¼ tsp. ground cloves	
6 Tbsp. butter, softened	½ cup coarsely chopped walnuts, hazelnuts (filberts), or pecans
1 cup sugar	
3 Tbsp. molasses	
2 eggs	1 recipe Pear Chips (optional)
2 cups unsweetened applesauce	Whipped cream (optional)

1. Preheat oven to 350° F. Grease and flour a 9-inch springform pan; set aside.

2. In a medium bowl stir together flour, cinnamon, baking soda, nutmeg, baking powder, salt, and cloves; set aside.

3. In a large mixing bowl combine butter, sugar, and molasses; beat with an electric mixer on medium speed until combined, scraping side of bowl constantly. Add eggs, one at a time, beating just until combined after each addition. Alternately add flour mixture and applesauce, beating on low speed until combined. Stir in orange peel.

4. Spoon the batter into the prepared pan. Arrange pear slices on top of the batter in one layer. Sprinkle with chopped chocolate and nuts. Bake about 1 hour or until the top springs back when gently touched and a toothpick inserted in the center comes out clean. Cool in pan on a wire rack for 10 minutes.

5. Remove side of pan. Serve cake warm with Pear Chips and whipped cream, if desired. Makes 10 servings.

Pear Chips: Using a mandoline or sharp knife, very thinly slice a small Bosc pear. Place pear slices on a large baking sheet lined with parchment paper. Bake in a 300° F oven for 20 to 25 minutes until golden brown and crisp, turning once.

Nutrition facts per slice: 359 cal., 15 g total fat (6 g sat. fat), 62 mg chol., 480 mg sodium, 55 g carbo., 3 g dietary fiber, and 5 g pro. Daily Values: 7% vit. A, 2% vit. C, 6% calcium, and 13% iron.

FROM THE FAMILY GARDEN

Although Jim Fobel—a food writer—hails from Ohio, he now lives near Central Park in New York City where he has a close-up view of the annual Macy's Thanksgiving Day Parade. He's never sure what he might bump into when he steps outside to watch the festivities. "Last year I came out to find three human cupcakes sitting on my front steps," he says.

When Jim was a youngster, he reaped the benefits of his family's peach orchard and enormous garden. His mother always baked bread, churned butter, put up preserves and canned fruits and vegetables. His Chocolate-Pear Spice Cake was inspired by his grandmother's spice cake, the orchard, and his own inclination to add a bit of fruit to his cake batters.

His recipe for Butterscotch Meringue Pie (page 224) came from his grandmother (below) who was on the road with her husband, an orchestra leader, sometime in the early 1900s. They had stopped at a restaurant, probably in Pennsylvania, where she ordered pie for dessert. It was so good that she asked for the recipe. The chef complied and the pie has been a family favorite ever since.

"My grandmother and Aunt Irma were avid recipe collectors," Jim Fobel says. "I have an old composition notebook—dated 1917—full of Aunt Irma's handwritten recipes" (below).

The penchant for keeping recipes was passed on through the generations. Jim started compiling his own assortment when he was a boy. "I began collecting my favorite recipes on cards," he says. "I didn't know if we'd ever have enough money to buy a cookbook, so this was how I put one together."

Visits to his aunt's house were times to scout out new recipes, and it was in her California kitchen that he learned the best way to prepare Thanksgiving dinner. He treasures this and many similar memories, which he shares in his book *Jim Fobel's Old-Fashioned Baking Book*, providing snippets of family tales, along with favorite recipes and old pictures from his photo album. He has also written *Jim Fobel's Big Flavors*.

new Caramel-Pecan Pumpkin Pie

Two favorite family pies—pecan and pumpkin—are layered in one flaky crust.

Prep: 25 minutes **Bake:** 45 minutes

2	eggs	¼	tsp. ground cinnamon
1	15-oz. can pumpkin	¼	tsp. ground nutmeg
¼	cup half-and-half, light cream, or milk	⅛	tsp. ground allspice
¾	cup granulated sugar	1	recipe Pastry for Single-Crust Pie (see recipe, page 301)
1	Tbsp. all-purpose flour		
1	tsp. finely shredded lemon peel	½	cup packed brown sugar
½	tsp. vanilla	½	cup chopped pecans
¼	tsp. salt	2	Tbsp. butter, softened

1. Preheat oven to 375° F. In a large bowl beat eggs; stir in pumpkin and half-and-half. Stir in granulated sugar, flour, lemon peel, vanilla, salt, cinnamon, nutmeg, and allspice.

2. Pour pumpkin mixture into Pastry for Single-Crust Pie. To prevent overbrowning, cover edge of pie with foil. Bake for 25 minutes.

3. Meanwhile, for topping, in a medium bowl stir together brown sugar, pecans, and butter until combined.

4. Remove foil from pie. Sprinkle topping onto pie. Bake about 20 minutes more or until a knife inserted near the center comes out clean and topping is golden and bubbly. Cool on a wire rack. Cover; refrigerate within 2 hours. Makes 8 servings.

Nutritional facts per slice: 386 cal., 19 g total fat (5 g sat. fat), 64 mg chol., 204 mg sodium, 52 g carbo., 3 g fiber, and 5 g pro. Daily Values: 239% vit. A, 5% vit C, 5% calcium, and 12% iron.

> ## "I began collecting my favorite recipes on cards as a boy, so I could put a cookbook together."
>
> —Jim Fobel

Butterscotch Meringue Pie

Jim Fobel played with his grandmother's homey pie recipe by topping it with a brown sugar meringue, although he says a traditional meringue also works well. You can simplify it even more by topping it with whipped cream instead of meringue.

Prep: 50 minutes **Bake:** 15 minutes **Chill:** 3 hours

3	egg whites	3	egg yolks
¼	tsp. cream of tartar	1	cup milk
¼	cup granulated sugar	3	Tbsp. butter, sliced
1	cup packed brown sugar	1	tsp. vanilla
¼	cup cornstarch	1	recipe Flaky Pecan Pastry
¼	tsp. salt		
1	12-oz. can (1½ cups) evaporated whole milk		

1. Preheat oven to 350° F. For meringue, in a large bowl combine egg whites and cream of tartar; whisk to blend. In a small bowl combine granulated sugar and ¼ cup brown sugar; set aside. Beat egg whites with an electric mixer on medium speed about 5 minutes or until peaks form (tips curl). Gradually add sugar mixture, 2 tablespoons at a time, beating on high speed about 5 minutes more or until stiff peaks form (tips stand straight). Let stand at room temperature while making filling.

2. For filling, in a medium saucepan combine remaining ¾ cup brown sugar, cornstarch, and salt. Whisk in about ½ cup evaporated milk; whisk in the egg yolks. Whisk in remaining evaporated milk and the 1 cup milk. Cook over medium heat, whisking constantly, until mixture is thickened and bubbly.

3. Remove pan from heat; stir in butter and vanilla until blended. Pour into Flaky Pecan Pastry. Spoon meringue over top, spreading evenly and sealing to pie shell. Bake 15 minutes.

4. Cool pie on a wire rack away from drafts for 1 hour. Chill for 3 to 6 hours. Serve cold. Makes 8 servings.

Flaky Pecan Pastry: In a medium bowl stir together 1⅓ cups flour and ¼ teaspoon salt. Using a pastry blender, cut in ¼ cup shortening and ¼ cup butter until pieces are pea-size. Stir in ⅓ cup finely chopped pecans. Combine 2 tablespoons cold water and 2 teaspoons vinegar; sprinkle over flour mixture. Gently toss with a fork. Repeat with additional 2 tablespoons cold water until dough is moistened.

Form dough into a ball. Wrap and chill for 1 hour. Preheat oven to 425° F. On a lightly floured surface roll pastry into a circle about 12 inches in diameter. Wrap pastry around rolling pin. Unroll pastry into a 9-inch pie plate. Ease pastry into plate. Trim to ½ inch beyond edge of pie plate. Fold under extra pastry; flute edge. Line with double thickness of foil. Bake for 12 minutes. Carefully remove foil. Bake for 8 to 10 minutes more or until golden brown. Cool on a wire rack.

Nutirtion facts per slice: 507 cal., 26 g total fat (12 g sat. fat), 125 mg chol., 354 mg sodium, 60 g carbo., 1 g fiber, and 9 g pro. Daily Values: 14% vit. A, 3% vit. C, 21% calcium, and 12% Iron.

Butterscotch Meringue Pie

Go for drama when you're spreading the meringue—create lots of dreamy swirls, swoops, and peaks. The only rule is to be sure to spread it to the edge so the meringue will protect the butterscotchy filling as it bakes.

Winter Squash

Summer's heat wave accelerates the growing season for squash, resulting in an abundance of winter squash that'll stick around into the winter season. As pretty as it is, squash looks great piled up as a long-term centerpiece—the hard, thick shells act as "storage containers" for sweet flesh, lasting 30 to 180 days. But cook 'em up to take full advantage of this seasonal bounty—and don't forget to save the seeds for roasting. Here are some of the more popular varieties.

Red kuri squash: The red-orange skin of this squash houses a finely textured flesh reminiscent of sweet potatoes. Red Kuri is delicious baked or steamed. Its flesh is also a great candidate for puréeing for a soup. Scrape the cooked flesh into a blender, and add seasonings and a liquid such as chicken broth, water, or cream. Then just hit the "blend" button.

Acorn squash: This favorite shows up in outfits of gold, green, and white, with wide ribs. It has tender, fine-textured flesh with a nutty, peppery taste. Serve this small, versatile squash quartered and baked, mashed, or puréed. Or create an edible bowl by halving it crosswise and baking, then filling it with cooked rice or stuffing.

Green buttercup squash: Use this for stress relief: a knife should be lightly pounded into its thick skin to aid slicing. The rewards for this effort are worth it. Its deep-yellow flesh eats like a sweet potato and holds up well through long cooking, so consider it for braising, roasting, and stewing.

Turban squash: Here are more color variations—from bright orange to green or white. Its oversized cap can be sliced off, hollowed, and used for serving soup. The seed cavity is small, which leaves room for plenty of sweet, hazelnut-flavored flesh to bake into tarts, pies, and breads.

Red Kuri Squash

PHOTOGRAPHS: JOYCE OUDKERK POOL. STORY: STEPHEN EXEL.

Acorn Squash

Green Buttercup Squash

 Squash, Pear, and Onion au Gratin

Prep: 25 minutes **Bake:** 60 minutes

1½ lb. acorn, buttercup, or turban squash	3 slices bacon, crisp-cooked, drained, and crumbled
1 large onion, sliced and separated into rings (1 cup)	2 Tbsp. chopped walnuts
1 Tbsp. butter or margarine	1 Tbsp. grated Romano cheese
1 medium pear, peeled and thinly sliced (1 cup) Salt	1 Tbsp. melted butter or margarine
3 Tbsp. fine dry bread crumbs	2 Tbsp. snipped fresh parsley (optional)

1. Preheat oven to 350° F. Slice squash in half lengthwise. Remove and discard seeds. Remove peel, if desired. Cut crosswise into ½-inch-thick slices. Set aside.

2. In a large skillet cook onion rings in 1 tablespoon hot butter for 5 to 10 minutes or until tender.

3. Arrange half of the squash slices in an 8x8x2-inch baking dish. Top with half of the pear slices. Repeat layers. Sprinkle with salt. Cover with the cooked onions. Bake, covered, about 45 minutes or until nearly tender.

4. Meanwhile, for topping, in a small bowl stir together bread crumbs, bacon, walnuts, Romano cheese, and 1 tablespoon melted butter.

5. Sprinkle topping over vegetables. Bake, uncovered, about 15 minutes more or until tender. If desired, sprinkle with parsley. Makes 6 servings.

Nutrition facts per serving: 153 cal., 8 g total fat (3 g sat. fat), 14 mg chol., 270 mg sodium, 20 g carbo., 1 g fiber, and 3 g pro. Daily Values: 146% vit. A, 35% vit. C, 7% calcium, and 6% iron.

SQUASH TIPS

■ Choose a well-shaped squash with good color for the variety. It should be heavy for its size, dry, and free from heavy bruising or cracks.

■ Store whole winter squash in a cool, dry place for up to 2 months.

■ Once you cut it, you can tightly wrap winter squash and store it for up to 4 days in the refrigerator.

■ Always scrape out the seed cavity before cooking.

■ Pierce the skin with a knife.

■ Whenever possible, cook squash, quartered or halved, in its skin. This makes it easier to peel or scrape the flesh out of the shell.

■ Steaming, microwave cooking, baking, and braising are the most effective ways to get the biggest flavor out of winter squash. Avoid boiling it.

■ In general, baked, cubed winter squash has about 40 calories for each ½-cup serving.

Turban Squash

Nuts about Nuts

PHOTOGRAPHS: COLLEEN DUFFLEY. FOOD STYLIST: BROOKE LEONARD. STORY: JOHN SCHIESZER.

Munching on a handful of nuts

not only gets you through a snack attack, but provides a batch of health benefits. Nuts—from almonds to pistachios—may protect your brain as well as your heart. They're a good source of dietary fiber, antioxidant vitamins, minerals, and other substances.

New studies suggest that chomping on nuts reduces your chances of developing heart disease and perhaps Alzheimer's disease. Researchers at Brigham and Women's Hospital in Boston recently reported that eating a handful of nuts two or more times a week may drop a person's risk of sudden cardiac death by 47 percent. The Boston researchers looked at more than 21,000 male physicians between the ages of 40 and 84. Researchers theorize that alpha-linolenic acid, a component of nuts (especially walnuts), may protect the heart by preventing a rhythm disturbance called ventricular fibrillation that causes sudden death.

The Chicago Health and Aging Project (CHAP) found that a diet rich in foods containing vitamin E may reduce the risk of Alzheimer's disease. Lead researcher Martha Clare Morris says the study showed that the more vitamin E a person consumed from food, the lower the risk of developing Alzheimer's disease. Nuts especially high in vitamin E include almonds, walnuts, hazelnuts, and pecans.

GO NUTS

Lola O'Rourke, a registered dietitian with the American Dietetic Association, recommends eating an ounce or so of nuts—a small handful—daily. Keep in mind that all nuts are high in total fat and calories. O'Rourke suggests using nuts to replace other fats in your diet. For example, try sprinkling toasted, slivered almonds onto green beans instead of butter.

For an adult nut nosh, toast 2 cups of walnut pieces in a 350° F oven about 10 minutes.

- Toss with ⅓ cup or so of golden raisins.
- Serve with tiny wedges of cheese.
- Pair the nuts with your favorite red wine.
- Munch along with a beautiful bunch of grapes.

30 Toasted Nuts with Rosemary

Start to finish: 20 minutes

Nonstick cooking spray
1 egg white
2 tsp. snipped fresh rosemary or 1 tsp. dried rosemary, crushed
½ tsp. salt
½ tsp. coarsely ground black pepper
3 cups walnuts, hazelnuts (filberts), and/or whole almonds

1. Preheat oven to 350° F. Line a 13x9x2-inch pan with foil; lightly coat the pan with cooking spray and set aside.

2. In a medium bowl lightly beat egg white with a fork until frothy. Add rosemary, salt, and pepper; beat with the fork until combined. Add the nuts; toss to coat.

3. Spread nut mixture in an even layer in the prepared pan. Bake for 15 to 20 minutes or until golden brown, stirring once.

4. Remove foil with nuts from pan; set aside to cool. Break up any large pieces. Store in an airtight container in freezer for up to 1 month. Makes about 3 cups.

Nutrition facts per tablespoon: 50 cal., 5 g total fat (1 g sat. fat), 0 mg chol., 25 mg sodium, 1 g carbo., 1 g fiber, and 1 g pro. Daily Values: 1% calcium and 2% iron.

In a nutshell (per 1-ounce serving)

ALMONDS
175 calories, 14.4 g fat,
6 g protein, 3.1 g fiber,
73 mg calcium, 7.5 mg vit. E

CASHEWS
163 calories, 13.2 g fat,
4.4 g protein, .90 g fiber,
13 mg calcium, .41 mg vit. E

HAZELNUTS (FILBERTS)
179 calories, 17.8 g fat,
3.7 g protein, 1 g fiber,
53 mg calcium, 4.4 mg vit. E

MACADAMIA NUTS
199 calories, 20 g fat,
2.4 g protein, 2.2 g fiber,
20 mg calcium, .30 mg vit. E

PEANUTS
164 calories, 13.9 g fat,
8 g protein, 2.5 g fiber,
28 mg calcium, 2.1 mg vit. E

PECANS
187 calories, 18.4 g fat,
2.3 g protein, 2.6 g fiber,
10 mg calcium, 3.5 mg vit. E

PISTACHIOS
164 calories, 13.7 g fat,
5.8 g protein, 3 g fiber,
38 mg calcium, .60 mg vit. E

WALNUTS
172 calories, 16.1 g fat,
6.9 g protein, 1.7 g fiber,
16 mg calcium, 4 mg vit. E

These sweetly flavored little cakes and cookies know their place: high on a pedestal. Just slather a generous pat of butter onto one of these spicy muffins while it's still warm, and call it dessert. Or grab a good cup of cappuccino, and start dunking the spritz cookies.

The sweet flavor comes from maple sugar, made from natural maple syrup. It may take a little effort to track down the maple sugar, but it's worth it. Look for the brownish granulated sugar in specialty food stores. Or you can order it from The Baker's Catalogue at 800/827-6836 or www.bakerscatalogue.com.

Once you buy a bag of maple sugar, you'll want to start playing with it. Try it in simple recipes to let the subtle maple flavor come through. Or stir it into tea. For starters, try these two naturally sweet recipes.

Tapping Into
Maple
Sugar

PHOTOGRAPH (MUFFINS): CHARLES SCHILLER. FOOD STYLIST: WILLIAM SMITH. PHOTOGRAPH (SUGAR): JOYCE OUDKERK POOL. FOOD STYLIST: POUKÉ. STORY JEANNE AMBROSE.

Maple Sugar
Muffins

30 Maple Sugar Muffins

Prep: 15 minutes **Bake:** 12 minutes

2¼ cups all-purpose flour
¾ tsp. baking soda
⅛ tsp. salt
1 egg
1 8-oz. carton dairy sour cream

1 cup maple granulated sugar or ¾ cup granulated sugar plus ¼ tsp. maple flavoring
½ tsp. ground allspice

1. Preheat oven to 375° F. Grease a large baking sheet. In a bowl stir together flour, baking soda, and salt. Set aside.

2. In a bowl beat egg; stir in sour cream, maple sugar, and allspice. Add flour mixture all at once; stir just until combined.

3. Turn dough out onto a well-floured surface. Knead for 10 to 12 strokes. Pat or lightly roll dough to a ½-inch thickness. Cut dough with a floured 2½-inch round cutter. Arrange muffins on the prepared baking sheet.

4. Bake for 12 to 15 minutes or until bottoms of muffins are brown. Transfer to a wire rack. Serve warm. Makes 14 muffins.

Nutrition facts per muffin: 148 cal., 4 g total fat (2 g sat. fat), 22 mg chol., 102 mg sodium, 25 g carbo., 1 g dietary fiber, and 3 g pro. Daily Values: 2% calcium and 5% iron.

new Maple Sugar Spritz

When making spritz, use only butter and do not chill the dough.

Prep: 25 minutes
Bake: 8 minutes per batch

1½ cups butter, softened
1 cup maple granulated sugar
1 tsp. baking powder
1 egg
3½ cups all-purpose flour
1 recipe Vanilla Glaze (recipe, page 233) (optional)

1. Preheat oven to 375° F. In a large mixing bowl beat butter with an electric mixer on medium to high speed for 30 seconds. Add maple sugar and baking powder. Beat until combined, scraping side of bowl occasionally. Beat in egg until combined. Beat in as much of the flour as you can with mixer. Stir in any remaining flour.

2. Force unchilled dough through a cookie press onto an ungreased cookie sheet. Bake for 8 to 10 minutes or until edges are firm but not brown. Cool on a wire rack.

3. If desired, dip tops into Vanilla Glaze. Makes about 84 cookies.

Nutrition facts per cookie: 57 cal., 4 g total fat (2 g sat. fat), 12 mg chol., 41 mg sodium, 6 g carbo., 0 g fiber, and 1 g pro. Daily Values: 3% vit. A, 1% calcium, and 2% iron.

Apricot Cherry
Slab Pie

Pie for a party

A bit sturdier than typical pies, this over-sized baking-sheet version can be eaten out of hand. Slice yourself a slab and sneak out of the kitchen without even dirtying a plate. An apple version has been around for decades, but this sweet and puckery apricot-cherry rendition will knock your socks off.

Making the fruity filling and the pastry is a snap. But rolling out the large, rectangular pastry and transferring it to the pan requires a little concentration.

A lightly floured pastry cloth is the ideal surface for rolling out the dough, but a countertop dusted with flour works too. Start by using your hands to pat the dough into a flat rectangle. Then let the rolling begin.

Flour the rolling pin, place it in the center of the dough, and roll from the center to the edges. Add just enough flour to the rolling surface to prevent the dough from sticking.

To transfer the dough to the pan, use the rolling pin method as directed in the recipe, right. Or try this: Sprinkle flour on top of the dough, brush off excess flour, then gently fold the dough in half; then fold in half again. Carefully place the dough into the pan and unfold. Patch any cracks with pastry scraps before adding the filling.

Apricot-Cherry Slab Pie

Keep a can of apricots and cherries on hand and you're ready to bake this when the pie mood strikes.

Prep: 30 minutes **Bake:** 40 minutes

3¼	cups all-purpose flour	3	15¼-oz. cans unpeeled apricot halves, drained and cut into quarters
1	tsp. salt		
1	cup shortening		
1	egg yolk	1	16-oz. can pitted tart red cherries, drained
	Milk		
½	cup sugar	1	recipe Vanilla Glaze
3	Tbsp. cornstarch		

1. For pastry, in a large mixing bowl stir together the flour and salt. Using a pastry blender, cut in shortening until pieces are pea-size. Set aside.

2. Lightly beat egg yolk in a glass measuring cup. Add enough milk to egg yolk to make ¾ cup total liquid; mix well. Stir egg yolk mixture into flour mixture; mix well. Shape one-third of the dough into a ball; set aside.

3. Form remaining two-thirds of dough into a ball. On a lightly floured surface use your hands to flatten dough. Roll dough from the center to edges into an 18x12-inch rectangle. Wrap pastry around the rolling pin; unroll into a 15x10x1-inch baking pan (pastry will hang over edges of pan).

4. Preheat oven to 375° F. In a large bowl combine sugar and cornstarch. Stir in apricots and cherries. Spoon into the crust.

5. Roll the remaining dough into a 16x11-inch rectangle; place over fruit. Bring bottom pastry up and over top pastry. Seal edges with the tines of a fork. Prick top pastry over entire surface with the tines of a fork.

6. Bake about 40 minutes or until golden brown. Cool in pan on a wire rack. Drizzle with Vanilla Glaze. Serve warm or cool. Cut into 2x3-inch bars. Makes 25 bars.

Vanilla Glaze: In a small bowl stir together 1¼ cups sifted powdered sugar and ½ teaspoon vanilla. Stir in enough milk (5 to 6 teaspoons) to make a glaze of drizzling consistency.

Nutrition facts per bar: 230 cal., 8 g total fat (2 g sat. fat), 9 mg chol., 104 mg sodium, 37 g carbo., 1 g dietary fiber, and 2 g pro. Daily Values: 16% vit. A, 3% vit. C, 2% calcium, and 8% iron.

Best-Ever **Chocolate**Cake

We tested and retested chocolate cake recipes to come up with the moistest, richest, chocolatiest cake ever. Then, we tasted chocolate frosting recipes and came up with the best of each. After we calmed down, we fine-tuned the recipe some more. Here's the result: our Best-Ever Chocolate Cake with your choice of frosting. It's so good, we made it THE chocolate cake in our just-released 12th edition of the *Better Homes and Gardens® New Cook Book*. Plus we put it on the cover of this book. So if chocolate cravings are part of your family's genetic blueprint, you'll want to end your holiday feast with this incredible cake. After all, chocolate is thicker than water.

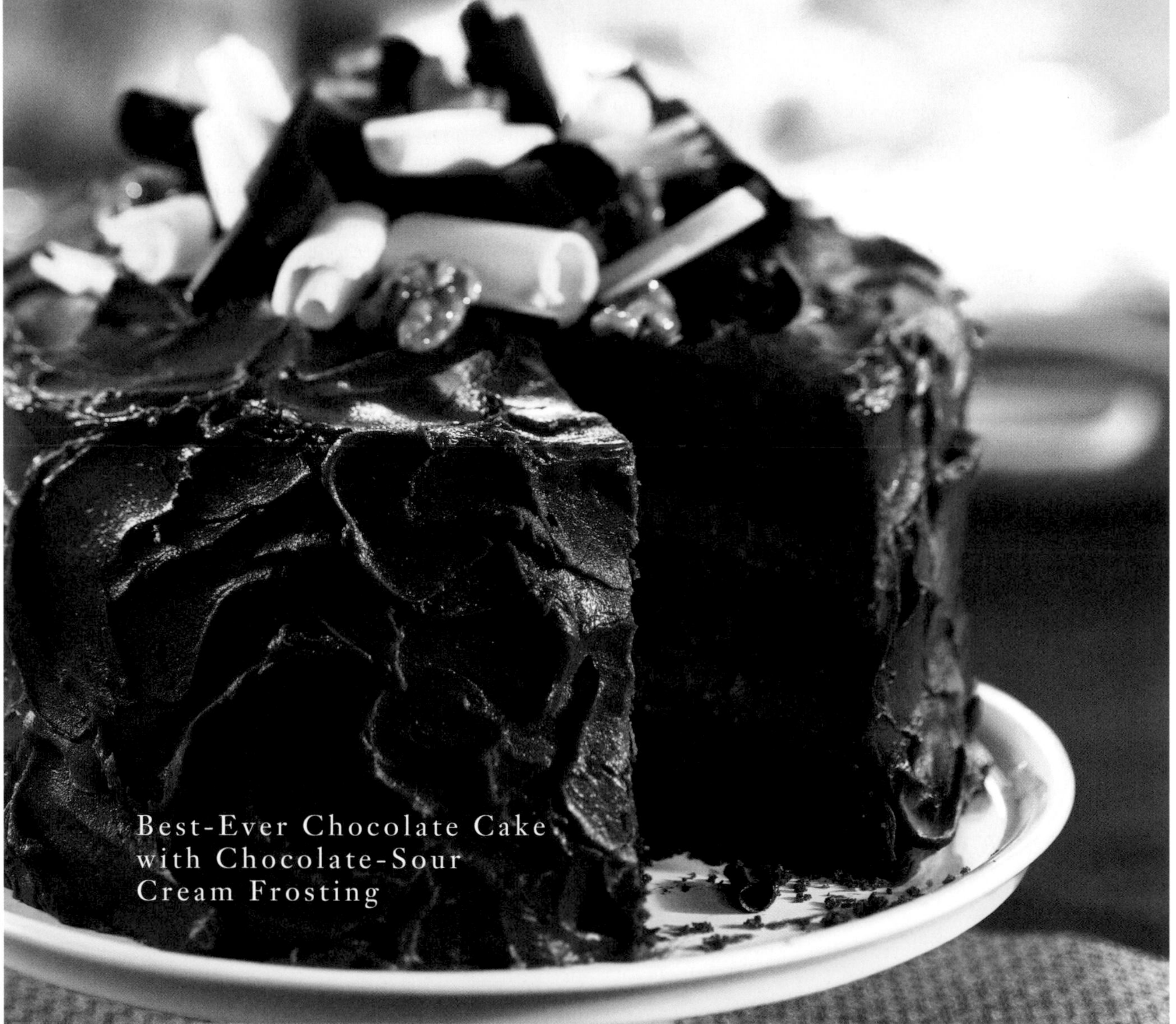

Best-Ever Chocolate Cake with Chocolate-Sour Cream Frosting

PHOTOGRAPH: MIKE DIETER. FOOD STYLIST: CHARLES WORTHINGTON. STORY STEPHEN EXEL.

Best-Ever Chocolate Cake

We pictured our best-loved cake opposite and on the cover with the Chocolate-Sour Cream Frosting and chocolate curls, but you can choose any of the frostings to the right.

Prep: 30 minutes **Bake:** 30 minutes **Cool:** 1 hour

¾	cup butter, softened	2	tsp. vanilla
3	eggs	1½	cups milk
2	cups all-purpose flour	1	recipe desired frosting
¾	cup unsweetened		(see right)
	cocoa powder		White and dark chocolate
1	tsp. baking soda		curls* (optional)
¾	tsp. baking powder	1	recipe Candied Nuts
½	tsp. salt		(optional)
2	cups sugar		

1. Allow butter and eggs to stand at room temperature for 30 minutes. Meanwhile, lightly grease bottoms of three 8x1½-inch round cake pans or two 9x1½-inch round cake pans or 8x8x2-inch cake pans. Line bottoms of pans with waxed paper. Grease and lightly flour bottoms and sides of pans. Or grease one 13x9x2-inch baking pan. Set pan(s) aside.

2. Preheat oven to 350° F. In a mixing bowl stir together flour, cocoa powder, baking soda, baking powder, and salt; set aside.

3. In a mixing bowl beat butter with an electric mixer on medium to high speed for 30 seconds. Gradually add sugar, about ¼ cup at a time, beating on medium speed for 3 to 4 minutes or until combined. Scrape side of bowl; continue beating on medium speed for 2 minutes. Add eggs, one at a time, beating after each addition (1 minute total). Beat in vanilla.

4. Alternately add flour mixture and milk to beaten mixture, beating on low speed after each addition just until combined. Beat on medium to high speed for 20 seconds more. Spread batter evenly into the prepared pan(s).

5. Bake round cake pans for 30 to 35 minutes; bake square or rectangular pan(s) for 35 to 40 minutes. The cake is done when a wooden toothpick inserted in center comes out clean.

6. Cool cake layers in pans for 10 minutes. Remove from pans. Peel off waxed paper. Cool on wire racks. Or place 13x9x2-inch cake in pan on a wire rack; cool. Frost with desired frosting. Cover and store cake in refrigerator. If desired, top with chocolate curls and Candied Nuts. Makes 12 to 16 servings.

*****Test Kitchen Tip:** To make chocolate curls, warm a chocolate bar in your apron pocket while frosting. Draw a vegetable peeler across the broad surface of the slightly warm bar.

Candied Nuts: In a 10-inch heavy skillet cook 1½ cups nuts, ½ cup sugar, 2 tablespoons butter, and ½ teaspoon vanilla until sugar begins to melt, shaking occasionally (do not stir). Cook over low heat until sugar is golden brown, stirring often. Pour onto a well-greased baking sheet. Cool. Break up.

Nutrition facts per slice with Chocolate-Sour Cream Frosting: 760 cal., 35 g total fat (20 g sat. fat), 118 mg chol., 475 mg sodium, 99 g carbo., 5 g fiber, and 7 g pro. Daily Values: 21% vit. A and 14% calcium.

 OUR FAVORITE CHOCOLATE FROSTINGS

Chocolate-Sour Cream Frosting: In a large saucepan melt one 12-ounce package (2 cups) semisweet chocolate pieces and ½ cup butter over low heat, stirring frequently. Cool for 5 minutes. Stir in one 8-ounce carton dairy sour cream. Gradually add 4½ cups sifted powdered sugar (about 1 pound), beating with an electric mixer until smooth. This frosts the tops and sides of two or three 8- or 9-inch cake layers. (Halve recipe to frost the top of a 13x9x2-inch cake.) Makes 4½ cups.

Chocolate Butter Frosting: In a very large mixing bowl combine ¾ cup softened butter and ½ cup unsweetened cocoa powder; beat with an electric mixer until smooth. Gradually add 2 cups sifted powdered sugar, beating well. Slowly beat in ¼ cup milk and 2 teaspoons vanilla. Gradually beat in 6½ cups sifted powdered sugar. Beat in enough additional milk to reach spreading consistency. This frosts the tops and sides of two or three 8- or 9-inch cake layers. (Halve the recipe to frost the top of a 13x9x2-inch cake.) Makes about 4 cups.

Chocolate-Buttermilk Frosting: In a medium saucepan combine ¼ cup butter or margarine, 3 tablespoons unsweetened cocoa powder, and 3 tablespoons buttermilk. Bring to boiling. Remove from heat. Beat in 2¼ cups sifted powdered sugar and ½ teaspoon vanilla until smooth. If desired, stir in ¾ cup chopped pecans. This frosts the tops of two or three 8- or 9-inch cake layers or a 13x9x2-inch cake. Makes about 3 cups.

Chocolate-Cream Cheese Frosting: In a large bowl combine one 8-ounce package softened cream cheese, ½ cup softened butter or margarine, ½ cup unsweetened cocoa powder, and 2 teaspoons vanilla; beat with an electric mixer until light and fluffy. Gradually add 2 cups sifted powdered sugar, beating well. Gradually beat in 3¼ to 3¾ cups sifted powdered sugar to reach spreading consistency. This frosts the tops and sides of two or three 8- or 9-inch layers. (Halve the recipe to frost a 13x9x2-inch cake.) Makes about 3⅔ cups.

Coconut-Pecan Frosting: In a medium saucepan slightly beat 1 egg. Stir in one 5-ounce can (⅔ cup) evaporated milk, ⅔ cup sugar, and ¼ cup butter. Cook and stir over medium heat for 6 to 8 minutes or until thickened and bubbly. Remove from heat; stir in 1⅓ cups flaked coconut and ½ cup chopped pecans. Cover and cool thoroughly. This frosts the tops of two or three 8- or 9-inch cake layers or a 13x9x2-inch cake for a German chocolate-style cake. Makes about 3 cups.

a gift of HOT CHOCOLATE

Finish off a cup of this outrageously chocolaty hot chocolate, and you'll want to stretch out on the couch with a sigh. Or maybe you'd rather go back for another steamy cup. Either way, you'll want to keep a pretty good stash of this handy drink mix for yourself or your very, very good friends.

A sprinkling of cinnamon added to the mix of chocolate chunks plus cocoa powder intensifies the flavor big time. Include a little toasted anise seed for its subtle licorice hint, and you'll stir up a combo like none you've ever tasted. This was intended as a homemade holiday gift, but chances are you'll want it all for yourself. Or maybe you'll succumb to the spirit of the season and share it with someone special.

If you do decide to make a gift of it, package it prettily, perhaps in a shiny silver tin wrapped in an oversized ribbon. You can also tuck in some interesting and whimsical stir sticks. How about candy canes, or stick candy, cinnamon sticks, colorful plastic spoons dipped into chocolate, or stick-style rolled wafer cookies?

Be sure to include the simple instructions for preparing the hot chocolate mix. Or, if you forget, maybe the recipients of your gift will invite you over to show them exactly how it's made. Nice trick.

All-Is-Calm Hot Chocolate Mix
Start to finish: 20 minutes

8   oz. semisweet or bittersweet
    chocolate chunks or pieces
⅔   cup sugar
½   cup unsweetened cocoa powder
½   tsp. anise seed, toasted*
    and crushed
½   tsp. ground cinnamon

1. For mix, in a large bowl combine chocolate chunks or pieces, sugar, cocoa powder, anise seed, and cinnamon. Spoon into a container, jar, or self-sealing plastic bag. Cover or seal. Makes 12 servings. Include the following directions:

All-Is-Calm Hot Chocolate: In a medium saucepan combine ⅔ cup mix and ¼ cup water. Stir over medium heat until chocolate is melted and mixture is smooth. Whisk in 4 cups milk, half-and-half, or light cream (you'll get a richer result using half-and-half or light cream); heat through, whisking occasionally. Pour into four mugs. Makes 4 servings.

***Test Kitchen Tip:** To toast anise seed, place anise in a shallow baking pan. Bake in a 350° F oven about 5 minutes or until toasted and aromatic.

Nutirtion facts per serving: 272 cal., 11 g total fat (6 g sat. fat), 18 mg chol., 122 mg sodium, 30 g carbo., 3 g fiber, and 9 g pro. Daily Values: 4% vit. C, 34% calcium, and 4% iron.

All-Is-Calm Hot Chocolate

Dec

Smoky Mountain Holiday

Plus...

With the holidays coming, our to-do-list is long: baking homemade gifts, gathering greens, trimming the tree, and making it all fun.

e m b e r

Grits with
Smoked Oysters
recipe on page 243

Collard Greens
with Tasso Ham

Braised Fresh Pork Hocks
with Bourbon Gravy

Smoky Mountain

Holiday

Grab a coat and a walking stick. You're all set to enjoy the
simple earthy cuisine of a cozy inn in Tennessee, and
celebrate the holidays with down-home country style.

PHOTOGRAPHS: COLLEEN DUFFLEY. FOOD STYLIST: BROOKE LEONARD. PROP STYLISTS: KAREN JOHNSON, JAMES PRINE, MARY CELESTE BEALL. STORY: NANCY WALL HOPKINS.

Braised Fresh Pork Hocks
with Bourbon Gravy

Start the gravy by lifting the tasty browned bits from the pan with a generous splash of smooth Southern whiskey.

Prep: 30 minutes **Bake:** 2½ hours

6	fresh pork hocks (about 5½ lb.)	1	small leek, coarsely chopped
¾	tsp. salt	1	small stalk celery, coarsely chopped
¾	tsp. pepper		
¾	cup all-purpose flour	1	small carrot, coarsely chopped
3	Tbsp. olive oil		
¼	cup bourbon whiskey	4	cloves garlic, peeled
1	14-oz. can beef broth	3	sprigs fresh thyme
3	Tbsp. (¼ of a 6-oz. can) tomato paste	1	bay leaf
		Fresh sage leaves (optional)	
1½	cups coarsely chopped sweet onion, such as Vidalia (see page 279)	Roasted garlic bulb (see page 211) (optional)	

1. Preheat oven to 325° F. Tie each pork hock tightly around the middle with 100-percent-cotton string. Season meat with salt and pepper. Place flour in a shallow dish. Add pork; turn to coat with flour, shaking off excess. Discard any extra flour.

2. In a 10- to 12-quart stewpot brown pork on all sides in hot oil over medium heat; remove from pan. Drain off excess oil.

3. To deglaze pan, carefully add bourbon, using a wooden spoon to scrape browned bits off the bottom of the pan and continuing to cook until nearly all of the liquid is gone.

4. Add beef broth and tomato paste, whisking together until smooth. Bring to boiling. Return pork to pan along with onions, leek, celery, carrot, garlic, thyme, and bay leaf. Return to boiling. Cover with oven-going lid or foil; bake for 2½ to 3 hours or until meat pulls apart easily with a fork.

5. Transfer pork to a serving platter; remove string. For sauce, skim fat from vegetable mixture; discard bay leaf and thyme sprigs. Season meat with salt and pepper. Spoon sauce over pork. If desired, garnish with sage leaves and roasted garlic. Makes 6 servings.

Nutrition facts per serving: 351 cal., 19 g total fat (5 g sat. fat), 55 mg chol., 611 mg sodium, 20 g carbo., 2 g fiber, and 19 g pro. Daily Values: 34% vit. A, 12% vit. C, 4% calcium, and 13% iron.

30 Collard Greens with Tasso Ham

Tasso is a Louisianan ham—usually pork shoulder that's richly seasoned. You can substitute another spiced ham.

Start to finish: 30 minutes

4½	lb. collard greens	⅓	cup packed brown sugar
1½	cups finely chopped tasso ham or Cajun-spiced cooked ham	⅓	cup red wine vinegar
		1	tsp. salt
2	Tbsp. clarified butter or butter	1	tsp. pepper

1. Remove stems and thick ribs from collard greens. In a 4-quart Dutch oven immerse greens, one-third at a time, in boiling water for 30 seconds. Remove with tongs or slotted spoon; drain well in a colander. Coarsely chop greens; set aside.

2. In a 12-inch skillet cook and stir tasso ham in hot butter over medium-high heat for 1 minute. Add brown sugar and vinegar; stir until sugar is dissolved. Add greens, salt, and pepper. Cook and stir until heated through. Serve warm. Makes 6 to 8 servings.

Nutrition facts per serving: 218 cal., 9 g total fat (1 g sat. fat), 22 mg chol., 998 mg sodium, 23 g carbo., 7 g fiber, and 13 g pro. Daily Values: 141% vit. A, 63% vit. C, 28% calcium, and 7% iron.

Grits with
Smoked Oysters

Pictured upper left: Mary Celeste Beall and daughter Cameron. Above: Chef John Fleer. Right: Local storyteller, Willard M. Abbott, and guest, Sam Carroll.

Grits with Smoked Oysters
Prep: 45 minutes **Bake:** 30 minutes

4	cups reduced-sodium chicken broth	6	Tbsp. butter
1⅓	cups stone ground yellow grits	4	egg yolks
½	tsp. ground red pepper	½	cup grated dry Monterey Jack or Parmesan cheese
1¼	cups chopped red sweet pepper	2	Tbsp. all purpose flour
1	cup chopped celery	12	oz. smoked oysters*, canned or fresh, drained and coarsely chopped
½	cup bias-sliced green onions	4	egg whites
1	Tbsp. snipped fresh parsley		Nonstick cooking spray

1. Preheat oven to 350° F. In a large saucepan bring chicken broth to boiling. Gradually whisk in grits and ground red pepper. Reduce heat. Cook, uncovered, about 25 minutes or until mixture is very thick, stirring frequently.

2. Meanwhile, in a large skillet cook and stir red sweet pepper, celery, green onions, and parsley in 1 tablespoon hot butter over medium heat about 5 minutes or just until tender; set aside.

3. In a small mixing bowl beat egg yolks; set aside. Remove cooked grits from heat; stir in remaining butter until melted. Gradually stir about 1 cup of the grits into the egg yolks. Return yolk mixture to the remaining grits. Stir in cooked vegetables, cheese, and flour. Gently stir in oysters; set aside.

4. In a mixing bowl beat egg whites with an electric mixer on high speed until stiff peaks form (tips stand straight); fold egg whites, one-third at a time, into the grits mixture. Lightly coat a 3-quart rectangular baking dish with cooking spray. Spoon grits mixture into baking dish.

5. Bake, uncovered, about 30 minutes or until a knife inserted off center comes out clean. Makes 10 to 12 servings.

*Test Kitchen Tip: If smoked oysters are unavailable, you can smoke the oysters at home. Soak 2 cups hickory or mesquite wood chips in enough water to cover for 1 hour. Drain before using. Place 1½ pounds drained, shucked oysters, half at a time, in a single layer in an 11x8-inch foil pan or grill pan. In a charcoal grill, arrange medium-hot coals around the outside edge of the grill. Test for medium heat in the center of the grill. Sprinkle the drained wood chips over the coals. Place the pan with the oysters in the center of the grill rack. Cover and smoke for 10 to 12 minutes or until edges of oysters begin to curl. Repeat with remaining oysters.

Nutrition facts per serving: 291 cal., 16 g total fat (8 g sat. fat), 114 mg chol., 513 mg sodium, 24 g carbo., 1 g fiber, and 14 g pro. Daily Values: 35% vit. A, 54% vit. C, 8% calcium, and 33% iron.

AT HOME ON THE FARM

Way down a winding hollow, along the foothills of the Great Smoky Mountains, there's a country house hotel in Walland, Tennessee, known as Blackberry Farm. Even when hunger beckons, there's plenty to do—a homey feast under a cottage roof, a luncheon hike up a rocky path, a cookie-and-nog storytelling session, and a quiet breakfast by a cozy crackling fire. After welcoming guests for nearly 30 years, proprietors Kreis and Sandy Beall want to make folks feel comfortable from the moment they arise from their fluffy feather beds until they've eaten their last bite of dessert. At Christmastime, this translates to greenery dripping from doorways, freshly cut trees, heirloom decorations, and heady aromas of baked breads, cookies, cider, and candies.

"A Tennessee Christmas is simple and relaxed. Ideally, it's about great food and how many extended kin you can gather in one place for great food," says executive chef John Fleer. "We believe that great cooking is nourishment for the soul. It should never intimidate and should always satisfy. My grandmother called it comfort food; I call it foothill's cuisine." Like Christmas at Blackberry, Fleer describes his cuisine as wandering a fine line between familiar and new, refined and rugged, and straightforward and simple. It's humble and always delicious. "We don't float up into the never land of gourmet but stay rooted in what makes sense."

Fleer often relies on an old Irish proverb, "The laughter is brightest where the food is best." He says, "While guests celebrate the holidays with us, we hope they experience the table as a place where the spirit of the season is rekindled."

Kreis Beall adds, "The main thing is: there is no right or wrong way to relish the season. It's the spirit behind the effort that becomes memory."

CHRISTMAS EVE FEAST

Braised Fresh Pork Hocks with Bourbon Gravy (recipe, page 241)

Grits with Smoked Oysters (recipe, left)

Collard Greens with Tasso Ham (recipe, page 241)

Orange Chess Pie (recipe, page 247)

Chocolate Chess Pie (recipe, page 247)

Wine or sparkling water

Peanut Soup

Even though it's native to Williamsburg, this soup has been a must-have for Chef Fleer's family and for Blackberry guests. "It's how my family has always started Christmas dinner," says Fleer.

Prep: 30 minutes **Bake:** 25 minutes **Cook:** 30 minutes

1 cup chopped shallots (two 3-oz. pkg.)	2 Tbsp. chopped unsalted raw Spanish peanuts
1 cup finely chopped celery	1 49-oz. can chicken broth (6 cups)
¼ cup butter	½ cup whipping cream
2 Tbsp. all-purpose flour	Ground red pepper
¾ cup creamy peanut butter	1 cup Red Spiced Peanuts

1. In a large saucepan cook shallots and celery in hot butter over medium heat about 5 minutes or until tender, stirring occasionally. Stir flour into shallot mixture; cook and stir about 2 minutes or until flour starts to brown.

2. Stir in peanut butter and peanuts; cook until peanut butter melts. Gradually whisk in chicken broth. Bring to boiling (watch carefully to prevent soup from boiling over); reduce heat. Simmer, uncovered, for 30 minutes, stirring occasionally.

3. Stir in cream and ground red pepper. Garnish with Red Spiced Peanuts. Makes 8 servings.

Nutrition facts serving: 396 cal., 34 g total fat (12 g sat. fat), 42 mg chol., 1,008 mg sodium, 17 g carbo., 3 g fiber, and 12 g pro. Daily Values: 16% vit. A, 4% vit. C, 5% calcium, and 8% iron.

Red Spiced Peanuts: Preheat oven to 350° F. Line a 15x10x1-inch baking pan with foil; grease the foil and set aside. In a large skillet melt ¼ cup butter over medium heat. Stir in ¼ cup granulated sugar, ¼ cup packed brown sugar, ½ teaspoon salt, and ¼ teaspoon ground red pepper. Stir in ¼ cup water. Cook and stir until sugars dissolve. Add 2 cups unsalted raw Spanish peanuts. Bring to boiling. Boil gently, uncovered, for 5 minutes. Transfer nut mixture to the prepared pan, spreading in an even layer. Bake, uncovered, for 25 minutes, stirring occasionally. Transfer foil lining to a wire rack. Cool completely. Break nut mixture into small clusters. Store in an airtight container for up to 2 weeks. Freeze for longer storage. Makes 3½ cups (28 servings).

Nutrition facts serving: 89 cal., 7 g total fat (2 g sat. fat), 5 mg chol., 62 mg sodium, 5 g carbo., 1 g fiber, and 3 g pro. Daily Values: 1% vit. A, 1% calcium, and 3% iron.

 ### Smoked Trout Club Sandwiches
Prep: 20 minutes **Chill:** up to 8 hours

12 slices firm-textured white bread (Pain de Mie), toasted	8 slices bacon, crisp-cooked, drained, and halved crosswise
1 cup Scallion Mayonnaise	1 to 1½ cups arugula
1 lb. smoked trout or smoked white fish, bones removed and broken into chunks	½ cup Pecan Sweet Hot Mustard Sauce or honey mustard

1. Spread one side of 4 bread slices with ½ cup of the Scallion Mayonnaise. Top, mayonnaise side up, with half of the trout. Top each with 2 bacon half-pieces and half of the arugula.

2. Spread both sides of 4 more bread slices with Pecan Sweet Hot Mustard Sauce. Lay slices on top of the bacon layer. Top with remaining trout, bacon pieces, and arugula.

3. Spread one side of remaining 4 bread slices with remaining ½ cup of the Scallion Mayonnaise. Place, mayonnaise side down, onto bacon. Wrap in plastic wrap; chill for up to 8 hours. Before serving, cut sandwiches in half. Makes 8 servings.

Nutrition facts per serving: 419 cal., 26 g total fat (4 g sat. fat), 77 mg chol., 789 mg sodium, 33 g carbo., 1 g fiber, and 15 g pro. Daily Values: 2% vit. A, 5% vit. C, 14% calcium, and 10% iron.

Scallion Mayonnaise: In a small saucepan cook 6 chopped green onions in 1 teaspoon hot cooking oil for 1 to 2 minutes or until bright green and just tender. Remove from heat and cool. In a blender container or food processor bowl combine cooked green onions, 6 chopped fresh green onions, 1 cup mayonnaise or salad dressing, 1½ teaspoons lemon juice, ½ teaspoon kosher salt, and ¼ teaspoon pepper. Cover and blend or process until smooth. Cover and store in the refrigerator for up to 1 week. Makes 1½ cups.

Nutrition facts per tablespoon: 70 cal., 8 g total fat (1 g sat. fat), 3 mg chol., 91 mg sodium, 1 g carbo., 0 g fiber, and 0 g pro. Daily Values: 2% vit. C and 1% iron.

Pecan Sweet Hot Mustard Sauce: In a medium bowl stir together 1½ cups packed brown sugar; ½ cup chopped pecans, toasted; ½ cup Dijon-style mustard; ½ cup stone ground mustard; 2 tablespoons cider vinegar; and ½ teaspoon bottled hot pepper sauce. Cover and store in the refrigerator for up to 1 week. Makes 1½ cups.

Nutrition facts per tablespoon: 44 cal., 2 g total fat (0 g sat. fat), 0 mg chol., 99 mg sodium, 6 g carbo., 0 g fiber, and 1 g pro. Daily Values: 2% calcium and 2% iron.

Smoked Trout Club
Sandwiches, Peanut Soup,
and Pear Isaacs, recipe, page 248

Orange and Chocolate Chess Pies

Can't decide which kind of pie to have? Stack 'em high and slice through two or three. Of course, your slices would be extra-thin.

Orange Chess Pie

Prep: 25 minutes **Bake:** 40 minutes

4	eggs	1	Tbsp. finely shredded orange peel
1¼	cups sugar		
⅓	cup butter, melted	1	Tbsp. orange liqueur
¼	cup buttermilk	¼	tsp. salt
2	Tbsp. cornmeal	⅛	tsp. ground nutmeg
2	Tbsp. vanilla	1	recipe Sweet Pastry Crust

1. Preheat oven to 325° F. For filling, in a medium mixing bowl slightly beat eggs with a rotary beater or fork. Stir in sugar, butter, buttermilk, cornmeal, vanilla, orange peel, orange liqueur, salt, and nutmeg.

2. Pour filling into partially baked Sweet Pastry Crust. Bake about 40 minutes or until edges are puffed and golden (center may still shake a bit). Cool in pan on a wire rack. Refrigerate within 2 hours; cover pie for longer storage. Makes 8 servings.

Sweet Pastry Crust: Preheat oven to 375° F. In a medium bowl stir together 1¼ cups all-purpose flour, 1 tablespoon sugar, and ¼ teaspoon salt. Using a pastry blender, cut in ⅓ cup shortening until pieces are pea-size. Sprinkle 1 tablespoon cold water over part of the mixture; gently toss with a fork. Push moistened dough to the side of the bowl. Repeat, using 1 tablespoon cold water at a time, until all the dough is moistened (4 to 5 tablespoons water total).

Form dough into a ball. On a lightly floured surface flatten dough. Roll out dough to a 12 inch circle. Transfer pastry to a 9-inch pie plate. (If stacking pies, line the bottom of the pie plate with foil. Lightly coat foil and sides of plate with cooking spray. Line the pie plate with pastry.)

Trim pastry to ½ inch beyond edge of pie plate. Fold extra pastry under and crimp edge as desired. Cover pastry with a double thickness of foil. Bake for 10 minutes. Remove foil cover from top. Bake about 5 minutes more or until set and dry.

Nutrition facts per slice: 401 cal., 19 g total fat (8 g sat. fat), 128 mg chol., 268 mg sodium, 50 g carbo., 1 g fiber, and 6 g pro. Daily Values: 10% vit. A, 3% vit. C, 4% calcium, and 8% iron.

Chocolate Chess Pie

Prep: 30 minutes **Bake:** 40 minutes

3	oz. bittersweet chocolate, chopped	¼	tsp. salt
		2	Tbsp. whipping cream
6	Tbsp. butter, cut up	1	Tbsp. bourbon whiskey
4	eggs	1½	tsp. vanilla
1⅓	cups sugar	1	recipe Sweet Pastry Crust
2	Tbsp. all-purpose flour		

1. Preheat oven to 325° F. For filling, in a small, heavy saucepan combine chocolate and butter; cook and stir over low heat until melted.

2. Meanwhile, in a medium mixing bowl slightly beat eggs with a rotary beater or fork. Beat in sugar, flour, and salt. Stir in whipping cream and melted chocolate mixture. Stir in bourbon and vanilla.

3. Pour filling into partially baked Sweet Pastry Crust. Bake about 40 minutes or until set (top will puff and fall on cooling, leaving a slightly crackled crust). Cool the pie in pan on a wire rack. Refrigerate within 2 hours; cover pie for longer storage. Makes 8 servings.

Nutrition facts per slice: 469 cal., 25 g total fat (12 g sat. fat), 136 mg chol., 273 mg sodium, 56 g carbo., 1 g fiber, and 6 g pro. Daily Values: 11% vit. A, 1% vit. C, 3% calcium, and 10% iron.

Test Kitchen Tip: For a tip-top serving idea, prepare 2 Orange Chess Pies and 1 Chocolate Chess Pie. Carefully remove whole pies from each pie plate, using foil liners. Stack the pies on a platter with the chocolate pie in the center; sprinkle with fresh blackberries.

Cranberry-Black Walnut Coffee Cake

Prep: 45 minutes **Bake:** 1 hour 15 minutes

2 cups dried cranberries (8 oz.)	2 tsp. baking powder
1 cup apple cider	1 tsp. ground cinnamon
½ cup packed brown sugar	¼ tsp. salt
½ cup water	4 eggs
1 2-inch piece stick cinnamon	1 cup whole milk
3 cups all-purpose flour	1 cup butter, melted
1 cup granulated sugar	1 tsp. vanilla
1 cup black or English walnuts, toasted and ground	1 recipe Walnut Streusel Topping

1. In a medium saucepan combine cranberries, cider, brown sugar, water, and cinnamon stick. Bring to boiling, stirring to dissolve sugar. Remove from heat. Cover; let stand 10 minutes.

2. Preheat oven to 325° F. Grease a 10-inch springform pan; set aside. Drain cranberries; discard liquid and cinnamon stick. Coarsely chop cranberries; set aside.

3. In a large mixing bowl stir together flour, granulated sugar, nuts, baking powder, ground cinnamon, and salt. In a medium bowl lightly beat eggs; stir in milk, melted butter, and vanilla. Add egg mixture to flour mixture; stir just until moistened. Spoon batter into prepared pan. Sprinkle center with cranberries to within 1 inch of the outside edge.

4. Sprinkle Walnut Streusel Topping evenly over top. Bake, uncovered, for 1 hour and 15 minutes or until a wooden toothpick inserted near the center comes out clean. Remove and cool for 15 minutes in the pan on a wire rack. Before serving, remove side of springform pan. Serve warm. Makes 12 servings.

Walnut Streusel Topping: In a food processor bowl combine ⅔ cup all-purpose flour, ⅓ cup packed brown sugar, ¼ cup sugar, ¾ teaspoon ground cinnamon, ¼ teaspoon salt, and ¼ teaspoon vanilla. Cover and process several seconds or until combined. Cut up ⅓ cup butter; add to flour mixture. Cover and process with several on-off turns until crumbly. (Or in a medium mixing bowl stir together flour, sugars, cinnamon, salt, and vanilla. Using a pastry blender, cut in butter until crumbly.) Stir in ¼ cup chopped black or English walnuts.

Nutrition facts per slice: 619 cal., 32 g total fat (15 g sat. fat), 132 mg chol., 422 mg sodium, 77 g carbo., 3 g fiber, and 10 g pro. Daily Values: 20% vit. A, 1% vit. C, 11% calcium, and 16% iron.

⬛ Pear Issacs

Chef Fleer named these pear cookies "Isaacs" since "Newton" was already taken by figs. Pictured on page 245.

Prep: 1 hour **Chill:** 2 hours **Bake:** 20 minutes per batch

6 medium pears, peeled, cored, and cut into eighths	½ cup sugar
	1 tsp. finely chopped crystallized ginger
1 tsp. finely shredded lemon peel	½ tsp. vanilla
1 Tbsp. lemon juice	1 recipe Cream Cheese Pastry
3 Tbsp. butter	Coarse sugar

1. For filling, in a large bowl toss together pears, lemon peel, and juice. In a large skillet, melt butter. Add pear mixture, sugar, and ginger. Stir gently until sugar is dissolved. Cook over medium heat for 15 to 20 minutes or until pears are translucent, stirring occasionally. Strain pears in colander, reserving syrup; transfer pears to a bowl. Return syrup to skillet. Heat to boiling; reduce heat and simmer syrup, uncovered, about 5 minutes or until slightly thick and golden brown. Stir in ½ teaspoon vanilla. Stir into pears; cover and chill.

2. Preheat oven to 350° F. On a lightly floured surface roll one portion of Cream Cheese Pastry into a 9-inch square. Transfer to a cookie sheet, placing dough near one end of sheet. Spoon one-fourth of the pear mixture (about ½ cup) over half of the dough to within ½ inch of edges. Brush edges with water. Fold uncovered dough over filling; press edges to seal. Brush top of dough with water; sprinkle with coarse sugar. Repeat with another portion of dough and one-fourth of the filling, placing second rolled dough near the other end of cookie sheet. Bake for 20 minutes or until light brown and edges are firm. Cool on wire rack. Repeat with remaining dough and filling.

3. With a serrated knife, trim edges to make a smooth edge. Cut each portion crosswise into 6 cookies. Makes 24 cookies.

Cream Cheese Pastry: In a medium bowl stir together 3 cups all-purpose flour, 1 teaspoon baking powder, ½ teaspoon salt, ½ teaspoon ground cinnamon, and ¼ teaspoon baking soda. In a large mixing bowl combine one 3-ounce package cream cheese, softened, and ¼ cup softened butter; beat with an electric mixer on medium speed for 30 seconds. Add 1 cup packed brown sugar; beat until fluffy. Beat in 2 egg whites and 1 teaspoon vanilla. Beat or stir in flour mixture. Divide dough into fourths; wrap each portion in plastic wrap. Chill for 2 to 3 hours or until firm enough to handle.

Nutrition facts per cookie: 182 cal., 5 g total fat (3 g sat. fat), 13 mg chol., 133 mg sodium, 32 g carbo., 1 g fiber, and 2 g pro. Daily Values: 4% vit. A, 3% vit. C, 3% calcium, and 6% iron.

Cranberry-Black Walnut Coffee Cake

Baking this fruit-studded coffee cake in a springform pan produces a cake that serves a crowd. Set it out warm on your breakfast buffet and watch it disappear.

Tennessee Orange
Biscuits with
Blackberry Gravy

Jackson's
Cereal Blend

Wake-Up
Smoothies

Tennessee Orange Biscuits with Blackberry Gravy

The farm uses its namesake blackberries in dishes year-round, including the sauce for these tender biscuits.

Prep: 30 minutes **Bake:** 12 minutes

3½	cups sifted cake flour	¼	cup whipping cream
3	Tbsp. sugar	1	Tbsp. orange juice
4	tsp. baking powder	1	Tbsp. water
1	Tbsp. finely shredded orange peel		Granulated sugar or extra-fine granulated sugar
1	tsp. salt	1	cup fresh or frozen blackberries, thawed
½	cup butter, chilled		
3	eggs	1	cup Blackberry Jam
½	cup whole milk	¼	cup butter, softened

1. Preheat oven to 400° F. In a large mixing bowl stir together cake flour, 3 tablespoons sugar, baking powder, orange peel, and salt. Using a pastry blender, cut in the ½ cup butter until mixture resembles coarse crumbs. In a medium bowl whisk together 2 of the eggs, milk, whipping cream, and orange juice. Add to dry ingredients; stir just to combine.

2. Turn dough out onto a well-floured surface (the dough will be slightly sticky). Knead by folding and pressing dough 10 to 12 strokes or until nearly smooth. Roll out dough to ¾-inch thickness. Cut with a floured 2- or 3-inch round cutter.

3. On a greased baking sheet arrange cutouts 1 inch apart. In a small bowl beat the remaining egg and water. Brush tops of cutouts with egg mixture; sprinkle with additional sugar. Bake for 12 to 14 minutes or until golden.

4. For blackberry gravy, stir blackberries into blackberry jam. Transfer biscuits to a wire rack; cool slightly. To serve, spread tops of biscuits with softened butter; top with blackberry gravy. To store leftover gravy, cover and refrigerate for up to 2 weeks. Makes 12 small or 8 large biscuits.

Nutrition facts per small biscuit: 337 cal., 16 g total fat (9 g sat. fat), 94 mg chol., 475 mg sodium, 43 g carbo., 2 g fiber, and 5 g pro. Daily Values: 13% vit. A, 6% vit. C, 13% calcium, and 16% iron.

30 low fat Fresh Blackberry Jam

Start to finish: 15 minutes

1. In a large saucepan combine 3 cups fresh or frozen blackberries, ⅓ cup sugar, ¼ cup sorghum or molasses, and 3 tablespoons blackberry brandy or orange juice. Bring to boiling; reduce heat. Cook, uncovered, over medium heat for 5 minutes, stirring occasionally. In a small bowl stir together ¼ cup orange juice and 3 tablespoons cornstarch; add to berry mixture in saucepan. Cook and stir until thickened and bubbly. Cook and stir for 2 minutes more. Remove from heat; cool slightly. To store, cover and chill for up to 2 weeks. Makes 2 cups.

Nutrition facts per tablespoon: 33 cal., 0 g total fat (0 g sat. fat), 0 mg chol., 1 mg sodium, 8 g carbo., 1 g fiber, and 0 g pro. Daily Values: 2% vit. C, 1% calcium, and 1% iron.

30 low fat Jackson's Cereal Blend

John Fleer's 10-year-old son, Jackson, created the farm's most popular cereal—a mix of sweet crunch and healthful bran.

Prep: 10 minutes

1	18.3-oz. pkg. whole bran cereal (about 8 cups)	1	14-oz. pkg. seven grain and sesame cereal (about 7 cups)
1	18-oz. pkg. low-fat granola (about 6 cups)	2	cups dried cranberries and/or raisins
1	16-oz. pkg. Grape Nuts® cereal (about 4 cups)		

1. In a very large storage container toss together cereals and cranberries. Cover tightly; store at room temperature for up to 2 weeks. For longer storage, seal in freezer bags and freeze for up to 3 months. Makes about 36 servings.

Nutrition facts per serving: 193 cal., 2 g total fat (0 g sat. fat), 0 mg chol., 143 mg sodium, 45 g carbo., 8 g fiber, and 5 g pro. Daily Values: 10% vit. A, 12% vit. C, 8% calcium, and 33% iron.

30 low fat Wake-Up Smoothies

Prep: 10 minutes

1	8-oz. carton plain low-fat yogurt	2	Tbsp. honey
1	cup apple cider, chilled	¼	tsp. ground white pepper (optional)
1	cup fat-free milk	¼	tsp. ground cinnamon
1	banana, sliced	¼	tsp. ground allspice
½	cup fresh blackberries	⅛	tsp. ground nutmeg

1. In a blender container combine all ingredients. Cover; blend until smooth. Pour into tall glasses. Makes 4 servings.

Nutrition facts per serving: 156 cal., 1 g total fat (1 g sat. fat), 5 mg chol., 74 mg sodium, 32 g carbo., 2 g fiber, and 6 g pro. Daily Values: 4% vit. A, 14% vit. C, 19% calcium, and 3% iron.

HOLIDAY BREAKFAST BUFFET

Jackson's Cereal Blend (recipe, above)

Tennessee Orange Biscuits
with Blackberry Gravy (recipe, left)

Cranberry-Black Walnut Coffee Cake (recipe, page 248)

Fresh fruit plate

Wake-Up Smoothies (recipe, above)

Coffee or tea

White Chocolate and Jam S'Mores

Sorghum laces together the blackberry jam in ooey gooey, kid-pleasing s'mores. With homemade Chocolate Graham Crackers, white chocolate, and blackberry jam, s'mores have just never been so good.

30 White Chocolate and Jam S'Mores
Prep: 8 minutes

1 oz. white baking bar
2 Chocolate Graham Crackers (see recipe, right)
3 marshmallows, toasted*

2 Tbsp. Fresh Blackberry Jam (see recipe, page 251) or purchased blackberry jam

1. For each s'more, place the white baking bar on top of one of the Chocolate Graham Crackers. Place marshmallows on top of the bar. Spoon Fresh Blackberry Jam over the marshmallows; top with remaining cracker.

*Test Kitchen Tip: To toast marshmallows, place marshmallows on the end of a long skewer and hold over a campfire flame or hot coals for 30 to 60 seconds, turning frequently. Makes 1 serving.

Broiler method: For 4 s'mores, place 4 Chocolate Graham Crackers on a foil-lined baking sheet. Top each with 1 ounce white baking bar. Top each with 3 marshmallows. Broil 4 inches from the heat for 30 to 60 seconds or until marshmallows are toasted and chocolate softens and begins to melt. Remove from broiler; add 2 tablespoons Fresh Blackberry Jam to each. Top with another Chocolate Graham Cracker. Makes 4 servings.

Nutrition facts per serving: 465 cal., 14 g total fat (9 g sat. fat), 15 mg chol., 199 mg sodium, 80 g carbo., 1 g fiber, and 4 g pro. Daily Values: 3% vit. A, 6% vit. C, 6% calcium, and 5% iron.

Alphabet Chocolate Graham Crackers

Sorghum Gingersnaps
"I'm completely infatuated with sorghum." says Chef Fleer. It appears here and in his blackberry jam.

Prep: 25 minutes **Bake:** 12 minutes per batch

2 cups sugar
1 cup shortening
2 eggs
½ cup sorghum or mild-flavored molasses
3½ cups all-purpose flour

2 tsp. baking soda
2 tsp. ground ginger
1¼ tsp. ground cinnamon
1 tsp. ground cloves
Sugar

1. Preheat oven to 350° F. In a large mixing bowl beat the 2 cups sugar and shortening with an electric mixer on medium speed until fluffy. Beat in eggs and sorghum.

2. In a medium mixing bowl stir together flour, baking soda, ginger, cinnamon, and cloves. Gradually beat or stir flour mixture into egg mixture. Shape dough into 1-inch balls; roll in additional sugar.

3. Arrange dough balls on an ungreased cookie sheet. Bake about 12 minutes or until bottoms are light brown. Cool on wire racks. Makes about 7 dozen cookies.

Nutrition facts per cookie: 66 cal., 3 g total fat (1 g sat. fat), 5 mg chol., 32 mg sodium, 10 g carbo., 0 g fiber, and 1 g pro. Daily Values: 1% calcium and 2% iron.

low fat Chocolate Graham Crackers
Prep: 30 minutes **Chill:** 1 hour **Bake:** 8 minutes per batch

⅓ cup milk
¼ cup honey
2 oz. bittersweet chocolate, chopped
2 cups all-purpose flour
1 cup packed brown sugar

½ cup whole wheat flour
1 tsp. baking soda
½ tsp. salt
½ cup butter
1 Tbsp. vanilla

1. In a small saucepan combine milk, honey, and chocolate; cook and stir over low heat just until chocolate is melted. Let cool about 15 minutes.

2. Meanwhile, in a food processor bowl combine all-purpose flour, brown sugar, whole wheat flour, baking soda, and salt. Cover; pulse to combine. Add butter; pulse until mixture resembles coarse crumbs. (Or place in a large bowl; cut in butter using a pastry blender until it resembles coarse crumbs.)

3. Stir vanilla into chocolate mixture; add to flour mixture. Pulse (or stir) until just combined. If necessary, knead dough gently to form a ball. Divide into fourths. Wrap each portion in plastic wrap; chill about 1 hour or until easy to handle.

4. Preheat oven to 350° F. On a lightly floured surface roll one portion of dough to ⅛-inch thickness. Cut with a 3-inch scalloped round cutter. Arrange on ungreased cookie sheets. Mark cracker tops in a snowflake pattern, using tines of a fork.

5. Bake for 8 to 10 minutes or until edges are firm. Transfer to a wire rack; cool. Makes about 4½ dozen crackers.

Alphabet Chocolate Graham Crackers: Prepare as directed above, except cut dough using 3-inch letter-shaped cutters. Bake as directed for 8 to 10 minutes.

Nutrition facts per cracker: 63 cal., 2 g total fat (1 g sat. fat), 5 mg chol., 66 mg sodium, 10 g carbo., 0 g fiber, and 1 g pro. Daily Values: 1% vit. A, 1% calcium, and 2% iron.

Spicy Bittersweet Cocoa
Start to finish: 25 minutes

½	cup unsweetened cocoa powder	5	oz. bittersweet chocolate, chopped
½	cup sugar	1	2-inch piece stick cinnamon
6½	cups whole milk	1½	tsp. vanilla
1½	cups whipping cream		Whipped cream (optional)

1. In a large saucepan stir together cocoa powder and sugar. Using a whisk, stir in milk, cream, chocolate, and cinnamon stick. Heat and stir over medium heat until just boiling. Remove cinnamon stick. Stir in vanilla. Serve warm topped with whipped cream, if desired. Makes 10 servings.

Nutrition facts per serving: 348 cal., 24 g total fat (15 g sat. fat), 71 mg chol., 92 mg sodium, 28 g carbo., 1 g fiber, and 8 g pro. Daily Values: 15% vit. A, 3% vit. C, 27% calcium, and 6% iron.

30 **Holiday Blackberry Nog**
Prep: 15 minutes **Chill:** 4 hours

4	egg yolks	1	cup whipping cream
1¾	cups milk	2	tsp. vanilla
⅓	cup sugar	1½	cups fresh blackberries (6 oz.) (optional)
¼	tsp. ground nutmeg		

1. In a medium, heavy saucepan beat egg yolks; stir in milk, sugar, and nutmeg. Cook and stir over medium heat until mixture just coats a metal spoon. Remove from heat.

2. Place pan in a sink or bowl of ice water; stir for 2 minutes. Stir in whipping cream and vanilla. Cover and chill for 4 to 24 hours.

3. To serve, place berries in gift bottles or a glass pitcher, if desired. Pour eggnog over berries. Serve immediately. Makes 8 servings.

Nutrition facts per serving: 194 cal., 15 g total fat (8 g sat. fat), 151 mg chol., 42 mg sodium, 12 g carbo., 0 g fiber, and 4 g pro. Daily Values: 14% vit. A, 1% vit. C, 10% calcium, and 2% iron.

low fat **Buttery Blackberry or Green Apple Lollipops**
Prep: 20 minutes **Cook:** 45 minutes **Cool:** 20 minutes

1	cup water	6	drops purple or 2 drops green gel food coloring (optional)
2	cups sugar		
¾	cup light-colored corn syrup	18	to 20 lollipop sticks or clean maple twigs
1	Tbsp. butter		
¼	tsp. blackberry flavoring oil or ½ tsp. apple flavoring		

1. In a medium saucepan bring the 1 cup water to boiling. Stir in sugar, corn syrup, and butter. Cook and stir over medium-high heat until mixture boils, stirring to dissolve sugar (about 7 minutes).

2. Clip a candy thermometer to the side of the pan. Reduce heat to medium; continue boiling at a moderate, steady rate, stirring occasionally until thermometer registers 300° F, hard-crack stage (45 to 50 minutes).

3. Remove saucepan from heat; stir in blackberry flavoring oil or apple flavoring and gel food coloring, if desired. Let stand until candy thermometer registers 220° F (about 20 minutes). Meanwhile, butter 2 large baking sheets. Place lollipop sticks 4 inches apart on the prepared baking sheets.

4. Working quickly, spoon 1 tablespoon of the candy mixture over the top 1 inch of each lollipop stick (do not spread; mixture will flow out). Cool completely. To store, wrap each lollipop in plastic wrap. Store at room temperature for up to 2 weeks. Makes 18 to 20 lollipops.

Nutrition facts per lollipop: 127 cal., 1 g total fat (0 g sat. fat), 2 mg chol., 24 mg sodium, 32 g carbo., 0 g fiber, 0 g pro. Daily Values: 1% vit. A.

Buttery Blackberry or Green Apple Lollipops

Holiday
Blackberry Nog

Spicy Bittersweet Cocoa

Pistachios with
a Kick

Add
Pizzazz
to
Pistachios

Thanks to the vending machine, pistachio nuts are pretty plentiful in America. When the machines began offering up nuts for coins—around about the 1930s—pistachios gained in popularity. However, it wasn't until 40 years later that the first commercial crop of pistachios was harvested in this country. Up until that time, most pistachios were imported from the Middle East.

Lucky for you, pistachio nuts today are readily available in supermarkets across the country—shelled and unshelled. Pistachio shells split open naturally as the nut inside grows to maturity. So if you find a shell that has no split, throw it away. The nut inside is not mature. Store pistachio nuts in a covered container or sealed plastic bag because they tend to absorb moisture from the air and may lose their crunch. Count on two cups of pistachios in their shells giving you about a cup of shelled nuts when you're making any of the pistachio recipes below.

30 Pistachios with a Kick
Prep: 5 minutes **Bake:** 20 minutes

2 Tbsp. butter or margarine, melted
1 tsp. ground coriander
½ tsp. salt
¼ tsp. ground cloves
¼ tsp. ground red pepper
1½ cups pistachio nuts

1. Preheat oven to 350° F. In a 9x9x2-inch baking pan combine melted butter, coriander, salt, cloves, and ground red pepper. Add nuts; toss to coat.

2. Bake, uncovered, for 20 to 25 minutes or until toasted, stirring occasionally. Spread on foil; cool. Store in an airtight container. Makes 1½ cups nuts.

Nutrition facts per ¼-cup serving: 212 cal., 18 g total fat (2 g sat. fat), 0 mg chol., 239 mg sodium, 9 g carbo., 3 g fiber, and 7 g pro. Daily Values: 3% vit. C, 4% calcium, and 8% iron.

Smoky Cheese Ball
Stand: 30 + 15 minutes
Prep: 15 minutes **Chill:** 4 hours

2 8-oz. pkg. cream cheese
2 cups finely shredded smoked Swiss, cheddar, or Gouda cheese
½ cup butter or margarine
2 Tbsp. milk
2 tsp. steak sauce
1 cup finely chopped pistachio nuts, toasted
Assorted crackers

1. In a large bowl let cream cheese, shredded cheese, and butter stand at room temperature for 30 minutes. Add milk and steak sauce; beat until fluffy. Cover and chill for 4 to 24 hours.

2. Shape mixture into a ball; roll in nuts. Let stand for 15 minutes. Serve with crackers. Makes 3½ cups spread.

Freeze-ahead directions: Prepare as above, except do not roll in nuts. Wrap cheese ball in moisture- and vaporproof plastic wrap. Freeze for up to 1 month. To serve, thaw cheese ball in the refrigerator overnight. Roll in nuts. Let stand for 30 minutes at room temperature before serving.

Nutrition facts per 1 tablespoon spread: 73 cal., 7 g total fat (4 g sat. fat), 17 mg chol., 71 mg sodium, 1 g carbo., 0 g fiber, and 2 g pro. Daily Values: 5% vit. A, 4% calcium, and 1% iron.

Lemon-Pistachio Biscotti
Prep: 35 minutes **Bake:** 36 minutes
Cool: 30 minutes

⅓ cup butter, softened
⅔ cup sugar
2 tsp. baking powder
½ tsp. salt
2 eggs
1 tsp. vanilla
2 cups all-purpose flour
4 tsp. finely shredded lemon peel
1¼ cups pistachio nuts
1 recipe Lemon Icing

1. Preheat oven to 375° F. Lightly grease 2 cookie sheets; set aside. In a large bowl beat butter with an electric mixer on medium to high speed for 30 seconds. Add sugar, baking powder, and salt. Beat until combined, scraping side of bowl occasionally. Beat in eggs and vanilla. Beat in as much flour as you can. Stir in any remaining flour and lemon peel. Stir in pistachio nuts.

2. Divide dough into 3 equal portions. Shape each portion into an 8-inch-long roll. Place at least 3 inches apart on prepared cookie sheets; flatten slightly until about 2½ inches wide.

3. Bake for 20 to 25 minutes or until golden brown and tops are cracked (loaves will spread slightly). Cool on cookie sheet for 30 minutes.

4. Reduce oven temperature to 325° F. Use a serrated knife to cut each roll diagonally into ½-inch-thick slices. Place slices, cut sides down, on ungreased cookie sheets. Bake for 16 to 18 minutes or until dry and crisp (do not overbake), turning after 8 minutes. Cool a wire rack.

5. Drizzle cookies with Lemon Icing. Makes about 36 cookies.

Lemon Icing: Prepare Lime Icing as directed on page 295, except substitute lemon peel and juice for the lime.

Nutrition facts per cookie: 95 cal., 4 g total fat (1 g sat. fat),17 mg chol., 76 mg sodium, 13 g carbo., 1 g fiber, and 2 g pro. Daily Values: 2% vit. A, 1% vit. C, 2% calcium, and 3% iron.

Easy Phyllo Pastries

Repeat after me: Phyllo (FEE-loh) is fun. It really is. And festive too. These finished phyllo bundles, full of sliced pears and caramel, have phyllo's characteristic flaky-crisp crunch. And, you've got to admit, the presentation is pretty darn stunning too.

There's no need to fear phyllo dough, especially when you use packaged phyllo, available in most supermarkets. Here are tips to bear in mind while fooling with phyllo.

■ Allow frozen phyllo dough to thaw while it is still wrapped and sealed. It's best to let it thaw overnight in the refrigerator.

■ Once you unwrap them, sheets of phyllo dough dry out quickly and crumble. If that starts to happen, keep the opened stack of phyllo sheets covered with a slightly damp cloth or plastic wrap until you need it.

■ If a phyllo sheet tears a little, don't worry; just gently brush tear with butter to seal the edges back together. With so many layers, the tear will soon be covered by another flaky layer.

Santa's Pear Pouches

Looking a little like Santa's sack, these flaky phyllo bundles bulge with a pleasant present of spiced pears.

Prep: 30 minutes **Bake:** 20 minutes

3	medium red or green skinned pears, cored and thinly sliced (about 3½ cups)
1	Tbsp. sugar
1	Tbsp. all-purpose flour
¼	tsp. ground cardamom
⅓	cup butter, melted
4	sheets frozen phyllo dough (18x14-inch rectangles), thawed
¼	cup caramel ice cream topping
	Sugar or coarse sugar
	Bay leaves (optional)*
	Dried cranberries (optional)

1. Preheat oven to 375° F. For filling, in a medium mixing bowl combine pears, 1 tablespoon sugar, flour, and cardamom. Toss to combine; set aside.

2. Brush four 6-ounce custard cups with some of the melted butter; set aside. Place 1 sheet of phyllo dough on a flat surface. (Cover remaining phyllo with plastic wrap to prevent it from becoming dry.) Lightly brush the sheet with some of the melted butter. Place another phyllo sheet on top; brush with butter. Repeat with 2 more phyllo sheets. Cut stack in half lengthwise and then in half crosswise to form 4 rectangles.

3. Ease a stack of phyllo into bottom and up sides of a custard cup (phyllo will hang over edge). Spoon about ¾ cup pear filling into center. Drizzle 1 tablespoon of caramel topping over pears. Bring phyllo up over filling, pinching together to form a ruffled edge. Secure pouch with 100-percent-cotton string. Brush again with butter. Sprinkle with sugar. Repeat to make 3 more pouches. Place custard cups in a 15x10x1-inch baking pan.

4. Bake for 20 minutes or until phyllo is golden brown. Cool for 5 minutes; remove bundles from cups. Serve warm. If desired, tuck bay leaves under string; arrange cranberries on plate. Makes 4 servings.

*Test Kitchen Tip: Bay leaves are for decorative purposes only in this recipe. Do not eat them.

Nutrition facts per serving: 364 cal., 18 g total fat (10 g sat. fat), 43 mg chol., 310 mg sodium, 51 g carbo., 4 g fiber, and 2 g pro. Daily Values: 13% vit. A, 8% vit. C, 3% calcium, and 6% iron.

PHOTOGRAPH: COLLEEN DUFFLEY. FOOD STYLIST: BROOKE LEONARD. STORY: JEANNE AMBROSE.

Santa's Pear
Pouches

Prize Tested

Our monthly recipe contest has been going since 1923. Turn to see the winners from 2002, plus earlier favorites.

Recipes®

Cheesy Appetizers

Feta Custard in Phyllo Cups

Fruited Cheese Log

Feta Custard in Phyllo Cups

Prep: 30 minutes **Bake:** 15 minutes

30	Phyllo Cups (see right) or 1¾-inch baked miniature phyllo shells (two 2.1-oz. pkg.)
1	4-oz. pkg. crumbled feta cheese
1	3-oz. pkg. cream cheese, softened
1	egg
2	tsp. lemon juice
1	tsp. all-purpose flour
⅓	cup pitted kalamata olives, chopped
½	tsp. dried oregano, crushed
½	tsp. olive oil
¼	tsp. balsamic vinegar
1	clove garlic, minced
	Dash ground cumin
	Dash ground red pepper

1. Preheat oven to 325° F. Place Phyllo Cups on a large baking sheet. Set aside.

2. For filling, in a bowl combine feta cheese, cream cheese, egg, lemon juice, and flour. Beat with an electric mixer until nearly smooth. Spoon into cups, using a scant 2 teaspoons for each cup. Bake for 15 to 17 minutes or until golden and crisp.

3. For topping, in a bowl stir together olives, oregano, olive oil, vinegar, garlic, cumin, and red pepper; sprinkle evenly over custards. Serve warm. If desired, sprinkle with snipped fresh parsley or oregano. Makes 30 appetizers.

Nutrition facts per appetizer: 49 cal., 3 g total fat (1 g sat. fat), 14 mg chol., 79 mg sodium, 3 g carbo., 1 g pro. Daily Values: 2% vit. A, 1% vit. C, 2% calcium, 1% iron.

Fruited Cheese Log

Prep: 20 minutes **Stand:** 1 hour **Chill:** 4 hours

½	cup snipped dried apricots
8	oz. shredded Monterey Jack cheese (2 cups)
½	of an 8-oz. pkg. cream cheese
2	Tbsp. orange juice
⅓	cup golden raisins, chopped
¼	cup pitted whole dates, snipped
¼	tsp. salt
	Chopped toasted almonds (optional)
	Assorted crackers and/or apple slices

1. In a bowl soak apricots in 1 cup water about 1 hour or until softened. Drain well; set aside. Let cheeses stand in a bowl 30 minutes or until room temperature.

2. Add orange juice to cheese mixture. Beat with an electric mixer on medium speed until combined. Stir in apricots, raisins, dates, and salt. Divide mixture in half.

3. On a large piece of waxed paper, shape each portion into a 5-inch-long log. Wrap in plastic wrap; chill for 4 to 24 hours. If desired, roll in nuts before serving. Serve with assorted crackers and/or apple slices. Makes 32 servings.

Nutrition facts per serving: 53 cal., 3 g total fat (2 g sat. fat), 10 mg chol., 67 mg sodium, 4 g carbo., 0 g fiber, 2 g pro. Daily Values: 5% vit. A, 1% vit. C, 6% calcium, 1% iron.

Phyllo Cups

Prep: 30 minutes **Bake:** 8 minutes

1. Preheat oven to 350° F. Grease thirty-six 1¾-inch muffin cups; set aside. Cover 4 sheets of frozen phyllo dough (18x14-inch rectangles), thawed, with plastic wrap to prevent them from becoming dry and brittle. Lightly brush 1 sheet of phyllo dough with some of ¼ cup melted butter. Stack 3 more sheets, brushing between each layer with melted butter.

2. Cut phyllo stack lengthwise into six 18-inch-long strips. Cut each strip crosswise into six 3-inch-long rectangles. Press each rectangle into a prepared cup, pleating as needed to fit. Bake for 8 to 10 minutes or until golden. Fill and bake as directed for Feta Custard in Phyllo Cups (see left). (Wrap and freeze any leftover cups for up to 3 months.) Makes 36.

Savory Baked Brie

Prep: 20 minutes **Bake:** 20 minutes

1	13½-oz. round Brie cheese
2	Tbsp. snipped fresh thyme or oregano
¼	cup pine nuts, toasted
3	slices provolone cheese (about 2½ oz.)
	Crackers, toasted baguette slices, and/or apple or pear slices

1. Unwrap Brie. Using a sharp knife, slice off the top of the rind. Set in a 9-inch glass pie plate. Sprinkle with thyme and pine nuts. Overlap provolone slices on Brie; tuck ends underneath, if necessary.

2. Place pie plate in a cool oven. Turn oven to 325° F. Bake for 20 to 25 minutes or cheese is softened.

3. Serve with crackers, baguette slices, and apple or pear slices*. Makes 8 servings.

***Test Kitchen Tip:** To prevent discoloration, treat apple or pear slices with citric acid color keeper or dip into a mixture of lemon juice and water.

Nutrition facts per serving: 215 cal., 18 g total fat (10 g sat. fat), 53 mg chol., 374 mg sodium, 1 g carbo., 0 g fiber, and 13 g pro. Daily Values: 8% vit. A, 2% vit. C, 16% calcium, and 5% iron.

Feta-Olive Wafers

Prep: 20 minutes **Chill:** 4 hours
Bake: about 15 minutes

- 1 4-oz. pkg. crumbled feta cheese (1 cup)
- ½ cup butter, softened
- 1 egg
- 1 Tbsp. dried Greek seasoning, crushed
- 1⅔ cups all-purpose flour
- ¼ cup pitted kalamata olives (about 10 olives), drained and finely chopped
- 1 Tbsp. oil-packed dried tomatoes, drained and finely chopped

1. In a large mixing bowl beat feta cheese and butter with an electric mixer on medium speed until combined. Beat in egg and Greek seasoning. Beat in as much of the flour as you can with the mixer. Stir in the remaining flour.

2. With your hands, knead in the olives and tomatoes. Divide dough in half; shape each portion into a 5½-inch-long log. Wrap in plastic wrap or waxed paper; chill for 4 to 24 hours.

3. Preheat oven to 375° F. Cut each log into ¼-inch-thick slices. Place 1 inch apart on an ungreased baking sheet. Bake about 15 minutes or until edges begin to brown. Serve warm or at room temperature. Makes about 40 wafers.

Nutrition facts per wafer: 50 cal., 3 g total fat (2 g sat. fat), 14 mg chol., 74 mg sodium, 4 g carbo., 0 g fiber, 1 g pro. Daily Values: 2% vit. A, 2% calcium, and 1% iron.

Goat Cheese and Spinach Pesto Bites

Prep: 25 minutes **Bake:** 12 minutes

- ¾ cup packed fresh basil leaves
- ⅔ cup packed fresh spinach leaves
- 2 Tbsp. pine nuts
- 1 Tbsp. olive oil
- 4 oz. soft goat cheese (chèvre)
- ¼ cup hazelnuts, toasted and very finely chopped
- 2 Tbsp. grated Parmesan cheese
- 8 sheets frozen phyllo dough (18x12-inch rectangles), thawed
- ⅓ cup butter, melted

1. Preheat oven to 400° F. For filling, in a food processor bowl or blender container combine basil, spinach, and pine nuts. Cover and process or blend with several on/off turns until paste forms, stopping machine several times and scraping sides down as needed. With machine running, slowly add the olive oil and process until almost smooth. Transfer to a bowl; stir in goat cheese, hazelnuts, and Parmesan cheese. Set aside.

2. Cover phyllo with plastic wrap to prevent it from becoming dry and brittle. Lightly brush a sheet of phyllo with some of the melted butter. Place another sheet of phyllo on top; brush with butter. Cut crosswise into eight 12-inch-long strips. Spoon a well rounded teaspoon of filling about 1 inch from an end of each dough strip. To fold into a triangle, bring a corner over filling so it lines up with the other side of the strip. Continue folding strip in a triangular shape. Repeat with remaining sheets of phyllo, melted butter, and filling.

3. Place triangles on an ungreased baking sheet; brush with any remaining butter. Bake for 12 to 15 minutes or until golden. Serve warm. Makes 24 servings.

Nutrition facts per serving: 76 cal., 6 g total fat (3 g sat. fat), 10 mg chol., 84 mg sodium, 4 g carbo., 0 g fiber, and 2 g pro. Daily Values: 4% vit. A, 1% vit. C, 2% calcium, and 3% iron.

Pear-Walnut Cheese Spirals

Soften Armenian cracker bread to roll into this pretty spiral. You'll find it in the cracker or specialty bread section of your supermarket. You can also use a couple of 8-inch flour tortillas.

Stand: 45 minutes **Prep:** 25 minutes
Cook: 5 minutes **Chill:** 4 hours

- 1 15-inch round Armenian cracker bread (lahvosh)
- 6 cups fresh spinach leaves
- 1 medium pear
- ⅓ cup finely chopped green onion or shallots
- 2 Tbsp. butter
- ⅓ cup finely chopped walnuts, toasted
- 1½ 8-oz. tubs cream cheese with chive and onion
- ½ tsp. salt
- ¼ to ½ tsp. freshly cracked pepper
- Fresh spinach leaves (optional)

1. Thoroughly wet both sides of the cracker bread by holding it under cool running water. Place between wet kitchen towels; let stand about 45 minutes or until soft enough to fold without breaking.

2. Meanwhile, finely chop spinach; set aside. Peel, core, and finely chop pear. In a large skillet cook and stir spinach, pear, and green onion or shallot in hot butter over medium heat until spinach is wilted and pear is tender. Stir in walnuts. Remove from pan; cool.

3. In a medium bowl combine cream cheese, salt, and pepper; spread onto cracker bread. Carefully spread spinach mixture onto cream cheese. Roll up cracker bread in a spiral; wrap in plastic wrap. Chill for 4 to 24 hours.

4. To serve, cut roll into ½-inch-thick slices. If desired, arrange on a platter lined with spinach. Makes about 20 servings.

Nutrition facts per serving: 117 cal., 8 g total fat (5 g sat. fat), 20 mg chol., 180 mg sodium, 8 g carbo., 2 g fiber, and 2 g pro. Daily Values: 16% vit. A, 5% vit. C, 4% calcium, and 12% iron.

Best Bread Machine Breads

Cranberry-Peanut Butter Bread

Salsa Bread

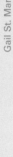
30 Cranberry-Peanut Butter Bread

No bread machine? No worries. Just follow the conventional directions at right.
Prep: 10 minutes

¾	cup water	3	cups whole wheat flour
½	cup milk	2	Tbsp. gluten flour*
1	egg	1½	tsp. salt
½	cup creamy peanut butter	2¼	tsp. active dry yeast or bread
3	Tbsp. honey		machine yeast
1	Tbsp. butter or margarine	1	cup dried cranberries

1. Add ingredients to a 1½- or 2-pound loaf bread machine according to manufacturer's directions. (The pan must have a capacity of 10 cups or more.) Select the basic white bread cycle and, if available, the light setting. Makes 1 loaf (16 slices).

*Test Kitchen Tip: Look for gluten flour in health food stores or the baking aisle. You need this high-protein, hard-wheat flour to give the bread elasticity.

Nutrition facts per slice: 179 cal., 6 g total fat (2 g sat. fat), 16 mg chol., 274 mg sodium, 28 g carbo., 4 g fiber, and 6 g pro. Daily Values: 1% vit. A, 2% calcium, and 7% iron.

30 low fat Salsa Bread

Make a tasty Tex-Mex sandwich with cream cheese, chicken, and roasted peppers.
Prep: 10 minutes

1	cup bottled chunky salsa	½	tsp. ground cumin
⅓	cup water	½	tsp. chili powder
1	Tbsp. cooking oil	¼	to ½ tsp. ground red pepper
	Dash bottled hot pepper sauce	2	tsp. active dry yeast or bread
3	cups bread flour		machine yeast
1	Tbsp. sugar		

1. Add ingredients to a 1½- or 2-pound loaf bread machine according to manufacturer's directions. Select the basic white bread cycle and desired color setting. Makes 1 loaf (10 to 12 slices).

Nutrition facts per slice: 172 cal., 2 g total fat (0 g sat. fat), 0 mg chol., 59 mg sodium, 32 g carbo., 1 g fiber, 5 g pro. Daily Values: 3% vit. A, 3% vit. C, 1% calcium, 12% iron.

Cranberry-Peanut Butter Bread

Prep: 30 minutes **Stand:** 2 hours
Bake: 30 minutes

Conventional Method:

1. In a large mixing bowl stir together 1¼ cups all-purpose flour and yeast; set aside (omit the gluten flour).

2. In a small saucepan heat and stir the water, milk, only ⅓ cup peanut butter, the honey, butter, and salt just until warm (120° to 130° F) and butter almost melts.

3. Add warm mixture to dry mixture; add egg. Beat with an electric mixer on low to medium speed for 30 seconds, scraping bowl. Beat on high speed for 3 minutes. Using a wooden spoon, stir in only 1½ cups whole wheat flour, cranberries, and enough all-purpose flour (about ½ cup) to make dough easy to handle.

4. Turn out onto a floured surface. Knead in ⅓ to ⅔ cup more all-purpose flour to make a moderately soft dough that is smooth and elastic (3 to 5 minutes total). Shape into a ball. Place in a greased bowl; turn once. Cover; let rise in a warm place until double in size (1 to 1¼ hours).

5. Punch dough down. Turn out onto a lightly floured surface. Cover and let rest 10 minutes. Lightly grease an 9x5x3-inch loaf pan. Shape dough into a loaf. Place in pan. Cover; let rise in a warm place until nearly double (about 45 minutes).

6. Preheat oven to 375° F; bake for 30 to 35 minutes or until top sounds hollow when tapped (if necessary, cover loosely with foil the last 10 minutes of baking to prevent overbrowning). Immediately remove from pan. Cool on a wire rack. Makes 1 loaf (16 slices).

Salsa Bread

Prep: 30 minutes **Stand:** 1½ hours
Bake: 30 minutes

Conventional Method:

1. In a large mixing bowl combine 1 cup of the bread flour (use 2½ to 3 cups total bread flour), yeast, cumin, chili powder, and ground red pepper; set aside.

2. In a small saucepan heat and stir salsa, water, sugar, oil, and hot pepper sauce just until warm (120° to 130° F).

3. Add to dry mixture. Beat with an electric mixer on low to medium speed for 30 seconds, scraping sides of bowl constantly. Beat on high speed for 3 minutes. Using a wooden spoon, stir in as much of the remaining flour as you can.

4. Turn the dough out onto a lightly floured surface. Knead in enough of the remaining flour to make a moderately stiff dough that is smooth and elastic (6 to 8 minutes total). Shape into a ball. Place in a lightly greased bowl, turning once to grease surface. Cover; let rise in a warm place until double (45 to 60 minutes).

5. Punch dough down. Turn dough out onto a lightly floured surface. Cover; let rest 10 minutes. Meanwhile, lightly grease one 8x4x2-inch loaf pan. Shape dough into a loaf. Place in the prepared pan. Cover and let rise in a warm place until nearly double in size (about 30 minutes).

6. Preheat oven to 375° F; bake about 30 minutes or until bread sounds hollow when lightly tapped (if necessary, cover loosely with foil the last 10 minutes of baking to prevent overbrowning). Immediately remove from pan. Cool on a wire rack. Makes 1 loaf (10 to 12 slices).

Stout Asiago Foccacia Bread

Prep: 15 minutes **Stand:** 20 minutes
Bake: 20 minutes

1	cup stout or dark beer
1	Tbsp. butter
2½	cups bread flour
2	Tbsp. sugar
1	tsp. salt
2¾	tsp. active dry yeast
2	tsp. olive oil
¼	cup finely shredded Asiago cheese
½	tsp. dried Italian seasoning, crushed
1	clove garlic, minced
¼	tsp. coarsely ground black pepper

1. Add beer, butter, flour, sugar, salt, and yeast to a 1½- or 2-pound loaf bread machine according to manufacturer's directions. Select the dough cycle. When the cycle is complete, transfer dough to a lightly floured surface. Cover and let rest for 10 minutes.

2. Preheat oven to 350° F. Transfer dough to a large greased baking sheet or 14-inch pizza pan. Pat dough into a 12-inch circle. Brush with olive oil. With floured fingers, make ½-inch-deep indentations every 2 inches on the surface.

3. In a small mixing bowl combine cheese, Italian seasoning, garlic, and pepper. Sprinkle onto dough. Cover and let stand in a warm place for 20 minutes (for conventional method, let stand for 30 to 40 minutes or until puffed).

4. Bake in the preheated oven for 20 to 25 minutes or until golden brown. Serve warm. Makes 8 to 10 servings.

Conventional Method:

1. In a large mixing bowl stir together 1 cup of the bread flour (use 2½ to 2¾ cups total flour) and yeast.

2. In a medium saucepan heat and stir stout, butter, sugar, and salt until warm (120° to 130° F) and butter almost melts.

3. Add to flour mixture. Beat with an electric mixer on low speed for 30 seconds, scraping sides of bowl. Beat on high speed for 3 minutes. Using a wooden spoon, stir in as much of the flour as you can.

4. Turn dough out onto a lightly floured surface. Knead in enough of the remaining flour to make a moderately stiff dough that is smooth and elastic (6 to 8 minutes total). Shape into a ball. Place in a lightly greased bowl, turning once to grease surface. Cover; let rise in a warm place until double in size (about 1 hour).

5. Punch dough down. Cover and let rest for 10 minutes. Continue as directed from Step 2 of the recipe above.

Nutrition facts per slice: 225 cal., 5 g total fat (2 g sat. fat), 8 mg chol., 347 mg sodium, 36 g carbo., 1 g fiber, and 7 g pro. Daily Values: 1% vit. A, 3% calcium, 12% iron.

30 low fat Honey Dijon Bread

Prep: 10 minutes

1	cup water
2	Tbsp. honey
2	Tbsp. Dijon-style mustard
1	Tbsp. olive oil or cooking oil
3	cups bread flour
½	tsp. dried thyme, crushed
¾	tsp. salt
½	tsp. dry mustard
1¼	tsp. bread machine yeast or active dry yeast

1. Add ingredients to a 1½- or 2-pound loaf bread machine according to manufacturer's directions. Select the basic white bread cycle. Makes 1 loaf (12 slices).

Conventional Method:

1. Use ingredients as above, except use 2⅔ to 3 cups all-purpose flour instead of bread flour, 1 package active dry yeast, and warm water (105° to 115° F).

2. In a large mixing bowl combine 1¼ cups all-purpose flour, yeast, thyme, salt, and dry mustard. Add water, honey, Dijon-style mustard, and olive oil. Beat with an electric mixer on low to medium speed for 30 seconds, scraping the sides of the bowl constantly. Beat on high speed for 3 minutes. Using a wooden spoon, stir in as much of the remaining flour as you can.

3. Turn out onto a lightly floured surface. Knead in enough of the remaining flour to made a moderately stiff dough that is smooth and elastic (6 to 8 minutes total). Shape dough into a ball. Place in a lightly greased bowl, turning once to grease the surface. Cover; let rise in a warm place until double (1 to 1¼ hours).

4. Punch dough down. Turn out onto a lightly floured surface. Cover and let rest 10 minutes. Meanwhile, lightly grease one 9x5x3-inch loaf pan. Shape dough into a loaf. Place in the prepared pan. Cover and let rise in a warm place until nearly double in size (45 to 60 minutes).

5. Preheat oven to 375° F; bake for 30 to 35 minutes or until bread sounds hollow when tapped (if necessary, cover loosely with foil last 10 minutes of baking). Remove bread from pan. Cool on a wire rack. Makes 1 loaf (12 slices).

Nutrition facts per slice: 150 cal., 2 g total fat (0 g sat. fat), 0 mg chol., 161 mg sodium, 28 g carbo., 1 g fiber, and 4 g pro. Daily Values: 1% vit. A, 1% calcium, and 9% iron.

Waffles and French Toast

Berry-Nut French Toast

Waffles with Salsa

30 Berry-Nut French Toast

Prep: 10 minutes **Cook:** 4 minutes

2 cups multi-grain flakes with oat clusters, cranberries, and almonds	4 ¾-inch-thick slices French bread or Italian bread
4 eggs	2 Tbsp. butter
½ tsp. ground cinnamon	Fruit-flavored syrup, maple syrup, or apricot preserves, warmed
¼ tsp. ground nutmeg	

1. In a shallow dish coarsely crush cereal; set aside. In another dish beat eggs; stir in cinnamon and nutmeg. Dip bread slices into egg mixture until moistened, turning to coat. Dip both sides into crushed cereal until coated.

2. In a large skillet or griddle cook bread in hot butter over medium-low heat about 2 minutes on each side or until golden. Serve with syrup. Makes 2 servings.

Nutrition facts per serving: 606 cal., 27 g total fat (11 g sat. fat), 458 mg chol., 765 mg sodium, 72 g carbo., 5 g fiber, and 21 g pro. Daily Values: 37% vit. A and 26% iron.

Waffles with Salsa

Prep: 25 minutes **Bake:** 3 minutes per waffle

1 cup all-purpose flour	1 cup buttermilk
½ cup yellow cornmeal	2 Tbsp. cooking oil
2 Tbsp. sugar	1 4-oz. can diced green chili peppers, drained
1 Tbsp. baking powder	1 recipe Jicama-Bean Salsa
2 tsp. chili powder	¾ cup bottled salsa
½ tsp. salt	Dairy sour cream (optional)
1 egg	

1. Combine flour, cornmeal, sugar, baking powder, chili powder, and salt. Beat together egg, buttermilk, and oil; add to flour mixture. Stir until mixed. Stir in peppers.

2. Pour batter onto grids of a preheated, lightly greased waffle baker. Bake according to manufacturer's directions. Serve warm with Jicama-Bean Salsa and bottled salsa. If desired, top with sour cream. Makes 10 to 12 (4-inch) waffles.

Jicama-Bean Salsa: Halve, seed, peel, and chop 1 avocado. Coarsely chop 1 medium tomato. In a medium bowl combine avocado; tomato; ½ of a 15-ounce can black beans, rinsed and drained; ¼ cup chopped, peeled jicama; ¼ cup chopped red onion; and 1 tablespoon snipped fresh cilantro. Makes about 2½ cups.

Nutrition facts per waffle with salsa: 174 cal., 7 g total fat (1 g sat. fat), 22 mg chol., 403 mg sodium, 24 g carbo., 3 g fiber, and 6 g pro. Daily Values: 10% vit. A, 17% vit. C, 13% calcium, and 9% iron.

Peaches-and-Cream Stuffed French Toast

Prep: 30 minutes
Cook: 4 minutes per batch

- ¼ cup butter
- 1 8-oz. pkg. reduced-fat or regular cream cheese, softened
- ¼ cup sifted powdered sugar
- 1 tsp. vanilla
- 1 29-oz. can peach slices, drained
- 16 ½-inch-thick slices challah bread or French bread
- 6 eggs
- 1 cup half-and-half, light cream, or whipping cream
- ¼ tsp. ground cinnamon
- 2 Tbsp. butter or cooking oil
- 1 recipe Spiced Peach Sauce

1. In a saucepan melt ¼ cup butter over medium heat. Cook and stir about 5 minutes until golden brown. Let cool.

2. For filling, in a medium mixing bowl combine cream cheese, powdered sugar, and vanilla; beat until smooth. Gradually beat in cooled butter. Chop enough of the peaches to equal ½ cup; stir into filling. Reserve remaining peaches for sauce.

3. Spread about 3 tablespoons filling onto one side of half of the bread slices. Top with remaining bread slices. (You will have eight "sandwiches" total.)

4. In a shallow dish beat eggs; stir in half-and-half and cinnamon. Dip sandwiches into egg mixture about 15 seconds on each side or until moistened.

5. In a large skillet or griddle cook sandwiches in the 2 tablespoons hot butter or oil over medium heat for 2 to 3 minutes on each side or until golden, adding more butter, if needed. Serve warm with Spiced Peach Sauce. Makes 8 servings.

Spiced Peach Sauce: In a medium saucepan stir together ¼ cup packed brown sugar, 2 tablespoons cornstarch, and ¼ teaspoon ground cinnamon. Stir in 2 cups peach nectar. Cook and stir over medium heat until thickened and bubbly. Cook and stir for 2 minutes more. Stir in ½ teaspoon vanilla and reserved peach slices. Heat through. Makes 2¼ cups.

Test Kitchen Tip: To keep French toast warm, place it on a baking sheet in a 300° F oven.

Nutrition facts per serving with sauce: 505 cal., 25 g total fat (14 g sat. fat), 237 mg chol., 494 mg sodium, 58 g carbo., 3 g fiber, 13 g pro. Daily Values: 31% vit. A, 10% vit. C, 13% calcium, and 14% iron.

30 low fat Baked French Toast with Orange-Maple Sauce

Prep: 15 minutes **Bake:** 11 minutes

- 2 Tbsp. butter, cut up
- 3 eggs
- ¼ cup milk
- 2 Tbsp. sugar
- 2 Tbsp. frozen orange juice concentrate, thawed
- ¼ tsp. ground cinnamon
- ¼ tsp. almond extract
- 8 ¾-inch-thick slices firm-textured French bread
- 1 recipe Orange-Maple Sauce
- 1 recipe Almond Whipped Cream (optional)
- ¼ cup sliced almonds, toasted

1. Preheat oven to 400° F. Place butter in a 15x10x1-inch baking pan. Heat in oven for 2 to 3 minutes or until butter is melted. Carefully remove from oven with pot holders, tilting pan to coat.

2. Meanwhile, in a shallow dish beat eggs; stir in milk, juice concentrate, sugar, cinnamon, and almond extract. Dip bread into egg mixture about 30 seconds on each side or until moistened.

3. Arrange bread in a single layer in the prepared pan. Bake, uncovered, about 6 minutes or until golden. Turn bread; bake 5 to 8 minutes more or until golden.

4. Serve warm with Orange-Maple Sauce. If desired, top with Almond Whipped Cream. Sprinkle with almonds. Makes 8 servings.

Orange-Maple Sauce: In saucepan heat and stir 1 cup pure maple syrup or maple-flavored syrup, ¼ cup orange marmalade, and a dash ground cinnamon. Stir in one 11-ounce can mandarin orange sections, drained; heat through. Makes 2 cups.

Almond Whipped Cream: In a chilled bowl combined ½ cup whipping cream, 1 tablespoon sifted powdered sugar, and several drops almond extract. Beat with chilled beaters of an electric mixer until soft peaks form (tips curl). Makes 1 cup.

Nutrition facts per serving with sauce: 324 cal., 8 g total fat (3 g sat. fat), 88 mg chol., 222 mg sodium, 59 g carbo., 2 g fiber, and 6 g pro. Daily Values: 12% vit. A, 24% vit. C, 8% calcium, and 10% iron.

Praline-Glazed French Toast

Prep: 20 minutes
Cook: 4 minutes per batch
Broil: 2 minutes

- 6 1-inch-thick slices French bread
- ¼ cup butter, softened
- ¼ cup packed brown sugar
- 1 Tbsp. light-colored corn syrup
- ⅛ tsp. ground cinnamon
- ¼ cup chopped pecans
- 3 eggs
- 1 cup half-and-half, light cream, or whipping cream
- ½ tsp. vanilla
- ¼ tsp. ground cinnamon
- ¼ tsp. ground nutmeg
  Fresh peach slices (optional)
  Whipped cream (optional)

1. Preheat broiler. Arrange bread slices on a baking sheet. Broil 4 inches from the heat about 1 minute per side or until toasted. Set aside.

2. For topping, in a small bowl stir together softened butter, brown sugar, corn syrup, and ⅛ teaspoon cinnamon. Stir in pecans; set aside.

3. In a shallow dish beat eggs; stir in 1 cup half-and-half, vanilla, ¼ teaspoon cinnamon, and nutmeg until blended. Dip bread into egg mixture about 30 seconds on each side or until moistened.

4. In a lightly buttered skillet or griddle cook bread slices over medium heat for 2 to 3 minutes on each side or until golden. Arrange cooked slices on baking sheet. Spread with topping.

5. Broil slices 4 inches from the heat about 2 minutes or until topping is golden and bubbly. Serve warm with fresh peach slices and whipped cream, if desired. Makes 6 servings.

Nutrition facts per serving: 306 cal., 19 g total fat (9 g sat. fat), 143 mg chol., 290 mg sodium, 27 g carbo., 1 g fiber, and 7 g pro. Daily Values: 13% vit. A, 1% vit. C, 9% calcium, and 8% iron.

30 Pumpkin Waffles with Maple-Pecan Cream

You can also serve the creamy caramel sauce over plain waffles, pancakes, pound cake, or ice cream.

Prep: 15 minutes
Bake: 3 minutes per waffle

- 2 cups all-purpose flour
- 4 tsp. baking powder
- ½ tsp. baking soda
- ½ tsp. pumpkin pie spice
- ¼ tsp. salt
- 2 8-oz. cartons vanilla-flavored yogurt
- 1 15-oz. can pumpkin
- 4 beaten eggs
- ¼ cup butter or margarine, melted
- ¼ cup sugar
- 2 tsp. vanilla
- 1 recipe Maple-Pecan Cream

1. In a medium mixing bowl stir together flour, baking powder, baking soda, pumpkin pie spice, and salt. Stir in yogurt, pumpkin, eggs, butter, sugar, and vanilla. Stir until just combined.

2. Spread 1½ cups of the batter onto grids of a preheated, lightly greased waffle baker (use less batter if using a round or heart-shaped waffle baker). Bake according to manufacturer's directions. When done, use a fork to lift waffle off grid. Repeat with remaining batter.

3. Serve warm with Maple-Pecan Cream. Makes 16 (4-inch) waffles.

Maple-Pecan Cream: In a medium saucepan melt 1 tablespoon butter or margarine over medium heat. Stir in ¾ cup coarsely chopped pecans. Cook and stir for 1 to 2 minutes or until toasted. Stir in 1½ cups pure maple syrup or maple-flavored syrup and ½ cup whipping cream; heat through. Makes 2½ cups.

Nutrition facts per waffle with sauce: 295 cal., 12 g total fat (5 g sat. fat), 75 mg chol., 256 mg sodium, 42 g carbo., 2 g fiber, and 6 g pro. Daily Values: 124% vit. A, 2% vit. C, 15% calcium, and 10% iron.

Chicken Salads

Grilled Chicken Salad

Mediterranean Chicken Salad

30 Grilled Chicken Salad

Prep: 15 minutes **Cook:** 12 minutes

4	skinless, boneless chicken breast halves (1¼ to 1½ lb.)
	Montreal or Kansas City steak seasoning
8	cups torn mixed salad greens
¾	cup seedless red grapes, halved
⅓	cup crumbled goat cheese (chèvre)
¼	cup pine nuts, toasted
1	recipe Dill Vinaigrette

1. Sprinkle chicken with seasoning. Grill on rack of uncovered grill directly over medium coals for 12 to 15 minutes or until no longer pink (170° F), turning once.

2. Arrange greens on four plates; top with grapes, cheese, and nuts. Slice chicken; arrange on salads. Shake Dill Vinaigrette; drizzle over salads. Makes 4 servings.

Dill Vinaigrette: In a screw-top jar combine ¼ cup grapeseed oil or olive oil; 3 tablespoons balsamic vinegar; 1 tablespoon dried dillweed; 1 large clove garlic, minced; ¼ teaspoon pepper; and ¼ teaspoon dried oregano, crushed. Cover and shake well to mix; let stand for 1 hour. Makes ½ cup.

Nutrition facts per serving: 400 cal., 23 g total fat (4 g sat. fat), 86 mg chol., 167 mg sodium, 12 g carbo., 2 g fiber, and 38 g pro. Daily Values: 22% vit. A, 21% vit. C, 9% calcium, and 18% iron.

30 Mediterranean Chicken Salad

Prep: 30 minutes **Chill:** up to 2 hours

1	lb. cooked chicken, shredded or cut into bite-size strips (3 cups)
½	of a medium cucumber, halved lengthwise, seeded, and sliced
1	cup chopped celery
½	cup sliced pitted kalamata olives
½	cup chopped walnuts
1	13¾-oz. can artichoke hearts, drained and quartered
⅓	cup sliced green onion
1	recipe Sherry-Lemon Vinaigrette (see right)
2	cups fresh spinach leaves
	Snipped fresh parsley (optional)

1. In a large mixing bowl combine chicken, cucumber, celery, olives, walnuts, artichokes, and green onion. Stir Sherry-Lemon Vinaigrette; pour over chicken mixture. Toss gently to coat. Cover and chill for up to 2 hours.

2. Arrange spinach on six salad plates. Top with chicken mixture. If desired, sprinkle with parsley. Makes 6 servings.

Nutrition facts per serving: 451 cal., 32 g total fat (5 g sat. fat), 67 mg chol., 628 mg sodium, 17 g carbo., 5 g fiber, and 25 g pro. Daily Values: 18% vit. A, 25% vit. C, 7% calcium, and 18% iron.

30 Cherry-Cashew Chicken Salad

Prep: 25 minutes **Chill:** 2 hours

½	cup light mayonnaise dressing or salad dressing
¼	cup orange marmalade
1	Tbsp. lemon juice
¼	tsp. salt
¼	tsp. ground nutmeg
¼	tsp. pepper
5	cups cubed cooked chicken
⅓	cup dried tart red cherries
¼	cup thinly sliced green onion
1½	cups cubed cantaloupe
½	cup cashews
1	medium orange, peeled and sliced
6	cups shredded fresh spinach

1. In a large bowl stir together dressing, marmalade, lemon juice, salt, nutmeg, and pepper. Fold in chicken, cherries, and green onion. Cover; chill for 2 to 24 hours.

2. Before serving, fold in cantaloupe and cashews. Quarter orange slices; fold in. Serve atop spinach. Makes 8 servings.

Nutrition facts per serving: 329 cal., 16 g total fat (4 g sat. fat), 83 mg chol., 277 mg sodium, 20 g carbo., 3 g fiber, and 28 g pro. Daily Values: 47% vit. A, 48% vit. C, 5% calcium, and 19% iron.

30 Sherry-Lemon Vinaigrette

Prep: 10 minutes

1. In a blender container or food processor bowl combine ½ of a small lemon, seeded and cut into 6 wedges; ½ cup olive oil; ¼ cup sugar; ¼ cup sherry vinegar or white wine vinegar; ½ teaspoon salt; and ¼ teaspoon pepper. Cover; blend until nearly smooth. Makes 1 cup.

Thai Chicken Salad

For this and many other salads, you can make the dressing ahead and let it chill for up to two days to blend the flavors.

Prep: 30 minutes **Marinate:** 2 hours
Cook: 12 minutes

4   skinless, boneless chicken breast halves (1¼ to 1½ lb.)
2   Tbsp. rice vinegar
1   Tbsp. reduced-sodium soy sauce
1   tsp. toasted sesame oil
¼   tsp. grated fresh ginger
⅛   tsp. ground white pepper
2   cups fresh pea pods, trimmed and strings removed
8   cups torn mixed salad greens
1   recipe Peanut-Sesame Vinaigrette
Toasted sesame seed (optional)

1. Place chicken breast halves in a plastic bag. For marinade, combine rice vinegar, soy sauce, sesame oil, ginger, and white pepper; pour over chicken. Close bag; marinate in the refrigerator for 2 to 24 hours, turning bag occasionally.

2. Drain chicken; discard marinade. Grill chicken on the rack of an uncovered grill directly over medium coals for 12 to 15 minutes or until tender and no longer pink (170° F), turning once.

3. Meanwhile, in a saucepan cook pea pods in a small amount of boiling water for 1 to 2 minutes or until crisp-tender; drain.

4. To serve, diagaonally cut chicken breast halves into thin slices. Arrange greens on a serving platter or four salad plates. Top with sliced chicken and pea pods. Stir Peanut-Sesame Vinaigrette; pour over salad. If desired, sprinkle with sesame seed. Makes 4 servings.

Peanut-Sesame Vinaigrette: In a small bowl whisk ¼ cup salad oil into 2 tablespoons peanut butter. Stir in 3 tablespoons rice vinegar, 1 tablespoon reduced-sodium soy sauce, 1 teaspoon brown sugar, ½ teaspoon toasted sesame oil, and ¼ to ½ teaspoon crushed red pepper. Makes ½ cup.

Nutrition facts per serving: 407 cal., 23 g total fat (4 g sat. fat), 82 mg chol., 419 mg sodium, 9 g carbo., 3 g fiber, and 38 g pro. Daily Values: 11% vit. A, 14% vit. C, 7% calcium, and 13% iron.

30 Greek Chicken Salad

Prep: 30 minutes **Chill:** up to 2 hours

1   9-oz. pkg. frozen artichoke hearts
2   cups cubed cooked chicken
1   cup cherry tomatoes, halved
1   small red onion, cut into slivers
1   recipe Honey-Mustard Vinaigrette
8   cups torn mixed salad greens
3   Tbsp. pine nuts, toasted
¼   cup crumbled feta cheese

1. Cook artichokes according to package direction; drain. In a large salad bowl combine artichokes, chicken, tomatoes, and red onion. Shake Honey-Dijon Vinaigrette; pour over salad and toss to coat. Cover and chill for up to 2 hours.

2. Toss chicken mixture with greens and pine nuts. Sprinkle with feta cheese. Makes 4 servings.

Honey Mustard Vinaigrette: In a screw-top jar combine ¼ cup olive oil; ¼ cup balsamic vinegar; 2 tablespoons honey mustard; 1 clove garlic, minced; ¼ teaspoon salt; and ⅛ teaspoon pepper. Cover; shake well to mix. Makes ⅔ cup.

Nutrition facts per serving: 405 cal., 24 g total fat (5 g sat. fat), 69 mg chol., 363 mg sodium, 22 g carbo., 6 g fiber, and 27 g pro. Daily Values: 16% vit. A, 34% vit. C, 10% calcium, and 18% iron.

Orange-Barley Chicken Salad

Prep: 25 minutes **Chill:** 1 hour

½   cup quick-cooking barley
Leaf lettuce
1   9-oz. pkg. frozen cooked chicken breast strips, thawed
1   cup halved seedless grapes
1½ cups cubed fresh pineapple
1   recipe Orange-Basil Vinaigrette
2   Tbsp. chopped pecans, toasted

1. Cook barley according to package directions. Drain. Rinse under cold water; drain again. Cover; chill for at least 1 hour.

2. Line four plates with lettuce. Top with chicken, grapes, and pineapple. Shake Orange-Basil Vinaigrette; pour on salad. Top with pecans. Makes 4 servings.

Orange-Basil Vinaigrette: In a screw-top jar combine 1 teaspoon finely shredded orange peel; ¼ cup orange juice; ¼ cup salad oil; 2 tablespoons white balsamic vinegar or white wine vinegar; 2 tablespoons snipped fresh basil or 1 teaspoon dried basil, crushed; and 1 tablespoon honey. Cover and shake to mix. Makes ½ cup.

Nutrition facts per serving: 381 cal., 20 g total fat (3 g sat. fat), 45 mg chol., 379 mg sodium, 36 g carbo., 4 g fiber, and 19 g pro. Daily Values: 6% vit. A, 41% vit. C, 4% calcium, and 7% iron.

Hazelnut and Jerusalem Artichoke Chicken Salad

Start to finish: 45 minutes

2   7½- to 10-oz. pkg. lemon-herb seasoned skinless, boneless chicken breast halves (4 halves total)
1   lb. Jerusalem artichokes, peeled and thinly sliced*
6   oz. fresh green beans, cut into 1-inch pieces
1   tsp. finely shredded lemon peel
¼   cup lemon juice
¼   cup hazelnut oil or olive oil
½   tsp. salt
¼   tsp. pepper
¾   cup hazelnuts (filberts) or almonds, toasted, skinned, and coarsely chopped**
¼   cup snipped fresh parsley
Butterhead lettuce leaves

1. Cook chicken breast halves according to package directions.

2. Meanwhile, in a steamer basket over boiling water, steam artichokes and green beans, covered, for 5 to 7 minutes or until crisp tender.

3. For dressing, in a screw-top jar combine lemon peel, juice, oil, salt, and pepper. Cover and shake well to mix.

4. Transfer vegetables to a large bowl. Add half of the dressing; toss to coat. Add hazelnuts and parsley; toss to combine.

5. Line four salad plates with lettuce leaves. Add a chicken breast half to each. Divide artichoke mixture evenly among the plates. Drizzle with remaining dressing. Makes 4 servings.

*Test Kitchen Tip: To keep Jerusalem artichokes from darkening, place in a bowl with 2 cups water and 2 tablespoons lemon juice until ready to use.

**Test Kitchen Tip: To toast and peel hazelnuts, preheat oven to 350° F. Spread in a shallow baking pan. Bake about 8 minutes or until toasted, stirring once. Spread on a clean kitchen towel. Fold towel over and gently rub to remove skins.

Nutrition facts per serving: 491 cal., 32 g total fat (3 g sat. fat), 80 mg chol., 950 mg sodium, 23 g carbo., 6 g fiber, and 36 g pro. Daily Values: 14% vit. A, 42% vit. C, 7% calcium, and 26% iron.

Dinner in a Bowl

Confetti Chicken Big Bowl   Italian Three-Bean Chili

Julie DeMatteo, Clementon, N.J.

$400 WINNER

Confetti Chicken Big Bowl

Prep: 30 minutes **Cook:** 6 minutes

1	lb. skinless, boneless chicken breasts, cut into 1-inch cubes
2	Tbsp. cooking oil
4	tsp. minced garlic (8 cloves)
4	tsp. grated fresh ginger
1	Tbsp. red curry paste
1	tsp. ground cumin
1	14-oz. can unsweetened coconut milk
2	cups shredded carrot
2	cups small broccoli florets
1	medium red sweet pepper, cut into bite-size strips
2	3-oz. pkg. chicken-flavored ramen noodles, coarsely broken
2	cups snow pea pods, halved
2	Tbsp. soy sauce
4	tsp. lime juice
1	cup slivered fresh basil
⅓	cup snipped fresh cilantro

1. In a 4-quart Dutch oven cook chicken in 1 tablespoon hot oil for 3 to 4 minutes or until no longer pink. Remove; set aside. Add remaining oil to pan. Add garlic, ginger, curry paste, and cumin; cook and stir for 30 seconds.

2. Stir in 4 cups water, milk, carrot, broccoli, pepper, and noodles (reserve seasoning). Bring to boiling; reduce heat. Simmer, covered, 3 minutes. Stir in chicken, pea pods, seasoning, soy, and lime. Stir in basil and cilantro. Makes 6 servings.

Nutrition facts per serving: 454 cal., 25 g total fat (12 g sat. fat), 44 mg chol., 1,087 mg sodium, 33 g carbo., 4 g fiber, and 26 g pro. Daily Values: 246% vit. A, 143% vit. C, 8% calcium, and 15% iron.

Lauri Sadorus, Everett, Wash.

$200 WINNER

low fat Italian Three-Bean Chili

Prep: 20 minutes **Cook:** 30 minutes

½	cup chopped red onion
1	clove garlic, minced
2	Tbsp. olive oil
1	15-oz. can tomato sauce
1	15-oz. can black beans, rinsed
1	15- to 16-oz. can great northern beans, rinsed and drained
1	14½-oz. can diced tomatoes
1	cup frozen green soybeans
1	4½-oz. can diced chili peppers
1	Tbsp. balsamic vinegar
⅓	cup sliced pitted ripe olives
2	Tbsp. snipped fresh cilantro
	Hot cooked rice, pasta, or couscous

1. Cook and stir onion and garlic in hot oil until tender. Add ½ cup water, tomato sauce, beans, tomatoes, soybeans, peppers, and vinegar. Bring to boiling; reduce heat. Simmer, covered, 20 minutes, stirring often. Stir in olives and cilantro; simmer 5 minutes. Serve over rice; top with cheese, if desired. Makes 6 servings.

Nutrition facts per serving: 436 cal., 12 g total fat (3 g sat. fat), 11 mg chol., 828 mg sodium, 62 g carbo., 10 g fiber, and 23 g pro. Daily Values: 6% vit. A, 42% vit. C, 33% calcium, and 29% iron.

Sausage Tortellini Soup

Prep: 15 minutes **Cook:** 20 minutes

	Nonstick cooking spray
1	lb. smoked, fully cooked chicken sausage, halved lengthwise, then sliced crosswise into 1-inch pieces
1	large onion, cut into thin wedges
2	cloves garlic, minced
2	14-oz. cans chicken broth
1	14½-oz. can diced tomatoes with basil, oregano, and garlic
1	cup water
2	9-oz. pkg. refrigerated mushroom or cheese tortellini
1	10-oz. pkg. frozen baby lima beans
¼	cup slivered fresh basil
2	Tbsp. freshly shredded Parmesan cheese

1. Lightly coat a Dutch oven with nonstick cooking spray. Cook sausage, onion, and garlic over medium heat until sausage is brown and onion is tender. Drain off fat.

2. Add broth, tomatoes, and water. Bring to boiling; reduce heat. Simmer, covered, for 10 minutes. Add tortellini and lima beans. Return to boiling; reduce heat. Simmer, uncovered, for 5 to 6 minutes or until pasta and beans are tender.

3. Stir in basil. Ladle into six bowls. Sprinkle each serving with Parmesan cheese. Makes 6 to 8 servings.

Nutrition facts per serving: 527 cal., 18 g total fat (6 g sat. fat), 62 mg chol., 1.636 mg sodium, 60 g carbo., 4 g fiber, and 32 g pro. Daily Values: 12% vit. A, 18% vit. C, 25% calcium, and 26% iron.

Easy Moroccan Stew

Prep: 40 minutes **Bake:** 1 hour 20 minutes

- 2   lb. boneless pork shoulder
- 3   Tbsp. all-purpose flour
- 1   tsp. ground cumin
- 2   Tbsp. cooking oil
- ½   cup chopped onion
- 2   14½-oz. cans diced tomatoes
- 1   tsp. salt
- 1   tsp. ground ginger
- 1   tsp. ground cinnamon
- ½   tsp. sugar
- ½   tsp. pepper
- 2   medium carrots, sliced
- 2   medium red potatoes, chopped
- 1   medium sweet potato, peeled and chopped
- 2   cups frozen cut green beans
- 1½ cups frozen baby lima beans
- 2   Tbsp. snipped fresh cilantro or parsley
- ½   cup plain yogurt
   Pita bread (optional)

1. Preheat oven to 350° F. Trim fat; cut pork into ¾-inch pieces. Combine flour and cumin; toss meat cubes with flour mixture. In a 4- to 5-quart oven-proof Dutch oven brown meat and onion, half at a time, in hot oil. Drain fat. Return all meat and onion to the pan.

2. Stir in ⅓ cup water, undrained tomatoes, salt, ginger, cinnamon, sugar, and pepper. Add carrot, potatoes, green beans, and lima beans. Bring just to boiling.

3. Cover; bake 1 hour and 20 minutes or until meat and vegetables are tender. Spoon into bowls. Sprinkle with cilantro or parsley; top with yogurt. If desired, serve with bread. Makes 6 servings.

Nutrition facts per serving: 400 cal., 23 g total fat (4 g sat. fat), 86 mg chol., 167 mg sodium, 12 g carbo., 2 g fiber, and 38 g pro. Daily Values: 22% vit. A, 21% vit. C, 9% calcium, and 18% iron.

low fat Green Chili Stew

This Tex-Mex favorite won hands down in October of 1998, and it's still a champion.

Prep: 15 minutes **Cook:** 1¾ hours

- 2   lb. beef stew meat
- ¼   cup all-purpose flour
- ¼   cup margarine or butter
- 6   cloves garlic, minced
- 3   cups beef broth
- 1   12-oz. bottle dark (Mexican) beer
- 1   cup bottled green salsa
- 2   Tbsp. snipped fresh oregano or 2 tsp. dried oregano, crushed

- 1   tsp. ground cumin
- 3   medium potatoes, cubed
- 1   14½-oz. can hominy, drained
- 2   4½-oz. cans diced green chili peppers, drained
- 12 green onions, bias-sliced into 1-inch pieces
- ½   cup snipped fresh cilantro

1. Toss beef cubes with flour. In a 4½-quart Dutch oven brown beef cubes, half at a time, in hot margarine or butter. Using a slotted spoon, remove meat from Dutch oven.

2. Add garlic to Dutch oven; cook for 1 minute. Stir in broth, beer, salsa, oregano, and cumin. Return meat to Dutch oven. Bring to boiling; reduce heat. Cover and simmer about 1¼ hours or until meat is nearly tender.

3. Add potatoes; simmer about 30 minutes more or until meat and potatoes are tender. Stir in hominy, chili peppers, green onions, and cilantro; heat through. Spoon into eight bowls. Makes 8 servings.

Nutrition facts per serving: 392 cal., 16 g total fat (4 g sat. fat), 82 mg chol., 720 mg sodium, 28 g carbo., 1 g fiber, and 32 g pro. Daily Values: 189% vit. A, 49% vit. C, 7% calcium, and 38% iron.

low fat Turnip and Barley Stew

Prep: 25 minutes **Cook:** 15 minutes

- 1   large onion, cut into wedges
- 4   cloves garlic, minced
- 1   Tbsp. olive oil or cooking oil
- 2   tsp. dried sage, crushed
- 1   tsp. ground cumin
- 2   medium turnips, peeled and cut into ½-inch cubes
- 1   small rutabaga, peeled and cut into ½-inch cubes
- 3   14-oz. cans vegetable broth
- ¾   cup quick-cooking barley
- 1   15-oz. can white kidney beans, rinsed and drained
- ⅓   cup snipped fresh parsley
- ½   tsp. pepper

1. In a 4-quart Dutch oven cook onion and garlic in hot oil over medium heat until onion is tender. Stir in sage, cumin, turnips, and rutabaga; cook and stir for 1 minute more.

2. Add broth and barley; bring to boiling. Reduce heat; simmer, covered, about 15 minutes or until tender.

3. Stir in beans, parsley, and pepper; heat through. To serve, spoon into six bowls. Makes 6 servings.

Nutrition facts per serving: 157 cal., 4 g total fat (0 g sat. fat), 0 mg chol., 955 mg sodium, 34 g carbo., 7 g fiber, and 7 g pro. Daily Values: 6% vit. A, 26% vit. C, 6% calcium, and 11% iron.

Creamy Cajun Shrimp with Pasta

Prep: 25 minutes **Cook:** 30 minutes

- 1   lb. fresh or frozen medium shrimp in shells, peeled and deveined
- ½   cup chopped onion
- 2   cloves garlic, minced
- 1   Tbsp. butter
- 1   Tbsp. olive oil
- 2   tsp. Cajun seasoning*
- 4   oz. fresh mushrooms, sliced (about 1½ cups)
- 1   medium zucchini, cut into ¼-inch-thick slices (about 1⅓ cups)
- 1   medium yellow summer squash, cut into ¼-inch-thick slices
- 1   medium red sweet pepper, cut into bite-size pieces
- 1   medium carrot, thinly sliced
- 1¼ cups chicken broth
- 1   cup whipping cream
- 6   oz. angel hair pasta, broken up
- 2   Tbsp. grated Parmesan or Romano cheese
   Freshly ground black pepper

1. Thaw shrimp, if frozen.

2. In a 12-inch skillet cook and stir onion and garlic in hot butter and oil until tender but not brown.

3. Stir in shrimp and Cajun seasoning*. Add mushrooms, zucchini, yellow summer squash, sweet pepper, and carrot; cook and stir for 3 minutes.

4. Add broth and whipping cream; bring to boiling. Gradually add pasta, stirring so pasta does not stick together. Cover and simmer for 3 to 5 minutes or until pasta is tender.

5. Sprinkle with Parmesan or Romano cheese. Season to taste with pepper. Spoon into four bowls. Makes 4 servings.

***Test Kitchen Tip:** If using salt-free Cajun seasoning, add ½ tcaspoon salt with the shrimp.

Nutrition facts per serving: 584 cal., 33 g total fat (17 g sat. fat), 222 mg chol., 572 mg sodium, 45 g carbo., 4 g fiber, and 29 g pro. Daily Values: 134% vit. A, 96% vit. C, 17% calcium, and 24% iron.

Dinnertime Sandwiches

Spanish Grilled Sandwiches Cobb Salad Hoagies

Spanish Grilled Sandwiches

Prep: 30 minutes **Chill:** 8 minutes **Cook:** 8 minutes

4 sandwich rolls, such as pan cubano, bolillos, teleras (about 6½x3 inches), hoagie buns, or two 8-inch Italian flat breads (focaccia), split in half horizontally

1 recipe Artichoke-Pepper Relish
1 lb. thinly sliced deli roast beef or roast pork
8 oz. sliced provolone cheese
4 tsp. olive oil

1. If using focaccia, cut in half crosswise. Arrange Artichoke-Pepper Relish, meat, and cheese over bottom halves of rolls. Add tops of rolls.

2. Coat a very large skillet with 2 teaspoons of the oil; heat. Add 2 sandwiches; cover with foil; press with a heavy skillet. Cook for 8 to 10 minutes or until heated through, turning once. Cut in half; keep warm. Repeat. Makes 8 servings.

Artichoke-Pepper Relish: Drain one 6½-ounce jar marinated artichoke hearts, reserving marinade; thinly slice artichokes. Combine artichokes; reserved marinade; one 7-ounce jar roasted red sweet peppers, drained and cut into strips; ⅔ cup jalapeño-stuffed olives, sliced; 1 medium onion, thinly sliced into rings; 1 clove garlic, minced; 1 tablespoon snipped fresh parsley; ⅛ teaspoon dried oregano, crushed; and ⅛ teaspoon ground cumin. Cover; chill 2 to 24 hours, tossing often.

Nutrition facts per serving: 417 cal., 16 g total fat (7 g sat. fat), 59 mg chol., 794 mg sodium, 38 g carbo., 2 g fiber, and 30 g pro. Daily Values: 7% vit. A, 97% vit. C, 24% calcium, and 22% iron.

Cobb Salad Hoagies

Start to finish: 35 minutes

1⅓ cups cubed cooked chicken
2 plum tomatoes, chopped
4 slices bacon, crisp-cooked, drained, and crumbled
½ cup crumbled blue cheese

1 recipe Avocado Vinaigrette
4 Boston lettuce leaves
4 hoagie buns, split, hollowed out, and toasted
2 hard-cooked eggs, chopped

1. In a bowl combine chicken, tomatoes, bacon, and blue cheese. Add Avocado Vinaigrette; toss to coat. Place lettuce leaves on bottom halves of buns. Add chicken mixture; top with chopped eggs and top halves of buns. Makes 4 sandwiches.

Avocado Vinaigrette: Whisk together 3 tablespoons olive oil, 1 tablespoon white wine vinegar, 1 teaspoon Dijon-style mustard, ½ teaspoon salt, and ½ teaspoon pepper. Stir in 1 avocado, halved, seeded, peeled, and finely chopped; set aside.

Nutrition facts: 659 cal., 35 g total fat (9 g sat. fat), 165 mg chol., 1,214 mg sodium, 55 g carbo., 5 g fiber, 32 g pro. Daily Values: 18% vit. A, 18% calcium, and 21% iron.

30 Roast Beef and Mango Hoagies

Start to finish: 25 minutes

1 medium onion, thinly sliced
¼ cup olive oil
½ of a medium red and/or green sweet pepper, cut into thin strips
½ tsp. curry powder
¼ cup red wine vinegar or cider vinegar
¼ tsp. dried thyme, crushed
⅛ tsp. ground black pepper
¼ cup tub light cream cheese
6 kaiser rolls, split and toasted
2 cups arugula
12 oz. thinly sliced fully cooked roast beef
1 mango, seeded, peeled, and sliced

1. In a medium skillet cook onion in olive oil until tender. Add sweet pepper and curry powder; cook and stir for 1 minute more. Stir in vinegar, thyme, and black pepper. Set aside.

2. Spread cream cheese onto cut side of each bun bottom. Line with arugula. Divide beef and mango slices among sandwiches. Top with curry mixture; add bun tops. Makes 6 sandwiches.

Nutrition facts per sandwich: 399 cal., 16 g total fat (4 g sat. fat), 44 mg chol., 399 mg sodium, 39 g carbo., 2 g fiber, and 24 g pro. Daily Values: 44% vit. A, 46% vit. C, 9% calcium, and 19% iron.

30 Reuben Quesadillas

Prep: 15 minutes **Bake:** 10 minutes

½ of a sweet onion, such as Vidalia or Walla Walla, halved and thinly sliced (about 1½ cups)
2 Tbsp. cooking oil
1 cup sauerkraut, drained
1 tsp. caraway seed
4 10-inch flour tortillas
¼ cup bottled Thousand Island salad dressing
8 oz. thinly sliced corned beef, cut into strips
1 cup shredded Swiss cheese (4 oz.)

1. Preheat oven to 375° F. In a medium skillet cook onion in 1 tablespoon of the cooking oil until tender. Add sauerkraut and ½ teaspoon of the caraway seed; cook for 2 to 3 minutes or until any liquid is evaporated.

2. Brush some of the remaining oil onto 2 of the tortillas. Place, oiled side down, on two large pizza pans or baking sheets. Spread salad dressing onto tortillas. Top with corned beef, onion mixture, and Swiss cheese. Top with remaining tortillas. Brush with remaining oil; sprinkle with remaining caraway seed.

3. Bake about 10 minutes or until cheese is melted. Cut into wedges to serve. Makes 16 wedges.

Nutrition facts per wedge: 132 cal., 9 g total fat (3 g sat. fat), 21 mg chol., 304 mg sodium, 8 g carbo., 1 g fiber, and 6 g pro. Daily Values: 1% vit. A, 3% vit. C, 8% calcium, and 4% iron.

30 Asian Chicken Wraps

Start to finish: 30 minutes

1 2- to 2¼-lb. cooked roasted chicken (from deli)
8 8- to 10-inch flour tortillas
½ cup hoisin sauce
¼ cup finely chopped peanuts
¼ cup finely chopped green onion
½ cup shredded daikon, well drained
1 recipe Soy Dipping Sauce

1. Remove skin from chicken and discard. Remove chicken from bones; shred chicken (you should have about 4 cups). Set aside.

2. Spread one side of each tortilla with some of the hoisin sauce; sprinkle with peanuts and green onion. Top with shredded chicken and daikon. Roll up; halve crosswise. Serve with Soy Dipping Sauce. Makes 8 servings.

Soy Dipping Sauce: In a small bowl combine 3 tablespoons soy sauce, 3 tablespoons Chinese black vinegar or rice vinegar, 1 tablespoon water, and 1 teaspoon chili oil or toasted sesame oil. Makes ⅓ cup.

Nutrition facts per sandwich: 283 cal., 9 g total fat (2 g sat. fat), 50 mg chol., 869 mg sodium, 26 g carbo., 1 g fiber, and 20 g pro. Daily Values: 1% vit. A, 5% vit. C, 5% calcium, and 10% iron.

30 Grilled Chicken Sausage Sandwiches

Start to finish: 30 minutes

1 medium sweet onion, such as Vidalia or Walla Walla, halved and thinly sliced (½ cup)
4 cloves garlic, minced
2 Tbsp. olive oil
1 large yellow summer squash, halved lengthwise and thinly sliced (about 2 cups)
1 cup sliced fresh mushrooms
2 Tbsp. balsamic vinegar
2 tsp. snipped fresh rosemary or ½ tsp. dried rosemary, crushed
½ cup quartered cherry tomatoes
6 cooked chicken sausage links or cooked smoked sausage links
6 hoagie buns
½ cup shredded fresh spinach

1. In a large skillet cook onion and garlic in hot oil over medium-high heat for 3 minutes. Stir in squash and mushrooms. Cook and stir for 4 to 5 minutes more or until vegetables are tender. Stir in vinegar and rosemary. Remove from heat. Stir in quartered cherry tomatoes.

2. Meanwhile, pierce skin of sausage several times with a fork. Grill sausages on the rack of an uncovered grill directly over medium coals about 7 minutes or until sausages are browned and heated through, turning once halfway through grilling.

3. Halve the buns lengthwise, cutting to but not through the other side. Toast cut sides of hoagie buns alongside the sausage.

4. Place a grilled sausage in each bun; top with mushroom mixture. Sprinkle with spinach. Makes 6 sandwiches.

Nutrition facts per sandwich: 466 cal., 19 g total fat (5 g sat. fat), 20 mg chol., 1,007 mg sodium, 55 g carbo., 4 g fiber, and 20 g pro. Daily Values: 6% vit. A, 18% vit. C, 10% calcium, and 16% iron.

Tropical Turkey Sub with Mango Salsa

Stir together the mango salsa next time you grill chicken or fish.

Start to finish: 45 minutes

1 16-oz. loaf French bread or Italian bread
Leaf lettuce
1 recipe Mango Salsa
12 oz. thinly sliced cooked turkey
4 oz. thinly sliced provolone cheese
3 Tbsp. mayonnaise or salad dressing
¼ tsp. Jamaican jerk seasoning

1. Slice bread in half lengthwise. Using a spoon, hollow out bottom half, leaving a ½-inch-thick shell. Line bottom half with leaf lettuce. Using a slotted spoon, place Mango Salsa atop lettuce. Add a layer of turkey and cheese.

2. Stir together mayonnaise and jerk seasoning; spread onto cut side of bread top. Place top on sandwich. Slice to serve. Makes 6 servings.

Mango Salsa: In a medium bowl gently toss together 1 small mango, seeded, peeled, and finely chopped (1 cup); ½ cup finely chopped red onion; ¼ cup snipped fresh cilantro; 2 tablespoons fresh lime juice; 1 fresh jalapeño pepper, seeded and very finely chopped*; 2 teaspoons brown sugar; and 2 teaspoons grated fresh ginger. Season to taste with salt and pepper. Cover and chill up to 8 hours. Makes 1½ cups.

*Test Kitchen Tip: Because chili peppers contain volatile oils that can burn your skin and eyes, avoid direct contact with them as much as possible. When working with chili peppers, wear plastic or rubber gloves. If your bare fingers touch the chili peppers, wash your hands well with soap and water.

Nutrition facts per serving: 453 cal., 16 g total fat (5 g sat. fat), 58 mg chol., 718 mg sodium, 48 g carbo., 4 g fiber, and 29 g pro. Daily Values: 36% vit. A, 27% vit. C, 23% calcium, and 19% iron.

Egg Stratas & Casseroles

Bagel, Lox, and Egg Strata   Margaret's Citrus Raisin Strata

Bagel, Lox, and Egg Strata

Prep: 30 minutes **Chill:** 4 hours **Bake:** 45 minutes **Stand:** 10 minutes

¼	cup butter or margarine, melted
4	to 6 plain bagels, cut into bite-size pieces (8 cups)
1	3-oz. pkg. thinly sliced smoked salmon (lox-style), cut into small pieces

8	oz. Swiss cheese or Monterey Jack cheese, shredded (2 cups)
¼	cup snipped fresh chives
8	eggs
2	cups milk
1	cup cream-style cottage cheese
¼	tsp. pepper

1. Place melted butter in a 3-quart rectangular baking dish; spread to cover the bottom. Spread bagel pieces evenly in the prepared dish. Sprinkle lox, cheese, and chives evenly over bagel pieces.

2. In a large bowl beat eggs; stir in milk, cottage cheese, and pepper. Pour over layers in dish; press down gently with the back of a wooden spoon to moisten all of the ingredients. Cover and chill for 4 to 24 hours.

3. Preheat oven to 350° F. Bake, uncovered, about 45 minutes or until center is set and edges are puffed and golden. Let stand for 10 minutes. Makes 12 servings.

Nutrition facts per serving: 267 cal., 14 g total fat (8 g sat. fat), 176 mg chol., 497 mg sodium, 16 g carbo., 1 g fiber, and 17 g pro. Daily Values: 13% vit. A, 2% vit. C, 28% calcium, and 8% iron.

Margaret's Citrus Raisin Strata

Prep: 10 minutes **Bake:** 45 minutes **Stand:** 15 minutes

10	slices cinnamon-raisin bread
3	eggs
2	cups half-and-half or light cream
⅔	cup sugar

1½	tsp. finely shredded orange peel
1	tsp. vanilla
	Vanilla yogurt (optional)

1. Preheat oven to 350° F. Tear bread into bite-size pieces. Place in a greased 2-quart square baking dish. In a medium bowl beat eggs; stir in half-and-half, sugar, orange peel, and vanilla. Pour over bread in baking dish.

2. Bake, uncovered, about 45 minutes or until a knife inserted near the center comes out clean. Let stand for 15 minutes before serving. If desired, serve with vanilla yogurt. Makes 6 servings.

Nutrition facts per serving: 345 cal., 14 g total fat (7 g sat. fat), 136 mg chol., 233 mg sodium, 48 g carbo., 2 g fiber, and 9 g pro. Daily Values: 10% vit. A, 2% vit. C, 13% calcium, and 9% iron.

Artichoke and Mushroom Bake

Turn this Greek-inspired dish into brunch by serving with a Greek salad.

Prep: 25 minutes **Bake:** 35 minutes

	Nonstick cooking spray
1½	cups sliced fresh mushrooms
½	cup finely chopped onion
1	Tbsp. olive oil
8	eggs
2	cups cream-style cottage cheese
½	cup all-purpose flour
4	oz. crumbled feta cheese
1	14-oz. can artichoke hearts, rinsed, drained, and chopped
½	cup grated Parmesan cheese
	Tomato wedges (optional)

1. Preheat oven to 350° F. Lightly coat a 2-quart rectangular baking dish with cooking spray; set aside.

2. In a large skillet cook mushrooms and onion in hot oil until tender; set aside.

3. In a large bowl beat eggs; stir in cottage cheese and flour. Stir in feta cheese, artichoke hearts, Parmesan cheese, and mushroom mixture. Pour mixture into the prepared dish.

4. Bake about 35 minutes or until a knife inserted near the center comes out clean. If desired, top with tomato wedges. Makes 8 servings.

Nutrition facts per serving: 257 cal., 14 g total fat (7 g sat. fat), 238 mg chol., 707 mg sodium, 12 g carbo., 2 g fiber, and 20 g pro. Daily Values: 12% vit. A, 2% vit. C, 23% calcium, and 13% iron.

Potato and Onion Breakfast Casserole

Serve with fresh tomatoes or melon or scramble a few eggs for a heartier meal.

Prep: 25 minutes **Chill:** Overnight
Bake: 40 minutes **Stand:** 15 minutes

- 4 slices bacon
- 3 cups thinly sliced sweet onion, such as Vidalia or Walla Walla
- 3 cups frozen loose-pack diced hash brown potatoes with onion and peppers (12 oz.)
- 1 Tbsp. balsamic vinegar
- Nonstick cooking spray
- 6 eggs
- 1½ cups milk
- 1 cup shredded Swiss cheese (4 oz.)
- ½ tsp. salt
- ¼ tsp. pepper

1. In a large skillet cook bacon until crisp. Drain on paper towels; reserve 2 tablespoons drippings in the skillet.

2. Add onion; cover and cook over medium-low heat for 10 minutes, stirring occasionally. Uncover; cook for 3 minutes more or until onions are tender.

3. Stir in hash brown potatoes. Remove from heat. Crumble bacon; stir bacon and balsamic vinegar into potato mixture.

4. Lightly coat a 2-quart rectangular baking dish with cooking spray. Spread potato mixture in the baking dish.

5. In a medium mixing bowl beat eggs; stir in milk, cheese, salt, and pepper. Pour evenly over potato mixture. Cover and chill overnight.

6. Preheat oven to 350° F. Uncover potato mixture. Bake about 40 minutes or until a knife inserted near the center comes out clean. Let stand for 15 minutes before serving. Makes 6 to 8 servings.

Nutrition facts per serving: 263 cal., 14 g total fat (6 g sat. fat), 238 mg chol., 412 mg sodium, 18 g carbo., 2 g fiber, and 16 g pro. Daily Values: 12% vit. A, 13% vit. C, 29% calcium, and 7% iron.

Southwestern Breakfast Casserole

Prep: 30 minutes **Chill:** 2 hours
Bake: 45 minutes **Stand:** 10 minutes

- Nonstick cooking spray
- 6 cups cubed firm-textured white bread
- 6 oz. uncooked chorizo sausage or bulk pork sausage*, crumbled
- 1 cup chopped onion
- ½ cup chopped red sweet pepper
- 1 cup frozen whole kernel corn
- ½ tsp. ground cumin (optional)
- ¼ tsp. salt
- Dash bottled hot pepper sauce
- 6 eggs
- 2 cups milk
- 4 oz. Queso Fresco, crumbled, or Monterey Jack cheese, shredded (1 cup)
- 1 to 2 Tbsp. snipped fresh cilantro or parsley (optional)
- Bottled salsa, dairy sour cream, chopped tomato, and/or sliced jalapeño peppers (optional)

1. Lightly coat a 2-quart rectangular baking dish with cooking spray; set aside. Place bread in a large bowl; set aside.

2. In a large skillet cook sausage, onion, and sweet pepper until meat is brown and onion is tender, stirring to break up sausage. Drain off any fat. Stir in corn, cumin (if using), salt, and hot pepper sauce; cook for 1 minute more. Add sausage mixture to bread mixture.

3. In a large bowl beat eggs; stir in milk. Pour egg mixture over bread mixture. Toss gently to moisten. (The mixture will be wet.) Spoon half of the bread mixture into prepared dish; sprinkle with half of the cheese. Cover with remaining bread mixture. Cover; chill for 2 to 24 hours.

4. Preheat oven to 350° F. Uncover baking dish; bake for 30 minutes. Sprinkle with remaining cheese; bake for 15 to 20 minutes more or until a knife inserted near the center comes out clean. Let stand 10 minutes before serving. If desired, sprinkle with cilantro; serve with salsa, sour cream, chopped tomato, and sliced jalapeño peppers. Makes 8 servings.

*Test Kitchen Tip: If using pork sausage, add ½ teaspoon ground cumin.

Nutrition facts per serving: 302 cal., 16 g total fat (6 g sat. fat), 187 mg chol., 569 mg sodium, 24 g carbo., 1 g fiber, and 16 g pro. Daily Values: 20% vit. A, 30% vit. C, 16% calcium, and 10% iron.

Prosciutto & Pasta Egg Casserole

It tastes like fettuccine alfredo, only baked with bow tie pasta! Serve this hearty dinner with a tossed green salad.

Prep: 25 minutes **Bake:** 35 minutes
Stand: 10 minutes

- ½ cup chopped onion
- 1 cup sliced fresh mushrooms
- 2 Tbsp. butter
- 3 oz. prosciutto, thinly slivered
- 2 cups cooked bow tie pasta
- 2 Tbsp. snipped fresh basil or 1½ tsp. dried basil, crushed
- 8 eggs
- 2 cups milk
- 1 cup finely shredded mozzarella cheese (4 oz.)
- ½ cup finely shredded Parmesan cheese
- Finely shredded Parmesan cheese (optional)

1. Preheat oven to 350° F. Grease a 2-quart rectangular baking dish; set aside.

2. In a large skillet cook onion and mushrooms in hot butter until tender. Stir in prosciutto; cook for 1 minute more. Remove from heat; stir in cooked pasta and basil. Spread in the prepared dish.

3. In a large bowl beat eggs; stir in milk. Stir in cheeses; pour over pasta mixture.

4. Bake, uncovered, about 35 minutes or until a knife inserted near center comes out clean. If desired, sprinkle with additional Parmesan cheese. Let stand for 10 minutes before serving. Makes 8 servings.

Nutrition facts per serving: 270 cal., 15 g total fat (7 g sat. fat), 247 mg chol., 552 mg sodium, 15 g carbo., 1 g fiber, and 19 g pro. Daily Values: 15% vit. A, 2% vit. C, 26% calcium, and 9% iron.

Entrées for Entertaining

Citrus Duck with Orange-Ginger Glaze

Apricot Chicken Roll-Ups

Citrus Duck with Orange-Ginger Glaze

Marinate: 4 hours **Prep:** 25 minutes **Cook:** 35 minutes **Roast:** 15 minutes

6	6- to 8-oz. duck breast halves	4	Tbsp. grated fresh ginger
1	Tbsp. finely shredded orange peel	¼	cup chicken broth
1	cup orange juice	1	Tbsp. soy sauce
1	cup dry white wine	1	Tbsp. olive oil
6	Tbsp. honey	3	cups hot cooked rice

1. Trim duck fat; score skin. In a bag mix peel, juice, ½ cup wine, ¼ cup honey, and 3 tablespoons ginger. Add duck; seal. Marinate 4 to 24 hours, turning often.

2. In a saucepan combine 1¾ cups marinade and ½ cup wine; bring to boiling. Reduce heat; simmer, uncovered, for 20 to 25 minutes or until reduced to 1¼ cups. Add 2 tablespoons honey, 1 tablespoon ginger, broth, and soy sauce. Return to boiling; cook and stir about 15 minutes or until reduced to ⅔ cup. Meanwhile, in a 12-inch skillet cook duck in hot oil about 10 minutes or until brown, turning once.

3. Preheat oven to 425° F. In 13x9x2-inch baking pan roast duck about 15 minutes or until 170° F. Serve sliced duck and glaze with rice. Makes 6 servings.

Nutrition facts per serving: 469 cal., 15 g total fat (4 g sat. fat), 154 mg chol., 402 mg sodium, 46 g carbo., 1 g fiber, 31 g pro. Daily Values: 3% vit. A, 45% vit. C, 28% iron.

Apricot Chicken Roll-Ups

Prep: 40 minutes **Bake:** 35 minutes

	Nonstick cooking spray	6	medium skinless, boneless
1	6- or 7-oz. pkg. dried apricots, snipped (about 1⅓ cups)		chicken breast halves (about 2 lb.)
½	cup dried cranberries	1½	tsp. ground ginger
3	Tbsp. honey	2	eggs, beaten
		1	recipe Herb Coating

1. Preheat oven to 350° F. Coat a 3-quart rectangular baking dish with spray; set aside. For filling, stir together apricots, cranberries, honey, and ginger; set aside.

2. Pound breasts to ¼-inch thickness. Spoon ¼ cup filling in centers. Fold in bottoms and sides; roll up. Secure with toothpicks. Dip into egg; coat in Herb Coating. Arrange in dish. Bake 35 to 40 minutes or until no pink remains. Serves 6.

Herb Coating: Stir together ⅔ cup fine dry bread crumbs; 2 tablespoons snipped fresh parsley; 1 tablespoon all-purpose flour; 1 tablespoon finely shredded Parmesan cheese; 1 teaspoon paprika; ½ teaspoon sugar; ½ teaspoon dried oregano, crushed; ½ teaspoon salt; ¼ teaspoon garlic powder; ¼ teaspoon onion powder; and ¼ teaspoon pepper. Cut in 2 tablespoons shortening to resemble fine crumbs.

Nutrition facts per serving: 405 cal., 9 g total fat (2 g sat. fat), 159 mg chol., 546 mg sodium, 43 g carbo., 4 g fiber, 40 g pro. Daily Values: 50% vit. A, 8% calcium, 20% iron.

low fat Stuffed Pork Tenderloin with Apple-Cranberry Glaze

Prep: 20 minutes **Roast:** 20 minutes

2	cups torn fresh spinach
½	cup frozen artichoke hearts, thawed and chopped
⅓	cup finely shredded Parmesan cheese
1	tsp. snipped fresh rosemary or ¼ tsp. dried rosemary, crushed
1	1-lb. pork tenderloin
½	cup frozen apple-cranberry juice concentrate, thawed
¼	cup balsamic vinegar

1. Preheat oven to 425° F. For stuffing, in a large skillet cook spinach in a small amount of water until just wilted; drain well. In a small bowl combine spinach, artichoke hearts, cheese, and rosemary.

2. Slice tenderloin lengthwise, almost all the way through, making a pocket. Spoon stuffing into the pocket (the filling will be exposed). Place in a shallow roasting pan, stuffing side up. Insert a meat thermometer. Roast, uncovered, for 20 to 25 minutes or until thermometer registers 160° F. (The temperature of the meat will rise 5° to 10° F during standing.)

3. Meanwhile, for glaze, in a small saucepan combine apple-cranberry juice concentrate and balsamic vinegar. Bring to boiling. Simmer, uncovered, about 15 minutes or until mixture measures ⅓ cup. Spoon over pork during the last 10 minutes of roasting. Makes 4 servings.

Nutrition facts per serving: 270 cal., 6 g total fat (3 g sat. fat), 81 mg chol., 181 mg sodium, 24 g carbo., 3 g fiber, 28 g pro. Daily Values: 20% vit. A, 58% vit. C, 12% calcium, and 15% iron.

Beer-Brined Turkey

Soaking turkey overnight in beer, salt, and herbs really adds flavor before roasting.

Prep: 25 minutes **Chill:** overnight
Roast: 1¼ hours **Stand:** 15 minutes

- 1 1¾- to 2-lb. bone-in turkey breast portion
- 3 12-oz. cans beer
- ¼ cup coarse salt
- 4 cloves garlic, peeled and sliced
- 4 fresh rosemary sprigs
- 6 bay leaves
   Water
- 1 Tbsp. butter, melted
- 2 cloves garlic, minced
- 1 tsp. dried thyme, crushed
- 1 tsp. paprika
- ½ tsp. onion powder
- ½ tsp. ground sage
- ¼ tsp. pepper

1. Place turkey in a very large bowl. Pour beer over turkey. Add salt, sliced garlic, rosemary sprigs, and bay leaves. If necessary, add enough water to just cover. Cover; chill overnight in the refrigerator.

2. Preheat oven to 325° F. Remove turkey from brine; discard the brine. Place turkey on a rack in a shallow roasting pan. In a small bowl stir together butter and minced garlic; brush onto roast. In another small bowl stir together thyme, paprika, onion powder, sage, and pepper; sprinkle onto turkey.

3. Insert a meat thermometer into thickest part of the breast, without touching bone. Roast turkey, uncovered, for 1¼ to 1¾ hours or until thermometer registers 170° F. Cover and let stand for 15 minutes. Makes 6 servings.

Nutrition facts per serving: 198 cal., 10 g total fat (3 g sat. fat), 78 mg chol., 846 mg sodium, 1 g carbo., 1 g fiber, and 25 g pro. Daily Values: 7% vit. A, 1% vit. C, 3% calcium, and 9% iron.

Chicken Chili Rellenos

Prep: 45 minutes **Bake:** 20 minutes

- 6 fresh poblano peppers*
- 2 cups shredded or chopped cooked chicken
- 1 cup shredded Monterey Jack cheese (4 oz.)
- ½ cup frozen whole kernel corn, thawed
- ½ of an 8-oz. tub cream cheese with chives
- 2 Tbsp. snipped fresh cilantro
- 1 cup thinly sliced sweet onion
- 3 cloves garlic, thinly sliced
- 1 Tbsp. olive oil
- 1 15-oz. can tomato sauce
- 1½ tsp. ground cumin
- ½ tsp. ground coriander
- ¼ tsp. salt
- ¼ tsp. ground red pepper
- 2 Tbsp. snipped fresh cilantro

1. Preheat oven to 350° F. Cut a lengthwise slice from one side of each pepper, leaving stems intact. Chop pepper slices; set aside. Remove seeds and membranes from peppers. In a large saucepan cook peppers, half at a time, in boiling water for 2 minutes. Drain well.

2. Meanwhile, for filling, combine chicken, ½ cup shredded cheese, corn, cream cheese, and 2 tablespoons cilantro.

3. For sauce, in a skillet cook chopped pepper, onion, and garlic in hot oil over medium-low heat about 5 minutes or until tender, stirring occasionally. Stir in tomato sauce, cumin, coriander, salt, and ground red pepper. Cook and stir until bubbly.

4. Spoon filling into poblano peppers; arrange in a greased 3-quart rectangular baking dish. Top with sauce. Bake, covered, for 20 to 25 minutes or until heated through. Sprinkle with remaining ½ cup cheese. Bake, uncovered, 2 minutes more or until cheese is melted. Before serving, sprinkle with remaining 2 tablespoons cilantro. Makes 6 servings.

*Test Kitchen Tip: Because chili peppers, such as poblanos, contain volatile oils that can burn your skin and eyes, wear plastic or rubber gloves when working with them. If your bare hands do touch the chili peppers, wash your hands well with soap and water.

Nutrition facts per serving: 327 cal., 18 g total fat (8 g sat. fat), 78 mg chol., 657 mg sodium, 20 g carbo., 2 g fiber, and 23 g pro. Daily Values: 28% vit. A, 553% vit. C, 20% calcium, and 24% iron.

 Mediterranean Jambalaya

A little eggplant and a few olives take a Cajun favorite to the riviera.

Prep: 30 minutes **Cook:** 25 minutes

- 1 lb. fresh or frozen medium shrimp in shells
- 1 cup long grain rice
- 2 medium green sweet peppers, chopped
- 1 large onion, chopped
- 2 stalks celery, sliced
- 2 Tbsp. cooking oil
- 1 14½-oz. can diced tomatoes with basil, oregano, and garlic
- 1 8-oz. can tomato sauce
- ¼ tsp. ground red pepper
- 2 cups chopped, peeled eggplant
- 1 medium zucchini or yellow summer squash, halved lengthwise and sliced
- 1½ cups cubed cooked ham
- ½ cup pitted kalamata olives, halved
- ⅓ cup snipped fresh Italian flat-leaf parsley

1. Thaw shrimp, if frozen. Peel, devein, and rinse shrimp; set aside. Cook rice according to package directions.

2. Meanwhile, in a Dutch oven cook sweet pepper, onion, and celery in hot oil until tender. Stir in tomatoes, tomato sauce, and ground red pepper. Bring to boiling; reduce heat. Cover and simmer for 10 minutes.

3. Stir in shrimp, eggplant, zucchini, and ham. Return to boiling; reduce heat. Cover and cook for 5 minutes more, stirring once. Stir in rice; heat through. Sprinkle each serving with olives and parsley. Makes 6 to 8 servings.

Nutrition facts per serving: 370 cal., 11 g total fat (2 g sat. fat), 108 mg chol., 1,320 mg sodium, 42 g carbo., 4 g fiber, and 25 g pro. Daily Values: 22% vit. A, 76% vit. C, 11% calcium, and 27% iron.

Grilled Chops & Steaks

Ribeye Steaks with Chipotle Butter

Mustard-Rosemary Grilled Lamb

Ribeye Steaks with Chipotle Butter

Prep: 20 minutes **Grill:** 14 minutes

2 tsp. ground cumin	¼ tsp. adobo sauce
1 tsp. paprika	4 8- to 10-oz. boneless beef ribeye
½ tsp. salt	steaks, cut 1 inch thick
½ tsp. pepper	1 recipe Chipotle Butter
1 Tbsp. olive oil	Fresh basil or cilantro

1. In a bowl stir together cumin, paprika, salt, and pepper. Stir in olive oil and adobo sauce (from the canned chipotle pepper used in Chipotle Butter) until a paste forms. Spread spice mixture onto both sides of steaks.

2. Grill steaks on rack of an uncovered grill directly over medium coals to desired doneness, turning once. Allow 14 to 18 minutes for medium. Serve with Chipotle Butter. If desired, garnish with fresh basil or cilantro. Makes 4 servings.

Chipotle Butter: Stir together ¼ cup butter, softened; 1 tablespoon finely chopped shallots; 2 teaspoons snipped fresh basil or cilantro; 1½ teaspoons lime juice; and 1 teaspoon finely chopped chipotle pepper in adobo sauce (reserve sauce for meat).

Nutrition facts per serving: 416 cal., 27 g total fat (12 g sat. fat), 118 mg chol., 519 mg sodium, 2 g carbo., 1 g fiber, 40 g pro. Daily Values: 17% vit. A, 4% vit. C, 19% iron.

Mustard-Rosemary Grilled Lamb

Prep: 20 minutes **Marinate:** 2 hours **Grill:** 12 minutes

8 lamb rib or loin chops, cut 1 inch thick (about 2 lb.)	3 cloves garlic, minced
¼ cup stone-ground mustard	1 tsp. snipped fresh rosemary
2 green onions, thinly sliced (¼ cup)	1 tsp. honey
2 Tbsp. dry white wine	½ tsp. salt
1 Tbsp. balsamic vinegar	½ tsp. pepper

1. Trim fat from chops; set chops aside. In a small bowl stir together mustard, green onion, wine, vinegar, garlic, rosemary, honey, salt, and pepper. Spread mixture evenly onto both sides of chops. Place chops on a large plate; cover loosely with plastic wrap. Chill for 2 to 3 hours.

2. Grill chops on the rack of an uncovered grill directly over medium coals to desired doneness, turning chops once halfway through grilling. Allow 12 to 14 minutes for medium-rare and 15 to 17 minutes for medium. Makes 4 servings.

Nutrition facts per serving: 194 cal., 9 g total fat (3 g sat. fat), 64 mg chol., 557 mg sodium, 4 g carbo., 21 g pro. Daily Values: 1 % vit. A, 4% vit. C, 4% calcium, 12% iron.

Curried Steaks with Mango-Cucumber Relish

Prep: 35 minutes **Grill:** 11 minutes

½ tsp. curry powder
⅛ tsp. salt
⅛ tsp. crushed red pepper
1 Tbsp. cooking oil
4 boneless beef top loin steaks, cut 1 inch thick (2¼ lb. total)
1 recipe Mango-Cucumber Relish

1. In a small bowl stir curry powder, salt, and red pepper into oil; set aside.

2. Grill steaks on rack of uncovered grill directly over medium coals to desired doneness, turning once halfway through cooking and brushing steak lightly with oil mixture. Turn steaks; brush again with oil mixture. Grill to desired doneness. Allow 11 to 15 minutes for medium-rare or 14 to 18 minutes for medium.

3. Serve steaks with Mango-Cucumber Relish. Makes 4 servings.

Mango-Cucumber Relish: In a bowl combine 1 small ripe mango, seeded, peeled, and chopped (¾ cup); 1 small cucumber, seeded and coarsely chopped (1¼ cups); ⅓ cup chopped red onion; ⅓ cup chopped red or green sweet pepper; ⅓ cup chopped, peeled jicama; 2 tablespoons snipped fresh mint or parsley; 2 tablespoons seasoned rice vinegar; ½ teaspoon curry powder; ⅛ teaspoon salt; and ⅛ teaspoon crushed red pepper. Cover; chill up to 8 hours. Makes 3 cups.

Nutrition facts per serving: 391 cal., 14 g total fat (4 g sat. fat), 155 mg chol., 348 mg sodium, 9 g carbo., 1 g fiber, and 55 g pro. Daily Values: 32% vit. A, 60% vit. C, 3% calcium, and 41% iron.

Ribeye Steaks with Glazed Sweet Onions

Most sweet onions are grown from fall to spring in warm-weather states. Look for Vidalia, Maui, Walla Walla, AmeriSweet, Imperial, Oso, or Texas sweet onions.

Prep: 25 minutes **Grill:** 11 minutes

- 1 tsp. coarse salt
- ¾ tsp. cracked black pepper
- ½ tsp. mustard seeds, coarsely ground
- 4 8- to 10-oz. boneless beef ribeye steaks, cut 1 inch thick
- 1 Tbsp. olive oil
- 1 medium sweet onion, halved and thinly sliced
- 1 clove garlic, minced
- ¼ cup chopped red sweet pepper
- 1 fresh jalapeño pepper*, seeded and finely chopped
- 2 Tbsp. balsamic vinegar
- 1 tsp. brown sugar
- ½ tsp. dried sage, crushed

1. In a small bowl combine salt, pepper, and mustard seeds; divide mixture in half. Rub half of the mustard mixture onto one side of the steaks; set aside.

2. In a large skillet heat olive oil; add onion and garlic. Cook and stir over medium heat about 5 minutes or until onion is tender. Add red sweet pepper and jalapeño pepper; cook and stir for 1 minute more. Add balsamic vinegar, brown sugar, sage, and remaining half of the mustard mixture; cook and stir for 1 minute more. Cover and keep warm.

3. Meanwhile, for a charcoal grill, grill steaks on the rack of an uncovered grill directly over medium coals until desired doneness, turning once halfway through grilling. Allow 11 to 15 minutes for medium-rare and 14 to 18 minutes for medium. (For a gas grill, preheat grill. Reduce heat to medium. Place steaks on rack over heat. Cover; grill as above.) Serve with onion mixture. Makes 4 servings.

*Test Kitchen Tip: Because chili peppers, such as jalapeños, contain volatile oils that can burn your skin and eyes, avoid direct contact with them as much as possible. Wear plastic or rubber gloves. If your bare hands do touch the peppers, wash your hands well with soap and water.

Nutrition facts per serving: 320 cal., 14 g total fat (4 g sat. fat), 81 mg chol., 575 mg sodium, 8 g carbo., 1 g fiber, and 38 g pro. Daily Values: 11% vit. A, 38% vit. C, 3% calcium, and 18% iron.

Grilled Steak and Mango Salad

Chill: 4 hours **Prep:** 20 minutes
Cook: 15 minutes

- 12 oz. boneless beef top loin steak, cut 1 inch thick
- 1 Tbsp. olive oil or cooking oil
- ½ tsp. salt
- ¼ tsp. cracked black pepper
- 1 10-oz. pkg. torn mixed salad greens
- 2 medium mangoes, seeded, peeled, and chopped
- 1 medium pear, peeled, cored, and chopped
- 1 recipe Blue Cheese Dressing
Cracked black pepper

1. Rub steak with oil; sprinkle both sides with salt and ¼ teaspoon pepper.

2. Grill steak on rack of an uncovered grill directly over medium coals to desired doneness, turning once. Allow 11 to 15 minutes for medium-rare; 14 to 18 minutes for medium.

3. To serve, thinly slice steak across grain. Arrange greens on a platter; top with meat, mangoes, and pear. Stir Blue Cheese Dressing; pour over salad. Sprinkle with pepper. Makes 4 servings.

Blue Cheese Dressing: Stir together ½ cup light mayonnaise dressing or salad dressing; 2 tablespoons dairy sour cream; 1½ teaspoons snipped fresh parsley; ¾ teaspoon lemon juice; ¾ teaspoon Worcestershire sauce; 1 clove garlic, minced; dash pepper; and dash bottled hot pepper sauce. Gently stir in ¼ cup crumbled blue cheese. Cover and chill for 4 to 6 hours. Makes ¾ cup.

Nutrition facts per serving: 456 cal., 30 g total fat (10 g sat. fat), 73 mg chol., 632 mg sodium, 30 g carbo., 4 g fiber, and 19 g pro. Daily Values: 88% vit. A, 58% vit. C, 8% calcium, and 12% iron.

30 Apple Butter Chops

Prep: 10 minutes **Grill:** 11 minutes

- 4 pork loin or rib chops, cut ¾ inch thick
- ½ tsp. Kansas City or Montreal steak seasoning
- ½ cup bottled chili sauce
- ¼ cup apple butter
- ½ tsp. apple pie spice, pumpkin pie spice, or ground cinnamon
- 2 medium zucchini or yellow summer squash, halved lengthwise

1. Sprinkle chops with seasoning. Mix sauce, apple butter, and spice; set aside.

2. Grill chops and zucchini on rack of an uncovered grill directly over medium coals for 11 to 14 minutes or until chops are slightly pink in center and zucchini is tender, turning once and brushing with sauce last 5 minutes. Makes 4 servings.

Nutrition facts per serving: 378 cal., 9 g total fat (3 g sat. fat), 110 mg chol., 622 mg sodium, 33 g carbo., 4 g fiber, and 39 g pro. Daily Values: 10% vit. A, 20% vit. C, 5% calcium, and 12% iron.

low fat Grilled Pork Chops with Honey-Orange Glaze

Prep: 20 minutes **Marinate:** 2 hours
Grill: 30 minutes

- 6 boneless pork loin chops, cut 1 to 1¼ inches thick
- 2 Tbsp. honey
- 1 Tbsp. finely shredded orange peel
- ¼ cup orange juice
- 2 Tbsp. Dijon-style mustard
- 2 Tbsp. soy sauce
- 6 cloves garlic, minced (1 Tbsp.)
- 2 tsp. grated fresh ginger
- 1 recipe Honey-Orange Glaze

1. Trim fat from chops; place in a plastic bag set in a shallow dish. For marinade, stir together honey, peel, juice, mustard, soy sauce, garlic, and ginger. Pour over chops; seal. Marinate in refrigerator for 2 hours, turning often. Drain, discarding marinade.

2. Arrange medium-hot coals around a drip pan. Test for medium heat above pan. Place chops on grill rack over pan. Cover; grill for 30 to 35 minutes or until slightly pink in the center and juices run clear, turning once halfway through grilling and brushing with Honey-Orange Glaze the last 5 minutes. Spoon on any additional glaze before serving. Makes 6 servings.

Honey-Orange Glaze: In a 2-quart saucepan combine 6 tablespoons honey, ¼ cup orange juice, 2 tablespoons soy sauce, and 4 teaspoons ground ginger. Bring to boiling; reduce heat. Boil gently, uncovered, for 5 minutes or until reduced by half (slightly less than ½ cup), stirring frequently. (Watch carefully because mixture will bubble up.) Set aside.

Nutrition facts per serving: 372 cal., 11 g total fat (4 g sat. fat), 103 mg chol., 552 mg sodium, 23 g carbo., 0 g fiber, and 43 g pro. Daily Values: 1% vit. A, 15% vit. C, 2% calcium, and 8% iron.

Five-Ingredient Dinners

Spicy Jalapeño-Shrimp Pasta

Southwest Pork Chops

Hyun C. Eom, Sunnyvale, Calif.

$400 WINNER

30 low fat Spicy Jalapeño-Shrimp Pasta

Start to finish: 30 minutes

12	oz. fresh or frozen large shrimp in shells	½	tsp. salt
8	oz. dried linguine	¼	tsp. pepper
1	or 2 fresh jalapeño chili peppers	2	cups chopped tomatoes and/or cherry tomatoes, quartered
2	Tbsp. olive oil		Finely shredded Parmesan cheese (optional)
2	cloves garlic, minced		

1. Thaw shrimp, if frozen. Peel and devein shrimp. Cook linguine according to package directions. Chop jalapeños finely (see tip, page 279).

2. In a large skillet heat oil over medium-high heat. Add jalapeños, garlic, salt, and pepper; cook and stir for 1 minute. Add shrimp; cook and stir about 3 minutes more or until shrimp turn opaque. Stir in tomatoes; heat through.

3. Drain linguine; toss with shrimp mixture. If desired, top with Parmesan cheese. Makes 4 servings.

Nutrition facts per serving: 363 cal., 9 g total fat (1 g sat. fat), 97 mg chol., 396 mg sodium, 48 g carbo., 3 g fiber, and 21 g pro. Daily Values: 14% vit. A, 39% vit. C, 5% calcium, and 20% iron.

Shannon Martinez, Winters, Calif.

$200 WINNER

low fat Southwest Pork Chops

Prep: 15 minutes **Cook:** 3 hours

6	pork rib chops, cut ¾ inch thick (about 2½ lb.)	1	cup fresh or frozen whole kernel corn
1	15½-oz. can Mexican-style or Tex-Mex-style chili beans	2	cups hot cooked rice
1¼	cups bottled salsa		Snipped fresh cilantro (optional)

1. Trim excess fat from chops. Place chops in a 3½- or 4-quart crockery cooker. Add chili beans and salsa. Cover; cook on high-heat setting for 2½ hours or on low-heat setting for 5 hours. Turn to high-heat setting. Stir in corn. Cover and cook for 30 minutes more. Serve over rice. If desired, sprinkle each serving with cilantro. Makes 6 servings.

Test Kitchen Tip: To cook all day, substitute 8 boneless pork chops for the 6 rib chops. Cover and cook on low-heat setting for 9½ hours. Turn to high-heat setting. Stir in corn. Cover and cook for 30 minutes more. Serve as above.

Nutrition facts per serving: 334 cal., 7 g total fat (2 g sat. fat), 77 mg chol., 716 mg sodium, 34 g carbo., 4 g fiber, and 33 g pro. Daily Values: 5% vit. A, 13% vit. C, 6% calcium, and 19% iron.

30 Salmon with Oriental Noodles

Prep: 15 minutes **Broil:** 8 minutes

4	fresh or frozen skinless, boneless salmon fillets, cut 1 inch thick (about 1¼ lb.)
1	Tbsp. olive oil
¼	tsp. pepper
5	Tbsp. bottled plum sauce
1	3-oz. pkg. ramen noodles (any flavor)
5	cups coarsely shredded Chinese cabbage
2	Tbsp. sliced almonds, toasted

1. Thaw fish, if frozen. Preheat broiler. Rinse salmon fillets; pat dry. Arrange fillets on the greased unheated rack of a broiler pan, tucking under any thin edges. Brush with the olive oil. Sprinkle with pepper. Broil 4 inches from the heat for 5 minutes. Using a wide spatula, carefully turn fish. Remove 1 tablespoon of the plum sauce; lightly brush onto salmon. Broil for 3 to 7 minutes more or until fish flakes easily with a fork.

2. Meanwhile, cook noodles according to package directions; drain.

3. Place shredded cabbage in a large bowl. Toss hot cooked noodles and remaining plum sauce with cabbage until combined. Serve salmon fillets over noodle mixture; sprinkle with sliced almonds. Makes 4 servings.

Nutrition facts per serving: 439 cal., 23 g total fat (3 g sat. fat), 87 mg chol., 464 mg sodium, 25 g carbo., 4 g fiber, and 36 g pro. Daily Values: 28% vit. A, 44% vit. C, 10% calcium, and 8% iron.

30 Salmon with Pesto Mayo

Make your own pesto or buy some for this September 2000 champion.

Start to finish: 20 minutes

- 4 5- to 6-oz. fresh or frozen skinless, boneless salmon fillets
- 2 Tbsp. crumbled firm-textured bread
- ¼ cup mayonnaise or salad dressing
- 3 Tbsp. basil pesto
- 1 Tbsp. grated Parmesan cheese

1. Thaw fish, if frozen. Preheat broiler. Place the bread crumbs in a shallow baking pan. Broil 4 inches from heat for 1 to 2 minutes or until lightly toasted, stirring once. Set bread crumbs aside.

2. Measure thickness of fish. Arrange fish on the greased unheated rack of broiler pan, tucking under any thin edges. Broil 4 inches from heat for 4 to 6 minutes per ½-inch thickness or until fish begins to flake easily with a fork. Turn 1-inch-thick fillets halfway through broiling.

3. Meanwhile, in a small bowl stir together mayonnaise and pesto; set aside. Combine toasted bread crumbs and cheese. Spoon mayonnaise mixture over fillets. Sprinkle with crumb mixture. Broil 1 to 2 minutes more or until crumbs are light brown. Makes 4 servings.

Nutrition facts per serving: 363 cal., 24 g total fat (3 g sat. fat), 84 mg chol., 309 mg sodium, 5 g carbo., 0 g fiber, and 31g pro. Daily Values: 6% vit. A, 4% calcium, and 7% iron.

30 Curried Shrimp on Rice

Start to finish: 25 minutes

- 1 10-oz. container refrigerated Alfredo sauce (1⅛ cup)
- 2 to 3 tsp. curry powder
- 12 oz. peeled, deveined, cooked medium shrimp*
- 3 cups hot cooked rice
- ¼ cup slivered almonds, toasted

1. In a large saucepan combine Alfredo sauce and curry powder. If necessary, add 1 or 2 tablespoons water to thin. Cook and stir over medium heat just until boiling. Add shrimp. Cook and stir 2 to 3 minutes more or until heated through. Serve shrimp mixture over rice; sprinkle with almonds. Makes 4 servings.

*Test Kitchen Tip: If tails are present on the shrimp, remove them before using.

Nutrition facts per serving: 550 cal., 29 g total fat (1 g sat. fat), 206 mg chol., 426 mg sodium, 41 g carbo., 2 g fiber, and 32 g pro. Daily Values: 4% vit. A, 4% vit. C, 10% calcium, and 27% iron.

30 new Lamb and Peppers

Toss some couscous with a little butter and some finely shredded lemon peel to serve alongside.

Start to finish: 25 minutes

- 8 lamb rib or loin chops, cut 1 inch thick
- 3 small green, red, and/or yellow sweet peppers, cut into 1-inch pieces
- 2 cloves garlic, minced
- 1 Tbsp. snipped fresh oregano
- 1 Tbsp. olive oil or cooking oil
- ¼ cup sliced pitted green or ripe olives

1. Preheat broiler. Place chops on the unheated rack of a broiler pan. Broil 3 to 4 inches from heat for 10 to 15 minutes for medium (160° F), turning meat over after half of the broiling time. Transfer to a serving platter.

2. Meanwhile, in a large skillet cook sweet peppers, garlic, and oregano in hot oil for 8 to 10 minutes or until sweet peppers are crisp-tender. Add olives. Cook and stir until heated through. Spoon over chops. Makes 4 servings.

Nutrition facts per serving: 186 cal., 10 g total fat (2 g sat. fat), 60 mg chol., 257 mg sodium, 4 g carbo., 1 g fiber, and 20 g pro. Daily Values: 7% vit. A, 72% vit. C, 3% calcium, and 12% iron.

TAKE FIVE

For our five-ingredient category, we decided not to count optional ingredients or very common staples, since we all have them in the kitchen. So when you see six ingredients in a recipe, chances are one of them might be cooking oil, nonstick cooking spray, salt, pepper, water, or ice. Any other ingredients count for this easy-on-the-shopper category.

---

30 Turkey and Cucumber Blue Cheese Salad

Start to finish: 25 minutes

- 8 cups torn mixed salad greens
- 8 oz. deli-sliced pepper turkey
- 1 small cucumber, thinly sliced (1 cup)
- 2 medium pears, nectarines, and/or plums, thinly sliced (about 2 cups)
- ½ cup bottled blue cheese salad dressing

1. Divide salad greens among four plates. Roll the turkey slices; divide among salads. Add cucumber and fruit slices.

2. Drizzle each salad with blue cheese salad dressing. Makes 4 servings.

Nutrition facts per serving: 282 cal., 18 g total fat (4 g sat. fat), 39 mg chol., 373 mg sodium, 18 g carbo., 4 g fiber, and 15 g pro. Daily Values: 10% vit. A, 16% vit. C, 7% calcium, and 9% iron.

30 Spicy Tex-Mex Pizza

Serve this September 2000 winner as an appetizer or main dish.

Prep: 10 minutes **Bake:** 20 minutes

- 1 12-inch thin-crust Italian bread shell (10-oz. Boboli) or Italian flat bread (12½-oz. focaccia)
- 2 cups shredded Monterey Jack cheese with jalapeño peppers or Monterey Jack cheese (8 oz.)
- 1 15-oz. can black beans, rinsed and drained
- 1 11-oz. can whole kernel corn with sweet peppers, drained
- 2 to 4 Tbsp. chopped pickled jalapeño peppers (optional) (see tip, page 279)

1. Preheat oven to 425° F. Place crust on an ungreased pizza pan or baking sheet. Sprinkle with half of the Monterey Jack cheese, all of the black beans, the drained corn, and, if desired, jalapeño peppers. Top with remaining cheese.

2. Bake about 20 minutes or until heated through and cheese is melted. Cut into wedges to serve. Makes 6 servings.

Nutrition facts per serving: 413 cal., 17 g total fat (8 g sat. fat), 48 mg chol., 971 mg sodium, 12 g carbo., 4 g fiber, and 24 g pro. Daily Values: 12% vit. A, 2% vit. C, 40% calcium, and 7% iron.

Holiday Ham

Harvest Holiday Ham
with Cider Glaze

Ham with Ginger-Pear Relish

Betty Nichols, Eugene, Oregon
$400 WINNER

low fat Harvest Holiday Ham with Cider Glaze

Prep: 20 minutes **Bake:** 1½ hours **Cook:** 20 minutes

1 5- to 6-lb. cooked ham, rump or shank portion	¼ cup Dijon-style mustard
2 cups apple cider or apple juice	2 tsp. chili powder
1 cup honey	1 Tbsp. butter
½ cup cider vinegar	½ tsp. apple pie spice

1. Preheat oven to 325° F. Trim fat from ham. Score with diagonal cuts in a diamond pattern. Place on a rack in a shallow roasting pan. Insert a meat thermometer. Roast, uncovered, about 1½ to 2¼ hours or until thermometer registers 140° F.

2. Meanwhile, for sauce, in a large saucepan combine apple cider, honey, vinegar, mustard, and chili powder. Bring to boiling; reduce heat. Simmer, uncovered, about 15 minutes or until reduced to 2 cups, stirring frequently. Transfer half of the mixture to a small bowl; stir in butter and ¼ teaspoon apple pie spice. Set aside.

3. For glaze, return remaining mixture in saucepan to boiling; reduce heat. Simmer gently about 5 minutes or until mixture is thickened and reduced to about ½ cup, stirring frequently. Stir in remaining ¼ teaspoon apple pie spice.

4. Brush ham with glaze the last 20 to 30 minutes of roasting. Transfer to a platter. Reheat sauce, if necessary; pass with ham. Makes 16 to 20 servings.

Nutrition facts per serving: 384 cal., 13 g total fat (5 g sat. fat), 138 mg chol., 126 mg sodium, 22 g carbo., 0 g fiber, and 44 g pro. Daily Values: 3% vit. A, 2% vit. C, 2% calcium, and 11% iron.

Betty Nichols, Eugene, Oregon
$200 WINNER

30 Ham with Ginger-Pear Relish

Prep: 25 minutes **Chill:** 1 hour

⅓ cup dried cranberries	1 Tbsp. olive oil
2 pears, cored and chopped	1 Tbsp. lime juice
4 green onions, thinly sliced	1 Tbsp. honey
3 Tbsp.. finely chopped crystallized ginger	1 tsp. snipped fresh rosemary
	1 2-lb. cooked boneless ham

1. Place cranberries in a small bowl; add boiling water to cover. Let stand for 10 minutes; drain and return to bowl.

2. Add remaining ingredients; toss gently to coat. Cover and chill for 1 to 3hours. Heat ham, if desired; serve with relish. Makes 8 servings (2⅓ cups).

Nutrition facts per serving: 279 cal., 14 g total fat (4 g sat. fat), 65 mg chol., 1,496 mg sodium, 18 g carbo., 0 g fiber, and 20 g pro. Daily Values: 1% vit. A, 6% vit. C, 2% calcium, and 8% iron.

30 Ham Bites with Cranberry-Apple Sauce

Remember fondue? Ham cubes make the perfect dipper. You can also serve the fondue as a sauce for baked ham.

Start to finish: 30 minutes

1 cup fresh or frozen cranberries
1 tsp. finely shredded orange peel
1 cup orange juice
1 medium apple, cored and finely chopped (1 cup)
⅓ cup packed brown sugar
1 jalapeño pepper, seeded and finely chopped (1 to 2 Tbsp.) (see tip, page 279)
⅛ tsp. ground cloves
1 2-lb. cooked boneless ham, cut into ¾-inch cubes
½ of a medium fresh pineapple, peeled, cored, and cut into 1-inch cubes

1. For sauce, in a medium saucepan combine cranberries, orange peel, and juice. Bring to boiling; reduce heat. Simmer gently, uncovered, for 1 minute. Add apple, brown sugar, jalapeño pepper, and cloves. Return to boiling; reduce heat and boil gently, uncovered, for 2 minutes more. Let cool for 10 minutes.

2. Place cranberry mixture in a food processor or blender; cover and process or blend until nearly smooth. Transfer to a fondue pot or chafing dish to keep warm.

3. Dip ham and pineapple cubes into warm sauce. Makes 16 appetizer servings.

Nutrition facts per serving: 141 cal., 5 g total fat (2 g sat. fat), 33 mg chol., 853 mg sodium, 10 g carbo., 1 g fiber, and 13 g pro. Daily Values: 1% vit. A, 20% vit. C, 1% calcium, and 5% iron.

Marinated Ham with Spiced Pineapple Sauce

Prep: 15 minutes **Marinate:** 4 hours
Roast: 1 hour

1¼	cups pineapple juice
¾	cup packed brown sugar
3	Tbsp. white wine vinegar
2	Tbsp. Dijon-style mustard
½	tsp. chili powder
⅛	to ¼ tsp. ground cloves
1	3- to 4-lb. cooked boneless ham
2	Tbsp. cornstarch

1. For marinade, in a medium bowl combine 1¼ cups pineapple juice, brown sugar, vinegar, mustard, chili powder, and cloves. Prick the ham all over with a long-tined fork. Place ham in an extra-large self-sealing plastic bag set in a shallow dish. Pour marinade over meat; close bag. Refrigerate for 4 to 24 hours.

2. Preheat oven to 325° F. Remove ham from marinade. Set aside 1¾ cups of the marinade for sauce. Place ham on a rack in a shallow roasting pan. Insert a meat thermometer into the thickest portion of the ham. Roast, uncovered, for 1 to 1¾ hours or until the thermometer registers 140° F, spooning some of the remaining marinade over the ham twice.

3. Meanwhile, for sauce, in a medium saucepan stir together reserved marinade and cornstarch. Cook and stir over medium heat until thickened and bubbly. Cook and stir for 2 minutes more.

4. Transfer ham to a serving platter. Spoon some sauce over ham; pass remaining sauce. Makes 12 to 16 servings.

Nutrition facts per serving: 278 cal., 10 g total fat (4 g sat. fat), 67 mg chol., 1,722 mg sodium, 19 g carbo., 0 g fiber, and 26 g pro. Daily Values: 1% vit. A, 5% vit. C, 3% calcium, and 11% iron.

Ham and Sweet Potatoes with Cranberry-Raspberry Sauce

Prep: 25 minutes **Roast:** 1¼ hours

1	3- to 4-lb. cooked boneless ham
6	medium (about 3 lb.) sweet potatoes, peeled and halved lengthwise
2	medium onions, cut into wedges
½	cup packed brown sugar
½	cup Champagne
1	recipe Cranberry-Raspberry Sauce

1. Preheat oven to 325° F. Slice ham into ¼-inch-thick slices. Arrange in the center of a shallow roasting pan. Arrange sweet potatoes and onion wedges around ham. Pour ¼ cup Champagne over ham. In a cup stir together brown sugar and ¼ cup Champagne; drizzle over potatoes and onion. Cover tightly with foil. Bake about 1¼ hours or until potatoes and onion are tender.

2. Transfer ham and vegetables to a serving platter. Pass Cranberry-Raspberry Sauce. Makes 12 to 16 servings.

Cranberry-Raspberry Sauce: Drain one thawed 10-ounce package frozen red raspberries in syrup, reserving liquid. Set the raspberries aside. In a small saucepan combine ⅓ cup packed brown sugar, 4 teaspoons cornstarch, and ¼ teaspoon ground allspice. Stir in the reserved raspberry liquid, ½ cup Champagne and 1¾ cups fresh or frozen cranberries. Cook and stir over medium heat until thickened and bubbly. Cook and stir for 2 minutes more. Remove from heat. Stir in ½ cup chopped walnuts and reserved raspberries.

Nutrition facts per serving: 480 cal., 14 g total fat (4 g sat. fat), 67 mg chol., 1,729 mg sodium, 57 g carbo., 5 g fiber, and 29 g pro. Daily Values: 432% vit. A, 41% vit. C, 26% calcium, and 17% iron.

new Prosciutto-Stuffed Mushrooms

Prep: 25 minutes **Bake:** 8 minutes

24	large fresh mushrooms, 1½ to 2 inches in diameter
¼	cup sliced green onion
1	clove garlic, minced
¼	cup butter or margarine
⅔	cup fine dry bread crumbs
⅓	cup chopped prosciutto or cooked ham
¼	cup shredded provolone cheese
½	tsp. dried Italian seasoning, crushed

1. Preheat oven to 425° F. Rinse and drain mushrooms. Remove stems; reserve caps. Chop enough stems to make 1 cup.

2. In a medium saucepan cook chopped stems, green onion, and garlic in hot butter until tender. Stir in bread crumbs, prosciutto or ham, cheese, and seasoning. Spoon mixture into mushroom caps.

3. Arrange stuffed mushrooms in a 15x10x1-inch baking pan. Bake for 8 to 10 minutes or until heated through. Makes 24 mushrooms.

Nutrition facts per mushroom: 42 cal., 3 g total fat (2 g sat. fat), 7 mg chol., 97 mg sodium, 2 g carbo., 0 g fiber, and 2 g pro. Daily Values: 2% vit. A, 2% calcium, and 2% iron.

new Ham-Asparagus Strata

Prep: 25 minutes **Chill:** 2 hours
Bake: 1 hour **Stand:** 10 minutes

4	English muffins, torn or cut into bite-size pieces (4 cups)
2	cups cubed cooked ham
1	10-oz. pkg. frozen cut asparagus or frozen cut broccoli, thawed and well drained, or 2 cups cut-up fresh cooked asparagus or broccoli
4	oz. process Swiss cheese, torn
4	eggs
1¼	cups milk
2	Tbsp. finely chopped onion
1	Tbsp. Dijon-style mustard
⅛	tsp. pepper

1. In a greased 2-quart square baking dish spread half of the English muffin pieces. Top with ham, asparagus or broccoli, and cheese. Top with the remaining English muffin pieces.

2. In a bowl whisk eggs; whisk in sour cream. Stir in milk, onion, mustard, and pepper. Pour evenly over layers in dish. Cover and chill for 2 to 24 hours.

3. Preheat oven to 325° F. Bake, uncovered, for 60 to 65 minutes or until the internal temperature registers 170° F on an instant-read thermometer. Let stand for 10 minutes. Makes 6 servings.

Nutrition facts per serving: 349 cal., 16 g total fat (7 g sat. fat), 193 mg chol., 1,224 mg sodium, 25 g carbo., 2 g fiber, and 26 g pro. Daily Values: 20% vit. A, 26% vit. C, 32% calcium, and 15% iron.

Skillet Dinners

Pesce Italiano

Tortellini and Veggies

30 Pesce Italiano

Start to finish: 30 minutes

1 cup dried penne pasta	2 tsp. drained capers
1 cup sliced fresh mushrooms	2 6-oz. salmon, tuna, or swordfish
⅓ cup dry white wine	steaks, cut ¾ inch thick
2 Tbsp. basil pesto	1 tsp. Creole seasoning
1 Tbsp. lemon juice	1 Tbsp. olive oil

1. In a large saucepan cook pasta in lightly salted boiling water for 4 minutes. Drain pasta (it will not be tender). In a medium bowl combine partially cooked pasta, mushrooms, wine, pesto, lemon juice, and capers; set aside.

2. Rinse fish; pat dry. Sprinkle fish with Creole seasoning. (If seasoning is salt free, sprinkle with ¼ teaspoon salt.) In a large skillet cook fish in hot oil over medium-high heat for 1 minute; turn and cook 1 minute more. Reduce heat to medium.

3. Spoon pasta mixture around fish in skillet. Bring to boiling; reduce heat. Simmer, covered, for 6 to 9 minutes or until fish flakes easily. Makes 2 servings.

Nutrition facts per serving: 627 cal., 30 g total fat (5 g sat. fat), 109 mg chol., 352 mg sodium, 36 g carbo., 2 g fiber, and 46 g pro. Daily Values: 6% vit. A, 7% vit. C, 11% calcium, and 17% iron.

Tortellini and Veggies

Start to finish: 40 minutes

1 large onion, coarsely chopped	2 tsp. dried Italian seasoning,
1 8-oz. pkg. fresh mushrooms, such	crushed
as crimini or white, halved	¼ tsp. ground black pepper
1 medium red sweet pepper, cut into	1 9-oz. pkg. refrigerated cheese-filled
¾-inch pieces (¾ cup)	tortellini
2 cloves garlic, minced	4 small zucchini, halved lengthwise
2 Tbsp. olive oil	and cut into ½-inch-thick slices
1 14½-oz. can diced tomatoes	½ cup shredded Asiago or Parmesan
¼ cup dry red wine	cheese (2 oz.)

1. In a large skillet cook onion, mushrooms, sweet pepper, and garlic in hot oil until tender. Stir in ½ cup water, undrained tomatoes, wine, seasoning, and black pepper. Add tortellini. Bring to boiling; reduce heat. Simmer, covered, 10 minutes.

2. Stir in zucchini. Cook, uncovered, about 5 minutes more or until zucchini is crisp-tender. Remove from heat. Sprinkle with cheese. Makes 4 to 6 servings.

Nutrition facts per serving: 414 cal., 18 g total fat (6 g sat. fat), 45 mg chol., 566 mg sodium, 46 g carbo., 4 g fiber, and 18 g pro. Daily Values: 38% vit. A, 118% vit.C, 32% calcium, and 19% iron.

low fat Flounder Mediterranean

Prep: 15 minutes **Cook:** 25 minutes

8 oz. sliced fresh mushrooms
2 shallots or half of a small onion, sliced (¼ cup)
4 cloves garlic, minced
2 Tbsp. olive oil
2 14½-oz. cans diced tomatoes with basil, oregano, and garlic
½ cup dry white wine
¾ cup roasted red sweet peppers, cut into strips (about ¾ of a 7-oz. jar)
¼ cup oil-packed dried tomatoes, drained and chopped
1 Tbsp. capers
6 4-oz. flounder, haddock, or cod fillets, cut ½ inch thick
¼ tsp. crushed red pepper
3 cups hot cooked rice
Snipped fresh Italian flat-leaf parsley

1. In a 10-inch skillet cook mushrooms, shallots, and garlic in hot olive oil about 4 minutes or until tender.

2. Stir in undrained diced tomatoes and wine. Bring to boiling; reduce heat. Simmer, uncovered, for 15 minutes. Stir in sweet peppers, dried tomatoes, and capers.

3. Rinse fish. Place atop sauce; sprinkle with red pepper. Simmer, covered, for 4 to 6 minutes more or until fish flakes easily.

4. Divide rice among six shallow bowls. Place a fish fillet on rice. Divide tomato mixture among bowls. Sprinkle with parsley. Makes 6 servings.

Nutrition facts per serving: 345 cal., 7 g total fat (1 g sat. fat), 64 mg chol., 845 mg sodium, 40 g carbo., 2 g fiber, and 28 g pro. Daily Values: 21% vit. A, 113% vit. C, 15% calcium, and 28% iron.

low fat Curried Chicken and Couscous

Prep: 15 minutes **Cook:** 17 minutes
Stand: 5 minutes

1 Tbsp. curry powder
½ tsp. ground ginger
¼ tsp. ground cumin
⅛ tsp. salt
⅛ tsp. pepper
1 6-oz. pkg. quick-cooking roasted garlic-flavored couscous or 1 cup plain couscous
4 skinless, boneless chicken breast halves (about 1¼ to 1½ lb.)
1 Tbsp. lime juice
2 Tbsp. cooking oil
½ cup sliced fresh mushrooms
¼ cup thinly sliced carrot
¼ cup sliced celery
¼ cup chopped red onion
2 cloves garlic, minced
1 14-oz. can reduced-sodium chicken broth
¼ cup mango chutney
1 Tbsp. snipped fresh cilantro
Lime wedges (optional)

1. In a small mixing bowl stir together curry powder, ginger, cumin, salt, pepper, and the seasoning packet from the couscous mix, if using.

2. Drizzle chicken with lime juice. Sprinkle 1½ teaspoons of the spice mixture onto both sides of chicken. Set remaining spice mixture aside.

3. In a large skillet brown chicken breasts on both sides in hot oil; set aside. Add mushrooms, carrot, celery, onion, garlic, and remaining spice mixture; cook 5 minutes or until vegetables are tender. Return chicken to skillet. Carefully add broth. Heat to boiling; reduce heat. Simmer, covered, for 12 to 15 minutes or until chicken is tender and no longer pink; remove chicken.

4. Stir couscous and chutney into cooking liquid. Return chicken to skillet. Remove from heat. Cover and let stand for 5 minutes or until couscous is done. Sprinkle with cilantro. If desired, serve with lime wedges. Makes 4 servings.

Nutrition facts per serving: 439 cal., 10 g total fat (2 g sat. fat), 82 mg chol., 796 mg sodium, 48 g carbo., 4 g fiber, and 41 g pro. Daily Values: 55% vit. A, 23% vit. C, 6% calcium, and 13% iron.

low fat Corn and Beans with Cornmeal Dumplings

Start to finish: 35 minutes

2 14½-oz. cans diced tomatoes with onions and garlic
1 15-oz. can black beans, rinsed and drained
1 cup frozen whole kernel corn
1 4-oz. can chopped green chili peppers
½ cup chopped green sweet pepper
½ cup chopped carrot
½ tsp. ground cumin
¼ tsp. ground black pepper
1 recipe Cornmeal Dumplings
½ cup shredded Monterey Jack cheese with jalapeño peppers
Dairy sour cream (optional)

1. In a very large skillet combine undrained tomatoes, beans, corn, green chili peppers, green sweet pepper, carrot, cumin, and black pepper. Bring to boiling.

2. Drop Cornmeal Dumplings from a tablespoon to make 10 to 12 mounds atop bubbling mixture in skillet. Reduce heat and simmer, covered, for 10 to 15 minutes or until a toothpick inserted in dumpling comes out clean. Sprinkle with cheese.

3. If desired, serve with a dollop of sour cream. Makes 5 to 6 servings.

Cornmeal Dumplings: In a medium bowl stir together ½ cup all-purpose flour, ⅓ cup cornmeal, ¼ cup shredded Monterey Jack cheese with jalapeño peppers, 2 tablespoons thinly sliced green onion, 1 teaspoon baking powder, ¼ teaspoon salt, and a dash ground black pepper. In a small mixing bowl beat 1 egg. Stir in 2 tablespoons milk and 2 tablespoons cooking oil; add all at once to the flour mixture. Stir just until combined.

Nutrition facts per serving: 375 cal., 13 g total fat (5 g sat. fat), 61 mg chol., 1,481 mg sodium, 54 g carbo., 7 g fiber, and 17 g pro. Daily Values: 91% vit. A, 57% vit. C, 34% calcium, and 29% iron.

30 Sweet Roast Beef Hash

Start to finish: 30 minutes

1 medium sweet potato, peeled
3 medium potatoes (1 lb.), peeled
½ cup chopped onion
⅓ cup chopped red sweet pepper
2 Tbsp. cooking oil
8 oz. cooked beef, cubed
4 eggs
2 green onions, chopped

1. Dice potatoes. In a large saucepan cook potatoes in a small amount of boiling water for 3 minutes. Drain; cool slightly.

2. In a large nonstick skillet cook onion and sweet pepper in hot oil until tender. Stir in potatoes. Cook and stir about 5 minutes or until just tender. Stir in beef.

3. With back of a large spoon, make 4 depressions in hash. Break an egg into each depression. Cook, covered, over medium-low heat about 5 minutes or until whites are completely set and yolks begin to thicken but are not hard. Sprinkle with green onion. Season to taste with salt and pepper. Makes 4 servings.

Nutrition facts per serving: 420 cal., 19 g total fat (5 g sat. fat), 257 mg chol., 154 mg sodium, 38 g carbo., 4 g fiber, and 25 g pro. Daily Values: 225% vit. A, 78% vit. C, 6% calcium, and 21% iron.

30 Pork and Mango Picadillo

Pronounced pee-kah-DEE-yoh, this tangy spiced meat mixture won in March, 1999. It's a popular topping or filling in many Spanish-speaking countries.

Start to finish: 30 minutes

1 lb. lean ground pork
⅓ cup thinly sliced green onion
2 cloves garlic, minced
1 tsp. ground cinnamon
1 tsp. ground coriander
1 tsp. ground cumin
1 tsp. dried oregano, crushed
1 tsp. dried thyme, crushed
1 cup bottled thick-and-chunky salsa
1 mango, seeded, peeled, and cubed
2 Tbsp. smoked or plain almonds, chopped
2 Tbsp. snipped fresh cilantro
Hot cooked white or yellow rice (optional)

1. In a large skillet cook meat until no longer pink. Drain off fat.

2. Stir in onion, garlic, cinnamon, coriander, cumin, oregano, and thyme. Cook and stir for 2 minutes more.

3. Gently stir in salsa and mango. Cover and cook for 1 to 2 minutes or until heated through. Spoon into a serving dish. Sprinkle with almonds and cilantro. If desired, serve with rice. Makes 4 servings.

Nutrition facts per serving: 223 cal., 12 g total fat (4 g sat. fat), 53 mg chol., 268 mg sodium, 16 g carbo., 2 g fiber, and 16 g pro. Daily Values: 30% vit. A, 58% vit. C, 5% calcium, and 20% iron.

Canned & Frozen Vegetables

East-West Veggies

Great Greek Green Beans

30 low fat East-West Veggies

Start to finish: 20 minutes

- 1 medium onion, cut into thin wedges (½ cup)
- 1 Tbsp. butter or margarine
- 1 Tbsp. olive oil
- 6 green onions, cut into 1-inch pieces (½ cup)
- 3 Tbsp. hoisin sauce
- 1 tsp. paprika
- 1 15¼-oz. can whole kernel corn, drained
- 1 15-oz. can black beans, rinsed and drained
- ¾ cup chopped celery
- ½ cup finely chopped red sweet pepper

1. In a large skillet cook and stir onion wedges in hot butter and oil over medium heat about 4 minutes or until tender but not brown. Stir in green onions, hoisin sauce, and paprika. Cook and stir for 1 minute more.

2. Add corn, beans, celery, and red sweet pepper. Cook and stir until heated through. Transfer to a serving bowl. Makes 6 servings.

Nutrition facts per serving: 166 cal., 5 g total fat (2 g sat. fat), 5 mg chol., 574 mg sodium, 28 g carbo., 5 g fiber, and 6 g pro. Daily Values: 21% vit. A, 47% vit. C, 4% calcium, and 6% iron.

30 Great Greek Green Beans

Start to finish: 25 minutes

- ½ cup chopped onion
- 1 clove garlic, minced
- 2 Tbsp. olive oil
- 1 28-oz. can diced tomatoes
- ¼ cup sliced pitted ripe olives
- 1 tsp. dried oregano, crushed
- 2 9-oz. pkg. or one 16-oz. pkg. frozen French-cut green beans, thawed and drained
- ½ cup crumbled feta cheese (2 oz.)

1. In a large skillet cook onion and garlic in hot olive oil about 5 minutes or until tender but not brown. Add undrained tomatoes, olives, and oregano. Bring to boiling; reduce heat. Simmer gently, uncovered, for 10 minutes.

2. Add beans. Return to boiling. Boil gently, uncovered, about 8 minutes or until desired consistency and beans are tender.

3. Transfer to a serving bowl; sprinkle with feta cheese. If desired, serve with a slotted spoon. Makes 6 servings.

Nutrition facts per serving: 132 cal., 7 g total fat (2 g sat. fat), 8 mg chol., 419 mg sodium, 15 g carbo., 5 g fiber, and 4 g pro. Daily Values: 9% vit. A, 32% vit. C, 11% calcium, and 8% iron.

30 Brussels Sprouts with Lemon-Dijon Sauce

Start to finish: 20 minutes

- 1 10-oz. pkg. frozen brussels sprouts or cut broccoli or one 9-oz. pkg. frozen cut green beans
- 2 slices bacon
- ½ cup thinly sliced green onion (6 onions)
- 2 cloves garlic, minced
- 2 Tbsp. Dijon-style mustard
- 2 tsp. all-purpose flour
- ½ tsp. finely shredded lemon peel
- ¼ tsp. pepper
- 1 cup half-and-half, light cream, or milk

1. Cook brussels sprouts, broccoli, or green beans in lightly salted water according to package directions. Drain; set aside.

2. Meanwhile, in a medium skillet cook bacon until crisp. Drain bacon on paper towels, reserving 1 tablespoon drippings in skillet. Crumble bacon; set aside.

3. Add green onion and garlic to drippings in skillet; cook over medium heat for 1 minute. Stir in mustard, flour, lemon peel, and pepper. Add half-and-half, light cream, or milk all at once. Cook and stir until thickened and bubbly. (Sauce may appear slightly curdled before it bubbles.) Cook and stir for 1 minute more.

4. Add vegetables to lemon sauce; heat through, tossing gently to combine. Transfer to a serving bowl. Sprinkle with crumbled bacon. Makes 4 servings.

Nutrition facts per serving: 175 cal., 13 g total fat (6 g sat. fat), 28 mg chol., 126 mg sodium, 12 g carbo., 3 g fiber, and 6 g pro. Daily Values: 17% vit. A, 71% vit. C, 10% calcium, and 7% iron.

30 low fat Golden Sunset Soup

Prep: 15 minutes **Cook:** 10 minutes

- 1 15-oz. can pumpkin
- 1 14-oz. can unsweetened light coconut milk
- 1 14-oz. can chicken broth
- 2 Tbsp. brown sugar
- 1 medium jalapeño pepper, seeded and finely chopped (see tip, page 279)
- ¾ tsp. salt
- 1 16-oz. pkg. frozen yellow, red, and green peppers and onion stir-fry vegetables, thawed and drained
- 3 Tbsp. snipped fresh cilantro or parsley
- Toasted large flaked coconut (optional)

1. In a large saucepan stir together pumpkin, coconut milk, broth, brown sugar, jalapeño pepper, and salt.

2. Coarsely chop thawed vegetables; add to saucepan. Bring mixture to boiling; reduce heat. Simmer, uncovered, for 10 minutes or until vegetables are heated through, stirring frequently.

3. Stir in cilantro or parsley. Spoon soup into eight to twelve soup bowls. If desired, garnish with toasted coconut. Makes 8 to 12 appetizer servings.

Nutrition facts per serving: 83 cal., 3 g total fat (2 g sat. fat), 0 mg chol., 397 mg sodium, 12 g carbo., 2 g fiber, and 2 g pro. Daily Values: 243% vit. A, 40% vit. C, 2% calcium, and 9% iron.

Artichoke-Spinach Dip

Prep: 30 minutes **Bake:** 25 minutes

- 2 10-oz. pkg. frozen chopped spinach, thawed and well drained
- 1 6-oz. jar marinated artichoke hearts, drained and finely chopped
- 1½ cups shredded Monterey Jack cheese (6 oz.)
- 1 8-oz. carton dairy sour cream
- ¾ cup mayonnaise or salad dressing
- ¼ cup thinly sliced green onion
- ¼ cup finely shredded or grated Parmesan cheese
- 2 Tbsp. finely shredded or grated Romano cheese
- 2 cloves garlic, minced
- ½ tsp. fajita seasoning
- 1 recipe Fajita Pitas

1. Preheat oven to 350° F. Grease a 2-quart square baking dish; set aside.

2. In a large bowl combine spinach, chopped artichoke hearts, Monterey Jack cheese, sour cream, mayonnaise, green onion, Parmesan cheese, Romano cheese, garlic, and fajita seasoning. Transfer to prepared baking dish.

3. Bake, uncovered, for 25 to 30 minutes or until bubbly. Serve with Fajita Pitas. Makes 64 servings (4 cups).

Fajita Pitas: Preheat oven to 400° F. Using a sharp knife, split 4 large pita rounds in half horizontally (8 rounds total). Brush tops of pita bread rounds evenly with 2 tablespoons olive oil. Sprinkle with ¼ cup finely shredded Parmesan cheese, 1 teaspoon fajita seasoning, and 1 teaspoon cracked black pepper. Using a sharp knife, carefully cut each pita round into 8 wedges (64 wedges total). Arrange wedges on ungreased baking sheets. Bake for 6 to 8 minutes or until golden brown. Let cool. (Pita chips will crisp upon standing.)

Nutrition facts per tablespoon with wedge: 59 cal., 5 g total fat (2 g sat. fat), 6 mg chol., 82 mg sodium, 3 g carbo., 0 g fiber, and 2 g pro. Daily Values: 14% vit. A, 3% vit. C, 5% calcium, and 2% iron.

30 Peas with Prosciutto and Pine Nuts

Start to finish: 20 minutes

- 1 Tbsp. olive oil
- ¼ cup pine nuts
- 1 16-oz. pkg. frozen peas
- 1 oz. very thinly sliced prosciutto, cut into thin strips
- 2 cloves garlic, minced
- ½ tsp. salt
- ¼ tsp. pepper
- 2 cups sliced fresh mushrooms

1. In a large skillet heat oil over medium heat. Add nuts to skillet. Cook and stir for 1 to 2 minutes until nuts are lightly browned. Remove nuts with a slotted spoon, reserving oil in skillet.

2. Add peas, prosciutto, garlic, salt, and pepper to skillet; stir gently to coat. Cook, covered, over medium-low heat for 5 minutes.

3. Add mushrooms. Cook and stir, uncovered, for 3 to 5 minutes more or until tender and heated through. Stir in toasted pine nuts. Makes 6 servings.

Nutrition facts per serving: 130 cal., 6 g total fat (1 g sat. fat), 3 mg chol., 406 mg sodium, 12 g carbo., 4 g fiber, and 8 g pro. Daily Values: 10% vit. A, 20% vit. C, 2% calcium, and 11% iron.

low fat Sauerkraut-Rye Bread

Prep: 30 minutes **Stand:** 1¾ hours **Bake:** 30 minutes

- 2 cups bread flour
- 2 tsp. active dry yeast or bread machine yeast
- ⅔ cup water
- 2 Tbsp. brown sugar
- 2 Tbsp. olive oil or cooking oil
- 2 Tbsp. molasses
- ½ tsp. salt
- 1 8-oz. can sauerkraut, rinsed, drained, and finely snipped (1 cup)
- 1 cup rye flour
- 1 Tbsp. caraway seed

1. In a large mixing bowl combine 1 cup of the bread flour and yeast; set aside.

2. In a small saucepan combine water, brown sugar, oil, molasses, and salt; heat and stir until warm (120° to 130° F).

3. Add molasses mixture all at once to flour mixture. Beat with an electric mixer on low to medium speed for 30 seconds, scraping side of bowl constantly. Beat on high speed for 3 minutes. Using a wooden spoon, stir in sauerkraut, rye flour, and caraway seed. Stir in as much of the remaining bread flour as you can.

4. Turn the dough out onto a lightly floured surface. Knead in enough of the remaining flour to make a moderately stiff dough that is smooth and elastic (6 to 8 minutes total). Shape dough into a ball. Place in a lightly greased bowl; turn once to grease surface. Cover; let rise in a warm place until double (about 1 hour).

5. Punch dough down. Turn dough out onto a lightly floured surface. Cover and let rest for 10 minutes. Meanwhile, lightly grease a 9x5x2-inch loaf pan. Shape dough into a loaf. Place in the prepared pan. Cover and let rise in a warm place until nearly double in size (30 to 45 minutes).

6. Preheat oven to 375° F. Bake for 30 to 35 minutes or until bread sounds hollow when tapped. Immediately remove bread from pan. Cool on a wire rack. Makes 1 loaf (16 servings).

Nutrition facts per slice: 119 cal., 2 g total fat (0 g sat. fat), 0 mg chol., 169 mg sodium, 22 g carbo., 3 g fiber, 4 g pro. Daily Values: 4% vit. C, 2% calcium, and 10% iron.

Fall Salads

Butternut Squash Salad
with Sage Vinaigrette

Marinated Beet Salad

Red Pepper and
Brussels Sprout Salad

Elizabeth Davis, Notre Dame, Ind.

$400 WINNER

30 Butternut Squash Salad with Sage Vinaigrette

Prep: 20 minutes **Cook:** 10 minutes

1	lb. butternut squash, peeled, halved lengthwise, seeded, and cut into ½-inch-thick slices (3 cups)
1	Tbsp. olive oil
¼	cup chicken or vegetable broth
1	Tbsp. snipped fresh sage or ½ tsp. dried sage, crushed
¼	tsp. salt
¼	tsp. pepper
6	cups torn mixed salad greens
½	medium red onion, thinly sliced
1	apple, cored and cut into chunks
1	recipe Sage Vinaigrette
2	oz. goat cheese (chèvre), crumbled

1. In a large skillet cook squash in hot oil about 5 minutes or until golden brown, turning occasionally. Add broth, sage, salt, and pepper. Cover and cook about 5 minutes longer or until squash is just tender, turning slices once or twice.

2. In a large salad bowl combine greens, onion, and apple. Drizzle Sage Vinaigrette over greens; toss gently. Top with squash and cheese. Makes 8 servings.

Sage Vinaigrette: In a screw-top jar combine 3 tablespoons balsamic vinegar; 3 tablespoons olive oil; 1 tablespoon snipped fresh sage or 1 teaspoon dried sage, crushed; ¼ teaspoon salt; and ¼ teaspoon pepper. Cover; shake well to mix.

Nutrition facts per serving: 130 cal., 9 g total fat (2 g sat. fat), 3 mg chol., 203 mg sodium, 11 g carbo., 2 g fiber, and 3 g pro. Daily Values: 66% vit. A, 29% vit. C, 5% calcium, and 6% iron.

Kathie Gill, St. Joseph, Mich.

$200 WINNER

Marinated Beet Salad

Prep: 30 minutes **Chill:** Overnight

1	cup chopped, peeled beet (5 oz.)
1	cup chopped, peeled turnip (5 oz.)
1	cup sliced carrot (2 medium)
1	small sweet onion, cut into thin wedges and separated (½ cup)
½	cup thinly shredded cabbage
⅓	cup olive oil
¼	cup lemon juice
2	Tbsp. sugar
1	tsp. salt
½	tsp. pepper
10	cups torn mixed salad greens
¼	cup dried tart cherries
¼	cup sunflower seeds, toasted

1. In a medium bowl stir together beet, turnip, carrot, onion, and cabbage. In a small bowl combine oil, lemon juice, sugar, salt, and pepper. Add to vegetable mixture; toss gently to coat. Cover and chill overnight.

2. Arrange greens on six salad plates. Using a slotted spoon, top with beet mixture. Sprinkle with cherries and sunflower seeds. Makes 6 servings.

Nutrition facts per serving: 216 cal., 15 g total fat (2 g sat. fat), 0 mg chol., 437 mg sodium, 19 g carbo., 4 g fiber, and 4 g pro. Daily Values: 120% vit. A, 31% vit. C, 5% calcium, and 8% iron.

Red Pepper and Brussels Sprout Salad

Prep: 25 minutes **Cook:** 8 minutes
Chill: 4 hours

12	oz. fresh brussels sprouts, stems trimmed and outer leaves removed (3 cups)
6	cups torn fresh romaine lettuce or spinach
2	cups torn radicchio
1	medium red sweet pepper, cut into thin bite-size strips (1 cup)
1	recipe Honey-Dijon Vinaigrette

1. In a steamer basket over boiling water, steam brussels sprouts, covered, for 8 to 10 minutes or until crisp-tender. In a colander, run brussels sprouts under cold running water to cool. Drain. Cut sprouts in half. Cover and chill.

2. In a large salad bowl combine brussels sprouts, romaine or spinach, radicchio, and pepper strips. Shake Honey-Dijon Vinaigrette; drizzle over salad. Toss to coat. Makes 4 servings.

Honey-Dijon Vinaigrette: In a screw-top jar combine ¼ cup white wine vinegar; 2 tablespoons olive oil; 1 tablespoon champagne mustard or Dijon-style mustard; 1 tablespoon honey; 1 green onion, chopped; 2 cloves garlic, minced; and ⅛ teaspoon pepper. Cover and shake well to mix. Chill for 4 to 24 hours.

Nutrition facts per serving: 148 cal., 8 g total fat (1 g sat. fat), 0 mg chol., 54 mg sodium, 18 g carbo., 6 g fiber, and 5 g pro. Daily Values: 99% vit. A, 249% vit. C, 8% calcium, and 14% iron.

Fennel Waldorf Salad

Prep: 30 minutes **Chill:** 2 hours

- 2 medium fennel bulbs (about 2 lb.)
- 4 medium apples, cored and chopped
- 2 cups seedless red grapes, halved
- 1 recipe Spiced Cream Dressing
- 1 cup chopped hazelnuts (filberts), toasted

1. Cut off and discard upper stalks of fennel, reserving feathery leaves. Snip enough of the leaves to equal 1 tablespoon. Discard remaining leaves. Remove any wilted outer layers; cut off a thin slice from fennel bases. Wash fennel and coarsely chop (should have about 3 cups).

2. Add fennel, 1 tablespoon snipped fennel leaves, apples, and grapes to Spiced Cream Dressing; stir to coat well. Cover and chill for 2 to 24 hours. Before serving, stir in hazelnuts. Makes 12 servings.

Spiced Cream Dressing: In a large bowl stir together ⅓ cup dairy sour cream; ⅓ cup light mayonnaise dressing or salad dressing; 2 tablespoons milk; 2 teaspoons coarse-grain brown mustard; 2 teaspoons lemon juice; 1½ teaspoons sugar; ½ teaspoon fennel seed, crushed; ½ teaspoon salt; ¼ teaspoon ground cinnamon; and a dash ground white pepper.

Nutrition facts per serving: 167 cal., 11 g total fat (2 g sat. fat), 5 mg chol., 173 mg sodium, 18 g carbo., 4 g fiber, and 3 g pro. Daily Values: 3% vit. A, 19% vit. C, 5% calcium, and 6% iron.

Apple-Fennel Salad with Spiced Cider Vinaigrette

Prep: 25 minutes **Bake:** 20 minutes

- ¼ cup olive oil
- ¼ cup cider vinegar
- 1 Tbsp. brown sugar
- 1 tsp. pumpkin pie spice
- 4 cups torn fresh spinach and/or romaine lettuce
- 1 medium fennel bulb, thinly sliced
- 1 medium apple, cored and coarsely chopped
- 1 medium pear, cored and coarsely chopped
- 1 cup Pumpkin Pie Nuts
- ⅓ cup dried cranberries

1. For dressing, in a screw-top jar combine oil, vinegar, brown sugar, and pumpkin pie spice. Shake until combined.

2. In a salad bowl combine spinach or romaine, fennel, apple, pear, Pumpkin Pie Nuts, and cranberries. Shake dressing; drizzle over salad. Toss gently to coat. Makes 4 to 6 servings.

Pumpkin Pie Nuts: Preheat oven to 350° F. In a large bowl combine 1 egg white and 2 teaspoons water; stir in 2 cups pecan halves and 2 cups walnut halves or pieces, tossing to coat with egg white mixture. Spread in a foil-lined 13x9x2-inch baking pan. Combine ¾ cup sugar and 1½ teaspoons pumpkin pie spice; sprinkle evenly over nuts. Bake for 20 minutes. Lift foil out of pan. Let nuts cool. Break apart if necessary. Store in an airtight container. Makes 4 cups.

Nutrition facts per serving: 445 cal., 34 g total fat (4 g sat. fat), 0 mg chol., 56 mg sodium, 38 g carbo., 13 g fiber, and 5 g pro. Daily Values: 35% vit. A, 23% vit. C, 8% calcium, and 19% iron.

Roasted Potato Salad

Prep: 20 minutes **Bake:** 25 minutes

- 1 lb. tiny new potatoes
- 1 lb. sweet potatoes
- 1 medium onion, cut into wedges
- 4 cloves garlic, minced
- ¼ cup olive oil
- 8 oz. fresh crimini or button mushrooms, halved
- 2 Tbsp. balsamic vinegar or red wine vinegar
- ½ tsp. salt
- ½ tsp. pepper
- 4 cups torn fresh spinach

1. Preheat oven to 425° F. Halve new potatoes; peel and cut sweet potatoes into 1-inch pieces. In a shallow roasting pan combine potatoes and onion. Combine garlic and oil; toss with potato mixture.

2. Roast, uncovered, for 15 minutes; add mushrooms. Gently stir mixture to coat mushrooms with oil. Roast for 10 to 15 minutes more or until potatoes are just tender. Combine vinegar, salt, and pepper; drizzle atop roasted vegetables.

3. Place spinach in a large salad bowl; carefully add roasted vegetables. Toss gently to mix. Makes 8 servings.

Nutrition facts per serving: 164 cal., 8 g total fat (1 g sat. fat), 168 mg chol., 168 mg sodium, 23 g carbo., 3 g fiber, and 4 g pro. Daily Values: 175% vit. A, 32% vit. C, 4% calcium, and 9% iron.

Spinach Beet Salad with Roasted Shallot Dressing

Using foil packets to roast the vegetables makes cleanup a snap.

Prep: 20 minutes **Bake:** 25 minutes
Cool: 25 minutes

- 2 shallots
- 3 small parsnips, peeled and sliced ½ inch thick
- ⅓ cup olive oil
- 2 small beets, peeled and quartered
- 2 Tbsp. balsamic vinegar
- 2 tsp. finely snipped fresh sage or ¼ tsp. dried sage, crushed
- ¼ tsp. salt
- ¼ tsp. pepper
- 6 cups fresh baby spinach
- ¼ cup coarsely chopped walnuts, toasted
- 1 oz. blue cheese or feta cheese, crumbled

1. Preheat oven to 450° F. Tear off two 18x12-inch pieces of heavy-duty foil. Peel shallots. Place shallots and parsnips in the center of one piece of foil. Drizzle with 1 tablespoon of the olive oil. Seal foil to make a packet. Make a packet of beets with the remaining foil; drizzle with 1 tablespoon of the olive oil before folding.

2. Place packets in a shallow baking pan. Roast for 25 minutes, turning once. Remove from oven; cool for 25 minutes.

3. For dressing, chop shallots. In a screw-top jar combine remaining olive oil, vinegar, sage, salt, and pepper.

4. Toss greens with half of the dressing. Divide among six salad plates. Slice beets. Divide beets and parsnips among the salads. Drizzle with remaining dressing. Sprinkle with walnuts and cheese. Makes 6 servings.

Nutrition facts per serving: 217 cal., 17 g total fat (3 g sat. fat), 4 mg chol., 235 mg sodium, 15 g carbo., 6 g fiber, and 4 g pro. Daily Values: 17% vit. A, 24% vit. C, 8% calcium, and 16% iron.

Homemade Relishes & Pickles

Peach and Pear Chili Sauce

Pickled Radishes

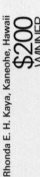

Cynthia C. Saunders, Westbrook, Conn.

$400 WINNER

low fat Peach and Pear Chili Sauce

Prep: 45 minutes **Cook:** 2 hours **Process:** 15 minutes

4½	lb. tomatoes	1	to 2 red or green fresh serrano
4	medium pears, peeled, cored, and		chili peppers, seeded and finely
	cut into ½-inch chunks (4 cups)		chopped (1 to 3 tsp.)*
4	medium peaches, peeled, pitted,	3	cups sugar
	and cut into ½-inch chunks	1½	cups cider vinegar
3	medium green sweet peppers,	4	tsp. salt
	seeded and chopped (2¼ cups)	2	tsp. ground nutmeg
4	medium onions, chopped (2 cups)	1	tsp. whole cloves
¾	cup chopped red sweet pepper	6	inches stick cinnamon

1. Wash tomatoes. Remove peels, stem ends, and cores. Cut tomatoes into chunks (you should have about 6¾ cups). In a 6- or 8-quart stainless steel, enamel, or non-stick Dutch oven or kettle combine tomatoes, pears, peaches, green sweet peppers, onions, red sweet pepper, and chili peppers. Stir in sugar, vinegar, salt, and nutmeg.

2. Tie cloves and cinnamon in 100-percent-cotton cheesecloth; stir into vegetable mixture. Bring to boiling; reduce heat to medium. Simmer, uncovered, about 2 hours or until thick, stirring occasionally.

3. Discard spice bag. Immediately ladle mixture into hot, clean pint canning jars, leaving ½-inch headspace. (Refrigerate any extra chili sauce; use within 3 days.) Wipe jar rims and adjust lids. Process in a boiling-water canner for 15 minutes (start timing when water begins to boil). Remove jars from canner; cool on racks. Makes 4 pints.

Nutrition facts per ¼-cup serving: 116 cal., 0 g fat, 0 mg chol., 300 mg sodium, 29 g carbo., 2 g fiber, 1 g pro. Daily Values: 15% vit. A, 47% vit. C, 1% calcium, 3% iron.

Rhonda E. H. Kaya, Kaneohe, Hawaii

$200 WINNER

low fat Pickled Radishes

Prep: 20 minutes **Chill:** 8 hours

2	cups sliced radishes (8 oz.)	½	cup white vinegar
1	small onion, cut into thin wedges	½	cup sugar
	and separated	1½	tsp. salt

1. Slice radishes. In a large bowl or crock combine radish slices and onion wedges.

2. In another bowl stir together vinegar, sugar, and salt until sugar is dissolved. Pour over radish mixture. Cover and chill for 8 to 24 hours. (The radish mixture will have a very pungent aroma.) Makes 2 cups.

Nutrition facts per 2-tablespoon serving: 25 cal., 0 g total fat (0 g sat. fat), 0 mg chol., 219 mg sodium, 6 g carbo., 0 g fiber, and 0 g pro. Daily Values: 1% vit. C.

low fat Mixed Fruit and Pepper Relish

Be sure to use a non-aluminum kettle for cooking because the acid in the vinegar can react with aluminum. Serve the relish with grilled pork or chicken.

Prep: 20 minutes **Cook:** 1¼ hours
Chill: 30 minutes

2	cups chopped red sweet pepper (1½ medium peppers)
1	7-oz. pkg. tropical blend mixed dried fruit bits, finely chopped (1⅓ cups)
1	fresh large anaheim pepper, finely chopped (⅓ cup)*
1	large shallot, finely chopped (⅓ cup)
¾	cup sugar
¾	cup cider vinegar
¼	cup raspberry wine vinegar
½	tsp. dry mustard
¼	tsp. salt
¼	tsp. ground cumin
⅛	tsp. lemon-pepper seasoning

1. In a medium stainless steel, enamel, or nonstick saucepan combine all ingredients. Bring to boiling; reduce heat to low and simmer for 1¼ hours or until almost all liquid is evaporated, stirring every 10 to 15 minutes.

2. Transfer pepper relish to a storage container; cool, uncovered, for 30 minutes. Cover and chill for up to 2 weeks. Makes about 2 cups.

Nutrition facts per 2-tablespoon serving: 76 cal., 0 g total fat (0 g sat. fat), 0 mg chol., 48 mg sodium, 20 g carbo., 1 g fiber, and 1 g pro. Daily Values: 21% vit. A, 63% vit. C, 1% calcium, and 3% iron.

Spiced Cucumber and Zucchini Relish

What a great way to use your neighbors' zucchini! Just remember to give them a jar and tell them to serve it with grilled brats or hot dogs.

Prep: 1 hour **Chill:** overnight
Cook: 5 minutes **Process:** 10 minutes

2½ lb. zucchini, chopped (8 cups)
2   lb. cucumber, seeded and chopped (5⅓ cups)
8   medium onions, chopped (4 cups)
⅓   cup pickling salt
2   large red and/or green sweet peppers, chopped (2 cups)
4   cups sugar
2½ cups cider vinegar
1   Tbsp. finely shredded lemon peel
½   cup lemon juice
2   Tbsp. celery seed
1   tsp. ground nutmeg
1   tsp. ground cinnamon
½   tsp. ground turmeric
½   tsp. ground black pepper

1. In a very large glass or plastic bowl combine zucchini, cucumber, onion, and salt. Cover and chill overnight.

2. Drain and rinse vegetables. Transfer to an 8- to 10-quart stainless steel, enamel, or nonstick kettle. Stir in sweet pepper, sugar, vinegar, lemon peel, lemon juice, celery seed, nutmeg, cinnamon, turmeric, and black pepper. Bring to boiling; reduce heat to medium. Simmer, uncovered, for 5 minutes.

3. Ladle pepper mixture into hot, sterilized pint canning jars, leaving ½-inch headspace. Wipe jar rims and adjust lids. Process the filled jars in a boiling-water canner for 10 minutes (start timing when the water returns to boil). Remove jars from canner; cool on wire racks. Makes about 7 pints.

Nutrition facts per ¼-cup serving: 66 cal., 0 g total fat (0 g sat. fat), 0 mg chol., 126 mg sodium, 17 g carbo., 1 g fiber, and 0 g pro. Daily Values: 7% vit. A, 21% vit. C, 1% calcium, and 2% iron.

Curried Jicama Confetti Relish

Prep: 20 minutes **Chill:** 4 hours

3   medium oranges, peeled, sectioned, and chopped
½   cup finely chopped peeled jicama
⅓   cup finely chopped red sweet pepper
⅓   cup finely chopped green sweet pepper
2   Tbsp. finely chopped red onion
2   Tbsp. balsamic vinegar
1   Tbsp. orange juice
1   tsp. curry powder
¼   tsp. salt
¼   tsp. ground black pepper

1. In a medium bowl combine all ingredients. Cover and chill for 4 to 24 hours. Serve with a slotted spoon. Makes about 1½ cups.

Nutrition facts per 2-tablespoon serving: 17 cal., 0 g total fat (0 g sat. fat), 0 mg chol., 49 mg sodium, 4 g carbo., 1 g fiber, and 0 g pro. Daily Values: 6% vit. A, 36% vit. C, 1% calcium, and 1% iron.

Pickled Star Fruit

Serve with grilled meats or fish.

Prep: 20 minutes **Cook:** 8 minutes
Chill: 4 hours

8   cardamom pods
3   Tbsp. sugar
3   Tbsp. white wine vinegar
2   tsp. grated fresh ginger
¼   tsp. crushed red pepper
2½ cups sliced, seeded carambola, (star fruit) (about 4)

1. Remove seeds from cardamom pods; discard hulls. Crush seeds (you should have about ⅜ teaspoon).

2. In a medium stainless steel, enamel, or nonstick saucepan combine sugar, vinegar, ginger, red pepper, and cardamom; add star fruit. Bring to boiling, stirring occasionally; reduce heat. Simmer, covered, about 8 minutes or until fruit begins to soften.

3. Transfer to a nonmetal bowl; cover and chill at least 4 hours or up to 3 days. Makes about 2 cups.

Nutrition facts per ¼-cup serving: 35 cal., 0 g total fat (0 g sat. fat), 0 mg chol., 1 mg sodium, 8 g carbo., 1 g fiber, and 0 g pro. Daily Values: 4% vit. A, 15% vit. C, and 1% iron.

Sweet Jalapeño Slices

Pick these hot pickled peppers to top nachos, Tex-Mex salads, or casseroles.

Prep: 30 minutes **Chill:** 2 hours
Cook: 9 minutes **Cool:** 30 minutes

1   lb. fresh jalapeño peppers, stemmed, halved, seeded, and cut into ½-inch-thick slices* (about 3 cups)
½   cup chopped onion
1   large red sweet pepper, cut into ¼-inch-wide strips
1   Tbsp. pickling salt
    Crushed ice
1¼ cups sugar
½   cup cider vinegar
1   tsp. mustard seeds
½   tsp. celery seed
¼   tsp. ground turmeric

1. In a large bowl combine jalapeño peppers, onion, red sweet pepper, and pickling salt. Cover with crushed ice; chill for 2 hours.

2. Drain pepper mixture in a colander; rinse well (remove any ice that remains). In a large stainless steel, enamel, or nonstick saucepan combine sugar, vinegar, mustard seeds, celery seed, and turmeric. Bring to boiling. Stir in drained pepper mixture. Return to boiling.

3. Ladle pepper mixture into hot, clean half-pint canning jars. Cool, uncovered, for 30 minutes. Cover and chill for at least 24 hours. Store in the refrigerator for up to 3 weeks. Makes 3 to 4 half-pints.

Nutrition facts per 1-tablespoon serving: 20 cal., 0 g total fat (0 g sat. fat), 0 mg chol., 73 mg sodium, 5 g carbo., 0 g fiber, and 0 g pro. Daily Values: 4% vit. A, 16% vit. C, and 1% iron.

***Test Kitchen Tip:** When you're working with hot peppers for any of the recipes on these pages, remember—because chili peppers, such as jalapeños, contain volatile oils that can burn your skin and eyes, avoid direct contact with them as much as possible. When working with chili peppers, wear plastic or rubber gloves. If your bare hands do touch the chili peppers, wash your hands well with soap and water.

Rice on the Side

Butternut Risotto

Guacamole Rice Salad

Butternut Risotto

Prep: 20 minutes **Cook:** 25 minutes

5	cups reduced-sodium chicken broth
3	cloves garlic, minced
2	Tbsp. olive oil
1	lb. butternut squash, peeled, seeded, and cut into ¼- to ½-inch cubes (about 3 cups)
1½	cups uncooked arborio rice
¼	tsp. thread saffron, crushed, or ground turmeric
2	Tbsp. butter or margarine
2	Tbsp. finely shredded Parmesan cheese
⅛	tsp. pepper

1. In a medium saucepan bring broth to boiling. Cover and reduce heat until broth just simmers. Meanwhile, in a large nonstick skillet cook garlic in hot oil for 15 seconds. Add squash and rice; cook and stir for 1 minute more.

2. Carefully add ½ cup of the hot broth and saffron or turmeric to rice mixture, stirring constantly. Cook and stir over medium heat until broth is absorbed. Continue adding broth, ½ cup at a time, stirring constantly until broth has been absorbed, but mixture is creamy. (This should take about 25 minutes total.) Remove from heat; stir in butter or margarine, cheese, and pepper. Makes 8 to 10 servings.

Nutrition facts per serving: 183 cal., 7 g total fat (3 g sat. fat), 10 mg chol., 440 mg sodium, 27 g carbo., 1 g fiber, and 5 g pro. Daily Values: 85% vit. A, 19% vit. C, 4% calcium, and 11% iron.

Guacamole Rice Salad

Prep: 30 minutes **Chill:** 2 hours

3	cups cooked basmati rice
1	large tomato, seeded and chopped (⅔ cup)
¾	cup chopped sweet onion, such as Vidalia or Walla Walla
3	Tbsp. snipped fresh cilantro
2	to 3 Tbsp. seeded and finely chopped fresh jalapeño pepper (see tip, page 291)
3	Tbsp. lemon juice
2	Tbsp. olive oil
½	tsp. salt
¼	tsp. pepper
1	avocado, halved, seeded, peeled, and chopped
2	Tbsp. lime juice
	Shredded romaine lettuce
	Lime wedges

1. In a large bowl combine rice, tomato, onion, cilantro, and jalapeño pepper. Stir together lemon juice, olive oil, salt, and pepper; stir into rice mixture. Toss avocado with lime juice; stir into rice mixture. Cover and chill for 2 to 8 hours. To serve, spoon atop shredded lettuce. Serve with lime wedges. Makes 6 servings.

Nutrition facts per serving: 233 cal., 10 g total fat (1 g sat. fat), 203 mg sodium, 34 g carbo., 3 g fiber, 4 g pro. Daily Values: 24% vit. A, 39% vit. C, 3% calcium, 13% iron.

30 Lemon Pesto Rice with Sugar Snap Peas

Start to finish: 30 minutes

¼	cup dry sherry
3	Tbsp. basil pesto
1	tsp. finely shredded lemon peel
1	Tbsp. lemon juice
1	cup sliced celery
1	Tbsp. olive oil
¾	cup coarsely chopped almonds
3	cloves garlic, minced
½	tsp. salt
8	oz. fresh sugar snap peas, halved crosswise, if desired
3	cups hot cooked rice
	Finely shredded Parmesan cheese
	Pepper

1. In a small bowl stir together dry sherry, basil pesto, lemon peel, and lemon juice; set aside.

2. In a large skillet cook and stir celery in hot oil over medium-high heat for 3 to 4 minutes or until tender. Stir in walnuts, garlic, and salt; cook and stir for 30 seconds. Add snap peas; cook and stir about 2 minutes more or until peas are crisp-tender.

3. Stir cooked rice into vegetable mixture. Add pesto mixture; stir to coat. Heat through. Sprinkle with cheese and pepper. Makes 8 servings.

Nutrition facts per serving: 234 cal., 13 g total fat (3 g sat. fat), 4 mg chol., 242 mg sodium, 23 g carbo., 2 g fiber, and 6 g pro. Daily Values: 12% vit. A, 13% vit. C, 9% calcium, and 8% iron.

30 Fruit, Wild Rice, and Spinach Salad

Start to finish: 30 minutes

- 6 cups torn fresh spinach
- 2 cups cooled, cooked wild rice
- 1 cup seedless green grapes, halved
- ¼ cup shelled sunflower seeds
- ¼ cup white balsamic vinegar or cider vinegar
- ¼ cup olive oil
- 1 Tbsp. honey
- 2 tsp. snipped fresh basil or ½ tsp. dried basil, crushed
- ¼ tsp. salt
- ¼ tsp. pepper
- 1 cup raspberries
- 2 oranges, peeled and sectioned

1. In a large salad bowl combine spinach, rice, grapes, and sunflower seeds.

2. For dressing, in a screw-top jar combine vinegar, oil, honey, basil, salt, and pepper. Cover and shake well to mix.

3. Pour dressing atop spinach mixture; toss gently to coat. Fold in raspberries and orange sections. Makes 6 servings.

Nutrition facts per serving: 235 cal., 13 g total fat (2 g sat. fat), 0 mg chol., 139 mg sodium, 28 g carbo., 7 g fiber, and 5 g pro. Daily Values: 36% vit. A, 44% vit. C, 5% calcium, and 18% iron.

low fat Curried Mango Rice

Prep: 15 minutes **Cook:** 20 minutes

- 1 cup uncooked basmati rice
- 1 Tbsp. margarine or butter
- 1½ tsp. curry seasoning blend, garam marsala, or Thai seasoning blend
- 2⅓ cups reduced-sodium chicken broth or vegetable broth
- 1 medium onion, coarsely chopped (½ cup)
- ⅓ cup golden raisins
- ¼ cup chopped dried mango or apricot
- ⅛ tsp. sea salt or coarse salt
- ¼ cup sliced almonds, toasted
- 2 Tbsp. snipped fresh cilantro
- 2 Tbsp. coconut, toasted (optional)

1. In a medium saucepan cook and stir rice in hot margarine or butter for 1 minute. Stir in seasoning blend; cook and stir for 1 minute.

2. Carefully add broth, onion, raisins, mango, and salt. Bring to boiling. Reduce heat and simmer, covered, for 18 to 20 minutes or until rice is tender and liquid is absorbed.

3. Sprinkle almonds, cilantro, and toasted coconut (if using) over the rice. Makes 4 to 6 servings.

Nutrition facts per serving: 318 cal., 8 g total fat (2 g sat. fat), 8 mg chol., 448 mg sodium, 56 g carbo., 4 g fiber, and 7 g pro. Daily Values: 13% vit. A, 6% vit. C, 4% calcium, and 7% iron.

Apple and Walnut Brown Rice Pilaf

Prep: 15 minutes **Cook:** 47 minutes

- 1 cup uncooked regular brown rice
- 2 cloves garlic, minced
- 2 Tbsp. butter or olive oil
- 2 cups water
- ⅔ cup apple juice
- ¾ tsp. salt
- 2 medium apples and/or pears, peeled and chopped
- ¼ cup dried apricots, cut into strips
- 1 tsp. grated fresh ginger or ¼ tsp. ground ginger
- ½ cup chopped walnuts, toasted

1. In a medium saucepan cook and stir brown rice and garlic in hot butter or olive oil for 2 minutes. Carefully add water, juice, and salt. Bring to boiling; reduce heat. Simmer, covered, for 40 minutes.

2. Add apples, apricots, and ginger. Return to boiling; reduce heat. Simmer, covered, 5 minutes more or until rice is tender. Stir in nuts. Makes 6 to 8 servings.

Nutrition facts per serving: 267 cal., 12 g total fat (3 g sat. fat), 11 mg chol., 338 mg sodium, 38 g carbo., 3 g fiber, and 4 g pro. Daily Values: 11% vit. A, 3% vit. C, 3% calcium, and 6% iron.

Bulgur-Wild Rice Casserole

This versatile side dish won in November, 1999, but it's so healthful and easy, it bears repeating.

Prep: 20 minutes **Bake:** 30 minutes

- ¼ cup margarine or butter
- 1 cup bulgur
- 1 cup chopped celery
- ½ cup chopped onion
- 3 cups chicken broth
- 1½ cups cooked wild rice
- ½ cup snipped fresh parsley
- ¼ tsp. pepper
- 1 Tbsp. snipped fresh basil or 1 tsp. dried basil, crushed
- 2 tsp. snipped fresh oregano or ½ tsp. dried oregano, crushed
- 2 cups sliced fresh mushrooms
- 1 cup chopped pecans, toasted

1. Preheat oven to 350° F. In a large saucepan melt margarine over medium heat. Add bulgur; cook for 2 minutes. Stir in celery and onion. Cook and stir 3 minutes more or until just tender.

2. Stir in chicken broth, cooked wild rice, parsley, pepper, and, if using, dried basil and oregano. Bring to boiling; reduce heat. Cover and simmer for 10 minutes.

3. Stir in mushrooms, walnuts, and, if using, fresh basil and oregano. Transfer to a 2-quart casserole. Bake, covered, about 30 minutes or until liquid is absorbed. Makes 8 to 10 servings.

Nutrition facts per serving: 266 cal., 16 g total fat (2 g sat. fat), 0 mg chol., 381 mg sodium, 26 g carbo., 6 g fiber, and 8 g pro. Daily Values: 12% vit. C, 3% calcium, and 12% iron.

Festive Pepper Rice

Serve this colorful March, 1997 winner with any Tex-Mex dish.

Prep: 15 minutes **Bake:** 20 minutes

- 1 cup chopped sweet pepper (red, yellow, and/or green)
- ½ cup chopped onion
- 2 to 3 medium jalapeño peppers, seeded and finely chopped (see tip, page 291)
- 2 cloves garlic, minced
- 1 Tbsp. cooking oil
- 1½ cups chopped tomatoes
- 2 to 3 Tbsp. snipped fresh cilantro
- ¼ tsp. salt
- 2 cups cooked regular brown rice (⅔ cup uncooked rice)
- 1 15-oz. can garbanzo beans, rinsed and drained
- 1 cup shredded Monterey Jack cheese (4 oz.)

1. Preheat oven to 350° F. In a large saucepan cook sweet pepper, onion, jalapeño peppers, and garlic in hot oil 5 minutes or until tender, stirring often.

2. Stir in tomatoes, cilantro, and salt; simmer, uncovered, for 5 minutes.

3. Add rice, garbanzo beans, and ½ cup of the cheese; stir gently until combined.

4. Turn mixture into a 1½-quart casserole. Sprinkle with remaining ½ cup cheese. Bake, covered, about 20 minutes or until heated through. Makes 8 servings.

Nutrition facts per serving: 189 cal., 8 g total fat (3 g sat. fat), 13 mg chol., 347 mg sodium, 24 g carbo., 4 g fiber, and 8 g pro. Daily Values: 7% vit. A, 47% vit. C, 11% calcium, and 12% iron.

Best Cake Mix Fix-Ups

Pumpkin Spice Whoopies

Easy Lemon Sugar Snaps

Lisa Volpe Hachey, Hopkinton, Mass.

$400 WINNER

Pumpkin Spice Whoopies

Prep: 20 minutes **Bake:** 15 minutes per batch

1	cup canned pumpkin	½ cup milk
⅓	cup butter, softened	1 recipe Marshmallow-Spice Filling
1	pkg. 2-layer-size spice cake mix	(see right)
2	eggs	

1. Preheat oven to 375° F. In a large mixing bowl beat pumpkin and butter with an electric mixer on medium speed until smooth. Add cake mix, eggs, and milk; beat with mixer on low speed until combined, then on medium speed for 1 minute.

2. Line a cookie sheet with parchment paper or foil (grease foil, if using). Drop batter by heaping tablespoons 3 inches apart onto cookie sheet; keep remaining batter chilled. Bake 15 minutes or until set and light brown around edges. Carefully remove from parchment or foil; cool on a wire rack. Repeat.

3. Spread about 2½ tablespoons Marshmallow-Spice Filling onto the flat side of one cookie; top with a second cookie. Repeat. Serve immediately or cover and chill for up to 2 hours. Makes 15 cookie sandwiches.

Nutrition facts per cookie: 379 cal., 19 g total fat (11 g sat. fat), 75 mg chol., 387 mg sodium, 49 g carbo., 1 g fiber, 3 g pro. Daily Values: 86% vit. A, 10% calcium, 6% iron.

Gloria Kirchman, Eden Prairie, Minn.

$200 WINNER

Easy Lemon Sugar Snaps

Prep: 25 minutes **Bake:** 9 minutes per batch

¾	cup butter, softened	1 cup yellow cornmeal
1	egg	2 Tbsp. finely shredded lemon peel
1	pkg. 2-layer-size lemon cake mix	Coarse sugar or granulated sugar
	(with pudding in mix)	

1. Preheat oven to 375° F. In a large mixing bowl beat butter and egg with an electric mixer on medium speed for 30 seconds. Gradually beat in cake mix until combined; stir in cornmeal and lemon peel. Knead in cornmeal until combined.

2. Using 1 tablespoon of dough for each cookie, roll dough into 1-inch balls. Roll in sugar. Arrange balls, 2 inches apart, on ungreased cookie sheets.

3. Bake for 9 to 10 minutes or until bottoms are lightly browned. Cool on cookie sheet for 1 minute. Transfer to wire rack; cool. Makes 3½ dozen cookies.

Nutrition facts per cookie: 99 cal., 5 g total fat (2 g sat. fat), 14 mg chol., 114 mg sodium, 14 g carbo., 0 g fiber, 1 g pro. Daily Values: 3% vit. A, 1% vit. C, 3% calcium, 2% iron.

30 Marshmallow-Spice Filling

Start to finish: 15 minutes

1. For Pumpkin Spice Whoopies (see left), combine ½ cup softened butter and one 8-ounce package softened cream cheese; beat until smooth. Beat in 2 cups sifted powdered sugar, ½ of a 7-ounce jar marshmallow creme, 1 teaspoon vanilla, and ½ teaspoon each ground cinnamon and ground nutmeg. Makes about 4 cups.

low fat Berry Good Banana Bread

Prep: 15 minutes **Bake:** 45 minutes

1	pkg. 2-layer-size white cake mix
1¾	cups mashed ripe banana (4 to 5)
1½	tsp. apple pie spice
2	eggs
1	cup fresh blueberries
¾	cup dried cranberries

1. Preheat oven to 350° F. Grease the bottom and ½ inch up the sides of two 8x4x2-inch loaf pans; set aside.

2. In a bowl combine cake mix, banana, spice, and eggs; stir until moistened. Beat by hand 1 minute (batter will be lumpy). Fold in blueberries and cranberries.

3. Divide batter between prepared loaf pans; spread evenly. Bake for 45 to 50 minutes or until a wooden toothpick inserted near centers comes out clean. Cool in pans on wire racks for 10 minutes. Remove from pans; cool completely on wire racks. Wrap and store overnight. Makes 2 loaves (20 slices).

Nutrition facts per slice: 156 cal., 3 g total fat (1 g sat. fat), 21 mg chol., 188 mg sodium, 31 g carbo., 1 g fiber, and 2 g pro. Daily Values: 1% vit. A, 5% vit. C, 3% calcium, and 4% iron.

Praline Crunch Cake

Prep: 25 minutes **Bake:** 30 minutes

2 Tbsp. molasses
1 Tbsp. instant coffee crystals
1 pkg. 2-layer-size yellow cake mix
3 eggs
⅓ cup cooking oil
1 recipe Coffee Frosting
1 recipe Pecan Crunch

1. Preheat oven to 350° F. Grease a 13x9x2-inch baking pan; set aside.

2. In a 2-cup glass measure combine molasses and coffee crystals. Add water to equal 1⅓ cups; stir to combine. Transfer to a bowl. Add cake mix, eggs, and oil. Beat with an electric mixer on low speed until combined. Beat on medium for 2 minutes.

3. Pour into prepared pan. Bake about 30 minutes or until a wooden toothpick inserted in the center comes out clean. Cool in pan on a wire rack. Frost cooled cake with Coffee Frosting; sprinkle with Pecan Crunch. Makes 16 servings.

Coffee Frosting: In a large mixing bowl beat ¼ cup butter with an electric mixer on low speed for 30 seconds. Add 1 cup sifted powdered sugar; beat until combined. Combine ¼ cup half-and-half, light cream, or milk; 1 teaspoon instant coffee crystals; and 1 teaspoon vanilla. Stir until dissolved. Add to powdered sugar mixture; beat until combined. (Mixture may appear curdled.) Gradually add 2½ cups sifted powdered sugar, beating until smooth and spreadable. If necessary, beat in additional half-and-half.

Praline Crunch: Preheat oven to 350° F. In a small mixing bowl stir together ⅓ cup all-purpose flour, 1 tablespoon brown sugar, and ½ teaspoon ground cinnamon. Cut in 3 tablespoons butter until crumbly. Stir in ⅓ cup chopped pecans. Knead until mixture starts to cling together. (Mixture should form small moist clumps.) Spread clumps in an even layer in a 15x10x1-inch baking pan. Bake about 10 minutes or until golden. Transfer to a piece of foil to cool.

Nutrition facts per serving: 354 cal., 15 g total fat (5 g sat. fat), 56 mg chol., 272 mg sodium, 53 g carbo., 0 g fiber, and 3 g pro. Daily Values: 6% vit. A, 8% calcium, and 6% iron.

Double Chocolate Cake

Prep: 30 minutes **Bake:** 50 minutes

1 pkg. 2-layer-size yellow, French vanilla, or vanilla cake mix
⅔ cup sugar
⅓ cup unsweetened cocoa powder
½ cup butter
1 cup chopped walnuts
1 cup semisweet chocolate pieces
¼ cup cooking oil
2 eggs
1 recipe Chocolate Icing

1. Preheat oven to 350° F. Grease and flour a 9x9x2-inch baking pan; set aside.

2. In a medium bowl combine 1½ cups cake mix, sugar, and cocoa powder. Cut in butter until crumbly; stir in walnuts and chocolate pieces. Press onto bottom of pan. Bake 15 minutes. Cool 15 minutes.

3. Combine remaining cake mix, oil, ⅔ cup water, and eggs; beat 2 minutes. Pour onto crust. Bake 35 minutes or until a toothpick inserted near center comes out clean. Cool on a wire rack. Top with Chocolate Icing. Makes 12 servings.

Chocolate Icing: In a small saucepan combine ½ cup semisweet chocolate pieces and 3 tablespoons light cream or milk; heat and stir until smooth.

Nutrition facts per serving: 532 cal., 31 g total fat (12 g sat. fat), 59 mg chol., 372 mg sodium, 61 g carbo., 2 g fiber, and 6 g pro. Daily Values: 8% vit. A, 1% vit. C, 6% calcium, and 12% iron.

Lemon-Lime Cake

Prep: 25 minutes **Bake:** 45 minutes
Cool: 10 minutes

1 pkg. 2-layer-size lemon cake mix
2 3-oz. pkg. cream cheese, softened
2 Tbsp. butter, softened
1 Tbsp. cornstarch
½ cup sweetened condensed milk
1 egg
2 tsp. finely shredded lime peel
3 Tbsp. lime juice
Few drops green food coloring (optional)
1 recipe Lime Icing

1. Preheat oven to 350° F. Grease and flour a 10-inch fluted tube pan. Prepare batter according to package directions; pour into prepared pan.

2. Beat cream cheese, butter, and cornstarch until combined. Beat in condensed milk, egg, lime peel, lime juice, and coloring, if desired. Spoon evenly onto batter.

3. Bake about 45 minutes or until toothpick inserted near center comes out clean. Cool on a wire rack for 10 minutes. Remove from pan. Cool completely. Top with Lime Icing. Makes 12 servings.

Lime Icing: In a small bowl stir together 1 cup sifted powdered sugar, 1 teaspoon finely shredded lime peel, 1 tablespoon lime juice, and several drops green food coloring, if desired. Stir in enough water (2 to 3 teaspoons) to make an icing of drizzling consistency.

Nutrition facts per serving: 321 cal., 12 g total fat (6 g sat. fat), 43 mg chol., 354 mg sodium, 52 g carbo., 0 g fiber, and 4 g pro. Daily Values: 7% vit. A, 4% vit. C, 13% calcium, and 6% iron.

Harvest Pudding

Prep: 25 minutes **Bake:** 45 minutes

⅓ cup quick-cooking rolled oats
¼ cup all-purpose flour
2 Tbsp. brown sugar
⅛ tsp. ground cinnamon
¼ cup butter
2 Tbsp. chopped hazelnuts or pecans
1 pkg. 2-layer-size sour cream white cake mix
3 eggs
Dairy sour cream
Pear nectar
2 medium pears, cored and finely chopped (2 cups)
1 medium cooking apple, cored and finely chopped (⅔ cup)

1. Preheat oven to 350° F. Grease a 3-quart rectangular baking dish; set aside.

2. For topping, combine oats, flour, sugar, and cinnamon. Cut in butter until pieces are pea-size. Stir in nuts. Set aside.

3. Prepare cake mix according to package directions, except use whole eggs instead of egg whites, sour cream instead of oil, and half water and half pear nectar for the water. Stir in pears and apple. Pour into baking dish; spread evenly.

4. Bake for 20 minutes. Carefully sprinkle topping over cake. Bake for 25 to 30 minutes more or until a wooden toothpick inserted near the center comes out clean. Cool on a wire rack for 30 minutes. Serve warm. Makes 12 servings.

Nutrition facts per serving: 333 cal., 12 g total fat (5 g sat. fat), 66 mg chol., 431 mg sodium, 53 g carbo., 1 g fiber, and 5 g pro. Daily Values: 6% vit. A, 3% vit. C, 8% calcium, and 7% iron.

Cheesecakes

Apricot Cheesecake   Banana Cheesecake

Apricot Cheesecake

Prep: 30 minutes **Bake:** 50 minutes **Chill:** 4 hours

1 15¼-oz. can unpeeled apricot halves	3 eggs
3 8-oz. pkg. cream cheese, softened	1 recipe Cookie Crust (see right)
1 cup sugar	1 10-oz. jar low-calorie apricot spread
1½ tsp. vanilla	¼ cup apricot nectar

1. Preheat oven to 325° F. For filling, drain apricots, reserving 3 tablespoons syrup; coarsely chop. In a bowl combine reserved syrup, cream cheese, sugar, and vanilla; beat until combined. Add eggs all at once; beat just until combined. Stir in apricots.

2. Pour filling into Cookie Crust. Place on a shallow baking pan in oven. Bake about 50 minutes or until center is nearly set. Cool in pan on a wire rack for 15 minutes. Loosen side of pan; cool for 30 minutes more. Remove side of pan; cool.

3. For topping, melt apricot spread over low heat; stir in apricot nectar. Spread onto cheesecake. Cover and chill at least 4 hours before serving. Makes 16 servings.

Nutrition facts per slice: 333 cal., 22 g total fat (13 g sat. fat), 108 mg chol., 213 mg sodium, 31 g carbo., 1 g fiber, and 2 g pro. Daily Values: 26% vit. A, 9% vit. C, 5% calcium, and 5% iron.

Banana Cheesecake

Prep: 30 minutes **Bake:** 35 minutes **Chill:** 4 hours

3 8-oz. pkg. cream cheese, softened	1 recipe Pecan Crust (see right)
¾ cup sugar	1 8-oz. carton dairy sour cream
1 tsp. vanilla	2 Tbsp. white crème de cacao
3 eggs	2 Tbsp. rum
1 cup mashed banana (2 medium)	1½ cups flaked coconut, toasted

1. Preheat oven to 350° F. For filling, in a large mixing bowl combine cream cheese, sugar, and vanilla; beat with an electric mixture on medium speed until combined. Add eggs; beat on low speed just until combined. Stir in banana.

2. Pour filling into Pecan Crust. Bake about 30 minutes or until center is set. Meanwhile, for topping, in a small bowl stir together sour cream, crème de cacao, and rum. Spread evenly onto filling; bake 5 minutes more. (The topping may crack slightly.)

3. Cool in pan on a wire rack for 15 minutes. Loosen side of pan; cool 30 minutes more. Remove side of pan; cool. Cover and chill for 4 to 24 hours. To serve, sprinkle with toasted coconut. Makes 16 servings.

Nutrition facts per slice: 472 cal., 35 g total fat (22 g sat. fat), 109 mg chol., 270 mg sodium, 33 g carbo., 1 g fiber, and 7 g pro. Daily Values: 20% vit. A, 3% vit. C, 7% calcium, and 10% iron.

Cookie Crust

Start to finish: 20 minutes

1. Preheat oven to 325° F. In a medium mixing bowl combine 2 cups finely crushed butter cookies (about 30 cookies) and ⅓ cup melted butter. Press crumb mixture evenly onto bottom and 2 inches up the side of a 9-inch springform pan. Bake for 8 to 10 minutes or until golden. Use crust for Apricot Cheesecake (see left). Makes 1 crust.

Pecan Crust

Start to finish: 10 minutes

1. In a medium mixing bowl combine 2 cups finely crushed graham crackers, ¼ cup sugar, and ½ cup finely chopped pecans. Stir in ½ melted butter. Press crumb mixture evenly onto bottom of a 13x9x2-inch baking pan. Use for Banana Cheesecake (see left). Makes 1 crust.

Mango Swirl Cheesecake

Prep: 1 hour **Bake:** 1 hour
Chill: 4 hours

- 3 8-oz. pkg. cream cheese or reduced-fat cream cheese (Neufchâtel), softened
- 1 cup sugar
- 2 Tbsp. all-purpose flour
- 1 tsp. finely shredded orange peel
- 1 tsp. vanilla
- 3 eggs
- ¼ cup orange juice
- 1 recipe Coconut-Graham Crust
- 1 recipe Mango Curd

1. Preheat oven to 325° F. For filling, in a large mixing bowl combine cream cheese, sugar, flour, orange peel, and vanilla; beat until combined. Add eggs all at once; beat on low speed just until combined. Stir in orange juice.

2. Pour filling into Coconut Graham Crust. Drizzle with Mango Curd; swirl gently with a knife to marble, being careful not to disturb crust.

3. Bake about 1 hour or until center appears nearly set when shaken. Cool in pan on a wire rack for 15 minutes. Loosen side of pan; cool for 30 minutes more. Remove side of the pan; cool completely on rack. Cover and chill at least 4 hours before serving. Makes 16 servings.

Coconut-Graham Crust: Preheat oven to 350° F. In a food processor bowl combine 24 broken cinnamon graham crackers, ½ cup toasted coconut, and 2 tablespoons sugar. Process mixture to fine crumbs. Stir in 4 tablespoons melted butter. (Or place the graham crackers in a resealable plastic bag and crush with a rolling pin. Chop the coconut finely. Stir together graham cracker cumbs, coconut, sugar, and melted butter.) Press evenly onto bottom and about 2 inches up the side of a 9-inch springform pan. Bake for 5 minutes.

Mango Curd: Seed, peel, and chop 1 medium mango. Place in a blender container or food processor bowl; cover and blend or process until smooth. In a small heavy saucepan combine mango puree, ¼ cup sugar, ¼ cup orange juice, and 1 tablespoon butter. Cook and stir over medium heat until bubbly. Stir half of the mixture into 1 slightly beaten egg yolk. Return egg mixture to saucepan. Cook and stir until bubbly; cook and stir 2 minutes more. Transfer to a small bowl. Cover surface with plastic wrap; chill for 1 hour.

Nutrition facts per slice: 335 cal., 22 g total fat (13 g sat. fat), 110 mg chol., 241 mg sodium, 31 g carbo., 1 g fiber, and 6 g pro. Daily Values: 27% vit. A, 13% vit. C, 5% calcium, and 7% iron.

Brownie Caramel Cheesecake

Prep: 30 minutes **Bake:** 45 minutes
Chill: 4 hours

- 1 14-oz. pkg. vanilla caramels (about 48 caramels)
- 1 5-oz. can (⅔ cup) evaporated milk
- 3 8-oz. pkg. cream cheese, softened
- 1 14-oz. can sweetened condensed milk
- 3 eggs
- 1 recipe Brownie Crust
- ⅓ cup chopped chocolate-covered English toffee (one 1.4-oz bar)

1. Preheat oven to 350° F. In a medium saucepan cook and stir caramels and evaporated milk over medium-low heat until caramels are melted and smooth; remove from heat. Remove ½ cup of the melted caramel for topping. Cover and chill until serving time.

2. For filling, in a large mixing bowl combine cream cheese and sweetened condensed milk; beat with an electric mixer on medium speed until combined. Add eggs, all at once; beat on low speed just until combined.

3. Pour filling into Brownie Crust. Drizzle with remaining caramel mixture; swirl gently with a knife to marble, being careful not to disturb crust. Bake about 45 minutes or until center appears nearly set when shaken.

4. Cool in pan on a wire rack for 15 minutes. Loosen side of pan; cool for 30 minutes more. Remove side of pan; cool completely on rack. Cover and chill at least 4 hours before serving. (Cake may crack where caramel mixture is swirled in.)

5. Before serving, heat the reserved caramel topping, drizzle over cheesecake. Sprinkle with chopped toffee bar. Makes 16 servings.

Brownie Crust: Preheat oven to 350° F. In a medium bowl beat 1 egg; stir in one 8-ounce package brownie mix and 1 tablespoon water. Press evenly onto the bottom of a greased 10-inch springform pan. Bake for 15 minutes.

Nutrition facts per slice: 433 cal., 24 g total fat (14 g sat. fat), 111 mg chol., 316 mg sodium, 48 g carbo., 1 g fiber, and 9 g pro. Daily Values: 16% vit. A, 1% vit. C, 20% calcium, and 9% iron.

Malt Shop Cheesecake

Prep: 30 minutes **Bake:** 40 minutes
Chill: 4 hours

- 3 8-oz. pkg. cream cheese, softened
- ¼ cup sugar
- ¾ cup instant malted milk powder
- ¼ cup milk
- 4 eggs
- ½ cup red maraschino cherries, drained and quartered
- ¾ cup chocolate instant malted milk powder
- ½ cup chocolate-flavored syrup
- 1 recipe Chocolate Cookie Crust Whipped cream (optional)
- ½ cup malted milk balls, chopped

1. Preheat oven to 350° F. In a large bowl beat cream cheese and sugar until smooth. Transfer half (about 1½ cups) to a medium bowl; set aside.

2. For cherry malt filling, to cream cheese mixture in the large bowl, add instant malted milk powder and 2 tablespoons milk; beat on medium speed until combined. Add 2 eggs; beat just until combined. Stir in cherries; set aside.

3. For chocolate malt filling, to cream cheese mixture in medium bowl, add chocolate instant malted milk powder, 2 tablespoons of the chocolate syrup, and remaining 2 tablespoons milk; beat until combined. Add remaining 2 eggs and beat on low speed just until combined.

4. Pour chocolate malt filling into Chocolate Cookie Crust. Carefully spoon cherry malt filling evenly over chocolate layer. Place pan in a 15x10x1-inch baking pan. Bake for 40 to 45 minutes or until center appears nearly set when shaken.

5. Cool in pan on wire rack 15 minutes. Loosen side of pan; cool for 30 minutes more. Remove side of pan; cool. Cover and chill at least 4 hours before serving.

6. If desired, top each serving with whipped cream, chocolate syrup, and malted milk balls. Makes 16 servings.

Chocolate Cookie Crust: In a medium bowl combine 1¾ cups finely crushed chocolate wafers (32 wafers) and ⅓ cup melted butter. Press evenly onto bottom and 1½ inches up side of an ungreased 9-inch springform pan. Chill.

Nutrition facts per slice: 360 cal., 23 g total fat (14 g sat. fat), 114 mg chol., 188 mg sodium, 32 g carbo., 1 g fiber, and 7 g pro. Daily Values: 25% vit. A, 12% vit. C, 10% calcium, and 10% iron.

Easy Cookies and Bars

Chocolate Caramel-Nut Bars

Banana Crunch Bars

Chocolate Caramel-Nut Bars

Prep: 20 minutes **Bake:** 30 minutes

Nonstick cooking spray
1   pkg. 2-layer-size white cake mix
1   cup quick-cooking rolled oats
½ cup peanut butter
1   egg
2   Tbsp. milk

1   8-oz. pkg. reduced-fat cream cheese (Neufchâtel)
1   12¼-oz. jar caramel ice cream topping
1   11½-oz. pkg. milk chocolate pieces
1   cup cocktail peanuts

1. Preheat oven to 350° F. Coat a 13x9x2-inch pan with spray; set aside. In a bowl combine cake mix and oats; cut in peanut butter to resemble fine crumbs. Beat egg with milk; stir into crumb mixture. Reserve ¾ cup mixture; press remaining into pan.

2. For filling, beat cream cheese until smooth. Add caramel topping; beat until mixed. Spread onto crumb mixture. Sprinkle chocolate on top; add nuts. Top with reserved crumb mixture. Bake 30 minutes. Cool on a wire rack. Makes 24 bars.

Nutrition facts per bar: 311 cal., 14 g total fat (5 g sat. fat), 16 mg chol., 273 mg sodium, 41 g carbo., 1 g fiber, and 7 g pro. Daily Values: 2% vit. A, 6% calcium, and 4% iron.

Banana Crunch Bars

Prep: 20 minutes **Bake:** 10 minutes **Chill:** 4 hours **Stand:** 20 minutes

1¾ cups crushed chocolate wafers (about 36 wafers)
½ cup sugar
¼ cup unsweetened cocoa powder
1   tsp. vanilla
½ cup butter, melted
3   Tbsp. light-colored corn syrup

2   Tbsp. butter
2   medium bananas, sliced (1½ cups)
1   tsp. rum flavoring
½ cup semisweet chocolate pieces
½ cup peanut butter-flavored pieces
1   tsp. shortening

1. Preheat oven to 350° F. Grease an 8x8x2-inch baking pan; set aside. In a bowl combine crushed wafers, sugar, cocoa powder, and vanilla; stir in ½ cup melted butter. Press onto bottom of pan. Bake for 10 minutes. Cool on a wire rack for 10 minutes.

2. In a saucepan combine corn syrup and 2 tablespoons butter; cook and stir until melted. Stir in bananas and rum flavoring; spoon into an even layer on baked crust.

3. In a small saucepan combine chocolate, peanut butter pieces, and shortening; stir over low heat until melted. Drizzle onto banana mixture. Cover and chill until set. Let stand for 20 minutes before cutting into bars. Makes 16 to 20 bars.

Nutrition facts per bar: 253 cal., 14 g total fat (8 g sat. fat), 22 mg chol., 204 mg sodium, 31 g carbo., 1 g fiber, 3 g pro. Daily Values: 6% vit. A, 3% vit. C, 3% calcium, 5% iron.

low fat Easy Chocolate-Peanut Butter Bars

Prep: 15 minutes **Bake:** 25 minutes

1¼ cups graham cracker crumbs
⅓ cup sugar
½ cup chopped nut topping or finely chopped peanuts
½ cup butter, melted
1   18-oz. roll refrigerated peanut butter cookie dough
40 bite-size chocolate-covered peanut butter cups (about a 13-oz. pkg.)

1. Preheat oven to 350° F. Line a 13x9x2-inch baking pan with foil; set aside.

2. For crust, in a medium bowl combine graham cracker crumbs, sugar, and nut topping or peanuts. Add butter; mix well. Press into a foil-lined 13x9x2-inch baking pan. Bake for 5 minutes. Cool on a wire rack for 10 minutes.

3. Cut cookie dough into ½-inch-thick slices; arrange on crumb crust and press together to make an even layer. (Slightly wet your hands to prevent dough from sticking to your fingers.) Unwrap peanut butter cups; arrange evenly on dough, pressing lightly.

4. Bake for 20 to 25 minutes or until a wooden toothpick inserted in center of cookie (not into a candy) comes out clean. Cool on a wire rack. Cut between candies into bars. Makes 40 bars.

Nutrition facts per bar: 164 cal., 4 g total fat (8 g sat. fat), 10 mg chol., 118 mg sodium, 16 g carbo., 1 g fiber, and 3 g pro. Daily Values: 2% vit. A, 2% calcium, and 2% iron.

30 Date-with-an-Angel Cookies

Dates and nuts swirled into crisp clouds of billowy meringue taste just heavenly.

Prep: 15 minutes **Bake:** 8 minutes
Stand: 1 minute

Nonstick cooking spray
- 3 egg whites
- 1 tsp. vanilla
- 1 cup sugar
- 1 cup all-purpose flour
- 1 cup chopped pitted dates
- 1 cup chopped walnuts or pecans, toasted

1. Preheat oven to 350° F. Lightly coat cookie sheets with cooking spray; set aside.

2. In a large mixing bowl beat egg whites and vanilla with an electric mixer on medium speed until soft peaks form (tips curl). Slowly add sugar, 2 tablespoons at a time, beating on high speed until stiff peaks form and sugar is almost dissolved. Fold in flour, dates, and nuts.

3. Drop by rounded teaspoons 2 inches apart onto prepared cookie sheets. Bake about 8 minutes or until bottoms are lightly browned.

4. Let cool on cookie sheets for 1 minute; transfer to wire racks to cool completely. Makes about 36 cookies.

Nutrition facts per cookie: 69 cal., 2 g total fat (0 g sat. fat), 0 mg chol., 5 mg sodium, 12 g carbo., 1 g fiber, and 1 g pro. Daily Values: 1% calcium and 2% iron.

30 Easy Gingerbread Bars

Prep: 10 minutes **Bake:** 20 minutes

- 1 14½-oz. pkg. gingerbread mix
- ¾ cup water
- 1 egg
- 1 7-oz. pkg. tropical blend mixed dried fruit bits
- 1 cup chopped pecans
- 1 recipe Ginger Glaze

1. Preheat oven to 350° F. Grease a 13x9x2-inch baking pan; set aside.

2. In a medium mixing bowl combine gingerbread mix, water, egg, fruit bits, and pecans; stir until just blended. Spread batter in prepared pan.

3. Bake for 20 to 25 minutes or until a toothpick inserted near the center comes out clean. Cool completely on a wire rack.

4. Drizzle Ginger Glaze over top. Cut into bars. Makes 24 bars.

Ginger Glaze: In a small bowl stir together 1 cup sifted powdered sugar, ⅛ teaspoon ground ginger, and enough milk (3 to 4 teaspoons) to make a glaze of drizzling consistency.

Nutrition facts per bar: 148 cal., 6 g total fat (1 g sat. fat), 9 mg chol., 123 mg sodium, 24 g carbo., 0 g fiber, and 2 g pro. Daily Values: 1% calcium and 3% iron.

Layered Shortbread

Prep: 20 minutes **Bake:** 35 minutes

Nonstick cooking spray
- 1 cup butter (no substitutes), softened
- ⅓ cup sugar
- ½ tsp. almond extract
- 2 cups all-purpose flour
- 3 1½-oz. bars dark sweet chocolate
- 3 1½-oz. bars milk chocolate

1. Preheat oven to 325° F. Coat an 8x8x2-inch baking pan with cooking spray; set aside.

2. In a large mixing bowl beat butter with an electric mixer on medium to high speed for 30 seconds. Add sugar and almond extract; beat until smooth. Beat in flour until a dough forms. (Mixture will appear very crumbly at first, but will cling together with continued beating.) Divide dough into thirds.

3. Press one portion of dough onto the bottom of prepared pan. Break two dark chocolate bars at perforations and arrange in a single layer atop the dough in pan. Press another portion of dough atop the dark chocolate. Break two milk chocolate bars at perforations and lay atop dough. Press remaining dough portion over milk chocolate layer (top layer will be uneven).

4. Bake about 35 minutes or until top is golden and set. Cool in pan on a wire rack for 10 minutes. Cut into 25 bars. Cool completely in pan.

5. In 2 separate small saucepans melt remaining chocolate bars over low heat. Drizzle each chocolate over shortbread bars. Makes 25 bars.

Nutrition facts per bar: 169 cal., 11 g total fat (6 g sat. fat), 22 mg chol., 84 mg sodium, 16 g carbo., 1 g fiber, and 2 g pro. Daily Values: 6% vit. A, 1% calcium, and 3% iron.

Maui Wowie Bars

A few macadamia nuts, some pineapple, and a little coconut and you can almost feel the sand in your toes—almost!

Prep: 20 minutes **Bake:** 30 minutes

- 1 cup quick-cooking rolled oats
- 1 cup all-purpose flour
- 1 3½-oz. jar macadamia nuts, finely chopped (¾ cup)
- ¼ cup sugar
- ½ cup butter, melted
- 2 tsp vanilla
- 1 12-oz. jar pineapple ice cream topping (1 cup)
- ¾ cup dried pineapple, finely chopped
- ¾ cup flaked coconut
- ¾ cup white baking pieces

1. Preheat oven to 350° F. Line a 9x9x2-inch baking pan with foil. Grease foil on bottom and sides. Set aside.

2. For crust, in a medium bowl stir together oats, flour, nuts, and sugar. Stir in melted butter and vanilla until combined (mixture will be crumbly). Press 2 cups of the crumb mixture onto the bottom of prepared pan. Set remaining mixture aside.

3. In a medium bowl stir together pineapple topping, dried pineapple, and coconut.

4. Sprinkle crust with baking pieces. Spoon pineapple mixture evenly atop. Sprinkle with reserved crumb mixture.

5. Bake about 30 minutes or until bubbly around edges and crumb topping is golden. Cool on a wire rack. Use the foil to lift the bars out of the pan onto a cutting surface; cut into bars. Makes 25 bars.

Nutrition facts per bar: 195 cal., 10 g total fat (5 g sat. fat), 12 mg chol., 65 mg sodium, 26 g carbo., 1 g fiber, and 2 g pro. Daily Values: 3% vit. A, 18% vit. C, 2% calcium, and 4% iron.

Pumpkin Desserts

Creamy Pumpkin Strudels

Harvest Pumpkin Trifle

Creamy Pumpkin Strudels

Prep: 35 minutes **Bake:** 15 minutes

1	15-oz. can pumpkin
½	cup packed brown sugar
4½	tsp. ground cinnamon
½	tsp. salt
¼	tsp. ground nutmeg
¼	tsp. ground ginger

12	sheets frozen phyllo dough (18x14-inch rectangles), thawed
⅔	cup butter, melted
1	cup granulated sugar
1	cup coarsely chopped pecans
1	8-oz. pkg. cream cheese

1. Preheat oven to 400° F. For filling, in a small bowl combine pumpkin, brown sugar, ½ teaspoon cinnamon, salt, nutmeg, and ginger. Set aside.

2. Stack 2 sheets of phyllo; brush with butter. Mix granulated sugar and 4 teaspoons cinnamon; sprinkle onto phyllo. Top with pecans. Cut into two 18x7-inch strips. Cut cheese into 12 slices; place a slice about 2 inches from end of each strip. Spoon filling atop cream cheese. Fold bottom edge of phyllo up and over filling. Fold in sides; roll up to encase filling. Place on a baking sheet, seam side down. Brush with melted butter. Repeat with remaining ingredients. Sprinkle with sugar-cinnamon mixture. Bake about 15 minutes or until phyllo is golden. Serve warm. Makes 12 servings.

Nutrition facts per serving: 391 cal., 25 g total fat (12 g sat. fat), 50 mg chol., 359 mg sodium, 40 g carbo., 3 g fiber, 4 g pro. Daily Values: 170% vit. A, 12% iron.

Harvest Pumpkin Trifle

Prep: 30 minutes **Chill:** 2 hours

1	10¾-oz. frozen pound cake
2 to 4	Tbsp. cream sherry
1	16-oz. can whole cranberry sauce
⅓	cup orange marmalade
1	15-oz. can pumpkin
1	4-serving-size pkg. instant vanilla pudding mix

1	cup milk
1	tsp. ground cinnamon
1	tsp. ground ginger
1	cup whipping cream
2	Tbsp. sugar
½	tsp. vanilla
½	cup chopped walnuts, toasted

1. Cut cake into ½-inch cubes; divide among eight 10- to 12-ounce glasses. Sprinkle with sherry. Combine cranberry sauce and marmalade; spoon over cake. Combine pumpkin, pudding mix, milk, cinnamon, and ginger; spoon over top.

2. In a chilled bowl combine whipping cream, sugar, and vanilla; beat with chilled beaters of an electric mixer until soft peaks form. Spread onto pumpkin layer. Cover and chill for 2 to 5 hours. Before serving, top with walnuts. Makes 8 servings.

Nutrition facts per serving: 532 cal., 25 g total fat (12 g sat. fat), 86 mg chol., 381 mg sodium, 73 g carbo., 3 g fiber, and 5 g pro. Daily Values: 249% vit. A, 6% vit. C, 10% calcium, and 9% iron.

Peach and Pumpkin Mousse

Stand: 5 minutes **Prep:** 20 minutes **Chill:** 4 hours

½	cup water
1	envelope unflavored gelatin
1	15-oz. can pumpkin
2	cups peach ice cream, softened
½	cup peach preserves
¼	cup packed brown sugar
1	tsp. ground coriander
1	tsp. pumpkin pie spice
1½	cups whipping cream
1	Tbsp. granulated sugar

1. In a small saucepan combine water and gelatin. Let stand for 5 minutes. Cook and stir over medium heat until gelatin is dissolved. Set aside to cool.

2. In a large mixing bowl combine pumpkin, peach ice cream, peach preserves, brown sugar, coriander, and pumpkin pie spice; beat with an electric mixer on low speed until combined. Stir in the gelatin mixture. Set aside.

3. In a chilled medium mixing bowl, with chilled beaters, beat 1 cup of the whipping cream on medium speed until soft peaks form (tips curl). Fold into the pumpkin mixture. Pour into a glass bowl. Cover and chill for 4 to 24 hours.

4. Before serving, in a chilled small mixing bowl combine ½ cup whipping cream and 1 tablespoon granulated sugar. Beat with chilled beaters of an electric mixer until soft peaks form (tips curl). Spoon onto mousse. Makes 12 servings.

Nutrition facts per serving: 220 cal., 14 g total fat (8 g sat. fat), 51 mg chol., 34 mg sodium, 24 g carbo., 1 g fiber, and 2 g pro. Daily Values: 167% vit. A, 5% vit. C, 6% calcium, and 4% iron.

Pumpkin Tiramisù

This Thanksgiving take-off on the traditional coffee-flavored dessert adds pumpkin to the creamy layer.

Prep: 40 minutes **Chill:** 6 hours

⅔ cup hot brewed coffee
2 Tbsp. packed brown sugar
½ cup brewed coffee, cooled
1 envelope unflavored gelatin
1 8-oz. carton mascarpone cheese
1 15-oz. can pumpkin
½ cup granulated sugar
2 tsp. ground cinnamon
¼ tsp. ground nutmeg
1½ cups whipping cream
2 3-oz. pkg. ladyfingers, split (24)
Ground cinnamon

1. Combine ⅔ cup hot coffee and brown sugar; stir to dissolve. Set aside.

2. In a small saucepan combine cooled coffee and gelatin. Let stand for 5 minutes. Cook and stir over medium heat until gelatin is dissolved. Set aside.

3. In a large mixing bowl combine mascarpone cheese, pumpkin, granulated sugar, 2 teaspoons cinnamon, and nutmeg; beat with an electric mixer on medium speed until combined. Stir in the gelatin mixture. Set aside.

4. In a chilled medium mixing bowl, with chilled beaters, beat 1 cup of the whipping cream on medium speed until soft peaks form (tips curl). Fold into the pumpkin mixture.

5. Arrange one-third of the ladyfinger halves in the bottom of a 2-quart square baking dish. Drizzle with one-third of the coffee-brown sugar mixture. Top with one-third of the pumpkin mixture. Repeat layers twice. Cover; chill for 6 to 24 hours.

6. Before serving, in a chilled small mixing bowl beat ½ cup whipping cream with chilled beaters of an electric mixer on medium speed until soft peaks form (tips curl). Spoon over pumpkin layer. Top with cinnamon. Makes 9 servings.

Nutrition facts per serving: 391 cal., 28 g total fat (17 g sat. fat), 156 mg chol., 63 mg sodium, 32 g carbo., 2 g fiber, and 9 g pro. Daily Values: 222% vit. A, 5% vit. C, 6% calcium, and 9% iron.

Harvest Pumpkin Upside-Down Cake

Prep: 25 minutes **Bake:** 35 minutes

¾ cup packed brown sugar
⅓ cup butter
1 cup whipping cream
1 cup snipped dried cranberries
¾ cup chopped hazelnuts (filberts) or pecans, toasted
1¾ cups all-purpose flour
¾ cup granulated sugar
½ cup packed brown sugar
2 tsp. baking powder
2 tsp. pumpkin pie spice
1 tsp. baking soda
4 eggs, beaten
1 15-oz. can pumpkin
¾ cup cooking oil
2 Tbsp. sifted powdered sugar

1. Preheat oven to 350° F. Grease a 13x9x2-inch baking pan; set aside.

2. In a small saucepan combine ¾ cup brown sugar, butter, and 3 tablespoons of the whipping cream. Cook and stir over medium heat until sugar is dissolved and butter is melted. Spoon mixture into prepared baking pan, tilting pan to distribute evenly. Sprinkle evenly with cranberries and chopped hazelnuts; set aside.

3. In a large mixing bowl stir together flour, granulated sugar, ½ cup brown sugar, baking powder, pumpkin pie spice, and baking soda. Stir in eggs, pumpkin, and oil until combined. Evenly spread batter in the prepared pan.

4. Bake for 30 to 35 minutes or until a wooden toothpick inserted near the center comes out clean. Cool on a wire rack for 10 minutes. Loosen sides of cake from pan; invert onto cooling rack. Replace any cranberry mixture that sticks in pan. Cool thoroughly on rack.

5. Before serving, in a chilled large mixing bowl combine remaining whipping cream and powdered sugar. Beat with chilled beaters of an electric mixer on medium speed until soft peaks form (tips curl). Top each serving of cake with whipped cream. Makes 12 servings.

Nutrition facts per serving: 561 cal., 34 g total fat (11 g sat. fat), 113 mg chol., 267 mg sodium, 63 g carbo., 3 g fiber, and 6 g pro. Daily Values: 168% vit. A, 5% vit. C, 12% calcium, and 15% iron.

Raisin-Ricotta Pumpkin Pie

Prep: 30 minutes **Bake:** 45 minutes

1 cup ricotta cheese
¾ cup packed brown sugar
½ tsp. ground ginger
¼ tsp. salt
¼ tsp. ground cinnamon
3 eggs
1 cup canned pumpkin
1 cup milk
¼ cup slivered almonds, toasted and chopped
¼ cup golden raisins
1 tsp. finely shredded orange peel
1 tsp. vanilla
1 recipe Pastry for Single-Crust Pie or 1 unbaked 9-inch pastry shell

1. Preheat oven to 375° F. In a large bowl combine ricotta cheese, brown sugar, ginger, salt, and cinnamon; beat with an electric mixer on medium speed for 2 minutes. Add eggs, 1 at a time, beating well after each. Stir in pumpkin, milk, almonds, raisins, orange peel, and vanilla. Pour into Pastry for Single-Crust Pie.

2. To prevent overbrowning, cover edge of the pie with foil. Bake for 25 minutes. Remove foil. Bake 20 to 25 minutes more or until a knife inserted near the center comes out clean. Cool on a wire rack. Refrigerate within 2 hours; cover for longer storage. Makes 8 servings.

Pastry for Single-Crust Pie: In a medium mixing bowl stir together 1¼ cups all-purpose flour and ¼ teaspoon salt. Using a pastry blender, cut in ⅓ cup shortening until pieces are pea-size. Sprinkle 1 tablespoon of cold water over part of the mixture; gently toss with a fork. Push moistened dough to the side of the bowl. Repeat, using 3 to 4 more tablespoons cold water, until dough is moistened.

Form dough into a ball. On a lightly floured surface use your hands to flatten dough. Roll dough from center to edges into a circle about 12 inches in diameter. Wrap pastry around the rolling pin. Unroll pastry into a 9-inch pie plate. Ease pastry into pie plate. Trim to ½ inch beyond edge of pie plate. Fold under extra pastry.

Nutrition facts per serving: 367 cal., 17 g total fat (6 g sat. fat), 98 mg chol., 222 mg sodium, 44 g carbo., 2 g fiber, and 1 g pro. Daily Values: 142% vit. A, 3% vit. C, 15% calcium, and 13% iron.

Hot or Sweet Peppers

Pepper Stromzoni

Mini Cherry Pepper Quiches

Pepper Stromzoni

Prep: 30 minutes **Bake:** 15 minutes **Stand:** 10 minutes

3	medium red, yellow, and/or green sweet peppers, chopped (3 cups)
1	Tbsp. minced garlic (6 cloves)
1	Tbsp. butter
¼	to ½ tsp. crushed red pepper
¾	cup shredded mozzarella cheese
½	cup ricotta cheese
2	Tbsp. snipped fresh basil
1	10-oz. pkg. refrigerated pizza dough
1	egg, slightly beaten

1. Preheat oven to 400° F. Line a large baking sheet with foil; grease. Set aside.

2. For filling, in a skillet cook sweet peppers and garlic in hot butter for 5 minutes or until tender, stirring often. Stir in crushed pepper, ½ teaspoon salt, and ¼ teaspoon pepper; cool. Stir in mozzarella, ricotta, and basil. Set aside.

3. On a lightly floured surface roll dough to a 16x10-inch rectangle. Cut into two 8x10-inch rectangles. For each loaf, spoon half the filling into a 3-inch width along a long side of one dough rectangle, leaving a 1-inch border on long side and a ½-inch border along short side. Fold one long side over filling; seal. Place on baking sheet. Cut 4 diagonal slits in loaf tops; brush with egg. Bake for 15 to 18 minutes or until golden. Let stand 10 minutes. Slice in half; serve warm. Makes 4 servings.

Nutrition facts per serving: 365 cal., 14 g total fat (7 g sat. fat), 89 mg chol., 855 mg sodium, 42 g carbo., 3 g fiber, and 17 g pro. Daily Values: 107% vit. A, 243% vit. C, 23% calcium, and 13% iron.

Mini Cherry Pepper Quiches

Prep: 25 minutes **Bake:** 15 minutes **Cool:** 5 minutes

24	fresh red mild cherry peppers
1	egg
½	cup whipping cream
1	green onion, finely chopped
¼	cup finely chopped fresh mushrooms
½	tsp. Dijon-style mustard
⅓	cup shredded Swiss cheese

1. Preheat oven to 375° F. Cut tops off peppers; remove seeds. Place each pepper in a 1¾-inch muffin cup, using crumpled foil to keep peppers upright.

2. In a bowl beat egg; stir in cream, onion, mushrooms, mustard, ¼ teaspoon salt, and ⅛ teaspoon pepper. Stir until combined. Spoon about 1½ teaspoons filling into each pepper. Sprinkle tops with cheese. Bake about 15 minutes or until filling is puffed and golden brown. Cool for 5 minutes. Serve warm. Makes 24 appetizers.

Nutrition facts per appetizer: 30 cal., 3 g total fat (1 g sat. fat), 17 mg chol., 32 mg sodium, 1 g carbo., 1 g pro. Daily Values: 16% vit. A, 34% vit. C, 2% calcium, 1% Iron.

Jalapeño Popper Pizza

Prep: 35 minutes **Bake:** 15 minutes **Stand:** 5 minutes

1	16-oz. pkg. Italian bread shell (Boboli)
½	of an 8 oz. pkg. cream cheese, softened
¼	cup mayonnaise or salad dressing
⅛	tsp. ground red pepper (optional)
1½	cups shredded Mexican blend cheese (6 oz.)
8	fresh jalapeño peppers*, seeded and coarsely chopped

1. Preheat oven to 400° F. Place bread shell on a baking sheet; set aside.

2. In a medium bowl combine cream cheese, mayonnaise, ground red pepper (if using), and ½ cup of the cheese blend. Spread atop bread shell; arrange peppers atop. Sprinkle with remaining cheese.

3. Bake for 15 minutes or until golden. Let stand for 5 minutes before serving. To serve, cut into thin wedges. Makes 30 appetizers.

*Test Kitchen Tip: When working with chili peppers, wear plastic gloves because chili peppers, such as jalapeños, contain volatile oils that can burn your skin and eyes. Avoid direct contact with them as much as possible. If your bare hands do touch the chili peppers, wash your hands well with soap and water.

Nutrition facts per appetizer: 91 cal., 6 g total fat (2 g sat. fat), 10 mg chol., 152 mg sodium, 7 g carbo., 1 g fiber, and 3 g pro. Daily Values: 1% vit. A, 6% vit. C, 5% calcium, and 2% iron.

Hot and Sweet Pepper Enchiladas

Prep: 30 minutes **Bake:** 30 minutes

Nonstick cooking spray
10 7- or 8-inch flour tortillas
1 medium green sweet pepper, chopped
1 medium red sweet pepper, chopped
1 medium yellow sweet pepper, chopped
1 to 2 fresh jalapeño peppers*, seeded and finely chopped
¾ cup bottled picante sauce
¼ cup thinly sliced green onion
1 15-oz. can black beans or pinto beans, rinsed and drained
1 10-oz. can enchilada sauce
2 Tbsp. canned tomato paste
1 cup shredded extra-sharp cheddar cheese (4 oz.)
¼ cup thinly sliced green onion (optional)
Lime wedges (optional)
Dairy sour cream (optional)

1. Preheat oven to 350° F. Coat a 3-quart rectangular baking dish with cooking spray; set aside. Stack tortillas; wrap tightly in foil. Bake about 10 minutes or until warm.

2. Meanwhile, for pepper filling, coat a large nonstick skillet with cooking spray. Cook sweet peppers, jalapeño peppers, ½ cup of the picante sauce, and ¼ cup green onion, uncovered, over medium heat for 4 to 5 minutes or until peppers are just tender, stirring occasionally. Remove from heat; set aside.

3. For bean filling, in a medium saucepan combine black or pinto beans and remaining picante sauce. Cook and stir over medium heat until heated through. Remove from heat.

4. Spoon about ¼ cup of the bean filling onto one edge of each tortilla. Top with about ½ cup of the pepper filling; roll up. Place, seam side down, in the prepared baking dish. In a small bowl combine enchilada sauce and tomato paste; spoon evenly over filled tortillas.

5. Bake, covered, about 25 minutes or until heated through. Top with cheese. Bake 5 minutes more or until melted. If desired, top with green onion, lime, and sour cream. Makes 5 servings.

Nutrition facts per serving: 374 cal., 13 g total fat (6 g sat. fat), 24 mg chol., 1,271 mg sodium, 51 g carbo., 7 g fiber, and 17 g pro. Daily Values: 38% vit. A, 102% vit. C, 29% calcium, and 22% iron.

Stuffed Pizza Peppers

Prep: 40 minutes **Bake:** 45 minutes

4 medium red and/or yellow sweet peppers (6 to 8 oz. each)
8 oz. bulk Italian sausage or sweet Italian sausage
1 cup chopped fresh mushrooms
1 cup marinara pasta sauce
⅓ cup sliced pitted ripe or kalamata olives
¼ tsp. ground black pepper
1 cup soft bread crumbs*
¼ cup shredded mozzarella cheese
¼ cup shredded Parmesan cheese
3 Tbsp. pine nuts

1. Preheat oven to 350° F. Grease a 3-quart rectangular baking dish; set aside. Cut tops from peppers; remove seeds. Chop pepper tops; set aside. Halve peppers lengthwise. Set pepper halves, cut side up, in the prepared baking dish.

2. For filling, in a large skillet cook sausage until meat is brown; drain off fat. Stir in chopped pepper and mushrooms; cook and stir until vegetables are tender. Stir in marinara sauce, olives, and black pepper; heat through. Remove from heat. Stir in bread crumbs.

3. Spoon about ⅓ cup filling into each pepper half. Bake stuffed peppers, covered, for 40 to 45 minutes or until tender. Sprinkle with mozzarella, Parmesan cheese, and pine nuts. Bake, uncovered, about 5 minutes more or until cheese is melted. Makes 4 to 6 servings.

*Test Kitchen Tip: To make soft bread crumbs, tear 1½ slices white bread into large chunks; place in a food processor bowl or blender container. Cover and process or blend to make crumbs.

Nutrition facts per serving: 365 cal., 23 g total fat (8 g sat. fat), 49 mg chol., 837 mg sodium, 22 g carbo., 4 g fiber, and 18 g pro. Daily Values: 137% vit. A, 330% vit. C, 17% calcium, and 17% iron.

low fat Red Pepper and Apricot Chutney

Serve this sweet-sour relish with grilled pork or chicken.

Prep: 25 minutes **Cook:** 20 minutes

3 large red sweet peppers, roasted,* peeled, and chopped (1¼ cups)
1 cup finely chopped red onion
½ cup dried apricots, snipped
⅓ cup golden raisins
⅔ cup cider vinegar
¼ cup granulated sugar
¼ cup packed brown sugar
3 cloves garlic, minced
1 Tbsp. grated fresh ginger
1 tsp. crushed red pepper
½ tsp. salt
½ tsp. dry mustard

1. In a medium saucepan combine all ingredients. Bring to boiling; reduce heat. Simmer, uncovered, about 20 minutes or until slightly thickened. Let mixture cool (it will continue to thicken as it cools).

2. Transfer to a nonmetal container; cover and chill for up to 1 week. Makes about 1¾ cups (about 8 servings).

Red Pepper and Apricot Chutney Spread: In a mixing bowl stir together 2 to 4 tablespoons Red Pepper and Apricot Chutney and half of an 8-ounce tub cream cheese. Serve with crackers.

*Test Kitchen Tip: To roast peppers, quarter peppers; remove seeds and membranes. Place peppers, skin side up, on a foil-lined baking sheet. Bake in 425° F oven about 20 minutes or until skins are charred. Wrap peppers in foil; let stand for 20 to 30 minutes or until cool enough to handle. Peel off skin.

Nutrition facts per serving: 116 cal., 0 g total fat (0 g sat. fat), 0 mg chol., 153 mg sodium, 29 g carbo., 3 g fiber, and 1 g pro. Daily Values: 61% vit. A, 123% vit. C, 2% calcium, and 6% iron.

Mango Magic

Salmon-Mango Pockets

Mango Green Salad with Mango Vinaigrette

Salmon-Mango Pockets

Prep: 40 minutes **Bake:** 25 minutes

1	lb. fresh or frozen skinless salmon fillets, thawed, cut into 4 pieces
⅓	cup chopped onion
1	Tbsp. olive oil
½	cup finely chopped mango
½	cup walnuts, finely chopped
12	sheets frozen phyllo dough (18x14-inch rectangles), thawed
½	cup butter, melted
¼	cup Mango-Curry Mayonnaise (see right)

1. Preheat oven to 375° F. Rinse salmon; pat dry. Sprinkle with salt and pepper.

2. For filling, in a skillet cook onion in hot oil over medium-high heat for 3 minutes. Stir in mango, walnuts, ½ teaspoon pepper, and ¼ teaspoon salt. Set aside.

3. Unfold phyllo; cover with plastic wrap, then a damp towel. Lay 1 phyllo sheet on a surface, with short side facing you. Brush with butter. Add 2 more sheets, brushing each with butter. Spoon ¼ cup filling in center about 4 inches from bottom. Place a salmon piece lengthwise on filling. Fold bottom phyllo edge over salmon. Fold in long sides. Roll up. Place, seam side down, on a greased 15x10x1-inch baking pan. Brush with butter. Repeat with remaining phyllo, butter, filling, and salmon.

4. Bake for 25 to 30 minutes or until phyllo is golden and fish flakes easily when tested with a fork. Serve with Mango-Curry Mayonnaise. Makes 4 servings.

Nutrition facts per serving: 685 cal., 47 g total fat (18 g sat. fat), 126 mg chol., 921 mg sodium, 39 g carbo., 3 g fiber, and 29 g pro. Daily Values: 42% vit. A, 14% vit. C, 5% calcium, and 19% iron.

30 Mango Green Salad with Mango Vinaigrette

Start to finish: 25 minutes

1	head red or green leaf lettuce, torn into bite-size pieces (10 cups)
3	oz. arugula, trimmed and torn into bite-size pieces (about 2½ cups)
½	cup watercress leaves
3	Tbsp. snipped fresh basil
3	mangoes
1	recipe Mango Vinaigrette (see right)

1. In a large salad bowl toss together lettuce, arugula, watercress, and basil; set aside. Seed, peel, and slice mangoes; chop enough to make ½ cup for dressing.

2. Drizzle about half the Mango Vinaigrette over greens; toss gently to coat. Arrange salad on eight to ten individual plates. Top with mango slices, remaining dressing, and pepper. Makes 8 to 10 servings.

Nutrition facts per serving: 130 cal., 6 g total fat (0 g sat. fat), 0 mg chol., 29 mg sodium, 21 g carbo., 3 g fiber, and 2 g pro. Daily Values: 93% vit. A, 61% vit. C, 7% calcium, and 7% iron.

30 Mango-Curry Mayonnaise

Start to finish: 5 minutes

1. Stir together ½ cup light mayonnaise dressing or salad dressing and ½ teaspoon curry powder. Add 1 cup coarsely chopped mango; stir to coat. Cover and chill. Serve with Salmon-Mango Pockets (see left). Makes 1½ cups.

30 Mango Vinaigrette

Start to finish: 10 minutes

1. In a blender container combine ½ cup chopped mango, ¼ cup rice vinegar, 3 tablespoons salad oil, 2 tablespoons honey, 1 teaspoon snipped fresh mint, and 1 teaspoon snipped fresh chives. Cover and blend until smooth. Season with salt and pepper. Serve with Mango Green Salad (see left). Makes 1 cup.

low fat Mango-Raspberry Pie

Prep: 30 minutes **Cook:** 10 minutes
Chill: 4 hours

4	mangoes, seeded, peeled, and coarsely chopped (4 cups)
¾	cup sugar
¼	cup quick-cooking tapioca
1	Tbsp. lemon juice
½	tsp. ground ginger
1	9-inch baked pastry shell
1½	cups fresh raspberries
	Whipped cream (optional)

1. In a medium saucepan combine mangoes, 1 cup water, sugar, tapioca, lemon juice, and ground ginger. Bring to boiling; reduce heat. Cover and simmer for 10 minutes, stirring often. Remove from heat. Set aside to cool slightly.

2. Fold half of the raspberries into mango mixture. Pour into pastry shell. Arrange remaining berries on top. Cover and chill for 4 to 24 hours or until set.

3. If desired, serve with whipped cream. Makes 8 servings.

Nutrition facts per serving: 309 cal., 9 g total fat (2 g sat. fat), 0 mg chol., 76 mg sodium, 57 g carbo., 4 g fiber, and 3 g pro. Daily Values: 81% vit. A, 59% vit. C, 2% calcium, and 6% iron.

Five-Spice Mango Macadamia Bread

Prep: 25 minutes **Bake:** 30 minutes

2¼	cups all-purpose flour
¼	cup packed brown sugar
1	tsp. five-spice powder
2	Tbsp. butter
⅓	cup chopped macadamia nuts or walnuts
1½	tsp. baking powder
½	tsp. baking soda
¼	tsp. salt
1	egg
⅔	cup milk
⅓	cup packed brown sugar
¼	cup cooking oil
1	large mango, seeded, peeled, and chopped (1 cup)

1. Preheat oven to 350° F. Grease two 7½x3½x2-inch loaf pans; set aside.

2. For streusel, in a medium bowl stir together ¼ cup flour, the ¼ cup brown sugar, and ¼ teaspoon five-spice powder; cut in butter until mixture resembles coarse crumbs. Stir in nuts. Set aside.

3. In a large mixing bowl stir together 2 cups flour, baking powder, baking soda, ¾ teaspoon five-spice powder, and salt. In a small mixing bowl beat egg; stir in milk, ⅓ cup brown sugar, and oil. Add all at once to dry mixture; stir just until moistened (batter should be lumpy). Fold in mango. Spread in prepared pans; sprinkle with streusel topping.

4. Bake about 30 minutes or until a wooden toothpick inserted near centers comes out clean. Cool in pans on wire racks for 10 minutes. Remove from pans. Cool completely on wire rack. Makes 2 loaves (20 servings).

Nutrition facts per slice: 135 cal., 6 g total fat (2 g sat. fat), 15 mg chol., 119 mg sodium, 18 g carbo., 1 g fiber, and 2 g pro. Daily Values: 8% vit. A, 4% vit. C, 4% calcium, and 5% iron.

Mango Coffee Cake

Look for fresh mangoes from March to September or buy slices in a jar.

Prep: 40 minutes **Bake:** 45 minutes
Chill: 4 hours

¼	cup sugar
1	Tbsp. cornstarch
¼	cup orange juice
2	mangoes, seeded, peeled, and chopped (2 cups)
2¼	cups all-purpose flour
¾	cup sugar
½	cup butter
½	tsp. baking powder
½	tsp. baking soda
1	egg
½	cup dairy sour cream
1	tsp. vanilla
1	8-oz. pkg. cream cheese, softened
¼	cup sugar
1	egg
½	cup chopped macadamia nuts

1. Preheat oven to 350° F. Grease and flour a 9-inch springform pan; set aside.

2. For sauce, in a medium saucepan stir together ¼ cup sugar and cornstarch. Stir in orange juice and mango. Cook and stir over medium heat until thickened and bubbly. Set aside to cool.

3. In a large mixing bowl stir together flour and ¾ cup sugar. Using a pastry blender, cut in butter until mixture resembles coarse crumbs. Remove 1 cup of the crumb mixture for topping; set aside.

4. For crust, in a medium bowl stir together remaining crumb mixture, baking powder, and baking soda. In a small bowl beat egg; stir in sour cream and vanilla until combined. Stir egg mixture into baking powder mixture until moistened. Using moistened fingers, spread mixture onto the bottom and 1½ inches up sides of the prepared pan; set aside.

5. For filling, in a medium mixing bowl beat cream cheese and ¼ cup sugar with an electric mixer until combined. Add 1 egg; beat just until combined. Spoon into crust-lined pan.

6. Spoon mango sauce onto cream cheese layer. Sprinkle with the 1 cup reserved crumb topping; top with nuts.

7. Place pan in a 15x10x1-inch baking pan. Bake about 45 minutes or until top and edges of crust are golden.

8. Cool in pan on a wire rack for 15 minutes. Loosen crust from sides of pan. Cool for 30 minutes more. Remove sides of pan; cool completely. Cover and chill for 4 to 24 hours. Serve chilled or at room temperature. Makes 12 servings.

Nutrition facts per serving: 392 cal., 22 g total fat (11 g sat. fat), 82 mg chol., 238 mg sodium, 45 g carbo., 2 g fiber, and 6 g pro. Daily Values: 41% vit. A, 20% vit. C, 5% calcium, and 8% iron.

Mango Cream Tart

Prep: 30 minutes **Bake:** 10 minutes
Chill: 4 hours

2	mangoes, seeded and peeled
1	8-oz. pkg. cream cheese, cut up and softened
2	Tbsp. brown sugar
1½	tsp. finely shredded lemon peel
1	cup fresh blueberries
1	Tbsp. coarse sugar
1	recipe Coconut-Macadamia Crust

1. For filling, place one mango in a food processor bowl or blender container. Cover and process or blend until pureed. Add cream cheese, brown sugar, and ½ teaspoon of the lemon peel. Cover and process or blend until just combined, scraping sides occasionally (the mixture will not be smooth).

2. Spoon filling into cooled Coconut-Macadamia Crust; spread evenly. Cover and chill for 2 to 4 hours or until firm.

3. To serve, slice remaining mango; arrange slices and blueberries atop filling. Combine coarse sugar and 1 teaspoon peel; sprinkle on top. Makes 8 servings.

Coconut-Macadamia Crust: Preheat oven to 375° F. In a medium mixing bowl combine ½ cup very finely chopped macadamia nuts, ½ cup all-purpose flour, ½ cup finely chopped flaked coconut, ⅓ cup brown sugar, and ½ teaspoon ground cinnamon. Using a pastry blender, cut in 6 tablespoons butter until mixture starts to cling together. Pat dough onto the bottom and up the sides of a 9-inch tart pan with a removable bottom. Bake for 10 to 12 minutes or until golden. Cool on a wire rack.

Nutrition facts per serving: 379 cal., 27 g total fat (14 g sat. fat), 56 mg chol., 207 mg sodium, 33 g carbo., 3 g fiber, and 4 g pro. Daily Values: 56% vit. A, 29% vit. C, 5% calcium, and 8% iron.

Pear-fect

Pork with Pears and Barley

Gingerbread-Pear Dessert

low fat Pork with Pears and Barley

Prep: 20 minutes **Roast:** 35 minutes **Cook:** 10 minutes

1	1-lb. pork tenderloin
2	cloves garlic, minced
2	Tbsp. snipped fresh sage
6	oz. boiling onions, peeled, halved
2	medium red and/or yellow sweet peppers, cut into bite-size pieces
1	29-oz. can pear halves in light syrup, drained (reserve syrup)
¼	cup balsamic vinegar
1	cup quick-cooking barley
2	tsp. snipped fresh sage
½	tsp. salt

1. Preheat oven to 425° F. Split pork horizontally, almost to opposite side. Rub on garlic and 2 tablespoons sage. In a baking pan combine meat, onions, and peppers. Slice pears; add to pan. Add vinegar. Roast, uncovered, 35 minutes or until 160° F.

2. Meanwhile, add water to reserved pear syrup to equal 2 cups. In a saucepan combine syrup mixture, barley, 2 teaspoons sage, and salt. Bring to boiling; reduce heat. Simmer, covered, 10 to 12 minutes or until barley is tender and liquid is nearly absorbed. Slice meat; serve with barley and vegetables. Makes 4 to 6 servings.

Nutrition facts per serving: 431 cal., 4 g total fat (1 g sat. fat), 73 mg chol., 354 mg sodium, 72 g carbo., 9 g fiber, and 29 g pro. Daily Values: 62% vit. A, 159% vit. C, 5% calcium, and 18% iron.

Gingerbread-Pear Dessert

Prep: 45 minutes **Bake:** 1 hour **Cool:** 1 hour **Chill:** 2 hours

1	cup sugar
2	Tbsp. lemon juice
5	pears, peeled, cored, and sliced
⅓	cup seedless red raspberry jam
1	14½-oz. pkg. gingerbread mix
½	cup butter, cut up
4	eggs
1	8-oz. pkg. cream cheese, softened
1	tsp. finely shredded lemon peel
½	tsp. vanilla

1. In a large saucepan bring 2 cups water, ½ cup of the sugar, and lemon juice to boiling. Add pears. Simmer, uncovered, for 5 minutes. Stir in jam. Let cool.

2. Preheat oven to 375° F. In a bowl place gingerbread mix; cut in butter until pea size. Stir in 1 egg yolk just until combined. Discard ½ cup mixture. Press remaining mixture onto bottom of a 10-inch springform pan. Bake 25 minutes. Cool.

3. Beat cheese for 30 seconds. Add ⅓ cup sugar; beat until light. Add 3 eggs, peel, and vanilla; beat until combined. In crust, layer half the cheese mixture, pears, and remaining cheese mixture. Bake at 325° F for 35 to 40 minutes or until set. Cool 30 minutes. Loosen pan sides. Cover; chill 2 to 24 hours. Remove sides. Serves 10.

Nutrition facts per serving: 424 cal., 22 g total fat (12 g sat. fat), 133 mg chol., 402 mg sodium, 52 g carbo., 2 g fiber, 6 g pro. Daily Values: 16% vit. A, 7% calcium, 14% iron.

low fat Pear, Mango, and Radish Salsa

Serve this spunky salsa along with grilled chicken, pork, or fish, or in flour tortillas with grilled chicken strips.

Prep: 25 minutes **Chill:** 2 hours

2	Tbsp. honey
2	Tbsp. lime juice
1	tsp. grated fresh ginger
1	tsp. toasted sesame oil
⅛	tsp. salt
	Dash pepper
3	medium pears, peeled, cored, and coarsely chopped
1	mango, seeded, peeled, and chopped
6	medium radishes, halved lengthwise and thinly sliced (1 cup)
¼	cup finely chopped red onion
1	or 2 fresh jalapeño peppers, seeded and finely chopped*

1. In a medium bowl combine honey, lime juice, ginger, oil, salt, and pepper. Add pears, mango, radishes, onion, and jalapeño peppers; toss to coat. Cover and chill for 2 to 4 hours.

2. Stir before serving. Makes 3½ cups.

***Test Kitchen Tip:** When working with chili peppers, wear plastic gloves because chili peppers, such as jalapeños, contain volatile oils that can burn your skin and eyes. Avoid direct contact with them as much as possible. If your bare hands do touch the chili peppers, wash your hands well with soap and water.

Nutrition facts per tablespoon: 11 cal., 0 g total fat, 0 mg chol., 6 mg sodium, 3 g carbo., 0 g fiber, and 0 g pro. Daily Values: 2% vit. A and 3% vit. C.

White Chocolate Cheesecake Pearadise

Prep: 30 minutes **Bake:** 45 minutes
Cool: 1¾ hours **Chill:** 4 hours

- 1 6-oz. pkg. white chocolate baking squares or white baking bars, chopped
- ¼ cup whipping cream
- 2 8-oz. pkg. cream cheese, softened
- ½ cup sugar
- 2 eggs
- 1 medium pear, peeled and finely chopped (1 cup)
- 1 recipe Macadamia Nut Crust
- ½ cup caramel ice cream topping
- 1½ tsp. rum or pear nectar

1. Preheat oven to 350° F. In a small saucepan combine chopped white baking squares or bars and whipping cream; cook and stir over low heat until baking squares or bars are melted. Cover and keep warm.

2. In a large mixing bowl beat cream cheese and ½ cup sugar with an electric mixer on medium speed until combined. Add eggs all at once; beat on low speed just until combined. Stir in cream mixture and chopped pear. Pour into Macadamia Nut Crust. Place in a shallow baking pan in oven. Bake about 45 minutes or until center appears nearly set when shaken.

3. Cool in pan on a wire rack for 15 minutes. Loosen crust from sides of pan; cool 30 minutes more. Remove sides of pan; cool cheesecake completely. Cover and chill at least 4 hours before serving.

4. In a small mixing bowl stir together caramel ice cream topping and rum or pear nectar. Drizzle over slices of cheesecake. Makes 12 servings.

Macadamia Nut Crust: In a medium mixing bowl combine 1¼ cups all-purpose flour, ¼ cup sugar, and ½ teaspoon ground cinnamon. Cut in ⅓ cup butter until pieces are the pea-size. Stir in ⅓ cup finely chopped macadamia nuts, toasted. Add 1 egg yolk and 1 teaspoon vanilla; stir to combine. Press onto bottom and 2 inches up the sides of an 8-inch springform pan. Chill.

Nutrition facts per slice: 465 cal., 29 g total fat (17 g sat. fat), 121 mg chol., 231 mg sodium, 43 g carbo., 1 g fiber, and 7 g pro. Daily Values: 18% vit. A, 1% vit. C, 7% calcium, and 7% iron.

Pear-isian Dessert Pizza

Prep: 15 minutes **Bake:** 45 minutes

- ½ cup granulated sugar
- ½ tsp. ground cinnamon
- 4 egg whites
- ½ tsp. cream of tartar
- 1 recipe Dessert Pizza Crust
- 1 29-oz. can pear slices, drained

1. Preheat oven to 350° F. In a small bowl combine ½ cup granulated sugar and cinnamon; set aside.

2. For meringue, in a medium bowl beat egg whites and cream of tartar with an electric mixer on medium speed until soft peaks form (tips curl). Gradually add sugar mixture, 1 tablespoon at a time, beating on high about 4 minutes or until mixture forms stiff, glossy peaks (tips stand straight) and sugar is dissolved.

3. Arrange pear slices in a circle on top of the hot Dessert Pizza Crust. Top with meringue. Bake, uncovered, about 25 minutes more or until meringue is golden. Serve warm. Makes 8 servings.

Dessert Pizza Crust: Preheat oven to 350° F. Grease a 12-inch pizza pan; set aside. In a medium mixing bowl beat ¾ cup butter with an electric mixer on medium speed for 30 seconds. Beat in ½ cup sifted powdered sugar. Gradually add 2 cups all-purpose flour and ¼ teaspoon salt, beating until mixed. (The mixture may be crumbly.) Pat evenly onto prepared pan. Bake about 20 minutes or until golden.

Nutrition facts per slice: 408 cal., 19 g total fat (11 g sat. fat), 49 mg chol., 292 mg sodium, 57 g carbo., 3 g fiber, and 5 g pro. Daily Values: 14% vit. A, 1% vit. C, 2% calcium, and 9% iron.

30 Brie-Pear Canapés

Start to finish: 25 minutes

- 8 oz. sweet bread (such as Portuguese sweet bread, brioche, or Hawaiian king's bread)
- 2 Tbsp. butter or margarine, melted
- 1 medium pear, peeled, cored, and finely chopped
- 1 Tbsp. brown sugar
- 1 Tbsp. lime juice
- ½ tsp. ground cinnamon
- ¼ tsp. ground allspice
- 3 oz. Brie cheese, cut into 24 pieces
- ⅓ cup finely chopped macadamia nuts

1. Preheat oven to 350° F. Cut bread into ½-inch-thick slices. Trim off crusts. Brush both sides of bread with melted butter; cut into 2-inch squares. Place on a baking sheet. Bake about 10 minutes or until lightly toasted, turning once.

2. Meanwhile, in a mixing bowl combine chopped pear, brown sugar, lime juice, cinnamon, and allspice.

3. Top each bread square with a piece of cheese, a little pear mixture, and a few nuts; press lightly to secure nuts on top. Broil 4 to 5 inches from heat for 2 to 3 minutes or until cheese begins to melt and nuts are lightly toasted. Makes 24 appetizers.

Nutrition facts per appetizer: 70 cal., 4 g total fat (2 g sat. fat), 10 mg chol., 62 mg sodium, 7 g carbo., 1 g fiber, and 2 g pro. Daily Values: 2% vit. A, 1% vit. C, 1% calcium, and 2% iron.

low fat Golden Pear Chutney

Slather this fruity spread onto cream cheese and bagels.

Prep: 20 minutes **Cook:** 15 minutes
Cool: 15 minutes **Chill:** 2 hours

- 1¼ cups pear nectar or apple juice
- ⅔ cup water
- ¼ cup cider vinegar
- 4 oz. dried pear halves, snipped (1 cup)
- 2 oz. dried apricots, snipped (⅓ cup)
- ½ cup very finely chopped onion
- ⅓ cup golden raisins
- 1 Tbsp. sugar
- 1 Tbsp. grated fresh ginger
- ¼ tsp. crushed red pepper
- 1 Tbsp. finely chopped crystallized ginger

1. In a medium saucepan combine pear nectar or apple juice, water, vinegar, dried pears, dried apricots, onion, raisins, sugar, grated fresh ginger, and red pepper. Bring to boiling; reduce heat. Simmer, uncovered, for 15 to 20 minutes until fruit is soft, onion is tender, and most of the liquid is absorbed, stirring occasionally.

2. Remove from heat; cool for 15 minutes. Stir in crystallized ginger. Cover and chill for 2 hours. Transfer to a storage container; store for up to 5 days. Makes about 2 cups.

Nutrition facts per 1-tablespoon serving: 56 cal., 0 g total fat (0 g sat. fat), 0 mg chol., 3 mg sodium, 15 g carbo., 1 g fiber, and 0 g pro. Daily Values: 5% vit. A, 2% vit. C, 1% calcium, and 3% iron.

Strawberry Treats

Strawberry Italian Ice

Strawberry-Mango Milk Shake

low fat Strawberry Italian Ice

Prep: 25 minutes **Freeze:** 6 hours **Stand:** 20 minutes

1	cup sugar	
¾	cup water	
1	Tbsp. finely shredded orange peel	
2	tsp. finely shredded lemon peel	
1½	tsp. finely shredded lime peel	

⅓	cup orange juice
3	Tbsp. lemon juice
2	Tbsp. lime juice
4	cups sliced fresh strawberries

1. In a medium saucepan combine sugar, water, and peels. Bring to boiling; reduce heat. Simmer, uncovered, for 5 minutes. Cool slightly. Strain and discard peels. Stir in orange, lemon, and lime juices.

2. In a blender container or food processor bowl combine half of the juice mixture and 2 cups of the strawberries. Cover and blend or process with several on/off turns or until nearly smooth (leave some small chunks of strawberries). Transfer to a 2-quart freezer container. Repeat with remaining juice mixture and strawberries. Cover and freeze for 6 hours or overnight, stirring once after freezing for 3 hours.

3. Let stand at room temperature for 20 to 30 minutes or until soft enough to scrape. To serve, scrape across frozen mixture with a large spoon. Scoop into eight individual serving dishes. Makes 8 servings.

Nutrition facts per serving: 123 cal., 0 g total fat (0 g sat. fat), 0 mg chol., 2 mg sodium, 31 g carbo., 2 g fiber, 1 g pro. Daily Values: 1% vit. A, 86% vit. C, 2% calcium, 2% iron.

30 low fat Strawberry-Mango Milk Shake

Start to finish: 15 minutes

2	cups halved fresh strawberries
1	cup chopped mango
1½	cups vanilla frozen yogurt

¼	cup milk
	Sliced fresh strawberries (optional)
	Sliced mango (optional)

1. In a blender container combine the 2 cups berries, chopped mango, frozen yogurt, and milk. Cover and blend until smooth.

2. Divide mixture between two tall glasses. Top each serving with strawberry and mango slices. Makes 2 servings.

Nutrition facts per serving: 262 cal., 5 g total fat (3 g sat. fat), 17 mg chol., 63 mg sodium, 50 g carbo., 5 g fiber, and 5 g pro. Daily Values: 69% vit. A, 175% vit. C, 74% calcium, and 4% iron.

low fat Strawberry-Filled Sweet Rolls

Prep: 25 minutes **Rise:** 30 minutes
Bake: 25 minutes **Stand:** 15 minutes

½	cup dried strawberries
1	cup boiling water
½	cup coarsely chopped pecans
⅓	cup strawberry preserves
⅓	cup packed brown sugar
2	Tbsp. butter
1	Tbsp. light-colored corn syrup
16	oz. frozen white roll dough, thawed (12 rolls)

1. In a small bowl combine dried strawberries and boiling water; let stand for 5 minutes. Drain. Coarsely snip strawberries. In the small bowl combine berries, ¼ cup pecans, and strawberry preserves.

2. In a small saucepan combine brown sugar, butter, and corn syrup. Heat and stir over medium heat until combined. Spread in a 9x1½-inch round baking pan. Sprinkle with remaining pecans. Set aside.

3. On a lightly floured surface roll each thawed roll into a 4-inch circle. Place about 1 rounded teaspoon of strawberry mixture in the center of each; pull edges to center and pinch to seal, shaping into a ball. Place, seam side up, in prepared pan. Cover; let rise in a warm place until nearly double in size (30 to 45 minutes).

4. Preheat oven to 375° F. Bake for 25 minutes or until golden. Carefully invert onto serving plate. Let stand for 15 minutes before serving. Makes 12 rolls.

Nutrition facts per roll: 220 cal., 7 g total fat (2 g sat. fat), 5 mg chol., 177 mg sodium, 34 g carbo., 2 g fiber, and 4 g pro. Daily Values: 2% vit. A, 1% vit. C, 1% calcium, and 8% iron.

Strawberry Marzipan Tart

Prep: 40 minutes **Bake:** 13 minutes
Chill: 1 hour

1   7- or 8-oz. container marzipan (not almond paste)
Sifted powdered sugar
1   recipe Rich Tart Crust
3   Tbsp. light-colored corn syrup
6½   cups small fresh strawberries, hulled
¼   cup apple juice
2   Tbsp. granulated sugar
1   Tbsp. cornstarch
Several drops red food coloring (optional)
Whipped cream (optional)

1. Roll marzipan between two sheets of waxed paper that have been lightly dusted with powdered sugar to a 9-inch circle. Remove top sheet. Brush Rich Tart Crust with 1 tablespoon of the corn syrup. Invert marzipan onto crust bottom; remove second sheet of waxed paper.

2. In a blender container or food processor bowl combine 1 cup of the strawberries and apple juice. Cover and blend or process until smooth. If necessary, add more juice to equal 1 cup.

3. In a saucepan combine granulated sugar and cornstarch; stir in berry mixture and remaining corn syrup. Cook and stir over medium heat until thickened and bubbly. Cook and stir for 2 minutes more. Remove from heat. If desired, stir in red food coloring. Cool for 10 minutes without stirring.

4. Carefully spread ¼ cup of the strawberry mixture atop the marzipan layer. Arrange small strawberries, point side up, in the tart shell. Spoon on remaining strawberry mixture, covering each berry. Chill for 1 to 2 hours before serving. (After 2 hours, filling may begin to water out.) If desired, serve with whipped cream. Makes 10 to 12 servings.

Rich Tart Crust: Preheat oven to 450° F. In a medium mixing bowl stir together 1¼ cups all-purpose flour and 2 tablespoons sugar. Cut in ½ cup cold butter until pieces are pea-size. In a small bowl stir together 1 beaten egg yolk, 1 tablespoon cold water, and 1 teaspoon vanilla. Gradually stir egg yolk mixture into flour mixture. Add 2 to 3 more tablespoons cold water, 1 tablespoon at a time, until dough is moistened.

Gently knead dough until a ball forms. If necessary, cover dough with plastic wrap; chill about 30 minutes or until dough is easy to handle.

On a lightly floured surface, slightly flatten dough. Roll dough from center to edges into a circle 12 inches in diameter. Wrap pastry around rolling pin and transfer to a 10-inch tart pan with a removable bottom. Ease pastry into pan, being careful not to stretch pastry. Press pastry into fluted sides of tart pan; trim edges. Line pastry with a double thickness of foil. Bake for 8 minutes. Remove foil. Bake for 5 to 8 minutes more or until golden. Transfer to a wire rack.

Nutrition facts per serving: 311 cal., 15 g total fat (7 g sat. fat), 90 mg chol., 114 mg sodium, 42 g carbo., 3 g fiber, and 4 g pro. Daily Values: 10% vit. A, 89% vit. C, 7% calcium, and 7% iron.

30 Strawberries with Lemon Cream

A few snips of lemon basil top this simple, elegant dessert. If you can't find lemon basil, use plain basil and add a pinch more finely shredded lemon peel.

Prep: 10 minutes

3   cups halved fresh strawberries
1   cup whipping cream
2   Tbsp. sifted powdered sugar
⅛   tsp. ground cardamom
¼   tsp. finely shredded lemon peel
1   Tbsp. snipped fresh lemon-basil or basil

1. Divide berries among six dessert dishes; set aside.

2. In a chilled medium mixing bowl beat cream, sugar, and cardamom with an electric mixer on medium speed until soft peaks form (tips curl). Fold in lemon peel. Spoon cream onto berries. Sprinkle each serving with basil. Makes 6 servings.

Nutrition facts per serving: 168 cal., 15 g total fat (9 g sat. fat), 55 mg chol., 16 mg sodium, 8 g carbo., 2 g fiber, and 1 g pro. Daily Values: 12% vit. A, 69% vit. C, 4% calcium, and 2% iron.

Strawberry Flan

Prep: 25 minutes **Bake:** 30 minutes
Chill: 1 hour **Stand:** 20 minutes

2   cups half-and-half or light cream
5   egg yolks
⅓   cup sugar
1   Tbsp. orange-flavored liqueur or orange juice
⅛   tsp. salt
1   cup sliced fresh strawberries
¼   cup sugar

1. Preheat oven to 325° F. In a heavy small saucepan heat half-and-half or light cream over medium-low heat just until bubbly, stirring often. Remove from heat.

2. In a medium mixing bowl beat egg yolks with a wire whisk; beat in the ⅓ cup sugar, liqueur or orange juice, and salt. Slowly beat warm half-and-half into egg mixture until combined.

3. Arrange five ¾-cup soufflé dishes or 6-ounce custard cups in a 13x9x2-inch baking pan. Set pan on oven rack. Pour custard mixture evenly into dishes. Pour enough boiling water into baking pan around dishes to reach halfway up sides.

4. Bake custards for 30 to 35 minutes or until a knife inserted near the center of each custard comes out clean. Remove custards from the water bath; cool on a wire rack. Cover and chill for 1 to 8 hours.

5. Before serving, arrange berries on chilled custards. Let stand at room temperature for 20 minutes.

6. Meanwhile, in a heavy 8-inch skillet heat ¼ cup sugar over medium-high heat until sugar begins to melt, shaking occasionally to heat evenly. Do not stir. Once sugar starts to melt, reduce heat to low; cook about 5 minutes more or until sugar is melted and golden, stirring as needed with a wooden spoon.

7. Quickly drizzle the caramelized sugar over custards. (If sugar starts to harden in skillet, return to heat, stirring until melted.) Makes 5 servings.

Nutrition facts per serving: 288 cal., 16 g total fat (8 g sat. fat), 248 mg chol., 105 mg sodium, 30 g carbo., 1 g fiber, and 6 g pro. Daily Values: 15% vit. A, 29% vit. C, 13% calcium, and 4% iron.

Good Ol' Buttermilk
Fried Chicken, page 75

Lavender Crème
Brûlée, page 33

Mai Tai Me,
page 132

Celeb

Guacamole Rice Salad,
page 292

PACIFIC RIM BUFFET

Whether it's a promotion, a retirement, or other good fortune, mark the event with this Oriental-style buffet that feeds a crowd.

Pork and Chicken BBQ Sticks, page 18

Soy-Glazed Squash, page 21

Egg Rolls, page 56

Chilled Thai Tenderloin and
Pasta with Tons of Basil, page 143

Curried Green and Yellow Bean Salad, page 143

Mango Cream Tart, page 305

Mai Tai Me, page 132

Tea or coffee

HOT-STUFF SUPPER

Perfect for a housewarming, this casual party menu will keep the conversation hot and spicy.

Jalapeño Popper Pizza, page 302

Beef and Red Bean Chili, page 51

Guacamole Rice Salad, page 292

Salsa Bread, page 264

Praline Crunch Cake, page 295

Mojito Sparklers, page 132

ELEGANT SIT-DOWN DINNER

Celebrate an anniversary or other occasion with a candlelit multi-course supper among the best of friends.

Golden Sunset Soup, page 287

Apple-Fennel Salad with
Spiced Cider Vinaigrette, page 289

Grilled Pork Chops
with Honey-Orange Glaze, page 279

Bulgur-Wild Rice Casserole, page 293

Asparagus with Almond Sauce, page 63

Dinner rolls

Lavender Crème Brûlée, page 33

Wine or coffee

POTLUCK IN THE PARK

Invite the folks for a family reunion. Ask everyone to bring a dish to keep this down-home picnic real friendly.

Artichoke-Spinach Dip, page 287

Good Ol' Buttermilk Fried Chicken, page 75

Tangy Barbecue Beef, page 52

Onion Gratin with Country Ham, page 159

Spinach Beet Salad with
Roasted Shallot Dressing, page 289

Red Pepper and Brussels Sprout Salad, page 288

Sauerkraut-Rye Bread, page 287

Rhubarb Pie, page 115

Chocolate Caramel-Nut Bars, page 298

Hit-the-Spot Lemon Water, page 121

ration
MENUS

Special occasions call for special food. When it's time to gather for a big anniversary, a birthday, or a shower to toast the bride and groom, choose from the menus on the following pages and rise to the occasion.

The Mount Everest of
Spice Cake, page 179

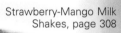

Lumpy PB&J Rooster,
page 126

Strawberry-Mango Milk
Shakes, page 308

Birth

Tandoori Chicken
Burgers, page 79

FUN FARMYARD FEST

Turn the backyard into a barnyard for your little one's birthday. Pull out the stuffed animals and top the cake with animal designs.

Lumpy PB&J Roosters, page 126

Shoestring potato chips

Carrots with Dried Fruit Confetti, page 126

Lemon-Lime Cake, page 295

Strawberry-Mango Milk Shakes, page 308

SPACE-AGE BASH

Your 'tweens will will think this star-gazing cookout is far out with saucer-shaped burgers and martian juice. Countdown to blastoff.

Tandoori Chicken Burgers, page 79

Sliced cucumbers and tomatoes

Double Chocolate Cake, page 295

Mad Mad Martian Juice, page 144

SWEET SIXTEEN PARTY

How do you make a teen party happen? Let 'em do their own kabobs and just hang back.

Chicken and Sausage Kabobs, page 76

Hot cooked rice

Cut-up vegetables and dip

Easy Chocolate-Peanut Butter Bars, page 298

Sweetheart Shakes, page 39

DINNER ON THE DECK

When your husband, dad, or grandfather celebrates a milestone, light the coals and offer up some manly fare with a surprising kick.

Pear, Mango, and Radish Salsa, page 306

Tortilla chips

Ribeye Steak with Glazed Sweet Onions, page 279

Texas toast

Caramel-Bourbon Upside-Down Cake, page 30

Basil Martinis, page 133

LADIES' NIGHT IN

Even if we've stopped counting, we still want to celebrate with our best girlfriends. And do we know how—a heap of salad and a bite (or two) of a really yummy dessert.

Feta-Olive Wafers, page 263

Thai Chicken Salad, page 269

Grilled Steak and Mango Salad, page 279

Crusty whole-grain rolls

White Chocolate Cheesecake Pearadise, page 307

Ultra Alexanders, page 133

day MENUS

Happy birthday! Whether we're celebrating a first or a fortieth, birthdays are the best time to round up friends and family for a little party. There's a menu here to appeal to just about any age. Many happy returns!

SOUTHWEST SAMPLER

The fruity ice dessert tempers the heat of this Tex-Mex stew. You can make and freeze the ice the night before.

Green Chili Stew, page 271

Warm tortillas

Jicama, carrot, and pepper sticks

Stawberry Italian Ice, page 308

Limeade

HEARTLAND DINNER

What could be better than home-cooked pot roast like Grandma's, only with half the fat?

Pork with Pears and Barley, page 306

Big Green Salad with Two-Pepper Dressing, page 177

Berry Good Banana Bread, page 294

Skim milk

NORTHWEST SOUP SUPPER

Salmon, berries, and sourdough bring the flavors of the Pacific Northwest to this stir-together meal.

Salmon Confetti Chowder, page 41

Fruit, Wild Rice, and Spinach Salad, page 293

Sourdough bread

Mango-Raspberry Pie, page 304

Cider or coffee

A TASTE OF FRANCE

Who said French cooking was all rich sauces and cream? Taste the lightness of the Loire tonight. C'est magnifique!

Flounder Mediterranean, page 284

Honey Dijon Bread, page 265

Strawberry Soufflé, page 29

Red wine or grape juice

THE ORIENT EXPRESS

It's Moo-Shu chicken with a tortilla twist for this Chinese-inspired meal. Now where are those chopsticks?

Asian Chicken Wraps, page 273

East-West Veggies, page 286

Hot cooked rice

Easy Gingerbread Bars, page 299

Hot green tea

Low-

When you're watching your fat intake, but want something a little special for dinner, look to these low-fat menus for inspiration. They'll take you around the country or around the world with flavor and style.

East-West Veggies,
page 286

Strawberry Soufflé,
page 29

Big Green Salad with Two-Pepper
Dressing, page 177

Fat
MENUS

Strawberry
Italian Ice,
page 308

index

30-minute or less recipes indicated with a •
Low-fat recipes indicated with a •
Recipes from the 2002 New Cook Book indicated with a •

I–n

t–z

tips

menus

Nutrition Information

With each recipe, we give you useful nutrition information you easily can apply to your own needs. First, read "What You Need" (below) to determine your dietary requirements. Then refer to the Nutrition facts listed with each recipe. You'll find the calorie count and the amount of fat, saturated fat, cholesterol, sodium, carbohydrates, fiber, and protein for each serving. In most cases, along with the Nutrition facts per serving, you'll find the amount of vitamin A, vitamin C, calcium, and iron noted as a percentage of the Daily Values. The Daily Values are dietary standards set by the Food and Drug Administration. To stay in line with the nutrition breakdown of each recipe, follow the suggested number of servings.

How We Analyze

The Better Homes and Gardens® Test Kitchen computer analyzes each recipe for the nutritional value of a single serving.

- The analysis does not include optional ingredients.
- We use the first serving size listed when a range is given.
  For example: If we say a recipe "Makes 4 to 6 servings," the Nutrition facts are based on 4 servings.
- When ingredient choices (such as margarine or butter) appear in a recipe, we use the first one mentioned for analysis. The ingredient order does not mean we prefer one ingredient over another.
- When milk and eggs are recipe ingredients, the analysis is calculated using 2-percent (reduced-fat) milk and large eggs.

What You Need

The dietary guidelines below suggest nutrient levels that moderately active adults should strive to eat each day. As your calorie levels change, adjust your fat intake too. Try to keep a percentage of calories from fat to no more than 30 percent. There's no harm in occasionally going over or under these guidelines, but the key to good health is maintaining a balanced diet *most of the time*.

Calories: About 2,000
Total fat: Less than 65 grams
Saturated fat: Less than 20 grams
Cholesterol: Less than 300 milligrams
Carbohydrates: About 300 grams
Sodium: Less than 2,400 milligrams
Dietary fiber: 20 to 30 grams

Low-Fat Recipes

For recipes that meet our low-fat criteria, each serving must contain three or fewer grams of fat for every 100 calories. These recipes are flagged with a low-fat symbol.

Emergency Substitutions

If you don't have:	Substitute:
Bacon, 1 slice, crisp-cooked, crumbled	1 tablespoon cooked bacon pieces
Baking powder, 1 teaspoon	½ teaspoon cream of tartar plus ¼ teaspoon baking soda
Balsamic vinegar, 1 tablespoon	1 tablespoon cider vinegar or red wine vinegar plus ½ teaspoon sugar
Bread crumbs, fine dry, ¼ cup	¾ cup soft bread crumbs, or ¼ cup cracker crumbs, or ¼ cup cornflake crumbs
Broth, beef or chicken, 1 cup	1 teaspoon or 1 cube instant beef or chicken bouillon plus 1 cup hot water
Butter, 1 cup	1 cup shortening plus ¼ teaspoon salt, if desired
Buttermilk, 1 cup	1 tablespoon lemon juice or vinegar plus enough milk to make 1 cup (let stand 5 minutes before using), or 1 cup plain yogurt
Chocolate, semisweet, 1 ounce	3 tablespoons semisweet chocolate pieces, or 1 ounce unsweetened chocolate plus 1 tablespoon granulated sugar, or 1 tablespoon unsweetened cocoa powder plus 2 teaspoons sugar and 2 teaspoons shortening
Chocolate, sweet baking, 4 ounces	¼ cup unsweetened cocoa powder plus ⅓ cup granulated sugar and 3 tablespoons shortening
Chocolate, unsweetened, 1 ounce	3 tablespoons unsweetened cocoa powder plus 1 tablespoon cooking oil or shortening, melted
Cornstarch, 1 tablespoon (for thickening)	2 tablespoons all-purpose flour
Corn syrup (light), 1 cup	1 cup granulated sugar plus ¼ cup water
Egg, 1 whole	2 egg whites, or 2 egg yolks, or ¼ cup refrigerated or frozen egg product, thawed
Flour, cake, 1 cup	1 cup minus 2 tablespoons all-purpose flour
Flour, self-rising, 1 cup	1 cup all-purpose flour plus 1 teaspoon baking powder, ½ teaspoon salt, and ¼ teaspoon baking soda
Garlic, 1 clove	½ teaspoon bottled minced garlic or ⅛ teaspoon garlic powder
Ginger, grated fresh, 1 teaspoon	¼ teaspoon ground ginger
Half-and-half or light cream, 1 cup	1 tablespoon melted butter or margarine plus enough whole milk to make 1 cup
Molasses, 1 cup	1 cup honey
Mustard, dry, 1 teaspoon	1 tablespoon prepared (in cooked mixtures)
Mustard, prepared, 1 tablespoon	½ teaspoon dry mustard plus 2 teaspoons vinegar
Onion, chopped, ½ cup	2 tablespoons dried minced onion or ½ teaspoon onion powder
Sour cream, dairy, 1 cup	1 cup plain yogurt
Sugar, granulated, 1 cup	1 cup packed brown sugar or 2 cups sifted powdered sugar
Sugar, brown, 1 cup packed	1 cup granulated sugar plus 2 tablespoons molasses
Tomato juice, 1 cup	½ cup tomato sauce plus ½ cup water
Tomato sauce, 2 cups	¾ cup tomato paste plus 1 cup water
Vanilla bean, 1 whole	2 teaspoons vanilla extract
Wine, red, 1 cup	1 cup beef or chicken broth in savory recipes; cranberry juice in desserts
Wine, white, 1 cup	1 cup chicken broth in savory recipes; apple juice or white grape juice in desserts
Yeast, active dry, 1 package	about 2¼ teaspoons active dry yeast

Seasonings

Apple pie spice, 1 teaspoon	½ teaspoon ground cinnamon plus ¼ teaspoon ground nutmeg, ⅛ teaspoon ground allspice, and dash ground cloves or ginger
Cajun seasoning, 1 tablespoon	½ teaspoon white pepper, ½ teaspoon garlic powder, ½ teaspoon onion powder, ½ teaspoon ground red pepper, ½ teaspoon paprika, and ½ teaspoon black pepper
Herbs, snipped fresh, 1 tablespoon	½ to 1 teaspoon dried herb, crushed, or ½ teaspoon ground herb
Poultry seasoning, 1 teaspoon	¾ teaspoon dried sage, crushed, plus ¼ teaspoon dried thyme or marjoram, crushed
Pumpkin pie spice, 1 teaspoon	½ teaspoon ground cinnamon plus ¼ teaspoon ground ginger, ¼ teaspoon ground allspice, and ⅛ teaspoon ground nutmeg

DATE DUE			
DEC 4			
MAY 9			
OCT 31			
DEC 2			
APR 21			
MAY 3			

Personality and Social Systems

EDITED BY

Neil J. Smelser

Professor of Sociology
University of California, Berkeley

William T. Smelser

Assistant Research Psychologist
Institute of Human Development
University of California, Berkeley

John Wiley and Sons, Inc.

New York · London · Sydney

PERSONALITY AND

SOCIAL SYSTEMS

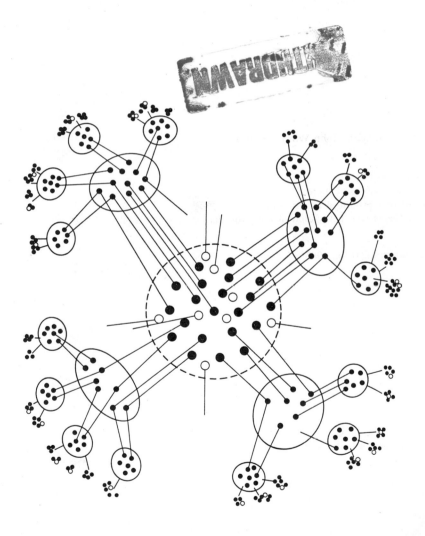

Copyright © 1963 by John Wiley & Sons, Inc.

THIRD PRINTING, JUNE, 1965

Library of Congress Catalog Card Number: 63-16021
Printed in the United States of America

Preface

WE CONCEIVE this book to have two objectives, one academic and one pedagogic. On the *academic* side, the study of the relations between personality and social systems—like much of social psychology in general—has a "shreds and patches" quality. Many disciplined and theoretically relevant items of research appear in the learned journals, but seldom are they organized systematically. Most books of selected articles reflect this undisciplined character of the field. We hope we have achieved a somewhat tighter conceptual framework in organizing this book of selections. We lay out the broad lines of this framework in the Introduction and attempt to adhere to it consistently in assigning articles to their appropriate place throughout the volume.

On the *pedagogic* side, courses in personality and society sprawl awkwardly over a number of college and university departments—psychology, social psychology, anthropology, and sociology. Teachers from each department view the subject from their own particular vantage point and sometimes neglect contributions from other areas. In this book we attempt to cover all the areas of the social sciences in which research on the relations between personality and social systems is currently proceeding. Our modest hope is that we have been able thereby to broaden the scope of many teachers.

We should like to express our appreciation to Mrs. Pauline Ward, who typed the letters of permission and attended to a thousand other details for us.

NEIL J. SMELSER
WILLIAM T. SMELSER
Berkeley, California
March, 1963

Contents

vii

PART ONE

Introduction: Analyzing Personality and Social Systems

F OR TENS of centuries civilized man has recognized that he is a social animal. Much of the history of theology and philosophy reveals his attempt to fathom the moral and political implications of this fundamental fact. In this effort thinkers have generated hundreds of speculations about the ideal and actual relations between man and society. Only in very recent times—roughly the past two hundred years—have man as an individual and his society become subjects of disciplined scientific investigation. As for the scientific study of the *relations* between the individual and his social surroundings, this endeavor has barely begun.

Personality and Social Systems as Levels of Analysis

Like many infant bodies of knowledge, moreover, the scientific study of these relations has been spotty in its development. Knowledge still rests on two legs— first, imaginative speculations (such as Freud's essays on man and civilization) that command respect because of their ingenuity and comprehensiveness, but do not rest on rigorous research; and second, bits of carefully conducted research that do employ both psychological and social variables, but have unknown or limited theoretical relevance and empirical generalizability. Despite these limitations, studies that link personality and social systems have yielded many promising developments in recent decades. We attempt to record and organize a representative sampling of these developments in this volume. In these introductory remarks we shall specify some of the dimensions for analyzing the relations between personality and social systems.

PERSONALITY AND SOCIAL SYSTEMS AS BODIES OF CONSTRUCTS. The study of *personality* focuses on the individual as a system of needs, feelings, aptitudes, skills, defenses, etc.; or on one or more processes, such as the learning of skills, considered in detail. In all cases the organizing conceptual unit is the person. The study of *social systems* focuses on certain relations that emerge when two or more persons interact with one another. Thus

1

the units of analysis of a social system are not persons as such, but selected aspects of interaction among persons, such as roles (e.g., husband, church-member, citizen) and social organization, which refers to clusters or roles (e.g., a clique, a family, a bureaucracy).

Ultimately, conceptualizations of both personality and social systems are based on inferences from a common body of behavioral data. The investigator of human affairs is confronted with a complex variety of phenomena: verbal and nonverbal communications, expressive movements, physiological states, interactions, etc. To organize these at the *personality* level, he infers or posits that more or less repeated patterns of behavior—e.g., restlessness, searching, eating, quiescence—can be characterized as signifying a "need" for the person. It is convenient to use this term to describe the person's activities, because it organizes many discrete items of behavior under one construct. In addition, the investigator may generate constructs about "attitudes," "defense mechanisms," and so on. To facilitate analysis further, he may posit certain relations among such constructs, and the result is a "personality system." Thereafter, any datum interpreted in terms of this system of constructs is significant at the "personality level."

Similarly, to make sense of behavior at the *social* level, the investigator infers that certain more or less repeated events —performances, interactions, expressions of sentiments, attempts of one person to influence another—can be characterized as signifying a "role." Such a term simplifies the process of describing thousands of discrete events individually. Constructs such as "norm," "sanction," and "clique" also may be developed. Then, when several of these constructs are set into logical relations with one another, the result is a "social system." Thereafter, any datum interpreted in terms of this system of constructs is significant at the "social level."

Any given behavioral datum is inher-

ently neither "psychological" nor "social"; indeed, the same event may be both, depending on the body of constructs within which it is interpreted. An outburst of anger, for instance, may be "psychological" in the sense that it gives rise to recriminations of conscience and subsequent adaptations to these recriminations by the individual. The same outburst may also be "social" in the sense that it strains family relations. The analytic status of a datum, then, is determined by the conceptual system to which it is referred for assessment.

Analytically, these frames of reference— the personality and the social—should be kept distinct. A description of a social system cannot be reduced to the psychological states of the persons in that system; a social system must be described in terms of roles, organizations, norms, etc. Similarly, a description of a personality system cannot be reduced to the social involvements of the person; it must be described in terms of distinctive psychological units. Empirically, however, the two frames of reference articulate in many ways. A social role may integrate many of an individual's drives, skills, attitudes and defenses; an individual's motivational predispositions determine in large part whether a system of roles (e.g., a friendship) will persist or not; a social role (e.g., that of parent) may be internalized to become part of a child's personality. The main objective of this volume is to investigate the many ways in which these two analytically distinct levels affect one another empirically.

We may distinguish between two uses of "personality" and "social system" constructs. The first is as independent variables that bear on the explanation of empirical regularities; the second is as dependent variables, which other sets of variables affect. Let us examine each of these uses.

PERSONALITY AND SOCIAL SYSTEM AS INDEPENDENT VARIABLES. Both personality and social system variables have been used in attempts to explain—i.e., to establish necessary and sufficient conditions for some behavioral regularity. Let us suppose, for instance, that the relevant problem is to account for different proportions of income saved by a group of individuals. In using the "personality" level as a source of explanation, we might make recourse to the conscious or unconscious meaning of saving to the individual. Some independent measure of this meaning (such as a defense mechanism of retentiveness) is then related to the differential saving behavior. In using the "social" level, we might refer to individuals' different positions in the society's income distribution to account for the same phenomenon. In both cases we are attempting to establish independent explanatory conditions.

Sometimes personality and social variables are seen as *competing* explanatory constructs. In such cases we can legitimately ask which does the better job. Suppose, for instance, we wish to predict the intellectual attainment of an individual or group of individuals. Can the prediction be made more accurately from a knowledge of the individuals' fantasies, defense systems (e.g., intellectualization) and intellectual capacities or from a knowledge of the parents' intellectual attainments or the intellectual opportunities afforded by relevant social structures?

On other occasions personality and social variables have been *combined* to yield a better explanation than is possible by using one set of variables alone. For instance, the prediction of delinquency is contingent in part on a measure of "ego control of impulse" among a population of individuals, but this measure is insufficient. By including data concerning the individuals' positions in the class structure of the community, it might be possible to account for still more of the variation in delinquent behavior. Part Five of this volume includes a number of

research items in which the social and psychological levels are combined to increase explanatory power.

In combining variables at two or more different analytic levels, it is important that these variables be defined independently of one another. If one variable— e.g., the psychological—turns out to be a mere restatement of the other variable, the addition of the psychological variable yields no independent explanatory value.

On still other occasions personality and social variables are viewed as *operating independently* as explanatory principles, since they bear on different aspects of behavior. For example, the incidence of intact marriages might be best predicted by comparing the marital partners' relative social class origins. This predictor, however, might prove to be of little value in accounting for the style or idiom of intact marriages. By adding some psychological measure—e.g., attitudes toward the opposite sex—it might be possible to distinguish intact marriages which are mutually gratifying from those which are not.

Personality and social-system theories can be conceptualized as independent (a) if they do not even concern themselves with common data because neither theory is comprehensive enough to cover all facets of behavior or (b) if they have such loose formal aspects (e.g., clarity and explicitness) that it is not evident whether both theories concern the same empirical data.

Finally, the use of variables at one analytic level frequently involves *implicit assumptions* about the status of variables at the other level. Suppose we predict that as an individual occupies a higher position in the distribution of incomes, the proportion of his savings rises. This is an appeal to a social variable. Suppose the justification for this hypothesis lies in an assertion that at higher income levels his more vital needs (e.g., hunger, food) become satisfied and that he can now lay aside a greater proportion of his income for the future. Such a justification reveals an unexamined assumption that certain needs (needs for food and warmth stemming from biological exigencies) are more fundamental than other needs (e.g., needs for security). Sometimes such unexamined assumptions turn out to be questionable on psychological grounds. On other occasions two explanatory theories might appear to be independent because of the lack of clarity concerning the implicit assumptions inherent in, or generated by, the theories. On closer inspection, there may be latent hypotheses concerning a common empirical domain. In examining any hypothesis involving variables at one level, then, it is important to locate the number and kinds of assumptions concerning variables at other analytic levels.

In sorting out these different explanatory roles of personality and social variables, we do not mean to obscure one essential feature of social life: Any concrete social situation always involves the operation of variables at both social and psychological levels and complicated feedback relations between the levels. In developing explanatory models, however, it is often necessary to ignore these complications for purposes of analytic simplicity, and introduce them only after establishing relations among a few major variables.

PERSONALITY AND SOCIAL SYSTEM AS DEPENDENT VARIABLES. In addition to serving as explanatory constructs, both personality and social variables can be conceived as themselves requiring explanation. At the *personality* level many questions arise: What is the genesis of motivational structures? How do a person's social involvements affect his attitudes? Under what conditions are skills acquired most rapidly? Why do people hold prejudices? Why do they act on these prejudices on some occasions and not others? In attempting to generate explanations for such problems, investigators appeal to

many types of variables—the individual's biological needs and capacities; the situational obstacles he confronts; the cultural traditions that bear on him, etc. *One* major class of variables that influence personality is the system of social interactions in which the individual is implicated. We wish to emphasize these distinctively social determinants of personality in this book; accordingly, Part Three contains research that treats social variables as independent and personality variables as dependent.

At the *social* level an equally complex array of problems arises: Why are role structures (e.g., authority relations) patterned in the ways they are? Under what conditions can conformity to roles be expected? When can deviance be expected? What directions does deviance take, and why does one type of deviance rather than another arise? What are the consequences of different kinds of deviance for the social system? Under what conditions is deviance controlled? As with personality, the variables that influence systems of social interaction are manifold; they include biological limitations, the level of resources in society, the cultural traditions of society, and so on. *One* major set of determinants that influence social systems is the personalities of actors that are implicated in these systems. We wish to emphasize these personality factors in this volume; accordingly, Part Four contains research that treats personality variables as independent and social variables as dependent.

The Personality System

Having noted some of the *uses* of variables at the personality and social levels, let us now consider the *composition* of systems at each level. What are the major classes of variables that constitute personality and social systems, respectively? What are the relations among these variables at each level? Or, to put these questions slightly differently, what are the major systems of variables that enter propositions at each level? In the pages that follow we shall outline these variables, first at the personality and then at the social level. We shall see that the same conceptual issues arise at each level, and that personality theories bear many formal resemblances to social theories. Having identified the major personality and social variables, we shall then be in a better position to examine how the two kinds of systems interact empirically.

In the following discussion, we are not attempting to formulate our own personality or social theory, but merely to outline several critical classes of variables. Not all these types of variables we mention, moreover, are found in all theories; in addition, some personality theories emphasize certain variables more than others. The following classifications of variables, then, constitute a sampling of the taxonomies currently emphasized in theories at each analytic level.

DIRECTIONAL TENDENCIES OF THE PERSONALITY. What kinds of forces give rise to purposive behavior in human beings? What motivates them? What makes them strive? Or, more specifically, what internal motivational processes give direction, intensity, and persistence to behavior? Such issues preoccupy many personality theorists; accordingly, their theories reveal recurrent attempts to solve them. The usual method of attacking these issues is to posit or infer certain directional tendencies—or needs—that provide the broadest guiding principles for behavior. A corollary assumption made by many theorists is that unless the demands of these directional tendencies are met in a relatively satisfactory manner, disequilibrium of the individual's personality will result.

Examples of these systems of directional tendencies are found in Freud's instincts, Murray's needs, Lewin's valences and vectors, and Miller and Dollard's primary drives. Unfortunately the field of personality psychology does not reveal anything like consensus on the number and kind of these internal tendencies. Freud, for instance, postulates sex and aggression as the two central instincts; in McDougall's theory, on the other hand, important instincts proliferate almost without limit. Again, some theorists find most of the central directional tendencies rooted in the biological requirements of the organism; others give a much more prominent place to social needs.

CAPACITIES OF THE PERSONALITY. Given a set of drives, needs, or instincts, what capacities does the individual possess for arriving at some resolution of tensions resulting from these motivating forces? What are his resources for engaging in successful commerce with his environment?

Personality theorists vary greatly in their treatment of capacities. Those with a more academic (as opposed to clinical) background tend to emphasize cognitive capacities: examples are Cattell's ability traits, Tolman's sign-Gestalts, and Murphy's cognitive and perceptual habits. Other theorists conceive of capacities more broadly. Jung posits four functions or inherent capacities—thinking, feeling, sensing, and intuiting—some of which may be developed at the expense of others. Murray includes intellectual and social abilities (e.g., leadership) in his discussion of those capacities that mediate between needs and the goal-objects of needs.

The capacities of the personality are conceptualized in two ways—as the *potential* of the organism to develop certain skills and abilities and as the *current status* of the individual's performance level. Empirically it is often difficult to distinguish between these two conceptualizations; controversies in the study of intelligence, for instance, revolve around the issue of whether intelligence tests (such as the Terman-Binet or Weschler) tap the individual's underlying potential or reflect the current state of his intellectual ability.

PERSONALITY STRUCTURE. The individual, according to the concepts just outlined, is motivated by certain directional tendencies and gifted with certain kinds of capacities. The concept of "personality structure" refers to relatively established adaptations that link an individual's needs, his environment, and his capacities. Different elements of personality structure range widely in their relative fixity and flexibility; "deep" structures such as an individual's basic mode of relating to parental figures, for instance, contrast with transient, attitudinal responses to temporary situations.

Freud's trichotomization of the personality into id, ego, and superego is an example of an overall formulation of personality structure. In his version the ego mediates between the demands of the id (directional tendencies) and the incorporated sanctions and prohibitions of society (superego); in so doing it utilizes the individual's capacities to assess reality, devise strategies, and so on. Similarly, Jung characterizes the displacement of psychic energy from one structure to another; in sublimating, for instance, the individual displaces energy from a primitive, undifferentiated state to a more rational, differentiated state.

One type of personality structure frequently studied empirically is a person's attitudes toward himself and others. Such a study marks a very important point of articulation between a personality and a social system. Attitudes, while clearly a part of personality structure, are a function both of "deeper" personality structures (such as infantile love-attachments) and the individual's contemporary involvements in social situations. Too often, unfortunately, investigators focus exclusively on one or the other of these classes of determinants, thus closing off the more fruitful question of the interaction between personality and social variables in the formation of attitudes and opinions.

UNIFYING PRINCIPLES OF PERSONALITY. Many personality theorists have set forth conceptual schemes to emphasize the integration of specific structures into unified, coherent patterns of personality. Adler's concepts of "style of life" and "the creative self" are both unifying principles that give man's life meaning and purpose. Adler stresses the uniqueness of each individual's style and gives great emphasis to man's ability to fashion his own personality. Other theorists are more specific than Adler. Murray, for instance, maintains that many needs operate in the service of definite values, such as physical well-being, knowledge, and esthetic sensitivity. Spranger postulated a number of underlying value orientations (e.g., the theoretical, the political, the economic) that operate as unifying principles for an individual's striving; his scheme has been translated into an empirical measure of an individual's hierarchy of values (the Allport-Vernon-Lindzey profile).

Other theorists resemble Adler in their emphasis on the "self" as a unifying principle; examples are Goldstein's concept of self-realization, Roger's concept of the ideal self, and Jung's concept of self. Jung envisions that the individual's self emerges as a result of religious experience that culminates in an awareness of the oneness of the self and the world. Fromm, finally, stresses broad unifying values such as the self (need for identity), belonging, a sense of uniqueness (creativity and transcendence), as well as theoretical and ideological values. Moreover, he, unlike many other personality theorists, attempts to relate these values to the individual's social context; he argues, for instance, that certain social arrangements, such as capitalism or communism, tend to frustrate individual needs.

Unifying principles may be negative as well as positive. Freud concerned himself with the punitive aspects of the superego; Sullivan dealt with the anxiety experienced when a person perceives or anticipates censure from others; one of Horney's list of irrational solutions to basic anxiety is the need for perfection and unassailability. Any one of these styles of coping with real or imagined censure from others may become a permanent establishment in the personality system and govern many kinds of behavior and thinking.

We now turn to several classes of variables that represent attempts to classify, describe, and account for processes of change in the personality. The degree to which a given theorist lays stress on change depends in large part on his fundamental assumptions concerning man; the theorist who sees personality in homeostatic balance, for instance, will be less likely to emphasize processes of change than one who sees personality as a creative development of emergent factors. Some theorists (e.g., Eysenck, Sheldon) have not treated change as a major dimension, while others (e.g., Freud, Murphy, Erikson) make change a central issue of personality.

The analysis of change at the personality level can be broken into four sub-variables—sources of strain, responses to strain, attempts to control responses to strain, and emergent processes of change. Let us consider each of these briefly.

SOURCES OF STRAIN. Sources of strain arise both from without and from within the personality. Examples of externally-generated strain are the loss of a significant figure, the prospect of death or injury in combat, the presence of an ambiguous environment, or the presence of environmental demands that exceed the individual's capacities. Examples of strain arising within the personality are conflicts between the perceived self and the ideal self (which Rogers has stressed), the overdevelopment of one personality function at the expense of another (which Jung emphasizes), the conflict between the instinctual demands of the id and the moral restraints of the superego (which Freud considers central). Adler's and Horney's emphasis on helplessness and isolation, and Sullivan's concern with disruptive anxiety and the failure of interpersonal communication are further attempts to conceptualize the problem of sources of strain.

RESPONSES TO STRAIN. The immediate response to strain involves subjective feelings of discomfort and unpleasantness (anxiety); frequently these feelings give rise to behavior which proves in many ways to be nonadaptive at the personality level (e.g., regression) and disruptive at the social level. Responses to strain that are especially relevant to social interaction are certain types of "acting out," such as suicide, anti-social behavior, or excessive drinking. Withdrawal from interpersonal involvement as a response to strain may be less immediately threatening publicly, but such a response often disrupts close social relations, such as those in the family.

ATTEMPTS TO CONTROL RESPONSES TO STRAIN. The classic attempt to conceptualize the attempts to deal with responses to strain is found in Freud's theory of the defense mechanisms. These strategies on the part of the ego represent an attempt to remove anxiety from awareness by denying the strain, by projecting the source of strain to external events, or by repressing the disturbing source of strain from memory. Adler sets forth the device of compensation to handle the disruptive effects of helplessness, and Horney describes such defensive strategies as submission or hostility.

Another set of attempts to control reactions to strain involves the reduction or removal of the source of strain itself. Internally this means some reorganization of the personality. Freud, for instance, speaks of bringing conflicts into awareness at one stage of sexual development so as to permit advance to the next stage. Jung postulates a redistribution of psychic energy so that the individual may pursue spiritual and cultural as well as biological needs. *Externally* the individual may attack the source of strain either by changing the environment or by withdrawing from it. An example of the latter is seen in Clark's article, "The 'Cooling-Out' Function in Higher Education," reprinted in this volume; in this case the educational counselor "eases out" the student from a competitive academic situation that would, in the counselor's judgment, be potentially disruptive to the person with limited capacities.

EMERGENT PROCESSES OF CHANGE. Processes of personality change frequently emerge from the delicate balance between responses to strain and attempts to control these responses. Such changes have been attacked generally under three major conceptual rubrics: theories of disorganization and integration, learning theories, and developmental theories.[1] We have discussed some aspects of disorganization in the paragraphs immediately above. Miller and Dollard are the foremost advocates of a learning theory of personality, and concern themselves with socialization as a form of learning. They postulate both the principles of learning (e.g., secondary generalization) as well as the conditions of learning (e.g., the social matrix). Freud, Erikson, Adler, and Sullivan are among those who stress the developmental aspects of change. Freud casts his theory in terms of the differential unfolding of the sexual drive; adult character structures are described in terms of fixation at various developmental stages. Adler deals with early family relations as they influence the individual's sense of power. Erikson and

[1] We do not envision this typology of approaches as either exhaustive or mutually exclusive. A theory of disorganization and integration, for instance, may in some cases be an integral part of a larger theory of development.

Sullivan both stress adolescent development more than Freud, and posit interpersonal relations as central influences in the development of identity (Erikson) or the self-system (Sullivan).

The major classes of personality variables we have reviewed—directional tendencies, capacities, structure, unifying principles, strain, responses to strain, attempts to control these responses, and processes of change—are present, though often implicitly, in most descriptions and explanations of personality. Most theorists, moreover, argue that these variables stand in systematic relation to one another. For the most part, however, the specifics of these complex interrelations have not been formulated on a scientific basis.

The Social System

Let us now attempt to identify analogous classes of variables at the social system level.

DIRECTIONAL TENDENCIES OF SOCIAL SYSTEMS. A fundamental set of concepts employed in analyzing social systems concerns the general orientations of social life. Or, as the question is often put, what are the exigencies that must be met in order for the social system to continue functioning? Evidently the search for functional tendencies of social systems parallels the search for basic needs at the personality level.

Analysts who attempt to identify the basic directional tendencies of social systems utilize terms such as "functional exigencies," "functional imperatives," "functional prerequisites," and so on.[2] Typical

[2] Perhaps the best-known discussion of the directional tendencies in society is found in D. F. Aberle, *et al.*, "The Functional Prerequisites of a Society," *Ethics*, Vol. 60 (1950), pp. 110–111; elaborated in Marion J. Levy, Jr., *The Structure of Society* (Princeton, 1952), Ch. III. Somewhat different considerations on the same subject are found in Talcott Parsons, *The Social System* (Glencoe, Ill., 1951), Ch. II.

exigencies that are listed include: (a) the production, allocation, and consumption of scarce commodities (sometimes called the economic function); (b) the creation, maintenance, and implementation of norms governing interaction among members in a system (sometimes called the integrative function); (c) the creation, maintenance, and transmission of the cultural values of a system; and so on. Around these exigencies social life revolves; certain amounts of social resources are devoted to each exigency. Some analysts maintain, moreover, that unless these exigencies are met satisfactorily, disequilibrium of the system will result.

CAPACITIES OF SOCIAL SYSTEMS. Given some conceptualization of basic directional tendencies, a second set of variables that enter propositions about social systems concerns the capacities or resources available to the system. In economics the importance of capacities has found expression in the "factors of production." Given the general objective of producing goods and services, capacities of the economy are found in (a) land, or the state of the natural resources, technical knowledge, etc.; (b) labor, or the level of motivation and skill of human beings; (c) capital, or the level of resources available for devotion to future production rather than immediate consumption; and sometimes (d) organization, or the ability to combine and recombine the other factors.

The importance of resources arises in areas other than the economic. Always relevant to social-system performance is the level of literacy and training of its population, the level of information available for action, the physical fitness of the actors, and so on. Clearly the concern with resources at the social level parallels the concern with ability, aptitude, and skill at the personality level.

It is useful to distinguish between two aspects of capacities: (a) obstacles that limit the performance of a system. Examples are the limited number of hours in a day, and the limited physical energy that people can expend before becoming exhausted; (b) means that facilitate the performance of a system. Examples are a high level of skill of the actors, a high level of knowledge about the social situation at hand, etc. The distinction between means and obstacles is always relative, for any set of means always approaches a point of limited effectiveness, at which point it becomes significant as a set of obstacles.[3]

SOCIAL STRUCTURE. The concept of "social structure" refers to roles and organizations oriented to the functional objectives of a social system. The business firm, for instance, is a structure devoted primarily to the production of scarce goods and services. The nuclear family is a set of institutionalized roles, one major function of which is to socialize the young in the cultural values of a society. In contributing to such functions, these structures utilize the resources of social systems. Firms utilize the factors of production. Families utilize some of the motivational energy of adults and some of the family income in socializing children. Thus "social structure" is an interstitial concept in that it links the notion of basic directional tendencies of a social system and the notion of the capacities of the system. In this sense "social structure" parallels "personality structure"—that complex of attachments, attitudes, interests, habits, etc., organized around the needs of the personality and utilizing the individual's resources.

UNIFYING PRINCIPLES OF SOCIAL SYSTEMS. Social systems are more than scattered roles and organizations, just as personality systems are more than scattered object-attachments and habits. At both levels

[3] For a discussion of the differences between means and conditions in social action, cf. Talcott Parsons, *The Structure of Social Action* (New York, 1937), Ch. II.

these ingredients are unified into larger patterns. At the social level values and norms are two unifying principles. Values refer to broad general conceptions of desirable social ends; these conceptions legitimize and rank into hierarchies certain classes of social activities.[4] Examples of general values in the American social system are equality of opportunity, occupational achievement, justice before the law, etc.[5] Values at the social level parallel elements such as a philosophy of life or ego-ideal at the personality level.

Norms concern the implementation of values in concrete interactive settings. Whereas the "value" is the conception of the general desirability of preserving individual life, the "norm" is the specific commandment, "Thou shalt not kill." Whereas the "value" legitimizing economic activity is the conception of free enterprise, the "norms" are specific property laws and contractual regulations of market activity. Norms, then, are more specific in their integration of social activity than values.

Norms, like values, parallel certain aspects of personality systems. Absolute norms, such as religious commandments, resemble the prohibitions and exhortations of the relatively inflexible superego. Contingent norms, such as the expectation that a married couple should reciprocate a social invitation to another couple's home, are less absolute and less tightly binding; thus they resemble more the regulation of the personality exercised by flexible ego control.

The constructs listed thus far—directional tendencies, capacities, social structure, and unifying principles—are used mainly to describe social systems stati-

cally. They do not provide hypotheses about processes of social adjustment and change. To generate such hypotheses it is necessary to take account of several other classes of variables:

SOURCES OF STRAIN. Social systems, like personality systems, vary in their degree of integration. The sources of malintegration, moreover, may arise from outside or inside the system. An example of externally-imposed strain is social disorganization arising from bombing attacks in wartime. An example of internally-generated strain is the build-up of contradictions such as those envisioned by Marx in his model of capital accumulation. The general presumption underlying the concept of "strain" is that such a condition imposes integrative problems on the system and subsequently gives rise either to restorative adjustments, some new form of integration, or breakdown in the system.

The types of strain arising in social systems are many.[6] Examples are ambiguity in role expectations (in which information regarding expectations is unclear or lacking altogether); conflict among roles (in which role-expectations call for incompatible types of behavior); discrepancies between role-expectations and actual social situations (for example, an unemployment level of fifteen per cent in a society committed to high levels of employment); presence of widespread conflicts of values in a system (which may result, for instance, from rapid migration of large numbers of ethnically alien persons into a system).

RESPONSES TO STRAIN. The initial responses to situations of strain tend to be disturbed reactions which are frequently (but not always)[7] deviant and malinte-

[4] For a general discussion of values, cf. C. Kluckhohn, "Values and Value-Orientations," in Talcott Parsons and Edward A. Shils (eds.), Toward a General Theory of Action (Cambridge, Mass., 1951).

[5] Robin Williams, American Society (New York, 1961), Ch. 11.

[6] William J. Goode, "A Theory of Role Strain," American Sociological Review, Vol. 25 (1960), pp. 483–496.

[7] For an attempt to catalogue the beneficent consequences of conflict (which often arises in situations of strain), cf. Lewis Coser, The

grative from the standpoint of the social system.[8] Though the exact number and types of deviance have never been catalogued fully, the following directions of deviance are relevant: evasion of norms, compulsive conformity, ritualism, automatism, rebellion, and withdrawal. Specific social problems that arise from deviance are crime, alcoholism, hoboism, suicide, addiction, mental disorders, outbursts of violence, and social movements. Each of these responses, while it involves the operation of personality variables, is social insofar as it has consequences for the structure and functioning of social systems.

ATTEMPTS TO CONTROL REACTIONS TO STRAIN. Given some strain and some threat of deviant behavior, two lines of attack are available at the social system level to reduce the possibly disruptive consequences. (a) Structuring the social situation so as to minimize strain. Examples are the institutionalization of priorities (so that conflicting expectations are ranked in a hierarchy of importance for the actor); the scheduling of activities (so that demands that would conflict if made simultaneously may be worked out serially); the shielding of evasive activity (so that illegitimate behavior is permitted so long as it does not openly disrupt the legitimately structured role-expectations); the growth of ideologies that justify certain types of deviance as "exceptions" while reaffirming, perhaps by paying lip service, the dominant norms of the situation.[9] (b) Attempting to control reactions to strain once they have arisen. This involves the activities of various agencies of social control, such as the police, the courts, social welfare agencies, mental hospitals, the press, and so on. These lines of attack are analogous to the operation of defense mechanisms at the personality level.

PROCESSES OF CHANGE AT THE SOCIAL LEVEL. Not all attempts to control strain and reactions to strain restore the social system to some previous equilibrium state. The interactions among strain, reactions to strain, and social control frequently give rise to changes in which the system proceeds to a new type of equilibrium. The movement to this new equilibrium may be controlled (for instance, when a new law is passed by the constituted authorities to meet a pressing social problem) or uncontrolled (for instance, when a revolutionary party overthrows the authorities and sets up a new constitution and government). The new equilibrium, moreover, need not be stable; recent changes may set up pressures for further change in the system. Finally, when attempts at social control fail repeatedly, the system may experience outright deterioration.

Such are some of the major ingredients —directional tendencies, capacities, social structure, unifying principles, strain, reaction to strain, attempts to control these reactions, and processes of change —that enter propositions about social systems. These ingredients constitute a conceptual system in the sense that changes in one ingredient affect the other ingredients. A reorganization in social

Functions of Social Conflict (Glencoe, Ill., 1956).

[8] In recent times the subject of deviance has accumulated a theoretically viable "literature," among which the following items are central: Robert K. Merton, _Social Theory and Social Structure_ (revised and enlarged edition) (Glencoe, Ill., 1957), Chs. IV–V; Parsons, _The Social System_, Ch. IX; Robert Dubin, "Deviant Behavior and Social Structure," _American Sociological Review_, Vol. 24 (1959), pp. 147–164. See also Albert K. Cohen, "The Study of Social Disorganization and Deviant Behavior," in Robert K. Merton, Leonard Broom and Leonard S. Cottrell, Jr. (eds.), _Sociology Today_ (New York, 1959).

[9] Treatments of these kinds of protection are found in Goode, "A Theory of Role Strain," _op. cit._, and Robert K. Merton, "The Role Set," _British Journal of Sociology_, Vol. 8 (1957), pp. 106–120.

structure, for instance, reallocates the resources of the system, and this reallocation frequently sets up strains, which in turn feed back into new processes of structural reorganization. At the present state of the social sciences, however, these systematic relations are understood only in dim outline.

The Relations between Personality and Social Systems

At this point it is essential to distinguish among three related conceptual operations: analogy, reduction, and empirical interaction between two system levels:

(a) Analogy. In the discussion just concluded we have pointed out a number of analogies between the personality and the social levels—between personality needs and functional exigencies, between psychological mechanisms of defense and social controls, and so on.[10] In drawing these analogies we are attempting simply to demonstrate that parallel conceptual problems and solutions arise in analyzing personality and social systems. Moreover, we are making no substantive claim that any of the personality constructs are determinants of any of the social constructs, or vice versa.

In addition to the analogies between major variables in personality and social systems, analogies may be made between the descriptive and explanatory *models*

[10] Analogies could be identified at even more detailed levels. It appears, for instance, that the "unconscious" in Freudian psychology is conceptually very close to "latent function" as considered especially by Merton (*Social Theory and Social Structure*, Ch. I). In both cases an attempt is made to indicate that certain unanticipated and unintended consequences of action, to be rendered intelligible, must be interpreted in terms of exigencies that are not recognized by the actor(s) but which are nonetheless important for the functioning of the system.

used at each level—e.g., mechanistic models, evolutionary models, literary models, etc. Finally, analogies may be drawn between social and personality systems with reference to their scientific adequacy; in such cases we would compare the systems on grounds such as the logical cohesiveness of their explanatory schemes, their scope and complexity, the operational definability of their terms, and so on.

(b) Reduction. This marks an attempt to translate, without loss, all statements at one analytic level into statements regarding the operations of variables at another level. Examples of reductionism would be the statements that "personality is nothing more than the subjective manifestation of social structure" or "social systems are nothing more than the objective manifestations of personality states." The general consequence of reductionist reasoning, if pushed far enough, is to deny the independent conceptual status of one level. In this respect reductionist reasoning is the opposite of reasoning by analogy. Analogy involves *no* claim of causal influence between two analytically independent levels; reductionism involves a claim of *total* determination of processes at one level by reference to variables at another level. The status of the reduced process is that of an epiphenomenal by-product with no causal feedback.

(c) Empirical interaction between two levels. This involves the construction of hypotheses in which the dependent variables are located at one analytic level and the independent variables at another level. Suppose, for instance, that we wish to account for the determinants of the internalization of a strong superego (a personality variable); suppose further that we possess some adequate measure of superego strength. Certain differences in superego strength can be explained by referring to individuals' different social-class positions; middle-class persons tend to be characterized by stronger superegos than lower-class persons. Such a finding should not, however, be pushed to the point of reductionism. Not all middle-class persons have strong superegos. Furthermore, all the variables that determine superego strength are not at the social level; independent reference must be made to processes of adjustment and change within the personality itself. Similar examples could be adduced for the influence of personality variables on social systems, as well as for interactive models containing independent variables at both analytic levels. The essential point is that in the analysis of empirical interaction the investigator *both* searches for determinants at several levels *and* simultaneously respects the analytic independence of each level.

Social System as Source of Independent Variables and Personality as Dependent

In this volume we have collected many items of research that show the empirical interaction between personality and social variables. We begin with the influences of social variables on personality. In order to disentangle the bewildering array of dozens of relevant variables and hundreds of connections among variables, we shall organize the discussion in terms of the ingredients of a personality theory.

THE SOCIAL DETERMINANTS OF BASIC PERSONALITY NEEDS. As the selections by Talcott Parsons in this book reveal ("Social Structure and the Development of Personality" and "The Incest Taboo in Relation to Social Structure and Socialization of the Child"),[11] even extremely fundamental personality needs, such as dependency, security, and sexuality, are shaped

[11] An even more detailed presentation of the arguments in these articles is found in Talcott Parsons, Robert F. Bales, *et al., Family, Socialization and Interaction Process* (Glencoe, Ill., 1955).

in large measure by the early role involvements of the child in the family. The original discovery and formulation of these insights belong to Freud; but Parsons has attempted to make the precise influence of social structural elements more determinate.

SOCIAL DETERMINANTS OF AN INDIVIDUAL'S CAPACITIES. The level and rate of acquisition of knowledge and skills by the individual depends in part on his motivation and general intelligence; the degree to which these psychological factors reach fruition, however, depends in turn on the social settings through which he passes in his formative years. To show the importance of these settings, we reprint two articles concerning the influence of educational structures on the development of an individual's talents. James S. Coleman, in "Academic Achievement and the Structure of Competition," also discusses the relations between student culture and learning. In "The 'Cooling-Out' Function in Higher Education," Burton R. Clark attempts to assess the influences, especially of the junior colleges, in selecting individuals for future training by subtle processes of encouragement and discouragement.

SOCIAL DETERMINANTS OF PERSONALITY STRUCTURE. It is possible to distinguish between *basic needs* (dependency, security, etc.) and *personality structure,* or that set of variables that involve a channeling of needs (motivational structures, object-attachments, conceptions of self, attitudes, etc.). Empirically, of course, the development of these two ingredients of personality blends in a continuous process of socialization.

A number of reprinted articles involve the *direct* influence of social determinants on personality structure. These include "Sports and Socialization," by R. Helanko; "The Influence of Peer Groups upon Attitudes toward the Feminine Role," by Lionel J. Nieman; "The Effects of Changes in Roles on the Attitudes of

Role Occupants," by Seymour Leiberman; and a number of others.

Some social determinants, while important in influencing personality structure, work their effects more *indirectly*. Social class, for instance, is a critical variable in conditioning family structure; family structure in turn affects personality structure more intimately. In this way the effect of class is mediated through the family. Several reprinted articles demonstrate this indirect effect: "Social Class, Child Rearing Practices, and Child Behavior," by Martha Sturm White; "Social Class and Parental Authority," by Melvin L. Kohn; "Schizophrenia in the Youngest Male Child of the Lower Middle Class," by Bertram H. Roberts and Jerome K. Myers; and "Social Change and Social Character: The Role of Parental Mediation," by Alex Inkeles.

SOCIAL DETERMINANTS OF UNIFYING PRINCIPLES. Empirically, again, the social influences of philosophies of life, ego-ideals, and other unifying principles overlap with the social influences on personality structure in general. Several reprinted articles, however, are of particular relevance to the incorporation of integrative personality patterns. These include "The Problem of National Character: A Methodological Analysis," by Maurice L. Farber, and "American Indian Personality Types and Their Sociocultural Roots," by George Spindler and Louise S. Spindler.

SOCIAL DETERMINANTS OF PSYCHOLOGICAL STRAIN. Many types of social strain—role ambiguity, role conflict, etc.—may give rise to psychological strain. The effects of these social factors, however, are always relative to the type of personality upon which they impinge. One unemployed worker, for instance, may be flooded with anxiety because losing his job is threatening to his masculine self-picture. Another may view unemployment as a temporary hardship to be endured calmly

until business improves. So we cannot always argue directly from the social to the psychological level. Still, social strain is important as a source of personality strain. Articles that bear on this determinant are "Some Consequences of Deindividuation in a Group," by Leon Festinger, Albert Pepitone, and Theodore M. Newcomb, and "The Skidder: Ideological Adjustments of Downward Mobile Workers," by Harold L. Wilensky and Hugh Edwards.

SOCIAL DETERMINANTS OF REACTION TO STRAIN. Although psychological variables —such as the intensity of stress and the adequacy of individual controls—determine in large part the kinds of reactions to strain, the social situation of the individual is also important. The effects of different social situations on reactions to stress is seen in "Social Stratification and Psychiatric Disorders," by August B. Hollingshead and Frederick C. Redlich; "Hypertension and Arteriosclerosis in Executive and Nonexecutive Personnel," by Richard E. Lee and Ralph F. Schneider; and "The Effects of Parental Role Model on Criminality," by Joan McCord and William McCord.

SOCIAL DETERMINANTS IN THE CONTROL OF REACTION TO STRAIN. Again, psychological variables such as defense mechanisms influence the management of anxiety, the tendency to deviance, and other responses to stress. But in this matter, too, the social setting of the individual is relevant. The following sample of reprinted articles analyzes the role of the social setting from a number of different angles: "Group Cohesiveness and the Expression of Hostility," by Albert Pepitone and George Reichling; "The Relation between Overt and Fantasy Aggression as a Function of Maternal Response to Aggression," by Gerald A. Lesser; "Mental Patients in the Community: Family Settings and Performance Levels," by Howard E. Freeman and Ozzie G.

Simmons; and "Suicide, Homicide, and Social Structure in Ceylon," by Jacqueline H. Straus and Murray Straus.

Personality as Source of Independent Variables and Social System as Dependent

In the section just concluded we have considered the impact of social variables on personality structure and process. Now we turn to the reverse—the impact of personality variables on social structure and process.[12] Again, to sort out the many points of connection between these two levels, we shall organize the discussion in terms of the ingredients of a theory of social systems.

PERSONALITY DETERMINANTS OF DIRECTIONAL TENDENCIES IN SOCIAL SYSTEMS. No author included in our selections addresses himself formally to the question of what features of social systems are geared to meet personality exigencies.[13] It is apparent, however, that societies must "take account" of such obvious psychological features as the long period of emotional dependency during childhood. As Parsons argues in his article on the incest taboo, the general structure of the family cannot be understood without reference to the personality needs of its members, particularly the very young. Further investigation will probably show that even very transient social systems—

[12] Alex Inkeles has noted a dearth of research that treats personality variables as genuinely independent influences on social structure and process: "Personality and Social Structure," in Merton, et al. (eds.), Sociology Today, op. cit., pp. 251–256. In our own search for articles to be incorporated into Parts Four and Five, we came to agree with Inkeles' conclusion.

[13] In The Social System (pp. 29–32) Parsons notes some of the ways in which personality constitutes "functional exigencies" for social systems.

such as experimental small groups—tend to develop structural features that accommodate the personality demands (e.g., the need for tension release) of their individual members.

PERSONALITY DETERMINANTS OF SOCIAL RESOURCES AND CAPACITIES. One article ("Effects of a Deviant Student's Power and Response to a Teacher-Exerted Control Technique," by William L. Gnagey) takes the personality of the deviant student as an independent variable; the author demonstrates how the power and the response of the deviant affects the other pupils' perception of the effectiveness of the teacher. The variables isolated by this author influence the effectiveness of teaching in the classroom.

PERSONALITY DETERMINANTS OF SOCIAL STRUCTURE. Much research on experimental small groups deals with the systematic introduction of an independent personality variable and the attempt to assess this variable's influence on group structure. In this volume we reprint two such articles. Arthur R. Cohen (in "Experimental Effects of Ego-Defense Preference on Interpersonal Relations") deals with the influence of psychosexual defenses on the attitudes, perceptions, and performances of paired interacting individuals. Finally, the article by Edgar F. Borgatta, Robert F. Bales, and Arthur R. Couch ("Some Findings Relevant to the Great Man Theory of Leadership") attempts to assess personality factors in leadership and the impact of leaders on group functioning. These small-group studies have advantages and disadvantages. Investigators are able to exercise statistical and experimental control over critical variables; but small groups lack many of the central features (e.g., institutionalization of authority) of large-scale social units such as bureaucracies.

In addition to the small-group studies, we reprint several selections concerning the impact of personality on large-scale social structure. In a general article ("Role, Personality, and Social Structure in its Organizational Setting"), Daniel J. Levinson investigates personal role definition as a linking concept between personality and social structure. Victor H. Vroom ("Some Personality Determinants of the Effects of Participation") assesses the impact of the need for independence and authoritarianism on the level of participation in a large company. Guy E. Swanson ("Agitation Through the Press") postulates that the choice of occupation is in part a reflection of psychosexual stages of development, so that participation in a particular occupation permits expression (and perhaps working through) of early unresolved conflicts.

PERSONALITY DETERMINANTS OF UNIFYING PRINCIPLES. Just as the personalities of individual participants influence social structures, so they influence the norms and values that integrate these structures. Three reprinted studies show the relevance of personality to the norms and values of a political system. The articles by Morris Janowitz and Dwaine Marvick ("Authoritarianism and Political Behavior") and by Robert E. Lane ("Political Character and Political Analysis") suggest that the personalities of political agents bear intimately on the existing political atmosphere. In a related analysis, Herbert E. Krugman ("The Appeals of Communism to American Middle Class Intellectuals and Trade Unionists") argues that the strength of movements that challenge political values depends in part on the appropriateness of these movements' messages to the personality needs of potential adherents.

PERSONALITY DETERMINANTS OF SOCIAL STRAIN AND ATTEMPTS TO CONTROL REACTIONS TO STRAIN. In all cases the degree of social strain depends on an interaction between objective social events (e.g., the proportion of unemployed workers in a society) and the attitudes that members of social systems bring to these events (e.g., the expectation of full employment as a "normal" state of affairs). In this sense attitudes operate as independent variables in the determination of social strain. In addition, processes of adjustment or maladjustment at the personality level come to constitute foci of strain for social systems. In the article by Marian R. Yarrow, John A. Clausen, and Paul R. Robbins ("The Social Meaning of Mental Illness"), for instance, the authors argue that the loss of personality organization places strain on the social structures of family and community. Erving Goffman (in "Embarrassment and Social Organization") traces other consequences of personality disruption for the structure of personal interaction. In "The Adjustment of the Family to Alcoholism," Joan K. Jackson posits a series of cumulative stages of family reorganization in response to the husband's chronic drinking. Finally, Ross Stagner (in "Personality Dynamics and Social Conflict") investigates several alternative dynamic formulations of personality to account for international conflict; he postulates that perceptual factors are important in both blocking effective communication and directing irrational behavior.

PERSONALITY DETERMINANTS OF EMERGENT PROCESSES OF SOCIAL CHANGE. As we have seen, different processes of social change may result from the delicate interplay among strain, reactions to strain, and attempts to control these reactions. Variables at the personality level are important in determining the character, timing, and content of these emergent changes. Three articles bear on the operation of such variables. Edward M. Bruner (in "Cultural Transmission and Cultural Change") argues that personality characteristics formed in earliest childhood pose the most formidable resistances to processes of cultural change. As the analysis of Krugman shows, however, "depth'" variables such as free-floating hostility may also be operative in determining who joins movements designed to change social systems radically. Finally, in their analysis of entrepreneurship, John W. Atkinson and Bert F. Hoselitz ("Entrepreneurship and Personality") stress the importance of personality variables in selecting and determining the behavior of those who lead the way in massive social changes.

Plan of the Volume

The first major section of the book (Part Two) is mainly theoretical and methodological. Authors in this section pose the fundamental questions involved in analyzing the relations among personality and social systems. What is a personality system? What is a social system? Can the two be conceived as analytically distinct from one another? What pitfalls arise in reducing social to psychological states, and vice-versa? What is the methodological status of concepts such as "national character" and "modal personality"? What are the empirical relations between social and psychological variables? What dangers arise in inferring individual psychological correlations from ecological associations? As the authors struggle with these and other questions, the reader will no doubt come to appreciate the headaches that develop in the attempt to deal with two systems of variables simultaneously.

Parts Three through Five form the heart of the volume. In these sections we arrange research items according to the interactive relations between personality and social systems. In Part Three we treat social variables as independent and psychological variables as dependent. After a brief section on the implications of small-group research, we organize the selections according to the life-cycle of the individual, beginning with the influence of family structure on personality, then moving to the influence of school,

peer group, and adult roles. A final few selections concern the influence of social change on personality.

In Part Four we turn the tables, making personality independent and social system dependent. The organization parallels Part Three, beginning with small-group research, moving through the life-cycle of the individual, and concluding with a few selections on the role of personality in social change.

Having considered personality and social variables each as independent, we turn in Part Five to research in which both classes of variables are employed in generating explanations for empirical data. Such research, based on increasingly complex relations among variables, poses extremely difficult problems of design. Consequently, examples of first-class research that varies both personality and social factors are relatively few. In Part Five we reprint studies in five research areas: the determinants of behavior in experimental small-group settings; the determinants of behavior in non-experimental face-to-face interaction; the determinants of educational performance; the determinants of occupational choice and social mobility; and the determinants of deviant behavior.

A final section (Part Six) contains articles on social structures that are devoted primarily to the rehabilitation of personality. In this section we include selections on the psychotherapeutic situation, the mental hospital, the social work situation, and the "therapeutic" aspects of religious leadership.

Criteria Employed for Selecting Articles

The first criterion for deciding on a selection was its *excellence*. In general, we found four kinds of desirable writings in the literature on personality and social systems: (a) rigorously designed and carefully conducted empirical studies; (b) sophisticated theoretical writings; (c) careful case studies, usually reported by psychiatrists, psychologists, social workers, or anthropologists; (d) sensitive speculative or programmatic essays. Examples of each are found in the volume. In selecting we tended to emphasize the first two. One consequence of this is that clinical reports by psychiatrists and other psychotherapists, as well as field studies on culture and personality by anthropologists, are somewhat under-represented, though by no means absent in this book.

A second criterion that came to be important was *recency of publication*. Mere recency, of course, does not guarantee high quality. In many cases, however, an author writing in recent years has been able to utilize an improved conceptual framework or research design. In addition, the author of a recent article often relates his findings to a major or minor "tradition" of research in his particular problem-area. By including such an article we were able to incorporate many summaries or references to past articles and books. To have included only an article many years old, however excellent,

would have neglected recent research; to have included both past and recent articles would have pushed us beyond our space limitations.

Representativeness of salient developments was a third criterion. It seemed important to have selections representing the influence of the authoritarian personality studies, Hollingshead's work on mental illness, McClelland's work on the achievement motive, Miller and Swanson on child-rearing, etc., even though in some cases the writings of the original authors do not appear.

Two final criteria were *brevity* and *controversial impact*. If two articles were of equal quality, we tended more often to choose the shorter. And if two articles were of equal quality in the same general area, we tended more often to choose the one that had stirred more critical attention.

We have reprinted all the articles without abridgment. In addition, we have left the notation system and bibliographical references as they appeared originally, even though this makes for slight discontinuity.

PART TWO

Theoretical and Methodological Issues

AS NOTED in the Introduction, the study of the relations between personality and social systems is in its infancy both theoretically and empirically. On the *theoretical* side, the major concepts for relating the two systems have yet to be identified. This failure results in part from the fact that personality psychology, sociology, and anthropology are themselves lacking in theoretical sophistication. In addition, the poverty of theory results from the fact that to relate two distinct levels of analysis poses many problems not encountered if the analyst remains at one conceptual level. On the *empirical* side, some rigorous research is being conducted, but this work is piecemeal and sprawling. This failure results in part from difficulties in quantifying and experimentally manipulating many psychological and social variables. In addition, research is weak because the major variables—and the relations among them—are only vaguely known; hence they cannot provide a guide to disciplined and theoretically relevant research.

Because of the underdeveloped state of the study of personality and social systems, analysts are likely to spend much of their time and energy in methodological exploration. They must pose the basic questions. They must ask if the relationship between personality and social systems is really a viable area for study at all, and if so, what sort of area it is. At the *theoretical* level, methodological exploration resolves into an attempt to identify the major variables, to set up conceptual boundaries around them, and to establish relations among them. What is a social system? What are its units? What is a personality system? What are its units? How can we conceive of a personality system affecting a social system, and vice versa? What sorts of hypotheses can be derived from what we know about each system, and vice versa? At the *empirical* level, methodological exploration resolves into an attempt to establish rules for assessing evidence regarding the mutual influence between personality and social variables. What kinds of experimental design are appropriate for assessing the impact of social factors on personality, and vice versa? Can we infer

19

personality states from the examination of social data, and vice versa? The authors we have included in Part Two address themselves to these kinds of questions.

The selections by George Devereux and Talcott Parsons involve the attempt to carve out distinctively psychological and social levels of analysis. But the emphases of the two men differ. Devereux asks how we can use the personality and the social levels to account for variations in behavior; Parsons explores the intermeshing of personality and social systems in the process of socialization.

Devereux first warns against reductionism—developing a psychological model of man solely by knowing social facts or developing a model of society solely by knowing individual psychological states. Further, he makes the telling point that even though a given social event (e.g., a revolution) excites similar behavior on the part of many individuals, the psychological significance of this behavior differs greatly among them. On the basis of these points, Devereux argues for a view of modal personality based on those socially legitimate types of needs into which actual psychological motives are channeled and gratified.

Taking Freudian psychology as a springboard, Parsons argues that the major stages of socialization envisioned by Freud can be interpreted as an interaction between the psychological and the social levels. At the psychological level socialization involves the familiar mechanisms of learning, identification, generalization, and so on. But the lever by which this psychological result is achieved is found in the interaction between the child and significant others (especially family members) in his social environment. In fact, according to Parsons' reinterpretation of Freud, the individual's personality takes shape as elements of his social environment are *internalized*. Parsons' theory of socialization, therefore, preserves the analytic distinction between personality and social system, but suggests that social objects are systematically introduced to become part of the personality.

The next two selections—by Dennis Wrong and Reinhard Bendix—voice apprehensions about two types of reductionism in treating personality and social systems. Wrong protests against "sociologistic" reductionism—the excessive reliance on variables at the social level to account for psychological processes. An example of this type of reductionism is the emphasis on internalized social roles as the sole determinant of personality processes. (In fact, Wrong chooses Parsons' theory of socialization as one of his main targets.) Another example is the emphasis on conformity to existing role expectations (which may or may not be internalized) as the sole determinant of personality processes. Bendix warns against the opposite, or "psychologistic" reductionism. An example of this is to account for the character of religious life in society solely by referring to the psychological significance of religion for individuals (e.g., as fantasy projections).

Three final articles in this methodological section deal with the assessment of evidence relevant to the study of the relations between personality and social systems. Maurice Farber's article, an early critical piece on the notion of national character, questions the empirical basis for this concept. What do we assert, he asks, when we say that a nation or a culture has a character? Is national character a viable construct? How can we speak of a stable national character in the face of great instability in national experiences and great heterogeneity within nations? In addition, Farber asks whether the concept of national character should represent merely a distribution of character traits of the individuals in a society or should it include reference to social and cultural institutions as well. Farber raises but does not solve these issues; in fact they have been at the forefront of the methodological exploration into the concepts of "national character" and "model personality" during the past decade.[1]

In 1950 W. S. Robinson published a methodological article on the ecological fallacy,[2] in which he pointed up the errors involved in arguing directly from ecological distributions of data to individual personality states. Using Robinson's argument as a starting point, John Clausen and Melvin Kohn examine the methodological problems involved in drawing conclusions from the fact that certain mental disorders cluster in definite geographical areas (such as sec-

tions of cities). On the whole, Clausen and Kohn would hesitate to draw any causal inferences concerning the genesis of mental disorders from ecological studies. In a comment H. Warren Dunham—whose own work has utilized the ecological method extensively—challenges their conclusions. Then, in a more general methodological article, Dunham re-examines not only the ecological method, but also suggests several other approaches —the clinical and the cultural—by which mental disorders might be studied.

The reader should be reminded that the several articles in this section on theory and method scarcely exhaust the issues that arise in the study of the relations among personality and social systems. Many of these issues have yet to be aired in the literature; still others have been raised, but only in very limited ways. In short, Part II should be viewed as a sampling of those issues that arise in a sub-field of investigation that is struggling to find a scientifically legitimate sphere of interest and study.

[1] For the most thorough discussion of these and other methodological issues, see Alex Inkeles and Daniel J. Levinson, "National Character: The Study of Modal Personality and Sociocultural Systems," in Gardner Lindzey (ed.), *Handbook of Social Psychology* (Cambridge, Mass., 1954), Vol. II, pp. 977–1020.

[2] W. S. Robinson, "Ecological Correlations and the Behavior of Individuals," *American Sociological Review*, Vol. 15 (1950), pp. 351–357.

A · PERSONALITY AND SOCIAL SYSTEM AS LEVELS OF ANALYSIS

1 · The Character of Explanation at Each Level

TWO TYPES OF MODAL PERSONALITY MODELS

by George Devereux

It is one of the hallmarks of a maturing science that each empirical problem which it solves creates new questions concerning the nature of the science itself. This essay reappraises the view that the basic construct of culture and personality studies—the socio-psychological conception of the personality—represents a true synthesis of the data and frames of reference of both psychology and social science. This new conceptual model is usually supposed to be a homogeneous, structurally integrated and coherent whole, equally relevant, *in the same way,* for the social scientist and for the psychologist. Logical qualities supposedly characterize all personality models of this type, regardless of variations in their actual form, content or theoretical orientation. Thus, regardless of whether a given (psychoanalytic, Hullian, Tolmanian, etc.) model represents the "modal" personality of Mohaves, of males, of shamans, or of old persons, or the much more concrete and specific "modal" personality of old Mohave male shamans, it is usually supposed to possess all the above men-

SOURCE: Bert Kaplan (ed.), *Studying Personality Cross-Culturally* (Elmsford, N.Y.: Row, Peterson and Co., 1961), pp. 227–241.

tioned criteria of homogeneity, coherence and dual relevance. Finally, it has been claimed that all such personality models are identical types of logical constructs and belong to the same universe of discourse, in the broad sense in which triangles, squares, pentagons . . . and circles are all polygons belonging to the domain of plane geometry.

This chapter seeks to disprove the belief that all "modal" personality constructs used in culture and personality studies are, in fact, specimens of one and the same category of logical constructs. It will be demonstrated that there are actually at least two ways in which current models of "modal" personalities have been constructed and that each of these two procedures produces a distinctive, *sui generis* model of the "modal" personality. These two models do not differ from each other in form and content only, the way the model of the "Mohave male" may differ from the conjugate model of the "Mohave female," or from the non-conjugate model of the "Hottentot female." Actually these models belong to wholly different conceptual species, having different relevances and demanding to be used in wholly different ways. It is unfortunate that there should

—almost inevitably—exist two logically distinct types of models of the "modal" personality. It is infinitely worse that this fact is so systematically ignored, that the two models are treated as interchangeable. Yet, because social scientists and psychologists ask entirely different questions, they must, of necessity, construct different models of the "modal" personality, if they are to find meaningful answers within their own frames of reference.

Those social scientists who are not exponents of the extreme culturological position and take cognizance of the existence of real people, seek to develop the kind of model of "modal" personality which will explain the type of cooperative, or conjugate, or parallel action on the part of many individuals, which permits the unfolding of social and cultural processes. The question such social scientists ask, with various degrees of sophistication, is: "Given all the known facts about society and culture, what characteristics must I *impute* to real people to make their actualization of social and cultural processes understandable?" A typical "modal" personality model evolved in order to answer this question is "the economic man," whom no one ever met in the flesh, for the good and sufficient reason that he does not exist. The logical construction process which culminates in the model of "the economic man" is fundamentally the same as the one which culminated in certain learning theorists' model of the "stat rat," which, even though it does not exist, is a construct or "thought token" enabling one to build one type of logically coherent pattern out of disparate facts related to "learning."

The psychologist who is not too biologically oriented, nor too individual-centered, to ignore society and culture is faced with one of two tasks:

(1) Whenever he observes certain biologically inexplicable congruences between the behavior of two or more individuals, he seeks to develop the kind of model of society and culture which renders these congruences understandable. In so doing he may develop models of society and culture which are quite as esoteric and quite as unsociologistic and unculturalistic as the social scientist's concept of "economic man" is unpsychologistic. He may then, by circular reasoning, explain these psychological uniformities of behavior in terms of a psychologistic model of society and culture, exactly as the naïve social scientist circularly explains socio-cultural uniformities in terms of a sociologistic model of man.

(2) The more sophisticated psychologist, aware of society and culture, will construct a "modal" personality which, by social and cultural means, can be made to fit the prevailing socio-cultural climate and to operate in a manner which implements social and cultural processes. The key characteristic ascribed to this model is socio-cultural teachability, reinforced by a primary orientation to society and culture.

This model of man is definitely psychologistic though its systematic use tends to produce, in the long run, a habitual lack of concern with the non-socio-cultural aspects of the personality. Where the "stat rat" of at least some extreme learning theorists has practically no sensorium and is made up almost entirely of an imaginary sort of "inner motor," which has only the remotest connection with the real neurophysiology of living rats, the "stat human" of the culture-and-personality extremist seems to be all sensorium and no "inner works" or backbone. At this point the extremist, though remaining a psychologist, comes singularly close to the exponent of superorganic or culturalistic extremism.[1] The extreme culturalist position in culture and personality studies is held by the neo-Freudians. Probably because they can do so only by fleeing everything reminding them of the non-socio-cultural segment of man's personality, they have managed to be accepted by many anti-psychological anthropologists and sociologists as more "modern" and more "realistic" than Freud. At this point it seems expedient to turn to a set of carefully documented facts, obtained from a group of some seventy recent Hungarian refugees by a multidisciplinary team which included the present writer.

The Relationship between Psychological and Social Analyses of Actual Behavior

The type of motivation in terms of which certain historians and political scientists tried to explain the participation of *actual* persons in the 1956 Hungarian Revolution (see Society for the Investigation of Human Ecology, 1958) proved, on careful psychological scrutiny, to have played an almost negligible role in the case of those individuals who actively participated in that struggle. Whenever such a discrepancy between the explanations of two types of behavioral scientists occurs, it is a methodological error—especially at first—to tackle the problem primarily in terms of concrete facts. Such discrepancies are best approached by determining the actual relationship between the divergent frames of reference with which the contending disciplines operate.

In such cases one deals essentially with the vexing problem of the real relationship between psychological–psychiatric (subjective) and socio-cultural-historical-economic-political (collective) explanations of human phenomena. These two sets of disciplines study radically different phenomena. The basic difference between the two subject matters can be clarified most easily by means of an analogy from physical science. (1) The behavior of the individual, when seen as an *individual,* and not in terms of his membership in human society, is under-

standable only in a specifically psychological frame of reference and in terms of psychological laws *sui generis*. In the same sense, the behavior of the *individual molecule* in a given gas model must be understood in terms of classical mechanics, dealing with reversible phenomena. (2) The behavior of a group, seen as *a group,* and not primarily as an aggregate of discrete individuals, is understandable only in terms of a specific sociologistic frame of reference and in terms of socio-cultural laws *sui generis*. In the same sense, the behavior of the gas model as a whole must be understood in terms of statistical mechanics pertaining to irreversible phenomena (Devereux, 1940).

Somewhere between these two extremes lies a borderline or transitional set of phenomena, whose usual locus is the small group. We may define as "small" any group in which the over-all interaction pattern is about equally determined by, or equally understandable in terms of, the individual makeup of the individuals composing it *and* in terms of the fact that these discrete individuals constitute a group. In such cases it is possible to explain even certain group events equally satisfactorily in exclusively social-collective *and* in exclusively psychological-individual terms. The extent to which this is possible depends primarily on the number of the members. As their number increases, exclusively psychological-individual explanations account for increasingly smaller, and more and more peripheral, portions of the total group behavior, causing the explanations to become increasingly vague. A good physical analogy is the fact that the behavior of two bodies in relative motion to each other can be fully and precisely accounted for in terms of classical mechanics. By contrast, the behavior of three or more bodies can be described only approximately in terms of classical mechanics because the problem of three bodies has never been solved in general terms. Moreover, such approximations become less and less accurate as the number of bodies in relative motion to each other increases. Hence, at the point where the number of bodies to be studied becomes unmanageably large, it becomes more efficient, economical and accurate to ignore the individual particles and to study instead the system, or aggregate itself, in terms of statistical mechanics. In so doing, one not only shifts one's frame of reference, but even seeks to obtain new and different kinds of results. The relevance of this analogy for an understanding of the difference between the psychological and the social is obvious (Devereux 1940, 1945, 1955, 1958).

Thus, in abstract terms, the question is never: "At what point do individuals and individual phenomena become irrelevant and society and social phenomena all important?"—nor vice versa, of course. The real question is simply this: "At what point is it more economical to use the sociological, rather than the psychological approach?" The same is true, *mutatis mutandis,* in regard to the nature-nurture controversy (Devereux 1945).

Where only individuals and relatively small groups are concerned, the actual outcome of a given process can be equally effectively predicted and equally fully explained either sociologically or psychologically. Thus, it was possible to show (Devereux 1960) that the self-incited (provoked) murder of a Mohave lesbian witch was as absolutely inevitable in terms of Mohave cultural mandates as in terms of that witch's distinctive and unique personality makeup. Moreover, in this case, and in numerous others as well, there is an almost incredibly compendious, perfect and subtle dovetailing of individual and sociocultural processes: each intrapsychic development mobilizes certain reinforcing cultural mandates and each cultural response mobilizes reinforcing subjective motives and processes. The real objective is not to determine whether the phenomenon is "ultimately" a psychological or a socio-cultural one, but to analyze, as precisely as possible, the dovetailing, interplay and mutual reinforcement (most often through a "feedback") of the psychological and socio-cultural factors involved.

The possibility of adequately predicting and understanding an event in terms of a particular frame of reference, such as psychology, does not mean in the least that the phenomenon is primarily a psychological one and that equally satisfactory explanations and predictions could not have been formulated in socio-cultural terms. Indeed, even though any frame of reference necessarily uses and operates in terms of *partial* abstractions, it can, nonetheless, provide an *operationally* satisfactory and "complete" explanation and prediction of a given phenomenon. A failure to grasp this point is largely responsible for Kroeber's (1948) recurrent objections to alleged attempts to "reduce" anthropology to psychology.

Even more important perhaps is the fact that there appears to obtain a quite genuine complementarity relationship between the individual (psychological) and the socio-cultural (collective) understanding of a given phenomenon (Devereux 1945, 1958). Thus, the more fully I understand John Doe's anger over the arrival of his mother-in-law in socio-cultural terms (autonomy of the U.S. nuclear family, the traditional stereotype of the mother-in-law, etc.) the less I can understand it *simultaneously* in psychological terms (John's irritability, his wife's infantile dependency on her mother, the mother-in-law's meddlesomeness, etc.)— and vice versa, of course. It is logically impossible to think simultaneously in terms of two different frames of reference, especially if, in terms of one of these, the key explanation is: "All mothers-in-law are defined by our culture as nuisances," while in the other system the key explanation is: "Mrs. Roe systematically interferes with her daughter's marriage."

Needless to say, the same complementarity relationship also obtains between the sociological and the psychological understanding of phenomena involving large groups and nations. This accounts for many of the exquisite complexities of problems involving "national character" and of many problems in social psychology as well. The difficulty is simply that *consistent* thinking in terms of, for instance, the psychological frame of reference makes it impossible to think, *at the same moment,* also in *consistently* socio-cultural terms.

The social scientist is, thus, literally forced to develop an individual "psychology" to fit his data. In order to understand how a large scale phenomenon can be produced by an inherently heterogeneous collection of individuals, he must assume that these individuals function in accordance with a series of pseudo psychological specifications. This "as if" approach is quite legitimate, but only in regard to that particular set of phenomena,[2] and only as long as one knows that one is dealing with "thought tokens" and "thought experiments." What is *not* legitimate—though it is done day after day—is to go one step further and ascribe or impute to the real and living individual members of that group the specific characteristics ascribed to the explanatory *model* of man. Such a procedure is as scurrilous as though a student of statistical mechanics said: "Since certain gas molecules go from the denser segments of the gas model to the less dense portions thereof, they obviously wish to escape crowding." This is strange reasoning indeed. Yet, it is precisely the type of reasoning used by some historians and political scientists who assume that everyone who rebels and fights against an economically unfair and politically oppressive system has been personally underpaid and harassed. No matter how sophisticated the manner in which such a statement is made, it is still factually incorrect and logically fallacious.

The reverse process—psychologistic sociologizing—is equally illegitimate. Since man is, both actually and by definition, a social being, even the student of the individual must learn to view him as part of a society and as the product of a culture. For example, if one is a Freudian, one must explore and clarify the nexus between the superego, the ego ideal and the patterning of ego functions on the one hand, and the structure of the socio-cultural matrix on the other hand. This is both necessary and legitimate. What is by no means legitimate, however, is the transposition of conceptual models pertaining to the individual to the socio-cultural system as a whole, and the interpretation of the socio-cultural structure and process *purely* in terms of the psychology of the individual, even if he does happen to belong to the society whose structure and processes one "interprets" in this manner. Specifically, and in simplest terms, the Constitution of the United States *is* not and can never *be* the "superego" or the "ego ideal" of American society. Moreover, it can never *function* in that capacity within that—or any other—society, for the good and sufficient reason that society does not have a superego or an ego ideal, any more than the psyche of an individual has a Constitution or a Supreme Court. What can and does happen, is that a particular individual may *incorporate* into his psyche—but only in the form of psychological materials—certain aspects of his society and culture and then *assign* these incorporated psychic representations of outer socio-cultural realities to the sphere of his superego or of his ego ideal. A jurist may subjectively adapt his superego to the Constitution, while a pious Catholic may adapt his to the Creed of the Apostles. Conversely, in times of stress, society may change its formal tenets to fit the average superego needs of the citizen. All this does not make the Constitution a social superego, nor the superego a psychic Constitution.

The social scientist must view his conception of "modal" man as a model valid only in the study of social phenomena, just as the psychologist must view his conception of society and culture as valid only in the study of individual phenomena. In the individual–psychological universe of discourse, society and culture are simply means for the implementation of subjective needs and psychic mechanisms, just as in the collective–sociological universe of discourse individual psychic structures and processes are simply means for the implementation of the collective needs and mechanisms of the socio-cultural system.

A summary analysis of facts and fancies regarding the actual motivation of individual Hungarians—as distinct from the "motivation" of the Hungarian people—who revolted against the system under which brute force on the part of their enemies and timid tergiversation on the part of their friends obliged them to live —will demonstrate with striking clarity the points just made.

Motivation of the Hungarian Freedom Fighter

A tabulation of the conscious motivation of individual Hungarian freedom fighters revealed that many of them had no genuinely personal experiences with cynical exploitation and brute oppression. In fact, quite a few of them were in relatively privileged positions and, externally at least, better off than they might have been under the Horthy regime. Hence, some political scientists held that those fighters who had no *private* grievances of a tangible type—and may even have had much to lose by participating in the revolution—were effectively and subjectively actuated by their indignation over the inherent viciousness of the system and the brazenness of alien rule, or else by national pride and the like. In so interpreting the motivation of

these *individuals,* these political scientists actually ascribed to individuals certain characteristics of a sociologistic "modal" personality construct, developed strictly in order to account for collective participation in mass movements and social processes.

It is true, of course, that some of those who had no real personal grievances did, themselves, interpret their conduct in terms of sociologistic and socially respectable motives, such as patriotism, love of freedom and the like. It would, indeed, be quite fallacious to deny that they were in part actuated by such motives, which are essentially components of the sociologistically conceived motivational structure of the sociologist's construct of the "modal" personality.

Unfortunately, this explanation of the active fighting in which these persons had voluntarily engaged, raises more questions than it solves. It leaves unexplained at least the following challenging facts:

(1) Those fighters who did have private and personal grievances and did cite these grievances in explanation of their participation in combat did not, in general, explain their own conduct *also* in terms of patriotism and the like, or at least did not explain it *primarily* and *convincingly* on those terms. This raises the question whether admittedly gallant fighters, who did have personal grievances, were simply unpatriotic and unidealistic individuals, seeking to exact an eye for an eye and a tooth for a tooth. A supplementary question is whether those who, despite unpleasant personal experiences with the Communist system, did *not* fight, were unidealistic, unpatriotic, or cowardly, or else simply pious Christians, who refuse to kill and who leave vengeance to the Lord.

(2) The second, and theoretically more relevant, question is whether it has not become customary to cite sociologistically conceived motives *only* where *no information* about the individual's subjective motivation is available. In practice, it is

precisely this criterion which is used in courts of law to determine the legitimacy of a plea of "not guilty by reason of insanity." A careful scrutiny of what actually happens when such a plea is made, shows that the plea is accepted only if the judge and the jury do *not* seem able to "understand" what could cause a person to commit such a crime. The accused is held to be "not guilty by reason of insanity" if his judges *cannot empathize* with his *deed, as distinct from his motivation.* Once the court feels that the *deed* itself is understandable in terms of the layman's conception of "common sense" (i.e., sociologistically defined) motives, the plea of insanity is nearly always rejected. Hardly ever is there an attempt to inquire into the accused's *real,* instead of *imputed,* motivation. Yet, only an understanding of the accused's real motives enables one to determine in a valid manner whether or not his seemingly "understandable" deed *actually* had the "sane" motivation *imputed* to it by judge and jury.

The fact is that if the list of non-subjective reasons for the individual fighter's participation in the revolution is supplemented by certain psychiatric insights, derived from data provided by the same informants to the interviewing psychiatrist (Dr. F. Kane) and to the present writer, one suddenly realizes that even these socio-culturally motivated individuals were also motivated in a highly subjective manner, though their motivation may not have been entirely conscious to them, and may have had no direct relationship to the social issues of the 1956 revolution.

The simple fact is that, as a Roman common sense psychologist pointed out long ago: *"Si bis faciunt idem, non est idem"* (If two people do the same thing, it is not necessarily the same thing). Where one man revolts because he had been exploited, another because, twelve years earlier, the Russians had raped his wife, another because he hates all author-

ity, still another may revolt because he wishes to impress his girl friend with his patriotism and valor. All these men may fight with equal ardor, kill an equal number of secret police and Russians, and therefore achieve *militarily and socially identical results. Psychologically, however, the results may not be the same.* Thus the one who thought that he fought from idealism may, in the long run, experience fewer guilt feelings than will the one who sought to destroy a hated father image by killing a secret police captain or the one who, at great personal risk and with conspicuous courage, blew up a Russian tank to impress his girl friend or to reaffirm his membership in a nation noted for its valor.

An interesting case is that of a gentle, well-behaved and well-brought-up, teenage Jewish girl, who, at the risk of her life, carried hand grenades to the active fighters. Except for the routine nationalization of her father's luxury goods store, this girl's family had not been particularly persecuted by the Communists. On the other hand, while she was still quite small, this girl and her family had been cruelly persecuted by the Nazis, and had twice escaped execution at the very last moment. Speaking in terms of so-called common sense (sociologistic) psychology, the last person on earth who had real and "obvious" reasons to risk her life in the revolutionary fighting was this girl. Moreover, given her sweet and gentle disposition, she was the last person one would —using a "common sense" conception of the personality—have expected to engage in violence, be it but to the extent of carrying hand grenades to the fighters.

On closer scrutiny, however, it became obvious that this girl, who had been a helpless child during the Nazi regime, was abreacting, twelve years later, her hatred of oppression and of oppressors. The most telling proof of this is the fact that she merely *carried* grenades to the fighters, but—unlike some other teen-age girls—did not lob them personally at the foe, though, in so doing, she would have incurred little additional risk. In other words, she functioned in the revolution simply as a gallant *child*, doing what even a child can do: bring ammunition to adult fighters, as did countless children raised on the American frontier.

Many other examples of unconscious motivations of an authentically subjective nature, hiding behind a conscious façade of sociologistic motivation, could be given. This, however, would represent only a laboring of the obvious.

The real point to be stressed is that *both organized and spontaneous social movements and processes are possible not because all individuals participating in them are identically* (and sociologistically) *motivated, but because a variety of authentically subjective motives may seek and find an ego syntonic outlet in the same type of collective activity.* This is equally true of spontaneous revolutionary movements and of extreme conformity. Indeed, there are few groups so rent by internecine squabbles as revolutionary cells and hyperconformist organizations. Moreover, just as a revolutionary may fight because he hates father figures, or because he has personal grievances, or else because he wishes to impress his girl friend, so a man may be a hyperconformist from sheer opportunism, from a fear of his own spontaneity, or else because emotionally he still needs his mother's approval.

The way in which the subjective motivations of various individuals find an outlet in the same type of activity, be it revolutionary or conventional, is rather uniform, as far as social effects are concerned. Individual differences in real motivation find a behavioral expression only in differences in the specific details of one's fighting pattern or conformity. Yet, though socially often unimportant, these individual motivational differences may determine intense psychological reactions to the deed which one has performed as a member of a collectivity. Just as the

conscious idealist among revolutionaries will, in the long run, probably experience fewer guilt feelings and self punitive urges than the one who killed an anonymous oppressor *instead* of killing his father, so the conformist actuated by a loyalty to the existing system will feel less shame in an hour of lonely self-appraisal than will the cowardly opportunist.

The real theoretical import of the finding that many, highly divergent, types of conscious and unconscious subjective motives can impel people to seek gratification through participation in a given social process is that it *simplifies* rather than *complicates* the possibility of obtaining a *psychological* understanding of the motivational structure of participation. Indeed—taking the Hungarian Revolution of 1956 as our paradigm—were we to assume that all freedom fighters were identically "motivated" (in the sociologistic sense of that term) we would have "solved" the problem of motivation only to be confronted with an even more complex problem. We would have to explain the mystery of a sudden and synchronous mass intensification of one type of motivation or need at a given point in history. At the same time, we would also have to account for its prolonged latency and non-exacerbation from 1944 to 1956. Figuratively speaking, we would have to imagine a single, massive, but subterranean torrent erupting suddenly and inexplicably from the ground, in a single huge explosion. By contrast, if we use the model of multiple psychologistic motivations, all of which can derive a certain amount of gratification from a given collective act, we have to imagine only a very commonplace river, fed by a variety of tiny tributaries coming from various directions.

Hence, it is sufficient to postulate that a large number of differently motivated persons may come to perceive a given historical moment or event as *suitable* for the gratification of their various subjective needs. In the psychological frame of reference, this position enables us to see the Hungarian Revolution of October 1956 as a sudden opportunity and means for the actualization and gratification of a variety of private needs, which had been present all along. Moreover, we can visualize various items of "motivation" formulated by some sound sociologists, historians and political scientists—nationalism, class struggle, resistance to oppression, idealism, etc.—as psychologically *instrumental* motives, which render ego syntonic, and not *only* socially acceptable, the acting out of certain needs. Were these needs acted out privately, they would not only be unsanctioned socially, but would also be highly anxiety arousing and productive of intense guilt feelings. Conversely, in the sociologistic frame of reference, this position permits us to view the variety of preexisting and highly individualized needs and motives as the raw material from which a social process, spontaneous or traditional, can crystallize just as a variety of fuels, when thrown in the same furnace, can heat the same boiler.

These considerations do not imply that one must discard, as useless and senseless, the sociologistic motivational structure of a given model of the "modal personality." Indeed, a variety of differently and highly subjectively motivated individuals may find that one and the same process in society at large can provide certain long desired gratifications. If they gratify their needs by participation in this social process, they may be able to render the necessary gratifying acts more ego syntonic than if these acts had to be performed privately. Thus, people go to church for many reasons: to seem respectable; because of piety, and all that piety implies in the unconscious; to show off a new Easter bonnet, and so on. All derive some gratification from this act, even though they are not actuated by a homogeneous set of motives, nor by one massive social motive. Their actual motives, when juxtaposed, form nothing

more than a conglomerate, which can be studied only as a conglomerate and not as a motivational torrent, since each qualitatively different motivational "unit" present in that conglomerate will be gratified by the collective act in a different way, and to a different extent.

The difference in the degree of gratification obtainable in this manner is of some importance. One young Hungarian freedom fighter, who fought with real courage and efficiency, would certainly have been a great deal happier had he been able to fight from the deck of a battleship flying the banner of the Holy Virgin, "Patrona Hungariae," not because he was an expert sailor or a religious traditionalist, but for purely subjective reasons. He could think of nothing more glorious than Naval Service (Horthy was an admiral!) unless it was a holy and virginal woman. Yet, this naïve worshipper of the Navy and of virgins fought as well as another, almost delinquent, young worker, who simply hated fathers and father representatives, or as well as still another worker, who was angry over Rakosi's betrayal of the idealistic-socialistic "essence" of communism, or another who had actually suffered persecution. The Russians which each of these men killed were, moreover, equally dead.

In brief, one must sharply differentiate between psychologistic conceptions of motivation and sociologistic conceptions of motivation, both in the construction of models of "modal personality" and in the interpretation of participation in social movements.

In the psychologistic model the motivation is and must be subjective. Hence, the motivational structure of the "modal" personality of a given group must be made up of motives and needs which are systematically stimulated—either through constant and expectable gratification or through systematic frustration—in that society. In the sociologistic model, the motivation must be collective and the motivational structure of the "modal" personality of a given group must be constructed out of the type of "common sense" motives which the social scientist must impute to all members of a given group in order to be able to explain their participation in collective activities: patriotism, economic self-interest, idealism, traditional conformism and the like.

In a sound culture-and-personality theory, the psychologist's conception of the "modal" personality's motivation will be considered as "operant" and the sociologistic conception of the "modal" personality's motivation will be considered as "instrumental." In interpretations, these two sets of motives will be brought into play only consecutively, because one cannot think of the same phenomenon simultaneously both in sociologistic and in psychologistic terms. The common denominator of individual motivations which are statistically frequent in a given society will be *defined* as the true operant mainsprings of social actions. The sociologistic type of motivation obtaining in that culture and society—and closely related to its value system—will be *defined* as the instrumental motivational means for the gratification of the more basic needs.

This theory *does not* undermine the sociologistic interpretation of collective events. It *does* show that the psychologistic definition of the "modal" personality's motivation leads to a science of operant motives, whereas its sociologistic definition forms the basis of a science of instrumental motives, or of "outlets." This view implies that society and culture provide, by means of something like a feedback mechanism, supplementary motivations which do not modify the initial operant motivation of the personalities but reinforce, trigger and channel them, by making their implementation ego syntonic and by providing the occasion, and often also the means for their implementation and gratification. This explains why a single exasperated but decent man may *not* be able to bring himself to shoot down secretly the Gestapo, MVD or AVO man representing a hated father figure, although he *will* be able to do so if society provides him with the means of defining his act as an ethical and patriotic one. Psychologically, this way of defining the situation may be a simple "rationalization," facilitating the performance of acts leading to gratification. Sociologically, however, this definition of the act represents also its sanctioning. Thereafter the sanctioning itself functions as a *bona fide* motive, but only instrumentally, and only insofar as the *execution* of a subjectively desired act is concerned.

This thesis implies, in turn, that one must sharply differentiate between substantive, subjective and operant motives which are often quite unconscious, and externally provided instrumental motives pertaining to the actualization of behavior permitting need gratification. The psychologizing social scientist must know that his proper universe of discourse, in the psychological frame of reference, is the problem of instrumental motives. The sociologizing psychologist must know that his proper sociological universe of discourse is the actualization of substantive basic needs, representing operant motives, through socially provided means, which, in sociology but not in psychology, can also function as instrumental motives.

Conclusion

Any explanation of behavior which uses the conceptual structures known as models of "modal personality" must consist of a series of steps:

(1) The first, psychologistic, step is the listing of the real motives of the actual participants in a given collective activity. These motives may be discovered through interviewing techniques, psychological tests, psychoanalytic procedures and other psychological means.

(2) This list serves as a basis for the construction of a psychologistic model

of the modal personality, whose need-and-motivation structure is limited to those needs which are statistically prevalent in, and appear to be closely linked to the structure of a particular society-and-culture.

(3) Next, it must be specified that the needs-and-motivations ascribed to this model of the "modal" personality can be, jointly and severally, gratified in various social or cultural sub-contexts such as participation in rituals, in parties, in revolutions, in counter-revolutions, or in the acceptance of certain mandates of culture, in certain attitudes, and so forth.

(4) Next, a sociologistic model of the modal personality must be constructed, to which are *ascribed* needs-and-motives that explain sociologically—in terms of a social "common sense" psychology related to value systems—the actual participation of individuals in a given social process. This list may include terms like economic interest, patriotism, piety, class consciousness, or conformism.

(5) This list of sociologically meaningful "motives" is then psychologized, by being redefined as "instrumental." These motives then serve to sanction actual individual maneuvers seeking to gratify subjective and genuinely psychologically "operant" needs and motives; they are also means for the actualization of gratification seeking behavior.

Of these five steps only the fifth and last permits the formulation of statements genuinely pertaining to, and relevant in terms of, the culture-and-personality frame of reference.

NOTES

1. It is probably more than a coincidence that the most extreme current exponent

of the culturological position took his Master's degree in psychology at a time when the most primitive sort of behaviorism dominated all learning theory and most of American psychology.

2. In order to grasp the significance of this specification, it suffices to imagine what would happen were an economist to decide to fill in existing "gaps" in the present model of "economic man" and wrote a paper on "The sexual and love life of economic man." His essay would be too weird even for a science fiction magazine.

REFERENCES

1. Devereux, George.: "A Conceptual Scheme of Society." *American Journal of Sociology*, 1940, 54:687–706.
2. ———.: "The Logical Foundations of Culture and Personality Studies." *Transactions of the New York Academy of Sciences*, Series II, 1945, 7:110–130.
3. ———.: *A Study of Abortion in Primitive Societies.* New York: Julian, 1955.
4. ———.: "The Anthropological Roots of Psychoanalysis." In Masserman, J. H. (ed.), *Science and Psychoanalysis, I: Integrative Studies.* New York: Grune and Stratton, 1958, pp. 73–84, 171–173.
5. ———.: *Mohave Ethnopsychiatry and Suicide.* Bureau of American Ethnology, Bulletin No. 175. Washington: Government Printing Office, 1960.
6. Kroeber, Alfred L.: *Anthropology.* (New, revised edition.) New York: Harcourt, Brace and Co., 1948.
7. Society for the Investigation of Human Ecology: Second Seminar on the Hungarian Revolution of October 1956. Forest Hills, L.I., N.Y.: Society for the Investigation of Human Ecology, Inc., 1958. (Mimeographed). (See papers by Hinkle and by Stephenson and discussion by Devereux.)

2 · The Interpenetration of the Two Levels

SOCIAL STRUCTURE AND THE DEVELOPMENT OF PERSONALITY:
FREUD'S CONTRIBUTION TO THE INTEGRATION
OF PSYCHOLOGY AND SOCIOLOGY

by Talcott Parsons

Perhaps for reasons connected with the ideological needs of the intellectual classes, the primary emphasis in interpreting Freud's work—at least in the United States—has tended to be on the power of the individual's instinctual needs and the deleterious effects of their frustration. Thus on the recent centenary of Freud's birth there were a number of statements to this effect.[1] The consequence of such a trend is to interpret Freud as a psychologist who brought psychology closer to the biological sciences and to suggest the relative unimportance of society and culture, except as these constitute agencies of the undesirable frustration of man's instinctual needs.

There is, however, another side to Freud's thinking, which became, I think, progressively more prominent in the course of the complicated evolution of his theoretical scheme, culminating in the works dealing with the structural differentiation of the personality into id, ego, and superego, and in his late treatment of anxiety. This trend concerns two main themes: the *organization* of the personality as a system; and the relation of the individual to his social milieu, especially in the process of personality development. This, in psychoanalytic terminology, is the field of "object-relations"—the most important area of articulation between the psychoanalytic theory of the personality of the individual and the sociological theory of the structure and functioning of social systems.

It is this latter aspect of Freud's thought which will form the subject of this paper.[2] It will be my main thesis

[1] Notable ones were made by Lionel Trilling in *Freud and the Crisis of our Culture;* Boston, Beacon Press, 1955; and by Alfred Kazin in "The Freudian Revolution Analyzed," *The New York Times Magazine,* May 6, 1956; p. 22. It is perhaps significant that this view is particularly strong in literary circles.

SOURCE: *Psychiatry,* Vol. 21 (1958), pp. 321–340. Reprinted by special permission of The William Alanson White Psychiatric Foundation, Inc.

[2] This paper belongs in a series of my own writings which have a major concern with the relations between psychoanalytic theory and the theory of social systems. The most important of these are: "Psychoanalysis and the Social Structure," *Psychoanal. Quart.* (1950) 19:371–384, reprinted in *Essays in Sociological Theory* (revised edition), Glencoe, Ill.: The Free Press, 1954. "The Superego and the Theory of Social Systems," PSYCHIATRY (1952) 15: 15–25. With Robert F. Bales, *Family, Socialization and Interaction Process,* Glencoe, Ill.: The Free Press, 1955. "Psychoanalysis and Social Science," pp. 186–215; in *Twenty Years of Psychoanalysis,* edited by Franz Alexander and Helen Ross, New York: Norton, 1953. "The Incest Taboo in Relation to Social Structure and the Socialization of the Child," *British J. Sociology* (1954) 5:101–117. "An Approach to Psychological Theory in Terms of the Theory of Action," to appear in *Psychology, Study of a Science,* Vol. III, edited by Sigmund Koch, New York: McGraw-Hill, 1958.

that there is, in the structure of Freud's own theoretical scheme, a set of propositions which can, with relatively little reinterpretation, be very directly integrated, first, with the sociological analysis of the family as a small-scale social system, and, further, with the problems of the child's transition from membership mainly in his own family to participation in wider circles which are not, in Western societies, mainly organized in terms of kinship. Freud's own contribution here centers chiefly in the earlier stages of socialization, through the Oedipal resolution, but the same principles of analysis can be extended to the later stages.

The most important of Freud's concepts in this respect are identification, object-cathexis, internalization or introjection, and the superego. Most attention has been given to the concept of the superego. Although many difficult problems of interpretation cluster about that concept, there is no doubt that it refers to the internalization, to become a constitutive part of the structure of the personality itself, of aspects of the normative culture of the society in which the individual grows up.

Very important clues, on which the present analysis builds, are given by the remarkable convergence between Freud's views on internalization and those developed, independently and at nearly the same time, in sociological quarters, by Emile Durkheim in France and by Charles H. Cooley and George Herbert Mead in the United States. I should regard this convergence as one of the few truly momentous developments of modern social science, comparable perhaps to the convergence between the studies of experimental breeding in the tradition of Mendel and the microscopic studies of cell division from which the conception of the chromosomes as the vehicles of biological heredity developed. The two together produced the modern science of genetics.

In another direction, however, the basic principle on which Freud's conception of the superego was based can be extended, not merely across disciplines to the relations between social structure and personality, but within the personality, to the constitution of its other sectors and structural components. Some have tended to treat the superego as a very special case within the personality, as the only point at which the norms of the culture enter. A major objective of the present paper, however, is to show that the whole logic of Freud's later position implies that the same is true for the structure of the ego also. Indeed it follows from Freud's whole main treatment of the process of socialization—and was, at least at one point, explicitly stated in his writings—that the major structure of the ego is a precipitate of the object-relations which the individual has experienced in the course of his life history.[3] This means that internalization of the sociocultural environment provides the basis, not merely of one specialized component of the human personality, but of what, in the human sense, is its central core. From the standpoint of the main traditions of modern psychology this is a very radical position, so radical that its import has not yet been very widely appreciated.

The final question inevitably arises as to whether even the id should be completely exempt from this central interpretation of the importance to the theory of personality of object-relations and internalization. In the final section of the paper I shall argue very briefly that the interpretation of the id as a manifestation of "pure instinct" is, in Freud's own terms, untenable. Although of course it is the primary channel of transmission of instinctual energy and more particularized impulses into the personality, it also is structured through internalized

[3] Sigmund Freud, *The Ego and the Id*, London: Hogarth Press, 1935; p. 36. The relevant passage is quoted later in this paper.

object-relations. This time, however, it involves, above all, the residues of the earliest object-relations of the life history of the individual, which have had to be rather drastically reorganized in the course of later life experience.

The analysis to follow is carried out in terms of an explicit theoretical frame of reference which I am accustomed to calling the "theory of action." This is a scheme for the analysis of *behavior* as a system, but broken down in terms of the analytical independence and interpenetration of four major subsystems which it is convenient to call the behavioral organism, the personality, the social system, and the cultural system.[4]

The distinction between, first, the aspects of the system of action centering on the individual and the determinants of his behavior, and, second, the transindividual factors of society and culture, is a very old one, stemming, in one major tradition at least, from the problems of Darwinian biology as applied to human behavior. More recently it has seemed necessary to draw lines within each of the two categories resulting from that distinction—namely, between cultural and social systems, on the one hand, and between organism and personality, on the other.

I shall stress the importance of the latter distinction—between organism and personality—which seems to me to be

emergent in Freud's own work.[5] This distinction is, I think, crucial to the understanding of the place of the theory of instincts in Freud's total psychological theory, and of the role of pleasure and of eroticism. My main emphasis, however, will be on the relations between personality and social system. My view will be that, while the main content of the structure of the personality is derived from social systems and culture through socialization, the personality becomes an independent system through its relations to its own organism and through the uniqueness of its own life experience; it is not a mere epiphenomenon of the structure of the society. There is, however, not merely interdependence between the two, but what I call *interpenetration*. At all stages of the socialization process, from the sociological side the essential concept of *role* designates this area of interpenetration. From the personality side, a corresponding concept of *relational needs* may be used, of which the psychoanalytically central one of the need for love may serve as an example.

The Oral Stage and the Process of Identification

Let me now turn to Freud's theory of object-relations. There are two main approaches to the nature of personality development. One may be illustrated by analogy with the plant. The main characteristics of the mature organism—for example, the number and qualities of wheat grains produced, or the brilliance

[4] These have been delineated in a number of places, for example: *Toward a General Theory of Action*, edited by Talcott Parsons and Edward A. Shils, Cambridge: Harvard University Press, 1951. Talcott Parsons, Robert F. Bales, and Edward A. Shils, *Working Papers in the Theory of Action*, Glencoe, Ill.: The Free Press, 1953. The most recent statements about the four systems are in Talcott Parsons, "An Approach to Psychological Theory in Terms of the Theory of Action," reference footnote 2; and in A. L. Kroeber and Talcott Parsons, "The Concepts of Culture and of Social System," *Amer. Sociological Rev.* (1958) 23:582–583.

[5] See Lord Adrian, Review of Ernest Jones, *The Life and Work of Sigmund Freud*, Vol. 1, in *The Observer*, London, November, 1953. This stands in contrast to the interpretation of many other commentators less qualified in biology than Lord Adrian. Compare also the formula that the instinct is the "representative" of the needs of the organism to the "psychic" apparatus.

and shape of the flowers—are predetermined in the genetic constitution of the species. There will, however, be differences in outcome as a function of the favorableness or unfavorableness of the environment. This process of interaction with the environment, however, does not determine the main pattern, but only the degree of excellence with which it "comes out."

The other view sees the genetic constitution as a *nonspecific* base from which the pattern of the adult personality will be evolved,[6] and, as the main pattern-setting components, the *values* of the culture and the *meanings* of social objects experienced in the course of personality development.

These two approaches are not mutually exclusive, although they may be given different relative emphasis. But it is my contention that the main significance of Freud's work for the social sciences consists in the seriousness and the fruitfulness with which he explored the *second* avenue; and, moreover, that the theory of object-relations—while not necessarily more important than the theory of instincts—colors Freud's whole theory of personality, including the theory of instincts.[7]

[6] This, for example, is clearly what happens in the learning of intellectual content. This requires "capacity"; but a textbook of algebra, for example, to one not previously trained in the subject is not just a "relatively favorable influence" on the outcome, but the primary source of the content of the learned pattern.

[7] In this connection I am particularly indebted to an as yet unpublished paper by John Bowlby, "The Nature of the Child's Tie to its Mother," and to personal discussions with Dr. Bowlby. In terms of relevance to the present context, the most essential point is that there are two main levels in Freud's treatment of the problem of instinct, one of which tended to predominate in his earlier work, the other in the later. The first is closer to the main biological tradition in emphasizing relatively specific inborn pat-

As noted above, three of Freud's concepts bear most directly on the problem of object-relations—identification, object-cathexis (or object-choice), and internalization or introjection. Freud associated these concepts particularly, although by no means exclusively, with three different levels of the process of socialization. Identification referred in the first instance to the relation established between mother and child in the oral phase. Object-cathexis was used preponderantly to characterize the relation of mother and child in the phase between the oral and the Oedipal; while internalization or introjection referred mainly to the establishment of the superego in the Oedipal

terns of behavior which do not need to be learned. It is a type of mechanism prominently emphasized by current "ethologists" such as Karl Lorenz and Nikolaas Tinbergen. Bowlby emphasizes five such "instinctual responses," as he calls them, which figure prominently in the first year or so of life—namely, sucking, crying, smiling, clinging, and following. The second level concerns the more diffuse "motivational energy" which is particularly involved in Freud's later conception of the id.

The role attributed by Bowlby to the more specific instinctual responses does not seem to me to be incompatible with the general thesis of this paper. That these and other patterns are definitely inborn is not to be doubted. But the higher level of organization of the behavioral system which is thought of as the personality cannot be derived from the organization of these responses without reference to the influence of object-relations in the course of socialization. It has, however, been necessary to revise a number of statements made in an earlier draft of this paper in the light of these considerations. Essentially, the "instinctual responses" may be thought of as a set of mechanisms of behavior which operate at a level intermediate between the metabolic needs of the organism, on which Freud himself and many later psychoanalysts have laid such great emphasis, and the higher-order mechanisms of control of behavior through internalized objects.

phase. It will be my thesis that each of these concepts, in different ways, designates an aspect of the integration of the personality in a social system, an integration which is characterized by a particular process of *learning* in a particular context of object-relations.

Therefore, I suggest, first, that Freud tended to confuse the genetic and the analytical uses of these concepts, and, second, that for the general purposes of the theory of personality, the analytical meaning of them is more important than the genetic.[8]

I shall now attempt to sketch these processes, mainly in my own terms, although with continual references to Freud, in order to establish a basis for clarifying some theoretical implications of Freud's treatment of them.

Freud, in common with many other writers, maintained that the starting point for what I would call the process of socialization was the action of persons responsible for child care—in the first instance, the mother—as agents for the gratification of organic needs.[9] Of such needs, in the earliest phases that for nutrition is paramount. In addition, the mother is the primary object for gratifi-

[8] There is a notable parallel in this respect between Freud and Durkheim. Although the empirical subject-matters of their concern are miles apart, Durkheim, in his treatment of the relations of mechanical and organic solidarity, particularly in his *The Division of Labor in Society* (Glencoe, Ill.: The Free Press, 1947) tended to treat them as associated with stages in the evolution of social systems, but also tried to put them in the context of an analytical theory of social systems. See my paper, "Durkheim's Contribution to the Theory of the Integration of Social Systems," to appear in *Emile Durkheim, 1858–1917. A Collection of Essays with Translations and a Bibliography,* edited by Kurt Wolff, Columbus: The Ohio State University Press, 1958.

[9] The thesis is perhaps most clearly stated in *The Problem of Anxiety,* New York: Norton, 1936.

cation of a series of instinctual responses at the behavioral level.[10]

The psychological importance of this physiological dependence on a human agent is partly a consequence of the "satisfaction" of the inborn needs. But there are also physiological mechanisms by which this satisfaction becomes a *reward*.[11] In order for it to acquire this meaning, the child must learn that instinctual gratifications are in some sense contingent *both* on the action of the mother *and* on that of the child. For example, it seems to be established that there is an inborn sucking response, but the child early learns to suckle better than he is equipped to do by sheer "instinct." He learns how to move his lips, what posture is best, when to exert effort, when to relax, and so on, for the amount of milk he gets and the ease with which he gets it are contingent to an appreciable degree on his own goal-oriented action.[12] This holds even apart from any influence he may exert on when and under what circumstances the breast or bottle will be presented to him.

On the mother's side also, feeding a baby is by no means purely instinctive but involves elements of skill and "intentional"—not necessarily conscious—regulation. She tries to "get him" to nurse properly, by her manner of holding him, by her sensitivity to his "need to rest," and by her judgment as to how far to "force" him and when he has "had enough." In addition, she is the primary agent of imposition of any sort of sched-

[10] Reference footnote 7.

[11] In this connection I am particularly indebted to the work of James Olds, who strongly emphasizes the independence of pleasure-reward mechanisms from the instinctual needs, frustration of which is closely associated with pain and other compulsive mechanisms. See James Olds, "Self-Stimulation of the Brain," *Science* (1958) 127:315.

[12] See Roy R. Grinker, *Psychosomatic Research,* New York: Norton, 1953.

ule on the feeding, and she determines the "picking up" and the "setting down" of the baby and the way he is dressed, covered, bathed, cleaned, and so on.

Thus even at this very elementary level, the relations between mother and infant constitute a genuine process of *social interaction,* of which "care" in the sense of sheer attending to physiological needs, is clearly only one component. The child, from the beginning, is to some degree an active agent who "tries" to do things and —increasingly with time—is rewarded or punished according to his "success" in doing them. The mother, on her side, actively manipulates the situation in which this learning takes place. However genuine the process of interaction as such, she is in the overwhelmingly predominant position of power, controlling the timing of feeding and other acts of care— indeed, the whole setting of the experience of being cared for. The child develops an attachment to her as an object in such a way that the *organization* of the emerging motivational system is a function, not simply of his own independently given needs, but of the way in which her responses to these needs have themselves been organized.[13]

Thus the infant in the first few weeks, if not days, of life comes to be integrated into a social system. Relatively definite expectations of his behavior are built up, not only in the predictive sense, but in the normative sense. He nurses "well" or

[13] Part, however, of the mother's position of power vis-à-vis the child is not a matter of sheer freedom of action on her part, but is determined by third parties involved in the relationship. For instance, the father may not participate very actively in early child care, but the fact that the mother lives with him in a common household greatly affects her treatment of her child. There may also be older siblings. Then, of course, this family is part of a larger society which imposes both relational constraints and a set of values which, among many other things, provide certain norms for what is considered *proper* treatment of infants.

"badly"; he cries only when he "should" and is quiet the rest of the time, or he cries "when there isn't any good reason." Inevitably, the behavior of adults takes on the character of rewarding him for what *they* feel to be "good" behavior and punishing him—including omitting reward—for what they feel to be "bad" behavior, and otherwise manipulating sanctions in relation to him.

From the point of view of the infant, there are two particularly crucial aspects of his situation which present cognitive problems to him. The first is the problem of "understanding" the conditions on which his gratifications and frustrations depend—the cues, or conditional stimuli, which indicate the consequences, for him, of acting in a given way. The psychology of learning shows that a high level of "rationality" or "higher mental process" is not required for significant learning to take place, if the situation is structured so that certain modes of action consistently produce rewards, while others do not. The second problem presented to him is the focus of *organization* of this system of cues. This is not simply the question of what specific cues indicate probable gratification or deprivation of specific needs, but rather, of what more general *formula* of action can serve to improve the chances of generalized gratification.

Here again, it is not necessary to assume any rationalistic hypotheses. If the pattern of sanctions imposed is *consistent* over a range of more specific actions, it may be assumed, on learning theory grounds, that there will be generalization from the more specific items to the *pattern.*[14] Thus, where the child "tries" to nurse properly in the sense of "cooperating" with the mother, he is more likely to be gratified. This is perhaps to say that

[14] The presumption is that the generalized pleasure mechanism plays a crucial part in this learning process and that this is, as will be noted below, a primary reason for the importance of childhood eroticism.

she presents prominently displayed cues and supplementary rewards. It is not a very long step from this level to thinking of the organized pattern of sanctions in terms of the *intentions* of the mother. The significance of this step derives from the fact that there is generally a *single* primary agent of early child care,[15] and that in a variety of significant respects the actions of this agent come to be *contingent* on what the child does. In these circumstances, the learning of the *meaning* of a cue is, I think, synonymous with the imputation of intention to the agent.

The concept of intention as here used involves two central components. The first is the *contingency* of what alter (the agent of care) does on what ego (the child) has done or is expected to do, so that alter's action may be treated as a sanction in relation to ego's action. The second is the component of *generalization*. There exist not merely discrete, disconnected sanctions, but a pattern of relatively systematic and organized sanctions which eventually leads to the learning of a complementary pattern of responses, which is also organized and generalized. In its relation to discrete, particularized acts on either side of the interaction process, the pattern of the sanction system acquires the character of a set of values or norms which define the relation between acceptable, rewarded behavior on the one hand, and unacceptable, nonrewarded, or punished behavior on the other.

Because of the immense inequality of the power relationship, the most important change brought about by this early phase of the process of interaction is the change in the personality of the child, although there is presumably a secondary one in the mother. The primary change in the child is the introduction into his personality, as a behavior system, of a new level of *organization*. In his orienta-

tion to the external world, it is a new level of capacity for organized behavior, for successfully attaining his goals and for coping with a variable situation. Internally, it is a new level of organization of his motivational or instinctual impulses or needs which, in one of its aspects, introduces a system of *control over* these impulses, but in another provides a pattern for their utilization in the interest of the newly learned goals and interests. In Freud's famous metaphor, this new organization derived from contact with objects—the ego—was likened to a rider on the impulse system, the id, a horse which may ordinarily do the rider's bidding, but on occasion may be difficult or impossible to control.[16]

The essential point here is that this system of internal control over the child's own instinctual or impulse system has become established through a generalized pattern of sanctions imposed by the mother, so that the child learns to respond, not simply to specific proffered rewards, but to "intentions," and thereby learns to "conform" to her wishes or expectations. In so doing he has learned a new *generalized goal,* which is no longer simply to gratify his constitutionally given instinctual needs, especially for food, but to "please" his mother. It is the attainment of this new level of organization, including a new goal, which I think Freud primarily designated as *identification.* This is a mode of *organization* of the ego with reference to its *relation* to a social object. One can clearly say that, at the same time, it is learning to act in conformity with a set of norms.

To sum up the main characteristics of

---

[15] This proposition needs qualification for certain types of variability in the structure of social situations, such as kinship systems.

[16] Freud, *New Introductory Lectures on Psychoanalysis*, New York: Norton, 1933, p. 108. It goes without saying that in terms of "motivational force" the id is "stronger" than the ego, as a horse is far stronger than its human rider. The ego, however, is not an energy system but a "cybernetic" type of *control* system. For this function relatively little energy is needed.

this learning process, its basis is the establishment of a determinate set of relations between a set of inborn mechanisms of the organism, on both metabolic and behavioral levels, and a set of stimuli from the environment. There are particularities, of organic and instinctual gratification and of practices of care, but equally on both sides there is *generalization*. There is reason to believe that, on the side of the learning infant, the most important vehicle of generalization is the pleasure mechanism,[17] which must not be confused with sheer organic or instinctual gratifications in the particularized sense; whereas it is quite clear that on the environmental side it is the *patterning* of the system of sanctions which constitutes the element of generalization.

The *correspondence* of these two patterns of generalization is the essential basis of the beginning of a new motivational structure, which can be called the ego. This new structure, in its external, environment-oriented process—which may be called "goal-gratification"—concerns the relation of the child to a social object outside himself. In its internal, organism-oriented process, it concerns his relation to a generalized neurological mechanism by which a plurality of gratification is organized to produce—perhaps to maximize—what has come to be called pleasure.

In Freud's view, it is fundamental that the external situation and the internal physiological system are to an important degree independent of each other. This is the basis of Freud's contention that the pleasure principle and the reality principle must be treated as analytically independent. At the same time, their integration is the most fundamental condition of the functioning of a personality as a system at this nodal point of articulation between the organism at one of

its boundaries and the external world at another.

Freud's commonest formula for instinctual impulse—governed by the pleasure principle—is that it is the "representative" of the needs of the organism to the psychic apparatus—the ego, as he referred to it in his later work.[18] This formula seems to be acceptable in the present terms. The point further to emphasize is that the most crucial part of "reality" even at the oral level is *social;* it is the mother as a social object, acting in a role in a system of social interaction. While one aspect of reality is nonsocial—that is, milk as food-object—it is the *agency* of the mother as the source of the milk which organizes the learning process. It is in terms of generalization that the social qualities of the significant object become crucial.

I should now like to look at the structure of this aspect of the mother-child system. The step to identification implies that the child's "interest" in the mother is, after a time, no longer exhausted by the fact that she acts as an instrumentality of discrete organically or instinctually significant goal-gratifications—food, clinging, and so on. *She, as role-person, becomes* on a higher level a meaningful object. Inevitably, in the learning process, the meaning of the mother as object must be established *through generalization from* gratification—and deprivation—experiences on nonsocial levels. But once this meaning has become established, then in a sense the tables are turned; the discrete, instinctually significant gratifications and deprivations become *symbols* of the intentions or attitudes of the mother. Food then is no longer sought only because it produces specific organic pleasure; and—perhaps just as important—it is no longer rejected simply because of alimentary discomfort. More generally,

---

[17] For some purposes it may well be necessary to distinguish different kinds of pleasure; for instance, erotic pleasure may be a special type.

[18] In somewhat different and more strictly theoretical terms one might say that it constitutes an *input* from the organism to the personality system.

a primary—indeed *the* primary—goal of the developing personality comes to be to secure the favorable attitude of the mother or, as it is often called, her love. Specific gratifications on lower levels, then, have become part of an organization on a wider level, and their primary meaning derives from their relation to the paramount goal of securing or maximizing love. Indeed, I think it a legitimate interpretation of Freud to say that only when the *need for love* has been established as the paramount *goal* of the personality can a genuine ego be present. This need, then, in an important sense comes to control the ontogenetically older goal-needs of the organism, including, eventually, that for pleasure. There must be provision for the adequate gratification of the latter, but, at the same time, each must take its place in an organized system of gratifications.

What, now, of the internal aspect at the level of oral generalization? Undoubtedly one of Freud's greatest discoveries was that of the significance of childhood eroticism and its beginnings in the oral stages of development.[19] I have suggested that the integration of external and internal references, of reality principle and pleasure principle, is the most important single condition of attainment of an organized ego. Although Freud was not able to spell out the physiological character of childhood eroticism very far, I think it can be regarded as, essentially, a built-in physiological mechanism of the *generalization* of internal reward, which matches the generalization of external goal-gratification. Erotic pleasure seems to be essentially a diffuse, generalized "feeling" of organic well-being which is not attached to any one discrete, instinctual need-fulfillment. When one is hungry, eating produces gastric pleasure;

when one is cold, being warmed produces another specific feeling of pleasure. But erotic pleasure is not, as such, dependent on *any one* of these or *any specific combination* of them. The mouth is, Freud held, an erogenous zone; thus oral stimulation through sucking is one important, specific source of this more generalized erotic pleasure. Yet oral stimulation produces a pleasure which is *independent* of that produced by the ingestion of food; and, moreover, this pleasure is capable of generalization to a higher level. Organically, the main manifestation of oral eroticism seems to be the capacity for pleasure in diffuse bodily contact, which is connected by generalization with stimulation of the mouth,[20] so that being held, fondled, and so on produce pleasure as a fundamental type of generalized reward.

Thus certain capacities of the organism operate as mechanisms which facilitate the generalization of cathexis, and hence of goals, from the goal-objects which immediately gratify particularized needs, to the *agent* of these gratifications, this agent coming to be treated as an organized system of sanctioning behavior. Eroticism, whatever the physiological processes involved,[21] is a mechanism of internal reward by which fixation on the more specific instinctual gratifications is overcome in favor of pleasure in the diffuse and generalized relationship to a nurturing social object.

I have suggested that this establishment of an organized ego in the personality through a pattern of sanctions desig-

[19] My own previous views on eroticism and its functions have been stated most fully in "The Incest Taboo in Relation to Social Structure and the Socialization of the Child," reference footnote 2.

[20] It may be that a special connection is thus established between the independent instinctual responses of sucking and clinging. Such a connection between discrete gratifications would imply a generalized medium analogous to money in social systems. It is as such a medium that I conceive pleasure. See, for example, Olds, reference footnote 11.

[21] Old's work implies that these processes operate at the level of the central nervous system, not of the "erogenous" peripheral areas alone. Reference footnote 11.

nates essentially what Freud meant by identification. Several of Freud's own formulations of the concept stress the striving to be *like* the object. This emphasis requires elucidation and some qualification. Only in a very qualified sense can one say that an infant learns to be like his mother. Rather, he learns to play a social role *in interaction* with her; his behavior—hence his motivation—is organized according to a generalized pattern of norms which define shared and internalized meanings of the acts occurring on both sides. Together, that is, mother and child come to constitute a *collectivity* in a strict sociological sense. But this does not mean that the two members of the collectivity are alike, in the sense that they play identical roles; on the contrary, their roles are sharply differentiated, as are the norms which define the respective expectations. Thus I should like to speak of identification as the process by which a person comes to be inducted into membership in a collectivity through learning to play a role complementary to those of other members in accord with the pattern of values governing the collectivity. The new member comes to be *like* the others with respect to their common membership status and to the psychological implications of this—above all, the common values thereby internalized. Psychologically, the essential point is that the process of ego development takes place through the learning of social roles in collectivity structures. Through this process, in some sense, the normative patterns of the collectivity in which a person learns to interact become part of his own personality and define *its* organization.[22] At the same time, however, by internalizing the reciprocal role-interaction pattern he lays the foundation of

[22] Freud clearly recognized the duality of being both like and unlike the object in speaking of the boy's identification with the father, and the girl's with her mother in the Oedipal period. See *The Ego and the Id*, reference footnote 3; pp. 44–45.

capacity to assume alter's role as well as his own.

Object-Choice and Internalization

The other two of Freud's basic concepts in this area are object-choice, or cathexis, and internalization, or what is sometimes called by Freud's translators introjection.[23] I have emphasized that for the infant the mother is a *social* object and becomes the most important part of "reality"—that is, of the environment external to him. But although he comes to be profoundly "attached" to her—that is, to "cathect" her as an object—he can scarcely be said to have chosen her. Object-choice is an act of the ego, and the neonate does not yet have an ego. He can be rejected by the mother, but he can neither choose nor reject her at first.

In the phase of primary identification, the infant is learning a role in, and the values of, a collectivity. There is, of course, an essential element of spontaneity or autonomy in response to the actions of alter. Yet the motivation to action in conformity with the expectations of the new role is still, for a time, directly dependent on the sanctions appropriate to the learning process; ego is able to fulfill alter's expectations in anticipation of reward. But now the capacity develops to implement autonomously the newly learned values in the absence of the accustomed rewards—as Freud clearly recognizes when he speaks of identification as having fully taken place only when the object has been renounced or lost.[24]

I spoke of the process of learning a role vis-à-vis the mother[25] as involving

[23] The German term used by Freud is *Introjektion*.

[24] Reference footnote 3; pp. 36–37.

[25] Throughout this discussion I speak of the mother as the primary object of cathexis. More strictly, one should refer to a generalized parent, since before the Oedipal transition the category of sex has presumably not

at least *two levels* of generalization and organization. The pattern of sanctions imposed by the mother incorporates and expresses the *higher* of these two levels. The consequence of successful identification is to develop the capacity to implement this higher pattern level in one's autonomous behavior, and not merely in response to the expected rewards of another. This capacity is perhaps the most important respect in which the child has through identification come to be like the mother.

If, however, action in accordance with the newly acquired value-pattern is to be reality-directed, it must establish goals in relation to objects. Here the object-world is not to be treated merely as given, taking over the care of the helpless infant. Instead, the new ego actively "tries out" its capacity for organized behavior in its object-environment. Object-choice, in Freud's sense, is the "spontaneous" investment of libido by the ego in seeking attachment to an object in the external world.

Typically, at the first stage of this process, the object "chosen" is the mother, who was the primary agent of care in the oral phase. But it is a mother who comes to play a different *role* vis-à-vis her child. She shifts from rewarding his conformity with the minimum expectations of being a "good child" to rewarding his attempts to perform above that minimum. The emphasis of his role shifts, in turn, from ascription to achievement. The minimum base is taken for granted, but beyond that his rewards depend far more heavily on *how well* he performs.

In one sense this shift involves a turning of the tables. If the *diffuse* attitude of the mother toward her child in the oral phase could be called love, then one may say that now, by his identification, the child has become capable of displaying and acting upon a similar attitude—

———

yet been fully internalized, nor the agency-roles of the two parents fully discriminated.

that he can love an object, normally his mother.

If the child's need to love and have this love reciprocated is strongly attached to an object, then this object gains a very strong point of leverage for motivating him to new levels of achievement. This is because the mother cannot only dispense specific rewards for specific performances, but she can treat these as *symbols* of her acceptance of the attachment of the child to her as a love-object—that is, of her reciprocation of his love.

The period when the love-attachment to the mother is paramount is the period of learning the basic *skills* of action—walking, which is, in a sense, the foundation of all the motor skills, and talking, which is the foundation of skills in communication. Object-choice, then, is the motivational foundation of that aspect of socialization in which basic performance patterns are learned. The diffuse attachment to the object of cathexis is the basis for the motivational meaning of the more specific rewards for specific performances.

It is worthwhile here to note the double reference of *meaning*. In speaking of the process by which identification is established, I discussed the organized pattern of sanctions as establishing the generalized meaning of the specific acts of the child and the mother. Now, in speaking of the process of achievement-learning, I refer to the diffuse love-attachment as the basis for the primary meaning of particular rewards—and of course of ego's own acts of performance in relation to these rewards. This, essentially, is what I mean by the internalization of a value-pattern—that it comes to define meanings for the personality system as such. The first set of meanings is organized about the sanctions applied to the child, the second about a set of performances he has spontaneously tried out and learned successfully to complete.

Freud's concept of object-cathexis designates the primary basis on which *one* type of process of differentiation in the structure of the personality takes place.[26] The starting point for this process is the "internalized mother" established through the previous identification. But from this base comes to be differentiated an autonomous subsystem of the personality oriented to active manipulation of the object-world. The dependency component of the personality then becomes the re-structured residue of the internalized mother, which gives a more diffuse and generalized *motivational* meaning to the specific acts and rewards involved in the exercise of motor and communication skills. On the other hand, the "self," or the ego in a more differentiated sense than at the oral level, is the part which assumes the role of autonomous initiative in the performance process.

The great increases in performance capacity which occur in this pre-Oedipal love-attachment period lead to an immense widening of the child's range of contacts with the world in which he lives. He is continually engaged in trying out new motor skills and in learning about his world, both by direct observation and by insistent questioning through the newly learned medium of language.

In relation to the infant, the mother played a role which was to a very important degree determined by her other roles—those of wife, of mother of older siblings of the infant, and of member of the household as a system, as well as her various extrafamilial roles. One may presume that these other involvements appeared mainly, from the point of view of the infant, as restrictions on her exclusive devotion to him. But with his growing mobility and communication, the other persons to whom his mother is related become more and more clearly

[26] I have analyzed this elsewhere at considerably greater length. See Parsons and Bales. *Family, Socialization and Interaction Process,* reference footnote 2; especially Ch. 2. This book may be used for general reference, although in a few respects my views have changed since its writing.

defined objects. These other persons, typically his father and his siblings—including, perhaps, by now a younger sibling—form the primary focus of this new structuring of the situation in which he acts and learns.

Thus a new phase in the processes of identification emerges, focused on the assumption of membership in the child's total nuclear family of orientation. This is a far more complex process than the original identification with the mother, since it involves at least three such identifications which are interdependent but also partially independent—namely, identification with the family as a collectivity, identification in terms of sex, and identification by generation.

What is required at this stage is the child's internalization of a *higher level* of generality or organization. In his relation with his mother, he has already learned the fundamentals of reciprocal role-behavior in a *dyadic* relationship, the simplest type of social system. But the circumstances of this early socialization have stacked the cards in favor of dependency, and so the problem of *independence training* is now, in the pre-Oedipal period, a focal one. The fundamental question is the balance between dependency and autonomy, the ranges within which the child can take independent initiative and those within which he must give way to the wishes and sanctions of his role-partner.

With the Oedipal period the child begins to have a plurality of dyadic relations—with his mother, father, sister, brother; and these, in turn, must be organized into a higher-order system, the family as a whole. It is in this context that Freud most prominently raises the problems of the superego and its place in the personality. Just as he treats identification with the mother as producing an internalized base from which object-choices are made, so he speaks of the superego as providing, for the latency period and later, the internal surrogate of the *parental function* as it operated in the control of the pre-Oedipal child.[27]

The situation of the primitive mother-identification was sociologically very simple, because the child was primarily related to a single person as object; the essential points were that it was a social object, and that mother and child together formed a collectivity. Now the situation has become much more complex, but nevertheless the same basic principles obtain. What Freud refers to as the parental function may be interpreted to mean a function of the family as a system, and moreover to include the functions of *both* parents as the leadership coalition of the family. Seen in these terms, *the family* is an object with which the child identifies, and through this identification he becomes a full-fledged member of that family; he and its other members come to constitute a collectivity which, if not new, is at least, through his altered status and the adjustments made by other members, a changed one.

The superego, then, is primarily the *higher-order* normative pattern governing the behavior of the different members in their different roles in the family as a system. This pattern is first impressed upon the child through the sanctions applied to his behavior—through the rewards and punishments which, although administered by different members of the family in different ways, presumably have a certain coherence as a system, deriving mainly from the co-ordinated leadership roles of the parents. Therefore, a new element of organization is introduced into the personality of this process of identification, an organization on a higher level of generality and complexity than before, giving the child new goals and values.

The child through this process comes to be 'like' the object of his identification in the same essential sense, and with the same qualifications, as he earlier came to be like his mother. He has acquired a pattern of orientation which he holds in common with the other, more socialized, members of his family. When this pattern has been internalized, he can act, in relation to the extrafamilial world, in terms of that pattern without reference to the earlier system of sanctions. In the same sense in which the oral mother became a lost object, so the latency child's family of orientation eventually becomes a lost object—a process normally completed in late adolescence.

Within the family, the child's role has become far more complex than it was earlier; he has as many subroles as there are dyadic relations to other family members. But from the point of view of the wider society he plays *one* role—that defined by his age-status as latency-period child of his family, and by his sex.[28]

Sex Role, Eroticism, and the Incest Taboo

One aspect of the greater complexity of the new system of identifications and object-relations is the fact that the child cannot identify indiscriminately with all the available objects of his nuclear family. Two of the subsidiary identifications within the family, by sex and by generation, are to become structurally constitutive for his status in the wider society, and these are cross-cutting. It is essential to the understanding of the differential impact of the Oedipal situation on the sexes that for the boy the tie to his mother—the original object of identification and of subsequent object-cathexis—is not included in either of these new identifications; whereas for the girl the tie to the mother is included in the identification by sex.

[27] See *New Introductory Lectures,* reference footnote 16; p. 91.

[28] See Robert K. Merton, "The Role Set," *British J. Sociology* (1957) 8:106–120, for an excellent discussion of the complexity of role-constellations.

Hence the girl can, in relation to her mother, repeat on a higher level the infantile identification, and can to a degree take over the mother's role as an apprentice in the household and in doll-play. She is, however, precluded from taking over the mother's role in relation to the father by her categorization as belonging to the child generation.

The boy, on the other hand, must break radically with his earlier identification pattern; he cannot turn an object-cathexis into an identification except on the familial level, which has to be shared with the other members. He is blocked by the importance of the sex categorization from identifying with the mother in intrafamilial function, and he is blocked by the generation categorization from taking a role like the father's in relation to her. Moreover, the father is a more difficult object of identification, because so much of his role is played outside the household. While the boy's subjection to his father's authority has often been considered the central factor in explaining the boy's ambivalent attitudes toward the father, it is only one component in a larger complex; the other considerations I have mentioned are perhaps equally important. The authority factor does, however, gain significance from the fact that at the Oedipal period the child begins to have much more important relations outside his family; in a sense, the father is the primary representative of the family to the outside society, and of the latter to the family.

Another important feature of the complexity in the Oedipal period is that the ascribed identification is *selective*—except for the over-all familial identification—among the members of the family. In particular, the very important possibility of the child's object-choice of the parent of opposite sex, and vice versa, is *excluded* from the main formal identification structure and relegated to the status of "secondary" or informal attachments; and such an attachment, if it be-

comes too strong, can be both disruptive of the family as a system and a distorting factor in the personality development of the child.

This relates to two fundamental and interrelated sociological problems in which Freud took a considerable interest but on which further light can now be thrown—the roles of the sexes, and the incest taboo. Freud is clear and insistent about the existence of what he calls constitutional bisexuality, and hence about the fact that the motivational structure of sex role is importantly influenced by object-relations in the course of the person's life history. One can extend the argument by noting that the learned aspect of sex role provides an essential condition for the maintenance of the family as an integral part of the social structure, and hence of its functions in the socialization of the child.

The feminine role is primarily focused on the maternal function. The crux of this is, through the *combination* of instrumental child care and love, to provide a suitable object for the child's earliest identification, and subsequently for the child's autonomous object-cathexis. The agent of these functions must be anchored in an organizational unit of the larger society, otherwise the leverage for socialization beyond the earliest stage would not be adequate.

The masculine role, on the other hand, is not primarily focused on socialization, but on the performance of function in the wider society—economic, political, or otherwise. If boys are to achieve in this arena, they must make the proper set of transitions between the intrafamilial context of early socialization and the larger societal context. The coalition of the *two* parents in the family leadership structure is the main sociological mechanism which makes this possible.[29] Clearly, also, the

[29] See R. F. Bales, "The Equilibrium Problem in Small Groups," pp. 111–163; in Parsons, Bales, and Shils, *Working Papers in the Theory of Action*, reference footnote 4.

relation of girls to their fathers, and hence to men in general, is just as important as that of boys to their mothers in balancing these forces as they are involved in the functioning of human society.

Consideration of the incest taboo brings up again the problem of the role of eroticism in the socialization process. Throughout the stages of this process so far considered—the oral stage, the stage of first object-choice, and the Oedipal stage—the main principle operating is the internalization, through successive identifications, of social object-systems and cultural patterns of the organization of behavior on progressively higher levels of complexity and generalization. These new identifications lead to new object-choices and new definitions of goals in relation to these objects.

I have suggested that at the oral level eroticism is primarily significant as a vehicle for the generalization of reward in its internal, physiological aspect. Apparently there is a duality of levels of the object-relation to the mother corresponding to the duality of hedonistic rewards— that is, rewards in the form of stimulation of erogenous zones and in the form of a general sense of well-being. It is this correspondence that makes oral eroticism so important. I am not competent to follow the subsequent course on a physiological level, but I would like to suggest that, with a difference, there is probably a repetition of this pattern in the "phallic" stage. The essential point here is the erotization of the genital organs, which is presumably partly instinctive and partly learned, either through masturbatory activities or through some kind of adult stimulation, or both.

This is the period during which the differentiation of personalities by sex role first becomes of critical significance. The genital organs are clearly, in the prepubertal period, the primary anatomical differentiae by sex. Hence they are particularly appropriate as *symbols* of sex-iden-

tification. The erotic gratification attained through genital stimulation then becomes a type of internal pleasure which can become directly associated with learning to act *in the role* of a member of the appropriate sex group. The diffuse sense of bodily well-being, which is the critical feature of erotic gratification in its generalized aspect, may then come to be associated with proper fulfillment of the expectations of sex role.

These considerations seem to be essential as background for the discussion of the incest taboo. In the period of identification with the mother, eroticism operated through affectionate physical contact with the object—through the stimulation of erogenous zones and through the induction of a diffuse sense of bodily well-being. The object was a single person, and the physical contact with her—being caressed or fondled—becomes the prototype of erotic gratification on the more generalized level.

In the Oedipal period, however, the significant object for identification is not an individual, but a collectivity, and tender physical contact with a complex collectivity is clearly not possible; thus eroticism cannot serve as a socialization mechanism as it did in the pre-Oedipal period. Indeed, the necessity to achieve a fundamental identification without the help of this internal reward may constitute one of the main sources of strain in this stage. This, more than the punishing aspects of paternal authority, may be why the superego stands out as being peculiarly impersonal and in some respects threatening.

From the point of view of the process of socialization, the incest taboo functions primarily as a mechanism by which the child is both forced and enabled to internalize value systems of a *higher order* than those which could be exclusively embodied in a dyadic two-person relation or in a social system as simple and diffuse as the nuclear family. The tendency of erotic relations is to reinforce solidarity *à deux,* to give the single person as object priority over the larger collectivity or system of collectivities in which the dyad is embedded. If the child is to internalize these higher-order value-systems, he must learn, in the requisite contexts, to do without the crutch of erotic gratification.

From the point of view of the society as a system, the incest taboo has another order of functional significance which is closely linked with the above. It serves to maintain a diversity of cultural patterns on the lowest level of internalization in personalities; thus the combination of these patterns takes place on a higher level of generality, where there is not so strong a tendency to "reduce" them to a less general common denominator. In other words, the incest taboo insures that new families of procreation will be set up by persons socialized in two distinct families of orientation. The culture internalized in the early stages by the children of the new family will then have a dual origin, and will in certain respects constitute a new variant a little different from either of the parental ones, as they are from each other. The argument is not that the crossing of familial cultures reduces them to greater uniformity; on the contrary, by *preserving variability* at the lower levels of generality, it prevents the establishment of a uniformity which might lessen the pressure to achieve higher levels of generality capable of including *all* the variable versions as instances.

Another aspect of the problem, which ties these two together, is the bearing of the incest taboo on the internal structure of the nuclear family. The erotic relation of the parents to each other is a primary focus of their solidarity. Its exclusiveness—even in comparison with the mother's relation to the small child—tends to symbolize their solidarity vis-à-vis third persons. As the child becomes more active and develops higher capacities for performance, there is a strong pressure for him to develop or reinforce erotic relationships to his parents, to both of them in different ways. The developing importance of sex as an ascribed focus of status then makes for attachment to the parent of opposite sex, thereby implicitly challenging the parent of the same sex. But the erotic solidarity of the parents tends to lead to rejection of the child's advances in this direction, so that his *primary* new identification is forced into the mold of member of the family as a whole, and into his sex and generation roles within it. The parent's erotic solidarity thereby forces him to a higher level of value-internalization than that governing *any* dyadic relation within the family and prepares him, in his latency period and in subsequent orientations outside his family, to internalize still higher-level patterns of value.

These considerations alone do not adequately account for the brother-sister aspect of the incest taboo. While this is the weakest of the three taboos within the nuclear family, it is none the less very strong. I suggest that this version of the taboo is internalized, at least in part, by emphasis on *generation* as an institutionalized status-component. The main focus of the prohibition of erotic relations to the Oedipal child is on his *age* status. He is too old for infantile erotic gratifications, and too young for adult. He must be classed with the parent of the same sex with respect to sex, but he cannot presume to the adult privilege of genital eroticism. The identifications with the family as a whole and by sex create a configuration in his environment which leaves no place for an erotic relation to a sibling of the opposite sex—indeed, for any overt erotic relation at all. Closely related is the fact that the two siblings who have both internalized the same "generalized parent" have substantially less psychological protection against dependency than if, as is the case with the unrelated partners, their parental figures are independent of each other. Finally, the one-sex peer group is, for the latency child, the primary heir of the earlier security-base in the family of orientation. Brother-sister incestuous needs would cut across this basis of solidarity.

More generally, in one major aspect the significance of the Oedipal transition lies in the fact that the child reaches a level of internalized values and a complex structure of identifications which enable him to dispense with erotic rewards as a primary mechanism of further socialization. The basic difference between the pre-Oedipal stages within the family and the post-Oedipal stages mainly without it is that, in the former, identification and object-choice involve an erotic attachment to a primary personal object, whereas later they do not. This shift is, as I have suggested, essential if the internalization of social value systems on high levels of generality is to be achieved.[30]

At the same time, the immediately pre-Oedipal attachment of erotic significance to sex-role, and the symbolization of this by the awakening of genital eroticism at the phallic level, has laid the foundations for the formation later by the individual, through his marriage, of a new family in which he will play conjugal and parental roles. But the erotic need, thus restructured, is allowed expression only in the context of an adult personality in which the higher-level value-patterns have had an opportunity to develop and consolidate their position. It is only through this non-erotic component of the parent's personality structure that he has a sufficiently strong superego and a sufficiently mature ego to be able to serve as a model for identification for his children, and that hence socialization beyond the stages of early childhood becomes possible.

[30] The taboo on homosexuality is dynamically closely related to that on incest. It applies, however, mainly to emancipation from the latency-period one-sex peer group, not from the family of orientation. Homosexuality would be the most tempting latency-period form of eroticism.

In the light of these considerations Freud's famous view about the sexual genesis of all the neuroses may perhaps be interpreted in a sense acceptable in current sociopsychological terms. The most important point is that the personality structure, as a precipitate of previous identifications and of lost objects, develops by a process of *differentiation* from the earliest and simplest identification with the mother. Both this early relationship of identification and the succeeding object-choice relationship contain in their motivation an essential erotic component. Without the element of erotic attachment, sufficient motivational leverage could not have existed to bring about the learning processes involved in the identification and in the performance learning later based upon it. Moreover, the evidence is that the erotic needs thus built up are never extinguished, but remain permanent parts of the personality structure.

The reason why neuroses, like other disturbances of personality functioning, involve important regressive components is essentially that the more generalized *motivational* structures—as distinguished from social values, where the order of generality is the reverse—are laid down in early childhood. Regression to deep enough levels, then, will always involve motivational structures in which erotic needs form an essential component. Hence in a neurosis which pervades the personality as a whole, an erotic component will always be present, not to say prominent, and by the same token, there will of necessity be a prominent component of erotic disturbance in its etiology.

This is not at all to say that all motivation is, in the last analysis, sexual. It is rather to say that, on the genetically earliest and hence in one sense most fundamental levels, the sexual—or better, erotic—element is always prominently involved, both symptomatically and etiologically. But this does not in any way contradict the importance of the capacity to develop and operate motivational structures which are *not* primarily oriented to erotic gratifications, but rather to impersonal or "affectively neutral" patterns of behavior. This occurs by the process which Freud usually refers to as sublimation.[31]

Post-Oedipal Object-Relations

Freud treated the relation between the Oedipal and latency periods as essentially parallel with that between the earlier oral and object-choice periods. The Oedipal period involves an identification process through which the "parental function" is internalized to form the superego. The identification, I have argued, must be interpreted to refer to membership in the nuclear family as a collectivity, and within that, to the child's own sex and generation roles. But once this process of identification has been completed, the child can turn to a new process of object-choice, this time in relationships primarily outside his family of orientation. What may be called his dependency base still remains inside that family: he lives with his parents and siblings, and they remain responsible for his subsistence and for a general protective function toward him; moreover, his place in the community is still defined primarily by his family membership.

But from this base, which is analogous to his identification with his mother at the earlier period, he ventures out to establish important relations outside the family. In a differentiated society of the modern Western type, this occurs typically in two overlapping contexts—the school, in which his formal education begins, and the informal peer group, usually composed of age-mates of his own sex. There are two particularly prominent

features of these new object-relations: None of them is overtly erotic in content or tone—hence Freud's concept of latency; and the pattern of relationship is, for the first time, not ascribed in advance. Age and sex status are ascribed, but the level of performance and the rewards for it which are accessible to the child are not, either in the school or in the display of various kinds of prowess in his relations with his peers. He is exposed, within the limits permitted in the community, to open competition with his age-peers, from which a significant structuring of the social groups will emerge, independent of the structure of the families from which the competitors come.[32]

This structuring seems to revolve about two axes. The first, achievements which can be evaluated by universalistic standards, has as its prototype the mastery of the intellectual content of the school curriculum, but other things, such as athletic prowess, fall into the same category. It is certainly of significance that the foundations of the skills involved in intellectual function are laid down in the latency period—notably the use of *written* language and the skills of abstract reasoning, as Piaget has so fully shown.[33]

The second axis is the establishment of position in more-or-less organized groups where status is not ascribed in advance. The focus here is on the assumption of such roles as leadership and followership, and of primarily task-oriented or primarily integrative roles in relation to one's fellows. The context in which this learning takes place range from the school class itself, under the direct supervision of the teacher, to

[31] Freud's own analysis of this process is, in my opinion, considerably less satisfactory than his analysis of the earlier ones.

[32] For a discussion of the sociological significance of this transition, see S. N. Eisenstadt, *From Generation to Generation*, Glencoe, Ill.: The Free Press, 1956, especially Chs. 1 and 3.

[33] See Barbel Inhelder and Jean Piaget, *The Growth of Logical Thinking from Childhood to Adolescence*, New York: Basic Books, 1958.

wholly informal peer activities entirely removed from adult participation.

It is a striking fact, perhaps particularly striking in the United States with its tradition of coeducation in the schoolroom, that in the latency period the peer group is overwhelmingly a *one*-sex peer group. The child is here "practicing" his sex role in isolation from the opposite sex. When this isolation begins to break down and cross-sex relations assume a prominent place, this is in itself a sign of the approach of adolescence. With this a further differentiation begins to take place, into, first, a sphere in which erotic interests are revived—which leads into marriage and eventually the establishment of a family of procreation; and, second, a sphere of organizations and associations in which the direct expression of erotic interests remains tabooed.[34] The essential point is the discrimination of the contexts in which erotic interests are treated as appropriate from those in which they are not. Their appropriateness is clearly confined to a single role-complex within a much larger context, most of which is treated as nonerotic.

It is my principal thesis that, in the analysis of object-relations, there is complete continuity in the basic conceptual framework appropriate to identification in the oral stage, and object-choice in the post-oral stage, on the one hand; and the latency period and adolescent socialization, on the other hand. The learning of roles in school and peer group occurs through the mechanisms of object-choice, motivated by prior identifications; but, in the first instance, collectivities rather than persons are clearly the most significant objects. Then—just as within the nuclear family significant new dyadic relations besides that with the mother develop—significant new dyads form in school and peer groups, with the teacher and with particular age-mates. But the

[34] Same-sex friendship seems to occupy an intermediate position between these two types. See footnote 30.

significance of these dyads must be understood *within the context of the new collectivity structures* in which the child is learning to play a role, or a complex of roles.

Similarly, this later process of object-choice leads to a new set of identifications, which involve the collectivity-types outside his family in which the child acquires memberships and roles. As in the case of the mother-child dyad and of the nuclear family, he internalizes the values of these collectivities as part of the process of identification with them and assumption of a role in them. The differences lie in the greater diversity of memberships the child acquires, the higher level of generality of the values he internalizes, and the absence of erotic rewards in the learning process. The direct involvement of such rewards is no longer necessary, because of the more highly differentiated and organized personality structure which the post-Oedipal child brings to his object-relations; in fact, the regressive associations of erotic experience would militate against his attaining the higher disciplines which are now needed.

By the completion of the major phase of adolescence, the normal child has presumably achieved, outside the family of orientation, identification with four main types of collectivity, and has hence internalized their values and become capable of pursuing the goals appropriate to them independent of the detailed pattern of sanctions which have operated during the internalization process. These are: (1) the subsociety of his age-peers as a whole, embodying the values of the so-called youth culture; (2) the school, which is the prototype of the organization dedicated to the achievement of a specified goal through disciplined performance; (3) the peer-association, the prototype of collective organization to satisfy and adjust mutual interests; and (4) the newly emerging cross-sex dyad, the prototype of the sole adult relationship in which erotic factors are allowed an overt part.

These identifications form the main basis in personality structure on which adult role-participations are built. Through at least one further major step of generalization of value-level, participation in the youth culture leads to participation in the values of the society as a whole. Participation in the school leads to the adult occupational role, with its responsibility for independent choice of vocation, a productive contribution, and self-support. The peer-association identification leads to roles of cooperative memberships in a variety of associations, of which the role of citizen in a democratic society is perhaps the most important. Finally the dating pattern of adolescence leads to marriage and to the assumption of parental responsibilities.[35]

I emphasize this continuity from the objects of identification in childhood to the role and collectivity structure of the adult society in order to bring out what is to me the central point of the whole analysis. This is that Freud's theory of object-relations is essentially an analysis of the relation of the individual to the *structure of the society* in which he lives. Freud analyzed this relation from the point of view of the individual rather than from the point of view of the structure of the social systems concerned. His perspective also was primarily developmental in the psychological sense; sociologically stated, he was mainly concerned with the processes by which the individual comes to acquire membership in social collectivities, to learn to play roles in them, and to internalize their values, and he was most interested in the identifications entered into in early childhood.

But throughout the course of personality development, identification, object-choice, and internalization are processes of relating the individual to and integrating him in the social system, and, through

[35] These two paragraphs constitute the barest sketch, which I hope to elaborate and verify further in a later publication.

it, the culture. Since these processes are a relational matter, eventually technical analysis has to be applied to both sets of relata, as well as to the relationship itself. Had Freud lived long enough to enter more deeply into the technical analysis of the object-systems to which the individual becomes related, he would inevitably have had to become, in part, a sociologist, for the structure of these object-systems is—not merely is influenced by—the structure of the society itself. Essentially, Freud's theory of object-relations is a theory of the relation of the individual personality to the social system. It is a primary meeting ground of the two disciplines of psychology and sociology.

Conclusion

In the introductory section of this paper, I suggested that if the individual's object-relations in the course of his life history are as important as they seem to be, then the significance of internalized social objects and culture cannot, as some psychoanalysts have tended to assume, be confined mainly to the content of the superego. On the contrary, it must permeate the whole personality system, for, with all Freud's emphasis on differentiation within the personality, he consistently treated it as an integrated whole.

In certain respects the ego should provide the test case of this hypothesis. Indeed, the increasing attention of Freud himself in his later years to problems of ego psychology, an area which has been considerably further explored by such authors as Heinz Hartmann and Ernst Kris, seems to be closely related to his increasing attention to the field of object-relations. At the same time, I do not think that the id should be exempt from the logic of this development.

First, however, let me say something about the ego. Since the ego is the primary location of interchange between the personality and the outside world of reality, and since the most important aspect of reality itself is social, the conclusion is inescapable that the ego is "socially structured." It is a particularly welcome confirmation of this hypothesis —much of which has been worked out from a sociological point of view—to find that Freud himself explicitly recognized it. The most striking passage I have found deserves to be quoted at length:

> When it happens that a person has to give up a sexual object, there quite often ensues a modification in his ego which can only be described as a reinstatement of the object within the ego, as it occurs in melancholia; the exact nature of this substitution is as yet unknown to us. It may be that by undertaking this introjection, which is a kind of regression to the mechanism of the oral phase, the ego makes it easier for an object to be given up or renders that process possible. It may even be that this identification is the sole condition under which the id can give up its objects. At any rate the process, especially in the early phases of development, is a very frequent one, and *it points to the conclusion that the character of the ego is a precipitate of abandoned object-cathexes* and that it contains a record of past object choices.[36]

I think it can, then, quite safely be said that object-cathexes and identifications do not, in Freud's own mature view, simply "influence" the development of the ego, in the sense in which temperature or moisture influences the growth of a plant, but that the structure of the object-relations a person has experienced is directly *constitutive* of the structure of the ego itself.

[36] Reference footnote 3; p. 36. The italics are mine. The relation of this passage to Freud's late view of the role of anxiety (*The Problem of Anxiety;* reference footnote 9), as concerned primarily with the fear of object-loss, is clear.

If it can be said of the ego that it is a precipitate of abandoned object-cathexes, there does not seem to be any serious doubt that the superego is primarily social and cultural in origin. Indeed, this has been clearly recognized by psychoanalysts ever since the introduction of the concept by Freud. Freud's formula that the superego represents the parental function is to my mind the most adequate one. He also quite explicitly refers to it as the focus of "that higher nature" representing the "moral, spiritual side of human nature," [37] which we have taken into ourselves from our parents.

The role of the id is focal to the issue with which the present discussion started —namely, the relative importance of "instinctive" as compared with cultural, social, and other "environmental" influences in the motivation of personality. The concept of the id in Freud's later work is, of course, one primary heir, although by no means the only one, of such concepts as the unconscious, the primary process, and the libido in his earlier work. Furthermore, in the enthusiasm of discovery, Freud tended to contrast the id as sharply as possible with the ego, which seemed to be the closest, of all the components of the personality, to traditionally rationalistic common sense—as, for instance, when he spoke of the id as entirely lacking in organization.[38]

Against the tendency to highlight the conflicts between the ego and id must be set the view implied in the metaphor of the horse and rider, the conception of the ego as a system of control. Furthermore, the id is treated at many points in specific relation to the pleasure principle, and I have suggested various reasons for assuming that pleasure is an organizing mechanism which integrates diverse motives at lower levels of organization.

A still further consideration which points in this direction is the progressive

[37] Reference footnote 3; pp. 46–47.

[38] For example, *New Introductory Lectures,* reference footnote 16; p. 103.

increase in the generality which Freud attributed to the basic instinctual urges, ending up with only a single underlying duality. This is not inconsistent with Bowlby's views of the importance, in more specialized contexts, of various more particularized instinctual responses.[39] But it does imply that, from a very early phase of development, the basic *organization* of the motivational system cannot be derived from instinctual sources, but must come from identifications and internalized objects.

It is my own view that the distinction between instinctual and learned components of the motivational system cannot legitimately be identified with that between the id, on the one hand, and the ego and superego on the other. Rather, the categories of instinctual and learned components cut across the id, the ego, and the superego. The id, like the other subsystems, is organized about its experience in object-relations. It differs, however, in two fundamental respects from the other subsystems. First, it is oriented, as the other two are not, to the person's own organism as object. This seems to me to be the essential significance of the pleasure principle as the governing principle of the id. Secondly, however, the object-cathexes which are constitutive of the structure of the id are predominantly those of the earlier phases of the process of socialization, so that in any internal conflicts involving the problem of regression, id-drives represent the regressive side of the conflict.

However true it may be that advancing beyond certain early levels of development requires transcending the fixation on these early cathexes, and however much the mature personality must control them through ego and superego mechanisms, it still remains true that these are particular cases of identification and internalization of objects—not the leading example of motivation in their absence.

[39] Reference footnote 7.

Thus it seems to me that the general principles of object-relations through identification, object-cathexis, and internalization must be extended to the *whole* psychoanalytic theory of personality. Indeed, this is the position Freud eventually, in all essential respects, came to, even though he had not ironed out all of the inconsistencies in his treatment of these matters, nor reconciled many of his earlier statements with his later ones.

There are two particular virtues of this position. First, it formulates psychoanalytic theory in such terms that direct and detailed articulation with the theory of social systems is enormously facilitated. This is of the first importance to the theory of the motivation of social behavior, and hence, in my opinion, is an essential prerequisite of the advance of sociology in certain connections. But at the same time there are reciprocal benefits for psychoanalysis—for example, this formulation suggests ways in which personality theory must take account of variations in the structure of the social system on which it impinges.

On a more general level, however, this view should do much to relieve psychoanalytic theory of involvement in a false dilemma in its use of the categories of heredity and environment. As general biology is showing with increasing clarity, it is not a question of whether or how much one or the other factor influences outcomes—in this instance, in the field of behavior. The trend is strongly away from a "predominant-factor" explanation of the phenomena of life toward a more analytical one. Analytically conceived variables are, except for limiting cases, always *all* important. The salient technical problems concern their clear definition and the working out of their intricate modes of *interrelationship* with each other. This paper has, in this respect, been meant as a contribution to what I conceive to be the major trend of psychoanalytic theory in this same direction.

B · THE PITFALLS OF REDUCTIONISM

1 · Personality Reductionism

COMPLIANT BEHAVIOR AND INDIVIDUAL PERSONALITY [1]

by Reinhard Bendix

During the last two decades there have been increasing efforts to integrate the various fields of study in the social sciences and related disciplines. A case in point is the study of society and the study of the individual. Many promising areas of research have been opened up, because sociology and psychiatry [2] have been related one to the other. On the other hand, there are many pitfalls in

[1] For the last year and a half the author has attended the staff meetings of the Psychiatric Annex to Cowell Hospital on the University of California campus. During this period he has also served as a psychotherapist, working under the supervision of a staff psychiatrist. His debt to Dr. Saxton Pope, the director of the clinic, is acknowledged.

[2] The following essay makes only reference to the body of theories which is sometimes designated as "depth psychology" and which has grown out of the pioneering work of Sigmund Freud. The terms "psychiatry" or "psychiatric theory" will be used in this general sense. The term "therapy" will be used for the empirical base on which psychiatry rests. The term "psychodynamic" is commonly used to single out those emotional processes, often unconscious, which can be traced to childhood experience and which in their entirety constitute the character structure or personality of an individual.

SOURCE: *American Journal of Sociology*, Vol. 58 (1952), pp. 292–303.

applying the concepts and theories of one discipline to another field. Hence, work designed to integrate the social sciences not only calls for an understanding of the indivisibility of the subject matter but also for an acute awareness of the differences which exist between the disciplines. How, then, does the study of society and culture relate to the problems with which psychiatry deals? And how does the study of psychiatry relate to the problems with which sociology deals? I shall attempt to answer these questions under five headings: (1) the orientation of propositions in sociology; (2) the orientation of propositions in psychiatry; (3) culture patterns and the response of the individual; (4) the psychological insignificance of compliant behavior; and (5) culture and personality reconsidered.

I. The Orientation of Sociological Propositions

Sociology aims at general propositions which are true of large numbers of people, considered as social groups. From the viewpoint of psychiatry such propositions are necessarily "superficial" and largely beside the point.

For example, it is well established that income and size of family are inversely related in the countries of the Western world. Sociologists have attempted to account for this relationship in a fairly consistent manner. Some years ago Alva Myrdal pointed out that modern civilization had fostered individualistic beliefs which prompted many families to restrict the number of their children. Family limitations seemed best suited to satisfy the desire of every family member for the development of each individual's personality. Child-bearing involved pain and discomfort for the mother; her desire for a career of her own would be frustrated for a longer or shorter period of time. Both parents would have other reasons for family limitation: children cause the interruption of sexual life, they reduce their parents' mobility, they interfere with social and cultural interests, they cause an increase in the family's expenses and a decrease in its standard of living, and they consequently expose the family as a whole to greater economic insecurities. Finally, there is the unwillingness of parents to have more children than they can properly care for, and the costs of what is thought of as "proper care" increase with each increase in income.[3]

Mrs. Myrdal's keen insights have been made the basis of several extensive research projects. In the studies of the Milbank Memorial Fund these basic ideas were elaborated into twenty-three formally stated hypotheses.[4] These hypotheses are of interest here as illustrations of the type of question a sociologist might ask. For example, the greater the adherence to tradition, the lower the proportion of families practicing contraception. At one level of analysis this is a useful abstraction. Yet a psychiatrist examining the same families would think that "adherence to tradition" is a phrase emptied of psychological meaning. Such significant questions as those pertaining to the history of the parent-child relation in each case are obviously left unanswered. Or, again, the dominant member of a family tends to be dominant also in determining the use of contraceptives and the size of the family. Yet the psychiatrist would think such a finding "superficial," since the fact of dominance suggests further questions, concerning the genesis of such dominance and its relation to the corresponding submissiveness of the other partner.

It may be objected that this statement is true as far as it goes but that there are certain propositions in sociology which are of great significance to psychiatry, nevertheless. I choose an example from the work of Georg Simmel to illustrate this point. Simmel states that adornment "singles out its wearer whose self-feeling it embodies and increases at the cost of others . . . while (at the same time) its pleasure is designed for others, since its owner can enjoy it only insofar as he mirrors himself in others." [5] Now, this juxtaposition of egoistic and altruistic elements in the use of adornments is certainly familiar in psychiatry. Yet, even here the proposition of the sociologist is "superficial" from the standpoint of psychiatry, in that it necessarily omits the biographical dimension. The interplay of egoistic and altruistic elements is of interest to the psychiatrist in terms of the meaning which it has for the individual as a result of his personal history. The

[3] See the extended discussion of these problems in Alva Mydral, *Nation and Family* (New York: Harper and Bros., 1941), Ch. iv; cf. also Guy Chapman, *Culture and Survival* (London: Jonathan Cape, 1940), pp. 160–179, and the excellent overall discussion by Frank Notestein, "Population—the Long View," in Theodore W. Schultz (ed.), *Food for the World* (Chicago: University of Chicago Press, 1945), pp. 36–69.

[4] P. K. Whelpton and Clyde V. Kiser, "Social and Psychological Factors Affecting Fertility," *Milbank Memorial Fund Quarterly* (October, 1945), XXIII, 147–149.

[5] Kurt H. Wolff, *The Sociology of Georg Simmel* (Glencoe, Ill.: Free Press, 1950), p. 339.

same interplay is of interest to the sociologist in terms of the way in which adornment may aid a group of individuals to strengthen its internal cohesion as well as deepen the cleavage between itself and others. My point is that the sociologist, in focusing his attention on this latter aspect, must necessarily ignore the psychological meaning of adornment to the individual.

II. The Orientation of Psychiatric Propositions

Propositions advanced in the field of psychiatry may be examined also from the viewpoint of the sociologist. Take the example of maternal overprotection. Psychiatrically speaking, there is a clear syndrome of character traits which *may* arise from this source. Among these are unsolved conflicts with regard to the individual's tendencies toward dependence, weak superego formation, ambivalence with regard to the masculine or feminine components of the personality, and so on. That is to say, these and other traits have been repeatedly observed in persons whose mothers were overprotective. There is very little that the sociologist can infer from these observations. Schematically put, he could utilize this insight only in so far as he could be sure of two conditions: (*a*) that maternal overprotection is a phenomenon universally present (in varying degrees) in some sociologically defined groups and (*b*) that it elicits, whenever it is present, the same syndrome of responses in the male child. Yet, neither of these conditions can be verified. On the first point the sociologist does observe that the daily absence of the father from the home is a characteristic feature of urban family life and leads to a predominance of mother-child (as compared with father-child) contacts. But he *cannot* observe that the predominance of mother-child contacts leads in fact to maternal overprotection,

nor can he be sure that the physical absence of the father is synonymous with the absence of psychologically effective father-figures. From the psychiatric viewpoint another uncertainty is added on the second point, since maternal overprotection need not lead to the syndromes described above; it only makes them possible to an indeterminate degree.

It is apparently difficult to arrive at sociological propositions when we utilize psychiatric theories. Part of this difficulty arises from the nature of therapy, whose aim is to cure not to establish valid generalizations. But since the theories of psychiatry are based on the empirical evidence derived from therapy, they run the danger of retrospective determinism, and this for two reasons. First, the personal history of every patient is determined by his cumulative experiences, and these account for the formation of specific symptoms. But it is deceptive to believe that the same experiences will lead to similar symptoms in other cases. Second, the therapist sees a sample of people who are distinguished from the population by the fact that they have decided to seek his help. He has little opportunity to compare his patients with a "control group" of persons who decide that they can manage their problems without such help. Both factors, the biographical determinability of neurotic symptoms in the individual case and the exclusion of "negative" cases by the very nature of therapy, lead to a systematic bias in favor of determinism and against a recognition of the important role which choices and accidents play in the development of the human personality.[6]

The difficulty of arriving at sociological propositions on the basis of psychiatric theories cannot be attributed solely to the nature of therapy, to the way in

[6] The danger of retrospective determinism is not unique to psychiatric theory; cf. Reinhard Bendix, "Social Stratification and Political Power," *American Political Science Review*, XLVI (June, 1952), pp. 357–375.

which the evidence for these theories is gathered. It may be attributed rather to the indeterminacy of each individual's development, which Erikson has formulated in the following terms: "While it is quite clear what *must* happen to keep the baby alive (the minimum supply necessary) and what *must not* happen, lest he die or be severely stunted (the maximum frustration tolerable), there is increasing [understanding of the] leeway in regard to what *may* happen."[7] In accordance with this model Erikson has constructed eight stages of the individual's development, each of which constitutes a phase of physiological and social maturation.[8] Thus the child is confronted at each stage with the task of resolving a developmental problem. His resolution will fall somewhere between the extremes if he is to be free to proceed to the next phase. It will be *his* resolution, and the therapist can only infer what this resolution has been from a knowledge of its consequences and of the familial setting.

This conceptualization of an individual's development clarifies the way in which social forces may affect his personality. In so far as these forces can be shown to have a widespread and relatively uniform effect on family life they pose for the child the perennial problems of psychological development in a special way. If, for example, the child is repeatedly shamed in his first efforts at independence, or autonomy, and if the same

is true for a large number of children, then we may say that these children have "to come to terms" with this problem or challenge of their familial environment. Some children will fail in their efforts to develop autonomy in such an environment, others will succeed. But it should be apparent that we cannot infer the response of the whole group from a knowledge of the challenge or from a knowledge of these who failed.[9] Yet the propositions of psychiatry concentrate on those that fail;[10] they deal with the origin of neurotic symptoms. These symptoms are an individual's way of expressing and disguising his failure to solve successfully the problems of shame, guilt, doubt, and so on which are posed for him at different stages of his development. They are evidence of an impairment in a person's ability to relate himself to others.

It is apparent that this characterization of propositions in psychiatry is evaluative. It implies that a person's full ability to relate himself to others is normal and good, while his failure to do so is neurotic and bad.[11] My point is not to criticize

[7] Erik H. Erikson, *Childhood and Society* (New York: W. W. Norton, 1950), p. 68. The author adds to this that "culture" largely determines the actual methods of child-rearing, which the members of the society "consider workable and insist on calling necessary." The later discussion will show why I do not share this view.

[8] *Ibid.*, Ch. vii. The stages are called: trust vs. basic mistrust, autonomy vs. shame and doubt, initiative vs. guilt, industry vs. inferiority, identity vs. role diffusion, intimacy vs. isolation, generativity vs. stagnation, ego integrity vs. despair.

[9] It is often easier to anticipate the pathological rather than the nonpathological resolutions, and because of this "pathological" bias the theories of psychiatry have frequently underestimated the uncertainty or indeterminacy of the individual's development. For an interesting attempt to incorporate this perspective in the "psychiatric image of man" see Alexander Mitscherlich, *Freiheit und Unfreiheit in der Krankheit* (Hamburg: Classen and Goverts, 1946).

[10] Cf. the critical evaluation of modern psychiatry by Jean MacFarlane in "Looking Ahead in the Fields of Orthopsychiatric Research," *American Journal of Orthopsychiatry*, XX (January, 1950), 85–91.

[11] These judgments can be stated in a factual manner, and they have a specific empirical content. A person's ability to relate himself to others and his manner of doing so are observable facts. The value element enters in when a given action is judged in terms of its meaning for, and its effect on, a per-

this value judgment but to stress that it is indispensable in therapy and psychiatric theory. Every theory is based on some judgment of relevance. It is such a judgment which prompts the psychiatrist to analyze the psychodynamic factors which have led to the impairment of a person's relatedness to others. Other disciplines have other value orientations which also emerge out of the order of facts with which they are concerned. Thus, the sociologist's approach to the value orientation of the psychiatrist would be to question the distinction between normal and neurotic. He would question it, because he denies its sociological, though not its psychiatric, relevance. That is to say, the psychiatrist could easily persuade his sociological colleague that the impairment or distortion of an individual's ability to relate himself to others is evidence of his neurosis. But the sociologist would consider that the neurotic symptoms which may drive a person to see a therapist are also evidence of his creative or destructive effect on the society of which he is a member.[12] The sociologist would view a person's inability to relate himself to others as of interest only if it were a group phenomenon. And, if it is a group phenomenon, then the question arises whether psychodynamic factors can be cited to account for it.

***

son's relations to others. And such judgments are made as a result of the patient's decision to request therapy in order to improve his relations to others.

[12] I am not suggesting that therapy necessarily kills a person's creative ability in the effort of making him "normal," though the problem is frequently discussed in professional circles. It is interesting, however, that this discussion often ends with the assertion that a person's creative ability which is adversely affected by his therapy was probably not worth preserving. At any rate, psychiatrists are certainly troubled by this problem.

III. Cultural Patterns and the Response of the Individual

This analysis raises important questions for the psychological interpretation of cultural patterns. Retrospective interpretations of *individual* case histories are probably quite reliable. But generalizations based on them imply that the difficulties which have created neurotic symptoms in the one case will do the same in most cases. In fact we know that they will not. Nevertheless, these generalizations of psychiatry are often applied to large numbers of people in an attempt to explain cultural phenomena in psychodynamic terms. Nazi propaganda, for example, placed a decided emphasis on such traits as will power, endurance, hardness, discipline, devotion, hard work, sacrifice, and many others. Kecskemeti and Leites have shown that these traits correspond to the "compulsive character" type of the psychoanalytic literature.[13] But how are we to interpret such a correspondence? The authors of the article here examined state the following reservations: One cannot say (1) that psychological causes (especially infantile experiences) alone or even primarily have caused the widespread development of compulsive traits among Germans; (2) how propaganda themes are related to psychological traits which are "fully ascertainable only in the psychoanalytic interview situation"; [14] (3) that the compulsive themes of Nazi propaganda and the inferred frequency of compulsive personality traits in the German population are valid for the periods before or after the Nazi regime; (4) that "major transformations of the political structure of Germany are incompatible

[13] Paul Kecskemeti and Nathan Leites, "Some Psychological Hypotheses on Nazi Germany," *Journal of Social Psychology*, XXVI (1947), 141–183; XXVII (February, 1948), 91–117; (May, 1948), 241–270; (August, 1948), 141–164.
[14] *Ibid.*, XXVI (1947), 142.

with present (and frequently compulsive) character structures"; [15] (5) that there were no other (than the compulsive) types of character structure among the adherents or the opponents of the Nazis.[16] Considering these reservations, we can only say that Nazi propaganda will have a special appeal to people whose personalities predispose them to accept its slogans. The authors make several educated guesses concerning those segments of the German people most likely to exhibit the syndrome of the compulsive personality.

> It may be safely said that it was more widely diffused among *lower middle class* persons than among persons higher up or lower down in the class system; among *males* than among females; among those who had been adolescents *before or around* 1933 than among those who were so afterwards; in *Northern Germany* than in Southern Germany; among Protestants than among Catholics; among city people than among country people; among *political followers* than among political leaders.[17]

Yet, despite these careful reservations, the authors attribute a character structure to a group of people who adhere to a set of cultural symbols. This character structure *would* correspond to these symbols *only if* all the personal histories of these people had actually led to the development of compulsive traits. That is to say, the authors substitute psychological traits for cultural symbols because it is *logically*

[15] *Ibid.,* p. 143.

[16] These reservations are listed in the introductory section of the article by Kecskemeti and Leites, and others are added which concern the provisional character of psychoanalytic findings in the field of compulsion neurosis. I should add that this article differs strikingly from most other writings in this field in terms of the care with which these reservations are stipulated.

[17] Kecskemeti and Leites, *op. cit.* p. 143.

possible to specify an analogous psychological syndrome for this, as for every other, set of cultural symbols which we could name.[18]

On the surface, this is a purely logical point. Yet, to attribute to psychological disposition what is in fact the result of economic pressure, political power, or historical tradition has a number of unexpected results. If we say that a cultural complex, e.g., the Nazi propaganda of the "strenuous life," attracts certain social groups whose members have compulsive personalities, we imply that people respond to cultural symbols because of their character structure. For instance, people with compulsive character traits will respond favorably to propaganda praising such traits. This statement implies that specific neurotic symptoms of individuals are widespread and therefore both cause and consequence of certain cultural symbols. Hence neurotic symptoms are here treated as an attribute of a culture. Certain symbols of a culture (e.g., Nazi propaganda) are the basis on which the character structure of particular groups in German society is inferred, and this inference is then used to show why the symbols had such wide appeal.

This circular reasoning rests on the assumption that people act as they do because their personality traits predispose them to do so. Indeed, if this could be proved, it would follow that a person's participation in a culture by itself reveals his character structure. Yet, people may respond favorably to such cultural symbols as propaganda slogans because of fear, apathy, acquiescence, greed, and many other reasons *in spite of,* as well as *because of,* their psychological dispo-

[18] This has incidentally the added fascination of personalizing cultural abstractions, which makes these abstractions much more plausible in an intuitive way; cf. the typology of cultures in Ruth Benedict, *Patterns of Culture* (New York: Penguin Books, Inc., 1946), Ch. iii, which goes back to the work of Nietzsche and Spengler.

sition.[19] This assertion may appear as a logical contradiction at first glance. How can it be said that people respond favorably to a slogan despite, rather than because of, their psychological disposition? Of necessity every response reflects that disposition, including responses to cultural symbols. But their meaning for the individual is not revealed in the responses themselves. Both persons of compulsive disposition and those of permissive disposition may respond favorably to the slogans of the "strenuous life," the one because he agrees with them, the other because he has to. Now the second person, who feels forced to respond as he does, will be affected by his action; it is certainly revealing that he complies rather than revolts or emigrates. *But for our purposes it is sufficient to state that he has responded favorably, although his psychological disposition would prompt him to respond unfavorably.* If cultural symbols are analyzed in terms of psychological analogies, then we obscure this characteristic disjunction between the symbol pattern of a culture and the ordinary lives of the people who are only partially involved with the historic traditions, the institutions, and the creative

[19] And those who do respond to these symbols in accordance with a compulsive disposition do not necessarily respond in the same way. There are significant differences, for example, between the responses of a Prussian Junker, a Nazi functionary, a Bavarian separatist, and a German Communist, yet all may have compulsive personalities. And, even if we take only Nazi functionaries, their differences in rank within the party would probably account for significant differences in their response to the Nazi slogans of the "strenuous life." Hannah Arendt has pointed out that cynicism with regard to the professed ideals of a totalitarian movement is great among persons who hold high rank in such a movement, while these ideals are believed most fervently by the average members or sympathizers. See Arendt, *The Origins of Totalitarianism* (New York: Harcourt, Brace and Co., 1951), pp. 369–371.

activities that give rise to these symbol patterns. If the symbols of a culture are taken as a clue to the characteristic personality types of its participants, then we underestimate the incongruity between institutions, culture patterns, and the psychological habitus of a people and we ignore an important source of social change.

IV. The Psychological Insignificance of Compliant Behavior

Modern psychiatry in all its various schools asserts that the personality of an individual reveals an internally consistent pattern of responses to the most varied stimuli and that this pattern is in large part an outgrowth of early experience. This statement is intended to be true of all men. If it is to be utilized in sociology we would have to know: (*a*) what cultural or social conditions existed at a given time; (*b*) that these conditions have had a pervasive effect on the early familial environment of children; (*c*) that it is reasonable to attribute certain widespread personality syndromes in a culture to this configuration of the familial environment. Now psychiatric theory supports the view that a configuration of the familial environment tends to perpetuate itself from generation to generation; that is, parents treat their children in response to their own childhood experience, and so on for successive generations.[20] But before we can accept

[20] This assertion is not without ambiguity. Parents treat their children in response to their own childhood experience, but it does not follow that this response is one of simple imitation. Parents might also try to raise their children contrary to the way they were raised themselves. However, psychiatrists would contend that the overt treatment of children, whatever it may be, would always reveal the unresolved conflicts of the parents' own childhood experience. In this sense the psychodynamic significance of both imitation and opposition would be the same.

this view of the relation between society and personality formation, a number of questions need to be answered.

It is obviously difficult to understand the effect which given social conditions have on family life and, especially, on the way in which parents treat their children. The impact of specific social events always comes "too late" really to affect family life, at any rate from a psychiatric point of view. Schematically put, an overwhelming event occurs in year x which affects all families. But those people whose personalities are already formed (i.e., the parents) will not be changed profoundly, because their response to the event is predetermined by the familial environment of their own childhood. And the children will not be changed profoundly either, because they will take their cue from their parents' response to the event.[21]

These considerations make it appear doubtful that changes in family life occur as a direct response to catastrophic social experiences.[22] And recent historical ex-

perience demonstrates, I think, that this view is mistaken. Take, for example, the authoritarian pattern of German family life, which was mentioned previously. Several attempts have been made to "explain" the rise of naziism in Germany by reference to the German national character.[23] Because naziism was authoritarian, it was related to other authoritarian aspects of German society such as the so-called "authoritarian" family. Yet this entire literature makes no mention of the fact that the Nazis took a very dim view of the political reliability of the authoritarian family pattern. They organized children into para-military formations. They subjected them (or they encouraged their submission) to authority figures which were outside the family and could be controlled politically. And they used the children systematically to spy on their parents in order to control children and parents alike. It may well be that the Nazis effected a culmination of that generational conflict which had been in the making in Germany since before the first World War. But if that is the fact, the result has been to undermine the authoritarian family pattern, not to strengthen it or to rely upon it.[24] This

[21] Cf. the instructive studies of Anna Freud, who has shown that separation from the parents had a more traumatic effect on the children during the London blitz than the direct experience with death and destruction and that the effect of the latter depended on the response of the parents to the same experiences. See Anna Freud and Dorothy T. Buelingham, *War and Children and Infants without Families* (New York: International Universities Press, 1944). A similar point concerning the lack of effect of political catastrophe is made in G. W. Allport *et al.*, "Personality under Social Catastrophe: Ninety Life Histories of the Nazi Revolution," in C. Kluckhohn and H. A. Murray (eds.), *Personality in Nature, Society and Culture* (New York: A. A. Knopf, 1948), pp. 347–366. See also the earlier monographs of the Social Science Research Council on the superficial effects of the depression on family life.

[22] The origin of observed characteristics of present-day family life has sometimes been inferred from certain social conditions which are known historically. See, e.g., Erikson,

op. cit., pp. 244–265, where the author imputes the American mother's encouragement of a competitive spirit in her son to the conditions of the frontier, when self-reliance was an essential condition. This imputation is mistaken, and a number of other historical explanations would do equally well. After all, there are a large number of factors other than the frontier which have contributed to the competitiveness of American life.

[23] A survey of these and similar studies is contained in Otto Klineberg, *Tensions Affecting International Understanding* (New York: Social Science Research Council, 1950), pp. 36–46.

[24] The leaders of totalitarian movements apparently regard the family as a seedbed of resistance, even if it is of an authoritarian pattern, and we cannot suppose that millions of German parents suddenly decided to abdicate their authority over their children.

evidence suggests that the authoritarian family stood opposed to a major social and political change and that it cannot be cited as a reason for that change. Far from explaining the rise of fascism in Germany, the authoritarian family pattern stands out as a bulwark against it.[25]

The fact is that this authoritarian family pattern has been undermined as a result of the experiences of parents and children under the Nazi regime. And once the traditional pattern of family life

is seriously disrupted—as a result of major historical changes—one may expect the emergence not of one but of *many* new patterns.[26] The preceding discussion of the relation between society and the pattern of family life leads to the rather traditional view that the family is a conservative element which tends to stand opposed to major changes in the society.[27] People will accommodate themselves to these changes as best they can, but they will resist as long as possible any transformation of their familial way of life. If such transformation is forced upon the family, nevertheless, then its members will respond in a variety of ways which will depend on local conditions, on the development of fashions, on individual idiosyncrasies, and so on. Hence there is no reason to expect that the Nazi regime, for example, has had a clearly discernible effect on German family life other than the destruction of its traditional patterns.

This view is clearly not in keeping with some of the most widely accepted theories of "social psychiatry." The most

---

There is evidence, on the other hand, to indicate that the Nazi movement was in part an outgrowth of the many youth movements, which had developed since the beginning of the twentieth century, and which were inspired by an anti-bourgeois, anti-authoritarian ideology. Of course, the psychiatrist would regard this anti-authoritarianism as evidence of the authoritarian personality, which illustrates once more that his level of abstraction differs from that of the sociologist. It illustrates also that the psychiatrist can "prove anything" when he deals with groups rather than individuals, because his generalizations are not checked by negative cases.

[25] The organization of German youth under Communist leadership in East Germany is a continuation of the Nazi pattern under different auspices. The political *Gleichschaltung* of a reluctant adult population is being accomplished by making their children enthusiastic supporters of the regime. The regime offers these young people occupational opportunities by depriving their elders of their jobs through the imputation of political unreliability. In view of these methods of the Nazis and the Communists it is not illuminating to suggest that the "authoritarian family pattern" made Germans yield readily to totalitarian rule, even though this pattern by itself may not have contributed to the rise of totalitarianism. We do not know that "permissive family patterns" enable people to resist a dictatorial rule effectively, at least for a time; we do know that it would be easy to exploit the conflict between the young and the old generation for political purposes in a society in which age does not carry much prestige anyway.

[26] The recent history of child-rearing practices illustrates the rapid change in fashions which may occur once traditional methods are abandoned. (See Clark E. Vincent, "Trend in Infant Care Ideas," *Child Development*, XXII [September, 1951], 199–209.)

[27] Social reformers for the last 3,000 years have held the view that marriage and the family are antisocial in that they prevent a man from doing his duty. It is characteristic of Plato and the ascetic tradition beginning with Jesus and the Apostle Paul and reflected in the views of the socialists of the nineteenth century. Fourier, for example, held that each man considered himself justified in any swindle because he was working for his wife and children. Cf. Alexander Gray, *The Socialist Tradition: Moses to Lenin* (London: Longmans, Green and Co., 1947 ed.), pp. 191–192. A similar view is expressed, though on different grounds, in Sigmund Freud, *Civilization and Its Discontents* (London: Hogarth Press, 1937), 65–77.

clear-cut statement of these theories may be found in the work of Erich Fromm.

> In studying the psychological reactions of a social group we deal with the character structure of the members of the group, that is, of individual persons; we are interested, however, not in the peculiarities by which these persons differ from each other, but in that part of their character structure that is common to most members of the group. We can call this character the *social character*.[28]

This formulation makes it apparent that "social character" is a scientific fiction. Is it a useful fiction? The ideas and actions which a group of people have in common are described in the terminology of psychiatry and are thereby made to appear as the traits of an individual person. The conventional patterns of behavior which people share are necessarily "superficial," from the standpoint of psychiatry. Therefore, the theory of "social character" must maintain, if it is to be consistent, that the shared conventions of a culture are in fact indicative of the character structure of a people. This is indeed what Fromm asserts:

> If we look at social character from the standpoint of its function in the social process, we have to start with the statement that has been made with regard to its function for the individual that by adapting himself to social conditions man develops those traits that make him *desire* to act as he *has* to act. . . . In other words, *the social character internalizes external necessities and thus harnesses human energy for the task of a given economic and social system*.[29]

I believe this view to be erroneous. The evidence of friction between the individual and the external necessities to which

[28] Erich Fromm, *Escape from Freedom* (New York: Farrar and Rinehart, 1942), p. 277.

[29] *Ibid.*, pp. 283, 284.

he is continually subjected does not make it appear probable that people desire to act as they have to act. Fromm is, in fact, aware of this friction, but he merely suggests that people "internalize external necessities" *in the long run,* even if they fail to do so in the short run.[30]

But the friction between the social environment and the prevailing pattern of family life cannot be dismissed so easily. People do *not* always or even eventually desire to act as they have to act. It is quite possible that external necessities are *not* internalized but are endured, even in the long run. Instead, I submit the view that the external necessities of a country may acquire distinctive traits and may impose distinctive psychological burdens on the people. I believe it is to these burdens that we refer, somewhat vaguely, when we talk about a "social" or a "national" character. The concluding section of this essay is devoted to a discussion of this approach.

V. Culture and Personality Reconsidered

It may be useful to recapitulate the preceding discussion. Psychiatric theory has emphasized the importance of childhood for the formation of the adult personality. It has emphasized also the tendency of familial patterns to perpetuate themselves from generation to generation. It is probable (*a*) that catastrophic events as such will not have fundamental psychological effects and (*b*) that historical changes which transform the prevailing patterns of family life are likely to destroy them rather than to establish new patterns.[31] People tend to resist major

[30] *Ibid.*, pp. 284–285.

[31] As applied to the German case this would mean that the destructive effect of the Nazi experience on German family life is of much greater interest and relevance (for theoretical reasons) than is the supposed contribution of German family life to the rise of fascism.

changes of their character structure and of their familial way of life. Many social and cultural changes are possible without major psychological transformations.

But, although it will not do to attribute a character structure to a cultural pattern, it is still possible to investigate the relation between these patterns and the psychological responses of large numbers of people. The traditions of a country, its institutions and ideologies, the experiences of its people with war and peace, with depression and prosperity, *have* significant psychological repercussions. How shall we interpret these if we do not resort to analogies from the psychodynamics of the individual?

The specific example chosen previously may serve as an illustration. It is probably true that Germans are more authoritarian than Americans are. But this statement refers to the whole complex of traditions and institutions in the two countries. There is no evidence to date that the *proportion* of people with compulsive traits is significantly larger among Germans than among Americans. People may be compulsive in their adherence to various forms of conduct, whether the prevailing culture pattern is authoritarian or otherwise.[32] But in each society people confront very distinct problems with which they have to cope, e.g., it is certain that questions of authority present different problems in Germany and the United States. It is merely a sophisticated ethnocentrism, which ignores this situational difference and which applies to the people of one society standards of mental health pertaining to the people of another society. Hence we must guard carefully against the fallacy of attributing to character structure what may be a part of the social environment. And we must resist the temptation of attributing to the people of another culture a psychological uniformity which we are unable to discover in our own.[33]

In terms of the preceding discussion I believe it to be more in keeping with the observed incongruity between institutions and psychological habitus to assume that all cultures of Western civilization have the same range of personality types. The differences between these cultures must then be accounted for at a level of abstraction with which the psychiatrist is not equipped to deal. In his study of a Mexican community Oscar Lewis has suggested recently that we might call this psychological dimension the "public personality" which is characteristic of a society.[34] When we study different societies or the same society over time, we notice differences in conventional conduct and in the expecta-

[32] The literature which deals with these matters is noticeably ambiguous when it treats the conventionality of American life, which is so strongly anti-authoritarian, since conventionality is quite compatible with compulsive personality traits. By the same token, writers have often ignored the strong individualism of German life, which is combined with being "authoritarian." This confusion is rather marked in Fromm, *op cit.,* pp. 240–256, but absent from Adolf Lowe, *The Price of Liberty* (London: Hogarth Press, 1937).

[33] Because of this we should attempt to discover in each society the diversity of responses which is hidden beneath the uniformity of conventional behavior that is "apparent" to the outside observer. Cases in point are two recent books on Germany: Bertram Schaffner's *Father Land* (New York: Columbia University Press, 1948) and David Rodnick's *Postwar Germans* (New Haven: Yale University Press, 1948). One author finds that the father is dominant, the child insecure and starved for affection; the other finds that the mother is dominant, the child secure and much loved. It is notable that both authors find it easy to relate their conflicting data to the "authoritarian pattern." Further research along these lines might be improved methodologically, but I doubt whether it would reveal a more consistent pattern of family life than these two studies taken together.

[34] Oscar Lewis, *Life in a Mexican Village: Tepoztlan Restudied* (Urbana: University of Illinois Press, 1951), pp. 422–426.

tions with which people in a society regard one another. For example, it is probable that in the United States among middle-class circles intensive, lifelong friendships are relatively rare compared with some European countries. Now this fact, *if* it is a fact, *could* be related to many aspects of American middle-class culture. Great mobility, a large number of relatively casual personal contacts, the degree to which the expression of personal feelings is restrained, the relative absence of social distance between people in different walks of life—these and many other aspects of the culture discourage intensive friendships between people of the same sex.[35] This fact and the conventional optimism and friendliness of interpersonal relations which is its related opposite are aspects of the "public personality" in the United States which differ from the character structure of the individual. They refer to a "public personality" in the sense that conventional behavior patterns (the type of conduct which we engage in because others expect it of us) make demands upon the emotions of the individual. I believe that two conclusions follow from this analysis.

The first is that we must avoid the idea, which Fromm has suggested, that men "desire to act as they have to act." It does not follow, for example, that Americans could not form intensive friendships under other circumstances; and the rela-

tive absence of such relations probably exacts its emotional toll. Nor is it convincing to argue, as Fromm seems to do, that Americans have "adjusted" to this situation and now do not want the kind of friendship which the circumstances of American life seem to have discouraged. Nor does it follow, finally, that the absence of friendship and the prevalence of friendliness are total liabilities, since this pattern makes for considerable ease in interpersonal relations, though it may give rise to a feeling of emptiness among a minority of especially sensitive people.[36] All this need not mean that men never desire to act as they have to act. It implies, rather, that men accommodate themselves to their circumstances and to social change as best they can. The conflicts which frequently arise between their desires and their conduct are reflected in the psychological tensions of everyday living. Different individuals will show greater or less tolerance for them, depending on their character structure as this is related to childhood experience. Hence, particular social changes will not lead to a determinable psychological response among masses of people. Rather, such changes will impose particular emotional burdens which some people can tolerate more easily than others, and those who can will have a greater opportunity for action.[37]

---

[35] The external factors which might account for the absence of friendship, such as distance and the infrequency of seeing the same friend often enough in a country of great geographic mobility, do not really explain much. My father, who was a lawyer in Germany, maintained a friendship with a fellow-student over a period of over sixty years, with an occasional exchange of letters, although this friend was a medieval historian, although they did not meet more than six times during this whole period, although they lived at a considerable distance most of their lives, and despite the interruption caused by an official (Nazi) prohibition of their correspondence.

[36] Much impressionistic evidence seems to point to a reversal of this pattern in the "public personality" that characterizes German life, namely, intense friendships but an absence of friendliness and a considerable distance in the casual contacts of everyday life. See, e.g., David Rodnick, *op. cit.*, pp. 1–8. See also the striking discussion of Kurt Lewin, *Resolving Social Conflicts* (New York: Harper and Bros., 1948), pp. 3–33, where the author contrasts these conventional patterns (in the United States and Germany) in terms of the different degrees to which the individual's privacy is accessible to another person.

[37] As an example of this type of analysis, though it is not consistently carried through,

This interpretation leads to a second conclusion. We can infer the emotional problems with which masses of people were faced as a result of specific historical experiences; we cannot infer the emotional meaning of their response. An example from the preceding discussion may make this point clearer. The superficial friendliness of interpersonal relations was discussed as a characteristic of American middle-class culture. This conventional behavior pattern which makes superficial contacts between people easy and pleasant, while it makes deeply personal relationships appear difficult and full of risk, does not reveal what meaning it has for the individual. There will be those who take it seriously and make it a way of

---

I cite Norbert Elias, *Ueber den Prozess der Zivilisation* (Basel: Haus zum Falken, 1942) in which the author shows strikingly the emotional burdens which frequent exposure to physical aggression imposed on the nobility in early medieval France. The implication of this analysis is that only those were successful in this struggle who were equal to it emotionally. Elias shows that the concentration of power in the hands of the king forced the nobility, if it wanted favors from the court, to adopt the manners of polite society. But it does not follow, as Elias seems to imply, that the people who developed these polite manners at court were somehow the same people who had, not long before, excelled in physical aggression. Rather, the new circumstances of the court favored those who excelled at the subtleties of courtly behavior, while those who excelled in aggression were kept away from the court, or did not attend, and were unsuccessful in the supercilious maneuvers of a court society when they did attend. In this sense it is possible to speak of psychological aptitudes which given historical conditions probably favored without implying that those who were ill-adapted emotionally disappeared because they now desired to act as they had to act. It is more probable that they tried to act as they had to act, without desiring it and without being too good at it either.

life, for example, the "typical" salesman or public relations man. There will be others who respond to this friendliness with cynicism. Others yet will enjoy being friendly but will not take it seriously. People who despair of its superficiality will seek intensive friendship, while others really enjoy the ease in casual personal contacts. Indeed, it would be rewarding to analyze the variety of responses which this behavior pattern elicits. But, for our purposes, it is sufficient to remark that large numbers of people have certain problems and certain conventional behavior patterns in common; they *do not* make a common response to these problems or conventions.

When we analyze the "social character" of a society, we are in fact characterizing the emotional problems with which the people are typically faced and which arise out of the institutions and historical traditions of that society. These institutions and traditions always elicit certain conventions, but they also elicit a wide range of responses to the conventions themselves, roughly corresponding to the range of personality types. We should therefore be properly sensitized to the emotional burdens *and* opportunities, to the psychological liabilities *and* assets, which every culture pattern entails. And we should learn to recognize that the traditions and institutions of every society present each of its members with peculiar emotional problems which he must resolve for himself in keeping with his psychological disposition. Hence, when we contrast one culture with another we refer to the typical psychological burdens which the demand for conformity imposes on the people. And if we attribute to these people a "social character" or a "national character" or a "basic personality type," we simply confuse the response with the stimulus and attribute to the people a uniformity of response which is contrary to all observed facts.

2 · Social Reductionism

THE OVERSOCIALIZED CONCEPTION
OF MAN IN MODERN SOCIOLOGY

by Dennis H. Wrong

Gertrude Stein, bed-ridden with a fatal illness, is reported to have suddenly muttered, "What, then, is the answer?" Pausing, she raised her head, murmured, "But what is the question?" and died. Miss Stein presumably was pondering the ultimate meaning of human life, but her brief final soliloquy has a broader and humbler relevance. Its point is that answers are meaningless apart from questions. If we forget the questions, even while remembering the answers, our knowledge of them will subtly deteriorate, becoming rigid, formal, and catechistic as the sense of indeterminacy, of rival possibilities, implied by the very putting of a question is lost.

Social theory must be seen primarily as a set of answers to questions we ask of social reality. If the initiating questions are forgotten, we readily misconstrue the task of theory and the answers previous thinkers have given become narrowly confining conceptual prisons, degenerating into little more than a special, professional vocabulary applied to situations and events that can be described with equal or greater precision in ordinary language. Forgetfulness of the questions that are the starting points of inquiry leads us to ignore the substantive assumptions "buried" in our concepts and commits us to a one-sided view of reality.

Perhaps this is simply an elaborate way of saying that sociological theory can

SOURCE: *American Sociological Review*, Vol. 26 (1961), pp. 183–193.

never afford to lose what is usually called a "sense of significance"; or, as it is sometimes put, that sociological theory must be "problem-conscious." I choose instead to speak of theory as a set of answers to questions because reference to "problems" may seem to suggest too close a linkage with social criticism or reform. My primary reason for insisting on the necessity of holding constantly in mind the questions that our concepts and theories are designed to answer is to preclude defining the goal of sociological theory as the creation of a formal body of knowledge satisfying the logical criteria of scientific theory set up by philosophers and methodologists of natural science. Needless to say, this is the way theory is often defined by contemporary sociologists.

Yet to speak of theory as interrogatory may suggest too self-sufficiently intellectual an enterprise. Cannot questions be satisfactorily answered and then forgotten, the answers becoming the assumptions from which we start in framing new questions? It may convey my view of theory more adequately to say that sociological theory concerns itself with questions arising out of problems that are inherent in the very existence of human societies and that cannot therefore be finally "solved" in the way that particular social problems perhaps can be. The "problems" theory concerns itself with are problems *for* human societies which, because of their universality, become intellectually problematic for sociological theorists.

Essentially, the historicist conception

of sociological knowledge that is central to the thought of Max Weber and has recently been ably restated by Barrington Moore, Jr. and C. Wright Mills [1] is a sound one. The most fruitful questions for sociology are always questions referring to the realities of a particular historical situation. Yet both of these writers, especially Mills, have a tendency to underemphasize the degree to which we genuinely wish and seek answers to transhistorical and universal questions about the nature of man and society. I do not, let it be clear, have in mind the formalistic quest for social "laws" or "universal propositions," nor the even more formalistic effort to construct all-encompassing "conceptual schemes." Moore and Mills are rightly critical of such efforts. I am thinking of such questions as, "How are men capable of uniting to form enduring societies in the first place?"; "Why and to what degree is change inherent in human societies and what are the sources of change?"; "How is man's animal nature domesticated by society?"

Such questions—and they are existential as well as intellectual questions—are the *raison d'être* of social theory. They were asked by men long before the rise of sociology. Sociology itself is an effort, under new and unprecedented historical conditions, to find novel answers to them. They are not questions which lend themselves to successively more precise answers as a result of cumulative empirical research, for they remain eternally problematic. Social theory is necessarily an interminable dialogue. "True understanding," Hannah Arendt has written, "does not tire of interminable dialogue and 'vicious circles' because it trusts that imagination will eventually catch at least

a glimpse of the always frightening light of truth." [2]

I wish briefly to review the answers modern sociological theory offers to one such question, or rather to one aspect of one question. The question may be variously phrased as, "What are the sources of social cohesion?"; or, "How is social order possible?" or, stated in social-psychological terms, "How is it that man becomes tractable to social discipline?" I shall call this question in its social-psychological aspect the "Hobbesian question" and in its more strictly sociological aspect the "Marxist question." The Hobbesian question asks how men are capable of the guidance by social norms and goals that makes possible an enduring society, while the Marxist question asks how, assuming this capability, complex societies manage to regulate and restrain destructive conflicts between groups. Much of our current theory offers an oversocialized view of man in answering the Hobbesian question and an overintegrated view of society in answering the Marxist question.

A number of writers have recently challenged the overintegrated view of society in contemporary theory. In addition to Moore and Mills, the names of Bendix, Coser, Dahrendorf, and Lockwood come to mind.[3] My intention, therefore, is to

[1] Barrington Moore, Jr., *Political Power and Social Theory,* Cambridge: Harvard University Press, 1958; C. Wright Mills, *The Sociological Imagination,* New York: Oxford University Press, 1959.

[2] Hannah Arendt, "Understanding and Politics," *Partisan Review,* 20 (July–August, 1953), p. 392. For a view of social theory close to the one adumbrated in the present paper, see Theodore Abel, "The Present Status of Social Theory," *American Sociological Review,* 17 (April, 1952), pp. 156–164.

[3] Reinhard Bendix and Bennett Berger, "Images of Society and Problems of Concept Formation in Sociology," in Llewellyn Gross, editor, *Symposium on Sociological Theory,* Evanston, Ill.: Row, Petersen and Co., 1959, pp. 92–118; Lewis A. Coser, *The Functions of Social Conflict,* Glencoe, Ill.: The Free Press, 1956; Ralf Dahrendorf, "Out of Utopia: Towards a Re-Orientation of

concentrate on the answers to the Hobbesian question in an effort to disclose the oversocialized view of man which they seem to imply.

Since my view of theory is obviously very different from that of Talcott Parsons and has, in fact, been developed in opposition to his, let me pay tribute to his recognition of the importance of the Hobbesian question—the "problem of order," as he calls it—at the very beginning of his first book, *The Structure of Social Action*.[4] Parsons correctly credits Hobbes with being the first thinker to see the necessity of explaining why human society is not a "war of all against all"; why, if man is simply a gifted animal, men refrain from unlimited resort to fraud and violence in pursuit of their ends and maintain a stable society at all. There is even a sense in which, as Coser and Mills have both noted,[5] Parsons' entire work represents an effort to solve the Hobbesian problem of order. His solution, however, has tended to become precisely the kind of elaboration of a set of answers in abstraction from questions that is so characteristic of contemporary sociological theory.

We need not be greatly concerned with Hobbes' own solution to the problem of order he saw with such unsurpassed clarity. Whatever interest his famous theory of the origin of the state may still hold for political scientists, it is clearly inadequate as an explanation of the origin of society. Yet the pattern as opposed to the details of Hobbes' thought bears closer examination.

The polar terms in Hobbes' theory are the state of nature, where the war of all against all prevails, and the authority of Leviathan, created by social contract. But the war of all against all is not simply effaced with the creation of political authority: it remains an ever-present potentiality in human society, at times quiescent, at times erupting into open violence. Whether Hobbes believed that the state of nature and the social contract were ever historical realities—and there is evidence that he was not that simple-minded and unsociological, even in the seventeenth century—is unimportant; the whole tenor of his thought is to see the war of all against all and Leviathan dialectically, as coexisting and interacting opposites.[6] As R. G. Collingwood has observed, "According to Hobbes . . . *a body politic is a dialectical thing*, a Heraclitean world in which at any given time there is a negative element."[7] The first secular social theorist in the history of Western thought, and one of the first clearly to discern and define the problem of order in human society long before Darwinism made awareness of it a commonplace, Hobbes was a dialectical thinker who refused to separate answers from questions, solutions to society's enduring problems from the conditions creating the problems.

What is the answer of contemporary so-

___

Sociological Analysis," *American Journal of Sociology*, 64 (September, 1958), pp. 115–127; and *Class and Class Conflict in Industrial Society*, Stanford, Calif.: Stanford University Press, 1959; David Lockwood, "Some Remarks on The Social System," *British Journal of Sociology*, 7 (June, 1956), pp. 134–146.

[4] Talcott Parsons, *The Structure of Social Action*, New York: McGraw-Hill Book Co., 1937, pp. 89–94.

[5] Coser, *op. cit.*, p. 21; Mills, *op. cit.*, p. 44.

[6] A recent critic of Parsons follows Hobbes in seeing the relation between the normative order in society and what he calls "the substratum of social action" and other sociologists have called the "factual order" as similar to the relation between the war of all against all and the authority of the state. David Lockwood writes: "The existence of the normative order . . . is in one very important sense inextricably bound up with potential conflicts of interest over scarce resources . . . ; the very existence of a normative order mirrors the continual potentiality of conflict." Lockwood, *op. cit.*, p. 137.

[7] R. G. Collingwood, *The New Leviathan*, Oxford: The Clarendon Press, 1942, p. 183.

ciological theory to the Hobbesian question? There are two main answers, each of which has come to be understood in a way that denies the reality and meaningfulness of the question. Together they constitute a model of human nature, sometimes clearly stated, more often implicit in accepted concepts, that pervades modern sociology. The first answer is summed up in the notion of the "internalization of social norms." The second, more commonly employed or assumed in empirical research, is the view that man is essentially motivated by the desire to achieve a positive image of self by winning acceptance or status in the eyes of others.

The following statement represents, briefly and broadly, what is probably the most influential contemporary sociological conception—and dismissal—of the Hobbesian problem: "To a modern sociologist imbued with the conception that action follows institutionalized patterns, opposition of individual and common interests has only a very limited relevance or is thoroughly unsound." [8] From this

[8] Francis X. Sutton and others, *The American Business Creed*, Cambridge: Harvard University Press, 1956, p. 304. I have cited this study and, on several occasions, textbooks and fugitive articles rather than better-known and directly theoretical writings because I am just as concerned with what sociological concepts and theories are taken to mean when they are actually used in research, teaching, and introductory exposition as with their elaboration in more self-conscious and explicitly theoretical discourse. Since the model of human nature I am criticizing is partially implicit and "buried" in our concepts, cruder and less qualified illustrations are as relevant as the formulations of leading theorists. I am also aware that some older theorists, notably Cooley and MacIver, were shrewd and worldly-wise enough to reject the implication that man is ever fully socialized. Yet they failed to develop competing images of man which were concise and systematic enough to counter the appeal of the oversocialized models.

writer's perspective, the problem is an unreal one: human conduct is totally shaped by common norms or "institutionalized patterns." Sheer ignorance must have led people who were unfortunate enough not to be modern sociologists to ask, "How is order possible?" A thoughtful bee or ant would never inquire, "How is the social order of the hive or ant-hill possible?" for the opposite of that order is unimaginable when the instinctive endowment of the insects ensures its stability and built-in harmony between "individual and common interests." Human society, we are assured, is not essentially different, although conformity and stability are there maintained by non-instinctive processes. Modern sociologists believe that they have understood these processes and that they have not merely answered but disposed of the Hobbesian question, showing that, far from expressing a valid intimation of the tensions and possibilities of social life, it can only be asked out of ignorance.

It would be hard to find a better illustration of what Collingwood, following Plato, calls *eristical* as opposed to dialectical thinking: [9] the answer destroys the question, or rather destroys the awareness of rival possibilities suggested by the question which accounts for its having been asked in the first place. A reversal of perspective now takes place and we are moved to ask the opposite question: "How is it that violence, conflict, revolution, and the individual's sense of coercion by society manage to exist at all, if this view is correct?" [10] Whenever a one-sided answer to a question compels us to raise the opposite question, we are

[9] Collingwood, *op. cit.*, pp. 181–182.

[10] Cf. Mills, *op. cit.*, pp. 32–33, 42. While Mills does not discuss the use of the concept of internalization by Parsonian theorists, I have argued elsewhere that his view of the relation between power and values is insufficiently dialectical. See Dennis H. Wrong, "The Failure of American Sociology," *Commentary*, 28 (November, 1959), p. 378.

caught up in a dialectic of concepts which reflects a dialectic in things. But let us examine the particular processes sociologists appeal to in order to account for the elimination from human society of the war of all against all.

The Changing Meaning of Internalization

A well-known section of *The Structure of Social Action,* devoted to the interpretation of Durkheim's thought, is entitled "The Changing Meaning of Constraint." [11] Parsons argues that Durkheim originally conceived of society as controlling the individual from the outside by imposing constraints on him through sanctions, best illustrated by codes of law. But in Durkheim's later work he began to see that social rules do not "merely regulate 'externally' . . . they enter directly into the constitution of the actors' ends themselves." [12] Constraint, therefore, is more than an environmental obstacle which the actor must take into account in pursuit of his goals in the same way that he takes into account physical laws: it becomes internal, psychological, and self-imposed as well. Parsons developed this view that social norms are constitutive rather than merely regulative of human nature before he was influenced by psychoanalytic theory, but Freud's theory of the superego has become the source and model for the conception of the internalization of social norms that today plays so important a part in sociological thinking. The use some sociologists have made of Freud's idea, however, might well inspire an essay entitled, "The Changing Meaning of Internalization," although, in contrast to the shift in Durkheim's view of constraint, this change has been a change for the worse.

What has happened is that internali-

zation has imperceptibly been equated with "learning," or even with "habit-formation" in the simplest sense. Thus when a norm is said to have been "internalized" by an individual, what is frequently meant is that he habitually both affirms it and conforms to it in his conduct. The whole stress on inner conflict —on the tension between powerful impulses and superego controls, the behavioral outcome of which cannot be prejudged—drops out of the picture. And it is this that is central to Freud's view, for in psychoanalytic terms to say that a norm has been internalized, or introjected to become part of the superego, is to say no more than that a person will suffer guilt-feelings if he fails to live up to it, not that he will in fact live up to it in his behavior.

The relation between internalization and conformity assumed by most sociologists is suggested by the following passage from a recent, highly-praised advanced textbook: "Conformity to institutionalized norms is, of course, 'normal.' The actor, having internalized the norms, feels something like a need to conform. His conscience would bother him if he did not." [13] What is overlooked here is that the person who conforms may be even more "bothered," that is, subject to guilt and neurosis, than the person who violates what are not only society's norms but his own as well. To Freud, it is precisely the man with the strictest superego, he who has most thoroughly internalized and conformed to the norms of his society, who is most wracked with guilt and anxiety.[14]

Paul Kecskemeti, to whose discussion I owe initial recognition of the erroneous view of internalization held by sociologists, argues that the relations between

[11] Parsons, *op. cit.,* pp. 378–390.

[12] *Ibid.,* p. 382.

[13] Harry M. Johnson, *Sociology: A Systematic Introduction,* New York: Harcourt, Brace and Co., 1960, p. 22.

[14] Sigmund Freud, *Civilization and Its Discontents,* New York: Doubleday Anchor Books, 1958, pp. 80–81.

social norms, the individual's selection from them, his conduct, and his feelings about his conduct are far from self-evident. "It is by no means true," he writes, "to say that acting counter to one's own norms always or almost always leads to neurosis. One might assume that neurosis develops even more easily in persons who *never* violate the moral code they recognize as valid but repress and frustrate some strong instinctual motive. A person who 'succumbs to temptation,' feels guilt, and then 'purges himself' of his guilt in some reliable way (e.g., by confession) may achieve in this way a better balance, and be less neurotic, than a person who never violates his 'norms' and never feels conscious guilt." [15]

Recent discussions of "deviant behavior" have been compelled to recognize these distinctions between social demands, personal attitudes towards them, and actual conduct, although they have done so in a laboriously taxonomic fashion. [16] They represent, however, largely the rediscovery of what was always central to the Freudian concept of the superego. The main explanatory function of the concept is to show how people repress themselves, imposing checks on their own desires and thus turning the inner life into a battlefield of conflicting motives, no matter which side "wins," by successfully dictating overt action. So far as behavior is concerned, the psychoanalytic view of man is less deterministic than the sociological. For psychoanalysis is primarily concerned with the inner life, not with overt behavior, and its most funda-

mental insight is that the wish, the emotion, and the fantasy are as important as the act in man's experience.

Sociologists have appropriated the superego concept, but have separated it from any equivalent of the Freudian id. So long as most individuals are "socialized," that is, internalize the norms and conform to them in conduct, the Hobbesian problem is not even perceived as a latent reality. Deviant behavior is accounted for by special circumstances: ambiguous norms, anomie, role conflict, or greater cultural stress on valued goals than on the approved means for attaining them. Tendencies to deviant behavior are not seen as dialectically related to conformity. The presence in man of motivational forces bucking against the hold social discipline has over him is denied.

Nor does the assumption that internalization of norms and roles is the essence of socialization allow for a sufficient range of motives underlying conformity. It fails to allow for variable "tonicity of the superego," in Kardiner's phrase. [17] The degree to which conformity is frequently the result of coercion rather than conviction is minimized. [18] Either someone has internalized the norms, or he is "unsocialized," a feral or socially isolated child, or a psychopath. Yet Freud recognized that many people, conceivably a majority, fail to acquire superegos. "Such people," he wrote, "habitually permit themselves to do any bad deed that procures them something they want, if only they are sure that no authority will discover it or make them suffer for it; their anxiety relates only to the possibility of detection. Present-day society has to take into account the prevalence of this state of mind." [19] The last sentence suggests

---

[15] Paul Kecskemeti, *Meaning, Communication, and Value*, Chicago: University of Chicago Press, 1952, pp. 244–245.

[16] Robert Dubin, "Deviant Behavior and Social Structure: Continuities in Social Theory," *American Sociological Review*, 24 (April, 1959), pp. 147–164; Robert K. Merton, "Social Conformity, Deviation, and Opportunity Structures: A Comment on the Contributions of Dubin and Cloward," *Ibid.*, pp. 178–189.

[17] Abram Kardiner, *The Individual and His Society*, New York: Columbia University Press, 1939, pp. 65, 72–75.

[18] Mills, *op. cit.*, pp. 39–41; Dahrendorf, *Class and Class Conflict in Industrial Society*, pp. 157–165.

[19] Freud, *op. cit.*, pp. 78–79.

that Freud was aware of the decline of "inner-direction," of the Protestant conscience, about which we have heard so much lately. So let us turn to the other elements of human nature that sociologists appeal to in order to explain, or rather explain away, the Hobbesian problem.

Man the Acceptance-Seeker [20]

The superego concept is too inflexible, too bound to the past and to individual biography, to be of service in relating conduct to the pressures of the immediate situation in which it takes place. Sociologists rely more heavily therefore on an alternative notion, here stated—or, to be fair, overstated—in its baldest form: "People are so profoundly sensitive to the expectations of others that all action is inevitably guided by these expectations." [21]

[20] In many ways I should prefer to use the neater, more alliterative phrase "status-seeker." However, it has acquired a narrower meaning than I intend, particularly since Vance Packard appropriated it, suggesting primarily efforts, which are often consciously deceptive, to give the appearance of personal achievements or qualities worthy of deference. "Status-seeking" in this sense is, as Veblen perceived, necessarily confined to relatively impersonal and segmental social relationships. "Acceptance" or "approval" convey more adequately what all men are held to seek in both intimate and impersonal relations according to the conception of the self and of motivation dominating contemporary sociology and social psychology. I have, nevertheless, been unable to resist the occasional temptation to use the term "status" in this broader sense.

[21] Sutton and others, op. cit., p. 264. Robert Cooley Angell, in Free Society and Moral Crisis, Ann Arbor: University of Michigan Press, 1958, p. 34, points out the ambiguity of the term "expectations." It is used, he notes, to mean both a factual prediction and a moral imperative, e.g. "England expects every man to do his duty." But this very

Parsons' model of the "complementarity of expectations," the view that in social interaction men mutually seek approval from one another by conforming to shared norms, is a formalized version of what has tended to become a distinctive sociological perspective on human motivation. Ralph Linton states it in explicit psychological terms: "The need for eliciting favorable responses from others is an almost constant component of [personality]. Indeed, it is not too much to say that there is very little organized human behavior which is not directed toward its satisfaction in at least some degree." [22]

The insistence of sociologists on the importance of "social factors" easily leads them to stress the priority of such socialized or socializing motives in human behavior.[23] It is frequently the task of the

ambiguity is instructive, for it suggests the process by which behavior that is non-normative and perhaps even "deviant" but nevertheless "expected" in the sense of being predictable, acquires over time a normative aura and becomes "expected" in the second sense of being socially approved or demanded. Thus Parsons' "interaction paradigm" provides leads to the understanding of social change and need not be confined, as in his use of it, to the explanation of conformity and stability. But this is the subject of another paper I hope to complete shortly.

[22] Ralph Linton, The Cultural Background of Personality, New York: Appleton-Century Co., 1945, p. 91.

[23] When values are "inferred" from this emphasis and then popularized, it becomes the basis of the ideology of "groupism" extolling the virtues of "togetherness" and "belongingness" that have been attacked and satirized so savagely in recent social criticism. David Riesman and W. H. Whyte, the pioneers of this current of criticism in its contemporary guise, are both aware, as their imitators and epigoni usually are not, of the extent to which the social phenomenon they have described is the result of the diffusion and popularization of sociology itself. See on this point Robert Gutman and Dennis H. Wrong, "Riesman's Typology of Char-

sociologist to call attention to the intensity with which men desire and strive for the good opinion of their immediate associates in a variety of situations, particularly those where received theories or ideologies have unduly emphasized other motives such as financial gain, commitment to ideals, or the effects on energies and aspirations of arduous physical con-

---

acter" (forthcoming in a symposium on Riesman's work to be edited by Leo Lowenthal and Seymour Martin Lipset), and William H. Whyte, *The Organization Man,* New York: Simon and Schuster, 1956, Chs. 3–5. As a matter of fact, Riesman's "inner-direction" and "other-direction" correspond rather closely to the notions of "internalization" and "acceptance-seeking" in contemporary sociology as I have described them. Riesman even refers to his concepts initially as characterizations of "modes of conformity," although he then makes the mistake, as Robert Gutman and I have argued, of calling them character types. But his view that all men are to some degree both inner-directed and other-directed, a qualification that has been somewhat neglected by critics who have understandably concentrated on his empirical and historical use of his typology, suggests the more generalized conception of forces making for conformity found in current theory. See David Riesman, Nathan Glazer, and Reuel Denny, *The Lonely Crowd,* New York: Doubleday Anchor Books, 1953, pp. 17 ff. However, as Gutman and I have observed: "In some respects Riesman's conception of character is Freudian rather than neo-Freudian: character is defined by superego mechanisms and, like Freud in *Civilization and Its Discontents,* the socialized individual is defined by what is forbidden him rather than by what society stimulates him to do. Thus in spite of Riesman's generally sanguine attitude towards modern America, implicit in his typology is a view of society as the enemy both of individuality and of basic drive gratification, a view that contrasts with the at least potentially benign role assigned it by neo-Freudian thinkers like Fromm and Horney." Gutman and Wrong, "Riesman's Typology of Character," p. 4 (typescript).

ditions. Thus sociologists have shown that factory workers are more sensitive to the attitudes of their fellow-workers than to purely economic incentives; that voters are more influenced by the preferences of their relatives and friends than by campaign debates on the "issues"; that soldiers, whatever their ideological commitment to their nation's cause, fight more bravely when their platoons are intact and they stand side by side with their "buddies."

It is certainly not my intention to criticize the findings of such studies. My objection is that their particular selective emphasis is generalized—explicitly or, more often, implicitly—to provide apparent empirical support for an extremely one-sided view of human nature. Although sociologists have criticized past efforts to single out one fundamental motive in human conduct, the desire to achieve a favorable self-image by winning approval from others frequently occupies such a position in their own thinking. The following "theorem" has been, in fact, openly put forward by Hans Zetterberg as "a strong contender for the position as the major Motivational Theorem in sociology": [24]

> An actor's actions have a tendency to become dispositions that are related to the occurence [sic] of favored uniform evaluations of the actor and-or his actions in his action system.[25]

Now Zetterberg is not necessarily maintaining that this theorem is an accurate factual statement of the basic psychological roots of social behavior. He is, characteristically, far too self-conscious about the logic of theorizing and "concept formation" for that. He goes on to remark that "the maximization of favorable attitudes from others would thus be the counterpart in sociological theory to the

[24] Hans L. Zetterberg, "Compliant Actions," *Acta Sociologica,* 2 (1957), p. 189.
[25] *Ibid.,* p. 188.

maximization of profit in economic theory." [26] If by this it is meant that the theorem is to be understood as a heuristic rather than an empirical assumption, that sociology has a selective point of view which is just as abstract and partial as that of economics and the other social sciences, and if his view of theory as a set of logically connected formal propositions is granted provisional acceptance, I am in agreement. (Actually, the view of theory suggested at the beginning of this paper is a quite different one.)

But there is a further point to be made. Ralf Dahrendorf has observed that structural-functional theorists do not "claim that order *is based on* a general consensus of values, but that it *can be conceived of in terms of* such consensus and that, if it is conceived of in these terms, certain propositions follow which are subject to the test of specific observations." [27] The same may be said of the assumption that people seek to maximize favorable evaluations by others; indeed this assumption has already fathered such additional concepts as "reference group" and "circle of significant others." Yet the question must be raised as to whether we really wish to, in effect, define sociology by such partial perspectives. The assumption of the maximization of approval from others is the psychological complement to the sociological assumption of a general value consensus. And the former is as selective and one-sided a way of looking at motivation as Dahrendorf and others have argued the latter to be when it determines our way of looking at social structure. The oversocialized view of man of the one is a counterpart to the overintegrated view of society of the other.

Modern sociology, after all, originated as a protest against the partial views of man contained in such doctrines as utilitarianism, classical economics, social Darwinism, and vulgar Marxism. All of the great nineteenth and early twentieth century sociologists [28] saw it as one of their major tasks to expose the unreality of such abstractions as economic man, the gain-seeker of the classical economists; political man, the power-seeker of the Machiavellian tradition in political science; self-preserving man, the security-seeker of Hobbes and Darwin; sexual or libidinal man, the pleasure-seeker of doctrinaire Freudianism; and even religious man, the God-seeker of the theologians. It would be ironical if it should turn out that they have merely contributed to the creation of yet another reified abstraction in socialized man, the status-seeker of our contemporary sociologists.

Of course, such an image of man is, like all the others mentioned, valuable for limited purposes so long as it is not taken for the whole truth. What are some of its deficiencies? To begin with, it neglects the other half of the model of human nature presupposed by current theory: moral man, guided by his built-in superego and beckoning ego-ideal.[29] In

[26] *Ibid.*, p. 189.

[27] Dahrendorf, *Class and Class Conflict in Industrial Society*, p. 158.

[28] Much of the work of Thorstein Veblen, now generally regarded as a sociologist (perhaps the greatest America has yet produced), was, of course, a polemic against the rational, calculating *homo economicus* of classical economics and a documentation of the importance in economic life of the quest for status measured by conformity to arbitrary and shifting conventional standards. Early in his first and most famous book Veblen made an observation on human nature resembling that which looms so large in contemporary sociological thinking: "The usual basis of self-respect," he wrote, "is the respect accorded by one's neighbors. Only individuals with an aberrant temperament can in the long run retain their self-esteem in the face of the disesteem of their fellows." *The Theory of the Leisure Class*, New York: Mentor Books, 1953, p. 38. Whatever the inadequacies of his psychological assumptions, Veblen did not, however, overlook other motivations to which he frequently gave equal or greater weight.

[29] Robin M. Williams, Jr. writes: "At the present time, the literature of sociology and

recent years sociologists have been less interested than they once were in culture and national character as backgrounds to conduct, partly because stress on the concept of "role" as the crucial link between the individual and the social structure has directed their attention to the immediate situation in which social interaction takes place. Man is increasingly seen as a "role-playing" creature, responding eagerly or anxiously to the expectations of other role-players in the multiple group settings in which he finds himself. Such an approach, while valuable in helping us grasp the complexity of a highly differentiated social structure such as our own, is far too often generalized to serve as a kind of *ad hoc* social psychology, easily adaptable to particular sociological purposes.

But it is not enough to concede that men often pursue "internalized values" remaining indifferent to what others think of them, particularly when, as I have previously argued, the idea of internalization has been "hollowed out" to make it more useful as an explanation of conformity. What of desire for material and sensual satisfactions? Can we really dispense with the venerable notion of material "interests" and invariably replace it with the blander, more integrative "social values"? And what of striving for power, not necessarily for its own sake—that may be rare and pathological —but as a means by which men are able to *impose* a normative definition of reality on others? That material interests, sexual drives, and the quest for power

have often been over-estimated as human motives is no reason to deny their reality. To do so is to suppress one term of the dialectic between conformity and rebellion, social norms and their violation, man and social order, as completely as the other term is suppressed by those who deny the reality of man's "normative orientation" or reduce it to the effect of coercion, rational calculation, or mechanical conditioning.

The view that man is invariably pushed by internalized norms or pulled by the lure of self-validation by others ignores—to speak archaically for a moment—both the highest and the lowest, both beast and angel, in his nature. Durkheim, from whom so much of the modern sociological point of view derives, recognized that the very existence of a social norm implies and even creates the possibility of its violation. This is the meaning of his famous dictum that crime is a "normal phenomenon." He maintained that "for the originality of the idealist whose dreams transcend his century to find expression, it is necessary that the originality of the criminal, who is below the level of his time, shall also be possible. One does not occur without the other." [30] Yet Durkheim lacked an adequate psychology and formulated his insight in terms of the actor's cognitive awareness rather than in motivational terms. We do not have Durkheim's excuse for falling back on what Homans has called a "social mold theory" of human nature.[31]

Social but not Entirely Socialized

I have referred to forces in man that are resistant to socialization. It is not my purpose to explore the nature of these

social psychology contains many references to 'Conformity'—conforming to norms, 'yielding to social pressure,' or 'adjusting to the requirements of the reference group' . . . ; the implication is easily drawn that the actors in question are *motivated* solely in terms of conformity or non-conformity, rather than in terms of 'expressing' or 'affirming' internalized values . . ." (his italics). "Continuity and Change in Sociological Study," *American Sociological Review*, 23 (December, 1958), p. 630.

[30] Emile Durkheim, *The Rules of Sociological Method,* Chicago: University of Chicago Press, 1938, p. 71.

[31] George C. Homans, *The Human Group,* New York: Harcourt, Brace and Co., 1950, pp. 317–319.

forces or to suggest how we ought best conceive of them as sociologists—that would be a most ambitious undertaking. A few remarks will have to suffice. I think we must start with the recognition that *in the beginning there is the body*. As soon as the body is mentioned the specter of "biological determinism" raises its head and sociologists draw back in fright. And certainly their view of man is sufficiently disembodied and non-materialistic to satisfy Bishop Berkeley, as well as being de-sexualized enough to please Mrs. Grundy.

Am I, then, urging us to return to the older view of a human nature divided between a "social man" and a "natural man" who is either benevolent, Rousseau's Noble Savage, or sinister and destructive, as Hobbes regarded him? Freud is usually represented, or misrepresented, as the chief modern proponent of this dualistic conception which assigns to the social order the purely negative role of blocking and re-directing man's "imperious biological drives."[32] I say "misrepresented" because, although Freud often said things supporting such an interpretation, other and more fundamental strains in his thinking suggest a different conclusion. John Dollard, certainly not a writer who is oblivious to social and cultural "factors," saw this twenty-five years ago: "It is quite clear," he wrote, ". . . that he (Freud) does not regard the instincts as having a fixed social goal; rather, indeed, in the case of the sexual instinct he has stressed the vague but powerful and impulsive nature of the

drive and has emphasized that its proper social object is not picked out in advance. His seems to be a drive concept which is not at variance with our knowledge from comparative cultural studies, since his theory does not demand that the 'instinct' work itself out with mechanical certainty alike in every varying culture."[33]

So much for Freud's "imperious biological drives!" When Freud defined psychoanalysis as the study of the "vicissitudes of the instincts," he was confirming, not denying, the "plasticity" of human nature insisted on by social scientists. The drives or "instincts" of psychoanalysis, far from being fixed dispositions to behave in a particular way, are utterly subject to social channelling and transformation and could not even reveal themselves in behavior without social molding any more than our vocal chords can produce articulate speech if we have not learned a language. To psychoanalysis man is indeed a social animal; his social nature is profoundly reflected in his bodily structure.[34]

But there is a difference between the Freudian view on the one hand and both sociological and neo-Freudian conceptions of man on the other. To Freud man is a *social* animal without being entirely a *socialized* animal. His very social nature is the source of conflicts and an-

---

[32] Robert K. Merton, *Social Theory and Social Structure*, Revised and Enlarged Edition, Glencoe, Ill.: The Free Press, 1957, p. 131. Merton's view is representative of that of most contemporary sociologists. See also Hans Gerth and C. Wright Mills, *Character and Social Structure*, New York: Harcourt, Brace and Co., 1953, pp. 112–113. For a similar view by a "neo-Freudian," see Erich Fromm, *The Sane Society*, New York: Rinehart and Co., 1955, pp. 74–77.

[33] John Dollard, *Criteria for the Life History*, New Haven: Yale University Press, 1935, p. 120. This valuable book has been neglected, presumably because it appears to be a purely methodological effort to set up standards for judging the adequacy of biographical and autobiographical data. Actually, the standards serve as well to evaluate the adequacy of general theories of personality or human nature and even to prescribe in part what a sound theory ought to include.

[34] One of the few attempts by a social scientist to relate systematically man's anatomical structure and biological history to his social nature and his unique cultural creativity is Weston La Barre's *The Human Animal*, Chicago: University of Chicago Press, 1954.

tagonisms that create resistance to socialization by the norms of any of the societies which have existed in the course of human history. "Socialization" may mean two quite distinct things; when they are confused an oversocialized view of man is the result. On the one hand socialization means the "transmission of the culture," the particular culture of the society an individual enters at birth; on the other hand the term is used to mean the "process of becoming human," of acquiring uniquely human attributes from interaction with others.[35] All men are socialized in the latter sense, but this does not mean that they have been completely molded by the particular norms and values of their culture. All cultures, as Freud contended, do violence to man's socialized bodily drives, but this in no sense means that men could possibly exist without culture or independently of society.[36] From such a standpoint, man may properly be called as Norman Brown has called him, the "neurotic" or the "discontented" animal and repression may be seen as the main characteristic

of human nature as we have known it in history.[37]

But isn't this psychology and haven't sociologists been taught to foreswear psychology, to look with suspicion on what are called "psychological variables" in contradistinction to the institutional and historical forces with which they are properly concerned? There is, indeed, as recent critics have complained, too much "psychologism" in contemporary sociology, largely, I think, because of the bias inherent in our favored research techniques. But I do not see how, at the level of theory, sociologists can fail to make assumptions about human nature.[38] If our assumptions are left implicit, we will inevitably presuppose a view of man that is tailor-made to our special needs; when our sociological theory over-stresses the stability and integration of society we will end up imagining that man is the disembodied, conscience-driven, status-seeking phantom of current theory. We must do better if we really wish to win credit outside of our ranks for special understanding of man, that plausible creature [39] whose wagging tongue so often hides the despair and darkness in his heart.

See especially Chs. 4–6, but the entire book is relevant. It is one of the few exceptions to Paul Goodman's observation that anthropologists nowadays "commence with a chapter on Physical Anthropology and then forget the whole topic and go on to Culture." See his "Growing up Absurd," *Dissent*, 7 (Spring, 1960), p. 121.

[35] Paul Goodman has developed a similar distinction; *op. cit.*, pp. 123–125.

[36] Whether it might be possible to create a society that does not repress the bodily drives is a separate question. See Herbert Marcuse, *Eros and Civilization*, Boston: The Beacon Press, 1955; and Norman O. Brown, *Life Against Death*, New York: Random House, Modern Library Paperbacks, 1960. Neither Marcuse nor Brown are guilty in their brilliant, provocative, and visionary books of assuming a "natural man" who awaits liberation from social bonds. They differ from such sociological Utopians as Fromm, *op. cit.*, in their lack of sympathy for the de-sexualized man of the neo-

Freudians. For the more traditional Freudian view, see Walter A. Weisskopf, "The 'Socialization' of Psychoanalysis in Contemporary America," in Benjamin Nelson (ed.), *Psychoanalysis and the Future*, New York: National Psychological Association For Psychoanalysis, 1957, pp. 51–56; Hans Meyerhoff, "Freud and the Ambiguity of Culture," *Partisan Review*, 24 (Winter, 1957), pp. 117–130.

[37] Brown, *op. cit.*, pp. 3–19.

[38] "I would assert that very little sociological analysis is ever done without using at least an implicit psychological theory." Alex Inkeles, "Personality and Social Structure," in Robert K. Merton and others, editors, *Sociology Today*, New York: Basic Books, 1959, p. 250.

[39] Harry Stack Sullivan once remarked that the most outstanding characteristic of human beings was their "plausibility."

C · SOME PROBLEMS IN RESEARCH METHOD

1 · The Analysis of National Character

THE PROBLEM OF NATIONAL CHARACTER:
A METHODOLOGICAL ANALYSIS

by Maurice L. Farber

Some six years have elapsed since Klineberg's (10) pioneering article, among psychologists, treating with the science of national character. Since then, there has been a burgeoning of investigation in this area, making it advisable, perhaps, on the basis of the additional perspective gained, to examine the salient methodological difficulties that have been revealed and to evaluate the prospects for future development.

The reasons for the expansion of this area constitute a problem for the sociology of knowledge, but one might speculatively suggest as a hypothesis the convergence during this period of the following trends: (*a*) the increased acceptance of the Freudian psychodynamics as an explanation of personality formation; (*b*) the development of projective methods of personality study with promise of intercultural adaptability; (*c*) the need, during the last war, for understanding the character of enemy and friendly nations, as well as our own, for the purpose of predicting and influencing morale; (*d*) a similar need, during the post-war period, for knowledge both leading to international understanding so that the possibility of war is mitigated, and, at the same time, providing am-

SOURCE: *The Journal of Psychology,* Vol. 30 (1950), pp. 307–316.

munition for the current "cold war" or a potential future one; and (*e*) the virtual exhaustion by cultural anthropologists of available un-described preliterate societies, with their subsequent turning to literate ones.

An interesting preliminary question is whether we are dealing here with pure or applied science. It is clear that the distinction is, in the social sciences, rather arbitrary. A nation represents one empirically observed type of human grouping and the character of such groupings may be studied as a problem in social organization in the investigatory spirit of pure science. On the other hand, if the scientist is primarily concerned in his research with the application of his findings to practical problems, such as international propaganda, then we are dealing with applied science. The distinction here would appear to revolve around the aims of the investigator, and these are rarely unmixed.

It should prove useful, at the outset, to examine the broad setting in which the problem rests.

Nations and Cultures

The problem of the measurement of differences between large groups of mankind is not, for social psychology, a new one. Psychological differences between the sexes, or among races, have been subject to researches for a good number of years. The demarcation of these groups, based upon anatomical differences, has been simple with regard to sex and not insurmountably difficult, once the anatomical criteria have been decided upon, with regard to race.

Unlike sex and race, which are physiological-anatomical concepts, the concept of *nation* is essentially political-geographical. We are dealing, in the case of a nation, with *a sub-division of mankind living under a sovereign government and within a circumscribed geographical area.* Fairly frequently, to be sure, other properties characterize the people of a nation: blood-ties; common mores, language and religion; a sense of social homogeneity and common interest. None of these, however, is a *sine qua non.*

It is clear that such a grouping need not—and frequently does not—correspond with cultural groupings. And yet, *it is in relation to a particular culture pattern that one might expect to find a particular character structure.* Eastern Poles of similar culture may live in Poland or over the border in the Soviet Union; the Tyrolese of northern Italy are part of the same culture group as the Tyrolese just over the Austrian border, and were, in fact, under the Austrian-Hungarian flag until after World War I. The very formulation of our problem, then, immediately reveals rather awkward dimensions.

Not only do national and cultural boundaries often fail to correspond, but we are confronted with the further difficulty of nations containing several cultures. Is it possible, for example, to make a general statement about the character structure of the people of the Soviet Union? Such a statement would have to include reference to Ukranians, Letts, Armenians, Mongols, and a large number of other culturally diverse groups. A

Canadian national character would need to include French and British Canadians, as well as, to an extent, Indians and Eskimos. It is dubious that any meaningful residuum of character structure could encompass such groups. It becomes clear that we cannot speak of a national character in multi-cultural nations, or stated positively, that the concept offers promise only in uni-cultural ones. It may be possible, to be sure, to speak of a nation having several subnational characters, but such a procedure appreciably modifies our present concept.

Geoffrey Gorer (11), although entitling his book *The American People,* with the sub-title *A Study in National Character,* states in his foreword that his study excludes the southern states, Texas, rural New England, and California, together with the obvious ethnic, religious and social minorities in the remaining area. Actually, then, he attempts to deal merely with the largest of the American subnational cultures.

Then there are nations of a different type, rare perhaps, but worth mentioning for methodological reasons. Consider a new nation like Israel, consisting of a *mélange* of peoples from various countries of Eastern Europe, from Germany, from the United States, added to older native groups. No describable culture seems yet to have emerged and it would be pursuing a will-o-the-wisp to seek a national character in such a culturally unstructured nation. A period of historical continuity for a nation would seem to be necessary before uniformities in character might be expected.

The Instability of Nations

It has been objected by Fyfe (3) for example, that the entire concept of national character is untenable because nations exhibit marked historical changes in behavior and attitudes. The national character of modern Greece is doubtless not that of Ancient Greece, of the Japanese of 1850 not that of the partially Westernized Japanese of today. There is every reason to believe that as a culture changes historically personality structure within it is concomitantly altered. In this connection, Kardiner and Linton (9) have demonstrated, in a happily discovered "natural experiment," how an economic shift from a dry-rice culture to a wet-rice culture apparently caused marked shifts in character structure in Tanala-Betsileo of Madagascar.

If we grant, then, this instability, what remains of our concept of national character? Clearly, we cannot insist upon descriptions that are true for all eternity: they are at best valid for only certain historical periods. If one were given a description of a national character, it would be difficult to state with certainty for how long that character had existed and impossible to state for how long it will continue to exist. Our concept is history-bound.

It must be pointed out that changes which are historically dramatic need not cause changes in national character structure. A nation may fight a war, suffer a change in government, or ally itself with a different power bloc without marked effect upon the character of its people.

There are, moreover, psychological aspects of nations that one would not want to include in the national character concept. Recently, for example, a trans-Atlantic plane crashed, killing a popular French boxing champion and plunging many French into a day or two of depression. It would be patently inadvisable to include "depression" as a component of the French character as it would be to ascribe "anxiety" to the Germans on the basis of their post-war state of mind. Short duration mood fluctuations, while they may well be related to character structure in the types of stimuli to which they are responses, for instance, or in the style of response, are not in themselves the psychological variables in which we are interested.

A concept of national character then, can neither on the one hand insist upon long-range stability nor accept on the other short-range fluctuations of a noncharacterological type. The implied problem of precisely what levels of personality are optimally to be probed is beyond the limits of the present paper.

The Heterogeneity of Nations

Strictly speaking, there are probably as many personalities in a nation as there are individuals. Even if we ignore large areas of individual differences, we still find sharp differences between rural and urban dwellers, and among classes within a nation. Yet the concept of national character would attempt a single general description which covers the bulk of individuals as well as all classes. Consider, for example: "the French character structure" would need satisfactorily to include Leon Blum and Charles deGaulle, peasants of Normandy and fishermen of Brittany, Communist auto workers of the Paris suburbs, the smart society of the Faubourg St. Honoré, inn-keepers of the Midi, and so on. Somehow, a lowest common denominator, or a modal personality must be extracted from this potpourri.

It has been suggested, indeed, that class differences within a nation may be greater than differences between given classes in different nations, for instance, that French and German industrialists might be more alike than are French industrialists and French peasants. This may well be true, though it does a certain violence by pulling out of context aspects of fairly integrated national constellations. It nevertheless dramatizes the awkwardness of our problem.

There has been a tendency in some anthropological circles, particularly by

Mead,[1] to minimize this problem, apparently on the theoretical ground that every member of a nation necessarily exhibits the national character, so that it matters little which particular individuals one studies. To simplify, it is as if all members of a nation were envisaged as having been immersed in the homogeneous fluid of national culture, with the soaked-up fluid readily identifiable by a trained observer on the person of each individual of the nation.

A more scientific analogy would perhaps be with the Spearman theory of intelligence: though there are individual differences (s factors) there is a general national character (g factor) common to all.

Such a view would seem to the present writer untenable. There may well be little general factor of any consequence running through all classes and groups of a nation; class characters may be interrelated in complex, perhaps complementary, ways. Methodologically, how could one ascertain, by examining a few members of a given class, where their class characteristics ended and their national characteristics began? One could not, without sampling and inter-class comparisons.

The concept of "the basic personality structure" of Kardiner (8) was designed for extremely broad cultural comparisons and not for the study of national differences. Kardiner maintains, for example, that the basic personality structure of Sophocles was essentially the same as that of modern Western man. Its possible applicability to the present problem, is, however, readily apparent, and Linton (11) has indeed suggested its use with nations.

Substantially the same difficulties as encountered in connection with Mead's approach would seem to be involved here. One of the underlying postulates of the

concept is "that the techniques which the members of any society employ in the care and rearing of children are culturally patterned and will tend to be similar, although never identical for various families within the society." Aside from the possibility, with which we are not here primarily concerned, that child-rearing practices may be overstressed as cause, this postulate is certainly inaccurate for modern Western nations. Ericson (2) has shown, for example, that there are important differences in child-rearing practices between social classes in the United States. Kardiner (8, p. 38) seems aware of the necessity of considering differentiations due to status, but feels (p. 365) that the basic character in the United States is uniform and does not follow class lines. Thus he attempts to designate the basic personality structure of "Plainville," a rural American community, and to treat it as if it were the character structure of Western culture.

It would seem that approaches such as Kardiner's and Mead's run the risk of assuming what is to be proved by spreading a homogeneous semantic veneer over the cracks in the social structure of nations. There would seem to be no substitute, if we are to know the character of nations, for the laborious task of considering classes and other groupings within nations.

Kaldegg (7) has recently compared English and German secondary school pupils, employing a projective test. While running the risk of failing to touch certain aspects of adult personality, this method, provided the social backgrounds of the student groups are comparable, would appear to be a useful one. Before generalizing about the entire nations, however, it would be desirable to sample students at several social levels.

The present writer has experimented with the method of comparing similar occupational groups in different countries, i.e., insurance clerks in England

---

[1] Personal communication.

and the United States. While such a method appears to keep many factors constant, the greatest caution should certainly be employed in generalizing observed differences to "the British" or "the Americans" as nations. Other occupational groups may differ along quite other dimensions. Nevertheless, this method offers a preliminary approach to an admittedly baffling problem.

In connection with the heterogeneity of nations, there is a special problem concerning the relation of élites or policy-makers of a nation to the population at large.

The Policy-Makers and the People

A headline like "Britain Recognizes Red China" semantically analyzed, means, of course, that the British Foreign Secretary, on the basis of consultation with his advisers, has extended recognition. Nevertheless, the tendency to impute certain characteristics to the British people on the basis of such a governmental act is very great. Can we generalize about the Russian character structure from the acts of the Politburo? It would be extremely foolhardy, and yet some relation of considerable subtlety doubtless exists, for are these political leaders not Russians living in the context of a Russian culture? And do not their policy decisions in turn mold the institutions of Russia and thus modify the Russian character structure? As an élite, are their attitudes and behavior not imitated? Are their decisions, and more particularly the decisions of policy makers in democratic countries, not limited by what "public opinion" will tolerate?

Let us keep in mind, on the other hand, that policy-makers are atypical members of a nation who have risen to their positions partially on the very basis of these atypical characteristics. Moreover, their governmental rôles expose them to different stimulus constellations as well as modify their motivational systems. Whatever their relation to the governed might be, it is certainly too complex to allow for easy transformation of descriptions between the two. One would surely wish to make more direct observation of the larger population itself.

Since policy is made by élites operating within a special psychological context, a pragmatic objection to the whole notion of national character arises from the viewpoint of applied psychology: that a description of a national character would be of little value in predicting the international political acts of a nation. Inkeles (6), for example, has made this point.

Even if of no primary interest to the pure scientist, this objection is a serious one to those more practically oriented. It would surely be perilous to predict whether a particular nation will attack by unannounced *Blitzkrieg* or only after a formal declaration of war, purely on the basis of national character data. Factors such as relative strengths, types of armaments, and geographical positions definitely are involved. Nonetheless, taken in conjunction with such variables, a knowledge of the national character would in all probability be of value.

Assuming, for instance, that Mead's (13) "chip on the shoulder" description of the American character is valid, one would be more apt to expect the United States to fight only after it has been attacked or declared war upon, though it may possibly have maneuvered the opposing nation into a position in which it felt that it had to attack. Benedict's (1) observations on the rôle of authority and hierarchy in the Japanese character have been useful in predicting the docility of the Japanese under occupation. In general, then, without insisting upon national character as the sole determinant of national policy, one can still insist upon its potential value when considered in conjunction with other variables.

Personality Structure or Social Structure?

The term "national character" has thus far in this discussion been deliberately employed in a rather loose and undefined way so that various facets of it might be examined. A serious problem must now, however, be faced. Is it profitable to deal in this connection with personality structure in the narrowly psychological sense of an organization of traits? Or is it necessary, on a national stage, to employ a broader concept which includes personality together with descriptions of certain important social institutions of the nation?

Would it be meaningful, for example, to talk of the religiosity of the Spaniards without description of the officially monopolistic position of the church in Spain, or of the irreligiosity of the Russians without considering the attitude of the Soviet government toward religion? Would it not constitute a distorting removal from context to speak of American extraversion without reference to our market, pecuniary economy? Extraversion in Italy, for instance, would have quite a different meaning.

No sharp lines can be drawn here, but it would seem advisable, on the basis of such considerations, to include aspects of the national institutions and ways of life along with the more narrow description of psychological personality traits. That some of these institutions may contribute causally to the personality structure does not eliminate the necessity for their inclusion.

A recent development in research technique is relevant here. That is, the use of what Klineberg (9) has called "cultural products," e.g., literature, art, and humor as an index of national character.

McGranahan and Wayne (12) have, for instance, compared the German and American character through analysis of popular plays. That the successful plays of a nation bear some relation to the national character is undeniable, but that this relation is sufficiently direct to allow easy inferences is another question.

Consider something of the life history of a successful play. It is written by a rare member of a nation, who selects and organizes certain aspects of experience based upon deep personal motives yet in accordance with certain literary conventions. His work must convince a producer that its production will be profitable, and then it must in actuality attract certain publics who are willing to pay to see it. A series of selective processes is involved here, and the play succeeding in passing through them may reflect only narrowly and distortedly particular aspects of the national character. Plays may merely tell élite classes what they would like to hear, or mirror them as they would like to be. Plays may fail to touch upon huge segments of the national character because these are taken for granted in the nation, unverbalized, and not viewed as dramatic material.

Cultural products, then, must be analyzed with delicacy. If we can tease out something of the selective processes involved we may gain valuable insights into national character. McGranahan's stimulating findings indicate that there is rich material here. The difficulty is rather that cultural products may be too rich after passing through a series of social processes, furnishing at best hypotheses rather than verifications.

The Methodology of Verification

Investigators trained in a rigorously empirical, experimentalist tradition are apt to find themselves ill-at-ease and inhibited in confronting the problem of national character. Non-scientific writers, in contrast, have been relatively free of paralyzing cautions in their sweeping, impressionistic generalizations. Somewhere between these two extremes has been the recent work carried out in certain anthropological circles, best exemplified, perhaps, by Gorer's (4) report on the American character. It should prove of value to examine methodologically this widely publicized book. That its title is rather too sweeping has already been indicated.

At first glance the experimentalist is nonplussed by the total lack of the kinds of scientific controls he has come to consider necessary. There is no systematic method of investigation; no description of the numbers or kinds of people interviewed, if any; no quantification; no deductions that follow with necessity from particular arrangements of data. There are only stated conclusions, in terms, to be sure, of some ethnological and psychoanalytic sophistication, but in the final analysis essentially impressionistic.

And yet, the conclusions possess a certain plausibility, and even brilliance. There can be no doubt that the very experience of "plausibility" needs analysis. For a scientifically trained person plausibility probably involves some swift mental manipulations which attempt to fit the hypothesis into accepted frames of reference, thus roughly testing it, and finding that it does violence to none of these frames and indeed fits some fairly well. In the present case, some of the material seems to correspond with the reader's own informal observations, but there is probably also another reason for the plausibility. That is, *that a single concept appears successfully to subsume a number of descrete social phenomena, or at least to interrelate them.* Specifically, Gorer relates to American rejection of immigrant fathers such characteristics as our contempt of Europe, of politicians, our dislike of military officers, of social

planning, etc. In mature sciences, such subsumption is successful and precise. Newton's Gravitational Law, for instance, explains specific phenomena like falling bodies, the movements of planets, and the rise and fall of tides.

The problem here is first to ascertain whether Gorer's specific assertions are in the main true, and secondly to note whether his generalization succeeds in subsuming them. Unfortunately, unlike the case of the phenomena of physics, no firm evidence is adduced to indicate the extent, or indeed the very existence of the American characteristics he describes. On the other hand, as already indicated, the general concept does succeed with a certain plausibility in subsuming and relating many of the specific descriptions of American character.

Methodological evaluation of this curious state of affairs is difficult. In the study of "the seamless web of culture" the method of plausible subsumptions may indeed be a valuable social science research tool. In the present case, one is, to be sure, disturbed by such considerations as the necessity for explaining the apparent dislike of authority in nations like France and Italy, where the causality could not be the same as in the United States. One would demand in addition, of course, evidence for the existence of the American characteristics as described. One is, moreover, *a priori* suspicious of the monolithic causal scheme presented. There is, however, no necessity for a dichotomous structuring which would either totally reject or totally accept Gorer's material or any other which uses a similar approach. There are provacative hypotheses here, which must be subjected to more rigorous test.

In conclusion, one can only point to the subtle and tenuous nature of the problem of national character. We are beset, particularly in this area of social research, by methodological riddles not easily susceptible of solution. We cannot plead, as is now being done, that the urgent need for results in a tense world justifies speedy but superficial work.

Is a science of national character possible? Yes, if we remain methodologically alert and are sufficiently un-compulsive to face the possibility that our laborious digging along this vein may never produce more than low-grade ore.

REFERENCES

1. Benedict, R. F.: *The Chrysanthemum and the Sword*. Boston: Houghton Mifflin, 1946.
2. Ericson, M. C.: "Quantified Interview Data at Two Class Levels. . . ." Paper read at American Psychological Association's 1946 meeting.
3. Fyfe, H.: *The Illusion of National Character*. London: Watts, 1946.
4. Gorer, G.: *The American Character: A Study of National Character*. New York: Norton, 1948.
5. ———: "Themes in Japanese culture." *Trans. New York Acad. Sci.*, 1943, II, 5, 105–124.
6. Inkeles, A.: Sigma Xi Lecture delivered at University of Connecticut, January 11, 1950.
7. Kaldegg, A.: "Responses of German and English secondary school boys to a projection test." *Brit. J. Psychol.*, 1948, 39, 30–53.
8. Kardiner, A., et al.: *The Psychological Frontiers of Society*. New York: Columbia Univ. Press, 1945.
9. Kardiner, A., and Linton, R.: *The Individual and his Society*. New York: Columbia Univ. Press, 1939.
10. Klineberg, O.: "A Science of National Character." *J. Soc. Psychol.*, 1944, 19, 147–162.
11. Linton, R.: Speech delivered at University of Connecticut, December 5, 1949.
12. McGranahan, D. V., and I. Wayne: "German and American Traits Reflected in Popular Drama." *Human Rel.*, 1948, 1, 429–455.
13. Mead, M.: *And Keep Your Powder Dry*. New York: Morrow, 1942.

2 · The Analysis of Ecological and Statistical Distributions of Personality Variables

THE ECOLOGICAL APPROACH IN SOCIAL PSYCHIATRY

by John A. Clausen and Melvin L. Kohn

The great increase of interest in social psychiatry prompts us to take a long and hard look at the method upon which many studies of the relationship between social factors and mental illness have relied—the ecological method. Several writers have examined the method, but from different points of view and with diverse conclusions. Robinson, treating ecological correlations solely as a substitute for individual correlations, has dis-

SOURCE: *American Journal of Sociology*, Vol. 60 (1954), pp. 140–151.

missed the method entirely.[1] Faris has assessed ecological studies in this and other content areas in the light of the proposition that, in societies in transition, "natural areas" are carved out which favor the development of certain abnormal behavior traits.[2] Dunham has

[1] W. S. Robinson, "Ecological Correlations and the Behavior of Individuals," *American Sociological Review*, XV (June, 1950), 351–357.

[2] Robert E. L. Faris, "Ecological Factors in Human Behavior," in J. McV. Hunt (ed.),

examined some of the technical and interpretative problems of the ecological method from the point of view of the researcher already committed to the method who is intent on maximizing its effectiveness for research on mental disturbance.[3]

Our interest in the ecological method is primarily in its usefulness for generating and testing hypotheses about the *etiology* of mental disturbances. We shall be concerned with two types of problems: (1) What interpretations can legitimately be made from ecological correlations? (2) How can we move from ecological correlations to the systematic testing of hypotheses about the etiology of mental disorders?

Assumptions Underlying Ecological Research in Mental Illness

The search for differences in the frequency of mental illness in population groups residing in different areas of the city is based upon several assumptions. In this section we shall deal at some length with these assumptions and with the data in hand which would permit us to assess them.

Assumption 1. That there is a direct relationship between the characteristics of a population group (or the conditions of life of that group) and the number of persons in that group who become mentally ill. In other words, rate differences among groups are not simply the reflection of ecological segregation or "drift-

---

ing" of the mentally ill after the onset of illness.[4]

Ever since the appearance of the first studies in this field, the "drift" hypothesis has been invoked as an explanation of the residential concentration of mental patients at the time of hospitalization. The high degree of concentration of alcoholics and paretics in hobohemia and the cheaper rooming-house areas seems without question to represent a sifting downward of individuals whose life-patterns and personalities have been formed in far different settings long before. Whether the same tendency is reflected in the distribution of schizophrenics is less clear. In part, the problem is one of assessing the nature of the disease process in schizophrenia. There is an ever increasing body of clinical evidence which points to the importance of early life-experience in predisposing an individual toward schizophrenia. At the same time it seems quite clear that many individuals whose early life-experiences may have predisposed them to schizophrenia manage in the absence of extreme stress to achieve reasonably normal role performance. Thus, depending on whether one is seeking knowledge of predisposing or of precipitating factors, the test of the drift hypothesis either requires data on area of residence in early childhood or at the time of the first clear signs of overt disorder (anywhere from a few days to several years prior to hospitalization).

Faris and Dunham argued that, since the distribution of older schizophrenics is no more heavily concentrated in the central areas of the city than is that of younger schizophrenics, there is no evidence for drift.[5] Gerard and Houston, on

---

Personality and the Behavior Disorders (2 vols.; New York: Ronald Press, 1944), II, 736–757.

[3] H. Warren Dunham, "Some Persistent Problems in the Epidemiology of Mental Disorders," *American Journal of Psychiatry,* CIX (February, 1953), 567–575. See also "The Current Status of Ecological Research in Mental Disorder," *Social Forces,* XXV (March, 1947), 321–326.

[4] This assumption has been the starting hypothesis to be tested in one or two recent studies, but it is most often assumed or asserted without attempting a thorough evaluation of its tenability.

[5] Robert E. L. Faris and H. Warren Dunham, *Mental Disorder in Urban Areas* (Chicago: University of Chicago Press, 1939), pp. 164–169.

the other hand, found that for Worcester, Massachusetts, almost all the concentration of high rates of schizophrenia could be accounted for by the concentration of highly mobile, unattached individuals.[6] They computed separate rates for men living in family groups and for men living alone, using as a base, however, the total male population of the ecological areas. Their findings are rendered inconclusive by virtue of the assumption they had to make that the proportion of men living alone does not vary by area—clearly an untenable assumption. Their data, nevertheless, add further plausibility to the drift hypothesis. So also does Schwartz's finding that schizophrenics tend to go down in the occupational scale prior to hospitalization.[7] On the other hand, in a recent study conducted in New Haven by Hollingshead and Redlich, preliminary analysis of data on schizophrenics failed to reveal any decline in status as between the parental family and the patient at the time of hospitalization.[8]

Assumption 2. That it is possible to determine which variables, of a cluster of variables that characterize an area, are responsible for its high or low rate of mental disorder.

Here we encounter the general problem of interpreting the relationship of a large number of intercorrelated variables with a criterion variable. For example, the areas in which highest rates of hospitalization for schizophrenia occur are characterized by high population mobility, by low socioeconomic status, by high proportions of foreign-born population, and by a high incidence of social and health problems. The imputation of etiological significance to any of these variables stems, for the most part, not from the ecological findings themselves, but from general theoretical formulations or from hunches derived from clinical study or life-history materials. The interpretation of ecological correlations is further complicated by the fact which Robinson has so well demonstrated—that ecological correlations tend to overstate the relationship between variables in so far as those variables can also be assessed as they relate to individuals.[9] This problem relates also to the next assumption.

Assumption 3. That the known characteristics of the area or of the general population residing in the area adequately reflect the characteristics or conditions of life of those individuals in the area who become ill. This involves two related assumptions. The first is that the particular local neighborhoods from which the "cases" come are representative of the larger ecological areas in which they are located. The second is that mentally disturbed individuals are either typical of their neighborhoods or sufficiently exposed to be influenced by the social characteristics of their neighbors.

The degree of area homogeneity is always a relative matter. Even in a slum area there are variations in rental, in condition of dwellings, and in composition of population. The general social climate may be grossly different from that of high rental districts or suburban neighborhoods but, like smoke and soot in the air, subject to eddies and pockets. To pursue the simile further, however, gets us into difficulties, for, despite the pockets and eddies that influence concentration of air pollutants, it is not too gross an assumption to take the atmosphere breathed by inhabitants of a census tract as relatively constant for all. The relevant social climate, on the other hand, whether viewed as the matrix of

[6] Donald L. Gerard and Lester G. Houston, "Family Setting and the Social Ecology of Schizophrenia," *Psychiatric Quarterly*, XXVII (January, 1953), 90–101.

[7] Morris S. Schwartz, "The Economic and Spatial Mobility of Paranoid Schizophrenics and Manic-Depressives" (unpublished Master's thesis, University of Chicago, 1946).

[8] Personal communication from Dr. A. B. Hollingshead.

[9] Robinson, *op. cit.*

family relationships, peer-group activities, or dominant value systems, is much more subject to variation as it impinges upon any individual.[10]

The extent to which one may proceed as if this assumption were valid will depend then somewhat on the nature of the ecological areas delineated in any particular study but even more upon the nature of those characteristics of ecological areas that the researcher postulates are implicated in the etiology of the illness. If, for example, socioeconomic status as such is regarded as a possible determinant of mental illness, an *ecological* correlation between rates of psychosis and some index of socioeconomic status is seldom defensible. The relationship postulated is one which can only be assessed by data on the socioeconomic and mental status of individuals. If, on the other hand, one postulates that the segregation of population, largely on an economic basis, leads to certain distinctive subcultures shared by neighborhood groups, then an ecological correlation may be the best means of assessing which clusters of variables are related to the incidence of mental illness. Socioeconomic status is in this instance being used as an index of something vastly more complex than occupation and earnings.[11]

Relatively few ecological studies have been adequately buttressed with evidence as to how area characteristics impinged on persons who became ill. Dunham's study of the social personality of the catatonic schizophrenic attempts to show how the character of life in the slum area intensifies anxieties in the sensitive, self-con-

scious, and timid child.[12] This finding raises several new questions for further research: What is the relative incidence of such children in various areas of the city? To what extent are the particular kinds of developmental problems described typical of catatonics from other settings? Furthermore, though it is clear that the tensions and conflicts reported by these patients accurately reflect their own perceptions of other peoples' responses to their deviant behavior, the problem remains as to whether or not these responses pushed the patients over the tenuous line between being deviant and being psychotic.

Assumption 4. That the probability of being labeled a "case" is not itself affected by the characteristics of the area.

This assumption raises somewhat different problems for studies using first admissions to mental hospitals as the index of mental disorder from the problems it raises for studies using psychiatric screening approaches. In the first instance, the problem is whether the same behavior is perceived as mental disorder by residents of all areas of the city and whether the same action is taken with respect to the mentally ill person. Clearly, differences exist: behavior that would go unnoticed in a rooming-house neighborhood would stand out in a suburban neighborhood; on the other hand, some forms of illness with which a family might attempt to cope at home would lead to the prompt commitment of an individual who was not living in a family setting.

Psychiatric screening avoids these problems but faces another: Is behavior that can be interpreted in one segment of the community as indicative of mental disorder necessarily indicative of mental disorder in another? It is quite possible that present screening techniques are even more "culture-bound" to middle-

[10] Kobrin has effectively described the problem in terms of the conflicting value systems to which the nondelinquent is subjected in areas of high delinquency rates (Solomon Kobrin, "The Conflict of Values in Delinquency Areas," *American Sociological Review,* XVI [October, 1951], 653–661).

[11] In the writers' opinion, this is a point which Robinson failed to make clear in his otherwise excellent analysis.

[12] H. Warren Dunham, "The Social Personality of the Catatonic-Schizophrene," *American Journal of Sociology,* XLIX (May, 1944), 508–518.

class values and verbalizations than are intelligence tests.[13] We shall not attempt to discuss the problem of defining what constitutes a psychiatric case in this paper but will merely note the importance of this problem for the interpretation of ecological findings.

Frames of Reference for the Interpretation of Ecological Findings

From the discussion of the assumptions underlying ecological analysis, we arrive at the position that none of these assumptions is wholly tenable, yet none can be dismissed as completely lacking in validity. Whether or not the reader accepts this position himself, let us consider the problem of interpreting the data, if it be granted temporarily that the consistent patterning of high rates of first hospital admission for schizophrenia that has been found in ecological studies of large cities is not merely an artifact of improper statistical method or the result of downward drifting by the sick.[14]

What theoretical bases or frames of reference lend themselves to an interpretation of the ecological distributions? In his Introduction to Faris and Dunham's volume, Ernest W. Burgess emphasized that the authors set forth their explanation in terms of social isolation "as a hypothesis rather than as a generalization established by the study."

It is a theoretical position congenial to the sociological student and consistent with a great body of sociological theory.

This hypothesis should, however, be confronted with the entire range of facts now available in the field of mental disorder and be oriented within the group of hypotheses suggested by other theoretical viewpoints.[15]

Burgess then went on to consider the possible roles of constitutional, psychological, and sociological factors in mental disorder, drawing upon the then available research literature.

In the light of more recent research, we shall briefly consider some alternative hypotheses that may be offered to explain the ecological findings, with the object of suggesting problems for further research.

The major frames of reference to be considered here are: (1) the genetic; (2) the ecological or interactional (e.g., the role of social isolation);[16] and (3) the cultural, as exemplified by social class and ethnic group differentials in value systems, in goals, and especially in socialization processes. Early papers on ecological theory and method pointed up the distinction between the symbiotic basis of the ecological order and the consensual basis of the cultural order. In recent years it has been recognized that the cultural order both influences and is influenced by the ecological. At the same time a distinction may be made between those characteristics of local life which tend to be shared as common beliefs, expectations, or values and those which relate most directly to the sifting process —economic level, mobility, heterogeneity of origin, prevalence of various forms of social disorganization, etc. It is by no means paradoxical for a population of a given area of the city to be so heterogeneous and "disorganized" as to be incapable of imposing effective social controls upon behavior regarded by the larger society as illegal, immoral, or other-

[13] See Frank Auld, Jr., "Influence of Social Class on Personality Test Responses," *Psychological Bulletin*, XLIX (July, 1952), 318–332.

[14] See Dunham's discussion of the criticisms that have been made of statistical methods used in ecological studies in "Some Persistent Problems," *op. cit.*, p. 568.

[15] Ernest W. Burgess, in Faris and Dunham, *op. cit.*, p. xi.

[16] For the sense in which ecological is here used see the treatment by Faris in "Ecological Factors in Human Behavior," *op. cit.*

wise deviant and yet at the same time to be relatively homogeneous as to aspirations and value systems. For this reason, and because of the somewhat different etiological implications of the two related frames of reference, we shall give separate attention to the ecological or interactional order and the cultural order.

The Genetic Interpretation

In his twin and proband studies Kallmann has produced substantial evidence for the hypothesis that vulnerability to schizophrenia is inherited.[17] According to this hypothesis, the particular symptomatology and severity of symptoms depend upon interaction of a specific biochemical dysfunction with general constitutional modifiers and precipitating (psychological or social) factors outside the individual.

Family studies by Kallmann and others have indicated that the expectancy of schizophrenia among children of schizophrenics is about 16 per cent—or about twenty times as high as in the general population. Roughly 10 per cent of all schizophrenics have at least one schizophrenic parent and another 5 per cent at least one schizophrenic grandparent. Since there is substantial evidence that this illness handicaps an individual in occupational competition, we may assume that a substantial proportion of those parents and grandparents of schizophrenics who were themselves affected were reduced in socioeconomic status, or prevented from rising, by virtue of the same genetic factor which produced the vulnerability to schizophrenia in the child.

Over a number of generations one might well anticipate substantial differentials in incidence rates for schizophrenics in areas of differing socioeconomic status.

This explanation, clearly plausible and at least potentially subject to empirical test, is not necessarily inconsistent with sociological and psychological interpretations. If a genetically derived tendency toward schizophrenia is activated only under certain social and psychological conditions, then the character of local life may decide whether those persons who possess the tendency will develop schizophrenia.

The Hypothesis of Social Isolation

Faris and Dunham's preferred explanation of the ecological findings focuses on the particular quality of social interaction in the local neighborhood.[18] They suggest that life in certain neighborhoods, at least for some residents, inhibits intimate interpersonal relations. And they believe that the incidence of schizophrenia in these neighborhoods is high because of the very high probability that these socially isolated residents become schizophrenic.

The range of experiences believed to be socially isolating is indeed wide:

a. Life in some neighborhoods—those with large numbers of rooming-houses and hotels—is believed to be conducive to social isolation because the residents are constantly on the move.[19] Even the relatively stable resident cannot form lasting relationships, because his neighbors

[17] Franz J. Kallmann, *Heredity in Health and Mental Disorder* (New York: W. W. Norton and Co., 1953), esp. pp. 178–181. See also Kallmann's *The Genetics of Schizophrenia* (New York: J. J. Augustin, 1938) and J. A. Book's "A Genetic and Neuropsychiatric Investigation of a North-Swedish Population," *Acta genetica et statistica medica*, IV (1953), 1–100.

[18] See Faris and Dunham, *op. cit.*, and Robert E. L. Faris, "Cultural Isolation and the Schizophrenic Personality," *American Journal of Sociology*, XXXIX (September, 1934), 155–169; Robert E. L. Faris, *Social Psychology* (New York: Ronald Press, 1952), pp. 338–365.

[19] Faris and Dunham, *op. cit.*, pp. 40–43, 100–109.

change so rapidly. Thus the resident of such an area simply does not meet the same neighbors in the hall for a long enough period of time to develop more than a nodding acquaintance and, as an *adult,* experiences a marked degree of social isolation.

b. In other areas the ethnic group status of particular residents is crucial: Negroes living in white areas of the city (and whites living in Negro areas) are believed to show high rates of schizophrenia because they are unable to form any but superficial relationships with their neighbors.[20] Thus both adults and children are markedly isolated.

c. In the foreign-born slum communities the harsh, competitive character of life is regarded as conducive to social isolation, particularly of the person who is already sensitive, self-conscious, or timid.[21] Whether child or adult, he cannot cope with the rugged competitive world about him and so retires from the struggle.

d. Finally, in lower-class neighborhoods generally, the somewhat less assertive *child,* whose personality does not match that of his peer group apparently is either dropped from the gang or never gains admission.[22]

The result of each of these diverse processes is believed to be that the individual is significantly cut off from the social relationships presumed to be essential for the maintenance of a nonschizophrenic personality. The social isolation hypothesis can thus be seen to encompass a great range of empirical data unearthed by the ecological studies. But the hypothesis is extremely ill defined. For predictive purposes, several questions must be answered:

[20] *Ibid.,* pp. 173–177

[21] Dunham, "Current Status of Ecological Research in Mental Disorder," *op. cit.,* pp. 323–324.

[22] Faris, "Ecological Factors in Human Behavior," *op. cit.*

1. What constitutes *sufficient* attenuation of interpersonal relationships to be called "isolation"? Only very rarely is anyone totally socially isolated. This means that for predictive purposes it is necessary to determine what degree of attenuation in range and intensity of social relations we may take as a cutting point for differentiating isolated from nonisolated persons.

2. What are the distinguishable types of isolating experiences? It is possible to distinguish several quite different isolating experiences even at a single age level. Some children are raised in isolated areas where there are no accessible playmates. Others move so frequently that they have little opportunity to develop close or lasting friendships. Still others are prevented from playing with their age mates, or forced to break off friendships, by overstrict or overprotective parents; others become so enmeshed in close family relationships that they do not seek friendship outside the family; and some are rejected by their peer groups. Among the type first mentioned, differences between areas of the city will be considerable. For types related to family structure and functioning, correlations with area of residence have not been established. The more subtle aspects relating to family influences upon extrafamilial interaction patterns are probably fully as important as are the physical availability and continuity of playmates for the child.

3. What are the differential consequences of attenuated social relationships in different situational contexts and for different temperamental types? One child rebuffed by his local peer group will turn his energies toward competition in school, perhaps thereby finding at least a few congenial spirits. Another may work doggedly to achieve success in some activity highly esteemed in the peer group. Still another may withdraw and sulk, developing a feeling of inferiority and a marked hostility to others. Under what circumstances do satisfying relationships in one

context compensate for inadequacy of relationships in other contexts? To what extent are the compensating relationships differentially available by ecological area or by social class?

4. At what period or periods in the individual's life does the experience of isolation have the greatest effect? In some of the examples cited, isolation is experienced in adolescence; in others, in adult life. If, as personality theory would indicate, the experience takes on a different quality for persons at different stages of personality development, prediction of the consequences of isolation requires exact knowledge of its timing.

5. Finally, how does the experience of social isolation fit into the development of schizophrenia? Is isolation a symptom of already-developing illness; is it an essential condition for the subsequent development of illness; or is it, possibly, both symptomatic of the beginning of the illness and a cause of its further development? In some instances the question is easily answered: the child who is cut off from his age mates by prolonged physical illness or by living on an isolated farm is certainly not isolated because of aberrant behavior. But most instances are considerably more complex. Is the child rejected by his age mates because he manifests signs of illness? Or can the behavior that causes his rejection be unrelated to the presence or absence of the schizophrenic process? The answer requires extremely precise and detailed investigation to determine the temporal sequence of isolating experiences and of manifestations of aberrant behavior.

The Cultural Frame of Reference

It is now generally recognized that ecological processes tend to sort out not only subcommunities but also subcultures. In the days of heavy immigration, ethnic group membership was frequently the most important basis for subcultural classification. At present social class is more generally the concept of choice. That ecological sifting tends to create areas in which the population is relatively homogeneous in socioeconomic status is now established by research; indeed, area of residence is frequently used as a major basis of classification in constructing indexes of social class.

Ecological studies of mental disturbance demonstrate clearly that the areas of the city populated by individuals and families at the bottom of the class hierarchy show the highest rates of schizophrenia. More direct evidence of the relationship between social class and the frequency of schizophrenia has been established in a recent study by Hollingshead and Redlich.[23] They compared the social class distribution of New Haven psychiatric patients with that of a representative sample of the adult population of the city. The prevalence of schizophrenia was approximately eleven times as high in the lowest socioeconomic class (composed of unskilled workers with an elementary-school education or less who live in the poorest areas of the community) as in the highest (comprised of families of wealth, education, and the highest social prestige).

Recent research has also shown that on

[23] A. B. Hollingshead and F. C. Redlich, "Social Stratification and Psychiatric Disorders," *American Sociological Review*, XVIII (April, 1953), 163–169. It should be noted that the New Haven study deals with prevalence (the number of mentally ill persons as of a given date) and not with incidence (the number of persons becoming mentally ill during a given period). Prevalence is a function of incidence and duration. Thus, a higher prevalence rate may reflect more frequent occurrence of mental illness in a given setting, or a longer duration of illness, or both. The index most frequently used in ecological studies is rate of first admissions to a hospital for mental illness during a given period. This approximates an incidence measure but is not wholly adequate as such.

most personality tests lower-class subjects attain significantly lower scores than do upper-class and middle-class subjects.[24] Whether this reflects the middle-class bias of the test constructor of real differences in degree of mental health is not yet entirely clear. More and more of the evidence now accruing suggests, however, that the background of lower-class rearing does not prepare the individual for self-confident participation in a social order that is predominantly oriented toward middle-class values.

There are a number of aspects of social stratification which may be regarded as of potential etiological significance for mental illness. Studies of the personality development of children from the lowest status levels of American society indicate that they typically face intense value conflicts, especially from the time they enter the middle-class-oriented school. The instability of the expectations developed by such children (and the deprecatory self-conceptions built up through internalizing the judgments of others) likewise may be expected to lead to the development of personalities which are highly vulnerable to stress.[25]

Findings of studies of social class differences in child-rearing practices have been inconclusive. Earlier studies tended to concentrate upon such items as age of weaning and toilet training. Recently, psychologists and sociologists have raised serious questions as to the assumptions

involved in much of the theoretical discussion of infant disciplines.[26] It would be folly, however, to assume that the nature of the parent-child relationship in connection with early training can be ignored in seeking to understand personality development. A more recent study, which appears to have been far more thorough and psychologically sophisticated than its predecessors, is summarized as follows: "In contrast with some previously published research, we find that the upper-middle class mothers are consistently more permissive, less punitive and less demanding than upper-lower class mothers." [27]

Finally, there is evidence from psychiatric research that particular types of interpersonal patterns in the family may be of significance in the etiology of schizophrenia.[28] In general, it is found, the mother tended to be the dominant figure in the household, and she typically over-

---

[24] Auld, *op. cit.*

[25] Though the difficulties peculiar to lower-class status are most striking, it should not be forgotten that the middle and upper classes produce their own varieties of stress. The incidence of manic-depressive psychosis is relatively higher for these segments of the population, and quite possibly certain types of neurotic manifestation have their highest incidence in the middle and upper classes. Data thus far available do not permit conclusive answers because of the great differences that exist in ease of access to treatment facilities.

[26] See, e.g., Harold Orlansky, "Infant Care and Personality," *Psychological Bulletin,* XLVI (January, 1949), 1–48; William Sewell, "Infant Training and the Personality of the Child," *American Journal of Sociology,* LVIII (September, 1952), 150–159.

[27] Eleanor E. Macoby and Patricia K. Gibbs, "Social Class Differences in Child Rearing," *American Psychologist,* VIII (August, 1953), 395 (abstract).

[28] See, e.g., Donald L. Gerard and Joseph Siegel, "The Family Background of Schizophrenia," *Psychiatric Quarterly,* XXIV (January, 1950), 47–73; Ruth W. Lidz and Theodore Lidz, "The Family Environment of Schizophrenic Patients," *American Journal of Psychiatry,* CVI (November, 1949), 332–345; Curtis T. Prout and Mary Alice White, "A Controlled Study of Personality Relationships in Mothers of Schizophrenic Male Patients," *American Journal of Psychiatry,* CVII (October, 1950), 251–256; Suzanne Reichard and Carl Tillman, "Patterns of Parent-Child Relationships in Schizophrenia," *Psychiatry,* XIII (May, 1950), 247–257; Trudy Tietze, "A Study of Mothers of Schizophrenic Patients," *Psychiatry,* XII (February, 1949), 55–65.

protected the child who subsequently became schizophrenic. Data on the promising subject of the frequency and functional relevance of such patterns for various social and cultural groupings are not yet available.

This discussion has centered on differences in the lives of children in different class groups. But it is possible to view the relationship between social class and the production of mental illness in two distinct ways: there are class differences in the degree to which children are made vulnerable to potential stress (presumably because of differences in early deprivations and frustrations) and differences in the degree to which adults are exposed to actual stress. There are a number of different ways that vulnerability may come about, and there are also many types of defenses which individuals may develop to minimize their vulnerabilities. It seems to us more feasible to study such phenomena than to attempt to relate each of the specific variables associated with social class to the incidence of mental illness. An example of such research is a project now in process which seeks to ascertain the methods used by children of lower-class and of middle-class origins in resolving conflicts and thereby defending themselves against anxiety.[29]

The Problem of Validating Interpretations

The fact that there are so many possible interpretations of the ecological findings—each consonant with the data, and each supported by other types of research data—poses an important problem: How can these interpretations be

[29] D. R. Miller and G. E. Swanson, "A Proposed Study of the Learning of Techniques for Resolving Conflicts of Impulses," in *Interrelations between the Social Environment and Psychiatric Disorders* (New York: Milbank Memorial Fund, 1953).

validated? All the general hypotheses stated may have some validity. Conceivably the variables included in these several clusters may tend to cancel each other out in some settings and to reinforce each other in others. One point seems abundantly clear: further ecological studies which do not secure data permitting the evaluation of several alternative hypotheses are not likely to add to our knowledge.

It should be emphasized that the major problem for further research is not to establish which hypotheses contribute most to explaining the ecological distribution but rather under what circumstances factors involved in any of these hypotheses actually contribute to the production of schizophrenia. Two alternative methods of testing the interpretations here considered suggest themselves as most promising. The first would be to concentrate on securing sufficiently intensive data to test a single hypothesis, or a set of related hypotheses, independently of all alternative hypotheses. This is essentially the approach that has been used by Kallmann in his studies of identical twins; these studies are designed to test the genetic hypothesis independently of any social or psychological hypotheses. Similarly, the authors of the present paper are investigating the relationship between social isolation in childhood and the subsequent development of schizophrenia by securing retrospective information about their childhood social relations from a group of former schizophrenic patients and a group of controls (matched as of several years prior to the onset of the patients' illnesses). Another research team is investigating hypotheses about the relations of variables associated with social class to the development of both schizophrenia and psychoneurosis by making systematic comparisons of patients drawn from two social classes.

An alternative is to utilize jointly the

several frames of reference here discussed. The ecological mode of investigation might be retained, not simply to repeat the ecological studies of the past, but to design interdisciplinary studies aimed at seeing how genetic and social variables are interrelated within a specified context. A study should not necessarily begin with the computation of incidence rates for different areas of the city; there is, however, considerable insight to be gained from intensively investigating how the quality of neighborhood life enters into the development of illness. For example, there exists a good deal of evidence that both genetic and social factors enter into schizophrenia, but we have only the vaguest notion of how they are related to each other in producing a given case of illness. Furthermore, we have almost no knowledge of how the effects of either can be intensified or mitigated by factors peculiar to a particular neighborhood. Is isolation, for example, easier to bear in a rooming-house neighborhood where it is the norm than in a suburban neighborhood where it is a sign of queerness? Is a genetic vulnerability more likely to result in schizophrenia in a "tough" neighborhood than in other neighborhoods? These questions require considerably more intensive study than has been done in any ecological study to date, but it seems clear that they can be answered more concretely in a study that proceeds within an ecological context than in one that does not.

We have attempted to examine the ecological method in terms of its assumptions and its implications for research on the etiology of mental illness. Briefly, our position is that ecological studies can serve as a useful steppingstone but that too often they have left the investigator stranded in the middle of the stream. If one wishes to cross the stream, other stones are needed, and they must be large enough to provide a stable base and a secure footing above water.

COMMENT

by H. Warren Dunham

Professors Clausen and Kohn, in attempting critically to scrutinize the use of the ecological method in the study of mental disease, have not succeeded in arriving at a fair judgment concerning its present and perhaps future utility at the present stage of research. They state that their interest in the ecological method "is primarily in its usefulness for generating and testing hypotheses about the etiology of mental disturbances." That the ecological method can and has done this is documented, at least partially, in the final section of their paper. But they fail to show the manner in which the ecological method can be extended in the investigation of mental disturbances to provide not only hypotheses which will explain the ecological distributions (in which Clausen and Kohn disclaim interest) but also evidence for establishing the validity of one kind of interpretation as over against another. For it seems reasonable to point out that, if the factors which contribute to the production of the schizophrenias are ever isolated, then we will probably also have some adequate explanation of their spatial distributions.

However, it is particularly in their assumptions that the authors have been obfuscating. In the first place, they set up their assumptions underlying this method to apply only to the investigation of mental illness, without indicating anywhere that the method has proved of value in the investigations of numerous other kinds of human and group behavior. True, there are certain assumptions in using it to investigate mental illness or any other type of behavioral phenomenon, but they are of a much more general character than they have indicated. In fact, as the literature shows, it is unwarranted to imply that investigators who have used this method in the study of mental illness have made these particular assumptions. They seem to overlook the fact that this mapping device for the study of both the community and human behavior was used extensively during the nineteenth century in western Europe. In the twenties Robert E. Park and others began to develop in some systematic form the discipline of human ecology as a framework for the study of the human community. The mapping of various social and economic characteristics of the community led quickly to the study of the distributions of various forms of behavior at first to provide indexes of "metabolic" changes in the community but later as a means for obtaining some insight into the behavior being studied and the factors which might account for it. It is, then, ecological theory which furnishes the central assumptions that underscore this research method. These assumptions, it seems to me, are:

1. That human communities have a certain organic character in that they expand, change, and decline with the probability that this process will be repeated. This cycle constitutes a dynamic equilibrium.
2. That in this expansion a process of distribution takes place which sorts and relocates individuals and groups by residence and occupation over a given land area. In ecological theory this expansion was a function of competition, and it has been demonstrated that certain conscious motives often operate in the relocation of persons.
3. That this selective process creates "natural areas" which develop their own characteristics and can be delimited.
4. That each area with its particular characteristics leaves its cultural "stamp" upon the people who reside there and affects them in numerous and diverse ways.

5. That this cultural "stamp" will be registered in each area by frequencies of numerous types of both acceptable and unacceptable behavior which will differ according to the character of the area.

Within these assumptions it seemed feasible to investigate numerous forms of behavior: delinquency, race prejudice, voting patterns, family behavior, suicide, vice, crime, and even mental disorder with the additional assumption that certain aspects of these interpersonal and cultural environments, in all probability, are relevant to the production of these behaviors.

Under these assumptions the first two assumptions of Clausen and Kohn might be fitted, but their third and fourth assumptions, as they themselves argue cogently, are highly questionable. These latter assumptions are not necessary, and in fact it can be argued that the ecological method might be used to shed some light upon them. The use of the method is not to assume that the characteristics of the population residing in the area reflect the characteristics of those persons in the area who became ill but rather that hypotheses may be developed about the relationship between the characteristics of the area and the types of experiences of persons who become mentally ill.

Likewise the assumption that the probability of being labeled a "case" is not itself affected by the characteristics of the area is not only inconsistent with the first assumption but also suggests that there are specific objectively determined means for diagnosing a functional disorder. In terms of our present knowledge, this is, of course, not valid, and especially so in the case of schizophrenia, around which the authors center much of their discussion. Bellak in his recent review of the literature of schizophrenia describes the emergent conception of this disorder in the following manner: "We believe that it may be helpful to conceive of any given case [schizophrenia] as actually occurring on some point of a continuum from a hypothetical point of complete psychogenicity to a hypothetical point of complete organicity." [1]

Now, if what passes as schizophrenia means all these things, one would hardly expect an investigator using the ecological method to assume that the probability of being a "case" would not be affected by the characteristics of an area. In fact, skilful use of this method might point to discrepancies between a societal judgment and a psychiatric judgment as to what constitutes a "case." Ecological studies of mental disease have already brought insight into this problem.

The authors' discussions of the various interpretative frames for the ecological studies is very much to the point. Any knowledge available with respect to any mental disturbance must be related to the pattern of distribution of the disease in the community. Their critical consideration of their three interpretative frames points to the need for a comparative examination of communities with high and low rates.

Ecological correlations, as Robinson has shown, cannot be substituted for correlations using individuals. Any area percentage or rate measuring some economic or movement factor is a quantitative index which stands for "something," as Clausen and Kohn point out, vastly more complex than the measure considered alone or apart from all other measures. The difficulty is that the researcher does not very clearly discern, in most cases, what this "something" is. In fact, ecological correlations skilfully developed provide a basis for predicting high or low incidence of specific behavior in other but similar situations. Gruenberg and his associates in New York have investigated the index correlated with a mental dis-

ease rate to discover if the correlated index is characteristic of the mental cases or the noncases in the community.[2] This may prove helpful even though not conclusive.

REJOINDER

by John A. Clausen and Melvin L. Kohn

Professor Dunham states that we "have not succeeded in arriving at a fair judgment" concerning the utility of the ecological method at this stage of research in mental health. He goes on to say that we "fail to show the manner in which the ecological method can be extended to provide . . . evidence for establishing the validity of one kind of interpretation as over against another." Our point is precisely that the ecological approach alone cannot provide validation for interpretations or hypotheses on the etiology of mental illness. If Professor Dunham thinks it can, we should welcome his suggestions along this line. We would not, however, accept additional ecological correlations as validating evidence.

Dunham seems to have missed the main point of our discussion of assumptions underlying ecological research. These are not "Clausen and Kohn's assumptions" but rather those necessarily implicit in causal explanations in sociological terms of the ecological distributions of mental patients. We do not believe that the long-standing use of ecological mapping or the fact that some investigators were not aware of assumptions implicit in their own research in any way contradicts our statement that "the search for differences in the frequency of mental illness in population groups residing

[1] See L. Bellak, *Dementia Praecox: The Past Decades Work and Present Status—a Review and Evaluation* (New York: Grave and Stratton, 1948), p. 444.

[2] E. M. Gruenberg, "Community Conditions and Psychosis of the Elderly" (presented at the American Psychiatric Association Meeting in Los Angeles, California, May 5, 1953).

in different areas of the city is based upon several assumptions."

The five statements which Professor Dunham presents as the central assumptions of the method are hardly assumptions but rather descriptive generalizations derived from research in human ecology. We fully agree that ecological studies of many social phenomena have added to our understanding of these phenomena and of social processes. A general evaluation of human ecology was not, however, the focus of our paper.

Finally, we find it difficult to assess Professor Dunham's assertion that the third and fourth assumptions listed by us are unnecessary when his further observations seem to us to support our own. His suggestion that the ecological method might be used to develop hypotheses "about the relationship between the characteristics of the area and the types of experience of persons who become mentally ill" quite clearly assumes that there *is* a relationship.

In view of our rather tart rejection of Professor Dunham's charge that we have been unfair to the ecological approach, we wish to add that we believe the careful and thoughtful ecological studies by himself and Professor Faris have had a most beneficial effect on research in social psychiatry. This, however, is one area where much replication has taken place without much further illumination. We reiterate, then, our hope that future research will advance beyond past achievements.

3 · Comparison of Different Research Methods

METHODOLOGY OF SOCIOLOGICAL INVESTIGATIONS
OF MENTAL DISORDERS

by H. Warren Dunham

The purpose of this paper is to make explicit certain methodological considerations in sociological investigations of mental disorder. Mental disorder, of course, includes many different types and a great variety of observable deviations in the mental, emotional and behavioural spheres. Certain of these deviations, where ætiology is still obscure, may prove to be grounded in the genetic structure, others in injuries or infections in the organism after birth, and still others in the nature of the ties that bind men to one another. Then, too, some mental deviations may be the resultant of certain

SOURCE: *International Journal of Social Psychiatry*, Vol. 3 (Summer, 1957), pp. 7–17.

social relationships acting upon specific kinds of biological organisms. The presence of these latter areas, which are of concern to the social scientist, emphasize the need for a careful statement of his methodological position. Such a statement is also necessary to bring about a more meaningful communication on research in mental disorder between psychiatrists and psychologists on the one hand and anthropologists and sociologists on the other. Their difficulties in communication are mainly due to differing conceptions concerning the natures of man, society and the bond between them.

A recent controversy (4) concerning the assumptions underlying the ecological approach to mental disorder has served further to point up the need for such a statement. Clausen and Kohn have attempted to state what they consider to be the assumptions among research workers using the ecological approach to mental disorder. These assumptions, which are not derived from human ecological theory as they should be, imply that investigators using this method have attempted to make it do something for which it is not designed and cannot do. However, instead of making clear its value in sociological investigations of mental disorder, they appear to challenge the sociologists who have used the method because it seems to leave them "stranded in the middle of the stream" rather than bringing them close to the ætiological issues.

To avoid such confusions in the future, to facilitate interdisciplinary communication and to provide a theoretical basis for the areas of sociological concern, then, require the careful formulation of a methodology for sociological research into mental disorder. Such a statement should include the central standpoints, the underlying assumptions, the basic theoretical concepts, the various approaches with their interrelationships and the unresolved central hypotheses.

Perspectives and Assumptions

This methodological statement has been constructed from the following general standpoints:

1. That the central objective in the sociological study of mental disorder is twofold: (a) to isolate those social variables that are causative or predisposing in the ætiology of the several types of mental disorder, and (b) to isolate those complexes of social conditions that are associated with high incidence as against low incidence rates of the various mental disorders.
2. That the achievement of this two-fold objective necessitates the utilization and integration of clinical, ecological and cultural approaches.
3. That empirically developed sociological generalizations must eventually square with validated theory stemming from biological, physiological and psychological investigations of mental disorder in human society.

From these standpoints the assumptions behind sociological enquiry into the nature of mental disorder can be stated. These assumptions serve not only to underscore the essential concepts, but also to point up the approaches necessary for sociological enquiry. These assumptions (3) are the following:

1. That symbolic communication and interpersonal relationships which have a relevance in accounting for normal mentality and behaviour must also have some relevance in accounting for abnormal mentality and behaviour.
2. That the interconnectedness of external events and their internalization in the person encompass a set of factors which will account for great variability in feeling, mentality and behaviour.
3. That the personality of a person and the culture of his society constitute interrelated systems that are in a constant process of change. Both personality and culture in a given society will manifest greater stability at some historical periods in contrast to others, but such stability as does occur will be temporary, never permanent.
4. That variations in the dynamics of any social system in time and space will make for significant differences in the feeling, thinking and acting of persons in that system.

These assumptions embody the sociological theory to account for variabilities in feeling, thought and action of persons in human groups. These variabilities may or may not be found eventually to represent the incipient stages of recognizable types of mental disorder. If it is assumed that the first possibility will happen, then the following hypotheses can be stated:

1. The bizarre, integrated and organized distortions in varying degrees of feeling, thought and conduct which can be observed in persons can be classified, systematized and objectified sufficiently for the development of differential diagnoses. This hypothesis focuses attention on the need for clinical study of the case from biological, physiological, psychological and sociological perspectives.

2. That a given culture in the functioning of its social system through time will show significant correlations between its incidence rate of mental disorder and certain kinds of cultural change.

3. That any given heterogeneous culture—one with two or more bodies of custom—will show significant differences in the incidence of mental disorders among its various subcultures.

4. That selected homogeneous cultures when compared will differ significantly in their incidence of mental disorder and will have either higher or lower incidence rates when compared with such rates in the subcultures of heterogeneous cultures. These hypotheses point to the utilization of an ecological approach.

5. The manner in which elements of the culture and events of the social situation make their ingression into the human organism and the manner in which the human organism organizes, integrates and utilizes these elements to form his ongoing experience, will produce certain emerging configurations of mentality and behaviour that will not meet with acceptance by the social group. This hypothesis sets the stage for a cultural approach.

Basic Theoretical Concepts

We turn now to a discussion of the central concepts contained in our assumptions. These concepts essential to our analysis are culture, socialization, cultural internalization and social system.

When one speaks of culture, he is speaking of a thing that makes man unique among all other animals. For man alone possesses culture. This culture which literally pervades every aspect of his existence is an accumulated product which has been passed down through the generations and had its beginning at that point of time in the development of man when symbolic communication first appeared. When symbolic communication first appeared among interacting mammals, the human mind, the human self and the early crude forms of culture also appeared. These crude forms are mutual expectancies which men develop with respect to physical things, social situations and conceptual objects. Culture, then, is this accumulated body of mutual expectancies, ideas and ideologies which men, in any society, "carry around in their heads." In short, they are the customs of the group. These elements become hardened into language, norms, rules, laws and institutions which are observable and make for the tenacious quality of any culture. The nature and amount of these mutual expectancies, ideas and ideologies will differ from one society to another and from the various status and role positions within the same society. The level of development in tools and technology is an objective and external aspect of any culture, but these things emerge as products of the heritage of subjective elements and gain their significance for the society in the action patterns men develop in relation to them. A person is culturally at home when he shares with others these subjective elements and action patterns; he finds himself uncertain, insecure and confused when placed in situations where he does not share them.

Let us turn now to the nature of socialization.* This is the process by which

* In attempting to describe the process of socialization, we have included what some-

the new-born child is moulded into the culture of his group and hence becomes an acceptable person in that society. The family provides the first situation from which the human organism takes on the initial rudiments of the culture. In any society there are numerous possibilities with respect to the completeness of socialization. Some persons may take over not enough of the culture to function properly, others may take over deviant versions which make their behaviour unacceptable in the light of the norms of their respective groups, and still others may take over just enough of the culture to enable them to function in relation to others with a minimum of acceptance and effectiveness. There are still others —perhaps those designated as the well adjusted—whose absorption of the culture is so complete that they are able to maintain an extremely even balance between their mental life and conduct and the customs and conventions of their social groups. Finally, there are the creative ones who internalize numerous and large segments of the total culture and then refashion these materials in such a way that new ideas and relationships emerge that are expressed in science, invention and art to become a part of the cultural heritage.

Human experience can be regarded, for the most part, as the internalization of culture. Human experience encom-

passes, of course, more than this. It is deeper and more complex, for it also refers to the manner in which the person organizes the internalized cultural forms both with respect to his own individuality and his previously acquired cultural values. The person internalizes the culture of his group by means of learning, both conscious and unconscious. Thus, through intensive and extensive contacts with persons, things and ideas, he has a high probability of internalizing enough of his culture to enable him to enter into a mutually satisfactory social existence with other human beings.

A social system is an organized structure of human beings which functions towards the ends of maintenance and survival. It must also satisfy certain needs of those humans composing it. It is held together through symbolic communication which makes culture possible. If an increasing number of persons in the structure have difficulties in adaptation, we say the structure functions badly; if these numbers decrease markedly we think the structure is moving towards a greater maximum efficiency.

Theoretical Approaches and Some Derived Hypotheses

In attempting to analyse the various approaches significant for sociological study of mental disorder, we wish to make it clear that we are operating within the assumptions that we have laid down. Of the approaches useful to sociological study, the clinical approach is the oldest, perhaps because it lies closest to a commonsense level. For it is the person with his variant behaviour and distorted mentality who is more easily observed, and such observation, to the trained and perceptive mind, points immediately to the need for some kind of systematic examination.

THE CLINICAL APPROACH. Our concern with the clinical approach is primarily

times has been referred to as the process of culturalization. In making observations of child growth and development, it is extremely difficult to separate the two processes. Socialization may be more significant in the pre-lingual period of the child, but after beginning to use words the process of culturalization is in full swing. Socialization produces the social self and culturalization the moral or cultural self, concepts comparable to Freud's *ego* and *superego*. The cultural self is also an extension of the *social self* and gives it content. For a good statement of this distinction, J. S. Slotkin, *Personality Development* (New York: Harper and Brothers, 1952), Paris II and III.

in terms of its research value, although in psychiatry, as in other branches of medicine, its use is intimately tied up with the pressing need for therapy which aims to correct any pathology which is demonstrated or inferred. The clinical method in medicine is naturally preferred because it brings the physician into first-hand contact with the patient who requires treatment.

Here, we are concerned with the clinical method as used in psychiatry, psychology and sociology, and particularly the extent to which the method as used by these disciplines can be fused into an instrument which will be useful for the sociological study of mental disorder. The development of the clinical method in psychiatry has been both descriptive and analytical. It has been descriptive in the sense that careful case examinations have been used to build up various schemes of classification on the basis of symptoms which could be observed and at least partially objectified. It has been analytical to the extent that various investigators have attempted to make the observed data secured from examination support or fit into some ætiological theory.

It is natural and expected that the clinical method, favoured by medical research and practice, would prove useful in psychiatry. Kraepelin's (15) work in psychiatry is a demonstration of the clinical method. Kraepelin and others through this method have attempted to build up a careful accounting of specific symptoms appearing in the various mental-diseased conditions and to develop precise methods for their observation and examination. These methods constituting the core of the psychiatric examination have been the essential framework for the practice of psychiatry. However, the examination carried out in an objective spirit has never succeeded in transcending the necessity for numerous subjective interpretations.

The static psychiatry, which still is strong in state mental hospitals, revealed its weaknesses in its atomistic conception of mental life, its methods of examinations, and its view of man which failed to take account of the fact that man wherever he is found leads a group existence. The atomization of the emotional and mental life into such entities as mood, thought content, orientation, remote memory, recent memory, retention, recall, thinking capacity, general knowledge, intelligence, insight and judgment did provide the basis for a psychiatric diagnosis, but did not provide much which could be turned to therapeutic value. Then, too, the methods for getting at these entities were simple and direct. They provided no check on their validity and gave no conception of their inter-relationships in the total personality.

The discoveries concerning man's mental life by Sigmund Freud were eventually to challenge this static conception of psychiatry. In his psychoanalytic theory, Freud provided a closed psychological system wherein certain observable mental symptoms could be explained by the damage, restrictions and pressures that Western culture placed in the way of the unfolding sexual instinct. These cultural harassments of man's sexual nature were described by careful clinical accounts of the playing out of the family drama where emotional growth would be either facilitated or arrested. This image of man and society proved not to have the universality ascribed to it, but it did furnish the means for breaking through the static quality of previous psychiatry by encompassing the total changing life of man as he moved from uninhibited infancy to controlled and responsible adulthood. Through its techniques of free association and dream analysis it provided in one blow a method both of research and therapy.

Clinical psychology in its development has supported and paralleled the development of clinical psychiatry. The construction of the first mental tests by Binet during World War I not only gave an impetus for the emergence of clinical psychology but also, and more important, created an objective measure for one aspect of the mental life with which the psychiatrist was concerned in his examination. If intelligence could be determined objectively it seemed only logical that many other mental and emotional characteristics could eventually be identified and described in objective terms. Thus, during the past forty years certain psychologists have directed their energies towards the perfection of various instruments which would provide objective measurements for such clinical inferences as reaction time, attitudes, personality traits, aptitudes, perceptions, educational level, interests, values, neurotic tendency and personality type.

Psychiatry, sensing some value in this work, turned increasingly to clinical psychology for objective measures of certain mental and emotional characteristics. As psychiatry moved from its early static conception to a dynamic view, clinical psychology attempted to keep pace by constructing instruments which would in an objective manner lay bare the richness, movement, content and conflicts of the mental life. The development of such clinical instruments as the Rorschach, thematic apperception and the Szondi tests emphasize this change of pace. These tests have been regarded in some quarters as providing an objective check upon the psychiatric diagnosis.

In general, the clinical approach as used in psychiatry and clinical psychology has the following purposes: (1) to lay bare the intercorrelation of physiological and mental mechanisms in order to account for subjective outlook and behaviour, and (2) to develop measures for objectively determining certain discrete but subjective characteristics. From some perspectives in these disciplines the assumption is made that cause is found in the interaction or combinations of those physiological and psychological elements found in the person.

The clinical approach is also found in sociology, but from quite an altered perspective concerning the nature of man and his relationship to society. Here, the clinical approach is best seen in the developed use of the life history document. The life history method has two major functions. It is a technique for studying the process involved in the internalization of experience with its meaning to the person in terms of his self-conception and his orientation to the world. Again, it can be and has been used as a means for gaining insight into the organization and functioning of certain aspects of a given culture, as viewed through one human experience.

Twenty years ago when Dollard (6) stated his criteria for judging the adequacy of the life history document, he emphasized as one of them that "the person should be considered a specimen in a cultural series." This criterion actually states the very essence of the differences between the clinical approach as described above and as used by the social scientist. From this perspective the person does not stand in opposition to his culture, nor does he create the culture on the basis of his biopsychic endowment, but rather is the person both a creature of and a creator of culture. Thus, it follows that the clinical approach in the study of mental disorder or any deviant behaviour should aim at the examination of the case from different theoretical positions. Further, as a research technique for analysing human personality and behaviour, it should not be used as a test or a proof of the correctness of any one theory. Thus, with every person who is identified as having distortions in the thinking, feeling or acting spheres, the examiner should attempt in his clinical study to answer the following questions. Does the evidence secured by the clinical examination provide plausible support for a biological, psychological or sociological explanation for the maladjustment in question? Does the burden of the evidence favour one type of explanation as against the other types? Are there elements from all three sources which form some integration to produce the complete clinical picture? What are the specific evidences which point to the selected alternative? The answers to these questions are all important, for they determine the next steps not only in research but also in treatment.

In considering the clinical approach to mental disorder, we have noted that the examination might proceed within a biological, a psychological or a sociological framework of theory. We concluded by indicating that the clinical examination of a case should not be used to test the correctness of any one theory. Rather, it should assemble the pertinent data from all three theoretical positions in order to form a diagnostic judgment which would contain statements not only of the immediate condition but also of the best theoretical interpretation of the findings in terms of biological, psychological or sociological theory, or a combination of all three.

THE ECOLOGICAL APPROACH. In this approach we are concerned with analysing the distribution of various types of mental disorder in time and space (7, 9, 11, 16, 17, 18). In such studies the investigator is immediately faced with the question as to whether or not any one distribution contains the same type of cases. If various bits of evidence can give him assurance on this point, then he can proceed to look for significant rate variations for a given type of case either in time or social space.

Let us consider, for the moment, significant rate variations for schizophrenia in a community or social space. What do such rate variations signify? At present there are, at least, two possible explanations. First, local areas in the community where rates are high have a greater prevalence of social conditions and characteristics which are schizophrenically inducing than is the case in areas where rates are low. Two assumptions are implicit here: (a) the social conditions and characteristics favourable to the disorder are relatively constant over a long period of time in the life of the community, and (b) the persons who make up the rate in the local area have been subjected to these conditions rather consistently through their growth years. A second explanation states that certain areas have disproportionately high rates because the social conditions and characteristics of these areas are favourable for selecting out and bringing to official attention numerous schizophrenic persons who, if they give no trouble, are left to the care of family or friends. This explanation implies that a societal judgment, in contrast to a psychiatric judgment, is crucial in determining who gets labelled as schizophrenic. In both explanations we are assuming an equal accessibility to hospital and clinical facilities. This is probably not the case in countries as large and as varied as the United States. The marked variation in first admission rates in the forty-eight states of the United States may be only a reflection of unequal facilities and not variations in true incidence. However, until we have more adequate checks, we cannot determine what the actual situation is. Unequal facilities may be a fact that can explain some rate variations, but it hardly can be said to constitute a theory.

A theory of social selection is found in the Hollingshead-Redlich hypothesis of differential treatment (14). Their findings support the hypothesis that "current prevalence is a measure of the responses patients in the several classes make to the treatment process," although they are quick to point out that it does not shed any light on why, from the beginning of treatment, schizophrenic patients are highly concentrated in the lower class. An acceptance of this hypothesis requires assurance on two counts. Under the condition that no treatment was available, what would be the prevalence index by social class? What evidence do we have that current treatment techniques available to upper-class persons actually arrest the development of schizophrenia?

Let us return to our two theoretical explanations. Significant rate differentials for areas within a community might be explained by either of these theories. But the ecological technique, even though skilfully used, is not likely to provide much of a basis for determining which theory is the more valid.

These two theories are also relevant in examining those studies dealing with the distributions of new mental cases through time. Does the functioning of a social system through time have a greater pathic effect during some periods than at others, or do merely more cases come to be selected out for psychotic designation at these pathic periods? Goldhamer and Marshall (2) in their recent study present statistical evidence to the effect that there has been no marked increase in the psychoses of the central age groups over the past century. Their findings, they think, serve to refute the view current in some quarters that there has been a marked increase in mental disease during the twentieth century and that such an increase is related to the "killing pace" of contemporary civilization. Now, if these findings are finally accepted it means, as Goldhamer and Marshall point out, that the particular stress factors relevant to the production of psychosis have not increased over the past century or that if they have, they do not have the particular pathic effect which has been attributed to them. One might also infer that short-term increase in rates, which Goldhamer and Marshall see as a possibility, means that at particular stress periods more persons are selected out and defined as psychotic than at other non-stress periods.

Now these inferences from the findings of this study have a direct bearing upon the community and social class distribution studies. For there would seem to be

no question that stress and strain are distributed differentially in the various parts of any social structure. This reasoning leads us to the original explanations. Does maximal social stress in an area operate in the production of psychotics or merely in the selection and designation of more persons as psychotic compared to the areas where social stress is minimized?

It is my judgment that this issue will not be resolved very quickly or easily. To aid in its resolution three possible procedures are available. Here, let us again use schizophrenia because it really represents the number one mental health problem. One procedure is to perfect clinically the diagnosis of schizophrenia. This may mean eventually the breaking up of this present diagnostic category into several entities (1). It would be necessary here, of course, to develop objective procedures for determining a diagnosis for each of these new entities. Another alternative, if no headway is made in this direction, is to assume that schizophrenia is in reality socially induced. If persons in the family or neighbourhood say a person is mentally unbalanced, then we may have to conclude after careful screening that this is a schizophrenic. This means, of course, that the social definition of schizophrenia will vary in the different areas of a community structure, and thus we have an understanding of the schizophrenic rate differentials in various communities. Schizophrenia, then, might be regarded as a joint product of social stress and social judgment.

Still a third procedure is to locate some community in Western culture that has been rather stable over a generation and influenced little by in or out migration. If such a community could be located, an investigator could then proceed to locate the areas of conflict, stress and tension. After delimiting such areas within the community, he would then proceed to examine the schizophrenic rate. If the rate was significantly higher in areas of high social stress, as compared to those of low social stress, then he might be in a stronger position for asserting the role of social stress factors in the ætiology of schizophrenia.

Ecological findings of distribution and correlation always face two questions: (1) What theoretical principle provides the most valid explanation for the findings? (2) How can such findings be most effectively utilized for the development of hypotheses about mental disorders which then must be studied by other methods?

THE CULTURAL APPROACH. This approach is closely linked with the ecological. To the extent that the ecological area can be said to encompass a subculture, the two approaches have a close working affinity. For in it are the elements of the subculture that a person internalizes and utilizes in coming to terms with other subcultures within the larger cultural framework. Some investigators have tended to concentrate on the observation and study of child training techniques when working within a cultural approach. Findings from these studies (8, 13, 19) have been more eloquent in reporting differences in child training techniques than they have been in showing their significance for mental disturbances.

However, the significance of the cultural approach is not reflected adequately in these studies but lies rather in the cross-cultural observations in studies of mental disorder. The person who proposes to investigate mental disorder from a cross-cultural perspective should be concerned with seeking answers to the following questions:

First, do the kinds of behaviour and syndromes which constitute various abnormal mental states show incidence variations within a given cultural system?

Secondly, are there significant variations in the incidence of mental disorder between different cultural systems?

Thirdly, does a given culture have significance for both the form and content or only the content of abnormal mental states?

Fourthly, are there marked variations between cultures in terms of the presence or absence of psychotic-inducing elements?

Finally, are the strains and stresses or the general ethos of a given culture significant for the development of mental disorders?

The significance of these questions can be seen more clearly by making certain assumptions about culture and then attempting to point to some logical consequences that follow from each assumption.

Because cultural relativism is still a prevailing doctrine among many anthropologists, let us start here. Cultural relativism as an intellectual position in anthropology asserts that the values and practices observed in any culture are to be understood and evaluated only in terms of the total framework of that particular culture. To be sure, there has been some concern among some anthropologists to find universal moral values but this problem, while it may cross the mind of a cultural relativist, is seldom confronted as a problem that can be solved.

Thus, starting from a position of cultural relativism in attempting to explain functional mental disorder, the following propositions would be expected to have validity. First, both form and content of functional mental disorder would vary in different cultures. Secondly, certain cultures would have a greater incidence of their particular mental disorders than other cultures would have of the mental disorders peculiar to them. This is equivalent to saying that some cultures contain more psychotic-inducing elements than do other cultures. Thirdly, the incidence rate of mental disorder in a given culture would be relatively constant during periods of stability, but would rise or fall with swift and sharp changes in the cultural system.

Let us now make the opposite assumption—namely, that there is a psychic unity of mankind which is independent of any particular cultural system. The following conclusions would then logically follow. First, functional mental disorders are present and found among people in every culture. Secondly, the content of a psychosis would vary from culture to culture, but not its form. Thirdly, variations in the incidence of mental disorder between different cultures would be accounted for either by (a) a given culture providing acceptable roles for certain psychotics (defined in Western diagnostic terms) in terms of its functioning, or (b) a given culture containing within it more psychotic-inducing elements or traits than another culture. If (a), as above, accounts for differential incidence, then by taking account of such cases one might expect to bring the rate of functional psychoses in that culture up to a rate parity found in other cultures. If significant variations still exist between cultures, one would then be in a more confident position for asserting the validity of the (b) alternative.

Let us make one final assumption that the incidence of functional disorders among different cultures is approximately equal but in any given culture sharp increases or decreases are observed. Where would one look for explanations for such occurrences? Current theory already suggests certain possibilities for enquiry and so we will do no more than make brief mention of them here. First, if a given culture develops sharply contradictory definitions in certain areas of behaviour, one might expect such contradictions to be registered in a differential rate of functional mental disorder. Secondly, if a culture is in the process of acculturation due to penetrating contacts from a culture outside of it, one might

again expect an increase in rate. Thirdly, if a culture shows sudden and quick social changes from within, one deals with another possibility for a rate increase. Finally, if a given culture is threatened in its peace and security from a force or forces outside of it, one deals with a situation where the mental disorder rate would be expected to decrease significantly.

In dealing with these logical possibilities we are well aware of the empirical difficulties. Most cultural barriers may be swept away before the means can be developed to test these hypotheses. Two surveys of observations and investigations of mental disease among so-called primitives (2, 5) have served to focus either directly or indirectly on the issues raised in attempting to explore the possible relationships between culture and mental disease. Benedict and Jacks contend that while abnormal mental states peculiar to individual cultures have been reported, the more penetrating analysis of individual dynamics along with the awareness of the cultural context demonstrate the "underlying similarities of these mental disorders among primitive peoples to those seen in the West." They call for more detailed and systematic investigations of mental disorders among non-Western societies. Their conclusion is much the same as Felix and Bowers made five years before when they called for more intensive studies of the development and breakdown of personality in differing cultural milieus (10).

In elaborating these various approaches, we have been especially concerned to sharpen the issues that they raise and to use our theory for pointing to those areas where sociological investigations will be most rewarding. We have seen that the great obstacle to more fruitful sociological investigations revolves around the lack of agreement as to what constitutes a case of schizophrenia or other functional disorders. It is possible that the present schizophrenic category contains many different entities with differing ætiologies. If in the future ways can be found for breaking up the current schizophrenic grouping and for determining objectively a diagnosis of schizophrenia, psychiatric medicine will have achieved its greatest triumph. If this does not take place, then we will be thrown back upon social judgments in diverse cultural milieus for determining just exactly who is "crazy." Even so, while a disturbance may take similar form in different cultural milieus, the level of tolerance of a culture then becomes relevant in determining who will be selected out to fill the role of the "psychotic" person. A resolution of this issue will greatly help to determine the relevance of the various sociological approaches for shedding light on mental disorder.

Summary

In this paper we have attempted to formulate a methodology for the sociological investigations of mental disorder. We have emphasized the necessity for such a methodology not only to guide subsequent sociological investigations in this area, but also to bring about more fruitful collaboration between the scientific disciplines concerned. We began our statement by attempting to make clear the general standpoints for sociological investigation. From there we formulated the assumptions which embody much of the theory for giving direction to sociological enquiry. We further elaborated the basis for sociological investigation by a statement of some essential concepts—culture, socialization, cultural internalization, and social system—that are essential for encompassing the reality embodied in man's relationship with his fellows. Finally, we examined the theoretical approaches essential for sociological investigations of mental disorder, attempting to show the manner that they can be integrated together for a total attack on the sociological side. It was further shown how these approaches made possible the derivation of certain specific hypotheses which might well serve as a starting point for future sociological research into the problems posed by mental disorder in human society.

It is hoped that this statement of methodology will serve to pin down to some extent both the limitations and opportunities for sociological research in this area.

REFERENCES

1. Bellak, L.: Concluding comment after reviewing the research in schizophrenia is very pertinent in this connection. "We believe that it may be helpful to conceive of any given case [schizophrenia] as actually occurring on some point of a continuum from a hypothetical point of complete psychogenicity to a hypothetical point of complete organicity." *Dementia Præcox: The Past Decade's Work and Present Status—A Review and Evaluation.* New York: Groves and Stratton, 1948, p. 444.
2. Benedict, P., and I. Jacks: "Mental illness in primitive societies." *Psychiatry,* November, 1954, 17, 377–389.
3. Caldwell, M. G., and Lawrence Foster (editors). Harrisburg, Pennsylvania: Stackpole Company, 1954, p. 322, for my first attempt at making these assumptions explicit.
4. Clausen, John A., and Melvin Kohn: "The ecological approach in social psychiatry," with Comment by H. Warren Dunham and Rejoinder by J. A. Clausen and M. Kohn. *American Journal of Sociology,* September, 1954, 60, 140–151.
5. Demerath, N. J.: "Schizophrenia among primitives." *American Journal of Psychiatry,* 1942, 98, 703–707.
6. Dollard, J.: *Criteria for the Life History.* New Haven: Yale University Press, 1935.
7. Elkind, Henry B., and M. Taylor: "The

alleged increase in the incidence of the major psychosis." *American Journal of Psychiatry,* January, 1936, 92.

8. Ericson, M. C.: "Child rearing and social status." *American Journal of Sociology,* November, 1946, 52, 190–192.

9. Faris, Robert E. L., and H. Warren Dunham: *Mental Disorders in Urban Areas.* Chicago: University of Chicago Press, 1939.

10. Felix, R. H., and R. V. Bowers: "Mental hygiene and socio-economic factors." *Milbank Memorial Fund Quarterly,* 1948, 26, 125–147.

11. Goldhamer, H., and A. Marshall: *Psychosis and Civilisation.* Glencoe, Illinois: The Free Press, 1953.

12. Op. cit., pp. 95–96.

13. Green, A. W.: "The middle-class male child and neurosis." *American Sociological Review,* February, 1946, 11, 31–41.

14. Hollingshead, A. B., and F. C. Redlich: "Social stratification and schizophrenia." *American Sociological Review,* June, 1954, 19, 302–306.

15. Kraepelin, E.: *Dementia Præcox and Paraphrenia.* Translated by R. Mary Barclay. Edinburgh: E. and S. Livingstone, 1919.

16. Malzberg, B.: *Social and Biological Aspects of Mental Disease.* Utica, New York: State Hospital Press, 1940.

17. Mowrer, E.: *Disorganisation—Personal and Social.* New York: J. B. Lippincott Co., 1942, Chs. 15 and 16.

18. Schroeder, C. W.: "Mental disorders in cities." *American Journal of Sociology,* July, 1942, 47, 40–47.

19. Sowell, W. H.: "Infant training and personality development." *American Journal of Sociology,* September, 1952, 8, 130–139.

Social System as Source
of Independent Variables and
Personality Variables as Dependent

SINCE we have attempted to identify the distinctive analytic differences between the personality and social-system levels in Parts One and Two, we now come to the substantive question: How do variables at these two levels affect one another empirically? This question dominates Parts Three, Four, and Five.

Part Three concerns the influence of social variables on personality. This influence can be characterized in several different ways. Social variables can affect the *formation* of personality characteristics, as in socialization; or they can affect the *expression* of already formed characteristics, as in social control. Social variables can act *directly* on the personality, as in the internalization of a parental role in the formation of the superego; or social variables can operate *indirectly,* as when the occupational role of the father places certain restrictions on his family life, and this family structure in turn influences the development of the child's personality. All these kinds of influence are seen in the selections in Part Three.

To organize Part Three we begin by considering that special body of research on experimental small groups—research on how group characteristics condition the emergence of personality characteristics. Then we turn to the life-cycle of the individual, viewed in terms of the social structures that impinge on his personality—the family, the school, the peer group, and finally adult roles. Toward the end of Part Three we examine some of the effects on personality when social structures themselves change.

In a way, small-group research is an artificial setting for studying the effects of social systems on personality, because small groups are very special types of social systems. They do not have to face many exigencies—birth of new members, prolonged periods of socializing children, institutionalization of complex systems of authority, and so on—that large-scale, more enduring social structures face. Nevertheless, by modifying relevant features of small groups experimentally, it is possible to isolate certain variables that influence the degree to which certain personality characteristics will be expressed. In this section we include two such experimental studies. Albert Pepitone and George Reichling investigate the influence of group cohesiveness (a social variable) on the expression of hostility (a personality variable) within the group. Their general conclusion is that highly cohesive groups, being more flexible, can "afford" more hostility, by contrast with groups that lack cohesion, whose brittleness presumably makes them more vulnerable to hostility. In a related article, Leon Festinger, Albert Pepitone, and Theodore Newcomb examine the effects of anonymity (or de-individuation) on personal behavior. The hypothesis tentatively supported in this study is that social anonymity tends to reduce inner restraints and to permit otherwise prohibited behavior to emerge. This finding is related to the phenomenon of extreme behavior that sometimes occurs in anonymous crowd situations.

Six selections deal with the impact of the family on the development of personality. Three deal with the genesis of "normal" motivational patterns and three involve the genesis of "mental disorders" and "deviance." For the first three we move from very general to very specific concerns. Talcott Parsons attempts to show the importance of having a *nuclear* family (one adult of each sex and young children), rather than some other type of family, as the core socializing unit for children. Parsons rests his case in part on the assertion that this type of family is optimum for inculcating male and female sex identification. Using such argumentation, Parsons attempts to rewrite the classic Freudian stages of socialization in terms of the distinctive role structures that impinge on the child at each stage. The concern of George de Vos in his article on Japanese family life is narrower than that of Parsons, though he, too, is interested in explaining adult personality characteristics (specifically, attitudes toward achievement and arranged marriages) in terms of the distinctive features of Japanese family life. It might be added that these attitudes, generated in the family structure, feed back positively into this structure, and in this way reinforce some of those very patterns (e.g., arranged marriage) that generated the attitudes in the first place. Finally, in a more detailed article, Gerald Lesser investigates the effect of the mother-child relationship on the ways in which the child's aggression will be expressed—overtly or in fantasy.

Turning to the genesis of behavior that is defined socially as disturbed or deviant, we include first the theoretical article by Gregory Bateson, Don Jackson, Jay Haley and John Weakland.[1] These authors single out family situations that create a "double-bind" for the child—situations that enforce two conflicting injunctions and simultaneously prevent him from escaping from either injunction. In such situations, it is argued, schizophrenic fantasies are likely to develop. In the selection by Bertram Roberts and Jerome Myers, the dependent variable is again schizophrenia, but the independent variables are defined more specifically. Roberts and Myers suggest that a combination of an overprotective mother and an inadequate but sadistic father—a pattern perhaps frequently found in the lower middle class—is typically schizophrenogenic. If properly established and interpreted, it might be that the Roberts-Myers finding would turn out to be a special case of the more general "double-bind" situation discussed by Bateson, *et al.* Finally, Joan and William McCord investigate the importance of the family situation for the genesis of criminality. Starting with the ancient belief that criminal fathers breed criminal sons, the McCords argue that only if other factors *plus* a criminal father are present will this be

[1] We wish to thank Dr. Harvey Peskin for suggesting this selection, which escaped our attention in our original search through the literature.

true. Among these other factors are parental rejection and erratic parental discipline.

One final article on the family—by Howard Freeman and Ozzie Simmons—concerns not so much the *genesis* of personality disturbances as the degree to which *existing* disturbances are expressed. In particular, the type of family to which a mental patient returns has much to do with whether he will be re-committed to the hospital. Freeman and Simmons produce findings that suggest that the patient who returns to a home in which he occupies the position of a child (i.e., when parental figures are present) will be less likely to be re-committed than the patient who returns to the responsibilities of a conjugal family.

After early childhood experiences in the family, the next critical social structures that impinge on the personality of the child are the school and the peer group. We include two articles on each. James Coleman stresses the largely negative influence of high-school student culture on achievement motivation. Coleman concludes with a critique of institutionalized competition in American high schools. In the final selection on education, Burton Clark investigates the effects of certain features of higher education on achievement motivation. In particular, he concentrates on the problem of how students judged to be inferior are "eased out" of higher education without undue damage to their self-picture.

Sports and games are an almost universal feature of peer groups, but the significance of these for personality development is little understood. R. Helanko, in his study of the sequences of sports participation among Scandinavian children, suggests that sports introduce children to new types of norms and to progressively more complicated social settings. In a second selection on the influence of peer groups on personality, Lionel Nieman argues that the adoles-

cent peer group is an important lever in modifying adolescent girls' views of femininity.

With respect to the influence of adult role memberships on personality, we include research on two social settings—bureaucratic structure and social class position. Robert Merton's article is a classic discussion of the consequences of bureaucratization for the personalities of bureaucrats—consequences such as trained incapacity, overconformity, and excessive impersonality. Merton's general article is followed by two revealing items of empirical research on bureaucratic roles. The selection by Seymour Lieberman, one of the few studies in this volume that employs longitudinal research methods, show the power of situational role involvements in conditioning attitudes; in particular, he demonstrates how the attitudes of workers change rapidly as they move to and from the positions of foreman and steward in an industrial bureaucracy. The selection by Richard Lee and Ralph Schneider introduces the problem of psychosomatic disorders. Using a particularly large sample, the authors compare the incidence of hypertension and arteriosclerosis in executive and nonexecutive personnel (clerks, secretaries, supervisors, etc.). Contrary to popular impression, the nonexecutive classes showed a significantly higher incidence of these disorders. While the authors offer only minimal interpretation of their findings, these results cast doubt on the traditional view that the more responsible is the executive, the more he will be plagued by chronic psychosomatic disorders.

Much research has accumulated in the past several decades on the influence of social class position on child-rearing practices, and through these practices on the personality development of the child. The results of this research are far from uniform. We include only a few samples in this volume. The selection by Martha

Sturm White compares her own research findings on differences in permissiveness between middle- and working-class parents with several past studies. The White article and its predecessors concentrate mainly on feeding, toilet training, and punishment for aggression. Melvin Kohn, in a more subtle study, inquires not only into the differences in behavior among classes in modes of punishment but also into the different reasons why such behavior occurs. Kohn suggests that working-class parents tend to utilize physical punishment in order to prevent the immediate consequences of disruptive behavior, whereas middle-class parents tend to punish physically only after they have assessed the child's motivation or intention in such behavior. Kohn's finding, if definitely established, would give us reason to suspect why it is that middle-class children typically develop stronger superegos than working-class children. In the final article on social class and personality, August B. Hollingshead and Frederick Redlich discover that *frequency* of diagnosed personality disorders, *type* of diagnosed disorders, and *treatment* received for disorders are all significantly associated with an individual's class position. One interesting problem that arises from their research is whether these associations reflect the true incidence of mental disorders or reveal some social class relationship between the diagnosers and the diagnosed.

We conclude Part Three with several articles on the effects of social change on personality. The first two selections—by Norman A. Scotch and by Harold Wilensky and Hugh Edwards—concern the personality effects that occur when individuals move into new social structures, as in migration or social mobility. Scotch attempts to relate differences in degree of blood pressure between migrant urban and traditional rural Zulu to the kinds and degrees of social stress experienced by each group. Wilensky and Edwards find that downwardly mobile workers (i.e., those with higher-class parents) tend to hold more conservative political beliefs and tend to be steadier and more committed employees than other workers. Wilensky and Edwards' interpretation is that the downwardly mobile "bring" their attitudes and habits with them into their new social environment.

The remainder of the selections deal with changing social structures themselves. In a thorough survey, Urie Bronfenbrenner attempts to assess recent changes in the American family structure and the consequences of these changes for child-rearing. Alex Inkeles, in an ingenious research into the family histories of Russian emigrants, shows how the values of parents are modified in periods of cataclysmic social change and how these changes are reflected in the ways they socialize their children. Turning to a completely different social context, George D. Spindler and Louise S. Spindler attempt to relate the different "national characters" of several American Indian tribes to the degree to which each has been acculturated to American society.

A · SMALL-GROUP RESEARCH AND ITS IMPLICATIONS

GROUP COHESIVENESS AND THE EXPRESSION OF HOSTILITY

by Albert Pepitone and George Reichling [1]

The field of interpersonal and intergroup hostility embraces several interlocked problem areas. There is, for example, the question of the conditions giving rise to hostility in the individual or group— the factors, in other words, that determine the hostile impulse. There is also the question—given the hostile impulse —of the conditions that govern the direction and quantity of its overt expression. A third question concerns the "fate" of the hostile impulse, particularly in relation to expression or lack of it. The phenomenon of "catharsis" illustrates this phase of the problem.

The present study is principally relevant to the problem of hostility expression. In particular, the experiment is concerned with the effect of group cohesiveness—as empirically defined in terms of the mutual attraction of members—upon the volume and direction of expressed hostility. The most pertinent data on this problem stem from an experiment by Wright (5). This investigator frustrated the play activity of paired chil-

[1] The authors are indebted to W. Wallace and E. Galanter, who participated in the experiment as the Assistant and Instigator, respectively.

SOURCE: *Human Relations*, Vol. 8 (1955), pp. 327–337.

dren between three and six years of age, who had been previously classified by their nursery school teacher as being Strong or Weak friends. The observed behavior of these children under conditions of frustration showed that the pairs of Strong friends expressed more aggression than the pairs of Weak friends, and that such aggression involved a greater incidence of physical attacks against the experimenter, e.g. kicking, biting.

If it is assumed that the two children in their play activity during the experiment constituted a group, and if preexisting friendship affected *only* the cohesiveness of this group, we may propose a formulation that is suggested by the data and that seems well in line with everyday observation: Members of cohesive groups provide each other with strength and support, which enables them to overcome internal and external restraints against retaliation in the event of attack. Highly cohesive groups, in other words, will be less restrained when under attack than relatively less cohesive groups. This greater ability of highly cohesive groups to reduce restraints will be reflected, we hypothesize, in a greater volume of expressed hostility and a more direct expression of hostility with respect to its source.

Method

Male volunteers were recruited from introductory psychology classes by an Assistant, who announced that a national organization was conducting an intensive survey of student attitudes toward various social and academic phases of campus life. The kinds of questions germane to the study were colorfully illustrated, and the fact that the Ss were to participate as a group was carefully explained. As an added incentive, it was indicated that several universities were participating in the survey and that a published copy of the comparative results would be furnished to all volunteers. Prospective Ss then indicated their free hours on a prepared form, and, for purposes of creating the cohesiveness variable, checked a list of assorted personality traits in accordance with: (a) the type of person they thought they were, and (b) the type of person with whom they would most like to work. A few additional questions bearing on their interest in school activities were also included on the form.

Ss recruited from *different* classes were paired and assigned at random to the High or Low Cohesiveness Conditions (Hico and Loco Groups). There were 13 groups in each condition. Upon being ushered into a conference room used for the experiment, the purposes of the survey were reviewed. Particular stress was placed upon the necessity for participation as a group. Then, in accordance with their designation as a Hico or Loco Group, the following treatments were given in a manner designed to maximize the effect of the formal content.

THE CREATION OF COHESIVENESS

Hico treatment: ". . . another factor in the selection of participants is that we try to get people who are basically compatible in their personalities, that is, who get along well together. We do this by matching people in terms of the traits

they possess with the traits of people they like. You probably remember doing this on the application form. I must say that, in your case, we were able to make an exceptionally good matching, so you should make an exceptional team."

Loco treatment: ". . . another factor . . . (exactly the same as the Hico treatment) . . . Unfortunately, we weren't able to make a good matching in your case, so I'm afraid you won't get along very well together."

The foregoing procedure is virtually identical with that successfully employed by Back for the purpose of inducing differential levels of group cohesiveness (1).

Following the cohesiveness treatment, the Assistant told the Ss that the "discussion leader" would arrive immediately.

THE CREATION OF HOSTILITY. On the basis of pilot studies, a technique was evolved that successfully aroused mild to strong hostility in these groups. In essence, the procedure was to treat the groups in an unjust, arbitrary, and insulting manner. The exact procedure followed was based wholly upon a well-rehearsed script, which was acted out in as natural and convincing a manner as possible.[2]

Instigator. (Enters after a deliberate, three-minute delay. To Assistant.) "Hello." (Looks annoyed.) "I see these groups finally got here. Do you have their application forms?"

Assistant. "Yes, here they are."

Instigator. (Looks through forms.) "This is terrible. How did these people get here?"

Assistant. "The campus doesn't have much to offer."

Instigator. "I can see that." (To one of the Ss.) "What's your name?" (To other S.) "And yours is?" (To one S.) "How old are you?" (Sarcastically, before S answers.) "We don't want kids for this

[2] Frequent checks by an independent observer indicated that the script was, in fact, being followed exactly as written.

survey—we need mature adults." (To second S.) "What's your age?" (Disgustedly, after S responds.) "That's just fine! Do either of you take part in any activities?" (Aside to Assistant.) "These people won't have any idea what's going on around campus." (To one S.) "Do you ever go out with girls? How often?" (After response, cynically.) "Great!" (To other S.) "And you?" (Moans as answer is given.) (To apparently poorer-dressed S.) "Do you always come to appointments dressed like that?" (To Assistant.) "Well, let's see if we can use these groups anyway. I'll give them a sample question." (To one S.) "How do you feel about student-faculty relations on campus?" (S is cut off before completing the answer. To other S.) "How about you?" (After response.) "Well, that's a profound observation!" (To Assistant.) "I can't waste the Association's time and money on drivel like this. I can't give them lab credit." (Volunteers had been promised an excuse from one lab paper.) "You might check with Professor Jason (fictitious) to find out if he can use them. He'll use almost anyone." (Exit.)

To eliminate external restraints from the situation, the Instigator severs his formal connection with the group and leaves. However, so as not to terminate the proceedings altogether, the possible use of the group by another person is suggested. Finally, to block any interpretation of official, repressive action toward the "bad" group, the Instigator is described by the Assistant as having relatively low status:

Assistant. "By the way, that was one of the graduate students in the department. These discussion groups are usually led by Professor Arnold Welch (fictitious), but he's attending a conference in New York today. I'll check with Professor Jason to find out if he can use you. I'll be back in about ten minutes."

There followed a "free" period of approximately six minutes, in which the groups were entirely alone. During this time, an observer in an adjacent room recorded various categories of motor and verbal behavior, which could be seen through a one-way-vision glass and heard through a sound-amplification system.

OBSERVATIONS. A schedule of observation categories was developed on the basis of pilot studies included were:

1. *Hostility.* All implicitly or explicitly negative statements were directed toward: the Instigator, the treatment and procedures employed by the Instigator or the Assistant, psychology and psychologists, the physical setting. In addition, there was a sub-category of general suspicion, which included all negatively toned statements of doubt, mistrust, and inquiry, without reference to any particular target.

2. *Mutual background.* All statements intended to enhance the Ss' knowledge about each other's "background," including interests, courses, and activities.

3. *Silence.*

4. *Physical gestures and movements.* The observations were made in terms of the number of seconds in which a statement occupied *one* of the above categories. The one exception was in the case of Physical Movements; here, word-descriptions were recorded. The categories were treated as mutually exclusive, i.e. there was no multiple coding. The Ss were not distinguished as individuals, since our major interest was focused on the group as a unit. For purposes of temporal analysis of the observed behavior, the schedule was divided into six sections of approximately one-minute duration.[3]

---

[3] Actually, adding the time it took the Assistant to walk from the "one-way" room to the conference room, the free period was for all groups somewhat over six minutes. In addition, the observer tended to overestimate the length of statements. Presumably, this error was constant for all groups.

QUESTIONNAIRE. At the end of the free period of observation, the Assistant reappeared. On an ambiguous pretext that additional information was needed by the "Association," a three-item questionnaire was administered. Each S recorded his response on a six-point rating scale.

1. Frankly, how much interest do you have in the proposed discussion? (Point 1, absolutely not interested; Point 6, extremely interested.)

plete explanation of the purposes of the experiment. Before the Ss were dismissed, apologies were tendered and, happily, in all cases accepted.

Results

The mean number of seconds of group behavior in the three observation categories employed during the free period are presented in *Table 1*.

TABLE 1. *Mean Seconds of Observed Behavior in the Hico and Loco Groups*

BEHAVIOR CATEGORY	HICO GROUPS N = 13	LOCO GROUPS N = 13	$SE_{diff.}$	t
Hostility	95.7	43.6	19.7	2.64 *
Mutual Background	145.6	179.0	37.7	0.89
Silence	75.7	105.5	29.0	1.03

* $p < .01$, one-tailed test

2. What is your feeling toward Professor Welch (the Instigator's name was substituted here) as a discussion leader? (Point 1, would dislike him thoroughly; Point 6, would like him pretty much.)
3. How do you feel towards your partner? How well would you get along in prolonged discussions and many meetings? (Point 1, would dislike him thoroughly; Point 6, would like him pretty much.)

GROUP INTERVIEW. Some thirty seconds after the questionnaires had been collected, the Instigator entered the room and announced to the Ss that they had been participating in an experiment and that it was all over. He then proceeded with a brief interview designed to uncover unexpressed feelings that Ss had during the experiment as well as their present sentiments. Responses to the standard set of open-ended questions were recorded verbatim by the Observer.

At the conclusion of the interview, appropriate time was taken for a com-

Table 1 shows that the only category significantly differentiating the Hico and Loco groups is that which reflects the amount of expressed hostility. The Hico groups, as predicted, release on the average more than twice as great a volume of hostility as the Loco groups. There is no significant difference between the experimental groups in the amount of mutual background behavior and in the time they were completely silent.

The three categories listed in Table 1, of course, did not exhaust the behavior that occurred during the free period. There were several other forms of verbal behavior not recorded. Also, throughout the free period there were physical movements and gestures of various sorts. These were described by the Observer as they appeared. For example, there were instances of laughter, changing seats, smiling, finger-drumming, throwing legs on table, sighing, looking under table, walking around the room.

A comparison of the Hico and Loco groups with respect to the total frequency

of these items reveals no difference. Further analysis, however, discloses a relevant finding. The Observer, the Assistant, and the Experimenter, with perfect agreement, sorted all the items into a dichotomy representing unrestrained and relatively restrained physical behavior.[4] For example, standing up, laughing, walking around the room were considered to be less inhibited behavior than smiling, drumming fingers, etc. The percentages of the total frequency of physical behavior thus characterized as relatively unrestrained are: 76 per cent for the Hico groups, and 47 per cent for the Loco groups. The difference, employing the standard error of P based upon the Hico

these precategorized objects of hostility included on the observation schedule.

It can be seen that, on the average, the Hico groups express significantly more hostility than the Loco groups toward the Instigator and toward the treatment accorded them by the Instigator and the Assistant. The groups do not differ in the hostility directed toward psychology, psychologists, and various features of the physical situation. There is also no difference with respect to general, nondirected suspicion. This result confirms our second prediction regarding the directness with which hostility is expressed. Presumably, the Instigator, the treatment, or both constitute the sources of hostility. As

TABLE 2. *Mean Seconds of Hostility Expressed toward Specified Objects by Hico and Loco Groups*

OBJECTS OF HOSTILITY	HICO GROUPS N = 13	LOCO GROUPS N = 13	$SE_{diff.}$	t
Instigator	55.7	11.5	11.6	3.81 *
Treatment	24.2	7.5	8.0	2.09 †
Psychology	3.8	8.8	4.4	1.14
Physical Setting	1.1	4.8	4.2	0.9
General Suspicion	10.9	10.6	7.0	0.04

* $p < .001$, one-tailed test
† $p < .03$, one-tailed test

and Loco groups combined, is significant at the .04 level of confidence, considering both tails of the normal probability distribution. The finding that highly cohesive groups are relatively less restrained in their physical behavior appears to be coordinate with the finding that these groups release more hostility than the less cohesive groups.

The hostility released by the groups was usually directed toward particular targets within and outside the immediate experimental situation. *Table 2* indicates the amount of hostility expressed toward

[4] The classifying procedure, of course, was accomplished independently of the consideration as to whether the Hico and Loco groups showed differential frequencies.

such, expression of hostility toward these objects may be considered to be more directed than toward other objects.

Since these sub-categories representing objects of hostility are exhaustive with respect to the amount of hostility released, a comparison of the Hico and Loco groups in terms of absolute mean values may not be an accurate reflection of true differences. The proportion of the total hostility released by the Hico and Loco groups that is directed toward the Instigator and the treatment may be compared. Eighty-three per cent of the hostility released by the Hico groups is in the direction of the Instigator or the treatment, while in the Loco groups forty-four per cent takes the same direction.

The difference between these percentages is significant at the .03 level of confidence, considering both tails of the probability distribution.

Throughout the course of the free period the amount of hostility released by the groups fluctuated from moment to moment. Fig. 1 pictures the amount of hostility expressed by the average Hico and Loco groups during each one-minute interval of the free period.

The curves representing both Hico and Loco groups are higher at the beginning than at the end of the free period. For the Hico groups, the reduction in the amount of expressed hostility is very steady over the whole time span. The mean of the difference from the first interval to the last is significant (t = 4.10, p < .01). The curve of the Loco groups begins with a slow decline, then drops sharply and significantly between the second and third minutes (t = 3.08, p < .01). Thereafter, the curve is essentially flat at about the level of five seconds' hostility.

There are several hypotheses that might reasonably account for these curves. One possibility may be briefly indicated. It should be borne in mind that the curves in Fig. 1 represent a succession of averages and not necessarily theoretical functions.

The general diminution of expressed hostility is due to a reduction in the amount of hostility that is available for release. Hostility expressed during any interval leaves a lesser amount to be released during subsequent intervals of the free period. As for the Loco groups, it has already been shown that they are not able to release as much hostility as the Hico groups. When interpreted in a temporal sense this would imply that they more quickly exhaust the amount of hostility they can release than the Hico groups.

Apart from whether this particular hypothesis is correct, there is no doubt that during the free period the Hico groups released a greater amount of hostility than the Loco groups. Making the reasonable assumption that the same amount of hostile impulse was generated in both groups, it might be expected that after the free period the Hico groups would display more favorable attitudes toward

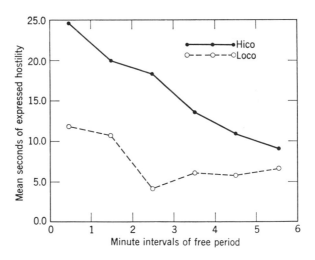

Fig. 1. Mean seconds of hostility expressed during each minute interval of the free period by the Hico and Loco groups.

environmental objects than the Loco groups. Table 3 presents data relevant to this point.

It can be seen that the Hico groups give a higher average questionnaire rating on Instigator attractiveness than the Loco groups. The difference between the groups in this respect is statistically significant. Although this finding appears to be understandable in terms of a greater catharsis of hostile impulses in the Hico groups, strictly speaking we cannot demonstrate catharsis without proof that the Loco groups did not become less favorably disposed toward the Instigator owing to their relatively low amount of expressed hostility.[5]

tility show no net change in cohesiveness (3).

There are no differences between the Hico and Loco groups in the degree of interest they had toward the proposed discussion. Such a motivational factor, therefore, cannot be used to explain the differential attitude toward the Instigator or the difference in cohesiveness.

When the Instigator informed the groups that they had been in an experiment and that they could relax, the Ss issued a variety of responses, which were recorded by the Observer. There were shouts of surprise, moans, hostile oaths, as well as stretches, smiles, etc. Although the Hico groups tended to make more of

TABLE 3. *Mean Ratings (Ss Pooled) on Questionnaire Items by Hico and Loco Groups*

QUESTION	HICO GROUPS N = 13	LOCO GROUPS N = 13	SE$_{diff.}$	t
Interest	8.4	9.1	.57	1.23
Liking of Instigator	6.8	6.2	.25	2.40 *
Liking of Partner	11.7	10.2	.32	4.69 †

* p < .02, both tails
† p < .001, both tails

Table 3 also shows a significantly greater degree of mutual attraction between the Hico pairs of Ss than between the Loco pairs. This result presumably confirms the different cohesiveness treatments given to the two experimental groups. To interpret this finding as due, not to the original cohesiveness treatment, but only to the differential amount of hostility released by the two groups would be difficult. In fact, there are data showing that groups in which hostility remains relatively unexpressed tend to show an *increase* in cohesiveness, while groups that express relatively more hos-

[5] See (4) for a critical discussion of this problem.

these "cathartic" responses than the Loco groups, the difference was not statistically significant. Further analysis, however, did reveal an interesting finding. It had been observed that in some groups the foregoing responses were made by both Ss, while in other groups, only one S responded—often in the manner of a spokesman—or there was no observable response at all. When the experimental groups are compared, we find that the number of groups in which *both* Ss respond occurs twice as often under the Hico condition as under the Loco condition. The difference is significant by chi-square test at about the .06 level of confidence. This result, although based upon relatively small frequencies, suggests that cohesiveness, in providing group members with more mutual support, enables a greater number of them to express their feelings.

Discussion

An increasing body of experimental evidence points to a close causal relationship between the cohesiveness of a group and the amount of mutual influence that is achieved among the members of that group (1, 2). In somewhat oversimplified terms, the theoretical basis for this relationship is essentially as follows: to the degree that, for whatever reason, members desire to remain in a given group, they will tend to originate and to accept pressures that are designed to preserve the group or to advance the group toward its goals. Thus, it may be said that the greater the cohesiveness of a group, the greater the power of that group to bring about change in its members. We propose a simple extension of this theory so that it may embrace phenomena other than influence pressures: The more cohesive the group, the greater the tendency for members to provide and accept support designed to overcome restraints that bar the removal of a threat to the group or that otherwise bar the locomotion of the group toward its goal. In other words, we may say that cohesiveness increases the group's "capacity" as well as its "power."

The foregoing general statement fits the results of the present experiment reasonably well. The members are attacked by the Instigator individually and collectively. They seek to remove this threat or at least retaliate against it. However, internal and perhaps external restraints tend to bar the expression of their hostility. The greater ability to reduce restraints assumed to characterize the Hico groups would account for the greater volume of hostility expressed, the greater directness with which hostility is expressed, and the apparently less restrained physical behavior.

Summary

1. The purpose of this experiment was to test the hypothesis that High cohesive groups are able to express more hostility than Low cohesive groups and that the hostility expressed by High cohesive groups will be more direct than that expressed by Low cohesive groups. Results tend to confirm these predictions at acceptable levels of confidence.

2. The Hico groups' physical behavior tended to be less restrained than that of the Loco groups.

3. There was some evidence supporting the psychoanalytic concept of catharsis. Having released a greater amount of hostility during a free period, the Hico groups rated the Instigator more favorably than the Loco groups.

4. In line with the proposed effect of cohesiveness in terms of the provision and acceptance of mutual support, the number of groups in which both Ss showed cathartic responses was significantly greater under the Hico than under the Loco condition.

5. A general theoretical statement was offered to integrate the findings.

REFERENCES

1. Back, K.: "Influence through social communication." *J. abnorm. soc. Psychol.,* 1951, 46, 9–23.
2. Festinger, L.: "Informal social communication." *Psychol. Rev.,* 1950, *57,* 271–282.
3. Thibaut, J.: "An experimental study of the cohesiveness of underprivileged groups." *Hum. Relat.,* 1950, 3, 251–278.
4. Thibaut, J., and J. Coules: "The role of communication in the reduction of Interpersonal hostility." *J. abnorm. soc. Psychol.,* 1952, 47, 770–777.
5. Wright, M. E. "The influence of frustration upon the social relations of young children." *Character and Pers.,* 1943, 12, 111–122.

SOME CONSEQUENCES OF DE-INDIVIDUATION IN A GROUP

by Leon Festinger, Albert Pepitone, and Theodore M. Newcomb

Anyone who observes persons in groups and the same persons individually is forced to conclude that they often behave differently in these two general kinds of situations. Casual observation would seem to indicate that one kind of behavior difference stems from the fact that people obtain release in groups, that is, are sometimes more free from restraints, less inhibited, and able to indulge in forms of behavior in which, when alone, they would not indulge.

The most-often noted instance of such freedom from restraint is the behavior of persons in crowds. In a crowd, persons will frequently do things which they would not allow themselves to do under other circumstances. In fact, they may even feel very much ashamed later on. Such behavior is not, however, limited to crowds. It occurs regularly in groups of all sizes and of many different types. For example, a group of boys walking down the street will often be wilder and less restrained than any of them individually would be; at an evening party persons who are usually very self-conscious and formal will sometimes behave quite freely; the delegates to an American Legion convention, all dressed in the same uniform manner, will sometimes exhibit an almost alarming lack of restraint. The question with which we will concern ourselves is: *when does this kind of behavior occur and why does it occur?*

There occurs sometimes in groups a state of affairs in which the individuals act as if they were "submerged in the group." Such a state of affairs may be

SOURCE: *Journal of Abnormal and Social Psychology,* Vol. 47 (1952), pp. 382–389.

described as one of de-individuation; that is, individuals are not seen or paid attention to as individuals. The members do not feel that they stand out as individuals. Others are not singling a person out for attention nor is the person singling out others.

We would like to advance the theory that, under conditions where the member is not individuated in the group, there is likely to occur for the member a reduction of inner restraints against doing various things. In other words, many of the behaviors which the individual wants to perform but which are otherwise impossible to do because of the existence, within himself, of restraints, become possible under conditions of de-individuation in a group.

If individuals, then, have needs which they are generally unable to satisfy because of the existence of inner restraints against doing certain things, a state of de-individuation in a group makes it possible for them to obtain satisfaction of these needs. A group situation where de-individuation does occur will consequently be more satisfying, other things being equal, than one where de-individuation never takes place. We would expect groups which do occasionally provide conditions of de-individuation to be more attractive to their members.

The satisfaction obtained during states of de-individuation is only one of many kinds of satisfactions which persons obtain in groups. Groups help people achieve goals which require joint or cooperative action, they provide support for opinions and behavior patterns, they sometimes satisfy persons' needs for approval and status, and the like. Many kinds of satisfactions which groups provide and which, consequently, make groups attractive to members may be put into two incompatible classes:

1. *Those which necessitate individuation in the group.* Prestige and status in a group, for example, require singling out an individual and behaving toward him in a special manner. Helping members achieve certain of their goals requires paying attention to the individual and to his particular needs.

2. *Those which necessitate de-individuation in the group.* These are the satisfactions which result from the lessening of inner restraints which we have discussed above.

It is clear that these two classes are incompatible in the sense that groups cannot provide both individuation and de-individuation at the same time. Groups can, however, provide both on different occasions.

Groups which can provide only states of de-individuation are probably not very stable. Crowds are a good example of this kind of group. The momentary and evanescent existence of crowds is probably due to the inability of this type of group to satisfy needs requiring individuation. On the other hand, groups which can provide only conditions of individuation are probably not very satisfying to their members. A group, for example, in which members were constantly being singled out for praise, approval and attention would most likely prove frustrating in the long run. Groups which succeed in being very attractive to their members probably provide both types of situations on different occasions.

As a beginning toward support of this theory concerning the consequences of de-individuation we set out, in the present study, to demonstrate:

1. That the phenomenon of de-individuation in the group occurs and is accompanied by a reduction in inner restraint for the members.

2. That groups in which inner restraints are reduced are more attractive to their members than groups in which this does not occur.

The attempt was made, in a laboratory situation, to provide conditions which would facilitate de-individuation in the group and would also provide adequate opportunities for measurement. To do this, we wanted to create a situation in which there would be a strong force acting on the members to engage in some behavior against which there were strong inner restraints. Under such conditions some groups would be better able to create de-individuation situations than others. If de-individuation in the group did occur it would seem, from our theory regarding the phenomenon, that during such periods of de-individuation individuals in the group would not be paying particular attention to other individuals *qua* individuals. If this were true then, while being attentive to (and consequently well able to remember) what was done in the group, they should be less attentive to and less well able to remember which particular member had done what.

The extent to which inner restraints against engaging in the particular behavior were reduced should be reflected in the extent to which the members showed the behavior in question. This measure would undoubtedly be subject to error because of variation from group to group in the strength of the force acting on the members to engage in the behavior. If, however, we find a positive correlation between the extent to which the behavior in question was produced and the extent to which they were unable to identify who did what, this would be evidence supporting our theory of de-individuation in the group.

In those groups in which the restraints against engaging in the particular behavior were reduced the members would have obtained more satisfaction from the group situation. From our theoretical considerations we would consequently expect that the groups which did provide the conditions for de-individuation would be more attractive to their members.

Procedure

The subjects (Ss) for the study were males who volunteered in various undergraduate classes at the University of Michigan to participate in a group experiment. Seven volunteers were scheduled for each session, but for various reasons (study pressures, forgetfulness, etc.) all seven rarely appeared for the discussion meeting. Our sample consists of 23 groups, ranging in size from 4 to 7.[1]

When they arrived at the discussion room, Ss were seated around a conference table and were engaged by the observer in mildly cheerful small talk. This procedure was adopted to prevent excessive prediscussion interaction among Ss which we felt might introduce additional factors.

When all Ss had arrived, the experimenter (E) directed them to print their first names on cards so that each could be identified by the others in the discussion, and then proceeded to read aloud the following statement. The alleged survey and its findings are, needless to say, entirely fictitious.

The following statement represents a summary of an important research project that has recently come to the attention of psychiatrists and social scientists concerned with problems of personal adjustment among students. Although the results are demonstrably

[1] Eight female discussion groups were also conducted. These are not included with our experimental sample of male groups because of their considerably poorer memory with respect to who said what during the discussion. The results for these female groups, however, are in the same direction as those herein reported for the males.

reliable, it is believed that additional implications can be brought to light by having small groups of students discuss their personal views relating to these results.

A highly representative sample of 2365 students (1133 female and 1232 male) on 14 campuses, from all social-economic classes and several nationality backgrounds, was subjected to an intensive three-week psychiatric analysis consisting of repeated depth interviews and a battery of sensitive diagnostic tests. The results show unequivocally that 87 per cent of the sample possessed a strong, deep-seated hatred of one or both parents, ranging from generalized feelings of hostility to consistent fantasies of violence and murder. A finding of further significance was that those individuals who at first vehemently denied having such hostile impulses or who were unwilling to discuss their personal feelings in the matter were subsequently diagnosed as possessing the most violent forms of hostility. In other words, conscious denial, silence, or embarrassment were found to be almost sure signs of the strongest kind of hatred. Of the 13 per cent in whom no trace of hostility was found, the great majority thought they probably hated their parents and were willing to discuss every aspect of their feelings with the investigator.

In summary, 87 per cent were found by modern psychiatric techniques to possess deep-seated resentments and hostilities toward one or both parents. Individuals in this category who most vigorously denied that they had such feelings revealed, at the conclusion of analysis, the strongest degree of hatred. Thirteen per cent were found to be free of such aggressive impulses. Most of these individuals at first thought they were basically hostile and were interested in discussing their feelings toward their parents freely.

Discuss in detail your own personal feelings toward your parents in the light of these results. Try to analyze yourself in such a way as to get at the basic factors involved.

The Ss were each given a copy of the above statement and were asked to start discussing the matter. The discussion lasted 40 minutes.

The discussion material was designed to create conditions in which the phenomenon of de-individuation might occur. The particular topic was chosen because it was felt that most people would have inner restraints against expressing hatred of their parents and, in fact, many would not even want to admit it to themselves. In preliminary experiments, the statement given to Ss did *not* include the part which indicated that those who initially denied it later turned out to be the ones with the strongest hatred toward their parents. In these preliminary experiments the most frequent occurrence was complete avoidance of the topic they had been asked to discuss. Including this statement provided a force on Ss to talk about it. In other words, to the degree that Ss accept the statement, they experience a more or less strong pressure to reveal negative feelings toward their parents. This, together with the inner restraints against saying such things, provided the conditions that we wished to create.

OBSERVATION METHODS

During the 40-minute discussion an observer categorized statements in terms of whether they reflected positive or negative attitudes toward parents in the present or the past; positive or negative attitudes of others toward their parents; impersonal theories about parent-child relationships; and whether they expressed concern with the interaction of group members and the discussion procedure. Each contribution to the discussion was categorized and recorded next to the name of the person who made it together with the length of the contribution in seconds. Pauses which lasted for 20 seconds or longer were also recorded. In order to permit a detailed analysis of the discussion, the observations were divided into 3-minute sequential frames.

Of particular relevance to the hypothesis being tested are those contributions which expressed existing negative or positive attitudes that the group members have toward their own parents, since from these we can infer the degree to which there was a reduction in the inner restraint against expressing negative feelings.

Experience in our preliminary experiments indicated that each contribution would have to be categorized as an entity. Frequently a statement would begin with the implication that the person loved his parents deeply and end with an explicit denunciation of them. The reverse also appeared quite often—the group member would begin to describe various hostilities he feels toward his parents, only to end with a highly favorable over-all estimate of them. Such examples made it clear that expressions of attitudes toward parents could be coded meaningfully only in terms of the contribution as a whole rather than in terms of specific and often contradictory statements within the contribution. When the observer could not make a judgment of the total unit, that is, whether the basic feeling revealed toward parents was positive or negative, she categorized it as "questionable."

To represent the degree to which inner restraint against expressing "hatred of parents" was reduced in the group, we calculated the difference between the number of contributions which expressed negative attitudes (categorized as N) and the number of contributions which expressed positive attitudes (categorized as P). The number of P contributions was subtracted from the number of N contributions because it was felt that P contributions were indications of the nonreduction of restraint. The larger the difference, the more successful the group had been in reducing restraint against the expression of negative attitudes toward their parents. Statements categorized as "questionable" were omitted from this calculation. Examples of statements falling into the two major observation categories follow:

Negative attitudes (N)

"Frequently I get very angry at my mother and seemingly there's a good reason; but I don't get angry that way with others."

"There are times when my parents are so stubborn and bull-headed; they think they know best. Sometimes I don't think so."

"No matter how much I try to think that my folks are good to me, the fact remains that they've done me wrong."

Positive attitudes (P)

"I respect my father because he's got a head on his shoulders; he's more of a leader and a man."

"I feel toward my father that if I could be half the man he is, I'd be a great success."

"I respect my parents for understanding how important independence is for the person."

The observer [2] was trained intensively in preliminary experiments and in informal practice sessions. To check reliability, the experimenter independently observed one of the discussion groups. Calculating reliability by correlating the number of seconds of N in each of the 3-minute observation frames for the two observers yields a coefficient of .91. A correlation could not be computed for P because, in that group, it occurred too infrequently. One would expect it to be of comparable magnitude.

THE RECORDING OF STATEMENTS

To obtain a measure of Ss' ability to identify who had said what in the dis-

cussion, the experimenter recorded, as nearly verbatim as possible, 10 statements made by the group members during the discussion.[3] The following criteria were employed in selecting these statements from the discussion:

1. The content of the statement should be distinct enough to permit identification of the person who made it, i.e., the statement should be as dissimilar as possible from those made by other group members.

2. The statement should be about a sentence in length.

3. The statement should be grammatically coherent.

4. The 10 statements should come from as many group members as possible.

5. The 10 statements should be distributed over the entire 40-minute discussion period.

At the conclusion of the discussion, E made sure that the name cards were visible, and separated Ss to prevent copying. He then distributed a form and gave the following instructions:

I am going to read off some statements that were made in the discussion and some that were not made. If you do not remember the statement having been made, place a check in the first column next to the appropriate number. If you remember the statement, but offhand you do not recall who made it, place a check in the second column next to the appropriate number. Finally, if you recall who made the statement write the first name of that person in the third column. This is not a memory test of any kind, and there is no need to guess.

The statements were then read off in the same temporal order in which they were

---

[2] Miss Dorothy Peterson, a graduate student in Sociology.

[3] In 7 of the groups only 8 or 9 statements were recorded. This was occasioned by a lack of statements which fitted the criteria employed.

made in the discussion. Interspersed among the 10 statements, in constant order for all groups, were 5 statements that were not made in the discussion. These were included so as to provide a basis for comparing "Identification Errors," i.e., errors in recalling who said what, with "Memory Errors," i.e., errors in remembering the content of the discussion.

The Ss' responses to the statements were scored in the following way. If, on any of the 10 statements actually made in the discussion, the person failed to recall who had made it or if he attributed the statement to the wrong person, he was given an error. The average number per person of these "Identification Errors" was calculated for each group. Errors of general memory were calculated similarly: Whenever an S thought that a given statement had been made which actually had not or whenever an S thought that a given statement had not been made which actually had, he was given an error. As with "Identification Errors" these "Memory Errors" were averaged for the group.

The E, in recording the statements, frequently had trouble meeting the criteria mentioned above. The statements recorded varied greatly in their identifiability. Sometimes a statement would be recorded and later on others would make very similar statements, thus making the identification ambiguous and difficult for Ss. Sometimes, when the discussion was proceeding rapidly the experimenter would not be able to record the statement accurately and consequently the recorded statement would be quite different from what was actually said. To cope with these difficulties some of the statements were eliminated from the analysis when there were good grounds for believing they were poor statements.

The specific criteria used to eliminate the statement were as follows: In groups of five persons or more a statement was eliminated if: (a) all or all but one S made errors on it, or (b) all but two made errors and the S who made the statement erred himself.

In groups of four Ss a statement was eliminated if all or all but one, including the S who made the statement, made errors on it.

When statements had been eliminated the average number of "Identification" (I) and "Memory" (M) errors was corrected so as to make all groups comparable with respect to number of statements. The correction consisted of multiplying the number of I and M errors, respectively, by 10 and 15 and dividing by the number of statements actually used in the counting of errors, i.e., the number of statements recorded and not eliminated.

The measure used to represent the ability of the group to identify who said what was the average number of "I-errors" minus the average number of "M-errors." The average number of "M-errors" is subtracted in order to correct for general memory level of the group.

THE MEASUREMENT OF ATTRACTION TO THE GROUP

A postsession questionnaire included an item designed to measure the attractiveness of the group for the members. The question and the possible responses are as follows:

"Frankly, how much would you like to return for further discussions of similar topics with this same group (assuming your schedule to be free)?"
...... definitely want to return
...... fairly strong desire to return
...... feel neutral about it
...... fairly strong desire not to return
...... definitely do not want to return

Numerical values were assigned to each alternative (1 for "definitely do not want to return"; 5 for "definitely want to return") and an average attraction score was computed for each group.

EXPLANATION TO THE SUBJECTS

In each group, after the questionnaire had been administered, E explained the purposes of the study in detail to Ss. They were told that the data presented for the discussion topic were entirely fictitious and the reasons for using it, together with the reasons for the rest of the procedure, were discussed with them. Sufficient time was spent in this manner with each group for them to leave with a good understanding of the experiment. They were also asked not to tell others about the experiment since we did not want future Ss to know what was going to happen in the group. As far as the experimenters know, Ss faithfully kept silent about it.

Results

There are two relationships with which we will be primarily concerned in examining the results of this experiment: (a) the relation between the frequency of negative attitudes toward parents re-

vealed in the discussion and the ability to identify who said what, and (b) the relation between the frequency of negative attitudes revealed in the discussion and the attractiveness of the group for its members. After examining the evidence on these two points we will look at possible alternative explanations of the data and evidence for or against such alternatives.

DE-INDIVIDUATION AND REDUCTION OF
INNER RESTRAINT

It will be recalled that our measure of de-individuation in a group was the extent to which the members of the group were unable to identify who said what during the discussion (I-errors — M-errors). The measure of the extent to which inner restraints were reduced is the frequency of negative attitudes toward parents revealed in the discussion ($N - P$). Figure 1 shows the scatter diagram of the obtained relation between these two measures. From the theory we elaborated above we would expect to find them positively correlated.

Figure 1 shows the scatter diagram of the obtained positive correlation between these two variables. The correlation, in-

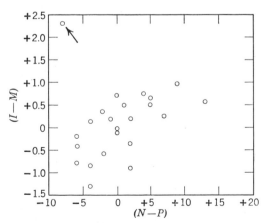

Fig. 1. Relationship between reduction in restraint and ability to identify who said what.

cluding all of the groups, is only .22. One of the groups, however, indicated on the figure by an arrow, is considerably off the scale on poorness of identification of who said what. There are grounds for believing that this group was affected by a very different factor, namely, disinterest in the experiment and in the discussion.

The major grounds for asserting this are the great number of pauses in the discussion for this group. Observing pauses only of 20-second duration or longer, this group had a total of over 5 minutes of complete pauses during the 40-minute discussion. No other group had pauses totaling more than one and a half minutes. Most of the groups had no pauses at all lasting as long as 20 seconds.

If we can take this as indicative of disinterest and, consequently, attribute the poor memory in this group to disinterested inattentiveness to people, then, considering how far off the scale of the other groups it is, it may be legitimate to omit this group from the calculations. Omitting this group, the correlation between the two variables in Fig. 1 is .57. This correlation is significant at the .01 level of confidence. Our further presentation and discussion of the data will omit this deviant group.

It is also instructive to examine the relations between the measure of reduction in restraint and the I-errors and M-errors separately. We would expect the reduction in restraint to be positively correlated with the average number of I-errors alone, although this correlation should be lower because of the uncontrolled general memory factor which enters. The correlation obtained between $N - P$ and I-errors is .31.

Perhaps a more accurate way to eliminate the general memory factor from this correlation would be to calculate the partial correlation of $N - P$ with I-errors, holding M-errors constant. Table 1 shows the intercorrelations among the three variables involved in this partial correlation.

TABLE 1. *Intercorrelations among I-Errors, M-Errors and N − P*

	M-ERRORS	$N - P$
I-errors	.24	.31
M-errors		−.39

The partial correlation of $N - P$ with I-errors, holding M-errors constant, is .45.

It is interesting to understand why the measure of reduction in restraint $(N - P)$ correlates negatively with the number of M-errors. This is probably due to the fact that the less the members of a group revealed negative attitudes and the more they tended to skirt the real discussion topic, the less distinctive were the statements which E was able to record verbatim during the discussion. Consequently, the greater the number of negative contributions, the better were they able to recall what was said. It is also possible that the greater the extent to which negative attitudes were revealed in the discussion, the more attentive were the members to what was being said and, consequently, the more adequate their memory. It then appears that an increase in the expression of negative attitudes toward parents is accompanied by an increase in the inability to identify who said what, *in spite of* a general improvement in memory.

REDUCTION OF INNER RESTRAINT AND
ATTRACTION TO THE GROUP

Since the reduction of inner restraints allows the group member to behave more freely and to satisfy needs which would otherwise be difficult to satisfy, groups in which reduction of restraint occurs should be more attractive to their members. We should then expect to find a positive correlation between the measure of the reduction of restraint $(N - P)$ and the average attraction to the group as measured on the postsession questionnaire. This correlation turns out to be .36, which is significant at almost the 10 per cent level of confidence considering both tails of the probability distribution.

There is evidence, then, supporting the two major derivations stemming from the theory about de-individuation in a group, namely, that it does tend to result in the reduction of inner restraints and that its occurrence does tend to increase the attractiveness of the group for its members.

POSSIBLE ALTERNATIVE EXPLANATIONS

In connection with any set of data for which a specific theoretical explanation is given the question arises: are there alternative and perhaps simpler explanations of the data? This question is especially pertinent in connection with a study such as the present one since a relatively new theory is being presented. We will consequently present possible alternative explanations which various persons have suggested to the authors and discuss whether or not these explanations are compatible with the data.

1. Can the results be explained in terms of theories of repression or selective forgetting? The Ss have been put in a situation where they were virtually forced to reveal attitudes which they perhaps considered shameful. It is plausible to expect that under these conditions they would tend to repress the shameful material and, consequently, the more shameful material is expressed in a group, the poorer is their ability to identify who said what.

It seems to the authors that any theory of repression would predict that the content of what was said would be forgotten as well as, or even sooner than, who said it. The data, however, indicate that the more "shameful material" expressed in the group the *better* is the members' memory for what was said. It is *only* the ability to identify who said what which is worse. It would seem further that if something like "shame" were the determining variable, those groups which produced more shameful content would be *least* attractive to their members. The data show exactly the opposite result. One may conclude that a theory of repression cannot adequately explain the results.

2. Can the results be explained in terms of the Ebbinghaus laws of forgetting? Those groups which followed the experimental instruction best stated more instances of negative attitudes toward their parents and said more things of a personal nature. This means they produced more statements of the kind that E recorded verbatim and tested them on. From experiments on forgetting we know that the more statements there are to be remembered, the poorer will the memory be.

This type of explanation again would predict poorer memory for what was said in those groups who revealed a lot of negative attitudes toward their parents. This is contrary to the facts. It would also seem that this explanation cannot handle the obtained positive relation with the attractiveness of the group.

3. Can the results be explained in terms of division of attention? It is plausible to suppose that in those groups where more negative attitudes were revealed, the members became correspondingly more interested and engrossed in the content of the discussion. Since they were paying so much attention to what was said they could not pay attention to who was saying it. This theory would account for the fact that there is a negative correlation between the frequency of negative attitudes revealed and number of M-errors while a positive correlation exists between the former variable and number of I-errors. This theory would also explain the relation with attraction to the group. Those groups in which more interesting discussions took place were more attractive to their members.

This theory has one additional implication. It would imply that one should obtain a sizeable negative correlation between the number of I-errors and the number of M-errors. This should certainly be the case if it is a matter of division of attention and the more one pays attention to content the less attention is it possible to pay to who is saying what. The actual result is that there is a correlation of .24 between these two kinds of errors. This would seem definitely to refute the division of attention explanation.

4. Can the results be explained simply in terms of individual reactions rather than as a group phenomenon? Perhaps those individuals who revealed negative attitudes toward their parents tended to ignore who was speaking because of the shameful nature of the content.

This possible explanation can be refuted by an analysis of the data in terms of individuals within each group. If it is a matter of individual reaction, then, within each group, the same relationship should hold that we find when we use the group as the unit of analysis. Accordingly, we ranked the members of each group on the basis of the extent to which each member made contributions to the discussion which revealed negative attitudes toward their parents $(N - P)$. We then examined the measure of ability to identify who said what (I-errors $-$ M-errors) in relation to these ranks.

If we split each group in half on the basis of the $N - P$ measure there is no consistent difference between the upper and lower halves on the ability to identify who said what. In 10 of the groups those who contributed more negative statements made more identification errors and in the other 12 groups the relationship is reversed.[4] In other words, the analysis on an individual basis reveals no relationship at all between the two measures.

It might be argued that dividing each group into two parts is a rather gross analysis and might obscure an existing relationship. We consequently also analyzed the data dividing each group into four parts. This required some arbitrary

[4] This analysis continues to exclude the extremely deviant group. If this group were included it would make 13 groups where the relationship was reversed.

decisions as to the division when there were actually more than four $N - P$ scores in a group, but these decisions could be made fairly easily. When there were only three different $N - P$ scores in a group, they were analyzed as belonging to the top three quartiles when groups were combined. When there were only two different $N - P$ scores in a group they were analyzed as belonging to the middle two quartiles. In this manner all groups could be combined and the average calculated for each quartile of I-errors minus M-errors. The following tabulation shows these data:

QUARTILE DIVISION ON $N - P$	N	AVERAGE I-ERRORS $-$ M-ERRORS
highest quartile	25	.32
second quartile	32	$-.42$
third quartile	34	.44
fourth quartile	23	.37

It is clear that there is no relationship between the two measures when analyzed in this manner. The variation within any quartile is quite large and none of the differences even approach statistical significance.

It might also be argued that this analysis does not dispose of the notion that it may be individual reaction rather than a group phenomenon because this analysis obscures the absolute magnitude of the $N - P$ measure which may be important. The data were accordingly also analyzed by individuals simply on the basis of absolute amount of $N - P$. The following tabulation presents the results of this analysis:

ABSOLUTE SCORE ON $N - P$	N	AVERAGE I-ERRORS $-$ M-ERRORS
greater than zero	42	.27
zero	28	.04
less than zero	43	.25

None of these differences are appreciable or statistically significant. Once more it is clear that analyzing the data by individuals does not show the same relationship which was found when the data were analyzed by groups. This certainly lends support to the theory which explains the results as a group phenomenon.

Summary

A group phenomenon which we have called de-individuation has been described and defined as a state of affairs in a group where members do not pay attention to other individuals *qua* individuals, and, correspondingly, the members do not feel they are being singled out by others. The theory was advanced that such a state of affairs results in a reduction of inner restraints in the members and that, consequently, the members will be more free to indulge in behavior from which they are usually restrained. It was further hypothesized that this is a satisfying state of affairs and its occurrence would tend to increase the attactiveness of the group.

A laboratory study was conducted to test this theory and the data from this study tend to support it. Other possible explanations of the obtained results have been considered and found inadequate.

B · THE FAMILY AND PERSONALITY

1 · The Genesis of Motivational Patterns

THE INCEST TABOO IN RELATION TO SOCIAL STRUCTURE
AND THE SOCIALIZATION OF THE CHILD

by Talcott Parsons

After something like a generation in which the attention of anthropologists and sociologists has been focused on the phenomena which differentiate one society from another and the different structures within the same society from each other, in recent years there has been a revival of interest in the problem of what features are common to human societies everywhere and what are the forces operating to maintain these common features. One reason for my present interest in the incest taboo is that it is one of the most notable of these common features. With all the variability of its incidence outside the nuclear family, there is the common core of the prohibition of marriage and in general of sexual relationships between members of a nuclear family except of course the conjugal couple whose marriage establishes it.

In the older discussions the prevailing tendency was to attempt to find a specific "cause" of the taboo, thus instinctive aversion or Westermarck's contention that aversion was acquired through being brought up in the same household. As our empirical information and theoretical re-

SOURCE: *British Journal of Sociology*, Vol. 5 (1954), pp. 101–117.

sources have accumulated, however, it seems less and less likely that this is the most fruitful approach. On the contrary anything so general as the incest taboo seems likely to be a resultant of a constellation of different factors which are deeply involved in the foundations of human societies. Analysis in terms of the balance of forces in the social system rather than of one or two specific "factors" seems much more promising. Furthermore, it seems highly probable that a combination of sociological and psychological considerations is involved; that a theory which attempts to by-pass either of these fields will find itself in difficulties.

The element of constancy clearly focuses in the nuclear family. Perhaps the most recent authoritative survey is that of Murdock, [1] and we have his authority that no society is known where incest between mother-son, father-daughter or full brother-sister is permitted except the few cases of brother-sister marriage in royal families, but never for the bulk of the people. There are a few cases of marriage permitted between half-brother and half-sister, and similar cases of closeness, but only a few. I shall therefore take the nuclear family as my point of departure and attempt to review a few highlights of it as a sub-system of the society. But the nuclear family is, in my opinion, only the focus of the structural problem, not the whole of it. I shall therefore next attempt to link with the relevant considerations about the family, a series of problems about its place in and articulation with the rest of the society. Then, given this wider setting of social structure, I will attempt to analyse some of the relevant problems of psychological mechanism in terms of the characteristics and significance of eroticism in personal relationships and in the personality itself.

I. The Structure and Functions of the Nuclear Family

The universality of some order of incest taboo is of course directly connected with the fact that the nuclear family is also universal to all known human societies. The minimal criteria of the nuclear family are, I suggest, first that there should be a solidarity relationship between mother and child lasting over a period of years and transcending physical care in its significance. Secondly, in her motherhood of this child the woman should have a special relationship to a man *outside her own descent group* who is sociologically the "father" of the child, and that this relationship is the focus of the "legitimacy" of the child, of his referential status in the larger kinship system. [2]

The common sense of social science has tended to see in the universality and constancy of structure of the nuclear family a simple reflection of its biological function and composition; sexual reproduction, the generation difference and the differentiation by sex in the biological sense. While I in no way question the importance of this biological aspect and am in agreement with the view that the human family is an "extension" of a subhuman precultural entity, on the human-cultural levels there is, I am sure, another

aspect of the problem of constancy. The two biological bases of differentiation, sex and generation, may be regarded, that is, as "points of reference" of a type of social organization the sociological significance of which is general in the structure of small groups.

Evidence from the experimental laboratory study of small groups [3] has shown first that small groups with no prior institutionalized differentiation of status, differentiate spontaneously on a hierarchical dimension, which I may call "power" in the sense of relative influence on the outcome of processes in the system. This is the case when this differentiation is measured by any one of a variety of possible measures, both from the point of view of the observer and that of participants in group process. We may say there is a differentiation between "leaders" and "followers."

Secondly, there appears a differentiation which cuts across this one, with reference to qualitative *type of function* in the group. The first broad qualitative type of differentiation which appears in this sense is what Bales and I have called that between primarily "instrumental" function in the group and primarily "expressive" function. An instrumental function is one primarily concerned with the relations of the group to the situation external to it, including adaptation to the conditions of that situation and establishment of satisfactory goal-relations for the system vis-à-vis the situation. Expressive function on the other hand is concerned primarily with the harmony or solidarity of the group, the relations internally of the members to each other and their "emotional" states of tension or lack of it in their roles in the group.

Level of differentiation is of course a function of size of the group. By the time we reach a membership of four there can be a typical four-role pattern, differentiated hierarchically into leadership and followership roles, and qualitatively into more instrumental and more expressive roles. I would like to suggest that it is fruitful to treat the nuclear family as a special case of this basically four-role pattern, with generation as the main axis of superior-inferior or leader-follower differentiation, sex the axis of instrumental-expressive differentiation. Obviously the helplessness of the child, particularly in the first years, is the main basis of the former. The universal fact that women are more intimately concerned with early child care than are men (with lactation playing a very fundamental part) is the primary reason why the feminine role, in the family as well as outside, tends to be *more* expressive in this sense than the masculine. [4]

My first point is thus that the nuclear family has certain characteristics common to small groups in general. The effectiveness of its performance of function as a family is, I think, dependent on its having these characteristics. The primary functions I have in mind are a certain significance for maintaining the emotional balances of all members of the family including the adults, and its paramount role as an agency for the socialization of children. The general characteristics I have in mind are three. The first is that it should be a *small* group, especially in its higher status-echelon. Given age-specific death rates as well as birth rates, presumably in no society does the effective nuclear family average more than about seven members, and generally fewer. The second characteristic is that the main structural differentiation of the family as a group should be along these two axes, namely that of power or hierarchy and the instrumental-expressive distinction. The third is that *both* the latter should be represented in the "leadership" structure and that there should be a strong "coalition" between them. [5] The fact that the two parents are of opposite sex and that marriage, though with variations, always constitutes an important structural bond of solidarity transcending the parental functions, in a broad way

insures this. It should be clear from the above that sex role differentiation in its more generalized sense which impinges on many contexts other than the structure of the nuclear family itself is importantly involved in this structural complex.

But this does not mean that just any kind of small group which met these specifications could perform the functions of the family. It clearly has to be a group which has relatively long duration—a considerable span of years. But it is not indefinite duration. One of its most important characteristics is that the family is a self-liquidating group. On attainment of maturity and marriage the child ceases in the full sense to be a member of his family of orientation; instead he helps in the establishment of a new one. The implications of this basic fact will be briefly discussed in the next section.

Secondly, it must be a group which permits and requires a high level of diffuse affective involvement for its members; though this of course varies with the different roles, being highest for the young child. Clearly no evanescent experimental group could perform the functions of a family. The fact that with few exceptions the nuclear family is the main unit of residence is of critical importance in this connection.

Finally, third, I suggest that it is essential to the family that more than in any other grouping in societies, overt erotic attraction and gratification should be given an institutionalized place in its structure. But when we say this is institutionalized we mean that eroticism is not only permitted but carefully regulated; and the incest taboo is merely a very prominent negative aspect of this more general regulation.

This aspect will be more fully discussed in the third section of the paper. But at this point it does seem worth while to summarize the familiar features of the erotic organization of the family. First genital eroticism is both permitted to and expected of the marital pair. Only in certain special religious groups is its justification even in theory confined to the direct procreative function; it is itself a bond and a very important symbol of the solidarity of the marriage pair as responsible for a family. But at the same time—and this fact accentuates this meaning—the marital couple have a monopoly of the right to genital eroticism within the nuclear family, though of course not necessarily outside.

Secondly, pre-genital eroticism is positively institutionalized, always in the early mother-child relation, and probably usually to some extent in that of father and child. But clearly it is generally far more important in the case of mother and child.

Third, with probably few exceptions, overt erotic expression except possibly autoeroticism in some cases, is tabooed as between post-oedipal children and both parents, and in the relations of the children to each other, except where an older sibling plays a partly parental role to a small child. Finally, no homosexuality is permitted at all within the nuclear family unless we wish to call the attraction between mother and pre-oedipal daughter homosexual. In view of what we know on psychological levels of the erotic potentials of human beings this structure is clearly not one of unrestricted permissiveness, but of a systematic combination of controlled expression and regulatory prohibition. Moreover, in view of the wide variety of human customs in so many respects, its relative uniformity is impressive and deserves to be counted as one of the most important universals of human society.

It would be rash to suggest that the socialization of children could not be carried out except in a group of the specific biological composition of the family, or even without this specific set of erotic relationships. I think, however, that it is fairly safe to contend that the primary socializing agency must be a small group with broadly the sociological characteristics I have suggested, and that even the erotic factor could not vary extremely widely. For example, it could not be completely suppressed, by having all fertilization occur by artificial insemination, and by a careful policy of avoiding arousing any erotic interest on the part of children, or at the other extreme by removing all restrictions on fulfilment of any and all erotic impulses as and when they might be aroused.

II. The Family and the Wider Social Structure

One of the cardinal uniformities of social structure which is most intimately connected with the incest taboo is the fact that nuclear families are *never* found as independent total "societies" on a human cultural level. There is never simply extra-social biological mating outside the family, but the nuclear family is always a unit within a society which contains a plurality of other families, and other types of units; "solidarity" extends over these areas and the other groupings, and even where they are kinship groupings, sociologically they have characteristics very different from those of the nuclear family.

Undoubtedly one of the main characteristics of the more "primitive" societies lies in the fact that a far larger proportion of the total social structure is organized about kinship than is the case with the more "advanced" societies. Indeed there are some where it is difficult to speak of any "statuses" or groups which are not in some important respect kinship statuses and groups. But two main things need to be said. First, though always including nuclear families, the kinship system always also includes groups which differ fundamentally from nuclear families. Secondly, it can, following Leach, [6] probably be said that a kinship system cannot be a completely "closed" system in that features of it always have to be analysed with reference to economic, political and other considerations which are not peculiar to kinship relations, which do not disappear in social structures which have entirely cast loose from a kinship base.

Whether the groupings which transcend the nuclear family are organized about kinship or not, relative to the family they have in general—with a few exceptions like friendships—certain characteristics in common. They are groups in which the personal emotional interests of the individual are not so closely bound up as in the family; where the accent is more on impersonal functions of the group. A good kinship case of this type is the lineage as a corporate entity with reference to its political functions. The case of organizations composed primarily of occupational roles in modern society is one where kinship is not prominent. Broadly one may say that in such cases the role or the organization is characterized by primacy of functional responsibility on a social system level, and by relatively severe control of affective spontaneity—by what I have elsewhere [8] called "affective neutrality." These are the structures in which the main functions of direct maintenance and goal-attainment in the society are performed; viz. economic provision, political stabilization and defence, religious expression, etc.

Where the main basis of composition of such groupings rest in kinship, marriage has direct functional significance as a mechanism which establishes important direct ties of interpenetration of memberships between the different elements in the structural network. Under such circumstances marriage cannot be merely a "personal affair" of the parties to it. Where it is difficult to have solidary relationships which do not involve kinship the intermarriage between groups can establish a pattern of such solidarities cross-cutting those based directly or primarily on relationships by descent.

As Fortune was one of the first to emphasize, and Lévi-Strauss has developed farther, [8] in this kind of situation it is not so much the prohibition of incest in its negative aspect which is important as the positive obligation to perform functions for the subunit and the larger society by marrying out. Incest is a withdrawal from this obligation to contribute to the formation and maintenance of suprafamilial bonds on which major economic, political and religious functions of the society are dependent.

Where extended kinship groupings have a critical importance in the social structure, it is considerations of this kind which underlie the patterns of extension of the incest taboo beyond the nuclear family. Broadly the principles seem to be that intermarriage is forbidden within units which, first, are organized primarily as kinship units, second, have functions in the social system which transcend the personal interests of the members of small family groups, which therefore involve a more impersonal set of disciplines and, third, groups within which, as kinship groups, daily interaction with reference to these interests is relatively close. The lineage and its segments and the male local succession group which Leach discusses are prototypes of such groups. Illustrating the last criterion it is typical that exogamy often breaks down within the most extensive lineage groups but is maintained within their lower-order segments. [9]

Recent work on kinship seems to indicate that in a very rough way it is possible to construct a series of types in this respect. At one end is the so-called Kariera type which is characterized by symmetrical cross-cousin marriage. This forms a very "tight" form of organization, but is very limited in the range of different kinds of social ties which can be established through it. It makes for a rigid social structure, though probably under certain conditions a relatively stable one.

Lévi-Strauss is probably right that the asymmetrical type of cross-cousin marriage which rests primarily on marriage with the mother's brother's daughter constitutes an important step towards a wider ranging and more flexible set of arrangements as compared both with the Kariera type and with marriage to the father's sister's daughter. It is interesting to note that this is connected with the asymmetry of the structure of the nuclear family itself as that was discussed above. If the masculine role is more instrumental than the feminine in the senses I have discussed, then the men should have more direct and important anchorages in the extended kinship groupings than the women. Then for a woman who has married out of her descent group, the strongest source of support would not be her sister but her brother. This is first because the sister may well have married either into ego's own post-marital group or into another controlled largely by her husband's agnatic kin and second because in the descent group the men have more control in extrafamilial affairs than the women.

The father's brother, on the other hand, is in a status directly similar to that of the father and not complementary to him, while the father's sister belongs to this same agnatic group. Put a little differently an alliance with the mother's brother is the stablest kind of alliance with a distinctly different group and at the same time bolsters the structure of the nuclear family in such a way as to redress the balance resulting from its internal asymmetry by giving the mother external support through a channel independent of her husband.

Lévi-Strauss therefore seems to be right in saying that asymmetrical cross-cousin marriage through the mother's brother's daughter relationship opens up a wider circle which is both stabler and more extensive than any alternative where the kin involved are so close. Leach, [10] however, has made an important additional contribution by showing that on such a basis the kinship system cannot be closed through marriage-exchange relations alone, but that there are several alternative ways in which such a system can work out. Which of them will develop will depend on the economic and political relations of the exchanging kinship units, and hence on the nature and values of the "considerations" which enter into the marriage arrangements other than the exchange of spouses as such.

But all this is compatible in a broad way with Lévi-Strauss' view that this makes women, though in somewhat different ways also men, a kind of symbolic "counters" in a process of exchange. Perhaps I may state it in somewhat different terms by saying that the woman or man, in marrying outside his own descent group, is performing a role-obligation in a social group or collectivity which transcends his own family of orientation, and one to which to some degree his family is subordinated; it is a superordinate unit in the social structure. He is no more free to marry whom he chooses in such a situation than is an industrial worker free within the organization to perform any job-task he chooses regardless of how it fits into the plan for how the total process is to be organized.

It is in this sense that incest would be socially regressive in the sense in which Lévi-Strauss analyses the problem. It would, in an area of the higher integrative structures of the society, constitute giving membership in the lower-level structure priority over that in the higher. It is only on the impossible assumption that families should constitute independent societies and not be segmental units of higher-level organizations, that incest as a regular practice would be socially possible.

These considerations give us the basis for a further generalization concerning the difference between extended exogamous systems and those found in modern societies. So far as the higher level functions of the society are performed by collectivities the composition of which is determined in kinship terms, there will be a tendency to extend the incest taboo to such collectivities. So far, however, as social function, economic, political and religious, comes to be organized in groups not put together out of kin, the whole issue of exogamy with reference to them will cease to be significant.

There is, however, complete continuity between these two types of cases so far as certain aspects of the social functions of the incest taboo are concerned. We may say that there are two primary interconnected but independent aspects of this function. In the first place, it is socially important that the nuclear family should not be self-perpetuating and hence that adults should have a personality structure which motivates them to found new and independent nuclear families. Erotic attraction to persons of opposite sex but outside the nuclear family is clearly a mechanism which aids in this. But, secondly, it is essential that persons should be capable of assuming roles which contribute to functions which no nuclear family is able to perform, which involve the assumption of non-familial roles. Only if such non-familial roles can be adequately staffed can a society function. I suggest that the critical roles in this class are roles in which erotic interests must be altogether subordinated to other interests.

I thus see the "problem" of the incest taboo in the following setting so far as social structure is concerned. It seems to be clear that human personalities are universally socialized in nuclear families, which are small groups of the special type sketched above. Included in their special characteristics is the role of erotic attraction between their members. The incest taboo operates to "propel" the individual out of the nuclear family, not in one but in two senses. He is propelled into a new nuclear family formed by his marriage. Here the erotic component of his personality is positively made use of. But also he is propelled into non-familial roles, which of course are differentiated by sex and other status-characteristics, but in some sense such roles must be assumed by all adults. This corresponds to the fact that every known society consists in a plurality of nuclear families the duration of which is limited to one generation and also the fact that these families are always relatively low-level units in a social structure the higher-level units of which have different functions in the society, functions which cannot be performed by family groups. [11] It is in this setting that I wish to discuss some of the problems of the psychological characteristics of eroticism and its place in the development of personality.

III. The Psychological Characteristics and Functions of Eroticism

After all, the most distinctive feature of the incest taboo is the regulation of erotic relationships, within the family and in relation to the establishment of new families. The considerations about social structure which I have advanced therefore need to be supplemented by a discussion of the nature of eroticism and its functions in the development of personality and in the personality of the adult. I shall here put forward a view which has three main emphases. First, eroticism will be held to play a very important part, probably an indispensable one, in the socialization of the child, in taking a raw organism and making a "person" out of it. Second, however, the awakening of erotic interests not only performs functions, it creates problems. There are important psychological reasons why erotic needs seem to be particularly difficult to control. Making use of this instrument of socialization therefore constitutes a kind of "pact with the devil." Once present the question of what is to be done with this force is a serious problem. Finally, third, the view of eroticism I take here will dissociate it considerably from what is ordinarily meant by the "sex instinct" or the instinct of reproduction. Though the interest in genital eroticism of the post-adolescent is undoubtedly genuinely part of the erotic complex, and a very important part, it is only part, and the complex is far broader than such an instinct in two senses. On the one hand its childhood or pregenital aspects are of fundamental importance for our problem and presumably have nothing to do with the reproductive function. Secondly, though there undoubtedly must be a basis on constitutional predisposition, the aspects of eroticism which are important for our purposes involve a very large component which is learned rather than "instinctive" in the usual sense.

I shall rely heavily on Freud for my views of the erotic complex, though I think Freud can be supplemented by some considerations derived from the sociological study of the process of socialization. But after all one of the greatest of Freud's discoveries was the fundamental *importance* of the eroticism of childhood—the fact of its existence was not discovered by Freud, but as so often in the history of science well-known facts excited little interest because nobody knew how to assess their importance. Furthermore, Freud clearly saw the importance of the processes of learning in the development of erotic interests. I may recall his famous statement that "the infant is polymorph perverse." This I interpret to mean that any normal child has the potentiality of developing *any* of the well-known types of erotic orientation, homosexuality, autoeroticism and the perversions as well as what we think of as normal heterosexuality. This can only

mean that the latter is in considerable measure the product of the process of socialization, not simply the expression of an instinct. [12]

What, then, are the most important characteristics of eroticism? Erotic interest is, I think, the interest in securing a particular type of organic pleasure, which is in *one* aspect organically specific in a way comparable to the pleasure of hunger-gratification or warmth. But this is only one aspect of it. What is most important about eroticism is, I think, its dual character, the combination of this organic specificity, the possibility of intense pleasure through the stimulation of specific parts of the body, with a *diffuse* spreading into a general sensation of well-being. From stimulation of an erogenous zone then, it is not a very big step to learning that almost any type of bodily contact with the agent can come to be felt as a source of pleasure. I may take a specific example from early childhood. Being fed by the mother is a source not only of hunger-gratification but very early, according to psychoanalytic views, of oral-erotic gratification as well. But from stimulation of this oral-erotic interest there is generalization to pleasurable sensation from any physical contact with the source of the original oral gratification; hence being held and fondled by the mother, is a source of pleasure and a focus of an incipient system of expectations.

Put in psychological terms, erotic gratification is a peculiarly sensitive source of conditioning in the "classical" Pavlovian sense. From desiring the specific stimulation, the child comes to desire diffuse non-specific contact with the object which has served as agent of the original gratification. Eroticism is thus a major, in the earlier stages probably *the* major mechanism for the "generalization of cathexis" by which a diffuse attachment to an object comes to be built up. [13]

The great importance of diffuse attachment in this sense to the process of learning has come to be well-recognized. So long as a socializing agent is only a source of specific segmental gratifications, the omission of such gratification will cause the child very rapidly to lose interest in the object. But the process by which the deeper kind of learning [14] is possible involves the building up of need-systems and then their frustration as a preliminary to the learning of new goals and needs. [15] The essential point is that the socializing agent should be in a position to frustrate the child—really seriously—without losing control of him.

Another aspect of the point is that it is by this order of generalization of cathexis that the child is made sensitive to the *attitudes* of the socializing agent, say the mother. This sensitivity to attitude is possible only through transcending the specificity of interest in organic gratifications as such. What matters to the child is whether and how much he feels that his mother "cares." The very fact that erotic gratification is *not* essential to any of the basic physiological needs of the individual organism makes it a suitable vehicle for this generalization.

A further characteristic of eroticism seems to be important in the general situation, it is what underlies my reference above to its arousal constituting in a sense a "pact with the devil." Erotic need, that is, seems to have some of the characteristics of addiction. The erotic interests of childhood cannot be allowed to be dominant in later phases of development, and in normal development are not. But the evidence is that by and large they are not, as the psychologists put it, successfully "extinguished," but rather have to be repressed. From this it comes that the psychoanalysis of any "normal" adult will bring to light "infantile" erotic patterns which are still there, though they have not been allowed overt gratification for many years. The evidence is very clear that normal and pathological differ in this respect only in degree, not in terms of presence or absence. [16] If this general view is correct then the mechanisms for handling such permanently repressed material must be of great importance in the normal adult personality.

Let us look at the matter in more of a sociological perspective. A socializing agent at any given major stage of the process plays a dual role, in *two* systems of social interaction. On the one hand he—or she—participates with the child at the level which is appropriate to the beginning of the phase in question, as in the case of the mother-child love attachment of the immediately pre-oedipal period. On the other hand she—the mother in this case—also participates in the full four-role family system. In disturbing the equilibrium of the former interaction system she acts as an agent of the latter. This act of disturbance constitutes frustration to the child and produces among other things anxiety and aggression. If, on the other hand, there were no positive motivation in his involvement in the relationship other than what he is now denied expression, the attachment would simply break up and no progress could be made, since he is not yet motivated to assume his *new* role in the new and higher level interaction system.

But the specific part of the erotic attachment is a focus of precisely the element of "dependency"—at the relevant level—which has to be overcome if the new level is to be attained. Under the conditions postulated, however, the *diffuse* aspect of the erotic attachment can survive the frustration of the focal specific desire, and it can thus become a main lever by which the child is positively motivated to learn a new role which, it must be remembered, involves learning new goals, not merely new instrumental means for the attainment of given goals.

Thus the child's erotic attachment to

the mother is the "rope" by which she pulls him up from a lower to a higher level in the hard climb of "growing up." But because the points of attachment of this "rope" remain sensitive, interest in them is not extinguished, there is a permanent channel back into the still operative infantile motivational system. Serious disturbances of the equilibrium of the personality can always re-open these channels. This is what is ordinarily meant by "regression" and early erotic patterns always play a prominent part in regressive tendencies. [17]

There seem to be three stages at which the mother is the primary object of erotic attraction of the child; these are what Freud identified as the Oral, the Anal and the Phallic phases. They correspond to those relatively discontinuous "steps" in the process of learning new levels of personality organization; new goals, and capacities for independent and responsible performance. Each one leaves a residuum of the erotic structures which have been essential in order to make the step, but which if allowed to remain active would interfere with the subsequent steps. Thus there is in all personalities, granting my hypothesis of addiction, a channel through erotic associations, right down into the lowest and most primitive strata of the Id—the most regressive parts of the personality system. These can be reactivated at any time. The connection of this situation with the problem of the probable psychological significance of incest seems to be clear.

From this point of view the problem of incest fits into the larger context of the structuring of erotic motivation in the personality, over time and with reference to choice of objects. The context includes the problem of homosexuality and of the status of the perversions. The goal of socialization—with many variations but in its broad pattern universal —is to establish at least the primacy, if not the complete monopoly over other possibilities, of normal genital erotic attraction which includes choice of object outside the family, and stability of orientation to objects.

Only mother-son incest is as such directly involved in the constellation I have sketched. Here the regressive implications seem very clear. This agrees with psychoanalytic opinion that such incest, where it does appear in our society, is always deeply pathological, on both sides but particularly that of the son.

The case of the daughter vis-à-vis her father is somewhat different. But when she is forced to abandon her primary attachment to her mother, it should be clear that the next available alternative is the father. This is further made "plausible" by the fact that she is taught that it is normal for a female to have a primary attachment to a masculine object, but in this case erotic development of the attachment is blocked. This clearly has to do on one level with the internal equilibrium of the nuclear family as a system. The erotic attachment of the parents to each other is a primary focus and symbol of their coalition as the leadership element of the family as a system. To allow the child who has just been forced out of an erotic attachment to the mother to substitute one with the father would immediately weaken this coalition as a source of generalized pressure to grow up for children of both sexes.

But there is a broader "functional" aspect of the problem. If it is exceedingly important that the boy should find a feminine object outside the family, this is obviously only possible in a generalized way if girls also typically do so. Furthermore, in order to perform her functions as a socializing agent, as mother, it is extremely important that a woman's regressive need systems should be controlled. Indeed it is probably more important than in the case of the man, because as a mother the woman is going to have to enter into much stronger erotic reciprocities with her young children than is her husband, and at the same time she is in due course going to have to act as the agent of their frustration in these respects. If she is not able to control her own regressive needs, then the mother-child system is likely to get "stuck" on one of the early levels and be unable to take the next step. Indeed such phenomena are prominent in the pathology of family relations in relation to the genesis of mental disorders. Thus the "overprotective" mother, instead of, at the proper time, refusing to reciprocate her child's dependency needs, positively encourages them and thereby makes it more difficult for him to grow up.

Finally, there is the case of the prohibition of brother-sister incest. It seems to me that in the first instance this relates to the symmetry of the nuclear family. Once the oedipal crisis has been passed, the most symmetrical arrangement is that which reserves a monopoly of erotic relations within the family to the married couple. But in a broader context functionally the more important thing is at the relevant time to achieve complete—though temporary—repression of erotic needs for both sexes. Fulfilment of this requirement would be blocked by permissiveness for brother-sister erotic relations.

For childhood eroticism regardless of the sex of the child the original object is the mother. Once this attachment to the mother has ceased to be useful to the development of the personality it tends, I have noted, to be repressed altogether. This means that not only is the original object denied, but those "next in time," that is all other members of the original nuclear family, are tabooed. This in turn, it seems, is an aspect of what I referred to above as the process of self-liquidation of each particular nuclear family.

What Freud called the period of "latency," i.e. from the point of view of overt eroticism, thus seems to be the period in which the individual is above all learning to perform extrafamilial roles. Childhood erotic attachment has

played a part in laying the necessary foundations for these processes, but beyond a certain point it becomes a hindrance. Just a word may be said about the first of these steps which seems to have a bearing on the problem of brother-sister attachment.

One of the primary features of the oedipal transition in the course of which the last phase of childhood eroticism is normally repressed is the assumption of sex role, or the first major step in that process. Though the points of reference for the differentiation are unmistakably biologically given, there is strong reason to believe that the role, including the psychological categorization of the self, must be learned to a much greater extent than has ordinarily been appreciated. It seems to be significant that just at this period children begin to be much more independent of their families and to associate particularly with other children. There will be many variations as a function of the structure of extended kinship groups and the nature of residential communities, but it seems to be broadly true that there is a general tendency to segregation of the sexes at this period. The phenomenon so familiar in Western society of the one-sex peer group seems to have a nearly universal counterpart to some extent elsewhere. The turning of primary interests into the channel of relations to friends of the same sex and nearly the same age seems to have a dual significance. On the one hand it reinforces the individual's self-categorization by sex by creating a solidarity transcending the family between persons of the same sex. On the other hand, for the first time the individual becomes a member of a group which both transcends the family and in which he is not in the strongly institutionalized position of being a member of the *inferior* generation class. It is the first major step toward defining himself as clearly *independent* of the authority and help of the parental generation.

Adolescence comes only after a considerable period of this latency-level peer group activity. Along with the fact that the emerging genital erotic interest of adolescence and after involves symmetrical attraction to persons of opposite sex, it is of the first importance that now for the first time erotic attraction is experienced with an object which is broadly an equal, instead of a generation-superior. On both counts there must be a considerable reorganization of the erotic complex in the personality and its relations to the other components before mature erotic attachments become possible. It is a psychiatric commonplace that much of the pathology of marriage relationships and of the erotic interests of adults otherwise, has to do with inadequate solution of these two problems, namely how to form a stable attachment to a single person of opposite sex and how to treat the partner as fundamentally an equal, neither to be dependent on him or her in a childish sense nor, by a mechanism which includes reaction-formation to dependency, to take the parental role and have a compulsive need to dominate.

When all this has taken place the circle is closed by the individual's marriage and parenthood. He has had his erotic ties within the nuclear family of orientation broken. But he has also built up the nonerotic components of his personality structure with the double consequences of building a relatively secure dam against his still-present regressive needs, and building a positive set of motivational capacities for the performance of the non-familial roles without which no society could operate. Only when this process has reached a certain stage are the gates to erotic gratification re-opened, but this time in a greatly restructured way and carefully controlled.

Finally, it must not be overlooked that the erotic motivational component of the adult personality is used not only to motivate the marital attachment, but also constructively as itself an instrument of the socialization of the next generation.

For it is clear that eroticism is fundamentally a phenomenon of social relationships. Strong erotic motivation is built up in the child only because the mother, and to a lesser degree the father, *enjoys* reciprocal erotic relations with the child. But as in the case of the genital eroticism of marriage, this must be controlled by strong ego and super-ego structures in the personality, lest the parent be unable to renounce his own need when the time comes.

I expressed agreement above with the view of Fortune and Lévi-Strauss that on the social level incest must be regarded as a regressive phenomenon, a withdrawal from the functions and responsibilities on the performance and fulfilment of which the transfamilial structures of a society rest. The review of the role of eroticism in the development of the personality, which I have just presented, shows a striking parallel. Incestuous wishes constitute the very prototype of regression for the mature person, the path to the reactivation of the primitive layers of his personality structure. But surely this is more than merely a parallel. There is the most intimate causal interdependence. Societies operate only in and through the behaviour of persons, and personalities on the human sociocultural level are only possible as participants in systems of socially interactive behaviour, as these are related to the needs of human organisms.

I have argued that erotic gratification is an indispensable instrument of the socialization of the human child, of making a personality and a member of society of him. But equally, unrestricted erotic gratification stands directly in the way, both of the maturation of the personality, and of the operation of the society. Indispensable to certain processes of learning, it becomes probably the most serious impediment to further essential stages of maturity. The incest taboo is a universal of human societies. I suggest that this is because it constitutes a main focus of the *regulation* of the erotic factor. The institutionalization of the family provides the organized setting for the positive utilization of the erotic factor, both in socialization and in strengthening the motivation to the assumption of familial responsibility. But the taboo in its negative aspect is a mechanism which prevents this positive use from getting "out of hand," which ensures the self-liquidation of the particular family and the production of personalities by it which are capable of fulfilling the functions of transfamilial roles.

Admittedly, as far as origins are concerned, this is very largely a functional argument and does not solve the problems of how incest taboos came into being. It does, I think, serve to illuminate the manifold ways in which the incest taboo is involved in the functioning of any going society and gives a basis for prediction of the probable consequences of various forms of interference with it or modification of it. It places the problem in the context of analysis of the social system in such a way as also to show the interdependence of social systems with the processes of the personality. Once this level of analysis has been worked out the problem of origins assumes a lesser significance, but also can be approached with better hope of success.

There is one final important point. At the beginning of this paper I referred to the earlier tendency to attempt to find a specific explanation of the incest taboo, and expressed my own belief that an analysis of the interdependence of a number of factors in a system was much more promising. A common counterpart of this specific factor view, is the demand that an explanation in some one simple formula adequately explain all the variations of incidence of the taboo. It seems to me clear that, on the basis of the analysis I have presented, this is an illegitimate and unnecessary requirement. I have emphasized that there is a solid

common core of incidence, namely centering on the nuclear family. But we know that even this is broken through under *very* exceptional circumstances, namely the brother-sister marriage of a few royal families. This case is not an embarrassment for the kind of theory I have presented. For if the taboo is held to be the resultant of a balance of forces, then it is always possible that the balance should be altered so as to relax it under certain circumstances. As Fortune [19] correctly points out a better test case would be the full legitimation of morganatic marriages in royal families—i.e. as taking the place of politically significant alliances. Essentially the same holds where it is a question of variations of incidence outside the nuclear family. Only a sufficiently full analysis of the conditions of stability of the *particular* social system in question can furnish an adequate answer to the question of why this rather than a different pattern is found in a particular case. But such variations, and the elements of contingency involved in them, do not alter the importance of the massive fundamental facts that no human society is known without an incest taboo, and in no case does the taboo fail, for a society as a whole, to include all the relationships within the nuclear family. It is to the understanding of these massive facts that this analysis has been primarily directed.

NOTES

1. *Social Structure*, 1949. Ch. 10.
2. It will be noted that I deliberately assume the incest taboo as part of the constitution and the family itself.
3. See R. F. Bales, "The Equilibrium Problem in Small Groups," in Parsons, Bales and Shils, *Working Papers in the Theory of Action*, 1953.
4. The best documentation of this generalization available so far is I think a paper by M. Zelditch, Jr., "Role Differentiation in the Nuclear Family," to appear as Ch.

III of Parsons, Bales, Zelditch and Olds, *Family, Socialization and Interaction Process* (to be published during 1954 by The Free Press). Zelditch studied a sample of fifty-five societies and found first an overwhelming preponderance of relative instrumentalism in the father role, second no cases where the available evidence was unequivocal that the mother role in the nuclear family is *more* instrumental than that of the father. The greatest difficulties for this thesis occur in the cases of matrilineal kinship systems where the mother's brother takes over some of the functions of the father in other systems. The weight of Zelditch's evidence, however, suggests that even in these cases the *relative* differentiation on this axis holds, though the span of it is greatly narrowed.

The importance of these four roles for family structure is, I think, emphasized by kinship terminology. I believe it is true that, with all the variation of kinship terminology, there is no known system where these four roles, namely mother, father, brother, sister and, conversely, self, spouse, son, daughter, are not discriminated from each other. Of course frequently incumbents of these roles are classified together with other kin, as father with his brothers. But there is no known system which fails to discriminate the four cardinal roles in the nuclear family from each other. This is to say that generation and sex within the family are universally made bases of discrimination. There is no other set of roles in kinship systems of which this is true.

5. The connection between the leadership coalition of the small group and the erotically bound marriage partners was first stated by Bales, "The Equilibrium Problem in Small Groups," in Parsons, Bales and Shils, *op. cit.*, Ch. IV.

6. E. R. Leach, *The Structural Implications of Matrilineal Cross-Cousin Marriage,* Royal Anthropological Society, London, 1951.

7. Cf. Parsons, *The Social System,* Ch. II.

8. R. F. Fortune, "Incest," in *Encyclopedia of the Social Sciences,* edited by Seligman and Johnson, and Claude Lévi-Strauss, *Les structures élémentaires de la parenté.*

9. For a recent survey, cf. Murdock, *op. cit.,* Ch. X.

10. *Op. cit.*

11. There are good reasons for believing that there is an intimate connection between the overcoming of the excessive autonomy of the nuclear family and the possibility of a cultural level of social development. In the first place such a group is apparently too small to support an independent language with its minimum of extensity of generalization and communicative range. It is also probable that it is too "ingrown," culturally rather than biologically. One of the important consequences of the incest taboo is to enforce the mixing of family cultures (on the distinctiveness of the cultures of particular households, see J. M. Roberts, *Three Navaho Households,* Peabody Museum Monographs, Cambridge, Mass.). There is an analogy here to the biological functions of sexual reproduction. If, therefore, I may hazard an extremely tentative hypothesis about socio-cultural origins it would be that the earliest *society* had to be a multifamily unit which enforced an incest taboo.

12. The best general reference for this aspect of Freud's work is his *Three Contributions to Sexual Theory.*

13. Freud's views on this problem are most fully developed in the late paper, *Hemmung, Symptom und Angst:* English title: *The Problem of Anxiety.*

14. Meaning the internalization of cultural values—cf. Parsons, *The Social System,* chap. VI.

15. This involves what Olds calls the "law of motive growth." See James Olds, *Psychological Papers in the Theory of Action,* Chs. I and II, 1954.

16. Eroticism in this respect seems to be a member of a larger class of strong affective interests. Thus the work of Solomon and Wynne on conditioned anxiety in dogs has shown that a sufficiently acute anxiety is almost impossible to extinguish.

17. This sociological aspect of the socialization process is much more fully analysed in Parsons, Bales, *et al., Family Socialization and Interaction Process,* The Free Press, 1954, especially Chs. IV and VI.

18. *Op. cit.*

THE RELATION OF GUILT TOWARD PARENTS TO ACHIEVEMENT
AND ARRANGED MARRIAGE AMONG THE JAPANESE *

by George De Vos

This paper, based on research materials gathered in Japan, suggests certain interpretations concerning the structuring of guilt in Japanese society. Especially pertinent are Thematic Apperception Test (TAT) materials in which the subjects in-

* The author is indebted to Hiroshi Wagatsuma for his able assistance and collaboration in the analysis and interpretation of basic materials. The materials on which the following interpretations are based were obtained by the author as a member of a large interdisciplinary project in cooperation with the Human Relations Interdisciplinary Research Group of Nagoya under the direction of Dr. Tsuneo Muramatsu, Professor of Psychiatry, Nagoya National University. This research, which is continuing in Japan under Professor Muramatsu's direction, was sponsored in part by the Center for Japanese Studies of the University of Michigan, the Foundation Fund for Research in Psychiatry, and the Rockefeller Foundation. The author, who takes full responsibility for the views expressed in the present paper, based on material from a single village, participated in the Human Relations Interdisciplinary Research Group as a Fulbright research scholar in Japan from September, 1953, to July, 1955. Subsequent research on these psychological materials in the United States was assisted in various stages by a faculty research grant from the University of Michigan, the Behavioral Science Division of the Ford Foundation, and the National Institute of Mental Health. The Human Relations group hopes to be able to make more definitive statements than those of the present paper upon completion of its analysis of comparable primary material taken from three villages and two cities.

SOURCE: *Psychiatry*, Vol. 23 (1960), pp. 287–301. Reprinted by special permission of The William Alanson White Psychiatric Foundation, Inc.

vent stories about a series of ambiguous pictures, which were taken from Niiike, an agricultural village of central Honshu. It is possible to obtain from the stories involving themes of achievement and marriage relationships indirect verification of hypotheses concerning the nature of internalization of the Japanese social sanctions that have been influenced by the traditional neo-Confucian ethics sustained by the dominant samurai class in the past.

A central problem to be considered is whether the Japanese emphasis on achievement drive and on properly arranged marriage may possibly have its motivational source in the inculcation of shame or guilt in childhood.[1] It is my contention that this emphasis is not to

[1] This paper will not discuss subcultural variations. Niiike village is representative of a farming community that has well internalized the traditional, dominant values held by the samurai during the Tokugawa period (about 1600–1868). Other local rural traditions emphasize other values. For example, material from a fishing community wherein the status position of women is higher than in the farming community considered shows far different results in the projective tests. Women are perceived in TAT stories as more assertive, even aggressive, toward their husbands. Guilt is not expressed in stories of self-sacrificing mothers. Love marriages are accepted and not seen in the context of remorse, and so on. A comparison of the attitudes of the farming village with those of the fishing village is presented in detail in the following article: George De Vos and Hiroshi Wagatsuma, "Variations in Traditional Value Attitudes Related Toward Status and Role Behavior of Women in Two Japanese Villages," submitted for publication, *Amer. Anthropologist*.

be understood solely as a derivative of what is termed a 'shame' orientation, but rather as stemming from a deep undercurrent of guilt developed in the basic interpersonal relationships with the mother within the Japanese family.

The characteristic beliefs, values, and obligatory practices that provide emotional security and are usually associated in the West with religious systems and other generalized ideologies—and only indirectly related to family life [2]—are related much more directly to the family system of the tradition-oriented Japanese. The structuring of guilt in the Japanese is hidden from Western observation, since there is a lack of empathic understanding of what it means to be part of such a family system. Western observers tend to look for guilt, as it is symbolically expressed, in reference to a possible transgression of limits imposed by a generalized ideology or religious system circumscribing sexual and aggressive impulses. There is little sensitivity to the possibility that guilt is related to a failure to meet expectations in a moral system built around family duties and obligations.

Piers and Singer, in distinguishing between shame and guilt cultures,[3] emphasize that guilt inhibits and condemns transgression, whereas shame demands achievement of a positive goal. This contrast is related to Freud's two earlier distinctions in the functioning of the conscience. He used *shame* to delineate a reaction to the ego ideal involving a goal of positive achievement; on the other hand, he related *guilt* to superego formation and not to ego ideal. A great deal of Japanese cultural material, when ap-

praised with these motivational distinctions in mind, would at first glance seem to indicate that Japanese society is an excellent example of a society well over on the shame side of the continuum.

Historically, as a result of several hundred years of tightly knit feudal organization, the Japanese have been pictured as having developed extreme susceptibility to group pressures toward conformity. This strong group conformity, in turn, is often viewed as being associated with a lack of personal qualities that would foster individualistic endeavor.[4] In spite of, or according to some observers because of, these conformity patterns, which are found imbedded in governmental organization as well as in personal habits, the Japanese—alone among all the Asian peoples coming in contact with Western civilization in the nineteenth century—were quickly able to translate an essentially feudal social structure into a modern industrial society and to achieve eminence as a world power in fewer than fifty years. This remarkable achievement can be viewed as a group manifestation of what is presumed to be a striving and achievement drive on the individual level.

Achievement drive in Americans has been discussed by Riesman,[5] among others, as shifting in recent years from Puritan, inner-directed motivation to other-directed concern with conformity and outer group situations. Perceived in this framework, the Japanese traditionally have had an other-directed culture. Sensitivity to 'face' and attention to protocol suggest that the susceptibility to social pressure, traced psychoanalytically, may possibly derive from underlying in-

[2] Abram Kardiner, *The Individual and His Society;* New York, Columbia University Press, 1939; pp. 89–91.

[3] Gerhart Piers and Milton B. Singer, *Shame and Guilt;* Springfield, Ill., Charles C Thomas, 1953. See also Thomas M. French, "Guilt, Shame, and Other Reactive Motives," an unpublished paper.

[4] See, for example, Lafcadio Hearn's statement that Japanese authoritarianism is that of "the many over the one—not the one over the many." *Japan, An Attempt at Interpretation;* New York, Macmillan, 1905; pp. 435 ff.

[5] David Riesman, *The Lonely Crowd;* New Haven, Yale University Press, 1950.

fantile fears of abandonment. Personality patterns integrated around such motivation, if culturally prevalent, could possibly lead to a society dominated by a fear of failure and a need for recognition and success.

Intimately related to a shift from Puritan patterns in America were certain changes in the patterns of child-rearing. Similarly, it has been observed in Japan that prevailing child-rearing practices emphasize social evaluation as a sanction, rather than stressing more internalized, self-contained ethical codes instilled and enforced early by parental punishment. In spite of some earlier contentions to the contrary based on a few retrospective interviews,[6] the child-rearing patterns most evident in Japan, in deed, if not in word, manifest early permissiveness in regard to weaning and bowel training and a relative lack of physical punishment.[7] There is, moreover, considerable emphasis on ridicule and lack of acceptance of imperfect or slipshod performance in any regard. There is most probably a strong relationship between early permissiveness and susceptibility to external social sanctions. In line with the distinctions made between shame and guilt, the Japanese could easily be classified as shame oriented, and their concern over success and failure could be explicable in these terms. Somehow this

[6] For example, Geoffrey Gorer, "Themes in Japanese Culture," *Transact. N.Y. Acad. Sciences* (1943) 2:106–124

[7] See, for example, the empirical reports by Betty B. Lanham, "Aspects of Child Care in Japan: Preliminary Report," pp. 565–583; and Edward and Margaret Norbeck, "Child Training in a Japanese Fishing Community," pp. 651–673; in *Personal Character and Cultural Milieu*, edited by Douglas G. Haring; Syracuse, Syracuse University Press, 1956. A forthcoming publication by Edward Norbeck and George De Vos, "Culture and Personality: The Japanese," will present a more comprehensive bibliography, including the works of native Japanese, on child-rearing practices in various areas in Japan.

formula, however, does not hold up well when reapplied to an understanding of individual Japanese, either in Japan or in the United States.[8] Emphasis on shame

[8] The five clinical studies of Japanese-Americans in *Clinical Studies in Culture Conflict* (edited by Georgene Seward; New York, Ronald Press, 1958) consistently give evidence of depressive reactions and an inability to express hostile or resentful feelings toward the parents. Feelings of guilt are strongly related to an inability to express aggression outwardly, leading to intrapunitive reactions. Feelings of worthlessness also result from the repression of aggressive feelings. The Nisei woman described by Norman L. Farberow and Edward S. Schneidman in Ch. 15 (pp. 335 *ff.*) demonstrates the transference to the American cultural situation of certain basic intrapunitive attitudes common in Japan related to woman's ideal role behavior. The Kibei case described by Marvin K. Opler in Ch. 13 (pp. 297 *ff.*) well demonstrates a young man's perception of the manifest "suffering" of Japanese women. The case described by Charlotte G. Babcock and William Caudill in Ch. 17 (pp. 409 *ff.*) as well as other unpublished psychoanalytic material of Babcock's, amply demonstrates the presence of deep underlying guilt toward parents. Such guilt is still operative in Nisei in influencing occupational selection and marriage choice. Seward in a general summary of the Japanese cases (p. 449) carefully points out the pervasive depression found as a cohesive theme in each of the cases. She avoids conceptualizing the problems in terms of guilt, perhaps out of deference to the stereotype that Japanese feel 'ashamed' rather than 'guilty.' She states, "Running through all five Japanese-American cases is a pervasive depression, in three reaching the point of suicidal threat or actual attempt." Yet she ends with the statement, "Looking back over the cases of Japanese origin, we may note a certain cohesiveness binding them together. Distance from parent figures is conspicuous in all as well as inability openly to express resentment against them. In line with the externalization of authority and the shame-avoidance demands of Japanese tradition, hostility is consistently turned in on the self in the *face-saving devices* of depression and somatic illness." (Italics mine.)

sanctions in a society does not preclude severe guilt. While strong feelings of anxiety related to conformity are very much in evidence, both in traditional as well as present-day Japanese society, severe guilt becomes more apparent when the underlying motivation contributing to manifest behavior is more intensively analyzed. Shame is a more conscious phenomenon among the Japanese, hence more readily perceived as influencing behavior. But guilt in many instances seems to be a stronger basic determinant.

Although the ego ideal is involved in Japanese strivings toward success, day-by-day hard work and purposeful activities leading to long-range goals are directly related to guilt feelings toward parents. Transgression in the form of 'laziness' or other nonproductive behavior is felt to 'injure' the parents, and thus leads to feelings of guilt. There are psychological analogs between this Japanese sense of responsibility to parents for social conformity and achievement, and the traditional association sometimes found in the Protestant West between work activity and a personal relationship with a diety.[9]

Any attempt to answer questions concerning guilt in the Japanese raises many theoretical problems concerning the nature of internalization processes involved in human motivation. It is beyond the scope of this paper to discuss theoretically the complex interrelationships between feelings of shame and guilt in personality development. But the author believes that some anthropological writings, over-

[9] Robert Bellah, in *Tokugawa Religion* (Glencoe, Ill., The Free Press, 1957), perceives, and illustrates in detail, a definite relationship between prevalent pre-Meiji Tokugawa period ethical ideals and the rapid industrialization of Japan that occurred subsequent to the restoration of the Emperor. A cogent application of a sociological approach similar to that of Max Weber allows him to point out the obvious parallels in Tokugawa Japan to the precapitalist ethical orientation of Protestant Europe.

simplifying psychoanalytic theory, have placed too great an emphasis on a direct one-to-one relationship between observable child-rearing disciplines culturally prevalent and resultant inner psychological states. These inner states are a function not only of observable disciplinary behavior but also of more subtle, less reportable, atmospheric conditions in the home, as well as of other factors as yet only surmised.

Moreover, in accordance with psychoanalytic theory concerning the mechanisms of internalizing parental identification in resolving the Oedipal developmental stage, one would presume on an a priori basis that internalized guilt tends to occur almost universally, although its form and emphasis might differ considerably from one society to another. This paper, while guided by theory, is based primarily on empirical evidence and a posteriori reasoning in attempting to point out a specifically Japanese pattern of guilt. Developmental vicissitudes involved in the resolution of Oedipal relationships are not considered. Concisely stated, the position taken in this paper is as follows:

Guilt in many of the Japanese is not only operative in respect to what are termed superego functions, but is also concerned with what has been internalized by the individual as an ego ideal. Generally speaking, the processes involved in resolving early identifications as well as assuming later adult social roles are never possible without some internalized guilt. The more difficult it is for a child to live up to the behavior ideally expected of him, the more likely he is to develop ambivalence toward the source of the ideal. This ideal need not directly emphasize prohibited behavior, as is the case when punishment is the mode of training.

When shame and guilt have undergone a process of internalization in a person during the course of his development, both become operative regardless of the relative absence of either external threats of punishment or overt concern with the opinions of others concerning his behavior. Behavior is automatically self-evaluated without the presence of others. A simple dichotomy relating internalized shame only to ego ideal and internalized guilt to an automatically operative superego is one to be seriously questioned.

Whereas the formation of an internalized ego ideal in its earlier form is more or less related to the social expectations and values of parents, the motivations which move a developing young adult toward a realization of these expectations can involve considerable guilt. Japanese perceptions of social expectations concerning achievement behavior and marriage choice, as shown in the experimental materials described in this paper, give ample evidence of the presence of guilt; shame as a motive is much less in evidence.

Nullification of parental expectations is one way to "hurt" a parent. As defined in this paper, guilt in the Japanese is essentially related either to an impulse to hurt, which may be implied in a contemplated act, or to the realization of having injured a love object toward whom one feels some degree of unconscious hostility.

Guilt feelings related to various internalization processes differ, varying with what is prohibited or expected; nevertheless, some disavowal of an unconscious impulse to hurt seems to be generic to guilt. In some instances there is also emphasis on a fear of retribution stemming from this desire to injure. Such seems to be the case in many of the Japanese. If a parent has instilled in a child an understanding of his capacity to hurt by failing to carry out an obligation expected of him as a member of a family, any such failure can make him feel extremely guilty.

In the following materials taken from the rural hamlet of Niiike,[10] an attempt

[10] See the comprehensive, five-year study of this village by means of various social sci-

will be made to demonstrate how guilt is often related to possible rebellion against parental expectations. Two possible ways for the male to rebel are: (1) Dissipating one's energies in some sort of profligate behavior rather than working hard, or neglecting the diligence and hard work necessary for obtaining some achievement goal. (2) Rejecting arranged marriage by losing oneself in a marriage of passion, a so-called "love marriage."

In women, guilt seems related to becoming selfish or unsubmissive in the pursuit of duties involved in their adult role possibilities as wife and mother. This could mean, as in the case of men, refusal to accept the parents' marriage arrangement, or, after marriage, failure to devote oneself with whole-hearted intensity, without reservations, to the husband and his purposes and to the rearing of the children. Failure to show a completely masochistic, self-sacrificing devotion to her new family is a negative reflection on the woman's parents. Deficiencies in her children or even in her husband are sometimes perceived as her fault, and she must intrapunitively rectify her own failings if such behavior occurs. TAT stories taken from the Niiike sample bring out in both direct and indirect fashion evidence to support these contentions.

The Relation of Guilt to Achievement

The Japanese mother has perfected the technique of inducing guilt in her children by quiet suffering. A type of American mother often encountered in clinical practice repeatedly tells her children how she suffers from their bad behavior but in her own behavior reveals her selfish motives; in contrast, the Japanese mother

ence disciplines by members of the Center for Japanese Studies of the University of Michigan. Richard K. Beardsley, Robert Ward, John Hall, *Village Japan;* Chicago, University of Chicago Press, 1959.

does not to the same extent verbalize her suffering for her children but lives it out before their eyes. She takes on the burden of responsibility for her children's behavior—and her husband's—and will often manifest self-reproach if they conduct themselves badly. Such an example cannot fail to impress. The child becomes aware that his mother's self-sacrifice demands some recompense. The system of *On* obligation felt toward the parents, aptly described by Ruth Benedict,[11] receives a strong affective push from the Japanese mother's devotion to her children's successful social development, which includes the standards of success set for the community. As discussed in a previous paper,[12] the educational and occupational achievements of Japanese-Americans also show this pattern, modified in accordance with American influences.

The negative side of accomplishment is the hurt inflicted on the parent if the child fails or if he becomes self-willed in marriage or loses himself in indulgence. Profligacy and neglect of a vocational role in Japan—and often in the West as well—is an attack on the parents, frequently unconsciously structured.

The recurrence of certain themes in the TAT data, such as the occurrence of parental death as a result of disobedience, suggests the prevalence of expiation as a motive for achievement.[13] Themes of illness and death seem to be used not only to show the degree of parental, especially maternal, self-sacrifice, but also seem to be used as self-punishment in stories of strivings toward an ideal or goal with a single-minded devotion so strong that its effects may bring about the ruin of one's health.

These attitudes toward occupational striving can also be seen in the numerous examples in recent Japanese history of men's self-sacrifice for national causes. The sometimes inexplicable—to Western eyes at least—logic of the self-immolation practiced in wartime by the Japanese soldier can better be explained when seen as an act of sacrifice not resulting only from pressures of group morale and propaganda stressing the honor of such a death. The emotions that make such behavior seem logical are first experienced when the child observes the mother's attitude toward her own body as she often exhausts it in the service of the family.

To begin the examination of TAT data, the relation of guilt to parental suffering is apparent in certain TAT stories in which the death of the parent follows the bad conduct of a child, and the two events seem to bear an implicit relationship, as expressed in the following summaries (*W* indicates a woman, *M* a man): [14]

> *W, age 16, Card J13:* A mother is sick; her son steals because of poverty; mother dies.
>
> *M, age 41, Card J6GF:* A daughter marries for love against father's will; she takes care of her father, but father dies.

[11] Ruth Benedict, *The Chrysanthemum and the Sword;* Boston, Houghton Mifflin, 1946.

[12] William Caudill and George De Vos, "Achievement, Culture, and Personality. The Case of the Japanese Americans," *Amer. Anthropologist* (1956) 58:1102–1126.

[13] Hiroshi Wagatsuma, *Japanese Values of Achievement—The Study of Japanese Immigrants and Inhabitants of Three Japanese Villages by Means of T.A.T.;* unpublished M.A. thesis, Dept. of Far Eastern Studies, University of Michigan, 1957.

[14] The TAT cards used in the Japanese research were in most instances modifications of the Murray cards, with changed features, clothing, and background to conform to Japanese experience. The situations in the original Murray set were maintained. New cards were added to the modified set to elicit reactions to peculiarly Japanese situations as well. The numbers given for the stories used illustratively in this paper refer to modified cards resembling the Murray set with the exception of J9 and J11, which represent original Japanese family scenes.

W, age 22, Card J6GF: A daughter marries against her father's opposition, but her husband dies and she becomes unhappy.

M, age 23, Card J18: A mother strangles to death the woman who tempted her innocent son; the mother becomes insane and dies. The son begs forgiveness.

In such stories one may assume that a respondent first puts into words an unconscious wish of some kind but then punishes himself by bringing the death of a beloved person quickly into the scene.

One could also interpret such behavior in terms of cultural traditions. Punishing or retaliating against someone by killing or injuring oneself has often actually been done in Japan in both political and social arenas. Such self-injury or death became an accepted pattern of behavior under the rigid feudal regime where open protest was an impossibility for the suppressed and ruled. Numerous works on Japanese history contain accounts of the severe limitations on socially acceptable behavior and spontaneous self-expression.

Understanding the 'emotional logic' of this behavior, however, requires psychological explanations as well as such valid sociological explanations. This "moral masochistic" tendency, to use Freud's terminology, is inculcated through the attitudes of parents, especially of the mother. Suffering whatever the child does, being hurt constantly, subtly assuming an attitude of "look what you have done to me," the Japanese mother often gains by such devices a strong control over her child, and by increasing overt suffering, can punish him for lack of obedience or seriousness of purpose. Three of the above stories suggest that a mother or father is 'punishing' a child by dying. Parents' dying is not only the punishment of a child, but also more often is the final control over that child, breaking his resistance to obeying the parental plans. This use of death as a final admonish-ment lends credence to a story concerning the Japanese Manchurian forces at the close of World War II. The young officers in Manchuria had determined to fight on indefinitely, even though the home islands had surrendered. A staff general was sent by plane as an envoy of the Emperor to order the troops to surrender. He could get nowhere with the officers, who were determined to fight on. He returned to his plane, which took off and circled the field, sending a radio message that this was the final directive to surrender. The plane then suddenly dived straight for the landing field, crashing and killing all on board. The troops then promptly surrendered.

It is not unknown for a mother to threaten her own death as a means of admonishing a child. In a therapy case with a delinquent boy,[15] the mother had threatened her son, with very serious intent, telling him that he must stop his stealing or she would take him with her to the ocean and commit double suicide. The mother reasoned that she was responsible and that such a suicide would pay for her failure as a mother, as well as relieve the world of a potentially worthless citizen. The threat worked. For the man, this kind of threat of possible suffering becomes related to the necessity to work hard in the adult occupational role; for the woman, it becomes related to working hard at being a submissive and enduring wife.

In other of the TAT stories the death of a parent is followed by reform, hard work, and success. Examples of these stories are:

W, age 16, Card J7M: A son, scolded by his father, walks out; the father dies; son works hard and becomes successful.

M, age 39, Card J5: A mother worries about her delinquent son, becomes sick and dies; the son reforms himself and becomes successful.

[15] Reported in unpublished material of a Japanese psychiatrist, Taeko Sumi.

M, age 54, Card J13: A mother dies; the son changes his attitude and works hard.

W, age 17, Card J7M: A father dies; son walks out as his mother repeatedly tells him to be like the father; when he meets her again, she dies; he becomes hard-working.

W, age 38, Card J9: Elder brother is going to Tokyo, leaving his sick mother; his sister is opposed to his idea; his mother dies; he will become successful.

M, age 15, Card J6M: A son becomes more thoughtful of his mother after his father's death; he will be successful.

Emphasis on hard work and success after the death of parents clearly suggests some expiatory meaning related to the "moral masochistic" attitude of the mother in raising her child. The mother's moral responsibility is also suggested by other stories, such as a mother being scolded by a father when the child does something wrong, or a mother—not the father—being hurt when the child does not behave well. The feeling experienced by the child when he realizes, consciously or unconsciously, that he has hurt his mother is guilt—because guilt is generated when one hurts the object of one's love. The natural ambivalence arising from living under close parental control supplies sufficient unconscious intent to hurt to make the guilt mechanism operative.

The expiatory emphasis on hard work and achievement is also evident as a sequel in TAT stories directly expressing hurt of one's mother or father:

M, age 17, Card J11: A child dropped his father's precious vase. The father gets angry and scolds the mother for her having allowed the child to hold it. The child will become a fine man.

M, age 53, Card J18: A child quarreled outside; his mother is sorry that his father is dead. The child makes a great effort and gets good school records.

M, age 24, Card J11: A mother is worrying about her child who has gone out to play baseball and has not yet come back. When he comes home he overhears his mother complaining about his playing baseball all the time without doing his schoolwork. He then makes up his mind not to play baseball any more and to concentrate on his studies.

Although the realization of having hurt one's parents by bad conduct is not stated in the following story, it is another example of the use of working or studying hard—obviously as the means to achievement—to expiate possible guilt:

W, age 17, Card J3F: A girl worries about the loss of her virginity, consults with someone and feels at ease. She studies hard in the future.

In the same context, if one fails to achieve, he has no way to atone. He is lost. The only thing left is to hurt himself, to extinguish himself—the one whose existence has been hurting his parents and who now can do nothing for them. Suicide as an answer is shown in the following stories:

M, age 57, Card 3BM (original Murray card): A girl fails in examination, kills herself.

W, age 32, Card J3F: Cannot write a reserach paper; commits suicide.

On the level of cultural conditioning, the traditional teaching of *On* obligations enhances the feeling of guilt in the child, who is repeatedly taught by parents, teachers, books, and so forth, that his parents have experienced hardship and trouble and have made many sacrifices in order to bring him up. For example, financial strain and, significantly, ill health because of overwork may haunt the parents because of this child. Of course the child did not ask for all this sacrifice, nor does he consciously feel that he has intentionally hurt the parents, but there seems no way out; all this suffering takes place somewhere beyond his control, and he cannot avoid the burden it imposes. Certainly the child cannot say to himself, "I did not ask my parents to get hurt. Hurt or not, that is not my business," because he knows his parents love him and are also the objects of his love. What can be done about it then? The only way open to the child is to attain the goal of highest value, which is required of him; by working hard, being virtuous, becoming successful, attaining a good reputation and the praise of society, he brings honor to himself, to his parents, and to his *Ie* (household lineage), of which he and his parents are, after all, parts. If he becomes virtuous in this way, the parents can also receive credit. Self-satisfaction and praise from society go to them for having fulfilled their duty to *Ie* and society by raising their children well. The pattern repeats itself; he sacrifices himself masochistically for his own children, and on and on.

My assumption is, therefore, that among many Japanese people such a feeling of guilt very often underlies the strong achievement drive and aspiration toward success. If this hypothesis is accepted, then it can easily be understood that the death of a parent—that is, the culmination of the parent's being hurt following some bad conduct of a child— evokes in the child a feeling of guilt which is strong enough to bring him back from delinquent behavior and to drive him toward hard work and success. This is what is happening in the TAT stories of parental death and the child's reform.

Guilt in Japanese Marriage Relationships

The feeling of *On* obligations generated in the family situation during childhood is also found to be a central focus in Japanese arranged marriages. This feeling of obligation is very pronounced in women. In a sense, a woman expresses her need for accomplishment and achievement by aiming toward the fulfillment of her roles as wife and mother within the new family she enters in marriage. The man does not face giving up his family ties in the same way. Interview data suggest that for a Japanese woman, failure to be a dutiful bride reflects on her parents' upbringing of her, and therefore any discord with her new family, even with an unreasonable mother-in-law, injures the reputation of her parents.

Marriages which go counter to family considerations and are based on individual passion or love are particularly prone to disrupt the family structure; they are likely to be of rebellious origin, and any subsequent stresses of adjustment to partner and respective families tend to remind the participants of the rebellious tone of the marriage and, therefore, to elicit guilt feelings.

The TAT stories give evidence of guilt in regard to both types of "unacceptable" marriage behavior—they show the wife's readiness for self-blame in marriage difficulties with her husband, and they express self-blame or blame of others, on the part of both men and women, for engaging in possible love marriages.

THE WIFE'S SELF-BLAME IN DIFFICULTIES WITH HER HUSBAND. Of the stories involving discord between a man and his wife, several indicate a woman's feeling herself to be wrong in a situation which in America would be interpreted as resulting from the poor behavior of the husband. There are no cases of the reverse attitude—of a man's being blamed in an even slightly equivocal situation.

Four of five such stories are given by women. The man's story involves a need for reform by both partners, who are united in a love marriage and therefore apparently conform to the guilt pattern of such marriages, which I shall discuss shortly. In summary, the four women's stories are:

W, age 26, Card J3F: A wife quarreled with her huband when he returned from drinking. She leaves her house to cry, feels guilty for the quarrel.

W, age 54, Card J4: A husband and wife quarrel because the former criticized her cooking. The wife apologizes to him.

W, age 37, Card J4: A husband and wife quarrel, and after it the wife apologizes to her angry husband.

W, age 22, Card J5: A husband comes home very late at night; the wife thinks it is for lack of her affection and tries hard; he finally reforms.

Such attitudes also seem to be reflected in other test data, such as the "Problem Situations" material [16] collected in Niiike village. It is especially interesting to note that a husband's profligacy can be attributed by women to the wife's failure. It seems that the husband's willfulness—as is also true of a male child—is in some instances accepted as natural; somehow it is not his business to control himself if he feels annoyed with his wife. The wife nonetheless has to take responsibility for her husband's conduct. In one therapy case of a psychotic reaction in a young wife,[17] the mother-in-law blamed the bride directly for her husband's extramarital activities, stating, "If you were a good and satisfying wife, he would have no need to go elsewhere."

In connection with this point it may be worth mentioning that on the deepest level probably many Japanese wives do not 'give' themselves completely to their husbands because the marriage has been forced on them as an arrangement between the parents in each family. Wives often may not be able to adjust their innermost feelings in the marital relationship so as to be able to love their husbands genuinely. They may sense their own emotional resistance, and believe that it is an evil willfulness that keeps them from complete devotion as dictated by ethical ideals of womanhood. Sensing in the deepest level of their minds their lack of real affection, they become very sensitive to even the slightest indication of unfaithful behavior by the husbands. They feel that the men are reacting to the wives' own secret unfaithfulness in withholding. They cannot, therefore, blame their husbands, but throw the blame back upon themselves. They may become very anxious or quickly reflect upon and attempt to remedy their own inadequacies—as when their husbands happen to be late in getting home. Another hypothetical interpretation is that, lacking freedom of expression of their own impulses, Japanese women overidentify with male misbehavior; hence, they assume guilt as if the misbehavior were their own.

This propensity for self-blame in women is not necessarily limited to the wife's role. In the following story a younger sister somehow feels to blame when an older brother misbehaves.

W, age 17, Card J9: An elder brother did something wrong and is examined by the policeman; he will be taken to the police station, but will return home and reform. The younger sister also thinks that she was wrong herself.

One might say, in generalization, that the ethical ideal of self-sacrifice and devotion to the family line—be it to father or elder brother before marriage, or to husband and children after marriage— carries with it internalized propensities to take blame upon oneself and to express a moral sensitivity in these family relationships which no religious or other cultural sanctions compel the men to share.

[16] This test included items specifically eliciting a response to a hypothetical disharmony between wife and mother-in-law. In such cases the results indicate that the wife often sees herself as to blame for failing in her duty as a wife. She "should" conduct herself so as to be above reproach.

[17] Described by the Japanese psychiatrist, Kei Hirano.

LOVE MARRIAGES AND OTHER HETEROSEXUAL RELATIONSHIPS. Of the Niiike village TAT stories involving marriage circumstances,[18] 13 directly mention an arranged marriage and 24 mention a love marriage. While 9 of the 13 arranged marriage stories show no tension or conflict between the people involved, only 2 of the 24 stories mentioning love marriage are tension-free. The rest all contain tension of some kind between parents and child or between the marriage partners. In other words, many of the men and women in Niiike who bring up the subject of love marriage still cannot see it as a positive accomplishment but rather see it as a source of disruption. As mentioned, love marriage carried out in open rebellion against the parents is punished in certain stories by the death of a beloved person.

M, age 41, Card J6F: They are father and his daughter. The mother has died. The daughter is sitting on a chair in her room. The father is looking in, and she is turning around to face him. He is very thoughtful of his daughter, and as she is just about of age [for marriage], he wants to suggest that she marry a certain man he selected. But she has a lover and does not want to marry the man her father suggests. The father is trying to read her face, though he does know about the existence of the lover. He brought up the subject a few times before, but the daughter showed no interest in it. Today also—a smile is absent in her face. The father talks about the subject again, but he fails to persuade her. So finally he gives in and agrees with her marrying her lover. Being grateful to the father for the consent, the daughter acts very kindly to him after her marriage. The husband and the wife get along very affectionately also.

[18] A total of 80 persons gave 807 stories; 33 persons gave one or more stories involving marriage circumstances.

But her father dies suddenly of apoplexy. The father was not her real father. He did not have children, so he adopted her, and accepted her husband as his son-in-law. But he died. He died just at the time when a baby was born to the couple.

W, age 22, Card J6: The parents of this girl were brought up in families strongly marked with feudal atmosphere—the kind of family scarcely found in the present time. So they are very feudal and strict. The daughter cannot stand her parents. She had to meet her lover in secret. She was seeing her lover today as usual, without her parents knowing it. But by accident her father came to find it out. She was caught by her father on the spot. When she returned home her father rebuked her severely for it. But she could not give up her lover. In spite of her parents' strong objection, she married him. [*Examiner:* Future?] The couple wanted to establish a happy home when they married. But probably she will lose her husband. He will die—and she will have a miserable life.

There are a number of stories about unhappy events in the lives of a couple married for love. Many of these are found in response to Card 13 of the TAT, which shows a supine woman, breasts exposed, lying on a bed. A man in the foreground is facing away from the woman with one arm thrown over his eyes. A low table with a lamp is also in the room. Since responses to this card bring out in clear focus some basic differences between guilt over sexuality in Americans and in the Japanese, it will be well to consider them in some detail. Card J13 in the Japanese series is a modification of the original Murray TAT Card 13, with furniture and facial features altered.

Comparing Japanese and American responses to Card 13, it is obvious that while Americans rarely express remorse in connection with a marriage, the Japanese of Niiike express remorse in a heterosexual situation *only* in the context of marriage. In Americans, Card 13 is apt to evoke stories of guilt related to intercourse between partners not married to each other, with the figure of the woman sometimes identified as a prostitute, or sometimes as a young girl. When the figures are identified by Americans as married, the themes are usually around the subject of illness. In contrast, in the sample of 42 stories given in response to this card in Niiike village, not one story depicts a theme of guilt over sexuality between unmarried partners. Remorse is depicted only when it is related to regret for having entered into a love marriage.

Most of the Japanese stories given about this card fall into one of three categories: sex and/or violence (10 stories); marital discord (10 stories); and sickness or death (20 stories). Some striking differences in themes are related to the age and sex of the subjects.

Card 13: Sex and/or violence.—Six stories involve themes of extramarital sexual liaison. In three, the woman is killed by the man. Five of the six stories are given by men, who were with one exception under 35 years of age, and one is given by a woman under 25. The young woman's story depicts a man killing a woman because she was too jealous of him. One young man sees a man killing an entertainer who rejects him. Another sees a man killing a woman who was pursuing him "too actively." Another young man gives the theme of a student and a prostitute. In this story the man is disturbed by the prostitute's nakedness, not by his feelings of guilt over his activity.

The man over 35 sees the picture as depicting disillusion in a man who unexpectedly calls on a woman with whom he is in love, only to find her asleep in a "vulgar" fashion. As is true in the stories of other men over 35, which pertain to marital discord, the man is highly censorious of the woman's position on the bed. The Japanese woman is traditionally supposed to be proper in posture even when asleep. To assume a relaxed appearance reflects a wanton or sluttish nature.

Japanese men are apt to split their relationships with women into two groups: those with the wife and those with entertainers. Other evidence, not discussed here, supports the conclusion that for many men genuine affection is directed only toward maternal figures. Conversely, little deep affection seems freely available toward women perceived in a sexual role. Moreover, the Japanese male must defend himself against any passivity in his sexual relationship, lest he fall into a dependent relationship and become tied. By maintaining a rude aloofness and by asserting male prerogatives, he contains himself from involvement.

Men can resort to a violent defense if threatened too severely. Younger women especially tend to see men as potentially violent. Three women under 35 see a man as killing a woman, in two cases his wife. In addition to the jealousy mentioned before, the motives are the wife's complaint about low salary (a man must be seen as particularly sensitive about his economic prowess if such a complaint results in murder), and regret for entering a love marriage. The latter story, which follows, is particularly pertinent to understanding how guilt is related not to sexuality per se but to becoming "involved."

W, age 22: He got married for love with a woman in spite of opposition by his parents. While they were first married they lived happily. But recently he reflects on his marriage and the manner in which he pushed his way through his parents' opposition— and the present wife—he wishes his present wife would not exist—he attempts to push away the feeling of blame within his breast. One night on the way home he buys some insect poison and gives it to his wife to drink and she dies. What he has done weighs on his mind. He gives himself up to the police. He trustfully tells his story to them. He reflects on how wicked he has been in the past. He completes his prison term and faces the future with serious intent.

This story indirectly brings out a feeling of guilt for attempting to carry out a love marriage. Since such a marriage is psychologically forbidden fruit, the tasting of it brings upon the transgressor punishment, much like what happens for sexual transgressions out of wedlock in the fantasies of some more puritanical Westerners.

Card 13: Marital discord.—The nature of the stories concerning marital discord is unique to the Japanese. Seven of the 21 Niiike men giving stories about Card 13 mention marital discord. Five of these men and all three women giving such stories are between 35 and 50 years of age. The men tend to see the marriage as ending badly, whereas the women are more optimistic about seeing the discord resolved. Both sexes usually place the blame for the discord on the women.

As in one of the stories mentioned previously, the men take a cue for their stories from the position of the woman in the bed. Rather than seeing the woman as ill, as do many of the women responding to this card, the men use the woman's posture as a basis for criticizing her. One of the chief complaints found in these stories is that such a woman obviously does not take "proper care" of her man. The following stories bring out the nature of some of the feelings leading to the castigation of the wife for "looseness" and lack of wifely concern for her husband. The man, too, is castigated in some of the stories, but not with the strength of feeling that is turned toward the woman.

M, age 39: This is also very difficult for me. What shall I say—I can't tell my impressions—what shall I say—it seems to me that they do not lead a happy life. The man often comes back home late at night, I suppose. But his wife does not wait for her husband. She has decided to act of her own accord, I suppose—he is back home late again, and his wife is already asleep. He thinks that it might be well to speak to her. I suppose there is always a gloomy feeling in this family. Well, if they lead a peaceful life, such a scene as this would never occur. It is customary that a wife takes care of her husband as she should when he comes home—and afterward she goes to bed. But, judging from this picture, I suppose this wife wouldn't care a bit about her husband. Such a family as this will be ruined, I think. They should change their attitude toward each other and should make happy home. [*Examiner:* What about the future?] They will be divorced. It will be their end. [*Examiner:* Do you have anything to add?] Well, I expect a woman to be as a woman should be. A man also should think more of his family.

M, age 41: This is also—this man is a drunkard, and his wife also a sluttish woman. And the man was drunk, and when he came back his wife was already asleep—and, well—finally, they will be ruined. They have no child. They will become separated from each other. This wife will become something like *nakai* or a procuress. The husband will be held in prison—and the husband will kill himself on the railroad tracks. And—the wife will work as a *nakai*, and after contracting an infectious disease will die. An infectious disease which attacks her is dysentery. They worked together in a company and were married for love. That is their past. [*Examiner:* What

does it mean that they will be ruined?]
He became desperate. He became separated from his wife, so that he became desperate. If a man committed
a bad thing, nobody cares for him. He
could not hope for any help, so that
he killed himself.

M, age 35: Well, this man and
woman married for love. The woman
was a café waitress and married the
man for love. But they have not lived
happily, so the man repents the marriage very much. Well, this man used
to be a very good man, but he was
seduced by the waitress and lost his
self-control, and at last he had a sexual
relationship with her. Afterwards, he
becomes afraid that he has to think
over their marriage. If their married
life has any future at all, I hope they
will maintain some better stability.
But if this woman doesn't want to do
so, he needs to think over their marriage, I suppose.

The latter story especially brings out
strong feelings of guilt related to an attempt to carry out a love marriage. The
story directly depicts the guilt as being
related to losing self-control and becoming involved with an unsuitable woman,
not with the sexual activity per se.

Implied, too, is the criticism that any
woman who would make a love marriage
is not really capable of being a very
worthy wife. Therefore, in addition to
depicting guilt for going counter to the
parents in a love marriage, Card 13 indicates the potential avenue for projecting guilt on to the woman who is active
enough to enter a love marriage. Such
a woman's conduct obviously does not include the proper submissiveness to parental wishes and attention to the needs
of her spouse.

This castigation of the woman is therefore directly related to an expectation
that the wife rather than being a sexual
object should be a figure fulfilling de-

pendency needs. The man sees his wife
in a maternal role and is probably quick
to complain if his wife renders him less
care and attention than were rendered
him by his mother. Since the wife-mother
image tends to be fused in men, there is
little concept of companionship per se,
or sharing of experience on a mutual
basis. Also, the wife's acting too free sexually excites aspects of sexuality toward
the mother that were repressed in childhood. The wife-mother image cannot be
conceived of in gross sexual terms. It is
speculated by some that the mistress is
a necessity to some men, because their
sexual potency toward their wives is
muted by the fused wife-mother image.
Certain free sexual attitudes on the part
of the wife would tend to change the
mother image of her to a prostitute image
and cause castigation of her as morally
bad.

One may say that this fusion of images
has a great deal to do with the conflict
often arising between the young bride
and her mother-in-law. The mother-in-
law's jealousy is partially due to her fear
of being directly replaced in her son's
affection by the bride, since they are essentially geared to similar roles rather
than forming different types of object
relationship with the man. The wife becomes more intimate with the husband
after she becomes a mother, and essentially treats him as the favorite child.

These sorts of attitudes were present in
Hirano's case, mentioned previously,
wherein a woman's psychotic episode was
precipitated by her mother-in-law's attacks, including the interpretation that
the dalliance of her son with other
women was further proof of the wife's
incompetence. It was interesting to note
that during the wife's stay in the hospital
the husband was able to express considerable feeling of concern for her. There
was no doubt that he loved her. In effect,
however, this feeling was more for her
as a maternal surrogate than as a sexual

partner. His mother knew she had more to fear from the wife in this respect than from liaisons with other women, with whom the husband never became too involved. He, on the other hand, had no manifest guilt for his sexual activities—in effect, they were approved of by his mother in her battle with the wife.

Card 13: Sickness or death of wife or mother.—In six instances (five women, three of them teen-agers), Card 13 is interpreted as a mother-son situation with the mother either sick or dead. The son is pictured specifically as working hard or studying; in one story the son steals because they are so poor. The younger girls especially seem to need to defend themselves from the sexual implications of the card by inventing a completely desexualized relationship. Unable to make the card into a marital situation, much less a more directly sexual one, some fall back on the favored theme of a sick mother and a distraught, but diligent, son. Emphasis on studying hard suggests the defensive use of work and study to shut out intrapersonal problems. Diligent work to care for the mother is again unconsciously used to avoid any feelings related to possible guilt. The way out is the one most easily suggested by the culture. Seeing Card 13 as a mother-son situation is rare in American records, even in aberrant cases.

Seeing Card 13 as illness or death of a wife is the most characteristic response of women; fourteen women, most of them over 35 years of age, gave such stories. Six men, including four of the five in the sample over 50, selected this theme. The middle-aged women were strongly involved in their stories about the death of a wife. Such stories were the longest of any given to the card. In sharp contrast to the derogatory stories directed toward the women by the men, the women use respectful concepts, such as *Otoko-naki* (manly tears), in referring to the men. On certain occasions it is expected that "manly tears" are shed. Although a man

is usually expected not to cry freely when sober, the death of a wife is an occasion on which he is expected to cry. Much emphasis is placed on the imagined love felt toward the wife by a husband, on his loneliness, and on his feeling of loss because of the absence of wifely care. Concern with potential loneliness and possible loss of such care is certainly reflected in the fact that the older men in most instances select similar themes. The women in all but one case see the wife as dead or dying; the man is frequently seen as remarrying. Conversely, the men are more optimistic about recovery of a wife from illness and more pessimistic about remarriage if she does not recover.

One woman constructs a story of the noble self-sacrifice of a sick wife who commits suicide so as not to be a burden to her husband. This type of story, which recalls many sentimental novels written in Japan, is considered very moving by the Japanese, since it is supposed to reflect the degree of devotion of a wife for her husband and his goals and purposes. Tears are brought to the eyes of the older members of a *Kabuki* audience when such a story unfolds. To the Westerner, the stories seem to be excessively masochistic and overdrawn. The Japanese ethical ideal of the self-sacrificing role of woman is here emphatically displayed.

The foregoing materials from a farming village, which other evidence suggests is deeply imbued with traditional attitudes, are consistent with the interpretation that the potentiality for strong guilt feelings is prevalent in the Japanese. Such feelings become evident when there is failure in the performance of expected role behavior. Guilt, as such, is not as directly related in the Japanese to sexual expression as it is in persons growing up within cultures influenced by Christian attitudes toward sexuality. As first pointed out by Benedict,[19] there is little pro-

[19] See footnote 11.

nounced guilt or otherwise negatively toned attitude directed toward physical expression of sexuality per se. Rather, there is concern with the possible loss of control suffered by becoming involved in a love relationship that interferes with the prescribed life goals of the individual.

From a sociological standpoint, Japanese culture can be considered as manifesting a particularistic or situational ethic as opposed to the more universalistic ethic built around moral absolutes found in Western Christian thought.[20] This evaluation can be well documented, but does not mean that the Japanese evidence a relative absence of guilt in relation to moral transgressions. Whereas the applicability of the more universalistic Western ethic in many aspects may tend to transcend the family, the Japanese traditional ethic is actually an expression of rules of conduct for members of a family, and filial piety has in itself certain moral absolutes that are not completely situationally determined even though they tend to be conceptualized in particularistic terms. This difference between family-oriented morality and a more universalistic moral system is, nevertheless, a source of difficulty in thinking about guilt in the Japanese.

Another reason for the failure to perceive guilt in the Japanese stems from the West's customary relation of guilt to sexuality. Missionaries in particular, in assessing the Japanese from the standpoint of Protestant moral standards, were often quoted as perplexed not only by what they considered a lack of moral feelings in regard to nonfamilial relationships, but also—and this was even worse in their eyes—by a seeming absence of any strong sense of 'sin' in their sexual relationships. It seems evident that the underlying emotional content of certain

aspects of Christianity, in so far as it is based on specific types of repression and displacement of sexual and aggressive impulses, has never appealed to the Japanese in spite of their intellectual regard for the ethics of Christianity. Modern educated Japanese often recognize Christianity as advocating an advanced ethical system more in concert with modern universalized democratic ideals of man's brotherhood. As such, Christianity is favored by them over their more hierarchically oriented, traditional system with its rigidly defined, particularistic emphasis on prescribed social roles. To the educated Japanese, however, the concept of sin is of little interest in their attitudes toward Christianity. The lack of interest in sin is most probably related to the absence of childhood disciplines that would make the concept important to them.

Traditional Western disciplinary methods, guided by concern with the inherent evil in man, have been based on the idea that the child must be trained as early as possible to conquer evil tendencies within himself. Later, he learns to resist outside pressures and maintain himself as an individual subject to his own conscience and to the universalist laws of God. The traditional Western Protestant is more accustomed in certain circumstances to repress inappropriate feelings. 'Right' thoughts are valued highly and one generally tries to repress unworthy motives toward one's fellow men. Justice must be impartial, and one must not be swayed by the feelings of the moment or be too flexible in regard to equity.

In Japanese Buddhist thought one finds a dual concept of man as good and evil, but in Shinto thought, and in Japanese thinking about children generally,[21]

---

[20] See Talcott Parsons, *The Social System;* Glencoe, Ill., The Free Press, 1951; p. 175, for a description of the particularistic achievement pattern. This category suits traditional Japanese culture very well.

[21] It is significant that the Japanese usually use Shinto ceremonials in regard to marriage and fertility, and to celebrate various periods in childhood, whereas Buddhist ceremonials are used mainly in paying respect to the parents—that is, in funerals and in memorial

the more prevailing notion is that man's impulses are innately good. The purpose of child training is merely the channeling of these impulses into appropriate role behavior.

The definitions of proper role behavior become increasingly exacting as the child grows and comes into increasing contact with others as a representative of his family. As such, he learns more and more to be diplomatic and to contain and suppress impulses and feelings that would be disruptive in social relations and put him at a disadvantage. He is not bringing a system of moral absolutes into his relations with others any more than the usual diplomat does in skillfully negotiating for the advantage of his country. The Japanese learns to be sensitive to 'face' and protocol and to be equally sensitive to the feelings of others. He learns to keep his personal feelings to himself as a family representative. It would be just as fallacious to assume, therefore, that the Japanese is without much sense of guilt, as it would be in the case of the private life of a career diplomat.

The fact that so much of conscious life is concerned with a system of social sanctions helps to disguise the underlying guilt system operative in the Japanese.

This system, which severely represses unconscionable attitudes toward the parents and superiors, is well disguised not only from the Western observer but also from the Japanese themselves. The Westerner, under the tutelage of Christianity, has learned to 'universalize' his aggressive and other impulses and feel guilt in regard to them in more general terms. The modern Japanese is moving toward such an attitude, but is affected by the traditional moral structure based on the family system, or if expanded, on the nation conceived of in familial terms.

Lastly, some difficulty in perceiving Japanese guilt theoretically, if not clinically, is due to the fact that psychoanalysis—the psychological system most often consulted for help in understanding the mechanisms involved in guilt—tends to be strongly influenced by Western ethical values. Psychoanalytic writers, in describing psychosexual development, tend to emphasize the superego on the one hand and concepts of personal individuation and autonomy on the other. A major goal of maturation is freedom in the ego from irrational social controls as well as excessive internalized superego demands. In understanding the Japanese this emphasis is somewhat out of focus. Maturational ideals valued by the traditional Japanese society put far more emphasis on concepts of 'belonging' and adult role identity.

In studying the Japanese, it is helpful, therefore, to try to understand the nature of internalization of an ego ideal defined in terms of social role behavior. Concern with social role has in the past been more congenial to the sociologist or sociologically oriented anthropologist,[22] who in examining human behavior is less specifically concerned with individuation and more concerned with the patterning of

---

services at specified times after death. It must be noted that the material in this paper does not include any reference to fear of punishment in an afterlife; although present in traditional Buddhism in the past, such feelings are not much in evidence in modern Japan. Relatively few modern Japanese believe in or are concerned with life beyond death. (See George De Vos and A. Wagatsuma, "Psycho-cultural Significance of Concern over Death and Illness Among Rural Japanese," *Internat. J. Social Psychiatry* (1959) 5:6–19; especially pp. 13 *ff.*) It is my contention that fear of punishment either by the parents, society, or God is not truly internalized guilt. Insofar as the punishment is perceived as external in source, the feeling is often fear or anxiety, as distinct from guilt.

[22] This approach is also evident in the theorist in religion. Also, the recent interest in existentialist psychiatry is one attempt to bring in relevant concepts of 'belonging' to the study of the human experience.

behavior within a network of social relations.

However, the sociological approach in itself is not sufficient to help understand the presence or absence of a strong achievement motive in the Japanese. It is necessary to use a psychoanalytic framework to examine the psychological processes whereby social roles are internalized and influence the formation of an internalized ego ideal. The ideas of Erikson,[23]

[23] Erik H. Erikson, "The Problem of Ego Identity," *J. Amer. Psychoanal. Assn.* (1956) 4:56–121.

in his exploration of the role of "self-identity" in the latter stages of the psychosexual maturation process, form a bridge between the psychoanalytic systems of thought and the sociological analyses which cogently describe the place of role as a vital determining factor of social behavior. The avenue of approach taken by Erikson is a very promising one in understanding the Japanese social tradition and its effect on individual development.

THE RELATIONSHIP BETWEEN OVERT AND FANTASY AGGRESSION AS A FUNCTION OF MATERNAL RESPONSE TO AGGRESSION

by Gerald S. Lesser

In recent years, a voluminous literature has developed around the problem of establishing relationships between fantasy behavior and overt behavior. Different researchers have used different drive areas, different populations, different theoretical bases, and different methods of measurement. The most conspicuous conclusion is that the empirical findings are not in agreement.

The importance of this area of investigation for both clinical practice and personality theory has been elaborated by Lindzey (12). He concludes that one of the most important and difficult problems is the "determination of the conditions under which inferences based upon projective material directly relate to overt behavior and the conditions for the reverse" (12, p. 18). The present study concerns the differential conditions under which aggressive behavior is learned that may allow prediction of how aggressive expressions in fantasy are related to those in overt behavior.

SOURCE: *Journal of Abnormal and Social Psychology*, Vol. 55 (1957), pp. 218–221.

Various studies (9, 13, 16, 18, 19) have demonstrated that the degree of correspondence between fantasy behavior and the associated overt behavior is greater for certain drives than for others. Significant positive correlations have been reported between TAT fantasy and overt behavior for variables such as abasement, achievement, creation, dependence, exposition, nurturance, etc. Significant negative correlations have been reported for sex, and inconclusive results have been obtained for a wide variety of other variables. For the variable of aggression, results include significant positive correlations between fantasy and overt expressions (8, 14), significant negative correlations (5, 16), and inconclusive findings (1, 2, 3, 4, 6, 10, 13, 15, 16, 18).

To resolve these inconsistent results, it has been suggested (13, 14, 16, 19) that motives that are culturally encouraged are ". . . likely to be as strong in their overt as in their covert manifestations" (13, p. 16), while motives that are culturally discouraged are apt to show little or no relationship between the strength of fantasy and overt expressions.

Mussen and Naylor (14) have attempted to test the first segment of this formulation. They contended that lower-class culture encourages aggression, and predicted that ". . . in a lower-class group, individuals who give evidence of a great deal of fantasy aggression will also manifest more overt aggression than those who show little aggression in their fantasies" (p. 235). A mixed group of white and Negro boys, ". . . almost all of whom had been referred to the Bureau of Juvenile Research for behaviors which brought them into conflict with school and court authorities . . ." (p. 236), were used as subjects. The authors report a statistically significant but not especially strong positive relationship between ratings of overt aggression and number of aggressive TAT themes. Further investigation of Mussen and Naylor's hypothesis would profit from more precise measurement of parental response to aggression, control comparisons, and a more representative sample.

The present study seeks to examine the comparative consequences of both encouragement and discouragement of aggression through the hypothesis that under conditions of maternal encouragement of aggression a greater degree of correspondence exists between fantasy and overt aggression of children than under conditions of maternal discouragement of aggression.

Method

SUBJECTS

The subjects (Ss) were 44 white boys (ages 10-0 to 13-2) and their mothers. The boys were drawn from one fifth grade and two sixth grades in two public schools. All of the boys and their mothers in these three classes participated except one mother who refused to be interviewed. The Kuhlmann-Anderson intelligence quotients of the boys ranged from 82 to 119, with a mean of 102. The two

schools are in adjacent districts and the families constitute a relatively homogeneous upper lower-class group.

MATERNAL ATTITUDES AND PRACTICES

Only one aspect of the environmental conditions of learning of aggressive behavior was measured, i.e., the maternal attitudes and practices supporting or prohibiting aggression. A structured questionnaire-interview schedule was orally administered to the mothers in their homes by a male interviewer. Questions regarding the support or prohibition of aggression constituted only one segment of the total interview; the entire interview schedule is described in detail elsewhere (11). Pertinent to the present study were eight items concerning the mother's attitudes toward aggression in children, and thirteen items about the mother's practices in dealing with the aggressive behavior of her child. An illustrative item measuring maternal attitudes toward aggression is: "A child should be taught to stand up and fight for his rights in his contacts with other children." The four response alternatives of agree, mildly agree, mildly disagree, and disagree were allowed for this item. An example of an item measuring maternal practices concerning aggression is: "If your son comes to tell you that he is being picked on by a bully at the playground who is his own age and size, there would be a number of different things you might tell him. Would you tell him to ignore him and turn the other cheek?" Response alternatives for this item were yes and no. Items that did not involve judgments on a four-point scale were transformed to have approximately the same range of scores as the items that involved four alternatives.

A single score was obtained for each mother by combining all items, assigning plus scores to the responses indicating support of aggression and minus scores to responses indicating discouragement of aggression. The range of scores was from

+9 to −7, with a median score of +2. The corrected odd-even reliability coefficient was .80.

The distribution of scores for maternal responses to aggression was dichotomized to form one group of mothers (with scores above or at the median) whose attitudes and practices were more supportive of aggressive behavior than those of the other group (with scores below the median). The hypothesis demands that the correlation between fantasy and overt aggression for the children of the mothers in the former group be significantly more positive than the corresponding correlation for the children of the mothers in the latter group.

FANTASY AGGRESSION

Fantasy aggression in the children was measured through an adaptation of the TAT procedure (13, p. 3–5). A set of ten pictures was designed. In each picture two boys are interacting. The pictures differed from one another in the degree to which the instigation to aggression was apparent.

To insure complete and accurate transcription of the stories, tape recordings were taken. An introductory period preceding the fantasy task served both to establish rapport between the child and the male examiner, and to familiarize the child with the recording device. Instructions were:

> I'm going to show you some pictures. These are pictures of two boys doing different things. What I'd like you to do is make up a story to each of these pictures. You can make up any story you wish; there are no right or wrong stories. Say what the boys are thinking and feeling and how the story will turn out.

The ten pictures, in the order of presentation, were:

1. One boy is holding a basketball and the other boy is approaching him with arms outstretched.
2. One boy is stamping upon an ambiguous object and the other boy is reaching for the object.
3. One boy is sitting behind the other boy in a classroom and is leaning toward him.
4. One boy is walking down the street and the other boy, with fists clenched, is glaring at him.
5. One boy, with fists clenched, is staring at the other boy who is sitting, head bowed, on a box.
6. One boy is sawing a piece of wood and the other boy is leaning on a fence between them, talking to him.
7. The two boys, surrounded by a group of other boys, are approaching each other with arms upraised and fists clenched.
8. The two boys are making a fire. One boy is kneeling to arrange the wood and the other boy is approaching, ladened with wood for the fire.
9. One boy, who is looking back, is running down a street and the other boy is running behind him.
10. Two boys are standing in a field. One boy, with his hand on the other boy's shoulder, is pointing off in the distance.

A fantasy aggression score was obtained for each S by counting the number of times the following acts appeared in his stories: fighting, injuring, killing, attacking, assaulting, torturing, bullying, getting angry, hating, breaking, smashing, bombing, destroying, scorning, expressing contempt, expressing disdain, cursing, swearing, insulting, belittling, repudiating, ridiculing.

Fantasy aggression scores ranged from 1 to 15, with a mean of 5.3. The corrected matched-half reliability coefficient was .86; the inter-judge scoring reliability coefficient was .92.

OVERT AGGRESSION

To measure overt aggression in the child, a modified sociometric device, the "Guess who" technique (7), was adopted.

The Ss were presented with a booklet containing a series of written descriptions of children, and asked to identify each of these descriptive characterizations by naming one or more classmates. Fifteen overt aggression items were used, such as "Here is someone who is always looking for a fight." A diversity of aggressive behaviors were included; items depicted verbal, unprovoked physical, provoked physical, outburst, and indirect forms of aggressive behavior.

An overt aggressive score was obtained for each subject by counting the number of times he was named by his classmates. There were substantial differences among the three classes in the distributions of the overt aggression scores; in order to combine into one distribution the scores of children in different classes, overt aggression raw scores were transformed into standard scores.

The biserial correlation coefficient between the overt aggression measures derived from the children and teacher entries for the same "Guess who" aggression items was .76 ($p < .01$).

Results

Two Pearson product-moment correlation coefficients were obtained. For boys ($N = 23$) whose mothers are relatively encouraging or supportive of aggression, the correlation between fantasy aggression and overt aggression is $+.43$ ($p < .05$, two-tailed test). For boys ($N = 21$) whose mothers are relatively discouraging of aggression, the corresponding correlation is $-.41$ ($p < .10$, two-tailed test). These coefficients are statistically different ($p = .006$, two-tailed test).

When the total sample is not separated into two groups on the basis of scores for maternal response to aggression, the overall Pearson product-moment correlation coefficient is $+.07$. This coefficient is not significantly different from zero.

Discussion

Confirmation is found for the hypothesis that under conditions of relative maternal encouragement of aggression, a greater degree of correspondence exists between the fantasy and overt aggression of children than under conditions of relative maternal discouragement of aggression. Thus, the direction and extent of the relationship between fantasy and overt aggression in the child is apparently influenced by the maternal attitudes and practices surrounding the learning of aggressive behavior.

It has been predicted (13, 16) that those tendencies which are negatively sanctioned or prohibited will be high in fantasy expression and low in overt expression. This association is premised upon a compensatory or substitutive role of fantasy where overt expression is not allowed. A scatter plot of the fantasy and overt aggression scores for the children whose mothers discourage aggression (from which the $-.41$ coefficient is derived) reveals a considerable number of such high fantasy aggression, low overt aggression scores. However, children with low fantasy aggression and high overt aggression scores are as well represented in this scatter plot as those with high fantasy aggression, low overt aggression scores. Although mothers of children in this group were classified (relative to the others) as discouraging aggression, perhaps certain of them do so ineffectively, and thus allow the child sufficient release of aggressive feelings in overt behavior so that he may not need to express aggression in fantasy. An alternative speculation regarding the concurrence of low fantasy aggression and high overt aggression in the group exposed to maternal discouragement of aggression suggests that a child with strong aggressive needs whose mother prohibits aggression may assign this prohibitory attitude to the adult experimenter and suppress fantasy aggression expressions in the testing situation; yet this child may find avenues for overt expression of aggression among his peers.

In the present study, only one condition related to the learning of aggressive responses and controls was assessed, maternal attitudes and practices. Other possibly critical determinants that remain to be explored include fathers' behavior and teachers' attitudes and practices. This study has sampled a limited range of maternal attitudes and practices concerning aggression. Although there is no direct manner of determining the absolute degree of punitiveness of the most prohibitive mother in this sample, it appears unlikely that extremely severe and continuous maternal punitiveness is represented. Such severe condemnation of aggression might so limit or restrict both the fantasy aggression and overt aggression expressions of the child that no correlational analysis within such a group would be possible. Both the extremes of unimpeded permissiveness and severe condemnation warrant further investigation.

Summary

The relationship between fantasy and overt expressions of aggression was studied as a function of the maternal attitudes and practices toward aggression. Subjects were 44 boys and their mothers. The boys' fantasy aggression was assessed through a modified TAT approach, their overt aggression was measured through a modified sociometric technique, and maternal attitudes and practices toward aggression were measured by use of a questionnaire-interview device.

Support was found for the hypothesis that under conditions of maternal encouragement of aggression, a greater degree of correspondence exists between fantasy and overt aggression of children than under conditions of maternal discouragement of aggression.

REFERENCES

1. Bach, G. R.: Young children's play fantasies. *Psychol. Monogr.*, 1945, 59, No. 2 (Whole No. 272).
2. Bialick, I.: The relationship between reactions to authority figures on the TAT and overt behavior in an authority situation by hospital patients. Unpublished doctor's dissertation, University of Pittsburgh, 1951.
3. Child, I. L., Kitty F. Frank, and T. Storm: Self-ratings and TAT: Their relations to each other and to childhood background. *J. Pers.*, 1956, 25, 98–114.
4. Davids, A., A. F. Henry, C. C. McArthur, and L. F. McNamara: Projection, self evaluation, and clinical evaluation of aggression. *J. consult. Psychol.*, 1955, 19, 437–440.
5. Fishbach, S.: The drive-reducing function of fantasy behavior. *J. abnorm. soc. Psychol.*, 1955, 50, 3–11.
6. Gluck, M. R.: The relationship between hostility in the TAT and behavioral hostility. *J. proj. Tech.*, 1955, 19, 21–26.
7. Hartshorne, H., and M. A. May: *Studies in the nature of character*. II. New York: MacMillan, 1929.
8. Kagan, J.: The measurement of overt aggression from fantasy. *J. abnorm. soc. Psychol.*, 1956, 52, 390–393.
9. Kagan, J., and P. H. Mussen: Dependency themes on the TAT and group conformity. *J. consult. Psychol.*, 1956, 20, 29–33.
10. Korner, Anneliese F.: *Some aspects of hostility in young children*. New York: Grune and Stratton, 1949.
11. Lesser, G. S.: Maternal attitudes and practices and the aggressive behavior of children. Unpublished doctor's dissertation, Yale University, 1952.
12. Lindzey, G.: Thematic Apperception Test: Interpretive assumptions and related empirical evidence. *Psychol. Bull.*, 1952, 49, 1–25.
13. Murray, H. A.: *Thematic Apperception*

Test Manual. Cambridge: Harvard University Press, 1943.

14. Mussen, P. H., and H. K. Naylor: The relationships between overt and fantasy aggression. *J. abnorm. soc. Psychol.*, 1954, 49, 235–240.

15. Pittlock, Patricia: The relation between aggressive fantasy and overt behavior. Unpublished doctor's dissertation, Yale University, 1950.

16. Sanford, R. N., Margaret M. Adkins, R. B. Miller, E. A. Cobb, *et al.*: Physique, personality, and scholarship: A cooperative study of school children. *Monogr. Soc. Res. Child Developm.*, 1943, 8, No. 1.

17. Sears, R. R.: Relation of fantasy aggression to interpersonal aggression. *Child Developm.*, 1950, 21, 5–6.

18. Symonds, P. M.: *Adolescent fantasy: An investigation of the picture story method of personality study*. New York: Columbia University Press, 1949.

19. Tomkins, S. S.: The *Thematic Apperception Test*. New York: Grune and Stratton, 1947.

2 • The Genesis of Mental Disorders and Social Deviance

TOWARD A THEORY OF SCHIZOPHRENIA

by Gregory Bateson, Don D. Jackson, Jay Haley, and John Weakland

This is a report [1] on a research project which has been formulating and testing a broad, systematic view of the nature,

[1] This paper derives from hypotheses first developed in a research project financed by the Rockefeller Foundation from 1952–1954, administered by the Department of Sociology and Anthropology at Stanford University and directed by Gregory Bateson. Since 1954 the project has continued, financed by the Josiah Macy, Jr. Foundation. To Jay Haley is due credit for recognizing that the symptoms of schizophrenia are suggestive of an inability to discriminate the Logical Types, and this was amplified by Bateson who added the notion that the symptoms and etiology could be formally described in terms of a double bind hypothesis. The hypothesis was communicated to D. D. Jackson and found to fit closely with his ideas of family homeostasis. Since then Dr. Jackson has worked closely with the project. The study of the formal analogies between hypnosis and schizophrenia has been the work of John H. Weakland and Jay Haley.

SOURCE: *Behavioral Science*, Vol. 1 (1956), pp. 251–264.

etiology, and therapy of schizophrenia. Our research in this field has proceeded by discussion of a varied body of data and ideas, with all of us contributing according to our varied experience in anthropology, communications analysis, psychotherapy, psychiatry, and psychoanalysis. We have now reached common agreement on the broad outlines of a communicational theory of the origin and nature of schizophrenia; this paper is a preliminary report on our continuing research.

The Base in Communications Theory

Our approach is based on that part of communications theory which Russell has called the Theory of Logical Types (17). The central thesis of this theory is that there is a discontinuity between a class and its members. The class cannot be a member of itself nor can one of the members *be* the class, since the term used for the class is of a *different level of abstraction*—a different Logical Type—from terms used for members. Although in formal logic there is an attempt to maintain this discontinuity between a class and its members, we argue that in the psychology of real communications this discontinuity is continually and inevitably breached (2), and that a priori we must expect a pathology to occur in the human organism when certain formal patterns of the breaching occur in the communication between mother and child. We shall argue that this pathology at its extreme will have symptoms whose formal characteristics would lead the pathology to be classified as a schizophrenia.

Illustrations of how human beings handle communication involving multiple Logical Types can be derived from the following fields:

1. *The use of various communicational modes in human communication.* Examples are play, non-play, fantasy, sacrament, metaphor, etc. Even among the lower mammals there appears to be an exchange of signals which identify certain meaningful behavior as "play," etc.[2] These signals are evidently of higher Logical Type than the messages they classify. Among human beings this framing and labeling of messages and meaningful actions reaches considerable complexity, with the peculiarity that our vocabulary for such discrimination is still very poorly developed, and we rely preponderantly upon nonverbal media of posture, gesture, facial expression, intonation, and the context for the communication of these highly abstract, but vitally important, labels.

2. *Humor.* This seems to be a method of exploring the implicit themes in thought or in a relationship. The method

[2] A film prepared by this project, "The Nature of Play; Part I, River Otters," is available.

of exploration involves the use of messages which are characterized by a condensation of Logical Types or communicational modes. A discovery, for example, occurs when it suddenly becomes plain that a message was not only metaphoric but also more literal, or vice versa. That is to say, the explosive moment in humor is the moment when the labeling of the mode undergoes a dissolution and resynthesis. Commonly, the punch line compels a re-evaluation of earlier signals which ascribed to certain messages a particular mode (e.g., literalness or fantasy). This has the peculiar effect of attributing *mode* to those signals which had previously the status of that higher Logical Type which classifies the modes.

3. *The falsification of mode-identifying signals.* Among human beings mode identifiers can be falsified, and we have the artificial laugh, the manipulative simulation of friendliness, the confidence trick, kidding, and the like. Similar falsifications have been recorded among mammals (3, 13). Among human beings we meet with a strange phenomenon—the unconscious falsification of these signals. This may occur within the self—the subject may conceal from himself his own real hostility under the guise of metaphoric play—or it may occur as an unconscious falsification of the subject's understanding of the other person's mode-identifying signals. He may mistake shyness for contempt, etc. Indeed most of the errors of self-reference fall under this head.

4. *Learning.* The simplest level of this phenomenon is exemplified by a situation in which a subject receives a message and acts appropriately on it: "I heard the clock strike and knew it was time for lunch. So I went to the table." In learning experiments the analogue of this sequence of events is observed by the experimenter and commonly treated as a single message of a higher type.

When the dog salivates between buzzer and meat powder, this sequence is accepted by the experimenter as a message indicating that "the dog has *learned* that buzzer means meat powder." But this is not the end of the hierarchy of types involved. The experimental subject may become more skilled in learning. He may *learn to learn* (1, 7, 9), and it is not inconceivable that still higher orders of learning may occur in human beings.

5. *Multiple levels of learning and the Logical Typing of signals.* These are two inseparable sets of phenomena—inseparable because the ability to handle the multiple types of signals is itself a *learned* skill and therefore a function of the multiple levels of learning.

According to our hypothesis, the term "ego function" (as this term is used when a schizophrenic is described as having "weak ego function") is precisely *the process of discriminating communicational modes either within the self or between the self and others.* The schizophrenic exhibits weakness in three areas of such function: (*a*) He has difficulty in assigning the correct communicational mode to the message he receives from other persons. (*b*) He has difficulty in assigning the correct communicational mode to those messages which he himself utters or emits nonverbally. (*c*) He has difficulty in assigning the correct communicational mode to his own thoughts, sensations, and percepts.

At this point it is appropriate to compare what was said in the previous paragraph with von Domarus' (16) approach to the systematic description of schizophrenic utterance. He suggests that the messages (and thought) of the schizophrenic are deviant in syllogistic structure. In place of structures which derive from the syllogism, Barbara, the schizophrenic, according to this theory, uses structures which identify predicates. An example of such a distorted syllogism is:

Men die.
Grass dies.
Men are grass.

But as we see it, von Domarus' formulation is only a more precise—and therefore valuable—way of saying that schizophrenic utterance is rich in metaphor. With that generalization we agree. But metaphor is an indispensable tool of thought and expression—a characteristic of all human communication, even of that of the scientist. The conceptual models of cybernetics and the energy theories of psychoanalysis are, after all, only labeled metaphors. The peculiarity of the schizophrenic is not that he uses metaphors, but that he uses *unlabeled* metaphors. He has special difficulty in handling signals of that class whose members assign Logical Types to other signals.

If our formal summary of the symptomatology is correct and if the schizophrenia of our hypothesis is essentially a result of family interaction, it should be possible to arrive a priori at a formal description of these sequences of experience which would induce such a symptomatology. What is known of learning theory combines with the evident fact that human beings use *context* as a guide for mode discrimination. Therefore, we must look not for some specific traumatic experience in the infantile etiology but rather for characteristic sequential patterns. The specificity for which we search is to be at an abstract or formal level. The sequences must have this characteristic: that from them the patient will acquire the mental habits which are exemplified in schizophrenic communication. That is to say, *he must live in a universe where the sequences of events are such that his unconventional communicational habits will be in some sense appropriate.* The hypothesis which we offer is that sequences of this kind in the external experience of the patient are responsible for the inner conflicts of Logical Typing. For such unresolvable sequences of experiences, we use the term "double bind."

THE DOUBLE BIND. The necessary ingredients for a double bind situation, as we see it, are:

1. *Two or more persons.* Of these, we designate one, for purposes of our definition, as the "victim." We do not assume that the double bind is inflicted by the mother alone, but that it may be done either by mother alone or by some combination of mother, father, and/or siblings.

2. *Repeated experience.* We assume that the double bind is a recurrent theme in the experience of the victim. Our hypothesis does not invoke a single traumatic experience, but such repeated experience that the double bind structure comes to be an habitual expectation.

3. *A primary negative injunction.* This may have either of two forms: (a) "Do not do so and so, or I will punish you," or (b) "If you do not do so and so, I will punish you." Here we select a context of learning based on avoidance of punishment rather than a context of reward seeking. There is perhaps no formal reason for this selection. We assume that the punishment may be either the withdrawal of love or the expression of hate or anger—or most devastating—the kind of abandonment that results from the parent's expression of extreme helplessness.[3]

4. *A secondary injunction conflicting with the first at a more abstract level, and like the first enforced by punishments or signals which threaten survival.* This secondary injunction is more difficult to describe than the primary for two reasons. First, the secondary injunction is commonly communicated to the child by nonverbal means. Posture, gesture, tone of voice, meaningful action, and the implications concealed in verbal comment may all be used to convey this more abstract message. Second, the secondary injunction may impinge upon any element of the primary prohibition. Verbalization of the secondary injunction may, therefore, include a wide variety of forms; for example, "Do not see this as punishment"; "Do not see me as the punishing agent"; "Do not submit to my prohibitions"; "Do not think of what you must not do"; "Do not question my love of which the primary prohibition is (or is not) an example"; and so on. Other examples become possible when the double bind is inflicted not by one individual but by two. For example, one parent may negate at a more abstract level the injunctions of the other.

5. *A tertiary negative injunction prohibiting the victim from escaping from the field.* In a formal sense it is perhaps unnecessary to list this injunction as a separate item since the reinforcement at the other two levels involves a threat to survival, and if the double binds are imposed during infancy, escape is naturally impossible. However, it seems that in some cases the escape from the field is made impossible by certain devices which are not purely negative, e.g., capricious promises of love, and the like.

6. Finally, the complete set of ingredients is no longer necessary when the victim has learned to perceive his universe in double bind patterns. Almost any part of a double bind sequence may then be sufficient to precipitate panic or rage. The pattern of conflicting injunctions may even be taken over by hallucinatory voices (14).

THE EFFECT OF THE DOUBLE BIND. In the Eastern religion, Zen Buddhism, the goal is to achieve Enlightenment. The Zen Master attempts to bring about enlightenment in his pupil in various ways. One

[3] Our concept of punishment is being refined at present. It appears to us to involve perceptual experience in a way that cannot be encompassed by the notion of "trauma."

of the things he does is to hold a stick over the pupil's head and say fiercely, "If you say this stick is real, I will strike you with it. If you say this stick is not real, I will strike you with it. If you don't say anything, I will strike you with it." We feel that the schizophrenic finds himself continually in the same situation as the pupil, but he achieves something like disorientation rather than enlightenment. The Zen pupil might reach up and take the stick away from the Master—who might accept this response, but the schizophrenic has no such choice since with him there is no not caring about the relationship, and his mother's aims and awareness are not like the Master's.

We hypothesize that there will be a breakdown in any individual's ability to discriminate between Logical Types whenever a double bind situation occurs. The general characteristics of this situation are the following:

1. When the individual is involved in an intense relationship; that is, a relationship in which he feels it is vitally important that he discriminate accurately what sort of message is being communicated so that he may respond appropriately.

2. And, the individual is caught in a situation in which the other person in the relationship is expressing two orders of message and one of these denies the other.

3. And, the individual is unable to comment on the messages being expressed to correct his discrimination of what order of message to respond to, i.e., he cannot make a metacommunicative statement.

We have suggested that this is the sort of situation which occurs between the preschizophrenic and his mother, but it also occurs in normal relationships. When a person is caught in a double bind situation, he will respond defensively in a manner similar to the schizophrenic. An individual will take a metaphorical state-ment literally when he is in a situation where he must respond, where he is faced with contradictory messages, and when he is unable to comment on the contradictions. For example, one day an employee went home during office hours. A fellow employee called him at his home, and said lightly, "Well, how did you get *there?*" The employee replied, "By automobile." He responded literally because he was faced with a message which asked him what he was doing at home when he should have been at the office, but which denied that this question was being asked by the way it was phrased. (Since the speaker felt it wasn't really his business, he spoke metaphorically.) The relationship was intense enough so that the victim was in doubt how the information would be used, and he therefore responded literally. This is characteristic of anyone who feels "on the spot," as demonstrated by the careful literal replies of a witness on the stand in a court trial. The schizophrenic feels so terribly on the spot at all times that he habitually responds with a defensive insistence on the literal level when it is quite inappropriate, e.g., when someone is joking.

Schizophrenics also confuse the literal and metaphoric in their own utterance when they feel themselves caught in a double bind. For example, a patient may wish to criticize his therapist for being late for an appointment, but he may be unsure what sort of a message that act of being late was—particularly if the therapist has anticipated the patient's reaction and apologized for the event. The patient cannot say, "Why were you late? Is it because you don't want to see me today?" This would be an accusation, and so he shifts to a metaphorical statement. He may then say, "I knew a fellow once who missed a boat, his name was Sam and the boat almost sunk, . . . etc.," Thus he develops a metaphorical story and the therapist may or may not discover in it a comment on his being late. The convenient thing about a metaphor is that it leaves it up to the therapist (or mother) to see an accusation in the statement if he chooses, or to ignore it if he chooses. Should the therapist accept the accusation in the metaphor, then the patient can accept the statement he has made about Sam as metaphorical. If the therapist points out that this doesn't sound like a true statement about Sam, as a way of avoiding the accusation in the story, the patient can argue that there really was a man named Sam. As an answer to the double bind situation, a shift to a metaphorical statement brings safety. However, it also prevents the patient from making the accusation he wants to make. But instead of getting over his accusation by indicating that this is a metaphor, the schizophrenic patient seems to try to get over the fact that it is a metaphor by making it more fantastic. If the therapist should ignore the accusation in the story about Sam, the schizophrenic may then tell a story about going to Mars in a rocket ship as a way of putting over his accusation. The indication that it is a metaphorical statement lies in the fantastic aspect of the metaphor, not in the signals which usually accompany metaphors to tell the listener that a metaphor is being used.

It is not only safer for the victim of a double bind to shift to a metaphorical order of message, but in an impossible situation it is better to shift and become somebody else, or shift and insist that he is somewhere else. Then the double bind cannot work on the victim, because it isn't he and besides he is in a different place. In other words, the statements which show that a patient is disoriented can be interpreted as ways of defending himself against the situation he is in. The pathology enters when the victim himself either does not know that his responses are metaphorical or cannot say so. To recognize that he was speaking metaphorically he would need to be aware that he was defending himself and therefore was afraid of the other person.

To him such an awareness would be an indictment of the other person and therefore provoke disaster.

If an individual has spent his life in the kind of double bind relationship described here, his way of relating to people after a psychotic break would have a systematic pattern. First, he would not share with normal people those signals which accompany messages to indicate what a person means. His metacommunicative system—the communications about communication—would have broken down, and he would not know what kind of message a message was. If a person said to him, "what would you like to do today?" he would be unable to judge accurately by the context or by the tone of voice or gesture whether he was being condemned for what he did yesterday, or being offered a sexual invitation, or just what was meant. Given this inability to judge accurately what a person really means and an excessive concern with what is really meant, an individual might defend himself by choosing one or more of several alternatives. He might, for example, assume that behind every statement there is a concealed meaning which is detrimental to his welfare. He would then be excessively concerned with hidden meanings and determined to demonstrate that he could not be deceived—as he had been all his life. If he chooses this alternative, he will be continually searching for meanings behind what people say and behind chance occurrences in the environment, and he will be characteristically suspicious and defiant.

He might choose another alternative, and tend to accept literally everything people say to him; when their tone or gesture or context contradicted what they said, he might establish a pattern of laughing off these metacommunicative signals. He would give up trying to discriminate between levels of message and treat all messages as unimportant or to be laughed at.

If he didn't become suspicious of meta-communicative messages or attempt to laugh them off, he might choose to try to ignore them. Then he would find it necessary to see and hear less and less of what went on around him, and do his utmost to avoid provoking a response in his environment. He would try to detach his interest from the external world and concentrate on his own internal processes and, therefore, give the appearance of being a withdrawn, perhaps mute, individual.

This is another way of saying that if an individual doesn't know what sort of message a message is, he may defend himself in ways which have been described as paranoid, hebephrenic, or catatonic. These three alternatives are not the only ones. The point is that he cannot choose the one alternative which would help him to discover what people mean; he cannot, without considerable help, discuss the messages of others. Without being able to do that, the human being is like any self-correcting system which has lost its governor; it spirals into never-ending, but always systematic, distortions.

A Description of the Family Situation

The theoretical possibility of double bind situations stimulated us to look for such communication sequences in the schizophrenic patient and in his family situation. Toward this end we have studied the written and verbal reports of psychotherapists who have treated such patients intensively; we have studied tape recordings of psychotherapeutic interviews, both of our own patients and others; we have interviewed and taped parents of schizophrenics; we have had two mothers and one father participate in intensive psychotherapy; and we have interviewed and taped parents and patients seen conjointly.

On the basis of these data we have developed a hypothesis about the family situation which ultimately leads to an individual suffering from schizophrenia. This hypothesis has not been statistically tested; it selects and emphasizes a rather simple set of interactional phenomena and does not attempt to describe comprehensively the extraordinary complexity of a family relationship.

We hypothesize that the family situation of the schizophrenic has the following general characteristics:

1. A child whose mother becomes anxious and withdraws if the child responds to her as a loving mother. That is, the child's very existence has a special meaning to the mother which arouses her anxiety and hostility when she is in danger of intimate contact with the child.

2. A mother to whom feelings of anxiety and hostility toward the child are not acceptable, and whose way of denying them is to express overt loving behavior to persuade the child to respond to her as a loving mother and to withdraw from him if he does not. "Loving behavior" does not necessarily imply "affection"; it can, for example, be set in a framework of doing the proper thing, instilling "goodness," and the like.

3. The absence of anyone in the family, such as a strong and insightful father, who can intervene in the relationship between the mother and child and support the child in the face of the contradictions involved.

Since this is a formal description we are not specifically concerned with why the mother feels this way about the child, but we suggest that she could feel this way for various reasons. It may be that merely having a child arouses anxiety about herself and her relationships to her own family; or it may be important to her that the child is a boy or a girl, or that the child was born on the anniversary of one of her own siblings (8), or the child may be in the same sibling position in the family that she was, or the child may be special to her for other reasons related to her own emotional problems.

Given a situation with these characteristics, we hypothesize that the mother of a schizophrenic will be simultaneously expressing at least two orders of message. (For simplicity in this presentation we shall confine ourselves to two orders.) These orders of message can be roughly characterized as (*a*) hostile or withdrawing behavior which is aroused whenever the child approaches her, and (*b*) simulated loving or approaching behavior which is aroused when the child responds to her hostile and withdrawing behavior, as a way of denying that she is withdrawing. Her problem is to control her anxiety by controlling the closeness and distance between herself and her child. To put this another way, if the mother begins to feel affectionate and close to her child, she begins to feel endangered and must withdraw from him; but she cannot accept this hostile act and to deny it must simulate affection and closeness with her child. The important point is that her loving behavior is then a comment on (since it is compensatory for) her hostile behavior and consequently it is of a different *order* of message than the hostile behavior—it is a message about a sequence of messages. Yet by its nature it denies the existence of those messages which it is about, i.e., the hostile withdrawal.

The mother uses the child's responses to affirm that her behavior is loving, and since the loving behavior is simulated, the child is placed in a position where he must not accurately interpret her communication if he is to maintain his relationship with her. In other words, he must not discriminate accurately between orders of message, in this case the difference between the expression of simulated feelings (one Logical Type) and real feelings (another Logical Type). As a result the child must systematically dis-

tort his perception of metacommunicative signals. For example, if mother begins to feel hostile (or affectionate) toward her child and also feels compelled to withdraw from him, she might say, "Go to bed, you're very tired and I want you to get your sleep." This overtly loving statement is intended to deny a feeling which could be verbalized as "Get out of my sight because I'm sick of you." If the child correctly discriminates her metacommunicative signals, he would have to face the fact that she both doesn't want him and is deceiving him by her loving behavior. He would be "punished" for learning to discriminate orders of messages accurately. He therefore would tend to accept the idea that he is tired rather than recognize his mother's deception. This means that he must deceive himself about his own internal state in order to support mother in her deception. To survive with her he must falsely discriminate his own internal messages as well as falsely discriminate the messages of others.

The problem is compounded for the child because the mother is "benevolently" defining for him how he feels; she is expressing overt maternal concern over the fact that he is tired. To put it another way, the mother is controlling the child's definitions of his own messages, as well as the definition of his responses to her (e.g., by saying, "You don't really mean to say that," if he should criticize her) by insisting that she is not concerned about herself but only about him. Consequently, the easiest path for the child is to accept mother's simulated loving behavior as real, and his desires to interpret what is going on are undermined. Yet the result is that the mother is withdrawing from him and defining this withdrawal as the way a loving relationship should be.

However, accepting mother's simulated loving behavior as real also is no solution for the child. Should he make this false discrimination, he would approach her; this move toward closeness would provoke in her feelings of fear and helplessness, and she would be compelled to withdraw. But if he then withdrew from her, she would take his withdrawal as a statement that she was not a loving mother and would either punish him for withdrawing or approach him to bring him closer. If he then approached, she would respond by putting him at a distance. *The child is punished for discriminating accurately what she is expressing, and he is punished for discriminating inaccurately—he is caught in a double bind.*

The child might try various means of escaping from this situation. He might, for example, try to lean on his father or some other member of the family. However, from our preliminary observations we think it is likely that the fathers of schizophrenics are not substantial enough to lean on. They are also in the awkward position where if they agreed with the child about the nature of mother's deceptions, they would need to recognize the nature of their own relationships to the mother, which they could not do and remain attached to her in the *modus operandi* they have worked out.

The need of the mother to be wanted and loved also prevents the child from gaining support from some other person in the environment, a teacher, for example. A mother with these characteristics would feel threatened by any other attachment of the child and would break it up and bring the child back closer to her with consequent anxiety when the child became dependent on her.

The only way the child can really escape from the situation is to comment on the contradictory position his mother has put him in. However, if he did so, the mother would take this as an accusation that she is unloving and both punish him and insist that his perception of the situation is distorted. By preventing the child from talking about the situation, the mother forbids him using the metacommunicative level—the level we use to correct our perception of communicative behavior. The ability to communicate about communication, to comment upon the meaningful actions of oneself and others, is essential for successful social intercourse. In any normal relationship there is a constant interchange of metacommunicative messages such as "What do you mean?" or "Why did you do that?" or "Are you kidding me?" and so on. To discriminate accurately what people are really expressing we must be able to comment directly or indirectly on that expression. This metacommunicative level the schizophrenic seems unable to use successfully (2). Given these characteristics of the mother, it is apparent why. If she is denying one order of message, then any statement about her statements endangers her and she must forbid it. Therefore, the child grows up unskilled in his ability to communicate about communication and, as a result, unskilled in determining what people really mean and unskilled in expressing what he really means, which is essential for normal relationships.

In summary, then, we suggest that the double bind nature of the family situation of a schizophrenic results in placing the child in a position where if he responds to his mother's simulated affection her anxiety will be aroused and she will punish him (or insist, to protect herself, that *his* overtures are simulated, thus confusing him about the nature of his own messages) to defend herself from closeness with him. Thus the child is blocked off from intimate and secure associations with his mother. However, if he does not make overtures of affection, she will feel that this means she is not a loving mother and her anxiety will be aroused. Therefore, she will either punish him for withdrawing or make overtures toward the child to insist that he demonstrate that he loves her. If he then responds and shows her affection, she will not only feel endangered again, but she may resent the fact that she had to force him to respond. In either case in a relationship, the most important in his life and the model for all others, he is punished if he indicates love and affection and punished if he does not; and his escape routes from the situation, such as gaining support from others, are cut off. This is the basic nature of the double bind relationship between mother and child. This description has not depicted, of course, the more complicated interlocking gestalt that is the "family" of which the "mother" is one important part (11, 12).

Illustrations from Clinical Data

An analysis of an incident occurring between a schizophrenic patient and his mother illustrates the "double bind" situation. A young man who had fairly well recovered from an acute schizophrenic episode was visited in the hospital by his mother. He was glad to see her and impulsively put his arm around her shoulders, whereupon she stiffened. He withdrew his arm and she asked, "Don't you love me any more?" He then blushed, and she said, "Dear, you must not be so easily embarrassed and afraid of your feelings." The patient was able to stay with her only a few minutes more and following her departure he assaulted an aide and was put in the tubs.

Obviously, this result could have been avoided if the young man had been able to say, "Mother, it is obvious that you become uncomfortable when I put my arm around you, and that you have difficulty accepting a gesture of affection from me." However, the schizophrenic patient doesn't have this possibility open to him. His intense dependency and training prevents him from commenting upon his mother's communicative behavior, though she comments on his and forces him to accept and to attempt to deal with the complicated sequence. The

complications for the patient include the following:

1. The mother's reaction of not accepting her son's affectionate gesture is masterfully covered up by her condemnation of him for withdrawing, and the patient denies his perception of the situation by accepting her condemnation.

2. The statement "don't you love me any more" in this context seems to imply:

a. "I am lovable."

b. "You should love me and if you don't you are bad or at fault."

c. "Whereas you did love me previously you don't any longer," and thus focus is shifted from his expressing affection to his inability to be affectionate. Since the patient has also hated her, she is on good ground here, and he responds appropriately with guilt, which she then attacks.

d. "What you just expressed *was not* affection," and in order to accept this statement the patient must deny what she and the cultures have taught him about how one expresses affection. He must also question the times with her, and with others, when he thought he was experiencing affection and when they *seemed* to treat the situation as if he had. He experiences here loss-of-support phenomena and is put in doubt about the reliability of past experience.

3. The statement, "You must not be so easily embarrassed and afraid of your feelings," seems to imply:

a. "You are not like me and are different from other nice or normal people because we express our feelings."

b. "The feelings you express are all right, it's only that *you* can't accept them." However, if the stiffening on her part had indicated "these are unacceptable feelings," then the boy is told that he should not be embarrassed by unacceptable feelings. Since he has had a long training in what is and is not acceptable to both her and society, he again comes into conflict with the past. If he is unafraid of his own feelings (which mother implies is good), he should be unafraid of his affection and would then notice it was she who was afraid, but he must not notice that because her whole approach is aimed at covering up this shortcoming in herself.

The impossible dilemma thus becomes: "If I am to keep my tie to mother I must not show her that I love her, but if I do not show her that I love her, then I will lose her."

The importance to the mother of her special method of control is strikingly illustrated by the interfamily situation of a young woman schizophrenic who greeted the therapist on their first meeting with the remark, "Mother had to get married and now I'm here." This statement meant to the therapist that:

1. The patient was the result of an illegitimate pregnancy.

2. This fact was related to her present psychosis (in her opinion).

3. "Here" referred to the psychiatrist's office and to the patient's presence on earth for which she had to be eternally indebted to her mother, especially since her mother had sinned and suffered in order to bring her into the world.

4. "Had to get married" referred to the shot-gun nature of mother's wedding and to the mother's response to pressure that she must marry, and the reciprocal, that she resented the forced nature of the situation and blamed the patient for it.

Actually, all these suppositions subsequently proved to be factually correct and were corroborated by the mother during an abortive attempt at psychotherapy. The flavor of the mother's communications to the patient seemed essentially this: "I am lovable, loving, and satisfied with myself. You are lovable when you are like me and when you do what I say." At the same time the mother indicated to the daughter both by words

and behavior: "You are physically delicate, unintelligent, and different from me ('not normal'). You need me and me alone because of these handicaps, and I will take care of you and love you." Thus the patient's life was a series of beginnings, of attempts at experience, which would result in failure and withdrawal back to the maternal hearth and bosom because of the collusion between her and her mother.

It was noted in collaborative therapy that certain areas important to the mother's self-esteem were especially conflictual situations for the patient. For example, the mother needed the fiction that she was close to her family and that a deep love existed between her and her own mother. By analogy the relationship to the grandmother served as the prototype for the mother's relationship to her own daughter. On one occasion when the daughter was seven or eight years old the grandmother in a rage threw a knife which barely missed the little girl. The mother said nothing to the grandmother but hurried the little girl from the room with the words, "Grandmommy really loves you." It is significant that the grandmother took the attitude toward the patient that she was not well enough controlled, and she used to chide her daughter for being too easy on the child. The grandmother was living in the house during one of the patient's psychotic episodes, and the girl took great delight in throwing various objects at the mother and grandmother while they cowered in fear.

Mother felt herself very attractive as a girl, and she felt that her daughter resembled her rather closely, although by damning with faint praise it was obvious that she felt the daughter definitely ran second. One of the daughter's first acts during a psychotic period was to announce to her mother that she was going to cut off all her hair. She proceeded to do this while the mother pleaded with her to stop. Subsequently the mother would show a picture of *herself* as a girl and explain to people how the patient would look if she only had her beautiful hair.

The mother, apparently without awareness of the significance of what she was doing, would equate the daughter's illness with not being very bright and with some sort of organic brain difficulty. She would invariably contrast this with her own intelligence as demonstrated by her *own* scholastic record. She treated her daughter with a completely patronizing and placating manner which was insincere. For example, in the psychiatrist's presence she promised her daughter that she would not allow her to have further shock treatments, and as soon as the girl was out of the room she asked the doctor if he didn't feel she should be hospitalized and given electric shock treatments. One clue to this deceptive behavior arose during the mother's therapy. Although the daughter had had three previous hospitalizations the mother had never mentioned to the doctors that she herself had had a psychotic episode when she discovered that she was pregnant. The family whisked her away to a small sanitarium in a nearby town, and she was, according to her own statement, strapped to a bed for six weeks. Her family did not visit her during this time, and no one except her parents and her sister knew that she was hospitalized.

There were two times during therapy when the mother showed intense emotion. One was in relating her own psychotic experience; the other was on the occasion of her last visit when she accused the therapist of trying to drive her crazy by forcing her to choose between her daughter and her husband. Against medical advice, she took her daughter out of therapy.

The father was as involved in the homeostatic aspects of the intrafamily situation as the mother. For example, he stated that he had to quit his position as an important attorney in order to bring his daughter to an area where competent psychiatric help was available. Subsequently, acting on cues from the patient (e.g., she frequently referred to a character named "Nervous Ned") the therapist was able to elicit from him that he had hated his job and for years had been trying to "get out from under." However, the daughter was made to feel that the move was initiated for her.

On the basis of our examination of the clinical data, we have been impressed by a number of observations including:

1. The helplessness, fear, exasperation, and rage which a double bind situation provokes in the patient, but which the mother may serenely and un-understandingly pass over. We have noted reactions in the father that both create double bind situations, or extend and amplify those created by the mother, and we have seen the father passive and outraged, but helpless, become ensnared in a similar manner to the patient.

2. The psychosis seems, in part, a way of dealing with double bind situations to overcome their inhibiting and controlling effect. The psychotic patient may make astute, pithy, often metaphorical remarks that reveal an insight into the forces binding him. Contrariwise, he may become rather expert in setting double bind situations himself.

3. According to our theory, the communication situation described is essential to the mother's security, and by inference to the family homeostasis. If this be so, then when psychotherapy of the patient helps him become less vulnerable to mother's attempts at control, anxiety will be produced in the mother. Similarly, if the therapist interprets to the mother the dynamics of the situation she is setting up with the patient, this should produce an anxiety response in her. Our impression is that when there is a perduring contact between patient and family (especially when the patient lives at home during psychotherapy), this leads

to a disturbance (often severe) in the mother and sometimes in both mother and father and other siblings (10, 11).

Current Position and Future Prospects

Many writers have treated schizophrenia in terms of the most extreme contrast with any other form of human thinking and behavior. While it is an isolable phenomenon, so much emphasis on the differences from the normal—rather like the fearful physical segregation of psychotics—does not help in understanding the problems. In our approach we assume that schizophrenia involves general principles which are important in all communication and therefore many informative similarities can be found in "normal" communication situations.

We have been particularly interested in various sorts of communication which involve both emotional significance and the necessity of discriminating between orders of message. Such situations include play, humor, ritual, poetry, and fiction. Play, especially among animals, we have studied at some length (3). It is a situation which strikingly illustrates the occurrence of metamessages whose correct discrimination is vital to the cooperation of the individuals involved; for example, false discrimination could easily lead to combat. Rather closely related to play is humor, a continuing subject of our research. It involves sudden shifts in Logical Types as well as discrimination of those shifts. Ritual is a field in which unusually real or literal ascriptions of Logical Type are made and defended as vigorously as the schizophrenic defends the "reality" of his delusions. Poetry exemplifies the communicative power of metaphor—even very unusual metaphor—when labeled as such by various signs, as contrasted to the obscurity of unlabeled schizophrenic metaphor. The entire

field of fictional communication, defined as the narration or depiction of a series of events with more or less of a label of actuality, is most relevant to the investigation of schizophrenia. We are not so much concerned with the content interpretation of fiction—although analysis of oral and destructive themes is illuminating to the student of schizophrenia—as with the formal problems involved in simultaneous existence of multiple levels of message in the fictional presentation of "reality." The drama is especially interesting in this respect, with both performers and spectators responding to messages about both the actual and the theatrical reality.

We are giving extensive attention to hypnosis. A great array of phenomena that occur as schizophrenic symptoms—hallucinations, delusions, alterations of personality, amnesias, and so on—can be produced temporarily in normal subjects with hypnosis. These need not be directly suggested as specific phenomena, but can be the "spontaneous" result of an arranged communication sequence. For example, Erickson (4) will produce a hallucination by first inducing catalepsy in a subject's hand and then saying, "There is no conceivable way in which your hand can move, yet when I give the signal, it must move." That is, he tells the subject his hand will remain in place, yet it will move, and in no way the subject can consciously conceive. When Erickson gives the signal, the subject hallucinates the hand moved, or hallucinates himself in a different place and therefore the hand was moved. This use of hallucination to resolve a problem posed by contradictory commands which cannot be discussed seems to us to illustrate the solution of a double bind situation via a shift in Logical Types. Hypnotic responses to direct suggestions or statements also commonly involve shifts in type, as in accepting the words "Here's a glass of water" or "You feel tired" as external or internal reality, or in literal response to metaphorical statements, much like schizophrenics. We hope that further study of hypnotic induction, phenomena, and waking will, in this controllable situation, help sharpen our view of the essential communicational sequences which produce phenomena like those of schizophrenia.

Another Erickson experiment (12) seems to isolate a double bind communicational sequence without the specific use of hypnosis. Erickson arranged a seminar so as to have a young chain smoker sit next to him and to be without cigarettes; other participants were briefed on what to do. All was ordered so that Erickson repeatedly turned to offer the young man a cigarette, but was always interrupted by a question from someone so that he turned away, "inadvertently" withdrawing the cigarettes from the young man's reach. Later another participant asked this young man if he had received the cigarette from Dr. Erickson. He replied, "What cigarette?", showed clearly that he had forgotten the whole sequence, and even refused a cigarette offered by another member, saying that he was too interested in the seminar discussion to smoke. This young man seems to us to be in an experimental situation paralleling the schizophrenic's double bind situation with mother: An important relationship, contradictory messages (here of giving and taking away), and comment blocked—because there was a seminar going on, and anyway it was all "inadvertent." And note the similar outcome: Amnesia for the double bind sequence and reversal from "He doesn't give" to "I don't want."

Although we have been led into these collateral areas, our main field of observation has been schizophrenia itself. All of us have worked directly with schizophrenic patients and much of this case material has been recorded on tape for detailed study. In addition, we are recording interviews held jointly with patients and their families, and we are taking sound motion pictures of mothers and disturbed, presumably preschizophrenic, children. Our hope is that these operations will provide a clearly evident record of the continuing, repetitive double binding which we hypothesize goes on steadily from infantile beginnings in the family situation of individuals who become schizophrenic. This basic family situation, and the overtly communicational characteristics of schizophrenia, have been the major focus of this paper. However, we expect our concepts and some of these data will also be useful in future work on other problems of schizophrenia, such as the variety of other symptoms, the character of the "adjusted state" before schizophrenia becomes manifest, and the nature and circumstances of the psychotic break.

Therapeutic Implications of This Hypothesis

Psychotherapy itself is a context of multilevel communication, with exploration of the ambiguous lines between the literal and metaphoric, or reality and fantasy, and indeed, various forms of play, drama, and hypnosis have been used extensively in therapy. We have been interested in therapy, and in addition to our own data we have been collecting and examining recordings, verbatim transcripts, and personal accounts of therapy from other therapists. In this we prefer exact records since we believe that how a schizophrenic talks depends greatly, though often subtly, on how another person talks to him; it is most difficult to estimate what was really occurring in a therapeutic interview if one has only a description of it, especially if the description is already in theoretical terms.

Except for a few general remarks and some speculation, however, we are not yet prepared to comment on the relation of the double bind to psychotherapy. At present we can only note:

1. Double bind situations are created by and within the psychotherapeutic setting and the hospital milieu. From the point of view of this hypothesis we wonder about the effect of medical "benevolence" on the schizophrenic patient. Since hospitals exist for the benefit of personnel as well as—as much as—more than—for the patient's benefit, there will be contradictions at times in sequences where actions are taken "benevolently" for the patient when actually they are intended to keep the staff more comfortable. We would assume that whenever the system is organized for hospital purposes and it is announced to the patient that the actions are for *his* benefit, then the schizophrenogenic situation is being perpetuated. This kind of deception will provoke the patient to respond to it as a double bind situation, and his response will be "schizophrenic" in the sense that it will be indirect and the patient will be unable to comment on the fact that he feels that he is being deceived. One vignette, fortunately amusing, illustrates such a response. On a ward with a dedicated and "benevolent" physician in charge there was a sign on the physician's door which said "Doctor's Office. Please Knock." The doctor was driven to distraction and finally capitulation by the obedient patient who carefully knocked every time he passed the door.

2. The understanding of the double bind and its communicative aspects may lead to innovations in therapeutic technique. Just what these innovations may be is difficult to say, but on the basis of our investigation we are assuming that double bind situations occur consistently in psychotherapy. At times these are inadvertent in the sense that the therapist is imposing a double bind situation similar to that in the patient's history, or the patient is imposing a double bind situation on the therapist. At other times therapists seem to impose double binds, either deliberately or intuitively, which force the patient to respond differently than he has in the past.

An incident from the experience of a gifted psychotherapist illustrates the intuitive understanding of a double bind communicational sequence. Dr. Frieda Fromm-Reichmann (5) was treating a young woman who from the age of seven had built a highly complex religion of her own replete with powerful Gods. She was very schizophrenic and quite hesitant about entering into a therapeutic situation. At the beginning of the treatment she said, "God R says I shouldn't talk with you." Dr. Fromm-Reichmann replied, "Look, let's get something into the record. To me God R doesn't exist, and that whole world of yours doesn't exist. To you it does, and far be it from me to think that I can take that away from you, I have no idea what it means. So I'm willing to talk with you in terms of that world, if only you know I do it so that we have an understanding that it doesn't exist for me. Now go to God R and tell him that we have to talk and he should give you permission. Also you must tell him that I am a doctor and that you have lived with him in his kingdom now from seven to sixteen—that's nine years—and he hasn't helped you. So now he must permit me to try and see whether you and I can do that job. Tell him that I am a doctor and this is what I want to try."

The therapist has her patient in a "therapeutic double bind." If the patient is rendered doubtful about her belief in her god then she is agreeing with Dr. Fromm-Reichmann, and is admitting her attachment to therapy. If she insists that God R is real, then she must tell him that Dr. Fromm-Reichmann is "more powerful" than he—again admitting her involvement with the therapist.

The difference between the therapeutic bind and the original double bind situation is in part the fact that the therapist is not involved in a life and death struggle himself. He can therefore set up relatively benevolent binds and gradually aid the patient in his emancipation from them. Many of the uniquely appropriate therapeutic gambits arranged by therapists seem to be intuitive. We share the goal of most psychotherapists who strive toward the day when such strokes of genius will be well enough understood to be systematic and commonplace.

REFERENCES

1. Bateson, G.: "Social planning and the concept of "deutero-learning." *Conference on Science, Philosophy, and Religion, Second Symposium.* New York: Harper, 1942.
2. ———.: "A theory of play and fantasy." *Psychiatric Research Reports,* 1955, 2, 39–51.
3. Carpenter, C. R.: "A field study of the behavior and social relations of howling monkeys." *Comp. Psychol. Monogr.,* 1934, 10, 1–168.
4. Erickson, M. H.: Personal communication, 1955.
5. Fromm-Reichmann, F.: Personal communication, 1956.
6. Haley, J.: Paradoxes in play, fantasy, and psychotherapy. *Psychiatric Research Reports,* 1955, 2, 52–58.
7. Harlow, H. F.: The formation of learning sets. *Psychol. Rev.,* 1949, 56, 51–65.
8. Hilgard, J. R.: Anniversary reactions in parents precipitated by children. *Psychiatry,* 1953, 16, 73–80.
9. Hull, C. L., et al.: *Mathematico-deductive theory of rote learning.* New Haven: Yale University Press, 1940.
10. Jackson, D. D.: An episode of sleepwalking. *J. Amer. Psychoanal. Assn.,* 1954, 2, 503–508.
11. ———.: Some factors influencing the Oedipus complex. *Psychoanal. Quart.,* 1954, 23, 566–581.
12. ———.: The question of family homeostasis. Presented at the Amer. Psychiatric Assn. Meeting, St. Louis, May 7, 1954.
13. Lorenz, K. Z.: *King Solomon's ring.* New York: Crowell, 1952.
14. Perceval, J.: A narrative of the treatment experienced by a gentleman during a state of mental derangement, designed to explain the causes and nature of insanity, etc. London: Effingham Wilson, 1836 and 1840.
15. Ruesch, J., and G. Bateson: *Communication: the social matrix of psychiatry.* New York: Norton, 1951.
16. von Domarus, E.: The specific laws of logic in schizophrenia. In J. S. Kasanin (Ed.), *Language and thought in schizophrenia.* Berkeley: University of California Press, 1944.
17. Whitehead, A. N., and B. Russell: *Principia mathematica.* Cambridge: Cambridge University Press, 1910.

SCHIZOPHRENIA IN THE YOUNGEST MALE CHILD
OF THE LOWER MIDDLE CLASS

by Bertram H. Roberts and Jerome K. Myers

Since 1866 there have been many studies dealing with the relationship between family ordinal position and the incidence of mental illness (8, 19). The early em-

SOURCE: *American Journal of Psychiatry,* Vol. 112 (1955), pp. 129–134.

phasis placed on the difficulties of the only child and the first-born engendered a long dispute which was terminated with more advanced statistical techniques when Malzberg demonstrated that previous investigators had failed to consider the prevalency of the first-born in the general population (16). With the correction of this bias, the previous conceptions were largely discredited, leading to the current belief that ordinal position, by itself, does not determine a predisposition to mental illness.

Accompanying the incidence studies there has been continuous interest in the relationship between ordinal position and various traits of personality (12). However, when Murphy et al. reviewed several hundred of these studies in 1937, they stated that the findings were highly contradictory and noncommittal. They felt that in the future it would be essential to relate the psychological study of ordinal position to broader aspects of family interaction (20). This policy has lead to the separate analyses of ordinal position according to sex, consideration of the order and spacing of the siblings, and studies of the relationship between the ordinal position and particular family contacts (18).

A further refinement has come with the recognition of the interplay of cultural factors in family interaction. For example, it has been demonstrated that our concepts of normality and preventive child-rearing practices have been influenced by the middle-class values of the clinician (13). Several important studies dealing with the rearing practices in the social classes of our society have shown that there is a wide difference between the middle and lower classes (1, 5). These trends in ordinal and class studies were combined by Sears in 1950 in his conception that ordinal position forms the basis of familial role differentiation calling forth a set of parent-child attitudes and practices; this role was then found to vary with the social class of the family (27).

The study to be described is oriented within this conceptual framework, as we attempted to locate a syndrome of conditions involving the individual when sex, social class, mental illness, and ordinal position are controlled. This analysis is part of a larger investigation of the relationship between social stratification and psychiatric disorder. The first phase of the research dealt with the treated prevalence of psychiatric disorder in metropolitan New Haven. In the second phase, reported here, several theoretical ideas emerging from the statistical findings were explored through a controlled case survey (11, 24, 25).

Method

This investigation has been called a controlled case survey since the cases were selected in the design of a 4-cell table split one way into 2 social classes and the other way into 2 diagnostic groups. Fifty cases were gathered, of which half were diagnosed as schizophrenic disorder excluding the latent state, and the other half as psychoneurotic disorder, using the latest official nomenclature. From the standpoint of social class the cases were drawn equally from 2 nonadjacent social classes, class III, the lower middle class, and class V, the lower class.[1] In addition the patients were white, between the ages of 22 and 44, and equally divided between the sexes. These 50 cases were found to constitute a representative sample of the total psychiatric population of New Haven in terms of religion, ethnic origin and exact age distribution.

The method of inquiry consisted of a 129-page schedule of questions built around 14 areas of interest, including

[1] The population of New Haven was divided into 5 classes using Hollingshead's *Index of Social Position* which is based upon education, occupation, and area of residence. According to this system, 3% are class I; 8%, class II; 21% class III; 50% class IV; and 18% class V. Class III includes proprietors, white-collar workers, and some skilled workers; they are mostly high school graduates. Class V includes unskilled and semi-skilled laborers, who have a grade school education or less, and who live in the poorest areas of the community.

psychiatric and medical history, attitude towards psychiatry, family dynamics, sexual history, religion, ethnic origin, occupation, housing, education, recreation, class status, social mobility, and social identification. The schedule was constructed so that the questions were directed to the informant judged most capable of responding. Some items were duplicated to check the validity of the responses. Data for the schedule were gathered by a team of psychiatrists and sociologists in 5 or more interviews with the patient, at least 2 members of his family, and the therapist. Also, an unstructured clinical interview was conducted with the patient, and his clinical records were abstracted. Finally, Rorschach examinations were carried out for 9 patients in each class.

When the interviews were completed the raw data were transferred to an assessment schedule, and each case was considered entirely in terms of its own dynamic development (21). In the next stage, the individual areas of interest were compared between social classes and diagnostic categories. We are preparing a monograph dealing with the patient's development in the family; one aspect of ordinal position in the family structure is presented here and the other positions will be described in later papers.

Findings

In reviewing the 50 cases it was found that 10 of the 13 males in class III were youngest boys, while only 4 of the 13 females were the youngest girl. In class V, 4 of the 12 males were the youngest boy and 3 of the 12 females were the youngest girl. In this paper we are concerned with the 10 youngest boys in class III, 5 of whom were schizophrenics and 5 psychoneurotic.

To explore the conditions surrounding the 10 patients, data from the assessment schedules were abstracted under the fol-

lowing broad headings: (1) relationship with mother; (2) relationship with father; (3) relationship with other siblings; (4) contact with peer groups in the community; and (5) age and stage of assuming responsibility. Approximately 50 common phenomena which we call attributes were located among the 5 schizophrenic cases. These attributes were then sought among the 5 neurotic cases and the remainder of the male cases in the series. The reliability of judgments concerning the presence or absence of the attributes was checked by 4 independent judges. After discarding 15% of the attributes, the level of agreement between the judges reached 93%. The findings are reported in terms of the percentage of cases in 4 subgroups: the youngest male, class III; other males, class III; youngest male, class V; and other males, class V, with the diagnostic dichotomy contained in each. By comparing these percentages it is possible to determine whether the attribute is related to ordinal position, class status, or diagnostic category.[2]

[2] The Chi-square test was used to determine whether significant differences existed between frequency distributions. Actual numbers were used in the computations, and significance was defined at the .05 level.

Examples of the method of analysis follow. The attribute "patient spent more time with the mother than did the other siblings" occurred among 90% of class III and 100% of class V youngest males. However, it was found among only 50% of the other males in class III and 25% of those in class V. Since there is a significant difference in the occurrence of this attribute between youngest males and other males regardless of social class status, we conclude that the attribute is related to the patient's ordinal position. The attribute "mother had mobility aspirations" was found among 100% of the youngest and 67% of other class III males, but among only 25% and 0% of the corresponding ordinal positions in class V. Therefore, this attribute is associated with class III status rather than ordinal position. The attribute "father was inadequate" occurred in the following percentages among schizo-

Space precludes the presentation of the separate attributes; however, to provide an example, one attribute referable to the mother will be discussed in detail. This attribute is "spent more time with the mother than did the other siblings." This was based upon the following type of information in a condensed form: in the M Case, the patient was considered backward from his early years while his mother was very ambitious for his progress. Since the siblings were more sociable and active in the community and the mother extremely devoted to her tasks at home, the patient was left with her a great deal of the time. In the C Case the mother was a very ambitious and aggressive person who pushed all of the members of her family, especially the patient, who was the slowest of the siblings. On these grounds the mother was forced to work with him for a longer period of time leading to the attribute. In the I Case the mother was very closely attached to the children, being described as perfectly devoted to them. In the midst of this situation, the patient adopted the role of "his mother's right-hand man," which was apparently acceptable to her. The attribute was derived from such data as observed in these and other cases.

The Syndrome

Instead of presenting the remaining attributes in detail, a summary in the form of a coherent picture will be described representing the 42 attributes which were characteristic of the schizo-

---

phrenic males: youngest class III, 100%; other class III, 67%; youngest class V, 100%; other class V, 60%. The corresponding percentages for neurotics were 33, 0, 0, and 0. Therefore, this attribute is characteristic of schizophrenics, regardless of ordinal or class position. All other attributes were analyzed in similar fashion to determine the relative influence of ordinal position, social class, and type of psychiatric disorder.

phrenic cases who were class III youngest males. Thirty-seven of the attributes were found in 100% of the schizophrenic cases and the remaining 5 in over 60%. A very similar pattern was found in the neurotic cases with 31 of the attributes occurring in at least 75% of the cases. Starting with the attributes referable to the mother, it was found that there was a close and distorted relationship with the mother which might be described as symbiotic, although the mother's reward was not very apparent (6). The mother's personality was distinctive as a rigid perfectionist who stressed disciplinary compliance. She was highly ambitious for her family's social advancement in the community. The patient spent more time with her than did the other siblings and in turn she devoted more attention to him. He became conforming to her demands and very dependent upon her, eventually assuming her social values as his own. As time passed the two formed a diffuse temperamental affinity in their emotional contact. With the onset of the illness, 3 of the 5 schizophrenics discarded their mother's value system in a brief rebellion.

In the relationships involving the father, there was tension and poor communication between the parents. The mother was the dominant partner as was clearly demonstrated at times of family crisis. In the community the father was an unsuccessful man who had trouble making friends and getting along with people, while at home he was quite uninvolved in household activities except as the executor of the most severe punishment. In the absence of actual achievements he tended to stress manly characteristics, especially in the demands he made of his slow-moving son. Hostility was exchanged between father and son as the father excluded the patient from his activities and concern. On the surface the patient was completely obedient to the father, but actually he rejected the father's values; at the last moment, however, he grasped for a few fragments of the father's characteristics as he descended into the illness.

A comparison of the patient's achievements with the older siblings showed that the latter were more successful in education, occupation, and social participation. In the developmental years the patient became submissive to them and much hostility was exchanged. An exception was found in a very close positive attachment to one sister which had a direct sexual expression in a few cases.

The analysis of his external relations showed that the patient lacked intimate friends which was quite apparent during adolescence when his previous acquaintances moved on to wider activities. Although he belonged to organizations, he formed no friendships in them. Over the years, his isolation increased, as his interests and hobbies grew more solitary. Sexual activity was extremely limited since there was little social dating or direct heterosexual contact. In terms of maturity and responsibility, the patient was noticed to be slower and more passive than the other children from early childhood, a status which was supported by illness and other physical handicaps in this period. During the school years, the patient did not exert adequate effort so that family support was continually required.

This description represents what we have called the social syndrome of schizophrenia in the youngest male of the lower middle class. However, the general trend towards interpersonal isolation with increased withdrawal was found to be a characteristic of the entire series of schizophrenic and neurotic patients.

The next stage in the analysis was to determine whether the attributes were related to ordinal position, social class, or schizophrenia. The patient's position as the youngest male child was related to the excessive time spent with the mother and the close dependent attachment which led to the assumption of her social values. In addition position seemed to account for the close attachment to the sister and the inferior, submissive feelings directed toward the other siblings.

Lower-middle-class status was correlated with the personality of the mother and the inadequacy of the father. Also, the sibling's achievements in education and occupation were typical of the social class as were the organizational activities of the patient. The general mobility of the patient's middle-class friends contributed to his isolation. Finally, the family's awareness of the patient's passivity seems to be a type of perception limited to the middle and upper classes.

It will be recalled that the syndrome was largely applicable to both schizophrenic and neurotic patients, but more intact in the schizophrenic. In comparing these 2 groups it was found that the characteristics of the father constituted a decisive difference in that his lack of participation in the home and hostile expression were much more apparent in the schizophrenic cases. Furthermore, the schizophrenics made only a preliminary approach to heterosexual relations. Finally, there was considerable difference in their achievement as compared with their siblings, since the patients never became established in adult pursuits.

Discussion

Since the syndrome merely represents an attempt on our part to establish a coherent logical connection between the attributes, an effort was made to locate comparable studies in order to assess the relevancy and importance of this picture.

In 7 studies we found descriptions which bear a close resemblance to our group, the most extensive being David Levy's monograph on the overprotective mother. To select a few points of similarity, he stated that these mothers had a personality resembling an obsessive neurotic. He described the parents' lack of a shared social life and the wholesale isolation of the patient (15). Tietze mentions the overprotective perfectionism of the mother, the compliance of the son, and his close attachment to an elder sibling. She also stresses the general inadequacy of the patient's heterosexual development (28). McKeown found an antagonistic-demanding relationship with the father who stressed athletic and occupational achievement while the mother failed to provide adequate support for the child throughout his development (17). One-half of the children whom Kasanin found were later to become psychotic had been considered queer, peculiar, and passive in their early years, calling for the protective solicitude of the mother and older siblings (13). Bowman found that there was a great distance between the patient and the other siblings with the exception of 1 or 2 close attachments. He also remarks on the patient's increase of solitary reaction in adulthood (4). Gerard and Siegel stressed the dependency and general incapability of their patients of accepting adult responsibility. The mother was the dominant person in the family and the father weak, immature, and passive (9). Reichard and Tillman found that the mothers of schizophrenic patients who were overtly rejecting or smothering were married to men who were quiet and ineffective. A separate category was established for domineering sadistic fathers whom they called schizophrenogenic. They found, as in our study, that the family conditions were more severe in the schizophrenic cases than in the neurotic (26). This cursory review of the literature represents a very small fraction of the findings of these studies. From this comparison we conclude that the syndrome we described conforms with an evolving delineation of the social-personal relations concomitant with the development of schizophrenia in male patients.

Within this syndrome it is now our task to consider the significance of the variables held under control: ordinal position, social class, and diagnosis. The previous studies of the families of schizophrenics made very little mention of ordinal position, with the exception of Gerard and Siegel, who stated that their patients generally held a special position in the family referring in part to ordinal status (9). Our findings indicate that the intensity and extent of contact with the mother were supported by the ordinal position as the mother seems prone to act in a protective manner when she observes slowness and passivity in her youngest boy. Also it might be expected that the youngest boy will have submissive and inferior feelings for his older siblings at some stage of his development; our patients were never able to overcome this handicap.

The significance of social class has widespread importance in our findings. Early studies of mother-child relationships in mental illness emphasized the rejecting actions of the mother, but as stated by Meltzer, we found that this type of overt aggressive behavior is probably limited to the lower class (18, 22, 23). Supporting this we found that the mothers in David Levy's series who were overprotective rather than rejecting were mainly middle class according to a close examination of his sample (15). In considering the relationship of social class to the fathers' behavior we found that their failure to advance in the occupational and social activities of the middle class tended to support the general impression they created of being failures as men. Aberle and Naegle have described the manner in which middle class fathers establish an identification with their sons and strive for their advancement; our cases demonstrate the consequences of the failure of this aspiration (2).

In a negative direction we observed that differences in family interaction based on ethnic origin were reduced in the middle class as the family presses for assimilation into the American system (3). However, middle class status does provide the educational and occupational objectives of the siblings' superior achievement. Also, middle class emphasis on social activities runs contrary to the solitary tendency of the patients. Finally, social class was found to be related to the perfectionistic disciplinary attitude of the mother and her mobility strivings. This raises the interesting question of the relationship between social class and character structure as the obsessive character of the mother apparently finds this form of expression in the middle class where ample time is available for household duties and the care of the children.

A comparison of the schizophrenic and neurotic patients indicates that there is a gradient into the syndrome with more severe interpersonal relationships in the schizophrenics followed by a more regressed decompensation. The punitive hostile relationships with the father was the principal difference between these diagnostic categories. This is of importance as the paternal role is changing with the rising status of women and the increase of leisure time bringing the father in closer contact with the rearing of the children. The remaining findings dealing with the sexual retardation and the immature social accomplishments of the schizophrenic are generally regarded to be secondary manifestations of the disease process.

We believe that the implications of our study with reference to the validity of psychoanalytic theory are minimal, since there is very little information dealing with the first 5 years when the fixations are believed to occur. From Freud's earliest writings, references were made to the consequences of the fixations on family interaction, and Flugel has expanded this suggestion into an integrated picture of family life. We did not find any significant conflict between Flugel's theoretical scheme and the syndrome which has been described. Of crucial importance to us is his suggestion that a parent's ill-feelings for a child can be converted into an identification with the child which would explain the mother's pressure on her passive son (7).

In summary it is our opinion that there is sufficient similarity between our cases in important elements to support the delineation of a social-psychiatric situation. The method described has made it possible to isolate aspects of the situation related to family structure and the social environment. In this analysis the unexpected finding regarding the role of the father in the schizophrenic cases was demonstrated. It is our opinion that this set of findings is still the material of hypotheses calling for further investigation which we hope to follow or stimulate among those who read this paper.

BIBLIOGRAPHY

1. Anderson, John E.: *Young Child in the Home.* New York: Appleton-Century, 1936.
2. Aberle, David F., and Kaspar D. Naegel: *Am. J. Orthopsychiat.*, 22:366, 1952.
3. Barrabee, Paul, and Otto von Mering: *Social Problems*, 1:48, 1953.
4. Bowman, Karl M.: *Am. J. Orthopsychiat.*, 4:473, 1934.
5. Davis, A., and R. J. Havighurst: Pp. 252–264 in *Personality in Nature Society and Culture*, edited by C. Kluckhohn and H. A. Murray. New York: Knopf, 1948.
6. Dunbar, F.: *Am. J. Orthopsychiat.*, 22:809, 1952.
7. Flugel, J. C.: *The Psycho-analytic Study of the Family.* London: The International Psycho-Analytical Library, Hogarth Press, 1929.
8. Galton, F.: *English Men of Science: Their Nature and Nurture.* London, 1929.
9. Gerard, Donald L., and Joseph Siegel: *Psychiat. Quart.*, 24:47, 1950.
10. Henry, Jules: *Am. J. Orthopsychiat.*, 19:665, 1949.
11. Hollingshead, A. B., and F. C. Redlich: *Am. J. Psychiat.*, 110:695, 1954.
12. Jones, Harold E.: Pp. 204–224 in *Handbook of Child Psychology*, edited by Carl Murchison. Worcester: Clark University Press, 1931.

13. Kasanin, J., Elizabeth Knight, and Priscilla Sage: *Nerv. and Ment. Dis.*, 79:249, 1934.
14. Krout, M. H.: *J. Gene. Psychol.*, 55:3, 1939.
15. Levy, D. M.: *Maternal Over Protection.* New York: Columbia University Press, 1943.
16. Malzberg, Benjamin: *Am. J. Phys. Anthrop.*, 24:91, 1938.
17. McKeown, James E.: *Am. J. Sociol.*, 56:175, 1950.
18. Meltzer, H.: *Am. J. Orthopsychiat.*, 6:590, 1936.
19. Mitchell, A.: *Edinburgh Med. J.*, 11:639, 1866.
20. Murphy, G., L. Murphy, and T. Newcomb: *Experimental Social Psychology.* New York: Harper, 1937.
21. Myers, J. K., and B. H. Roberts: *Sociol. and Socl. Res.*, 39:11, Sept. 1954.
22. Newell, H. W.: *Am. J. Orthopsychiat.*, 4:387, 1934.
23. ————.: *Am. J. Orthopsychiat.*, 6:576, 1936.
24. Redlich, F. C. *et al.*: *Am. J. Psychiat.*, 109:729, 1953.
25. Roberts, B. H., and J. K. Myers: *Am. J. Psychiat.*, 110:759, 1954.
26. Reichard, C. T., and C. Tillman: *Psychiatry*, 13:247, 1950.
27. Sears, Robert R.: *Am. Sociol. Rev.*, 15:397, 1950.
28. Tietze, Trude: *Psychiatry*, 12:55, 1949.

THE EFFECTS OF PARENTAL ROLE MODEL ON CRIMINALITY

by Joan McCord and William McCord

Those who are at all familiar with criminology no longer question the importance of the family environment in the causation of crime. Among the many factors in the home which are known to be related to crime are the parents' attitudes toward their children, their methods of discipline, and their attitudes toward society. This last factor, the parental role model—the behavior and attitudes of the parents—is the focus of this paper. Many criminologists have emphasized the importance of the paternal role model in the making of criminals.[1] The aim of this paper is a more detailed investigation of the ways in which paternal role models affect criminality.

The present research is an outgrowth

of the Cambridge-Somerville Youth Study, designed by Dr. Richard Clark Cabot for the prevention of delinquency. In 1935, Dr. Cabot and his staff selected 650 lower- and lower-middle-class boys from Cambridge and Somerville, Massachusetts, as participants in the project. Half of these boys were referred to Dr. Cabot as pre-delinquents, and the other half (added to avoid stigmatizing the group) were considered "normal" by their teachers and community officers. The average age of these boys was seven. After interviews, physical examinations, and psychological testing, each boy was matched to another as nearly similar in background and personality as possible. One from each pair (determined by toss of a coin) was placed in a treatment group; the remaining boys constituted the control group.

The treatment program began in 1939 and continued (on the average) for five years. Counselors gathered information from teachers, ministers, parents, and neighbors detailing the backgrounds of each of their boys. More importantly, the

[1] See for example: William Healy and Augusta F. Bronner. *Delinquents and Criminals.* New York: Macmillan, 1926; and Sheldon Glueck and Eleanor T. Glueck. *Unraveling Juvenile Delinquency.* New York: The Commonwealth Fund, 1950.

SOURCE: *Journal of Social Issues*, Vol. 14, No. 3 (1958), pp. 66–75.

counselors repeatedly visited the boys and their families. Although two books have been written which point to the failure of this treatment as a preventive to crime,[2] the comprehensive reports written by the counselors provide a fund of information on the backgrounds of these boys who are now men.

Seventy-two boys who died, moved away from the area, or were dropped from the project near its beginning have been omitted from the present study. For the remaining 253 boys, running records had been kept which depicted each boy as he acted in his family and among his peers. The records describe conversations overheard by the counselors and discussions with the counselors; they report casual and formal interviews with or about the boys and their families.

In 1955 a staff of trained workers read these voluminous case records and recorded data pertaining to the behavior of each boy's parents. Thus, information on family background was based on direct, repeated observations by a variety of investigators, over an extended period of time.

Also in 1955, the names of the subjects and their parents were sent through the Massachusetts Board of Probation. In this way, we learned which of our subjects and which of their parents had acquired criminal records either in Massachusetts or Federal courts. For the purpose of this study, we defined as criminal anyone who had been convicted at least once for a crime involving violence, theft, drunkenness, or sexual violations. We recognize, of course, the deficiencies in this standard: some criminals may escape detection, and a number of cultural variables inter-

cede between the committing of a crime and subsequent conviction. Nevertheless, as we have argued elsewhere in more detail, we believe that this is the most objective standard available.

The information produced by the Cambridge-Somerville Youth Study enabled a unique longitudinal analysis of the causes of crime: the boys averaged seven years of age when the data was first collected, while their average age was twenty-seven when their criminal records were gathered. Moreover, since all of the boys came from the relatively lower-class, disorganized urban areas, they were all exposed to the delinquent sub-culture described by James Short and Albert Cohen. Since this factor was held constant, we could concentrate our attention on those variables which differentiate among boys living in transitional areas.

In the study of the relation between role models and crime, we focused on three interacting variables in the familial environment of the boys: the role model of the parents, the attitudes of the parents toward the child, and the methods of discipline used by the parents.

The *parental role model* was, of course, our basic variable. Information about this factor was ascertained from two sources. First, the verbatim records kept by the observers contained direct evidence of the everyday behavior of the parents. Second, reports from the Boston Social Service Index and the Massachusetts Board of Probation reported all contacts between the parents and community agencies. We classified each parent into one of three groups: (1) those who had been convicted by the courts for theft or assault or who had spent time in a state or Federal prison; (2) those who, though they were non-criminal by our definition, were known to be alcoholic (many had records for repeated drunkenness) or were sexually promiscuous in a blatant fashion; and (3) those who were neither criminal nor alcoholic nor sexually un-

---

[2] Edwin Powers, and Helen Witmer. *An Experiment in the Prevention of Delinquency.* New York: Columbia University Press, 1951; William McCord, and Joan McCord, with Irving Zola. *Origins of Crime,* New York: Columbia University Press, 1959.

faithful. These we considered as non-deviant. Two raters independently checking the same randomly selected cases agreed on 90 per cent.

In addition, information was gathered concerning the *attitudes of each parent toward the subject*. Previous research has linked parental rejection and crime; consequently, we expected that the influence of the parental role model might well depend on the emotional relation between the child and his parents. A parent was considered "warm" if he or she generally enjoyed the child and showed affectionate concern for him. A parent was considered "passive" if he or she had very little to do with the child. And a parent was considered "rejecting" if he or she gave primarily negative attention to the child. Finally, of course, there were a number of absent parents. (We rated step-parents in families where they had replaced the natural parents.) Using these classifications, three judges agreed in their ratings on 84 per cent of the fathers and on 92 per cent of the mothers in the cases selected at random from the sample.

Disciplinary methods, as well as parental attitudes, have often been cited as an important variable in the causation of crime. Since discipline can be regarded as the mediator between parental values and the child's learned behavior, we naturally wished to investigate the importance of this factor. The classification of discipline rested upon a theoretical division between techniques which depended upon the physical strength of the parent for effectiveness, and those techniques which utilized withdrawal of love. Verbal or physical attacks upon the child—beatings, displays of violent anger, and aggressive threats—constituted our "punitive discipline" category. Use of approval and verbal disapproval, reasoning, and withholding privileges were considered "love-oriented" discipline. If both parents regularly used one or the other of these basic methods, we classified the discipline

as consistent. If one or both parents were erratic in their discipline or if they disagreed in their techniques, we considered the discipline inconsistent. Only if there was evidence that almost no restraints of any kind were used by the family did we consider the discipline to be "lax." Thus we arrived at five classifications of discipline: (1) consistently punitive, (2) consistently love-oriented, (3) erratically punitive, (4) erratically love-oriented, and (5) lax. Three raters agreed in the classification of 88 per cent of the cases they read.

In our sample of 253 subjects, we found that 45 boys had been raised by criminal fathers, and of these boys 56 per cent had themselves been convicted of crimes. Sixty-nine boys had alcoholic or sexually promiscuous fathers, and of these boys 43 per cent had themselves been convicted of crimes. Of the remaining 139 boys, only 35 per cent had received criminal convictions. These differences are significant at the .05 level.

Clearly, paternal deviance tends to be reflected in criminality among the sons. As a next step, we wished to determine whether paternal rejection of the son aggravated or hindered the boy's tendency to imitate the father. Two conflicting hypotheses appeared reasonable. One might hypothesize that boys would be more likely to imitate or "identify" with their fathers if these fathers were affectionate towards them. (If this were true, the highest criminal rates would appear among boys having criminal, but "warm" fathers.) On the other hand, one could hypothesize that criminality is primarily an aggressive response to emotional deprivation—and that a criminal model serves to channel aggression against society. (If this second hypothesis were true, one would expect the highest criminal rates among boys having criminal, rejecting fathers.) To check which hypothesis was more adequate, we held constant the fathers' attitudes toward their sons and found the following pattern:

TABLE 1. *Per Cent Convicted of Crimes*

FATHER'S ROLE MODEL

Father's Attitude Toward Boy	Criminal	Alcoholic or Promiscuous	Non-deviant
Warm	(N: 13) 46	(N: 15) 27	(N: 67) 33
Passive	(N: 6) 50	(N: 15) 40	(N: 16) 13
Rejecting	(N: 13) 85	(N: 25) 60	(N: 30) 40

(Absent fathers and 8 about whom there was inadequate information are omitted.)

This analysis suggests that *both* paternal rejection and a deviant paternal model tend to lead to criminality. Holding constant rejection by the father, sons of criminals had a significantly [3] higher incidence of criminality than did sons of non-deviants. Holding constant paternal criminality, subjects raised by rejecting fathers had a significantly higher rate of criminality than did those raised by warm or passive fathers. *Criminal rates were highest among paternally rejected boys whose fathers were criminal.*

closeness with his father, or maternal rejection increases aggression and a criminal role model channels aggression against society. Because the criminal rates for sons of passive women approximated those for maternally rejecting women, the second explanation seems more adequate.

The importance of maternal warmth to the process of gaining acceptance of the rules of society can be seen in Table 2. Even among boys whose fathers presented non-deviant role models, absence of ma-

TABLE 2. *Per Cent Convicted of Crimes*

FATHER'S ROLE MODEL

Mother's Attitude Toward Boy	Criminal	Alcoholic or Promiscuous	Non-deviant
Warm	(N: 27) 41	(N: 45) 42	(N: 102) 28
Passive	(N: 6) 83	(N: 4) 25	(N: 12) 50
Rejecting	(N: 9) 89	(N: 19) 53	(N: 19) 53

(Absent mothers and 2 about whom there was inadequate information are omitted.)

What effect does the mother's attitude have on the boy's tendency to imitate his father's behavior? One would naturally assume that rejecting mothers would have a relatively high proportion of criminal sons. Two theories might account for this expected result: either maternal rejection tends to "push" a boy toward greater

[3] Tests of significance were two-tailed, using P < .05 as the minimum standard for asserting significance.

ternal warmth resulted in significantly higher criminal rates.

From this analysis we conclude: (1) Maternal affection decreases criminality, while maternal rejection or passivity increases criminal tendencies. (2) The criminal-producing effect of a criminal role model is aggravated by absence of maternal warmth. The combination of a criminal father and a passive or rejecting mother is strongly criminogenic.

Next, we investigated the effects of disciplinary methods upon the child's tendency to imitate his father's behavior. One of the questions we had in mind concerned the conscious values of criminal fathers. Assuming that discipline accorded with conscious values, we could test the nature of these values through analysis of the interrelationship of discipline and role model. If the conscious values of criminals supported criminality, one would anticipate that the highest criminal rates would occur among sons of criminals who were disciplined consistently. If the conscious values of criminals supported the non-criminal values of society, however, one would expect relatively low criminality among this group.

Quite clearly, this analysis indicates that the conscious values of criminals support the non-criminal values of society. Of those boys raised by criminal fathers, a significantly *lower* proportion whose discipline had been consistent became criminal. This agrees with the findings of Maccoby, Johnson, and Church.

Unfortunately, the distribution according to techniques of discipline permits only very tentative answers to our second question. Although there is a tendency, holding constant erratic administration, for punitive techniques to correspond with higher criminal rates, the difference is not statistically significant. Comparing criminal rates between the two techniques in instances where these were ad-

TABLE 3. *Per Cent Convicted of Crimes*

| | FATHER'S ROLE MODEL | | |
Discipline	Criminal	Alcoholic or Promiscuous	Non-deviant
Consistent:			
Punitive	(N: 2) 0	(N: 1) 100	(N: 11) 18
Love-oriented	(N: 11) 18	(N: 8) 25	(N: 41) 29
Erratic:			
Punitive	(N: 17) 76	(N: 26) 54	(N: 41) 44
Love-oriented	(N: 3) 67	(N: 14) 43	(N: 23) 26
Lax	(N: 12) 75	(N: 20) 35	(N: 20) 50

A second question we hoped to answer dealt with the relative effectiveness of punitive as opposed to love-oriented techniques in the prevention of criminality. While the evidence generally supports the theory that love-oriented techniques have superior effectiveness in transmitting the values of society, we wished to check the relationship of disciplinary technique to criminality among our sample of (largely) lower-class subjects who were exposed to a deviant subculture.

The figures which help to answer both of these questions are presented in Table 3.

ministered consistently, we find a tendency for punitiveness to result in lower criminal rates (though this difference, too, is not statistically significant). The relationship between techniques of discipline and consistency is, however, very strong and may, perhaps, account for some previous findings which have indicated that love-oriented discipline tends to deter criminality.

Our results suggest: (1) Conscious values, even within a deviant sub-culture, support the non-criminal values of general society. (2) Consistent discipline effectively counteracts the influence of a criminal father. (3) Consistency of discipline is more strongly related to transmission of values than is the technique of discipline.

In these analyses of the effect of the paternal role model in the causation of crime, we have seen that the father's criminal behavior, paternal rejection, absence of maternal warmth, and absence of consistent discipline are significantly related to high crime rates. To ascertain the interrelationship among these factors, we computed the criminal rates for each category of familial environment.

crime rates among sons of two loving parents were significantly lower than for those who had only one or neither parent loving.

Thus, we see that consistent discipline or love from both parents mediates against criminality, whereas absence of parental love tends to result in crime. The paternal role model seems to be most crucial for boys who are raised by only one loving parent and whose discipline is not consistent.

TABLE 4. *Per Cent Convicted of Crimes*

Father's Role Model	TWO LOVING PARENTS Discipline		ONE LOVING PARENT Discipline		NO LOVING PARENT Discipline	
	Consistent	Erratic or Lax	Consistent	Erratic or Lax	Consistent	Erratic or Lax
Criminal	(N: 5) 40	(N: 8) 38	(N: 8) 0	(N: 9) 100		(N: 12) 92
Alcoholic or Promiscuous	(N: 5) 40	(N: 16) 38	(N: 5) 20	(N: 28) 43		(N: 15) 60
Non-deviant	(N: 29) 28	(N: 37) 30	(N: 18) 13	(N: 30) 37	(N: 3) 33	(N: 16) 75

(Passive fathers were considered as "loving"; passive mothers were grouped with absent and rejecting women.)

Several interesting relationships emerge from Table 4:

1. Boys reared by parents both of whom were loving were generally not criminal. In this group of boys, neither the paternal role model nor disciplinary methods bore a significant relation to crime.
2. Boys reared in families where only one parent was loving were strongly affected both by methods of discipline and by the paternal role model.
3. In families where neither parent was loving, the crime rate reached a high level regardless of the paternal model.
4. Among subjects whose discipline had not been consistent, parental affection seemed to have a stronger influence on criminality than the paternal model. Holding constant paternal criminality,

Theoretically, one might assume that the father's role model would be more important than the mother's in determining the criminal behavior of the sons. In the above analyses, we have not considered the influence of the mother's role model. Yet criminal rates, computed on the basis of the mother's role model, indicated that this might be a critical variable.

Fifteen of our subjects had mothers who were criminal, by our definition, and of these boys 60 per cent had themselves been convicted of crimes. Thirty boys had mothers who were alcoholic or promiscuous, and 67 per cent of these boys had received criminal convictions. Of the remaining 208 boys, only 36 per cent had criminal convictions. These differences are significant at the .01 level.

The interaction of the mother's and

father's role model can be seen clearly in Table 5. In this table mothers who were criminal, alcoholic, or promiscuous are grouped together as "deviant."

If either the mother or the father was non-deviant, crime rates were not significantly related to the role model of the other parent. Yet, if the mother was deviant, crime rates varied significantly according to the father's role model; and if the father was criminal, the mother's role model seemed to be strongly influential in determining the behavior of the son.

greatly increases the likelihood of criminality.

To put these conclusions regarding the influence of a criminal father in another form, one could say that the son is extremely likely to become criminal unless either (a) both parents are loving and the mother is non-deviant, or (b) parental discipline is consistent and one parent is loving. *Twenty-four of the twenty-five boys whose fathers were criminal and whose backgrounds evidenced neither of these mitigating circumstances had criminal records as adults.*[4]

TABLE 5. *Per Cent Convicted of Crimes*

FATHER'S ROLE MODEL

Mother's Role Model	Criminal	Alcoholic or Promiscuous	Non-deviant
Deviant	(N: 16) 88	(N: 17) 59	(N: 12) 42
Non-deviant	(N: 29) 31	(N: 52) 42	(N: 127) 34

As a summary of these many factors which mediate between the parental role model and criminality, we present in Table 6 the interrelationships of these variables as they affect criminality.

This final analysis regarding the relationship of the paternal role model to criminality suggests several conclusions:

1. If the father is criminal and the mother is also a deviant model, criminality generally results regardless of parental affection.

2. If the father is criminal but the mother is non-deviant, and only one parent is loving, consistent discipline apparently deters the son from becoming criminal.

3. If the father is criminal but the mother is non-deviant (holding discipline constant), parental affection seems to be crucial: two loving parents apparently counteract the criminogenic force of a criminal father.

4. If the father is criminal and both parents are loving, the mother's deviance

Summary

This paper, an outgrowth of a larger longitudinal study of the causes of crime, has been concerned with the effects of the parental role model on crime. Over a five year period, observations were made of the day-to-day behavior of 253 boys and their families. These observations are relatively valid, for the investigators had no chance of learning the eventual outcome of their subjects' lives. Twenty years later, the criminal records of these boys, now adults, were examined. The backgrounds of the men were independently categorized and compared to their rates of crime. All of the men came from relatively lower-class, urban areas;

[4] Although the distribution of other factors among alcoholic or promiscuous fathers is quite poor, we may perhaps stretch the evidence to suggest that paternal alcoholism and promiscuity are not nearly so criminogenic as popular literature would have us believe.

TABLE 6. *Per Cent Convicted of Crimes*

Parental Role Model	TWO LOVING PARENTS Discipline		ONE LOVING PARENT Discipline		NO LOVING PARENT Discipline	
	Consistent	Erratic or Lax	Consistent	Erratic or Lax	Consistent	Erratic or Lax
Father criminal Mother deviant	(N: 1) 100	(N: 3) 100	(N: 1) 0	(N: 4) 100		(N: 7) 86
Father criminal Mother non-deviant	(N: 4) 25	(N: 5) 0	(N: 7) 0	(N: 5) 100		(N: 5) 100
Father alcoholic or promiscuous Mother deviant	(N: 1) 0	(N: 1) 0	(N: 1) 0	(N: 5) 60		(N: 9) 78
Father alcoholic or promiscuous Mother non-deviant	(N: 4) 50	(N:15) 40	(N: 4) 25	(N:23) 39		(N: 6) 33
Father non-deviant Mother deviant	(N: 3) 33	(N: 4) 25	(N: 1) 0	(N: 2) 50		(N: 2) 100
Father non-deviant Mother non-deviant	(N:26) 27	(N:33) 30	(N:17) 18	(N:28) 36	(N:3) 33	(N:14) 71

thus one major factor in the causation of crime, the influence of a delinquent subculture or tradition, was held constant.

The following conclusions emerge from this paper:

1. The effect of a criminal father on criminality in the son is largely dependent upon other factors within the family.

2. If paternal rejection, absence of maternal warmth, or maternal deviance is coupled with a criminal role model, the son is extremely likely to become criminal.

3. Consistent discipline in combination with love from at least one parent seems to offset the criminogenic influence of a criminal father.

4. The conscious values, even among criminals, seem to support the noncriminal norms of society. These conscious values are transmitted through consistent discipline.

More generally, we conclude:

First, the old adage, "like father, like son," must be greatly qualified—at least when one is talking about criminality. Children imitate their father's criminality when other environmental conditions (rejection, maternal deviance, erratic discipline) tend to produce an unstable, aggressive personality.

Second, in terms of crime, it seems fallacious to assume that sons imitate their criminal fathers because they have established an affectionate bond with the fathers and "identify" with them. Rather, it would appear that rejection by the father creates aggressive tendencies in the child who, having witnessed a crimi-

nal model in childhood, tends to channel aggression into criminal activities.

Third, again in terms of crime, the parents' conscious values can affect the child's behavior if these values are impressed upon the child by consistent discipline. Even though the actual behavior of the parent contradicted his conscious values, the consistently disciplined son tended more often to follow the expressed values, instead of the behavior, of the parent. This finding opposes those who maintain that children will follow their parents' values only if the parents' actions reinforce their values.

Thus, this study casts serious doubt on some of the more popular opinions concerning the causes of crime.

3 · The Manifestation of Personality Disorders as Conditioned by Family Structure

MENTAL PATIENTS IN THE COMMUNITY: FAMILY SETTINGS AND PERFORMANCE LEVELS

by Howard E. Freeman and Ozzie G. Simmons

Shorter periods of hospitalization and longer periods of community living between hospitalizations are among the notable trends in the treatment of psy-

The research reported here is being undertaken by the Community Health Project of the Harvard School of Public Health, under the direction of Dr. Ozzie G. Simmons, and is supported by a grant (M 1627) from the National Institute of Mental Health. We are grateful for the advice provided during the design phase of the study by Dr. James A. Davis of the University of Chicago. Mrs. Marilyn Plath and Mr. Bernard Bergen assisted during data collection and analysis phases of the study.

SOURCE: *American Sociological Review,* Vol. 23 (1958), pp. 147–154.

chotics, particularly those with functional disorders. Although the extensive employment of tranquilizing drugs has discernibly increased the length of community experience of patients, the largest proportion of those ever exposed to hospital treatment remained in the community for substantial periods of time, even prior to the advent of tranquilizers.[1]

[1] Adler, for example, found that one year after release from a state hospital, almost three-fourths of the patients in her cohort were still in the community. Leta M. Adler, "Patients of a State Mental Hospital: The Outcome of Their Hospitalization," in Arnold Rose (editor), *Mental Health and Mental Disorder,* New York: Norton, 1955, pp. 501–523.

There is considerable evidence, however, that improved functioning is not a necessary requisite for "success," i.e., remaining in the community. The clinical impression that former patients frequently reside in the community while actively psychotic and socially withdrawn is supported by studies employing modes of interpersonal performance as criteria of level of functioning.[2] As Clausen has noted, some released patients are "fully as ill as many patients currently in hospitals."[3]

Explanation of the continued existence in the community of a large number of patients who are less than well must be made with reference to the nature of their interpersonal relations in the posthospital situation. Patients are able to avoid the hospital when their interpersonal performance is within the range of behaviors expected by those with whom they interact. Tolerance of deviant behavior, on the part of the patient's "significant others," is a key factor affecting the process of posthospital experience and crucial to whether or not the patient succeeds in remaining in the community.

By tolerance of deviant behavior we mean the continued acceptance of the former patient by his significant others even when he fails to perform according to the basic prescriptions of his age-sex roles, as these are defined by the society. In our society, access to status is very largely determined by occupational achievement, and the strong emphasis on this factor, and to a lesser extent on other instrumental orientations, tends to be reasonably constant in American society.[4] Consequently, whatever the areas in which deviant behavior is likely to become a critical issue between the patient and those who comprise his world, instrumental performance is one of the most strategic, and acceptance of *non*-instrumental performance may be said to constitute substantial evidence of high tolerance of deviance.[5]

The familial network in which the patient resides and his status within this network thus assume considerable importance. Not only is tolerance by other household members directly related to "success" in remaining out of the hospital, but since familial expectations affect the patient's participation in other interpersonal networks, acceptance of the patient as a deviant restricts his exposure to others usually less tolerant of non-instrumental performance.[6] If those with

---

[2] For example, in Adler's cohort, less than one-fourth of the patients were regularly employed and socially active one year after release. *Ibid.*

[3] John A. Clausen, *Sociology and the Field of Mental Health,* New York: Russell Sage Foundation, 1956, p. 9.

[4] Cf. Talcott Parsons, "An Analytical Approach to the Theory of Social Stratifica-

tion," *Essays in Sociological Theory; Pure and Applied,* Glencoe, Ill.: Free Press, 1949, p. 174.

[5] In the longitudinal studies of rehabilitative process that constitute one of our principal research activities, we are working with a much broader concept of deviance than that implemented in the survey research reported in this paper. We are here concerned only with the tolerance of non-instrumental performance in role relationships where instrumental behavior is ordinarily prescribed. The objectives of our processual studies are to discern, along a time axis, what becomes viewed as deviant behavior on the part of the patient, by the patient himself as well as by his significant others: how much of this is viewed as problematic and by whom; the ways in which the problems are handled; and the thresholds or points at which deviance is no longer tolerated and cannot be handled within the network. It would be inappropriate to elucidate this statement here, but a paper on the conceptual analysis of deviance for purposes of our research is now in preparation.

[6] This observation is an illustration of the point advanced by Merton that the social structure may tend to insulate the individual from having his activities observed by those who would normally be his peers. Such insulation obviously results in a reduction of

whom the patient resides place little emphasis upon his being gainfully employed and, moreover, make few demands upon him to be socially active, he can exist as if in a one-person chronic ward, insulated from all but those in the highly tolerant household.

Investigation of the relationship between level of performance and structural and status variations in the residential settings of successful patients was a major purpose of a pilot investigation of a small number of patients and their families.[7] One of the principal findings of this exploratory study was that low levels of interpersonal performance are most tolerated in parental families where the patient occupies the status of "child." When patients were divided by level of performance into high and low groups, high level patients clustered in conjugal families or non-familial residences, while those with low levels were concentrated in parental families.[8] Further analysis indicated that this correlation between family type and performance level was not an artifact of associations between family type and either pre-

_____

pressures for prescribed performance. Robert K. Merton, "The Role Set: Problems in Sociological Theory," *British Journal of Sociology*, 8 (June 1957), pp. 106–121.

[7] James A. Davis, Howard E. Freeman, and Ozzie G. Simmons, "Rehospitalization and Performance Level of Former Mental Patients," *Social Problems*, 5 (July, 1957), pp. 37–44.

[8] The patients were dichotomized so that those rated high: (1) worked full time or were solely responsible for the care of the home; (2) participated in informal and social activities about as often as other family members; (3) were able to relate well in the interview situation (as judged by a clinically sophisticated interviewer); and (4) were reported by their relatives to be recovered, active in the life of the family, and without such symptoms as periods of depression or hallucinations.

hospital psychiatric state or psychiatric state at the time of release.

The finding was amplified by comparing, within the same cohort, those low level patients who were successful with those who were rehospitalized. Among the rehospitalized group, about as many came from parental families as there were low level patients living with parental families in the community. In contrast, there were four times as many returned to the hospital from conjugal families or non-familial settings as there were low level patients living in such settings in the community.

The finding that patients with a low level of performance who succeed in remaining in the community cluster in parental families is consistent with the fact that the role of the child in the parental family is the only social-biological role without expectations of instrumental performance. The child's role, regardless of age, consists largely of affective relations with parents and, compared with other family roles, is less concerned with instrumental performance.

To the extent that the grown-up "child" in the parental family has specific prescriptions built into his role, the structure of such families usually provides for alternate actors who can replace or supplement his performance when it is below expectation. Unlike spouses or those who live in non-familial settings, "children" are free of many of the stresses that accompany every other kin or household status.

On the basis of these findings, as well as upon differences in attitudes found to exist between relatives of patients with high and low levels of performance, a large-scale survey of female relatives of successful male patients was undertaken. In this paper, the first report of the survey, we report replication of the association between structural differences in the family settings of patients and performance levels.

Methodology

The female informants interviewed were all relatives, predominantly wives and mothers, of male patients who have succeeded in remaining in the community since their latest release from a mental hospital sometime between November, 1954 and December, 1955. Every male patient with the following characteristics was included in the potential drawing group: between 20 and 60 years of age; white; native-born; living in the Boston area at the time of release; hospitalized more than 45 days prior to release; not physically handicapped to the extent of being unemployable; not addicted to narcotics; and not hospitalized primarily for acute alcoholism. By diagnosis, all were psychotics with non-organic, functional disorders, the majority diagnosed as schizophrenic. Each patient selected was last hospitalized in one of thirteen hospitals in the Boston area, of which nine are State, three Veterans Administration, and one private.

Preliminary screening of the patients was accomplished by examining the discharge forms at the State's central reporting agency.[9] The hospital records of all patients who initially met the criteria were thoroughly reviewed. From this more detailed source of information, it became clear that a number of patients who appeared eligible on the State forms actually did not meet all the criteria, and the drawing group was reduced to 294. We planned to interview a female relative in the household of each patient.[10]

Except in cases where the hospital record clearly indicated that the patient was not living with his family, attempts were made to locate a female relative.[11]

Interviews were attempted in 209 of the 294 cases. The remaining cases consisted of five patients who lived in all male households, 64 who lived in non-familial settings, and 16 where the location of neither the patient nor his family could be discovered. It is probable that most of these 16 patients, even if living with families, no longer reside in the interviewing area, which comprises the whole of metropolitan Boston. Of the 209 interviews attempted, 182 were completed.[12] Thus 88 per cent of the attempted interviews were completed and, even if the 16 cases that could not be located are included, the loss rate is still under 20 per cent.[13]

[9] The cooperation of the Massachusetts Department of Mental Health, Dr. Jack Ewalt, Commissioner, is gratefully acknowledged, as is the advice and assistance provided by Dr. Thomas Pugh of the Department and his staff, and by the superintendents of the 13 cooperating hospitals.

[10] The difficulty of rating instrumentality of the "homemaker" role was only one of the reasons for restricting the informants to female relatives of male patients. These requirements also reduced variability in terms of both informants and patients. In addition, as survey research studies indicate, females are more likely to be at home and less likely to refuse to be interviewed.

[11] The informants were notified in advance by mail that they were to be interviewed. The letters were sent ordinary mail but the envelopes were stamped "Postmaster: DO NOT FORWARD, RETURN TO SENDER." Each one returned to us was sent out certified mail with a request for the new address. In this way it was possible to reach all cases in which there was a forwarding address on file. A second source of locating cases was the social service exchange.

[12] The important role of our eighteen interviewers is acknowledged. Most were social workers, though there were two resident psychiatrists and two social scientists.

[13] This loss rate is exceptionally low. In our exploratory study it was 45 per cent and in other cases of interviewing patients and their families, loss rates over 50 per cent are not unusual. Our refusal rate compares favorably with those encountered in studies of normal populations and in marketing research.

Interviews averaged two hours and were conducted with a standardized schedule which contained items to elicit social data, particularly regarding family structure; attitudes toward mental hospitals, treatment and illness, and "personality" measures such as the "F" scale. In addition, the schedule included items to obtain information about the patient's pre- and posthospital work history and social life. For each of the 182 completed cases, the data available from the interview and hospital record occupy nearly 1,000 IBM columns. For all the cases, information on 15 background variables is available. There are no differences on these 15 variables between the 182 cases completed and the 27 refusals.

Performance Level and Family Setting

The relationship between family setting and performance level uncovered in the exploratory study is clearly substantiated in this survey. Two separate measures of performance are employed

TABLE 1. *Relationship between Level of Work Performance and Family Setting*

LEVEL OF PERFORMANCE		FAMILY SETTING *			
		Parental		Conjugal	
		N	%	N	%
(High)	1	20	20.0	45	66.2
	2	11	11.0	14	20.6
	3	7	7.0	2	2.9
	4	5	5.0	4	5.9
	5	13	13.0	1	1.5
(Low)	6	44	44.0	2	2.9
	Total	100	100.0	68	100.0

$$r_{pbs} = .83$$

* 14 cases living with siblings not included.

which are modifications of work and social participation scales originally developed by Adler.[14] The high end of the six-point work performance scale includes those patients who have been continuously employed since their release, the low end those who have never worked since their release. As Table 1 indicates, patients who are husbands are almost exclusively concentrated on the high side and, conversely, patients who are sons cluster on the low side.

TABLE 2. *Relationship between Level of Social Participation and Family Setting*

LEVEL OF PERFORMANCE		FAMILY SETTING *			
		Parental		Conjugal	
		N	%	N	%
(High)	1	2	2.0	4	5.9
	2	16	16.0	23	33.8
	3	9	9.0	18	26.4
	4	18	18.0	8	11.8
	5	13	13.0	5	7.4
	6	11	11.0	4	5.9
(Low)	7	31	31.0	6	8.8
	Total	100	100.0	68	100.0

$$r_{pbs} = .53$$

* 14 cases living with siblings not included.

When social participation is employed as the measure of interpersonal performance, the same results occur. The highest category is composed of patients who belong to one or more voluntary associations and attend their meetings regularly, and who visit and are visited at least twice a month and at least as often as the rest of the household. Former patients in the lowest category do not belong to any voluntary associations, visit and are visited less than once a month and less frequently than other household members. Once again the results are strik-

[14] Adler, *op. cit.*

ing, particularly when the cases are dichotomized.

The Pearsonian correlation between the work and social participation ratings of interpersonal performance is .51. The magnitude of this correlation indicates that the two ratings are manifestations of a more general mode of interpersonal performance.[15] This is evident when the two ratings are dichotomized and then combined.

in remaining in the community receives additional support when we consider patients from the cohort who were released during the same time period but subsequently rehospitalized. In the course of collecting information on the successful patients in the cohort, a record check was made of the "failures." These failures, it should be noted, include only patients released to the community and returned to the hospital after having been dropped

TABLE 3. *Relationship between Combined Work and Social Level of Performance and Family Setting*

		FAMILY SETTING *			
LEVEL OF PERFORMANCE		Parental		Conjugal	
Work	Social	N	%	N	%
High (1–3)	High (1–3)	19	19.0	43	63.2
High (1–3)	Low (4–7)	19	19.0	18	26.5
Low (4–6)	High (1–3)	8	8.0	2	2.9
Low (4–6)	Low (4–7)	54	54.0	5	7.4
Total		100	100.0	68	100.0
	$r_{pbs} = .60$				

* 14 cases living with siblings not included.

Our thesis regarding the relationship between the differential tolerance of family members and variations in levels of performance of patients who succeed

[15] For purposes of future, more quantitative aspects of data analysis, distributions on the work and social participation ratings have been normalized, added together, and distributed into categories. The intercorrelations of either the raw or normalized work and social participation scores with this combined standarized level of performance measure range between .80 and .90.

We wish to stress, however, that this study deals with level of performance as defined in terms of performance in work and social participation. The relationship between performance as so defined and the level of functioning of the patients from a psychiatric viewpoint has not been assessed. But it is our belief, based on our exploratory study where patients as well as relatives were interviewed and on the field work experience

from the hospital's books. Most of the patients not voluntarily committed are so dropped only after leaving bed and successfully remaining on trial visit in the community for one year. There are other variations in the release practices of hospitals. For example, patients whose prognosis is doubtful are sometimes released on extended leaves of absence and then discharged if they succeed in remaining in the community. However, if they "fail," it is not reflected in the records used to select the cohort. The failures whose records are available thus consist of the "best" of the failures in the sense that patients officially discharged are in the community the longest time

and judgments of our clinical staff, that the bulk of the "low" patients would be judged seriously disturbed by a psychiatrist, although we cannot present empirical evidence of this.

of all hospitalized patients given an opportunity to "leave bed." [16]

In Table 4, the family settings of the low level patients are compared with the settings at the time of rehospitalization of the official failures. Many more patients who last lived with conjugal families are back in the hospital in comparison with parents are back in the hospital in comparison with low level patients presently living in parental families. Table 4 presents these findings for each rating of performance level.

These results are consistent with our introductory remarks regarding more tolerant expectations toward those who

TABLE 4. *Family Setting of Patients Rehospitalized and Those with Low Level of Performance Who Remain in the Community*

	FAMILY SETTING				
	Parental		Conjugal		
	N	%	N	%	r
Work Rating					
Low level in community (4–6)	62	65.3	7	25.9	
Rehospitalized	33	34.7	20	74.1	
Total	95	100.0	27	100.0	.33
Social Rating					
Low level in community (4–7)	73	68.9	23	53.5	
Rehospitalized	33	31.1	20	46.5	
Total	106	100.0	43	100.0	.15
Combined Work-Social Rating					
Low level in community	54	62.1	5	20.0	
Rehospitalized	33	37.9	20	80.0	
Total	87	100.0	25	100.0	.35

son with successful low level patients presently living with wives. In contrast, few patients whose last residence was

[16] The problem of the use of legal definitions as criteria has been amply evaluated by the criminologist whose comments are directly applicable to the field of mental health. It was possible, in our definition of success, to employ the more realistic one of the date the patient "left bed." It was more difficult to distinguish "failures" from patients not ever returned to the community. The hospitals are required to indicate the "left bed" date only when the case is officially "dropped" from the books.

occupy the status of "child." Over time it appears that a greater proportion of patients are returned to hospitals from conjugal families. In their entirety, these findings support the earlier exploratory study.

Influence of Prior Conditions

Considering the replicative nature of the investigation and the magnitude of the correlation, it is quite certain that the relationship between performance level and family setting is a stable one. Explanation of the differential performance of former patients, however, in terms of tolerance of deviance on the part of their significant others could represent an overemphasis upon the posthospital situation and a neglect of prehospital and hospital conditions. Our analysis of the influence of prior conditions has to depend upon hospital record data and retrospective information from the relative interviewed. Within the limits of accuracy and reliability of these types of data, our explanation of tolerance is not vitiated by this additional information.

Information from the hospital record eliminates the possibility that differences in hospital experience offer a satisfactory alternative explanation. There are no significant differences in performance level which can be accounted for in terms of such variables as type of hospital, diagnosis, type of psychiatric treatment, and ward mobility.

The influence of the prehospital condition of the patient presents a more complex set of relationships for analysis. There is considerable evidence that patients from parental families are more ill when hospitalized than those from conjugal families. Without reference to the data of this study, the argument can be advanced that marriage serves a screening function and "sicker" persons cluster in parental families before hospitalization since the "healthier" of the mentally ill are more likely to marry. Actually, in terms of similar measures of level of performance employed in the previous section of our analysis, but with reference to prehospital history, patients from parental families do have a lower performance level than do those from conjugal families.[17] Furthermore, the obvious point that patients "sicker" when hos-

[17] Differences in number of times hospitalized and number of months hospitalized since first admitted to a mental hospital also suggest that patients from parental families tend to have lower prehospital levels of performance.

pitalized are generally "sicker" after release is confirmed by the correlation among patients studied between pre- and posthospital level of performance. On the basis of these findings, is the relationship between level of posthospital performance and family setting perhaps an artifact of differences in prehospital level of functioning of the patients?

While differences in prehospital levels of performance partly explain our findings, several considerations strongly support the relevance of differential tolerance of deviance as a key variable in accounting for the range of variation in performance of successful patients during the posthospital period. First, the magnitude of the correlations between prehospital level of performance and family setting are substantially lower than those between posthospital level of performance and family setting. Second, if low level patients do cluster in parental families before as well as after hospitalization, a higher proportion of patients should be rehospitalized from parental as compared with conjugal families, unless rehospitalization is associated with differential conditions in posthospital settings. The same proportion are rehospitalized from the two types of settings, however, supporting our explanation of tolerance of deviance on the part of family members in the posthospital period. Moreover, as already reported in Table 4, the number of failures in relation to the number of patients rated "low" is much higher among those from conjugal settings.

Finally, when prehospital level of performance is controlled in the cross-tabulations, posthospital level of performance remains associated with family type, *within* prehospital level of performance groups, indicating that prehospital functioning, in itself, is an insufficient explanation.

Actually, the correlation between prehospital level of performance and family setting is support for our contention that tolerance of deviance is a key varia-ble. While of special significance during the posthospital period, undoubtedly the importance of the tolerance of family members is not unique to this period but crucial to understanding the process of hospitalization as well as rehospitaliza-tion. Mothers, compared with wives, are more likely to tolerate deviant perform-ance before the admission of the patient to the hospital, as well as between subse-quent readmissions.[18] The person with a low level of interpersonal performance is probably less likely to be hospitalized if living in a parental family, as well as less likely to be rehospitalized if returned to the community in a similar state.

Conclusions

In this survey of families of male men-tal patients living in the community, we have found a high correlation between level of performance and family setting. Unlike the exploratory study upon which this survey is based, we have attempted to control variations which might ac-count for the relationship. This replica-tion, with its added controls, convinces us of the stability of the finding. How-ever, several qualifications regarding its generality should be noted:

[18] The tolerance of wives, compared with mothers, probably decreases after the pa-tient's first hospital experience. Wives, eman-cipated from the patient during hospitaliza-tion, are more likely to find, in terms of complementary systems of emotional gratifi-cation as well as everyday activities, that they can get along as well or better without their mates. Mothers could not as easily move to such a position. Clausen and Yarrow imply that wives are likely to regard the behavior of husbands, after release, without much tolerance, and the recurrence of the hus-band's illness as "the last straw." John A. Clausen and Marian Radke Yarrow, "Further Observations and Some Implications," *Jour-nal of Social Issues*, 11 (1955), p. 62.

1. With the exception of the few cases where an interview was refused, the re-sults are based upon all cases in a pre-selected cohort of patients. Unlike most survey research, where a sample is inter-viewed and findings generalized to a population, our findings are limited, in the strict sense, to the cases at hand.

2. Clearly, generalization to groups of patients excluded from the cohort—such as Negroes, foreign-born, and psychotics with organic disorders—is precarious. Al-though female patients were not in-cluded in this research, they were con-sidered in the earlier, exploratory study. On the basis of the results of the earlier study, we believe that the present find-ings and their implications also apply to female patients.

3. A number of patients who do not live with their families succeed in re-maining in the community. Of male pa-tients whose social background and diag-nosis are similar to those studied here, probably only 70 or 80 per cent live with their families. Questions regarding the relationship between performance level and residential setting of some twenty to thirty per cent remain unanswered. Nevertheless, we believe that non-familial settings provide functional equivalents in the form of surrogate mothers and wives, and that patterns would be found similar to those depicted in this study of patients with families.

Future reports of the analysis of the survey will amplify the data discussed here by specification of structural dis-tinctions *within* parental and conjugal settings. Though we have confined this report to structural differences, data processing has advanced considerably fur-ther. The additional analysis supports the basic proposition underlying the sur-vey, namely that differences in family structure and attitudes, personality, and behavior of family members are asso-ciated with level of performance of mental patients who succeed in remaining in the community.

We believe that the findings reported here, in themselves, are of considerable interest from both a psychiatric and sociological point of view. The relationship between family setting and performance level should be of concern to practitioners associated with mental hospitals in planning the release of the patient and in prognosticating his posthospital behavior. If the goal of treatment is only the permanent or semi-permanent separation of hospital and patient, the release of patients to parental families would appear to be an efficient practice. While effective in freeing a hospital bed, however, releasing the patient to the tolerant milieu which tends to predominate in the parental family may be the most inadequate community setting if movement toward instrumental performance is a desired outcome of hospitalization. Return of the patient to the parental family, where there is less likely to be an expectation of instrumental performance, may well occasion regression from, rather than movement toward, better functioning, and eliminate any gains of a therapeutic hospital experience.

The findings are particularly relevant for the sociological study of deviance. In terms of our measures of instrumental performance—work and social participation—the question can be raised whether differences between mothers and wives in tolerance of deviance is peculiar to the perception of the person as a mental patient. Are mothers and wives of, e.g., drug addicts, alcoholics, and the physically handicapped differentially distributed in degree of tolerance when the definition of deviance is with respect to instrumental performance?

Finally, we are convinced that it is the differential *quality* of the role relationships which is critical to understanding the influence of significant others in the posthospital experience of the patient. For example, with respect to the role of the patient in the family, there is the question of the availability of functionally equivalent actors to occupy the normally prescribed roles. Patients who are husbands probably are tolerated more often in non-instrumental roles when there are other adult males in the household to occupy the instrumental roles. Conversely, sons who are patients are probably least tolerated in the parental family when no other male actors are available to take instrumental roles. Such speculations can be partly verified and assessed by further analysis of our survey data, but problems of this order also require longitudinal investigations that employ repeated interviewing. Our research strategy includes cross-sectional surveys, of the kind reported here, and processual studies for observation and assessment of change. Both are necessary for systematic inquiry into the posthospital experience of former mental patients.

C · THE SCHOOL AND PERSONALITY

ACADEMIC ACHIEVEMENT AND THE STRUCTURE OF COMPETITION

by James S. Coleman

In secondary education (and to a lesser extent in lower grades), we are beset by a peculiar paradox: in our complex industrial society, there is increasingly more to learn, and formal education is ever more important in shaping one's life chances; at the same time, there is coming to be more and more an independent "society of adolescents," an adolescent culture which shows little interest in education and focuses the attention of teenagers on cars, dates, sports, popular music, and other matters just as unrelated to school. Thus while it is becoming more important that teenagers show a desire to learn, the developing adolescent culture shifts their interest further and further away from learning.

Are these conflicting tendencies "natural" ones, irreversible processes resulting from changes in society? Is the nonchalance of the adolescent culture toward scholastic matters, its irresponsibility and hedonism, simply because "teenagers are that way"? Is it something which must be accepted? If so, then the hope of developing students truly interested in learning lies in "rescuing" from the adolescent culture a few students who accept adult values, set their sights on long-range goals, and pay little attention to the frivolous activities of their fellows.

SOURCE: *Harvard Educational Review*, Vol. 29 (1959), pp. 330–351.

This approach is very nearly the one we take now, in our emphasis on special programs for "the gifted child," our concern with selecting the most intelligent and setting them apart with special tasks which will further separate them from their fellows.

This is one approach to the problem, but I think a too-simple one, which refuses to face the serious problem of raising the level of training of the less-than-gifted child, one which in effect says that we must accept the hedonism and lack of interest in learning of the adolescent culture, a hedonism which drains off the energies of the majority of high school students. And this is an approach which can fail even in its attempt to develop the potentialities of the gifted child, for it depends completely on the selection process, and at its best probably misses far more potential scientists and scholars than it finds.

If we answer the question differently, if we refuse to accept as inevitable the irresponsibility and educational unconcern of the adolescent culture, then this poses a serious challenge. For to change the norms, the very foci of attention, of a cultural system is a difficult task—far more complex than that of changing an individual's attitudes and interests. Yet if the challenge can be met, if the attention of the adolescent culture can be directed toward, rather than away from, those educational goals which adults hold for children, then this provides a far more fundamental and satisfactory solution to the problem of focusing teenagers' attention on learning.

Norms and Values in the Adolescent Culture

For the past two years, I have been conducting a study in nine public high schools of the "climate of values" which exists among the students in each school, and the effects of the different value climates upon achievement in school.* The schools, all located in the Midwest, include small-town schools, suburban schools (one—School F in Table 1—a

were studied in several ways, among them a questionnaire filled out by every student in each school.[1] To help get a picture of his general interests and activities, each student was asked:

What is your favorite way of spending your leisure time?

The responses are given in Table 2.

These responses indicate that boys like to spend a great deal of their time in fairly active outdoor pursuits, such as organized sports, boating, and just going around with the fellows. They spend it on hobbies, too (the most frequent of which is working on their car) and on such passive pursuits as movies, television, records, and the like. Being with girls does not, as adults sometimes think,

TABLE 1. *Summary Data of General Characteristics of the Nine Schools*

| | | | | SCHOOL | | | | | |
GENERAL CHARACTERISTIC	A	B	C	D	E	F	G	H	I
Number of students [a]	200	400	500	400	500	1100	1400	1900	1900
Location	town	town	town	town	town	suburb	city	city	suburb
Average family income [b]	6000	6400	6400	6400	5800	6200	5400	7200	11400

[a] Given to the nearest hundred of students.
[b] Given to the nearest hundred of dollars.

working class school from which about 25 per cent of the graduates attend college, and one—School I—an especially well-equipped upper-middle class school about 85 per cent of whose graduates attend college), and two schools (Schools G and H) in cities of about 100,000. Thus the range in social class, in size of school, in type of community, and in parental style of life is very great. Consequently, the schools, though far from constituting any cross-section or sample of American schools, cover a broad range of social contexts, a range which includes a large proportion of American schools.

The interests of these teenagers, and the values of the adolescent culture itself,

* This research was carried out under a grant from the U. S. Office of Education.

occupy a large part of their time (though, to be sure, it comes to occupy more time as they go from the freshman year to the senior year).

The comparison with girls' leisure-time activities shows a sharp contrast in some categories. Girls spend far less time in the active outdoor ways that boys en-

[1] The problem of getting straightforward responses in such a questionnaire is extremely difficult. To help insure this, members of our staff administered the questionnaires in the absence of the teacher, and students were assured that no one in the school would see their responses. The responses we obtained were undoubtedly adult-oriented, but appeared, by all the criteria at our disposal, to give us as accurate a picture as adults are likely to obtain of the values current among the adolescents.

TABLE 2. *Percentage Distributions of the Favorite Leisure Time Activities Mentioned by Boys and Girls*

FAVORITE LEISURE TIME ACTIVITY	BOYS [a] (N = 4,021)	GIRLS [a] (N = 4,135)
1. Outdoor sports	36.7	18.2
2. Being with the group, riding around, going up town, etc.	17.2	32.5
3. Attending movies and spectator events (athletic games, etc.)	8.5	10.4
4. Dating or being out with opposite sex, or going dancing	13.6	23.6
5. Hobby (working on cars, bicycles, radio, musical instruments, etc.)	22.5	20.1
6. Indoor group activities (bowling, playing cards, roller skating, etc.)	8.0	8.1
7. Watching television	19.4	23.6
8. Listening to records or radio	11.2	31.7
9. Reading	13.7	35.5
10. Other	7.1	9.3
11. No answer	8.1	3.7

[a] Percentages add to more than 100 per cent because some students mentioned more than one activity as their "favorite."

NOTE: For all those readers who use statistical tests of significance to evaluate the results of such tables as this, it should be stated that all the differences discussed in the text from this and succeeding tables are significant at more than the .01 level. This does not imply, of course, that the inferred difference is an important one. It should also be recognized that the assumptions behind significance tests are not met in such survey statistics.

joy themselves, more time "just being with their friends," and far more time in vicarious pleasures: reading, listening to records, watching television, movies, attending games.

The general pattern of these leisure pursuits, showing considerably more activity among the boys, is indicative of something which seems to be quite general in the adolescent community: boys have far more to *do* than girls have. Whether it is athletics or cars or hunting or model-building, our society seems to provide a much fuller set of activities to engage the interests of boys than of girls. Thus when girls are together they are much more often just "with the gang" than are boys (one of their frequent afternoon activities being simply "going up town" to window-shop and walk around).

There is a particular point of interest in these responses, thinking about their relation to the school. Few of these categories have any relation to things which go on in school. Some of the hobbies may, of course, have their genesis in school, and some sports are centered around the school, but, except for these, school activities are missing. No one responds that doing homework is his favorite way of spending his leisure time. To be sure, this is at least in part because homework is not viewed as leisure, but as work. Yet athletics manages to run over into leisure time, breaking the barrier that separates work from leisure. Perhaps it is not too much to expect that scholastic activities could also—if the right way were found to take them out of the category of pure work and allow them to spill over into leisure.

In a sense, we have spread out before us in Table 2 the activities which capture the energies and interests of teenagers, and the question we are asking is

ing friendly." Not only is this mentioned most often overall, but it is mentioned most often in seven of the nine schools. The importance of having a good personality or, what is a little different, "being friendly" or "being nice to the other kids," in these adolescent cultures is something which adults often fail to realize. Adults often forget how "person-oriented" children are: they have not yet moved into the world of cold impersonality in which many adults live. This is

TABLE 3. *Percentage Distributions of the Criteria for Membership in the Leading Crowd Perceived by Boys and Girls*

CRITERION FOR MEMBERSHIP IN THE LEADING CROWD [a]	BOYS [b] $(N = 4,021)$	GIRLS [b] $(N = 4,135)$
Good personality, being friendly	26.6	48.7
Good looks, beauty	14.3	28.9
Having nice clothes	9.0	27.4
Good reputation	17.9	25.9
Having money	7.7	14.2
Good grades, being smart	11.9	11.6
Being an athlete (boys only)	16.3	——
Having a car (boys only)	10.7	——

[a] Only categories which were mentioned 10 per cent of the time or more are included.

[b] Percentages add to more than 100 per cent because some students responded with more than one criterion.

NOTE: In computing averages each of the nine schools was considered as a unit.

how schools can come to capture those energies and interests in a way that they presently fail to do.

The values of the adolescent subcultures in these schools were studied in several ways, including questions asked of each student. One question asked: "What does it take to get to be a member of the leading crowd?" The major categories of response are tabulated in Table 3, for boys and girls separately.

Consider first the girls' responses, at the right of the table. Most striking in these responses is the great importance of "having a good personality" or "be-

probably due to the limits on their range of contacts—for in the limited world of a grade school, a boy or girl *can* respond to his classmates as persons, with a sincerity which becomes impossible as one's range of contacts grows. One of the transitions for some children comes, in fact, as they enter high school and find that they move from classroom to classroom and have different classmates in each class.

After "a good personality" come a wide range of attributes and activities. A flavor of them is indicated by the collection of responses listed below—some hostile to the leading crowd (and in their hostility, often seeing it as immoral), others friendly to it (and in their friendliness, attributing positive virtues to it).

What does it take to get into the leading crowd in this school?

"Wear just the right things, nice hair, good grooming, and have a wholesome personality."

"Money, clothes, flashy appearance, date older boys, fairly good grades."

"Be a sex fiend—dress real sharp—have own car and money—smoke and drink—go steady with a popular boy."

"Have pleasant personality, good manners, dress nicely, be clean, don't swear, be loads of fun."

"A nice personality, dress nice without over-doing it."

"Hang out at _____'s. Don't be too smart. Flirt with boys. Be cooperative on dates."

Among these various attributes, the table shows some mention of "good looks" to be second to "personality" in frequency. Having nice clothes, or being well-dressed, is also important in most of the schools, as the responses above suggest and as Table 3 indicates. What it means to be well-dressed differs sharply in a well-to-do suburb and in a working-class school, of course. Nevertheless, whether it is the number of cashmere sweaters a girl owns, or simply having neat, clean, pastel frocks, the matter of "having good clothes" is an important one in the value systems to which these girls pay heed.

In part, the importance of having good clothes appears to derive from its use as a symbol of family status and general opulence. But in some part, it appears to derive from the same source that gives importance to "good looks": these items are crucial in making a girl attractive to boys. Thus in this respect the values of the girls' culture are molded by the presence of boys—and by the fact that success with boys is itself of over-riding importance in these cultures.

Another element in the constellation of attributes required if one is to be in the leading crowd is indicated by the class of responses labelled "having a good reputation." In all these schools, this item was often mentioned (though in each school, a disgruntled minority saw the leading crowd as composed of girls with bad reputations and immoral habits). A girl's "reputation" is a crucial matter among adolescents. A girl is caught in a dilemma, a dilemma suggested by the importance of good looks on the one hand, and a good reputation on the other. A girl must be successful with the boys, says the culture, but in doing so she must maintain her reputation. In some schools, the limits defining a good reputation are stricter than others —but in all the schools, the limits are there, and they define what is "good" and what is "bad." The definitions are partly based on behavior with boys, but they also include drinking, smoking, and other less tangible matters—something about the way a girl handles herself, quite apart from what she actually *does*.

Another criterion by which a girl gets into the leading crowd or fails to get in is expressed by a girl who responded simply, "Money, fancy clothes, good house, new cars, etc. (the best)."

These qualities are all of a piece: they express the fact that being born into the right family is a great help to a girl in getting into the leading crowd. It is expressed differently in different schools and by different girls, sometimes as "parents having money," sometimes as "coming from the right neighborhood," sometimes as "expensive clothes."

These qualities differ sharply from some of those discussed above, for they are not something a girl can *change*.[2]

[2] To be sure, she sometimes has a hard time changing her looks or her personality; yet these are her own personal attributes, which she can do something about, except in extreme situations.

Her position in the system is ascribed according to her parents' social position, and there is nothing she can do about it. If criteria like these dominate, then we would expect the system to have a very different effect on the people than if other criteria, which a girl or boy could hope to achieve, were the basis of social comparison—just as in the larger society, a caste system has quite different effects on individuals than does a system with a great deal of mobility between social classes.

It is evident that these family-background criteria play some part in these schools, but—at least, according to these girls—not the major part. (It is true that the girls who are *not* in the leading crowd more often see such criteria, which are glossed over or simply not seen by girls who are in the crowd.) Furthermore, these criteria differ sharply in their importance in different schools. In the working-class suburban schools (F), for example, they are almost never mentioned. They are mentioned most often in Schools B, D, and H—three schools in stable communities in which middle class families are somewhat more predominant (and more dominant) than in the other towns.

Another criterion for being in the leading crowd is scholastic success. According to these girls, good grades, or "being smart" or "intelligent," has something to do with membership in the leading crowd. Not much, to be sure—it is mentioned less than 12 per cent of the time, and far less often than the attributes of personality, good looks, clothes, and the like. Doing well in school apparently counts for something, though. It is surprising that it does not count for more, because in some situations, the "stars," "heroes," and objects of adulation are those who best achieve the goals of the institution. For example, in the movie industry the leading crowd is composed of those who have achieved the top roles —they are by consensus the "stars." Or

in a graduate school, the "leading crowd" of students ordinarily consists of the bright students who excel in their studies. Not so for these high school girls. The leading crowd seems to be defined primarily in terms of *social* success: their personality, beauty, clothes—and in communities where social success is tied closely to family background, their money and family are important, too.

For the boys, a somewhat different set of attributes is important for membership in the leading crowd. The responses below give some idea of the things mentioned.

> "A good athlete, pretty good looking, common sense, sense of humor."
> "Money, cars and the right connections and a good personality."
> "Be a good athlete. Have a good personality. Be in everything you can. Don't drink or smoke. Don't go with bad girls."
> "Athletic ability sure helps."
> "Prove you rebel the police officers. Dress sharply. Go out with sharp Freshman girls. Ignore Senior girls."
> "Good in athletics; 'wheel' type; not too intelligent."

By categories of response, Table 3 shows that "a good personality" is important for the boys, but of less prominence than it is for the girls. Being "good-looking," having good clothes, and having a good reputation are similarly of decreased importance. Good looks in particular are less important for the boys than for the girls. Similarly for the items which have to do with parents' social position—having money, coming from the right neighborhood, and the like.

What then are the criteria which are more important for boys than for girls? The most obvious is, as the table indicates, athletics. The role of athletics as an entree into the leading crowd appears to be extremely important. Of the things that a boy can *do*, of the things he can *achieve*, athletic success seems the clearest and most direct way to gain membership in the leading crowd. Having good grades, or doing well academically, appears to be a much less safe path to the leading crowd than does athletics (and sometimes it is a path away, as the final quotation listed above suggests).

An item which is of considerable importance for the boys, as indicated in Table 3, is a *car*—just having a car, according to some boys, or having a *nice* car, according to others. But whichever it is, a car appears to be of considerable importance in being part of the "inner circle" in these schools. In four of the five small-town schools—but in none of the larger schools—a car was mentioned more often than academic achievement. When this is coupled with the fact that these responses include not only juniors and seniors, but also freshmen and sophomores, who are too young to drive, the place of cars in these adolescent cultures looms even larger.

Several other questions in the questionnaire present the same general picture that this "leading crowd" question reveals: social success with the opposite sex (to which good looks, a good reputation, good clothes, and a car contribute), athletic achievement for boys, a few school activities such as cheerleading for girls, being willing to "have a good time" for both boys and girls, are the attributes and activities which are highly valued among teenagers. Far less important to the adolescent community are the activities which school is ostensibly designed for: scholastic achievement, leadership of academic clubs, and the like. For example, the question:

> If you could be remembered here at school for one of the three things below, which one would you want it to be: brilliant student, star athlete, or most popular?

Boys responded star athlete over 40 per cent of the time, and brilliant student less than 30 per cent of the time. This despite the fact that the boy is asked how he would like to be remembered *in school,* an institution explicitly designed to train students, not athletes.

It is clear from all these data that the interests of teenagers are not focused around studies, and that scholastic achievement is at most of minor importance in giving status or prestige to an adolescent in the eyes of other adolescents. This is perhaps to be expected in some areas, where parents place little emphasis on education. Yet the most striking result from these questions was the fact that the values current in the well-to-do suburban school (I) were no more oriented to scholastic success than those in the small-town schools or the working-class school.

There were differences in the value climates, but not at all in expected directions. And the differences were dwarfed by the similarities. For example, in every school, more boys wanted to be remembered as a star athlete than as a brilliant student. And in six of the nine schools, "good looks" was first, second, or third in importance as a criterion for being in the leading crowd of girls. Having good grades almost always occupied roughly the same place for girls. It was seventh in seven schools, fifth in one (B), and eighth in one (F). That is, in eight schools, it ranked below some of the less-frequently mentioned items not included in Table 3. For boys, the average was higher, and the variation was the greater: it was fifth in three schools (F, G, and I), sixth in two (C and E), third in one (H), fourth in one (B), seventh in one (D), and eighth in one (A). In all schools athletic achievement held a high place for the boys (it was first, second, or third in six of the nine schools).

In short, despite wide differences in parental background, type of community, and type of school, there was little difference in the standards of prestige, the activities which confer status, and the values which focus attention and interest. In particular, good grades and academic achievement had relatively low status in all schools. If we add to this the fact that these responses were given in school classrooms, under adult (though not teacher) supervision, and to questions which referred explicitly to the school, then the true position of scholastic achievement in the adolescent culture appears even lower.

In fact, there is a good deal of evidence that special effort toward scholastic success is *negatively* valued in most teenage groups. Scholastic success may, in the minor way indicated by the data above, add to a student's status among his fellows; but the success must be gained without special efforts, without doing anything beyond the required work. For example, along with nine public schools, the research mentioned above included a private university laboratory school whose average IQ level is probably surpassed by few schools in the country. This school should be an extreme example of the academically-inclined school. It is, and many students individually pursue their studies with intensive effort. Yet student leaders of the school reported that the "thing to do" to be part of the crowd was to get reasonably good grades *without* expending special efforts in doing so. In other words, even at this extremely scholastically-oriented school, there are group norms in the direction of holding down effort. How effective they are at this high school is unimportant. The important point is that despite the academic inclinations and background of the students, there is a norm against working too hard on one's studies.

A pair of questions asked in the questionnaire gives some indication of the lack of encouragement teenagers give to scholastic effort. Boys were put in a pair of hypothetical situations, one having to do with an academic course, biology, and the other having to do with a non-academic course closely related to the adolescent culture, auto shop. (Some of the schools had no auto shop, but the hypothetical situation seemed to be understood well in all schools.) [3]

The situations, as posed in the questionnaire, were:

Bill was going well in biology class, because he had a hobby of collecting and identifying insects. One day his biology instructor asked Bill if he would act as the assistant in the class. Bill didn't know whether this was an honor to be proud of or whether he would be the "teacher's pet." How would you feel—that it would be something to be proud of, or wouldn't it matter?

something to be proud of
something I wouldn't care for
I'd have mixed feelings

Tom had always liked to fool around with cars and tear down engines and was very good at it. Because of this, the shop teacher singled him out to act as his special assistant. Tom didn't know what to do, since he had no use for boys who hung around the teacher. If you were in Tom's place what would you do?

I would agree to be assistant.
I wouldn't agree to be assistant.
I am not sure.

After each of these questions, a second part was asked:

Now suppose you decided to agree to be the assistant in biology. What would your friends think when they found out about it?

They would envy me and look up to me.
They would kid me about it, but would still envy me.
They would look down on me.

[3] Girls were asked a similar pair of questions, the first one the same biology question, and the second a question about sewing class. The results were essentially the same as those for the boys presented below, so that they are omitted for simplicity.

They wouldn't care one way or the other.

If you did become the assistant in the auto-shop class, would your friends look up to you for it, or would they look down on you?

They would envy me and look up to me.

They would kid me about it, but would still envy me.

They would look down on me.

They wouldn't care one way or the other.

The distributions of responses on these two questions were as follows:

TABLE 4. *Percentage Distributions of Friend's Reactions to the Biology Assistantship and Auto Shop Assistantship Perceived by Boys (N = 3,830)* [a]

FRIEND'S REACTION	BIOLOGY ASSISTANT	AUTO SHOP ASSISTANT
Envy and look up to me	5.3	18.6
Kid me about it, but envy me	50.0	42.0
Look down on me	3.9	5.7
Wouldn't care	37.3	28.8
No answer	3.5	4.9
Total	100.0	100.0

[a] The number of cases is only 3830 rather than 4120 as in the previous tabulation because these questions were in a second questionnaire administered in the Spring of the school year (1957–58). The difference is due primarily to drop-outs.

Only 5.3 per cent of these boys felt that their friends would unambiguously look up to them for being biology assistant; over three times as many, 18.6 per cent felt that their friends would unambiguously look up to them for the nonscholastic activity, assisting in the auto shop.

Both these situations, however, involve special effort toward goals defined by the school. And in both these cases, the largest category of response (50 per cent for the biology assistant, 42 per cent for the shop assistant) is the ambivalent one: friends will kid him for becoming the teacher's assistant, but will nevertheless privately envy him. This ambivalent response illustrates the conflicting feelings of adolescents about scholastic success: privately wanting to succeed and be recognized themselves, but (in most adolescent groups) publicly making fun of the success of others, and disavowing interest in scholastic success. Thus it is not only that scholastic success counts for little in the adolescent culture; extra effort devoted to scholastic matters often counts negatively, and is discouraged.

It is true, as suggested above, that some students may be partially "immunized" to this culture, either by the attention of adults who have singled them out for special attention, or by their own concentration upon career aims. Yet in most schools, such a move is almost completely isolating, for the student must cut himself off from the activities of his friends, and in effect remove himself from the pursuits which would make him "part of the crowd." It is not a move easily made, and certainly not one frequently made in the schools I have been studying.

The question, then, is the one posed earlier: Is the nonchalance of the adolescent culture toward scholastic matters something which must be accepted? Or, on the contrary, is it possible for the school itself, or the community, to modify these values in such a way that they will reinforce, rather than conflict with, educational goals? The first step in answering these questions is to analyze the source of the existing norms of the adolescent culture—to refuse to explain away these values by asserting that "teenagers are that way," and instead to inquire how the social demands and constraints to which adolescents are subject may help generate these norms.

Institutional Demands and Group Response

There is a class of institutions which are essentially composed of an administrative corps and a larger group of persons subject to such administration. Schools are one such institution, the teachers of course being the "administrative corps" and the students subject to their ministrations.

The armed services are another example, the officers and enlisted men composing the two groups. Many factories, which have a great number of workers doing roughly similar tasks under the authority of management, are institutions of this sort. Jails are perhaps the most extreme example, for in jails the constraints placed upon the inmates by the guards are maximal, and there is no period of escape from the demands of the institution.

To be sure, these institutions have many differences. The demands placed upon prisoners by the warden, or the demands placed upon workers by management, are very different from those placed on teenagers by the school. Yet the fact remains that the school is an institution designed by the adult society to transmit adult values and skills to children. To transmit these values and skills, the school makes demands upon its students.

In all such institutions, the administrative corps makes certain demands upon, and places certain constraints upon, those under them. In some institutions, the demands and constraints are great; in others they are less so. A kind of continuum could be conceived, with jails at the one extreme of maximal demands and constraints, with the army somewhere in the middle, and schools and factories located further from the maximal extreme (though differences among schools and differences among factories are so great that both can vary

almost from one extreme of the continuum to the other). The demands made by management upon workers are essentially that they work and produce, in return for which they receive pay. Similarly, in schools, the demands are that the students study and learn, in return for which they receive grades and are promoted.

The second characteristic of such institutions of importance to the present discussion is not part of the formal rules and regulations, and cannot be found in books of standard practice nor in the school principal's handbook of administration. Yet it is no less there. This is the collective response to the demands and constraints, the collective response made by the group upon which these demands and constraints are thrust. In jails, the codes and the norms to which the inmates hold each other, sharply divergent from the goals and aims of the prison, are well known. The fact that prisons do not rehabilitate, but largely confirm offenders in criminal ways, is almost solely attributable to the fact that each prisoner is subject to the society of the inmates, with its deviant norms and values, and cannot be reached by the professed goals of the prison.[4] A caveat must be entered at this point, however. Not *all* the prisoners adhere to the strong group values and norms of the body of prisoners; some isolates either go wholly their own way or go along with the administration.

The jail is an extreme case, of course.

[4] There are several interesting researches which show the values of the prisoners. A classic is Donald Clemmer's *The Prison Community* (Boston: Christopher, 1940). Richard Cloward, reporting upon intensive research in an army prison, shows well the norms which develop among prisoners in response to the demands of the prison. He shows also the different modes of response of different prisoners to the rehabilitative aims of the prison. This is reported in *Social Control and Anomie: A Study of a Prison Community* (to be published by The Free Press).

But it illustrates the kinds of processes which occur in other institutions. In factories, among groups of workers, the same process has been documented by much research.[5] Work groups develop norms about how much work is "appropriate," norms against working for employers who pay low rates, norms against taking the jobs of men protesting against an employer. The rules of unions against such practices are merely the formalization of these norms.

These norms are reinforced by all the means groups have at their disposal— ridicule, ostracism, loss of prestige, even physical violence. The "rate-buster" is only one of many epithets which serve to set apart the worker who refuses to reduce his pace to meet the norms.[6]

The defensiveness of these work groups of course varies quite radically from industry to industry and employer to employer. The organization of workers in response to employers' demands ranges from the most militant unions with their arsenal of defense weapons to nonunionized informal work groups which

[5] A classic study is F. J. Roethlisberger and W. J. Dickson, *Management and the Worker* (Cambridge: Harvard University Press, 1939). A recent study of a number of work groups gives considerable insight into the conditions which generate norms of defensiveness among workers. See Leonard R. Sayles, *Behavior of Industrial Work Groups: Prediction and Control* (New York: John Wiley and Sons, Inc., 1958).

[6] This is not to say that there are not sometimes pressures in the opposite direction— to work harder, faster. But these are pressures from the other workers as *individuals,* in the absence of group formation. Peter Blau shows this well in his *Dynamics of Bureaucracy* (Chicago: University of Chicago Press, 1955), in which he shows that one interviewing section in a welfare agency develops group norms which modify the demands upon them, while the other never develops such a group. Instead, each individual, in direct competition with the others, exerted a pressure for more and faster work.

have no dispute with their employer and use only the mildest means to constrain their over-eager fellows. It is true also, as in the jail, that despite the strength of these informal norms among workers, some workers isolate themselves from the group constraints and set their own pace.

The same process which occurs among prisoners in a jail and among workers in a factory is found among students in a school. The institution is different, but the demands are there, and the students develop a collective response to these demands. This response takes a similar form to that of workers in industry— holding down effort to a level which can be maintained by all. The students name for the rate-buster is the "curve-raiser" or the "D.A.R.—damned average raiser," and their methods of enforcing the work restricting norms are similar to those of workers—ridicule, kidding, exclusion from the group.

Again it is true that not all the students give in to this group pressure. In particular, scholastically-oriented subgroups can form in large schools and insulate their members against the larger group. It is true also that many students, preparing for college, may work intensely in preparation for a competitive examination for college entrance. Nevertheless, the results of the research discussed above suggest that for most students such intense efforts remain within the framework laid down by the group, interfering little with social activities, sports, or dates.

Looking generally now at this class of institutions, it is characterized by demands on the one hand, and group norms resisting these demands on the other. What is the source of the group norms? Are they purely a social irrationality, a means by which workers foolishly reduce their own pay, as the employer would argue, a means by which teenagers impede their own development, as teachers would insist? Hardly so.

Such norms seem quite rational, given

a goal of maximum rewards for minimum effort. If the employer sees what speed is possible, for one man at least he is likely to revise the work standards upward, or more informally to expect more work from the others. Thus the majority is protecting itself from extra work by constraining the fast minority. Since work rates are necessarily relative, and cannot be judged except in relation to the rates of other men, then one man's gain is another's loss. Consequently such norms, holding down the fastest men, act as a collective protection, to keep within reasonable bounds the effort each worker must expend on his job.

In a high school, the norms act to hold down the achievements of those who are above average, so that the school's demands will be at a level easily maintained by the majority. Grades are almost completely relative, in effect ranking students relative to others in their class. Thus extra achievement by one student not only raises his position, but in effect lowers the position of others.

Again the response of the group is purely rational. By holding down efforts and achievements of those who might excel, the general level of effort required to keep an average position is reduced. The group's effort can be seen as one of "combining to prevent excessive competition," and is precisely parallel to the trusts and combines of industries, which attempt by price-fixing and other means to prevent excessive competition. The structure of the situation is the same in both cases: the teacher (or the customer) is attempting to deal with each student (or manufacturer) independently, to obtain his best effort (or his lowest price). In response, the students (or manufacturers) combine, placing constraints on one another, so that the effort (or price) may be kept at a level which is comfortable for most members.[7]

[7] The way in which a modification in the structure of institutional demands and re-

The school creates, with its grading system, what an economist would call a "free-market" situation, with each student a competitor against all his classmates for scholastic position. This un-

wards creates a modification in the group response is well illustrated by the following comment. It was written by a colleague (Jan Hajda) who had attended a Czechoslovakian gymnasium, upon reading a draft of this paper.

In the European gymnasium system, both the institutional demands and the group response to them are different. First, the levels of achievement are set by impersonal standards established by the Ministry of Education or a comparable distant supervisory body. Consequently, the standards themselves cannot be manipulated by students nor, for that matter, by their teachers. Theoretically, all students in a given class can pass a course on the highest level or fail to pass. Ideally, the performance of students is judged individually in terms of the set standards and not in comparison with the performance of his peers. This fact tends to minimize—although it does not eliminate—interpersonal competition.

Nobody benefits from holding down effort to a lower level and consequently there is no reason for protecting the collectivity from superior achievement of a few students. The group solution is not in "price-fixing" but in establishing a holding operation which benefits all participants—institutionalized cheating. The informal group norms demand that the top students help the mediocre ones by letting them copy their assignments or by circulating correct answers to a written class examination while the examination is in progress. In a way, the top student is giving up his chance to outdistance others without lowering his own performance. In return, he gets not only recognition for his cooperative behavior but also for his scholastic performance. The better his own performance, the higher the survival chance of his peers.

Thus it is in the interest of the collectivity that there be at least a few outstanding achievers. The top students be-limited competition, to be sure, may operate without restraint in a few schools, and it is this "free-market" which has led some educators and laymen to attempt to reduce competition. In the large majority of schools, however, there is the collective protection, the defense against excessive effort by group norms which restrain efforts. The schools in which such norms do not exist are few indeed. My research included, as mentioned earlier, one elite suburban school from which 85 per cent of the graduates attended college; even in this school, good grades were certainly *not* an important means of prestige, and extra effort devoted to scholastic matters brought on the usual kidding or ridicule. And the example of the university high school in which a norm of "good grades without extra effort" exists amid one of the most achievement-oriented student bodies in the country suggests that the school's demands seldom fail to create such a response from the adolescent society.

The result of these norms produces in students a conflict of motivation: put very simply, to be one of the fellows and not work too hard in school, or to work hard in school and ignore the group. Different teenagers resolve this conflict in different ways. Whichever way it is resolved, it sets an artificial dilemma. On the one hand are sociable average students (who could do far better); on the other hand are a few academically-oriented, highly competitive isolates. A boy

or girl can be oriented to academic achievement *or* to being popular, but it is hard to be both. This is almost puzzling, because in certain activities (e.g., athletics), achievement generates popularity rather than scorn.

The question raised by this situation is whether such a conflict is necessary. Is it impossible to have the group's informal norms positively *reinforce* (or at least not conflict with) scholastic achievement? To answer this question it will be useful to go a roundabout way and to examine an experiment carried out by a social psychologist some years ago.

Deutsch's Experiment: "Competition vs. Cooperation"

Morton Deutsch carried out an experiment to show effects of a "competitive situation" and a "cooperative situation" upon achievement, cohesion, and other matters.[8] The experiment went roughly as follows: Classes in industrial psychology were given hypothetical human relations problems to discuss and solve. There were two different reward structures: (a) In some classes, each member was told that he and his four fellow students would each be ranked from 1 to 5 according to the contribution of each to the discussion and to the problem's solution. At the end of the semester, each student's grade was based upon the average of his ranks through the semester. (b) In five other classes, each class was told that it would be ranked as a class from 1 to 5 on the basis of its solution to the problems. At the end of the semester, the ranks of the five classes were averaged, and the members of each class graded according to their class's average rank. Thus in condition (a), each stu-

come symbols of collective security. In turn, academic achievement becomes highly desirable, since it represents the safest way to informal leadership and prestige. The exception to this rule arises only in case the top students refuse to cooperate in cheating, i.e., refuse to share the product of their labors with their peers. In such instances the high achiever is ostracized, ridiculed, and stereotyped as teacher's pet, and his peers do their best to prevent him from making the grade he is aiming for.

[8] Morton Deutsch, "The Effects of Cooperation and Competition upon Group Process," in D. Cartwright and A. Zander (eds.), *Group Dynamics* (Evanston: Row Peterson, 1953), pp. 319–353.

dent was being compared with his class-mates. In condition (b), each class was being compared with other classes.

Deutsch found several things, all favoring condition (b). He found that the solutions to the problems were better among the classes in condition (b); the class members impeded one another in the discussion under condition (a), but aided one another under condition (b); the feeling of class members toward one another was more positive under condition (b) than (a).

The structure of rewards under conditions (a) and (b) is simple to state: in condition (a), individuals were compared with others in the same group and rewarded relative to these others. This produced competition between individuals. In condition (b), groups were compared with other groups and rewarded relative to the other groups. This produced competition between groups. But although there was competition in both cases, the second kind of competition produced very different consequences from the first: in achievement, in the group members' feelings toward one another, in the unity of the group. So long as the group was competing against other groups, one man's achievement benefited, rather than lowered, the position of other members of his group; consequently, the group's response to his achievement was positive rather than negative.

When the competition was between individuals, the fact that one individual's achievement lowered the position of other group members generated *interference* with one person's efforts by other members, though the interference was perhaps unconscious and subtle. When the competition was between groups, there was *support* of one person's efforts by others in the group. In effect, then, Deutsch's experiment answers the question raised earlier: whether it is possible for the group's informal rewards to reinforce the formal rewards from the outside. When competition was no longer between individuals, but instead between groups, this reinforcement occurred.

An excellent example of the group's norms reinforcing achievement rather than inhibiting it may be found within the high school itself. Athletics is the activity. In high school athletics, there is no epithet comparable to curve-raiser, there is no ostracism for too-intense effort or for outstanding achievement. Quite to the contrary, the outstanding athlete is the "star," extra effort is applauded by one's fellows, and the informal group rewards are for positive achievement, rather than for restraint of effort.

Why the difference between athletics and studies? The athletic team is competing as a team against another school. Thus any achievement by one person benefits those around him—who in turn encourage his efforts, rather than discourage them. His efforts benefit the team, and fellow-team members encourage his efforts. They bring prestige to the school, and other students encourage and look up to him. His achievements give a lift to the community as a whole, and the community encourages his efforts. The basketball player or aspirant who shoots baskets at lunch period in school is watched with interest and admiration, not with derision. This is in direct opposition to achievement in the classroom, which does not benefit the school and puts one's fellows at a disadvantage. A boy or girl who studies at lunch period is regarded as someone a little odd, or different, or queer.

A passage from a recent novel about a high school illustrates the general process:

> In his home room Trent [a star halfback] received his schedule, made out for him while he was at football camp.
>
> "Are we going to have a good football team this year?" Miss Vereen asked, as she handed him his schedule slip.
>
> "Yes ma'am, I hope so."

"Well, that's fine. That's certainly fine." Miss Vereen knew nothing about football and probably had never seen a game, but anything which increased the stature of Harrison [High School], to which she was fanatically devoted, had her loyal support.[9]

When I write to one of the principals in the schools I am studying and want to say something good or congratulatory about his school, what can I comment on? Nothing scholastic, for his school has little or no opportunity to do anything *as a school* in scholastic directions. I can congratulate him on the basketball team's success, for this is an achievement of the school. When I talk to a class of students and want to compliment their school, the same conditions hold—I can only congratulate them on what the school has done *as a school,* which is ordinarily some athletic success in interscholastic competition. Only when I am talking to one student, alone, can I congratulate him on his excellent grades.

Such congratulations and support of activities of the school as a whole, multiplied many times from persons inside and outside the school, persons inside and outside the community, encourage a school to do more and better in directions which bring on such encouragement. Thus in spite of itself the school's energies are channeled into these directions—the directions which generate support for the school, which make others look up to the school, and give the school a pride in itself for its achievements.

One finding from the research discussed earlier is relevant here. The students' school spirit or feeling of identification with the school was indicated by answers to several questions in the questionnaire. It was highest in those schools which had winning athletic teams, and lowest in schools whose teams had not been successful for several years. But lowest of all was the university high school mentioned earlier, which had a minimal athletic program and discouraged any sort of interscholastic competition. In this school there was seldom an activity which the students could "get behind" as a body.

The peculiar power of interscholastic competition to generate encouragement and support for achievement lies in two directions. First, competition with other groups has a magic ability to create a strong group goal. While some group projects succeed without the added incentive of competition, others would hopelessly flounder if it were not for the chance of winning. This has been the fate of many well-intentioned and well-planned group projects in high schools—projects which have failed to capture the energies of the group.

Secondly, interscholastic competition generates support at levels which intergroup competition within the school can never reach. Until now, I have discussed the social support given by other "group members," with no further differentiation. But consider the difference between interscholastic competition, on the one hand, and competition between two teams into which a school class has been divided, on the other. In the latter case, there will be support and encouragement only from fellow team members. In the former case, there will be support first from other team members, then from other non-participating students, and finally from persons in the community. That is, if the school's winning gives the community pride in itself and its school, they will encourage its efforts; if the team's winning gives the student body pride in their school, they will encourage its efforts.[10]

[9] John Farris, *Harrison High* (New York: Rinehart, 1959), p. 5.

[10] To be sure, there are interscholastic games between schools which are ignored by student body and community alike; but this is less true than is usually realized when such games are given attention and encouragement by the school administration.

In other words, when competition is interscholastic, the social support and encouragement begins at the level of the school itself, thus permeating the whole social milieu surrounding the team members. When it is intramural, social support begins only at the level of the team, or the subgroup it represents, resulting in a much less supportive social environment for the team member.

An Alternative to Interpersonal Competition

The structure of competition in high schools—interpersonal competition in scholastic matters, interscholastic competition in athletics (and sometimes in music, and occasionally in a few fringe activities)—presents a curious picture. It undermines a student's efforts in scholastic directions (where he is working only for himself), and encourages his efforts in these other, tangential directions (where he is striving for team and school as well as himself). The interests of the adolescent community, emphasizing sports and ignoring studies, must be attributed in large part to this structure of competition—something for which adults, not adolescents, are wholly responsible.

One obvious solution is to substitute interscholastic (and intramural) competition in scholastic matters for the interpersonal competition for grades which presently exists. Such a substitution would require a revision of the notion that each student's achievement must be continually evaluated or "graded" in every subject. It would instead make such evaluations infrequent, and subsidiary to the group contests and games, both within the school and between schools.

Such a change from interpersonal to intergroup competition would also make it necessary to create, with considerable inventiveness, the vehicles for competition: intellectual games, problems, group and individual science projects, and other

activities. Yet there are some examples which show that it can be done: debate teams, group discussion tournaments, drama contests, music contests, science fairs (though science fairs as now conducted lack one crucial element, for they are ordinarily competitions between individuals, and not competitions between schools, thus lacking the group reinforcement which would go along with "winning for the school"). There are, in one place and another, math tournaments, speaking contests, and other examples of interscholastic competition.

In other places, one can find the bases from which to develop new kinds of scholastic competition. For example, at Rand Corporation sociologists have developed "political gaming," in which teams represent policy-makers in various countries. An international situation is set up, the policy-making teams respond to it and to one another's moves (under the supervision of referees), and a game is pursued in earnest. It is not too difficult to see how this, and modifications of it to include legislative politics, union-management bargaining, and other such situations, could be brought to the high school level and used in interscholastic competition. (Rand reports that an experiment in political gaming at MIT induced such interest among the student players and spectators that for weeks afterwards they avidly followed international news events, to see how their moves corresponded with actual policies as they developed.)

As another example, business executives are now being trained in a few companies by "management games," in which hypothetical situations are set up requiring teams of executives to make decisions and observe the consequences. Electronic computers provide the hypothetical situation and the economic environment, so that the executive in a sense is playing against the computer. With effort and ingenuity, such games could be adapted to training in high school, not only in business economics, but in other areas.

There are many examples in high schools which show something about the effects such competitions might have. As an example, one of the schools I have been studying is too small to compete effectively in most sports, but participates with vigor each year in the state music contests. It nearly always wins a high place in the statewide contest. The striking result of this successful competition is the high status of music among the adolescents themselves. It is a thing of pride to be a trombone soloist in this school, and the leading boys in the school are also leading musicians—not, as in many schools, scornful of such an unmanly activity. This is despite the fact that the school serves a largely farming community.

It is true that many of the examples mentioned above have had far less effect in bringing informal social rewards, encouragement, and respect to participants than the present analysis would suggest. The reason is clear, however: such social rewards from the student body as a whole are only forthcoming in response to something the individual or team has done for *them*, such as bringing glory to the school by winning over another school. If the activity, whether it be debate or math competition or basketball, receives no publicity, no recognition in the newspapers and by the community generally, then its winning will have brought little glory to the school, and will bring little encouragement to the participants. (For example, basketball games at the University of Chicago have for years played to crowds of ten or twenty students.)

For this reason, sporadic and infrequent cases of interscholastic competition in non-athletic activities, with no attention to promotional activity, have little effect. However, if there were systematically organized competitions, tournaments, and meets in all activities ranging from mathematics and English through home economics and industrial arts to basketball and football, and if promotional skills were used, the resulting public interest and student interest in these activities would undoubtedly increase sharply. Suppose such a set of activities culminated in a "scholastic fair," which like a state fair included the most diverse exhibits, projects, competitions, and tournaments, not between individuals, but between *schools*. I suspect that the impact upon student motivation would be remarkably great—an impact due to the fact that the informal social rewards from community and fellow-students would reinforce rather than conflict with achievement.

These are simply examples of what might be done to change the structure of rewards in high school—to shift from interpersonal competition, with its conflict-producing effects, to intergroup competition, in which group rewards reinforce achievement. More important than these examples, however, is the general principle—that motivations may be sharply altered by altering the structure of rewards, and more particularly that among adolescents, it is crucial to use the informal group rewards to reinforce the aims of education rather than to impede them.

It is important, of course, that unintended consequences be taken into account in changing the reward structure in the ways that have been suggested. For example, in devising interscholastic games of an intellectual sort, it is important that they do in fact teach the skills desired. A carelessly-designed program of interscholastic games might result in nothing more than a series of quiz shows, which exercise no other mental activities than those of recall. It is for this reason that the recently developed "political gaming" and "management games" which use electronic computers to simulate the market seem particularly interesting. Like debate, and unlike quiz shows, these games teach skills and impel the participants to learn how the economic, political, or other system operates.

Perhaps the most important problems in devising such games would be to insure a balanced system of rewards among the various activities and to insure a balanced participation among the various students. As many schools have found with extra-curricular activities, participation becomes narrowly confined to a few unless rules are set up to prevent such concentration. If interscholastic games were to replace the present within-school competition for grades, such rules to distribute participation would become even more important.

These problems indicate that such changes should be made with care. But the general point is clear: the present structure of rewards in high schools produces a response on the part of the adolescent social system which effectively impedes the process of education. Yet the structure of rewards could be so designed that the adolescent norms themselves would reinforce educational goals.

THE "COOLING-OUT" FUNCTION IN HIGHER EDUCATION [1]

by Burton R. Clark

A major problem of democratic society is inconsistency between encouragement to achieve and the realities of limited opportunity. Democracy asks individuals to act as if social mobility were universally possible; status is to be won by individual effort, and rewards are to accrue to those who try. But democratic societies also need selective training institutions, and hierarchical work organizations permit increasingly fewer persons to succeed at ascending levels. Situations of opportunity are also situations of denial and failure. Thus democratic societies need not only to motivate achievement but also to mollify those denied it in order to sustain motivation in the face of disappointment and to deflect resentment. In the modern mass democracy, with its large-scale organization, elaborated ideologies of equal access and participation, and minimal commitment to social origin

as a basis for status, the task becomes critical.

The problem of blocked opportunity has been approached sociologically through means-ends analysis. Merton and others have called attention to the phenomenon of dissociation between culturally instilled goals and institutionally provided means of realization; discrepancy between ends and means is seen as a basic social source of individual frustration and recalcitrance.[2] We shall here

[1] I am indebted to Erving Goffman and Martin A. Trow for criticism and to Sheldon Messinger for extended conceptual and editorial comment.

SOURCE: *American Journal of Sociology*, Vol. 65 (1956), pp. 569–576.

[2] "Aberrant behavior may be regarded sociologically as a symptom of dissociation between culturally prescribed aspirations and socially structured avenues for realizing these aspirations" (Robert K. Merton, "Social Structure and Anomie," in *Social Theory and Social Structure* [rev. ed.; Glencoe, Ill.: Free Press, 1957], p. 134). See also Herbert H. Hyman, "The Value Systems of Different Classes: A Social Psychological Contribution to the Analysis of Stratification," in Reinhard Bendix and Seymour M. Lipset (eds.), *Class, Status and Power: A Reader in Social Stratification* (Glencoe, Ill.: Free Press, 1953), pp. 426–442; and the papers by Robert Dubin, Richard A. Cloward, Robert K. Merton, and Dorothy L. Meier, and Wendell Bell, in *American Sociological Review*, Vol. XXIV (April, 1959).

extend means-ends analysis in another direction, to the responses of organized groups to means-ends disparities, in particular focusing attention on ameliorative processes that lessen the strains of dissociation. We shall do so by analyzing the most prevalent type of dissociation between aspirations and avenues in American education, specifying the structure and processes that reduce the stress of structural disparity and individual denial. Certain components of American higher education perform what may be called the cooling-out function,[3] and it is to these that attention will be drawn.

The Ends-Means Disjuncture

In American higher education the aspirations of the multitude are encouraged by "open-door" admission to public-supported colleges. The means of moving upward in status and of maintaining high status now include some years in college, and a college education is a prerequisite of the better positions in business and the professions. The trend is toward an ever tighter connection between higher education and higher occupations, as increased specialization and professionalization insure that more persons will need more preparation. The high-school graduate, seeing college as essential to success, will seek to enter some college, regardless of his record in high school.

A second and allied source of public interest in unlimited entry into college is the ideology of equal opportunity.[4]

Strictly interpreted, equality of opportunity means selection according to ability, without regard to extraneous considerations. Popularly interpreted, however, equal opportunity in obtaining a college education is widely taken to mean unlimited access to some form of college: in California, for example, state educational authorities maintain that high-school graduates who cannot qualify for the state university or state college should still have the "opportunity of attending a publicly supported institution of higher education," this being "an essential part of the state's goal of guaranteeing equal educational opportunities to all its citizens."[5] To deny access to college is then to deny equal opportunity. Higher education should make a seat available without judgment on past performance.

Many other features of current American life encourage college-going. School officials are reluctant to establish early critical hurdles for the young, as is done in Europe. With little enforced screening in the pre-college years, vocational choice and educational selection are postponed to the college years or later. In addition, the United States, a wealthy country, is readily supporting a large complex of colleges, and its expanding economy requires more specialists. Recently, a national concern that manpower be fully utilized has encouraged the extending of college training to more and different kinds of students. Going to college is also in some segments of society

[3] I am indebted to Erving Goffman's original statement of the cooling-out conception. See his "Cooling the Mark Out: Some Aspects of Adaptation to Failure," *Psychiatry*, XV (November, 1952), 451–463. Sheldon Messinger called the relevance of this concept to my attention.

[4] Seymour Martin Lipset and Reinhard Bendix, *Social Mobility in Industrial Society* (Berkeley: University of California Press, 1959), pp. 78–101.

[5] *A Study of the Need for Additional Centers of Public Higher Education in California* (Sacramento: California State Department of Education, 1957), p. 128. For somewhat similar interpretations by educators and laymen nationally see Francis J. Brown (ed.), *Approaching Equality of Opportunity in Higher Education* (Washington, D.C.: American Council on Education, 1955), and the President's Committee on Education beyond the High School, *Second Report to the President* (Washington, D.C.: Government Printing Office, 1957).

the thing to do; as a last resort, it is more attractive than the army or a job. Thus ethical and practical urges together encourage the high-school graduate to believe that college is both a necessity and a right; similarly, parents and elected officials incline toward legislation and admission practices that insure entry for large numbers; and educational authorities find the need and justification for easy admission.

Even where pressures have been decisive in widening admission policy, however, the system of higher education has continued to be shaped partly by other interests. The practices of public colleges are influenced by the academic personnel, the organizational requirements of colleges, and external pressures other than those behind the open door. Standards of performance and graduation are maintained. A commitment to standards is encouraged by a set of values in which the status of a college, as defined by academicians and a large body of educated laymen, is closely linked to the perceived quality of faculty, student body, and curriculum. The raising of standards is supported by the faculty's desire to work with promising students and to enjoy membership in an enterprise of reputed quality—college authorities find low standards and poor students a handicap in competing with other colleges for such resources as able faculty as well as for academic status. The wish is widespread that college education be of the highest quality for the preparation of leaders in public affairs, business, and the professions. In brief, the institutional means of the students' progress toward college graduation and subsequent goals are shaped in large part by a commitment to quality embodied in college staffs, traditions, and images.

The conflict between open-door admission and performance of high quality often means a wide discrepancy between the hopes of entering students and the means of their realization. Students who pursue ends for which a college education is required but who have little academic ability gain admission into colleges only to encounter standards of performance they cannot meet. As a result, while some students of low promise are successful, for large numbers failure is inevitable and *structured*. The denial is delayed, taking place within the college instead of at the edge of the system. It requires that many colleges handle the student who intends to complete college and has been allowed to become involved but whose destiny is to fail.

Responses to Disjuncture

What is done with the student whose destiny will normally be early termination? One answer is unequivocal dismissal. This "hard" response is found in the state university that bows to pressure for broad admission but then protects standards by heavy drop-out. In the first year it weeds out many of the incompetent, who may number a third or more of the entering class.[6] The response of the college is hard in that failure is clearly de-

[6] One national report showed that one out of eight entering students (12.5 per cent) in publicly controlled colleges does not remain beyond the first term or semester; one out of three (31 per cent) is out by the end of the first year; and about one out of two (46.6 per cent) leaves within the first two years. In state universities alone, about one out of four withdraws in the first year and 40 per cent in two years (Robert E. Iffert, *Retention and Withdrawal of College Students* [Washington, D.C.: Department of Health, Education, and Welfare, 1958]; pp 15–20). Students withdraw for many reasons, but scholastic aptitude is related to their staying power: "A sizeable number of students of medium ability enter college, but . . . few if any of them remain longer than two years" (*A Restudy of the Needs of California in Higher Education* [Sacramento: California State Department of Education, 1955], p. 120).

fined as such. Failure is public; the student often returns home. This abrupt change in status and in access to the means of achievement may occur simultaneously in a large college or university for hundreds, and sometimes thousands, of students after the first semester and at the end of the freshman year. The delayed denial is often viewed on the outside as heartless, a slaughter of the innocents.[7] This excites public pressure and anxiety, and apparently the practice cannot be extended indefinitely as the demand for admission to college increases.

A second answer is to sidetrack unpromising students rather than have them fail. This is the "soft" response: never to dismiss a student but to provide him with an alternative. One form of it in some state universities is the detour to an extension division or a general college, which has the advantage of appearing not very different from the main road. Sometimes "easy" fields of study, such as education, business administration, and social science, are used as alternatives to dismissal.[8] The major form of the soft response is not found in the four-year college or university, however, but in the college that specializes in handling students who will soon be leaving—typically, the two-year public junior college.

In most states where the two-year college is a part of higher education, the students likely to be caught in the means-ends disjuncture are assigned to it in large numbers. In California, where there are over sixty public two-year colleges in a diversified system that includes the state university and numerous four-year state colleges, the junior college is unselective in admissions and by law, custom, and self-conception accepts all who wish to enter.[9] It is tuition-free, local, and under local control. Most of its entering students want to try for the baccalaureate degree, transferring to a "senior" college after one or two years. About two-thirds of the students in the junior colleges of the state are in programs that permit transferring; but, of these, only about one-third actually transfer to a four-year college.[10] The remainder, or two out of three of the professed transfer students, are "latent terminal students": their announced intention and program of study entails four years of college, but in reality their work terminates in the junior college. Constituting about half of all the students in the California junior colleges, and somewhere between one-third and one-half of junior college students nationally,[11] these students cannot be ignored by the colleges. Understanding their careers is important to understanding modern higher education.

The Reorienting Process

This type of student in the junior college is handled by being moved out of a transfer major to a one- or two-year program of vocational, business, or semi-professional training. This calls for the relinquishing of his original intention, and

[7] Robert L. Kelly, *The American Colleges and the Social Order* (New York: Macmillan Co., 1940), pp. 220–21.

[8] One study has noted that on many campuses the business school serves "as a dumping ground for students who cannot make the grade in engineering or some branch of the liberal arts," this being a consequence of lower promotion standards than are found in most other branches of the university (Frank C. Pierson, *The Education of American Businessmen* [New York: McGraw-Hill Book Co., 1959], p. 63). Pierson also summarizes data on intelligence of students by field of study which indicate that education, business, and social science rank near the bottom in quality of students (*ibid.*, pp. 65–72).

[9] Burton R. Clark, *The Open Door College: A Case Study* (New York: McGraw-Hill Book Co., 1960), pp. 44–45.

[10] *Ibid.*, p. 116.

[11] Leland L. Medsker, *The Junior College: Progress and Prospect* (New York: McGraw-Hill Book Co., 1960), Ch. iv.

he is induced to accept a substitute that has lower status in both the college and society in general.

In one junior college [12] the initial move in a cooling-out process is pre-entrance testing: low scores on achievement tests lead poorly qualified students into remedial classes. Assignment to remedial work casts doubt and slows the student's movement into bona fide transfer courses. The remedial courses are, in effect, a subcollege. The student's achievement scores are made part of a counseling folder that will become increasingly significant to him. An objective record of ability and performance begins to accumulate.

A second step is a counseling interview before the beginning of the first semester, and before all subsequent semesters for returning students. "At this interview the counselor assists the student to choose the proper courses in light of his objective, his test scores, the high school record and test records from his previous schools." [13] Assistance in choosing "the proper courses" is gentle at first. Of the common case of the student who wants to be an engineer but who is not a promising candidate, a counselor said: "I never openly countermand his choice, but edge him toward a terminal program by gradually laying out the facts of life." Counselors may become more severe later when grades provide a talking point and when the student knows that he is in trouble. In the earlier counseling the desire of the student has much weight; the counselor limits himself to giving advice and stating the probability of success. The advice is entered in the counseling record that shadows the student.

A third and major step in reorienting

the latent terminal student is a special course entitled "Orientation to College," mandatory for entering students. All sections of it are taught by teacher-counselors who comprise the counseling staff, and one of its purposes is "to assist students in evaluating their own abilities, interests, and aptitudes; in assaying their vocational choices in light of this evaluation; and in making educational plans to implement their choices." A major section of it takes up vocational planning: vocational tests are given at a time when opportunities and requirements in various fields of work are discussed. The tests include the "Lee Thorpe Interest Inventory" (given to all students for motivating a self-appraisal of vocational choice") and the "Strong Interest Inventory" ("for all who are undecided about choice or who show disparity between accomplishment and vocational choice"). Mechanical and clerical aptitude tests are taken by all. The aptitudes are directly related to the college's terminal programs, with special tests, such as a pre-engineering ability test, being given according to need. Then an "occupational paper is required of all students for their chosen occupation"; in it the student writes on the required training and education and makes a "self-appraisal of fitness."

Tests and papers are then used in class discussion and counseling interviews, in which the students themselves arrange and work with a counselor's folder and a student test profile and, in so doing, are repeatedly confronted by the accumulating evidence—the test scores, course grades, recommendations of teachers and counselors. This procedure is intended to heighten self-awareness of capacity in relation to choice and hence to strike particularly at the latent terminal student. The teacher-counselors are urged constantly to "be alert to the problem of unrealistic vocational goals" and to "help students to accept their limitations and strive for success in other worthwhile objectives that are within their grasp."

[12] San Jose City College, San Jose, Calif. For the larger study see Clark, *op. cit.*

[13] San Jose Junior College, Handbook for Counselors, 1957–58, p. 2. Statements in quotation marks in the next few paragraphs are cited from this.

The orientation class was considered a good place "to talk tough," to explain in an *impersonal* way the facts of life for the overambitious student. Talking tough to a whole group is part of a soft treatment of the individual.

Following the vocational counseling, the orientation course turns to "building an educational program," to study of the requirements for graduation of the college in transfer and terminal curriculum, and to planning of a four-semester program. The students also become acquainted with the requirements of the colleges to which they hope to transfer, here contemplating additional hurdles such as the entrance examinations of other colleges. Again, the hard facts of the road ahead are brought to bear on self-appraisal.

If he wishes, the latent terminal student may ignore the counselor's advice and the test scores. While in the counseling class, he is also in other courses, and he can wait to see what happens. Adverse counseling advice and poor test scores may not shut off his hope of completing college; when this is the case, the deterrent will be encountered in the regular classes. Here the student is divested of expectations, lingering from high school, that he will automatically pass and, hopefully, automatically be transferred. Then, receiving low grades, he is thrown back into the counseling orbit, a fourth step in his reorientation and a move justified by his actual accomplishment. The following indicates the nature of the referral system:

Need for Improvement Notices are issued by instructors to students who are doing unsatisfactory work. The carbon copy of the notice is given to the counselor who will be available for conference with the student. The responsibility lies with the student to see his counselor. However, experience shows that some counselees are unable to be sufficiently self-directive to seek aid. The counselor should, in such cases, send for the student, using the Request for Conference blank. If the student fails to respond to the Request for Conference slip, this may become a disciplinary matter and should be referred to the deans.

After a conference has been held, the Need for Improvement notices are filed in the student's folder. *This may be important* in case of a complaint concerning the fairness of a final grade.[14]

This directs the student to more advice and self-assessment, as soon and as often as he has classroom difficulty. The carbon-copy routine makes it certain that, if he does not seek advice, advice will seek him. The paper work and bureaucratic procedure have the purpose of recording referral and advice in black and white, where they may later be appealed to impersonally. As put in an unpublished report of the college, the overaspiring student and the one who seems to be in the wrong program require "skillful and delicate handling. An accumulation of pertinent factual information may serve to fortify the objectivity of the student-counselor relationship." While the counselor advises delicately and patiently, but persistently, the student is confronted with the record with increasing frequency.

A fifth step, one necessary for many in the throes of discouragement, is probation: "Students [whose] grade point averages fall below 2.0 [C] in any semester will, upon recommendation by the Scholarship Committee, be placed on probationary standing." A second failure places the student on second probation, and a third may mean that he will be advised to withdraw from the college altogether. The procedure is not designed to rid the college of a large number of students, for they may continue on probation for three consecutive semesters; its purpose is not to provide a status halfway out of the college but to "assist

[14] *Ibid.*, p. 20.

the student to seek an objective (major field) at a level on which he can succeed." [15] An important effect of probation is its slow killing-off of the lingering hopes of the most stubborn latent terminal students. A "transfer student" must have a C average to receive the Associate in Arts (a two-year degree) offered by the junior college, but no minimum average is set for terminal students. More important, four-year colleges require a C average or higher for the transfer student. Thus probationary status is the final blow to hopes of transferring and, indeed, even to graduating from the junior college under a transfer-student label. The point is reached where the student must permit himself to be reclassified or else drop out. In this college, 30 per cent of the students enrolled at the end of the spring semester, 1955–56, who returned the following fall were on probation; three out of four of these were transfer students in name.[16]

This sequence of procedures is a specific process of cooling-out; [17] its effect, at the best, is to let down hopes gently and unexplosively. Through it students who are failing or barely passing find their occupational and academic future

[15] Statement taken from unpublished material.

[16] San Jose Junior College, "Digest of Analysis of the Records of 468 Students Placed on Probation for the Fall Semester, 1956," September 3, 1956.

[17] Goffman's original statement of the concept of cooling-out referred to how the disappointing of expectations is handled by the disappointed person and especially by those responsible for the disappointment. Although his main illustration was the confidence game, where facts and potential achievement are deliberately misrepresented to the "mark" (the victim) by operators of the game, Goffman also applied the concept to failure in which those responsible act in good faith (op. cit., passim). "Cooling-out" is a widely useful idea when used to refer to a function that may vary in deliberateness.

being redefined. Along the way, teacher-counselors urge the latent terminal student to give up his plan of transferring and stand ready to console him in accepting a terminal curriculum. The drawn-out denial when it is effective is in place of a personal, hard "No"; instead, the student is brought to realize, finally, that it is best to ease himself out of the competition to transfer.

Cooling-out Features

In the cooling-out process in the junior college are several features which are likely to be found in other settings where failure or denial is the effect of a structured discrepancy between ends and means, the responsible operatives or "coolers" cannot leave the scene or hide their identities, and the disappointment is threatening in some way to those responsible for it. At work and in training institutions this is common. The features are:

1. *Alternative achievement.*—Substitute avenues may be made to appear not too different from what is given up, particularly as to status. The person destined to be denied or who fails is invited to interpret the second effort as more appropriate to his particular talent and is made to see that it will be the less frustrating. Here one does not fail but rectifies a mistake. The substitute status reflects less unfavorably on personal capacity than does being dismissed and forced to leave the scene. The terminal student in the junior college may appear not very different from the transfer student—an "engineering aide," for example, instead of an "engineer"—and to be proceeding to something with a status of its own. Failure in college can be treated as if it did not happen; so, too, can poor performance in industry.[18]

[18] *Ibid.*, p. 457; cf. Perrin Stryker, "How To Fire an Executive," *Fortune*, L (October, 1954), 116–117 and 178–192.

2. *Gradual disengagement.*—By a gradual series of steps, movement to a goal may be stalled, self-assessment encouraged, and evidence produced of performance. This leads toward the available alternatives at little cost. It also keeps the person in a counseling milieu in which advice is furnished, whether actively sought or not. Compared with the original hopes, however, it is a deteriorating situation. If the individual does not give up peacefully, he will be in trouble.

3. *Objective denial.*—Reorientation is, finally, confrontation by the facts. A record of poor performance helps to detach the organization and its agents from the emotional aspects of the cooling-out work. In a sense, the overaspiring student in the junior college confronts himself, as he lives with the accumulating evidence, instead of the organization. The college offers opportunity; it is the record that forces denial. Record-keeping and other bureaucratic procedures appeal to universal criteria and reduce the influence of personal ties, and the personnel are thereby protected. Modern personnel record-keeping, in general, has the function of documenting denial.

4. *Agents of consolation.*—Counselors are available who are patient with the overambitious and who work to change their intentions. They believe in the value of the alternative careers, though of lower social status, and are practiced in consoling. In college and in other settings counseling is to reduce aspiration as well as to define and to help fulfil it. The teacher-counselor in the "soft" junior college is in contrast to the scholar in the "hard" college who simply gives a low grade to the failing student.

5. *Avoidance of standards.*—A cooling-out process avoids appealing to standards that are ambiguous to begin with. While a "hard" attitude toward failure generally allows a single set of criteria, a "soft" treatment assumes that many kinds of ability are valuable, each in its place. Proper classification and placement are then paramount, while standards become relative.

Importance of Concealment

For an organization and its agents one dilemma of a cooling-out role is that it must be kept reasonably away from public scrutiny and not clearly perceived or understood by prospective clientele. Should it become obvious, the organization's ability to perform it would be impaired. If high-school seniors and their families were to define the junior college as a place which diverts college-bound students, a probable consequence would be a turning-away from the junior college and increased pressure for admission to the four-year colleges and universities that are otherwise protected to some degree. This would, of course, render superfluous the part now played by the junior college in the division of labor among colleges.

The cooling-out function of the junior college is kept hidden, for one thing, as other functions are highlighted. The junior college stresses "the transfer function," "the terminal function," etc., not that of transforming transfer into terminal students; indeed, it is widely identified as principally a transfer station. The other side of cooling-out is the successful performance in junior college of students who did poorly in high school or who have overcome socioeconomic handicaps, for they are drawn into higher education rather than taken out of it. Advocates of the junior college point to this salvaging of talented manpower, otherwise lost to the community and nation. It is indeed a function of the open door to let hidden talent be uncovered.

Then, too, cooling-out itself is reinterpreted so as to appeal widely. The junior college may be viewed as a place where all high-school graduates have the opportunity to explore possible careers and find the type of education appropriate to their individual ability; in short, as a place where everyone is admitted and everyone succeeds. As described by the former president of the University of California:

> A prime virtue of the junior college, I think, is that most of its students succeed in what they set out to accomplish, and cross the finish line before they grow weary of the race. After two years in a course that they have chosen, they can go out prepared for activities that satisfy them, instead of being branded as failures. Thus the broadest possible opportunity may be provided for the largest number to make an honest try at further education with some possibility of success and with no route to a desired goal completely barred to them.[19]

[19] Robert Gordon Sproul, "Many Millions More," *Educational Record*, XXXIX (April, 1958), 102.

The students themselves help to keep this function concealed by wishful unawareness. Those who cannot enter other colleges but still hope to complete four years will be motivated at first not to admit the cooling-out process to consciousness. Once exposed to it, they again will be led not to acknowledge it, and so they are saved insult to their self-image.

In summary, the cooling-out process in higher education is one whereby systematic discrepancy between aspiration and avenue is covered over and stress for the individual and the system is minimized. The provision of readily available alternative achievements in itself is an important device for alleviating the stress consequent on failure and so preventing anomic and deviant behavior. The general result of cooling-out processes is that society can continue to encourage maximum effort without major disturbance from unfulfilled promises and expectations.

D · PEER GROUPS AND PERSONALITY

SPORTS AND SOCIALIZATION

by R. Helanko

Introduction

In Scandinavia as well as in other countries of Western culture sports are today the most favoured leisure-time activity of youth. In the course of slightly more than one generation sports have become what may be called the greatest world movement of our time, the development and gradual organization of which can be easily traced historically. History has, however, been unable to offer an adequate explanation for the actual origin of sports. The old theory, connected with the name of Gulick (4), according to which sports have been elaborated out of the athletic games of our forefathers, who, in their struggle for existence, had to exercise their fighting capacity up to the point of utmost effectivity, has proved to be biologically as well as sociologically untenable. Deviating from this still fairly prevalent opinion I have endeavoured to show that sports, nowadays as well as in earlier times, are developed as part of a process of socialization. To express it more freely: if sports could suddenly be blotted out from the world and from people's consciousness, they would soon be born again and would perhaps even be recreated in the same forms as now, provided that the

SOURCE: *Acta Sociologica,* Vol. 2 (1957), pp. 229–240.

process of socialization and its influencing factors remained the same.

On undertaking to study the emergence and the development of sports the first step is to determine the criteria of sports. Searching for these it is immediately apparent that, descriptively seen, sports do not in any substantial degree differ from the type of activity displayed in children's games. As the child grows up, playing is gradually replaced by more strenuous sports and athletics. During this development the principal change occurs more in the attitudes of the individual than in the activity itself. Sports may be play as long as the person who engages in it takes a playing attitude towards them.

Bodily exercise and competition are the main elements in sports. The former has its roots in the individual's natural need for exercise, which he strives to satisfy within the possibilities provided by his physical make-up. Competition again is of a sociological origin, since the need for competition can arise only in a community. These needs are not particularly closely inter-related. Therefore, the nature of sports changes as one or the other of these needs becomes predominant. Because of this, different age-groups have different sporting habits. The athletic element is emphasized in sports when undertaken chiefly for the sake of physical exercise; the mainspring of competitive sports is, of course, competition. In group games, such as football, co-operation is an important additional factor.

If the element of bodily exercise is regarded as the main criterion of sports, then a definite turning-point between play and sports cannot be found in the life-history of the individual. If, on the other hand, the competitive attitude is chosen as a criterion, then the turning-point will be easy to find.

It has been shown that in all of the Scandinavian countries interest in sports continues to grow up to the age of 22–24 years after which it begins to decline. Similarly, it has been shown that joining in athletic organisations usually takes place before the age of 19. Accordingly, in searching for the origin of sports the investigation should be focused mainly on these young age-groups. In the following study the period of socialization will, to begin with, be divided into three phases, each of which will then be dealt with separately. They are: 1) the period preceding the gang age (0–8 years), 2) the gang age (9–16 years), and 3) the period following the gang age (17–24 years).

The Period Preceding the Gang Age

There are many different opinions as to the age when competitive tendencies begin to emerge in an individual. Depending largely on the methods of study used, and also on their definitions of the term competition, students of human development have pointed to various ages ranging from the first to the seventh year of an individual's life. Among these studies, only those by Piaget (8), dealing with the age when playing with marbles is learned, will be mentioned here. Piaget differentiates between four phases in the development of the child's behaviour in the game, and three phases with regard to his conception of the rules

of the game at different ages. The following table (p. 240) gives a survey of these phases. In order to facilitate comparison I have attached to the table a summary of the periods of development which I have found in the socialization process of boys. The most noteworthy point in this table is that group-formation and group-behaviour on the one hand, and playing marbles on the other hand, seem to call for the same mental and social qualifications in the participant. Thus, the ability to take part in group-behaviour may be seen as a kind of game, which has to be played according to certain rules. Among others Furfey (3) has observed that there exists a certain degree of dependence between the development of some generally known games and that of puberty (= socialization).

According to Piaget, competitive tendencies do not enter into the game of marbles until the age of 7–8 years, viz. at the age when co-operation begins to emerge. This is also the stage of life when primitive sports activities together with equally primitive group activities begin to appear, activities in which we can still observe traits of infantile egocentricity side by side with the co-operative characteristics of the gang-age. This is particularly evident when 7–8-year-old boys "play" football. The entire activity is characterized more by self-centered "kicking" of the ball than by actual "playing" for the sake of the team. Gulick (4), who is an expert on ball-games, has pointed out that the boys have an important lesson to learn: that there is something which is greater than the individual. This they have to learn from experience and if they have not grasped it earlier they will learn it when they begin to take part in group-games.

The Gang Age

The gang age (9–16 years) is a crucial phase in the process of socialization.

STAGES IN LEARNING HOW TO PLAY
MARBLES, ACCORDING TO PIAGET

AGE (YEARS)	PRACTICE OF RULES	CONSCIOUSNESS OF RULES	STAGES IN THE PROCESS OF SOCIALIZATION AMONG BOYS, ACCORDING TO THE AUTHOR
1	Stage I	Stage I	Yard-aggregation-stage
2	Motor behavior of an individualistic	No comprehension of rules	Egocentricity
			Primitive pairs appear
3	nature		No actual groups are formed
			No sports
4			
5	Stage II Egocentricity		
6			
7		Stage II	Play-gang stage
		Rules are regarded	Primitive groups are formed
8		as "sacred" and	Weak solidarity
	Stage III	absolute	Primitive sports
9	Co-operation		
			First period of gang age
10			Solid groups
			Strong in-group feeling
11			Centripetal interaction
			Clubs are formed within the gang
12		Stage III	Sports (ball-games) appear
	Stage IV	Rules are regarded	
	Codification of rules	as relative	Second period of gang age. At the
13			outset of this period solid groups still appear
14			At the termination of this stage interaction becomes centrifugal
15			Gangs and gang-clubs begin to dissolve
16	Termination of interest in marbles		Interest in sports continues, but becomes more individualistic
17			The gang age terminates
18			Individuals who have left their gangs form pairs which aggregate

During it the boys learn how to behave in primary groups in the company of their equals. In this study only boys' gangs can be dealt with, as the corresponding phase among girls has not yet been enough investigated.

A gang is always formed as an aggregation of *neighbourhood boys*. The first motives to gang-formation are usually provided by the yard-aggregates of small children. The gang age is clearly divisible into two sub-periods (5).

The first gang period (9–12 years, child-hood type of gang, Fig. 1) is characterised by introversive interaction, i.e. the boys find their interests exclusively within the closed circle of their own gang. This in-group force leads to the growth of a firm organisation, which is manifested in the formation of gang clubs and in a re-pellent attitude towards other neigh-bourhood gangs. The gangs of the first period usually consist of 6–7 boys.

Simultaneously with the beginning of the gang age a strong interest in sports awakens in the boys. About 90 % of the boys' gangs in Turku went in almost ex-clusively for sports, mainly ball-games (football, Tables 1 and 2).

According to Puffer (10), Furfey (2) and Thrasher (13) American gangs play ball games just as eagerly, although the game itself usually is baseball and not football.

TABLE 1. *Development of interest in gang and sports activities during the gang age among boys in the town of Turku*

AGE (YEARS)	9	10	11	12	13	14	15	16	17–20
Gang activity %	66	74	79	81	72	66	53	52	33
Sports activity %	66	70	74	83	79	78	72	78	57

The second gang period (adolescent type of gang, 12–16 years) is the time when interaction changes and becomes extroversive. This in its turn leads to a weakening of interaction within the gang itself. As a consequence, the organisation and the inner cohesion of the gang gradually weaken, gang clubs are dis-solved and older boys begin to withdraw from the gang. When the trend of inter-action is outward-going the gangs come into closer contact with each other than earlier, and the result is often that they merge and, thus, grow.

Sports are born in the gang. Accord-ingly, sports are originated at the stage of socialization at which the individual first learns the art of living in a group, when young boys are intensely interested in forming groups and when they have learned to comprehend rules as norm-systems of a relative nature. Learning to co-operate, which is closely connected with the factors mentioned above, has also been a necessary qualification for the development of sports and the forma-tion of the attitudes towards them.

The interests and activities of gang-

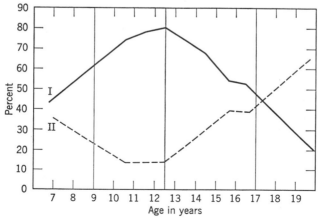

Fig. 1. I—*Graph showing membership in boys' gangs.* II—*Graph showing companionship of one friend only.*

agers can also be seen as answers to certain needs. From the data given in Table 1 it seems reasonable to assume that the predominant needs of the gang-ager are: (1) the need to satisfy his gregarious wishes, which leads to gang-formation (2) the need for exercise, which leads to sports. Group games, particularly football (which forms the main activity of boys' gangs in Turku) may be regarded as a common function of these two needs.

sports further the growing extrovertive tendencies in the gang. One of the consequences of this is that during the second gang period, if not earlier, different boys' gangs come into contact with each other which in turn often gives rise to secondary groups.

Since the boys' gangs gather for the purpose of sports, it follows that the norms of the gang coincide with the norms concerning sports. The nature as

TABLE 2. *The part played by sports (ball games) in the activities of boys' gangs in the town of Turku* *

Mean age (years) of the four oldest boys in the gang	Below 9	9	10	11	12	13	14	15	16	17–20
Number of gangs with sports as their main activity %	62	75	91	91	96	91	93	92	88	80

* The *n* values and methods of calculation are explained in *Helanko* (5) pp. 34, 84, 88.

As a matter of fact, the boys' gangs and sports are two different aspects of the same phenomenon. Sports are essentially the dynamics of the gang, a form of primitive group activity brought to perfection. The social mechanism of the gang is kept continuously at work by sports. Thus, it is as justifiable to speak of the birth of sports as of gang-formation. Accordingly, the sociology of the gang is an inseparable part of the sociology of sports. And the system found in sports must consequently be the same as the system of the gang. If the basic elements of the gang are interaction, control and a system of values and norms, then the same basic elements must also be found in sports. Thus, sports must be seen as a basically sociological phenomenon.

When a boy joins a gang he automatically comes within the influence of sports. The widening of the field of interaction, which takes place as the gang develops, is closely related to sports, since

well as the rules of sports are such that it is difficult to imagine them as having been created anywhere else except in a primary group such as the boys' gang. This provides a reasonable explanation of the fact that as far as the greater part of sports rules are concerned, there exist no written data documenting the earliest stages of development.

In the boys gang, as in other groups, the main activity around which the group is organised provides the means of defining the status of its members. When sports form the main activity of the gang, then the boy's status in the gang is usually determined by his skill in sports. This again is generally dependent on the boy's age, with the result that the status-rank of the boys usually coincides with their age-rank. Sports serve two functions in the gang: they are a source of pleasure and a means of status definition. Prizes are in such circumstances unnecessary. Sports and the gang together constitute the social milieu in which, for the first time in his life, the boy is called upon to create a social position for himself among his equals.

Control was mentioned above as a basic factor in the group. There can be no doubts about the effectual power of the control exercised by the gang, one need only listen to the noise produced by a gang playing football.

One may say that the boys' gang keeps on "producing sports" and that the sports movement of today is founded on and dependent upon this production. Naturally, the organised sports movement throws its reflection back upon the world of the gang-agers and influences in its turn his choice of sports. Thus, a mutual interrelationship, one might say a feed-back mechanism, is established between organised sports and the primitive form of sports engaged in by the boys' gangs. The sports movement will exist as long as this feed-back continues. The aim of the following chapter will be to elucidate how the primitive sports of boys' gangs develop their secondary characteristics.

The Period Following the Gang Age

Some boys begin to withdraw from gang life as early as at the age of 12–13 years, but in most cases the withdrawal takes place later, when the boys have attained the age of 14–16 years (Fig. 1). At this time their interest in sports diminishes although it still remains (in any case in the Scandinavian countries) the most favoured leisure-time activity of adult youth. It has been established that in Sweden (Skellefteå) 29% of all persons between the ages of 15 and 20 belong to sports clubs. The corresponding percentages for the age-groups 21–25 and 26–35 years are 34% and 37% (12).

Post-gang-age sports are, however, exercised in an environment totally different to that of the boys' gang. This in itself is likely to bring about a change in the sports activities. Now a more individual aspect enters into sports.

The young man, who has become estranged from his own gang, is now journeying across the no man's land that separates the world of the adult from that of the child. At this very stage these "vagabonds" probably have all the characteristics of marginal men; they are dissatisfied, embittered and always ready to revolt against the grown-ups. Although they are still at the age when "man is beloved by the gods," that is to say when they combine in themselves the open mind and attitudes of the child with the strength of the young adult, they feel that they are not allowed to put this enviable combination of powers into free use in society.

AGGREGATION. It can easily be shown that the pair is a typical social pattern during the period following the gang age (Fig. 1). These pairs—the partner being of either the same or the opposite sex— ramble over the social field in the manner of floating molecules. It is pertinent to ask, first, whether there is any regularity or pattern to be discerned in these ramblings and, secondly, whether there exists during the phase between the termination of the gang age and the beginning of the marriageable age, i. e., during the age-period 16–24 years, any group-forming tendency which is characteristic of this very age-group.

One can certainly not point to any group-formation which would be as clearly defined as during gang age, but the pairs do show an obvious tendency to aggregate (Fig. 2). This phenomenon can be noticed in all population centres. In rural areas aggregation takes place on the outdoor dance-floor of the village, in youth clubs, at the village swing, at a suitable crossroads, on a bridge or at some other central place. In towns young people gather in the same way in dance-halls, restaurants, cinemas, sports fields, certain streets or squares; and everywhere various kinds of business enterprises take advantage of this phenomenon.

It has also been shown that aggregation was typical of adult youth already in ancient times. This is indicated in, for instance, Unsener's, Hoffmann-Krayer's and Erixon's descriptions of customs among young people in ancient Scandinavia and Central Europe. It seems probable that some well-known historical events may be explained as natural consequences of the tendency among young peoples to aggregate. As such may be mentioned the gymnasiums of the ancient Greek cities, which grew to play an important part in Greek civilization, although on the other hand they also developed into hotbeds of vice.

Aggregation is a common phenomenon among modern as well as ancient nations and is to be found also among non-European civilized nations. Schurtz's study "Altersklassen und Männerbünde," published as early as 1912, gives ample proof for this. According to him it is customary among young, unmarried men to gather together in temporarily constructed sheds, under roofings, around bonfires and in other traditional and suitable gathering-places in order to be in each other's company. In many in-

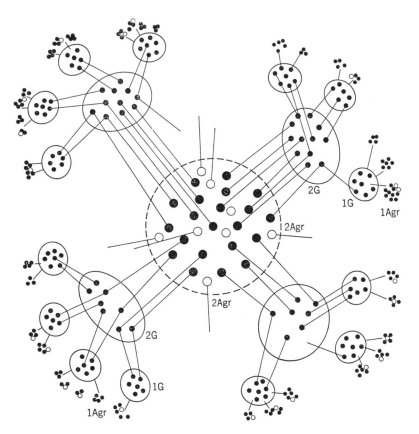

Fig. 2. Graphic representation of the formation of an aggregate of adult youth in the town of Turku. 1 Agr: yard aggregates of small children. 1 G: gang of 9–12 year old children (gang of the first period). 2 G: gang of 12–16 year old boys (gang of the second period). 2 Agr: aggregate of adult youth during the post-gang-age period. Black dots indicate boys, circles girls.

stances this habit has developed into a system according to which young men, after having reached maturity move away from their families and go and live together in the so called men's houses. Schurtz holds that among some tribes or nations the men's house has given rise to various institutions.

The termination of the gang age and the following aggregation show that the needs of the individual have undergone a change during this period. The predominant needs during this phase of socialization seem to be (1) finding a partner of the opposite sex and (2) reaching a social position. These needs colour the behaviour of adult youth and aim at the elimination of its marginal tendencies. Studies of young people's behaviour in different countries have shown that dancing and sports are their most favoured leisure-time activities. This is certainly due to the fact that these activities are most apt to satisfy the above-mentioned needs. As concurrent results of the process of socialization dancing and sports exhibit a certain affinity and a degree of mutual dependence. Both are ancient as young people's pastimes, and they may in aggregates develop in a "positive" as well as a "negative" direction. Negative effects closely connected with dancing are sexual dissipation, "night-prowling" and other unfavourable sides of free love. Likewise, fighting, more especially the so-called village fights, may be seen as a brutalized parallel phenomenon of sports.

ORGANIZATION OF THE AGGREGATE. Between the individuals belonging to an aggregate of young people interaction is soon developed and the aggregates are changed into groups. This process of transformation will in this study be called the organization of the aggregate. The manner in which this organization is effected depends on the current needs of the young people concerned. In their most primitive and typical form groups composed of aggregates have a weak degree of cohesion and they are often difficult to detect, as their members may in the intervals between aggregation be scattered over a wide geographical area. They are characteristically intermediary or secondary groups. To use an expression created by Tönnies (14) these groups, as well as the boys' gangs, are essentially *Gemeinschaften*, that is to say spontaneous social formations.

As these groups become organised they may turn into clubs or associations. This indicates that a common purpose, either recognised or subconscious, has become crystallized within the group. The leaders of the group play an important part with regard to this. According to Tönnies groups of this kind are *Gesellschaften*. If aggregates of adult youth organize themselves around a common belief or for the same purpose over a wide area it is justifiable to speak of a popular movement. I shall now examine two examples of such popular movements, the youth club movement and the sports movement, which have both during recent times been of considerable importance for Finnish youth.

There exists a very good history of the youth club movement (7) which shows that this movement has its origins in precisely the above described aggregates of adult youth. It goes without saying that groups composed of such aggregates existed already before the youth clubs came into being; such groups were well known in every village and town throughout the country. They had made themselves noticed through village fights, dances, "night-prowling" and other usually discreditable forms of behaviour through which young people attempted to satisfy their needs. It was no coincidence that the first youth club was formed at Kauhava on Midsummer day, which is known as the most favoured aggregation day of young people. The ideological basis of the youth club movement—which was not formulated until ten years after the first meeting had been held—could be *sociologically* defined as follows: the aim of the youth clubs is to further the need for aggregation, which is a characteristic of young people, by supplying them with suitable meetingplaces (houses) and by arranging such entertainment for them which will satisfy their current needs. All other activity within the youth clubs has been sociologically speaking of secondary importance.

As the sports movement grew, the youth club movement lost ground. To begin with in hundreds of youth clubs sports sections were formed and gradually became independent clubs. This did not change the process of socialization itself, since the secondary groups of adult youth now continued their existence within the frame-work provided by organized sports. In addition to furnishing opportunities for aggregation in the athletic clubs, organized sports provided a definite system through which a young man could rise to the position of the best sportsman not only in his own village but in the whole world as well. Could a young man wish for a better means of improving his status?

A study of how sports clubs were originated will shed light on the process of socialization. With this in view I have studied the origins of athletic clubs in the town of Turku. The 41 registered athletic associations in Turku may be divided into local ones, which are restricted to relatively small but natural suburban areas, and regional associations, that have members in all parts of the town. There are 15 of the former and 26 of the later type. I have been able to show that all local clubs have been formed by aggregates of adult youth and that the origins of the greater part of them can be traced all the way back to the numerous boys' gangs in the area. The birth process of an athletic club is graphically in Fig. 2. The aggregation has always taken place at the centre of the area, where a Workers' Hall or Temperance Hall or other gathering place could

be found. The two most important athletic associations in Turku were originated in this way and only later did they grow into great associations comprising the whole town. On the other hand, specialized clubs such as boxing, cycling or fencing clubs etc., have in most cases been formed by separating from some general field and track association or from some older specialized athletic clubs. A small group, going in for some special form for sports, has separated from the "mother-association" and then, finally, founded an independent club.

About half of all the members of athletic associations in Turku do not actually practise sports or take part in competitions and only one fourth of the total number of members did, when interviewed, mention sports as their main interest. If the chief function of the athletic associations is measured in terms of these facts, then it becomes clear that it does not consist merely in the furthering of sports, but also in providing an aggregation-centre for young people. An orthodox sports leader might by this statement be inspired to purge his association of this secondary phenomenon, whereby he would unwittingly do a great disservice to his club, because sports are necessarily closely connected with the above-mentioned phenomenon of aggregation. Sports always appear where youth aggregates. Primitive sports first flourished in aggregates of young people.

The Process of Socialization

The main tendency of socialization is a bio-sociological one. The needs governing the individual at different ages are basically biological and exert a strong influence upon his sociological behavior. The gregarious instinct compels individuals to aggregate. Thus, interaction begins and group-formation takes place within the aggregate.

The first attempt at aggregation among

age-mates occurs before the gang age and it assumes the form of, for instance, small children's gatherings around the sand-box in the back yard. In these aggregates pairs are gradually cyrstallized and these in their turn give rise to back-yard groups of a slightly cohesive character. Finally boys' gangs and the corresponding girls' groups appear. At this stage in the process of socialization boys and girls form, for the first time in their lives, true primary groups. Simultaneously sports, which may be looked upon as the dynamics of the boys' gang, are originated in this microcosm.

The need to find a partner of the other sex drives the boys who have attained the age of about 14–16 years to leave their gangs. Girls withdraw from their groups. Separate pairs appear. These pairs aggregate in the traditional meeting-places of the population centre where they live. With increasing interaction these aggregates may group together and in this phase they generally form groups which are called associations or clubs.

As the socialization process of these young people progresses, phases of aggregation and group-phases alternate, and this phenomenon may be called the *rhythm of socialization*.

During their socialization young people first learn how to behave in a system of pairs and then gradually in larger and larger groups, such as primary groups (small groups), intermediary groups and secondary groups. This development I have named the *expansion of socialization*. Naturally, the expansion concerns not only the size of the groups but also

their interaction and sphere of influence (area). Expansion and rhythm may be regarded as the main tendency of socialization.

REFERENCES

1. Erixon, Sigurd, Ynglingalaget: En gengångare i samhället, *Fataburen* 1–4, 1921.
2. Furfey, Paul Hanly: *The gang age.* New York, 1926.
3. Furfey, Paul Hanly: Pubescence and play behavior. *The American Journal of Psychology*, 41, 1929.
4. Gulick, L. H.: *A Philosophy of play.* New York, 1920.
5. Helanko, R.: *Turun Poikasakit* (with an English summary: *The boys' gangs of Turku*). Turku, 1953.
6. Hoffmann-Krayer, E.: Knabenschaften und Volksjustiz in der Schweiz. *Schweitzerisches Archiv für Volkskunde*, 8, 1904.
7. Hästesko, F. A.: *Suomen nuorisoseuraliikkeen historia.* Helsinki, 1931.
8. Piaget, Jean: *The moral judgment of the child.* London, 1932.
9. Pihkala, Lauri: Kulttuuri ja urheilu. *Keski-Suomea ja keskisuomalaisia*, II, 1951.
10. Puffer, J. Adams: Boys' gangs. *Pedagogical Seminary*, 12, 1905.
11. Reaney, M. J.: The psychology of the organized group game. *The British Journal of Psychology. Monograph Supplements*, IV, 1916.
12. *Svensk Idrott 1903–1953:* Malmö, 1953.
13. Thrasher, Frederic M.: *The gang.* Chicago, 1947.
14. Tönnies, Ferdinand: *Individuum und Gemeinschaft.* Berlin, 1927.
15. Andersen, Helge a.o.: *Sports and Games in Denmark.* Acta Sociologica, Vol. 2, fasc. 1, 1956.

THE INFLUENCE OF PEER GROUPS UPON ATTITUDES
TOWARD THE FEMININE ROLE

by Lionel J. Neiman

This paper, a pilot study, is concerned with the effect of peer groups on changing attitudes. There are two main objectives to this exploratory work: 1. That it will lead eventually to a series of inquiries into the areas of conflict, real or potential, which arise as a result of attempted adherence to divergent social norms. 2. That it will lead to quantitative substantiation for some of the now assumed sociological generalizations. For example, there has been presented, implicitly as well as explicitly, an emphasis to the effect that the roles which individuals play in married life, like other roles, have been previously learned. In addition there is the emphasis, in Burgess and Locke to cite one case, that the roles learned prior to marriage are learned in terms of broad generalizations which are then expressed in terms of specific social norms. (1) In other words, the individual first learns specific patterns of behavior and the concomitant attitudes, both of which are later incorporated into the particular social norm.

It has also been traditionally accepted that the roles which an individual learns in the family milieu are most important in determining the individual's later behavior. It is usually assumed that the child identifies himself with the parent of the same sex, and thus acquires the attitudes and expectancies which contribute to the individual's acceptance of the cultural norms and role behavior.

There is also evidence that some learning is acquired from the individual's peer group. Divergence in norms and attitudes

SOURCE: *Social Problems*, Vol. 2 (1954), pp. 104–111.

between those of the familial group and the peer group may, however, create conflict situations for the individual. Stouffer's article, while dealing primarily with methodology, points up this possible divergence. (5) Though the author apparently accepts it as a matter of fact, the evidence for the assumption is lacking. In a widely quoted article, (4) Margaret Mead discusses the potential inconsistency between family and peer group; unfortunately, little scientific evidence is offered for the existence of the inconsistency.

In the light of the above, there are three separate, but related questions raised which this research attempts to investigate:

One. Are the norms of the individual's own family of more importance to the individual than those of his peer group.* In other words, are the earliest roles and attitudes the roles which continue to be of prime importance to him in the process of continued interaction outside of the family circle?

Two. Related to the first, is the question: are the norms of the individual's family different from the norms of his peer group? That is to say, are there actually two sets of norms, a familial set and a peer group set, which may be divergent and which may be a potential source of conflict? The literature in the field suggests this is true; quantitative evidence is lacking. The corollary here is the question of the "conflict of ages."

* "Importance" in this usage means in terms of acceptance of the norms as his own, and carries with it the connotation of identification.

Three. Is there a time differential involved in the acceptance of norms and concomitant attitudes? That is to say, if one compares three groups of different ages, would one find an increased acceptance of peer group norms with a decreased acceptance of family norms; or would the reverse be true? In either case, would there be a potential source of intra-family conflict, to say nothing of personal conflict for the individual? A corollary question is: if the divergence appears, when does it become important to the individual?

The Study

The present study attempts to explore, at three different age-grade levels, the individual's awareness of, and conceptions of, differences and similarities between his attitudes and those of his parents and peers with regard to the feminine role.†

The theoretical frame of reference for this study is essentially a socio-psychologi-

† Attitudes toward the role women are permitted to play in the family specifically and the society in general is only one area which will eventually be explored. Conflicting norms regarding permissive and non-permissive sexual behavior, the "romantic complex," and levels of occupational aspirations are some of the other areas which need investigation. In all of these, as well as others, an individual as a member of two groups, playing different roles, may well be faced with incompatible and ambiguous norms. Some specific aspects of the larger problem have already been examined by the many adequate studies of language difficulties of second generation children, and by the study of the marginal positions of the foreman in industry, the non-commissioned officer in the army, *et cetera.* Likewise some areas of adolescent behavior have been investigated with signal success (e. g., juvenile crime and juvenile sex offenses); but with the exception of a few studies, most have been concerned with enumeration of the data.

cal one. It adheres more closely to a Dewey-Mead-Cooley approach to explanations of human behavior than to a synthetic biological-psychological frame. It is a basic assumption of the writer, for example, that an individual's role, and the relationship of his role to a complementary role, is contingent upon (a) his conception of his own attitudes; (b) the definition of the situation that he accepts; and (c) the degree of consensus between his own attitudes and those he attributes to others. Role, in this sense, is used as a synonym for delimited behavior in a specific situation or relationship. Attitudes are simply acquired verbal responses, to a variety of stimuli, learned in the social milieu.

RESEARCH AND HYPOTHESES: In the study 350 respondents were originally used; 28 cases were later discarded for various reasons—primarily incomplete returns. All of the subjects were lower socioeconomic class; the gross family incomes ranged from $500 to one case of $2800 per annum. (2) The three age-grades used were: a pre-adolescent group, which included subjects from 11 to 13 years of age, 51 males, 56 females; adolescent, 15 to 18 years of age, 58 males, 50 females; post-adolescent, 20 to 24 years of age, 53 males, 54 females. Random sampling of every seventh case was possible in the first two age-grades as these subjects were drawn from urban schools within a two hundred mile radius of the writer's home. The population in the third age-grade was contacted through, but did not include, students in an extension class in an urban community within the same radius. All subjects were single, white and Protestant.

From the above sample, data were gathered to bear upon the following hypotheses: 1. Similarities in the attitudes of ego, and those attributed to parents and peers represent identification with and acceptance of previously learned attitudes. Conversely, differences in attitudes attributed to parents and peers represents a shift away from the importance of the family in the process of learning social norms on the part of ego. 2. The influence of the peer group attitudes on the feminine role begins to have effect in the early adolescent years—effect in terms of contradiction of and divergence from earlier expressed attitudes. 3. The influence of the individual's conception of peer group attitudes is in direct proportion to the length of the post-adolescent years. Conversely, the influence of earlier learned attitudes lessens as the individual participates in peer group relationships with greater frequency and intensity. 4. The most significant sex difference in attitudes toward the feminine role will occur in the adolescent years where peer group identification is most intense. Conversely, the least significant sex difference will appear in the preadolescent years where parental influence is strongest.

Kirkpatrick's "A Belief-Pattern Scale for Measuring Attitudes Toward Feminism" (Form A) was revised so as to make 23 pairs of questions concerning permissive behavior and concomitant attitudes, with a vocabulary of sufficient ease for the youngest informants. (3) Each question was answered by the respondent as to (a) his own attitudes, (b) (as he put himself in the place of others) his conceptions of the attitudes of the parent of the same sex (Pas), (c) his conceptions of the attitudes of the parent of the opposite sex (Pos), and (d) his conceptions of the attitudes of his peers. Each section of the scale was given on different days with sufficient time gaps between to permit "forgetting" of the previous scoring.

Each of the four parts of the scale were scored algebraically, and could range from -46, indicating extremely permissive attitudes toward feminism, to $+46$, indicating no permissive attitudes toward feminism. The actual range of raw scores was from -34 to $+35$. Each of the age-grades were used in pre-testing but the results were not included in this study. Although the Kirkpatrick Scale had been proven both valid and reliable, the adaptation of the scale necessitated further assurance. A test of reliability for both males and females showed an identification of ego with his peer group and compared favorably with the original study by Kirkpatrick. Validity was attempted by the use of intensive interviews with the subjects randomly drawn from the sample. The Critical Ratio was used as a test of significance with a C.R. of 3 as being significant. The minus sign in some of the C.R.'s is due to the algebraic scoring.

FINDINGS. The statistical results of the four parts of the scale given to each respondent are shown in Table 1. In the first age-grade it was surprising, to the writer at least, to note the degree of permissiveness toward feminism found among these lower class males as indicated by the mean score of -2.5. The comparatively low positive scores at the other two age-grades, together with the above, certainly does not coincide with the stereotyped picture of lower class emphasis on hypermasculine values. For males in the first age-grade, the high critical ratio is taken as indication of the lack of males in the first age-grade. For both sexes there is significant divergence between the subject's conception of the feminine role and the concomitant attitudes and those of parents of both sexes.

In the second age-grade the C.R. of 1.0 for males and peers and of -2.3 for females and peers indicate the effect of peer groups upon attitudes toward feminism and the growing divergence between potentially conflicting norms. For both males and females there is significant difference between their own attitudes and those attributed to both parents. The highest C.R.'s between Self

TABLE 1. *Table of Age-Grades, Means and Critical Ratios for 322 Subjects*

	NO.	SEX	MEAN *		C. R. #	
1. Pre-adolescent 11–13 yrs.	51	M	1. —	2.5		
			2.	3.9	2.	7
			3. —	4.5	3.	—10
			4. —	4.65	4.	—10.8
1. Pre-adolescent 11–13 yrs.	56	F	1. —	7.95		
			2. —	5	2.	—13.4
			3.	3.45	3.	—21.3
			4. —	6.3	4.	— 7.5
2. Adolescent 15–18 yrs.	58	M	1.	7.25		
			2.	2.6	2.	24.4
			3.	—11.2	3.	— 6.6
			4.	7.05	4.	1
2. Adolescent 15–18 yrs.	50	F	1. —	4.9		
			2.	—10.1	2.	—26
			3.	2.6	3.	—10.9
			4. —	4.3	4.	— 2.3
3. Post-adolescent 20–24 yrs.	53	M	1.	8.95		
			2.	9.15	2.	1
			3. —	7.1	3.	8
			4.	7.7	4.	1.8
3. Post-adolescent 20–24 yrs.	54	F	1. —	5.3		
			2. —	4.9	2.	— 1.9
			3.	9.35	3.	10.2
			4. —	5.65	4.	— 1.6

* Mean 1. Self   #C. R. 2. Self-Pas
       2. Pas   3. Self-Pos
       3. Pos   4. Self-Peer
       4. Peer

Minus mean scores indicate permissive attitudes toward feminism;
Plus mean scores indicate non-permissive attitudes toward feminism.

and Pas (parent of the same sex) are found in this age-grade. Family conflict has a high potential.

In the third age-grade, the only significant C.R.'s are found between Self and Pos (parent of the opposite sex), for males, 8 and for female 10.2. For both males and females in this age level, the C.R.'s between Self and Peer and between Self and Pas remain on the level of chance. For males, there is a trend back to the masculine, anti-feminine attitudes which were consistently attributed to their fathers.

The imputation of divergent attitudes on the part of the individual with regard to parents and peers is certainly important in terms of analyzing the behavior of the individual and accounting for much of the real or potential conflict.* For example, the adolescent females with a mean score of −4.9 indicated a significantly different set of attitudes for their mothers (mean score −10.1). Item analysis helped clarify this. To illustrate, in scoring the statement, "It is naturally proper for parents to keep a daughter, on the average, under closer control than a son," 86% of the cases, or 43 subjects, disagreed. However, 82% scored the statement to indicate agreement in terms of mother's attitudes. But, lest one assume the subjects' scoring of the scale in terms of peer group attitudes to be mere repetition, or projection, of their own attitudes, it may be shown that for this same group of subjects in scoring the statement, "Women should have the right to compete with men for jobs," 88% agreed. Only 58% indicated agreement on this item when checking in terms of peer group attitudes.

In the adolescent and post-adolescent groups, for both males and females, there was some indication of consistent inconsistency in scoring some of the statements. The statement, "Women have as much right to have pre-marital sex relations, as men" was acceptable to 75% of the adolescent males and 85% of the post adolescent males. The statement, "The unmarried mother is morally a greater failure than the unmarried fa-

ther," was found agreeable to 87% of the adolescent males and 84% of the post-adolescent males. To say there is a slight male bias, and something of an inconsistency here, is perhaps an understatement.†

In addition to the four parts of the scale, the subjects also filled out a data sheet which yielded much information of value in the interviews. For example, in answer to the question, "Have you ever felt that you could discuss things better with your friends than you could with your parents?", 61% of the males in the first age-grade answered "yes"; 90% in the second, and 76% in the third. For females, the percentages were 55, 93 and 72 respectively. For both sexes the peak of peer group identification was the second age-grade, and in neither case did the percentages of the third age-grade drop below that of the first.

In answering the question, "Have you ever felt that your parents do not understand you as well as your friends?", the percentages of "yes" for males in the three age levels were 59, 88 and 77 respectively; for females in answer to the same question 54%, 89% and 74%.

The twenty-three pairs of questions were divided into four basic categories dealing with feminine and anti-feminine propositions. There were statements concerning legal-political rights, family authority and status, sexual behavior and morality, and some statements of a primarily economic nature. The latter propositions were the best discriminators of permissive and non-permissive attitudes toward the feminine role. In responding to the statement, "There should

---

* The point may be raised, for example, that actually the peer group was not subjected to the scale. The 47 interviews conducted to ascertain the validity of the scale included 18 cases where both the subject and his two closest friends had scored the scale. These 54 schedules were analyzed separately, as well as with the rest of the sample. There were no significant differences in Self-Peer critical ratios for these 54 cases when compared with 54 other cases randomly selected where ostensibly their closest friends had not been included.

† These same figures, however, may be interpreted to represent further evidence of the inherent validity of the conflicting norms and values of our culture, or are representative of what has been termed "our schizoid culture." In this light though the figures may represent male bias, and certainly an anti-feminine attitude, they cannot actually be called inconsistent.

always be equal pay for equal work for both men and women," there was a clear demarcation of the acceptability of the proposition. The figures for Self and Peer Group are shown in Table 2.

TABLE 2

AGE GRADE	SEX	% AGREED- SELF	% AGREED- PEER
I	M	35	39
	F	89	70
II	M	28	24
	F	90	92
III	M	30	26
	F	91	87

Responding to the statement, "Women should have the right to compete with men for jobs," the adolescent females indicated 58% agreement in terms of peer group attitudes; to the statement above, 92%. This interesting discrepancy is somewhat puzzling unless it is taken to mean that, in terms of peer group attitudes, women have the right to compete for jobs but should not receive the same pay for them as men.

Conclusions

One. The differences in attitudes attributed to parents by the subjects indicates a shift away from the importance of the family in the process of acquiring the attitudes and behavior concomitant to social norms. With the sample given in this study, this divergence away from the importance of the family patterns occurs as early as eleven to thirteen years of age. The first hypothesis is substantiated by the data obtained.

Two. The second hypothesis, dealing with the conceptions of peer groups and the changing attitudes is likewise substantiated for this sample. One possible exception, mentioned above, is that the influence of the peer group may be noted

much earlier than the period of adolescence as originally hypothecated. In fact, in the first age-grade the difference in attitudes between self and peer group was also significant. However it is possible that the C.R. at the first age level represents the individual faced with two divergent sets of norms and attitudes—the earlier of the two, the parental norms are being cast aside, and the more recent, the peer norms, are not yet internalized. It is evident from this study that two sets of norms are being presented to the subject in early adolescence. It is to be recognized that a sample of subjects drawn exclusively from middle or upper class environments may alter this picture considerably.

Three. The third hypothesis, the influence of the individual's conception of peer group attitudes is in direct proportion to the length of the post-adolescent years, is substantiated for this sample of lower class subjects. There is no evidence of significant differences occuring between the individual's conception of the attitudes of his peer group and his own for the adolescent and post-adolescent age-grades. Whether frequency of contact or intensity of the interpersonal relationships enters the picture, and to what extent it should be controlled, is difficult to say. A measure of frequency of self-peer contact was attempted during the interviews and was not adequate. Intensity of opinion as well as intensity of contact was also attempted; both were unsatisfactory.*

Four. The fourth hypothesis was found to be unsatisfactory. The greatest sex difference occured in the post-adolescent group; and coincides with the differences in attitudes attributed to both parents by the subjects of that age-grade.

* Intensity of opinion was attempted by asking the respondent to double check those statements about which he felt most strongly. Of the 322 cases only 21 double-checked any items. The mean number of double-checked items was 2.1.

Five. For males there was an increasing masculine, or unfavorable, attitude toward feminism in the trend of male mean scores from —2.5 through 7.25 to 8.95. Similarly, for the males' conceptions of their peer groups, the trend of mean scores was from —4.65 through 7.05 to 7.7. This might possibly negate the Freudian emphasis on the Oedipus complex as one would anticipate the reverse if there were identification with mother and rejection of father.

Most studies of this nature pose more problems for the researcher than are actually solved; this study is no exception. Although a longitudinal study in which the investigator follows the same sample of subjects through a given time span would undoubtedly result in greater validity and would permit greater generalization in terms of the sample, and the universe from which it is drawn, this scientific ideal was not possible in this pilot study. The three age-grades reported here did show demonstrable conflicting attitudes toward the feminine role, as an illustration of a social norm, resulting from increased identification with their peer groups. The original thesis of the effect of the individual's relationship to his peer groups on his changing attitudes is supported.†

† A cogent criticism by Wellman J. Warner, in personal conversation, offers the substitute hypothesis of discontinuities present in the learning of attitudes toward the feminine role and negates the effect of the peer group. The evidence for Dr. Warner's remarks can be ascertained by emphasis upon the algebraic signs of the mean scores (— or +). With the exception of the pre-adolescent males, both sexes in all age-grades indicated similar degrees of permissive or non-permissive attitudes for Self and Pas (parent of the same sex).

REFERENCES

1. Ernest W. Burgess and Harvey J. Locke: *The Family,* New York: American Book Company, 1945, Ch. 9. Although roles are called "habits," the same implication is found in Williard Waller and Reuben Hill, *The Family,* New York: Dryden Press, 1951, pp. 29–30, 87, 281–286.

2. Where the father was still living, whether employed or not, his occupation was used as a check on socio-economic status. If the father was not living, mother's occupation was used. See A. M. Edwards, *Comparative Occupation Statistics, U.S.,* 1870–1940, 16th Census, Washington, D. C.: United States Bureau of the Census, 1943, p. 179.

3. For a discussion of the construction of the original scale and the conceptual analysis see Clifford Kirkpatrick, "Construction of a Belief-Pattern Scale For Measuring Attitudes Toward Feminism," *Journal of Social Psychology,* 7 (1936), 421–437; Clifford Kirkpatrick, "Inconsistency in Attitudinal Behavior with Special Reference to Attitudes Toward Feminism," *Journal of Applied Psychology,* 20 (1936), 535–552; also, Clifford Kirkpatrick, "The Content of a Scale for Measuring Attitudes Toward Feminism," *Sociology and Social Research,* 20 (1935–36), 512–526.

4. Margaret Mead, "Social Change and Cultural Surrogates," *Journal of Educational Sociology,* 14 (1940), 92–110. Mead's thesis is that peer groups may stand *in loco parentis* to the individual and substitute standards for him. The result may be real or potential conflict. For an early work in this area, see Caroline McConn Tryon, *Evaluations of Adolescent Personality by Adolescents,* Washington, D. C.: 1939, National Research Council.

5. Samuel A. Stouffer, "An Analysis of Conflicting Social Norms," *American Sociological Review,* 14 (1949), 707–717.

E · ADULT ROLES AND PERSONALITY

1 · Occupational Roles

BUREAUCRATIC STRUCTURE AND PERSONALITY

by Robert K. Merton

A formal, rationally organized social structure involves clearly defined patterns of activity in which, ideally, every series of actions is functionally related to the purposes of the organization.[1] In such an organization there is integrated a series of offices, of hierarchized statuses, in which inhere a number of obligations and privileges closely defined by limited and specific rules. Each of these offices contains an area of imputed competence and responsibility. Authority, the power of control which derives from an acknowledged status, inheres in the office and not in the particular person who performs the official role. Official action ordinarily occurs within the framework of preexisting rules of the organization. The system of prescribed relations between the various offices involves a considerable degree of formality and clearly defined social distance between the occupants of these positions. Formality is manifested by means of a more or less complicated social ritual which symbolizes and supports the "pecking order" of the various offices. Such formality, which is integrated with the distribution of authority within the system, serves to minimize friction by largely restricting (official) contact to modes which are previously defined by the rules of the organization. Ready calculability of others' behavior and a stable set of mutual expectations is thus built up. Moreover, formality facilitates the interaction of the occupants of offices despite their (possibly hostile) private attitudes toward one another. In this way, the subordinate is protected from the arbitrary action of his superior, since the actions of both are constrained by a mutually recognized set of rules. Specific procedural devices foster objectivity and restrain the "quick passage of impulse into action."[2]

The Structure of Bureaucracy

The ideal type of such formal organization is bureaucracy and, in many respects, the classical analysis of bureaucracy is that by Max Weber.[3] As Weber indicates, bu-

[1] For a development of the concept of "rational organization," see Karl Mannheim, *Men and Society in an Age of Reconstruction*, New York: Harcourt, Brace and Company, 1949, esp. pp. 51 ff.

SOURCE: *Social Forces*, Vol. 17 (1940), pp. 560–568. Reprinted with minor modifications.

[2] H. D. Lasswell, *Politics*, New York: McGraw-Hill, 1936, pp. 120–121.

[3] H. H. Gerth and C. Wright Mills, translators and editors, *From Max Weber: Essays in Sociology*, New York: Oxford University

reaucracy involves a clear-cut division of integrated activities which are regarded as duties inherent in the office. A system of differentiated controls and sanctions is stated in the regulations. The assignment of roles occurs on the basis of technical qualifications which are ascertained through formalized, impersonal procedures (e.g. examinations). Within the structure of hierarchically arranged authority, the activities of "trained and salaried experts" are governed by general, abstract, clearly defined rules which preclude the necessity for the issuance of specific instructions for each specific case. The generality of the rules requires the constant use of *categorization*, whereby individual problems and cases are classified on the basis of designated criteria and are treated accordingly. The pure type of bureaucratic official is appointed, either by a superior or through the exercise of impersonal competition; he is not elected. A measure of flexibility in the bureaucracy is attained by electing higher functionaries who presumably express the will of the electorate (e.g. a body of citizens or a board of directors). The election of higher officials is designed to affect the purposes of the organization, but the technical procedures for attaining these ends are carried out by a continuous bureaucratic personnel.[4]

Most bureaucratic offices involve the expectation of life-long tenure, in the absence of disturbing factors which may decrease the size of the organization.

Bureaucracy maximizes vocational security.[5] The function of security of tenure, pensions, incremental salaries and regularized procedures for promotion is to ensure the devoted performance of official duties, without regard for extraneous pressures.[6] The chief merit of bureaucracy is its technical efficiency, with a premium placed on precision, speed, expert control, continuity, discretion, and optimal returns on input. The structure is one which approaches the complete elimination of personalized relationships and nonrational considerations (hostility, anxiety, affectual involvements, etc.).

With increasing bureaucratization, it becomes plain to all who would see that man is to a very important degree controlled by his social relations to the instruments of production. This can no longer seem only a tenet of Marxism, but a stubborn fact to be acknowledged by all, quite apart from their ideological persuasion. Bureaucratization makes readily visible what was previously dim and obscure. More and more people discover that to work, they must be employed. For to work, one must have tools and equipment. And the tools and equipment are increasingly available only in bureaucracies, private or public. Consequently, one must be employed by the bureaucracies in order to have access to tools in order to work in order to live. It is in this sense that bureaucratization entails separation of individuals from the instruments of production, as in modern capitalistic enterprise or in state communistic enterprise (of the 1951 variety),

---

Press, 1946, pp. 196–244. For a brief summary of Weber's discussion, see Talcott Parsons, *The Structure of Social Action*, Glencoe, Illinois: The Free Press, 1949, esp. pp. 506 ff. For a description, which is not a caricature, of the bureaucrat as a personality type, see C. Rabany, "Les types sociaux: le fonctionnaire," *Revue générale d'administration*, LXXXVIII (1907), 5–28.

[4] Karl Mannheim, *Ideology and Utopia*, New York: Harcourt, Brace, 1936, pp. 18n., 105 ff. See also Ramsay Muir, *Peers and Bureaucrats*, London: Constable, 1910, pp. 12–13.

[5] E. G. Cahen-Salvador suggests that the personnel of bureaucracies is largely constituted of those who value security above all else. See his "La situation matérielle et morale des fonctionnaires," *Revue politique et parlementaire* (1926), p. 319.

[6] H. I. Laski, "Bureaucracy," *Encyclopedia of the Social Sciences*. This article is written primarily from the standpoint of the political scientist rather than that of the sociologist.

just as in the post-feudal army, bureaucratization entailed complete separation from the instruments of destruction. Typically, the worker no longer owns his tools nor the soldier, his weapons. And in this special sense, more and more people become workers, either blue collar or white collar or stiff shirt. So develops, for example, the new type of the scientific worker, as the scientist is "separated" from his technical equipment—after all, the physicist does not ordinarily own his cyclotron. To work at his research, he must be employed by a bureaucracy with laboratory resources.

Bureaucracy is administration which almost completely avoids public discussion of its techniques, although there may occur public discussion of its policies.[7] This secrecy is confined neither to public nor to private bureaucracies. It is held to be necessary to keep valuable information from private economic competitors or from foreign and potentially hostile political groups. And though it is not often so called, espionage among competitors is perhaps as common, if not as intricately organized, in systems of private economic enterprise as in systems of national states. Cost figures, lists of clients, new technical processes, plans for production—all these are typically regarded as essential secrets of private economic bureaucracies which might be revealed if the bases of all decisions and policies had to be publicly defended.

The Dysfunctions of Bureaucracy

In these bold outlines, the positive attainments and functions of bureaucratic organization are emphasized and the internal stresses and strains of such structures are almost wholly neglected. The community at large, however, evidently emphasizes the imperfections of bureaucracy, as is suggested by the fact that the "horrid hybrid," bureaucrat, has become an epithet, a *Schimpfwort*. The transition to a study of the negative aspects of bureaucracy is afforded by the applications of Veblen's concept of "trained incapacity," Dewey's notion of "occupational psychosis" or Warnotte's view of "professional deformation." Trained incapacity refers to that state of affairs in which one's abilities function as inadequacies or blind spots. Actions based upon training and skills which have been successfully applied in the past may result in inappropriate responses *under changed conditions*. An inadequate flexibility in the application of skills will, in a changing milieu, result in more or less serious maladjustments.[8] Thus, to adopt a barnyard illustration used in this connection by Burke, chickens may be readily conditioned to interpret the sound of a bell as a signal for food. The same bell may now be used to summon the "trained chickens" to their doom as they are assembled to suffer decapitation. In general, one adopts measures in keeping with his past training and, under new conditions which are not recognized as *significantly* different, the very soundness of this training may lead to the adoption of the wrong procedures. Again, in Burke's almost echolalic phrase, "people may be unfitted by being fit in an unfit fitness"; their training may become an incapacity.

Dewey's concept of occupational psychosis rests upon much the same observations. As a result of their day to day routines, people develop special preferences, antipathies, discriminations and emphases.[9] (The term psychosis is used by Dewey to denote a "pronounced character of the mind.") These psychoses de-

---

[7] Weber, *op. cit.*

[8] For a stimulating discussion and application of these concepts, see Kenneth Burke, *Permanence and Change*, New York: New Republic, 1935, pp. 50 ff.; Daniel Warnotte, "Bureaucratie et Fonctionnarisme," *Revue de l'Institut de Sociologie*, XVII (1937), 245.

[9] *Ibid.*, pp. 58–59.

velop through demands put upon the individual by the particular organization of his occupational role.

The concepts of both Veblen and Dewey refer to a fundamental ambivalence. Any action can be considered in terms of what it attains or what it fails to attain. "A way of seeing is also way of not seeing—a focus upon object A involves a neglect of object B." [10] In his discussion, Weber is almost exclusively concerned with what the bureaucratic structure attains: precision, reliability, efficiency. This same structure may be examined from another perspective provided by the ambivalence. What are the limitations of the organization designed to attain these goals?

For reasons which we have already noted, the bureaucratic structure exerts a constant pressure upon the official to be "methodical, prudent, disciplined." If the bureaucracy is to operate successfully, it must attain a high degree of reliability of behavior, an unusual degree of conformity with prescribed patterns of action. Hence, the fundamental importance of discipline which may be as highly developed in a religious or economic bureaucracy as in the army. Discipline can be effective only if the ideal patterns are buttressed by strong sentiments which entail devotion to one's duties, a keen sense of the limitation of one's authority and competence, and methodical performance of routine activities. The efficacy of social structure depends ultimately upon infusing group participants with appropriate attitudes and sentiments. As we shall see, there are definite arrangements in the bureaucracy for inculcating and reinforcing these sentiments.

At the moment, it suffices to observe that in order to ensure discipline (the necessary reliability of response), these sentiments are often more intense than is technically necessary. There is a margin

[10] *Ibid.*, p. 70.

of safety, so to speak, in the pressure exerted by these sentiments upon the bureaucrat to conform to his patterned obligations, in much the same sense that added allowances (precautionary overestimations) are made by the engineer in designing the supports for a bridge. But this very emphasis leads to a transference of the sentiments from the *aims* of the organization onto the particular details of behavior required by the rules. Adherence to the rules, originally conceived as a means, becomes transformed into an end-in-itself; there occurs the familiar process of *displacement of goals* whereby "an instrumental value becomes a terminal value." [11] Discipline, readily interpreted as conformance with regulations, whatever the situation, is seen not as a

[11] This process has often been observed in various connections. Wundt's *heterogony of ends* is a case in point; Max Weber's *Paradoxie der Folgen* is another. See also, MacIver's observations on the transformation of civilization into culture and Lasswell's remark that "the human animal distinguishes himself by his infinite capacity for making ends of his means." See R. K. Merton, "The Unanticipated Consequences of Purposive Social Action," *American Sociological Review*, I (1936), 894–904. In terms of the psychological mechanisms involved, this process has been analyzed most fully by Gordon W. Allport, in his discussion of what he calls "the functional autonomy of motives." Allport emends the earlier formulations of Woodworth, Tolman, and William Stern, and arrives at a statement of the process from the standpoint of individual motivation. He does not consider those phases of the social structure which conduce toward the "transformation of motives." The formulation adopted in this paper is thus complementary to Allport's analysis; the one stressing the psychological mechanisms involved, the other considering the constraints of the social structure. The convergence of psychology and sociology toward the central concept suggests that it may well constitute one of the conceptual bridges between the two disciplines. See Gordon W. Allport, *Personality*, New York: Henry Holt and Co., 1937, Ch. 7.

measure designed for specific purposes but becomes an immediate value in the life-organization of the bureaucrat. This emphasis, resulting from the displacement of the original goals, develops into rigidities and an inability to adjust readily. Formalism, even ritualism, ensues with an unchallenged insistence upon punctilious adherence to formalized procedures.[12] This may be exaggerated to the point where primary concern with conformity to the rules interferes with the achievement of the purposes of the organization, in which case we have the familiar phenomenon of the technicism or red tape of the official. An extreme product of this process of displacement of goals is the bureaucratic virtuoso, who never forgets a single rule binding his action and hence is unable to assist many of his clients.[13] A case in point, where strict recognition of the limits of authority and literal adherence to rules produced this result, is the pathetic plight of Bernt Balchen, Admiral Byrd's pilot in the flight over the South Pole.

According to a ruling of the department of labor Bernt Balchen . . . cannot receive his citizenship papers. Balchen, a native of Norway, declared his intention in 1927. It is held that he has failed to meet the condition of five years' continuous residence in the United States. The Byrd antarctic voyage took him out of the country, although he was on a ship carrying the American flag, was an invaluable member of an American expedition, and in a region to which there is an American claim because of the exploration and occupation of it by Americans, this region being Little America.

The bureau of naturalization explains that it cannot proceed on the assumption that Little America is American soil. That would be *trespass on international questions* where it has no sanction. So far as the bureau is concerned, Balchen was out of the country and *technically* has not complied with the law of naturalization.[14]

Structural Sources of Overconformity

Such inadequacies in orientation which involve trained incapacity clearly derive from structural sources. The process may be briefly recapitulated. (1) An effective bureaucracy demands reliability of response and strict devotion to regulations. (2) Such devotion to the rules leads to their transformation into absolutes; they are no longer conceived as relative to a given set of purposes. (3) This interferes with ready adaptation under special conditions not clearly envisaged by those who drew up the general rules. (4) Thus, the very elements which conduce toward efficiency in general produce inefficiency in specific instances. Full realization of the inadequacy is seldom attained by members of the group who have not divorced themselves from the "meanings" which the rules have for them. These rules in time become symbolic in cast, rather than strictly utilitarian.

Thus far, we have treated the ingrained sentiments making for rigorous discipline simply as data, as given. However, definite features of the bureaucratic structure may be seen to conduce to these sentiments. The bureaucrat's official life is planned for him in terms of a graded

[12] See E. C. Hughes, "Institutional Office and the Person," *American Journal of Sociology,* XLIII (1937), 404–413; R. K. Merton, "Social Structure and Anomie," in *Social Theory and Social Structure,* Glencoe, Illinois: The Free Press, (1949); E. T. Hiller, "Social Structure in Relation to the Person," *Social Forces,* XVI (1937), 34–44.

[13] Mannheim, *Ideology and Utopia.*

[14] Quoted from the *Chicago Tribune* (June 24, 1931, p. 10) by Thurman Arnold, *The Symbols of Government,* New Haven: Yale University Press, 1935, pp. 201–208. (My italics.)

career, through the organizational devices of promotion by seniority, pensions, incremental salaries, *etc.*, all of which are designed to provide incentives for disciplined action and conformity to the official regulations.[15] The official is tacitly expected to and largely does adapt his thoughts, feelings, and actions to the prospect of this career. But *these very devices* which increase the probability of conformance also lead to an over-concern with strict adherence to regulations which induces timidity, conservatism, and technicism. Displacement of sentiments from goals onto means is fostered by the tremendous symbolic significance of the means (rules).

Another feature of the bureaucratic structure tends to produce much the same result. Functionaries have the sense of a common destiny for all those who work together. They share the same interests, especially since there is relatively little competition insofar as promotion is in terms of seniority. In-group aggression is thus minimized and this arrangement is therefore conceived to be positively functional for the bureaucracy. However, the esprit de corps and informal social organization which typically develops in such situations often leads the personnel to defend their entrenched interests rather than to assist their clientele and elected higher officials. As President Lowell reports, if the bureaucrats believe that their status is not adequately recognized by an incoming elected official, detailed information will be withheld from him, leading him to errors for which he is held responsible. Or, if he seeks to dominate fully, and thus violates the sentiment of self-integrity of the bureaucrats, he may have documents brought to him in such numbers that he cannot manage to sign them all, let alone read them.[16] This

illustrates the defensive informal organization which tends to arise whenever there is an apparent threat to the integrity of the group.[17]

It would be much too facile and partly erroneous to attribute such resistance by bureaucrats simply to vested interests. Vested interests oppose any new order which either eliminates or at least makes uncertain their differential advantage deriving from the current arrangements. This is undoubtedly involved in part in bureaucratic resistance to change but another process is perhaps more significant. As we have seen, bureaucratic officials affectively identify themselves with their way of life. They have a pride of craft which leads them to resist change in established routines; at least, those changes which are felt to be imposed by coworkers. This nonlogical pride of craft is a familiar pattern found even, to judge from Sutherland's *Professional Thief,* among pickpockets who, despite the risk, delight in mastering the prestige-bearing feat of "beating a left breech" (picking the left front trousers pocket).

In a stimulating paper, Hughes has applied the concepts of "secular" and "sacred" to various types of divisions of labor; "the sacredness" of caste and *Stände* prerogatives contrasts sharply with the increasing secularism of occupational differentiation in our mobile society.[18] However, as our discussion suggests, there may ensue, in particular vocations and in particular types of organization, the

[15] Mannheim stresses the importance of the "Lebensplan" and the "Amtskarriere." See the comments by Hughes, *op. cit.,* 413.

[16] A. L. Lowell, *The Government of England* (New York, 1908), I, 189 *ff.*

[17] For an instructive description of the development of such a defensive organization in a group of workers, see F. J. Roethlisberger and W. J. Dickson, *Management and the Worker* (Boston: Harvard School of Business Administration, 1934).

[18] E. C. Hughes, "Personality Types and the Division of Labor," *American Journal of Sociology,* XXXIII (1928), 754–768. Much the same distinction is drawn by Leopold von Wiese and Howard Becker, *Systematic Sociology,* New York: John Wiley and Sons, 1932, pp. 222–225 *et passim.*

process of sanctification (viewed as the counterpart of the process of secularization). This is to say that through sentiment-formation, emotional dependence upon bureaucratic symbols and status, and affective involvement in spheres of competence and authority, there develop prerogatives involving attitudes of moral legitimacy which are established as values in their own right, and are no longer viewed as merely technical means for expediting administration. One may note a tendency for certain bureaucratic norms, originally introduced for technical reasons, to become rigidified and sacred, although, as Durkheim would say, they are *laïque en apparence.*[19] Durkheim has touched on this general process in his description of the attitudes and values which persist in the organic solidarity of a highly differentiated society.

Primary vs. Secondary Relations

Another feature of the bureaucratic structure, the stress on depersonalization of relationships, also plays its part in the bureaucrat's trained incapacity. The personality pattern of the bureaucrat is nucleated about this norm of impersonality. Both this and the categorizing tendency, which develops from the dominant role of general, abstract rules, tend to produce conflict in the bureaucrat's contacts with the public or clientele. Since functionaries minimize personal relations and resort to categorization, the peculiarities of individual cases are often ignored. But the client who, quite understandably, is convinced of the "special features" of *his* own problem often objects to such categorical treatment. Stereotyped behavior is not adapted to the exigencies of individual problems. The impersonal treatment of affairs which are at times of great personal significance to the client gives rise to the charge of "arrogance" and "haughtiness" of the bureaucrat. Thus, at the Greenwich Employment Exchange, the unemployed worker who is securing his insurance payment resents what he deems to be "the impersonality and, at times, the apparent abruptness and even harshness of his treatment by the clerks. . . . Some men complain of the superior attitude which the clerks have." [20]

Still another source of conflict with the public derives from the bureaucratic structure. The bureaucrat, in part irrespective of his position with*in* the hierarchy, acts as a representative of the power and prestige of the entire structure. In his official role he is vested with definite authority. This often leads to an actually or apparently domineering atti-

[19] Hughes recognizes one phrase of this process of sanctification when he writes that professional training "carries with it as a by-product assimilation of the candidate to a set of professional attitudes and controls, *a professional conscience and solidarity. The profession claims and aims to become a moral unit.*" Hughes, *op. cit.,* p. 762 (italics inserted). In this same connection, Sumner's concept of *pathos,* as the halo of sentiment which protects a social value from criticism, is particularly relevant, inasmuch as it affords a clue to the mechanisms involved in the process of sanctification. See his *Folkways,* Boston: Ginn and Co., 1906, pp. 180–181.

[20] " 'They treat you like a lump of dirt they do. I see a navvy reach across the counter and shake one of them by the collar the other day. The rest of us felt like cheering. Of course he lost his benefit over it. . . . But the clerk deserved it for his sassy way.' " (E. W. Bakke, *The Unemployed Man,* New York: Dutton, 1934, pp. 79–80). Note that the domineering attitude was *imputed* by the unemployed client who is in a state of tension due to his loss of status and self-esteem in a society where the ideology is still current that an "able man" can always find a job. That the imputation of arrogance stems largely from the client's state of mind is seen from Bakke's own observation that "the clerks were rushed, and had no time for pleasantries, but there was little sign of harshness or a superiority feeling in their treatment of the men."

tude, which may only be exaggerated by a discrepancy between his position within the hierarchy and his position with reference to the public.[21] Protest and recourse to other officials on the part of the client are often ineffective or largely precluded by the previously mentioned esprit de corps which joins the officials into a more or less solidary in-group. This source of conflict *may* be minimized in private enterprise since the client can register an effective protest by transferring his trade to another organization within the competitive system. But with the monopolistic nature of the public organization, no such alternative is possible. Moreover, in this case, tension is increased because of a discrepancy between ideology and fact: the governmental personnel are held to be "servants of the people," but in fact they are usually superordinate, and release of tension can seldom be afforded by turning to other agencies for the necessary service.[22] This tension is in

part attributable to the confusion of status of bureaucrat and client; the client may consider himself socially superior to the official who is at the moment dominant.[23]

Thus, with respect to the relations between officials and clientele, one structural source of conflict is the pressure for formal and impersonal treatment when individual, personalized consideration is desired by the client. The conflict may be viewed, then, as deriving from the introduction of inappropriate attitudes and relationships. Conflict with*in* the bureaucratic structure arises from the converse situation, namely, when personalized relationships are substituted for the structurally required impersonal relationships. This type of conflict may be characterized as follows.

The bureaucracy, as we have seen, is organized as a secondary, formal group. The normal responses involved in this organized network of social expectations are supported by affective attitudes of members of the group. Since the group is oriented toward secondary norms of impersonality, any failure to conform to these norms will arouse antagonism from those who have identified themselves with the legitimacy of these rules. Hence, the substitution of personal for impersonal treatment within the structure is met with widespread disapproval and is characterized by such epithets as graft, favoritism, nepotism, apple-polishing, etc. These epithets are clearly manifestations of injured sentiments.[24] The function of such

[21] In this connection, note the relevance of Koffka's comments on certain features of the pecking-order of birds. "If one compares the behavior of the bird at the top of the pecking list, the despot, with that of one very far down, the second or third from the last, then one finds the latter much more cruel to the few others over whom he lords it than the former in his treatment of all members. As soon as one removes from the group all members above the penultimate, his behavior becomes milder and may even become very friendly. . . . It is not difficult to find analogies to this in human societies, and therefore one side of such behavior must be primarily the effects of the social groupings, and not of individual characteristics." K. Koffka, *Principles of Gestalt Psychology*, New York: Harcourt, Brace, 1935, pp. 668–669.

[22] At this point the political machine often becomes functionally significant. As Steffens and others have shown, highly personalized relations and the abrogation of formal rules (red tape) by the machine often satisfy the needs of individual "clients" more fully than the formalized mechanism of government bureaucracy.

[23] As one of the unemployed men remarked about the clerks at the Greenwich Employment Exchange: " 'And the bloody blokes wouldn't have their jobs if it wasn't for us men out of a job either. That's what gets me about their holding their noses up.' " Bakke, *op. cit.*, p. 80.

[24] The diagnostic significance of such linguistic indices as epithets has scarcely been explored by the sociologist. Sumner properly observes that epithets produce "summary criticisms" and definitions of social situ-

"automatic resentment" can be clearly seen in terms of the requirements of bureaucratic structure.

Bureaucracy is a secondary group structure designed to carry on certain activities which cannot be satisfactorily performed on the basis of primary group criteria.[25] Hence behavior which runs counter to these formalized norms becomes the object of emotionalized disapproval. This constitutes a functionally significant defence set up against tendencies which jeopardize the performance of socially necessary activities. To be sure, these reactions are not rationally determined practices explicitly designed for the fulfilment of this function. Rather, viewed in terms of the individual's interpretation of the situation, such resentment is simply an immediate response opposing the "dishonesty" of those who violate the rules of the game. However, this subjective frame of reference notwithstanding, these reactions serve the latent function of maintaining the essential structural elements of bureaucracy by reaffirming the necessity for formalized, secondary relations and by helping to prevent the disintegration of the bureaucratic structure which would occur should these be supplanted by personalized relations. This type of conflict may be generically described as the intrusion of primary group attitudes when secondary group attitudes are institutionally demanded, just as the bureaucrat-client conflict often derives from interaction on impersonal terms when personal treatment is individually demanded.[26]

Problems for Research

The trend toward increasing bureaucratization in Western society, which Weber had long since foreseen, is not the sole reason for sociologists to turn their attention to this field. Empirical studies of the interaction of bureaucracy and personality should especially increase our understanding of social structure. A large number of specific questions invite our attention. To what extent are particular personality types selected and modified by the various bureaucracies (private enterprise, public service, the quasi-legal political machine, religious orders)? Inasmuch as ascendancy and submission are held to be traits of personality, despite their variability in different stimulus-situations, do bureaucracies select personalities of particularly submissive or ascendant tendencies? And since various studies have shown that these traits can be modified, does participation in bureaucratic office tend to increase ascendant tendencies? Do various systems of recruitment (*e.g.* patronage, open competition involving specialized knowledge or "general mental capacity," practical experience) select different personality types? Does promotion through seniority lessen competitive anxieties and enhance

---

ations. Dollard also notes that "epithets frequently define the central issues in a society," and Sapir has rightly emphasized the importance of context of situations in appraising the significance of epithets. Of equal relevance is Linton's observation that "in case histories the way in which the community felt about a particular episode is, if anything, more important to our study than the actual behavior. . . ." A sociological study of "vocabularies of encomium and opprobrium" should lead to valuable findings.

[25] Cf. Ellsworth Faris, *The Nature of Human Nature*, New York: McGraw-Hill, 1937, pp. 41 *ff.*

[26] Community disapproval of many forms of behavior may be analyzed in terms of one or the other of these patterns of substitution of culturally inappropriate types of relationship. Thus, prostitution constitutes a type-case where coitus, a form of intimacy which is institutionally defined as symbolic of the most "sacred" primary group relationship, is placed within a contractual context, symbolized by the exchange of that most impersonal of all symbols, money. See Kingsley Davis, "The Sociology of Prostitution," *American Sociological Review*, II (1937), 744–755.

administrative efficiency? A detailed examination of mechanisms for imbuing the bureaucratic codes with affect would be instructive both sociologically and psychologically. Does the general anonymity of civil service decisions tend to restrict the area of prestige-symbols to a narrowly defined inner circle? Is there a tendency for differential association to be especially marked among bureaucrats?

The range of theoretically significant and practically important questions would seem to be limited only by the accessibility of the concrete data. Studies of religious, educational, military, economic, and political bureaucracies dealing with the interdependence of social organization and personality formation should constitute an avenue for fruitful research. On that avenue, the functional analysis of concrete structures may yet build a Solomon's House for sociologists.

THE EFFECTS OF CHANGES IN ROLES ON THE ATTITUDES OF ROLE OCCUPANTS [1]

by Seymour Lieberman

Problem

One of the fundamental postulates of role theory, as expounded by Newcomb (2), Parsons (3), and other role theorists, is that a person's attitudes will be influenced by the role that he occupies in a social system. Although this proposition appears to be a plausible one, surprisingly little evidence is available that bears directly on it. One source of evidence is found in common folklore. "Johnny is a changed boy since he was made a monitor in school." "She is a different woman since she got married." "You would never recognize him since he became foreman."

As much as these expressions smack of the truth, they offer little in the way of systematic or scientific support for the proposition that a person's attitudes are influenced by his role.

Somewhat more scientific, but still not definitive, is the common finding, in many social-psychological studies, that relationships exist between attitudes and roles. In other words, different attitudes are held by people who occupy different roles. For example, Stouffer et al. (5) found that commissioned officers are more favorable toward the Army than are enlisted men. The problem here is that the mere existence of a relationship between attitudes and roles does not reveal the cause and effect nature of the relationship found. One interpretation of Stouffer's finding might be that being made a commissioned officer tends to result in a person's becoming pro-Army—i.e. the role a person occupies influences his attitudes. But an equally plausible interpretation might be that being pro-Army tends to result in a person's being made a commissioned officer—i.e. a person's attitudes influence the likelihood of his being selected for a given role. In the absence of longitudinal data, the relation-

[1] This study was one of a series conducted by the Human Relations Program of the Survey Research Center, Institute for Social Research, at the University of Michigan. The author wishes to express a special debt of gratitude to Dr. Gerald M. Mahoney and Mr. Gerald Gurin, his associates on the larger study of which the present one was a part, and to Dr. Daniel Katz, Dr. Theodore M. Newcomb, and Dr. Eugene Jacobson for their many useful suggestions and contributions.

SOURCE: *Human Relations*, Vol. 9 (1950), pp. 385–403.

ship offers no clear evidence that roles were the "cause" and attitudes the "effect."

The present study was designed to examine the effects of roles on attitudes in a particular field situation. The study is based on longitudinal data obtained in a role-differentiated, hierarchical organization. By taking advantage of natural role changes among personnel in the organization, it was possible to examine people's attitudes both before and after they underwent changes in roles. Therefore, the extent to which changes in roles were followed by changes in attitudes could be determined, and the cause and effect nature of any relationships found would be clear.

Method: Phase 1

The study was part of a larger project carried out in a medium-sized Midwestern company engaged in the production of home appliance equipment. Let us call the company the Rockwell Corporation. At the time that the study was done, Rockwell employed about 4,000 people. This total included about 2,500 factory workers and about 150 first-level foremen. The company was unionized and most of the factory workers belonged to the union local, which was an affiliate of the U.A.W., C.I.O. About 150 factory workers served as stewards in the union, or roughly one steward for every foreman.

The study consisted of a "natural field experiment." The experimental variable was a change in roles, and the experimental period was the period of exposure to the experimental variable. The experimental groups were those employees who underwent changes in roles during this period; the control groups were those employees who did not change roles during this period. The design may be described in terms of a three-step process: "before measurement," "experimental period," and "after measurement."

BEFORE MEASUREMENT. In September and October 1951, attitude questionnaires were filled out by virtually all factory personnel at Rockwell—2,354 workers, 145 stewards, and 151 foremen. The questions dealt for the most part with employees' attitudes and perceptions about the company, the union, and various aspects of the job situation. The respondents were told that the questionnaire was part of an overall survey to determine how employees felt about working conditions at Rockwell.

EXPERIMENTAL PERIOD. Between October 1951 and July 1952, twenty-three workers were made foremen and thirty-five workers became stewards. Most of the workers who became stewards during that period were elected during the annual steward elections held in May 1952. They replaced stewards who did not choose to run again or who were not re-elected by their constituents. In addition, a few workers replaced stewards who left the steward role for one reason or another throughout the year.

The workers who became foremen were not made foreman at any particular time. Promotions occurred as openings arose in supervisory positions. Some workers replaced foremen who retired or who left the company for other reasons; some replaced foremen who were shifted to other supervisory positions; and some filled newly created supervisory positions.

AFTER MEASUREMENT. In December 1952, the same forms that had been filled out by the rank-and-file workers in 1951 were readministered to:

1. The workers who became foremen during the experimental period (N = 23).
2. A control group of workers who did not become foremen during the experimental period (N = 46).
3. The workers who became stewards during the experimental period (N = 35).

4. A control group of workers who did not become stewards during the experimental period (N = 35).

Each control group was matched with its parallel experimental group on a number of demographic, attitudinal, and motivational variables. Therefore, any changes in attitudes that occurred in the experimental groups but did not occur in the control groups could not be attributed to initial differences between them.

The employees in these groups were told that the purpose of the follow-up questionnaire was to get up-to-date measures of their attitudes in 1952 and to compare how employees felt that year with the way that they felt the previous year. The groups were told that, instead of studying the entire universe of employees as was the case in 1951, only a sample was being studied this time. They were informed that the sample was chosen in such a way as to represent all kinds of employees at Rockwell—men and women, young and old, etc. The groups gave no indication that they understood the real bases on which they were chosen for the "after" measurement or that the effects of changes in roles were the critical factors being examined.[2]

Statistical significance of the results was obtained by the use of chi square.[3] The

[2] Some of the top officials of management and all of the top officers of the union at Rockwell knew about the nature of the follow-up study and the bases on which the experimental and control groups were selected.

[3] In those instances where there was a theoretical frequency of less than five in one or more cells, the following procedures, which are an adaptation of the rules of thumb suggested by Walker and Lev (6), were used:

a. If only one theoretical frequency was less than five but it was not less than two, and there were two or more degrees of freedom, then the chi-square test was used without combining any classes or applying any corrections.

probability levels that are differentiated in the tables are: less than .01, between .01 and .05, between .05 and .10, and N.S. (not significant—p is greater than .10).

Results: Phase 1

The major hypothesis tested in this study was that people who are placed in a role will tend to take on or develop attitudes that are congruent with the expectations associated with that role. Since the foreman role entails being a representive of management, it might be expected that workers who are chosen as foremen will tend to become more favorable toward management. Similarly, since the steward role entails being a representative of the union, it might be expected that workers who are elected as stewards will tend to become more favorable toward the union. Moreover, in so far as the values of management and of the union are in conflict with each other, it might also be expected that workers who are made foremen will become less favorable toward the union and workers who are made stewards will become less favorable toward management.

Four attitudinal areas were examined: 1. attitudes toward management and officials of management; 2. attitudes toward the union and officials of the union; 3. attitudes toward the management-sponsored incentive system; and 4. attitudes toward the union-sponsored seniority system. The incentive system (whereby workers are paid according to the number of pieces they turn out) and the seniority

b. If more than one theoretical frequency was less than five or if any theoretical frequency was less than two, then classes were combined to increase cell expectations before the chi-square test was applied.

c. If after combining classes, the theoretical frequency was still less than five and there was only one degree of freedom, then Fisher's exact test was used.

system (whereby workers are promoted according to the seniority principle) are two areas in which conflicts between management and the union at Rockwell have been particularly intense. Furthermore, first-level foremen and stewards both play a part in the administration of these systems, and relevant groups hold expectations about foreman and steward behaviors with respect to these systems. Therefore, we examined the experimental and control groups' attitudes toward these two systems as well as their overall attitudes toward management and the union.

The data tend to support the hypothesis that being placed in the foreman and steward roles will have an impact on the attitudes of the role occupants. As shown in Tables 1 through 4, both experimental groups undergo systematic changes in attitudes, in the predicted directions, from the "before" situation to the "after" situation. In the control groups, either no attitude changes occur, or less marked changes occur, from the "before" situation to the "after" situation.

Although a number of the differences are not statistically significant, those which are significant are all in the expected directions, and most of the nonsignificant differences are also in the expected directions. New foremen, among other things, come to see Rockwell as a better place to work compared with other companies, develop more positive perceptions of top management officers, and become more favorably disposed toward the principle and operation of the incentive system. New stewards come to look upon labor unions in general in a more favorable light, develop more positive perceptions of the top union officers at Rockwell, and come to prefer seniority to ability as a criterion of what should count in moving workers to better jobs. In general, the attitudes of workers who become foremen tend to gravitate in a pro-management direction and the attitudes of workers who become stewards tend to move in a pro-union direction.

A second kind of finding has to do with the relative *amount* of attitude change that takes place among new foremen in contrast to the amount that takes place among new stewards. On the whole, more pronounced and more widespread attitude changes occur among those who are made foremen than among those who are made stewards. Using a p-level of .10 as a criterion for statistical significance, the workers who are made foremen undergo significant attitude changes, relative to the workers who are not made foremen, on ten of the sixteen attitudinal items presented in Tables 1 through 4. By contrast, the workers who are made stewards undergo significant attitude changes, relative to the workers who are not made stewards, on only three of the sixteen items. However, for the steward role as well as for the foreman role, most of the differences found between the experimental and control groups still tend to be in the expected directions.

The more pronounced and more widespread attitude changes that occur among new foremen than among new stewards can probably be accounted for in large measure by the kinds of differences that exist between the foreman and steward roles. For one thing, the foreman role represents a relatively permanent position, while many stewards take the steward role as a "one-shot" job and even if they want to run again their constituents may not re-elect them. Secondly, the foreman role is a full-time job, while most stewards spend just a few hours a week in the performance of their steward functions and spend the rest of the time carrying out their regular rank-and-file jobs. Thirdly, a worker who is made a foreman must give up his membership in the union and become a surrogate of management, while a worker who is made a steward retains the union as a reference group and simply takes on new functions and responsibilities as a representative of it. All of these differences suggest that the change from worker to foreman is a more

TABLE 1. *Effects of Foreman and Steward Roles on Attitudes toward Management*

| | KIND OF CHANGE | | | | | |
	More Favorable to Management	No Change	More Critical of Management	Total	N	p
	%	%	%	%		
1. How is Rockwell as a place to work?						
New foremen	70	26	4	100	23	N.S.
Control group *	47	33	20	100	46	
New stewards	46	31	23	100	35	N.S.
Control group †	46	43	11	100	35	
2. How does Rockwell compare with others?						
New foremen	52	48	0	100	23	.01–.05
Control group	24	59	17	100	46	
New stewards	55	34	11	100	35	N.S.
Control group	43	46	11	100	35	
3. If things went bad for Rockwell, should the workers try to help out?						
New foremen	17	66	17	100	23	N.S.
Control group	17	66	17	100	46	
New stewards	26	74	0	100	35	N.S.
Control group	14	69	17	100	35	
4. How much do management officers care about the workers at Rockwell?						
New foremen	48	52	0	100	23	<.01
Control group	15	76	9	100	46	
New stewards	29	62	9	100	35	N.S.
Control group	20	80	0	100	35	

* Workers who did not change roles, matched with future foremen on demographic and attitudinal variables in the "before" situation.

† Workers who did not change roles, matched with future stewards on demographic and attitudinal variables in the "before" situation.

TABLE 2. *Effects of Foreman and Steward Roles on Attitudes toward the Union*

KIND OF CHANGE

	More Favorable to the Union	No Change	More Critical to the Union	Total	N	p
	%	%	%	%		
5. How do you feel about labor unions in general?						
New foremen	30	48	22	100	23	N.S.
Control group *	37	48	15	100	46	
New stewards	54	37	9	100	35	.01–.05
Control group †	29	65	6	100	35	
6. How much say should the union have in setting standards?						
New foremen	0	26	74	100	23	<.01
Control group	22	54	24	100	46	
New stewards	31	66	3	100	35	N.S.
Control group	20	60	20	100	35	
7. How would things be if there were no union at Rockwell?						
New foremen	9	39	52	100	23	.01–.05
Control group	20	58	22	100	46	
New stewards	14	86	0	100	35	N.S.
Control group	11	72	17	100	35	
8. How much do union officers care about the workers at Rockwell?						
New foremen	22	69	9	100	23	N.S.
Control group	15	78	7	100	46	
New stewards	57	37	6	100	35	.01–.05
Control group	26	68	6	100	35	

* Workers who did not change roles, matched with future foremen on demographic and attitudinal variables in the "before" situation.
† Workers who did not change roles, matched with future stewards on demographic and attitudinal variables in the "before" situation.

TABLE 3. *Effects of Foreman and Steward Roles on Attitudes toward the Incentive System*

| | KIND OF CHANGE | | | | | |
	More Favorable to Incentive System	No Change	More Critical of Incentive System	Total	N	p
	%	%	%	%		
9. *How do you feel about the principle of an incentive system?*						
New foremen	57	26	17	100	23	.01
Control group *	15	52	33	100	46	
New stewards	17	54	29	100	35	N.S.
Control group †	31	40	29	100	35	
10. *How do you feel the incentive system works out at Rockwell?*						
New foremen	65	22	13	100	23	.05–.10
Control group	37	41	22	100	46	
New stewards	43	34	23	100	35	N.S.
Control group	40	34	26	100	35	
11. *Should the incentive system be changed?*						
New foremen	39	48	13	100	23	.01
Control group	11	69	20	100	46	
New stewards	14	63	23	100	35	N.S.
Control group	20	60	20	100	35	
12. *Is a labor standard ever changed just because a worker is a high producer?*						
New foremen	48	43	9	100	23	.01
Control group	11	74	15	100	46	
New stewards	29	57	14	100	35	N.S.
Control group	26	65	9	100	35	

* Workers who did not change roles, matched with future foremen on demographic and attitudinal variables in the "before" situation.
† Workers who did not change roles, matched with future stewards on demographic and attitudinal variables in the "before" situation.

TABLE 4. *Effects of Foreman and Steward Roles on Attitudes toward the Seniority System*

KIND OF CHANGE

	More Favorable to Seniority System	No Change	More Critical of Seniority System	Total	N	p
	%	%	%	%		
13. *How do you feel about the way the seniority system works out here?*						
New foremen	0	65	35	100	23	.01–.05
Control group *	20	63	17	100	46	
New stewards	23	48	29	100	35	N.S.
Control group †	9	71	20	100	35	
14. *How much should seniority count during lay-offs?*						
New foremen	9	52	39	100	23	.05–.10
Control group	24	59	17	100	46	
New stewards	29	48	23	100	35	N.S.
Control group	29	40	31	100	35	
15. *How much should seniority count in moving to better jobs?*						
New foremen	17	44	39	100	23	N.S.
Control group	20	54	26	100	46	
New stewards	34	46	20	100	35	.01–.05
Control group	17	34	49	100	35	
16. *How much should seniority count in promotion to foreman?*						
New foremen	17	70	13	100	23	N.S.
Control group	15	52	33	100	46	
New stewards	31	35	34	100	35	N.S.
Control group	17	43	40	100	35	

* Workers who did not change roles, matched with future foremen on demographic and attitudinal variables in the "before" situation.

† Workers who did not change roles, matched with future stewards on demographic and attitudinal variables in the "before" situation.

fundamental change in roles than the change from worker to steward. This, in turn, might account to a large extent for the finding that, although attitude changes accompany both changes in roles, they occur more sharply among new foremen than among new stewards.

A third finding has to do with the *kinds* of attitude changes which occur among workers who change roles. As expected, new foremen become more pro-management and new stewards become more pro-union. Somewhat less expected is the finding that new foremen become more anti-union but new stewards do not become more anti-management. Among workers who are made foremen, statistically significant shifts in an anti-union direction occur on four of the eight items dealing with the union and the union-sponsored seniority system. Among workers who are made stewards, there are no statistically significant shifts in either direction on any of the eight items having to do with management and the management-sponsored incentive system.

The finding that new foremen become anti-union but that new stewards do not become anti-management may be related to the fact that workers who become foremen must relinquish their membership of the union, while workers who become stewards retain their status as employees of management. New foremen, subject to one main set of loyalties and called on to carry out a markedly new set of functions, tend to develop negative attitudes toward the union as well as positive attitudes toward management. New stewards, subject to overlapping group membership and still dependent on management for their livelihoods, tend to become more favorable toward the union but they do not turn against management, at least not within the relatively limited time period covered by the present research project. Over time, stewards might come to develop somewhat hostile attitudes toward management, but, under the conditions prevailing at Rockwell, there is appar-

ently no tendency for such attitudes to be developed as soon as workers enter the steward role.

Method: Phase 2

One of the questions that may be raised about the results that have been presented up to this point concerns the extent to which the changed attitudes displayed by new foremen and new stewards are internalized by the role occupants. Are the changed attitudes expressed by new foremen and new stewards relatively stable, or are they ephemeral phenomena to be held only as long as they occupy the foreman and steward roles? An unusual set of circumstances at Rockwell enabled the researchers to glean some data on this question.

A short time after the 1952 re-survey, the nation suffered an economic recession. In order to meet the lessening demand for its products, Rockwell, like many other firms, had to cut its work force. This resulted in many rank-and-file workers being laid off and a number of the foremen being returned to non-supervisory jobs. By June 1954, eight of the twenty-three workers who had been promoted to foreman had returned to the worker role and only twelve were still foremen. (The remaining three respondents had voluntarily left Rockwell by this time.)

Over the same period, a number of role changes had also been experienced by the thirty-five workers who had become stewards. Fourteen had returned to the worker role, either because they had not sought re-election by their work groups or because they had failed to win re-election, and only six were still stewards. (The other fifteen respondents, who composed almost half of this group, had either voluntarily left Rockwell or had been laid off as part of the general reduction in force.)

Once again, in June 1954, the researchers returned to Rockwell to readminister the questionnaires that the workers had filled out in 1951 and 1952. The instructions to the respondents were substantially the same as those given in 1952—i.e. a sample of employees had been chosen to get up-to-date measures of employees' attitudes toward working conditions at Rockwell and the same groups were selected this time as had been se-

throw some light on an important question suggests that a reporting of these results may be worthwhile.

Results: Phase 2

The principal question examined here was: on those items where a change in roles resulted in a change in attitudes

TABLE 5. *Effects of Entering and Leaving the Foreman Role on Attitudes toward Management and the Union*

	WORKERS WHO BECAME FOREMEN AND STAYED FOREMEN (N = 12)			WORKERS WHO BECAME FOREMEN AND WERE LATER DEMOTED (N = 8)		
	(W) 1951	(F) 1952	(F) 1954	(W) 1951	(F) 1952	(W) 1954
% who feel Rockwell is a good place to work	33	92	100	25	75	50
% who feel management officers really care about the workers at Rockwell	8	33	67	0	25	0
% who feel the union should not have more say in setting labor standards	33	100	100	13	63	13
% who are satisfied with the way the incentive system works out at Rockwell	17	75	75	25	50	13
% who believe a worker's standard will not be changed just because he is a high producer	42	83	100	25	63	75
% who feel ability should count more than seniority in promotions	33	58	75	25	50	38

lected last time in order to lend greater stability to the results.

In this phase of the study, the numbers of cases with which we were dealing in the various groups were so small that the data could only be viewed as suggestive, and systematic statistical analysis of the data did not seem to be too meaningful. However, the unusual opportunity to

between 1951 and 1952, how are these attitudes influenced by a reverse change in roles between 1952 and 1954?

The most consistent and widespread attitude changes noted between 1951 and 1952 were those that resulted when workers moved into the foreman role. What are the effects of moving out of the foreman role between 1952 and 1954? The data indicate that, in general, most of the "gains" that were observed when workers became foremen are "lost" when they become workers again. The results on six of the items, showing the proportions who take pro-management positions at various points in time, are presented in Table 5. On almost all of the items, the foremen who remain foremen

to the same levels as they had been in 1951, before they had ever moved into the foreman role.

The results on the effects of moving out of the steward role are less clearcut. As shown in Table 6, there is no marked tendency for ex-stewards to revert to earlier-held attitudes when they go from the steward role to the worker role. At the

TABLE 6. *Effects of Entering and Leaving the Steward Role on Attitudes toward Management and the Union*

	WORKERS WHO WERE ELECTED STEWARDS AND WERE LATER RE-ELECTED ($N = 6$)			WORKERS WHO WERE ELECTED STEWARDS BUT WERE NOT LATER RE-ELECTED ($N = 14$)		
	(W) 1951	(S) 1952	(S) 1954	(W) 1951	(S) 1952	(W) 1954
% who feel Rockwell is a good place to work	50	0	0	29	79	36
% who feel management officers really care about the workers at Rockwell	0	0	0	14	14	0
% who feel the union should not have more say in setting labor standards	0	17	0	14	14	14
% who are satisfied with the way the incentive system works out at Rockwell	17	17	0	43	43	21
% who believe a worker's standard will not be changed just because he is a high producer	50	50	17	21	43	36
% who feel ability should count more than seniority in promotions	67	17	17	36	36	21

either retain their favorable attitudes toward management or become even more favorable toward management between 1952 and 1954, while the demoted foremen show fairly consistent drops in the direction of re-adopting the attitudes they held when they had been in the worker role. On the whole, the attitudes held by demoted foremen in 1954, after they had left the foreman role, fall roughly

same time, it should be recalled that there had not been particularly marked changes in their attitudes when they initially changed from the worker role to the steward role. These findings, then, are consistent with the interpretation offered earlier that the change in roles between worker and steward is less significant than the change in roles between worker and foreman.

A question might be raised about what is represented in the reversal of attitudes found among ex-foremen. Does it represent a positive taking-on of attitudes appropriate for respondents who are re-entering the worker role, or does it constitute a negative, perhaps embittered reaction away from the attitudes they held before being demoted from the foreman role? A definitive answer to this question cannot be arrived at, but it might be suggested that if we were dealing with a situation where a reversion in roles did not constitute such a strong psychological blow to the role occupants (as was probably the case among demoted foremen), then such a marked reversion in attitudes might not have occurred.[4]

One final table is of interest here. Table 7 compares the attitudes of two groups of respondents: 1. the twelve employees who were rank-and-file workers in 1951, had been selected as foremen by 1952, and were still foremen in 1954; and 2. the six employees who were rank-and-file workers in 1951, had been elected as stewards by 1952, and were still stewards in 1954. At each time period, for each of the sixteen questions examined earlier in Tables 1 through 4, the table shows 1. the proportion of foremen or future foremen who took a pro-management position on these questions; 2. the proportion

[4] There were a number of reactions to demotion among the eight ex-foremen, as obtained from informal interviews with these respondents. Some reacted impunitively (i.e. they blamed uncontrollable situational determinants) and did not seem to be bothered by demotion. Others reacted extrapunitively (i.e. they blamed management) or intrapunitively (i.e. they blamed themselves) and appeared to be more disturbed by demotion. One way of testing the hypothesis that attitude reversion is a function of embitterment would be to see if sharper reversion occurs among extrapunitive and intrapunitive respondents. However, the small number of cases does not permit an analysis of this kind to be carried out in the present situation.

of stewards or future stewards who took a pro-management position on these questions; and 3. the difference between these proportions. The following are the mean differences in proportions for the three time periods.

1. In 1951, while both future foremen and future stewards still occupied the rank-and-file worker role, the mean difference was only −.1 per cent, which means that practically no difference in attitudes existed between these two groups at this time. (The minus signs means that a slightly, but far from significantly, larger proportion of future stewards than future foremen expressed a pro-management position on these items.)

2. In 1952, after the groups had been in the foreman and steward roles for about one year, the mean difference had jumped to +47.8 per cent, which means that a sharp wedge had been driven between them. Both groups had tended to become polarized in opposite directions, as foremen took on attitudes consistent with being a representative of management and stewards took on attitudes appropriate for a representative of the union.

3. In 1954, after the groups had been in the foreman and steward roles for two to three years, the mean differences was +62.4 per cent, which means that a still larger gap had opened up between them. Although the gap had widened, it is interesting to note that the changes that occurred during this later and longer 1952 to 1954 period are not as sharp or as dramatic as the changes that occurred during the initial and shorter 1951 to 1952 period.

These findings offer further support for the proposition that roles can influence attitudes. The data indicate that changes in attitudes occurred soon after changes in roles took place. And inside a period of three years those who had remained in their new roles had developed almost

TABLE 7. *Effects of Foreman and Steward Roles over a Three-Year Period: before Change in Roles, after One Year in New Roles, and after Two-Three Years in New Roles*

% Who Take a Pro-management Position on the Following Questions.†	BEFORE CHANGE IN ROLES (1951)			AFTER 1 YEAR IN NEW ROLES (1952)			AFTER 2–3 YEARS IN NEW ROLES (1954)		
	Workers Who Became Foremen	Workers Who Became Stewards	D%*	Workers Who Became Foremen	Workers Who Became Stewards	D%*	Workers Who Became Foremen	Workers Who Became Stewards	D%*
Question 1.	33	50	−17	92	0	+92	100	0	+100
Question 2.	33	33	0	75	33	+42	67	17	+50
Question 3.	92	83	+9	100	100	0	100	50	+50
Question 4.	8	0	+8	33	0	+33	67	0	+67
Question 5.	67	100	−33	67	17	+50	33	17	+16
Question 6.	33	0	+33	100	17	+83	100	0	+100
Question 7.	8	0	+8	50	0	+50	58	0	+58
Question 8.	75	67	+8	75	50	+25	58	17	+41
Question 9.	33	83	−50	83	17	+66	83	0	+83
Question 10.	17	17	0	75	17	+58	75	0	+75
Question 11.	17	17	0	25	0	+25	67	0	+67
Question 12.	42	50	−8	83	50	+33	100	17	+83
Question 13.	58	50	+8	100	17	+83	100	17	+83
Question 14.	33	67	−34	50	17	+33	75	17	+58
Question 15.	33	0	+33	58	0	+58	67	0	+67
Question 16.	67	33	+34	67	33	+34	67	67	0
No. of Cases	12	6		12	6		12	6	
Mean D%			−0.1			+47.8			+62.4

* Percentage of workers who became foremen who take a pro-management position minus percentage of workers who became stewards who take a pro-management position.

† Question numbers refer to the question numbers of the attitudinal items in Tables 1 through 4.

diametrically opposed sets of attitudinal positions.

Discussion

A role may be defined as a set of behaviors that are expected of people who occupy a certain position in a social system. These expectations consist of shared attitudes or beliefs, held by relevant populations, about what role occupants should and should not do. The theoretical basis for hypothesizing that a role will have effects on role occupants lies in the nature of these expectations. If a role occupant meets these expectations, the "rights" or "rewards" associated with the role will be accorded to him. If he fails to meet these expectations, the "rights" or "rewards" will be withheld from him and "punishments" may be meted out.[5]

A distinction should be made between the effects of roles on people's attitudes and the effects of roles on their actions. How roles affect actions can probably be explained in a fairly direct fashion. Actions are overt and readily enforceable. If a person fails to behave in ways appropriate to his role, this can immediately be seen, and steps may be taken to bring the deviant or non-conformist into line. Role deviants may be evicted from their roles, placed in less rewarding roles, isolated from other members of the group, or banished entirely from the social system.

But attitudes are not as overt as actions. A person may behave in such a way as to reveal his attitudes, but he can —and often does—do much to cover them up. Why, then, should a change in roles lead to a change in actions? A number of explanatory factors might be

suggested here. The present discussion will be confined to two factors that are probably generic to a wide variety of situations. One pertains to the influence of reference groups; the other is based on an assumption about people's need to have attitudes internally consistent with their actions.

A change in roles almost invariably involves a change in reference groups. Old reference groups may continue to influence the role occupant, but new ones also come into play. The change in reference groups may involve moving into a completely new group (as when a person gives up membership in one organization and joins another one) or it may simply involve taking on new functions in the same group (as when a person is promoted to a higher position in a hierarchical organization). In both situations, new reference groups will tend to bring about new frames of reference, new self-percepts, and new vested interests, and these in turn will tend to produce new attitudinal orientations.

In addition to a change in reference groups, a change in roles also involves a change in functions and a change in the kinds of behaviors and actions that the role occupant must display if he is to fulfil these functions. A change in actions, let us assume, comes about because these actions are immediately required, clearly visible, and hence socially enforceable. If we further assume a need for people to have attitudes that are internally consistent with their actions, then at least one aspect of the functional significance of a change in attitudes becomes clear. A change in attitudes enables a new role occupant to justify, to make rational, or perhaps simply to rationalize his change in actions. Having attitudes that are consistent with actions helps the role occupant to be "at one" with himself and facilitates his effective performance of the functions he is expected to carry out.

The reference-group principle and the self-consistency principle postulate some-

[5] An earlier discussion of the role concept, with particular reference to its application to the study of complex organizations, is found in Jacobson, Charters, and Lieberman (1).

what different chains of events in accounting for the effects of roles on attitudes and actions. In abbreviated versions, the different chains may be spelled out in the following ways:

1. Reference-group principle: A change in roles involves a change in reference groups . . . which leads to a change in attitudes . . . which leads to a change in actions.

2. Self-consistency principle: A change in roles involves a change in functions . . . which leads to a change in actions . . . which leads to a change in attitudes.

In the former chain, a person's attitudes influence his actions; in the latter chain, a person's actions influence his attitudes. Both chains might plausibly account for the results obtained, but whether either chain, both chains, or other chains is or are valid cannot be determined from the data available. A more direct investigation of the underlying mechanisms responsible for the impact of roles on attitudes would appear to be a fruitful area for further research.

But apart from the question of underlying mechanisms, the results lend support to the proposition that a person's attitudes will be influenced by his role. Relatively consistent changes in attitudes were found both among workers who were made foremen and among workers who were made stewards, although these changes were more clear-cut for foremen than for stewards. The more interesting set of results—as far as role theory in general is concerned—would seem to be the data on the effects of entering and leaving the foreman role. It was pointed out earlier that the foreman role, unlike the steward role, is a full-time, relatively permanent position, and moving into this position entails taking on a very new and different set of functions. When workers are made foremen, their attitudes change in a more pro-management and anti-union direction. When they are demoted and move back into the worker role, their attitudes change once again, this time in a more pro-union and anti-management direction. In both instances, the respondents' attitudes seem to be molded by the roles which they occupy at a given time.

The readiness with which the respondents in this study shed one set of attitudes and took on another set of attitudes might suggest either that 1. the attitudes studied do not tap very basic or deep-rooted facets of the respondents' psyches, or 2. the character structures of the respondents are such as not to include very deeply ingrained sets of value orientations. Riesman (4) deals with this problem in his discussion of "other-directedness" vs. "inner-directedness." How much the rapid shifts in attitudes observed here reflect the particular kinds of respondents who underwent changes in roles in the present situation, and how much these shifts reflect the national character of the American population, can only be speculated on at the present time.

Summary

This study was designed to test the proposition that a person's attitudes will be influenced by the role he occupies in a social system. This is a commonly accepted postulate in role theory but there appears to be little in the way of definitive empirical evidence to support it. Earlier studies have generally made inferences about the effects of roles on attitudes on the basis of correlational data gathered at a single point in time. The present study attempted to measure the effects of roles on attitudes through data gathered at three different points in time.

In September and October 1951, 2,354 rank-and-file workers in a factory situation were asked to fill out attitude questionnaires dealing with management and the union. During the next twelve months, twenty-three of these workers were promoted to foreman and thirty-five were elected by their work groups as union stewards. In December 1952, the questionnaires were re-administered to the two groups of workers who had changed roles and to two matched control groups of workers who had not changed roles. By comparing the attitude changes that occurred in the experimental groups with the attitude changes that occurred in their respective control groups, the effects of moving into the foreman and steward roles could be determined.

The results on this phase of the study men tended to become more favorable toward management, and the workers who were made stewards tended to be-showed that the experimental groups underwent systematic changes in attitudes after they were placed in their new roles, while the control groups underwent no changes or less marked changes from the "before" situation to the "after" situation. The workers who were made fore-come more favorable toward the union. The changes were more marked among new foremen than among new stewards, which can be probably accounted for by the fact that the change from worker to foreman seems to be a more significant and more meaningful change in roles than the change from worker to steward.

In the months following the second administration of the questionnaire, a number of the workers who had become foremen and stewards reverted to the rank-and-file worker role. Some of the foremen were cut back to non-supervisory positions during a period of economic recession, and some of the stewards either did not run again or failed to be re-elected during the annual steward elections. In June 1954, the questionnaires were once again administered to the same group of respondents. By comparing the attitude changes that occurred among foremen and stewards who left these roles with the attitude changes that occurred among foremen and stewards who re-

mained in these roles, the effects of moving out of these roles could be assessed.

The results of this phase of the study showed that foremen who were demoted tended to revert to the attitudes they had previously held while they were in the worker role, while foremen who remained in the foreman role either maintained the attitudes they had developed when they first became foremen or moved even further in that direction. The results among stewards who left the steward role were less consistent and less clear-cut, which parallels the smaller and less clear-cut attitude changes that took place when they first became stewards.

The findings support the proposition that a person's role will have an impact on his attitudes, but they still leave unanswered the question of what underlying mechanisms are operating here. A more direct investigation of these underlying mechanisms might comprise a fruitful area for further research.

REFERENCES

1. Jacobson, E., W. W. Charters, Jr., and S. Lieberman: "The Use of the Role Concept in the Study of Complex Organizations." *J. Soc. Issues*, Vol. 7, No. 3, pp. 18–27, 1951.
2. Newcomb, T. M.: *Social Psychology*. New York: The Dryden Press, 1950; London: Tavistock Publications, 1952.
3. Parsons, T.: *The Social System*. Glencoe, Ill.: The Free Press, 1951; London: Tavistock Publications Ltd., 1951.
4. Riesman, D.: *The Lonely Crowd*. New Haven: Yale University Press, 1950.
5. Stouffer, S. A., E. A. Suchman, L. C. DeVinney, S. A. Star, and R. M. Williams, Jr.: *The American Soldier: Adjustment During Army Life* (Vol. 1). Princeton: Princeton University Press, 1949.
6. Walker, H. M., and J. Lev: *Statistical Inference*. New York: Henry Holt and Co., Inc., 1953.

HYPERTENSION AND ARTERIOSCLEROSIS
IN EXECUTIVE AND NONEXECUTIVE PERSONNEL

by Richard E. Lee and Ralph F. Schneider

In relatively recent press reports, several writers have highlighted a close association between cardiovascular disease and the strains of executive responsibility. Popular novels have been devoted to this theme, and promotion with increase in executive load has been described as possibly a considerable threat to life. Few, if any, of these articles, however, contain objective and factual data to substantiate their theses. Workers in outstanding medical clinics have described their findings in relatively large numbers of executive individuals, particularly with regard to the incidence of various cardiovascular ailments,[1] but few have buttressed their findings with specific cardiovascular disease data on nonexecutive "office" personnel of comparable age and sex and working in the same or similar industrial environments. For that reason, the present study was carried out to obtain preliminary information as to whether there is any outstanding increase in the incidence of hypertensive and arteriosclerotic disease in executives as compared to nonexecutive personnel. In order to keep the study as uniform as possible, both groups examined included only "white-collar" employees of a large company, working in the same office buildings of a metropolitan area. Influential factors that might conceivably have resulted from differences in the type of work (such as heavy manual labor), geographical location, or climate were thereby ruled out as much as possible.

SOURCE: *Journal of the American Medical Association*, Vol. 167 (1958), pp. 1447–1450.

Methods

It is difficult to define an executive. Perhaps his greatest single general characteristic is that of policy formation and implementation. When the employment data on those subjects whose positions could be so described were collected and examined, it was found that three broad groupings could be established on the basis of job responsibilities. Those executives in the first group, consisting of members of boards of directors, corporate officers, and general managers, are referred to as "top executives." The second class, that of the middle management levels, is composed of department heads and assistants to corporate officers and is called the "executive" class. A third grouping of "minor executives" includes division heads, auditors, and others of lesser rank than a department head. It is possible that, in addition to these specific categories, there are certain other persons within the company that sometimes have occasional duties of policy-forming nature. Such would be few, however, and these positions were not included in the survey.

The findings in each executive class were compared with those of subjects with fewer responsibilities (such as stenographers, secretaries, clerks, assistant supervisors, and supervisors) in the same companies. This latter group was considered in entirety and, also, with regard to only males of an average age comparable in general to that of the executive group.

A total of 1,171 male executives and

TABLE 1. *Association between Executive Work and Hypertensive Disease*

	TOP EXECUTIVE (Av. Age, 52.4 Yr.)			EXECUTIVE (Av. Age, 50.6 Yr.)			MINOR EXECUTIVE (Av. Age, 48.6 Yr.)			TOTAL EXECUTIVE (Av. Age, 50.5 Yr.)			NONEXECUTIVE MALE — All (Av. Age, 39.5 Yr.)			NONEXECUTIVE MALE — Over 40 Yr. (Av. Age, 51.3 Yr.)			NONEXECUTIVE FEMALE (Av. Age, 35.9 Yr.)		
	No.	%	Av. Age, Yr.	No.	%	Av. Age, Yr.	No.	%	Av. Age, Yr.	No.	%	Av. Age, Yr.	No.	%	Av. Age, Yr.	No.	%	Av. Age, Yr.	No.	%	Av. Age, Yr.
Labile blood pressure	2	1.0	50.0	1	0.3	40.0	8	1.3	45.0	11	1.0	45.0	3*	0.4	41.0	1	0.3	...	2	0.3	44.0
Essential hypertension	10	5.0	56.5	15	5.0	53.9	42	7.0	48.0	67	6.1	52.8	29*	4.5	50.1	22	7.5	52.5	21*	3.7	47.1
Hypertensive vascular disease	3	1.6	51.0	5	1.7	58.2	17	2.8	58.2	25	2.2	55.8	11	1.7	52.6	10	8.4	52.7	3	0.4	48.0
Hypertensive cardiovascular disease	5	2.5	60.0	6	2.0	60.0	19	3.0	59.7	30	2.8	59.9	13	2.0	57.4	11	3.7	59.1	4	0.6	55.0
Totals	20	10.1		27	9.0		86	14.1		133	12.1		56	8.6		44	14.9		30	5.0	
No. examined	135			297			601			1,088			640			293			563		
Cardiovascular disease	48			62			141			251			142			111			59		

* Benign.

1,203 nonexecutives (of whom 563 were female) were studied for an average of five years. All were subjected periodically to a complete medical history, physical examination, urinalysis, complete blood cell count, chest x-ray, and electrocardiogram. Other laboratory data were obtained in accordance with the findings. When considered necessary, referral was made to specialists for further diagnostic evaluation and for treatment. With the exception of those few who died or retired, all persons are still on a program of active medical follow-up.

Blood pressures greater than 140/95 mm. Hg were considered elevated, and four major clinical categories of "hypertension" were considered. The first, labile blood pressure, was usually normal but could be found on occasional examinations at hypertensive levels. Persons in the second group, that of essential vascular hypertension, had a fixed blood pressure elevation but no evidence of vascular abnormality (for instance, the fundal vessels were normal). In contrast, those in the third group, that of hypertensive vascular disease, displayed grade 1 to grade 3 changes in the retinal vessels, and their urea clearance, when tested, was below 70% of normal. The fourth and last category, that of hypertensive cardiovascular disease, included individuals with vascular abnormalities in the fundi and objective evidence of cardiac involvement and three persons with "malignant hypertension."

Patients with arteriosclerosis were readily separated into three major groups. The first included those whose history, physical examination, and x-rays indicated generalized arteriosclerosis without evidence of cardiac involvement. The second included persons with arteriosclerosis with arteriosclerotic heart disease as evidenced by either angina or cardiac decompensation and cardiac enlargement or abnormal electrocardiograms. The third group was composed of those having generalized arteriosclerosis and heart involvement

with myocardial infarction. In each case the latter was documented by history, by a physical examination, and, in all instances, by specific changes in the electrocardiograms.

In each group and subgroup, the total number of individuals and the percentage having the various diseases were calculated, along with the average age, and the findings collected in tabular form. The nonexecutive males are presented in total and also in a subgroup including only those over 40 years of age, with a mean age equal generally to that of the average executive. For comparative purposes, the findings on nonexecutive females are also presented. Collected data were analyzed by the chi-square test.

Results

HYPERTENSION (Table 1). Lability of blood pressure was recorded relatively infrequently in all work classes, generally being noted in about 1% or less of individuals. Essential vascular hypertension was found in 5 to 7% of the various groups, although it was somewhat lower in nonexecutive females. Hypertensive vascular disease ranged from a low of 1.6% in the group of top executives to a high of 3.4% in the group of nonexecutive males of comparable age. Hypertensive cardiovascular disease in the group of nonexecutive males had an incidence of 3.7%, compared with 2.5% in the group of executives in the top levels of management. Analysis of data by the chi-square test reveals a p value of between 0.05 and 0.1, indicating lack of association between the executive state and hypertensive disease (Table 2). Actually, hypertension was almost significantly more frequent in nonexecutives. Of interest is the finding that females of a comparable average age to males generally have fewer hypertensive ailments.

TABLE 2. *Association Between Executive Work and Hypertension and Arterio-sclerosis (Total Groups)*

	TOP EXEC-UTIVE		EXEC-UTIVE		MINOR EXEC-UTIVE		TOTAL EXEC-UTIVE		NONEX-ECUTIVE (OVER 40 YR.)		p (Chi-Square)
	No.	%	No.	%	No.	%	No.	%	No.	%	
No. examined	185		297		601		1,083		293		
Hypertension	20	10.8	27	9.1	86	12.60	133	12.3	44	15.0	>0.05
Arteriosclerosis	22	11.9	23	7.7	40	6.56	85	7.8	45	15.4	<0.01
Myocardial infarction	8	4.3	12	4.0	20	3.30	40	3.7	15	5.1	<0.1

ARTERIOSCLEROTIC DISEASE (Table 3). In consideration of generalized arteriosclerosis, it is noted that the top executives had a somewhat greater incidence of this ailment than either of the other two executive classes. It is doubtful that this is related to their duties, however, for this vascular disorder was slightly more common in the nonexecutive males over 40 years of age than in persons in the top management levels. This latter is true, also, with regard to arteriosclerotic heart disease. Myocardial infarction also appeared slightly more frequently in the older nonexecutive males than in any of the three executive categories. A comparison of the groups with regard to total cases of arteriosclerotic disease demonstrates that the group of nonexecutive males over 40 years of age had the greatest percentage of subjects with this general disorder. Analysis of the differences in incidence of arteriosclerotic disease (all types) between executives as a whole and the nonexecutive males of comparable age by the chi-square test (Table 2) reveals a p value of less than 0.01. Its infrequency in executives is therefore considered to be significant. Evaluation of the incidence of "heart attacks" (myocardial infarction) in both groups (Table 2) by the same method revealed no relationship with the level of business responsibility (p value greater than 0.1).

Comment

The data in these tables are surprising, for, in spite of the implied relationship between executive responsibilities and increased cardiovascular ailments,[2] our data reveal no increase in incidence of either hypertensive or arteriosclerotic disease in the executive class. Hypertension generally appeared somewhat more frequently in subjects at lower levels of business duties. In considering arteriosclerotic disease as a whole, its occurrence among executives was significantly less than in persons in other work groups, of comparable age, and employed in the same office building.

The incidence of certain diseases in employed personnel as determined by different observers may vary as much as twelvefold.[3] For that reason, comparisons of the data obtained in the present study with those obtained by workers who were studying exclusively executive populations elsewhere must be made with this fact in mind. Nonetheless, in general terms, the incidence of hypertensive disease or arteriosclerotic disease in the executive and nonexecutive staffs studied herein compares favorably with or is generally somewhat below that found in other studies.[4]

It is tempting to consider the possible reasons why even the group of persons at the highest levels of executive respon-

TABLE 3. *Association between Executive Work and Arteriosclerotic Disease*

| | TOP EXECUTIVE (Av. Age, 52.4 Yr.) | | | EXECUTIVE (Av. Age, 50.6 Yr.) | | | MINOR EXECUTIVE (Av. Age, 48.6 Yr.) | | | TOTAL EXECUTIVE (Av. Age, 50.5 Yr.) | | | NONEXECUTIVE * | | | | | |
| | | | | | | | | | | | | | All (Av. Age, 39.5 Yr.) | | | Over 40 Yr. (Av. Age, 51.3 Yr.) | | |
	No.	%	Av. Age, Yr.	No.	%	Av. Age, Yr.	No.	%	Av. Age, Yr.	No.	%	Av. Age, Yr.	No.	%	Av. Age, Yr.	No.	%	Av. Age, Yr.
Generalized arteriosclerosis	8	4.3	63	5	1.7	59.0	7	1.16	60.5	20	1.8	60.8	15	2.3	59.5	15	5.1	58.2
Arteriosclerotic heart disease	6	3.2	55	6	2.0	60.0	13	2.10	57.6	25	2.3	57.3	16	2.4	55.6	15	5.1	56.1
Myocardial infarction	8	4.3	57	12	4.0	58.9	20	3.30	53.4	40	3.7	56.7	19	3.0	53.5	15	5.1	58.4
Totals	22	11.8		23	7.7		40	6.56		85	7.8		50	7.7		45	15.3	
No. examined	185			297			601			1,083			640			298		
Miscellaneous vascular disease	6			12			15			...			36			...		

* No women were found with arteriosclerotic disease.

sibility showed no increase in incidence of the vascular states described and had notably fewer subjects with arteriosclerotic disease, as compared to less demanding positions from the business viewpoint. There is always the possibility that success in career attainment goes hand in hand with good health; in other words, the healthier go higher. A second possibility is that, with greater financial income, a person is able to afford a higher standard of living and perhaps more complete medical care from private physicians. This latter is not likely a major factor in the present study, because all of the subjects concerned have available to them and maintain the same medical follow-up program regardless of the level of duties within the organization. A third consideration should be to the matter of executive education and insight. The majority are college graduates, and several have postgraduate degrees. As a part of their training in the past, they have perhaps learned to realize the value of "escape valves" and the need for outside avenues of expression, such as hobbies. The benefit that may be derived from such endeavors has been emphasized repeatedly.

The lack of an increased incidence of hypertension among executives as a "stress" phenomenon further emphasizes the importance of reaction by the individual to his environment, rather than the physical and intellectual demands of that environment per se. Stress is a relative and a subjective matter. When the inherent capacities of the individual to perform fail to measure up to the demands of his world, the harmonious balance between the subject and his environment is disrupted and a stress reaction takes place in the individual. This response occurs regardless of whether the factor in the external environment is a speedily approaching deadline for a frantic technical assistant or the threatened failure of a large business venture for the director in charge. From the medical viewpoint, one can therefore wonder whether at least a part

of the recent emphasis on dangers of executive life to the vascular system may be based more on knowledge of the exceptions rather than of the rule.

Summary and Conclusions

The health status of executives and non-executives (white-collar workers) of comparable age and sex, working in the same buildings, were compared with regard to the incidence of hypertension and of arteriosclerotic disease. There was, among the executives, significantly less of the arteriosclerotic phenomena studied than was expected. Analysis of group data revealed no relationship between the level of responsibility and the incidence either of hypertensive disease or of myocardial infarction.

REFERENCES

1. (a) Baker, J. P., and others: "Executive Health Examination," *South M. J.* 46:984–988 (Oct.) 1953. (b) S. C. Franco, and A. J. Gerl: "Periodic Health Examination —5-Year Survey." *Indust. Med.* 24:161–167 (April) 1955. (c) M. Fremont-Smith: "Periodic Examination of Supposedly Well Persons," *New England J. Med.* 248:170–173 (Jan. 29) 1953. (d) R. J. Bolt, C. J. Tupper, and O. T. Mallery, Jr.: "Appraisal of Periodic Health Examinations," *A. M. A. Arch. Indust. Health* 12:420–426 (Oct.) 1955. (e) J. P. Baker, and others: "Effectiveness of Periodical Medical Evaluation," *Indust. Med.* 25:248–250 (June) 1956. (f) S. C. Franco: "Early Detection of Disease by Periodic Examination." *Indust. Med.* 25:251–257 (June) 1956.
2. Alvarez, W. C.: "How to Care for Health of Executives," Chicago, Wilcox and Follet Co. P. Stocks: "Coronary Disease in Modern Stress," Letters to the Editor, *Lancet,* 1:351 (Feb. 10) 1951.
3. Densen, P. M., C. A. D'Alonzo, and M. G. Munn: "Opportunities and Problems in Study of Chronic Disease in Industry," *J. Chron. Dis.* 1:231–252 (March) 1955.

4. Morris, J. M., and others: "Coronary Heart-Disease and Physical Activity of Work," *Lancet* 2:1053–1057 (Nov. 21) 1953. R. P. McCombs, and J. J. Finn, Jr.: "Group Health Surveys in Diagnostic Center," *New England J. Med.* 248:165–170 (Jan.) 1953. H. M. Marvin: *Executive and His Heart Attack*, publications 11–17, Chicago, Chicago Heart Association, Nov., 1952. Commission on Chronic Illness:

"Chronic Illness in Large City, Baltimore Story," *Chronic Illness in United States*, vol. 4, Cambridge, Mass., Harvard University Press, 1957, p. 78. C. A. D'Alonzo, P. M. Densen, A. S. Fleming, and M. G. Munn: "Prevalence of Certain Diseases Among Executives in Comparison with Other Employees," *Indust. Med.* 23:357 (Aug.) 1954. Reference 1d and e.

2 · Social Class Position

SOCIAL CLASS, CHILD REARING PRACTICES, AND CHILD BEHAVIOR

by Martha Sturm White

Several recent studies have raised interesting questions about the relation of social class position to child-rearing practices. In particular there have been some challenges to the study reported on by Ericson and by Davis and Havighurst.[1] This study, carried out in Chicago in the early 1940's, found the middle class to be generally more severe in weaning and toilet training, and to restrict and put more demands upon the child. Later studies[2] have found several differences, primarily in the direction of more permissiveness by middle class mothers than the Chicago study described.

What are the causes of these differences? Are the samples not comparable? Are there regional differences? Or have mothers in different social class positions changed their child-rearing practices during the intervening decade? The study reported here pertains to these questions. During the first half of 1953, a group of mothers and their children were interviewed on two occasions in a study on the effects of sibling birth. An approximately equal number of middle- and working-class families were included, so that it was pos-

[1] Martha C. Ericson, "Social Status and Child Rearing Practices," in T. M. Newcomb and Eugene L. Hartley (eds.), *Readings in Social Psychology*, New York: Henry Holt and Company, pp. 494–501; A. Davis and R. J. Havighurst, "Social Class and Color Differences in Child Rearing," *American Sociological Review*, 11 (December, 1946), pp. 698–710. See also Robert J. Havighurst and Allison Davis, "A Comparison of the Chicago and Harvard Studies of Social Class Differences in Child Rearing," *American Sociological Review*, 20 (August, 1955), pp. 438–442.

[2] Ethelyn Henry Klatskin, "Shifts in Child Care Practices in Three Social Classes Under an Infant Care Program of Flexible Methodology," *The American Journal of Orthopsychiatry*, 22 (January, 1952), pp. 52–61; Eleanor E. Maccoby and Patricia K. Gibbs and the Staff of the Laboratory of Human Development, Harvard University, "Methods of Child Rearing in Two Social Classes," in *Readings in Child Development* edited by W. E. Martin and Celia Burns Stendler; New York: Harcourt, Brace and Company, 1954; Robert R. Sears, Eleanor E. Maccoby and Harry Levin, *Patterns of Child Rearing*, New York: Row, Peterson and Co., 1957.

SOURCE: *American Sociological Review*, Vol. 22 (1957), pp. 704–712.

sible to test several social class hypotheses.

The two hypotheses reported on in this article are: (1) child-rearing practices have changed since the earlier studies were made; (2) these changes are a result of the different reference groups used by the middle- and working-class mothers.

Comments on the changing fashions in child rearing are common in popular literature, particularly comments on the increase in permissiveness, and it is possible that these remarks are a reflection of changes in practice. It is of course difficult to demonstrate a change when knowledge of prior conditions is scanty. Davis and Havighurst, for example, stress the fact that theirs is not a representative sample. However, it has frequently been taken as representative of child training practices of the time,[3] and since we have no contrary knowledge, it will be accepted as such here. The method of testing is to compare the child training practices found in California in 1953 with those of Chicago in 1943 and of Boston in 1951–52.

How or why changes take place is another question. One possibility, tested here, is that the middle class is most responsive to new ideas in the environment, particularly those transmitted by experts and through mass media. To use Riesman's term, they are "other directed," i.e. they tend to rely on other people (outside of the family) in their environment, and on certain kinds of authority figures.[4] Although both classes rely on mass media, the middle class is more discriminating.

Other studies have established that expert ideas on child rearing have changed from decade to decade.[5] It seems conceiv-

able that if middle-class parents are responsive to certain sources of opinion, such as experts and other people, they also might be more apt to change their practices. On this basis, we would expect the middle-class to have changed their practices since the 1943 study.

Method

THE SAMPLE. The sample consisted of 74 mothers and 74 children. All of the mothers had only one child, and the child was between $2\frac{1}{2}$ and $5\frac{1}{2}$ years of age. These ages were chosen so that the children would be able to talk, and would be mainly under the influence of the family rather than the school. Additional requirements were that the parents be living together and be native-born.

The data were gathered during the first half of 1953 in California in the South San Francisco Peninsula area, which does not include San Francisco itself, but a string of suburban and industrial communities stretching from San Mateo to San Jose. Approximately 15 families each came from Palo Alto, Menlo Park, and San Jose, and the remainder from adjacent towns. Although the study was conducted from Stanford University, only a few families had any connection with the university.

The larger study on stress caused by the arrival of a second child in the family [6] of which this was a part required 50 of the mothers to be expecting a second child at the time of the first interview, and the remaining 24 control families (who were not expecting a baby) to be matched on a

[3] As in John W. M. Whiting and Irvin L. Child, *Child Training and Personality*, New Haven: Yale University Press, 1953, pp. 66–67.

[4] David Riesman, *The Lonely Crowd*, New Haven: Yale University Press, 1950, pp. 19–23, 36–55.

[5] See Martha Wolfenstein, "The Emergence of Fun Morality," in *The Journal of Social Issues*, 7 (No. 4, 1951), pp. 15–25; C. B. Stendler, "Sixty Years of Child Training Prac-

tices," *Journal of Pediatrics*, 36 (January, 1950), pp. 122–134.

[6] Frances Orr, "The Reactions of Young Children to the Birth of a Sibling," (In preparation) as a Genetic Psychology Monograph. More extensive information on the sample and method of obtaining it can be found here.

group basis by occupation of father, neighborhood, age and sex of child. Due to the difficulties of getting such a sample that could also be interviewed over a six month interval, referrals were secured in a variety of ways. They came from neighbors or friends of families already in the study, from Public Health Nurses, personnel managers in industry, from maternal prenatal exercise classes, from physicians and nursery school teachers, and from school district surveys. Only 14 women, or less than 6 per cent of the total 245 contacted, were uninterested or were unwilling to be interviewed. The remainder of those not used proved to be ineligible or had moved.

THE INTERVIEW. The interviewing was done in the home by two experienced psychologists. While one talked to the mother for a period of between one-and-a-half and three hours, the other "interviewed" the child in his room or in the kitchen by means of doll play. Draw-A-Man tests, and other standard situations. Standard questions were used in the mother interview with follow-up probes. Many of the questions asked were identical with those of the Boston study.[7] The replies of the mother were taken down as nearly verbatim as possible.

The Measures

SOCIAL CLASS. The occupation of the father in the family was rated on a Warner scale with an inter-rater reliability coefficient of .93.[8] A comparison of the occupation status of the two groups may be seen in Table 1. Groups were desig-

[7] Copies of the interview and codes used in the Boston study were made available by Robert S. Sears.

[8] W. Lloyd Warner, Marcia Meeker, Kenneth Eells, Social Class in America, Chicago: Science Research Associates, Inc., 1949, pp. 140–141.

nated as middle or working class on the basis of an index of occupation and income. Occupation was given a weight of two, income one. The resulting distribution was divided into nine socio-economic status levels; from 1 to 4 was designated middle class and from 5 to 9, working class. Thus 36 of the families were classified as middle class, 38 as working class.

This system of class placement has the advantage of making the data comparable to the Boston study, and seems a fair approximation to the Chicago data. It also rather accurately divides the group into white-collar and blue-collar occupations. Such a gross, dichotomous classification was used tentatively, but it proved to be meaningful, not unduly distorting the underlying structure, and seemed appropriate to the size of the sample and the statistical measures used.

MOTHER BEHAVIOR VARIABLES. The answers to the interview questions were coded using when possible the same codes as the Boston study. Reliabilities were computed on all, and only items on which satisfactory reliabilities (.72 or above) were found were used. No reliability rating was possible for personality ratings of mother and child since only one person conducted each interview; consequently these ratings were used as a supplement to the parent behavior data.

STATISTICAL ANALYSIS. Although other investigators have used the t test for comparison, preliminary study indicated that the variances were not homogeneous on several items, so that chi-square seemed more appropriate for these data. Four-fold tables were used and comparisons made of the number of middle- and working-class families above and below the median of the variable in question. The break was made at the point that most nearly divided the total group evenly. In some cases a "yes" or "no" classification was more appropriate than the median. In other cases the meaning of the scale

TABLE 1. *Socio-Economic Characteristics of the Sample*

| | CLASS | |
	Middle	Working
Father's occupation (Warner)		
1	15 (42%)	0
2	14 (39%)	1 (3%)
3	7 (19%)	4 (10%)
4	0	10 (26%)
5	0	17 (45%)
6 & 7	0	6 (16%)
Father's education		
Grade school	0	3
7–12 grades	2	19
Some college	34	16
Mother's education		
Grade school	0	1
7–12 grades	7	26
College or technical training	29	11
Occupation of father's father		
Middle (1–3)	26	4
Working (4–7)	10	34
Occupation of mother's father		
Middle (1–3)	22	13
Working (4–7)	14	25
Social class by self-placement		
Middle	32	13
Intermediate	1	4
Working	3	20
"None"		1
Salary		
$5000 or over	32	11
Under $5000	4	27
Age of mother		
28 or under	14	21
Over 28	22	17

was better served by a three-fold classification, the highs, the moderates, and the lows. In these cases such a comparison was first made. This often resulted in low cell frequencies, and the median comparison was substituted when it did no violence to the relationship as indicated by the three-fold break. The two-tailed test was used and a correction for continuity was employed, since many authorities consider it mandatory for four-fold tables. regardless of cell frequencies.[9]

[9] For example, Don Lewis and C. J. Burke, "The Use and Misuse of the Chi-Square Test," *Psychological Bulletin*, 46 (November, 1949), pp. 433–489; Frederick Mosteller and Robert R. Bush, "Selected Quantitative Techniques," p. 314 in *Handbook of Social Psychology*, edited by Gardner Lindzey, Cambridge, Mass.: Addison-Wesley, 1954.

Results

The comparison of middle and working class on oral behavior and feeding regimen are presented in Table 2. On the whole there are few social class differences.

TABLE 2. *Social Class Differences on Oral and Feeding Variables*

	MIDDLE No.	WORKING No.
	Total	Total
* Number of children ever breast-fed	25/36	24/38
Breast-fed one month or less	9/36	12/38
Weaned before 9 months †	7/32	2/36
Weaned after 12 months	18/32	19/36
Weaned after 18 months ‡	13/32	8/36
* Self demand or child set schedule	23/36	21/38
* Some feeding problems	12/36	17/38
Severe oral regimen	11/24	23/34
Report of child thumbsucking §	23/36	14/38
Report of child nailbiting §§	6/36	16/38
Miscellaneous oral activity	8/36	7/38
Child has or has had comfort object (blanket etc.)	24/36	23/38

* Indicates question identical with that used in Boston study.
† $x^2 = 2.92$.
‡ $x^2 = 2.07$.
§ $x^2 = 4.62$, p $< .05$.
§§ $x^2 = 4.84$, p $< .05$.

There are no significant differences in use of breast feeding, duration of breast feeding, age when weaning is completed, extent to which demand feeding is practiced,

or severity of feeding problems. There is a very slight tendency for middle-class children to have been weaned either younger or older than lower-class children (but no difference in average age of weaning), and for middle-class infant oral regimen (an overall measure scored by a rater) to have been less severe. As in the Chicago and Boston studies, middle-class mothers report significantly more thumbsucking. However, working-class mothers report significantly more nailbiting, or biting and chewing activity.

In toilet training (Table 3), no difference was found in age at which bowel training was begun, but working-class mothers were significantly more severe in toilet training.

TABLE 3. *Social Class and Toilet Training*

	MIDDLE No.	WORKING No.
	Total	Total
* Below median age at which bowel training begun	18/35	21/38
* Severity of toilet training Below median †	23/36	14/38

* Indicates question identical with that used in Boston study.
† $x^2 = 4.62$, p $< .05$.

As seen in Table 4, there were no significant differences in dependency—how much the child wanted to be near mother, wanted attention, objected to separation, or was judged dependent.

When we asked the mothers about obedience training (Table 5), one rather interesting significant difference was found. If the child did not do what was asked, middle-class mothers were significantly more inclined to drop the subject occasionally. However, there was no difference when they were asked if they expected immediate obedience. More mothers in both groups say the father is more strict than they, but there is no class difference.

TABLE 4. Social Class and Dependency

	MIDDLE No.	WORKING No.
	Total	Total
* Dependence of child (from mother's report)		
Lows	16/36	20/38
* How much mother keeps track of child		
Lows	12/36	13/38
* Amount of attention child wants		
Lows	20/34	17/35
* Objects to separation		
Lows	14/36	18/38
* Rater's judgment of amount of dependency (based on mother's report)		
Lows	15/36	12/38

* Indicates question identical with that used in Boston study.

In an area that might be described as mother's responsiveness to the child, Table 6, there was one significant difference—middle-class mothers were more responsive to their baby's crying. They did not differ in amount of fun taking care of the baby, in the amount of demonstrativeness shown, or in how much they kept track of the child.

Several of the questions were directed at the topic of aggression. Table 7 shows that there were no differences in parents' report of amount of aggression in the home, in their demands for aggression against other children, or in how much the child was encouraged to fight back. One highly significant difference was in permissiveness towards aggression against

TABLE 5. Social Class and Obedience

	MIDDLE No.	WORKING No.
	Total	Total
* Who is stricter with child		
Father	16/36	14/38
Mother	10/36	10/38
* Does mother carry through demands or occasionally drop the subject		
Occasionally drops subject †	23/36	12/37
* Strictness in requiring obedience		
Lows	22/34	18/35

* Indicates question identical with that used in Boston study.
† $x^2 = 6.36$, $p < .02$.

TABLE 6. Social Class and Mother's Responsiveness to Child

	MIDDLE No.	WORKING No.
	Total	Total
Tendency to pick up baby when he cried †		
Lows	16/36	27/38
Amount of fun taking care of baby		
Lows	23/36	22/38
* Warmth or demonstrativeness of mother		
Lows	22/35	18/37

* Indicates question identical with that used in Boston study.
† $x^2 = 4.58$, $p < .05$.

parents. Middle-class women were consistently above the median in feeling that expression of aggression should be allowed. There are some tendencies for the working-class children to be more severely punished for aggression against the parent, and to be reported as fighting more with other children.

TABLE 7. *Social Class and Aggression*

	MIDDLE No.	WORKING No.
	Total	Total
* Parent demand for aggression against other children		
Lows	17/35	24/37
* Extent parent encouraged child to fight back		
Lows	9/28	12/32
Amount of fighting with other children		
Lows †	17/32	10/32
* Amount of aggression within the home		
Lows	11/36	12/38
* Permissiveness for aggression against parents		
Lows ‡	8/36	24/37
* Severity of punishment for aggression against parents		
Lows	21/34	16/34

* Indicates question identical with that used in Boston study.

† $\chi^2 = 2.50$, p $< .20$.

‡ $\chi^2 = 12.22$, p $< .001$.

Did these differences in training methods result in any differences among the children? Practically no class differences were found in tests (such as ability to delay gratification, Draw-A-Man), personality ratings, or aggression in doll play.[10]

[10] One of the most interesting differences was found on the second visit, four months later, when the children were rated on their change in psychological health. They could be rated

Although there was no class difference on source of ideas about child rearing, the most frequently named source was the mother herself—her own ideas, her common sense, her trial and error. There was no class difference between mothers mentioning reading newspapers or magazines, but there was a significant difference if they mentioned a specific book by an expert (e.g., Spock or Gesell) rather than newspaper or magazine articles. Middle-class mothers mention the expert books more. They also mentioned other people or friends significantly more often as a source of ideas. There were slightly more middle-class women who got ideas from child-rearing authorities such as doctors or nursery instructors, and from parent education classes with other mothers. Although similar numbers of working- and middle-class mothers mention their own childhoods as sources of ideas, middle-class mothers more often mention practices used by their parents which they would modify or reject. Many more sources of ideas were mentioned by the middle-class mothers.

A number of questions in the interview were designed to extract explanatory concepts, as indicators of the mothers' frames of reference, goals, and personalities. They will not be developed in this paper, but some of the raw class differences are of interest.

When mothers were asked what kind of person they wanted their child to be, they tended to answer in terms of five general categories—they wanted him to be happy, well-adjusted, a nice or good person, independent, or liked. There were class differences on two of these. More middle-class mothers said well adjusted, and more working-class mothers said a nice or good child. There were no differences in the degree to which the mothers saw themselves as better, same, or worse. The middle-class children were most frequently rated better or same, while the working-class children were worse or same. The difference was highly significant.

selves as similar to others in strictness, whether they perceived themselves as similar to their own parents in strictness or in sympathetic understanding, the aspects of parenthood they found most and least enjoyable, or in their own self-descriptions, except that working-class women more often spontaneously mentioned that they were neat.

cord with those obtained in 1951–52 in Boston than with those of 1943 in Chicago. Of five variables on which the Chicago study found class differences, we found no difference. Of fourteen variables also used in the Boston study, we found essentially the same results on eleven, and slightly different results on three. Considering the smaller sample size, and the

TABLE 8. *Social Class and Sources of Ideas about Child-Rearing*

	MIDDLE N = 36	WORKING N = 35	x^2	p
Expert book (e.g. Spock, Gesell)	15	6	4.30	<.03 *
"Reading" (newspapers, magazines)	12	13		
Authorities (physicians, nursery teachers)	8	3	1.82	<.10 *
Class in child rearing	11	6	1.26	<.10 *
Friends, "other people in the neighborhood"	16	8	3.02	<.05 *
Own ideas, "just common sense"	25	22		
Learn from the child	3	2		
Husband	5	5		
Relatives	4	6		
Own childhood				
Positive feeling	6	9		
Negative or mixed feelings	9	3	2.34	<.20
Total	114	83		

* One-tail tests, since direction of differences was predicted.

The mothers were also rated by the interviewer on a number of personality variables. Middle-class mothers were significantly more secure, independent, and dominant. There was a tendency for them to be more controlled, but no differences in ratings of potential anxiety, hostility, ability to express affect, aggression, constriction, ability to accept dependency, or ability to accept aggression.

Discussion

These results may be compared to those found in Chicago and in Boston (see Table 9). The main topics which all three studies had in common are feeding and toilet training.

In general the results are more in ac-

conservatism of the statistical test, this is remarkable agreement. In addition, the over-all picture of the middle class as more permissive and less demanding of the child is in general agreement with the Boston study, rather than with the Chicago data.

The relevant question is, of course, whether these differences indicate changes in child-rearing over the decade, or whether they are artifacts of the methods and samples used. Havighurst and Davis have suggested that the differences may be due to sample differences, such as ethnic or religious differences, occupational classification, or regional characteristics of the country. In regard to ethnic and religious differences, the California sample had more native-born grandparents than either the Boston or Chicago studies, and

TABLE 9. *Extent of Agreement between the Three Studies of Social Class Differences*

	AGREEMENT WITH FINDINGS	
CALIFORNIA SOCIAL CLASS FINDINGS	Chicago 1943	Boston 1951–52
1. No class difference in per cent ever breast fed	Agree	Agree
2. No class difference in median duration of breast feeding	Agree	Agree
(Calif. sample:		
Middle—2.5 mon.		
Working—1.5 mon.)		
3. No difference in median age at completion of weaning	Disagree	Agree
(Calif. sample:		
Middle—13.9 mon.		
Working—12.8 mon.)		
4. No difference in number of children bottle or breast fed after 12 months	Disagree	
5. No difference in per cent of infants fed when hungry	Disagree	
6. No difference in strictness of scheduling of feeding		Agree
7. Middle class reported more thumbsucking	Agree	
8. No difference in age at which bowel training begun	Disagree	Agree
9. Working class more severe in toilet training	Agree	Agree
10. No difference in demonstrativeness of affection		Agree
11. No difference in which parent is stricter with child		Agree
12. No difference in strictness in requiring obedience		Agree
13. No difference in how much mother keeps track of child		Disagree
14. Middle-class mothers report more permissiveness for aggression against parents		Agree
15. No difference in how much parent encourages child to fight back if attacked		Agree
16. No difference in permission for aggression against other children (Question may not be comparable for Chicago)	Disagree	Disagree
17. No difference in severity of punishment for aggression against parents (Slight difference in same direction as Boston study, but not significant)		Disagree

there are probably as many or more Catholics as in the Boston study [11] and fewer Jewish families. We cannot say that ethnic and religious differences are not responsible for the Chicago-Boston differ-

[11] Contrary to Havighurst and Davis, *op. cit.* (1955), p. 439, Maccoby reports in a personal communication that the Boston sample does contain Catholic children, since many do not start in parochial school until the first grade.

ences, but the fact that our sample seems to be different from the Boston sample in having more native-born grandparents, more Catholics, and fewer Jews—and yet yields fairly similar results—makes less plausible any explanation depending upon these factors.

The occupational composition of the samples is not so similar as might be desired; the Boston sample contains fewer families from the lowest socio-economic levels than does the Chicago study, and there are still fewer in the California sample. Comparability of the working-class samples is, therefore, questionable, but the middle-class samples in the three studies seem to be reasonably comparable, and it is here that some of the greatest differences in findings occur. Regional differences seem a less likely explanation because similar practices to those in Massachusetts were found in California within a two-year period.

Still another possibility is that our sample might contain so many women with upward mobile aspirations, even though objectively classified as working class, that class differences might be obliterated. If so, this would account for lack of agreement with the Chicago data. We were able to check this hypothesis since our sample was asked the class they thought of themselves as belonging to—upper, lower, working, or middle. By comparing those who subjectively identify themselves as middle and working, we have one possible method of eliminating upward-mobile members of the working class from that group. There are some differences when this comparison, rather than the objective classification, is used, but the trend is still the same. In some cases, class differences are heightened.

One possible source of bias remains: both the Boston and California samples contain largely suburban respondents, families who prefer to live in residential areas and surrounding smaller towns rather than a metropolitan city. This may well be a point of difference from the Chicago sample.

This still leaves open the hypothesis that changes in child-rearing have taken place, and that differences in reference sources of the two social classes account for the differences in practices. As had been predicted, the reference sources for the two classes are different. The middle-class mothers refer to more sources and to specific experts such as Spock; they are attentive to what friends and other mothers do. The working-class mothers are more diffuse in approach; they "read" but no one author in particular; they seem to dip less into the larger cultural mainstream than into their own inclinations and upbringing.

Several problems present themselves before the difference in reference groups can be accepted as the cause of the differences in child-rearing. The first is that this is only a partial test of the reference group hypothesis. Comparative or standard setting reference groups have been studied rather than those with a normative function.[12] It may be that the latter are more relevant.

Secondly, although causal relationship is plausible, it has not actually been demonstrated. It is not impossible that some other factor is responsible for the use of certain child-rearing practices and choice of reference sources. Some such factors, primarily personality variables, are suggested by the data. These are being tested and will be reported on later.

Verification of the reference group hypothesis would still not constitute evidence that a real change in practice from 1943 to 1953 had taken place.[13] Actually,

[12] Harold H. Kelly, "Two Functions of Reference Groups," in *Readings in Social Psychology*, edited by Guy E. Swanson, T. M. Newcomb, and Eugene H. Hartley, New York: Henry Holt, 1952, pp. 410–414.

[13] Indirect supporting evidence comes from a study of Evelyn Millis Duvall, "Conceptions of Parenthood," *American Journal of Sociology*, 52 (November, 1946), pp. 193–203. She found two styles of child-rearing which she called *traditional*, characterized by respect and obedience, and *developmental*, characterized by emphasis on growth and development. The traditional way of thinking was more characteristic of mothers who had a child five years or older, and the developmental way of those who had a child under five years. She explained this in terms of the experience of the mother—those more experienced were more strict and less flexible. However, in the light of our change hy-

this can never be demonstrated unless additional data from these years are available. If social class behavior does indeed change over time, future studies should be expected to be *unable* to replicate these results. If similar results are obtained after a ten year period, this would be evidence against the hypothesis. If both the change and reference source hypotheses are true, then future practices of the suburban middle class should be in accord with what is being said then (or a few years earlier) in the child-rearing literature and sources of the time. These sources, incidentally, may also change.

The fact that no differences were found in the children themselves is of some interest. It may be that the measures used were insensitive. However, some of the same measures were useful and sensitive in the part of the study dealing with reaction to the birth of a sibling. It may well be that it takes longer than three or five years for class differences in the so-

---

pothesis, the difference might be explained by when the mother raised the children. Those with younger children might have been more influenced by newer ideas of the 1940's while the mothers with older children might have absorbed ideas current in the late 1930's.

A study which failed to find expected changes is reported by Charles E. Ramsey and Lowry Nelson, "Change in Values and Attitudes Toward the Family," *American Sociological Review*, 21 (October, 1956), pp. 605–609.

cializing process to make their mark. Perhaps it is because the majority of items reported here represent the mothers' *perceptions* of what they and the child do, and may not necessarily be descriptive of their true behavior. If the latter is so, it should be remembered that class differences in perception are an aspect of behavior worthy of study.

Summary

Thirty-six middle-class and 38 working-class mothers were interviewed in 1953 about their child-rearing practices. Significant differences were found in the following: middle-class mothers were less severe in toilet training, permitted more aggression against the parents, were more responsive to the baby's crying, less often carried through when they told a child to do something, reported more thumb-sucking and less nailbiting. The middle-class mothers more often mentioned experts, other mothers, and friends as their sources of ideas on child-rearing. The data show far more agreement with the Boston study of 1951–52 than with the Chicago study of a decade earlier.

The available evidence is consistent with the notion that a change in child-rearing practices has taken place, and that this change is due to the different reference groups used by the two classes. However the causal connection of the latter relationship awaits further verification.

SOCIAL CLASS AND THE EXERCISE
OF PARENTAL AUTHORITY *

by Melvin L. Kohn

Much past research on the relationship between social class and the exercise of parental authority has been concerned with the question of whether or not working-class parents typically employ different techniques from those used by middle-class parents in dealing with their children's misbehavior.[1] Bronfenbrenner has summarized the results of twenty-five years of investigation in this area as indicating that: "In matters of discipline, working-class parents are consistently more likely to employ physical punishment, while middle-class families rely

more on reasoning, isolation, appeals to guilt, and other methods involving the threat of loss of love." [2]

The studies to which Bronfenbrenner refers have relied primarily on parents' generalized statements about their usual or their preferred methods of dealing with discipline problems—irrespective of what the particular problem might be. But obviously not all discipline problems evoke the same kinds of parental response. In some sense, after all, the punishment fits the crime. *Under what conditions* do parents of a given social class punish their children physically, reason with them, isolate them—or ignore their actions altogether?

The present study attempts to specify the practices of middle- and working-class parents in various circumstances, and from this information to develop a more general interpretation of the relationship of social class to the exercise of parental authority.

Sample and Method of Data Collection

Washington, D.C.—the locus of this study—has a large proportion of people employed by government, relatively little

---

* This is the second report of a more general inquiry into the relationship of class and family directed by the author and John A. Clausen, with the collaboration and aid of Eleanor Carroll, Bernard Finifter, Mary Freeman, Paul Hanlon, Sylvia Marshall, Alexander Shakow, and Eleanor Wolff. Expert advice on sample design and statistical problems was generously provided by Samuel W. Greenhouse. The interviews were conducted during the period March, 1956 to March, 1957.

[1] Sometimes the question has been put as to whether or not working-class parents employ more "severe" techniques. This of course involves an *a priori* judgment as to which techniques are most "severe."

Another major question, arising out of studies of the training of infants and very young children (e.g., weaning, toilet training) has been: which social class is the more "permissive," which the more "rigid," in its training procedures? These terms lead to difficulty because of the ambiguity as to what behaviors may be regarded as constituting "permissiveness" and "rigidity."

SOURCE: *American Sociological Review,* Vol. 24 (1959), pp. 352–366.

[2] Urie Bronfenbrenner, "Socialization and Social Class Through Time and Space," in Eleanor E. Maccoby, Theodore M. Newcomb, and Eugene L. Hartley, editors, *Readings in Social Psychology,* New York: Holt, 1958, p. 424. This article provides a fine analytic summary of past research on class and family, as well as a bibliography of the major studies in this field.

heavy industry, few recent immigrants, a white working class drawn heavily from rural areas, and a large proportion of Negroes, particularly at lower economic levels. Generalizations based on this or any other sample of one city during one limited period of time are, of course, tentative.

Our intent in selecting the families to be studied was to secure approximately two hundred representative white working-class families and another two hundred representative white middle-class families, each family having a child within a narrowly delimited age range. We decided on fifth-grade children in order to be able to direct the interviews to relationships involving a child old enough to have a developed capacity for verbal communication.

The sampling procedure involved two steps: the first, selection of Census tracts. Tracts with 20 per cent or more Negro population were excluded, as were those in the highest quartile with respect to median income. From among the remaining tracts we then selected four with a predominantly working-class population, four predominantly middle-class, and three having large proportions of each. The final selection of tracts was based on their occupational distribution and their median income, education, rent (of rented homes), and property value (of owner-occupied homes). The second step in the sampling procedure involved selection of families. From records made available by the public and parochial school systems, we compiled lists of all fifth-grade children whose families lived in the selected tracts. Two hundred families were then randomly selected from among those in which the father had a "white-collar" occupation and another two hundred from among those in which the father had a manual occupation.

In all four hundred families, the mothers were to be interviewed. In every fourth family we also scheduled interviews with the father and the fifth-grade

child. (When a broken family fell into this sub-sample, a substitute was chosen from our overall sample, but the broken family was retained in the overall sample.)

When interviews with both parents were scheduled, two members of the staff visited the home together—a male to interview the father, a female to interview the mother. The interviews were conducted independently, in separate rooms, but with essentially identical schedules. The first person to complete his interview with the parent interviewed the child.

We secured the cooperation of 86 per cent of the families where the mother alone was to be interviewed, and 82 per cent of the families where mother, father, and child were to be interviewed. Rates of non-response do not vary by social class, type of neighborhood, or type of school. This of course does not rule out other possible selective biases introduced by the non-respondents.

INDEX OF SOCIAL CLASS. Each family's social class position was determined by the Hollingshead Index of Social Position, assigning the father's occupational status a relative weight of 7 and his educational status a weight of 4. Here we consider Hollingshead's Classes I, II, and III to be "middle-class," and Classes IV and V as "working-class." The middle-class sample is composed of two fairly distinct groups: Classes I and II are almost entirely professionals, proprietors, or managers, with at least some college training. Class III is made up of small shopkeepers, clerks, and salespersons, but includes a small number of foremen and skilled workers of unusually high educational status. The working-class sample is composed entirely of manual workers, but preponderantly those of higher skill levels. These families are of the "stable working class" rather than "lower class" in the sense that the men have steady jobs and in that their education, income, and skill levels are above those of the lowest socio-economic strata.

TABLE 1. *Mothers' Evaluations of the Decision-Making Process in Middle- and Working-Class Families*

PROPORTION OF MOTHERS WHO REPORT THAT:

| | DECISIONS ARE MADE PRIMARILY BY: | | | | PARENT PARTICIPATES IN DECISIONS: | | | |
| | MOTHER | | FATHER | | MOTHER | | FATHER | |
TYPE OF DECISION	Middle Class	Working Class	Middle Class	Working Class	Middle Class	Working Class	Middle Class	Working Class
Day-to-day decisions	.90	.82	.04	.05	.97	.95	.12	.20
Major family decisions	.05	.14	.22	.19	.81	.82	.95	.88
Decisions that affect the fifth-grade child most directly	.38	.43	.06	.08	.98	.95	.71	.68

Number of cases: 163 middle-class and 146 working-class. (This table is limited to mothers living with their husbands; the total sample is composed of 174 middle-class and 165 working-class families.)

The Context of Authority

The context for our study of parents' reactions to specific disciplinary situations is provided by a cursory examination of three general aspects of authority: the relative role of mother and father in making family decisions, the relative role

working-class parents and children (see Table 1).[3] Nor is there any appreciable difference between the social classes in mothers', fathers', or children's evaluations of which parent is stricter, more likely to restrict the children's freedom, "lay down the law" when the child misbehaves, or dominate the child (see Table 2). Finally, middle-class parents report

TABLE 2. *Middle- and Working-Class Mothers' Evaluations of Their Own and Their Husbands' Roles in Setting Limits upon Their Children's Freedom of Movement or Activity*

| | PARENTS' BEHAVIOR DIRECTED TO: | | | |
| | SONS | | DAUGHTERS | |
PROPORTION OF MOTHERS WHO REPORT THAT:	Middle Class	Working Class	Middle Class	Working Class
Mother is stricter than father	.32	.37	.32	.25
Father is stricter than mother	.44	.36	.40	.38
Mother is more likely to restrict child's freedom	.45	.39	.38	.36
Father is more likely to restrict child's freedom	.29	.40	.31	.29
Mother is more likely to "lay down the law" when child misbehaves	.34	.34	.43	.37
Father is more likely to "lay down the law" when child misbehaves	.37	.33	.27	.40
Mother is more likely to dominate the child	.34	.32	.41	.45
Father is more likely to dominate the child	.22	.16	.17	.21
Number of cases *	82	73	81	73

* Limited to intact families.

of mother and father in setting limits upon the children's freedom of movement or activity, and the frequency with which mother and father resort to physical punishment to enforce obedience. From none of these perspectives do we find any appreciable difference between middle- and working-class families. Middle-class parents' and children's evaluations of the extent to which each parent participates in the making of day-to-day decisions, major family decisions, and the decisions that affect the fifth-grade child most directly, are quite similar to those of

that they make use of physical punishment about as frequently as do working-class parents (see Table 3).

[3] Tables 1 and 2 present only the mothers' evaluations. The evaluations provided by fathers and children yield entirely consistent results. (Although there are no appreciable differences between middle- and working-class families with respect to which parent predominates in decision-making and limit-setting, it may be that working-class respondents are less likely to perceive the two parents as sharing equally in these functions. This question will be examined in another report.)

TABLE 3. *The Reported Use of Physical Punishment by Middle- and Working-Class Parents*

PROPORTION OF PARENTS WHO REPORT USING PHYSICAL PUNISHMENT:

	MOTHERS				FATHERS			
	Response to Sons		Response to Daughters		Response to Sons		Response to Daughters	
	Middle Class	Working Class	Middle Class	Working Class	Middle Class	Working Class	Middle Class	Working Class
Parent reports that he (or she) punishes child physically:								
Occasionally or frequently	.14	.16	.09	.16	.04	.04	.10	.00
Infrequently	.46	.44	.39	.42	.40	.40	.33	.36
Parent reports that he (or she) last punished child physically:								
Within past week	.16	.13	.13	.14	.00	.12	.14	.09
Within past month	.30	.28	.27	.32	.16	.28	.19	.27
Within past six months	.59	.55	.45	.56	.40	.44	.43	.36
Number of cases *	79	82	75	77	25	25	21	11

* These questions were not asked of the first 26 mothers interviewed.

Nevertheless, there are distinct differences in the conditions under which middle- and working-class parents resort to physical punishment. We shall see that parents of both social classes reserve physical punishment for fairly extreme circumstances. But even in these extreme circumstances, some actions that are intolerable to working-class parents are not punished by middle-class parents, and other actions intolerable to middle-class parents are not punished by working-class parents.

In attempting to specify the conditions under which middle- and working-class parents use physical punishment, we rely here on parent's reported reactions to eight types of situation: the child's wild play, fighting with his brothers and sisters, fighting with other children, really losing his temper, refusing to do what his parents tell him to do, "swiping" something from home or from other children, smoking cigarettes, and using language his parent doesn't want him to use.

Parents were questioned in some detail about each of these situations. We asked, for example, whether or not the fifth-grade child ever loses his temper; precisely what he does when he loses his temper; what the parent "generally does when he acts this way"; whether he "ever finds it necessary to do anything else" and, if so, "under what circumstances" and what else he does.[4]

Parents' reports on their reactions to

[4] Middle- and working-class mothers were equally likely to report that their children have lost their tempers, fought with others, refused to do what they were told, swiped something, smoked, or used disapproved language. Middle-class mothers, however, were more likely to tell us that their sons had played wildly (71 per cent *vs.* 52 per cent) and fought with their brothers or sisters (97 per cent *vs.* 87 per cent of those having brothers or sisters close to them in age). This does not mean that a disinterested observer would agree that working-class boys are less likely than are middle-class boys to play wildly or fight with their

their children's behavior were classified according to the following scheme:

1. Ignore: not doing anything about it.
2. Scold, admonish to be good, demand that he stop, inquire into causes of behavior, scream at him, threaten to punish him. (It has proved impossible to differentiate these several verbal reactions reliably from interview material.[5] We could not determine, for example, whether or not a parent's reported attempt to discover the causes of a fight was in fact a scolding. Therefore we have reluctantly decided to treat these several responses as a single category.)
3. Separate from other children or divert attention: removing the child from the situation or providing alternative activities.
4. Punish or coerce: (a) Punish physically—everything from a slap to a spanking. (b) Isolate—confining child *alone* for a period of time, for example, sending him to bed during the day. (c) Restrict usual activities—limiting his freedom of movement or activity short of isolation, for example, not letting him play outside.

brothers or sisters, or that working-class mothers have withheld information from the interviewers. Instead, it reflects the fact that mothers who said that these situations do *not* occur conceive of "wild play" in terms that we would classify as *aggressively* wild play (not boisterousness) and fighting in terms that we would classify as *physical combat* (not an argument).

In general, middle- and working-class mothers who say that any given situation does occur were likely to describe their children's specific actions in quite similar ways. Two notable exceptions are that working-class mothers were more apt to describe their sons' fights with brothers or sisters and their daughters' fights with other children as physical encounters, while middle-class mothers were more likely to describe them as arguments.

[5] The standard of coding reliability used here and throughout the study was 90 per cent inter-coder agreement on independent trials for each classification used.

The Exercise of Maternal Authority

Most mothers—in both social classes—report that their *usual* response in the eight situations about which we inquired is to ignore the child's actions altogether, or at most to admonish him (see Table 4). Few mothers isolate or restrict their children at this stage of things, and virtually none punishes them physically. One cannot conclude that mothers of either social class are especially quick to resort to physical punishment or to other forms of coercion.

But when their children persist in wild play, fighting with their brothers or sisters, or displays of temper, both middle- and working-class mothers are apt to turn to one or another form of punishment (see Table 5). Working-class mothers are more likely than are middle-class mothers to do so in the case of their sons' prolonged loss of temper; middle-class mothers, on the other hand, are more likely to punish their sons for refusing to do as they are told.[6]

Working-class mothers are more likely than are middle-class mothers to resort to *physical* punishment when their sons persist in wild play or fighting with brothers or sisters, or when their daughters fight with other children. There may be in addition a general, albeit slight, greater tendency for working-class mothers to resort to physical punishment no matter what the situation. (In thirteen of sixteen comparisons, a somewhat larger proportion of working-class than of middle-class mothers report using physical punishment, although only in the three comparisons noted above is the difference large enough for us to be confident that it is not simply a chance occurrence.) But we previously noted that middle-class mothers say they

[6] The criterion of statistical significance used throughout this paper is the five per cent level, based on the chi-square test.

use physical punishment about as *frequently* as do working-class mothers. Therefore, it is not likely that working-class mothers' propensity to use physical punishment is sufficiently greater than that of middle-class mothers to be of serious import. A more important difference lies in the conditions under which mothers of the two social classes punish their children physically.

THE CONDITIONS UNDER WHICH WORKING-CLASS MOTHERS PUNISH THEIR SONS PHYSICALLY. Working-class mothers are apt to resort to physical punishment when the immediate consequences of their sons' disobedient acts are most extreme, and to refrain from using punishment when its use might provoke an even greater disturbance.

We have noted two actions for which working-class mothers are more likely than are middle-class mothers to punish their sons physically: wild play and fighting with their brothers or sisters. In either situation, the more extreme their sons' actions, the more likely are working-class mothers to use physical punishment (see Table 6). Those whose descriptions of their sons' wild play indicate that it is nothing more than boisterousness or running around are no more apt to resort to physical punishment than are middle-class mothers in the same circumstances. But those whose descriptions of wild play include elements that we see as aggression or destruction are far more likely than are middle-class mothers to employ physical punishment. Similarly, working-class mothers are not appreciably more likely than are middle-class mothers to punish their sons physically for fights with brothers or sisters when the "fights" are no more than arguments, but they are more likely to resort to physical punishment when the fights involve physical combat.

This suggests that the more extreme forms of wild play and fighting are particularly intolerable to working-class

TABLE 4. *Mothers' Reported Responses to Their Children's Actions—under Usual Circumstances* *

PROPORTION OF MOTHERS WHO REPORT THAT THEY RESPOND BY:

WHEN CHILD:	IGNORING		SCOLDING OR ADMONISHING		SEPARATING THE CHILD FROM OTHERS		PUNISHING PHYSICALLY		ISOLATING OR RESTRICTING ACTIVITIES		NUMBER OF CASES	
	Middle Class	Working Class	Middle Class	Working Class	Middle Class	Working Class	Middle Class	Working Class	Middle Class	Working Class	Middle Class	Working Class
1. Plays wildly												
Sons	.31	.34	.42	.45	.17	.07	.00	.02	.10	.12	64	44
Daughters	.36	.56	.49 † .28		.10	.08	.00	.03	.05	.05	42	39
2. Fights with his brothers or sisters												
Sons	.13	.05	.54	.40	.18	.31	.02	.02	.13	.22	65	55
Daughters	.18	.10	.53	.60	.19	.08	.02	.06	.08	.16	68	50
3. Fights with children other than brothers or sisters												
Sons	.48	.44	.37	.36	.15	.08	.00	.00	.00 † .12		46	50
Daughters	.35	.29	.48	.46	.17	.19	.00	.00	.00	.06	42	41
4. Loses his temper												
Sons	.32	.30	.49	.41	.03	.01	.05	.09	.11	.19	81	74
Daughters	.41	.32	.40	.43	.00	.00	.06	.11	.13	.14	67	57
5. Refuses to do what his mother tells him to do												
Sons	.14	.19	.74	.77	.00	.02	.00	.00	.12	.02	56	43
Daughters	.30 † .09		.59	.77	.00	.00	.00	.06	.11	.08	37	35
6. Uses language that his mother doesn't want him to use												
Sons	.11	.03	.78	.86	.00	.00	.00	.05	.11	.06	48	36
Daughters	.04	.00	.89	.78	.00	.00	.00	.04	.07	.18	29	27
7. Smokes cigarettes												
Sons	.24	.27	.66	.73	.00	.00	.00	.00	.10	.00	21	15
Daughters	.64	.30	.36	.50	.00	.00	.00	.10	.00	.10	14	10
8. Swipes something from home or other children												
Sons	.12	.05	.76	.90	.04	.00	.00	.00	.08	.05	26	20
Daughters	.00	.08	.67	.67	.00	.00	.22	.08	.11	.17	9	12

* Limited to mothers who report that their children behave in the particular way.
† Social class differences statistically significant, .05 level or better, using chi-square test.

TABLE 5. *Mothers' Reported Use of Physical Punishment, Isolation, and Restriction—in Extreme Circumstances* *

PROPORTION OF MOTHERS WHO REPORT THAT THEY USE:

WHEN CHILD:	PHYSICAL PUNISHMENT		ISOLATION		RESTRICTION		PUNISHMENT OF ANY TYPE		NUMBER OF CASES	
	Middle Class	Working Class	Middle Class	Working Class	Middle Class	Working Class	Middle Class	Working Class	Middle Class	Working Class
1. Plays wildly										
Sons	.09 †	.23	.05	.02	.20	.18	.34	.43	64	44
Daughters	.02	.08	.12	.00	.17	.18	.31	.26	42	39
2. Fights with his brothers or sisters										
Sons	.17 †	.43	.34 †	.25	.06	.04	.57	.72	65	55
Daughters	.21	.26	.24	.26	.09	.14	.54	.66	68	50
3. Fights with children other than brothers or sisters										
Sons	.00	.02	.00	.06	.15	.12	.15	.20	46	50
Daughters	.00 †	.15	.02	.05	.14	.12	.16	.32	42	41
4. Loses his temper										
Sons	.20	.30	.14	.11	.06 †	.19	.40 †	.60	81	74
Daughters	.24	.26	.12	.12	.03	.09	.39	.47	67	57
5. Refuses to do what his mother tells him to do										
Sons	.12	.07	.04	.07	.18 †	.00	.34 †	.14	56	43
Daughters	.08	.23	.05	.06	.14	.06	.27	.35	37	35
6. Uses language that his mother doesn't want him to use										
Sons	.04	.11	.02	.00	.10 †	.00	.16	.11	48	36
Daughters	.00	.11	.03	.00	.07	.11	.10	.22	29	27
7. Smokes cigarettes										
Sons	.00	.00	.00	.00	.05	.00	.05	.00	21	15
Daughters	.00	.10	.00	.00	.00	.10	.00	.20	14	10
8. Swipes something from home or from other children										
Sons	.04	.00	.00	.00	.08	.05	.12	.05	26	20
Daughters	.12	.17	.11	.00	.00	.25	.23	.42	9	12

* Limited to mothers who report that their children behave in the particular way.
† Social class differences statistically significant, .05 level or better, using chi-square test.

TABLE 6. *Mothers' Reported Use of Physical Punishment, Isolation, and Restriction, in Extreme Circumstances—Controlled on Mother's Description of Her Child's Behavior*

	PROPORTION OF MOTHERS WHO REPORT THAT THEY USE:									
	PHYSICAL PUNISHMENT		ISOLATION		RESTRICTION		PUNISHMENT OF ANY TYPE		NUMBER OF CASES	
WHEN SON:	Middle Class	Working Class	Middle Class	Working Class	Middle Class	Working Class	Middle Class	Working Class	Middle Class	Working Class
1. Plays wildly										
a. Described as boisterousness or running around	.13	.11	.03	.04	.16	.18	.32	.33	38	28
b. Described as willful aggression or destruction	.04 *	.43	.08	.00	.26	.19	.38	.62	26	16
2. Fights with his brothers or sisters										
a. Described as argument	.10	.27	.30	.13	.10	.13	.50	.53	30	15
b. Described as physical encounter	.23 *	.50	.37	.30	.03	.00	.63	.80	35	40
3. Fights with children other than his brothers or sisters										
a. Described as physical encounter	.00	.02	.00	.07	.16	.12	.16	.21	31	42
4. Loses his temper										
a. Described as pouting, yelling, or, sulking	.15	.26	.12	.06	.06 *	.22	.33 *	.54	66	54
b. Described as a violent or aggressive outburst	.40	.40	.20	.25	.07	.10	.67	.75	15	20

* Social class differences statistically significant, .05 level or better, using chi-square test.

mothers, and less so to middle-class mothers. This impression is sustained by the fact that those working-class mothers who consider themselves unusually strict and "ready to lay down the law" are especially likely to punish their sons physically for physical combat with brothers or sisters. And those working-class mothers who describe themselves as easily angered by their sons' actions or unwilling to "give in" to them are especially likely to use physical punishment for aggressively wild play. They cannot or will not tolerate these forms of aggressive behavior.

But working-class mothers do not find all aggressive behavior intolerable. They are far less likely to punish their sons physically for fights with friends or neighbors than for equally serious fights with brothers or sisters. It would appear that it is not for aggressive behavior as such, but for the disturbances arising out of aggressive behavior, that working-class boys are punished. Their mothers seem unwilling or unable to tolerate the immediate consequences of their sons' aggressive acts.

The responsiveness of working-class mothers to immediate consequences is demonstrated anew by a consideration of the conditions under which they do *not* punish their sons. They shun punishment if it might provoke a disturbance more serious than that already underway.

There is ample evidence presented above that working-class mothers are prone to punish their sons physically for acts of disobedience. Futhermore, they are more likely than are middle-class mothers to report that on the last occasion they used physical punishment it was invoked in response to disobedience. But there is a world of difference between punishing a boy for violating a negative injunction and punishing him for not doing something he is positively enjoined to do. Working-class mothers appear to be far more likely to punish their sons for the former type of disobedience than for the latter. In fact, they are less likely than are middle-class mothers to punish their sons for refusing to do things they have been told to do (see Table 5).

The immediate consequences of acquiescing to a son's refusal may be trivial—often nothing more than doing a minor household chore when he will not comply. However, under some conditions—specifically, when the boy is adamant about his refusal—the consequences of forcing him to do as he is told may be serious. Working-class mothers are highly unlikely to punish their sons—physically or in any other way—in such circumstances (see Table 7). No working-class mother who described her son's refusals as prolonged delays under conditions where he had unquestionably heard the order, or as an act of outright defiance, told us that she punished him physically, restricted his activities, or isolated him. They were more likely than were middle-class mothers to tell us that they took no action at all under these circumstances. Nor does this indicate indifference. The interview reports indicate that these mothers do make an attempt to secure compliance, but then back down. This is especially true of those who say they are "easily upset" by their sons' actions. They seem unable to bring themselves to take strong action, but are hardly indifferent.

THE CONDITIONS UNDER WHICH MIDDLE-CLASS MOTHERS PUNISH THEIR SONS PHYSICALLY. It is clear that middle-class and working-class mothers make different discriminations in their use of physical punishment. Middle-class mothers seem to punish or refrain from punishing on the basis of their interpretation of the child's intent. Most indicative of this are their responses to wild play and loss of temper (see Table 6). They are not likely to punish their sons physically for wild play, however serious it may be. Nor are they particularly likely to punish them physically for loss of temper when it is manifested only as pouting, yelling, or sulking. But a violent or aggressive outburst of

TABLE 7. *Mothers' Reported Responses When Their Children Defiantly Refuse to Do What They Are Told to Do*

| | PROPORTION OF MOTHERS WHO REPORT THAT THEY RESPOND: | | | |
| | TO SONS | | TO DAUGHTERS | |
	Middle Class	Working Class	Middle Class	Working Class
BY:				
Punishing them physically	.13 ⎫	⎧ .00	.09	.25
Isolating them	.02 ⎬ * ⎨ .00		.04	.07
Restricting their activities	.17 ⎭	⎩ .00	.12	.07
Scolding, admonishing, insisting that child obey, threatening to punish	.59	.66	.63	.57
Not doing anything about it	.09 *	.34	.12	.04
	1.00	1.00	1.00	1.00
Number of cases	46	32	33	28

* Social class differences statistically significant, .05 level or better, using chi-square test.

temper is far more likely to elicit physical punishment. In these circumstances, middle-class mothers are as prone as their working-class counterparts to punish their sons physically.[7]

The descriptions of temper-loss classified here as "a violent or aggressive outburst" are quite similar to the descriptions of wild play classified as "willful aggression or destruction." Working-class

[7] We noted earlier (with reference to Table 5) that working-class mothers are more likely than are middle-class mothers to punish their sons for loss of temper. It is now clear that this difference obtains almost entirely among mothers who describe the child's loss of temper as pouting or yelling, for middle-class mothers are nearly as likely as are working-class mothers to punish a violent or aggressive outburst. This, too, we take as evidence (admittedly indirect) that working-class mothers are attuned to immediate consequences. Although yelling or pouting may not be of very serious import (in the sense that the child does not necessarily lose control over his actions), it is disconcerting, and working-class mothers do not abide it.

mothers respond to the one much as they do to the other. But middle-class mothers are far more likely to punish their sons physically for what they call loss of temper than for behavior defined as wild play. They appear to find the child's loss of temper, but not his wild play, particularly intolerable.

There is one salient respect in which an outburst of temper may be quite different from wild play: the outburst may be directed against the mother herself. Short of a frontal assault, however, this is largely a matter of the mother's interpretation. The interview reports indicate that the distinction between wild play and loss of temper was most often made in terms of the child's presumed intent, as judged by his preceding actions. If in the course of play he became very excited, this was not judged to be loss of temper—however extreme his actions. But if his actions seemed to stem from the frustration of not having his own way, they were judged to indicate loss of temper. The overt behavior in the two types of situation might be, and often was, nearly identical.

THE CONDITIONS UNDER WHICH MOTHERS PUNISH THEIR DAUGHTERS. Middle-class mothers appear to respond to their daughters' actions much as they do to their sons' (see Tables 5 and 7). But working-class mothers are more likely to use physical punishment when their sons play wildly or fight with brothers or sisters than when their daughters do so (see Table 5). This tendency, however, reflects the fact that boys' wild play and fighting are more apt to be extreme. Daughters are only slightly less likely to be punished physically for behavior which is actually similar. They are, in fact, *more* likely to be punished physically when they swipe something or fight with children other than brothers or sisters. (Nevertheless, working-class mothers are far less likely to punish their daughters physically for fights with friends than for equally serious fights with brothers or sisters. In this crucial respect, their treatment of boys and of girls is much the same.)

The most dramatic difference in the working-class mothers' response to boys and to girls occurs when the child defiantly refuses to do as he is told: boys are permitted to have their own way, while girls are punished physically (see Table 7). Something more is expected of a girl than of a boy—she must not only refrain from doing what she's not supposed to do, but must also carry out actions her mother wants her to do.

There is no indication in these data that working-class mothers are more prone to examine their daughters' than their sons' intent, but clearly, the actions are evaluated differently. We shall return to the question of why this is so.

HYPOTHETICAL REACTIONS. Whenever a mother told us that her child had *not* performed an action about which we inquired, we asked her what she thought she would do if the situation did occur. Middle-class mothers who said that a

given situation had not occurred thought that they would probably respond in ways almost identical to those noted by mothers who said that it had taken place. This is not the case for working-class mothers. Although no working-class mother who declared that her son had swiped something, smoked, or defiantly refused to carry out an order reported punishing him physically, roughly one-fifth of those who said that their sons had not done these things expected to use this sanction if the situation were to occur.

It is possible, of course, that those working-class mothers who are most prone to use physical punishment are unwilling to admit that their sons misbehave, or have somehow forestalled their sons' misbehavior. This does not seem likely, however, for in circumstances when working-class mothers are quite likely to use physical punishment—when their sons engage in aggressively wild play—those who say that they have not faced the situation are quite unlikely to predict that they would resort to physical punishment. (Roughly one-fifth of such mothers think that they would do so—about the same proportion as those who think that they would punish their sons physically for swiping something, smoking, or being defiant.)

It seems, then, that working-class mothers are unable to envisage either the conditions under which they would be very likely to use physical punishment or the conditions under which they would be very unlikely to do so. Considering the degree to which they are responsive to immediate circumstances, this conclusion should not be surprising.

Paternal Authority

In considering fathers' reactions to their children's behavior, we rely on interviews both with a sub-sample of eighty-two fathers and the much larger sample of mothers. The small number of interviews with fathers limits us severely in attempt-

TABLE 8. *Fathers' Reported Responses to Their Sons' Actions—under Extreme Circumstances* *

WHEN SON:	PHYSICAL PUNISHMENT		ISOLATION		RESTRICTION		PUNISHMENT OF ANY TYPE		NUMBER OF CASES	
	Middle Class	Working Class	Middle Class	Working Class	Middle Class	Working Class	Middle Class	Working Class	Middle Class	Working Class
1. Plays wildly	.07	.06	.07	.06	.07	.17	.21	.29	15	18
2. Fights with his brothers or sisters	.43	.50	.10	.25	.05	.06	.58	.81	21	16
3. Fights with children other than brothers or sisters	.00	.00	.00	.00	.00	.00	.00	.00	15	11
4. Loses his temper	.22	.16	.13	.11	.00 †	.16	.35	.43	23	19
5. Refuses to do what his father tells him to do	.19	.20	.06	.00	.13	.10	.38	.30	16	10

PROPORTION OF FATHERS WHO REPORT THAT THEY USE:

* Limited to fathers who report that their sons behave in the particular way.
† Social class differences statistically significant, .05 level or better, using chi-square test.

ing to take account of the sex of the child and the father's description of the child's behavior. Thus we are forced to interweave the analysis of fathers' self-reports with wives' reports on their behavior. This procedure is not entirely satisfactory, for reasons presented in the next section.

Working-class fathers are appreciably less likely than are their wives to say that they punish their sons physically for wild play (see Tables 5 and 8). In fact, they are no more likely than are middle-class fathers to report using physical punishment in this situation. This reflects the fact that few working-class fathers describe their sons' wild play as anything more than boisterousness—for which they are most unlikely to punish boys physically. However, those few working-class mothers who indicate that their husbands are exposed to *aggressively* wild play are far more likely than are middle-class mothers to report that in these extreme circumstances their husbands resort to physical punishment. It would appear that working-class fathers respond in two ways: if the child's behavior does not compel their attention, they are apt to ignore it; but if it is sufficiently disruptive, they are very likely to use physical punishment. They may be even more responsive to immediate consequences than are their wives.

Middle-class fathers apparently are a good deal more likely than are their wives to punish sons physically for fighting with their brothers or sisters (see Tables 5 and 8). This seems to be true however serious the fights. Thus, middle-class fathers are as likely as are working-class fathers to resort to physical punishment when their sons fight. Nevertheless, working-class fathers are somewhat more likely to report using physical punishment, and considerably more likely to report using isolation or restriction, when their sons' fights are *serious*. The wives' reports lead to the same conclusion.

In other respects as well, our information indicates that the major conclusions about the conditions under which mothers of the two social classes punish their children physically, noted above, also apply to fathers. In particular, middle-class mothers say that their husbands are far more likely to punish their sons physically for severe loss of temper than for aggressively wild play. (The small number of fathers' reports on reactions to severe loss of temper prevents our determining whether or not fathers agree.) Working-class mothers, furthermore, tell us that their husbands are not likely to punish their sons' defiant refusals to do as they are told, but are likely to punish their daughters physically for similar behavior. (The few fathers' reports relevant to this issue are consistent with this finding.)

Strengths and Limitations of the Data

Although we have reports from all three relevant persons in a representative sub-sample of these families, there remains the question as to whether or not disinterested observers would present similar descriptions. Moreover, interview responses are in their nature limited: we cannot differentiate reliably among various types of verbal behavior; we cannot tell whether or not a parent expresses his displeasure by grouchiness, assuming an air of martyrdom, or simply "acting differently"; and we do not know to what degree any of a parent's actions may be interpreted by his child as a withdrawal of love.

Each respondent has summarized a number of his own and another's actions. We do not know how frequently situations of a given type have occurred,[8] or how consistent a parent's reactions have been. Nor can we, for example, assume from a parent's description of his child's

[8] It is primarily for this reason that one cannot draw from our data on parents' reactions to specific types of situations the inference that working-class parents use physical punishment more often than do middle-class parents.

fights as arguments, that the child never fights physically.

On the other hand, the parents' ability to differentiate between what they generally do and what they do in more pressing circumstances gives reason for confidence in the findings. So does the fact that the relationships we have found between social class and mothers' reactions are not appreciably modified by controlling other relevant variables (including mother's age, size of the family, ordinal position of the child in the family, length of time the family has lived in the neighborhood, the socio-economic status of the neighborhood, whether or not the mother has a job, and if so what type of job, whether or not she has been socially mobile or feels socially mobile, her social class identification, her level of education, her religious background, whether her background is rural or urban, whether or not she reads popular literature on child-rearing, and whether or not her husband works for the government).

Furthermore, the information provided by the sub-sample of fathers and children enables us to check some of the inferences we have drawn from mothers' reports.[9] We asked each father, for example, "What does your wife generally do when [child] fights with his brothers or sisters?" Although the question parallels "What do *you* generally do . . . ?", it was put immediately after we asked him what he does in circumstances other than those that usually prevail. Most parents seem to have answered with the latter circumstances in mind. This precludes a comparison of what fathers say they do with what they say their wives do in exactly the same circumstances. But it does give us some basis for judging whether or not our inferences about social class differences in the conditions under which mothers use physical punishment are supported by what husbands tell us.

[9] In most instances the number of cases is so small as to preclude the possibility of statistical confirmation.

The only respect in which the fathers' reports of their wives' reactions raise a question about the inferences we have drawn is that two of the nine working-class fathers who say that their sons defiantly refuse to do as they are told also report that their wives punish the boys. Perhaps, then, we have overstated the case in concluding that working-class mothers are singularly unlikely to punish their sons for defiance.

Concerning the fathers' reactions, it appears that interviews with fathers and with mothers yield much the same conclusions. This holds even for the conclusion that working-class fathers are unlikely to punish their sons for a defiant refusal.

The children, too, were asked about their parents' reactions in three of the situations: fights with brothers and sisters, fights with other children, and loss of temper. The information provided by middle-class children, although based on few interviews, is entirely consistent with their parents' reports. But working-class boys are rather unlikely to tell us that their mothers punish them *physically* for fighting with brothers or sisters or for loss of temper. They acknowledge that their fathers do so, but they report that their mothers isolate or restrict them for such actions.

Interpretation

Neither middle- nor working-class parents resort to punishment as a first recourse when their children misbehave. It seems, instead, that parents of both social classes initially post limits for their children. But children sometimes persist in their misbehavior despite their parents' attempts to forestall them. At this juncture, parents may turn to physical punishment.

The conditions under which they punish their children physically, or refrain from doing so, appear to be quite different for the two social classes. *Working-class parents are more likely to respond in terms of the immediate consequences of the child's actions, middle-class parents in terms of their interpretation of the child's intent in acting as he does.*[10] This should not be interpreted to imply that while middle-class parents act on the basis of long-range goals for their children's development, working-class parents do not. On the contrary, we believe that parents of *both* social classes act on the basis of long-range goals—but that the goals are quite different.

In an earlier study we have examined the relation of social class to the values parents most wish to see incorporated into their children's behavior.[11] We concluded that parents are most likely to accord high priority to those values which seem both important, in the sense that failure to achieve them would affect the child's future adversely, and problematic, in the sense that they are difficult to achieve. For working-class parents, the "important but problematic" centers around qualities that assure *respectability;* for middle-class parents, it centers around *internalized standards of conduct.* In the first instance, desirable behavior consists essentially of not violating proscriptions; in the second, of acting according to the dictates of one's own principles. Here the act becomes less important than the actor's intent.

We believe that the reactions of parents of both social classes to their children's undesired behavior are entirely appropriate to their values. To say that working-class parents are particularly responsive to consequences and relatively unconcerned about intent, is equivalent to saying that their efforts are directed to enjoining disobedient, disreputable acts.

[10] This distinction, of course, is closely akin to that made by Piaget in his discussion of "moral realism." See Jean Piaget, *The Moral Judgment of the Child,* Glencoe, Ill.: Free Press, n.d., pp. 104–194.

[11] Melvin L. Kohn, "Social Class and Parental Values," *American Journal of Sociology,* 64 (January, 1959), pp. 337–351.

To say that middle-class parents are more concerned about intent is equivalent to saying that their efforts are directed to encouraging their children to develop internalized standards and to act on the basis of these standards rather than externally imposed rules.

To see parents' reactions to their children's misbehavior as a function of their values helps to answer several questions which otherwise may be perplexing.

First, why are working-class parents so much more likely to punish their children physically for fighting than for arguing with their brothers or sisters?—or for aggressively wild play than for boisterousness? The answer seems to be that disreputability is defined in terms of consequences: the measure of disreputability is the degree to which the act transgresses rules of propriety. Fighting and wild play are disobedient, disreputable behaviors only when sufficiently extreme to be seen as transgressions of rules.

Second, why are working-class parents more likely to administer physical punishment when their daughters fight with friends, swipe something, or defiantly refuse to do as they are told than when their sons act in these ways? The answer seems to lie in different conceptions of what is right and proper for boys and for girls. What may be taken as acceptable behavior (perhaps even as an assertion of manliness) in a pre-adolescent boy may be thought thoroughly unlady-like in a young girl. Working-class parents differentiate quite clearly between the qualities they regard as desirable for their daughters (happiness, manners, neatness, and cleanliness) and those they hold out for their sons (dependability, being a good student, and ambition). They want their daughters to be "little ladies" (a term that kept recurring in the interviews) and their sons to be manly. This being the case, the criteria of disobedience are necessarily different for boys and for girls. Obedience is valued highly for both. But working-class mothers who value obedience most highly punish their daughters physically

for refusing to carry out parental requests and orders, while they are much less likely to take any action when their sons do so.

Middle-class parents make little or no distinction between what they regard as desirable for boys and for girls—the issue for both sexes is whether or not the child acts in accord with internalized principles. Therefore, the conduct of both boys and girls should be judged by the same criterion: intent. Our evidence supports this interpretation.

Finally, why do middle-class parents react so differently to aggressively wild play and to outbursts of temper? Why do they interpret these overtly similar behaviors as implying radically different intent? The answer is provided by the fundamental importance they attach to internal standards for governing one's relationships with other people and, in the final analysis, with one's self.

Wild play, however extreme, does not necessarily represent a loss of *self*-control, although it may indicate that the parent has lost control over the child. It may be regarded as a childish form of emotional expression—unpleasant, but bearable, since there are virtues in allowing its free expression in a ten- or eleven-year-old. This is evidenced by the fact that those middle-class mothers who accord highest priority in their scheme of values to their children's happiness are least likely to punish wild play. An outburst of temper, however, may signal serious difficulty in the child's efforts at self-mastery; it is the type of behavior most likely to distress the parent who has tried to inculcate in his child the virtue of maintaining self-control. Again, the evidence supports the interpretation: those parents who value self-control most highly are most likely to punish their children for loss of temper.

If middle-class parents are to act in accord with their values, the must take explicit account of subjective and emotional factors, including the possible effects of punishment. They give considerable evidence that they so do. For example, when asked if there are any ways in which they would prefer to act differently toward the child, they are likely to cite the desirability of fuller understanding. When the child does poorly in school, they often try to be supportive, while working-class parents are likely to respond negatively. Of course, parents can rationalize. It is easy to believe that behavior which is at the moment infuriating ought to be punished. One gains the impression, however, that although middle-class parents may punish when angry, they try to restrain themselves—as they apparently do when they believe their children's actions to be wild play.[12]

The working-class orientation, on the other hand, excludes or minimizes considerations of subjective intent, and places few restraints on the impulse to punish the child when his behavior is out of bounds. Instead, it provides a positive rationale for punishing the child in precisely those circumstances when one might most like to do so.

[12] It is revealing that the middle-class mothers who are most apt to report the frequent use of physical punishment are those who have least confidence in their ability to assess the child's intent—that is, the mothers who say they are "unsure of themselves" in dealing with their children. The working-class mothers who are most likely to make frequent use of physical punishment are those who are most sensitive to the immediate situation—who say they are "easily upset" by their children's actions.

SOCIAL STRATIFICATION AND PSYCHIATRIC DISORDERS

by August B. Hollingshead and Frederick C. Redlich

The research reported here grew out of the work of a number of men, who, during the last half century, have demonstrated that the social environment in which individuals live is connected in some way, as yet not fully explained, to the development of mental illness.[1] Medi-

cal men have approached this problem largely from the viewpoint of epidemiology.[2] Sociologists, on the other hand, have

[1] For example, see A. J. Rosanoff, *Report of a Survey of Mental Disorders in Nassau County, New York*, New York: National Committee for Mental Hygiene, 1916; Ludwig Stern, *Kulturkreis und Form der Geistigen Erkrankung* (Sammlung Zwanglosen Abshandlungen aus dem Gebiete der Nervenund-Geiteskrankheiten), X, No. 2, Halle a. S:C. Marhold, 1913, pp. 1–62; J. F. Sutherland, "Geographical Distribution of Lunacy in Scotland," *British Association for Advancement of Science*, Glasgow, Sept. 1901; William A. White, "Geographical Distribution of Insanity in the United States," *Journal of Nervous and Mental Disease*, XXX (1903), pp. 257–279.

SOURCE: *American Sociological Review*, Vol. 18 (1953), pp. 163–169.

[2] For example, see: Trygve Braatoy, "Is it Probable that the Sociological Situation is a Factor in Schizophrenia?" *Psychiatrica et Neurologica*, XII (1937), pp. 109–138; Donald L. Gerard and Joseph Siegel, "The Family Background of Schizophrenia," *The Psychiatric Quarterly*, 24 (January, 1950), pp. 47–73; Robert W. Hyde and Lowell V. Kingsley, "Studies in Medical Sociology, I: The Relation of Mental Disorders to the Community Socio-economic Level," *The New England Journal of Medicine*, 231, No. 16 (October 19, 1944), pp. 543–548; Robert W. Hyde and Lowell V. Kingsley, "Studies in Medical Sociology, II: The Relation of Mental Disorders to Population Density," *The New England Journal of Medicine*, 231, No. 17 (October 26, 1944), pp. 571–577; Robert M. Hyde and Roderick M. Chisholm, "Studies in Medical Sociology, III: The Relation of Mental Disorders to Race and Nationality," *The New England Journal of Medicine*, 231, No. 18 (November 2, 1944), pp. 612–618; William Mala-

analyzed the question in terms of ecology,[3] and of social disorganization.[4] Neither

---

mud and Irene Malamud, "A Socio-Psychiatric Investigation of Schizophrenia Occurring in the Armed Forces," *Psychosomatic Medicine,* 5 (October, 1943), pp. 364–375; B. Malzberg, *Social and Biological Aspects of Mental Disease,* Utica, N. Y.: State Hospital Press, 1940; William F. Roth and Frank H. Luton, "The Mental Health Program in Tennessee: Statistical Report of a Psychiatric Survey in a Rural County," *American Journal of Psychiatry,* 99 (March, 1943), pp. 662–675; J. Ruesch and others, *Chronic Disease and Psychological Invalidism,* New York: American Society for Research in Psychosomatic Problems, 1946; J. Ruesch and others, *Duodenal Ulcer: A Socio-psychological Study of Naval Enlisted Personnel and Civilians,* Berkeley and Los Angeles: University of California Press, 1948; Jurgen Ruesch, Annemarie Jacobson, and Martin B. Loeb, "Acculturation and Illness," *Psychological Monographs: General and Applied,* Vol. 62, No. 5, Whole No. 292, 1948 (American Psychological Association, 1515 Massachusetts Ave., N.W., Washington 5, D.C.); C. Tietze, Paul Lemkau and M. Cooper, "A Survey of Statistical Studies on the Prevalence and Incidence of Mental Disorders in Sample Populations," *Public Health Reports,* 1909–27 58 (December 31, 1943); C. Tietze, P. Lemkau and Marcia Cooper, "Schizophrenia, Manic Depressive Psychosis and Social-Economic Status," *American Journal of Sociology,* XLVII (September, 1941), pp. 167–175.

[3] Robert E. L. Faris, and H. Warren Dunham, *Mental Disorders in Urban Areas,* Chicago: University of Chicago Press, 1939; H. Warren Dunham, "Current Status of Ecological Research in Mental Disorder," *Social Forces,* 25 (March, 1947), pp. 321–326; R. H. Felix and R. V. Bowers, "Mental Hygiene and Socio-Environmental Factors," *The Milbank Memorial Fund Quarterly,* XXVI (April, 1948), pp. 125–147; H. W. Green, *Persons Admitted to the Cleveland State Hospital,* 1928–1937, Cleveland Health Council, 1939.

[4] R. E. L. Faris, "Cultural Isolation and the Schizophrenic Personality," *American Journal of Sociology,* XXXIX (September, 1934), pp. 155–169; R. E. L. Faris, "Reflections of

psychiatrists nor sociologists have carried on extensive research into the specific question we are concerned with, namely, interrelations between the class structure and the development of mental illness. However, a few sociologists and psychiatrists have written speculative and research papers in this area.[5]

The present research, therefore, was designed to discover whether a relationship does or does not exist between the class system of our society and mental illnesses. Five general hypotheses were formulated in our research plan to test some dimension of an assumed relationship between the two. These hypotheses were stated positively; they could just as easily have been expressed either negatively or conditionally. They were phrased as follows:

I. The *expectancy* of a psychiatric disorder is related significantly to an individual's position in the class structure of his society.

II. The *types* of psychiatric disorders

Social Disorganization in the Behavior of a Schizophrenic Patient," *American Journal of Sociology,* L (September, 1944), pp. 134–141.

[5] For example, see: Robert E. Clark, "Psychoses, Income, and Occupational Prestige," *American Journal of Sociology,* 44 (March, 1949), pp. 433–440; Robert E. Clark, "The Relationship of Schizophrenia to Occupational Income and Occupational Prestige," *American Sociological Review,* 13 (June, 1948), pp. 325–330; Kingsley Davis, "Mental Hygiene and the Class Structure," *Psychiatry,* I (February, 1938), pp. 55–56; Talcott Parsons, "Psychoanalysis and the Social Structure," *The Psychoanalytical Quarterly,* XIX, No. 3 (1950), pp. 371–384; John Dollard and Neal Miller, *Personality and Psychotherapy,* New York: McGraw-Hill, 1950; Jurgen Ruesch, "Social Technique, Social Status, and Social Change in Illness," Clyde Kluckhohn and Henry A. Murray (editors), in *Personality in Nature, Society, and Culture,* New York: Alfred A. Knopf, 1949, pp. 117–130; W. L. Warner, "The Society, the Individual and his Mental Disorders," *American Journal of Psychiatry,* 94, No. 2 (September, 1937), pp. 275–284.

are connected significantly to the class structure.

III. The type of *psychiatric treatment* administered is associated with patient's positions in the class structure.

IV. The *psycho-dynamics* of psychiatric disorders are correlative to an individual's position in the class structure.

V. *Mobility* in the class structure is neurotogenic.

Each hypothesis is linked to the others, and all are subsumed under the theoretical assumption of a functional relationship between stratification in society and the prevalence of particular types of mental disorders among given social classes or strata in a specified population. Although our research was planned around these hypotheses, we have been forced by the nature of the problem of mental illness to study *diagnosed* prevalence of psychiatric disorders, rather than *true* or *total* prevalence.

Methodological Procedure

The research is being done by a team of four psychiatrists,[6] two sociologists,[7] and a clinical psychologist.[8] The data are being assembled in the New Haven urban community, which consists of the city of New Haven and surrounding towns of East Haven, North Haven, West Haven, and Hamden. This community had a population of some 250,000 persons in 1950.[9] The New Haven community was selected because the community's structure has been studied intensively by sociologists over a long period. In addition, it is served

[6] F. C. Redlich, B. H. Roberts, L. Z. Freedman, and Leslie Schaffer.

[7] August B. Hollingshead and J. K. Myers.

[8] Harvey A. Robinson.

[9] The population of each component was as follows: New Haven, 164,443; East Haven, 12,212; North Haven, 9,444; West Haven, 32,010; Hamden, 29,715; and Woodbridge, 2,822.

by a private psychiatric hospital, three psychiatric clinics, and 27 practicing psychiatrists, as well as the state and Veterans Administration facilities.

Four basic technical operations had to be completed before the hypotheses could be tested. These were: the delineation of the class structure of the community, selection of a cross-sectional control of the community's population, the determination of who was receiving psychiatric care, and the stratification of both the control sample and the psychiatric patients.

August B. Hollingshead and Jerome K. Myers took over the task of delineating the class system. Fortunately, Maurice R. Davie and his students had studied the social structure of the New Haven community in great detail over a long time span.[10] Thus, we had a large body of data we could draw upon to aid us in blocking out the community's social structure.

The community's social structure is differentiated *vertically* along racial, ethnic, and religious lines; each of these vertical cleavages, in turn, is differentiated *horizontally* by a series of strata or classes. Around the socio-biological axis of race two social worlds have evolved: A Negro world and a white world. The white world is divided by ethnic origin and religion into Catholic, Protestant, and Jewish con-

[10] Maurice R. Davie, "The Pattern of Urban Growth," G. P. Murdock (editor), in *Studies in the Science of Society*, New Haven: 1937, pp. 133–162; Ruby J. R. Kennedy, "Single or Triple Melting-Pot: Intermarriage Trends in New Haven, 1870–1940," *American Journal of Sociology*, 39 (January, 1944), pp. 331–339; John W. McConnell, *The Influence of Occupation Upon Social Stratification*, Unpublished Ph.D. thesis, Sterling Memorial Library, Yale University, 1937; Jerome K. Myers, "Assimilation to the Ecological and Social Systems of a Community," *American Sociological Review*, 15 (June, 1950), pp. 367–372; Mhyra Minnis, "The Relationship of Women's Organizations to the Social Structure of a City," Unpublished Ph.D. Thesis, Sterling Memorial Library, Yale University, 1951.

tingents. Within these divisions there are numerous ethnic groups. The Irish hold aloof from the Italians, and the Italians move in different circles from the Poles. The Jews maintain a religious and social life separate from the gentiles. The *horizontal* strata that transect each of these vertical divisions are based upon the social values that are attached to occupation, education, place of residence in the community, and associations.

The vertically differentiating factors of race, religion and ethnic origin, when combined with the horizontally differentiating ones of occupation, education, place of residence and so on, produce a social structure that is highly compartmentalized. The integrating factors in this complex are twofold. First, each stratum of each vertical division is similar in its cultural characteristics to the corresponding stratum in the other divisions. Second, the cultural pattern for each stratum or class was set by the "Old Yankee" core group. This core group provided the master cultural mold that has shaped the status system of each sub-group in the community. In short, the social structure of the New Haven community is a parallel class structure within the limits of race, ethnic origin, and religion.

This fact enabled us to stratify the community, for our purposes, with an *Index of Social Position*.[11] This *Index* utilizes three scaled factors to determine an individual's class position within the community's stratificational system: ecological area of residence, occupation, and education. Ecological area of residence is measured by a six point scale; occupation and education are each measured by a seven point scale. To obtain a social class score on an individual we must therefore know his address, his occupation, and the num-

[11] A detailed statement of the procedures used to develop and validate this *Index* will be described in a forthcoming monograph on this research tentatively titled *Psychiatry and Social Class* by August B. Hollingshead and Frederick C. Redlich.

ber of years of school he has completed. Each of these factors is given a scale score, and the scale score is multiplied by a factor weight determined by a standard regression equation. The factor weights are as follows: Ecological area of residence, 5; occupation, 8; and education, 6. The three factor scores are summed, and the resultant score is taken as an index of this individual's position in the community's social class system.

This *Index* enabled us to delineate five main social class strata within the horizontal dimension of the social structure. These principal strata or classes may be characterized as follows:

CLASS I. This stratum is composed of wealthy families whose wealth is often inherited and whose heads are leaders in the community's business and professional pursuits. Its members live in those areas of the community generally regarded as "the best"; the adults are college graduates, usually from famous private institutions, and almost all gentile families are listed in the New Haven *Social Directory*, but few Jewish families are listed. In brief, these people occupy positions of high social prestige.

CLASS II. Adults in this stratum are almost all college graduates; the males occupy high managerial positions, many are engaged in the lesser ranking professions. These families are well-to-do, but there is no substantial inherited or acquired wealth. Its members live in the "better" residential areas; about one-half of these families belong to lesser ranking private clubs, but only 5 per cent of Class II families are listed in the New Haven *Social Directory*.

CLASS III. This stratum includes the vast majority of small proprietors, white-collar office and sales workers, and a considerable number of skilled manual workers. Adults are predominately high school graduates, but a considerable percentage have attended business schools and small colleges for a year or two. They live in "good" residential areas; less than 5 per cent belong to private clubs, but they are not included in the *Social Directory*. Their social life tends to be concentrated in the family, the church, and the lodge.

CLASS IV. This stratum consists predominately of semi-skilled factory workers. Its adult members have finished the elementary grades, but the older people have not completed high school. However, adults under thirty-five have generally graduated from high school. Its members comprise almost one-half of the community; and their residences are scattered over wide areas. Social life is centered in the family, the neighborhood, the labor union, and public places.

CLASS V. Occupationally, class V adults are overwhelmingly semi-skilled factory hands and unskilled laborers. Educationally most adults have not completed the elementary grades. The families are concentrated in the "tenement" and "cold-water flat" areas of New Haven. Only a small minority belong to organized community institutions. Their social life takes place in the family flat, on the street, or in neighborhood social agencies.

The second major technical operation in this research was the enumeration of psychiatric patients. A Psychiatric Census was taken to discover the number and kinds of psychiatric patients in the community. Enumeration was limited to residents of the community who were patients of a psychiatrist or a psychiatric clinic, or were in a psychiatric institution on December 1, 1950. To make reasonably certain that all patients were included in the enumeration, the research team gathered data from all public and private psychiatric institutions and clinics in Connecticut and nearby states, and all private practitioners in Connecticut and the metropolitan New York area. It received the cooperation of all clinics and institutions, and of all practitioners except a small number in New York City. It can be reasonably assumed that we have data

comprising at least 98 per cent of all individuals who were receiving psychiatric care on December 1, 1950.

Forty-four pertinent items of information were gathered on each patient and placed on a schedule. The psychiatrists gathered material regarding symptomatology and diagnosis, onset of illness and duration, referral to the practitioner and the institution, and the nature and intensity of treatment. The sociologists obtained information on age, sex, occupation, education, religion, race and ethnicity, family history, marital experiences, and so on.

The third technical research operation was the selection of a control sample from the normal population of the community. The sociologists drew a 5 per cent random sample of households in the community from the 1951, New Haven *City Directory*. This directory covers the entire communal area. The names and addresses in it were compiled in October and November, 1950—a period very close to the date of the Psychiatric Census. Therefore there was comparability of residence and date of registry between the two population groups. Each household drawn in the sample was interviewed, and data on the age, sex, occupation, education, religion, and income of family members, as well as other items necessary for our purposes were placed on a schedule. This sample is our Control Population.

Our fourth basic operation was the stratification of the psychiatric patients and of the control population with the *Index of Social Position*. As soon as these tasks were completed, the schedules from the Psychiatric Census and the 5 per cent Control Sample were edited and coded, and their data were placed on Hollerith cards. The analysis of these data is in process.

Selected Findings

Before we discuss our findings relative to Hypothesis I, we want to reemphasize that our study is concerned with *diagnosed* or *treated* prevalence rather than *true* or *total* prevalence. Our Psychiatric Census included only psychiatric cases under treatment, diagnostic study, or care. It did not include individuals with psychiatric disorders who were not being treated on December 1, 1950, by a psychiatrist. There are undoubtedly many individuals in the community with psychiatric problems who escaped our net. If we had *true* prevalence figures, many findings from our present study would be more meaningful, perhaps some of our interpretations would be changed, but at present we must limit ourselves to the data we have.

Hypothesis I, as revised by the nature of the problem, stated: *The diagnosed prevalence of psychiatric disorders is related significantly to an individual's position in the class structure.* A test of this hypothesis involves a comparison of the normal population with the psychiatric population. If no significant difference between the distribution of the normal population and the psychiatric patient population by social class is found, Hypothesis I may be abandoned as unproved. However, if a significant difference is found between the two populations by class, Hypothesis I should be entertained until more conclusive data are assembled. Pertinent data for a limited test of Hypothesis I are presented in Table 1. The data included show the number of individuals in the normal population and the psychiatric population, by class level. What we are concerned with in this test is how these two populations are distributed by class.

When we tested the reliability of these population distributions by the use of the chi square method, we found a *very significant* relation between social class and treated prevalence of psychiatric disorders in the New Haven community. A comparison of the percentage distribution of each population by class readily indicates the direction of the class concentration of psychiatric cases. For example, Class I con-

tains 3.1 per cent of the community's population but only 1.0 per cent of the psychiatric cases. Class V, on the other hand, includes 17.8 per cent of the community's population, but contributed 36.8 per cent of the psychiatric patients. On the basis of our data Hypothesis I clearly should be accepted as tenable.

TABLE 1. *Distribution of Normal and Psychiatric Population by Social Class*

SOCIAL CLASS	NORMAL POPULATION *		PSYCHIATRIC POPULATION	
	Number	Per Cent	Number	Per Cent
I	358	3.1	19	1.0
II	926	8.1	131	6.7
III	2500	22.0	260	13.2
IV	5256	46.0	758	38.6
V	2037	17.8	723	36.8
Unknown †	345	3.0	72	3.7
Total	11,422	100.0	1,963	100.0

Chi square = 408.16, P less than .001.

* These figures are preliminary. They do not include Yale students, transients, institutionalized persons, and refusals.

† The unknown cases were not used in the calculation of chi square. They are individuals drawn in the sample, and psychiatric cases whose class level could not be determined because of paucity of data.

Hypothesis II postulated a significant connection between the *type* of psychiatric disorder and social class. This hypothesis involves a test of the idea that there may be a functional relationship between an individual's position in the class system and the type of psychiatric disorder that he may present. This hypothesis depends, in part, on the question of diagnosis. Our psychiatrists based their diagnoses on the classificatory system developed by the Veterans Administration.[12] For the purposes of this paper, all cases are grouped into

[12] *Psychiatric Disorders and Reactions,* Washington: Veterans Administration, Technical Bulletin 10A–78, October, 1947.

two categories: the neuroses and the psychoses. The results of this grouping by social class are given in Table 2.

TABLE 2. *Distribution of Neuroses and Psychoses by Social Class*

SOCIAL CLASS	NEUROSES		PSYCHOSES	
	Number	Per Cent	Number	Per Cent
I	10	52.6	9	47.4
II	88	67.2	43	32.8
III	115	44.2	145	55.8
IV	175	23.1	583	76.9
V	61	8.4	662	91.6
Total	449		1,442	

Chi square = 296.45, P less than .001.

A study of Table 2 will show that the neuroses are concentrated at the higher levels and the psychoses at the lower end economic considerations in determining the character of psychiatric intervention. This question therefore requires further research.

The high concentration of psychotics in the lower strata is probably the product of a very unequal distribution of psychotics in the total population. To test this idea, Hollingshead selected schizophrenics for special study. Because of the severity of this disease it is probable that very few schizophrenics fail to receive some kind of psychiatric care. This diagnostic group comprises 44.2 per cent of all patients, and 58.7 per cent of the psychotics, in our study. Ninety-seven and six-tenths per cent of these schizophrenic patients had been hospitalized at one time or another, and 94 per cent were hospitalized at the time of our census. When we classify these patients by social class we find that there is a very significant inverse relationship between social class and schizophrenia.

TABLE 3. *Comparison of the Distribution of the Normal Population with Schizophrenics by Class, with Index of Probable Prevalence*

SOCIAL CLASS	NORMAL POPULATION		SCHIZOPHRENICS		INDEX OF PREVALENCE
	No.	Per Cent	No.	Per Cent	
I	358	3.2	6	.7	22
II	926	8.4	23	2.7	33
III	2,500	22.6	83	9.8	43
IV	5,256	47.4	352	41.6	88
V	2,037	18.4	383	45.2	246
Total	11,077	100.0	847	100.0	

of the class structure. Our team advanced a number of theories to explain the sharp differences between the neuroses and psychoses by social class. One suggestion was that the low percentage of neurotics in the lower classes was a direct reaction to the cost of psychiatric treatment. But as we accumulated a series of case studies, for tests of Hypotheses IV and V, we became skeptical of this simple interpretation. Our detailed case records indicate that the social distance between psychiatrist and patient may be more potent than Hollingshead decided to determine, on the basis of these data, what the probability of the prevalence of schizophrenia by social class might be in the general population. To do this he used a proportional index to learn whether or not there were differentials in the distribution of the general population, as represented in our control sample, and the distribution of schizophrenics by social class. If a social class exhibits the same proportion of schizophrenia as it comprises of the general population, the index for that class is 100.

If schizophrenia is disproportionately prevalent in a social class the index is above 100; if schizophrenia is disproportionately low in a social class the index is below 100. The index for each social class appears in the last column of Table 3.

The fact that the Index of Prevalence in class I is only one-fifth as great as it would be if schizophrenia were proportionately distributed in this class, and that it is two and one-half times as high in class V as we might expect on the basis of proportional distribution, gives further support to Hypothesis II. The fact that the Index of Prevalence is 11.2 times as great in class V as in class I is particularly impressive.

Hypothesis III stipulated that the type of psychiatric treatment a patient receives is associated with his position in the class structure. A test of this hypothesis involves

organic treatment. Psychotherapy, on the other hand, was concentrated in the higher classes. Within the psychotherapy category there were sharp differences between the types of psychotherapy administered to the several classes. For example, psychoanalysis was limited to classes I and II. Patients in class V who received any psychotherapy were treated by group methods in the state hospitals. The number and percentage of patients who received each type of therapy is given in Table 4. The data clearly support Hypothesis III.

At the moment we do not have data available for a test of Hypotheses IV and V. These will be put to a test as soon as we complete work on a series of cases now under close study. Preliminary materials give us the impression that they too will be confirmed.

TABLE 4. *Distribution of the Principal Types of Therapy by Social Class*

	PSYCHOTHERAPY		ORGANIC THERAPY		NO TREATMENT	
SOCIAL CLASS	Number	Per Cent	Number	Per Cent	Number	Per Cent
I	14	73.7	2	10.5	3	15.8
II	107	81.7	15	11.4	9	6.9
III	136	52.7	74	28.7	48	18.6
IV	237	31.1	288	37.1	242	31.8
V	115	16.1	234	32.7	367	51.2

Chi square = 336.58, P less than .001.

a comparison of the different types of therapy being used by psychiatrists on patients in the different social classes. We encountered many forms of therapy but they may be grouped under three main types; psychotherapy, organic therapy, and custodial care. The patient population, from the viewpoint of the principal type of therapy received, was divided roughly into three categories: 32.0 per cent received some type of psychotherapy; 31.7 per cent received organic treatments of one kind or another; and 36.3 per cent received custodial care without treatment. The percentage of persons who received no treatment care was greatest in the lower classes. The same finding applies to

Conclusions and Interpretations

This study was designed to throw new light upon the question of how mental illness is related to social environment. It approached this problem from the perspective of social class to determine if an individual's position in the social system was associated significantly with the development of psychiatric disorders. It proceeded on the theoretical assumption that if mental illnesses were distributed randomly in the population, the hypotheses designed to test the idea that psychiatric disorders are connected in some functional way to the class system would not be found to be statistically significant.

The data we have assembled demonstrate conclusively that mental illness, as measured by diagnosed prevalence, is not distributed randomly in the population of the New Haven community. On the contrary, psychiatric difficulties of so serious a nature that they reach the attention of a psychiatrist are unequally distributed among the five social classes. In addition, types of psychiatric disorders, and the ways patients are treated, are strongly associated with social class position.

The statistical tests of our hypotheses indicate that there are definite connections between particular types of social environments in which people live, as measured by the social class concept, and the emergence of particular kinds of psychiatric disorders, as measured by psychiatric diagnosis. They do not tell us what these connections are, nor how they are functionally related to a particular type of mental illness in a given individual. The next step, we believe, is to turn from the strictly statistical approach to an intensive study of the social environments associated with particular social classes, on the one hand, and of individuals in these environments who do or do not develop mental illnesses, on the other hand. Currently the research team is engaged in this next step but is not yet ready to make a formal report of its findings.

F · SOCIAL CHANGE AND PERSONALITY

1 · The Effects of Migration and Social Mobility on Personality

A PRELIMINARY REPORT ON THE RELATION
OF SOCIOCULTURAL FACTORS TO HYPERTENSION AMONG THE ZULU

by Norman A. Scotch *

This paper represents a preliminary and partial analysis of data collected in an epidemiological study of hypertension in two African communities. The two groups studied are both Zulu communities in the Union of South Africa, the first in a rural native reserve, and the second in an urban "location" called Lamontville.†

This paper is based primarily on ethnological observation and on data collected in single interviews with 548 rural and 505 urban Zulu. The total study yielded considerably more data from a number of follow-up interviews, psychological tests, and medical examinations of a selected number of hypertensives matched with normal controls. This latter material will be reported at another time. The interview was conducted by Zulu trained especially for the project. In the urban area the interviewer was

* It is a pleasure to acknowledge the guidance and support of M. J. Herskovits and the Program of African Studies, Northwestern University, Evanston, Ill.

† Sampling techniques, basic data, and methodology will be reported elsewhere. More detailed analysis will be found in the *American Journal of Public Health*, August, 1963.

SOURCE: *Annals of The New York Academy of Sciences*, Vol. 84 (1960), pp. 1000–1009 (*abridged by the Editors*).

a Zulu nurse, whereas in the rural area the interviewers were Zulu medical assistants. All interviewers participated in a prestudy whereby their interviewing techniques could be checked and their readings of blood pressures could be standardized with those of European physicians.

The interviews were taken in the homes of the participants and consisted of the taking of three blood pressure determinations with five-minute intervals between and the measuring of height and weight. A number of questions were asked concerning features of the participants' background, such as age, income, religion, occupation, and marital status. For the analysis that follows the initial blood pressure reading was used.

Results

In general the mean blood pressure levels of both the rural and urban Zulu are relatively high. When these mean blood pressure levels are compared to Master's so-called representative sample of Americans, we find that the rural Zulu are somewhat below, and urban Zulu somewhat above, these United States mean values (Table 1). Another comparison with a

TABLE 1. *Zulu Urban and Rural, and Representative American,* and Georgia † American White and Negro Mean Blood Pressures by Age and Sex*

	SYSTOLIC PRESSURE									DIASTOLIC PRESSURE				
	Master's	Zulu			Georgia		Georgia			Master's	Zulu		Georgia	Georgia
AGE	American	Rural	N	Urban	N	White	N	Negroes	N	American	Rural	Urban	White	Negroes
Males														
20–24	123									76				
18–24		120	(30)	123	(23)	123	(44)	127	(37)		73	77	74	78
25–29	125									78				
25–34		120	(26)	122	(48)	122	(40)	133	(21)		78	77	79	81
30–34	126									79				
35–39	127									80				
35–44		116	(28)	130	(40)	124	(65)	143	(34)		74	82	83	92
40–44	129									81				
45–49	130									82				
45–54		127	(23)	153	(20)	133	(59)	151	(25)		82	92	86	96
50–54	135									83				
55–59	138									84				
55–64		129	(24)	149	(7)	138	(39)	167	(15)		76	91	79	96
60–64	142									85				
65+		127	(20)	147	(9)	148	(21)	147	(5)		77	85	84	82
Females														
20–24	116									72				
18–24		117	(82)	118	(76)	113	(56)	126	(37)		72	72	66	78
25–29	117									74				
25–34		115	(102)	135	(124)	113	(87)	125	(44)		74	79	72	80
30–34	120									75				
35–39	124									78				
35–44		118	(95)	133	(76)	121	(96)	146	(47)		76	84	77	91
40–44	127									80				
45–49	131									82				
45–54		128	(65)	149	(33)	136	(62)	158	(32)		82	94	83	94
50–54	137									84				
55–59	139									84				
55–64		140	(29)	146	(28)	147	(46)	170	(17)		85	89	82	97
60–64	144									85				
65+		136	(24)	156	(10)	157	(45)	173	(16)		83	92	82	89

* The American mean blood pressures are derived from Master's *et al.* study: Master, A. M., Garfield, C. I., and Walters, M. B., *Normal Blood Pressure and Hypertension* (Philadelphia, Pa.: Lea and Febiger, 1952).

† The data on the Georgia sample are derived from the study by G. W. Comstock, 1957, "An Epidemiologic Study of Blood Pressure Levels in a Biracial Community in the Southern United States." *Am. J. Hygiene.* 65: No. 3, 271–315. Note that the mean pressures in Master's sample are given in five-year intervals. Since Master does not give the sample size for his population, it is not possible to include this data.

United States sample studied by Comstock in Georgia, indicates that the rural Zulu, in general, have mean blood pressures somewhat below both his white and Negro groups, and that the urban Zulu, in general, have higher pressures than these American whites but not quite as high as United States Negroes (Table 1).

The contrast between rural and urban Zulu blood pressure is striking. This is shown in two ways:

(1) There is a greater frequency of elevated blood pressures (using a criterion of 90 mm. Hg diastolic) among urban Zulu for all age groups and both sexes. For males the difference between rural and urban is significant (0.10) only in the 25 to 44 age group (Table 2).

(2) Using mean blood pressure values urban males and urban females are significantly higher in all age groups.

Increasing age is associated with increasing frequency of elevated blood pressures and with higher mean blood pressures for both sexes and in both communities (Tables 2 and 3). Male frequency of elevated blood pressure approximates the female in the lower age groups, but in the 45 to 64 category the females appear considerably higher than the males (Table 2).

Discussion

How can we explain the difference in blood pressure found between rural and urban Zulu? Such factors as race and climate can be eliminated immediately. Two very promising factors that have received much attention recently are diet and social stress.

To examine the question of diet first,

TABLE 2. *Frequency of Elevated* * *Diastolic Blood Pressures of Rural and Urban Zulu, by Age and Sex*

AGE AND BLOOD PRESSURE	MALE				FEMALE			
	Rural		Urban		Rural		Urban	
	N	%	N	%	N	%	N	%
18–24								
Normal	27	(90)	19	(83)	75	(91)	70	(92)
Elevated *	3	(10)	4	(17)	7	(09)	6	(08)
	$\chi^2 = 0.67$		P > 0.10		$\chi^2 = 0.03$		P > 0.10	
25–44								
Normal	46	(88)	68	(77)	167	(85)	153	(73)
Elevated	6	(12)	20	(23)	30	(15)	58	(27)
	$\chi^2 = 3.46$		P < 0.10		$\chi^2 = 9.86$		P < .01	
45–64								
Normal	36	(74)	15	(56)	60	(63)	25	(41)
Elevated	13	(26)	12	(44)	34	(36)	36	(59)
	$\chi^2 = 2.62$		P > 0.10		$\chi^2 = 8.23$		P < 0.01	
65 and above								
Normal	16	(80)	6	(67)	15	(63)	4	(40)
Elevated	4	(20)	3	(33)	9	(37)	6	(60)
	$\chi^2 = 0.52$		P > 0.10		$\chi^2 = 1.52$		P > 0.10	

* The criteria for elevated diastolic blood pressure was 90 mm. Hg and above.

TABLE 3. *Zulu Urban/Rural Mean Blood Pressures by Age and Sex*

AGE RESIDENCE AND SEX	SYSTOLIC PRESSURE				DIASTOLIC PRESSURE		
	N	Mean	Standard deviation	F *	Mean	Standard deviation	F *
Male							
(25–44)				8.68 †			4.08
Rural	54	118	13.6		76	9.9	
Urban	88	125	14.6		80	11.8	
(45–64)				11.64 †			9.23 †
Rural	47	128	26.5		79	14.4	
Urban	27	151	32.3		92	22.2	
(All ages)				11.66 †			12.87 ‡
Rural	151	123	19.7		76	11.8	
Urban	147	131	22.7		82	14.9	
Female							
(25–44)				44.57 ‡			20.51 ‡
Rural	197	116	16.4		75	12.1	
Urban	211	128	19.3		81	15.3	
(45–64)				13.96 ‡			13.64 ‡
Rural	94	132	27.7		83	15.0	
Urban	61	148	24.6		92	15.4	
(All ages)				30.66 ‡			19.64 ‡
Rural	397	121	21.5		77	13.6	
Urban	358	130	21.9		81	15.8	

* Tests of significance based on analysis of variance.
† With P < 0.10.
‡ With P < 0.01.

it has been shown elsewhere § that urban diet is somewhat superior, although similar in terms of cereal variety and the consumption of animal tissues and other protective foodstuffs. However, in a small study of the diet of the same urban population on which I am now reporting it was found that there was no evidence of a relationship between the prevalence of hypertension and the consumption of a "superior" or "inferior" diet.

The possibility of a selective factor operating so that hypertensives would tend to gravitate toward the city does not receive support from the data.

§ "Observations on the Epidemiology of Hypertension in an Urban Zulu Community," by J. H. Abramson, E. Slome, B. Gampel, and N. Scotch. In preparation.

When participants in the study were asked where they would prefer to live, those who lived in the city and who would have preferred to live in the country had hypertension frequencies similar to those who lived in the city and preferred it to the country. The same was true of the rural area, there being no significant difference between those who prefer the city to the rural area.

A more convincing case can be made for social stress as a variable related to the prevalence of hypertension among the Zulu. It is hypothesized that stress is not only more frequent in the city but is much more severe as well.

Almost all rural informants said that poverty and migratory labor were the major problems of life. In the city, however, respondents went on and on when asked the same question. Not only was there poverty, but degradation and humiliation in the treatment of Africans by Europeans, frequent arrests, high rates of illegitimacy, divorce and separation, alcoholism, and open competition for few jobs. It is of interest that a significantly greater percentage of city dwellers expressed a preference for living in the country than the percentage of country dwellers who stated they would prefer to live in the city (Table 4).

certain measure of respect and continues to hear and judge tribal disputes. The family remains primarily an extended family and, although the authority of the headman has diminished in contrast with former times, it is still very much in existence.

The religious picture is somewhat complex. Due to the work and influence of missionaries representing several denominations, the great majority of the community are nominal Christians. Those who are not Christians retain much of the

TABLE 4. *Home Preference of Urban and Rural Females, by Frequency of Elevated Blood Pressure*

	LIVE IN URBAN		LIVE IN RURAL	
	Normal B.P.	Elevated B.P.	Normal B.P.	Elevated B.P.
Prefer urban	118	69	21	3
Prefer rural	44	31	185	47

NOTE: The higher frequency of those urbans who would prefer to live in the country over those rurals who would prefer to live in the city is significant at the 0.02-level, using Chi Square.

In the rural area the Zulu live in scattered homesteads consisting of fairly large extended families. The subsistence economy is basically agricultural supplemented by cattle keeping. Since not enough food is produced to feed the population, the people are forced to buy their food. Buying food, however, requires cash and the men are forced to the cities to work for a cash wage. Some men go to the city for a few years, save part of their salary, and then return to the rural community, but by far the majority of men prefer to work in the city for about nine to ten months a year, sending home a portion of their salary for their wives and children, returning occasionally for a few days, and then coming home for about two months every year for the planting season.

The social structure is undergoing a certain amount of change, although with certain continuations of native institutions. For example, the power of the chief is crumbling although he still receives a

traditional beliefs. This, however, is also true of the Christians and, despite the earnest efforts of the missionaries, much traditional belief is incorporated into the framework of native Christianity. For example, almost all of the community still retain their belief in witchcraft as the cause of not only all illness but all other sorts of misfortune as well. For this reason native doctors, called *inyangas* and *isangomas*, still retain a very prominent position within the social hierarchy.

In contrast to the dominant position of men in the traditional social structure the position of women is subservient. Whereas the men work hard only for a few months out of every year and spend the rest of the time in relative leisure, looking after cattle and in general supervising the output of the family unit, the women work extremely hard and have relatively little leisure. They are engaged in such matters as working in the fields, fetching water, and chopping and carrying firewood great distances. Women's position in this society involves difficult and arduous roles, which are nevertheless clearly defined and inculcated during childhood training. Furthermore the women know that as they grow older and their children reach adulthood, the rigors of their early adult life will be substantially ameliorated.

The aged of both sexes in the rural area are in a particularly favorable position. They are considered as elder statesmen and are accorded much respect and status. The Zulu aged have very little worry about providing for themselves since they occupy a still productive role in the family as the repositories of tribal custom and tradition.

Children are either sloughed off on relatives or friends, or they are left to fend for themselves in the streets of the location. Delinquent gangs, called *tsotsis,* roam the location causing damage and threatening the community.

The traditional extended family is the exception in the city rather than the rule, as it is in the reserve. Today the city family is nuclear, consisting of husband, wife, children, and lodgers, and occasionally unmarried relatives. The fact that there are no chiefs nor headmen in the city is not as significant as the lack of the traditional family. The high incidence of divorce, separation, and illegitimacy may be attributed to difficulties in adjustment to a new type of family.

TABLE 5. *Rural and Urban Females Who Admit to Being Bewitched by Frequency of Elevated Blood Pressure*

	RURAL		URBAN	
	Normal B.P.	Elevated B.P.	Normal B.P.	Elevated B.P.
Not bewitched	91	19	79	27
Bewitched	106	32	96	63

NOTE: Those urbanites who admit to being bewitched have a higher frequency of elevated pressures than those who do not admit to being bewitched. This is significant at the 0.02 level. There is no significant difference among the rurals. Chi Square was used in significance tests.

In contrast with this picture of a slowly changing, relatively stable rural community we must view the urban community as undergoing drastic change with accompanying problems and difficulties.

In the city the Africans live crowded together in "locations" that can charitably be described only as slums. The quality of the housing, the sanitation, and the space must be described as poor. The men work for low wages at the most menial tasks and under the most trying conditions. Moreover the men have to travel great distances to work with inadequate transportation. Since the men do not earn enough to support their families, it is customary for the women to take jobs as domestics, and this requires that they too travel long distances and spend the greater portion of their time away from the home.

Just as bewitchment and sorcery explain illness and misfortune in the reserve, so do they in the city. It is of interest that a greater proportion of city dwellers admit to being bewitched than do those in the reserve, despite some advance in sophistication of the urbanites. A belief in sorcery explains not only the timeless misfortunes of illness, unrequited love, and accidents, but is now extended to explain the failure to find or keep a job, the failure of avoiding arrest, and the failure to win money or break even at the race track. Higher rates of accusations of sorcery can also be partially explained by the fact that the Zulu now live in crowded flats rather than scattered homesteads, and that also living in these flats are Africans from other tribes, such as the Sutho, Swazi, and Xosa.

It is of interest that the proportion of urban women who admitted to being bewitched had significantly higher rates of elevated pressure than did those who did not admit to bewitchment. For the urban males the same trend is noted, but it does not quite reach levels of significance. This trend is not observable among the rural males and females (Table 5).

most of them do not appreciate the role of family head. It is of interest that, in our sample, widows had significantly higher rates of hypertension than nonwidows * of comparable ages (Table 6).

The men in the city, in contrast to the reserve, are subject to almost continual stress especially in their contact with Europeans. Employment is not always easy to

TABLE 6. *Married versus Separated and Widowed Zulu Women, by Residence, and by Frequency of Elevated Blood Pressure*

	RURAL		URBAN	
	Normal B.P.	Elevated B.P.	Normal B.P.	Elevated B.P.
Married	188	48	162	82
Separated or widowed	21	12	3	9

NOTE: Separated and widowed women had higher frequencies of elevated blood pressures than married women that were significant at the 0.05 level in the rural area, and 0.02 level in the urban area. However the higher frequency of elevated pressures among urban widows and separated women over rural counterparts was also significant at the 0.05 level. Chi Square was used in significance tests.

The position of the women has become less subservient though more ambiguous, and this increases tensions between man and wife. Now that many of the women are wage earners they have begun to emerge from their traditionally subordinate position. This is made easier by the fact that in the city a woman is no longer under the domination of her husband's mother and other in-laws, but this emergence is not without attendant difficulties. While working as domestics for European families the Zulu woman learns that she need not be completely subordinate to her husband. She also learns that the European husband and wife share many activities, but when she returns to the location she finds that her husband absolutely refuses to engage in joint activities and maintains tribal tradition to the extent of sharing his leisure with other men.

Many women become the heads of families at a comparatively early age, due to the high mortality rates of men in dangerous occupations, and due also to the high arrest and detention rates for trivial past offenses. Although the women are motivated toward elevating their status,

find, and with few exceptions even the regularly employed men fail to make a subsistence living. The work itself is most menial, with absolutely no opportunities for advancement and with long hard hours. Simply getting to the place of employment presents daily obstacles, waiting in line for long hours to get on crowded buses both to and from work. In his contact with the white man the African is in a completely inferior position, which is shown by continual overt acts of humiliation imposed on natives by whites. This continuous and daily frustration in relations with whites finds few opportunities for expression. The hostility must be displaced and eventually is expressed against wives (witness the high rate of broken homes), against other Africans (higher rates of sorcery and bewitchment), or against the self (alcoholism, hypertension). The situation in the city contrasts strikingly with the situation in the reserve as regards contacts with Europeans. While

* This is also true for rural widows, but even so the rates of elevated pressures are significantly higher for urban than for rural widows (Table 6).

the Zulu on the reserve knows full well the meaning of apartheid he comes in contact only infrequently with Europeans and does not face the constant day-to-day harassment of his urban counterpart.

The position of the aged in the urban area is decidedly inferior to the rural area, primarily because of the dissolution of the extended family. Rather than occupying a place of honor and respect, the aged, unable to provide for themselves, find themselves in the position of unwelcome guests in the already over-crowded homes of their sons.

Why, in the face of severe, constant stress, does the African remain in the city? One reason already noted is the need to earn a cash income simply to meet daily food needs. Aside from the question of need, however, it is interesting and significant that most of the Zulu interviewed *prefer* to live in the city. Primarily, Africans *do* want to acculturate themselves to Western culture, particularly as regards the European technology. Most are convinced that the tribal way of life is restrict-

ing and limited and that it is only a matter of time before its eventual disappearance. The eagerness and drive for formal education further illustrate the desire for acculturation. Again, this drive, since it is blocked as a result of the present political situation, leads only to further stress and frustration.

Thus we have seen in this brief analysis that there is considerably more stress for Zulu living in the city than for those that live in a reserve. Those stress factors that seem significantly related to greater urban Zulu hypertension are all derivable from social features of present South African Negro city life. Some of them are absent or insignificant in rural Zulu society, others are present in the rural milieu but in apparently less emphatic forms than in the cities. In addition, the rural culture has greater continuity with past tradition and greater stability of expected roles. This is in striking contrast to life in the city, where there is a complete break with tradition in many, although not all, areas of life that has resulted in anomie.

THE SKIDDER: IDEOLOGICAL ADJUSTMENTS
OF DOWNWARD MOBILE WORKERS

by Harold L. Wilensky and Hugh Edwards

This is a secondary analysis of data from a study of two large factories in a small Midwestern city. It seeks to demonstrate that in a period of prosperity (1) downward occupational mobility ("skidding") has a conservative impact on values and beliefs regarding the stratification order among urban workers; but (2) the strength of the relationship between mobility and ideology varies with age, type of mobility, and aspirations (situs *versus* stratum). Alternative explanations of the skidder's conservatism are tested. In the manner of

Sombart's *Why Is There No Socialism in the United States?* [1] the analysis underscores one cultural constraint on political extremism—the optimism of even those who have suffered status deprivation about their chances to re-coup losses.

Theory and Hypotheses

Since Durkheim called attention to the possible disruptive consequences of social

SOURCE: *American Sociological Review*, Vol. 24 (1959), pp. 215–231.

[1] Werner Sombart, *Warum gibh esinden Vereingten staaten keinen Sozialismus?* Tübingen: J. C. B. Mohr (Paul Siebeck), 1906.

mobility for person and society,[2] students of stratification have seen the mobile person as deviant from his status peers. Whether moving up or down, he tends to lack firm ties to either the groups he has left behind or those into which he is moving. This is reflected in the findings of the few systematic studies which contrast the patterns of behavior and belief of mobile and non-mobile persons. The differences show up in prejudice,[3] politics,[4] union membership and activity,[5] the control of family size,[6] marital adjustment,[7] mental disorder, social isolation, nervousness, and preoccupation with health,[8] tendencies to

suicide, homicide, and other crime.[9]

Investigators agree on the political effects of downward social mobility. Workers with white collar fathers are more conservative than those with blue-collar fathers. In the United States, Centers found that, of the 50 urban skidders in his national sample, 40 per cent were "conservative" (anti-New Deal liberal) as compared with 25 per cent of 236 nonskidders.[10] Lipset and Gordon indicate that mobile individuals in their Oakland, California sample are less likely than others to belong to or to report themselves as active in trade unions.[11] Three election studies give the same picture: intergenerational skidders are more likely to support the Republican candidate than two-generation workers, though the differences are not great.[12] In Europe, too, the

---

[2] Emile Durkheim, *Suicide*, Glencoe, Ill.: Free Press, 1951, pp. 242–254.

[3] B. Bettelheim and M. Janowitz, *The Dynamics of Prejudice*, New York: Harper, 1950; J. Greenblum and L. I. Pearlin, "Vertical Mobility Prejudice: A Socio-Psychological Analysis," in R. Bendix and S. M. Lipset, editors, *Class, Status and Power*, Glencoe, Ill.: Free Press, 1953, pp. 480–491.

[4] See, e.g., E. E. Maccoby, "Youth and Political Change," *Public Opinion Quarterly*, 18 (Spring, 1954), pp. 23–39; and E. Havemann and P. S. West, *They Went to College*, New York: Harcourt, Brace, 1952, pp. 117–120.

[5] S. M. Lipset and J. Gordon, "Mobility and Trade Union Membership," in Lipset and Bendix, *op. cit.*, pp. 491–500.

[6] R. Reimer and C. V. Kiser, "Economic Tension and Social Mobility in Relation to Fertility Planning and Size of Planned Family," in P. K. Whelpton and C. V. Kiser, editors, *Social and Psychological Factors Affecting Fertility*, Vol. IV, New York: Milbank Memorial Fund, 1954, pp. 1005–1068.

[7] J. Roth and R. F. Peck, "Class and Social Mobility Factors Related to Marital Adjustment," *American Sociological Review*, 16 (August, 1951), pp. 478–487.

[8] A. B. Hollingshead, R. Ellis, and E. Kirby, "Social Mobility and Mental Illness," *American Sociological Review*, 19 (October, 1954), pp. 577–584; E. Ellis, "Social Psychological Correlates of Upward Social Mobility Among Unmarried Women," *American Sociological Review*, 17 (October, 1952), pp. 558–563; E.

Litwak, "Conflicting Values and Decision Making," unpublished Ph.D. Dissertation, Columbia University, 1956.

[9] Inferences from A. F. Henry and J. F. Short, *Suicide and Homicide*, Glencoe, Ill.: Free Press, 1955; and L. N. Robins and P. O'Neal, "Mortality, Mobility, and Crime: Problem Children Thirty Years Later," *American Sociological Review*, 23 (April, 1958), pp. 162–171.

[10] R. Centers, *The Psychology of Social Classes*, Princeton: Princeton University Press, 1949, p. 180. Cf. Maccoby's finding that downward mobile persons conformed or over-conformed to middle class norms of Republican voting and affiliation (*op. cit.*, pp. 34–35).

[11] *Op. cit.* Cf. A. S. Tannenbaum and R. L. Kahn, *Participation in Union Locals*, Evanston, Ill.: Row, Peterson, 1958, pp. 142–148.

[12] Differences range from 8 to 21 per cent. Of 283 union auto workers in Detroit, 40 per cent of those from white collar families voted for Eisenhower in 1952, as compared with 29 per cent of the sons of farmers, 26 per cent of the sons of skilled workers, and 19 per cent of the sons of other manual workers. A. Kornhauser, H. L. Sheppard and A. J. Mayer, *When Labor Votes*, New York: University Books, 1956, p. 43. The 1952 Survey Research Center data on 156 urban

two available studies report the skidder as less prone to leftist politics than his non-mobile brethren. In an investigation in Germany, 64 per cent of 357 workers whose fathers were manual workers supported the Social Democratic party, compared to 52 per cent of the 58 workers with non-manual fathers.[13] In Finland, two-generation workers have been more likely to vote Communist than workers of middle class origin—a difference of 20 per cent.[14]

Speculations about the reasons for the ideological conservatism of the downward mobile worker are varied. The main arguments fall into two categories:

1. *Resistance to failure in a society which emphasizes success values and the belief in an open class system.* Skidders resist the status implications of downward mobility by denying failure and striving to succeed.[15]

2. *Early, retrospective, anticipatory, or later socialization.* (a) *Early:* Skidders have earlier absorbed inappropriate attitudes from a "middle class environment" or "white collar occupational culture." [16] (b) *Retrospective:* Skidders reject full participation in the working class and retrospectively come to value what they have lost—they adopt attitudes and practices of the middle class.[17] (c) *Anticipatory:* Skidders aspire and expect to return to their former status and so, in anticipation, take on the values of a middle class reference category.[18] (d) *Acculturation, or later socialiation:* Skidders lack firm integration with any social class, communicate little with other people, and receive little social support from them. "In the absence of extensive communication, [the mobile individual] cannot fully assimilate the style of life of the members of his new social class, with the result that his beliefs and practices are intermediate between theirs and those of the members of his class of origin." [19] Non-mobile

---

manual workers show that 46 per cent of the skidders and 38 per cent of the non-skidders favored the Republicans. The comparable difference is 18 per cent for the 1948 election. Based on tabulations by S. M. Lipset and H. L. Zetterberg in "A Theory of Social Mobility," *Transactions of the Third World Congress of Sociology,* III, London: International Sociological Association, 1956, p. 174.

[13] Based on a 1953 study by the UNESCO Institute of Social Science in Cologne, Germany, reported in *Ibid.*

[14] *Ibid.,* p. 174.

[15] Compare the conclusions of a study of class variations in defense mechanisms. The mechanism of denial in fantasy, a product of harsh, external child-rearing practices (e.g., beatings), is concentrated among children of working class parents (indexed by occupation and income). D. R. Miller and G. E. Swanson, *Inner Conflict and Defense,* New York: Holt, Chs. 8, 9, in press. One reason is that denial of reality is disfunctional for the maintenance and enhancement of social position, and middle class children are handled in ways that assure status continuity. According to this psycho-

logical hypothesis, when the man who has learned to favor the mechanism of denial fails and suffers status anxiety, he substitutes in fantasy a picture of success or of a system in which he is sure to rise. Some of our intergenerational skidders may have slipped not only because of bad breaks but because they were taught the "wrong" defense mechanisms; worklife skidders with working class parents are simply using the typical mechanism of the class (which handicapped them in their attempt to breach the class barrier).

[16] Lipset and Gordon, *op. cit.,* pp. 492 ff.

[17] *Ibid.,* p.. 496. "Retrospective" seems to imply "early" socialization; it may be distinguished on the assumption that the early experience did not fully penetrate but nevertheless the person is moved to conform to norms which by distasteful comparison he now realizes are prestigeful.

[18] *Ibid.,* pp. 493, 496.

[19] P. M. Blau, "Social Mobility and Interpersonal Relations," *American Sociological Review,* 21 (June, 1956), p. 292. Cf. H. H. Hyman, "The Value Systems of Different

workers, on the other hand, in frequent contact and communication with others like themselves and free from counteracting cross-class influences, acquire and maintain working class patterns of behavior and thought.[20] Differences between skidders and non-skidders, then, are a function of time for acculturation.

All of these explanations imply differences in class ideology between mobile and non-mobile workers: the skidder, more than the non-skidder, should adhere to the success ideology, cherish high occupational ambition, and be optimistic about the chance for himself and his children to return to white collar status. In short, he should be more "middle class" in what he believes, wants, and expects. The present study affords further test of this general hypothesis. (Hypothesis I in "Findings" below.)

The specific explanations—resistance to failure, class socialization—have further implications, however, which remain unexplored in the stratification literature. To tackle these, we must make certain distinctions between types of mobility, aspirations, and age.

One explanation of ideological conservatism among skidders pictures them as denying failure at the same time that they strive to regain what they have lost. For several reasons, this adherence to the tradition of opportunity should apply more

to young intergenerational skidders than to young worklife skidders; more to older worklife skidders than to older intergenerational skidders; and more to older worklife skidders than to young worklife skidders (Hypothesis II, in "Findings" below). First, the real worklife skidders are the *older* factory workers who were white collar employees before entering the plant; unlike the youngsters, their occupational history is long enough to make worklife skidding meaningful in failure-success terms. Moreover, skidders under 40 or 50, like those under 30, in fact have a good chance to regain lost status.[21] Finally, where lie the coercive comparisons that men make in evaluating their class situation? If the skidder adheres to the success ideology and has an occupational history, he is more likely to compare himself with his own white collar past than with his father's—and to find a spur to his ambition in the process. Contrast the youngster. In some cases the young white collar worker may have deliberately *chosen* the better starting wage of the workbench as a temporary expedient. Gripped for the moment by a young adult subculture with its call for cars, trips, tailormade suits, expensive outings with the girl friend or

Classes," in Lipset and Bendix, *op. cit.*, p. 441.

[20] Lipset and Gordon, *op. cit.*, p. 493; Blau, *op. cit.*, p. 291. At the logical extreme, we would find complete ecological segregation permitting communication only with those of identical occupation and social class. The militancy of miners, seamen, longshoremen, etc. throughout the Free West has often been explained in terms of this social isolation hypothesis. C. Kerr and A. Siegel, "The Interindustry Propensity to Strike—An International Comparison," in A. Kornhauser et al., editors, *Industrial Conflict*, New York: McGraw-Hill, 1954, pp. 189–212.

[21] While ". . . there is relatively little permanent crossing between manual and non-manual occupations . . . the temporary crossings occur more frequently downward than upward . . . from 40 to 80 per cent of [the non-manual workers in the Oakland, California, sample of men over 30] have at one time or another worked in the manual occupations." S. M. Lipset and R. Bendix, "Social Mobility and Occupational Career Patterns II," in Lipset and Bendix, *op. cit.*, pp. 455–456. Consistent with the Oakland findings are synthetic working life patterns constructed from data on urban workers from the Six City Study. A. J. Jaffe and R. O. Carleton, *Occupational Mobility in the United States 1930–1960*, New York: King's Crown Press, 1954, pp. 51—59. These studies tell us that worklife skidders in the second or third decade of their careers can still strive with justified optimism.

wife,[22] he shows up in our samples as a worklife skidder—but he feels little sense of failure and no need to resist its status implications. For the majority who have *not* chosen the downward path, worklife skidding should again count for little: the youngster has scanty labor market experience, and is fresh from the controls of a middle class family; the important comparison for him is the one in which he comes out second best to his father. As he grows older, however, the intergenerational skidder is moved to adapt to working class values and beliefs: the success ideology holds that what he is has nothing to do with his father's status; less and less will he remind himself or be asked by his peers, "What did your father do?" In sum, when we deal with the ideological conservatism of downward mobile workers, intergenerational mobility should count more for very young workers, while worklife mobility should have its most solid impact upon older workers (Hypothesis II below).

What about the explanations of ideological conservatism that point to class socialization—early, retrospective, anticipatory, or later? What do they imply for the differential effect of types of mobility on age categories? If socialization is early or retrospective, the implications follow our previous argument: as workers grow older and family values and beliefs are screened through labor market experience, worklife comparisons become salient and intergenerational comparisons fade into the background (as, indeed, they should in accordance with the success ideology). As our intergenerational skidder moves into his thirties and forties, if he remains in the working class, he adapts to working class culture and by the time we interview him as a downward mobile worker, the effect of mobility has been attenuated.

On the other hand, if the anticipatory socialization and later socialization arguments are valid, our predictions would be wrong: the skidder who wants and expects to move out and up can adopt the appropriate values, beliefs, and life style whatever his age, whatever the type of mobility. No differences would show up (contrary to Hypothesis II). And the worklife skidder who has spent ten or twenty years in the working class, according to this view, should surely learn working class ideology more thoroughly than the youngster fresh from a white collar job—which means that the differences between older worklife skidders and non-skidders (due to common later socialization) should be *less* than the differences between younger skidders and non-skidders (contrary to Hypothesis II 6).

Finally, in addition to making these distinctions between age and types of mobility, we must ask: In what system is the deprivation felt or the aspiration held? We cannot lump together the worker whose ambitions are limited to the next step on the shop ladder, a skilled worker's or foreman's job, and the worker whose gaze is directed toward higher rungs on quite different ladders—independent proprietorship or further training for a semi-professional career (see Hypothesis III).[23]

The specific hypotheses and indicators derived from these considerations are elaborated with the findings below.

Company, Setting, and Methods of Study

Data were derived from questionnaires using mainly fixed-alternative questions filled out anonymously under direction of the investigators by 2,499 non-supervisory

---

[22] Cf. D. Riesman and W. Bloomberg, "Work and Leisure: Fusion or Polarity?" in C. Arensberg et al., editors, *Research in Industrial Human Relations*, New York: Harper, 1957, pp. 75–78.

[23] See Ely Chinoy's sensitive discussion of the differences between workers whose ambitions are factory-bound and those who talk about escape. *Automobile Workers and the American Dream*, New York: Random House, 1955, pp. 47–95.

employees—virtually all of the manual workers in the "Rockwell Company." Our index of mobility is movement from white collar to manual occupations.[24] "Manual" applies to jobs coded as skilled, semi-skilled, unskilled (including service other than protective), and mining; the "white collar" categories are professional and semi-professional, office work, sales work, managers, officials, self-employed business-men or artisans, and protective service.[25] A worker reporting that his father was a white collar man when he was growing up is classified as an intergenerational skid-der. A worker who himself entered the factory from a white collar job is classified as a worklife skidder.[26] All others are non-skidders. On ideology, we used twelve items which seemed to us most unequivo-cally to reveal attitudes toward social class and job opportunities in the workplace.[27]

[24] The case for using this move as the best single index of social mobility is stated else-where. See, e.g., J. A. Kahl, *The American Class Structure*, New York: Rinehart, 1957, p. 46; Hans Speier, "The Worker Turning Bourgeois," in his *Social Order and the Risks of War*, New York: Stewart, 1952, p. 65. Among the well-known limits of this index is the fact that many of the jobs classified as white collar—especially "proprietor," "clerk," and "salesman"—carry only slightly more prestige than the jobs called "manual." For our purposes, this may not be so severe a limit: a status difference seen as real but small often pains more poignantly than a large one. As Lipset and Gordon (*op. cit.,* pp. 703–704) suggest, status panic may be inversely related to the decline in status.

[25] "Protective service" includes eight respond-ents and 22 fathers. Of the alternative as-sumptions about working class perspectives, it seemed that the move from fireman, po-liceman, regular army, etc. to factory worker was downward.

[26] The question: "If you had a job before you came to Rockwell, what kind of work did you spend most time at?"

[27] "Face validity" was the criterion for ac-ceptance or rejection of items. For example,

We label all workers under 30, "young," all those 30 and over, "older."

To permit tests of our hypotheses we eliminated the following categories: (1) Female workers, whose status is not de-rived mainly from employment. (2) Male workers whose fathers were farmers when they were growing up, or who had them-selves worked on farms before entering the factory. While most shifts from farm to factory in the course of early industrializa-tion are moves from low rural to low urban position (non-skidder), the situa-tion is probably more ambiguous for the midwest sample under consideration. (3) Workers who were students or had no occupation prior to entering the Rockwell Company. (4) All workers who failed to specify either their father's occupation or their own prior to employment at Rock-well. The study sample thus consists of male, urban, manual workers who had jobs elsewhere before entering this com-pany—495 in all.

In the fall of 1951 these men were work-ing in two separate plants, one new, one old, containing foundries, machine shops, and assembly units; most jobs were semi-skilled. The setting is a one-industry city of about 15,000 population, surrounded by farmland and located 35 miles from a metropolitan area. The Rockwell Com-pany, an established, family enterprise, manufacturing home appliances, is the largest single employer in the city, employ-ing about 4,000 people. In a tight labor market it competes for labor with the metropolis.

The union local is presently an affiliate of the UAW-AFL-CIO. Rockwell was originally organized by the United Elec-trical Workers in 1938, after a long, bitter strike. In 1951, after the UE was expelled

scious unionism," we rejected "Suppose you went to work in a company where the union was very weak and could not get anything for the workers. Do you think you would join anyway?" A class conscious worker who had experienced weak unionism or worse might well answer "no."

from the CIO for Communist domination, the local joined the UAW. A brief strike was called shortly thereafter—only a few months before data were collected. These events may have served to make ideological responses more readily available and to highlight contrasts between variously situated workers.

Rockwell's manual workers are quite stable. Most of them live in the city in which the plant is located and plan to remain at Rockwell "as long as I can work here." They are predominantly male (80 per cent), married (74 per cent), with at least one dependent (78 per cent). The median age for all manual workers is 35 and for the study sample, 30. (Only one in eight of the sample is older than 50.) A third have at least five years seniority; the comparable figure for the study sample is 39 per cent. Four in ten Rockwell workers grew up on a farm, three in ten in a small town; while those in the study sample are very much more urbanized.

This small city, ex-farm boy milieu should minimize class-conscious responses and hence reduce the differences between the mobile and non-mobile. Moreover, a quasi-company town like this one may afford more cross-class communication than, say Detroit, where more diversified work environments yield less basis for conversation between the classes, and where more homogeneous working class neighborhoods foster greater sharing of intra-class grievances. If recent events favor our general thesis, the social setting of the Rockwell Company works against it.

By our definitions, 19 per cent of the 495 men were intergenerational skidders, and 20 per cent were worklife skidders. There is reason to believe that in this respect our sample typifies national mobility patterns.[28]

[28] In the three national samples available, between one-sixth and one-fourth of the manual workers had non-manual fathers. We eliminated females and farmer sons and fathers, made minor adjustments, and retabu-

Since we predicted the relationships discussed above, we used chi square as a one-tailed test; percentage differences serve as a measure of the strength of relationships. Our argument rests not only upon the size but also upon the consistency of predicted differences within a homogeneous sample exposed to a common working class culture in the same workplace and community.

Findings

The data, presented in detail in Table 1, generally confirm our hypotheses. Of

lated to achieve some comparability with Rockwell. Of 288 manual worker sons in Centers' study (July, 1945, quota sample), 18 per cent reported white collar fathers (large business owners and managers; professional, small business owners and managers, and white collar). This is the only sample that excludes Negroes. Richard Centers, "Occupational Mobility of Urban Occupational Strata," *American Sociological Review*, 13 (April, 1948), p. 198. Of 256 sons in manual or farm labor occupations in the 1952 Survey Research Center election study (area-probability sample) 24 per cent had non-manual fathers. Based on tabulation by Lipset and Zetterberg, *op. cit.*, p. 165. Kahl's adaptation of census-classified NORC data (Spring, 1947, quota sample) eliminates service worker sons and counts the few service worker fathers with the unskilled. The further elimination of farm sons and fathers and "Don't Know's," yields 314 manual worker sons, of whom 24 per cent were skidders. "Jobs and Occupations: A Popular Evaluation," *Opinion News*, 9 (September 1, 1947), p. 12; and Joseph A. Kahl, *The American Class Structure*, New York: Rinehart, 1957, p. 260.

The size of our sample did not permit statistical analysis of categories combining mobility types (men who have experienced *both* intergenerational and worklife mobility). Only about one in four of our intergenerational skidders is also a worklife skidder. Tables comparing these two-time skidders with non-skidders, however, suggest a consistently additive effect on social class items for the two types of mobility within age categories.

48 possible comparisons of skidders and non-skidders called for by Hypotheses I and II (holding age and mobility type constant and counting aspiration for foremanship as middle class aspiration) only five comparisons show percentage differences in the unexpected direction (items 4, 6, 9, and 11 for the young intergenerational category and item 5 for the young worklife category). The net average difference in the predicted direction is 11 per cent.[29] The main findings are the following:

I. *Skidders are more conservative in their values and beliefs regarding the stratification order than non-skidders.* This appears for all attitudes toward social class and mobility. A larger proportion of workers who have moved downward reject identification with the working class (items 1 and 5); believe in an open class system and in ability as the proper basis for promotion (items 4 and 10); aspire to middle class position for themselves, attach importance to promotion opportunity, and say they would accept the job of foreman if offered (items 2, 9, and 12); anticipate leaving the factory soon (item 6); and expect their children to achieve middle class position (item 3). In general, the men who have lost status adhere more firmly to the free mobility ideology than those who have not.

Results which are statistically insignificant or contradictory can be explained with reference to our hypotheses about types of mobility, age differences, and, to some extent, by the distinction between situs and stratum aspirations.

II. *The ideological conservatism of skidders can be explained almost entirely by the presence of, first, older worklife*

[29] Applying hypothesis III, in which we count a desire to be a foreman as situs aspiration, less applicable to class ideology, the number of errors is 12 in 48; the average difference in the predicted direction is eight per cent.

skidders and, second, young intergenerational skidders. The following comparisons demonstrate the point:

1. *Older worklife skidders* (column 7) *versus non-skidders* (column 8). For all five items on social class there are significant differences in the predicted direction —a net average difference of 27 per cent. All seven items on inplant mobility conform in direction to our hypotheses, six of them significantly. The net average difference in predicted direction for all items is 21 per cent.

2. *Older intergenerational skidders* (column 5) *versus non-skidders* (column 6). The weaker impact of intergenerational comparisons for older workers is seen in the fact that the differences here are significant only on class identification and aspiration (items 1 and 2) and the foremanship items (11 and 12). The net average difference in predicted direction for social class items is 11 per cent, for all items nine per cent.[30]

3. *Young intergenerational skidders* (column 1) *versus non-skidders* (column 2). Significant differences appear in four of five social class items (item 4, belief in open class system, shows a seven per cent reversal). Differences are in the predicted direction in four of seven workplace items

[30] Our skidders, whatever their age, tend to have more education (e.g., some college for 22 per cent of intergenerational and 27 per cent of worklife skidders in contrast with eight and six per cent for comparable non-skidders). Therefore we tried to control for education, as an ideological force intervening between early socialization and labor market experience. Although the small N in some age-mobility categories limits the analysis, these tables suggest the following hypotheses: (1) education has very little effect on the relationship between worklife skidding and ideology; (2) a high school education or more strengthens the long-run impact of intergenerational skidding (older intergenerational skidders are more conservative than non-skidders); (3) little education slightly reduced the intergenerational effect for youngsters.

TABLE 1. *Distribution of Responses in Per Cent by Age and Type of Mobility Experience*

| | MOBILITY EXPERIENCE | | | | | | | | Significance Level | | |
| | YOUNG WORKERS, UNDER 30 | | | | OLDER WORKERS, 30 & OVER | | | | | | |
ITEM NUMBER / QUESTION	(1) Intergeneration Skidders N=24	(2) IG Non-Skidders N=193	(3) Worklife Skidders N=52	(4) WL Non-Skidders N=165	(5) IG Skidders N=66	(6) IG Non-Skidders N=212	(7) Worklife Skidders N=45	(8) WL Non-Skidders N=233	Comparison by Cols.	P<	Per Cent Difference in Predicted Direction
Social Class 1 / Class identification "If you were asked to use one of these four names for your social class, which would you say you belonged in?"									(1) vs. (2)	.01	35
Middle or upper class,	54	19	33	19	33	18	49	16	(3) vs. (4)	.05	14
Working class,	46	81	65	81	67	81	49	83	(5) vs. (6)	.01	15
Lower class,	—	—	2	—	—	1	2	1	(7) vs. (8)	.01	33
No answer									(1) vs. (5)	.05	21
									(3) vs. (7)	n. s.	16
2 / Class aspiration "Which social class would you *like* to belong in?"									(1) vs. (2)	.05	19
Middle or upper class,	79	60	63	62	59	44	78	42	(3) vs. (4)	n. s.	1
Working class,	21	35	29	35	39	53	22	55	(5) vs. (6)	.05	15
Lower class,	—	5	8	3	2	2	—	3	(7) vs. (8)	.01	36
No answer									(1) vs. (5)	.05	20
									(3) vs. (7)	n. s.	15
3 / Expectations for children "If you have children, which social class do you think they will belong in when they have families of their own?"									(1) vs. (2)	.05	23
Middle or upper class	71	48	65	46	50	47	71	43	(3) vs. (4)	.01	19
Working class,	16	36	17	39	38	41	18	45	(5) vs. (6)	n. s.	3
Lower class,	13	16	17	15	12	12	11	12	(7) vs. (8)	.01	28
No answer									(1) vs. (5)	.05	21
									(3) vs. (7)	n. s.	6

4 Belief in open class system

"Suppose a person belongs to one class and wants to belong in a different social class. If he has ability and works hard, what do you think his chances are for moving from one social class to another?"

	(1)	(2)	(3)	(4)	(5)	(6)	(7)	(8)			
Good or very good	63	70	69	69	79	67	87	66	(1) vs. (2)	n.s.	−7
Fair or not too good	38	26	25	28	20	27	11	28	(3) vs. (4)	n.s.	0
No answer	—	4	6	3	2	6	2	6	(5) vs. (6)	n.s.	12
									(7) vs. (8)	.01	21
									(1) vs. (5)	.05	−16
									(3) vs. (7)	.05	18

5 Support of class conscious unionism

"Suppose there is a section of the country where very few workers are unionized. A drive is started to try to unionize the companies there. Union workers all over the country are asked to give some money to help support the drive. Some union people think they should give money; others think they shouldn't. How do you think you would feel about this?"

	(1)	(2)	(3)	(4)	(5)	(6)	(7)	(8)			
Think would give	25	42	42	39	49	58	40	59	(1) vs. (2)	.05	17
Don't think would give or unsure	75	55	58	58	52	39	60	39	(3) vs. (4)	n.s.	−3
No answer	—	3	—	3	—	3	—	3	(5) vs. (6)	n.s.	9
									(7) vs. (8)	.01	19
									(1) vs. (5)	.05	24
									(3) vs. (7)	n.s.	2

TABLE 1. Distribution of Responses in Per Cent by Age and Type of Mobility Experience—Continued

	MOBILITY EXPERIENCE									Significance	
	YOUNG WORKERS, UNDER 30				OLDER WORKERS, 30 & OVER						Level	Per Cent Difference in Predicted Direction
	(1) Intergeneration Skidders N = 24	(2) IG Non-Skidders N = 193	(3) Worklife Skidders N = 52	(4) WL Non-Skidders N = 165	(5) IG Skidders N = 66	(6) IG Non-Skidders N = 212	(7) Worklife Skidders N = 45	(8) WL Non-Skidders N = 233	Comparison by Cols.	P <	
ITEM NUMBER / QUESTION											
Workplace											
6									(1) vs. (2)	n.s.	−10
Commitment to factory									(3) vs. (4)	n.s.	11
"About how long do you expect to be working at Rockwell?"									(5) vs. (6)	n.s.	0
As long as can	63	53	46	57	77	77	67	79	(7) vs. (8)	.05	12
A lesser time	38	44	50	41	18	20	29	18	(1) vs. (5)	.05	14
No answer	—	3	4	2	5	3	4	3	(3) vs. (7)	.05	−21
7									(1) vs. (2)	n.s.	5
Interest in other job in plant									(3) vs. (4)	n.s.	1
"Is there any other job in the plant you would rather have than the one you now have?"									(5) vs. (6)	n.s.	2
									(7) vs. (8)	.05	14
Yes	25	30	29	30	46	48	36	50	(1) vs. (5)	.05	21
No	75	69	71	69	54	43	62	43	(3) vs. (7)	n.s.	−7
No answer	—	1	—	1	—	9	2	8			
8									(1) vs. (2)	n.s.	12
Interest in higher wages									(3) vs. (4)	n.s.	6
"How important is it to you to be able to make higher wages on a job?"									(5) vs. (6)	n.s.	3
Very important	21	33	27	33	18	21	9	23	(7) vs. (8)	.05	14
Not too important	79	67	73	67	82	77	91	76	(1) vs. (5)	n.s.	−3
No answer	—	—	—	—	—	1	—	1	(3) vs. (7)	.05	18
9									(1) vs. (2)	n.s.	−14
Interest in promotion									(3) vs. (4)	n.s.	9
"Different people want different things out of their jobs. What are the things you yourself feel									(5) vs. (6)	n.s.	5
									(7) vs. (8)	.01	32

	(1)	(2)	(3)	(4)	(5)	(6)	(7)	(8)	Comparison	Sig.	Diff.
are *most important* in a job?"											
Promotion important	50	64	69	60	39	34	62	30	(1) vs. (5)	n.s.	11
Promotion not important (ranks 6–10)	50	35	29	39	52	59	36	61	(3) vs. (7)	n.s.	−7
No answer	—	1	2	1	9	8	2	9			
10 **Ability as criterion for promotion** "How much do you think seniority and ability *should* count in promotion to a higher job grade or transfer to a better job?"											
Seniority as important or more important than ability	67	68	64	69	70	72	58	74	(1) vs. (2)	n.s.	2
									(3) vs. (4)	n.s.	7
									(5) vs. (6)	n.s.	4
									(7) vs. (8)	.01	18
Ability more important than seniority	33	31	37	30	30	26	42	24	(1) vs. (5)	n.s.	3
									(3) vs. (7)	n.s.	5
No answer	—	1	—	1	—	2	—	2			
11 ***Importance of chance to become foreman** "How important is it to you to have a good chance of becoming a foreman?"											
Important	25	35	39	33	44	26	40	30	(1) vs. (2)	n.s.	−10
									(3) vs. (4)	n.s.	6
									(5) vs. (6)	.01	18
									(7) vs. (8)	n.s.	10
Not important	75	64	61	66	56	67	58	65	(1) vs. (5)	.05	−19
									(3) vs. (7)	n.s.	1
No answer	—	1	—	1	—	8	2	5			
12 ***Would accept foreman's job** "If you were offered the job of foreman, would you take it?"											
Yes	50	44	56	41	53	36	60	36	(1) vs. (2)	n.s.	6
									(3) vs. (4)	.05	15
									(5) vs. (6)	.01	17
									(7) vs. (8)	.01	24
No	42	51	38	54	42	57	38	57	(1) vs. (5)	n.s.	−3
									(3) vs. (7)	n.s.	4
No answer	8	5	6	6	5	7	2	7			

* Counted as indicators of situs aspiration, Hypothesis III. Because of the ambiguity of the foreman's position, results are reported in the text both ways. In the table items 11 and 12 are counted as class aspiration (Hypotheses I and II).

(7, 8, 10, 11), none of them significant. The net average difference in predicted direction for social class items is 17 per cent, for all items seven per cent.

4. *Young worklife skidders* (column 3) *versus non-skidders* (column 4). Significant differences emerge on only two of five social class items (1 and 3), and one of seven workplace items (12, accept foremanship). Relationships tend to be weak. The net average difference for social class items is seven per cent, the same as for all items. The impact of worklife skidding thus seems much greater for older men while intergenerational skidding is a bit more important for the young. This is not a product of our definition of "older," since drawing the line at 40 instead of 30 yields the same results.

Item 1 provides a striking example of how even these rough controls for type of mobility and age sharpen the contrasts between mobile and non-mobile workers. Centers found for a national sample that 34 per cent of intergenerational downward mobile workers identified with the middle or upper class as compared with 19 per cent of the non-skidders,[31] figures nearly identical with our distribution for young worklife and older intergenerational categories. But in our sample the differences double when the crucial skidder-non-skidder comparisons are made— young intergenerational (54 *versus* 19 per cent) and older worklife (49 *versus* 16 per cent).

5. *Young intergenerational* (column 1) *versus older intergenerational skidders* (column 5). If the early and retrospective socialization arguments are correct, this analysis should show decreasing ideological conservatism with age as the coercive effect of comparisons with father wears off and adaptation to working class culture begins. Significant differences in this direction appear for four of five class items (all but item 4) and for two of seven work-

[31] *Op. cit.*, p. 180.

place items (6, 7). There is almost no difference for items 8, 10 and 12. But two significant reversals appear: 19 per cent more of the older skidders stressed the importance of a chance for foremanship and 16 per cent more of them believe in an open class system. The net average difference in predicted direction for social class items is 14 per cent, for all items eight per cent.

6. *Older worklife skidders* (column 7) *versus young worklife skidders* (column 3). The explanation in terms of denial of failure predicts more ideological conservatism in the older category; on this score all five class items come out in the right direction, one significantly. The workplace items show an inconsistent picture. The net average difference in predicted direction for social class is 12 per cent, and for all items four per cent. In contrast, the later socialization hypothesis holds that the worklife skidder will in time become acculturated to the working class and will be less conservative than the young man who just took off the white collar; but all of the relevant comparisons tend to contradict this view. Older worklife skidders are clearly more "middle class" in what they believe, want, and expect than comparable non-skidders, and on the most directly relevant measures (1, 2, 3, 4, 10) they adhere more to the free mobility ideology than do the young worklife skidders. Finally, for all 12 items the size of predicted differences between older worklife skidders and non-skidders is greater than the size of differences which appear between young worklife skidders and non-skidders.

III. *Skidders, because of their adherence to the success ideology, are more interested in escape from the factory than movement within it; modest aspirations and expectations for in-plant mobility and bolder aspirations and expectations for out-plant mobility tend to be mutually exclusive. Using the concept of "situs"—*

a group of occupations whose status system may be considered a unit [32]—we hypothesized that workers who show little interest in inter-class mobility may still aspire to better themselves within the status system of the factory, and that workers who adopt the mobility stance of the middle class (for example, our skidders) are not likely to be interested in intra-situs movement. The two types of movement, we reasoned, call for incompatible kinds of behavior. Class mobility requires more detachment from the moral order of the plant and the working class sub-culture; situs mobility requires, or at least is compatible with, commitment to both (even the foreman must in some degree adhere to working class values and beliefs, as well as those work-place norms which cut across status levels). Accordingly, for the workplace items available, we predicted that our skidders would show more interest in getting out of the factory but less interest in current wages or some other job in the plant; more interest in promotions generally and ability as the criterion, but less interest in foremanship. Table 1 shows this reasoning to be correct for everything but the foreman's job. It accents further the salience of older work-life skidders as a source of ideological conservatism among workers.

Older worklife skidders were significantly less committed to Rockwell, less interested in workplace mobility (as indicated by the importance attached to high wages and the desire for another job in the plant). At the same time they rated "good chance for promotion" high in their evaluation of a job more often and displayed more opposition to seniority as a promotion criterion. Contrary to our predictions, however, the skidders showed

more desire for and willingness to accept a foreman's job. The foremanship issue also provides the only significant reversal for our point that intergenerational mobility should count for *less* than worklife mobility for older workers (see item 11) and *more* for young workers (see item 12).[33] The celebrated ambiguity of the foreman's position in the status system and the ambivalence of workers toward this "master and victim of double talk" may account for the ambiguity of our results whenever the foreman was mentioned.

A more direct test of Hypothesis III—relating situs aspiration (items 6, 7, 8, 11, 12) to class identification and aspiration (items 1 and 2)—shows that while the two are not mutually exclusive, there is no relation between them. Low and high class aspiration are equally compatible with strong situs aspiration. But cross-class identifiers (those who say they are working class but want to be middle class) tend to reject situs aspiration.

At best the data give Hypothesis III as stated only weak support. Better measures of types of aspiration would be desirable.

In summary, then, analysis of 495 Rockwell workers with urban background and previous occupational history shows that skidding has a conservative impact on values and beliefs regarding the stratification order. More precisely, those experiences which precede and accompany downward occupational mobility play a

[32] P. K. Hatt suggests the following situses: manual work, business, political, professional, recreation and aesthetics, service, agriculture, military. "Occupation and Social Stratification," *American Journal of Sociology*, 55 (May, 1950), p. 539.

[33] Answers to the question, "Would you take the job of foreman," consistently contradict our expectations: older skidders, especially worklife skidders, are more willing to accept foremanship than non-skidders, as are young worklife skidders. There is some indication that many of the disinterested young intergenerational skidders (75 per cent say the chance to become a foreman is not important) will end up as enthusiastic management men (only 42 per cent say they would not accept the job). See also footnote 35 below.

part in making the skidder more conservative than workers in his class of destination. (We lack comparisons with norms of class of origin—baseline data from which to measure changes in ideology.) The relationship between mobility and ideology was affected in the expected direction by age, type of mobility (intergenerational *versus* worklife), and to a lesser extent by type of mobility aspirations (situs *versus* stratum). The strongest and most consistent relationships prevail among older worklife skidders, whether the age split is made at 30 or 40.

The anomalous conservatism of the status-deprived can be understood with reference to early or retrospective socialization leading to denial of failure and individual striving. Like a man falling from a skyscraper, our skidder reaches not in the direction of his fall, but back up the structure. The values and beliefs of the middle class family or the white collar workgroup retain their force despite later status loss.

These explanations are borne out more than the later socialization hypothesis, which, contrary to our results, implies that older worklife skidders should be less conservative than young ones. There may be a general tendency, evident in these and other data, for most workers to give up hope of getting ahead as they approach the age of 40 and become embedded in the working class, but older skidders in Rockwell plainly resist this tendency.

Finally, our data provide no support for the anticipatory socialization argument. This is given further emphasis in a study of upward-moving workers—an ingenious natural experiment in the same company—in which Lieberman found that workers who become foremen or stewards do not adopt attitudes that "fit" the position until *after* the move.[34]

[34] Twenty-three Rockwell workers who became company foremen and 35 who were elected union stewards between the adminis-

Some Implications

Why so little anticipatory socialization —either for our mobility-oriented skidders or for Leiberman's mobility-oriented future foremen and stewards? An explanation is suggested by the following features of the organizational context: (1) industrial conflict is not severe enough and positions most readily available to mobile men—foreman, steward, or similar jobs out of the plant—are not authoritative enough to demand recruitment on the basis of "loyalty" criteria; (2) positions so strongly instituted, with relatively clear (if inconsistent) behavior directives, do not require prior attitudes that "fit" the positions; (3) anticipatory socialization is functional only where mobility channels

tration of questionnaires in the fall of 1951 and December, 1952, plus matched control groups were re-studied in December. Comparisons of the initial characteristics of workers who later moved up with the rest of Rockwell's workers measured anticipatory socialization; before-and-after comparisons of those who changed roles with control groups measured socialization in role. Lieberman found that workers who moved to foremanship were *not* initially pro-management (indicated by attitudes toward Rockwell, the union, the incentive and seniority systems); workers who became stewards were *not* initially pro-union. If anything, they were both somewhat anti-management and anti-union —that is, until they got their new jobs, whereupon the unseemly sentiments were quickly cast off. This study also found that foremen and stewards both tend to come from those elements of the rank and file who are more capable (educated, skilled, have read the contract), stable (integrated in community), dissident (active griper), younger (nine in ten were 20 to 40 years old), and mobility-oriented. Many of our skidders would fit. Seymour Lieberman, "The Relationship Between Attitudes and Roles," unpublished Ph.D. Dissertation, University of Michigan, 1954.

are wide open, while promotion possibilities at Rockwell are quite limited.[35]

Why so little acculturation? The findings on the conservatism of skidders must also be put in a larger social context. We deal here with the impact of regular patterns of urban occupational mobility at a time of sustained prosperity in a country at a high level of economic development. Structural and cultural conditions which might dispose our skidders to more radical political adjustments—for example, rejection of the stratification order—include: (1) the insecurities of early industrialization, with its painful transformations from peasant to proletarian, rural to urban, alien to citizen; [36] (2) economic slump in an advanced society accompanied by a widespread sense of declining opportunity; [37] (3) a structure of opportunity similar to that confronting Rockwell workers but cultural values which put less emphasis on an open class system and the urgency of success; (4) a society in which the working class has not moved up, relatively, in income, style of life, and sources of prestige other than occupation (a radical response would then be more available to the skidder).

Rockwell data remind us of promising leads for stratification research:

1. *The need to take account of types of mobility and aspirations in studies of the social and psychological consequences of mobility.* Few such studies have used work history as a variable; our analysis shows worklife mobility to be much more in-

---

[35] Cf. R. K. Merton and A. S. Kitt, "Contributions to the Theory of Reference Group Behavior," in R. K. Merton and P. F. Lazarsfeld, editors, *Studies in the Scope and Method of "The American Soldier,"* Glencoe, Ill.: Free Press, 1950, pp. 86 ff.

[36] W. E. Moore, *Industrialization and Labor,* Ithaca: Cornell University Press, 1951. Cf. H. L. Wilensky and C. N. Lebeaux, *Industrial Society and Social Welfare,* New York: Russell Sage Foundation, 1958, Chs. 3–5.

[37] We have been unable to locate directly relevant data. However, several students at the University of Michigan have been engaged in field explorations of the impact of unemployment. Among especially deprived segments of the population anti-system responses are common. For instance, J. C. Leggett, D. P. Street, and R. O. Richards have analyzed 121 interviews with three groups of Negroes who were hard hit by the recession of 1957–58. Fifty displaced Negroes in a study directed by H. L. Sheppard and L. A. Ferman of an auto plant shutdown were asked, "If a bad depression were to happen again what do you think would happen?" The modal responses were: (1) *Collective violence*—predicts revolution, rioting, etc., *28 per cent* (". . . we would have a revolution and knock out a few of these capitalists who dog it and hog it"; "I don't see much hope for the country. These youngsters aren't going to take what we took in the last depression. They will tear up the country"; etc.). (2) *Individual acts of violence*—assault, killing, etc., *18 per cent* ("We won't have no country. There'll be fighting, stealing, starving. No one will have no chance. Not even the rich man," etc.). These were high seniority semi-skilled workers who had achieved a foothold in Detroit industry and partial home ownership. Almost identical distribution of response—about half projecting violence—was found in two other Negro samples, one in a close-knit Negro neighborhood with radical leadership and younger population, half of which was unemployed (N = 32), the other in a neighborhood chosen for comparable deprivation but the absence of political organization (N = 39). Most of these 121 Negroes had experienced considerable recent unemployment or the threat of it by virtue of low seniority position; the data suggest that the most deprived are most prone to "violent" verbal responses. That depression makes a radical perspective more available to skidders and non-skidders alike is, of course, illustrated by some of the sociology of the 'thirties. See, e.g., A. W. Jones, *Life, Liberty and Property,* New York: Lippincott, 1941. Since all industrial societies are subject to economic instability, bringing with it variations in the incidence of status deprivation, it would seem wise to relate variations in the rates and effects of skidding to the business cycle.

fluential than intergenerational mobility in shaping the adult perspectives of all but very young workers and older educated workers. Still fewer studies have distinguished the status system of workplace from that of community and society. Our data here are equivocal. In fact, they contain a suggestion contrary to Hypothesis III but one consistent with two hypotheses in the literature of psychology and sociology: aspiration levels in different contexts are interdependent,[38] and status achievement in one system exerts a strain toward achievement in other systems.[39] Those who aim to move up aim at all rank systems possible; the worker who wishes to leave the factory for some other occupational ladder or who has in the past achieved a white collar position also wants to be foreman if that will yield a similar result by other criteria of status (income, style of life).

2. *The gains and costs of mobility and the need to consider descent as well as ascent.* Even where data have been collected on mobility patterns, the stratification literature attends more to the consequences of upward than downward mobility—a reflection, perhaps, of the relatively low rate of skidding in American society during the boom period when the research was under way.[40] Moreover, the

more systematic studies following Durkheim's lead have emphasized the consequences of rapid ascent for the *person*—disruption of primary relations is the main theme.[41] The impact of mobility upon larger *social structures* has received less systematic attention, although many writers have speculated imaginatively about possible social consequences of mobility. Rockwell data are indirectly relevant to one such speculation. Does a high rate of rapid social mobility produce a social category which powerfully reinforces the cult of optimism and gratitude, thereby deadening social criticism? [42] Or does it, on the contrary, develop a cadre of creative men of independent mind, released from traditional norms, ready to provide some needed novelty and flexibility? [43] The more skilled segments of the mobile population—the professional, scientist, artist—are under scrutiny here; but it is possible that those who have not made out so well nevertheless love the system. Indeed, our data picture the skidder as optimistic-grateful rather than creative-independent. In so far as lively debate about the social order is vital for the maintenance of a democratic society, this represents a loss. On the other hand, it seems likely that the presence of our skidders

---

[38] Kurt Lewin *et al.*, "Levels of Aspiration," in J. McV. Hunt, *Personality and the Behavoir Disorders*, New York: Ronald, 1944, Vol. I, pp. 333—378. G. H. Fenchel, J. H. Monderer, and E. L. Hartley, "Subjective States and the Equilibration Hypothesis," *Journal of Abnormal and Social Psychology,* 46 (October, 1951), pp. 476–479.

[39] The status consistency hypothesis is stated in a different context by G. C. Homans in "Status Among Clerical Workers," *Human Organization,* 12 (Spring, 1953), pp. 5–10. Cf. G. Lenski, "Status Crystallization: A Non-Vertical Dimension of Social Status," *American Sociological Review,* 19 (August, 1954), pp. 405–413.

[40] The "sociological" novels and TV shows about mobility are almost exclusively preoccupied with the psychological strains of

successful businessmen and professionals. Apparently even the "humanists" who make a business of expropriating then attacking social science for its ideological or methodological conservatism have seen richer material in the point of no return than in the death of a salesman.

[41] See two careful reviews of this literature: P. M. Blau, *op. cit.;* M. Janowitz, "Some Consequences of Social Mobility in the United States," *Transactions of the Third World Congress of Sociology,* III, London: International Sociological Association, 1956, pp. 191–201.

[42] M. M. Tumin, "Some Unapplauded Consequences of Social Mobility in a Mass Society," *Social Forces,* 36 (October, 1957), p. 35.

[43] Janowitz, *op. cit.,* p. 195. See also the several discussions of the "marginal man."

in the working class, with their adherence to the free mobility ideology, constrains tendencies toward political extremism among two-generation workers, who, sharing the same grievances and perspectives, if unexposed to deviant views of skidders would be more susceptible to totalitarian solutions.

In short, our skidders, along with other workers who escape from working class culture psychologically or actually, function to reduce working class solidarity and social criticism from below—and thereby slow down the push toward equality. But if the declassé were not optimistic-grateful, they might combine with normally apa-thetic workers to form the vanguard of extremist political movements. What American society loses in equality, it may gain in the maintenance of freedom.

Whatever its consequences, and whether we applaud or condemn them, we surely cannot ignore the fact of downward mobility. The Organization Man on the make, who has gained the center of the stage, represents a tiny fraction of the population. The skidder, as we have defined him, represents perhaps a fifth of the working class of urban background, almost a tenth of all urbanites in the labor force—in time of recession, more.

2 · The Effects of Social and Cultural Change on Personality

THE CHANGING AMERICAN CHILD—A SPECULATIVE ANALYSIS [1]

by Urie Bronfenbrenner

A Question of Moment

It is now a matter of scientific record that patterns of child rearing in the United States have changed appreciably over the past twenty-five years (Bronfenbrenner, 1958). Middle class parents especially have moved away from the more rigid and strict styles of care and disci-

[1] This paper draws heavily on results from a program of research being conducted by the author in collaboration with Edward C. Devereux and George J. Suci. The contribution of these colleagues to facts and ideas presented in this paper is gratefully acknowledged. The research program is supported in part with grants from the National Science Foundation and the National Institutes of Health.

SOURCE: *Journal of Social Issues,* Vol. 17, No. 1 (1961), pp. 6–18.

pline advocated in the early Twenties and Thirties toward modes of response involving greater tolerance of the child's impulses and desires, freer expression of affection, and increased reliance on "psychological" methods of discipline, such as reasoning and appeals to guilt, as distinguished from more direct techniques like physical punishment. At the same time, the gap between the social classes in their goals and methods of child rearing appears to be narrowing, with working class parents beginning to adopt both the values and techniques of the middle class. Finally, there is dramatic correspondence between these observed shifts in parental values and behavior and the changing character of the attitudes and practices advocated in successive editions of such widely read manuals as the Children's Bureau bulletin on *Infant Care* and Spock's *Baby and Child Care.* Such correspondence should not be taken to mean that the expert has now become the principal instigator and instrument of social change, since the ideas of scientists and professional workers themselves reflect in part the operation of deep-rooted cultural processes. Nevertheless, the fact remains that changes in values and practices advocated by prestigeful professional figures can be substantially accelerated by rapid and widespread dissemination through the press, mass media of communication, and public discussion.

Given these facts, it becomes especially important to gauge the effect of the changes that are advocated and adopted. Nowhere is this issue more significant, both scientifically and socially, than in the sphere of familial values and behavior. It is certainly no trivial matter to ask whether the changes that have occurred in the attitudes and actions of parents over the past twenty-five years have been such as to affect the personality development of their children, so that the boys and girls of today are somewhat different in character structure from those of a decade or more ago. Or, to put the question more succinctly: has the changing American parent produced a changing American child?

A Strategy of Inference

Do we have any basis for answering this intriguing question? To begin with, do we have any evidence of changes in the behavior of children in successive decades analogous to those we have already been able to find for parents? If so, we could take an important first step toward a solution of the problem. Unfortunately, in contrast to his gratifying experience in seeking and finding appropriate data on parents, the present writer has, to date, been unable to locate enough instances in which comparable methods of behavioral assessment have been employed with different groups of children of similar ages

over an extended period of time. Although the absence of such material precludes any direct and unequivocal approach to the question at hand, it is nevertheless possible, through a series of inferences from facts already known, to arrive at some estimate of what the answer might be. Specifically, although as yet we have no comparable data on the relation between parental and child behavior for different families at successive points in time, we do have facts on the influence of parental treatment on child behavior at a given point in time; that is, we know that certain variations in parental behavior tend to be accompanied by systematic differences in the personality characteristics of children. If we are willing to assume that these same relationships obtained not only at a given moment but across different points in time, we are in a position to infer the possible effects on children of changing patterns of child rearing over the years. It is this strategy that we propose to follow.

The Changing American Parent

We have already noted the major changes in parental behavior discerned in a recent analysis of data reported over a twenty-five year period. These secular trends may be summarized as follows:

1. Greater permissiveness toward the child's spontaneous desires
2. Freer expression of affection
3. Increased reliance on indirect "psychological" techniques of discipline (such as reasoning or appeals to guilt) *versus* direct methods (like physical punishment, scolding, or threats)
4. In consequence of the above shifts in the direction of what are predominantly middle class values and techniques, a narrowing of the gap between social classes in their patterns of child rearing.

Since the above analysis was published, a new study has documented an additional trend. Bronson, Katten, and Livson (1959) have compared patterns of paternal and maternal authority and affection in two generations of families from the California Guidance Study. Unfortunately, the time span surveyed overlaps only partially with the twenty-five year period covered in our own analysis, the first California generation having been raised in the early 1900's and the second in the late '20's and early '30's. Accordingly, if we are to consider the California results along with the others cited above, we must make the somewhat risky assumption that a trend discerned in the first three decades of the century has continued in the same direction through the early 1950's. With this important qualification, an examination of the data cited by Bronson et al. (1959) points to still another, secular trend—a shift over the years in the pattern of parental role differentiation within the family. Specifically:

5. In succeeding generations the relative position of the father vis-à-vis the mother is shifting with the former becoming increasingly more affectionate and less authoritarian, and the latter becoming relatively more important as the agent of discipline, especially for boys.

"Psychological" Techniques of Discipline and Their Effects

In pursuing our analytic strategy, we next seek evidence of the effects on the behavior of children of variations in parental treatment of the type noted in our inventory. We may begin by noting that the variables involved in the first three secular trends constitute a complex that has received considerable attention in recent research in parent-child relationships. Within the last three years, two sets of investigators, working independently, have called attention to the greater efficacy of "love-oriented" or "psychological" techniques in bringing about desired

behavior in the child (Sears, Maccoby, and Levin, 1957; Miller and Swanson, 1958; 1960). The present writer, noting that such methods are especially favored by middle class parents, offered the following analysis of the nature of these techniques and the reasons for their effectiveness.

Such parents are, in the first place, more likely to overlook offenses, and when they do punish, they are less likely to ridicule or inflict physical pain. Instead, they reason with the youngster, isolate him, appeal to guilt, show disappointment—in short, convey in a variety of ways, on the one hand, the kind of behavior that is expected of the child; on the other, the realization that transgression means the interruption of a mutually valued relationship. . . .

These findings [of greater efficacy] mean that middle class parents, though in one sense more lenient in their discipline techniques, are using methods that are actually more compelling. Moreover, the compelling power of these practices is probably enhanced by the more permissive treatment accorded to middle class children in the early years of life. The successful use of withdrawal of love as a discipline technique implies the prior existence of a gratifying relationship; the more love present in the first instance, the greater the threat implied in its withdrawal (Bronfenbrenner, 1958).

It is now a well established fact that children from middle class families tend to excel those from lower class in many characteristics ordinarily regarded as desirable, such as self-control, achievement, responsibility, leadership, popularity, and adjustment in general.[2] If, as seems plausible, such differences in behavior are attributable at least in part to class-linked variations in parental treatment, the strat-

[2] For a summary of findings on social class differences in children's behavior and personality characteristics, see P. H. Mussen, and J. J. Conger, *Child Development and Personality*. New York: Harper, 1956.

egy of inference we have adopted would appear on first blush to lead to a rather optimistic conclusion. Since, over the years, increasing numbers of parents have been adopting the more effective socialization techniques typically employed by the middle class, does it not follow that successive generations of children should show gains in the development of effective behavior and desirable personality characteristics?

Unfortunately, this welcome conclusion, however logical, is premature, for it fails to take into account all of the available facts.

Sex, Socialization, and Social Class

To begin with, the parental behaviors we have been discussing are differentially distributed not only by socio-economic status but also by sex. As we have pointed out elsewhere (Bronfenbrenner, 1961), girls are exposed to more affection and less punishment than boys, but at the same time are more likely to be subjected to "love-oriented" discipline of the type which encourages the development of internalized controls. And, consistent with our line of reasoning, girls are found repeatedly to be "more obedient, cooperative, and in general better socialized than boys at comparable age levels." But this is not the whole story.

> . . . At the same time, the research results indicate that girls tend to be more anxious, timid, dependent, and sensitive to rejection. If these differences are a function of differential treatment by parents, then it would seem that the more "efficient" methods of child rearing employed with girls involve some risk of what might be called "oversocialization" (Bronfenbrenner, 1961).

One could argue, of course, that the contrasting behaviors of boys and girls have less to do with differential parental treatment than with genetically-based maturational influences. Nevertheless, two independent lines of evidence suggest that socialization techniques do contribute to individual differences, *within the same sex*, precisely in the types of personality characteristics noted above. In the first place, variations in child behavior and parental treatment strikingly similar to those we have cited for the two sexes are reported in a recent comprehensive study of differences between first and later born children (Schachter, 1959). Like girls, first children receive more attention, are more likely to be exposed to "psychological" discipline, and end up more anxious and dependent, whereas later children, like boys, are more aggressive and self-confident.

A second line of evidence comes from our own current research. We have been concerned with the role of parents in the development of such "constructive" personality characteristics as responsibility and leadership among adolescent boys and girls. Our findings reveal not only the usual differences in adolescents' and parents' behaviors associated with the sex of the child, but also a striking contrast in the relationship between parental and child behaviors for the two sexes. To start on firm and familiar ground, girls are rated by their teachers as more responsible than boys, whereas the latter obtain higher scores on leadership. Expected differences similarly appear in the realm of parental behavior: girls receive more affection, praise, and companionship; boys are subjected to more physical punishment and achievement demands. Quite unanticipated, however, at least by us, was the finding that both parental affection and discipline appeared to facilitate effective psychological functioning in boys, but to impede the development of such constructive behavior in girls. Closer examination of our data indicated that both extremes of either affection or discipline were deleterious for all children, but that the process of socialization entailed somewhat different risks for the two sexes. Girls were especially susceptible to the detrimental influence of overprotection; boys to the ill effects of insufficient parental discipline and support. Or, to put it in more colloquial terms: boys suffered more often from too little taming, girls from too much.

In an attempt to account for this contrasting pattern of relationships, we proposed the notion of differential optimal levels of affection and authority for the two sexes.

The qualities of independence, initiative, and self-sufficiency, which are especially valued for boys in our culture, apparently require for their development a somewhat different balance of authority and affection than is found in the "love-oriented" strategy characteristically applied with girls. While an affectional context is important for the socialization of boys, it must evidently be accompanied by and be compatible with a strong component of parental discipline. Otherwise, the boy finds himself in the same situation as the girl, who, having received greater affection, is more sensitive to its withdrawal, with the result that a little discipline goes a long way and strong authority is constricting rather than constructive (Bronfenbrenner, 1960).

What is more, available data suggest that this very process may already be operating for boys from upper middle class homes. To begin with, differential treatment of the sexes is at a minimum for these families. Contrasting parental attitudes and behaviors toward boys and girls are pronounced only at lower class levels, and decrease as one moves up the socio-economic scale (Kohn, 1959; Bronfenbrenner, 1960). Thus our own results show that it is primarily at lower middle class levels that boys get more punishment than girls, and the latter receive greater warmth and attention. With an increase in the family's social position, direct discipline drops off, especially for boys, and indulgence and protectiveness decrease for girls. As a result, patterns of parental treatment for the two sexes begin to converge. In like manner, we find that the differential effects of parental behavior on the two sexes are marked only in the lower middle class. It is here that girls especially risk being over-protected and boys not receiving sufficient discipline and support. In upper middle class the picture changes. Girls are not as readily debilitated by parental affection and power; nor is parental discipline as effective in fostering the development of responsibility and leadership in boys.

All these trends point to the conclusion that the "risks" experienced by each sex during the process of socialization tend to be somewhat different at different social class levels. Thus the danger of over-protection for girls is especially great in lower class families, but lower in upper middle class because of the decreased likelihood of overprotection. Analogously, boys are in greater danger of suffering from inadequate discipline and support in lower middle than in upper middle class. But the upper middle class boy, unlike the girl, exchanges one hazard for another. Since at this upper level the more potent "psychological" techniques of discipline are likely to be employed with both sexes, the boy presumably now too runs the risk of being "oversocialized," of losing some of his capacity for independent aggressive accomplishment.

Accordingly, if our line of reasoning is correct, we should expect a changing pattern of sex differences at successive socio-economic levels. Specifically, aspects of effective psychological functioning favoring girls should be most pronounced in the upper middle class; those favoring boys in the lower middle. A recent analysis of some of our data bears out this expectation. Girls excel boys on such variables as *responsibility* and *social acceptance* primarily at the higher socio-economic levels. In contrast, boys surpass girls on such traits as *leadership, level of aspiration,* and *competitiveness* almost exclusively in lower middle class. Indeed, with a rise in a family's social position, the differences tend to reverse themselves with girls now excelling boys.[3]

Trends in Personality Development: A First Approximation

The implications for our original line of inquiry are clear. We are suggesting that the "love-oriented" socialization techniques, which over the past twenty-five years have been employed in increasing degree by American middle class families, may have negative as well as constructive aspects. While fostering the internalization of adult standards and the development of socialized behavior, they may also have the effect of undermining capacities for initiative and independence, particularly in boys. Males exposed to this "modern" pattern of child rearing might be expected to differ from their counterparts of a quarter century ago in being somewhat more conforming and anxious, less enterprising and self-sufficient, and, in general, possessing more of the virtues and liabilities commonly associated with feminine character structure.[4]

At long last, then, our strategy of inference has led us to a first major conclusion. The term "major" is appropriate since the conclusion takes as its points of departure and return four of the secular trends which served as the impetus for our inquiry. Specifically, through a series of empirical links and theoretical extrap-

[3] These shifts in sex difference with a rise in class status are significant at the 5% level of confidence (one-tailed test).

[4] Strikingly similar conclusions were reached almost fifteen years ago in a provocative essay by Arnold Green ("The Middle Class Male Child and Neurosis," *American Sociological Review*, 1946, 11, 31–41). With little to go on beyond scattered clinical observations and impressions, Green was able to detect many of the same trends which we have begun to discern in more recent systematic empirical data.

olations, we have arrived at an estimate of the effects on children of the tendency of successive generations of parents to become progressively more permissive, to express affection more freely, to utilize "psychological" techniques of discipline, and, by moving in these directions to narrow the gap between the social classes in their patterns of child rearing.

Family Structure and Personality Development

But one other secular trend remains to be considered: what of the changing pattern of parental role differentiation during the first three decades of the century? If our extrapolation is correct, the balance of power within the family has continued to shift with fathers yielding parental authority to mothers and taking on some of the nurturant and affectional functions traditionally associated with the maternal role. Again we have no direct evidence of the effects of such secular changes on successive generations of children, and must look for leads to analogous data on contemporaneous relationships.

We may begin by considering the contribution of each parent to the socialization processes we have examined thus far. Our data indicate that it is primarily mothers who tend to employ "love-oriented" techniques of discipline and fathers who rely on more direct methods like physical punishment. The above statement must be qualified, however, by reference to the sex of the child, for it is only in relation to boys that fathers use direct punishment more than mothers. More generally, . . . the results reveal a tendency for each parent to be somewhat more active, firm, and demanding with a child of the same sex, more lenient and indulgent with a child of the opposite sex. . . . The reversal is most complete with respect to discipline, with fathers being stricter with boys, mothers with girls. In the spheres of affection and protectiveness, there is no actual shift in preference, but the tendency to be especially warm and solicitous with girls is much more pronounced among fathers than among mothers. In fact, generally speaking, it is the father who is more likely to treat children of the two sexes differently (Bronfenbrenner, 1960).

Consistent with this pattern of results, it is primarily the behavior of fathers that accounts for the differential effects of parental behavior on the two sexes and for the individual differences within each sex. In other words, it is paternal authority and affection that tend especially to be salutary for sons but detrimental for daughters. But as might be anticipated from what we already know, these trends are pronounced only in the lower middle class; with a rise in the family's social status, both parents tend to have similar effects on their children, both within and across sexes. Such a trend is entirely to be expected since parental role differentiation tends to decrease markedly as one ascends the socio-economic ladder. It is almost exclusively in lower middle class homes that fathers are more strict with boys and mothers with girls. To the extent that direct discipline is employed in upper middle class families, it tends to be exercised by both parents equally. Here again we see a parellelism between shifts in parental behavior across time and social class in the direction of forms (in this instance of family structure) favored by the upper middle class group.

What kinds of children, then, can we expect to develop in families in which the father plays a predominantly affectionate role, and a relatively low level of discipline is exercised equally by both parents? A tentative answer to this question is supplied by a preliminary analysis of our data in which the relation between parental role structure and adolescent behavior was examined with controls for the family's social class position. The results of this analysis are summarized as follows: . . . Both responsibility and leadership

are fostered by the relatively greater salience of the parent of the same sex. . . . Boys tend to be more responsible when the father rather than the mother is the principal disciplinarian; girls are more dependable when the mother is the major authority figure. . . . In short, boys thrive in a patriarchal context, girls in a matriarchal. . . . The most dependent and least dependable adolescents describe family arrangements that are neither patriarchal nor matriarchal but equalitarian. To state the issue in more provocative form, our data suggest that the democratic family, which for so many years has been held up and aspired to as a model by professionals and enlightened laymen, tends to produce young people who "do not take initiative," "look to others for direction and decision," and "cannot be counted on to fulfill obligations" (Bronfenbrenner, 1960).

In the wake of so sweeping a conclusion, it is important to call attention to the tentative, if not tenuous character of our findings. The results were based on a single study employing crude questionnaire methods and rating scales. Also, our interpretation is limited by the somewhat "attenuated" character of most of the families classified as patriarchal or matriarchal in our sample. Extreme concentrations of power in one or another parent were comparatively rare. Had they been more frequent, we suspect the data would have shown that such extreme asymmetrical patterns of authority were detrimental rather than salutary for effective psychological development, perhaps even more disorganizing than equalitarian forms.

Nevertheless, our findings do find some peripheral support in the work of others. A number of investigations, for example, point to the special importance of the father in the socialization of boys (Bandura and Walters, 1959; Mussen and Distler, 1959). Further corroborative evidence appears in the growing series of studies of effects of paternal absence (Bach, 1946; Sears, Pintler and Sears, 1946; Lynn and

Sawrey, 1959; Tiller, 1958). The absence of the father apparently not only affects the behavior of the child directly but also influences the mother in the direction of greater over-protectiveness. The effect of both these tendencies is especially critical for male children; boys from father-absent homes tend to be markedly more submissive and dependent. Studies dealing explicitly with the influence of parental role structure in intact families are few and far between. Papanek (1957), in an unpublished doctoral dissertation, reports greater sex-role differentiation among children from homes in which the parental roles were differentiated. And in a carefully controlled study, Kohn and Clausen (1956) find that "schizophrenic patients more frequently than normal persons report that their mothers played a very strong authority role and the father a very weak authority role." Finally, what might best be called complementary evidence for our inferences regarding trends in family structure and their effects comes from the work of Miller, Swanson, and their associates (1958; 1960) on the differing patterns of behavior exhibited by families from *bureaucratic* and *entrepreneurial* work settings. These investigators argue that the entrepreneurial-bureaucratic dichotomy represents a new cleavage in American social structure that cuts across and overrides social class influences and carries with it its own characteristic patterns of family structure and socialization. Thus one investigation (Gold and Slater, 1958) contrasts the exercise of power in families of husbands employed in two kinds of job situations: (a) those working in large organizations with three or more levels of supervision; (b) those self-employed or working in small organizations with few levels of supervision. With appropriate controls for social class, equalitarian families were found more frequently in the bureaucratic groups; patriarchal and, to a lesser extent, matriarchal in the entrepreneurial setting. Another

study (Miller and Swanson, 1958) shows that, in line with Miller and Swanson's hypotheses, parents from these same two groups tend to favor rather different ends and means of socialization, with entrepreneurial families putting considerably more emphasis on the development of independence and mastery and on the use of "psychological" techniques of discipline. These differences appear at both upper and lower middle class levels but are less pronounced in higher socioeconomic strata. It is Miller and Swanson's belief, however, that the trend is toward the bureaucratic way of life, with its less structured patterns of family organization and child rearing. The evidence we have cited on secular changes in family structure and the inferences we have drawn regarding their possible effects on personality development are on the whole consistent with their views.

Looking Forward

If Miller and Swanson are correct in the prediction that America is moving toward a bureaucratic society that emphasizes, to put it colloquially, "getting along" rather than "getting ahead," then presumably we can look forward to ever increasing numbers of equalitarian families who, in turn, will produce successive generations of ever more adaptable but unaggressive "organization men." But recent signs do not all point in this direction. In our review of secular trends in child rearing practices we detected in the data from the more recent studies a slowing up in the headlong rush toward greater permissiveness and toward reliance on indirect methods of discipline. We pointed out also that if the most recent editions of well-thumbed guidebooks on child care are as reliable harbingers of the future as they have been in the past, we can anticipate something of a return to the more explicit discipline techniques of an earlier era. Perhaps the most important forces, however, acting to redirect both the aims and methods of child rearing in America emanate from behind the Iron Curtain. With the firing of the first Sputnik, Achievement began to replace Adjustment as the highest goal of the American way of life. We have become concerned —perhaps even obsessed—with "education for excellence" and the maximal utilization of our intellectual resources. Already, ability grouping, and the guidance counsellor who is its prophet, have moved down from the junior high to the elementary school, and parents can be counted on to do their part in preparing their youngsters for survival in the new competitive world of applications and achievement tests.

But if a new trend in parental behavior is to develop, it must do so in the context of changes already under way. And if the focus of parental authority is shifting from husband to wife, then perhaps we should anticipate that pressures for achievement will be imposed primarily by mothers rather than fathers. Moreover, the mother's continuing strong emotional investment in the child should provide her with a powerful lever for evoking desired performance. It is noteworthy in this connection that recent studies of the familial origins of need-achievement point to the matriarchy as the optimal context for development of the motive to excel (Strodtbeck, 1958; Rosen and D'Andrade, 1959).

The prospect of a society in which socialization techniques are directed toward maximizing achievement drive is not altogether a pleasant one. As a number of investigators have shown (Baldwin, Kalhorn and Breese, 1945; Baldwin, 1948; Haggard, 1957; Winterbottom, 1958; Rosen and D'Andrade, 1959), high achievement motivation appears to flourish in a family atmosphere of "cold democracy" in which initial high levels of

maternal involvement are followed by pressures for independence and accomplishment.[5] Nor does the product of this process give ground for reassurance. True, children from achievement-oriented homes excel in planfulness and performance, but they are also more aggressive, tense, domineering, and cruel (Baldwin, Kalhorn and Breese, 1945; Baldwin, 1948; Haggard, 1957). It would appear that education for excellence if pursued singlemindedly may entail some sobering social costs.

But by now we are in danger of having stretched our chain of inference beyond the strength of its weakest link. Our speculative analysis has become far more speculative than analytic and to pursue it further would bring us past the bounds of science into the realms of science fiction. In concluding our discussion, we would re-emphasize that speculations should, by their very nature, be held suspect. It is for good reason that, like "damn Yankees" they too carry their almost inseparable sobriquets: speculations are either "idle" or "wild." Given the scientific and social importance of the issues we have raised, we would dismiss the first of these labels out of hand, but the second cannot be disposed of so easily. Like the impetuous child, the "wild" speculation responds best to the sobering influence of friendly but firm discipline, in this instance from the hand of the behavioral scientist. As we look ahead to the next twenty-five years of human so-

[5] Cold democracy under female administration appears to foster the development of achievement not only in the home but in the classroom as well. In a review of research on teaching effectiveness, Ackerman reports that teachers most successful in bringing about gains in achievement score for their pupils were judged "least considerate," while those thought friendly and congenial were least effective. (W. I. Ackerman, "Teacher Competence and Pupil Change," *Harvard Educational Review*, 1954, 24, 273–289.)

cialization, let us hope that the "optimal levels" of involvement and discipline can be achieved not only by the parent who is unavoidably engaged in the process, but also by the scientist who attempts to understand its working, and who—also unavoidably—contributes to shaping its course.

REFERENCES

1. Bach, G. R.: "Father-Fantasies and Father-Typing in Father-Separated Children." *Child Development*, 1946, 17, 63–79.
2. Baldwin, A. L., J. Kalhorn, and F. H. Breese: "The Appraisal of Parent Behavior." *Psychological Monographs*, 1945, 58, No. 3 (Whole No. 268).
3. Baldwin, A. L., "Socialization and the the Parent-Child Relationship." *Child Development*, 1948, 19, 127–136.
4. Bandura, A., and R. H. Walters: *Adolescent Aggression*. New York: Ronald Press, 1959.
5. Bronfenbrenner, U.: "Socialization and Social Class Through Time and Space," in E. Maccoby, T. M. Newcomb, and E. L. Hartley, *Readings in Social Psychology*. New York: Holt, 1958, pp. 400–425.
6. Bronfenbrenner, U.: "Some Familial Antecedents of Responsibility and Leadership in Adolescents," in L. Petrullo, and B. M. Bass, *Leadership and Interpersonal Behavior*, New York: Holt, Rinehart, and Winston, 1961.
7. Bronson, W. C., E. S. Katten, and N. Livson: "Patterns of Authority and Affection in Two Generations," *Journal of Abnormal and Social Psychology*, 1959, 38, pp. 143–152.
8. Gold, M., and C. Slater: "Office, Factory, Store—and Family: A Study of Integration Setting." *American Sociological Review*, 1959, 23, 64–74.
9. Haggard, E. A.: "Socialization, Personality, and Academic Achievement in Gifted Children." *The School Review*, 1957, 65, 388–414.
10. Kohn, M. L., and J. A. Clausen: "Parental Authority Behavior and Schizo-

phrenia." *American Journal of Orthopsychiatry*, 1956, 26, 297–313.
11. Kohn, M. L., "Social Class and Parental Values." *American Journal of Sociology*, 1959, 44, 337–351.
12. Lynn, D. B., and W. L. Sawrey: "The Effects of Father-Absence on Norwegian Boys and Girls," *Journal of Abnormal and Social Psychology*, 1959, 59, 258–262.
13. Miller, D. R., and G. E. Swanson: *The Changing American Parent*. New York: John Wiley, 1958.
14. Miller, D. R., and G. E. Swanson: *Inner Conflict and Defense*, New York: Holt, 1960.
15. Mussen, P., and L. Distler: "Masculinity, Identification, and Father-Son Relationships." *Journal of Abnormal and Social Psychology*, 1959, 59, 350–356.
16. Papanek, M.: *Authority and Interpersonal Relations in the Family*. Unpublished doctoral dissertation on file at the Radcliffe College Library, 1957.
17. Rosen, B. L., and R. D'Andrade: "The Psychosocial Origins of Achievement Motivation." *Sociometry*, 1959, 22, 185–217.
18. Schachter, S., *The Psychology of Affiliation*. Stanford, California: Stanford University Press, 1959.
19. Sears, R. R., M. H. Pintler, and P. S. Sears: "Effects of Father-Separation on Preschool Children's Doll Play Aggression." *Child Development*, 1946, 17, 219–243.
20. Sears, R. R., Eleanor Maccoby, and M. Levin, *Patterns of Child Rearing*. Evanston, Illinois: Row, Peterson, 1957.
21. Strodtbeck, F. L., "Family Interaction, Values, and Achievement" in D. C. McClelland, A. L. Baldwin, U. Bronfenbrenner, and F. L. Strodtbeck. *Talent and Society*. Princeton, New Jersey: Van Nostrand, 1958, pp. 135–194.
22. Tiller, P. O., "Father-Absence and Personality Development of Children in Sailor Families," *Nordisk Psykologis Monograph Series*, 1958, 9.
23. Winterbottom, M. R., "The Relation of Need Achievement to Learning Experiences in Independence and Mastery," in J. W. Atkinson, *Motives in Fantasy, Action, and Society*. Princeton, New Jersey: Van Nostrand, 1958, pp. 453–494.

SOCIAL CHANGE AND SOCIAL CHARACTER:
THE ROLE OF PARENTAL MEDIATION [1]

by Alex Inkeles

In his general essay on national character Gorer (3) provides a clear and succinct formulation of one of the major premises underlying most of the related literature. Gorer indicated that we can deal with the simple but imposing fact that "societies continue, though their personnel changes" only because we can assume that "the present generation of adults will be replaced in due course by the present generation of children *who, as adults, will have habits very similar to their parents*." [2] Implicit in this general pattern, of course, is the further assumption "that the childhood learning of the contemporary adults was at least very similar to the learning which contemporary children are undergoing."

Gorer recognizes, and indeed states explicitly, that this model is probably not applicable to "societies which are in the process of drastic change." As Margaret Mead (8) points out, however, so few individuals may now hope to grow up under conditions of sociocultural stability

that we may regard this situation as almost unusual, and its products as in a sense "deviants." Gorer's model, therefore, requires elaboration, extension, and adjustment to enable it to deal adequately with national character as it develops and emerges under conditions of social change. The question is essentially this: Insofar as rapid social change interrupts the simple recapitulation of child training practices and produces new modal personality patterns, by what means are such changes mediated or effected?

The literature on national character contains several important and interesting efforts to answer this question. Margaret Mead (8), for example, has explored the significance for personality development of growing up in a culture that is no longer homogeneous, and posits the development under those circumstances of what she calls a "tentative" personality syndrome. Riesman (10), developing in full detail a point also made by Mead (7), has discussed the significance for social character of growing up under the strong influence of peer group pressures and standards. Erikson (2) has stated the implications for personality development that arise from the absence of adequate and valued role models with which to identify, and from the associated lack of roles through which the individual can find socially sanctioned and culturally meaningful outlets for the discharge of his emotions.

Despite the diversity of these studies they seem to have one element in common in their approach to the role of the parent as "child rearer" under conditions of social change. Implicitly, if not explicitly, the

[1] This paper was read by Alice Rossi and David Gleicher, to whom thanks are due for several valuable suggestions. The data reported on were collected as part of the Harvard Russian Research Center's Project on the Soviet Social System, under contract AF No. 33(038)-12909 with the Officer Education Research Laboratory at Maxwell Field, Alabama.

[2] Italics mine. For a detailed statement of the position that national character should be defined in terms of modal adult personality patterns rather than in cultural or structural terms see Inkeles and Levinson. (6)

SOURCE: *Journal of Social Issues*, Vol. 11 (1955), pp. 12–23.

parent is conceived as having available a relatively fixed repertory of child training procedures provided by his culture and learned by him in the period of his own childhood. Two main alternatives as to his utilization of those techniques are then generally considered. On the one hand, the parent is seen as acting as the passive agent of his culture, raising his children according to the procedures he had learned earlier in his own childhood, even though these techniques may have lost their appropriateness. It is assumed in that case, that as his children grow up the gulf between parent and child will rapidly grow great, and relations will become strained as the child meets and learns the conflicting behavior patterns and underlying values of his "own" new culture. On the other hand, the parent may know enough not to try to apply the training procedures under which he was raised, and in that case he either surrenders to other cultural surrogates such as peer group, teachers, mass media, etc., or borrows, and of course generally ineptly applies, some prefabricated set of rules. In the lower classes the borrowing might be from the local baby clinic, and in the upper classes from books and lectures on child rearing. In short the parents will manifest what Mead (8) terms "disturbed and inconsistent images of their children's future."

Without doubt these descriptions are faithful to the facts in many situations. Nevertheless, they seem to have made inadequate allowance for the positive adjustive capacity of human beings and for the process of continuous interaction that goes on between them and their sociocultural environment. Very often the global impact of Western contacts on a non-literate people may be almost totally disorienting, but parents need not be either unimaginative and passive agents of their culture, raising their children by rote, nor so disorganized and disoriented as is suggested by Mead's discussion. Although parents are adults, they may never-

theless still *learn*, and learn what they feel to be major "lessons," from their experiences under conditions of social change. This learning, furthermore, may influence the parents to seek purposefully to bring their children up in a way different from that in which they were raised, and in a manner intended better to suit the children for life in the changed social situation. This has been clearly recognized by Aberle and Naegele (1), who in a passage not easily duplicated elsewhere in the literature affirm that:

> All in all child rearing is future oriented to an important extent. The picture of the desired end product is importantly influenced by the parents' experiences in the adult world, as well as by their childhood experiences. When adult experience changes under the impact of major social change, there is reason to believe that there will ultimately, although not necessarily immediately, be shifts in the socialization pattern as well.

Of course, if either the parental experience of change or the response to it were purely idiosyncratic, then even where such experiences were widely distributed their effect on the character of the next generation would be essentially randomized. But it is in the nature of social structure, particularly in modern industrial society, that large groups of the population will be exposed to and perceive on-going change in similar fashion. Furthermore, it follows both from the existence of modal personality patterns and the shared cultural heritage of those in the subgroups of any population that they are very likely to react to this experience in systematically patterned ways. One very probable reaction to the experience of social change is to adjust the training of children to better prepare them for life in the future as the parent now anticipates that life in the light of his own experience. There is reason to assume, therefore, that the influence of large-scale social change occurring at any one time may be reflected in the character of the *next* generation because of mediation by parents living under and experiencing the change.

To test these assumptions one would ideally want a research design permitting the exploration of two distinct although intimately related questions. The first involves the hypothesis that parents who have experienced extreme social change seek to raise their children differently from the way in which they were brought up, purposefully adapting their child rearing practices to train children better suited to meet life in the changed world as the parent now sees it. To test this hypothesis we would need detailed information about the child rearing practices utilized by two consecutive generations of parents in the same culture, the first of which lived and raised its children in a period of relative stability, whereas the second lived and brought up its children under conditions of fairly extreme social change. A different requirement is posed by the question of how effective the parents in the second generation are in developing new traits or combinations of traits in their children. The extension of the ideal research design in this direction would require that we secure data on the modal personality patterns prevalent in the third generation. We would anticipate that as a result of their different socialization experience those in the third generation would manifest modal personality patterns different in important respects from those of their parents in the second generation.

Clearly such a design is extremely difficult to execute. Fortunately, however, we can approximate the ideal, although admittedly very imperfectly, through the utilization of some of the materials collected by the Harvard Project on the Soviet Social System. In that research program detailed life history interviews were conducted with about 330 former Soviet citizens, yielding a well-balanced sample in regard to such factors as age, sex, and occupation. The interview extensively explored the life of the respondent in both his family of orientation and procreation. Particular attention was paid to the values in regard to character development and occupational goals that dominated in child rearing as practiced by the respondent's parents and by the respondent himself in the role of parent. Through an exploration of these data we may hope to see some of the effects of social change in the Soviet Union as the parents who "lived" the change adjusted their child rearing practices in response to their own adult experiences, and thus acted as intermediaries in transmitting the effects of their current change to a future generation.

We may begin by testing the first assumption, namely that a generation experiencing extreme social change in adulthood will adapt the methods whereby it raises its children, and that as a result its children will be reared differently than it had been and yet more in keeping with the changed social realities. For our first generation, which we shall call the "Tsarist" generation, we need a group that raised its children during a period of relative social stability. The most recent period of that sort in Russia unfortunately falls as far back as the time immediately preceding the First World War, roughly from 1890 to 1915. Since we are interested in child rearing practices, and particularly of people who raised their children to adulthood (taken here as age 15) in those years, then eligible respondents would have been at least 33 by 1915 and at least 68 by the time of our interview in 1950. Indeed, most of those who could qualify as parents in our first generation were probably dead by 1950, and in any event only three of those living appear in our sample. We can learn about the child rearing practices utilized by that generation, therefore, only by relying on what their children report to have been true of the parents. The children of the Tsarist generation do, of course, appear in our sample. In this group we include all respondents over 45 in 1950,[3] and we call it the "Revolutionary" generation because its members, born in 1905 or before, were young adults at the time of the Revolution and lived as mature individuals through the subsequent Civil War and the later periods of momentous social change represented by the forced collectivization and industrialization programs. It was this second generation that was raising its children to adulthood during the main period of Soviet development.

It will be recognized, therefore, that, although dealing with the child rearing practices of two different generations of parents, we draw our information from but a single set of respondents, namely those in our sample over 45 years of age in 1950. In telling us how their parents brought them up they provide us with data about the child rearing practices of the Tsarist generation, whereas in describing the training of their own children, they provide our materials on the child rearing practices of the Revolutionary generation. Although limits of space do not permit presentation of the evidence, we have data that indicate that this procedure of ascertaining the child rearing values of an earlier generation by accepting the description given by those who had been the children of the group being

[3] The median age in the group was 52, and only six respondents were over 65. Such an age class admittedly does not represent a truly distinctive generation. In part this results because the limited number of cases we have forces us to use a gross dichotomization of those over 45 and under 35 in 1950. But even larger numbers and finer age gradations would not eliminate overlapping, because at any one time some children are being raised who are the *last* to be raised by a given generation of parents whereas others of the same age are the *first* to be raised by the next generation. Since we have no reliable absolute measure of generation, the respondent's own age is used as the basis for classifying the respondent's generation and that of his parent. We are not unaware of the complications thereby raised, but feel the procedure adequate for present purposes.

studied, is methodologically less suspect than might appear to be the case. The description by the youngest generation in our sample of the manner in which it was reared agrees so closely with the report of how the training was done as related by the middle generation, which actually reared the children, as to yield correlations of .89 and .95 on the two available comparisons.

Relative to the child rearing materials we have a detailed summary code of the dominant values governing child rearing, both as to character and occupational goals, characteristic for each generation acting as parents. In no case, however, is the rating of the parent based on his observed behavior, but only on the values deduced by us to have been operative on the basis of the interview. Furthermore, as already noted, the respondents from the prerevolutionary Tsarist generation could not speak for themselves and we had to rely on the retrospective report of their children.

In the following analysis a larger number of code categories had been grouped into a set of six major dimensions that were prominent value orientations in the child rearing efforts of those in our sample. The value of "tradition" was coded mainly for emphasis on religious upbringing, but it included as well references to maintenance of strong family ties and traditions; "adjustment" reflects emphasis on "getting along," staying out of trouble, keeping an eye on your security and safety, etc; "achievement" was coded when parents stressed attainment, industriousness, mobility, material rewards, and similar goals; "personalistic" was checked when the parent was concerned with such personal qualities as honesty, sincerity, justice, and mercy; "intellectuality," where the emphasis was on learning and knowledge as ends in themselves; and "political" when the focus was on attitudes, values, and beliefs dealing with government and particularly with *the* government of the land.

When we consider the profound differences, during their years of child rearing, in the life experience of the Revolutionary generation as contrasted with that of its parents in the Tsarist generation, what differences may we expect in their values with regard to child rearing? The revolutionary upheaval of 1917 and the subsequent programs of forced social change struck a great blow at the traditional structure of Russian society and profoundly altered it.[4] Massive programs of expansion were undertaken in industrialization, in urbanization, in formal organization and administration. The pattern of rural life, in which the bulk of the population was involved, was drastically revised through the forced collectivization of agriculture. Centralized political control and political terror were ruthlessly imposed. Opportunities for mobility increased greatly. Under these circumstances we might well expect the traditional values to suffer the greatest loss of emphasis, with a consequent shift to stress on either simple successful adjustment or the more secularized morality represented by the personalistic values and the pursuit of knowledge as an end in itself. In addition, our knowledge of the growing opportunities for advancement, associated with the generally expanded development of the formal occupational structure, leads us to anticipate that greatly increased weight would be given to achievement. Finally the central role played by the state in Soviet affairs, the existence of the political terror, and the additional fact that our respondents were disaffected from the political system, lead us to anticipate heightened concern with political considerations in child rearing.

In Table 1 we have indicated the distribution of emphasis among the dimensions in our set of dominant value orientations. The relative stability of the gross rank order is testimony to the fact that both generations of parents represented a

[4] See Moore (9) and Inkeles (5) for discussion of this process, and for evaluation of its significance as a program of planned social change.

TABLE 1. *Child Rearing Values of Parents in Russian Pre-revolutionary and Post-revolutionary Times*

AREAS	DISTRIBUTION [*] OF EMPHASIS IN:	
	TSARIST PERIOD	POST-REVOLUTIONARY PERIOD [†]
Tradition	75%	44%
Achievement	60	52
"Personalistic"	32	44
Adjustment	16	21
Intellectuality	12	22
Politics	12	20
Number of Respondents	77	78

[*] These percents total more than 100, since respondents were scored for as many themes as cited, but percentaging is on the basis of total respondents.

[†] The percentages in this column have been adjusted to equalize for the effect created by the larger number of responses given by our informants in describing their own activity as parents, as against the manner in which they had been raised by the Tsarist generation.

common cultural tradition which they carried forward through time. Nevertheless, it is clear that there have been very substantial shifts in the relative weight of several value orientations, and they go largely in the expected direction.[5] Perhaps the most striking finding is the sharp decrease in emphasis on the traditional values, accounted for overwhelmingly by the decreased emphasis on religious training and belief. Under the impact of industrialization and urbanization, perhaps

[5] There is some evidence that the strength of the shift varies by class on certain dimensions. Limits of space preclude the exploration of such differences. It must suffice to say that on the whole class differences represent only special cases of the general points being made here.

abetted by the antireligious and "proscientific" propaganda conducted by the regime, parents in the Revolutionary generation clearly shifted toward an emphasis on more secular values.[6] This shift is reflected in the increased emphasis on learning (intellectuality) and positive personal qualities *as ends in themselves* rather than as *means* to the attainment of the good life lived, as it were, "in the sight of God." Thus, secular morality replaced traditional and religiously based morality.

Perhaps most directly and explicitly related to the intervening experience of the parents under conditions of social change is the increased attention paid to political considerations in the education of one's children. The greater emphasis on political problems arises from the fact that the Soviet regime has progressively "politicized" more and more areas of human activity that in most Western societies fall outside the political realm. A person at all alert to his situation and surroundings could therefore hardly fail to realize that if he wished to prepare his child adequately for life under Soviet conditions he must train him to an awareness concerning the political realities of the system, even though such training had not been important in his own childhood. This interpretation is borne out by the statements made by our interviewers.

Finally, it is necessary to comment on the major instance in which the data fail to confirm expectation, namely in regard to emphasis on achievement values. This failure is, of course, only relative, since achievement was the most emphasized value in the rearing of children by those in the Revolutionary generation. Nevertheless, in absolute weight it declined in importance even though it had been expected to increase. It might be that since our respondents were refugees from the system, and since many of them looked

upon too active pursuit of a career as suggesting involvement with the regime, they did not admit fully the importance they actually attributed to inculcating achievement strivings in their children. On the other hand, it may be that the expectation was unrealistic quite apart from specific Soviet conditions. There is some evidence that values such as security, adjustment, and personal attractiveness are becoming ever more important foci in child rearing in the United States (10) and that stress on achievement *as an end in itself,* although still prevalent, has become somewhat old-fashioned. This pattern may be associated with the combination of mass industry, education and communication, and the consumer culture of which the Soviet Union is but one example.

All told, however, the data certainly seem strongly to support the assumption that the experience of extreme social change that the Revolutionary generation underwent did have a marked effect on that generation's approach to the rearing of its children. As compared with the way their parents raised them, they can hardly be assumed to have merely "recapitulated" the earlier pattern of child rearing. On the contrary, having experienced marked social change, they adjusted their child rearing practices, the better to prepare their children for the life they expected those children to lead.

To test the effectiveness of the changed general child rearing orientations of the Revolutionary generation, we would need data on the personality patterns prevalent among their children in the third generation, which we unfortunately do not have.[7] Nevertheless, we can make a very approximate approach to our second question concerning the effectiveness of the

---

[6] Alice Rossi (11) has prepared an outstanding analysis, as yet unpublished, on the declining importance of religious belief in a succession of Soviet Russian generations.

[7] The Harvard Project on the Soviet Social System did collect data on personality patterns among former Soviet citizens. However the small size of the clinical sample, and the nature of the personality variables investigated, largely rule out the possibility of an adequate test.

changed child rearing emphases if we shift our attention to the realm of occupational choices. In that area we have data not only on the values stressed by parents, but we also have information on the values which the individual held in regard to himself. In treating value orientations relative to the occupational world we are, of course, dealing not with personality patterns in a psychodynamic sense, but rather with something more closely akin to "social character" as it has been defined by Riesman (10) and Inkeles (4).

toward the occupational world. In addition it is reasonable to assume that economic and material rewards would have come to be much more stressed among the goals set before the child, as would the necessity of finding work that permitted an appropriate accommodation to the highly politicized occupational structure in Soviet society.

As a comparison of the first and second columns of Table 2 indicates, three of these four expectations are rather strongly supported by the responses of our inter-

TABLE 2. *Changing Values Concerning the Occupational Realm*

DISTRIBUTION OF EMPHASIS AMONG VALUES STRESSED

| VALUE AREAS | IN CHILD REARING BY: | | IN HYPOTHETICAL CHOICE BY "SOVIET" GENERATION |
	"TSARIST" GENERATION	"REVOLUTIONARY" GENERATION	
Rewards	41%	25%	14%
Tradition	35	14	11
Self-expression	21	38	62
Politics	3	23	13
Number of Responses (equal to 100%)	58	63	931

The influence of their experience with social change on the child training practices adopted by the Revolutionary generation is perhaps even more strikingly evident in the area of occupational choices. In addition to asking about the specific occupations for which parents wished to prepare their children, we asked the reasons for the selection. The reasons cited provide us with a guide to the values that were dominant in the home atmosphere created by the parent for the child. Considering the nature of the social change experienced by the Revolutionary generation and described above, we might again well expect that as part of the general weakening of the traditional way of life there would have been a decline in the importance of family tradition, as against self-expression or free choice, as values emphasized in orienting the child

viewees. We see, to begin, a sharp decline in the importance of family tradition as a criterion in shaping the child's occupational orientation, along with a marked increase in the role played by self-expression or free job choice. In addition, we may note the much greater emphasis on guiding the child toward a job that is politically desirable, which for our respondents generally meant one safe from danger of political arrest and not too directly involved in the regime's political objectives. Finally, it should be observed that here again the data fail to support our expectation that the material and psychic rewards on the job—roughly equivalent to earlier discussed achievement value—would be more emphasized by the Revolutionary generation than by the Tsarist generation. Indeed, the relative weight of such rewards as values to be emphasized in orienting children toward the occupational world declined markedly from the one generation to the next.

Now to return to our original research design, do we have any evidence that the different child rearing patterns utilized by the middle generation as a response to their experience of social change actually were effective? Or did the parents in that second generation, despite their apparent intention, act in fact as passive agents of the culture and, *nolens volens,* raise their children in their own image and much as the first generation would have done the job? For a proper answer to this question we should have access to the children of the Revolutionary generation, and to data on their job choices coded by the same categories used to describe the child training values of their parents. Unfortunately we can only approximate each requirement. Respondents on both our written questionnaire and oral interview remained anonymous, and we therefore have no way of identifying the actual children of the Revolutionary generation. But we can secure a reasonable equivalent of that third group, which we call the "Soviet" generation, by taking all respondents under 35 in 1950. Most of them were raised and reached adulthood in the same period in which the Revolutionary generation was acting in the parental role and could well have been their children. As for the values that governed their job choices, we are obliged to draw on our written questionnaire, which presented the respondents with a choice of precoded categories not strictly comparable with those used in assessing child training values.[8] For example the check list included the omnibus category "I feel suited to it," which we have equated here with "self-expression," but which obviously could have meant many more things to the respondents.

[8] The respondent was asked what job he would have chosen while in the U.S.S.R. if he had had a completely free choice, and was then asked to checked off the reason for his choice.

Quite apart from such methodological difficulties, it would be naive to expect a near-perfect correlation between the values that the parents in the Revolutionary generation stressed while they reared the Soviet generation and the ones which that generation emphasized in its own job choices. Such training always produces only an approximation of the parents' desire. More important, those in the Soviet generation have had their values shaped by many influences other than those exerted by their parents. Nevertheless, our expectation is that on the whole the pattern of value orientations of the Soviet generation will be quite close to those that were stressed in child training by their parents in the Revolutionary generation as contrasted with those inculcated in an earlier era by the Tsarist generation. The relative degree of fit between the two sets of orientations may be taken as a rough measure of how successful the Revolutionary generation was in training the Soviet generation to orient in new directions.

The appropriate comparison may be obtained by examining the third column of Table 2—which contains the distribution of emphasis in the operative values guiding the job choices of the younger generation—in relation to the first and second columns. The over-all comparison strongly suggests that those in the Revolutionary generation were highly successful in their purposive effort to shape the values their children would carry into adulthood. This is most evident in the marked emphasis that the Soviet generation places on self-expression rather than family tradition as a criterion for its job choices, much in keeping with the lesser emphasis that its parents had put on tradition in orienting their children's thoughts about the world of jobs and work. Even if we make allowance for the strong pull of the actual code category, "I feel suited for it," this interpretation would clearly not be materially affected.

It will be noticed, further, that in raising children those in the Tsarist generation gave extremely slight attention to political considerations, whereas those in the Revolutionary generation stressed it very heavily, indeed more heavily than tradition. In their own job choices, those in the Soviet generation again show the apparent influence of their parents' concern for this dimension, although in their own value scheme it does not loom quite so large as it did in their parents' efforts at socialization. Finally, we may note that material and psychic rewards such as income and prestige had roughly similar relative weight, as compared to politics and tradition, in the child rearing practices of the Revolutionary generation and in the actual job choices of the Soviet generation.

It seems reasonable to conclude again, therefore, that the Revolutionary generation did not merely act passively as the agent of the old culture, recapitulating in its own parental activities the socialization practices that had earlier been used by *its* parents. On the contrary, it may be said that the middle generation, responding to its experience of social change under the Soviet regime, in large measure turned away from the pattern of child rearing under which it had been raised earlier and in its approach to the new Soviet generation stressed goals and values of a different sort. It appears, furthermore, that this training of the youth in new value orientations was relatively successful.

Because the numbers are small and the sample unusual, the material presented here is perhaps little more than suggestive of the results that might be yielded by research specifically designed to increase our knowledge in this area. Indeed, a stronger case could have been made with the material at hand had not rigorous limits of space precluded the presentation of quotations from our interviews that show graphically the way in which conditions of social change experienced by the parents influenced their approach to raising their children. Nevertheless, the material presented should serve to alert us to the role that the parent plays, through both purposive and unconscious adjustments in his child rearing practices, in mediating the influence of social change to his children and consequently in better adapting them for the changed social conditions they may meet as adults. Furthermore, although the demonstration presented above dealt only with the more surface level of attitudes and value orientations, there is reason to believe that similar processes operate with regard to the development of personality at deeper levels.

REFERENCES

1. Aberle, D. F., and K. D. Naegele: "Middle-class fathers' occupational role and attitudes toward children." *American Journal of Orthopsychiatry*, 1952, *22*, 366–378.
2. Erikson, E. H.: *Childhood and society.* New York: Norton, 1950.
3. Gorer, G.: "The concept of national character." In J. L. Crammer (Ed.), *Science news.* Harmondsworth Middlesex: Penguin Books, 1950, No. 18, pp. 105–122.
4. Inkeles, A.: "Some sociological observations on culture and personality studies." In C. Kluckhohn, H. A. Murray, and D. M. Schneider (Eds.), *Personality in nature, society, and culture.* (2nd. ed.) New York: Knopf, 1953, pp. 577–592.
5. Inkeles, A.: "Social change in Soviet Russia." In M. Berger, T. Abel, and C. H. Page (Eds.), *Freedom and control in modern society.* New York: Van Nostrand, 1954, pp. 243–264.
6. Inkeles, A., and D. J. Levinson: "National character: The study of modal personality and sociocultural systems." In G. Lindzey (Ed.), *Handbook of social psychology.* Cambridge: Addison-Wesley, 1954, pp. 977–1020.
7. Mead, Margaret: "Social change and cultural surrogates." *Journal of Educational Psychology*, 1940, *14*, 92–110.
8. ———.: "The implications of culture change for personality development." *American Journal of Orthopsychiatry*, 1947, *17*, 633–646.

9. Moore, B.: *Soviet politics: The dilemma of power.* Cambridge: Harvard University Press, 1950.
10. Riesman, D.: *The lonely crowd.* New Haven: Yale University Press, 1950.
11. Rossi, Alice S.: *Generational differences in the Soviet Union.* Russian Research Center, Harvard University, 1954 (mimeographed).

AMERICAN INDIAN PERSONALITY TYPES
AND THEIR SOCIOCULTURAL ROOTS

by George D. Spindler and Louise S. Spindler

The questions with which we will be concerned in this paper are: what psychological characteristics may be considered universal among the Indian tribes of North America? What are some of the variations around these basic psychological themes? Does psychological structure act as a selective screen in culture change? What are some of the personality types cast up in the process of change as Indians in groups and as individuals adapt to the impact of twentieth-century American culture? Although each of these questions is indeed broad enough to justify a separate article, they belong together. We will place most emphasis on the last two questions. This is because psychological structures as selective screens and the psychological types cast up in culture change situations provide focus on relationships that will be of significance in new developments in the status or cultural position of American Indians.

We must at this point declare our hesitance about stating some of the generalizations it is necessary to make in the treatment of these questions. Although no area in the world has been so combed over by anthropologists as has North America, the combing has been done mainly with *cultural*, not *psychological*, tools. For large areas, psychological data—including impressionistic descriptions of character—

SOURCE: *Annals of the American Academy of Political and Social Science,* Vol. 311 (1957), pp. 147–157.

are lacking. What psychological data are available—and probably more is available for North America than for any other major culture area of the world—are frequently not comparable from one tribe to another because of differing theoretical orientations in their treatment, different levels of abstraction in interpretation, and the variant purposes of research.

Inference from cultural materials alone is frequently unsafe because the manifest aspects of culture sometimes vary from situation to situation without corresponding variations in psychological structure, and vice versa. We have used what is available in the literature of psycho-cultural studies among North American Indians, have inferred from cultural patterning to a limited extent and from life histories, and have projected from our own observations among Wisconsin Indians, particularly the Menominee. Much of what we will say in the following pages, however, must be regarded as constituting reasonable hypotheses rather than established fact.

Common Psychological Characteristics

As we checked through the psychologically oriented studies—including autobiographies and psychological "asides" in ethnographies—of Indian tribes representing all of the major culture areas in North America except the Southeastern

Woodlands, it seemed clear that some psychological characteristics are more widely shared than others, and that of these some may be regarded as representing modal tendencies. We regard them not as static, but as long-standing features of a relatively high degree of stability. They characterize in a very general sense limited aspects of the aboriginal personalities of American Indians and possibly characterize the pan-Indian psychological core of the least acculturated segments of contemporary tribes. We shall, therefore, describe these core psychological features, and later treat their variations, as though we were speaking of aboriginal America.

Without attempting to document the many sources from which inferences and data were drawn, we can tentatively describe the psychological features most widely exhibited among North American Indians as a whole in the following way: nondemonstrative emotionality and reserve accompanied by a high degree of control over interpersonal aggression within the in-group;[1] a pattern of generosity that varies greatly in the extent to which it is a formalized social device without emotional depth; autonomy of the individual, a trait linked with sociopolitical structures low in dominance-submission hierarchies; ability to endure pain, hardship, hunger, and frustration without external evidence of discomfort; a positive valuation of bravery and courage that varies sharply with respect to emphasis on

highly aggressive daring in military exploit; a generalized fear of the world as dangerous, and particularly a fear of witchcraft; a "practical joker" strain that is nearly everywhere highly channelized institutionally, as in the common brother-in-law joking prerogative, and that appears to be a safety valve for in-group aggressions held sharply in check; attention to the concrete realities of the present—what Rorschachists would call the "large D" approach to problem solving—practicality, in contrast to abstract integration in terms of long-range goals;[2] a dependence upon supernatural power outside one's self—power that determines one's fate, which is expressed to and can be acquired by the individual through dreams, and for which the individual is not held personally accountable, at least not in the sense that one's "will" is accountable for one's acts in Western culture.

Variations in Psychological Characteristics

Each of the items in the preceding list of "core" psychological features varies by context and serves somewhat different purposes in somewhat different ways in each culture. They are, therefore, in no sense fixed psychological constants. They are, rather, foci around which psychological and cultural elaboration has taken place in more or less unique ways in each culture. Study of this variation will lead to greater understanding of the behavior of American Indians, historically and in the present, than does the abstraction of common psychological denominators. If we analyze one of these foci— the handling of aggression—we find that

[1] There are exceptions to each of these descriptive statements. The Mohave and Navaho, for instance, are subject to abrupt swings of mood and are emotionally volatile, though the Navaho are described as outwardly impassive. See G. Devereux, "Mohave Culture and Personality," *Character and Personality*, Vol. 8 (1939–1940), pp. 91–109; A. Kroeber, "Mohave Disposition," *Handbook of the Indians of California*, Bureau of American Ethnology, Bulletin 78 (1925), pp. 729–731; C. Kluckhohn and D. Leighton, *The Navaho* (Cambridge: Harvard University Press, 1947).

[2] This may vary according to the extent to which a people are sedentary, accumulative, and status-oriented. It seems probable that nomadic hunting, and gathering peoples, as most North American Indians were, would usually exhibit this practical, reality-centered approach.

it is true that American Indian cultures as a whole tend to exercise sharp controls on interpersonal, in-group aggression; but that the kinds of controls, what is being controlled, and the purpose of controls vary impressively from situation to situation. The following is an attempt to sketch the salient features of aggression control and channelization in three culture types, corresponding to culture areas in North America, as examples of variation.[3]

On the Plains, for example, out-group aggression is highly channelized—among tribes like the Comanche, Sioux, Arapaho, Crow—by raids on other tribes for horses, scalps, and booty and with systems of status based on one's daring in these exploits. And here also in many tribes, in-group aggression is highly channelized—in legitimatized wife stealing by certain men's societies, highly aggressive sexual conquest with males "counting coup" on women in some tribes, very rough institutionalized practical joking on relatives and old people, and ritualized boasting about military, and frequently sexual, exploits.[4] We infer that these Plains Indians are high in aggression, but that their cultures pro-

vide channels for it so that random in-group expression of aggression was infrequent enough not to be a major cause of disruption.

Among the Algonquians of the Northeastern Woodlands—the Ojibwa of Ontario and Wisconsin, the Menominee, the Naskapi of Labrador—there are fewer outlets for the expression of aggression on out-groups. Only some of the southern tribes tortured prisoners of war as a public spectacle, or even had formal warfare. The primary outlet for aggression seems to have been, and still is among the least acculturated groups within tribes, witchcraft—just as it is, coupled with gossip, among the Pueblo peoples like the Hopi and Zuni of the Southwest.[5]

The sociocultural mechanisms centering on aggression are of a rather different order in the Northeast than on the Plains. Here there is great stress on kind words, on treating everybody nicely, on never giving offense, not gossiping and fighting, not "showing off," not stealing women, doing favors whenever you are asked for fear you might displease someone if you refused, and on being quiet. The emphasis is seen in the constant, carefully phrased exhortations: by parents to children, by elders to participants during ceremonials and feasts, and in folklore, as well as in everyday behaviors.[6]

This pattern within these Northeastern

---

[3] The definition of culture area terms for North America used in this paper is that of A. L. Kroeber, *Anthropology* (New York: Harcourt, Brace and Company, 1923), p. 337.

[4] There are a multitude of descriptions of Plains patterns along these lines in both popular and ethnographic literature. See, for instance, E. C. Parsons (Ed.), *American Indian Life* (New York: B. W. Huebsch, 1922) for short, vivid, fictionalized stories; and A. Wallace and E. A. Hoebel, *The Comanches* (Norman: University of Oklahoma Press, 1952) for an ethno-historical analysis. A. Kardiner, in *Psychological Frontiers of Society* (New York: Columbia University Press, 1945), provides a psychoanalytic interpretation of Comanche character, and G. Devereux, *Reality and Dream* (New York: International Universities Press, 1951) analyzes the neurosis of an anonymous Plains Indian in terms of an areal Plains personality.

[5] See D. F. Aberle, *The Psychosocial Analysis of a Hopi Life-History*, "Comparative Psychology Monographs" (Berkeley: University of California Press, 1951) for a discussion of the functions of witchcraft in Hopi society; and L. S. Spindler, "Witchcraft in Menomini Acculturation," *American Anthropologist*, Vol. 54, No. 4 (1952), pp. 593–602 for the Menominee.

[6] See A. I. Hallowell, "Some Psychological Characteristics of Northeastern Indians," in: F. Johnson (Ed.), *Man in Northeastern North America*, "Papers of the Robert S. Peabody Foundation for Archeology," Vol. 3 (1946), for an analytic description of the pattern.

societies can be regarded as functioning to control in-group aggressions in situations where formal sociopolitical control systems are almost nonexistent and decidedly atomistic. This does not mean that the Northeastern Algonquians are potentially, or latently, highly aggressive, hostile people.[7] It only means that a psycho-cultural system of controls over in-group aggression must be used as social insurance, in the absence of a formalized, authority-centered system of control.

Among the Southwestern Pueblo peoples, where a superficially similar pattern of restraints on the expression of interpersonal, in-group aggression operates, the sociocultural setting is quite different; and the psychological process becomes altered. These societies are highly organized into communities governed by differentiated theocracies and structured by various interlocking and overlapping categories of kin, maternal clans, and ceremonial societies. The stress is on conformity to the rules of the group, with the theocrats as censors. That all is not peaceful with the Pueblos is indicated by considerable bickering, gossip about even a light deviation from social norms, robust teasing of children by the special classes of relatives so privileged, and open breaks of intragroup hostility that have resulted from time to time in the splitting of villages, with one of the factions going off to establish a new community.[8]

In the Pueblos the stress on overt interpersonal amiability, on constraint of direct interpersonal aggression, on avoiding the spotlight and not boasting, on conformity, helps maintain a tightly organized system of sociopolitical controls, in contrast to the situation in the Northeast. This support apparently operates in part as a cultural compensation for the potentially disruptive effect of strong covert hostilities—and indeed the covert hostility may be in part a result of the tight system of controls—so the psychological and sociocultural systems interact to maintain each other. It thus appears that atomistic Algonquians and organized Pueblo peoples both exercise exceptionally strong psycho-cultural sanctions against the overt expression of interpersonal, in-group aggression; but these sanctions support different sociopolitical systems by controlling psychological processes of different intensity.

The point has been made that the mechanisms for releasing and controlling aggression must be formed out of cultural materials peculiar to each situation, irrespective of cross-tribal commonalities, but that the emphasis on control of aggression is a central focus in these highly diverse cultural situations.[9]

---

[7] The projective test data from this area do not indicate high aggressiveness or hostility, although tribes do apparently vary in the degree and pervasiveness of anxiety. See the several papers on this and related subjects in A. I. Hallowell, Culture and Experience, Philadelphia: University of Pennsylvania Press, 1955; and G. D. Spindler, Sociocultural and Psychological Processes in Menomini Acculturation, "Culture and Society Series," Vol. 5 (Berkeley: University of California Press, 1955).

[8] The social psychology of the Pueblos has been a matter of some dispute. For support of the interpretive sketch we are drawing

here, see Aberle, op. cit (note 5 supra); L. W. Simmons, Sun Chief (New Haven: Yale University Press, 1942); F. H. Ellis, "Patterns of Aggression and the War Cult in the Southwestern Pueblos," Southwestern Journal of Anthropology, Vol. 7, No. 2 (1951), pp. 177–201; W. Bennett, "The Interpretation of Pueblo Culture: A Question of Values," Southwestern Journal of Anthropology, Vol. 2, No. 4 (1946), pp. 361–374.

[9] We recognize that all psycho-cultural systems include mechanisms for handling aggression. What is uniquely Indian about this is that the controls of aggression are highly developed and are linked with a nondemonstrative emotional mode that results in at least an appearance of interpersonal amiability in many, if not most, tribal and areal personalities.

Psychological Structure and Culture Change

That the bio-emotional and cognitive-perceptual organization shared by a group of people, and often referred to as "basic personality structure," is quite stable over time and through different levels of manifest culture change is one of the better documented generalizations of significance to our topic. This stability of psychological pattern may be described, as did Scudder Mekeel in his study of the Teton Dakota, as a retention of "values and attitudes behind the concrete pattern of culture." [10] He demonstrates how bravery, generosity, fortitude, and moral integrity, basic values of the past embodied in the conception of the "good man," survive despite their dysfunctional role in the modern situation. For example, the very high value placed upon generosity expressed in the giving of goods at most important social occasions and in the hospitality extended to relatives and friends makes the accumulation of property necessary to the goal of material success in American culture very difficult. In fact, if a Teton Dakota does become successful in the white man's eyes and in terms of accumulation of property, he necessarily loses his security-giving membership in the Indian primary group, as long as that group lives by values derived from the Dakota past.[11] Unless white society has a rewarding place for him he will become an isolated and unhappy individual.

The stability of psychological pattern

may also be described in terms of highly generalized attitudes, such as the belief in immanent justice, which are considered indicative of basic world view. Laura Thompson explores to this purpose responses to psychological devices like the Thematic Apperception, Moral Ideology, and Emotional Responses tests by Indian children 6 to 18 years of age in five tribes: Zuni, Navaho, Papago, Dakota Sioux, Ojibwa. She finds evidence that world view in each tribe is congruent with the aboriginal mode of life and that these world views have apparently persisted despite great changes in the economy, social structure, and manifest culture.[12]

The most striking evidence for the persistence of psychological structure is provided by the work of A. Irving Hallowell. He administered Rorschach projective tests to several hundred Ojibwa men, women, and children living at three different levels of acculturation. These Indians varied in the degree to which their sources of subsistence, social organization, religion, and language approximated aboriginal or modern American culture. Hallowell's conclusion is dramatic; while the Ojibwa appear more and more like whites at the most acculturated levels in the manifest aspects of culture—dress, language, religion, and so forth—there is . . . "no evidence at all for a basic psychological shift in a parallel direction." [13] What shifts do occur are regressive and disintegrative. They do not fundamentally alter the basic psychological structure; they merely corrode it.

The Spindlers did a study along somewhat similar lines of Menominee Indians with four distinct levels of acculturation, from a native-oriented base to a thor-

[10] H. S. Mekeel, *The Economy of a Modern Teton Dakota Community*, "Yale University Publications in Anthropology," No. 6 (New Haven: Yale University Press, 1936).

[11] For an insightful discussion of the role of the primary group in a similar situation (Mandan-Hidatsa), see E. Bruner, "Primary Group Experience and the Process of Acculturation," *American Anthropologist*, Vol. 58, No. 4 (1956), pp. 605–623.

[12] Laura Thompson, "Attitudes and Acculturation," *American Anthropologist*, Vol. 50, No. 2 (1948), pp. 200–215.

[13] A. L. Hallowell, "Ojibwa Personality and Acculturation," in: Sol Tax (Ed.), *Proceedings and Selected Papers of the 29th International Congress of Americanists* (Chicago: University of Chicago Press, 1951), p. 112.

oughly acculturated, white-collar group. All the Menominee lived on the same reservation community. Without becoming involved with various other phases of the problems studied, we can note that the conclusions drawn concerning stability and retention of psychological structure were fundamentally the same as those of Hallowell, insofar as the samples are comparable. But there is this important difference: the Menominee situation provided a group of Indians who had attained occupational and social positions equivalent to those of high status in the nearby white towns. This was due to the presence of a Menominee-owned and managed lumber industry. The modal psychological structure exhibited by a sample of the men in this elite group departed dramatically from that exhibited in native-oriented and culturally transitional levels. It constitutes a psychological transformation, a reformulation of personality in successful adaptation to the demands of status achievement, punctuality, and the linkage of work and success appropriate to the middle-class American value system. This suggests that significant psychological changes do occur when the barriers to achievement on the white man's terms are broken down, and the new adaptation thereby becomes rewarding rather than punitive.[14]

Psychological Structure as a Perceptual Screen

What has already been said about the stability, sometimes dysfunctional stability, of psychological structure in culture change situations, suggests the determinant role of personality as a selective, perceptual screen. In the absence of clearcut and meaningful rewards for psychological readaptation, the psychological structure based upon the survival of attenuated tra-

[14] See G. D. Spindler, *op. cit.* (note 7 *supra*).

ditional culture will block out whole areas of the new cultural environment and makes possible the learning of only limited techniques of white culture as necessary accessories to getting along in today's world.[15] But the selective role of psychological structure goes beyond this. Two instances of those described in the literature will be noted.

Anthony Wallace cites the absence of fear of heights, a penchant for alcohol, and the lack of anal-reactive (retentive) traits (with the presence of so-called "oral" traits) in the modal personality structure of the Iroquoian Tuscarora as significant aspects of the "sorting screen," with the following results.[16] About one-third of the Tuscarora adult males are workers on high steel construction and are sought after by contractors because they lack the mildly phobic fear of heights normal in whites. The Baptist Church and Temperance Society flourish on the reservation to reduce the incidence and severity of drinking. The Tuscarora refuse to become "anal-reactive" whites. That is, they do not save money, keep appointments punctually, or compulsively tend to the maintenance of their possessions—fields, cars, homes, and equipment—despite one hundred and fifty years of attempts (by whites) by persuasion, example, and punishment, to make them do so.

In an interesting research, Evon Vogt and John Adair studied the attitudes towards veterans of World War II, the acceptance of the innovations they brought back with them, and the reintegration of the veterans in their home communi-

[15] This has also been noted by E. Bruner, *op. cit.* (note 11 *supra*), and for the Sioux by E. H. Erikson, *Childhood and Society* (New York: W. W. Norton and Company, 1950).

[16] A. F. C. Wallace, "Some Determinants of Culture Change in an Iroquoian Community," in: W. N. Fenton (Ed.), *Symposium on Local Diversity in Iroquoian Culture*, Bureau of American Ethnology, Bulletin 149 (1951), pp. 59–75.

372 Personality and Social Systems

ties among the Navaho and Zuni.[17] The Zuni requested large numbers of deferments for men in religious offices when the draft began; and when the draft board asked that deferments be requested only for men who held these offices for life, the Zuni filled lifetime offices that had not been occupied for years and revived ceremonials that had become defunct. When the Zuni veterans returned, they were met with a solid front of conservatism. Deviant behaviors of any sort were gossiped about, and strong pressures were exerted by the priests and others to make veterans conform to the traditional Zuni norms and reintegrate into the traditional statuses and roles provided by Zuni social structure. The veterans who could not conform left the community.

In contrast, hundreds of Navaho males enlisted, few deferments were requested, and there was no increase in ritual activity to keep medicine doctors or religious functionaries at home. When the Navaho veterans returned, they were greeted with interested curiosity, the pressures to conform were not intense, and some have been active innovators since then.

Adair and Vogt point to Zuni and Navaho differences in sociocultural systems, patterns of warfare, and degree of curiosity about the outside world as antecedents of the selectively variant responses to the contact processes of which returning veterans are a part. In short, the tightly organized and inflexible, community-oriented and centripetal Zuni selected differently from the same stimuli than did the more loosely organized, more flexible, more outward-oriented Navaho.

Psychological structure appears to be associated with differential selection of alternatives available in culture change situations. The process can be seen as large in scope as one views the adaptations of tribes in whole culture areas to

the impact of European-American culture. But space forbids further discussion except to note a word of caution—that the *conditions* of contact are often so massively determinant that the psychological structure of the people may affect the response to contact but not the end result, as in the numerous cases in North America where forcible removal, destructive forms of religious proselyting, epidemics, or military action virtually destroyed whole societies and cultures.

Psychological Types Generated in Culture Change

Now we reverse the relationship between psychological structure and culture change described so far. We will discuss certain personality types and psychological processes generated in the melee of culture change and culture conflict. While we will draw to a large extent from our own observations of Indians we have known and studied,[18] the parallels with other situations are such that generalization is possible.

The major criteria for similarity are that a "native-oriented" or "least acculturated" category of individuals, oriented predominantly towards the traditional culture, exist in the tribal community; that varying degrees of culturally transitional states be represented; and that some individuals or groups be so acculturated to white norms that they are potentially capable of being assimilated into the contemporary American social and occupational structure. These con-

[17] John Adair and Evon Vogt, "Navaho and Zuni Veterans: A Study of Contrasting Modes of Culture Change," *American Anthropologist*, Vol. 51, No. 4 (1949), pp. 547–561.

[18] The authors' major field work has been done with the Menominee. We have also made excursions of short duration to Chippewa reservations in Wisconsin, did a brief psychological study of Winnebago Peyotists in 1954, and visited the Walker River Paiute, and Eastern Pueblo peoples. Statements concerning Menominee personality are based on analysis of Rorschach tests, autobiographies, interviews, and participant observation.

ditions obtain in varying degrees and with unique ramifications on many, but not all, Indian reservations in this country.[19] In some cases whole tribal communities fall into one or another of these acculturative categories. The Western Pueblos, for example, can be considered native-oriented societies. And the Southern Ute appear to function, as a whole, at an apathetic, disorganized, transitional level of adaptation.[20] With this introduction, we will sketch some of the psychological types, representing kinds of personal-social adaptation to the conditions of life brought about by the impact of European-American culture upon American Indians.

Native Type

This type was raised as an Indian, had only marginal contacts with whites and white culture, and lives in a world perceived and patterned by the symbols and motivation of the traditional culture. He thinks and acts Indian, and speaks as one in both a figurative and literal sense. He will represent the modal, aboriginal personality type of whatever tribal group he is a member. As a Menominee, his emotional and intellectual range is limited without being attenuated, his emotional balance highly controlled without being constricted. He is sensitive to others' feelings, but not imputative. He accepts the dictates of fate, retains equanimity under duress, and achieves control under provocation. He avoids any action that will arouse another's anger or hostility, partly because he fears retaliation in the form of sorcery. His fantasy life is active and functions within a world where men and

[19] See, for example, F. Voget, "Crow Socio-Cultural Groups," in: Tax (Ed.), *op. cit.* (note 13 *supra*), pp. 88–93; and E. Bruner, *op. cit.* (note 11 *supra*).

[20] As described by O. C. Stewart, "Southern Ute Adjustment to Modern Living," in: Tax (Ed.), *op. cit.* (note 13 *supra*), pp. 80–87.

animals transform into each other, and where dreams provide inspiration and guidance drawn from the pool of supernatural power in which all beings and objects float. His personality is adequate within the traditional setting, but he is quite unequipped, psychologically and technologically, for competition in the modern socioeconomic system. He is aware of this, and is nostalgic for the life of the past, but regretfully comprehends the futility of wishing for its return. Almost by definition he is aged, and as an elder he constitutes part of the slim stock of leadership stemming from the past and providing continuity for the native-oriented group. With him, the ancient culture will die in its comparatively vigorous and comprehensible form.

Reaffirmative Native Type

This type is usually represented by younger men. He was raised Indian, and frequently by grandparents, but has experienced comparatively wide and intensive contact with white culture through years of boarding school, intermittent occupation with the white economic system, and usually has traveled outside the reservation. For one reason or another he encountered blocks in his adaptation to white culture, and may not have been strongly motivated to adapt in the first place. He has rebounded from white culture back to the tradition-oriented primary group maintained by geographical isolation and the influence of elders within the reservation community. His psychological position is, therefore, different from that of the first type, even though he is a member of the same primary group. He has some doubts about the traditional culture that he has to submerge by compensatory and self-conscious identification with the native-oriented group. Because of this, for him the native-oriented group and its affirmation in ceremonial form assumes some of the character of a "nativistic" movement.[21] He is ambivalent about whites and white culture, and unlike the elder, has some doubts about his personal adequacy in the Indian as well as in the white man's world. His personality, however, is modally like that of the native type, but clouded by his doubts and ambivalence, distorted somewhat by his compensations, and attenuated in some degree through cultural loss, since he has learned no one culture fully. This type probably constitutes the largest portion of most native-oriented groups existing in contemporary reservation communities.

Transitional Types

In one sense all Indians are in transition. Here we are referring to the types of individuals who are clearly suspended between the white and Indian ways of life, and are not identified strongly with either native-oriented or acculturated social primary groups. They are marginal men. There is no one transitional type, even in this restricted sense. But all of the discernible types are marked by at least one feature held in common; they are, as Hallowell concluded for the Ojibwa, still fundamentally Indians in basic psychological structure, even though this structure is badly corroded by regressive breakdown. The breakdown, among Menominee at least, is represented particularly in loss of emotional controls that are so important in the traditional setting, in a reduction of active fantasy life, and in the development of marked anxieties accompanied by outbursts of overt and sometimes very destructive hostility. These transitional people are unpredictable. They are capable of great generosity and hospitality and are also capable of dangerous violence, particularly when drinking —and they drink frequently. They are the unknown quotient in tribal decision-making and shift abruptly from one stance to another in general councils where problems of tribal policy are thrashed out. Since they constitute a sizable portion of most tribes today, their psychology must be taken into account in attempts to develop rational and progressive withdrawal programs designed to eventuate in completely independent status.

More space would allow us to describe the variants in transitional type. We can only note that the unpredictable, aggressive type probably represents the majority, but that passively withdrawn, and acculturation-oriented types also exist in significant numbers. One has given up and is vegetating; the other has set his sights on achievement in white terms and is trying to acquire the necessary techniques, with varying degrees of success.

A Special Deviant Type

In many reservation communities there exist various special religious bodies such as the Peyote Cult or Shaker Church.[22] These groups and the religious observances associated with them constitute a variant solution to the problems of culture conflict and self-doubt engendered by the culture change situation. They provide, through the primary groups they make available, a social reference point for the free-floating, marginal individual. They also provide a more or less coherent rationalization of the culture conflict itself, since in their religious observances and the premises behind them, white and Indian patterns of belief and behavior are intermingled.

The Peyotists among the Menominee represent, modally, a particular personality configuration. They exhibit a high de-

[21] The literature on "nativistic movements" is extensive. For recent analyses, see F. W. Voget, "The American Indian in Transition: Reformulation and Accommodation," *American Anthropologist*, Vol. 58, No. 2 (1956), pp. 249–263, and A. F. C. Wallace, "Revitalization Movements," *Ibid.*, pp. 264–281.

[22] Voget and Wallace, *Ibid.*; and G. D. Spindler, "Personality and Peyotism in Menomini Indian Acculturation," *Psychiatry*, Vol. 15, No. 2 (May 1952), pp. 151–159.

gree of self-involvement in their fantasy life, retrospect about their past lives, ruminate about their sins and about the hope of salvation, and are preoccupied with the symbols and meanings of Peyote ritual and rationale. They are anxious people, who introspect rather than project their anxieties in outbursts of violence. Though they exhibit a certain "schizoid" tendency in their intense self-concern and introspection, they are sufficiently reality-centered to earn a living and live lives that on the whole are better ordered than those of the ungrouped transitionals, with whom they share the experience of cultural disorganization and culture conflict.

Though the Shaker Church and other similar institutions are not directly comparable to the Peyote Cult in commandment or ceremonial, they satisfy many of the same needs in culture change among American Indians and may therefore be selective of, and support, some of the same personality traits, it is hypothesized.

Acculturated Types

Acculturation processes among American Indians do not necessarily eventuate in the emergence of middle-class American personalities or culture patterns, even when they run full course. Acculturative adaptation may occur to a middle-class standard, a laboring class pattern, or move in the direction of the cultural norms and values of variant local subgroups with whom Indians come into contact. Therefore, acculturated psychological types are not all the same.

We will describe a personality type that is represented modally among elite acculturated Menominee Indians who have adapted to a middle-class socio-economic and cultural pattern of norms. This acculturated type does not display the stoic control of emotions characteristic of the native type, nor does it exhibit the anxiety and unpredictable hostility of the transitional type, nor the self-involvement

and search for resolution of personal and cultural conflict of the Peyotists. In the psychological constellation of this type, emotions and aggressions are highly channelized toward the achievement of success, exhibited in economic and occupational attainments and the accumulation of property. Anxiety is present, but is integrated with the personality structure as generalized tension, which helps make the individual quick to respond and keeps him moving toward his goals. The range of intellectual interests is comparatively broad and the fantasy life vigorous, but not particularly introspective. In short, this type is the achievement-oriented middle-class American personality. It constitutes a marked psychological departure in the Menominee continuum of adaptations and requires a dramatic rechannelizing of energies and capacities. It is probably not represented in many reservation communities today, for when a person reaches this state in most situations, he leaves the reservation and is assimilated into the American social structure. The rewards at home must be high to keep him there.

Psychological Differences Between Males and Females

We have written as though all psychological types were males. This has been a necessary convenience, but the matter cannot be left there. Women, among the Menominee, exhibit consistent, over-all, differences from the men, in psychological adaptation to the exigencies of culture change. They are less anxious, less tense, react more quickly in problem-solving situations, exhibit less loss of emotional control, are more limited in intellectual interests and experience, and are less introspective.[23] The women also exhibit

[23] These statements are based on statistical tests of difference applied to male-female Rorschach scores and to comparative analyses of autobiographies. See L. S. Spindler (Mary L.), "Women and Culture Change: A Case

more consistent retentions of basic Menominee values through all levels of acculturation than do the men. These differences seem to be accounted for in part by the fact that the basic roles of women as mothers, wives, and social participants change less than do the subsistence-based and more public roles of men, so that the past and the present have greater continuity for women.

As a consequence of these significant and consistent differences, Menominee women within each acculturative category in the

---

Study of the Menomini Indians," unpublished Ph.D. dissertation, Stanford University, 1956, for these data and further analysis of psychological adaptations among Menominee Indian women.

reservation community exhibit psychological adaptations somewhat different from those of men in the same categories. Most of the intracategory differences can be traced to the greater continuity of women's roles and express various permutations of the over-all differences in psychological structure and value retention stated above. But limitations of space prevent further discussion.

To what extent the male/female differences in psychological adaptation to culture change exhibited among the Menominee are present in other tribal communities is an open question. Data available for a number of Indian tribes suggest that fairly wide generalization may be possible.

PART FOUR

Personality System as Source
of Independent Variables and
Social System Variables as Dependent

PART Three dealt with the influence of social variables on personality; this section presents articles illustrating the impact of personality variables on social variables. The ways that the latter process unfolds are diverse. Personality variables can influence the *direction* of group processes—its productivity, its playfulness, or its creativity. They can also influence the *style* of a group structure—its mode of communication, its cohesiveness, its disharmony, or its disintegration. Personality variables can also *alter* the formation or development of a group structure, for example when new aspirations or disenchantments of the group members emerge. Sometimes the particular *content* of a personality variable is the critical factor in affecting social processes, for example when different intellectual capacities of students come into contact with a teacher's expectations regarding the performance of the class.

Part Four begins with selections from small-group research; each of these studies examines the relation of selected personality variables to the structure of a temporary group formation (rather than a more permanent social system, such as a bureaucracy or a family). Next we organize the selections according to the life cycle of the individual, taking up in turn the impact of personality variables on the family, the school, and adult roles. At the end of Part Four we include a few items that deal with the influence of personality on social change.

Small-group studies are able to isolate (experimentally and statistically) both personality variables and the resultant social interaction, but there are definite limits to generalizing the findings of such studies, since it is possible to sample only a limited range of both personality and social variables. In small-group experiments, the investigator usually takes a very active part in posing his questions; he manipulates the conditions of interaction so that he can ascertain the impact of personalities on social behavior. Arthur Cohen investigates the influence of different psychosexual defenses of individuals (personality variable) on patterns of interaction (social variable). One of his general findings is that the interacting individuals who share a specific psychosexual disturbance experience a more negative relationship than paired subjects who do not share these disturbances. Edgar Borgatta et al. posit three different personality factors an individual must possess in order to become and remain a group leader. This study has the virtue of employing repeated measurements across time, so that a measure of the consistency of the impact of the leader on the group is given. Personality measures are not included for all the participants—as in the Cohen article—yet the presence of an effective leader is clearly related to differences between groups.

In contrast to the two small-group articles, the selections by Marian Yarrow et al. and Joan Jackson use as their independent variable *classes* of personality structures (the institutionalized and the alcoholic) instead of defining personality in terms of *specific* personality levels or dimensions (e.g., defenses, intellectual functioning, impulses). The impact of these personalities on the immediate family is then examined. The Jackson article contains a detailed account of the process of family members' adjustment to the alcoholic male; Yarrow et al. are concerned not only with the meaning of mental illness of a family member but also with the family's perception of its status in the community after the hospitalization of the adult male. Both these studies illustrate the selective patterns of communication that develop when a group or community is confronted with a "deviant." William Gnagey's article also studies (under more controlled but less representative conditions) the impact of a deviant's behavior on students' perception of the teacher's effectiveness in a classroom. The importance of individual assertiveness in the teacher's leadership and control reminds us of the findings of the article by Borgatta et al.

Next we turn to the ways in which personality affects the choice of adult roles and behavior in these roles. We first include a theoretical article by Daniel Levinson, who postulates *personal* role definition as a concept that links personality and social structure. His article bears directly on Guy Swanson's article, which is concerned with the personality dynamics operating to influence choice and participation in different occupations within a newspaper organization. Swanson does not concern himself with the possible incongruities between the instinctual demands of the worker and the formal requirements of the specific job, but rather maintains that the impulses expressed through activities of the work afford gratification for various psychosexual defenses and stages of development. Combining Levinson's and Swanson's emphases we might say that personal role definition is a mediator between the structural demands of an organizational role and the motivational demands of the individual. As a construct, then, personal role definition resembles Freud's characterization of the ego.

Levinson's article is also relevant to the empirical study of voting behavior by Morris Janowitz and Dwaine Marvick, who link the predispositions of the authoritarian personality to his relations with others (roles) and to his political behavior and attitudes. Robert Lane posits a theoretical model of different political roles, employing Riesman's taxonomy (among others) of personality types to explain and predict the formation of political factions. One of Lane's central theses is that the structure of a political organization is in part a function of the distribution of personality types within that organization.

We conclude Part Four with selections concerning the effects of personality on social change. Using anthropological studies of two native cultures, Edward Bruner advances the hypothesis that those values learned earliest in life are most resistant to change from social and cultural pressures. Ross Stagner, by contrast, does not rely on a genetic description of personality to explain the course of social conflicts and changes. He posits hostility, perceptual distortion, and generalization as personality variables that contribute to continued international misunderstanding and conflict. His emphasis on the notion of perceptual generalization is similar to Janowitz and Marvick's assertion that individuals employ a characteristic reaction pattern to a wide array of social situations.

John Atkinson and Bert Hoselitz set forth a programmatic research article on the role of achievement, affiliation and power motives of entrepeneurs in different institutional settings. They ask (and

offer research designs to answer) a fundamental question: What are the personality dynamics of leaders in industry who innovate change? Herbert Krugman concerns himself with the personality factors in individuals who are attracted to a political movement that advocates radical change. His analysis, based on interviews, suggests that many who join the Communist Party are attempting to resolve what Erik Erikson has termed the "identity crisis." [1]

[1] Erik Homburger Erikson, "The Problem of Ego Identity," *Journal of the American Psychoanalytic Association,* IV (1956), 56–121.

A · SMALL-GROUP RESEARCH
AND ITS IMPLICATIONS

1 · Cooperation

EXPERIMENTAL EFFECTS OF EGO-DEFENSE PREFERENCE
ON INTERPERSONAL RELATIONS

by Arthur R. Cohen

A central issue of contemporary social science has to do with the interrelationships between personality and social interaction. One important aspect of this problem is concerned with the quality of the interpersonal relations among different kinds of people. The present experiment is an attempt to relate the personality defenses of interacting individuals to a range of perceptions they may have concerning their interaction.

According to the most general dynamic interpretation, defenses are ways of handling unacceptable impulses which are striving for expression. The question may be by-passed as to whether they are successful or unsuccessful by viewing them as enabling the individual to function in the social world by turning his unacceptable impulses to channels of expression other than direct ones. Fenichel (6) distinguishes a number of ego defenses, among which the following were selected for study: projection, regression, reaction formation, avoidance (the repression-denial family), and intellectualization (a form of isolation).

SOURCE: *Journal of Abnormal and Social Psychology*, Vol. 52 (1956), pp. 19–27.

Individuals may differ in their disturbances related to various stages of psychosexual development and in the intensity of these disturbances. They may also differ, and differ independently, in their characteristic mode of defense against these disturbing impulses. Thus, each of the various psychosexual disturbances may be associated in a variety of individuals with each of the various defense patterns. Given two individuals with a disturbance in the same psychosexual area, their preferred defense in this area may be the same or quite different. Both may handle intense oral strivings, for example, by avoidance, or one may use reaction formation while the other projects his oral strivings.

At least in theory these defense patterns should influence interaction. If, for instance, the two individuals with oral disturbance are interacting and their oral strivings are aroused, their patterns of defense should have direct implications for the way they behave toward each other. Two avoiders may both bury their disturbing oral strivings and reach an amicable relationship with relative ease. On the other hand, if one avoids expression by reaction formation and the other expresses it by intellectualizing (i.e., by bringing up the oral strivings in discussion and isolating the affect connected with them), these two should develop a relatively tense and mutually hostile relationship. The simplest deductions from such reasoning would state that if the interaction of two persons centers around a psychosexual disturbance which they share, then similarity of defense should generate a different sort of relationship from that generated by dissimilar defense patterns.

It is also possible that certain dissimilar defenses, if complementary, could lead to a good deal of solidarity between two persons, whereas certain similar ones might produce considerable conflict. In this latter connection, psychoanalytic theory suggests that projection is particularly applicable. Freud (7) defines projection as the attribution to the external world of impulses unacceptable to the ego. If two people interact and both tend to project the same unacceptable, disturbing impulses, a potentially explosive relationship can be anticipated if these impulses are aroused by the content of their interaction. Both may be expected to express the disturbance and project it, each attributing his unacceptable impulse to the other, fighting against this impulse in the other, and tossing it back and forth in this fashion as long as the interaction continues in this context. These considerations generate the following major hypothesis: when two people who share a common psychosexual disturbance, which they tend to defend against by means of projection, interact concerning content which arouses this disturbance, they will experience more negative affect in their relationship than will people who share a psychosexual disturbance, but have differing defenses associated with that disturbance.

It may be (at least with regard to projection) that a characterization of defenses in interaction as congenial or uncongenial would be more accurate. Defenses might then be viewed as congenial or uncongenial whether they are similar or dissimilar. It should be noted that the concept of congeniality or uncongeniality of defense as it is discussed here is different from that of compatibility or incompatibility of defenses within a given person's hierarchy of defenses. Here the interactive factor is stressed: the congeniality or uncongeniality of defenses of two individuals who are involved in a specified social relationship.

The hostile or negative interactions which are expected to ensue when defenses are uncongenial are of a variety of orders, all stemming from a conception of threat in interpersonal relationships (3). When the two persons threaten one another, they may: (a) be relatively unattracted to the relationship, to the other person, and to the task around which they interact; (b) perceive the other as hostile, unfriendly, as not giving them social support, and as self-centered; (c) develop a negative self picture and feel that their partner is attempting to exert influence upon them; and (d) be unmotivated in the situation and disposed to avoid such situations in the future. Of course, all persons with uncongenial defenses may not respond in all these possible ways, but in general, the uncongenials may be expected to do so in this manner more than the congenials.

Method

To test the hypotheses suggested above, a research design was developed that: (a) provided for the interaction of persons with common conflicts and given defenses associated with those conflicts, (b) experimentally aroused the conflict, (c) focused the content of the interaction around the conflict, and (d) measured the individual's perception of a variety of aspects of that interaction.

The procedure and rationale for determining the degree and areas of psychosexual disturbance for each S and the nature of the defenses associated with his disturbances have been fully reported else-where (2). Here it will be sufficient to note that the Blacky Pictures, developed by Blum (1), were used to assess psychosexual conflicts. The Blacky test is a modified projective device consisting of a series of eleven pictures which can be shown to in-dividuals or groups. Each picture is geared to a major object relationship treated by psychoanalytic theory. From the S's re-sponses to the pictures, one may derive a series of scores indicating the degree of disturbance in such areas as oral, anal, oedipal, love object, superego, and so forth.

The major source of data for the assess-ment of defense was the Defense Prefer-ence Inquiry (DPI) for the Blacky Pic-tures. Some additional procedures were also used to assess defense but they were of relatively minor importance. The DPI taps defensive reactions to psychosexual stimuli in an indirect manner by having the S judge a series of alternatives in terms of the degree to which they represent the way "Blacky seems to be feeling or acting" in a particular picture (8). This encourages the S to identify with Blacky and thereby reveal his own personal reactions. Each alternative is an operational definition of a defense mechanism. The subject is asked to rank-order a given set of alternatives for each psychosexual dimension in a very short time, thus facilitating spontaneity of response.

For each S, then, a catalogue of his psy-chosexual disturbances and associated de-fenses was obtained. The next task was to group the Ss in some arrangement that would allow the testing of the hypotheses as well as maximize the possibility for new and unexpected findings. It was decided to confine the interaction to two people; pairs are the simplest interpersonal model and in addition are relatively easy to manipulate experimentally. The design also called for limitation of interaction to people paired on the basis of the same psychosexual dimension, thereby control-ling the variability which might result

from differences in area of disturbance.

The main criterion for pairing was di-rectly geared to the hypotheses of the study. The main hypothesis specified a difference between pairs of projectors and other pairs, and the secondary one a dif-ference between similar and dissimilar de-fenders. Therefore three general types of pairs were decided upon: pairs of projec-tors, pairs of other similars of all kinds, and pairs of dissimilars of all kinds.

Since the experimental arrangement provided an opportunity for testing the effects of such other factors as dimension and intensity of psychosexual conflict, these became additional criteria for pair-ing. Five dimensions were chosen; the choices were determined by the represent-atives of the dimension in psychosexual chronology as well as by its availability in the experimental population. For some dimensions, there were very few Ss who had a given degree of conflict and an associated defense, and this precluded their use. The five psychosexual dimen-sions decided upon were: oral sadism, anal expulsiveness, oedipal intensity, cas-tration anxiety, and sibling rivalry. Each S was used just once; he was paired with his partner on the basis of one of these dimensions, and one only.

Furthermore, each S had a certain de-gree of disturbance on the dimension on which he was paired. Some people had relatively little (indicated by 0) and others had a relatively intense disturbance (indi-cated by +). The projector, similar and dissimilar pairs were arranged so that in some cases both partners would have a high degree of disturbance (+, +) on the psychosexual dimension on which they were paired. In other cases, both partners had relatively little disturbance (0, 0). In still others one had a high degree of dis-turbance and the other relatively little (+, 0).

The final and limiting criterion for pairing was a sociometric one. No two Ss were paired if they had indicated one an-other as friends in a preliminary sociometric questionnaire. This procedure allowed some control over the effect of prior attitudes and past contacts.

The complete pairing arrangement for all Ss is given in Table 1.[1] Av designates avoidance; RF, reaction formation; Rg, regression; P, projection; and I, intellectualization.

of a pair taking a seat directly behind his partner.

The general experimental manipulations involved the following sequence:

1. *The creation of a state of high motivation in the subjects.* The Ss were told that they would be asked to interpret some

TABLE 1. *Arrangement of Experimental Pairs across Psychosexual Dimensions, Intensity of Conflict, and Type of Defense Preference*

PSYCHOSEXUAL DIMENSION	SIMILAR DEFENSES (BOTH HAVE +)	SIMILAR DEFENSES (BOTH HAVE 0)	SIMILAR DEFENSES (ONE HAS +, THE OTHER 0)	DISSIMILAR DEFENSES (BOTH HAVE +)
1. Oral sadism	+Av, +Av		+P, 0P	+Av, +Rg
	+RF, +RF		+P, 0P	
	+Rg, +Rg			
2. Anal expulsiveness		0RF, 0RF	+RF, 0RF	+RF, +Rg
		0RF, 0RF		+Av, +I
3. Oedipal intensity	+Av, +Av			+P, +Rg
				+P, +RF
4. Castration anxiety	+Av, +Av		+P, 0P	+Av, +I
5. Sibling rivalry	+P, +P		+Rg, 0Rg	+P, +Rg
	+P, +P		+RF, 0RF	

SUBJECTS. The Ss were 44 undergraduate members of a social fraternity at the University of Michigan who had made themselves available for a large program of testing and experimentation in connection with the psychoanalytic theory project. They were extremely homogeneous with regard to their interests and their educational, ethnic, and socioeconomic backgrounds.

PROCEDURE. The Ss were run in three large groups of 16, 20, and 8. The experimental setting for all groups was a rather large lecture hall over which the Ss were told to spread out in pairs, one member

[1] It should be noted that the possibilities for pairing were quite limited by the size of the sample on whom the personality assessments were obtained.

brief descriptions of the behavior of some individuals. The importance of the task as an index of sensitivity and intelligence was impressed upon them and they were emphatically urged to try as hard as they could to do well. They were also told that the experimenter was very interested in their performance.

2. *The arousal of the psychosexual disturbance in each partner separately so that the defenses associated with the disturbance would be stimulated.* Each S was given a series of written stories concerned with the psychosexual dimension on which he was paired. For each dimension three stories calculated to tap the disturbance were provided. One located the particular disturbance in a home context, one in a school context, and one in the context of a social group. This was

done because a representative selection of experiences seemed more likely to arouse the disturbance and stimulate the defense.

3. *The heightening of the disturbance by the motive interpretation class.* After the S had read the three conflict-arousal

S's known psychosexual disturbance, his disturbance was expected to be heightened and the associated defense stimulated. The motive interpretation blank contained two questions: "Why do you think _____ acted this way in this situation?" and

TABLE 2. *Projector Pairs versus Other Defense Pairs (Similar and Dissimilar) for Each Dependent Item*

DEPENDENT ITEMS	MEAN OF ALL INDIVIDUALS IN SIMILAR PAIRS $(++, +0, 00)$ $(N = 20)$	p VALUE OF DIFFERENCE BETWEEN SIMILARS AND PROJECTORS	MEAN OF ALL INDIVIDUALS IN PAIRS OF PROJECTORS $(++, +0)$ $(N = 10)$	p VALUE OF DIFFERENCE BETWEEN DISSIMILARS AND PROJECTORS	MEAN OF ALL INDIVIDUALS IN DISSIMILAR $(++)$ PAIRS $(N = 14)$
1. Attraction to interpersonal situation	9.1	<.001	5.6	<.001	9.3
2. Attraction to task	5.3	.08	4.2	.08	5.2
3. Attraction to other	10.3	<.001	6.4	<.001	9.4
4. Perceived success of team	4.6	<.001	3.0	<.001	4.9
5. Perception of individual success	4.1	ns	4.1	ns	4.4
6. Perception of others' success	3.4	.05	3.0	<.05	3.6
7. Perception of social support	4.2	.03	3.3	.05	3.8
8. Perception of partner's hostility	6.1	<.001	4.2	<.01	5.5
9. Perception of partner's self-interest	4.1	<.01	2.8	<.01	4.0
10. Security in relationship	5.6	<.001	3.5	<.001	5.9
11. Partner's attempted influence	5.3	.05	4.0	.04	5.3
12. Own attempted influence	5.0	<.01	3.2	<.01	5.5
13. Perceived quality of team	6.3	<.001	3.6	<.001	6.4
14. Desire to avoid such experiences	5.4	ns	5.2	ns	5.6
15. Motivation to do well	6.3	.04	5.2	<.05	6.2
16. Desire to organize work: independent cooperative extremely cooperative dependent	0 20	<.02	4 6	<.08	0 14

stories, they were collected and he was handed an "individual motive interpretation" blank. By having him write interpretations of the behavior of the "hero" of the stories when the behavior was directly concerned with the content of the

"What do you think are the underlying personality forces behind his behavior?"

4. *Interaction of the partners: their involvement by discussion of the disturbance-arousing material.* After finishing the individual motive interpretations the part-

ners were instructed to discuss the material for 15 minutes, preparatory to writing their common interpretations. They were also apprised of the fact that observers would be watching closely to gauge the quality of their discussions. The observer device was instituted in order to keep motivation high throughout the discussions.

5. *Interaction of the partners: their further involvement by having to work together over the disturbance-arousing material.* To further heighten the interactive aspect, the Ss were asked to produce a set of joint interpretations. They were given motive interpretation blanks identical to the individual ones, except that it was indicated that this was to be a team effort.

6. *The measurement of their perception of their interaction.* The dependent measures were all assumed to tap manifestations of threat in interpersonal relations. In most cases they involved ratings by the S on a series of seven- and eight-point a priori scales. Others involved scaling devices such as "pick two," and one measure gathered the Ss' responses into simple categories. Sixteen measures in all were used; they can be seen in Table 2.

Results

PROJECTION HYPOTHESIS. The major hypothesis specified a difference between projectors and all other pairs, both similar and dissimilar. Projectors were expected to have more negative and hostile interpersonal relationships than other pairs. The results confirm this hypothesis, as shown in Table 2. In this table, the mean response on each dependent item for the Ss who experienced the three main experimental arrangements is given; the lower the mean the more negative the interaction. The projector pairs are given in the middle column, with the dissimilars and similars on either side. The p values for the significance of the difference between the two other conditions and the

projectors are given in the two columns between the three conditions. The t test was used on all measures but the last one, where the Exact test was employed.

The results show that the pairs of projectors are far more negative concerning their interaction than are those whose defenses are also similar but are other than projection. They are also more negative about their interaction than are those with dissimilar defenses. On almost every index of interpersonal relations, they perceive a more hostile atmosphere than either of the other two groups. They perceive their team's success on the task to have been minimal, feel that they were members of a poor quality team, and even think that other people do not do well on such tasks. They are less attracted to the interpersonal situation in general, and to the task and to their partner specifically. They perceive less support from their partner, perceive him to be more hostile and more interested in his ideas only, and are more insecure in the relationship. They feel that he is attempting to influence them more and also that they themselves tried to exert more influence. They withdrew their motivation from the task presumably as a self-protective device. And finally, they prefer to have the work organized in a way that emphasizes more independence. These results provide verification for the major hypothesis concerning the projectors.

FURTHER EXPLORATION OF THE EFFECTS OF PROJECTION [2]

1. *Paired projectors vs. projectors paired with other defenders.* It appears that simply being a projector may not

[2] These analyses and the succeeding explorations were carried out by taking into account direction of difference, not magnitude. The comparisons between two given conditions were made by taking their means on all the dependent items and seeing which group had lower means (an indication of more hostile

lead to so much negatively laden interaction. On all 16 dependent items, the
projectors who were paired with other
projectors experience their interaction as
more negative than do the few projectors
who were paired with others of a different
defense. It may be expected then that if
one is a projector, more hostile interpersonal relationships tend to ensue when
the other person is also a projector.

2. *Effects of intensity of disturbance
within projection pairs.* The group of
paired projectors included pairs where
both had relatively high disturbance
(+ +) on the psychosexual dimension on
which they were paired and pairs where
one partner had high disturbance and the
other low (+ 0). The data show that there
is a trend for the pairs where both have
high disturbance to perceive a more hostile interrelationship than the pairs where
one partner is relatively disturbance-free.
The +, + group reported more negative
interaction on 10 out of the 16 items, the
+, 0 group on four. They were equal in
threat on two measures. It seems that even
among the projector pairs, those with more
disturbance tend to have more negative
interaction.

3. *Effects of intensity of disturbance in
projector pairs vs. pairs of other defenders.*
This comparison was made to check on
the possibility that it was only the projector pairs where both partners were highly

_____

interaction). By pointing to trends in this
manner, it was possible to isolate some of
the more specific conditions of defense and
disturbance under which negative interpersonal relationships take place. The important
point here is the consistency of the trends;
the preponderance of means indicating more
negative interaction among certain groups
suggests that the given group may be behaving differently from another group and
that this difference is meaningful. *p* values
for sign tests could be given here but it was
felt that the question of the independence of
measures of interaction could be raised.
Therefore, the more conservative course of
inspecting the distribution of means was
taken.

disturbed which caused the entire projector group to be more negative. Accordingly, the pairs where only one member
had a high degree of psychosexual disturbance were compared with all other
groups where only one member was highly
disturbed. The trends suggest that the
paired projectors where only one partner
has a high degree of psychosexual disturbance have more hostile interaction
(more threat on 11 items) than do other
pairs where only one partner is relatively
disturbed (more threat on four items; one
tie). Thus, though the former are less
threat-oriented than the pairs where both
projector partners are relatively disturbed,
they still are more so than the rest of the
population.

4. *Projectors paired with other defenders vs. dissimilar defender pairs excluding
projectors.* Finally, an exploration was
undertaken of the difference between the
projectors who were paired with someone
else and other members of dissimilar pairs
to see if projection alone led to negative
interaction. The data indicate that the
projectors when not paired with other
projectors are not more threat-oriented
than other dissimilar pairs.

It was seen earlier that paired projectors have more negatively toned interaction than other similar and dissimilar
pairs of all kinds. The data which followed suggest further that it may not be
projection alone, but being paired with
another projector which makes the difference. The pairs tend to be more negative
than those who are alone, and the latter
are not more negative than other people
who do not have partners with identical
defenses. Furthermore, there appear to be
differences even among the paired projectors: when both partners have a high degree of psychosexual disturbance, more
threat tends to be produced than when
only one is highly disturbed. Finally,
paired projectors with one having high
disturbance are more negative in their
perceptions than are pairs of other defenses where only one partner is disturbed.

SIMILARITY - DISSIMILARITY HYPOTHESIS. The possibility was also raised that people with dissimilar defenses associated with a common psychosexual disturbance might perceive their interaction differently from those with similar defenses. Accordingly, all those pairs with similar defenses (except for projectors) were compared with those with dissimilar defenses on each of the 16 dependent measures. The means for the similar group are given in Table 2, column 1, for the dissimilars in Table 2, column 5. When these comparisons were made, no differences what-

people who received oral sadism stories and those who received anal expulsiveness stories, oral sadism stories versus oedipal stories, and so on.[3] Ten comparisons were made; every dimension with every other, using the sign test model. They are too lengthy to be reported here in full and may be summarized.

Briefly, the dimensions can be ordered according to the degree to which people paired on them experienced negative interpersonal relationships when interacting around relevant disturbing material. It appears that those paired on sibling ri-

TABLE 3. *Comparison of Various Defense Pairs with Each Other*

(Projection, N = 10; Regression, N = 4; Reaction Formation, N = 10; Avoidance, N = 6)

PROJECTION VS. ALL OTHERS	NO. OF DE-PENDENT ITEMS	REGRESSION VS. OTHERS	NO. OF DE-PENDENT ITEMS	REACTION FORMATION VS. AVOIDANCE	NO. OF DE-PENDENT ITEMS
P's show more threat	16	Rg's show more threat	14	RF's show more threat	14
Av's show more threat	0	Av's show more threat	2	Av's show more threat	2
P's show more threat	16	Rg's show more threat	11		
RF's show more threat	0	Rg's and RF's equal	1		
		RF's show more threat	4		
P's show more threat	13				
P's and and Rg's equal	1				
Rg's show more threat	2				

soever were found; both groups perceived their interaction to have been relatively smooth and rewarding.

FURTHER EXPLORATIONS OF DISTURBANCE AND DEFENSE

1. *Comparison among Blacky dimensions in terms of perceived negative interaction.* Of further interest were the differences between people who were paired on the basis of different psychosexual dimensions. Disregarding specific defense and intensity of disturbance, one may also explore the effects of the various dimensions themselves. Comparisons on the 16 dependent items were made between those

valry had the most negatively toned interaction, compared with those people who were paired on the other four dimensions. On the other hand, pairing on oedipal intensity was related to the least threat-oriented interaction. The order determined by these 10 comparisons was as follows, from most negative to most positive:

1. Sibling rivalry
2. Castration anxiety
3. Oral sadism
4. Anal expulsiveness
5. Oedipal intensity

[3] The N's on these dimensions are: sibling rivalry, 10; and expulsiveness, 10; oral sadism, 12; oedipal intensity, 6; castration anxiety, 6.

Of course, the dimensions in the middle range shade into one another, but at the extremes the dimensions are clearly different in their evocation of interpersonal hostility. It may also be that the projector pairs are responsible for the negative effect of the sibling rivalry dimension since two pairs fall in this area. However, it is quite possible that sibling rivalry occupies the place it does in the hierarchy independently of projection. This is an interpersonal situation where two undergraduate peers are interacting around disturbing sibling rivalry content.[4]

2. *Hierarchy of defense preference according to perceived negative interaction.* Table 3 summarizes the comparisons made between the different types of defense pairs. In this analysis only pairs of similars were used; there were too few different types of dissimilars to permit their exploration. Intellectualization was omitted because there were no similar pairs using this defense.

[4] The question may also be raised as to the general effect of sibling rivalry. Is it possible that just having sibling rivalry may lead the individual to experience his relations with a peer as negative? If this is true, then perhaps it is disturbance on the dimension of sibling rivalry and not a projector paired with another projector which is generating differences in the perception of interaction. To answer this question, a differentiated analysis of sibling rivalry was undertaken. These results show that the mere presence of sibling rivalry does not seem to account for the differences found previously. It appears that those who had a disturbance on the dimension and also interacted around disturbance-arousing sibling rivalry material were more negative concerning their interaction than those who did not receive the stimulus, whether they had the disturbance or not. On the other hand, those who had the disturbances and did not get the sibling rivalry stories were no different from those who were free from sibling rivalry problems and did not get these stories. It may be said then that disturbance on this dimension is meaningful only when there has been some arousal of the disturbance.

The data strongly suggest a hierarchy of defenses in terms of their effect on the perception of interpersonal relationships. Pairs of projectors appear to be more negative concerning their interaction than pairs who had other defenses associated with psychosexual disturbances. This reflects the confirmation of the main hypothesis. Furthermore, regression appears to bring more negative interaction than reaction formation and avoidance, and reaction formation itself more than avoidance. The order is as follows from most negative to most positive:

1. Projection
2. Regression
3. Reaction formation
4. Avoidance

Thus, it appears that among people whose interaction is colored by a common psychosexual disturbance and who have similar defenses associated with that disturbance, there are distinct differences depending upon the defense. In general the defenses which stress the avoidance of an unacceptable impulse (avoidance and reaction formation) generate more cohesive interaction than those which permit the impulse to gain some sort of expression (projection and regression).

Discussion

The results of this investigation raise a number of interesting problems. It was seen that the hypothesis regarding the interaction of projectors was confirmed. The reasoning behind this hypothesis assumed that projectors in interaction around disturbing material would keep it in the open as a source of constant anxiety, thereby generating hostile interpersonal relationships. The person who uses projection (as well as any other defense) in conjunction with a given psychosexual disturbance is fighting against an unacceptable impulse. In the present situation he is in interaction with a partner who gives him a perfect opportunity for fighting the impulse by having it himself. And since the projector's characteristic mode of warding off unacceptable impulses is to perceive them in another person, the other person may become the symbol of these impulses. In effect, the projector may be said to fight against the impulse by fighting the other member of the pair.

Fenichel notes that the paranoid person who uses projection "is sensitized, as it were, to perceive the unconscious of others, wherever this perception can be utilized to rationalize his own tendency toward projection" (6, p. 147). The present experimental situation made it relatively easy for an individual to see his own unacceptable impulses in the other person, and to react negatively to them. This was expected, and found, to be easiest for the projected pairs, where the same processes obtained for both partners. In this manner, a mutually hostile interpersonal relationship was generated.

This line of reasoning also permits an explanation of some of the additional findings concerning projection. It was seen that more negative interaction resulted when both partners were projectors than when only one member of a pair used this defense. Here, of course, the fact that both partners are behaving in the fashion described above tends to increase the interpersonal conflict; when only one partner behaves this way, he may not receive so much additional support for his behavior through his partner's actions.

One may also view in this light the finding that more negative interaction ensues when both projector partners have a high degree of psychosexual disturbance than when only one member of the pair is highly disturbed. What may be happening here is that the defense of projection is not operating too effectively for the highly disturbed people and they may be driven to this interpersonal conflict as a way of working out the defense. It may

also be that when both partners have strong conflict the interaction will produce more expressions of the unacceptable impulse, thereby increasing the threat and the hostility and facilitating further projection. When both partners are engaged in such a struggle, the conflict may be raised to a higher pitch than when only one acts in this manner. It should be emphasized that the foregoing is largely speculative; it is, however, one way of explaining the present results.

It was also seen that while the projection hypothesis was confirmed, the secondary hypothesis concerning differences between similars and dissimilars was not. Though limited to the field of projection, the present evidence points to a theoretical position with regard to the interaction of people with given defenses which favors the congeniality-uncongeniality notion rather than that of similarity-dissimilarity. While groups of people with dissimilar and similar defenses other than projection reacted equally favorably to their experiences in this experimental situation, those groups of similars where both were projectors perceived their interaction in a more negative and threat-oriented fashion. Apparently, the use of such an expressive defense as projection by two individuals in interaction causes the maintenance and heightening of the disturbance and leads them to threaten one another. Other sorts of expressive defenses, as well as avoidance defenses which block the outlet of unacceptable impulses, whether people have them in common or in different combinations, appear to enable them to handle the disturbing material in a more efficient and rewarding manner.

The results also indicate the presence of a hierarchy of defenses with regard to perceived negative interaction among partners. The defenses associated with the most negative interaction were seen to be projection and regression in that order. These are defenses permitting the unacceptable impulse to gain an outlet. In the present situation such a mode of defense leads to many interpersonal complications. On the other hand, the avoidance mechanisms which appear to lead to smoother interaction are more easily accommodated by the experimental task. Those partners who use these defenses can avoid unpleasantness by virtue of their tendency to repress, deny or ignore disturbing material. Each, thereby, contributes to the increasing security of the other in the relationship.

Further evidence consistent with these findings is available. In a related investigation of personality and sociometric choice, within the same research project, the author (4) found that people who used projection against given disturbances underchose others who also used projection against these same disturbances. No other significant underchoices were found. In the same study, those people who used avoidance defenses were seen by their social group to be less deviant from the norms and values of that group. In addition, the use of the avoidance defenses was found (5) to be related to high self-esteem, whereas projection tended to be associated with low self-esteem. Thus, in an open friendship choice situation, and on a self-rating questionnaire, the different defenses appear to have differential consequences for social adjustment.

Summary

This experiment was designed to explore the connection between the personality defenses of interacting individuals and their attitudes toward and perceptions of their interaction. The reasoning behind the experiment assumed that two people in interaction who had a psychosexual disturbance in common would react to one another, when that disturbance was aroused, as a function of their defenses against that disturbance.

The assessment of psychosexual conflicts and ego-defense preferences specific to each individual was made prior to the experiment. The Blacky Pictures technique and its auxiliary Defence Preference Inquiry were used for this purpose. Five psychosexual dimensions were used: oral sadism, anal expulsiveness, oedipal intensity, castration anxiety, and sibling rivalry. The following defenses were studied: projection, avoidance, regression, reaction formation, and intellectualization.

The Ss were paired in terms of defense, psychosexual dimension and intensity of disturbance. The limiting criterion for pairing was a sociometric one which assured some control over the affective ties among the Ss. The basic pairs were of three kinds: pairs of projectors, pairs with similar defenses other than projection, and pairs where the defenses were dissimilar.

It was found that:

1. When in interaction involving a task which arouses a specific psychosexual disturbance they have in common, two people who tend to project this impulse will experience their interaction as more negative than pairs of people who utilize other defenses.

2. The mere presence of projection, however, may not be sufficient to lead to interpersonal hostility. Negative effects seem to be obtained only when two projectors are paired. Projectors interacting with people using other defenses tend to be no different from any other pairs having dissimilar defenses.

3. There may be differences among the pairs of projectors depending upon whether one partner or both has a high degree of psychosexual disturbance on the dimension along which they were paired. When both partners have high conflict, more negative interaction tends to result than when only one is highly disturbed.

4. Similarity or dissimilarity of defense per se appear to make no difference as far as quality of interpersonal relations is concerned.

5. Among those with similar defenses however, there appears to be a hierarchy of efficiency with regard to interpersonal relations. Pairs of avoiders reported more positive interaction than pairs of other defenses. Reaction formation was next best, regression next, and projection worst in this regard.

6. The psychosexual dimensions themselves were ordered in terms of the degree to which they stimulated negative interaction. The order from most negative to most positive was: sibling rivalry, castration anxiety, oral sadism, anal expulsiveness, and oedipal intensity.

REFERENCE

1. Blum, G. S.: "A study of the psychoanalytic theory of psychosexual development." *Genet. Psychol. Monogr.*, 1949, 39, 3–99.
2. ———.: Procedure for the assessment of conflict and defense. Unpublished manuscript, University of Michigan, 1954. (mimeographed)
3. Cohen, A. R.: Situational structure and individual self-esteem as determinants of threat-oriented reactions to power. Unpublished doctoral dissertation, University of Michigan, 1953.
4. ———.: Personality and sociometric choice. Unpublished manuscript, University of Michigan, 1954. (mimeographed)
5. ———.: Some explorations of self-esteem. Unpublished manuscript, University of Michigan, 1954. (mimeographed)
6. Fenichel, O.: *Psychoanalytic theory of neurosis.* New York: Norton, 1945.
7. Freud, S.: Psychological notes upon an autobiographical account of a case of paranoia. In *Collected papers,* London: Hogarth, 1925.
8. Goldstein, S.: A projective study of psychoanalytic mechanisms. Unpublished doctoral dissertation, University of Michigan, 1952.

2 · Leadership

SOME FINDINGS RELEVANT TO
THE GREAT MAN THEORY OF LEADERSHIP

by Edgar F. Borgatta, Robert F. Bales, and Arthur S. Couch

A central area of research and theory in social psychological science, particularly in group dynamics and small group research, is that of "leadership." The interest apparently lies in the expectation that the "effectiveness" of group performance is determined in large part by the leadership structure of the group. Effective performance is usually defined by the joint occurrence of high task accomplishment and high satisfaction of members of the group.

There are at least six types of thinking about the optimum leadership structure

SOURCE: *American Sociological Review*, Vol. 19, (1954), pp. 755–759.

of the group for effective performance. (1) The most effective group is the one which has the most adequate all-around leader ("great man"). (2) The most effective group is the one in which all members have been chosen according to ability for the specific task. (3) The most effective group is the one in which members are selected on the basis of their sociometric choices of each other as co-workers. (4) The most effective group is the one in which the various qualities of task ability and social ability are distributed among the members to allow or encourage role differentiation and division of labor. (5) The most effective group is one in which members are similar in values or some critical area of values. (6) The most effective group is the one in which members are selected primarily on the basis of compatibility of personality characteristics, such as authoritarianism, major mechanisms of defense, ascendance-submission, and the like.

Our concern here is with exploring some aspects of the first principle which we arbitrarily call the "great man theory of leadership." This is probably the oldest of the six theories and one which has received attention throughout the centuries. Such attention is understandable when one considers that history is frequently written from the reference point of "great men." It is equally understandable in terms of the implicit ease with which manipulation is possible if the organizational performance is determined by the single person in the top position. Much psychological research, assuming the great man theory, has been oriented to the problems of selecting persons who are best fitted for a top position of leadership. However, tests of the great man theory which involve the performance of groups rather than the consistency of the leader's behavior are relatively absent in the literature.

Procedure

The data to be presented, bearing on the great man theory, are based on 166 sessions of three man groups.[1] The subjects (N = 126) were male enlisted Air Force personnel assigned to the research project on temporary duty. They were recruited from different organizations, and acquaintance was minimal. The purpose of the testing was represented to the subjects as being the observation of how small groups work together, and presumably, this observation was to take place when they did some role playing. However, they were also observed in periods during which they planned the role playing session and periods of informal participation. It is these data which are analyzed in this experiment. Each of these 166 sessions was 24 minutes long. Every person participated in four sessions with two new co-participants in each session. The differences in enlisted grade were controlled by assignment of subject to session with persons of their own status.

Design

Couch and Carter [2] have demonstrated in a factor analysis of the rated behavior of individuals in group interaction that

[1] Other aspects of this research have been reported in other papers. Problems of reliability of scoring and consistency of subject performance were discussed in: E. F. Borgatta and R. F. Bales, "The Consistency of Subject Behavior and the Reliability of Scoring in Interaction Process Analysis," *American Sociological Review*, 18 (October, 1953), pp. 566–569. Problems concerning the effect of task differences of experience, and the "accumulation of a common culture" are discussed in: E. F. Borgatta and R. F. Bales, "Task and Accumulation of Experience as Factors in the Interaction of Small Groups," *Sociometry*, 16 (August, 1953), pp. 239–252. The effects of participation with various types of co-participants, and a rationale for reconstituting groups are presented in: E. F. Borgatta and R. F. Bales, "Interaction of Individuals in Reconstituted Groups," *Sociometry*, 16 (November, 1953), pp. 302–320. The relationships among sociometric measures, interaction performance, ratings by superiors, intelligence, and selected variables are discussed in: E. F. Borgatta, "Analysis of Social Interaction and Sociometric Perception," *Sociometry*, 17 (February, 1954), pp. 7–32.

[2] See: L. F. Carter, "Leadership and Small Group Behavior," in M. Sherif and M. O. Wilson, *Group Relations at the Crossroads*, New York: Harper, 1953.

three orthogonal factors account for the major portion of the variance in these ratings. The factors have been identified as: (1) *Group goal facilitation;* (2) *Individual prominence;* and (3) *Group sociability.* More simply, the factors may be identified as Task ability, Individual assertiveness, and Social acceptability. For this study, using the Couch and Carter experience, along with that accrued from other sources, we attempted to measure the factors as follows:

Factor I. *Task ability*—(a) leadership rating received from co-participants on a task criterion; (b) the I.Q. score as measured by the Science Research Associates Primary Mental Abilities.

Factor II. *Individual assertiveness*—the total activity rate of the individual in terms of the number of initiated acts per unit of time (using Bales' category system).[3]

Factor III. *Social acceptability*—the sociometric popularity as determined by choice received on a criterion of "enjoyed participation with."

It is our notion that a *great man* would need to possess each of the three independent qualities to a substantial degree. With this *fusion of qualities* the great man is able to satisfy the major role demands and personality needs of group members. In this study, we have defined the great man in terms of a product of the four measures mentioned above. The product of the scores is used rather than a sum to emphasize the requirement of a *simultaneous* occurrence of the qualities. Some sample computations of the product index used are shown in Table 1.

Great men were selected on the basis of their performance in the first session. The top eleven such persons were chosen, each participating in a separate group. That is,

[3] The observation system used was that of: R. F. Bales, *Interaction Process Analysis,* Cambridge: Addison-Wesley Press, 1950.

there was no case of two great men together in a first session. Our choice of eleven persons was arbitrary and based on the assumption that only about the top tenth of the total sample would satisfy the criterion of "greatness." In the three subsequent sessions when two great men participated together, that three man group was eliminated from the sample; this reduced our number from 33 to 25. We did this because the term "great man group" implies a group with a *single* great man as all-around leader.

Before examining other hypotheses, a point of concern for this study is whether a person who performs as a great man in the first session does so by virtue of the particular composition of his group, or whether it is a function of relatively stable characteristics of his personality which determine his "greatness" in any group in which he participates. If there is no stability in performance, our subsequent hypotheses are meaningless.

We have no post-meeting estimates of productivity or satisfaction. However, we have indices of interaction in the group which have face validity as bearing on productivity and satisfaction.

(a) For the satisfactory performance of a group in relation to a complex or general task, a large number of suggestions which are acceptable to the group must be made. An index which is a reasonable *a priori* estimate of this kind of task facilitation is the simultaneous presence of high rates of giving suggestion and showing agreement in the group as a whole. Again, for this index we use a product relationship so that both must be high in order for the index to be high. The total number of suggestions was multiplied by the total number of agreements (Bales' category 4 times category 3). This gives a rough measure of the degree to which a given group reaches consensus on proposed solutions to the task problem.

(b) A high rate of showing tension

TABLE 1. *Some Sample Factor Product Indices*

SUBJECT IDENTIFICATION	FACTOR I TASK ABILITY		FACTOR II INDIVIDUAL	FACTOR III SOCIAL	PRODUCT INDEX
(Ordered by Index)	(a) Leadership	(b) I. Q. (Percentile)	(c) Assertiveness	(d) Acceptability	(a) (b) (c) (d) (in 1,000's)
1	4	97	161	2	124.9
2	4	96	145	2	111.4
3	4	98	126	2	98.8
4	4	81	152	2	98.5
5	4	78	151	2	94.2
6	3	88	175	2	92.4
7	4	78	135	2	84.2
8	4	96	106	2	81.4
9	4	68	144	2	78.3
10	4	70	121	2	67.8
11	4	54	145	2	62.6
.					
.					
.					
102	1	4	117	2	0.9
103	3	2	94	1	0.6
104	1	4	46	2	0.4
105	1	1	99	2	0.2
106	0	8	75	0	0.0 *
107	0	1	25	1	0.0
108	0	12	16	0	0.0
.					
.					
.					

* There were twenty-one persons with a product-index of 0.

(Bales' category 11) is a fairly direct indication of difficulty in the interaction process. It is usually a sign of anxiety and withdrawal from participation by the individual. High rates of showing tension in the group are probably associated with low satisfaction, although the relationship may not be linear.

(c) An indication of a friendly atmosphere in a group is a high rate of interaction in the positive social emotional categories—showing solidarity and showing tension release. In this case, our measure is the sum of these (Bales' category 1 plus category 2), indicating the amount of warmth expressed in the group.

Hypotheses

Hypothesis 1. Great men will tend to remain great men over a series of sessions.

Hypothesis 2. Sessions in which great men participate will have a higher product rate of suggestion and agreement (index: time rate of giving suggestion times rate of giving agreement).

Hypothesis 3. Sessions in which great men participate will have lower time rates of showing tension than those in which they do not participate.

Hypothesis 4. Sessions in which great men participate will have higher time rates of showing solidarity and tension release than those in which they do not participate.

Results

Hypothesis 1. The top eleven persons (of a total sample of 123) defined by the product index of the first session were followed through the subsequent sessions, and the frequency with which they appeared within the top eleven ranks of the product index in the second, third and fourth sessions was noted. Of the eleven persons, eight were in the top ranks in the second and third sessions, and seven were still in top rank in the fourth session, which is a remarkably stable performance. This pattern, based on chi-square tests, is significant beyond .001 level. The hypothesis is emphatically supported.

The results of the remaining hypotheses are presented in Table 2.

Hypothesis 2. When the first sessions in which the great man participated were examined, it was found that they were significantly higher than the residual category of first sessions in terms of the product rate of agreement and suggestion. When subsequent sessions in which they participated were examined, it was found that the product index of agreement and suggestion for the sessions remained significantly higher than those in which the great men did not participate. The hypothesis is emphatically supported.

Hypothesis 3. Sessions from which great men were selected showed less tension than the residual first sessions as expected. The difference in the predicted direction was significant when subsequent sessions in which great men participated were compared to those in which they did not. The hypothesis is supported.

Hypothesis 4. When the first sessions in which great men participated were compared with the remaining first sessions with regard to amount of positive affect shown, it was found that the "great man" sessions were significantly higher. In the subsequent sessions, the difference remained significant. The hypothesis is emphatically supported.

TABLE 2. *Mean Rates of Interaction for Great Man Groups and Non-Great Man Groups: Identification of Great Men Based on First Session*

	Session 1	Sessions 2, 3, 4
Product rate of giving suggestion and agreement:		
Great man groups	867 (N = 11)	530 (N = 25)
Non-great man groups	566 (N = 31)	362 (N = 95)
(value of t)	(5.98) *	(2.43) *
Rate of showing tension		
Great man groups	9.4 (N = 11)	11.7 (N = 25)
Non-great man groups	14.1 (N = 31)	16.4 (N = 95)
(value of t)	(1.41)	(1.79) *
Rate of showing solidarity and tension release		
Great man groups	39.6 (N = 11)	28.6 (N = 25)
Non-great man groups	19.7 (N = 31)	22.2 (N = 95)
(value of t)	(3.98) *	(1.65) *

* $a \leq .05$, one-tail test.

Discussion

The stability with which great men, chosen on the basis of their first session performance, retain top position in subsequent groups is impressive. One is encouraged to believe that a single session may be adequate for the selection of great men.

To the extent that our hypotheses are supported, it is suggested that great men selected on the basis of their first session continue to have an influence on the relatively superior performance of the groups in which they subsequently participate.

The evidence is quite clear that those groups containing a great man have higher product-rates of giving suggestions and agreements. Insofar as one has any reason to believe that this is related to the quality of solutions, the "productivity" of these groups is likely to be increased relative to the groups without great men.

To the extent that a lack of showing tension is an indication of smooth functioning, groups with great men appear to show less inhibited response to the task situation with less anxiety and withdrawal from active participation. This may indicate greater satisfaction with the group. Further evidence of this is seen by the greater amount of positive social emotional behavior, reflecting friendly interpersonal relationships among the members of the group.

Thus, it may be said that great men tend to make "great groups" in the sense that both major factors of group performance—productivity and satisfaction of the members—are simultaneously increased.

Conclusion

In general, the great man principle of group composition appears to have much to recommend it. Further study [4] should focus on testing some of the underlying assumptions of the various principles of group composition, especially in terms of the differential effect of the leadership structures on group performance.

[4] A study is now in progress under the direction of Robert F. Bales in which groups composed according to the role differentiation principle will be compared with groups composed according to the great man rationale.

B · PERSONALITY AND FAMILY-COMMUNITY

THE SOCIAL MEANING OF MENTAL ILLNESS

by Marian Radke Yarrow, John A. Clausen, and Paul R. Robbins

The problems which mental illness precipitates are not confined within the family unit but are likely to have far-reaching implications for existing relationships between family members and persons outside. The mental illness of a family member can be regarded only partly as a "private affair." The patient's deviant behavior and (after hospitalization) his absence from home are sooner or later observed by others and necessitate some action or explanation. Unless all social contacts are cut off (a solution which has severe consequences and which is difficult to maintain), there must be communication with others about the patient's illness, even though communications about mental illness are likely to entail a variety of unpleasant and uncertain consequences for the communicator. After the patient's return from the hospital, further adjustments are required in the family's communication and relationships with others.

The present paper is concerned with the effects of the husband's mental illness upon the family's relationships with other persons. More specifically, it examines, from the perspective of the wife of the patient: (a) attitudes and expectations regarding the meaning or valuation of mental illness in our society and (b) the nature of communications concerning the mental patient which take place in his family and

SOURCE: *Journal of Social Issues*, Vol. 11, No. 4 (1955), pp. 33–48.

in his personal-social environment of friends, neighbors and co-workers.

Unlike other stressful situations which may befall the family, such as death or physical illness, in which expectations regarding behavior are relatively clear, and in which forms of help and sympathy from others are socially prescribed and formalized, no similarly clear guides or patterns for response are apparent in the case of mental illness. The heritage of attitudes and practices regarding the "insane" has been one of "putting the patient away." On the other hand, educational campaigns in the mental health field have long stressed the concept of "illness" rather than "insanity" and have emphasized the need for sympathetic care and treatment of the mentally ill rather than blame.

These educational endeavors do not yet appear to have made their point, however. Findings [1] from recent studies of public attitudes toward mental illness reveal confusions as to what is mental illness, and attitudes of fear and rejection toward the mentally ill. The questioning

[1] See for example: Julian Woodward, "Changing Ideas in Mental Illness and its Treatment." *American Sociological Review*, 16, 1951, 443–454. Other recent researches, presenting more detailed analysis of the problem, are those by the Survey Research Center, and by the National Opinion Research Center.

of persons not themselves faced with problems of mental illness indicates that a majority of the general public would be inclined not to reveal the existence of mental illness in their own family or to tell anyone that they are seeing a psychiatrist. The present study analyzes the extent and manner of communication about mental illness in the families of mentally ill persons.

Expectations of Social Reactions to Patient's Illness

Among the factors that influence the reactions of patients' families, their expectations regarding society's conceptions of mental illness are of great importance. There is one predominant expectation—that mental illness is regarded by others as a stigma. This feeling is expressed again and again, and spontaneously, in the interviews with the wives of the patients:

"I'm not ashamed, but people who don't know the hospital would take the wrong attitude about it . . . most people don't understand the type of hospital. They would be afraid he was there because there was something wrong with his mind. The ordinary run of people think Saint Elizabeths is a bug house. . . . You mention Saint Elizabeths and they throw up their hands in holy terror."

"I know things are changing but perhaps not fast enough. He feels it is a stigma to be in Saint Elizabeths. I personally don't feel there is a stigma to mental illness more than any other kind. But growing up in Washington, we always heard of Saint Elizabeths as a place you never got out of. I know that's not true."

"I live in a horror—a perfect horror —that some people will make a crack about it to Jim (child), and suppose after George gets out everything is going well and somebody throws it up

in his face. That would ruin everything. I live in terror of that—a complete terror of that."

The wives find it difficult to be explicit as to what they feel accounts for the expected hostilities and criticisms of society, or what they feel they forfeit with others' knowledge of the husband's mental illness. Some seem mainly concerned with a "psychological" stigma, i.e., they fear that people generally are suspicious, disrespectful or afraid of mental patients and that these attitudes will carry-over to their husbands. These wives ascribe to others stereotypes of the mentally ill as "crazy," "screaming and uncontrollable" and the like. They also express feelings of uncertainty as to what people *really* think, despite what they may say when they learn of the husband's illness.

Wives' fears are also of social discrimination, such as fears that their husbands' jobs may be endangered if people know of his illness, worries that they will be "avoided" by old friends, anxieties that their children will be excluded from play groups or will be taunted by other children about their father's illness.

Social status of the family is threatened in other respects as well. The "reputation" or the social "front" of the family as a congenial, happy group seems shattered. The marriage may be seen as a failure. As one wife describes this, "We've had a lot of false pride which prevented admitting it to ourselves or to others. It's hard to admit you can't manage on your own." Others fear pressure from family or friends to break up the marriage, to give up the husbands.

The stigma of the illness is sometimes a matter of the "family name" being at stake, not only that of the immediate family but of the extended family as well. Thus, "I don't know whether you know anything about Southern towns. There is still a lot of the old Southern pride. 'This couldn't happen to me'—that sort of attitude. 'Get him off to a hospital so that nobody will know about it'—that's the way his family felt."

Although concern about the reactions of others is expressed by nearly all of the wives, the greatest concern is manifested by wives who are attempting to maintain a relatively high social class position or are upwardly aspiring. The college trained women voiced greater fear about the status-damaging effects of hospitalization than the wives with high school education or less.

Patterns of Communications

The wives of patients differed measurably in the extent of their communication with others: roughly a third can be described as communicating minimally, predominantly motivated to conceal; another third as communicating extensively, with the others distributed between the extremes.

Anticipations of unfavorable reactions from others seem clearly to constitute a restraining influence on the wives' disclosures. At the same time, confronted with the many psychological and material problems precipitated by the husband's illness, these wives feel the need to turn to others for help. Almost without exception, and regardless of the extent to which they have informed others, signs of discomfort, uncertainty and unwillingness to reveal the situation to others occurred along with expressions of need and eagerness to talk about the illness. We may look upon the resulting patterns of communication as kinds of resolutions of conflict which the wives work out.

Several distinct patterns emerge as ways in which the conflict exists and is handled by the wife of the mental patient. One pattern of behavior is organized by an orientation of aggressive concealment. some of the wives responding in this way set about making drastic changes in living which serve to cut off as many former associations as possible. Living is rearranged

so as to minimize or avoid the problems or "threats" which may stem from others' knowledge of their husband's illness. Concealment is as overt and thorough as possible, but there are, inevitably, some "leaks." Concealment is never complete. It requires "patching up" of old explanations, inventing new "stories," making new moves; in other words, the concealment has to be kept up to date. In addition, the wife's image of having concealed her husband's illness does not correspond to reality. Many people *do* know something about her husband's hospitalization, and in many instances she has given the information herself. These wives develop an accentuated concern regarding "who knows," "how much they know," "how they found out," and what they will think of her. There is a tendency for the wife to feel that the information has spread, but she doesn't know how far.

With many stored-up feelings and problems, this wife is likely to look desperately for someone to listen to and be concerned with her problems. The characteristics of this pattern are illustrated in the following responses of one of the wives.

Elements of conflict

"Of course it was all new to me. I had never known anyone like this before. At first I was a little ashamed, but now I'm getting to understand it better. I know that mental illness is just like physical illness. I don't think people think about mental illness the way they used to. Of course, I have cut out seeing all but a couple of our friends. There are especially some I have cut out. In fact, Joe asked me not to tell his friends while he was in Saint Elizabeths Hospital.

Overt measures to conceal, and rationalization for action

There are two girl friends who know about it. One couple that we met and liked a great deal, they lived in the same apartment as us and know about it. He has been to see a psychiatrist and I know they would understand. There's another girl friend who used to live in this apartment house, too, and she knows about it. But I've cut off all our other friends. I didn't tell them that I was giving up the apartment and I had the phone disconnected without telling anyone so they don't know how to get in touch with me.

Withholding puts limits on wife's relationships

I haven't gotten too friendly with anyone at the office because I don't want people to know where my husband is. I figure that if I got too friendly with them, then they would start asking questions, and I might start talking, and I just think it's better if as few people as possible know about Joe."

Accentuated sensitivity to what others may be saying about her husband

She states that once when she was in the grocery store where her husband had been employed, while waiting in line to check out, she heard a clerk at the next counter talking to two customers, "You remember him—he was the red-head." The two customers had turned and looked at her inquiringly. "I am sure he was telling them about Joe."

Intensified need to find a sympathetic listener

She states that last Saturday when she was feeling very lonely and needed very much to talk to someone, she had seriously thought about coming to see the interviewer to talk to her at that time.

Other wives who are equally reluctant to communicate differ somewhat from the wife described above in the extent to which they are able to manipulate the situation to avoid communication. They are more likely to be pushed by circumstances to impart information which they had not intended giving. This imparting is often regretted, resented. Little in the

way of support or satisfaction derives from these discussions. When trapped by the situation, these wives still manage to maintain substantial reserve, not sharing with others or indicating the kind of personal impact which the husband's illness has. For instance, Mrs. R. had told only a few intimate friends about her husband's hospitalization. "It's foolish," she says, "to try to tell people who don't know him." At a point well into her husband's hospitalization, however, she was forced into making this information known. She tells it this way. "One of our men friends called and asked for Bill. He didn't ask where he was when I said he was away. Men aren't as inquisitive as women, and it was easy for me to say that. The other night, a woman friend called to ask us to a party. When I said that Bill was away, she wanted to know where he was, so I told her he was in the hospital."

Another wife indicates the stress under which information is imparted, even to a potential source of sympathy and understanding: "You were here, weren't you, when Reverend H. asked me about it? I almost died when he did, but I said, I can't tell the minister a lie. It took courage for me to do that, I tell you."

Another resolution of the conflict regarding communication is found in about half of the cases: Communication is determined on the basis of a clear demarcation of "ins" and "outs"; "There are certain people whom you tell, and not others." The "ins" are variously defined, (a) there are those who will know because they are part of the problem or have been involved in the hospitalization of the patient, or (b) they have a "right" to know, or (c) they are people who will "understand." Mrs. C. orders her communications in this way. She has told most of their friends of her husband's hospitalization, particularly the friends in the church where she and her husband are active members. She states that her neighbors knew about the patient and had visited him. On the other hand, she has carefully concealed the information in other directions. She has written to her husband's family and her family telling them that her husband is in the hospital for a "check-up." "They don't know what's wrong. They know he's in a hospital. They don't know where. The people at his work who know he is on two months sick leave are not told why. They think he is just off on a rest. My husband doesn't like for them to know."

Some wives seem not to consider seriously the feasibility of proceeding otherwise than with generally free reference to their husband's illness. This is not necessarily easy or pleasant, or free of conflict, but serves in a variety of ways to reduce tensions. Thus, some wives are able to circumvent discussing the husband's *mental* illness by restricting discussions to his organic problems, his "nervous exhaustion" and the like, communicating freely in this context. Mrs. S., for example, did not try to conceal her husband's illness and hospitalization. She talked to nearly everyone she knew. She centers on the physical side of her husband's difficulties, and this is quite feasible in light of her husband's case. His psychotic symptoms followed a cerebral injury. She was, herself, in chronic conflict in deciding whether his illness was "physical" or "mental." Only in passing does she suggest some feelings of misgiving about exposing her problems to others. She says she *could* go over and talk with her neighbors, but she doesn't do this much. Further she reflects, "maybe I feel guilty about having put him in the hospital."

The other wives who communicate extensively with others do not comprise a homogeneous group in terms of motivations. It appears that these wives expect less dire social consequences (at least, they voice such fears less often than others). But individualized needs to inform others rather than needs to conceal (sometimes to express their antagonisms toward their husbands, to lay claim to others' help,

and the like) seem the stronger determinants of their behavior.

Communication in Different Social Contexts

Discussions of the husband's illness occur in specific interpersonal relationships. The characteristics of these relationships may materially alter the meaning of the communication. For purposes of analysis, the wife's social environment has been differentiated in terms of her relationships with her children, the parental families, friends, neighbors, co-workers and professional persons. Communications follow very different patterns in each of these contexts. The sanctions and prohibitions which govern "normal" communication in these relationships, it is assumed, impose varying requirements on the wife which may be expected to influence communications involving the husband's illness. In the period of acute decisions, when hospitalization is being decided and arranged, the wife's discussions concerning her husband tend to be confined primarily to family members and to professional persons to whom he turns for counsel. Most often the latter is the family physician or a psychiatrist or both; occasionally the clergy. Rarely are friends or neighbors or co-workers summoned into this complex of decisions and conflicts. After hospitalization, however, there are changes both in the settings and in the purposes of the wife's communications.

Communication with the Parental Families

Communication among family members, as compared with communication beyond the family boundaries, occurs within a relatively "closed" system. By virtue of intra-family contacts and interdependencies, control over information is more limited than outside. If relatives are in close physical proximity, there is less possibility for the wife to avoid giving some kinds of information, for example, about the husband's absence from home.

In two-thirds of the cases studied, either or both of the parental families live in or near the District of Columbia, and, in the great majority of these cases, they were either involved in hospitalizing the patient or informed about it. Where the illness was concealed from family members, these relatives almost always live some distance away. Motives for concealment are tied up with the stigma expectation (discussed earlier), as well as with pre-existing states of feeling—knowledge that one's own parents had reservations about the spouse or had opposed the marriage, or that parents or siblings were privy to previous interpersonal difficulties which may have helped precipitate the patient's breakdown.

Distinctly different patterns of communication are associated with different roles and positions within the family— with the husband's family and wife's family, and with older and younger children. In the decision period before hospitalization, the wife tends to turn to the husband's family. Her questions of what to do about the husband, how to get him in the hospital, where to turn for help, are directed toward them. Directly and indirectly the wife communicates the idea, "Here, he's yours—. You have had something to do with it. You have a responsibility for him now." One wife, for example, sends her husband to his family just before hospital admission, as she says, in order that they may see just what she's had to put up with, so that they'll not blame her when she puts him in the hospital. She describes how they have made a "baby out of him" and have never been able to understand why she hasn't continued to baby him as they have. In 18 out of 29 cases with living

relatives, the husband's family is brought in to assume some responsibility at this time. This compares with only three cases in which the wife's family takes the same responsibility role.

Running through the communications between wife and husband's family in more than half the cases is a dominant theme of hostility. Accusations and counter accusations are made. Patience is short and criticisms are easy and frequent. Often the wife blames her husband's personality or character defects, if not his illness, on parent-child relationships in his early childhood. The husband's mother, on the other hand, may accuse the wife of keeping the husband in the hospital. The husband's illness seems to have the effect of consolidating or accentuating the prior relationships between the wife and the parental families. Even where prior relationships have been good, the wife and the husband's family are, with respect to each other, in roles which are most vulnerable for attack; i.e., they are the persons closest to the husband, and the persons, in the eyes of the other, most available for the ascription of guilt or responsibility for the illness.

A specialized role of the wife's family becomes apparent during the hospitalization period. While communication with them during the initial stage (when the *husband* has been the focus of trouble and problems) is extensive, it is only after the focus shifts to the wife's problems (to problems of finances, of caring for the children, of what the husband's illness has "done" to her), after the husband is in the care of the hospital, that the wife looks to her own family for help. In a sense, the wives assume the dependent daughter role. This shift within the families is documented in various ways: by sending the children (in some cases) to their family, by some of the wives moving in with their parents or married children, by expressing confidence in and receiving help from their family when financial problems arise. Financial help is offered by the wife's family in 17 cases out of 33; by the husband's family in 10: When financial help is given by the husband's family, there is often an undertone of hostility.

Visits to the hospitalized patient also reflect the differential responsibilities assumed by the two families. Of the husbands' families who have been informed about his illness and who live in the Washington area, 17 out of 18 visit the patient at least once, of the wives' families only 16 out of 27. The visits tend to produce many anxieties, and after one or two visits in the early weeks of hospitalization, most relatives other than wife and children, and sometimes the patient's mother, are unlikely to return. Seeing the patient "disturbs (them) too much," they "cannot bear to see what is happening" and they "don't want to be around him." A father who continues to visit his son comes each time only ten minutes before the close of visiting hours. This infrequency of visiting appears to be accepted by the wives with some understanding, and they seldom complain about relatives in this respect. Perhaps this reflects their own anxieties in visiting with the patient. The more frequent complaint about "in-laws" is that there has been little appreciation of the difficulty of this experience for the wife: "I feel hurt and feel they have not considered me. All they are concerned about is my husband."

Communication with the Children

Our sample of families provides us with enough cases for analysis in two age groups: 18 families in which there are children 6 years old or younger, and 12 families with children of adolescent or adult years. Adolescent and adult sons and daughters tend to share intimately with the mother the problems of the father's illness significantly more often

than any other group of persons. In 7 of 10 cases the children become the mother's confidants, carrying some of the load of responsibilities, sharing her uncertainties and anxieties. Reactions toward the father follow about equally frequently one of two patterns: (a) Either the children visit their father regularly and assume much the same role and attitude toward the illness as their mother or (b) they refuse to visit, expressing openly a great deal of hostility toward their father.

In interpreting the father's illness to younger children, almost all the mothers attempt to follow a course of concealment. The child is told either that his father is in a hospital (without further explanation) or that he is in the hospital suffering from a physical ailment (he has a toothache, or trouble with his leg, or a tummy ache, or a headache). Only one mother spoke frankly about the illness from the beginning, explaining to her five year old that her father "had gone to the hospital because he was nervous and upset and that they were giving him some treatment to make him feel better." While the mothers "protest" that theirs have been sufficient explanations, there is both insensitivity and uncertainty in their responses. ("She can't see that he is sick so I guess she just doesn't understand." "I think any child under ten wouldn't know what it's all about." "She never asks about it, I have never asked her what she thought was wrong, but I have often wondered what she thinks.") Mothers begin to look anxiously at the child in terms of his resemblance to the father, ("I hope he is not going to get real nervous like (his father)"); and to wonder about the "negative effect" of associating with the father before he was hospitalized or of seeing him or "bad cases" in the hospital.

Despite their resolutions to conceal as much as possible from their young children, sooner or later the mothers take them to visit the patient (14 of 18 cases). Following these visits, a few mothers become more candid. Thus, Mrs. Y. whose six year old had been told that her father was "sick in the hospital," later tells her daughter that her father had had "a nervous breakdown, that his head was tired and that his brain was tired from working too hard." Most mothers, however, stand by their original explanations, with minor embellishments. Mrs. F. told her five year old that daddy was in the hospital because of a toothache. After a visit to the hospital, she doubts her daughter's acceptance of this explanation and so adds that in addition to his teeth he has pneumonia, "and that's why he has to stay in the hospital. I've taken her over to the hospital grounds and she didn't say anything about it."

Communication Outside the Family

In a number of relationships outside the family, some explanation of the situation by the wife is virtually required, as for example in arranging her own employment, in explaining her husband's absence from work, in meeting financial obligations, in obtaining care for the children. Most often the wives define these circumstances as depersonalized "privileged communication." Thus, a wife explains her circumstances to her employer with the understanding that this communication is held in confidence. Occasionally these necessities for communication are manipulated as means to an end. The creditor, the grocer, and the like are told with the hope of gaining some special consideration (refinancing a mortgage, getting food at a lower price, etc.).

Information that wives allow friends and acquaintances is highly selective as to its content and the persons receiving it. Many persons are excluded who have normally shared other kinds of family information. While all wives disclose the husband's hospitalization to someone outside the family, approximately two-thirds of the wives deliberately conceal this in-

formation from particular persons or groups among their friends and neighbors and the persons with whom they work. (Extensive evasion is more frequent among the college trained wives than among wives with high school education or less.) In informing others of the fact of the husband's illness (but without discussing the details of his illness or emotional impact upon her) the wife more often turns to friends than to neighbors or co-workers. Similarly, she more often grossly misinforms co-workers and neighbors than personal friends. There are, however, many exceptions to this pattern, and it does not reflect the ambivalences which exist with regard to these communications. We shall examine this process by looking at the wives' behavior in greater detail.

As might be anticipated, it is difficult for the wife to conceal the husband's long absence, and her attempts to do so by avoidance and fabrication seriously threaten her relationships with others. Evasions, such as "my husband is in the hospital," tend to lead to an unstable situation and eventually either to giving out the truth or more frequently to more definite deliberate distortions ("He has physical complaints." "He is in the country, taking a rest."). Concealment often becomes cumbersome. Thus, to keep the neighbors from knowing the husband's hospital (having reported that he was in a hospital because of suspicion of cancer), Mrs. G. must rush to her apartment house to get the mail before her neighbors pick it up for her as they used to do. She has had to abandon second breakfasts at the drugstore with the women from neighboring apartments to avoid their questions. Before she can allow visitors in her apartment, she must pick up any material identifying the hospital, and so on.

While the most radical attempts at concealment remove the wife from the sources of embarrassing questions, they serve also to isolate her. By sharply limiting her interactions with others she has little basis for testing out her beliefs concerning their responses to her husband's illness, and she drifts away from a reality basis for her perception of others. Mrs. E. illustrates this tendency. She has told few people about her husband, yet somehow she expects that everybody knows about it. "I'm sure they (neighbors) know he's not here. They saw him go out with the police that night, I bet." She refers to "hundreds" of people at the church who must know it, though she has told none of them. Her evaluation of these people follows: "Nobody has called and asked me to have dinner or anything. Nobody comes over. They act like you are contagious or something. I don't understand people's attitudes at all. It makes me so mad." Much later, when her husband is home from the hospital, her hypersensitivity persists; she sees two people talking in the neighborhood and immediately assumes that they are talking about her and her family. Similar sensitivities play on many of the wives.

Somewhere in the course of the husband's hospitalization, for conditions individual to each case, tensions, isolation, and uncertainties are likely to build up beyond a bearable level. At such a time there is a strong desire to seek out someone to whom she can pour out her feelings. Many of the wives find such a confidant, a person who listens without blame. An enumeration of the persons who have filled this role reveals its own pattern: a new boarder, a fellow-worker, a sister-in-law with whom she had little acquaintance before the husband's illness, a neighbor who has a mentally ill relative, a minister, the interviewer, her grown children. Except for older children, the confidant is a person whose intimate role in the wife's life is (or can be) confined to the present situation. Often the confidant does not know the patient or the members of the parental family. The tangential characteristics of this relationship make it possible for the wife to terminate the intimate phase almost at will.

The Reactions of Others

To interpret the wives' behavior, it is necessary to take account of their experiences in making the husband's illness known to others. From the wives' reports on the reactions of others, it seems clear that people are puzzled and confused upon learning of a friend's or acquaintance's commitment to a mental hospital and that they lack any clearly defined socially appropriate responses. There are confused expectations as to how a friend's illness changes one's responsibilities and attitudes toward him, how it changes (if at all) the patient's relationships with his family, or how, indeed, it changes the patient.

When friends and neighbors learn of the illness, it is true, many come to help out—they take care of needed repairs in the house, or take in the child after school hours, or drive the wife to the hospital. Their more direct reactions to the illness, however, need examination. They take many forms: expressions of sympathy (three-fourths of the cases), "verifications" of the rightness of the wife's decision to hospitalize her husband or derogations of the patient (about half the cases), and reassurances to the wife that her husband will get well (often by relating accounts of others who have been ill and have recovered). This latter reaction is functionally an effective support to the wife and one which occurs with high frequency. In the experience of three-fourths of the wives in the study, people have told them about persons they have known (often their relatives) who have been in a mental hospital. One senses a kind of relief in the wife (and perhaps in her informant, too) in finding this avenue for discussing the husband's illness, and there are often repeated exchanges about the progress of his case. Here the wife seems to feel less restraint than in other settings.

After the patient is hospitalized, it would appear that people are less cautious than earlier in making critical evaluations of the patient or in commenting on his symptomatic behavior. Neighbors and friends now tell the wife what they observed or felt earlier. ("How could you have put up with him this long?" Friends who had noticed how "upset" he had been "weren't surprised he was hospitalized." A landlady now tells the wife of the husband's strange actions as he used to stand hidden to watch his wife when she came home from work each day.)

Incongruities and insensitivities mark many situations in which the wife has informed others about her husband. For example, her efforts to "keep things going" meet with reactions such as "kidding" by co-workers about her lack of sexual relations since her husband's hospitalization, advances from male friends since "she doesn't have a husband now" or joking remarks about mental hospitals and mental patients.

During the patients' hospitalization there was rather thorough-going avoidance by friends and acquaintances. Normal expressions of concern for the welfare of one who is ill such as visits, written messages or gifts are avenues little used for the mental patient. According to the wives' reports, 50% of the patients in this study had no visitors outside the family during all the months of hospitalization, 41% had only a single or a very occasional visitor, 9% had frequent visitors. Friends telephone the wife to inquire about her husband, with vague promises of "wanting to go to see him," which never materialize.

Communication after the Husband's Return Home

For the period following discharge, our data are still too limited to permit more than examples of reactions from acquaintances and friends. In a few cases (N-17) which have been followed up, it appears that in the early weeks or months, at least, social interaction seems to be faced by patient and wife with many of the same fears and conflicts which characterized the wife's reaction during the husband's hospitalization. Thus, the patient and his wife vacillate between escape (moving away, changing jobs) and "returning to normal" (going back to the same job, continuing old friendships and social participation). Again as during the hospitalization, there are social encounters which result in setbacks and which support the wives' prevalent generalization "you just don't know what people really think," "you just don't know what to expect."

Mrs. G., whose course of action during the hospitalization had been one of aggressive concealment (at her husband's urging), reports serious problems of social relationships for herself and her husband.

The interviewer asks, *How about your friends, have you picked up the ones that you knew previously?*—"Not a one, we've had a bad time with that." She describes a very close friend who called to say she was going to visit them on Tuesday and then called that Tuesday to break the appointment because she had to take her mother to the hospital. She made an appointment for the following Tuesday. She called the following week and broke the appointment again. Mrs. G. reported seeing the friend's mother downtown when she supposedly was in the hospital. Then Mrs. G. goes on to describe another friend, "She called to ask if we could come over for an evening. We went over and she and I were having a wonderful time in the kitchen talking and Joe and her husband sat in the living room. Joe told me later that they sat there for one and a half hours and that all Jimmie said to him was hello, and then he did not say one word."

There are stories of success for the patient returning to his former employment—

"He seems to have taken hold after he went back to work. He said it seems he was never away. I happened to talk to one of the fellows at work over the phone and he said that my husband acts just the same as before."

and of failure—

"He had a terrible fear of facing people when he first came out. And when he went up to . . . (where he worked before) they had to send him away from there. He went all to pieces and he couldn't work. I don't know if it was the fact of facing people who could ask him where he had been."

The systematic study of the post-hospital aspects of the social meaning of mental illness constitutes a continuing part of the present research project.

Psychological Factors underlying Communication about the Husband's Illness

The data which have been presented on the wives' communications present wide variations in kinds of disclosures about the husbands' mental illness and kinds of attitudes towards communicating this information. Not only do the wives differ with respect to this behavior, but the individual wife, too, shows many ambivalences and vacillations in her responses. If one considers in detail the various settings and circumstances of her communication, there is some predictability of disclosures and concealments in terms of several underlying psychological conditions. As we have seen, wives define their situation generally as one which carries a social stigma. By virtue of this definition, telling other persons of the husband's illness establishes a social relationship in which the wife (as well as the family) is placed in a disadvantaged position. This asymmetry of relationships is inherent in nearly all of the social settings in which the wife communicates, but it is intensified in some and lessened in others. The kind and amount of communication vary rather consistently with the kind and amount of asymmetry involved in the relationship. Just telling the fact of illness is not at all comparable to confiding the problems and injuries it entails; the two kinds of communication must be distinguished in our analysis.

Let us consider first the communications which are limited primarily to telling about the illness without the emotional components. Friends and family are recipients more often than neighbors or companions at work. While family and friends share the information regarding the illness, the wife does not usually confide the emotional significance of the experience. A judgmental role can readily be assumed by persons who have known the wife and husband over a long period of time, most readily of all by the parental families. Undoubtedly the judgmental interactions between wife and in-laws have been important factors in the wife's withholding of confidences. (Recall the counter-posed judgments of wife and husband's parents—with wife blaming husband's upbringing, and parents suggesting wife's responsibility for the husband's illness.)

The wives' reluctance to confide in their own parents sometimes stems from a somewhat different judgmental relationship. A wife recalls her expectations and the hopes of her family for her successful marriage. These have not come true. Her pride will not permit her to reveal the problems she has experienced with her husband.

Confidences tend also to be withheld from friends (couples with whom she and her husband shared a social life), the wife feeling keenly a threat with respect to her role as wife. These resistances are verbalized in the example below.

"It's hard to talk about it. When I am unhappy, I'd rather be my myself. I don't want people to know I am unhappy—we have lots of friends who could have been a help, but I just didn't turn to them. I was too jealous of them and their little smug lives. I'd hear one of my friends fussing because her husband had done something that had irritated her, or a husband telling me about something his wife had done, and I would think, you just don't know what you have."

We should, then, expect to find in the relationships in which the wife's behavior is confiding, conditions in which judgment or social disadvantage is minimal. Least likely to confront the wife with judgments of herself, and with her past errors, are the newcomers in her life. These are persons who will know the story only as she tells it, who can be involved intensively at the time but, if she wishes, her relationship with them can be time limited and need not continue into her future. This is very much the picture of the confidants who have been described earlier.

Confiding communications occur, too, in several settings in which relationships are continuing and intense. But in them the symmetry of the relationship is the important variable. Namely, grown children afford the wife's greatest relief from self-control. In a very special way she is at no special disadvantage sharing confidences with them for they are equally close to the problem and have lived through and perhaps participated in the progressive difficulties. One other relationship within which the wives communicate with lessened tension is with persons who have themselves experienced mental illness personally or close at hand.

Summary Interpretations

Through the perspectives of wives of mental patients, we have secured some understanding of the social meaning of mental illness to the family and to the persons in the familiar environment of the family and the patient. The generally conflictual aspects of the wives' communications about the illness—the needs for help and understanding but the unwillingness to reveal the nature of the illness and the anxieties associated with it—have been apparent in their reactions. What is perhaps an obvious consideration that should not be omitted in attempting to explain these reactions is the nature of any data about mental disturbance. Namely, that any discussion at all of the problems which led to the husband's hospitalization or which describe his current condition requires a revelation of many aspects of intimate, highly personal relationships between husband and wife. In any other context, we would not expect such personal problems to be aired and examined with others.

In asking the wives about their communications and expectations, we have directed their attention "outward," toward the impressions created and the responses forthcoming from the significant "others" who learn of the husband's illness. In so doing we have emphasized the social or cultural side of the process—the attempts at face saving, maintaining a front, etc. We have given little attention to the significance for husband-wife relationships of the information which is disclosed about the husband's illness. This information and the wife's expressed affect in giving it may serve to mobilize supportive understanding from others. It may, on the other hand, be used aggressively by the wife against the patient. Furthermore, discussion of the patient's illness while he is hospitalized may contribute in important ways to the psychological situation confronting him when he returns from the hospital. These problems require further study.

Certain practical implications which can be drawn from the present data for problems of patient rehabilitation, meeting the needs of relatives of patients and public education regarding the mentally ill have been touched upon elsewhere. The specific behavioral and attitudinal phenomena observed in the families of mental illness can be seen, too, in terms of more general social psychological theory. The social psychological situation of the family and the mechanisms of adjustment utilized by them in many ways parallel the dynamics of minority group-belonging, conceptualized by Lewin.[2] The position of the minority member is characterized by feelings of under-privilege and marginality. The social environment consists of many unknowns in reactions from others, as well as expected and experienced social distance. The minority member considers attempts at concealment (attempts to "pass"). His tendency to interpret ambiguous social contacts as rejection or hostility based on ethnic grounds dramatizes his hyper-sensitivity. Ambivalent acceptance of imposed negative evaluations by others exists side by side with his seeking out of we-groups for closer associations (others with the same characteristics or experience).

Each of these reactions has been manifested many times in the wives' responses to the husbands' mental illness. Similarly, there are close parallels between these data and the data reported in studies of adjustment problems of the physically injured and handicapped [3] which have also been systematized within the minority framework. Regardless of the setting, similar sensitivities in social communications and concerns are verbalized. The comparative findings from the several specific settings, therefore, suggest the applicability of an integrated theory which applies to various circumstances of social threat or social stigma. With a common theoretical orientation we may, on firmer ground, proceed with social action programs designed to help the individual (patient, family, minority member) and to change public attitudes.

[2] Lewin, K. "Self Hatred Among Jews," in G. Lewin (ed.), *Resolving Social Conflicts* (New York: Harpers, 1948), pp. 186–200.

[3] Barker, R. "The Social Psychology of Physical Disability," *The Journal of Social Issues*, 4, 1948, 28–34; and R. K. White, B. A. Wright, and T. Dembo, "Studies in Adjustment to Visible Injuries: Evaluation of Curiosity by the Injured." *Journal of Abnormal and Social Psychology*, 43, 1948, 13–28.

THE ADJUSTMENT OF THE FAMILY TO ALCOHOLISM

by Joan K. Jackson

There is a sizable literature on alcoholism and on families in crisis. However, there have been few publications dealing with families who are attempting to make an adjustment to the crisis of alcoholism.

Individual members of the families of alcoholics have been studied. Psychologists and social workers have evaluated the personalities of wives of alcoholics. While these studies offer descriptions of some of the characteristic behaviors involved in the crisis, they tend to conceptualize this behavior as arising from the pre-crisis personality pathology of the wives, and to focus on those personality attributes and behaviors which appear to prolong and intensify the crisis (1–4). Comments have been published on some effects of the alcoholic father on the personality development of children (1, 5).

Sociological studies of families in crisis (6) have concentrated on crises of a rather different nature from that precipitated by alcoholism. Such crises as bereavement and war separation and reunion are so-

SOURCE: *Marriage and Family Living*, Vol. 18 (1956), pp. 361–369.

cially acceptable and do not tend to involve a sense of shame, which is a major characteristic of the alcoholism-induced crisis. Unemployment and divorce, while less socially acceptable, are known by those affected by them to be crises which are shared by others in the society. The family of an alcoholic rarely knows that the problem is a common one until a relatively late stage in the crisis. The family crises referred to above tend to occur in a more or less pure form. This is very rarely true of the crisis of alcoholism. Uncontrolled drinking may be the important initial precipitant of the crisis; but, by the time the crisis has run its course, unemployment, desertion and return, nonsupport, infidelity, imprisonment, illness and progressive dissension have also occurred. It is, therefore, very difficult to separate out the particular aspect of the crisis which leads to any specific adjustive behavior on the part of the family unit.

A family crisis which is similar to that induced by alcoholism arises when a family member becomes mentally ill. A recently published report on the preliminary findings of a study of the impact of mental illness on the family (7) indicates that this crisis is similar in the type of confusion generated, its complexity, and in the way in which shame is felt and dealt with. The report is focussed on the way in which the wife defines the situation, and her resulting behavior from the first signs of bizarre behavior to the end of her husband's hospitalization.

Although the crisis induced by alcoholism is somewhat different from most other family crises which have been investigated, and is more complex, the method and theory of the earlier studies are directly applicable.

Method and Sample

The method of gathering data for the study of family adjustment to alcoholism had elements in common with that used by Koos in his investigation of the incidence and types of problems found in low-income families (8) and that used in the study of the impact of mental illness on the family (7). The investigator was associated in a friendship relationship with a group of wives of alcoholics over a prolonged period of time. At the time of the first report on this research, this association had been of three years' duration (9), and at present, of five years'. The women who contributed the data belong to the Alcoholics Anonymous Auxiliary in Seattle. This group is composed partly of women whose husbands are or were members of Alcoholics Anonymous, and partly of women whose husbands are excessive drinkers who have never contacted Alcoholics Anonymous. At a typical meeting one fifth would be the wives of Alcoholics Anonymous members who have been sober for some time; the husbands of another fifth would have recently joined the fellowship; the remainder would be divided between those whose husbands were "on and off" the Alcoholics Anonymous program and those whose husbands had not as yet had any contact with this organization. The meetings of this group, which usually take a form similar to a group psychotherapy session, were recorded verbatim in shorthand. In addition, the frequent informal contacts with past and present members were recorded. This group of approximately seventy-five women provided the largest body of data.

When the initial report was completed, it was read to members of the Auxiliary with a request for correction of errors in fact or interpretation. Corrections could be presented anonymously or from the floor. Only one change was suggested, that the family of the solitary drinker had some problems which were due to the in-the-home, rather than away-from-home locale of the drinking. This suggestion was incorporated. The investigator is certain that her relationship with the group is such that there was no reticence about offering suggestions for change in the formulation.

Additional information on family interactions and responses to the crisis was garnered from interviews with the relatives of hospitalized alcoholics. These data, gathered as one aspect of a larger study of alcoholism, were used to raise questions about the data derived from the Auxiliary group, and to give some indication of the degree to which these findings could be generalized to other samples of families undergoing a similar crisis.

It should be noted, however, that the findings of this research are applicable only to those families which are seeking help for the alcoholism of the husband. Other families are known to have divorced, often without having sought help for the drinking problem. It is known that some families never seek help and never disintegrate. While the wives of the hospitalized alcoholics gave substantially the same picture of the crisis as did the women from the Auxiliary, there is no evidence that the conclusions of this study can be generalized beyond these two groups. In addition, there are good theoretical reasons for believing that where the alcoholic family member is the wife or a child, the process of the crisis is substantially different.

Findings

The crisis induced by alcoholism goes through several stages. When the interactions of family members in respect to the excessive drinking per se are viewed, the crisis starts as a series of acute crises, probably widely spaced in time, passes into a progressive type of crisis in which the emotional involvement and hostility expressed are diminished, and finally, if the family has stayed together, into a habituated crisis. In the latter stage, the family is accustomed to the excessive drinking and the behavior surrounding it, has made its adjustment to it, and is concerned about it but not disrupted by it (10).

However, a characteristic of the overall crisis of alcoholism is that secondary crises arise from the very nature of the illness. Many of these crises, too, go through the same stages, beginning as sporadic acute crises, and gradually passing into progressive and finally habituated crises. For example, the nonsupport problem begins as a series of acute crises over the spending of money for drinking rather than for necessities. As time passes, the conflict over diminishing support becomes cumulative and persistent. Finally, the family adjusts by ceasing to expect support and makes other arrangements for subsistence. After this the crisis is of a habituated nature, being one element of a larger area of continued disagreement. At this latter stage, the disruptive effects of lack of support have been minimized.

The elements of the crisis of alcoholism, and each of the subsidiary crises, are similar to those of less complex crises. Throughout, all family members behave in a manner which they hope will resolve the crisis and permit a return to stability. Each member's actions are influenced by his previous personality, by his previous role and status in the family group, and by the history of the crisis and its effects on his personality, habit patterns, roles and status up to that point (6). Action is also influenced by the past effectiveness of that particular action as a means of social control or as an adjustive technique before and during the crisis. The behavior of the members of the family individually and as a unit during each phase of the crisis contributes to the form which the crisis takes in the following stages and sets limits on possibilities of behavior in subsequent stages.

In addition, family members are influenced strongly by the cultural definitions of alcoholism as evidence of weakness, inadequacy, or sinfulness; by the cultural prescriptions for the roles of family members; and by the cultural values of family solidarity, sanctity, and self-sufficiency. Alcoholism in a family poses a situation which the culture defines as shameful; but for the handling of which there are no prescriptions which are effective, or which permit direct action that is not in conflict with other cultural prescriptions. In crises such as physical illness or bereavement the family can draw on cultural definitions of appropriate behavior and on procedures which will terminate the crisis, but this is not the case when there is alcoholism in the family. The cultural view is that alcoholism is shameful and should not occur. Thus, in facing alcoholism, the family is in a socially unstructured situation and must find the techniques for handling it through trial and error. In this respect, there are marked similarities to the crisis of mental illness (7).

The over-all crises and each of the subsidiary crises go through the stages delineated by Hill (6), that is, crisis—disorganization—recovery—reorganization. As in other crises, and especially the bereavement crisis, there is an initial denial of the problem, followed by a downward slump in organization during which roles are played with less enthusiasm and there is an increase in tensions and strained relationships. Finally, as some of the adjustive techniques prove successful, an improvement occurs and family organization becomes stabilized at a new level. Characteristics of each stage of the crisis are: reshuffling of roles among family members, changes in status and prestige, changing "self" and "other" images, shifts in family solidarity and self-sufficiency and in the visibility of the problem to outsiders. In the process of the crisis, considerable mental conflict is engendered in all family members, and personality distortion occurs.

In evaluating the following presenta-

tion of the stages through which the family passes in adjusting to the alcoholism of the father, it should be kept in mind that we are dealing with the wife's definition of the situation. As most of the families investigated were composed of a wife, husband, and minor children, her definition of the situation was the relevant one.

Hill (6) points out that the way in which a family defines a given situation or event is an important element in whether or not a crisis results. He calls this the "c factor" in the development of a crisis. In the case of alcoholism in the family, it is difficult to envisage the possibility that there could be a family definition of excessive drinking behavior such that a crisis would not occur. In the experience of the investigator, excessive drinking tends to constitute a crisis even in the special case where both spouses are alcoholics.

However, the definition of the crisis and its nature by the family does determine in large measure the action which is taken to cope with it. Some families shorten the crisis by casting the alcoholic member out of their ranks at an early stage of excessive drinking; others prolong the crisis by continuing their attempts to adjust to the alcoholic member. The latter is particularly the case among the families who define the alcoholic as sick, thereby activating the cultural prescriptions for behavior in relation to the chronically and seriously ill.

The extent to which the family's definition of excessive drinking behavior contributes to the development of alcoholism or increases the probability of alcoholism is unknown. That the definition of the excessive drinker by others is an important factor in the process of becoming an alcoholic and in developing a conception of oneself as a problem drinker (a necessary first step towards the termination of alcoholism) is a hypothesis worthy of investigation.

STAGES IN FAMILY ADJUSTMENT TO AN AL-
COHOLIC MEMBER

The Beginning of the Marriage: At the
time marriage was considered, the drinking of most of the men was within socially acceptable limits. In a few cases the
men were already alcoholics but managed
to hide this from their fiancees. On dates
they drank only moderately or not at all
and often avoided friends and relatives
who might expose their excessive drinking. Those relatives and friends who were
introduced to the fiancee were those
who had hoped that "marriage would
straighten him out" and thus said nothing about the drinking. In a small number of cases the men spoke about their
alcoholism with their fiancees. The
women had no conception of what alcoholism meant, other than that it involved
more than the usual frequency of drinking. These women began marriage with
little more preparation than if they had
not been told anything about the drinking problem.

Stage 1: Attempts to Deny the Problem.
At some time during the marriage, incidents of excessive drinking begin. Although they are sporadic, these episodes
place strains on the husband-wife interaction and pose crises of the acute type.
After each drinking episode, the relationships of family members are redefined,
usually in a way that minimizes other
family problems which are not obviously
related to the drinking. Both spouses attempt to explain the drinking episode in
a manner which will permit them to regard it as "normal" behavior (7). Thereafter, as a kind of safety measure, situations or behavior which are thought to
be related to the onset of drinking are
avoided. During periods of reconciliation
when inappropriate drinking does not occur, both husband and wife feel guilty
about the thoughts they had had about
each other, about their behavior, and
about their impact on their mate. Each

tries to play "Ideal Spouse" roles in an
attempt to deny that strains exist in the
marriage.

As inappropriate drinking behavior becomes recurrent, initial explanations of
the reasons for this behavior as being
within the range of "normal behavior"
become unsatisfactory. The wife's definitions of the nature of the problem change
from one formulation to another, until
gradually she recognizes the behavior as
alcoholism. The process by which the
wife comes to recognize alcoholism is precisely the same as the process of recognizing mental illness. The report on the
Impact of Mental Illness on the Family
(7) points out that the problems in accurately and immediately defining the
situation are understandable within the
framework of perception theory. "Behavior which is unfamiliar and incongruent
and unlikely in terms of current expectations and needs will not be readily recognized, and stressful or threatening stimuli
will tend to be misperceived or perceived
with difficulty or delay." The same study
delineates the stages in defining the problems as follows:

1. The wife's threshold for initially
discerning a problem depends on the
accumulation of various kinds of behavior which are not readily understandable or acceptable to her.

2. This accumulation forces upon
the wife the necessity for examining
and adjusting expectations for herself
and her husband which permit her to
account for his behavior.

3. The wife is in an "overlapping"
situation, of problem—not problem,
or of normal—not normal. Her interpretations shift back and forth.

4. Adaptations to the atypical behavior of the husband occur. There is
testing and waiting for additional cues
in coming to any given interpretation,
as in most problem solving. The wife
mobilizes strong defenses against the

husband's deviant behavior. These defenses take form in such reactions as denying, attenuating, balancing and normalizing the husband's problems.

5. Eventually there is a threshold point at which the perception breaks, when the wife comes to the relatively stable conclusion that the problem is a psychiatric one and/or that she cannot alone cope with the husband's behavior.

In this initial stage of the crisis, both the husband and wife are concerned with the social visibility of the drinking behavior. They feel that if the nature and extent of the drinking become widely known, family status will be threatened. The wife tends to be the more concerned. The family's status in the community is dependent on the behavior of the husband, and the wife feels less in control of the situation than he. As a result she attempts to exert some control and is usually blocked in her efforts by the sacredness of drinking behavior to the male. The usual response of the husband to her efforts is to state no problem exists.

Friends contribute to her confusion. If she compares her husband with them, some show parallels to his drinking and others are in marked contrast. Depending on which friends she is comparing him with, her definition of his behavior is "normal" or "not normal." If she consults friends, they tend to discount her concern, thus facilitating her tendency to deny that a problem is emerging. As the report on the Impact of Mental Illness on the Family points out, "social pressures and expectations not only keep behavior in line, but to a great extent perceptions of behavior as well" (7).

Stage 2: Attempts to eliminate the problem. When incidents of excessive drinking multiply, the family becomes socially isolated. The isolation results partly from a voluntary withdrawal from extrafamily social interactions, and partly from ostracism by others. The increasing isolation magnifies the importance of intrafamily interactions and events. The behavior and thought of the husband and wife become obsessively drinking-centered. Drinking comes to symbolize all conflicts between the spouses, and even mother-child and father-child conflicts are regarded as indirect derivatives of the drinking behavior. Attempts to keep the social visibility of the excessive drinking at the lowest possible level increase. The children are shielded from the knowledge of their father's behavior; lies are told to employers and to others directly affected by the drinking.

During this stage the husband and wife draw further apart; the process of alienation (6) accelerates. Each spouse feels resentful of the other. When resentment is expressed, further drinking occurs. When it is not, tension mounts until another drinking episode is precipitated. Both search frantically for the reasons for the drinking, feeling that if the reason could be discovered, all family members could gear their behavior so as to make the drinking unnecessary. Such husband-wife discussions become increasingly unproductive as the alienation process continues.

In this stage the wife begins to feel increasingly inadequate as a wife, mother, woman, and person. She feels she has failed to meet her husband's needs, and to make a happy and united home for her children. Her husband's frequent comments to the effect that her behavior is the cause of his drinking intensify the process of self-devaluation, and leave her tense and frightened.

During this stage there are sporadic reconciliations. Usually an attempt has been made to maintain the illusion that there has been no change in husband-wife-children roles. As a result, the family organization is disrupted each time the husband drinks excessively

The maximum level of trial and error efforts to control the drinking occurs during this second stage of the crisis. At times it reaches a frantic level. Despite these efforts, or because of them, no consistency is achieved. All efforts to structure the situation and to stabilize the family appear to fail. No matter what action is taken, drinking occurs. Gradually all family goals, including permanent sobriety for the husband, become secondary to the short-term goal of having him sober today.

Stage 3: Disorganization. During Stage 3, attempts to control the drinking of the husband became sporadic, or are given up entirely. Family behavior is engaged in as a means of relieving tension, rather than as means to an end. Any techniques which diminished tension successfully in earlier stages of the crisis are used increasingly, with no other motive in mind. The wife adopts a "what's the use?" attitude and begins to think of her husband's drinking as a problem which is likely to be permanent. The demoralization of the family is also shown by the discontinuation of efforts to understand the alcoholic, by the cessation of efforts to keep the visibility of the problem at a minimum or to shield the children from a knowledge of their father's behavior. The myth that the alcoholic has his former status in the family is no longer upheld as he fails to support the family, to play husband or father roles, is imprisoned, sporadically disappears and returns, or is caught in infidelity. Although in actuality his roles have been dropped before this, the alcoholic resists the relinquishment of the myth. His efforts to have his importance to the family verbally recognized add to the general dissension. In addition, the sexual relationship between the spouses has been severely disturbed by this time. The family has also resorted to public agencies for aid, thereby further damaging its self-sufficiency and self-respect.

The wife begins to worry about her sanity during this stage, as she finds herself engaging in behavior which she knows to be senseless and random, and as she becomes more tense, anxious, and hostile. She regards her precrisis self as "the real me," and is frightened at the extent to which she has deviated from this earlier self.

Stage 4: Attempts to reorganize in spite of problems. Stage 4 usually begins when one of the subsidiary crises occurs and some action must be taken if the family is to survive as a unit. At this point some wives separate from their husbands and the family goes directly into Stage 5. Some families become stabilized at the Stage 4 level.

The major characteristic of this stage is that the wife takes over her husband's roles in action. The alcoholic husband is ignored or is assigned the status of a recalcitrant child by the wife and children. When the wife's obligations to her husband conflict with her obligations to her children, she decides in favor of the latter. As the husband becomes less disruptive to the on-going family organization and function, hostility toward him diminishes and feelings of pity and protectiveness arise. The husband's response is frequently intense; but sporadic efforts continue to be made to gain recognition as a husband and father, and to re-enter the family ranks which are being progressively closed to exclude him.

The reorganization of the family structure has a stabilizing effect on the children as they find their environment more consistent and predictable. They accept their mother's definition of the drinking as being unrelated to the behavior of family members, and guilt and anxiety diminish.

As the wife assumes more control of the family, she gradually regains her sense of worth and worries less about her sanity. Long-term family goals begin to emerge again, and plans are made to achieve them. Although by this time the family has been helped by innumerable agencies, this help has come to be accepted as necessary and ceases to be a source of shame. If, as a means of helping herself the wife contacts the Alcoholics Anonymous, she gains perspective on her problem, learns that it is one which is extremely common, and thereby loses much of her shame and her motivation for concealment. She also gains a definition of the illness, prescriptions for behavior in the situation, and a definition of the form which the illness can be expected to take. All this makes her feel that the situation has become structured, that the family is now part of a group, rather than alone, and that her behavior is purposeful. She can also renew extra-family social relationships with a group of people who are undisturbed by the drinking behavior and unpredictability of her husband.

Despite the greater stabilization of the family, subsidiary crises multiply. The violence or withdrawal of the alcoholic increases, so income is less certain; periods of unemployment, imprisonment, hospitalization, and other illness increase in frequency and duration. If the alcoholic formerly saw other women in secret, they may now be brought home. Each of these secondary crises is of an acute nature and is disruptive. The symbolization of these events as being caused by alcoholism, however, prevents the complete disruption of the family.

The most disruptive type of crisis during this stage is the husband's recognition of his drinking as a problem and his efforts to get treatment. Hope for his recovery is mobilized, and the family attempts to open its ranks and to reinstate him in his former roles in order to follow the recommendations of treatment agencies and in order to give the alcoholic the maximal chance for recovery. Roles are partially reshuffled, attempts at attitude-changes are made, only to be again disrupted if treatment is unsuccessful.

Stage 5: Efforts to escape the problems: The decision to separate from the alcoholic husband. The decision to separate from the husband is made in a manner

similar to the decision to separate for any other reasons. The wife seeks legal separation or divorce actively while the husband is the passive and resistant spouse. They play their roles and interact in substantially the same way as other separating couples (6). The problems of support, of depriving children of a father, of the attitudes of others toward the action, of conflicting advice by children, relatives, and social and treatment agencies are not unique to the alcoholism-induced crisis. However, there are problems which are more concentrated in this type of crisis. For example, in Stage 4 of the crisis the husband has contributed financially to the family from time to time, often as a means of temporarily regaining the favor of the wife, or of manipulating her in a quarrel. This motivation no longer exists to the same extent after a separation. The wife, in deciding to separate from him, cannot count on any money from him. The mental conflict about deserting a sick man must be resolved, as well as the wife's feelings of responsibility for his alcoholism.

By Stage 5, the family has often been threatened with physical violence or has experienced it. The appearance of this symptom of alcoholism is frequently the precipitant of the decision to separate. The possibility that separation may intensify the feelings behind the violence complicates the decision. The wife is afraid that if she goes to work, child-care personnel may be exposed to the violence, or that she may be absent when the children require protection, or that she will be unable to handle this behavior herself.

The previous tendency of family members to use excessive drinking as the symbolization of all other subsidiary crises and the accompanying conflicts also complicates the decision-making process. When the decision to separate is made, the alcoholic often gives up drinking temporarily, thereby removing what appears to be the major reason for the separation. This action tends to leave the wife feeling confused and bewildered.

While the definition of alcoholism as illness alleviates much of the personal involvement of the wife in the alienation process of earlier stages, at this stage it makes for additional difficulties. To separate from a husband who is a continually disruptive element in the family would be ethically possible; to desert an ill man in his hour of greatest need (as he and agencies treating him insist) leads to the mobilization of feelings of guilt. If alcoholism as an illness is defined to include the concept that no one can influence the outcome except the alcoholic himself, the guilt is less.

Events and experiences of Stage 4 have facilitated the decision-making process in many ways. Recurrent absences of the husband (due to desertion, imprisonment, or hospitalization) have indicated how smoothly the family can run without him. Taking over control of the family has bolstered the self-confidence of the wife. The orientation of the wife has switched from inaction to action, and this orientation adds to the pressure to make a decision. That she is now acquainted with public agencies which can provide help and that she has overcome her shame about using them are also helpful.

Stage 6: Reorganization of the family. The process of family reorganization after the separation or divorce is substantially similar to that experienced by families with other reasons for this action. Hill and Waller (6) describe this process as involving a reshuffling of family roles, changes in the habit patterns of individual family members, and emotional reactions similar to those in the midst of the bereavement process. The experiences of earlier stages of the crisis, in which the family has closed ranks against the alcoholic father, tend to minimize the disorganization following this subsidiary dismemberment crisis.

Reorganization is somewhat impeded if the alcoholic continues to attempt reconciliation or if he feels he must "get even" with the family for deserting him.

Stage 7: Reorganization of the whole family. Stage 7 is entered if the husband achieves sobriety, whether or not separation has preceded. It was pointed out that in earlier stages of the crisis most of the problems in the marriage were attributed to the alcoholism of the husband. Thus problems in adjustment which were not related directly to the drinking were unrecognized and unmet. The "sober personality" of the husband was thought of as the "real" personality, with a resulting lack of recognition of other factors involved in his sober behavior, for example, remorse and guilt over his actions, which led him to act like "the ideal husband" when sober. Lack of conflict and lack of drinking were defined as indicating a perfect adjustment. For the wife and husband facing a sober marriage after many years of an alcoholic marriage, the expectations of marriage without alcoholism are unrealistic and idealistic. The reality of marriage almost inevitably brings disillusionments.

The sobriety of the husband does not raise hope at first. The family has been through this before. They are, however, willing to stand by him in the new attempt. As the length of sobriety increases, so do the hopes for its permanence and the efforts to be of help.

With the continuation of sobriety, many problems begin to crop up. Mother has for years managed the family, and now father wishes to be reinstated in his former roles. Usually the first role reestablished is that of breadwinner. The economic problems of the family begin to be alleviated as debts are gradually paid and there is enough left over for current needs. With the resumption of this role, the husband feels that the family should reinstate him immediately in all his former roles. Difficulties inevitably ensue. For example, the children are often unable to accept his resumption of his father role. Their mother has played the roles of both parents for so long that it takes time to get used to the idea of consulting their father on problems and asking for his decisions. Often the father tries too hard to manage this change overnight, and the very pressure put upon the children toward this end defeats him.

The wife, who finds it difficult to conceive of her husband as permanently sober, feels an unwillingness to relinquish control, even though she believes that reinstatement of her husband in his family roles is necessary to his sobriety. She remembers events in the past when his failure to handle his responsibilities was catastrophic to the family. Used to avoiding anything which might upset him, the wife often hesitates to discuss problems openly. If she is successful in helping him to regain his roles as father, she sometimes feels resentful of his intrusion into territory she has come to regard as her own. If he makes errors in judgment which affect the family adversely, her former feelings of being superior to him may come to the fore and affect her interaction with him.

Often the husband makes demands for obedience, for consideration, and for pampering which members of the family feel unable to meet. He may become rather euphoric as his sobriety continues. He may feel superior and very virtuous for a time, which are difficult for the family to accept in a former alcoholic.

Gradually, however, the drinking problem sinks into the past and marital adjustment at some level is achieved. Even when this has occurred, the drinking problem crops up occasionally, as when the time comes for a decision about whether the children should be permitted to drink. At parties the wife is concerned about whether her husband will take a drink.

If sobriety has come through Alcoholics Anonymous, the husband frequently throws himself so wholeheartedly into A.A. activities that his wife sees little of him and feels neglected. As she worries less about his drinking, she may press him to cut down on these activities. That this is dangerous, since A.A. activity is highly correlated with success in Alcoholics Anonymous, has been shown by Lahey (11). The wife also discovers that, though she has a sober husband, she is by no means free of alcoholics. In his Twelfth Step work, he may keep the house filled with men he is helping. In the past her husband has avoided selfsearching; and now he may become excessively introspective.

If the husband becomes sober through Alcoholics Anonymous and the wife participates actively in groups open to her, the thoughts of what is happening to her, to her husband, and to her family will be verbalized and interpreted within the framework of the Alcoholics Anonymous philosophy; and the situation will probably be more tolerable and more easily worked out.

Summary

The onset of alcoholism in a family member has been viewed as precipitating a cumulative crisis for the family. Seven critical stages have been delineated. Each stage affects the form which the following one will take. The family finds itself in an unstructured situation which is undefined by the culture. Thus it is forced to evolve techniques of adjustment through trial and error. The unpredictability of the situation, added to its lack of structure, engenders anxiety in family members which gives rise to personality difficulties. Factors in the culture, in the environment, and within the family situation prolong the crisis and deter the working out of permanent adjustment patterns. With the arrest of the alcoholism, the crisis enters its final stage. The family then attempts to reorganize to include the ex-alcoholic and to make adjustments to the changes which have occurred in him.

REFERENCES

1. Baker, S. M.: Social case work with inebriates. In Alcohol, Science and Society, Lecture 27. New Haven: *Quarterly Journal of Studies on Alcohol,* 1945.
2. Futterman, S.: "Personality trends in wives of alcoholics." *J. Psychiat. Soc. Work,* 23:37–41, 1953.
3. Whalen, T.: "Wives of alcoholics: four types observed in a family service agency." *Quart. J. Studies Alcohol,* 14: 632–641, 1953.
4. Price, G. M.: "A study of the wives of twenty alcoholics." *Quart. J. Studies Alcohol,* 5:620–627, 1945.
5. Newell, N.: "Alcoholism and the father image." *Quart. J. Studies Alcohol,* 11: 92–96, 1950.
6. Waller, W.: (Revised by Reuben Hill). *The Family: a Dynamic Interpretation.* New York: The Dryden Press, 1951, pp. 453–561, for a resume of the major research on families in crisis.
7. "The impact of mental illness on the family." *Journal of Social Issues,* XI:4, 1955.
8. Koos, E. L.: *Families in Trouble.* New York: King's Crown Press, 1946.
9. Jackson, J. K.: The adjustment of the family to the crisis of alcoholism. *Quart. J. Studies Alcohol,* 15:562–586, 1954.
10. Folsom, J. K.: *The Family and Democratic Society.* New York: John Wiley and Sons, 1943, p. 447.
11. Lahey, W. W.: A Comparison of Social and Personal Factors Identified with Selected Members of Alcoholics Anonymous. Master's Thesis, University of Southern California, 1950.

C · PERSONALITY AND THE SCHOOL

EFFECTS ON CLASSMATES OF A DEVIANT STUDENT'S POWER AND RESPONSE
TO A TEACHER-EXERTED CONTROL TECHNIQUE

by William J. Gnagey

The purpose of this study was to further clarify some of the dynamics of discipline in the public school classroom. We were especially interested in the reaction of a misbehaving student (deviant) to a teacher-exerted control technique with respect to its effect upon the behavior of his onlooking nontarget classmates (audience). In addition, we wished to determine the influence of the deviant's status in the class power structure.

Two notable efforts in the area of discipline research have been concerned primarily with the effects of certain types of control efforts upon the deviant himself. Redl and Wineman (1951, 1952) pioneered in this field, reporting the results of a clinical study of ego damaged children. More recently Kounin and Gump (1958) published preliminary findings of a somewhat different nature. They were able to show that a teacher's control effort not only influences the behavior of the deviant who is its target, but significantly affects the behavior of students who are audience to but not targets of the disciplinary action. This phenomenon was called the ripple effect.

One of the factors influencing the ripple effect interested us especially. Kounin and Gump discovered that children who were connected in some way with the

SOURCE: *Journal of Educational Psychology*, Vol. 51 (1960), pp. 1–8.

deviant or deviancy before the control technique was emitted appeared to have been more influenced than those who had no such previous connection. This raised the question as to what the nature of some of these previous connections might be, other than those of attention or proximity at the time of the deviancy. We believed one might be social power status.

The impact of a powerful group member's behavior upon the other members of the group had previously been studied by Lippitt, Polansky, and Redl (1952) in two camp settings. They concluded that the behavior of a boy was more likely to spread to other members of the group when he had high power than when he had low power. The Lippitt group limited their study of contagion to overt behavior. We were interested in the possibility that the overt reaction of the deviant to the control technique might influence the perceptual behavior of the nontarget audience, as well as their overt actions, and possibly also their learning.

Theoretical Expectations

POWER OF THE TEACHER. Since the Lippitt group found that male members tended to identify more with a high influence peer than with a low influence peer, we believed that if a high-powered

420

deviant submitted to the teacher's control effort, his overt acceptance of the teacher's dominance would spread to the others in the class for whom the deviant was an identifying figure. Likewise, we predicted that a high-powered deviant's attitude of defiance toward the teacher would also spread to his classmates.

The responses of opposite sex members of the class were not clearly predictable. Even if girls should agree with the boys in attributing high power to a certain male deviant, it is doubtful if the identification dynamic would be of the same nature.

Though we expected little contagion from the behavior of the low-powered deviant, we entertained the possibility that the mere success or failure of the teacher to achieve submission from him might be used as a cue by the audience upon which they might base their judgments on the teacher's ability to control the class.

VALENCE OF THE TEACHER. French (1956) suggests that there are several "bases of power" when considering the influence of a leader over a group. These are: attraction, coercion, expertness, reward, and legitimacy. We hypothesized that any incident which influenced the total power attributed to the teacher by her class might influence their judgment of her power from each of these bases. In other words, we predicted that if the deviant's response tended to cause the audience to raise their appraisal of the teacher's ability to handle the class (i.e., themselves), it might also raise the level of her attractiveness to the group.

EXPERTNESS OF THE TEACHER. Following a line of reasoning parallel to that in the paragraph above, we predicted that whatever the experimental incident did to the audience judgment of the teacher's ability to handle the class, this would also be reflected in their judgment of her expertness, another of French's bases of social power.

FAIRNESS OF THE CONTROL TECHNIQUE. We anticipated a ripple effect concerning the apparent fairness of the control technique. The attitude of acceptance (submission) or rejection (defiance), conveyed to the audience by means of the deviant's overt response to the control technique, would be spread to others in the audience for whom the deviant was an identifying figure. We believed the effects of the low-powered deviant's response would be negligible, but were uncertain about the responses of members of opposite sex.

DIFFERENCES IN AUDIENCE LEARNING. In appraising defiance and submission as two responses which a deviant might act out, we believed that the former behavior was unusual enough so that the general expectation of the audience—that a student will do what a teacher tells him to —would be disrupted. If this happened, we believed an imbalance tension would result, cutting down the efficiency of recall in the audience. Heider (1946) has discussed balance in some detail.

In addition, we believed that the audience would be in a greater state of tension if the defiant class member had high power, since a greater sensitivity to his actions would be present in those for whom he was an identifying figure.

The Experimental Procedure

We accordingly devised an experimental design in which the independent variables were (a) the response of the deviant (defiance vs. submission) and (b) the power of the deviant (high power versus low power). As discussed above, the dependent variables were: (a) power of the teacher, (b) valence of the teacher, (c) expertness of the teacher, (d) fairness of the control technique (as qualitative characteristics of the audience perceptual behavior), and (e) audience learning. In brief, four classes of fifth graders were to be measured before and after the showing of a 10-minute film during which a male classmate, selected and trained secretly beforehand, misbehaved, became the target of a control technique executed by a new teacher, and reacted in a prearranged defiant or submissive manner.

SUBJECTS. Four classes of fifth graders ($N = 130$) were chosen from schools in the area around North Manchester, Indiana. Since it was our purpose to obtain "classroom reality," we chose intact homerooms which had operated as such from September of 1956 until May of 1957. We felt that the group structure would be more stabilized by the end of the school year than at the beginning. Table 1 summarizes the size, sex composition, and ability of each group. It was established that none of the differences existing among the average achievement of the groups favored the experimental hypotheses.

TABLE 1. *Several Characteristics of the Experimental Groups*

GROUP	NUMBER OF SUBJECTS			MEAN ACADEMIC GRADE [a]
	Boys	Girls	Total	
High-powered defiant	19	18	37	3.8
High-powered submissive	12	13	25	3.9
Low-powered defiant	18	15	33	3.5
Low-powered submissive	13	22	35	3.2

[a] Mean academic grade was computed by averaging the grade for all subjects (except art and music) for the preceding grading period. A five-point scale was used: A-5, B-4, C-3, D-2, F-1.

PRE-EXPERIMENTAL MEASUREMENTS. The experimenter administered the first questionnaire under the guise of one who was making a study of "how to make school more interesting." The students were provided with a list of their classmates' names, since part of the instrument was a sociogram constructed to measure the social power attributed to each boy by other members of his class. Such items as the following were used:

> When a bunch of kids from this class get together outside of school, which *three boys* nearly always get the others to do what they want to?
> Some boys are stronger and tougher than others. If it came to a fight, which *three boys* in this class could win over most of the rest, if they had to?

A second section measured the students' pre-experimental perceptions of the power, expertness, and valence of female teachers in general. Such questions as the following were used:

> How well can lady teachers handle the kids in this class?
> How much do lady teachers know about showing films?
> How well do you like most lady teachers?

Students registered each of their answers by drawing a vertical line across a 100 centimeter horizontal rating scale which had the extreme choices printed at the ends. Scores were ascertained by measuring the number of centimeters between the students' mark and the negative end of the scale.

SELECTION AND TRAINING OF DEVIANTS. On a subsequent day, the experimenter and T (a female elementary education major) secretly trained the boy who had been selected by means of the sociogram. In each of two classes a high-powered boy was chosen, and in the other two, low-powered boys were selected. Table 2 summarizes the *attributed power ratio* of each of the boys finally chosen. Other questions helped us avoid choosing deviants who were actively disliked. Each of these boys was secretly trained to play a specific part during the experimental situation in his own group. By means of role-play techniques, they were trained to execute the same deviancy (saying aloud, "Hey, is this film about over?") in each group.

TABLE 2. *Attributed Power Ratios of Deviants by Groups*

	ATTRIBUTED POWER RATIOS [a]		
GROUP	Girls' Ratings	Boys' Ratings	Combined Ratings
High-powered defiant	.82	.68	.75
High-powered submissive	.70	.75	.72
Low-powered defiant	.16	.03	.09
Low-powered submissive	.01	.03	.02

[a] Attributed power ratio computed by dividing actual number of power choices received, by most possible.

Two of the deviants were trained to react to the control technique in a submissive manner (hanging the head and saying, "Yes ma'am, I'm sorry ma'am," as each left the room). The other deviants were trained to react in a defiant manner (saying belligerently, "I'll leave the room, but I won't go to the principal's office. The heck with you!" as he left the room).

THE EXPERIMENTAL EPISODE. Some time after the newly trained deviant had returned to his room, the experimenter appeared officially. After the class had been seated in the projection room, the experimenter introduced the teacher by saying, "Yesterday I told you I would bring along a grade-school teacher who would show you a film. This is Miss Robe. She wants to talk to you about the film before she shows it, so I will turn the class over to her." At this, the experimenter left the room.

The teacher then said to the class, "I am very interested in finding out some things about films that we show in school. I have brought one with me today. I want you to watch it quietly, without talking, so that you can rate it accurately when it is over." She then turned out the light and began showing the film.

At a prearranged signal (the teacher scratched her head), the deviant talked aloud in the prescribed manner. The teacher immediately shut off the projector and said in an irritated voice, "Hey you, I told you not to talk. You leave the room and report to the principal's office." The deviant then reacted to this control technique in his prescribed defiant or submissive manner and left the room. The teacher then showed the rest of the film, turned on the light and left the room.

POSTEXPERIMENTAL MEASUREMENTS. Shortly, the experimenter re-entered the room and passed out the final questionnaire which ostensibly rated the film showing, but which also measured the dependent variables. The first part was a rating scale containing questions matched to those on the first instrument. These indicated the change in the dependent variables. The second section of the final measurement was an objective, multiple-choice test over many of the facts presented in the film. Some typical items were: "How many boys were working in the laboratory? (one, two, three, four, five)." "At the end of the film, the boy who held the microscope had: (black hair, red hair, blonde hair, brown hair, white hair)." Scores were ascertained by computing the number of correct responses.

Finally, a fairness question was added. It read: "How fair is it for the teacher to send a person to the principal's office for talking during a film?" The horizontal rating scale technique was used in this item.

Thus the effects of four separate conditions were measured, each one a unique combination of the social power and overt reaction of the deviant, that is, high-powered and defiant, high-powered and submissive, low-powered and defiant, low-powered and submissive. The deviancy, the control technique, the film, and the teacher were all constants in the situation.

Results and Discussion

With the exception of the questions that measured fairness and learning, scores on all items were derived from the differences between the matched items on the first and second measurements. These change scores were prefixed with a plus or minus sign to indicate the direction in which the subject's answer varied, and where treated by the chi square test.

how well they thought the teacher "could handle the kids in their class." Students (boys and girls combined) who saw deviants submit to the teacher's control effort rated her as significantly more capable of handling kids in their class than did students who saw deviants defy her ($x^2 = 16.55$, $p < .001$) (see Table 3).

In order to determine whether the power of the deviant influenced the effects on the audience, two other comparisons were completed. Because of the aforementioned possibility of an identification linked contagion effect, we compared male high-powered defiance scores with male high-powered submissive scores and found that boys who saw a high-powered deviant submit thought the teacher could handle the kids in the class

TABLE 3. *Effects of the Deviant's Reaction upon His Classmates' Perception of the Teacher's Power*

SUBJECTS	GROUPS	SCORES 0 and +	−	x^2 (1 df)	p
All	All defiant	40	31		
	All Submissive	54	6	16.55	<.001
Male Only	High-powered defiant	11	8		
	High-powered submiss.	12	0		.0095 [a]
Male Only	Low-powered defiant	11	12		
	Low-powered submiss.	12	1		.0524 [a]

[a] Fisher exact probability.

Due to an artifact of the measuring device, some of the scores on the premeasurement were seriously restricted from any possibility of shift. We therefore checked back on each apparently significant result to make sure that these frozen scores did not work against the null hypothesis. In cases where they favored the experimental hypotheses, Fisher exact probability test was used.

POWER ASCRIBED TO THE TEACHER. The students of each class were asked to rate

significantly better than did boys who saw a high-powered deviant defy ($p = .0096$, Fisher exact test) (see Table 3).

When a similar comparison was made between low-powered defiant and low-powered submissive scores, the difference was just below the .05 level of confidence ($p = .0524$, Fisher exact test) (see Table 3).

When male and female scores were lumped together, the high-powered defiant vs. the high-powered submissive and the low-powered defiant versus the low-powered submissive comparisons were both well above the .01 level of confidence.

This might indicate that while all onlookers used the deviant's reaction as a cue to the teacher's success as a disciplinarian, boys were somewhat more sensitive to the cues emitted by the high-powered deviants than those emitted by the low-powered deviants.

VALENCE OF THE TEACHER. Students were asked to indicate how much they liked the teacher. When male and female scores were lumped together, no significant difference was apparent between students who saw the deviant submit and those who saw deviants defy the teacher. No other comparisons produced significant differences.

who saw high-powered deviants defy ($x^2 = 14.10$, $p < .001$). A similar comparison done with those who saw low-powered deviants submit showed no significant difference ($x^2 = .007$, $p > .95$) (see Table 4).

This would tend to support the hypothesis that factors which influence the teacher's total ascribed power tend to influence audience perception of her expertness also. In addition, it would appear that students are more sensitive to cues emitted by high-powered deviants than those by low-powered deviants.

FAIRNESS OF THE CONTROL TECHNIQUE. The students were asked to indicate how fair they thought it was for a teacher to send a person to the principal's office. Those (boys and girls combined) who saw

TABLE 4. *Effects of the Deviant's Reaction upon His Classmates' Perception of the Teacher's Expertness*

| SUBJECTS | GROUPS | SCORES | | x^2 (1 df) | p |
		0 and +	—		
All	Defiant	40	30		
	Submissive	46	12		
				7.07	<.01
All	High-powered defiant	18	19		
	High-powered submiss.	22	1		
				14.10	<.001
All	Low-powered defiant	22	11		
	Low-powered submiss.	23	12		
				.007	>.95

EXPERTNESS OF THE TEACHER. The students were asked to indicate how much they thought the teacher knew about showing films. Students (boys and girls combined) who saw deviants submit to the teacher's control effort rated her as knowing more about showing films than did students who saw deviants defy her ($x^2 = 7.07$, $p < .01$) (see Table 4).

It was found that students who saw high-powered deviants submit rated the teacher as more expert than did students

deviants submit to the teacher's control effort rated the control technique as significantly fairer than did those who saw deviants defy ($x^2 = 8.96$, $p < .01$) (see Table 5).

In addition, while students who saw a high-powered deviant submit rated the control technique as fairer than did students who saw a high-powered deviant defy ($x^2 = 11.09$, $p < .001$), no significant difference was found between students who saw a low-powered deviant submit and those who saw a low-powered deviant defy ($\chi^2 = .09$, $p > .80$) (see Table 5).

This would tend to support the hypothesis that the deviant's attitude tended to spread to his classmates and that the effects were much stronger when he was high-powered than when he had low-power.

teacher caused enough disruption of the expectations of the other students that they were able to learn fewer facts from the film than those who saw deviants submit. As predicted, this effect appeared to be more pronounced on the male classmates when the deviants had high power than when deviants had lower power.

TABLE 5. *Effects of the Deviant's Reaction upon His Classmates' Perception of the Fairness of the Control Technique*

SUBJECTS	GROUPS	SCORES		χ^2 (1 df)	p
		0 and +	−		
All	Defiant	49	19		
	Submissive	49	3		
				8.96	<.01
All	High-powered defiant	19	16		
	High-powered submiss.	23	1		
				11.09	<.001
All	Low-powered defiant	30	3		
	Low-powered submiss.	26	2		
				.09	>.80

AUDIENCE LEARNING SCORES. Scores from the multiple-choice test were used to measure the students' recognition of film facts. Students (boys and girls combined) who saw deviants defy the teacher were able to recognize significantly fewer film facts than were students who saw deviants submit to the teacher's control effort ($t = 2.07$, $df = 129$, $p < .05$) (see Table 6).

In addition, while the boys who saw high-powered deviants submit were able to recognize significantly more film facts than were boys who saw high-powered deviants defy ($t = 2.08$, $df = 30$, $p < .05$), no difference was found between boys who saw low-powered deviants submit and boys who saw low-powered deviants defy ($t = 1.14$, $df = 30$, $p > .10$) (see Table 6).

This would tend to support the hypothesis that a deviant's defiance of a

Summary and Conclusions

Four classes of fifth-graders were shown a science film during which a male classmate misbehaved and became the target of a control technique exerted by a new teacher. The deviants (who were confederates of the experimenter) were selected on the basis of having high or low power among their peers and were trained to react in either a defiant or submissive manner. Classmates who saw deviants submit to a teacher's control technique perceived the teacher to be more expert and powerful, perceived the control technique to be fairer, and recognized more film facts than did classmates who saw deviants defy. These effects were more pronounced when deviants had high power than when they had low power.

TABLE 6. *Effects of the Deviant's Reaction upon His Classmates' Learning of Film Facts*

SUBJECTS	GROUP	N	MEAN SCORE [a]	S^2	t	p
All	Defiant	70	3.76	.471		
	Submiss.	60	4.10	1.31		
					2.07	<.05
Male Only	Hi-pow. Defiant	19	3.68	.784		
	Hi-pow. Submiss.	12	4.50	1.364		
					2.08	<.05
Male Only	Low-pow. Defiant	18	4.00	.796		
	Low-pow. Submiss.	13	4.46	1.603		
					1.14	>.10

[a] Mean score is average number of items marked correctly on film fact test.

It seems reasonable to conclude that the overt reaction of a male deviant student *does have* some measurable effects on the perceptual behavior and learning performances of his classmates and that these effects are influenced by the social power of the deviant.

REFERENCES

1. French, J. R. P., Jr.: "A formal theory of social power." *Psychol. Rev.*, 1956, 63, 181–194.

2. Heider, F.: "Attitudes and cognitive organization." *J. Psychol.*, 1946, 21, 107–112.

3. Kounin, J., and P. Gump: "The ripple effect in discipline." *Elem. sch. J.*, 1958, 59, 158–162.

4. Lippitt, R., N. Polansky, F. Redl, and S. Rosen: "The dynamics of power." *Human Relat.*, 1952, 5, 37–64.

5. Redl, F., and D. Wineman: *Children who hate.* Glencoe, Ill.: Free Press, 1951.

6. ———.: *Controls from within.* Glencoe, Ill.: Free Press, 1952.

D · PERSONALITY AND ADULT ROLES

1 · Roles in Formal Organizations

ROLE, PERSONALITY, AND SOCIAL STRUCTURE IN THE ORGANIZATIONAL SETTING

by Daniel J. Levinson

During the past twenty years the concept of role has achieved wide currency in social psychology, sociology, and anthropology. From a sociopsychological point of view, one of its most alluring qualities is its double reference to the individual and to the collective matrix. The concept of role concerns the thoughts and actions of individuals, and, at the same time, it points up the influence upon the individual of socially patterned demands and standardizing forces. Partly for this reason, "role" has been seen by numerous writers (e.g., Gerth and Mills, 1953; Gross, Mason, and McEachern, 1958; Hartley and Hartley, 1952; Linton, 1945; Mead, 1934; Merton, 1957; Parsons, 1951; Sarbin, 1954) as a crucial concept for the linking of psychology, sociology, and anthropology. However, while the promise has seemed great, the fulfillment has thus far been relatively small. The concept of role remains one of the most overworked and underdeveloped in the social sciences.

My purpose here is to examine role theory primarily as it is used in the analysis of organizations (such as the hospital, business firm, prison, school). The organi-

SOURCE: *Journal of Abnormal and Social Psychology*, Vol. 58 (1959), pp. 170–180.

zation provides a singularly useful arena for the development and application of role theory. It is small enough to be amenable to empirical study. Its structure is complex enough to provide a wide variety of social positions and role-standardizing forces. It offers an almost limitless opportunity to observe the individual personality *in vivo* (rather than in the psychologist's usual *vitro* of laboratory, survey questionnaire, or clinical office), selectively utilizing and modifying the demands and opportunities given in the social environment. The study of personality can, I submit, find no setting in which the reciprocal impact of psyche and situation is more clearly or more dramatically evidenced.

Organizational theory and research has traditionally been the province of sociology and related disciplines that focus most directly upon the collective unit. Chief emphasis has accordingly been given to such aspects of the organization as formal and informal structure, administrative policy, allocation of resources, level of output, and the like. Little interest has been shown in the individual member as such or in the relevance of personality for organizational functioning. The prevailing image of the organization has been that of a mechanical apparatus operating impersonally once it is set in motion by administrative edict. The prevailing conception of social role is consonant with this image: the individual member is regarded as a cog in the apparatus, what he thinks and does being determined by requirements in the organizational structure.

This paper has the following aims: (1) To examine the traditional conception of organizational structure and role and to assess its limitations from a sociopsychological point of view. (2) To examine the conception of social role that derives from this approach to social structure and that tends, by definition, to exclude consideration of personality. (3) To provide a formulation of several, analytically distinct, role concepts to be used in place of the global term "role." (4) To suggest a theoretical approach to the analysis of relationships among role, personality, and social structure.

Traditional Views of Bureaucratic Structure and Role

Human personality has been virtually excluded from traditional organization theory. Its absence is perhaps most clearly reflected in Weber's (1946, 1947) theory of bureaucracy, which has become a major source of current thought regarding social organization and social role. I shall examine this theory briefly here, in order to point up some of its psychological limitations but without doing justice to its many virtues. In Weber's writings, the bureaucratic organization is portrayed as a monolithic edifice. Norms are clearly defined and consistently applied, the agencies of role socialization succeed in inducing acceptance of organizational requirements, and the sanctions system provides the constraints and incentives needed to maintain behavioral conformity. Every individual is given a clearly defined role and readily "fills" it. There is little room in this tightly bound

universe for more complex choice, for individual creativity, or for social change. As Gouldner (1954) has said of the studies carried out in this tradition: "Indeed, the social scene described has sometimes been so completely stripped of people that the impression is unintentionally rendered that there are disembodied social forces afoot, able to realize their ambitions apart from human action" (p. 16).

For Weber, bureaucracy as an ideal type is administered by "experts" in a spirit of impersonal rationality and is operated on a principle of discipline according to which each member performs his required duties as efficiently as possible. Rationality in decision-making and obedience in performance are the pivots on which the entire system operates. In this scheme of things, emotion is regarded merely as a hindrance to efficiency, as something to be excluded from the bureaucratic process.

The antipathy to emotion and motivation in Weber's thinking is reflected as well in his formulation of three types of authority: traditional, charismatic, and rational-legal. The rational-legal administrator is the pillar of bureaucracy. He receives his legitimation impersonally, from "the system," by virtue of his *technical* competence. His personal characteristics, his conception of the organization and its component groupings, his modes of relating to other persons (except that he be fair and impartial)—these and other psychological characteristics are not taken into theoretical consideration. There is no place in Weber's ideal type for the ties of affection, the competitive strivings, the subtle forms of support or of intimidation, so commonly found in even the most "rationalized" organizations. It is only the "charismatic" leader who becomes emotionally important to his followers and who must personally validate his right to lead.

While Weber has little to say about the problem of motivation, two motives implicitly become universal instincts in his conception of "bureaucratic man." These are *conformity* (the motive for automatic acceptance of structural norms), and *status-seeking* (the desire to advance oneself by the acquisition and exercise of technical competence). More complex motivations and feelings are ignored.

There has been widespread acknowledgment of both the merits and the limitations of Weber's protean thought. However, the relevance of personality for organizational structure and role-definition remains a largely neglected problem in contemporary theory and research.[1] Our inadequacies are exemplified in the excellent *Reader in Bureaucracy,* edited by Merton, Gray, Hockey, and Selvin (1952). Although this book contains some of the most distinguished contributions to the field, it has almost nothing on the relation between organizational structure and personality. The editors suggest two lines of interrelation: first, that personality may be one determinant of occupational choice; and second, that a given type of structure may in time modify the personalities of its members. These are valuable hypotheses. However, they do not acknowledge the possibility that personality may have an impact on social structure. "The organization" is projected as an organism that either selects congenial personalities or makes over the recalcitrant ones to suit its own needs. This image is reflected in the editors' remark: "It would seem, therefore, that officials not initially suited to the demands of a bureaucratic position, progressively undergo modifications of personality" (p. 352). In other words, when social structure and personality fail to mesh, it is assumed to be personality alone that gives. Structure is the prime, uncaused, cause.

The impact of organizational structure on personality is indeed a significant problem for study. There is, however, a converse to this. When a member is critical of the organizational structure, he *may* maintain his personal values and traits, and work toward structural change. The manifold impact of personality on organizational structure and role remains to be investigated. To provide a theoretical basis for this type of investigation we need, I believe, to re-examine the concept of role.

[1] Contemporary organization theory has benefited from criticisms and reformulations of Weber's theory by such writers as Barnard (1938), Friedrich (1950), Gerth and Mills (1953), Gouldner (1954), Merton (1957), and Parsons (in his introduction to Weber, 1947). Selznick (1957) has recently presented a conception of the administrative-managerial role that allows more room for psychological influences, but these are not explicitly conceptualized. There is growing though still inconclusive evidence from research on "culture and personality" work (Inkeles and Levinson, 1954) that social structures of various types both "require" and are influenced by modal personality, but this approach has received little application in research on organizations. An attempt at a distinctively sociopsychological approach, and a comprehensive view of the relevant literature, is presented by Argyris (1957).

"Social Role" as a Unitary Concept

The concept of role is related to, and must be distinguished from, the concept of social position. A position is an element of organizational autonomy, a location in social space, a category of organizational membership. A role is, so to say, an aspect of organizational physiology; it involves function, adaptation, process. It is meaningful to say that a person "occupies" a social position; but it is inappropriate to say, as many do, that one occupies a role.

There are at least three specific senses in which the term "role" has been used, explicitly or implicitly, by different writers or by the same writer on different occasions.

a. Role may be defined as the *structurally given demands* (norms, expectations, taboos, responsibilities, and the like) associated with a given social position. Role is, in this sense, something outside the given individual, a set of pressures and facilitations that channel, guide, impede, support his functioning in the organization.

b. Role may be defined as the member's *orientation* or *conception* of the part he is to play in the organization. It is, so to say, his inner definition of what someone in his social position is supposed to think and do about it. Mead (1934) is probably the main source of this view of social role as an aspect of the person, and it is commonly used in analyses of occupational roles.

c. Role is commonly defined as the *actions* of the individual members—actions seen in terms of their relevance for the social structure (that is, seen in relation to the prevailing norms). In this sense, role refers to the ways in which members of a position act (with or without conscious intention) *in accord with or in violation of a given set of organizational norms.* Here, as in (*b*), role is defined as a characteristic of the actor rather than of his normative environment.

Many writers use a definition that embraces all of the above meanings without systematic distinction, and then shift, explicitly or implicitly, from one meaning to another. The following are but a few of many possible examples.[2]

[2] An argument very similar to the one made here is presented by Gross, Mason, and McEachern (1958) in a comprehensive overview and critique of role theory. They point up the assumption of high consensus regarding role-demands and role-conceptions in traditional role theory, and present empirical evidence contradicting this assumption. Their analysis is, however, less concerned than the present one with the converging of role theory and personality theory.

Each of the above three meanings of "role" is to be found in the writings of Parsons: (*a*) "From the point of view of the actor, his role is defined by the normative expectations of the members of the group as formulated in its social traditions" (Parsons, 1945, p. 230). (*b*) "The role is that organized sector of an actor's orientation which constitutes and defines his participation in an interactive process" (Parsons and Shils, 1951, p. 23). (*c*) "The status-role (is) the organized subsystem of acts of the actor or actors . . ." (Parsons, 1951, p. 26).

More often, the term is used in a way that includes all three meanings at once. In this *unitary,* all-embracing conception of role, there is, by assumption, a close fit between behavior and disposition (attitude, value), between societal prescription and individual adaptation. This point of view has its primary source in the writings of Linton, whose formulations of culture, status, and role have had enormous influence. According to Linton (1945), a role "includes the attitudes, values and behavior ascribed by the society to any and all persons occupying this status." In other words, society provides for each status or position a single mold that shapes the beliefs and actions of all its occupants.

Perhaps the most extensive formulation of this approach along sociopsychological lines is given by Newcomb (1950). Following Linton, Newcomb asserts, "Roles thus represent ways of carrying out the functions for which positions exist—ways which are generally agreed upon within (the) group" (p. 281). And, "Role is strictly a sociological concept; it purposely ignores individual, psychological facts" (p. 329). Having made this initial commitment to the "sociological" view that individual role-activity is a simple mirroring of group norms, Newcomb later attempts to find room for his "psychological" concerns with motivation, meaning, and individual differences. He does this by partially giving up the "unitary" concept of role, and introducing a distinction between "prescribed role" and "role behavior." He avers that prescribed role is a sociological concept, "referring to common factors in the behaviors required" (p. 459), whereas role behavior is a psychological concept that refers to the activities of a single individual. The implications of this distinction for his earlier general definition of role are left unstated.

Whatever the merits or faults of Newcomb's reformulation, it at least gives conceptual recognition to the possibility that social prescription and individual adaptation may not match. This possibility is virtually excluded in the definition of social role forwarded by Linton and used by so many social scientists. In this respect, though certainly not in all respects, Linton's view is like Weber's: both see individual behavior as predominantly determined by the collective matrix. The matrix is, in the former case, culture, and in the latter, bureaucracy.

In short, the "unitary" conception of role assumes that there is a 1:1 relationship, or at least a *high degree of congruence,* among the three role aspects noted above. In the theory of bureaucratic organization, the rationale for this assumption is somewhat as follows. The organizationally given requirements will be internalized by the members and will thus be mirrored in their role-conceptions. People will know, and will want to do, what is expected of them. The agencies of role socialization will succeed except with a deviant minority—who constitute a separate problem for study. Individual action will in turn reflect the structural norms, since the appropriate role-conceptions will have been internalized and since the sanctions system rewards normative behavior and punishes deviant behavior. Thus, it is assumed that structural norms, individual role-conceptions and individual role-performance are three isomorphic reflections of a single entity:

"the" role appropriate to a given organizational position.

It is, no doubt, reasonable to expect some degree of congruence among these aspects of a social role. Certainly, every organization contains numerous mechanisms designed to further such congruence. At the same time, it is a matter of common observation that organizations vary in the degree of their integration; structural demands are often contradictory, lines of authority may be defective, disagreements occur and reverberate at and below the surface of daily operations. To assume that what the organization requires, and what its members actually think and do, comprise a single, unified whole is severely to restrict our comprehension of organizational dynamics and change.

It is my thesis, then, that the unitary conception of social role is unrealistic and theoretically constricting. We should, I believe, eliminate the single term "role" except in the most general sense, i.e., of "role theory" as an over-all frame of analysis. Let us, rather, give independent conceptual and empirical status to the above three concepts and others. Let us investigate the relationships of each concept with the others, making no assumptions about the degree of congruence among them. Further, let us investigate their relationships with various other characteristics of the organization and of its individual members. I would suggest that the role concepts be named and defined as follows.

Organizationally Given Role-Demands

The role-demands are external to the individual whose role is being examined. They are the situational pressures that confront him as the occupant of a given structural position. They have manifold sources: in the official charter and policies of the organization; in the traditions and ideology, explicit as well as implicit, that help to define the organization's purposes and modes of operation; in the views about this position which are held by members of the position (who influence any single member) and by members of the various positions impinging upon this one; and so on.

It is a common assumption that the structural requirements for any position are as a rule defined with a *high degree of explicitness, clarity, and consensus* among all the parties involved. To take the position of hospital nurse as an example: it is assumed that her role-requirements will be understood and agreed upon by the hospital administration, the nursing authorities, the physicians, etc. Yet one of the striking research findings in all manner of hospitals is the failure of consensus regarding the proper role of nurse (e.g., Burling, Lentz, and Wilson, 1956; Argyris, 1957). Similar findings have been obtained in school systems, business firms, and the like (e.g., Gross et al., 1958; Kornhauser, Dubin, and Ross, 1954).

In attempting to characterize the role-requirements for a given position, one must therefore guard against the assumption that they are unified and logically coherent. There may be major differences and even contradictions between official norms, as defined by charter or by administrative authority, and the "informal" norms held by various groupings within the organization. Moreover, within a given-status group, such as the top administrators, there may be several conflicting viewpoints concerning long range goals, current policies, and specific role-requirements. In short, the structural demands themselves are often multiple and disunified. Few are the attempts to investigate the sources of such disunity, to acknowledge its frequency, or to take it into conceptual account in general structural theory.

It is important also to consider the specificity or *narrowness* with which the normative requirements are defined. Norms have an "ought" quality; they confer legitimacy and reward-value upon certain modes of action, thought and emotion, while condemning others. But there are degrees here. Normative evaluations cover a spectrum from "strongly required," through various degrees of qualitative kinds of "acceptable," to more or less stringently tabooed. Organizations differ in the width of the intermediate range on this spectrum. That is, they differ in the number and kinds of adaptation that are normatively acceptable. The wider this range—the less specific the norms—the greater is the area of personal choice for the individual. While the existence of such an intermediate range is generally acknowledged, structural analyses often proceed as though practically all norms were absolute prescriptions or proscriptions allowing few alternatives for individual action.

There are various other normative complexities to be reckoned with. A single set of role-norms may be internally contradictory. In the case of the mental hospital nurse, for example, the norm of maintaining an "orderly ward" often conflicts with the norm of encouraging self-expression in patients. The individual nurse then has a range of choice, which may be narrow or wide, in balancing these conflicting requirements. There are also ambiguities in norms, and discrepancies between those held explicitly and those that are less verbalized and perhaps less conscious. These normative complexities permit, and may even induce, significant variations in individual role-performance.

The degree of *coherence* among the structurally defined role-requirements, the degree of *consensus* with which they are held, and the degree of *individual choice* they allow (the range of acceptable alternatives) are among the most significant properties of any organization. In some organizations, there is very great coherence of role-requirements and a minimum of individual choice. In most cases, however, the degree of integration within roles and among sets of roles appears to be more moderate.[3] This structural pattern is of especial interest from a sociopsychological point of view. To the extent that the requirements for a given position are ambiguous, contradictory, or otherwise "open," the individual members have greater opportunity for selection among existing norms and for creation of new norms. In this process, personality plays an important part. I shall return to this issue shortly.

While the normative requirements (assigned tasks, rules governing authority-subordinate relationships, demands for work output, and the like) are of great importance, there are other aspects of the organization that have an impact on the individual member. I shall mention two that are sometimes neglected.

ROLE-FACILITIES. In addition to the demands and obligations imposed upon the individual, we must also take into account the techniques, resources, and conditions of work—the means made available to him for fulfilling his organizational functions. The introduction of tranquillizing drugs in the mental hospital, or of automation in industry, has provided tremendous leverage for change in organizational structure and role-definition. The teacher-student ratio, an ecological characteristic of every school, grossly affects the probability that a given teacher will work creatively with individual students. In other words, technological and ecological facilities are not merely "tools" by which norms are met; they are

often a crucial basis for the maintenance or change of an organizational form.

ROLE-DILEMMAS OR PROBLEMATIC ISSUES. In describing the tasks and rules governing a given organizational position, and the facilities provided for their realization, we are, as it were, looking at that position from the viewpoint of a higher administrative authority whose chief concern is "getting the job done." Bureaucracy is often analyzed from this (usually implicit) viewpoint. What is equally necessary, though less often done, is to look at the situation of the position-members from their own point of view: the meaning it has for them, the feelings it evokes, the ways in which it is stressful or supporting. From this sociopsychological perspective, new dimensions of role analysis emerge. The concept of role-dilemma is an example. The usefulness of this concept stems from the fact that every human situation has its contradictions and its problematic features. Where such dilemmas exist, there is no "optimal" mode of adaptation; each mode has its advantages and its costs. Parsons (1951), in his discussion of "the situation of the patient," explores some of the dilemmas confronting the ill person in our society. Erikson (1957) and Pine and Levinson (1958) have written about the dilemmas of the mental hospital patient; for example, the conflicting pressures (from without and from within) toward cure through self-awareness and toward cure through repressive self-control. Role-dilemmas of the psychiatric resident have been studied by Sharaf and Levinson (1957). Various studies have described the problems of the factory foreman caught in the conflicting cross-pressures between the workers he must supervise and the managers to whom he is responsible. The foreman's situation tends to evoke feelings of social marginality, mixed identifications, and conflicting tendencies to be a good "older brother" with subordinates and an "obedient son" with higher authority.

[3] The reduced integration reflects in part the tremendous rate of technological change, the geographical and occupational mobility, and the diversity in personality that characterize modern society. On the other hand, diversity is opposed by the standardization of culture on a mass basis and by the growth of large-scale organization itself. Trends toward increased standardization and uniformity are highlighted in Whyte's (1956) analysis.

Role-dilemmas have their sources both in organizational structure and in individual personality. Similarly, both structure and personality influence the varied forms of adaptation that are achieved. The point to be emphasized here is that every social structure confronts its members with adaptive dilemmas. If we are to comprehend this aspect of organizational life, we must conceive of social structure as having intrinsically *psychological* properties, as making complex psychological demands that affect, and are affected by, the personalities of its members.

Personal Role-Definition

In the foregoing we have considered the patterning of the environment for an organizational position—the kind of sociopsychological world with which members of the position must deal. Let us turn now to the individual members themselves. Confronted with a complex system of requirements, facilities, and conditions of work, the individual effects his modes of adaptation. I shall use the term "personal role-definition" to encompass the individual's adaptation within the organization. This may involve passive "adjustment," active furthering of current role-demands, apparent conformity combined with indirect "sabotage," attempts at constructive innovation (revision of own role or of broader structural arrangements), and the like. The personal role-definition may thus have varying degrees of fit with the role-requirements. It may serve in various ways to maintain or to change the social structure. It may involve a high or a low degree of self-commitment and personal involvement on the part of the individual (Selznick, 1957).

For certain purposes, it is helpful to make a sharp distinction between two levels of adaptation: at a more *ideational* level, we may speak of a role-conception; at a more *behavioral* level, there is a pattern of role-performance. Each of these has an affective component. Role-conception and role-performance are independent though related variables; let us consider them in turn.

INDIVIDUAL (AND MODAL) ROLE-CONCEPTIONS. The nature of a role-conception may perhaps be clarified by placing it in relation to an ideology. The boundary between the two is certainly not a sharp one. However, ideology refers most directly to an orientation regarding the entire organizational (or other) structure —its purposes, its modes of operation, the prevailing forms of individual and group relationships, and so on. A role-conception offers a definition and rationale for one position within the structure. If ideology portrays and rationalizes the organizational world, then role-conception delineates the specific functions, values, and manner of functioning appropriate to one position within it.

The degree of uniformity or variability in individual role-conceptions within a given position will presumably vary from one organization to another. When one or more types of role-conception are commonly held (consensual), we may speak of modal types. The maintenance of structural stability requires that there be at least moderate consensus and that modal role-conceptions be reasonably congruent with role-requirements. At the same time, the presence of incongruent modal role-conceptions may, under certain conditions, provide an ideational basis for major organizational change.

Starting with the primary assumption that each member "takes over" a structurally defined role, many social scientists tend to assume that there is great uniformity in role-conception among the members of a given social position. They hold, in other words, that for every position there is a *dominant, modal role-conception corresponding to the structural demands,* and that there is relatively little individual deviation from the modal pattern. Although this state of affairs may at times obtain, we know that the members of a given social position often have quite diverse conceptions of their proper roles (Greenblatt, Levinson, and Williams, 1957; Gross, Mason, and McEachern, 1958; Reissman and Rohrer, 1957; Bendix, 1956). After all, individual role-conceptions are formed only partially within the present organizational setting. The individual's ideas about his occupational role are influenced by childhood experiences, by his values and other personality characteristics, by formal education and apprenticeship, and the like. The ideas of various potential reference groups within and outside of the organization are available through reading, informal contacts, etc. There is reason to expect, then, that the role-conceptions of individuals in a given organizational position will vary and will not always conform to official role-requirements. Both the diversities and the modal patterns must be considered in organizational analysis.

INDIVIDUAL (AND MODAL) ROLE-PERFORMANCE. This term refers to the overt behavioral aspect of role-definition—to the more or less characteristic ways in which the individual acts as the occupant of a social position. Because role-performance involves immediately observable behavior, its description would seem to present few systematic problems. However, the formulation of adequate variables for the analysis of role-performance is in fact a major theoretical problem and one of the great stumbling blocks in empirical research.

Everyone would agree, I suppose, that role-performance concerns only those aspects of the total stream of behavior that are structurally relevant. But which aspects of behavior are the important ones? And where shall the boundary be drawn between that which is structurally relevant and that which is incidental or idiosyncratic?

One's answer to these questions probably depends, above all, upon his conception of social structure. Those who conceive of social structure rather narrowly in terms of concrete work tasks and normative requirements, are inclined to take a similarly narrow view of role. In this view, role-performance is simply the fulfillment of formal role-norms, and anything else the person does is extraneous to role-performance as such. Its proponents acknowledge that there are variations in "style" of performance but regard these as incidental. What is essential to role-performance is the degree to which norms are met.

A more complex and inclusive conception of social structure requires correspondingly multi-dimensional delineation of role-performance. An organization has, from this viewpoint, "latent" as well as "manifest" structure; it has a many-faceted emotional climate; it tends to "demand" varied forms of interpersonal allegiance, friendship, deference, intimidation, ingratiation, rivalry, and the like. If characteristics such as these are considered intrinsic properties of social structure, then they must be included in the characterization of role-performance. My own preference is for the more inclusive view. I regard social structure as having psychological as well as other properties, and I regard as intrinsic to role-performance the varied meanings and feelings which the actor communicates to those about him. Ultimately, we must learn to characterize organizational behavior in a way that takes into account, and helps to illuminate, its functions for the individual, for the others with whom he interacts, and for the organization.

It is commonly assumed that there is great uniformity in role-performance among the members of a given position. Or, in other words, that there is *a dominant, modal pattern of role-performance corresponding to the structural requirements.* The rationale here parallels that given above for role-conceptions. However, where individual variations in patterns of role-performance have been investigated, several modal types rather than a single dominant pattern were found (Argyris, 1957; Greenblatt et al., 1957).

Nor is this variability surprising, except to those who have the most simplistic conception of social life. Role-performance, like any form of human behavior, is the resultant of many forces. Some of these forces derive from the organizational matrix; for example, from role-demands and the pressures of authority, from informal group influences, and from impending sanctions. Other determinants lie within the person, as for example his role-conceptions and role-relevant personality characteristics. Except in unusual cases where all forces operate to channel behavior in the same direction, role-performance will reflect the individual's attempts at choice and compromise among diverse external and internal forces.

The relative contributions of various forms of influence to individual or modal role-performance can be determined only *if each set of variables is defined and measured independently of the others.* That is, indeed, one of the major reasons for emphasizing and sharpening the distinctions among role-performance, role-conception, and role-demands. Where these distinctions are not sharply drawn, there is a tendency to study one element and to assume that the others are in close fit. For example, we may learn from the official charter and the administrative authorities how the organization is supposed to work—the formal requirements —and then assume that it in fact operates in this way. Or, conversely, one may observe various regularities in role-performance and then assume that these are structurally determined, without independently assessing the structural requirements. To do this is to make structural explanations purely tautologous.

More careful distinction among these aspects of social structure and role will also, I believe, permit greater use of personality theory in organizational analysis. Let us turn briefly to this question.

Role-Definition, Personality, and Social Structure

Just as social structure presents massive forces which influence the individual from without toward certain forms of adaptation, so does personality present massive forces from within which lead him to select, create, and synthesize certain forms of adaptation rather than others. Role-definition may be seen from one perspective as an aspect of personality. It represents the individual's attempt to structure his social reality, to define his place within it, and to guide his search for meaning and gratification. Role-definition is, in this sense, an *ego achievement*—a reflection of the person's capacity to resolve conflicting demands, to utilize existing opportunities and create new ones, to find some balance between stability and change, conformity and autonomy, the ideal and the feasible, in a complex environment.

The formation of a role-definition is, from a dynamic psychological point of view, an "external function" of the ego. Like the other external (reality-oriented) ego functions, it is influenced by the ways in which the ego carries out its "internal functions" of coping with, and attempting to synthesize, the demands of id, superego, and ego. These internal activities —the "psychodynamics" of personality— include among other things: unconscious fantasies; unconscious moral conceptions and the wishes against which they are directed; the characteristic ways in which unconscious processes are transformed or deflected in more conscious though, feeling, and behavioral striving; conceptions of self and ways of maintaining or changing these conceptions in the face of changing pressures from within and from the external world.

In viewing role-definition as an aspect of personality, I am suggesting that it is, *to varying degrees,* related to and imbedded within other aspects of personality. An individual's conception of his role in a particular organization is to be seen within a series of wider psychological contexts: his conception of his occupational role generally (occupational identity), his basic values, life-goals, and conception of self (ego identity), and so on. Thus, one's way of relating to authorities in the organization depends in part upon his relation to authority in general, and upon his fantasies, conscious as well as unconscious, about the "good" and the "bad" parental authority. His ways of dealing with the stressful aspects of organizational life are influenced by the impulses, anxieties, and modes of defense that these stresses activate in him (Argyris, 1957; Erikson, 1950; Henry, 1949; Blum, 1933; Pine and Levinson, 1957).

There are variations in the degree to which personal role-definition is imbedded in, and influenced by, deeper-lying personality characteristics. The importance of individual or modal personality for role-definition is a matter for empirical study and cannot be settled by casual assumption. Traditional sociological theory can be criticized for assuming that individual role-definition is determined almost entirely by social structure. Similarly, dynamic personality theory will not take its rightful place as a crucial element of social psychology until it views the individual within his sociocultural environment. Lacking an adequate recognition and *conceptualization* of the individual's external reality—including the "reality" of social structure—personality researchers tend to assume that individual adaptation is primarily personality-determined and that reality is, for the most part, an amorphous blob structured by the individual to suit his inner needs.

Clearly, individual role-conception and role-performance do not emanate, fully formed, from the depths of personality. Nor are they simply mirror images of a mold established by social structure. Elsewhere (Levinson, 1954), I have used the term "mirage" theory for the view, frequently held or implied in the psychoanalytic literature, that ideologies, role-conceptions, and behavior are mere epiphenomena or by-products of unconscious fantasies and defenses. Similarly, the term "sponge" theory characterizes the view, commonly forwarded in the sociological literature, in which man is merely a passive, mechanical absorber of the prevailing structural demands.

Our understanding of personal role-definition will remain seriously impaired as long as we fail to place it, analytically, in *both intrapersonal and structural-environmental contexts.* That is to say, we must be concerned with the meaning of role-definition both for the individual personality and for the social system. A given role-definition is influenced by, and has an influence upon, the *psyche* as well as the *socius.* If we are adequately to understand the nature, the determinants, and the consequences of role-definition, we need the double perspective of personality and social structure. The use of these two reference points is, like the use of our two eyes in seeing, necessary for the achievement of depth in our social vision.

Theory and research on organizational roles must consider relationships among at least the following sets of characteristics: structurally given role-demands and -opportunities, personal role-definition (including conceptions and performance), and personality in its role-related aspects. Many forms of relationship may exist among them. I shall mention only a few hypothetical possibilities.

In one type case, the role-requirements are so narrowly defined, and the mechanisms of social control so powerful, that only one form of role-performance can be sustained for any given position. An organization of this type may be able selectively to recruit and retain only individuals who, by virtue of personality, find this system meaningful and gratifying. If a congruent modal personality is achieved, a highly integrated and stable structure may well emerge. I would hypothesize that a structurally congruent modal personality is one condition, though by no means the only one, for the stability of a rigidly integrated system. (In modern times, of course, the rapidity of technological change prevents long-term stability in any organizational structure.)

However, an organization of this kind may acquire members who are not initially receptive to the structural order, that is, who are *incongruent* in role-conception or in personality. Here, several alternative developments are possible.

1. The "incongruent" members may change so that their role-conceptions and personalities come better to fit the structural requirements.

2. The incongruent ones may leave the organization, by choice or by expulsion. The high turnover in most of our organizations is due less to technical incompetence than to rejection of the "conditions of life" in the organization.

3. The incongruent ones may remain, but in a state of apathetic conformity. In this case, the person meets at least the minimal requirements of role-performance but his role-conceptions continue relatively unchanged, he gets little satisfaction from work, and he engages in repeated "sabotage" of organizational aims. This is an uncomfortably frequent occurrence in our society. In the Soviet Union as well, even after 40 years of enveloping social controls, there exist structurally incongruent forms of political ideology, occupational role-definition, and personality (Inkeles, Hanfmann, and Beier, 1958).

4. The incongruent members may gain sufficient social power to change the or-ganizational structure. This phenomenon is well known, though not well enough understood. For example, in certain of our mental hospitals, schools and prisons over the past 20–30 years, individuals with new ideas and personal characteristics have entered in large enough numbers, and in sufficiently strategic positions, to effect major structural changes. Similar ideological and structural transitions are evident in other types of organization, such as corporate business.

The foregoing are a few of many possible developments in a relatively monolithic structure. A somewhat looser organizational pattern is perhaps more commonly found. In this setting, structural change becomes a valued aim and innovation is seen as a legitimate function of members at various levels in the organization. To the extent that diversity and innovation are valued (rather than merely given lip-service), variations in individual role-definition are tolerated or even encouraged within relatively wide limits. The role-definitions that develop will reflect various degrees of synthesis and compromise between personal preference and structural demand.

In summary, I have suggested that a primary distinction be made between the structurally given role-demands and the forms of role-definition achieved by the individual members of an organization. Personal role-definition then becomes a linking concept between personality and social structure. It can be seen as a reflection of those aspects of individual personality that are activated and sustained in a given structural-ecological environment. This view is opposed both to the "sociologizing" of individual behavior and to the "psychologizing" of organizational structure. At the same time, it is concerned with both the psychological properties of social structure and the structural properties of individual adaptation.

Finally, we should keep in mind that both personality structure and social structure inevitably have their internal contradictions. No individual is sufficiently all of a piece that he will for long find any form of adaptation, occupational or otherwise, totally satisfying. Whatever the psychic gains stemming from a particular role-definition and social structure, there will also be losses: wishes that must be renounced or made unconscious, values that must be compromised, anxieties to be handled, personal goals that will at best be incompletely met. The organization has equivalent limitations. Its multiple purposes cannot all be optimally achieved. It faces recurrent dilemmas over conflicting requirements: control and freedom; centralization and decentralization of authority; security as against the risk of failure; specialization and diffusion of work function; stability and change; collective unity and diversity. Dilemmas such as these arise anew in different forms at each new step of organizational development, without permanent solution. And perpetual changes in technology, in scientific understanding, in material resources, in the demands and capacities of its members and the surrounding community, present new issues and require continuing organizational readjustment.

In short, every individual and every sociocultural form contains within itself the seeds of its own destruction—or its own reconstruction. To grasp both the sources of stability and the seeds of change in human affairs is one of the great challenges to contemporary social science.

REFERENCES

1. Argyris, C.: *Human relations in a hospital*. New Haven: Labor and Management Center, 1955.
2. ———.: *Personality and organization*. New York: Harper, 1957.
3. Barnard, C. I.: *The functions of the executive*. Cambridge, Mass.: Harvard University Press, 1938.
4. Bendix, R.: *Work and authority in industry*. New York: Wiley, 1956.
5. Blum, F. H. *Toward a democratic work process*. New York: Harper, 1933.
6. Burling, T., Edith Lentz, and R. N. Wilson: *The give and take in hospitals*. New York: Putnam, 1956.
7. Erikson, E. H.: *Childhood and society*. New York: Norton, 1950.
8. Erikson, K. T.: Patient role and social uncertainty: A dilemma of the mentally ill. *Psychiatry*, 1957, 20, 263–274.
9. Friedrich, C. J.: *Constitutional government and democracy*. Boston: Little, Brown, 1950.
10. Gerth, H. H. and C. W. Mills: *Character and social structure*. New York: Harcourt, Brace, 1953.
11. Gouldner, A. W.: *Patterns of industrial bureaucracy*. Glencoe, Ill.: Free Press, 1954.
12. Greenblatt, M., D. J. Levinson, and R. H. Williams (Eds.): *The patient and the mental hospital*. Glencoe, Ill.: Free Press, 1957.
13. Gross, N., W. S. Mason, and A. W. McEachern: *Explorations in role analysis*. New York: Wiley, 1958.
14. Hartley, E. L., and Ruth E. Hartley: *Fundamentals of social psychology*. New York: Knopf, 1952.
15. Henry, W. E.: The business executive: the psychodynamics of a social role. *Amer. J. Sociol.*, 1949, 54, 286–291.
16. Inkeles, A., Eugenia Hanfmann, and Helen Beier. Modal personality and adjustment to the Soviet political system. *Hum. Relat.*, 1958, 11, 3–22.
17. Inkeles, A., and D. J. Levinson: National character: The study of modal personality and socio-cultural systems. In G. Lindzey (Ed.), *Handbook of social psychology*. Cambridge, Mass.: Addison-Wesley, 1954.
18. Kornhauser, A., R. Dubin, and A. M. Ross: *Industrial conflict*. New York: McGraw-Hill, 1954.
19. Levinson, D. J.: *Idea systems in the individual and society*. Paper presented at Boston University, Founder's Day Institute, 1954. Mimeographed: Center for Sociopsychological Research, Massachusetts Mental Health Center.
20. Linton, R.: *The cultural background of*

personality. New York: Appleton-Century, 1945.

21. Mead, G. H.: *Mind, self and society*. Chicago: University of Chicago Press, 1934.

22. Merton, R. K.: *Social theory and social structure*. (Rev. Ed.) Glencoe, Ill.: Free Press, 1957.

23. Merton, R. K., A. P. Gray, Barbara Hockey, and H. C. Selvin: *Reader in bureaucracy*. Glencoe, Ill.: Free Press, 1957.

24. Newcomb, T. M.: *Social psychology*. New York: Dryden, 1950.

25. Parsons, T.: *Essays in sociological theory*. (Rev. ed.) Glencoe, Ill.: Free Press, 1945.

26. ———.: *The social system*. Glencoe, Ill.: Free Press, 1951.

27. Parsons, T., and E. A. Shils (Eds.): *Toward a general theory of action*. Cambridge, Mass.: Harvard University Press, 1951.

28. Pine, F., and D. J. Levinson: Two patterns of ideology, role conception, and personality among mental hospital aides. In M. Greenblatt, D. J. Levinson, and R. H. Williams (Eds.), *The Patient and the mental hospital*. Glencoe, Ill.: Free Press, 1957.

29. ———.: *Problematic issues in the role of mental hospital patient*. Mimeographed: Center for Sociopsychological Research, Massachusetts Mental Health Center, 1958.

30. Reissman, L., and J. J. Rohrer (Eds.): *Change and dilemma in the nursing profession*. New York: Putnam, 1957.

31. Sarbin, T. R.: Role theory. In G. Lindzey (Ed.), *Handbook of social psychology*. Cambridge, Mass.: Addison-Wesley, 1954.

32. Selznick, P.: *Leadership in administration*. Evanston, Ill.: Row, Peterson, 1957.

33. Sharaf, M. R., and D. J. Levinson: Patterns of ideology and role definition among psychiatric residents. In M. Greenblatt, D. J. Levinson, and R. H. Williams, (Eds.), *The patient and the mental hospital*. Glencoe, Ill.: Free Press, 1957.

34. Weber, M.: *Essays in sociology*. Ed. by H. H. Gerth and C. W. Mills. New York: Oxford University Press, 1946.

35. ———.: *The theory of social and economic organization*. Ed. by T. Parsons. New York: Oxford University Press, 1947.

36. Whyte, W. F.: *The organization man*. New York: Simon and Shuster, 1956.

AGITATION THROUGH THE PRESS:
A STUDY OF THE PERSONALITIES OF PUBLICISTS

by Guy E. Swanson

This is a study of the need systems of journalists who are active in trying to influence their social worlds through the public press.[1] One variety of newspaperman is studied, not from a particular interest in him, but because he provides us with an operational definition of a role of increasing importance—the role of the publicist.

In 1930, Lasswell published a series of essays called *Psychopathology and Politics*.[2] His interest was "to discover what developmental experiences are significant for the political traits and interests of the mature: the agitators, administrators, theorists," and to "uncover the typical subjective histories of typical public ca-

[1] Several of my students shared in gathering the data for this study and in some parts of the planning and analysis. They are James Thompson, Irwin Goffman, Judith Levine, and Leonard Greenbaum. We are appreciative of the co-operation of the Editors and staffs of *The Michigan Daily* who provided us with these data.

SOURCE: *Public Opinion Quarterly,* Vol. 20 (1956), pp. 441–456.

[2] Lasswell, Harold D., Chicago: The University of Chicago Press, 1937.

reers."[3] Here, and in his later work, *Power and Personality*,[4] Lasswell began to outline the need systems that would predispose individuals to unusual interests in influencing others and to particular methods of wielding that influence.

In his early work, Lasswell distinguished political agitators from political administrators. He said:

> The essential mark of the agitator is the high value which he places on the emotional response of the public. Whether he attacks or defends social institutions is a secondary matter. The agitator has come by his name honestly, for he is enough agitated about public policy to communicate his excitement to those about him.[5]

Within this general picture, Lasswell suggests there are two sub-types: the oratorical agitator who tries to influence audiences through direct, face-to-face appeals, and the publicist who works through the press.

It seems appropriate to try to develop a theory of the need structure of the publicist from a "job analysis" of his role. First of all, the publicist deals with the controversial. Secondly, he takes a side. He is trying to influence the direction of decisions; not simply to see that they are made. In the light of these facts one would expect to find a disproportionate number of publicists who are unusually concerned about the problems of power and authority.

Such persons are likely to view the environment as filled with people who want to force their will on the self whether it likes it or not. This world must be controlled. The publicist takes an active rather than a passive approach to this problem of control. Instead of retreating from the world so it cannot touch him, he advances to direct it away from interference with his desires. Such a pattern of attitudes toward the world is called anal expulsiveness in psychoanalytic theory.

Some activists, however, are content to work behind the scenes. They are the powers behind thrones, the nameless, faceless movers of events. The publicist takes no such role. His name will be known. As Lasswell suggests, both orator and publicist are likely to be "strongly narcissistic types." They want a public validation of their competence, independence, and virility. This is the need pattern of the phallic character in psychoanalytic theory.

But publicists are not orators. They avoid the face-to-face contact with their audience. In this way, they avoid the approving roar of their audience, but, should they fail to persuade, they also avoid the cat-calls of rejection. There is a great need for support that can be satisfied in this way—a great dependency on the approval of others that requires protection. These are sensitive people. Behind the writing desk, they can nurse their rejections in private and gather strength to try again. This is the pattern of oral dependency in psychoanalytic theory.

In summary, it may be predicted that the publicist will have strong needs to take active steps to control his world, to be recognized as its master, while, at the same time, be protected from its unfavorable reactions. In psychoanalytic terms, we would expect him to have strong tendencies of an anal expulsive, phallic, and oral passive sort.

Rosten's 1937 study of the Washington political correspondents suggests that we may expect journalists covering general news about controversial public issues to be a special case of the empirical type of the publicist.[6] Limiting his observations to some 127 "active political corre-

---

[3] *Ibid.*, p. 8.

[4] New York: W. W. Norton and Co., Inc., 1948.

[5] *Psychopathology and Politics*, pp. 78–79.

[6] Rosten, Leo C., *The Washington Correspondents*. New York: Harcourt, Brace and Co., 1937.

spondents" who fit the categories of writers of news-dispatches or columns of national political content for daily United States newspapers or press associations of a large, general circulation, Rosten concludes:

> . . . the energies which lead men into newspapers are . . . the desire to startle and expose; the opportunity to project personal hostilities and feelings of injustice on public persons under the aegis of "journalistic duty"; the inner drives for "action," plus inner anxieties about accepting the consequences of action. The last is particularly important.
>
> There is a sense of invulnerability attached to newspaper work. Journalism represents a world within a world. Reporters derive a vicarious pleasure in experiencing the excitement of events as observers, not participants, without personal risk in the outcome of those events. . . .[7]

Again we have a prediction of strong tendencies toward the phallic, anal expulsive, and oral passive character levels.[8] The present study tests for these tendencies in publicists.

Populations Studied

The populations studied are the several staffs of *The Michigan Daily,* the student newspaper at the University of Michigan. The *Daily* tries to present the campus

[7] *Ibid.,* pp. 243–244.

[8] These concepts representing the character levels of psychoanalytic theory are used in this study to refer to patterns of attitudes. There is no necessary acceptance of the theory of generalization from body zones that is associated with them in psychoanalytic theory. For a recent description of the theory, see: Erik H. Ericson, *Childhood and Society.* New York: W. W. Norton and Co., 1950.

scene, but it also carries the principal stories of state, national, and international importance. Its editorial policy, set by the student staff, is liberal—probably Fair Deal in orientation. Publishing every day from Tuesday through Sunday during the time classes are in session, and paying its staff members little or no money for their services, the *Daily* offers long hours, hard work, and experience. It seemed reasonable to believe that any student who volunteered to serve on its staff must have strong personal needs for the kind of experience it provides. Here, then, was a "natural experiment" that might provide a test of hypotheses about the needs of persons trying to influence others through the press. If anything, it was a more ideal setting in which to test such hypotheses than could be provided by the usual newspaper staff, for these students were literally working for love, not money.

Four staffs operate the *Daily.* The editorial staff is responsible for covering general campus news, for writing editorials, for selecting and pursuing special issues of general interest (e.g., the civil liberties of students and faculty, discrimination in fraternities, the lengthening of the Thanksgiving holiday), and for selecting the news to be reprinted from the A.P. wire.

Business staff members begin their service by working on advertising. To help raise the $160,000 a year that it costs to run the paper, they contact possible advertisers, try to sell them space, help them make up their ads, and maintain happy relations with them. From advertising, the staffers move into circulation, where they answer phones, take care of complaints, or help in the secretarial work of sending out letters and promotional material. These general kinds of work may be followed later by experience in such specialties as taking care of classified advertising or national advertising, deciding on page layouts, sending bills, and paying salaries. The editorial and business staffs have both men and women students as members.

Sports and women's staff members have job assignments of the kind usually found on any newspaper, except, of course, that their coverage is focused on campus activities. The sports staff selects state, national, and international sports news for reprinting from the A.P. wire. All sportswriters are men; all members of the women's staff are female.

Coordinating Definitions

From these descriptions, it appears that the staff members whose motivations are most likely to fit those pictured in the theory of the publicist are the male members of the editorial staff. The theory is geared to the significance of the publicist's role for males in our culture. Later, we shall make some predictions for women publicists that differ from those for males.

When one predicts certain "strong tendencies" among publicists, he assumes some kind of standard of comparison, some kind of person in this case, that has weaker predispositions along these lines. The standard of comparison for our theory of the publicist, and for psychoanalytic theory generally, is the genital character. Genitality involves the expectation that, in most cases, the environment is a supportive, gratifying place that will satisfy many of the individual's demands. It means that the person expects that he is capable of modifying that environment and, if need be, controlling it, but that he does not have to watch it constantly in order to be free of unwanted restrictions and threats. It means that he has the ability to hold up the expression of impulses if the deprivation from their expression would be too great, but to let them pass into overt behavior when the opportunity permits. It means that he can give gratification to others without

immediate reward—though, presumably, with the expectation that others will reciprocate at some future time.

We have predicted that publicists will be different from this picture in some respects. We can now add that they will not deviate from it in certain other ways. Specifically, we find no special reason for expecting them to have stronger or weaker tendencies than the genital character on the remaining psychosexual character levels: oral sadism and anal retentiveness. Very briefly stated, oral sadism is a pattern of demanding that the environment care for one's needs; anal retentiveness is a pattern of protecting oneself from an environment perceived as hostile by withdrawing from it.

The problem, then, was one of choosing a population of males that might be expected to approach genitality more clearly than the publicists and might, consequently, represent a "control" group. The best readily available population was afforded by the sports staff of the *Daily*.

The job of the sports staff consists of a great deal of direct, informal contact with people in a peer relationship. Those contacts are not to expose or to influence, but to describe the technical qualities and problems of a skilled behavior. The subject-matter is largely non-controversial, or, at least, does not involve issues that will have much influence on the lives of most readers. Finally, the material involved and the contacts made are almost exclusively masculine in content and interest, but masculine in the sense of a common, positively sanctioned interest among males in this culture.

This is not to argue that sportswriters have no pregenital tendencies that exceed in strength those ascribed to the ideal genital character. What it does say is that, as compared with editorialists, those tendencies will not be in the areas of orality, anality, or phallic striving and ambition. They may be in the areas of phallic sex identification, but our data are not suitable to examine this possibility.

There are reasons to believe that the male members of the business staff will also differ from the sportswriters. They are selected through a successful apprenticeship in contacting advertisers, cooperating with advertisers, and keeping advertisers as regular patrons of the *Daily*. This must require considerable ease in meeting people and in developing a mutually pleasant relationship with them, and must demand a low level of hostility. Another part of the apprenticeship, however, consists of the rather routine desk

cies toward hostility and striving, that is toward oral sadism, anality, and phallic aspiration.

The Methods of Data Collection

Data for this study were obtained primarily through the administration of a questionnaire to *Daily* staff members at the time of regular staff meetings. The questionnaire included a personality rating instrument, a section of demographic data, questions about college life, and about attitudes toward the *Daily*, the

TABLE 1. *Questionnaire Returns by Staff*

STAFF	ESTIMATED NUMBER OF STAFF MEMBERS *			PERCENTAGE RETURNING QUESTIONNAIRES		
	Male	Female	Total	Male	Female	Total
Editorial	28	32	60	96	100	98
Business	23	25	48	91	68	80
Sports	27	0	27	81	—	81
Women's	0	21	21	—	90	90
Total	78	78	156	90	87	88

* There was uncertainty in these staffs as to the exact number of members at the time the study was made. The percentages had to be computed from membership lists compiled at the beginning of the semester. Since that time, some persons had dropped from participation, making the actual totals at the time of the study much smaller. As a consequence, these percentages should be considered as quite conservative estimates of the response.

chores of circulation. These tasks must require a willingness to submit to the very dependent role of the minor office clerk. It might be expected, in short, that these men are more dependent than the sportswriters, though, possibly, no more so than the editorialists. They should be more oral dependent and feminine than the sportswriters and less orally sadistic, anal, phallic aspiring and masculine.

Based on these job descriptions editorialists were predicted to be equal to businessmen in tendencies toward oral dependency, to be less masculine, and more feminine, and to have stronger tendencies

press, and toward current public issues. Table 1 shows what percentages of the several staffs returned the questionnaires.

To test the predictions about character level, the Krout *Personal Preference Scale* (PPS) [9] was included as part of the questionnaire. This instrument is a paper-and-pencil personality test consisting of 100 items "typical of the seven psychoanalytic stages (pre-natal, early oral, late

[9] Permission to use this instrument, and preliminary normative data for its interpretation, were kindly provided by one of its authors, Maurice H. Krout. His collaborator is Johanna Krout.

oral, early anal, late anal, early genital, and final genital)." The items, arranged in ten groups, refer to things and states that may be experienced. The subject is asked to respond to each item by circling one of the following responses: I like it, I feel indifferent to it. I dislike it. Each item is chosen because it is predicted in psychoanalytic theory to be a common symptom, at least among middle-class Americans, of an underlying attitude structure summarized in one of the psychosexual stages. For example, an item among the ten for oral passivity reads "Eating soft-boiled eggs" while a sample from the items under anal retentiveness is "Checking and re-checking for errors."

The split-half reliability of the whole form (by the Spearman-Brown prediction formula) is reported as .82 on a population of 1,340 subjects of both sexes and ranging in age from 17 through 45 years. The modal item reliability is reported as "being in the .70's." "Of 45 intercorrelations of subtest scores, all but three were significantly low, proving basic 'developmental' categories [to be] essentially independent."

The standard method for scoring each subtest is to give a weight of 2 to the "I like it" response, considered indicative of the tendency measured in the subtest, a weight of 1 to feelings of indifference, and a weight of 0 to a response of "I dislike it," which is always thought to be in the direction opposite to the tendency being measured. As is true of most other scoring techniques with data like these, such weights are purely arbitrary, assuming equality of units and the unidimensionality of the item as a measure. It seemed more conservative to tabulate the three possible types of response as attributes. Thus, for any given subtest, a subject's total number of like, of indifferent, and of dislike responses were recorded separately. Staff totals for each of these kinds of response were then obtained. Inspection of the resulting tables showed that, on some subtests, most subjects, re-

gardless of their particular staff affiliation on the *Daily,* used only the like and dislike responses. On others, only the like and indifferent responses were used, and, on still others, all three responses were used.

The second of five subtests, reported in Table 3, requires some explanation. Subtests VII and VIII seem, respectively, efforts to rate femininity and masculinity, in terms of the cultural norms of modern America. Subtest IX, said by its authors to provide ratings of emotional immaturity, consists of items that seem to reflect a preference for working with subordinates or in a dependent role as over against having contacts with one's equals.

The final subtest, originally labeled as a rating of social maturity, has a wider range of items. Some relate to an ability to face unpleasant realities without being overwhelmed. Others probably reflect tolerance for people. Still others try to tap a willingness to be ruthless if "reality" demands it. In total, they seem to be getting at a flexibility in the face of widely diverse and trying circumstances— the ability to face and do variously unpleasant things from dominating to submitting to suffering embarrassment to drudgery to putting up with petty annoyance to exploitation to being impartial under duress. The labels in the left-hand stub of Table 3 are phrased to suggest these interpretations. They are not those of the test's authors.

Social Origins and Interests of Male Staff Members

This material was gathered during the study and was not available at the time the hypotheses about the relative psychosexual character level patterns of the staffs were constructed. The social background of the male editorial staffer is very much like that of his business and sports colleagues in a number of ways. Men on these staffs do not differ significantly from one another in age, in the type of occupation of their fathers, the number of years of school completed by either their fathers or mothers, or in the political preferences of their parents.[10]

Only with respect to size of city of upbringing, amount of family income, and to certain features of family religious belief do we find some differences among the staffs. Businessmen tend to have spent more of their lives before age sixteen in larger cities than did editorialists ($p = < .10$) or sportswriters ($p = < .02$). The families of editorialists and sportswriters and of editorialists and businessmen do not differ in income, but businessmen's families tend to have larger incomes than those of sportswriters ($p = < .02$). The parents of editorialists and sportswriters are alike in their religious preferences, but editorialists, more than businessmen, come from Protestant and Jewish homes and fewer from Roman Catholic families ($p = < .05$). Further, the attitudes of editorialists' mothers toward the religious beliefs traditional in the family are less favorable than those of the mothers of sportswriters ($p = < .05$). There are no significant differences, among the several staffs, in the favorableness of the attitudes of fathers toward the family's traditional religious practices.

EDITORIALISTS AND SPORTSWRITERS. The differences between the attitudes and behaviors of editorialists and sportswriters are few and can be itemized quickly. Editorialists tend to be more liberal on a wide range of controversial public issues than are sportswriters ($p = < .01$). They are somewhat more likely to hope for a career in journalism, writing, or medicine ($p = < .10$). Consistent with this—they estimate spending a larger part of their time at work on the *Daily* ($p = < .001$). They are also different in the kind of arti-

[10] All p values reported in this paper were estimated by computing chi-square values for the significance of the difference in inter-staff distributions of questionnaire responses.

cles they prefer to write, being more likely to prefer editorial writing and, interestingly, less likely to choose straight news stories ($p = < .001$).

EDITORIALISTS AND BUSINESSMEN. Editorialists differ from businessmen on many more counts. Consistent with our picture of the male editorialist as interested in people, he is more likely to be a major in the social sciences or the humanities ($p = < .02$), and, less likely to center his study in the technicalities of business administration ($p = < .02$).

He estimates that he studies fewer hours ($p = < .01$), and tends to take part in fewer campus organizations and activities ($p = < .05$). By his own estimates, as compared with the estimates of businessmen, he spends less time in recreation and entertainment ($p = < .01$). (Time estimates like those for study and recreation may or may not be objectively correct. If they are false, they must reflect great pressures to feel that study and recreation time are short. These pressures are likely to spring from conditions that are fairly persistent for these men, since it is hard to believe they are coerced momentarily into distorting their estimates when the questionnaire they were completing was anonymous.)

Where is the editorialists' time going? By their estimates, the *Daily* is one important channel. Their reports show them spending more time working at the *Daily* ($p = < .05$). Further, the time they spend socially is more likely to be spent with other *Daily* staffers ($p = < .001$).

A second channel for their time is in reading. They tend to read more nonassigned books each month ($p = < .02$) and a larger number of daily newspapers ($p = < .02$). They are more likely to read *The New York Times* ($p = < .01$). The two staffs do not differ significantly in the number or types of magazines read. In both cases, there is a strong tendency to read *Time* and *Life* ($p = < .001$).

Editorialists differ from businessmen in

their post-college occupational preferences ($p = < .05$), and the major part of this difference is contributed by their choice of journalism or "writing" as occupational careers.

As might be expected, they choose to write articles different from those preferred by the businessmen ($p = < .001$). This difference is produced largely by greater preference among editorialists for writing editorials, human interest stories, special features, and by a lesser preference for writing straight news stories. The editorialists' view of the function of a newspaper fits this pattern of choice. When asked to say whether they felt that "the most important job a newspaper can do is: (a) to inform its readers about events or (b) to stir its readers to take action," male editorialists were more likely than businessmen ($p = < .01$) or sportswriters ($p = < .15$) to choose the latter.

Not only are more editorialists manipulatively oriented, but the direction of their manipulation is more likely to be what would be called "liberal" in modern American society. On a list of ten questions on currently controversial public issues, the editorialists were significantly ($p = < .01$) more liberal in their responses than the businessmen.

These formal, statistical results square nicely with the impression held by editorialists and other *Daily* staff members. The editorialists, everyone agrees, spend more time in the *Daily* building. Members of other staffs are not at all certain that all the time editorialists spend in the office is used for getting out the paper; it is often said that "horsing around" and "cementing the edit clique" are principal functions.

The *Daily* editorialists tend to be politically left of the other staffs, and, perhaps, of general campus sentiment, but there are no significant inter-staff differences in preferences for political parties even when the traditional "two" parties are broken down into their right and left wings. Perhaps the editorialists would

choose a program further to the left than the Fair Deal wing of the Democrats if they thought it had a chance of winning, or, perhaps, even on an anonymous questionnaire, there were hesitancies about expressing even more leftward tendencies.

There is some evidence that the *Daily's* editorials are less strongly identified with their parents than are other staff members. This evidence is their greater tendency ($p = < .001$) to have abandoned the religious beliefs traditional in their families for atheism or agnosticism. Neither businessmen nor sportwriters show any significant difference in their religious affiliations from those of their parents.

On several counts, the attitudes and practices of the editorial and business males are similar. Both tend to feel they are upper middle class, political independents instead of party adherents, and to prefer Fair Deal Democrats and Anti-Taft Republicanism to the conservative wings of the major parties.

BUSINESSMEN AND SPORTSWRITERS. To round out our picture, we will compare businessmen with sportswriters. In college, the businessman's major field of study is more likely to be business administration and less likely to be in the biological, physical, or social sciences ($p = < .05$). He belonged to fewer extracurricular activities in high school ($p = < .05$). In college, he spends more time with people who are not members of the *Daily* staff ($p = < .05$), and makes quite different choices of the type of articles he prefers to write ($p = < .001$). Most of this difference comes from less interest in writing straight news and human interest stories.

Social Origins and Interests of Female Staff Members

As we found for our male respondents, there are some differences in the demographic characteristics of the three populations of women on the *Daily*. Editorial women tend to be younger than those of either of the other staffs ($p = < .001$). They are more likely to have spent most of their years before age sixteen in larger cities than are members of the women's staff ($p = < .001$). They are more likely than are Women's staffers to be Jewish and less likely to come from Protestant or Roman Catholic families ($p = < .05$). Their fathers tend to be less favorable toward the religion traditional in the home as compared with the fathers of businesswomen ($p = < .05$) or of members of the Women's staff ($p = < .10$). Their mothers are also less favorable toward the family's religious beliefs ($p = < .01$) than the mothers of Women's staffers. On the other hand, there are no differences between the parents of these and the other women with respect to education, occupation, income, or political preferences.

FEMALE EDITORIALISTS AND OTHER FEMALE STAFF MEMBERS. Women editorialists participated in fewer extracurricular activities in high school than did members of the Women's staff ($p = < .05$). In college, they took part in fewer activities than businesswomen ($p = < .001$). They tend to spend fewer hours in study than members of the other two staffs ($p = < .05$), but show some tendency to read more non-assigned books during the semester than do businesswomen ($p = < .10$).

Looking into the future, their hopes for an occupation differ from the members of the other staffs ($p = < .05$). They are more likely than the businesswomen to choose journalism as a career, and exceed Women's staff members in choosing journalism and teaching as future occupations.

Like editorial men, women editorialists take more liberal attitudes toward controversial public issues than their colleagues. Their difference from businesswomen in this respect is slightly less

($p = < .05$) than from Women's staffers ($p = < .01$). They are far more likely than businesswomen to feel that they are independents in politics ($p = < .001$). Toward the religious beliefs traditional in their homes, they are less favorable ($p = < .05$) than the Women's staff and are more likely than the businesswomen ($p = < .10$) or Women's staffers ($p = < .05$) to be agnostic or Jewish; less likely to be Protestant or Roman Catholic. Again, like Editorial men, they are alone among the staff members of their sex to differ significantly ($p = < .01$) from the religious beliefs of their parents.

We have seen that male editorialists are more likely than other male staffers to see the primary function of a newspaper as one of stirring its readers to action as against simply informing them. This tendency is also present at the .01 level for female editorialits when they are compared with either of the other staff populations of their sex.

No differences appeared in the areas of study chosen for specialization, the number of hours estimated as spent in working on the *Daily* or used for recreation, in the number or kind of newspapers or magazines read, the type of articles these women prefer to write, or in their judgment of the social class to which they belong.

In a very general way, the *Daily* editorialists of *both* sexes departed further than their colleagues from conventional positions on controversial public issues and from an identification with the religious beliefs of their parents. They are more frequently committed to journalism as a profession and to the role of the press as an instrument of manipulation and control of reader behavior rather than as a means of assisting the reader to learn the facts.

It is probably important that the editorialists have come from homes in which religious beliefs were held in less favor than in the homes of other staffers. However, when this difference is controlled, editorialists remain just as significantly deviant from the faith of their fathers as before. It may, of course, be that the initial skepticism in the home helped in their moving toward disbelief.

BUSINESSWOMEN AND WOMEN'S STAFF MEMBERS. Businesswomen are quite like women's staffers. The only points of difference in these data are that they tend to have spent their early years in cities of larger population ($p = < .01$), to come

bers in the amount of time they spend socially with persons not on the staff.

Findings on Personality Hypotheses

Table 3 presents the results of a chi-square analysis of the difference in distribution of scores on the various Krout dimensions among the *Daily* staffs.[11] The values in these tables are one-tailed p values. Only one tail of the probability

TABLE 2. *Summary of Confirmations and Disconfirmations of Predictions of Inter-Staff Differences in Need Structure*

INTER-STAFF COMPARISONS

CHARACTER LEVEL	Male Editorial and Sports	Male Editorial and Business	Business and Sports	Female Editorial and Business	Female Editorial and Women's	Business and Women's
Oral: Dependent	> *	= *	> *	= *	N. P.	N. P.
Oral: Sadist	= *	> *	< *	> #	N. P.	N. P.
Anal: Expulsive	> *	> *	< *	> *	N. P.	N. P.
Anal: Retentive	= *	> *	< *	> *	N. P.	N. P.
Phallic: Aspiring	> *	> *	< *	> #	N. P.	N. P.
Phallic: Feminine	> *	> *	> #	< *	N. P.	N. P.
Phallic: Masculine	< *	< *	< #	> #	N. P.	N. P.

Key:
>—a prediction that the first staff listed would choose this category significantly more often than the second staff listed.
<—a prediction that the first staff listed would choose this category significantly less often than the second staff listed.
=—a prediction that there would be no significant difference in frequency of choice of this category between the two staffs listed.
N. P.—no prediction was made.
*—the prediction was confirmed.
#—the prediction was disconfirmed.

from Jewish rather than Protestant or Roman Catholic homes ($p = < .01$), and to have mothers with less favorable attitudes toward the family's religious group ($p = < .02$). They took part in fewer extracurricular activities in high school ($p = < .02$) and more ($p = < .02$) in college. They show a slight tendency ($p = < .10$) to exceed Women's staff mem-

distribution was used since the direction as well as the magnitude of the inter-staff differences was predicted. Table 2 is a summary of the predictions and of their confirmation or lack of it.

A prediction is said to be confirmed

[11] Table 3 reports only those p values that showed differences at or beyond the .10 level.

either if the p value in the "like," the "feel indifferent," or the "dislike" column is at, or less than, the .05 level of expectancy and is in the predicted direc-

editorialists' comparative under-choice of the "like" response or their over-choice of the "feel indifferent" or "dislike" responses.

TABLE 3. *Significance of Differences Between the Need Structures of Staff Members*

NO.	CHARACTER LEVEL	EDITORIAL MALES AND SPORTS STAFF			EDITORIAL MALES AND BUSINESS MALES			BUSINESS MALES AND SPORTS STAFF		
		Like	Indiff.	Dislike	Like	Indiff.	Dislike	Like	Indiff.	Dislike
I	Pre-Ego	.0005 *	.005		.0005 *	.01				
II	Oral: Dependent	.0005 *	.01			.025		.025 †		
III	Oral: Sadist			.005 *	.01 *			.10		.05 †
IV	Anal: Expulsive	.005 *	.0005		.0005 *	.0005				
V	Anal: Retentive			.10 *	.0005 *	.05		.01		
VI	Phallic: Aspiring	.05 *	.005		.025 *	.10				.05 †
VII	Phallic: Feminine	.025 *			.01 *	.05				
VIII	Phallic: Masculine			.0005 *		.05	.025 *			
IX	Genital: Ego Strength	.005	.05 *		.025	.01				.025 †
X	Genital: Reality Oriented	.025 *	.01 *							

NO.	CHARACTER LEVEL	EDITORIAL AND BUSINESS FEMALES			EDITORIAL FEMALE AND WOMEN'S STAFF			BUSINESS FEMALE AND WOMEN'S STAFF		
		Like	Indiff.	Dislike	Like	Indiff.	Dislike	Like	Indiff.	Dislike
I	Pre-Ego				.10 ‡					
II	Oral: Dependent							.05 #		
III	Oral: Sadist					.10 ‡				
IV	Anal: Expulsive	.005 ‡								
V	Anal: Retentive	.025 ‡						.05		
VI	Phallic: Aspiring				.025 ‡			.10 #		
VII	Phallic: Feminine	.05		.025 ‡	.025		.05 ‡			
VIII	Phallic: Masculine				.025			.025		
IX	Genital: Ego Strength		.01			.10 ‡		.10	.025	
X	Genital: Reality Oriented					.10 ‡				

* Editorial males more likely to choose this response.
† Business males more likely to choose this response.
‡ Editorial females more likely to choose this response.
# Business females more likely to choose this response.

tion. In the case of predictions of "no difference" between specified staffs, the prediction was confirmed if the p value was greater than the .05 level. Thus the prediction that editorial males would prefer fewer masculine responses than sportswriters could be confirmed either by the

Table 2 shows that a total of 21 predictions for male inter-staff patterns of character level were made. Of these, 19 were confirmed and 2 were disconfirmed. This large a number of confirmations could be obtained by chance less than once in one hundred times.

Great uncertainty about the job specifications of female staff members resulted in the making of only seven predictions. Of these, four were confirmed by the analysis of the data; three were disconfirmed. This number of confirmations does not exceed that to be expected by chance.

That these inter-staff differences in character level might be explained as products of differences in the social origins of the *Daily* populations was tested. Surprisingly, these two types of variables were found to be independent of each other in every case.

MALE EDITORIALISTS COMPARED WITH SPORTSWRITERS. We have predicted that editorialists, when compared with sportswriters, would show stronger tendencies toward oral passivity, and expulsiveness, and phallic aspiring, and equal tendencies toward oral sadism and anal retentiveness. The *p* values reported in the first column of Table 3 show that all five of the predictions were supported. It also shows additional supportive evidence for our interpretation of the dynamics of the editorialists' attitude structures. One would expect that their dependency would generalize to the several test categories strongly affected by such a tendency. The table shows that they have significantly deviant scores in the right direction on precisely such categories: pre-ego, femininity, and ego strength. The masculinity scores provide an interesting result. While there is no significant difference in the number of masculine items *liked* by editorialists and sportswriters, editorialists are very significantly more likely to *dislike* masculine items.

MALE EDITORIALISTS COMPARED WITH BUSINESSMEN. The second column of Table 3 repeats this kind of comparison for editorialists and businessmen. It will be remembered that we predicted that editorialists would show significantly stronger tendencies on all comparisons on pregenital dimensions except oral pas-

sivity and masculinity. These predictions are also borne out.

MALE EDITORIALISTS COMPARED WITH BUSINESSMEN AND SPORTSWRITERS. A more rigorous test of the hypothesis that editorialists will tend more often than sportswriters or businessmen to be strongly oral passive, anal expulsive, and phallic can now be made. We may count the number of men in each of these Daily staffs who have scores on all three personality characteristics that are above the median score for all males in the three staffs. Thirteen of the 27 editorialists and one each of the 22 sportswriters and the 21 businessmen have high scores on all three personality characteristics. Thus our prediction is confirmed at a point beyond the .005 level of confidence.

BUSINESSMEN COMPARED WITH SPORTS-WRITERS. Of the six comparative predictions made for these groups, four were supported by the data. No especially strong theoretical reasons appear for the failure of the predictions on sex role identification.

FEMALE EDITORIALISTS COMPARED WITH OTHER FEMALE STAFF MEMBERS. The leads provided by the work of Lasswell and Rosten predict only to males in our culture. The significance of a woman's entering the editorialist role is very different. She must quit the traditional prescriptions of dependence and passivity and must compete in a man's profession.

The role of the woman in many aspects of business is more common and accepted. The requirements of the work of the business staff of the *Daily* are much like those of many offices. The woman member can remain in a protected position. After her apprenticeship period, she is not required to go out and meet people or to sell her ideas. One might expect that, as compared with businesswomen, editorialists would be more hostile, less passive, and less feminine. In terms of character levels, they should have higher scores on anality, both expulsive and passive, and lower scores on femininity and passivity. Column 6 of Table 3 shows the findings.

The predictions of higher scores on anality are borne out completely. The prediction of lower feminine ratings also holds. Our passivity measures show a less clear confirmation of the hypothesis. There are no differences in the number of pre-ego items checked as "liked," but the tendency in the other "passive" categories is for editorialists to be less interested in such experiences, or to reject them by checking "dislike."

Since the job description for members of the women's staff was not very clear at the time data collection began, no personality predictions were made involving that staff. The empirical results are presented in the last two columns of Table 3.

Addenda

Most of the ideas about the social origins of publicists coming from Rosten's study of Washington political correspondents were clearly inapplicable to the populations studied. One lead that did seem reasonable to follow was the possibility that publicists tended to have fathers in those occupations and professions that deal more largely with words and concepts than with material objects, or that the fathers of publicists would be more likely to have occupations involving the symbolic manipulation of the behavior of others. These possibilities were not confirmed, there being no difference in the occupations of the fathers of the various staffs when coded into categories appropriate for these analyses.

The expectations, drived from predictions about their character levels, that publicists would be less likely to identify with their parents and that they would be more likely to see the newspaper as an instrument for manipulating rather than just informing its readers, are supported by these data.

Summary and Addenda

Those journalists who specialize in covering controversial issues (as contrasted with such persons as the writers of sports, or society, or cooking news) are here considered to represent a special case of the role of the publicist. They have been thought to be unique, as compared with orators and administrators, in their orientation to other people. It has been suggested that this orientation is, in part, a product of a peculiar set of unconscious needs (phrased in terms of psycho-sexual character levels).

This hypothesis was tested in the study of a population of general news reporters and other staff members working voluntarily on a college newspaper. The predictions about the personal needs of male publicists are generally supported by the data. The more tentative predictions of the need structures of female publicists receive less support.

Most of the ideas about the social origins of publicists coming from Rosten's study of Washington political correspondents were clearly inapplicable to the populations studied. One lead that did seem reasonable to follow was the possibility that publicists tended to have fathers in those occupations and professions that deal more with words and concepts than with material objects, or, that the fathers of publicists would be more likely to have occupations involving the symbolic manipulation of the behavior of others. These possibilities were not confirmed, there being no differences in the occupations of the fathers of the various staffs when coded into categories appropriate for these analyses.

The expectations, derived from predictions about their character levels, that publicists would be less likely to identify with their parents and that they would be more likely to see the newspaper as an instrument for manipulating rather than just informing its readers are supported by these data.

2 · Political Roles

AUTHORITARIANISM AND POLITICAL BEHAVIOR

by Morris Janowitz and Dwaine Marvick

In common sense language, the authoritarian is the individual who is concerned with power and toughness and who is prone to resolve conflict in an arbitrary manner. He is seen as having strong and persistent desires that others submit to his outlook. Social psychology in recent years has added the observation that the authoritarian person has another powerful desire of which he is not fully aware. He himself desires to submit to other individuals whom he sees as more powerful.

The predisposition of the authoritarian individual to conform to an "authority" is directly relevant to the study of political behavior in a democratic society. The "F" scale developed by the "Berkeley group" was designed specifically as a personality scale to identify "anti-democratic" individuals in a population.[1] Any reliable and valid method of analysis of such personality variables is of crucial importance in the study of political propaganda impact, the effectiveness of campaign arguments and appeals, the conditions under which political protest movements are likely to attract support, and a host of similar problems.

This paper reports the findings of an attempt to investigate (a) the extent of the authoritarian predispositions in two nation-wide samples and (b) the link between such predispositions and certain types of political behavior and attitudes.

[1] Adorno, T. W., *et al. The Authoritarian Personality* (New York: Harper and Brothers, 1950).

SOURCE: *Public Opinion Quarterly*, Vol. 17 (1953), pp. 185–201.

In the light of our present knowledge and research techniques, it is neither necessary nor feasible to postulate that we are concerned with authoritarian "personality." To talk about personality implies a comprehensive understanding of the life development of an individual's emotions. Instead, authoritarianism can be seen as a characteristic psychological reaction pattern to a wide variety of social situations. Since it is a characteristic reaction pattern of which the individual is not completely aware, only indirect approaches serve to reveal its presence.

Research into political behavior need not concern itself with all of the nine key dimensions which the Berkeley group included in the concept of authoritarianism.[2] In fact, two dimensions seem most directly relevant to political behavior research. One is "authoritarian submission," a tendency in an individual to adopt an uncritical and submissive attitude toward the moral authorities that are idealized

[2] The other key dimensions in the authoritarian syndrome are: conventionalism, authoritarian aggression, anti-intraception, superstition and stereotypy, destructiveness and cynicism, projectivity, and exaggerated concern with sex. Cf. Adorno, Frenkel-Brunswick, Sanford, and Levinson, *op. cit.*, pp. 228–229.

Individuals displaying a number of these characteristics in pronounced fashion were defined as highly authoritarian. The anti-democratic "F" scale was constructed as an instrument for tapping these deep-seated responses. This was accomplished by a series of attitude questions involving moral values and interpersonal relationships but without any specific political content.

by his in-group. The other dimension is "power and toughness," a preoccupation with considerations of strength and weakness, domination and subservience, superiority and inferiority. The authoritarian scale reported in this paper is designed especially to tap these two dimensions whereas the "F" scale of the Berkeley group sought to tap a fuller range.

It should be recalled that, in the population which they studied, the Berkeley group found significant correlations between high authoritarianism and both anti-semitism and ethnocentrism. At the same time, they found that the authoritarian syndrome had only a moderately close relation to political-economic conservatism. In part, this may have been due to the conception of politics on which they based their scale of liberalism-conservatism. Their scale did not permit a distinction between "conservatives" and "reactionaries," nor a distinction between "liberals" and "radicals." [3] The authoritarian predispositions would seem to be more closely linked with the reactionary and radical positions than with an overall ideological continuum from liberalism to conservatism.

However, the approach of this paper was based on the assumption that authoritarianism would be (a) more relevant for explaining political participation and feelings of self-confidence about politics, and (b) less relevant for explaining specific political attitudes and preferences. The hypothesis was investigated that high authoritarians would tend to participate less and have less political self-confidence than low authoritarians in politics as presently organized. In order to understand how authoritarianism might be related to specific political attitudes and preferences, however, it was necessary to assume that the social origins of authori-

[3] That the Berkeley group was aware of this problem is shown by their distinction between genuine conservatism and pseudo-conservatism, in their interpretative sections.

tarianism would differ for specific social groupings in the total population. Only by analyzing these social groupings individually would it be possible to relate adequately authoritarianism to specific political preferences and attitudes.

Research Design

In seeking to clarify the relation between such authoritarian traits and political behavior, the methods used by those interested in spelling out the nature of authoritarianism cannot readily be employed. If the problem is how to gain intensive access to individuals in order to chart in detail their authoritarian tendencies, the representativeness of the groups studied does not matter. In fact, for such research, representative cross sections are not likely to be studied.

In general, only the neurotic, the mentally disturbed, and specialized groups of students have made themselves available for prolonged psychological testing. Although the research of the Berkeley group achieved greater representativeness than usual, even there the samples examined were admittedly limited and self-selected.

Findings from their samples can hardly form the basis for a description of where in the American social structure authoritarian traits tend to predominate. Only by developing an instrument that might be administered through nation-wide surveys could more representative populations be investigated. This implied modifying the original "F" scale to make it suitable for inclusion in a typical attitude survey.

A battery of questions designed to measure authoritarianism had been developed by Fillmore Sanford for inclusion in an attitude survey in the Philadelphia area.[4] Most of the items for this personal-

[4] Sanford, Fillmore, *Authoritarianism and Leadership* (Philadelphia Institute for Research in Human Relations, 1950).

ity scale were selected from the long battery of the Berkeley "F" scale and modified. Since one of these items were subsequently discarded as manifestly making no contribution to the scale, the personality scale analyzed in this paper is based on six questions in the form developed by Sanford.[5]

In particular, these questions measure tendencies to respond to ambiguous social reality in terms that reveal attitudes of authoritarian submission and preoccupation with power and toughness. Drawing upon the theories of dynamic psychology, we assume that projective-like questions are likely to reveal underlying

[5] The wording of Sanford's statement is as follows: (a) Human nature being what it is, there will always be war and conflict; (b) A few strong leaders could make this country better than all the laws and talk; (c) Women should stay out of politics; (d) Most people who don't get ahead just don't have enough will power; (e) An insult to your honor should not be forgotten; and, with the responses scored inversely, (f) People can be trusted. Respondents were asked to agree or disagree and then permitted to state the intensity of their attitude. Thus a six point, Likert-type scale was obtained for each question.

These items are roughly comparable to the following Berkeley "F" scale items: (a) Human nature being what it is, there will always be war and conflict; (b) What this country needs most, more than laws and political programs, is a few courageous, tireless, devoted leaders in whom the people can put their faith; (c) No weakness or difficulty can hold us back if we have enough will power; (d) An insult to our honor should always be punished.

For the remaining items on Sanford's scale, no close analogue can be found in the Berkeley list, except for the following Berkeley item which parallels a Sanford question omitted by us in making the present scale: Obedience and respect for authority are the most important virtues children should learn. We discarded this measure because over 86% of our population gave at least some agreement with it.

psychological reactions of which the individual is not aware. The greater the tendency for an individual to agree with the ambiguous slogans and stereotyped sentiments in the attitude scale, the more authoritarian he is said to be.

Since 1945, the University of Michigan Survey Research Center has conducted a series of nation-wide surveys of public opinion on American foreign policy. In November 1949, the sixth of these studies took place. In May 1950, additional information was gathered by reinterviewing a sub-sample (58 per cent) of the group first interviewed in the previous November.[6] On this sub-sample, responses of 341 persons to Sanford's simplified battery of questions measuring authoritarian tendencies were gathered.[7] In another survey conducted by the Survey Research Center, at about the same time and largely concerned with economic attitudes,[8] the same battery of questions was included. Thus, in establishing the incident of authoritarian tendencies for

[6] Cf. "American's Role in World Affairs: Patterns of Citizen Opinion, 1949–50." (Survey Research Center, University of Michigan, 1952, mimeographed.) This survey was directed by Burton R. Fisher, George Belknap and Charles A. Metzner.

[7] The Survey Research Center, in conducting nation-wide surveys, employs a cross-sectional, area probability sample design with carefully controlled selection procedures. In both the November and May surveys such sampling controls were used, with an additional criterion introduced for the May sub-sample: only that portion of the original sample which scored "consistently" on a scale of intervention-isolation attitudes toward Europe was eligible for the May reinterviewing. Although a nation-wide sample was obtained, it was not necessarily a fully representative sample.

[8] Cf. Big Business from the Viewpoint of the Public. (Ann Arbor, Michigan: Survey Research Center, University of Michigan, 1951.) This survey was directed by Stephen Withey and Ivan Steiner. The sample for this study was both nation-wide and representative.

different social groups, a replicating group of 1227 cases was available. It is of central importance that in every single relevant social relationship the findings based on the second sample population confirmed the conclusions based on the first sample population—the political attitude survey sample.

a low authoritarian group was distinguished at one extreme, each member of which disagreed with at least four of the six slogans. A high authoritarian group was distinguished at the other extreme, each member of which agreed with at least four of the six. Finally, the intermediate group that remained was made

TABLE 1. *Distribution of Authoritarianism*

	POLITICAL SURVEY		REPLICATION SURVEY		TOTAL	
	No.	%	No.	%	No.	%
High authoritarian	107	32	262	23	369	25
Intermediate	117	34	437	39	554	38
Low authoritarian	117	34	430	38	547	37
	341	100	1129	100	1470	100

In both samples, each of the six questions elicited a wide range of responses. Conveniently, enough persons consistently agreed and enough consistently disagreed with the slogans about which they were questioned to permit division of the population into three groups of approximately equal size, without "watering down" the extremist groups.[9] Thus

[9] We used the six questions as a composite battery measuring "authoritarian tendencies" in both primary and secondary relationships. Three of the questions constitute what seems to be a "primary relations" authoritarianism index; none of these three makes *explicit* reference to a social context and all three suggest situations involving a face-to-face evaluation. The other three questions constitute what appears to be a "secondary relations" authoritarianism index; each of these three makes explicit reference to situations involving secondary social institutions.

Using the political attitude survey sample, the distribution of responses from strong agreement to strong disagreement on the two sub-indexes proved to be much alike. An analysis was made to ascertain whether or not the social characteristics (age, education, occupation, income, religion) of persons classed as "authoritarian" on the primary relations sub-index differed from the characteristics of those classed as authoritarian on the secondary relations sub-index. No important differences were found.

up of persons none of whom either agreed or disagreed with more than four of the six items in the index.[10]

[10] Our requirements for classification in one of the extreme categories are more rigorous than this summary statement might suggest. Two criteria were used: cumulative score on all six questions, and ratio of agree to disagree responses. Numerical equivalents from 1 to 6 were assigned to responses ranging from strong agreement to strong disagreement. A low cumulative score for all six responses—a score of less than 19—was necessary in order to be classed as a high authoritarian while a high cumulative score—a score of at least 25—was necessary for classification as low authoritarian. The intermediate group thus included persons whose scores ranged from 19 through 24. To be classed as low authoritarian, it was not enough to have disagreed with at least four of the six items; it was also necessary that the four disagreements be "strong" enough to yield a cumulative score of 25 or more when taken together with the two agreement responses. Similarly, to be classed as high authoritarian, both criteria had to be met: at least four agreement responses, and a cumulative score of less than 19. In the political survey sample, only six cases meeting the ratio of 4:2 failed to qualify for extreme classification because the cumulative score criterion was not met; in the replication survey sample, only the cumulative score criterion was applied.

This mode of analysis permits us to characterize an important predisposition in roughly one fourth of the adult population of the nation. Authoritarianism in these relative terms does not, therefore, refer to a marginal extremist group. The quarter of our nationwide samples classified as highly authoritarian is of crucial importance and direct relevance for understanding American political behavior.

Social Profile of the Authoritarian

Before relating personality traits to political behavior, it seems necessary to attempt to locate where in the social structure the authoritarian individuals are concentrated. What is the social setting in which the anti-democratic personality is most likely to be found?

In the Berkeley research, either the subjects or the voluntary associations through which they were recruited had to be persuaded to submit to investigation. "Save for a few key groups, the subjects were drawn almost exclusively from the middle socio-economic class." [11] As such, little could be said by them about the manner in which authoritarian tendencies would vary with age, education, or socio-economic class. Our more representative cross section of the American population makes it possible for these points to be investigated somewhat more adequately.

Age, education, occupation, and income emerge as key sociological indicators

locating the authoritarian in American society [12] (See Table 2).

First, there was a statistically significant tendency for younger people to register as "low authoritarians" more frequently than older people.[13] Also a clear and significant relationship between education and authoritarian tendencies emerged. Those with limited education tend more frequently to be high authoritarians while those with fuller education tend to be low authoritarians (See Table 2). These two finding are in line with the implications of the Berkeley group, and are what one would expect.

However, we did not find that middle class persons are the main carriers of authoritarianism.[14] The data from our samples suggest that middle-class persons were no more authoritarian than lower class persons. In fact, what differences were found indicated that high authoritarianism occurs more frequently in the lower class. Likewise, the middle class displayed a significantly greater concentration of individuals with low authoritarian scores than did the lower class [15] (See Table 2).

Next we attempted to locate more precisely the authoritarian by considering income differences within class strata.

[11] *Op. cit.*, p. 23. The Berkeley group administered questionnaires to a total of 2099 persons, the great majority of whom lived in San Francisco, with smaller groups sampled in Oregon and in the area around Los Angeles. Their population also included about as many college graduates as persons who had not completed high school. Moreover, the great majority were young people, ranging in age from 20 to 35. For the purpose of validation, approximately 100 subjects were given clinical interviews.

[12] For all analysis, Negroes and Jews were removed from the political survey sample, since they are the objects of much anti-democratic sentiment and constitute a special analytical problem. Negroes were also removed from the replication survey sample, but it was not possible to identify Jews for this population.

[13] Except where otherwise noted, all differences which are reported as statistically significant are at the one per cent level of confidence.

[14] In this respect, our findings closely support conclusions reached in the companion research to *The Authoritarian Personality*, namely, *The Dynamics of Prejudice*, by B. Bettelheim and M. Janowitz.

[15] In the replication survey, the difference is significant at the five per cent level.

TABLE 2. *Social Correlates of Authoritarianism*

AGE	POLITICAL SURVEY SAMPLE		REPLICATION SURVEY SAMPLE		COMPOSITE SAMPLE	
	Under 45	45 or Older	Under 50	50 or Older	Younger People	Older People
High authoritarian	31%	36%	21%	26%	24%	28%
Intermediate	30	37	38	41	36	40
Low authoritarian	39	27	41	33	40	32
	100	100	100	100	100	100
Number of cases:	(189)	(126)	(679)	(379)	(868)	(505)
EDUCATION *	Limited Education	Fuller Education	Limited Education	Fuller Education	Limited Education	Fuller Education
High authoritarian	42%	23%	25%	18%	28%	20%
Intermediate	33	33	40	36	39	35
Low authoritarian	25	44	35	46	33	45
	100	100	100	100	100	100
Number of cases:	(168)	(147)	(803)	(326)	(971)	(473)
SOCIAL ECONOMIC CLASS †	Lower Class	Middle Class	Lower Class	Middle Class	Lower Class	Middle Class
High authoritarian	35%	26%	26%	20%	28%	21%
Intermediate	37	29	37	36	37	35
Low authoritarian	28	45	37	44	35	44
	100	100	100	100	100	100
Number of cases:	(133)	(122)	(436)	(413)	(567)	(535)

* In the political survey, limited education means less than four years of high school; in the replication survey, a slightly different definition was necessary, viz., not more than four years of high school. Correspondingly, in the political survey, fuller education means at least high school graduation while in the replication survey it means more than high school graduation.

† In both surveys, by middle class is meant those persons engaged in non-manual occupations and by lower class those engaged in manual occupations. Farmers were excluded from this analysis.

Both the middle and the lower class were subdivided into upper and lower income groups, thereby delineating four socioeconomic strata.[16] From the data, it emerges that within the middle class the lower income group was considerably more vulnerable to authoritarianism than the upper income middle class group. This finding is in line with many contemporary studies of social stratification that point to the lower middle class as being particularly susceptible to authoritarianism because of their thwarted aspirations. Political scientists have often noted that extremist movements tend to attract such lower middle class authoritarians. As far as the lower class is con-

[16] By lower income is meant less than $3000 a year and by upper income is meant at least $3000 a year.

cerned, there too the lower income group displayed more authoritarianism than the more advantageously situated upper lower class group. However, the difference was not as striking as that found between the upper and lower middle class [17] (See Table 3).

binations of them have a particular tendency to produce authoritarianism. Although many more variables need to be investigated, one important pattern seems to emerge. The social circumstances that condition authoritarianism seem to differ for different social classes. Age and edu-

TABLE 3. *Authoritarianism by Class and Income Level*

| | LOWER CLASS | | MIDDLE CLASS | |
COMBINED SAMPLES:	Lower Income	Upper Income	Lower Income	Upper Income
High authoritarian	32%	24%	34%	18%
Intermediate	36	39	29	37
Low authoritarian	32	37	37	45
	100	100	100	100
Number of cases:	(253)	(319)	(130)	(395)

The question now emerges: was the lower middle class the most authoritarian of all the socio-economic groups? The answer is that the lower class was almost as authoritarian. It might be argued that because the lower middle class presumably includes more people who are politically articulate, the incident of authoritarianism in that group is more serious to the stability of American political life.

cation as correlates of authoritarianism appear to have a different significance for middle class and lower class people.

a. We have seen that age by itself was related to authoritarian tendencies; likewise that social class was related to authoritarianism. Within classes, however, age does not significantly affect authoritarianism. Only between classes is age significant. The older group in the lower

TABLE 4. *Authoritarianism by Class and Age*

| | MIDDLE CLASS | | LOWER CLASS | |
COMBINED SAMPLES:	Younger	Older	Younger	Older
High authoritarian	20%	25%	28%	30%
Intermediate	35	36	33	37
Low authoritarian	45	39	39	33
	100	100	100	100
Number of cases:	(343)	(167)	(371)	(171)

Since in actuality these sociological correlates do not work independently, the next step is to ascertain whether com-

class is significantly more authoritarian than the younger middle class group.[18] In fact, reading across the table, a consistent increase in authoritarianism emerges. It seems reasonable to interpret these

[17] All of the findings reported for the combined samples in Tables No. 3, 4, 5, 6 were also significant for each of the nation-wide samples taken separately.

[18] Significant at the 5 per cent level.

data as indicating that old age to a lower class person maximizes the social insecurity and frustration which presumably encourage authoritarian tendencies while youth to a middle class person minimizes this predisposition (See Table 4).

b. In a similar way educational status by itself was related to authoritarianism, just as was age. Yet the link between edu-

authoritarian tendencies (See Table 5).

c. Again, the link between authoritarianism and educational status emerges as operating differently for the lower and middle classes. For the middle class, fuller education brings about a significant drop in the level of authoritarianism while for the lower class more education appears to have no significant effect on

TABLE 5. *Authoritarianism by Age and Educational Status*

	YOUNGER PEOPLE		OLDER PEOPLE	
COMBINED SAMPLES:	Limited Education	Fuller Education	Limited Education	Fuller Education
High authoritarian	29%	16%	27%	31%
Intermediate	37	35	42	35
Low authoritarian	34	49	31	34
	100	100	100	100
Number of cases:	(540)	(342)	(400)	(127)

cation and authoritarianism is clarified by comparing people of different age groups with comparable educational status. The younger group with fuller education has a significantly lower concentration of high authoritarians than the older group with full education. On the other hand, despite the advantage of their youth, younger people with limited education display authoritarian tendencies significantly more often than younger people with fuller education. To older people, lack of education does not appear to be a significant factor encouraging

authoritarian tendencies. There can be little doubt that we are measuring more than formal educational training here. The educational system operates as part of the status system. In achieving the desired values and aspirations of American society, lack of education is obviously a disability in the middle class whereas it seems to make little difference in the lower class (See Table 6).

d. Finally, when educational status is considered in connection with a detailed breakdown of class strata, the social incidence of authoritarianism is thrown into

TABLE 6. *Authoritarianism by Class and Educational Status*

	LOWER CLASS		MIDDLE CLASS	
COMBINED SAMPLES:	Limited Education	Fuller Education	Limited Education	Fuller Education
High authoritarian	28%	31%	31%	16%
Intermediate	36	28	35	35
Low authoritarian	36	41	34	49
	100	100	100	100
Number of cases:	(446)	(96)	(220)	(290)

sharper relief.[19] We were able to compare the incidence of authoritarianism in "advantageously situated" social groups and in "disadvantageously situated" groups. Limiting ourselves to those groups with the lowest and the highest

cated lower lower class, where 33 per cent of the combined samples were highly authoritarian; and the poorly educated lower middle class, where 39 per cent of the combined samples were highly authoritarian (See Table 7).

TABLE 7. *Incidence of Authoritarianism by Social Groupings*

	WELL-EDUCATED UPPER MIDDLE CLASS	POORLY EDUCATED LOWER LOWER CLASS	POORLY EDUCATED LOWER MIDDLE CLASS
Combined Samples			
High authoritarian	13%	33%	39%
Intermediate	36	36	32
Low authoritarian	51	31	29
	100	100	100
Number of cases:	(236)	(224)	(75)
Political Survey Only			
High authoritarian	17%	42%	67%
Intermediate	30	27	22
Low authoritarian	53	31	11
	100	100	100
Number of cases:	(60)	(45)	(18)
Replication Survey Only			
High authoritarian	12%	31%	30%
Intermediate	39	38	35
Low authoritarian	49	31	35
	100	100	100
Number of cases:	(176)	(179)	(57)

concentrations of authoritarianism, we found that the lowest concentration of authoritarianism was in the well-educated upper middle class group. This was true for both samples. For the combined samples, only 13 per cent of such persons were highly authoritarian. On the other hand, and again for both samples, the highest concentration of authoritarianism appeared in two groups: the poorly edu-

[19] The detailed breakdown of class strata involved dividing both the lower and the middle class groups by level of income, as previously indicated. Thus we have four strata: upper middle, lower middle, upper lower, and lower lower.

First, let us compare the lowest authoritarian group—the well-educated upper middle class—with the poorly educated lower lower class. This is a comparison that cuts across class lines. It juxtaposes that portion of the middle class that is most advantageously situated against the group in the lower class that is most disadvantageously situated.

Authoritarianism in these terms is clearly and significantly linked to those social and economic class cleavages which have long been recognized by political scientists as pervasively affecting American politics.

Second, let us compare the least authoritarian group—the well educated upper middle class—with the poorly educated lower middle class group. This is a comparison within the middle class; the differences in authoritarian tendencies found were at least as great as the comparison was across class lines. One explanation could be that frustrated social mobility, thwarted status aspirations and inadequate purchasing power appear to produce in the poorly educated lower middle class the highest incidence of authoritarianism in any social group. Within this group, too, it seems likely that there are upwardly mobile individuals from the lower class whose adult psychological responses are linked to the problems they face of ridding themselves of values acquired previously and incorporating the values of their new middle class position.

We cannot explain why particular sets of social circumstances prove to be conducive to authoritarianism. It is hardly a simple matter of economic insecurity; on the other hand, it is clearly not frustration *per se* in a strictly psychological sense. Modern society apparently needs to be viewed in terms which interrelate functionally its various strata and status segments. There is no need either to single out the personality syndrome of authoritarianism or to point to the frustrating social circumstances in an effort to determine the cause. Our data in any case do not permit making such a refined judgment. The social and psychological elements of which the "authoritarian response pattern" is composed stand in mutual interdependence. A consistent pattern of authoritarian responses is then seen as a mode for the release of tensions created in persons who have accepted the goals of our society but who find it difficult to adapt to the democratic processes by which they are achieved.

The data from our political survey reveal the social profile of the authoritarian. These data, confirmed in every respect by the replication survey, help to identify the different social groups who display the highest concentration of this response pattern. On the basis of this social profile one can analyze the authoritarian's response to politics.

Political Perspective of the Authoritarian

Although a voter's view of a particular candidate may involve considerations that are both particularized and transitory, his attitudes toward "politics" are more likely to reflect his inner self. For example, participation in the political life of a democratic nation—even the minimum participation of voting—is both an expression of self-confidence and a calculation of self-interest. These facets of the individual are as deeply rooted in his personality as any syndrome of authoritarianism. This is what was encountered. Authoritarianism operated to condition a person's basic approach to politics as well as his general political attitudes.

TABLE 8. *Authoritarianism and Isolationism*

	HIGH AUTHOR- ITARIAN	INTER- MEDI- ATE	LOW AUTHOR- ITARIAN
Generally Isolationist	45%	34%	22%
Generally Interventionist	55	66	78
	100	100	100
Number of Cases:	(71)	(82)	(81)

Attitudes toward American foreign policy will illustrate the matter. Are persons who were generally isolationist in attitudes toward American relations with Europe more authoritarian than those persons who had a generally interventionist attitude? A series of questions were asked: Should we give the European countries money? Should we give them arms? And, strongest of all, should we aid them if they are threatened? Answers to these questions scaled well and served to distinguish isolationist proclivities from interventionist ones.

Although a significant link was found between authoritarianism and isolationism, the data confirm the frequently made observation that the isolationist is by no means always the "reactionary." Only that minority of the isolationists characterized by high authoritarianism seem appropriately classifiable as "reactionaries" (See Table 8).[20] Thirty-two individuals or less than one tenth of the total sample fell into the category of high authoritarian and generally isolationist. These individuals correspond to the "reactionaries" in terms of general political usage.[21]

Another type of question investigated was whether a person felt himself powerless in influencing government action, and what he thought could be done by groups he belonged to. Since these questions seek to tap basic political orientations, it is of high importance for political behavior research to note that authoritarianism is significantly and directly related to feelings of political ineffectiveness (See Table 9).

Perhaps the most crucial relation was found between authoritarian tendencies and voting behavior. The findings furnish a meaningful glimpse into certain dynamics of the political process. So far as the 1948 presidential election was concerned the authoritarian syndrome was less relevant in explaining party preference among those who voted than it was in predicting non-voting. Party preference involves not only the voter's basic

[20] Cf. "America's Role in World Affairs: Patterns of Citizen Opinion" op. cit., pp. 156–159.

[21] Political isolation again was associated with authoritarian tendencies when the question was whether America should admit at least some of Europe's war refugees.

approach to politics but a number of particular considerations about the issues and candidates as well. On the other hand, non-voting was expected to be closely linked to authoritarianism since authoritarianism was postulated to be an expression both of thwarted self-interest and lack of self-confidence. These are the two underlying facets of individual personality—self-interest and self-confidence—that receive expression partly through participation in the political processes.

TABLE 9. *Authoritarianism and Attitudes of Political Effectiveness*

	HIGH AUTHOR- ITARIAN	INTER- MEDI- ATE	LOW AUTHOR- ITARIAN
Believes influence is impossible	63%	59%	41%
Believes influence is possible	37	41	59
	100	100	100
Number of Cases:	(90)	(96)	(99)

In fact, in 1948 individuals with high authoritarian scores did vote significantly less than the rest of the population. Nevertheless, among those who did vote, the incidence of high authoritarianism was in no way significantly linked either to the Truman vote or the Dewey vote [22] (See Table 10).

[22] The incidence of low authoritarianism, on the other hand, was significantly related to a preference for Truman. By itself this relationship is difficult to explain and assumed significance only through more elaborate analysis. Methodologically, this table illustrates rather well the advantage of treating "high authoritarian" and "low authoritarian" groups separately, with "intermediates" in between. Had we worked with mean levels of authoritarianism, as in the previous research on this subject, differences due to the presence of many high authoritarians could not be distinguished from differences due to the absence of low authoritarians.

Another way of demonstrating the link between authoritarianism and non-voting emerges if the social groups in the population which were characterized either by very high or very low authoritarianism are examined. The well-educated upper middle class had the lowest incidence of authoritarianism, only 17 per cent in the political survey sample; this is the group with only 20 per cent non-voters. On the other hand, the poorly-educated groups in the lower middle class and lower lower

spectively, the same proportions voted for Dewey and for Truman. On the other hand, those who did vote in the other highly authoritarian group—the poorly-educated lower lower class—voted overwhelmingly for Truman [23] (See Table 11).

Support of the "liberal" policies of the Fair Deal was not incompatible with authoritarian tendencies in the lower lower class. On the other hand, neither Dewey nor Truman in 1948 presented a

TABLE 10. *Authoritarianism and Voting Behavior*

	DID YOU VOTE IN 1948?		FOR WHOM DID YOU VOTE?	
	Voters	Non-Voters	Truman	Dewey
High authoritarian	25%	40%	26%	26%
Intermediate	40	27	33	47
Low authoritarian	35	33	41	27
	100	100	100	100
Number of Cases:	(199)	(92)	(109)	(81)

TABLE 11. *Candidate Preference by Social Groups*

	WELL-EDUCATED UPPER MIDDLE CLASS	POORLY EDUCATED LOWER MIDDLE CLASS	POORLY EDUCATED LOWER LOWER CLASS
Voted for Truman	40%	22%	31%
Voted for Dewey	40	22	9
Non-voters	20	56	60
	100	100	100
Number of Cases:	(60)	(18)	(45)

class had the highest incidences of authoritarianism, 67 per cent and 42 per cent respectively in the political survey sample; each of these groups had at least 55 per cent non-voters.

For the nation-wide sample as a whole, authoritarianism helped very little to explain candidate preference in the 1948 presidential election. But for the three specific groups having the highest and the lowest incidences of authoritarianism, an important inference emerges. When we compared the two middle class groups with high and low authoritarianism re-

program overwhelmingly appealing to the disadvantageously placed persons in the middle class.[24] Since in 1952 the cam-

[23] This difference is significant at the one per cent level of confidence.

[24] These data suggest the hypothesis that personality reactions to "politics" are manifested not merely in the choice between participation or non-participation, but also depend upon the meaningfulness to the individual of the available political alternatives. In the 1948 election, both highly authoritarian groups—those in relatively disadvantageous circumstances manifested a similar lack of

paign issues were related as much to the tensions generated by external threats to national security as to socio-economic cleavages, the link between authoritarianism and political behavior seems certain to have changed. These changes are being investigated by the University of Michigan Survey Research Center.

In summary, the application to nationwide samples of the techniques used in this study indicates the feasibility of considering personality tendencies as dimensions of American political behavior. At least three conclusions underline the

participation. But the available political alternatives, emphasizing as they did socioeconomic cleavages, led those in the lower lower class who did vote to an overwhelming preference for Truman.

desirability of continued study of these personality tendencies in different political situations: (a) Personality tendencies measured by authoritarian scale served to explain political behavior at least as well as those other factors traditionally included in political and voting behavior studies (age, education, class); (b) It was possible to locate in the national population a number of social groupings characterized by very high and very low authoritarian reactions. The social origins of authoritarianism, however, varied for different classes and status groups; (c) The incidence of authoritarianism not only was significantly related to political isolationism and to feelings of political ineffectiveness, but also to non-voting. Authoritarianism was helpful in explaining candidate preferences.

POLITICAL CHARACTER AND POLITICAL ANALYSIS

by *Robert E. Lane*

The purpose of this paper is threefold: (1) it suggests the utility of the idea of political character in political analysis; (2) it attempts to show how three specific political problems can be illuminated by the use of models, or types, of political character; and (3) it tests the particular types of political character set forth in David Riesman's *The Lonely Crowd* [1] by using them in the analysis of certain political problems.

A person's political character may be defined as his habitual responses to political situations rooted at the personality level. These responses, of course, include a wide range of attitudes and traits—such as apathy or interest, submission or

[1] David Riesman, *The Lonely Crowd;* New Haven: Yale University Press, 1950.

SOURCE: *Psychiatry,* Vol. 16 (1953), pp. 387–398. Reprinted by special permission of The William Alanson White Psychiatric Foundation, Inc.

assertiveness towards authority, suspicion or trust of other groups, and so on. Persons having similar responses may be grouped together as a "type"; this is sometimes done on the basis of a single significant response pattern (ethnocentricity) and sometimes on the basis of a cluster of responses which are seen to go together (authoritarian personality). It is these various typologies which are at the focus of this paper.

The Idea of Political Character in Political Analysis

Since every kind of politics implies some psychological premises, political theory has always included assumptions about the nature of man—assumptions which were more often implicit than overtly stated. Political theorists, and economic theorists as well, have therefore created a range of characterological types to populate the systems they created. Aristotle's "good man," the Machiavellian personality, the law's "reasonable" man, the Marxian's "bourgeois" or class-bound personality, the Marshallian "economic man," Bentham's pleasure-seeking and pain-avoiding human register, and other familiar types all illustrate varieties of political character—some with sophistication but others with the implication that there is only one human nature.[2]

Contemporary insight into the nature of personality has made many of these types of political character seem archaic and quaint, thereby subverting the political theories with which they were associated. New typologies have been developed; some of them have been strictly for therapeutic reasons (such as manic depressives, schizoids, and paranoids), but there are other typologies which are more closely related to the above definition of political character. A few of these types are set forth below, with the definitions condensed from the various works cited:

automaton. A person who "escapes from freedom" by adopting culturally popular personality patterns, losing his sense of personal identity and re-

[2] In a sense many classic theoretical works may best be used to illustrate model communities wherein a single psychological orientation is made the premise and the governmental forms outlined may be considered the result. Thus Hobbes' *Leviathan* (Oxford: Blackwell, 1946) may be considered as a discussion of the society and government which would follow if human beings were sado-masochistic and paranoid; Machiavelli's *The Prince* (Chicago: Packard and Co., 1941) may be considered as a discussion of government where the elite is competitive, anxious, and possessed of psychopathic personalities; and J. S. Mill's *On Liberty and Considerations on Representative Government* (Oxford: Blackwell, 1946) represents a Utopia where men are assumed to have democratic personalities, are thought to have their libidinous drives well under control, and are guided by reason.

sponding to political stimuli without any individual or distinctive orientation. *Erich Fromm.*[3]

pseudo-conservative. A person who adopts the conservative's ideology at the verbal level but, because of underlying personality disorders, subconsciously seeks radical solutions—for example, the lynching of agitators in the name of law and order. *T. W. Adorno and associates.*[4]

authoritarian personality. A person who (among other things) perceives the world as made up of a small glorified in-group and despised out-groups, hierarchically arranged by power relationships, peopled by types rather than individuals. He cannot establish warm human relationships, judges people by exterior qualities, adopts a moralistic condemnatory tone toward deviant behavior, and so forth. *T. W. Adorno and associates.*[5]

political agitator. A political leader whose satisfactions are derived from arousing emotions in others and whose skills are greatest in this area of interpersonal contact. *Harold Lasswell.*[6]

political administrator. A person whose skill lies in the manipulation of things and situations and whose displacement of affect upon less remote objects is associated with a better adjustment to society. *Harold Lasswell.*[7]

political theorist. A person whose skill lies in the manipulation of ideas and who has displaced his private motives and emotions upon a system of abstract concepts. *Harold Lasswell.*[8]

bureaucratic personality. A person whose

[3] *Escape from Freedom;* New York: Rinehart, 1941; pp. 185–206.

[4] *The Authoritarian Personality,* New York: Harper, 1950; pp. 181 ff.

[5] Reference footnote 4; *passim.*

[6] *Psychopathology and Politics;* Chicago: University of Chicago Press, 1930; pp. 78–126.

[7] Reference footnote 6; pp. 127–152.

[8] Reference footnote 6; pp. 53–56.

interpersonal relations have been habitually formalized by the demands of his work-life and whose responses to new situations are governed by overvaluation of rules. *Robert Merton.*[9]

indifferent. A person either who has no emotional or mental relationship to politics or whose mobility or lack of orientation leads him to shun all political involvements. *David Riesman.*[10]

moraliser (indignant or enthusiast). A person whose responses to political situations are characterized by high affect and low competence. *David Riesman.*[11]

inside-dopester. A person with controlled (and low) affect and great desire to know and/or use political phenomena for his amusement and advantage. *David Riesman.*[12]

anomic. A person whose political style is inappropriate to the situations he faces and who shows other symptoms of disorientation. *David Riesman.*[13]

autonomous. A person who is neither dominated by parentally instilled conscientious views of politics nor by concern for the opinions of peer groups; a person, therefore, free to choose his own political opinions. *David Riesman.*[14]

Underlying the above political types conceived by David Riesman is another typology which has a much broader application than political phenomena. Riesman suggests a relationship between certain demographic situations and social character, and then proceeds to define three emergent types: (a) the *tradition-directed* person, who has no image of himself as in any way related to the world of government and politics; (b) the *inner-directed* person, whose orientation is given in childhood and who is not responsive to the changing moods and opinions of his associates; and (c) the *other-directed* person, whose means of dealing with each situation is determined by a sensitive screening of whatever doctrine or behavior prevails among the groups close to him at a given moment.[15]

These and other contemporary conceptions of political character have been employed to explain political phenomena in a limited but growing number of instances.[16] Their utility in political analysis is manifold, but four services seem to emerge as most important:

(1) *When it appears that socioeconomic and historic factors are relatively constant in two situations but the situations develop differently, the concept of political character may serve as an auxiliary explanation of social causation.* For example, the impact of a crisis situation has often presented socialist and communist groups with similar opportunities. Is it ideology alone, or may it also be a differential selection of per-

[15] Reference footnote 1; chap. 1.

[16] For a discussion of the political character of members of the Nazi elite, see G. M. Gilbert, *The Psychology of Dictatorship;* New York: Ronald Press, 1950. For a discussion of the traits of Nazi leaders among prisoners of war, see H. V. Dicks, "Personality Traits and National Socialistic Ideology," *Human Relations* (1950) 3:111–154. For a discussion of the political character of American Fascist agitators, see Leo Lowenthal and Norbert Guterman, *Prophets of Deceit;* New York: Harper, 1949. For a discussion of the political traits of Soviet elite and followers, see H. V. Dicks, "Observations on Contemporary Russian Behavior," *Human Relations* (1952) 5:111–176; and Margaret Mead, *Soviet Attitudes Toward Authority;* New York: McGraw-Hill, 1951. For a discussion of methodological problems, see Nathan Leites, "Psychocultural Hypotheses About Political Acts," *World Politics* (1948) 1:102–119.

[9] "Bureaucratic Structure and Personality," *Social Forces* (1940) 17:560–568.

[10] Reference footnote 1; pp. 184–190.

[11] Reference footnote 1; pp. 190–199.

[12] Reference footnote 1; pp. 199–210.

[13] Reference footnote 1; pp. 287–288.

[14] Reference footnote 1; pp. 295–299.

sonality types which causes the observable difference in reactions?[17] The West invaded China and Japan with a significantly different reception in each case.[18] Cultural and geographic distinctions may seem to explain these differences—but do not the concepts of comparative culture implicitly include the concept of difference in political character? The employees in a West Virginia mill staffed by workers with rural breeding react to exploitation in a manner different from that of metropolitan-bred workers. This is more than a difference of ideology and economic alternatives; it is a difference in habitual responses to social and political stimuli—that is, a difference in social and political character.

(2) *Hypotheses respecting the political character of the members of a social organization helps suggest the probable development, the tropisms, and the limitations of that organization.* One might, for example, upon seeing a high percentage of pseudo-conservatives (Adorno) in an organization dedicated to traditional values, anticipate internal friction on the appropriate means for defending these values. This would follow from the different political characters of the genuine conservatives and the pseudo-conservatives. Or it would be possible to predict that there will be recruitment difficulties in an organization that defends the in-

terests of groups which are populated by indifferents (Riesman). Or, to cite a third instance, it was just such an analysis of defective psychological substructure which Fromm employed in his explanation of the rise of Naziism in Germany.

(3) *The explicit use of types of political character in the construction of political and social models (Utopias) minimizes the use of concealed premises about the nature of man, and facilitates the use of these models to clarify social goals.* In the use of such models one follows in eminent footsteps. Thus Marx constructed his model community, the eventual classless communist society, on the basis of a compliant, unaggressive, self-controlled model of human nature.[19] Another Utopia may be seen in the atomized capitalist society conceived by Marshall and Mill, a Utopia populated entirely by rational and selfish versions of economic man.[20] A third model community is seen in Lasswell's garrison state, which is inhabited by paranoids and their captives.[21] Each such hypothetical so-

---

[17] See the forthcoming work by Gabriel Almond on the sources of Communist party membership. See also, Howard Wriggins, "The Ideal Image of the Communist Militant"; unpublished Ph.D. dissertation on file at Yale University Library, 1952, and Herbert Krugman, "The Appeal of Communism to American Middle Class Intellectuals and Trade Unionists," *Public Opinion Quart.* (1952) 16:331–355.

[18] See: Ruth Benedict, *The Chrysanthemum and the Sword;* Boston: Houghton Mifflin, 1946. J. K. Fairbank, *The United States and China;* Cambridge: Harvard University Press, 1948. D. N. Rowe, *China Among the Powers;* New York: Harcourt, Brace, 1945.

[19] Although Marxian literature does not provide a clear picture of the nature of the prophesied Utopia, a few suggestions by Marx and Engels can be found in Max Eastman (ed.), *Capital, the Communist Manifesto, and Other Writings;* New York: Modern Library, 1932; part 1, "Outlines of a Future Society." For a commentary on this and other Utopias, see Karl Mannheim, *Ideology and Utopia;* New York: Harcourt, Brace, 1944; pp. 173–236.

[20] Although Jevons presents the conceptualized analysis of economic man in its purest form, both Alfred Marshall (*Principles of Economics;* London: Macmillan, 1890) and John Stuart Mill (*Principles of Political Economy;* Boston: Little, Brown, 1845) give more rounded and complete presentations of the operation of the capitalist Utopia.

[21] See Harold Lasswell, "The Garrison State and Specialists on Violence," *Amer. J. Sociol.* (1941) 46:455–468 (reprinted in Lasswell, *The Analysis of Political Behavior;* London: Routledge and Kegan Paul, 1948; pp. 146–157).

ciety must include assumptions regarding the natures of the inhabitants, and it is an advance to recognize that these inhabitants are not live men but are stage characters borrowed from the cast made available by contemporary views of human nature.

(4) *The employment of alternate types of political character in the premises of classical political issues serves to give them a new dimension and to illuminate new aspects of these problems.* In this use, the concept of political character is employed on a hypothetical basis in such a way as to shed light where the nature of the participants has eluded attention. What one does, in effect, is to take a certain situation, make various assumptions regarding the type of political character of the participants in the situation, and then predict the results that would be likely to occur on the basis of these assumptions. For example, this might be done to shed light on the problems associated with force and revolution by comparing the typical responses of the pseudo-conservative with the genuine conservative (Adorno), the automaton with the spontaneous man (Fromm), or the indifferent with the inside-dopester (Riesman). By varying the type of political character assumed, our knowledge of a problem may be enriched and stale arguments given new meaning.

An Example of Political Character Analysis: Riesman's Typology and Interest Group Theory

The merits and defects of this last type of analysis may best be revealed by an example: the application of a political typology to the classic issues of interest group theory. "Interest group" is defined as a formally organized association exercising an influence on governmental policy; a few examples would be the American Medical Association, Americans for Democratic Action, locals of the United

Steel Workers of America, and the New Haven Chamber of Commerce.

In giving such an example of the application of a political typology, the selection of the typology offers a dilemma—for the solutions to the problems presented will depend upon the style and capacities of the characters introduced. Thus electoral behavior and the democratic processes will differ in their results in societies and groups inhabited by (a) pseudo-conservatives or (b) indifferents, and in societies and groups led by (c) agitators or (d) bureaucratic personalities.

For the purposes of this paper, I have selected Riesman's troupe, not because it is the closest to reality—probably the Adorno typology deserves this honor—but because it is a more complete group, offering more variety, and is particularly serviceable in opening up hidden but real issues in the area of interest group theory.[22] In what follows, three aspects of interest group theory are discussed: (1) the pluralistic problem; (2) the interpretation of group pressures; and (3) problems of representation in the leadership of interest groups.

THE PLURALISTIC PROBLEM. The interpretation of men's actual and potential relationship to government has formed the substance of political discussion in every arena and forum of Western culture. In broad and blunt outline, the units of observation are threefold: the individual, the group and constellation of groups, and what is usually termed "the state." Today, the focus of scholarly political science attention rests upon the middle category, the group and the constellation of groups which characterize

[22] Riesman's focus of attention in *The Lonely Crowd* (reference footnote 1) and *Faces in the Crowd* (New Haven: Yale University Press, 1952) is such that many of the classic problems of interest group theory are not treated there. But, with an autonomy of their own, his ideas may be made to grapple with these problems.

society. This mental focus is, of course, a reflection of the changing structure of society, as well as a sharpening of insight into what was, in reduced measure, always there. A society which recognizes the importance of these groups, as contrasted with a society which recognizes only the state and the individual, is termed a "pluralistic" society.

The nature and perspectives of individuals who elude affiliation with interest groups bear closer examination. In Riesman's terms, who are the isolates? Are they *anomic*—persons with no appropriate political style, lost in the maze of people and events? Or are they *inner-directed moralizers*—persons steered by a rigid conscience, who, in their isolation from others, may become a persistent and difficult force of political anomalies? Or are they *autonomous*—that is, self-possessed and in possession of a perspective which leads them to avoid close affiliations and political commitments? Of course the isolates are of all three types, but it appears from the observable evidence that they are more anomic than they are autonomous or inner-directed moralizers.[23] Analysis, prescription, and therapy must then proceed in part from this identification of isolate character. It should be understood that the problem here is one of giving guidance to disoriented people rather than one of providing opportunities for expression for oriented and politically stable citizens. And it is important to recognize that the prescription and therapy must depend upon

the differential analysis of the type of isolate under consideration. Solidarity and greater group integration may be prescribed as both an individual and a social cure for the anomic; but for the autonomous person, tenuous and lightly worn group relationships may indeed be socially healthy. For the moralizer, membership in groups of fellow indignants may serve to reinforce his indignation, while membership in multipurpose groups may dull the edge of his indignation, thwart its expression, and broaden its frame of reference.

If the nature of the isolate is a fractious problem, so also is the nature of group adherence. Political theorists have been inclined to regard the problem of group adherence in terms of the undifferentiated conception of "membership" in interest groups, without reference to the variety of meanings that membership may have for different people. This is a deficiency in conceptualization which any sophisticated approach to political character should seek to repair. The approach to the problem of group membership may also proceed through the use of Riesman's typology: *anomic, moralizer, autonomous,* and also, since this problem deals with affiliated individuals, the *inside-dopester* —the person who endows his politics with little affect, treats goals and ends casually, but possesses great technical (political) competence and seeks to employ it constantly to reorient himself with respect to other people's desires and ideas.

The typology is limited in its serviceability at this point. It fails to illuminate much of the significance of group membership: for example, it is not useful for distinguishing among, say, those veterans who join the American Legion in search of solidarity or because of a "need to avoid aloneness," to use Fromm's terminology; those who join in order to recapture status formerly accorded them by military rank; and those who join because of sympathetic responsiveness to hierarchical society (Adorno). To apply

[23] Membership in formal organized groups normally increases as one goes up the social scale. Political participation and interest also increase with socioeconomic status. But at any given socioeconomic level, those with greater group connections are likely to be more clearly oriented politically, more confirmed in their political beliefs, than those with fewer group connections. See P. F. Lasarsfeld, B. Berelson, and H. Gaudet; *The People's Choice;* New York: Columbia University Press, 1948; pp. 145–147.

Riesman's ideas on political character in an effort to develop those themes would be adventitious; it would overburden an already speculative line of argument.

But Riesman's typology does illuminate some aspects of group membership which might otherwise escape attention. I have before me the image of the New Haven League of Women Voters who recently mobilized for an all-out assault upon the weak-mayor form of government in that city in an effort to secure the adoption of a council-manager charter. For some of the members the League represented a reflection of their own strong consciences, a force for Right, and the opposition represented the incarnation of evil. These women may properly be designated "indignant moralizers" and the analysis of such a character type is fruitful and, indeed, pragmatic. For others in the League, the association offered sources of information, a little power, opportunities for the exercise of interpersonal skills— in short, a favorable milieu for the inside-dopester. A few of the League members seemed at the same time to have both political skills and a secure conviction of the direction in which they wished to go; for such autonomous persons, compromise, minor achievements, and the higgling ways of municipal democracy were admissible without defection or despair.

The significance of this breakdown of members into types lies in the destruction of the conception of an organization as a monolith, and in its re-creation in proper molecular terms. As a result, the respective sources of weakness and strength come more quickly to attention. The possibilities of compromise, the capacity for creating and holding allies, the stock pile of emotional fuel which may give staying power to the organizational effort, the capacity to sustain defeat, to change goals, and so forth—these may all be a reflection of the political character of the interest group membership or at least of the leadership.

It is not only societies that are plural-

ist, however; it is also individuals. A man belongs, inevitably, to many latent interest groups, even though he may be only dimly aware of them—his ethnic group (for the native white Protestant, often a group outlined only by the presence of other groups which he does recognize), his class group (ambiguous to most Americans), his religious group, his "cause" groups if any, his sectional group, and any number, variety, and complexity of others.[24] Normally, a person will be conscious of his group affiliation with men in similar occupations—professional, union, business, farm.

It is not surprising that such a multiplicity of group affiliations creates contradictions and conflicts for the individual— particularly when they present their claims for support simultaneously.[25] It has been said, therefore, that representation by interest groups fractionalizes a person—divides him into irreconcilable component parts so that he never becomes a whole man with an orientation that overrides his subordinate interests. The conclusion follows that political-party representation, because it presents a comprehensive, if vague, orientation, is superior to the atomistic representation of unreconciled interest groups.[26] Al-

[24] W. L. Warner and associates present a schematic version of an individual's formal group membership (*The Status System of a Modern Community*; New Haven: Yale University Press, 1942). The informal groups to which a person belongs are analyzed as voting determinants in several studies: see, for example, Angus Campbell and R. Kahn, *The People Elect a President*; Ann Arbor, Survey Research Center, 1952; pp. 20–39.

[25] See W. Y. Elliott, *The Pragmatic Revolt in Politics*; New York: Macmillan, 1928; pp. 95–99, 204. See also F. W. Coker, *Recent Political Thought*; New York: Appleton-Century, 1934, chap. 18.

[26] "It is clear that my underlying assumption in this critique is that the ultimate legal relationship between [group] members and the state could . . . only be one of citizenship made effective by political parties, al-

though the conclusion may be right, it follows too swiftly at this point, for it is precisely here that it may be useful to employ the concepts of political character.

The first revelation to appear from this psychologically oriented analysis is that the question has been miscast: psychologically the choice is not between party and interest group, but between whole-hearted devotion to a few interest groups or to a narrow third party, on the one hand, and, on the other hand, a sympathetic affiliation with a broad major party and a complex of interest groups. Riesman's indignant or enthusiast will find congenial representation in a goal-oriented organization (such as the Anti-Saloon League, Prohibition Party, Committee for Constitutional Government, People's Lobby, or Socialist Party) and will refuse to consider himself represented by other interest groups or parties. But the other-directed overpoliticized person will seek representation by many interest groups whose conflicting goals will not disturb him—since he will have a loose and tenuous interest in their goals. Such an other-directed person will also find satisfaction in representation by a broad and amorphous party whose orientation is toward power rather than toward program. Being himself a pluralist, he sees no threat in the pluralistic problem.

But the pluralistic problem has facets other than the nature of the isolate in a group-structured society, the nature of the linkage which binds men to their groups, and the nature of the role of political character in the conflict of interest groups and political parties. There is, also, the question of the relationship between social typologies and character typologies. One such social typology refers to the isolation and the group solidarity of the individuals in a given society. A society of isolated persons may be said to be atomistic; a society in which most persons have many and close group memberships may be said to be pluralistic.[27] What, then, would be the relationship of the inner-directed-other-directed character typology to such an atomistic-pluralistic social typology?

Theoretically, of course, it would be possible to have a fourfold classification (see Figure 1): pluralistic and inner-directed; pluralistic and other-directed; atomistic and inner-directed; atomistic and other-directed.

Inner-directed and Atomistic	Inner-directed and Pluralistic
Other-directed and Atomistic	Other-directed and Pluralistic

Fig. 1.

The logic of the typologies, however, is such that an atomistic other-directed society is impossible, and a pluralistic and inner-directed society is too explosive to exist in any other than transitional form. On the other hand, both an atomistic inner-directed society, such as those of earlier agrarian America, and a pluralistic other-directed society can logically exist. Perhaps with these particular variables there is no other logical choice.

[27] In addition to atomistic and pluralistic societies, there are monolithic societies where the nation is *the* group and the group is solidary and demanding. This represents the kind of homogeneous consensual society implied in the works of Plato, Rousseau, and Mussolini. For a different kind of scale—irrational to rational—see Karl Mannheim, *Man and Society in an Age of Reconstruction;* New York: Harcourt, Brace, 1948.

though this citizenship is now 'filtered' by group life. Political parties based on territorial representation must be the final means . . . of enforcing responsibility and registering public opinion." Elliott, reference footnote 25; p. 213.

The United States is a pluralistic society.[28] Furthermore, the predominant emphasis in the range of political character types seems to be other-directed: thus Mead refers to the American search for contemporary popular orientation that has resulted from distrust of tradition,[29] Jones reports on the centralist tendency in opinion formation—the fear of isolation from the median public opinion [30] —and Riesman, of course, develops the theme of American other-directedness at some length.[31] As a pluralistic other-directed society, however, the American nation—or at least the urban parts of it—may have found the best available basis for democracy, now that the earlier simpler agrarian and inner-directed basis is no longer generally available.

THE INTERPRETATION OF GROUP PRESSURES. The Constitution arranges the elements of government in such a manner that the translation of popular desires into law is difficult and often delayed; it

[28] See David Truman, *The Governmental Process;* New York: Knopf, 1951; and Earl Lathan, *The Group Basis of Politics;* Ithaca: Cornell University Press, 1952.

[29] Margaret Mead. *And Keep Your Powder Dry;* New York: Morrow, 1943; pp. 27–53. Almond seems to agree with Mead in her estimate of the "faddistic" nature of American orientation, but his stress upon the privatization of interests in the United States appears to qualify his conception of the other-directed American character. See Gabriel Almond, *The American People and Foreign Policy;* New York: Harcourt, Brace, 1950.

[30] See A. W. Jones, *Life, Liberty and Property;* Philadelphia: Lippincott, 1941; pp. 318–354.

[31] "Bearing [certain] qualifications in mind, it seems appropriate to treat contemporary metropolitan America as our illustration of a society—so far, perhaps, the only illustration—in which other-direction is the dominant mode of insuring conformity." Reference footnote 1; pp. 20–21; see also chaps. 10 and 12.

has created a situation where political parties, the vehicles of popular majorities, are weak, and the interest groups, the vehicles of minorities, are strong. Among the interest groups, those with independent sources of strength in the economy are in a relatively stronger position than those dependent upon governmental action for protection of their interests; this results from the fact that it is easier to block governmental action under a bicameral system endowed with a separation of powers than it is to advance governmental action in such a system. The result, of course, is that not only have interest groups flourished in such institutional soil, but they have developed chiefly along the lines of thwarting governmental action. Hence the term "veto groups," applied to them by Riesman and others, has some justice.

Institutional analysis of this variety offers a primer's answer to the question, "Why are interest groups so influential in the United States?"—a question to which I shall return. But one may as well ask, "Why, given their institutional leverage, do not interest groups achieve greater strength in the United States?" For both questions, the ideas associated with the concept of political character have relevance.

It is to this second question that Riesman addresses himself, applying his social schema to achieve an explanation of the relative restraint of interest group leaders. In summary, it appears that the inner-directed robber baron has now given way to the politically sensitive industrial statesman, frightened by the cautions of his public relations counsel, fearful lest he appear "exotic" to his fellows, anxious to avoid controversy—in short, all "radar" (other-directedness) and no "gyroscope" (inner-directedness). Furthermore, if the veto groups are acknowledged to exercise the really decisive influence in a wide range of social issues and if they restrain themselves from a blunt and overt exercise of this influence, there may be said to be a power vacuum at the top. Asking himself who is the ruling class in this situation, Riesman says there is none.[32]

But this does not dispose of the matter. In the very system that Riesman describes there are forces which sustain the power of the interest groups and impoverish the resistance which society can offer. Among the forces contributing to interest group influence is the character structure of the society Riesman describes, a society populated by men trained to yield to others' opinions, to exhibit "tolerance" towards diverse interests (within an approved framework), and to move cautiously towards acceptability by the more powerful agents of that society. Most of the remainder of the population is busily indifferent to political matters, and, of those few who are concerned, a large number possess political styles inappropriate to their times and so lack the competence to make themselves heard. Such a society offers itself helplessly to the rape of the interest group chieftain who overcomes his diffidence in this matter.

Nor can it be said that the interest group counselors are unaware of the milieu which offers them such advantages. For those interests which directly engage the public seem most often to select for emphasis themes that suggest the popularity, cultural approval, indigenous nature, and American Way of the proposed public policy. Not the merits but the orthodoxy of the proposal seems at stake, and in such manner the other-directeds, the inside-dopesters, the conformists of suburbia and pseudo-suburbia are moved to respond favorably.

Equally important is the anaesthetic appeal of the interest group which narcotizes potential indignation with "goodwill" advertising and stimulates indifference and apathy toward their loosely regulated activities by elaborate devices for turning public attention toward something else.[33] Furthermore, aggregates of enormous power attempt to masquerade as "just one of the boys" (the oligopolist as a small business man) or to deny their existence completely (the union leader whose followers act "spontaneously" to quit work). Using Riesman's model to reveal a possible truth, if not a present situation, it appears that an overpoliticized society under tension to return to a happier state of indifference will respond with quiet satisfaction to the narcotizing appeal of a number of interest groups.[34]

[32] Reference footnote 1; chap. 11, "Images of Power." In support of this position, it may be said that in all probability those interest groups with a stake in governmental decisions fail to treat lobbying costs as they would some other more explicit and formalized cost factor (such as wages or capital or advertising) and consequently underspend in this area. In further support, it appears that the failure of business to accept what may be called "Brady's solution"—the establishment of a hierarchical organization of business groups to absorb political power in their own interest, on a scale comparable to the German pattern of the 1920–1932 period—suggests indeed a marked restraint of these dominant veto groups. See Robert Brady, *Business as a System of Power;* New York: Columbia University Press, 1943.

[33] Thus Thurman Arnold suggests that the chief utility of the Sherman Anti-Trust Act has been to lull the public into a sense of security and permit the normal activities of trusts, cartels, and oligopolies to proceed without serious public concern or governmental interference. See Thurman Arnold, *The Folklore of Capitalism;* New Haven: Yale University Press, 1937; pp. 207–229.

[34] Kris and Leites found the German people generally seeking to escape the politicization of their lives during the Nazi era, and they suggest that this phenomenon is present in less degree in all Western countries. (E. Kris and N. Leites, "Trends in Twentieth Century Propaganda," pp. 393–409; in *Psychoanalysis and the Social Sciences,* edited by Géza Róheim; New York: International University Press, 1947.) Riesman argues that the mass media constantly present political stimuli to people who are constantly trying to escape it. (Reference footnote 1; pp. 224 ff.)

While some interest groups engage in this variety of persuasion and discussion among the public at large, most, being small, operate in more intimate relationships with such congressmen as seem vulnerable or at least approachable. The responses of congressmen, furthermore, are guided by their political characters, which may be stylized as other-directed raised to the second power—that is, politically sensitive men selected from constituencies heavily endowed with other-directed voters and letter writers. It is not over-reaching the argument to say that the tenderness of congressmen to pressures, many of which bear no conceivable relation to past or future electoral results, is partly due to this social sensitivity distilled from society and purified in the atmosphere of Washington.[35]

PROBLEMS OF REPRESENTATION: THE ELITE-CONSTITUENCY RELATIONSHIP. In addition to the pluralistic problem (the person, the group, and the state) and the interpretation of interest group strategy, there are problems emerging from the relationship of leaders to constituencies in the interest groups themselves which merit attention. Orthodox attention singles out certain aspects of this relationship: Is the leader responsible to the constituency and what are the sanctions to enforce such responsibility? Is he vested with the powers of discretion or must he act within a narrow prescription

of opinions upon which he has received instructions? Does he serve only the majority faction, if any, or does he modify his actions to suit a minority view? Is he permitted to transcend the bounds of the group's apparent interest to serve the interests of a larger group, perhaps the nation, when there is conflict between the two?

If these are classic questions, how may the classic answers be illuminated by reference to a typology of political character? In the first place, the relationship between the personality characteristics of the leaders and of the constituents—the "closeness of fit," to use Dicks' terminology [36]—is suggestive. Since leaders and delegates respond to issues with reference both to their internal personality pressures and external political pressures, the question arises of whether leaders whose personality characteristics differ from those of their constituents will validly represent their constituents. It is for this reason that, for example, leadership responding in terms of organizational advantage, public relations considerations, and strategic concepts (inside-dopesterism) runs afoul of the fraction of membership, large or small, which is purely goal-oriented (moralizers). If there is a systematic recruitment of inside-dopesters among the elite of an interest group, it is questionable whether the indignant and enthusiastic membership may be said to be adequately represented. Thus the anything-to-win psychology which seemed to be ascendant in the leadership group of Americans for Democratic Action at the 1948 Democratic Convention—on candidates, not issues—appeared hopelessly compromising to a portion of moralizing rank and file back home. On the other

---

Thus if interest groups can offer reassurance that attention is not needed, this theme will chime with an already present and poignant desire.

[35] The responsiveness of United States congressmen to pressure groups is often described, but any effort to appraise motivation or the role of personality and character requires more information than has hitherto been available. See L. E. Gleeck, "98 Congressmen Make Up Their Minds," *Public Opinion Quart.* (1940) 4:3–24; or Jerry Voorhis, *Confessions of a Congressman;* New York: Doubleday, 1947; *passim.*

[36] See H. V. Dicks, "Observations on Contemporary Russian Behavior," reference footnote 16; pp. 168–174. Much of Dicks' discussion centers on the problem of the divergent personality characteristics of the new Bolshevik elite and the mass of the Russian people.

hand, there are occasions when an indignant radical faction will achieve control of an organization, defy public opinion, and gladly crucify themselves and their organization on some principled issue which might, from an organizational point of view, better have been avoided. Thus recently a strong faction in a cooperative housing community, in demonstrating their breadth of view on racial matters, welcomed a mixed couple (Negro and white) into the group, heedless of the fact that the couple had not sanctified their union by marriage, and were defiant toward the probable legal action which would follow.

The psychological congruity of elite and constituency is more than a matter of the accuracy of the representation involved; it also raises a question of the significance of the various kinds of discrepancies. Thus a moralistic elite in a fraternal and other-directed community or group, will pursue the formal explicit goals of the organization at the expense of the implied and unconscious goals of solidarity and "escape from aloneness." The instrumentalist other-directed elite in a moralistic group, will preserve the organization and attend to its needs for cohesion and solidarity at the expense of the formal goals. In organizations where both elite and constituency consist of inside-dopesters, the survival instrumental values of the group will tend to be accentuated at the expense of the ideological values; and in organizations made up entirely of moralizers, it is the ideological values that will tend to be accentuated. In the former case, the organization will flourish to do nothing; in the latter, clear goals will be enthusiastically pursued by an organization of dwindling effectiveness.[37]

The case of an elite which represents a constituency of indifferent and apathetic members, neither concerned over the organization's goals nor linked to the organization by its opportunities for advancement or social stimulus, offers special problems.[38] This is, by and large, the nature of much union membership, except for bread-and-butter issues, and it is also reflected in the membership of a number of churches. It is, in fact, a special case of wide frequency. In such cases the personality responses of the leadership are given free rein and are neither confirmed nor restrained by membership responses. As a consequence of this absence of external pressures of all kinds—

_____

stage of the reasoning. Here, for example, it appears that the Anti-Saloon League, surely an indignant organization if there ever was one, was eminently successful in attracting adherents. (See Peter Odegard, _Pressure Politics;_ New York: Columbia University Press, 1928.) Furthermore it is at least possible that one reason Hitler achieved success was his obsessive, indignant nature. (See Gilbert, reference footnote 16; p. 295.) These two exceptions suggest a modification of the principles stated above: Where there is a constituency available with strong indignant feelings in certain areas, an indignant elite may be both uncompromising with respect to these areas and successful in attracting adherents.

[38] This is, of course, Michels' problem, although he deals with it in terms of divergent and conscious interests rather than in terms of divergent psychological referents. Much of Michels' argument rests upon the capacity of the elite to change from their revolutionary (and representative) position to their position of leaders with vested interests and conservative orientation. If this change is the product of material and status considerations, it may be easy and rapid. If, however, the change requires characterological changes as well, it will necessarily be a slower and more difficult process. See Robert Michels, _Political Parties;_ Glencoe, Ill.: Free Press, 1949 (first published in 1915); pp. 205–234.

[37] It is well to keep in mind throughout that this essay represents a stylized account of possible factors to take into consideration; it is not a descriptive account. Furthermore, there is an implied _ceteris paribus_ at every

ideological and social—the internal pressures of the character structure of the elite are released; the personalities of the leadership find their own media and style of expression. In the case of unions, because of the pragmatic nature of the leadership, the ideological content of the union program is apt to recede, *for both elite and constituency,* into a limbo of unmentioned topics; in the case of some of the churches, the indignation of leaders with a hyperdeveloped social conscience may alight upon convenient issues almost indiscriminately as they erupt in the news. In neither case does representation have anything to do with the event.

In addition to being important in the study of the degree to which the wishes of the constituency are accurately reflected by the leadership and the nature of the distortion of their wishes, if any, the psychological relationship of elite to constituency is also important in the treatment of the majority-minority problem. It is in the perspective of a range of values—consensus, heterodoxy, fear of authority, concern for economic privation, and so on—that this issue is usually argued,[39] but the problem has its psychological aspects as well.

A simple diagram of four possible situations, where there is only one minority group and where only Riesman's two major political character types are employed, is set forth in Figure 2.

The resolution of these situations of course is, in fact, unpredictable; but by using them as models, it becomes possible to suggest tendencies created by the conflict of political character:

1. Inside-dopester majority and inside-dopester minority: Both groups would

[39] See, for example: H. S. Commager, *Majority Rule and Minority Rights;* New York: Oxford, 1948. Edward Mims, *The Majority of the People;* New York: Modern Age, 1941. Willmoore Kendall, *John Locks and the Doctrine of Majority Rule;* Urbana: University of Illinois Press, 1941.

tend to compromise; the unity of the organization would be preserved at the expense of whatever principles were at issue. There would be consensual rule rather than majority rule, in conflict with minority rights.

Inside-dopester Majority and Inside-dopester Minority	Inside-dopester Majority and Moralizer Minority
Moralizer Majority and Inside-dopester Minority	Moralizer Majority and Moralizer Minority

Fig. 2.

2. Inside-dopester majority and moralizer minority: The majority would be inclined to yield to the resolute minority in order to save the organization from irreparable split (although the desire of the majority to be acceptable to the outside world might yet force the split). Temporarily, at least, the minority goals would be furthered and there would thus be a tendency toward minority rule.

3. Moralizer majority and inside-dopester minority: The minority would yield to the majority and the organization would pursue a strict majoritarian policy. This is the only situation conductive to strict majoritarian rule.

4. Moralizer majority and moralizer minority: Neither group would yield to the other and a split would almost inevitably follow. This would be a revolutionary situation.

There is, finally the question of the affinity of like-minded members of an organization—those with congenial personalities—at both the leadership and constituency levels. It often appears that intraorganizational disputes which turn on questions of "principle" generate more heat than the principles involved alone would call forth. Although there are many reasons for the intensity of feeling on trivial issues—including their symbolic value, the history of factional disputes in the organization, conflict between rival leaders, and so forth—one of the sources of emotion may be the unrecognized conflicts between types of political character. Furthermore, on such occasions, the leadership itself will be drawn into an apparent affiliation with those whose responses seem most reliable —that is, whose psychological referents are most like their own. The psychological faction, therefore, should be recognized along with the economic and ideological faction of a group. The fact that these cohesions are overlaid and reinforced by what is called "friendship" tends to divert attention from their more enduring and more fundamental causes.[40]

Summary

Every politics implies a psychology. Classic political theorists relied, implicitly or overtly, on assumptions regarding the plasticity, sociability, fearfulness, ambition, conscience of mankind. Sophisticated modern political theorists, more conscious of the many dimensions of human nature, may turn to the theories of contemporary psychology and psychiatry to inform their doctrines and make their conceptions more plausible. In both cases, the combinations of traits which are thought to go together create "types"— that is, persons with similar habitual responses to political stimuli, responses which have their sources in some aspect of personality.

[40] Friendship, itself, is a combination of many things, among them: "frequency of interaction" as the result of purely external pressures (Homans), common group memberships and identifications, common foci of attention (sports, shopping, and so on), and congenial response patterns to political and social stimuli (political and social character). See George C. Homans, *The Human Group;* New York: Harcourt, Brace, 1950.

The conscious employment of these types of political character can serve several useful purposes in political science:

1. They can offer auxiliary causal explanations for historical events.
2. They can help in the analysis of social and political organizations.
3. They can populate social science models and clarify social goals.
4. They can be inserted as data in the arguments over classic issues and thus give them a new dimension and new definiteness for political theory.

To illustrate the possibilities of the use of types of political character in political analysis, I have selected a typology from among those available (Fromm, Adorno et al., Lasswell, Merton, Riesman) and have employed it in the analysis of interest group theory. Employing Riesman's cast of political character types, the following hypotheses emerge:

Regarding the pluralistic problem— that is, the interrelationships of individual, group, and state:
1. Individual isolation from interest groups takes its meaning from the political character of the individual; it may be healthy or pathological for both society and the individual depending upon the individual's degree of "autonomy."
2. The nature of the adhesives which bind people, particularly the leadership, to their interest groups will determine the capacities of the interest group to compromise, endure, broaden its membership, define its goals, and so on.
3. A person's choice of agencies of representation—among political parties and the varieties of interest groups—is partly a search for means of expression congenial to his political character.
4. The nature of a person's response to the conflicts between groups with which he identifies depends upon the nature of his connection with social groups. For goal-oriented persons, the conflict will be severely felt.

5. The relationship between the "pluralistic-atomistic" social scale and the "inner-directed-other-directed" personality scale reveals how personality types must fit the social pattern and vice versa. A pluralistic, other-directed society may give democracy its most favorable environment.

Regarding the power of interest groups in American culture:

1. If it is assumed that the pattern of American social relations emphasizes the sensitive, "radar screening," other-directed type of response, it seems true that the interest groups themselves are restrained by this emphasis (Riesman).

2. The interest groups are assisted in their search for influence by the open-mindedness and other directedness of the population, as well as by the large residue of indifference.

3. The interest groups take advantage of these popular traits through stressing the "general acceptance" of their positions and through narcotizing public resistance with abundant "good-will" advertising.

4. The influence of interest groups upon Congress is accentuated by the distillation of other-directed attitudes through the electoral process and the consequent supersensitivity of congressmen to the pressures of interest groups.

Regarding problems of representation:

1. The relationship of men with different political characters in elite and constituency positions poses special problems of representation: (a) When the political character of members of the elite differs from the political character of their constituencies, the organization may be led along lines not desired by the membership. (b) When the political character of members of the elite is in harmony with the political character of their constituencies, the policy of the organization may tend, in Riesman's typology, either towards doctrinaire indignation or disoriented drift. (c) When the political character of the constituency group is apathetic and indifferent, the elite will be guided less by external pressures and more by internal (character) pressures.

2. In the controversy over majority rule and minority rights, the respective political character types of majority and minority factions may determine the outcome: where both groups are inside-dopesters, consensus is quickly achieved without majority enforcement; where both groups are moralizers, a split is almost inevitable; where the majority is composed of inside-dopesters and the minority is composed of moralizers, there is a tendency toward minority rule; only where the majority is composed of moralizers and the minority is composed of inside-dopesters is there likely to be a clear case of majority rule.

3. The intensity of factional conflict in an organization often has its source in the types of political character of the two groups, each employing psychological referents unfamiliar and uncongenial to the other group.

E · PERSONALITY AND SOCIAL CHANGE

1 · Resistance to Change

CULTURAL TRANSMISSION AND CULTURAL CHANGE

by Edward M. Bruner

Students of acculturation agree that in every contact situation some aspects of the native culture change more than others, but they do not agree on why this is so, nor on how to characterize that which has changed and that which has not in categories that have cross-cultural validity. Nor do they understand why a change in one area of culture sometimes precipitates radical change or disorganization throughout the entire culture pattern while other times a very modest or even negligible readjustment occurs.

Two recent surveys of the literature on acculturation [1] call for additional research on the problem of different rates of change in various aspects of culture. This paper explores a tentative general proposition, one not mentioned in the above surveys, which aids in the ordering of data gathered among the Mandan-Hidatsa Indians of North Dakota on differential culture change.

Differential Change

A rather striking pattern of differential change emerges from a comparison of the

[1] Keesing, 1953, pp. 82–84; The Social Science Research Council Summer Seminar on Acculturation, 1953, 1954, pp. 990–991.

SOURCE: *Southwestern Journal of Anthropology*, Vol. 12 (1956), pp. 191–199.

contemporary culture, as I observed it in 1951, 1952–1953, among the unacculturated segment [2] of the Mandan-Hidatsa population, with the aboriginal culture, described in the published ethnologies of Wilson, Lowie, Bowers, and others,[3] which refer to the time period of approximately 1850–1860. This division into contemporary and aboriginal periods is convenient and provides a time span of about one century.

Within the social organization the Crow type kinship system is still largely intact [4] but the entire age-grade society system, which was such a colorful feature of aboriginal life, has completely disappeared. The extended family has given way to the nuclear family, residence is no longer matrilocal, and the clans have diminished in importance.

Far-reaching economic changes have occurred, but there has not been change in the basic roles of male and female. The aboriginal Mandan-Hidatsa had a dual economy adjusted to the fertile river bottom lands. The women attended to household tasks, and engaged in maize,

[2] As defined in Bruner, ms., seventy percent of the total population of one village were found to be unacculturated.

[3] Wilson, 1914, 1917; Lowie, 1917; Bowers, 1950, ms.; Matthews, 1877; Will and Spinden, 1906.

[4] Bruner, 1955.

bean, and squash horticulture in small garden plots, while the men fought hostile nomads and hunted bison, antelope, deer, and small game. Fishing, gathering, and a wide network of trading relationships were important supplements to the economy. In the contemporary period major changes were precipitated by the dependency relationship to the government and by necessary adjustments to the American economy. Nevertheless, sexual role conceptions have persisted. Women see themselves as housekeepers, mothers, and gardeners, while Indian men derive most satisfaction from the roles of soldier, cowboy, athlete, and hunter. A relatively large non-cash income is derived from the woman's labor in small garden plots and in the gathering of wild fruits and berries, and from the man's ability as a hunter of deer and pheasant. Unacculturated Indian men have never taken to large-scale farming for the market nor have any but a few become economically successful cattlemen.

The aboriginal Mandan-Hidatsa had a very complex and highly developed ceremonial system, which no longer exists. Sacred public ceremonies are not performed in contemporary society, and everyone has been converted to the Congregational or Catholic Church. Christianity may not be deeply felt nor fully understood by the Indian people, but it has replaced the native religion. However, particular aspects of the religious system have persisted. Shamans continue to cure the sick with the aid of their medicine bundles, and there is a widely accepted belief in ghosts who are thought to be returning spirits of the dead.

The value system, as I have inferred it from my observations among the Mandan-Hidatsa and from the published ethnologies, shows a remarkable persistence. A good man was, and is, one who respects the old people, is brave and demonstrates fortitude, conforms to the obligations of the kinship system, is devoted to village coöperation and unity, is generous, gives away property in public, gets along well with others, and avoids overt expressions of aggression in interpersonal relationships.

Thus kinship, values, and traditional role conceptions have persisted virtually intact, despite vast change in the larger units of social organization, in the economy, and in most of the religious-ceremonial system. With the possible exception of values, there has been change and persistence within each aspect of culture.

Previous Hypotheses

Our problem becomes: What general propositions enable us to understand these results? The literature on acculturation contains a number of hypotheses which have been offered as explanations why some aspects of culture change more than others. A few will be mentioned here; all go beyond such notions as that of culture lag or survivals, which only identify the phenomenon but which do not explain it.

One is the principle of integration. Kroeber [5] feels this principle is most crucial and suggests that a practice will persist if it has become integrated into ". . . an organized system of ideas and sentiments . . . [if] it is interwoven with other items of culture into a larger pattern." This principle does not appear to apply to my data. The age-grade society system, for example, did not persist, yet it formed a large organized pattern.[6] It was the most highly developed graded society system on the Plains and was, in aboriginal times, interwoven with the warfare and hunting complex, the kinship system, and the social, educational, and religious structures.

A second principle is that of function. If a complex is functional, i.e., if its consequences are adaptive or adjustive for

[5] Kroeber, 1948, p. 402.

[6] Lowie, 1913.

a given system, supposedly it will not change.[7] There is a methodological difficulty in relating functionalism to culture change, a kind of circularity: one is tempted to identify that which is functional by the fact of its persistence. Nevertheless, I submit that the aboriginal ceremonial complex was functional, that its functions outweighed its dysfunctions, yet it did not persist. Nor do I see in contemporary Mandan-Hidatsa society any alternate forms which have replaced the vital functions performed by aboriginal ceremonialism.

Other principles to explain differential culture change have appeared in the literature[8] such as: the principle of utility, that a people will retain the old or accept the new depending upon which has greater usefulness; the principle of concreteness, the more concrete a complex the less its resistance to change; the principle of consensus, the more a pattern requires common consent within a culture the greater its tendency to persist. I am not suggesting, of course, that the principles mentioned here have not had validity and explanatory value in other acculturation situations, nor even that they have no relevance in this case. I do say that other general propositions do not explain as much of the Mandan-Hidatsa data as an alternate hypothesis which I should now like to suggest.

The Early Learning Hypothesis

That which was traditionally learned and internalized in infancy and early childhood tends to be most resistant to change in contact situations.[9] This sug-

gests that we view a culture from the perspective of cultural transmission, the process by which the content of culture is learned by and communicated to members of the society. It says that if we knew the point in the life career of an individual at which every aspect of culture was transmitted, we would find that what changes most readily was learned late in life and what was most resistant to change was learned early.

A re-examination of the Mandan-Hidatsa data from the perspective of cultural transmission and the early learning hypothesis reveals the following: that which persists, i.e., kinship, role conceptions and values, was learned early, and the primary agents of cultural transmission were members of ego's lineage. The age-grade society system and the religious complex, which no longer exist, were learned late, from agents of transmission who were not members of ego's lineage and who were all respect-relatives.

A widely extended kinship system was the basis of aboriginal Mandan-Hidatsa social structure; every interpersonal relationship was determined by kinship. Thus it was absolutely essential that the growing child learn kin terms and behavior early in life, so that he could relate properly to others. The kinship system was learned by a young boy mainly from his mother, older brother, maternal grandfather, and mother's brother who was classified as an older brother; and by a young girl mainly from her mother, older sister, and maternal grandmother. These are all members of the same lineage. The father took little part in routine economic and social training.

The Crow type kinship system is still learned early in contemporary Mandan-Hidatsa society. We studied kinship among children between the ages of six to ten, and found that unacculturated children knew how to behave toward their relatives in terms of the Crow pat-

[7] Merton, 1949, pp. 32–34.

[8] See the discussion in the references cited in footnote 2; also Keesing, 1949.

[9] In a suggestive paper, Hart, 1955, p. 143, presents a contradictory hypothesis. Also note Burrows, 1947, p. 9. Independently, and after this paper was completed, Spiro (1955, pp. 1249–1250) came to a similar conclusion

based upon a survey of the literature on American ethnic groups.

tern, although no child had any conception of the kinship system as a system. Some children did not know the correct behavior toward relatives with whom they interacted infrequently, as in the case of those who lived in another village, but no child behaved incorrectly toward a close relative with whom he had frequent contact.

Religious knowledge was learned late in life in aboriginal Mandan-Hidatsa society and is in sharp contrast with, for example, the practice among Catholics, where children begin religious training at a relatively early age. With few exceptions a man under the age of thirty did not and was not expected to know the traditions, origin myths, or religious rituals of the tribe. In Mandan-Hidatsa thought a man younger than thirty was not mature: he was thought to be reckless and irresponsible. Religious knowledge and lore were slowly revealed to a man after the age of thirty, and this process of religious learning continued throughout his entire life career.

The agents of religious transmission were primarily members of the father's lineage and clan, all of whom were respect-relatives. Religious knowledge was not freely given: it had to be purchased from selected ceremonial fathers. A man spent a considerable portion of his productive time in the acquisition of goods which he gave to ceremonial fathers in return for religious knowledge. An old man who had purchased many ceremonies had attained the cultural objective: he was successful and was respected by all. He subsisted in part on gifts and on the goods he received from the sale of religious knowledge to younger men.

Some evidence has been given that kinship persists and was learned early, and that religion did not persist and was learned late. Additional evidence to support the hypothesis could be offered from other segments of the culture. It is in the context of kinship and at the same point in the life career that role conceptions and the value system are internalized. The age-grade society system was not even entered by an individual until the age of seven to eight, and serious society activity did not begin for a boy until the age of fifteen to seventeen, with the first fasting experience. The graded structure of the societies was such that only an older person, who had passed through the entire system, had full knowledge and understanding of this aspect of aboriginal culture. Parts of religion that do persist, such as fear of ghosts, were learned early in that returning spirits of the dead were and are used in Mandan-Hidatsa society to frighten and discipline young children, and are comparable in function to our bogeyman and the Hopi Soyoko Kachinas.

That religion is learned after the age of thirty in Mandan-Hidatsa society should not be regarded as unique in cultural transmission. All cultures vary not only according to their culture patterns, but also according to the age-grading of the educational process, the age at which each aspect of culture is internalized.[10] The variation in this important dimension of culture is well-known in traditional anthropology, and is amply documented in the life cycle sections of many ethnological reports. For example, in Trukese society such key activities as weaving, canoe building, complex religious techniques, and genealogical knowledge are not acquired until about the age of forty.[11] It is frequently stated that in primitive society the social world of the child coincides with adult reality but the reverse may prove to be the case —that there will always be a discrepancy between childhood and adult learning. This may be universal, since the situation of the child is universally, by the biological nature of the case, different from the adult, and because this situational difference is intensified, universally, by cultural definition.

[10] Herskovits, 1955, pp. 326–329.

[11] Gladwin and Sarason, 1953, pp. 141–145.

Discussion

A final question concerns the applicability of the early learning hypothesis to cases of culture contact other than the Mandan-Hidatsa. If it is applicable it will have relevance to those applied programs in many parts of the world where the question is asked: What are the hard and soft parts of culture; what is most and what is least resistant to change?

As a working assumption, I submit that the early learning hypothesis is universal,[12] as it identifies one variable that may aid in the understanding of differential culture change everywhere, although its explanatory value and importance will vary considerably in different situations. Any principle must always be considered in conjunction with alternate hypotheses as no one principle will ever be sufficient to explain the totality of differential change in any given case. Even within the framework suggested here, resistance to change may be a function of other factors in addition to relative age of learning, such as the degree of affect and ego involvement in the learning situation.[13] The early learning hypothesis will work out differently in different cases as the acculturation process itself is selective. Cases vary according to the availability of alternatives, the extent and direction of pressures for change, and the general circumstances in which the people find themselves. *The early learning hypothesis simply orders the cultural content* [14]

[12] It may be noted that the hypothesis is consistent with learning theory and psychoanalysis (Child, 1954, pp. 678–679).

[13] Dorothy Eggan, who has kindly made her unpublished work on the Hopi available to me, is currently working on this problem. Also note Du Bois, 1955.

[14] The ordering of Mandan-Hidatsa cultural content into traditional categories of social organization, economy, religion, and values was done for convenience and because I could offer no substitute. It does not appear

in terms of potential resistance to change; the actual sequence of change is dependent upon a multiplicity of factors in the contact situation. Change in any segment of culture, whether learned early or late, will not occur unless there is a reason for it to change.[15]

Partial support for the universality of the early learning hypothesis is provided by two frequently stated anthropological findings as to which aspects of culture tend to persist longest in contact situations. One group of students has found that core culture, implicit values, cultural orientations, and personality are most resistant to change.[16] Another group of students interested in social structure suggests that family and kinship institutions tend to persist.[17]

These findings are not unrelated. Values and personality on the one hand and family and kinship on the other may well be aspects of life that are generally learned in infancy and early childhood and thus tend to be most resistant to change. Indeed, personality and kinship are usually separated by us as being in different categories, but from the point of view of the individual who internalizes them, both come across early in the socialization process and in the same bundle. Psychoanalysts tell us that the first self-other differentiation is basically, in our lingo, a kinship one, when the child differentiates self from mother and later mother from other objects.[18] This is how a kinship system is built into and internalized by an individual and how it, in turn, provides the context for the further development of personality.

to be the most appropriate way of categorizing culture from the point of view of learning. Cf. Kluckhohn, 1953.

[15] Hallowell, 1955, p. 308.

[16] Linton, 1936, p. 360; Vogt, 1951, p. 119; Spicer, 1954, p. 667; Hallowell, 1955, p. 351.

[17] Murdock, 1949, pp. 118–119; note Fortes, 1953, p. 23, and his references to the early work of Rivers.

[18] Fenichel, 1945, pp. 87–89.

But these are speculations and very general. The early learning hypothesis itself is, I trust, quite clear and specific. That which is learned and internalized in infancy and early childhood is most resistant to change in contact situations. The hypothesis directs our attention to the age in the individual life career at which each aspect of culture is transmitted as well as to the full context of the learning situation and the position of the agents of socialization in the larger social system. Its relevance to instances of culture contact other than the Mandan-Hidatsa will, I hope, become a problem for future research.

BIBLIOGRAPHY

1. Bowers, Alfred W.: *Mandan Social and Ceremonial Organization;* University of Chicago Press: Chicago, 1950.
   Ms. *Hidatsa Social and Ceremonial Organization.*
2. Bruner, Edward M.: "Two Processes of Change in Mandan-Hidatsa Kinship Terminology"; *American Anthropologist,* 1955, Vol. 57, pp. 840–850.
   Ms. "Primary Group Experience and the Processes of Acculturation"; *American Anthropologist,* in press.
3. Burrows, Edwin G.: *Hawaiian Americans.* Yale University Press: New Haven, 1947.
4. Child, Irvin L.: "Socialization" in *Handbook of Social Psychology,* ed. by Gardner Lindzey, 1954, pp. 655–692, Addison-Wesley: Cambridge.
5. Du Bois, Cora: "Some Notions on Learning Intercultural Understanding" in *Education and Anthropology,* ed. by George D. Spindler, pp. 89–126, Stanford University Press: Stanford, 1955.
6. Fenichel, Otto: *The Psychoanalytic Theory of Neurosis.* Norton: New York, 1945.
7. Fortes, Meyer: "The Structure of Unilineal Descent Groups." *American Anthropologist,* 1953, vol. 55, pp. 17–41.
8. Gladwin, Thomas, and Seymour B. Sarason: *Truk: Man in Paradise.* Viking Fund Publications in Anthropology, no. 20, 1953.
9. Hallowell, A. Irving: *Culture and Experience.* University of Pennsylvania Press: Philadelphia, 1955.
10. Hart, C. W. M.: "Contrasts Between Pre pubertal and Postpubertal Education" in *Education and Anthropology,* ed. by George D. Spindler, pp. 127–162, Stanford University Press: Stanford, 1955.
11. Herskovits, Melville J.: *Cultural Anthropology.* Knopf: New York, 1955.
12. Keesing, Felix M.: "Cultural Dynamics and Administration." *Proceedings, Seventh Pacific Science Congress,* 1949, Vol. 7, pp. 102–117.
   Culture Change. Stanford Anthropological Series, no. 1, 1953.
13. Kluckhohn, Clyde: "Universal Categories of Culture" in *Anthropology Today,* ed. by A. L. Kroeber, pp. 507–523, University of Chicago Press: Chicago, 1953.
14. Kroeber, A. L.: *Anthropology.* Harcourt, Brace and Company: New York, 1948.
15. Linton, Ralph: *The Study of Man.* Appleton-Century-Crofts: New York, 1936.
16. Lowie, Robert H.: "Societies of the Hidatsa and Mandan Indian." *Anthropological Papers, American Museum of Natural History,* 1915, Vol. 11, part 3, pp. 219–358.
   "Social Life of the Mandan and Hidatsa." *Anthropological Papers, American Museum of Natural History,* 1917, Vol. 21, pp. 7–52.
17. Matthews, Washington: "Ethnography and Philology of the Hidatsa Indians." *Miscellaneous Publications, United States Geological and Geographic Survey,* Vol. 7, 1877.
18. Merton, Robert K.: *Social Theory and Social Structure.* Free Press: Glencoe, 1949.
19. Murdock, George Peter: *Social Structure.* Macmillan: New York, 1949.
20. The Social Science Research Council Summer Seminar on Acculturation, 1953: "Acculturation: an Exploratory Formulation." *American Anthropologist,* 1954, Vol. 56, pp. 973–1002.
21. Spicer, Edward H.: "Spanish-Indian Acculturation in the Southwest." *American Anthropologist,* 1954, Vol. 56, pp. 663–684.

22. Spiro, Melford: "The Acculturation of American Ethnic Groups." *American Anthropologist*, 1955, Vol. 57, pp. 1240–1252.

23. Vogt, Evon Z.: "Navaho Veterans." *Papers, Peabody Museum of American Archaeology and Ethnology*, 1951, Vol. 41, no. 1.

24. Will, George P., and H. J. Spinden: "The Mandans." *Papers, Peabody Museum of American Archaeology and Ethnology*, Vol. 3, no. 4.

25. Wilson, Gilbert L.: *Goodbird the Indian.* Revell: New York, 1914.

"Agriculture of the Hidatsa Indians." *University of Minnesota Studies in the Social Sciences*, 1917, vol. 9.

2 · Conflict

PERSONALITY DYNAMICS AND SOCIAL CONFLICT

by Ross Stagner

"Wars begin in the minds of men" asserts the UNESCO charter. This is, of course, a view widely held outside of our profession as well as within it. Mr. George F. Kennan, distinguished analyst of foreign policy, has also stressed the psychological determinants of American activities. In 1954 he wrote, "It is precisely these subjective factors—factors relating to the state of mind of many of our own people —rather than the external circumstances, that seem to constitute the most alarming component of our situation. It is such things as the lack of flexibility in outlook, the stubborn complacency about ourselves and our society, the frequent compulsion to extremism, the persistent demand for absolute solutions . . . it is these things in the American character that give added gravity to a situation which would in any case be grave enough" (Kennan, 1954, p. 32).

We may appropriately enough note that Mr. John Foster Dulles, whose rigidity Kennan was implicitly criticizing, had in 1938 taken a stand on the same basis as Kennan. Dulles wrote, "there has been

SOURCE: *Journal of Social Issues*, Vol. 17, No. 3 (1961), pp. 28–44.

a grave misconception of the nature of peace. Peace has been identified with the status quo, stability with rigidity" (Dulles, 1939, p. ix). And elsewhere he stated, "The human race craves certainty and precision. . . . It treats the world as a basket in which are placed packages, each wrapped, labeled and tied in its separate container . . ." (Dulles, 1939, p. 156). "The ambitious and dynamic powers bitterly resent a dominant world philosophy under which peace and international morality are equated with the preservation of rigidities which for long operated, as they believe, to protect selfishness and to prolong inequities" (Dulles, 1939, pp. 162–163).

Some readers may suspect that I have chosen this quotation from our late Secretary of State because of his emphasis on the craving for certainty and related rigidity. This suspicion is justified. I want to deal with problems of social conflict in the framework of a homeostatic conception of human nature, and an emphasis on perception as a major process. Let me remind you of only a few basic assumptions which will assume considerable importance in the analysis.

A Homeostatic Conception of Human Nature

According to this view, the dominant principle in the behavior of living organisms is the maintenance of certain vital constancies of the internal environment—that is, the steady states of oxygen, food, water, and other essentials for survival. In the service of these constancies man creates a predictable environment, in the physical world, by way of agriculture, housing, economic systems, and the like; in his personal world by way of the perceptual constancies. He learns to adapt to the changing aspects of physical reality, *distorting* sensory inputs to correspond to the most probable physical object. He creates a *constant* perceptual environment, and as far as possible he stabilizes the physical and social milieu within which he lives. Some individuals even come to value the ideological environment which they associate with survival, and mobilize energy to resist change in this structure of institutions, beliefs, and values (Stagner, 1961, pp. 69–86).

The specific application of this thesis which I shall propose in this paper is that man comes to value his nation, or other social group, as an essential part of his environment, and mobilizes energy to protect it. Further, as a part of this process, he distorts the input of information in such a fashion as to protect valued aspects of his social environment, and these distortions contribute in no small degree to the intensity and bitterness of social conflicts. The rigidity referred to by Messrs. Kennan and Dulles is a key aspect of this distortion.

In this connection it is important, I think, to clarify a source of confusion which sometimes creeps into discussions of homeostasis. Man needs a *predictable environment*, a stable milieu, within which he can function. But this is not to say that he wants to make the same responses over and over. It is not uniformity of behavior, but an environment within which he can anticipate the consequences of behavior, which is essential.

In an agrarian civilization, man's need for such a stable environment was largely met by the uniformity of physical laws, the weather and the seasons, plants and lower animals. But as men multiplied and lived closer together, their very spontaneity and unpredictability as individuals compelled the creation of bureaucracy as a device for imposing some order upon chaos—for improving the stability of the milieu. Strong men imposed rules on their fellows to obtain predictability; but the strong man did not expect to, and generally did not, conform to the rules. As Dalton (1959) has pointed out, the efficient executive is one who knows when to ignore or circumvent rules. And unquestionably man will go on trying to evade bureaucratic controls, just as he has always sought to master the limitations imposed by physical and biological laws.

Ethnocentrism

It was over 60 years ago that Hobson, a British social scientist, wrote, "The actual direct efficient forces in history are human motives." Yet, despite sporadic efforts, psychologists as a group have contributed relatively little to the understanding of social conflict.

Some efforts, of course, have been made in this direction. SPSSI established in 1936 a Committee on War and Peace. In recent years, the American Psychological Association has created a committee to study the place of psychology in the maintenance of world peace. I should like to urge all of you to cooperate with this committee with suggestions, with questions, with research proposals.

I would like to hark back for just a moment to the work of the SPSSI Committee on War and Peace, whose labors were rudely interrupted by Pearl Harbor. A major conclusion had early been reached by this committee, on the basis of a careful study of the writings of historians, economists, and political scientists—viz., that the major psychological factor involved in the occurrence of international war was the attitude complex called "nationalism" (Stagner et al., 1942). The political scientists, for example, stressed the phenomenon of sovereignty; disputes could not be settled peacefully because nations recognized no higher authority to which they could be submitted. Blackstone's famous Commentaries referred to sovereignty as "the supreme irresistible, absolute, uncontrolled authority." Clearly persons who hold such a view cannot tolerate the notion of yielding to a court of justice; equally clearly there is an element here of psychotic delusions of grandeur. Similarly, in economic discussions of war stress was placed on a struggle for competitive advantage, with ruthless disregard for the welfare of other nations, through policies of economic nationalism (Stagner et al., 1942).

The defining features of nationalism are generally considered to be two in number: an exaggerated glorification of the nation, its virtues, its benefactions, its right to superiority; and an exaggerated denigration of nations perceived as being in opposition, these nations generally being seen as bad, cruel, vicious and untrustworthy.

When we look at this description, we readily observe that a similar pattern appears in other forms of social conflict. During the religious wars in Europe 300 years ago, a comparable glorification of one's in-group and vilification of the out-group were common; and anti-Semitism in this country shows this pattern in less bizarre form. The white supremacists of our southern states, and in extreme the Afrikaners of South Africa, hold similar delusions of racial grandeur and of the inferiority of colored races. Partisans of labor unions and of industrial owners

do not show quite the same extremes of grandeur and hostility, but certainly many of them suggest that all virtue is on their side, all stupidity, violence, or greed on the other. It seems, therefore, that this bi-polar attitude of grandeur and evil is a psychological feature of all social conflicts. It is unfortunate that we have no generally accepted term for labeling this pattern. Ethnocentrism is undoubtedly the most appropriate term, but it has become identified with religious and racial prejudice. I shall use ethnocentrism to identify this general trend toward group-centeredness, and nationalism for its specific form in international conflict, on which I shall focus.

The central problem, from the point of view of personality theory, is how the motives and perceptions of individuals influence their decisions on social issues. Psychoanalytic writers on these problems, such as Glover, Hopkins, Durbin and Bowlby, and Alix Strachey, have tended to emphasize the decisive influence of motivation, frequently in the form of a "death instinct." In opposition, I wish to stress the perceptual approach to these questions.

Hostility as a Critical Factor in Social Conflicts

Let me first deal with the argument that the decisive consideration in major social conflicts is the level of aggressive drive or hostility. I propose to argue that this is not an important consideration, and indeed that it can, in some degree, be ignored as both a theoretical and a practical problem.

As a theoretical problem aggression has mainly been conceptualized in one of two ways: first, as an instinctive drive, as in the nineteenth century "instinct of pugnacity" associated with the names of McDougall and James; and its modern variant, the "death instinct" proposed by Freud and still advocated by some orthodox analysts. Secondly, aggression has been conceptualized as a derivative of frustration—largely in a means-end relationship, proposed by John Dollard and the Yale School, and also in a tension-release formulation by Norman Maier (Dollard et al., 1939; Maier, 1949).

A hereditary conception of aggression leads nowhere with regard to social conflict. If man is born with a given potential for aggression, we must apparently assume that in the course of his life he will act out this potential in some form. But aggression, as even the Freudians agree, may be channeled into face-to-face hostility, into competitive behavior, and even into work, or it may be vented in group competition and conflict of a non-violent nature. Thus the theory cannot logically lead to any kind of prediction about the occurrence of violent social conflict, whether between nations, or classes, or races.

A similar conclusion must be reached with respect to the frustration-aggression hypothesis. This view is somewhat more directly relevant to problems of social interaction because it carries an important, sometimes unstated, assumption that the preferred outlet for aggression will be an attack on the frustrating agent. This would suggest that, if large numbers of individuals find themselves being frustrated by, let us say, communist tactics, they will become hostile to communists. The inadequacy of this approach is suggested by the fact that most of the applications of the theory to social problems make use of displaced aggression, as in the famous study of southern lynchings, in which it appeared that a drop in the price of cotton led to more aggressive outbursts. But opposed to this we have the observation of criminologists that crimes of violence for the entire population increase in times of prosperity, not in times of depression. It thus appears that the crucial question is not, what led to the increase in aggressive acts? The question must be phrased: what variables determine the direction to be taken in expressions of hostility? It seems likely that the groups perceived as "bad" and therefore suitable for attack, and preferably "weak," hence not in a position to retaliate, will be the objects of aggression.

As a practical problem neither an instinctivist nor an environmentalist theory of aggression has much value from the point of view of blunting or disarming social conflicts. Both the Freudians and the Yale School advocate reducing frustrations to a socially tolerable minimum, especially for young children; but this seems to be based on concern for the mental health of the individual more than for social health.

As a concrete example, let me say that many people suppose the level of hostile tension experienced by the leaders of the Soviet Union to be a factor of great importance as regards the possible outbreak of World War III. It is assumed that these men may allow, or even order, acts which will precipitate a nuclear war. But does the level of aggression have anything to do with such a decision? On the hereditary assumption, we must conclude that their tension levels are already determined and what we do is irrelevant. If we look at the problem in terms of a frustration theory, we must certainly conclude that the men in the Kremlin are not hungry, they are not cold and wretched, and they have tremendous gratifications for any drive toward power which may motivate them. Can we suppose, then, that their *personal* level of frustration is relevant to a decision on international policy? I think not.

There is, of course, the theory of leader behavior expressed variously by Plato, by Machiavelli, and by more recent advisors to rulers: if your people are aggressive, encourage them to hate a foreign enemy, thus displacing their hatred from yourself. But even on this kind of theorizing, it must be clear that the crucial consideration becomes this: what are the perceptual factors determining the *di-*

rection of aggression? The level of aggressive tension then becomes a remote rather than an immediate factor—not to be ignored, but not open to practical manipulation if we seek to reduce the probability of organized violence.

In opposition to those views of social conflict which stress drive, therefore, I want to talk about the decisive role of perception. Essentially, what I shall say is that for both theoretical and practical reasons, we should focus on how members of groups perceive other groups, and their goals and their tactics. To quote Kenneth Boulding (1959, p. 120), "the people whose decisions determine the policies and actions of nations do not respond to the 'objective' facts of the situation, whatever that may mean, but to their 'image' of the situation."

The Decisive Role of Perception

Perception can operate in the service of creating a predictable environment in at least three ways. First, it can magnify certain information inputs, giving them greater weight; and secondly, the obvious corollary, it can diminish the importance of other cues. Finally, actual distortions may occur in quality and magnitude. The phenomena of size constancy, for example, require that the individual differentiate among cues of apparent size, and weight them in such a fashion as to give the closest approximation to the assumed "real object."

Perception in social affairs shows the same attributes. The real virtues of our nation are magnified; our sins are blocked out. The evils of the enemy are exaggerated, and his virtues ignored. Finally, cues indicative of behavior contrary to our expectations are often distorted to support the rigid percepts already organized. The great British statesman, Edmund Burke, said a long time ago, "We can never walk surely but by being sensible of our blindnesses." We must

recognize our tendency to exclude certain information from consciousness. Another early insight on this topic comes from the Greek historian, Thucydides, who commented that, "Different eyewitnesses give different accounts of the same events, speaking out of partiality for one side or the other, or else from imperfect memories." Since memory distortions seem to obey the same dynamic principles as perceptual distortions, it appears that most erroneous reports stem from dynamic influences within the personalities of the reporters.

But let us not assume that only reporters and historians are guilty of partiality. Diplomats, presidents, and prime ministers likewise have their blind spots, their distortions, their misperceptions. So does the famous "man in the street." Each tends to see reality only in the manner which is compatible with his own motives and past experiences.

I propose this assertion as a starting point for my discussion of social conflict: social conflicts are rational if we grant the accuracy of the way in which the participants perceive the issues. It is easy enough for the detached observer to see the irrationality of both sides, let us say, in the Spanish-American War of 1898, in the 1959 steel strike, or in the religious wars of three hundred years ago. But if we learn to look at the matters in controversy as they were seen by the participants, it becomes clear that perceptual distortion was a fundamental process. Once given these misperceptions, given a distorted reality, the behavior of the participants was reasonable.

I shall propose, in other words, that the behavior of the Communist is rational once we grant his way of perceiving western democracy; the behavior of the white supremacist is rational if we accept his way of perceiving the Negro; the behavior of the steelworkers' union is rational if we grant this way of perceiving the companies' proposals in changes in work rules, and so on.

This view, in effect, says that it is inappropriate for psychologists to label other people as "good" or "bad," even if we do it in fancy terms like authoritarian aggression, austistic hostility, unresolved Oedipus complexes and the like. I suggest that the problem of psychological theory is not to pin labels on those persons who hold attitudes with which we disagree, but to analyze the processes by which certain distorted perceptions become established and to consider ways in which these ways of seeing reality might be modified.

Such an approach does not eliminate any occasion for concern with needs, desires, emotions and conflicts. It does shift the focus of theoretical exploration from the motivational state itself to the effects of motivation on perceiving—recognizing, of course, that any distinction between the two processes is logical, not functional.

We must be concerned not solely with the processes of perceptual distortion and rigidity, but also with content. Many perceptual distortions are strictly interpersonal and have no social implications. Some relate to religious, racial or industrial conflicts, others to national problems. I should like to illustrate my remarks primarily with reference to questions of international hostility.

Whittlesey (1942) reproduced a propaganda map issued by Nazi Germany early in the campaign against Czechoslovakia. It visualized that small nation as a dagger aimed at the heart of Germany, with bombers readily capable of saturating the German nation. What it ignored was the much greater extent to which Czechoslovakia was at the mercy of Germany, a fact which became apparent in 1938. One need not assume that the German author was aware of this distortion; consider the excitement in the USA today over the situation in Cuba, which is even less capable of mounting an assault on our country. Looked at from the other side, note that Americans approve strongly of the ring of air bases we have built around Russia, many of which are as close to that nation as Cuba is to ours.

The perceptual distortion here arises from the fact that we perceive our nation and its purposes as good and pure, hence our bases are no threat to anyone. Russia, on the other hand, is obviously bad, cruel and untrustworthy, hence Russian bases are a great menace to world peace. Please do not interpret my remarks as implying that a Russian base in Cuba would be innocent and virtuous; what I do want to observe is that objectively similar events look quite different when viewed through nationalistic spectacles.

We should also remember that a policy of secrecy is no monopoly of the Soviet Union. Just after World War II our futile efforts to keep the A-Bomb secret aroused antagonism even among our allies. It was undoubtedly perceived as extremely threatening by the Russians—as, indeed, we find their secrecy so alarming that we risk air flights over their territory to penetrate the curtain. Perhaps such efforts at secrecy are always interpreted as threats because of the phenomenon which Else Frenkel-Brunswik christened "intolerance of ambiguity"—the very common mechanism which treats an unclear situation as potentially dangerous. The individual who is extremely anxious is likely to show this intolerance of ambiguity in extreme form. This, clinicians tell us, leads to both perceptual rigidity and behavioral rigidity. It gives rise to the sharp polarization of good and bad which is so characteristic of nationalism, and to the inflexibility deplored by Mr. Kennan and Mr. Dulles.

The significance of this intolerance of ambiguity as regards foreign policy questions can readily be illustrated by a report by Lane (1955). In the Korean War of 1950–53, clear-cut choices were represented by "get out of Korea entirely" or by "bomb China and Manchuria," whereas an ambiguous policy was represented by "keep on trying to get a peaceful settlement." In a national sample, the high authoritarian cases chose either of the clear-cut choices much oftener than the middle choice; the low authoritarian cases avoided the extreme policies.

Perhaps this is a good point at which to say that I consider such findings to be important regardless of one's emphasis on leaders or on the general population as determinants of policy. Leaders have personalities too, and there is every reason to believe that they can be impatient, can seek for and push the quick, clear-cut alternative, can shy away from policies which appear weak and vacillating. Similarly, the populace can prod the government in certain directions. Our concern with perceptual dynamics is thus not tied to either alternative view of policy determination.

Rigidity on the part of a dominant group is perceived by others as an arbitrary frustration, and so gives rise to exceptionally strong hostility. The inflexible policy of *Apartheid* in South Africa is arousing violence on the part of the natives. Despite the examples of Algeria, Cyprus, and other former colonies, the Afrikaners cling blindly to their delusion that tyranny can work. Few of us will have doubts as to the tragic violence so elicited.

I have noted above the tendency to personalize the nation, to deal with it as a hero or as a villain. Sometimes the personalization is in terms of a specific individual: Churchill, Stalin, DeGaulle, Eisenhower, sometimes in terms of a mythical personage such as Uncle Sam. While psychologists have often deplored this because of the obvious distortion involved, I think we must accept it as inevitable. After all, our patterns of cognition are derived from experience—unless we wish to accept some Kantian absolutes. Since our experience of active agents has almost exclusively been with people, it is scarcely possible that we would think of nations except in a personalized way.

Certainly it is easier to build myths of grandeur and virtue about a nation-hero than about the oddly assorted characters we see on the bus going to work. And it is easier to project vicious, violent attitudes onto a foreign leader than onto the total foreign population which, even the relatively naive citizen realizes, must be much like ourselves. It is also true that the leader of a nation is more dangerous than the average citizen. By the demands of his social role, he must be more defensive of national honor, more suspicious of national enemies, more alert to exaggerate trivial actions into major threats. Should he underestimate a foreign danger he would be derelict in his duty. But by his actions he tends to magnify these delusions of persecution which are so widely held among the citizens.

The dilemma of the two World Powers today is that each is afraid to give up the ability to destroy the other. The best escape route available today seems to be this: the control of these destructive devices must be placed in other hands, so that Russia and the USA can withdraw gracefully from their hazardous positions. I think this is entirely possible; we have done little to explore the techniques for accomplishing it. Creative thinking along this line is urgently needed. C. E. Osgood (1959) has offered an intriguing suggestion in his recent article, "On winning the real war with communism."

The solution, according to the political scientists, calls for giving to an international force a monopoly on the instruments of violence. We clearly dare not allow sovereignty—with its concomitant right to unlimited violence—to the small countries of the world. As in the days of our own Wild West—at least as portrayed on TV—we must have a Wyatt Earp or Matt Dillon who will deny to small nations the right to shoot up the town. But such a plan can work only if the USA and the USSR will support it. Our picture of the Communists, and theirs of us, make such cooperation difficult.

The legal authority must not only have a monopoly of violence, but he must also be perceived as impartial. This calls for a body of law, a set of rules acceptable to the contesting parties, which he enforces. Labor unions would not give up what they considered the sovereign right to violence until law enforcement was less purely a defense of managerial rights. Religious wars continued until both Protestants and Catholics came to perceive the government as an impartial arbiter. Can we turn to international law as a body of doctrine which could provide this framework of impartiality? Unfortunately, nobody today knows just what international law is. Clearly we shall not be able to provide for peaceful settlement of national disputes until we get some legal framework within which the participants can expect to receive justice.

Some Principles of Perception

Before taking up the problem of what can be done to foster such a development let me return to the question of theory for a moment. I said that personification of the nation, while it is a distortion of reality, seems inevitable. In terms of the conceptualization I am offering, the individual's awareness of his nation is qualitatively similar to his perception of another person. This suggests that we may utilize the same principles of perception which have become well-accepted in our observations of physical objects and in face-to-face personal relations.

There are two possible approaches to this problem. One places emphasis on stimulus generalization or perceptual equivalence. That is, one may simply generalize from perceptions of persons to a percept of the nation as a person. This is known as the *generalization hypothesis*. A second approach stems from psychoanalytic theory and involves the notion that emotions such as hostility

may be repressed as regards persons near at hand, but are expressed toward foreign groups or personified nations. Christiansen (1959) has suggested that this be called the *latency hypothesis,* since its distinctive feature is that latent emotions are directed toward out-groups.

The empirical evidence, as collected both in this country and abroad, seems to favor the generalization hypothesis. An excellent study, within the limits of attitude scales and questionnaires, has recently been published in Norway by Christiansen (1959). He finds that persons who report aggressive behavior toward their fellows also endorse aggressive policies toward other nations by Norway. Persons reporting generally cooperative behavior endorse less aggressive policies. Those inclined to be self-critical and intropunitive are likely to assume that Norway may have committed errors in international dealings, whereas the extrapunitive individual usually assumes that Norway was right and the other nation guilty. I reported somewhat parallel findings on American subjects 20 years ago (Stagner, 1944a), and other researchers, e.g., Harry Grace (1949) have confirmed this.

The latency hypothesis, on the other hand, would predict a negative correlation between manifest behavior toward close associates and preferred behavior toward foreign nations, racial minorities, etc. This follows from the fact that the displaced emotion, either affection or hostility, leaves its opposite to govern behavior and perception. Thus the boy who resolves his Oedipus complex by repressing hostility to his father will presumably show affection and positive attitudes at home, but will project bad, tyrannical characteristics onto the evil rulers of foreign nations.

Limited evidence favoring the latency hypothesis is reported by Christiansen using the Blacky Pictures and the Rosenzweig P-F test as devices for getting at latent emotions. On the whole he confesses to disappointment that the evidence is not clear-cut. Similar, slightly favorable evidence has been reported by Krout and Stagner (1939), by Lasswell (1930) and others. No one has reported strong support for this point of view.

The complexity of the problem is exaggerated by variations in what may be called the range of stimulus generalization. This is important in connection with the role of reference groups in defining "good" and "bad" nations or social groups. The anthropologists tell us that isolated cultures quite commonly hold to the view that "only we are human." The Hebrews' perception of the Gentiles, like the Greek view of the barbarians, illustrates this. Growing up in an ethnocentric culture, we become alert to trivial cues which identify the in-group, but which enable us to label and reject the out-group. Various studies suggest that anti-Semites are more accurate at detecting Jewish facial characteristics than are their more tolerant peers. Whether this alleged sensitivity can hold up realistically is unimportant. The individual *believes* that he can perceive major differences between his fellows and the out-group; his gradient of generalization, and his responses of friendship and co-operation, are thus limited in scope. There is reason to believe, however, that some individuals are unable to perceive these allegedly differentiating cues, and thus may generalize responses of acceptance to humans beyond the in-group. These persons may manifest the cognitive style which George Klein (1951) has called "levelling"; i.e., they tend to iron out differences and to see *all* humans as basically similar.

A second factor which appears to play a part in the choice of such reference groups is also perceptual-cognitive in character. Helen Peak and her students (Peak et al., 1960) have been working with a cognitive style which they call *opposition*. Each of us, I am sure, knows one or more persons who have a consistent tendency to "see the other side" of any issue. They enjoy playing the devil's advocate; and often enough they are not playing. In contrast to this, of course, we have the response-set of *acquiescence*, which has received so much attention in the aftermath of the "Authoritarian Personality" and F-scale studies. A distribution of cases on a hypothetical continuum from extreme acquiescence to extreme opposition would, of course, reveal a skew toward the acquiescent end. And this confirms everyday experience; most children within a nation grow up to accept the nation's leaders as a reference group. But occasionally we get individuals who insist upon looking at the other side, who are not convinced that the policies of their nation are always just, the leaders necessarily paragons of virtue and wisdom. Such critics may become mere cranks and chronic objectors; they may, indeed, find some foreign reference group which is more acceptable. But another common outcome is that they choose an idealistic reference group, and perhaps contribute to the development of a body of advocates of an internationalist position. Peak cites some evidence to indicate that oppositionists are also "levellers"; they would thus be more likely to perceive all human beings as basically alike.

I assume that I need not expand on the application of this idea to parallel social conflicts. How did the Reformation start? Because some people rejected the leaders of the Catholic Church. How did feudalism begin its decline? When some individuals saw the possibility of rejecting feudal leaders and organizing a different social structure. Men such as Martin Luther, John Calvin, Descartes, and Spinoza were undoubtedly characterized by the tendency to ponder automatically the opposite of statements posed to them. (This does not suggest that such men reacted favorably to questioning of their own dogmas. On the contrary, such persons are often quite intolerant of "opposite thinking" when it is focused on their views.)

Given these facts regarding the ways in which decision-makers may act on biased information, and the psychological processes which lead to biasing, one must ask: what can we do about it? The physical scientists have already made it possible for all men to *die* together. The task of the social scientists is to seek ways by which we can *live* together.

In this paper, I can only suggest a line of approach. Let me mention a couple of suggestions which seem quite futile, and some which appear to have promise.

First of all, I see no point in the recommendation, offered in all seriousness by some psychoanalysts, that government leaders ought to be analyzed. Can we imagine a megalomaniac like Hitler, on the threshold of power, taking off a few years to be analyzed? Can we suppose the United Nations would demand that a Prime Minister come in for psychotherapy? Or that he would obey? I think not.

Secondly, I see little value in communications which focus on the horrors of war, and the devastation which would result from atomic war. It is clear that past decision-makers have in general found war and violence distasteful, but these alternatives have seemed to them less painful than the situations facing them. That is, if the Communist perceives capitalism as a deadly menace, he must eventually come to the point at which he will risk nuclear war because he is so hostile to the bad capitalist nations; the citizen of a capitalist nation must also come to such a point when he perceives communism as an intolerable threat.

Turning to the positive side, I would stress first the importance of *diluting sovereignty* by building up groups and institutions of a supranational character. As we cede a little bit of sovereignty to the International Postal Union, we get used to the idea that our nation cannot act in a completely unilateral manner,

without regard to other nations and their rights. More spectacular and more beneficial, of course, is the UN venture in the Congo. This enables people all over the world to get used to the idea that force might be removed from nationalistic controls and used for the welfare of the entire human race.

We need a much larger staff of persons who are agents of such supranational agencies. Ernst Haas (1958), in his recent book, *The Uniting of Europe,* shows the major contributions of the European Coal and Steel Community to developing an internationalist point of view. He speaks of the "spill-over" process, i.e., that men whose duty it is to run the ECSC organization efficiently find themselves forced to expand international cooperation in areas peripheral to the organization itself. I am reminded here of the observations reported by Melville Dalton (1959), describing industrial managers who, in their quest for personal power, go beyond assigned roles (treaties?) to activate new functions. Dalton's findings support Haas; they indicate that the creation of a few more supranational structures like ECSC may help tremendously in the task defined by Haas as "redirecting the loyalties and expectations of political actors" from one level of government (the national) to another (the European).

A more frequent suggestion is that we exchange more visitors with other countries. While this can be hardly undesirable, I think the benefits may easily be exaggerated. Unless personal motives become engaged in the perception of other persons and other nations, the effects are likely to be minimal.

We should keep in mind the rigidity of perceptual constancy, and the effectiveness of perceptual defense. Mere communication without involvement has little effect. A recent proposal by the well-known semanticist, S. I. Hayakawa (1960), for example, argues that we could make progress toward peace simply by listening, i.e., by inviting Russian speakers over and letting them state their case, if we were allowed to do likewise. It seems to me unlikely that this would have any effect.

The French have a phrase, *le dialogue des sourds*—the dialogue of the deaf—to refer to the fact that two people may talk to each other without either hearing what the other is trying to communicate. Clearly such dialogues make up a major portion of what passes for social communication. Consider, for example, the Negro-White colloquy in the southern United States. The Negro is talking about education to fit him for job opportunities, the opening up of these opportunities, the chance to participate in economic and political affairs. The White speaks of violence, immorality and other social problems. Neither listens to what the other has to say. We have had, of course, a more dramatic instance of the same kind in the recent interchanges between the USA and the Soviet Union over disarmament. The Russians speak in favor of complete disarmament, the Americans ask about controls and inspections. Since all of you are familiar with the defects of the Russian argument, let me point out a weakness in our own approach. The Russians propose that reports of violations of arms agreements go to the UN Security Council; we object that this would enable them to veto any resolution of condemnation. This utterly misses the point that we have been trying frantically, via U-2, RB-47, and heaven knows what other devices, to get information from inside Russia. If a UN inspection team reported a violation, does it matter who is condemned? We would have obtained vital information; effective counteraction must be taken by the United States, not by the UN.

Unless we take account of the different realities perceived by ourselves and the Russians, increased communication may lead only to increased *misunderstanding*. Let me cite a very simple case. The Yalta agreements provided for "free democratic elections" in Poland, Czechoslovakia, and other satellite nations. Ultimately we learned that these were to be "free and democratic" as in Russia, i.e., the voter was free to vote for the Communist slate or not to vote. The Russians were not hypocritical; the words did not convey the same "reality" to them as to us.

I hope I am making my point clear. I am trying to say that perceptual distortions and perceptual rigidities block communication between groups in conflict. Further, man's craving for a stable, predictable environment tends to force ambiguous data into the existing perceptual structure. All of you remember the Irishman who, when told that Ireland was neutral in the last war, said, "Yes, I know we are neutral, but who are we neutral against?" Thus many Americans assumed that a neutral India must be against us. Fortunately, it has become more clear in recent months that India is neutral against communism; however, this is not the crux of the matter. The psychological phenomenon here takes the form of a demand for a clearly-structured environment, one with a minimum of ambiguities. It has variously been discussed by Osgood (1955) as a need for congruity, by Festinger (1957) in terms of consonance and dissonance, and by Newcomb (1953) as a case of symmetry of meaning. Osgood points out that if an approved source, say ex-President Eisenhower, issues a statement favorable to a disapproved object, such as communism, incompatible responses are activated, and conflict occurs. Congruity is achieved by becoming less favorable to Eisenhower or more favorable to communism. However, there is another solution which is often adopted; this is to refuse, in effect, to receive the communication. The technique effectively blocks channels and makes possible the "dialogue of the deaf."

Let me say just a word about the role of *consciousness* in adaptation. Studies of subliminal perception make it clear that the organism can utilize information fed in under conditions operationally defined as unconscious, i.e., when the subject could not report verbally that he had received the information (Miller, 1939). But such utilization is at a very low level of efficiency. Material of which one is consciously aware can be used more effectively in guiding behavior; Norman Maier (1931) has shown that problem-solving goes on more expeditiously when the experimenter calls attention to significant cues. Finally, we have the widespread belief of clinicians that the resolution of a neurotic conflict requires that all of the significant components of the conflict become available to consciousness. If we are on firm ground in our assertion that social conflicts must be resolved—as they were initiated—in the minds of men, then it follows that men must become conscious of aspects of the social conflict which heretofore they have refused to see. Whether non-directive or directive psychotherapy is appropriate here we cannot say at this moment, but my prediction is that a vigorously directive approach will be necessary for effective treatment.

Is an attempt to understand the Russians, and to seek ways in which we might establish peaceful co-existence, a sign of national weakness? I do not think so. I am reminded of the fact that, 300 years ago, suggestions of religious tolerance were denounced as evidence of moral weakness. Today we consider religious *intolerance* a sign of moral decay. I think we may reach a point at which the delusions of national pride and national persecution will be looked upon with the same tolerance—when they no longer threaten us with the holocaust of nuclear war.

How Can Our Civilization Survive?

The illusory nature of perceived reality, our tendency to build up a dream-world based on wishful thinking, was brilliantly described by Matthew Arnold:

The world, which seems
To lie before us like a land of dreams,
So various, so beautiful, so new,
Hath really neither joy, nor love, nor light. . . .

Unconsciously we have deceived ourselves into the belief that we can have more chromium on our cars and fewer teachers in our schools; that we can afford the luxuries of nationalism and race prejudice, and dispense with the sacrifices of comfort and ego-expansion needed to resolve these social conflicts. But repression means wandering in the dark, denying ourselves the information essential to a problem solution. To complete Arnold's familiar passage,

We are here, as on a darkling plain
Swept with confused alarms of struggle and flight
Where ignorant armies clash by night.

This is the problem facing social psychologists; to devise methods by which we can break the darkness, enlighten the ignorant armies. At all levels of society there are psychological barriers to clear understanding of the social conflicts which plague us. Can we marry the skills and insights of social and clinical psychologists to aid this clarification? This is the specific version, for our profession, of the great question facing the West today: how can our civilization survive?

REFERENCES

1. Boulding, Kenneth E.: "National Images and International Systems." *Journal of Conflict Resolution*, 1959, 3, 120–131.
2. Christiansen, Bjorn: *Personality and Attitudes Toward Foreign Policy.* Oslo: University of Oslo Press, 1959.
3. Dalton, Melville: *Men Who Manage.* New York: John Wiley and Sons, 1959.
4. Dollard, John, et al.: *Frustration and Ag-*

gression. New Haven: Yale University Press, 1939.

5. Dulles, John Foster: *War, Peace and Change.* New York: Harper and Bros., 1939.

6. Durbin, E. F. M., and John Bowlby: *Personal Aggressiveness and War.* New York: Columbia University Press, 1939.

7. Festinger, Leon: *A Theory of Cognitive Dissonance.* Evanston, Ill.: Row, Peterson and Co., 1957.

8. Grace, Harry A.: *A Study of the Expression of Hostility in Everyday Professional, and International Verbal Situations.* New York: Columbia University, 1949.

9. Haas, Ernst B.: *The Uniting of Europe.* Stanford: Stanford University Press, 1958.

10. Hayakawa, Samuel I.: "Formula for Peace: Listening." *New York Times Magazine,* July 31, 1960, 10–12.

11. Janis, Irving L.: "Decisional Conflicts: a Theoretical Analysis." *Journal of Conflict Resolution,* 1959, 3, 6–27.

12. Kennan, George F.: "The Illusion of Security." *Atlantic Monthly,* August 1954, 31–34.

13. Klein, George S.: "The Personal World through Perception." In Robert R. Blake and Glenn Ramsey (eds.), *Perception: an Approach to Personality.* New York: Ronald Press, 1951.

14. Krout, Maurice H., and Ross Stagner: "Personality Development in Radicals: a Comparative Study." *Sociometry,* 1939, 2, 31–46.

15. Lane, Robert E.: "Political Personality and Electoral Choice." *American Political Science Review,* 1955, 49, 173–190.

16. Lasswell, Harold D.: *Psychopathology and Politics.* Chicago: University of Chicago Press, 1930.

17. Levinson, Daniel J.: "Authoritarian Personality and Foreign Policy." *Journal of Conflict Resolution,* 1957, 1, 37–47.

18. Maier, Norman R. F.: "Reasoning in Humans. II. The solution of a problem and its appearance in consciousness." *Journal of Comparative Psychology,* 1931, 12, 181–194.

19. ———.: *Frustration.* New York: McGraw-Hill Book Co., 1949.

20. Miller, James G.: "Discrimination without Awareness." *American Journal of Psychology,* 1939, 52, 562–578.

21. Newcomb, Theodore M.: "An Approach to the Study of Communicative Acts." *Psychological Review,* 1953, 60, 393–404.1.

22. Osgood, Charles E.: "Suggestions for Winning the Real War with Communism." *Journal of Conflict Resolution,* 1959, 3, 295–325.

23. Osgood, Charles E., and Percy Tannenbaum: "The Principle of Congruity in the Prediction of Attitude Change. *Psychological Review,* 1955, 62, 42–55.

24. Peak, Helen, et al.: "Opposite Structures, Defenses, and Attitudes." *Psychological Monographs,* 1960, 74, No. 8.

25. Stagner, Ross: "Studies in Aggressive Social Attitudes." I. *Journal of Social Psychology,* 1944a, 20, 109–120.

26. ———: "Studies in Aggressive Social Attitudes." III. *Journal of Social Psychology,* 1944b, 20, 129–140.

27. ———: *Psychology of Personality* (3rd ed.) New York: McGraw-Hill Book Co., 1961.

28. Stagner, Ross, Junius F. Brown, Ralph H. Gundlach, and Ralph K. White: "Analysis of Social Scientists' Opinions on the Prevention of War." *Journal of Social Psychology,* 1942, 15, 381–394.

29. Strachey, Alix: *The Unconscious Motives of War.* New York: International Universities Press, 1957.

30. Whittlesey, Derwent: *German Strategy of World Conquest.* New York: Farrar and Rinehart, Inc., 1942.

3 · Leadership in Change

ENTREPRENEURSHIP AND PERSONALITY

by John W. Atkinson and Bert F. Hoselitz

I

In the recent literature in social science increasing attention is being given to entrepreneurship as a factor in economic growth, but also as a special characteristic of the role structure in modern vigorous economies. It has sometimes been said that we witness a certain drying up of entrepreneurship and that this will have unfavorable consequences on the prospects of growth of the American economy. At the same time, studies are undertaken in which the attempt is made to discern whether entrepreneurship may have become routinized, whether the change—if any—in the supply of entrepreneurs is dependent upon changes in the facility of vertical social mobility, and what are the general social and some personal characteristics of entrepreneurs or business leaders. In all this literature, little attention has as yet been paid to the question of whether the successful performance of an entrepreneurial role is associated with certain personality traits. Yet some investigation of this problem would throw potentially valuable light on our understanding of the overall place of entrepreneurs in the process of economic development of relatively backward as well as economically advanced societies. On the one hand it might enlighten us on what changes in socialization processes have occurred in the period

SOURCE: *Explorations in Entrepreneurial History,* Vol. 10, (1958), pp. 107–112.

at least since the industrial revolution, which has seen the emergence of so many "new men" in entrepreneurial functions. On the other hand, it may contribute to our better understanding of the personality characteristics of persons performing entrepreneurial functions in our economy, and this in turn has intrinsic scientific interest, as well as practical interest, since it may contribute to a better knowledge of what to look for in the selection and training of persons who are destined to occupy roles of business leadership.

A study in which the relations between personality traits and entrepreneurship are explored more systematically appears to be indicated, moreover, by several additional reflections. In most of the existing literature on entrepreneurship, at least in the literature on the historical role entrepreneurs have played in economic development, little distinction has been made between entrepreneurs in different types of occupations, or in firms of different size. Even the typical behavioral characteristics of entrepreneurship have not been clarified. In the economic literature there exist at least three descriptions of the "entrepreneurial function." One which goes back to J. B. Say stresses the function of the entrepreneur as a co-ordinator and planner of the productive process. He brings together the factors of production and combines them into a product. He brings together, as it were, the suppliers of productive factors (including technological knowledge) and the buyers of finished products. This function of the entrepreneur in Say's view is well expressed when he says that the entrepreneur is "at the center of different relationships" (*au centre de plusiers rapports*).[1] Another view in economics, often associated with the work of F. H. Knight, stresses the function of uncertainty-bearing. This view has become widely accepted in a vulgarized form, when it is said that entrepreneurs are individuals who handle "venture capital." A somewhat more scholarly, partly psychological, exposition of this interpretation of the entrepreneurial function is to be found in some writings of Werner Sombart who depicted the spirit of adventure and the willingness of risk-taking as one of the ingredients of the capitalist spirit.[2]

Finally, J. A. Schumpeter developed a third view of the entrepreneurial function which has attained more and more vogue, especially among social and economic historians. In this interpretation the main function of the entrepreneur is the introduction of innovations. In some more recent works in entrepreneurial history this function has been seen as the chief role of entrepreneurs. However, as we will see later, the empirical determination of what specific behavior constitutes "innovation" presents very severe difficulties.[3]

Once some function, such as coordination and management, risk-taking, or innovating had been declared to be the central function of entrepreneurial activity, determining the entrepreneurial role, it was thought necessary to investigate more closely the precise environment in which some entrepreneurs operated. Each of the three functions listed could be carried out in a large or a small enterprise, each could be exercised in banking or financial institutions, in commerce, or in manufacturing. The nature of the productive process in which managerial or entrepreneurial activity was exercised, the size of the firm (i.e., the relative quantity of assets over which an entrepreneur disposed, as well as the degree of division of labor among several persons in entrepreneurial or quasi-entrepreneurial functions) were considered factors either of indifference or of secondary order. Finally, a tendency set in to confound entrepreneurship in the narrower sense of the term and business leadership in general.[4]

At this point, a critical revaluation of entrepreneurial "theory," as it stands today, should start. In the first place we must ask whether the kind of productive activity in which an entrepreneur operates is really without, or only of limited, significance. Could the same person be a successful banker and a successful manufacturer? Are the same qualities—and above all, is the identical personality structure—best adapted for success in entrepreneurial activity in finance or commerce as well as in heavy or light manufacturing? Finally, is the pattern of behavior characteristically performed by an entrepreneur in pursuit of his role the same whether he is guiding a financial institution or a commercial or manufacturing enterprise? Can a merchant whose innovations consist in the conquest of a new market be interchanged, as it were, with a manufacturer whose innovation consists in the devising of a new pattern of teamwork in his plant, or with an inventor whose innovation consists of a new device for a machine? These questions appear to suggest an almost obvious answer. One may say that this interchange between persons is impossible or very difficult because the different roles require for their adequate performance different previous training and different accumulations of knowledge. Yet we may add that a further difficulty arises because the persons performing these different roles may, in order to perform them successfully and with satisfaction to themselves, have to be endowed with different personality structures.

If the problem is posed in this way, three further problems emerge immediately. The first is the need of an accurate and detailed description of roles. To say that the entrepreneurial role consists in innovating, or managing, or risk-bearing, is a statement which is vague and can, at best, only be made *ex post facto*. We have scarcely a way of predicting whether any given action or set of actions of a person in an entrepreneurial position will result in an innovation or not. Once we have observed what result this action or set of actions has had, we can discern it as one which actually did (or did not) bring about an innovation. It is the same with risk-taking, and almost the same with managing. In this last instance, we can designate—at least ideally—a set of actions as constituting managing behavior. But here we run up against another multitude of problems which can easily be recognized if we consider the comparison between large firms with large managerial staffs as against smaller enterprises in which the management functions are performed by one or two persons. The distinction between managerial roles in large and small enterprises is not only based upon the fact that in the large enterprise there is more specialization than in the small enterprise, but also on the greater bureaucratic apparatus in the large enterprise. In a small firm managerial decisions, as well as decisions involving risk or leading to innovations, are usually—and perhaps only ideally—made by the entrepreneur himself. In a large firm the ideas and original implementation of innovations may be made by someone on one of the lower rungs of the bureaucratic ladder, and its actual adoption may then be the result of a long process of consultations, testing, conferences, and persuasion. Although it is probably true that the men "at the top" of a large firm make the ultimately most important decisions for the enterprise, the actual procedures by which they arrive at their decisions differ profoundly from the analogous activity in a smaller firm.

II

These reflections appear to indicate a series of important conditions for the design of a research project in the interrelations between entrepreneurship and personality. We have suggested in the preceding argument that a distinction should be made between entrepreneurs in large and small firms, that furthermore, criteria have to be developed for "successful performance" of an entrepreneurial role, and that, in order to appraise entrepreneurial performance in firms of different size, as well as in different fields of business specialization, a more detailed and accurate description has to be worked out of what are the roles of entrepreneurs in general, and the entrepreneurial specialist in particular. In a rough way, business leaders make decisions in the following general fields of activity: sales, purchasing, finance, personnel, production, and general overall coordination. A sales manager whose main effort consists in persuading others to buy the products of his firm may be—and probably is—engaged in activities which differ greatly from a production manager who is concerned primarily with the internal allocational and, in a narrower sense, engineering aspects of his enterprise. A financial manager who deals with paper claims is concerned with vastly different problems from a personnel manager who deals with people.

Now if such differences can be ascertained even on a superficial level, the question arises as to where the precise differences in roles of all of these men lie. The importance of these differences should not be lost sight of, especially if it is stipulated that entrepreneurial performance is related to personality structure. For it appears plausible that different managerial specialties may call for individuals with different personality structures, especially if as additional criteria the successful performance and satisfaction in an entrepreneurial or managerial role are stipulated.

If this should turn out to be the case, the study of entrepreneurs in small firms becomes particularly crucial. Since the entrepreneur of a small firm customarily is charged with performance in several fields of endeavor, is it probable that he will perform in all of them with equal success? May it not turn out that he will concentrate on sales, or personnel work, or supervision of production, and leave the other aspects of entrepreneurial-managerial activity either to someone else or at best perform them in a routinized cut-and-dried manner? Can we find persons who can and do perform these various tasks successfully, and if so, in what way are their personalities different from those of other entrepreneurs?

The actual evaluation of entrepreneurial success, as well as the choice of a particular specialty of managerial performance involves not only deeply rooted personality factors but also situationally defined (external) conditions which may be designated in their most general way as "cognitive orientations" and "values." A man who in the general social environment of the United States might—for personality reasons—become a successful production manager, would not do so in an underdeveloped country in which both the cognitive orientations—i.e., the technological environment—and the values—i.e., industrial entrepreneurship as a prestigeful role—are absent. This consideration is of particular importance if we wish to apply any findings of the relationship between entrepreneurial performance and personality to historical situations. But the cognitive orientations do not only affect the actual choice of career of a person, but also the kinds of emphasis expressed by parents in the socialization and education of children. Clearly, the child training patterns will differ in accordance with differences in the values and cognitive orientations of parents. And, since child training patterns affect subsequent personality developments, these factors are of double importance. They affect both the career lines which will be considered open (or desirable) for persons with a given personality structure to pursue, but they will also affect the relative frequency distribution of motivational dispositions which are forthcoming in a given society because of the valuations or cognitive orientations of the parents who tend to provide child training leading to certain personality structures.

III

Among psychologists, David McClelland has taken the lead in following through an hypothesis concerning a particular characteristic of personality and entrepreneurship as reflected in technological advance.[5] He has begun to accumulate an increasing amount of evidence that the association between the Protestant ethic and growth of capitalism, elaborated by Max Weber, may be mediated by the achievement motive. The need for achievement is fostered by the kinds of child-rearing practices consistent with the Protestant ethic, and it is both challenged and satisfied by the kinds of activity demanded of entrepreneurs. In the light of his lead and the progress that has been made in the development of valid methods of measuring the strength of the achievement motive [6] and other important social motives, e.g., affiliation [7] and power,[8] which also may be associated with degree of interest in entrepreneurial activity, we propose to emphasize the assessment of these three basic motives in the search for an association between type of personality and entrepreneurship. This decision is consistent with an hypothesis that motivational dispositions developed early in life define capacities for satisfaction and interest in certain kinds of activity for which opportunity arises later in life. Entrepreneurial activity is one of these.

In a number of empirical studies of achievement motivation,[9] McClelland has called attention to the correspondence between characteristics attributed to entrepreneurs and characteristics evinced by persons highly motivated to achieve. Their motive is not money for its own sake, but rather for generalized success where money is simply the objective measure of degree of success. They appear to be independent-minded and autonomous. They seek out situations which allow them to have a feeling of personal responsibility for the outcome and where the results of their efforts are clearly measurable. A theoretical model has been developed to explain why the person highly motivated to achieve should take "calculated risks." [10]

Illustrative case studies of successful and unsuccessful business executives reported recently by Warner and Abegglen [11] also contain suggestive evidence that motivation to achieve is one of the essential ingredients of entrepreneurship. Their analysis of several individual cases further suggests that singleness of purpose—to achieve above all else—may turn out to be the distinguishing feature of the successful entrepreneur. They call attention to the business executive who has advanced to a certain level but who then finds it impossible to move on to a new and more challenging position of responsibility in another place because he is torn between the desire for accomplishment and an equally strong tie to his home and community (the affiliation motive). For this reason, and because an analysis of entrepreneurial activity suggests various other facets of the role which may either attract or repel the person who is motivated to affiliate, i.e., to be warmly accepted by others, or for power, i.e., to control the means of influencing the behavior of others, we propose an assessment of the personality structure of entrepreneurs which will be amenable to an analysis searching for a distinctive configuration or pattern of these three motives: achievement, affiliation, power.

The theoretical basis for expecting an association between the motives of the individual and successful performance in an entrepreneurial role is relatively simple. If, as is generally supposed, individuals differ greatly in the strength of their motives for certain kinds of satisfaction, the person whose motives correspond to the kinds of satisfaction that are to be experienced in meeting the demands of entrepreneurship should be attracted to it and should perform the role with great efficiency and satisfaction. However, the individual who faces a discrepancy between the demands of an entrepreneurial role and his basic motives will either perform unsatisfactorily during the long training period in which selections for advancement occur or he will perform efficiently at such a great cost to himself in terms of personal satisfaction that he will ultimately choose to leave the path that leads eventually to an entrepreneurial position.[12]

Our emphasis on the motivational characteristics of the individual does not mean that we ignore the basic requirements for certain skills, a high level of intelligence, and certain shared cognitive orientations and values as outlined earlier. These factors are generally recognized. But a definitive study of the motivational characteristics of the entrepreneur has not been possible until now for the simple reason that a valid method of measuring socially significant human motives has been developed only within the past eight years.[13]

Our discussion of the relationship between personality and entrepreneurship can be reduced to two basic hypotheses: (1) successful entrepreneurs will differ significantly from a random sample of persons of comparable age in the strength of those motives which find satisfaction in the challenges of entrepreneurial activity; (2) to the extent to which there is specialization within the entrepreneurship (e.g., financial innovation versus technological invention), the motives of persons engaging in different kinds of entrepreneurial activities should differ. These hypotheses, as stated, assume that motivational differences discovered will be independent of other obvious differences that might be expected between entrepreneurs and non-entrepreneurs (e.g., education, opportunity, intelligence, etc.).

The kind of research design implied in the foregoing discussion can be outlined briefly. If there is greater specialization of entrepreneurial activity in the large business enterprise, this becomes the ideal situation in which to attempt to assess the different character of the various entrepreneurial roles and the motivations associated with each. Samples of executives whose major responsibilities are sales, purchasing, finance, personnel, production, or general coordination will constitute six groups of entrepreneurs who might be expected to differ in strength and configuration of motives. In addition, the assessment of each of the different roles in terms of objective descriptions of the job and its requirements and also more subtle assessments of the kinds of satisfactions and challenges associated with the activities of each should produce differences that are congruent with the assessment of motivation in persons filling those roles.

The strength of achievement, affiliation, and power motives can be assessed through content analysis of a short series of imaginative (thematic apperceptive) stories obtained in a half-hour test especially designed for this purpose. The experimental validity and reliability of the method to be employed has been established in numerous laboratory investigations and several cross-cultural and community studies which are surveyed in several places.[14] A more up-to-date review of this work appears in a forthcoming book by J. W. Atkinson, *The Assessment of Human Motives*.

The assessment of entrepreneurial role requires several innovations in method since there is still a surprising lack of agreement among sociologists and others interested in the concept of role as to how best to operationalize it. An adaptation of techniques which have been developed and refined in psychological investigations of the self-concept (a variable in psychological theory having properties analogous to those of the role concept) appears to show promise as a technique for this purpose.

A separate phase of the research will focus on the smaller business enterprise in which the role of entrepreneur appears to fall more into the classic mold. As argued earlier, it is expected that there is much less specialization of entrepreneurial activity in the small business where all entrepreneurial functions have to be performed by one or two persons. A fairly representative sample of small business activities will be chosen in terms of the following criteria which emerge from theoretical analysis of the classic conception of entrepreneurial role:

1. The business involves technological operations, physical transformation of objects, i.e., manufacturing.
2. The entrepreneurial functions are carried out by one or two persons.
3. The entrepreneur engages in face to face relationships with workers, i.e., he hires and fires.
4. The field of activity involves product differentiation short of monopoly, i.e., there is competition.
5. The entrepreneur need not be the supplier of capital.
6. All businesses in the sample are at a comparable stage of development.[15]

A variety of business enterprises which might meet these specifications are: garment industry, printing establishments, automobile repair shops, bakeries, canneries, candy manufacturers, instrument manufacturers, etc. It would be desirable to isolate a reasonable number of successful and relatively unsuccessful entrepreneurs within each category. Degree of success can be measured by comparing the profitability and/or the rate of growth of each firm to the average ratio of profit and/or rate of growth within that industry. In addition, ratings by competitors can provide a basis for determining the relative success of any particular enterprise.

The measurement of motives and assessment of the characteristics of the entrepreneurial role will proceed as in the larger firms. But here the theoretical expectation is that there will be less specialization and hence greater homogeneity in the entrepreneurial role, i.e., a greater tendency for the executive to perform *all* of the activities usually associated with the role of entrepreneur. The definition of the role within one industry might be compared with that of another industry to determine whether or not the nature of the enterprise tends to emphasize one rather than another of the entrepreneurial functions. If so, there might be some basis for expecting motivational differences among entrepreneurs engaged in different kinds of business activity. But the major hypothesis focuses attention upon motivational differences between relatively successful and unsuccessful entrepreneurs, and particularly between successful entrepreneurs and a control group representing a fairly random sample of persons of comparable age and intelligence within the society.

Obviously, the data collection in this research will involve other meaningfully related material such as ethnic, religious, and class background; educational opportunities; etc. This brief description of a plan for research has focused attention on what seem to us several of the most important issues which require clarification through empirical inquiry: the assessment of motivation and of role, and the possible distinction between entrepreneurial roles in large organizations and in small businesses.

REFERENCES

1. See Jean Baptiste Say, *Traité d'économie politique*, 6th ed., Paris, 1841, p. 371. On Say's theory and earlier theories of entrepreneurship see Bert F. Hoselitz; "The Early History of Entrepreneurial Theory," *Explorations in Entrepreneurial History*, 3 (1951), pp. 193–220.
2. See Frank H. Knight, *Risk, Uncertainty and Profit*, Boston, 1921, Ch. VII to IX.
3. See Joseph A. Schumpeter, *The Theory of Economic Development*, Cambridge, 1934, especially Ch. II. On innovations see Yale Brozen, "Invention, Innovation, and Imitation," *American Economic Review*, 41 (1951), 239–257; idem, "Adapting to Technological Change," *Journal of Business of the University of Chicago*, 24 (1951), 114–126; and idem, "Business Leadership and Technological Change," *American Journal of Economics and Sociology*, 14 (1953), 13–30.
4. See, for example, on the need for making sharper distinctions between the two concepts, Fritz Redlich, "The Origin of the Concepts of 'Entrepreneur' and 'Creative Entrepreneur,'" *Explorations in Entrepreneurial History*, 1 (No. 2, Feb. 1949), 1–7; and idem, "The Business Leader in Theory and Reality," *American Journal of Economics and Sociology*, 8 (1948–49), 223 ff.; also Bert F. Hoselitz, "Entrepreneurship and Economic Growth," *American Journal of Economics and Sociology*, 12 (1952), 97–110.
5. See David C. McClelland, "The Psychology of Mental Content Reconsidered," *Psychological Review*, 62 (1955), 297–302; idem, "Some Social Consequences of Achievement Motivation," in *Nebraska Symposium on Motivation, III*, Lincoln, Neb., 1955; idem, *Studies in Motivation*, New York, 1955; idem, "Interest in Risky Occupations among Subjects with High Achievement Motivation," unpublished paper, 156.
6. David C. McClelland, John W. Atkinson, R. A. Clark, and E. L. Lowell, *The Achievement Motive*, New York, 1953.
7. John W. Atkinson, R. W. Heyns, and J. Veroff, "The Effect of Experimental Arousal of the Affiliation Motive on

Thematic Apperception," *Journal of Abnormal and Social Psychology*, 49 (1954), 405–410.

8. J. Veroff, "Development and Validation of a Projective Measure of Power Motivation," unpublished doctoral dissertation, University of Michigan, Ann Arbor, 1956.

9. David C. McClelland, "Interest in Risky Occupations among Subjects with High Achievement Motivation," *op. cit.*

10. John W. Atkinson, "Individual Differences in Achievement Motive and Fear of Failure Related to Performance under Uncertainty and Level of Aspiration," unpublished paper, November, 1956.

11. W. L. Warner and J. Abegglen, *Big Business Leaders in America* (New York, 1955). See also W. E. Henry, "The Business Executive: The Psychodynamics of a Social Role," *American Journal of Sociology*, 54 (1949), 286–291.

12. It is immaterial, so far as the major hypothesis is concerned, whether persons having particular motives actively seek entrepreneurial roles or are recruited by others for such roles on the basis of demonstrated competence in certain lines of activity or possession of particularly desirable attributes of personality. In either case, the behavior of the individual which serves either directly or indirectly to bring him closer to an entrepreneurial role is influenced by his motives.

13. See the paper by Atkinson, Heyns, and Veroff cited in reference (7). See also Veroff's dissertation, cited in reference (8), and McClelland, Atkinson, *et al.*, cited in reference (6). Finally, see John W. Atkinson and David C. McClelland, "The Projective Expression of Needs, II: The Effect of Different Intensities of the Hunger Drive on Thematic Apperception," *Journal of Experimental Psychology*, 38 (1948), 642–658.

The discovery of an association between a particular kind of motivation and entrepreneurship does not, of course, prove the causal relationship implicit in our hypothesis. But placed in the context of other research findings which trace the development of motives and their influence on behavior, and in

light of the fairly wide acceptance among psychologists of the assumption that early childhood is the origin of relatively stable attributes of personality, a fairly strong argument can be presented that the motives of an individual are antecedent to occupational role and not the consequence of it. Ultimately, long-term studies which assess the strength of motives in college students and then follow up with assessment of occupation later in life will be needed to finally substantiate the point.

14. See, in addition to McClelland, *Studies in Motivation,* and McClelland and associates, *The Achievement Motive,* the following two essays: J. W. Atkinson, "Explorations Using Imaginative Thought to Assess the Strength of Human Motives," *Nebraska Symposium on Motivation, II* (Lincoln, Neb., 1954); and D. C. McClelland, "Measuring Motivation in Phantasy: The Achievement Motive," in H. Guetzkow, ed., *Groups, Leadership and Men,* Pittsburgh, 1951.

15. We are fully aware that a study which would produce "final and definitive" results would involve great complexities of sampling. There may doubtless exist significant differences in the personality structure of entrepreneurs in enterprises of different size; in firms located in different localities (either distinguished by population size, geographical location, or distance from metropolitan areas); in firms producing different commodities; and in managerial positions involving different tasks. In fact, we have suggested these differences by posing the question earlier of whether a successful financial entrepreneur would also be equally successful as a manufacturer and vice versa. A thorough investigation of these differences would require a research project of gigantic proportions. Moreover, it is very uncertain whether many truly significant differences would ensue. Hence it appears wise, at this stage, to treat entrepreneurs of all categories as a uniform class, and to refine the analysis at a later stage if the results obtained in this project appear to make it advisable to put more resources into a more refined and complex research design.

4 · Attraction to Change-Oriented Movements

THE APPEAL OF COMMUNISM TO AMERICAN MIDDLE CLASS
INTELLECTUALS AND TRADE UNIONISTS

by Herbert E. Krugman

In every country in which there is a communist party, large segments of the party's elite "hard core" of professional revolutionaries have been drawn not from the ranks of the proletariat but from the ranks of the bourgeois, particularly the intellectual bourgeois. To further our understanding of this phenomenon, it should be helpful to consider original motivations for joining as they differentiate between intellectuals and non-intellectuals. It should also be relevant to consider which aspects of their prior experience prepare members of both groups for party affiliation. What needs does party membership satisfy for them? To what extent and by what mechanisms does the party reshape the basic personality orientations of those who become part of the elite hard core?

Background of the Study: the Interviewees

The data to be discussed are fifty interviews with ex-members of the American Communist Party. These interviews, conducted in New York State within the period October 1950 to July 1951, typically required two three-hour sessions in order to cover the topics listed on a forty-seven item open-ended interview schedule. Interviews were usually conducted in the interviewee's home and were preceded by assurances of anonym-

SOURCE: *Public Opinion Quarterly*, Vol. 16 (1952), pp. 331–355.

ity and a description of the purposes and methods of the study.[1]

The number of interviews is not large, their representativeness is unknown, and their content cuts across several historical periods. We are dealing, furthermore, with data on the American Communist Party, a group which has always been looked upon as highly deviant. We are also dealing with ex-communists rather than present members. On the other hand it may be noted that, in view of the notoriously high turnover of members, the typical member at any given time may be fairly described as someone about to become an ex-member. Our group of interviewees were, however, members of much higher ranking, and longer tenure than any that might have been chosen randomly from among the committed membership for any stated period; they should, therefore, be qualified to report on party social structure and organization.

The optimum interview situation would

[1] The methods and hypotheses reported in this article were developed collaboratively by the members of the Appeals of Communism Project (under the direction of Gabriel A. Almond) of the Center of International Studies at Princeton University. The author had primary responsibility for gathering and analyzing the data on the American Party, and the present article represents a preliminary analysis of some of this material. The final report of the study will be based upon an interviewing program carried on in England, France, and Italy as well as in the United States.

have had the interviewee discussing his or her experiences fully for the first time. It was felt that spontaneity (i.e. lack of prior, overt rehearsal) would enable probing into more valid material and would allow the interviewer to observe more meaningful affect. Unfortunately such spontaneity could only be fully realized in a small proportion (about 25 per cent) of the interviews, and in inverse proportion to time elapsed after leaving the party. People who were known to have published, lectured, or testified about their experiences were by-passed. Most interviewees were referred by previous ones, and one-fourth of those approached refused cooperation. The refusal rate understandably increased with the passage of time.

Our 50 cases included 24 journalists, writers, artists, professionals, students, etc. who may be termed intellectuals, and 18 trade union officials who, for the most part, originally became officials with party help. The intellectuals were predominantly college graduates whereas the trade unionists had typically achieved less than a complete high school education. The intellectuals came predominantly from second-generation American, middle-class homes, while the trade unionists were largely foreign born and of poor homes. Half of the trade unionists but none of the intellectuals were religiously devout during the period of party membership. These trade unionists saw no conflict between party membership and religion, apparently because they literally did not "see" the party since their "duties" were generally confined to intra-union activities. Ten of the 18 trade unionists belonged to no party units except the party faction within their union, and they continued to think and talk primarily about local union matters throughout their period of party membership. All of the intellectuals at one time or another belonged to some party unit that did not overlap with their occupational group memberships.

The average age of our cases at the time they joined the party was 24 years. Nine intellectuals, but only one trade unionist, made an independent decision to join the party (i.e., under no pressure by members) and then went out to search for a place to do so or for members who would help them do so. The intellectuals tended to have joined between 1931 and 1936 when the party was sectarian and to have defected between 1937 and 1946; the trade unionists, on the other hand, seem to have been less selective about when they joined and more likely to have left after the war (e.g., during the C.I.O. fight of 1947–8). Intellectuals were members for an average of 5.4 years and trade unionists for 8.9 years. The intellectuals had their "first doubts" earlier and left the party sooner after having had them than did the trade unionists, but few in either group left abruptly at the time of a change in line.

Prior Experience and Party Attractions

In characterizing their lives during the years immediately prior to their joining the party, the interviewees mentioned various non-vocational but central themes. Table 1 indicates plainly that relatively more subtle and emotional factors underlay the party membership of the intellectuals.[2]

[2] In connection with the tables presented in this report, it should be noted that (a) those cases not classified as either trade union or intellectual are heterogeneous with regard to membership-type and attention will be focussed therefore on the first two columns only; (b) all data have been tallied and classified independently by two people familiar with the data, and inconsistencies have been adjusted on the basis of joint discussion; (c) although the use of only one interviewer prevented a check on the reliability of marginals as affected by possible interviewer bias, bias, if it operates at all, is at least held constant, and therefore cannot jeopardize

Of the 17 intellectuals who mentioned emotional adjustment problems, 13 referred to difficulties due to "parents." Eleven of these went on to specify the father as the source of their difficulties. Four of the 11 further identified the father's "weakness" as the source of their problem, while only one respondent indicated the father's tyranny as responsible. In no case was the mother mentioned in other than favorable terms.

a direct question on the party's attractions. It is clear that, in comparison with trade unionists, the intellectuals were more concerned with defiance of authority, excitement, and feelings of belonging to an elite group. The data in Table 3, drawn from a discussion of party attitudes toward danger, suggest not only that the trade unionists were less concerned with personal bravery (at least in *post hoc* discussion), but also that the intellectuals

TABLE 1. *Main Theme in Life Prior to Joining the Party*

| | FREQUENCY BY GROUPS | | | |
MAIN THEME	Intellectual (N = 24)	Trade Union (N = 18)	Unclassified (N = 8)	Total (N = 50)
Emotional adjustment problems	17	2	1	20
Under political pressure	1	7	2	10
Already political	4	4	3	11
Unemployed	1	4	2	7
Anger-fascism	1	—	1	2
Anger-depression	1	—	1	2
Dull, materialistic life	1	—	—	1
Life good	—	2	—	2
Total Themes *	26	19	10	55

* Multiple responses tallied.

Seven of the intellectuals spontaneously mentioned that they had received psychotherapeutic treatment before (3 cases) or after (4 cases) their period of party membership. Since this information was never directly sought by the interviewer, the seven cases may be considered as a minimum but not necessarily a maximum figure.

The emotional turbulence underlying the intellectuals' affiliation with the Communist Party is shown more explicitly in Table 2, which is based on responses to

―――――――
any cross-tabulations; and (d) for our purposes it is enough that the tables contain merely suggestive data. It is unnecessary to give them a perhaps undeserved dignity by reporting levels of significance of statistical differences.

tended to be split between the needs of being fearless on the one hand and cautious on the other. Neither over-all behavior evaluations by the interviewer nor the interviewees' comments about the "attractions" of the party constituted very satisfactory data on motivation. The interviewees' comments on the "attractions" of the party may have been invalid *post hoc* rationalizations. The danger of leaning too much on ready made evaluations, however, was lessened somewhat by obtaining a detailed biographical record. The "rationalizing attitude," if it existed at all, was most apparent when the acts of joining and leaving the party were discussed. In the larger biographical context, significant inconsistencies were noted. It therefore seemed safer to evaluate the functions rather than the attractions of

TABLE 2. *Attractions of the Party*

| | FREQUENCY BY GROUPS | | | |
ATTRACTION	Intellectual ($N = 24$)	Trade Union ($N = 18$)	Unclassified ($N = 8$)	Total ($N = 50$)
Idealistic; fight against injustice, fascism, poverty	10	6	7	23
Romantic; defy authority, participate in danger and excitement	11	1	1	13
Practical; seek knowledge, understanding, trade union skills, job	5	7	—	12
Escape; avoid loneliness, meaninglessness, competition	5	3	5	13
Status; constitutes an heroic, powerful, or Bohemian elite	7	1	—	8
Admiration; for members	4	3	3	10
Tradition	2	2	—	4
Other	—	2	—	2
Total Attractions *	44	25	16	85

* Multiple responses tallied.

TABLE 3. *Party Attitudes toward Danger*

| | FREQUENCY OF GROUPS * | | | |
RESPONSE	Intellectual ($N = 21$)	Trade Union ($N = 12$)	Unclassified ($N = 4$)	Total ($N = 37$)
Be brave, fearless	5	2	—	7
Be brave but not rash, consult superiors	6	—	—	6
Avoid danger	1	—	3	4
Protect leaders, let rank and file take risks	1	3	—	4
Arrests and bloody noses equal prestige	1	2	—	3
"Education committees," "shock troops" are available	1	2	—	3
I or most are willing to do anything	1	1	1	3
Provoke violence but turn other cheek	1	1	—	2
Only immigrants would be brave underground	1	—	—	1
Don't know, no particular policy	3	1	—	4

* This topic was omitted when time available for interview was limited. The total number of cases therefore is less than 50.

membership, and to define functions as apparent need-satisfying consequences.

The Functions of Party Membership

Two broad categories of functions— "conscious" and "unconscious"—were classified. The terms are adequate in the sense that the general tendency is for one group of functions to be associated with a low, and the other group with a high, level of consciousness. Six unconscious functions were classified. They included release of anxiety associated with feelings of (1) hostility, (2) unworthiness, (3) weakness, (4) apathy, (5) confusion, and (6) isolation. This is not to say that the party provides hostility-objects, prestige, power, etc.; our definition of function implies only that certain situational factors provided by the party satisfied previously existing needs which had been at least partially unsatisfied

The six conscious functions classified were also split into two groups of three each. The first group of self-oriented functions included: (1) career functions (jobs, training, etc.), (2) social relatedness functions ("belonging," etc.), and (3) intellectual functions (curiosity, interest, etc.).[3] The second group of other-oriented functions includes obligations to (1) trade unions, (2) ethnic minority groups, and (3) mankind (e.g. moral or humanitarian obligations).

The following excerpts from interviews are intended only to suggest the quality or affective tone associated with each function:

[3] Social relatedness differs from "isolation" in that no intrapersonal inhibitions (e.g. shyness) block satisfaction of similar social needs. Intellectual curiosity differs from "confusion" in that the former involves at least some genuine curiosity about the world per se in contrast with anxiety about the ambiguous role of the self in that world.

Hostility

"My family and father violently disapproved of my painting. I was going to be against everything he stood for."

"Had a martyr complex at the time . . . I was just a stupid militant agitator. . . . As soon as I joined (CP), I began to shoot my mouth off."

Unworthiness

"Very miserable and unhappy yet feeling superior because I could play Mozart and read poetry. . . . I was delighted to be accepted by (CP) adults. It gratified many of my superiority fantasies."

"I was at my most unattractive period . . . very unsure of myself as a woman. . . . I was kept very busy, flattered, made to feel important. . . . I began to develop a sense of identity. . . . They tried to convince me that I had great talents for organization and moving people . . . I believed it then . . ."

Weakness

"I was afraid of everyone in those days. I was very small."

"I saw that the YCL was the powerhouse. . . . Finally he said to me, 'Look, don't be a child . . . join the YCL.' . . . They decided to make me a real power."

Apathy

"The quiescent virtues were not stressed. . . . You were expected to talk, argue, etc. . . . You had to be on the go all the time."

"It was a rather dull life, a materialistic one . . . not very spiritual (before CP). It was a little sensational going into an underground movement."

Confusion

"I decided that to acquire some feeling of dignity I should go off alone and think. I went to X and then to Y . . . it didn't help. So I went to Z for two years. Z didn't solve anything. . . ."

"I have a lot of personal problems.

One of my peculiarities is that I must always be right, 100% right. . . ."

Isolation

"I was a very backward young man, shy, etc. . . . I was isolated . . . I got used to being isolated. . . . It's the only thing I ever joined in my life . . . don't like organizations—too shy, . . . a sense of commitment—belongingness—escape from loneliness."

"I used to fear (before YCL) that if I died in the gutter no one would care. I'm grateful to the YCL for giving me the ego pick-up I needed."

Career

"He asked me to help him with the (CP) magazine—to write for it. It was a godsend to me—in this cultural desert."

"Since I was young and the party saw I was ambitious they put me up for office (in the union). They said I was young, should join and be a leader."

Social relatedness

"Sort of drifted in—used to see a lot of X college girls and all their intellectual leaders were communists. I had a couple of little crushes there."

"One evening I got involved with a little house party of theirs—and I was treated very nicely. . . . Before I knew it I was a member."

Intellectual clarity

"I read like a maniac for two years —everything by Lenin et al. . . . annotated all the books. It seemed to answer certain questions. . . . Marxism said history was meaningful, had direction. It freed the individual from tyranny of haphazard fact."

"This communism thing for me was inseparable from a general intellectual awakening . . . communism offered a general theory—easy to grasp."

Trade-union obligations

"I joined because all the most interested, best, most effective union members were communists."

"To me joining the CP was some-

thing with which to arm myself in being a better trade union member."

Minority-group obligations

"I did feel the oppression on Jews and was all for equality and justice."

"I never had any contacts with whites that could be called decent until I met Commies. . . . I read their literature. With the ILD they were busy showing they were genuine friends of the negro people."

Humanitarian obligations

"We belonged to some group doing much reading on fascism. I had been to Germany several times . . . I think we got in (to CP) because there was so much wrong and poverty."

"I joined the party when it moved widows' evicted furniture back into the home. I thought it was right. That's why I joined."

Table 4 indicates in a summary way the frequency with which the several functions were mentioned by the interviewees. Note first that the satisfying consequence of party membership for those with prior feelings of unworthiness was prestige, whereas for those with feelings of weakness it was power. Note too that the low frequencies associated with minority-group obligations were indeed realistic. Although there were many minority group members among the interviewees, only the four negroes mentioned their minority group membership among their motivations for joining. The others subsumed their personal concern for minority rights under general humanitarian obligations. The one intellectual who did comment about anti-semitism said:

"Then there was the pain of being Jewish and the hurts suffered in X state. The first community we lived in was very hostile. My reaction was something like 'If I can't belong to any country then I'll belong to no country—therefore nobody should belong to a country,' or 'If I'm merely non-accepted by Gentiles why not join the most different group—give it some meaning rather than just non-acceptance—revel in isolation—so you don't have to wonder about the why of anti-semitism in the first place.'"

It should also be pointed out, in connection with the factors of isolation and

unconscious to conscious functions was almost 2 to 1 (51/29), whereas for the trade unionists the same ratio was almost 1 to 2 (18/32). We could infer, therefore, that communism among trade unionists is primarily related to rational interpersonal needs; e.g. group obligation. For intellectuals, however, we could infer that the rel-

TABLE 4. *Functions of Communism* *

	FREQUENCY BY GROUPS			
FUNCTION	Intellectual (N = 24)	Trade Union (N = 18)	Unclassified (N = 8)	Total (N = 50)
Unconscious				
Hostility	13	6	4	23
Unworthiness	13	2	2	17
Weakness	6	3	3	12
Apathy	8	4	3	15
Confusion	4	—	1	5
Isolation	7	3	3	13
Total	51	18	16	85
Conscious				
Self-oriented:				
Career	4	7	1	12
Social relatedness	6	7	3	16
Intellectual clarity	5	—	1	6
Other-oriented:				
Trade union	3	12	1	16
Minority group	2	2	3	7
Humanitarian	9	4	4	17
Total	29	32	13	74
Total Functions	80	50	29	159

* This classification of the functions of party membership was developed collaboratively on the Appeals of Communism Project and will appear in its fully elaborated form in the comparison of the American, British, French, and Italian case histories.

social relatedness, that none of the intellectuals, whether it bothered them or not, had voluntarily belonged to any organized groups prior to their political "awakening." This includes Boy Scouts, fraternities, social clubs, etc.

But the basic finding reflected in Table 4 is this: For the intellectuals the ratio of

evant needs are less rational, intra-personal factors. The most striking difference between intellectuals and trade unionists is related to status-anxiety.

This classification of functions was not without methodological pitfalls. It was observed, for example, that the interviewees seemed to take one of three different attitudes toward the interview task. These may be described, in order of prominence, as (1) soul searching, (2) reminiscing, and (3) answering questions. The first attitude was frequently associated with recent defection and/or intellectualism; the second with long past defection; the third with non-intellectualism, or with the very limited ideological commitment made to the party by some rank and file members. In the first case, clear insights were possible because rationalizations were still being struggled with and inconsistencies, as well as areas of tension, were very obvious. In the second case, a rationalization (if any were involved) had long since been smoothed out and crystallized. The whole biography by then may conceivably have been perceived by the interviewee through a screen provided by that rationalization. In the third case rationalization was less likely, and evaluation was therefore relatively simple. Many of our intellectuals fell into the second group, although there were a few who had been out of the party for a long time and were still struggling with rationalizations.

Despite the limitations of our various data summaries, taken as a whole they indicate that commitment to the goals of communism is, among trade unionists, exceedingly limited; among intellectuals it is based in large part on other than politico-economic factors. The differences between trade unionists and intellectuals, as they have been reported in this paper; (a) emphasize the relevance of these non-politico-economic factors, (b) provide us with a rationale for the collection of psychoanalytic data,[4] and (c) permit us to speak of communism as representing a more pronounced political deviation for intellectuals than for trade unionists. Specifically, intellectuals are apparently more likely than trade union communists to have:

1. been native born Americans
2. come from middle class homes

[4] To be reported in a subsequent paper.

3. belonged to regular party organizations
4. had emotional adjustment problems prior to joining the party
5. joined the party independently; i.e. without pressure
6. been attracted by the opportunity to defy authority, experience excitement, and belong to an heroic or other elite
7. been ambivalent about the topic of bravery
8. satisfied unconscious needs through the party
9. been status-anxious

As an institution, the Communist Party apparently serves a wide variety of functions for its members. These functions, furthermore, tend to differ markedly for different groups in the social structure. The nature of these differences, however, may challenge the too easy assumption of a necessary historical relationship between susceptibility to communism and certain groups, particularly Labor. In view of the Western world's exposure to the works of Marx, Engels, and Lenin, many quite anti-communist—even anti-socialist—individuals have associated Labor with Liberalism or (potential) communism. For these individuals, the conservatism of American trade unions was an exception to the rule. There is in the present study, however, an implication that the working classes are highly flexible politically in their pursuit of concrete necessities. Alexander's study of the Peronist movement in Argentina corroborates this finding in great detail; enthusiastic political support was given in return for concrete economic advantages.[5]

Our data on the intellectuals' lives prior to their joining the party, coupled with the data on attractions and functions of membership, strongly suggests that powerful emotional needs were satisfied by membership. It is reasonable to assume that in the process of gaining

[5] Alexander, R. J. *The Peron Era*, New York: Columbia University Press, 1951.

these satisfactions, the intellectual exhibits a greater malleability and striving for personal approval within the group. With this malleability in mind, we shall discuss certain aspects of party life in terms of the pressures put upon the intellectual to conform, to mobilize, to direct his hostility, and to exchange intellectual integrity for political power.[6]

Party Pressures and the Individual: the Unit Meeting

The agenda of a party unit meeting characteristically, though not always, follows a stereotyped pattern wide-spread throughout the communist parties of the world: so many minutes for the report of the financial secretary, so many for the educational director, etc. The heart of the agenda, however, is the political discussion of (and perhaps a "vote" on) a topic handed down from higher echelons. The topic is usually introduced by a "report" given by one of the members previously assigned to the task and perhaps helped in its preparation by one of the leaders. After the report is read, each member must comment in turn until at last the unit organizer makes his summary.

The original report is typically a strenuous attempt to represent the party line, and each of the commenting members will, of course, generally agree with and support its conclusions. There is for a group of intellectuals,[7] nevertheless, a tense competitiveness in the air. As one interviewee put it:

[6] The reliability of interview data used for this purpose is probably greater than the reliability of data on motivations. Materials used in this section were reported in a matter-of-fact atmosphere apparently devoid of those "rationalization" needs sometimes encountered in the discussion of motivations.

[7] As was previously noted, intellectuals are more likely than trade unionists to attend regular party unit meetings.

"The atmosphere of meetings was an attempt to prove that you were righter, more loyal than the next person. Each person had to say something to prove his rightness. If you spoke first at a meeting and were very sincere and right there was still the problem of the organizer speaking later on. He had to be just a bit righter since he was top man. Hence you were ipso facto slightly wrong. You worried about this if you were middle class."

Despite unanimous votes and other symbols of an apparent submissiveness, it would appear that intellectuality can be an active competitive tool within the party. For those who use it successfully enough to earn the compliments of the leader, there is a most marked (and temporary) experience of pleasure and prestige. But for those who are "wrong" by not being "right enough," there is a guilt defined as such by a very heavy weight of communist tradition. One is never wrong "accidentally":

"Their motto was 'there's no such thing as an intellectual error'—you must find out why and where it comes from—what bourgeois factors were responsible."

To be "wrong" therefore smacks of deviation and attracts as much (if not more) hostility within the party as without:

"Every deviation within the party is seen as a reflection of the class struggle. Hence one of the contestants unwittingly or wittingly represents the capitalist class viewpoint. Hence the rules of handling such problems outside get applied inside. Only 'liberals' distinguish between ideas and the man."

But not all kinds of "error" are equally risky, and one is safer discussing the evils of the local status quo than the virtues of the distant Utopia:

"Deviation of slightest amount on foreign policy brings you into much more trouble than deviation on domestic issues."

"In denouncing capitalism you can do it without restraint. In praising the Soviet Union you have to be more careful in how you do it—hence more time is spent denouncing capitalism—there's no mincing of words. In praising the Soviet Union you still need some diplomacy."

When these cautions are combined with the fact that there is no "blueprint" for the communist utopia—Marx wrote about capitalism, not communism, and Lenin said that the "dictatorship of the proletariat" was temporary and let it go at that—it may be said that the party structures verbal testaments of loyalty-correctness into hostile-denouncing channels. Thus, the status-seeking intellectual must use his intellectuality in a hostile manner regardless of whether his "hostility" existed prior to, or was released during, his life in the party. Intellectuality itself, furthermore, may be used as a tool with which to make the status-secure intellectual first insecure, and then hostile. This may best be demonstrated by examining party training techniques.

Party Schools

Since the Communist Party does not expect to recruit fully mature Marxists, it must and does offer many opportunities for training. This may be given by (1) the persons who do the recruiting, (2) new members' classes, (3) party units, (4) open schools and (5) secret party schools. The National Training School and the Lenin Institute (in Moscow) are at the top of the educational hierarchy, but the state schools in the United States and other party schools abroad all use the teaching techniques originally established at the Lenin Institute. These techniques are reflected to some extent at all levels of party training, particularly during "left" periods.

A typical party school on the state level runs two or three times a year for four to five weeks at a time. About twenty students are organized into groups of four or five, and the curriculum is broken down into daily units involving (1) a three hour morning lecture to the group as a whole, (2) an hour of reading both before and after lunch, (3) group discussions and the assignment of reports to sub-units (one person in each taking major responsibility), and (4) a conference of the whole group in which various reports are presented. The lectures are conventional. In group discussions, however, the emphasis is on searching for deviations among the group (with one of the four or five in charge of the search). In conferences, both the instructor and the director of the school (a non-instructor) take charge of the deviation-hunting. The treatment of the deviation is most important. It has to be intensively traced back to its "bourgeois" source—partially as a testament to the sinful basis of deviation, and partially as a means of expunging it. The technique used is "self-criticism," or critical self-analysis before the group, with the group and/or the instructor challenging the confessor from time to time. Although this confessional is very painful at times, it is nonetheless acceptable—perhaps especially to intellectuals—on the ground that reason is stronger than emotion, a central tenet of the idealized "good Bolshevik." As in most confessionals that take place before hostile audiences, however, the confessor either rebels (and leaves) or remains and goes through certain changes—changes which in this case involve an increased degree of submissive conformity to party norms. The most pertinent norms are concerned with deviation-hunting in self and others, a persistent party activity that both mitigates against status-security and conduces to the use of "challenges" in political or other discussions. And in the Communist Party the definition of "political" is broad enough to cover anything: any factor which keeps one from working effectively becomes "political":

> "If you were a homosexual then this interest detracted from your political interest. If you didn't know it you were 'confused'; if you knew it and didn't do anything about it you were a 'traitor.'"

The process of challenging people who are being "developed" seems to involve a conscious expectation that they will (or should) "crack," if vulnerable:

> "The way to develop people according to the CP is to pound them and guide the eruption when it takes place."
> "Pop Mindel[8] was a good teacher but used to enrage and attack people, then suddenly lighten up with a joke —then suddenly attack again. The object was to break down independence of judgment or character. Pop Mindel was a destroyer of individuality. Parroting would not do. The stress would only be withstood if you had a complete grasp of the material; one didn't think of it as cruel but as freeing them from bourgeois fetters. He usually picked on one or two people—made them the butt of the class. He usually picked on the (1) most alert and intellectual or (2) the most stupid or quiet."

Mindel was the ranking training expert of the American party and as such his teaching methods were widely respected. It is interesting to note that at one time his methods were attacked, publicly as "psychologizing" and privately as "sadistic." Mindel won out in the controversy on the grounds that his methods were those used in the Lenin Institute. Those of our interviewees who had attended the Lenin Institute confirmed this point.

[8] Instructor, National Training School.

High level training schools were to "proletarianize the leadership":

> "The party schools were supposed to give to the proletarian those verbal and intellectual skills that he of course lacked. You were not supposed to send non-proletarians to these schools, but of course you were not always able to do it that way."

The impression gained from our interviews is that the intellectuals were more likely to attend local or state schools, and trade unionists, Negroes, etc., were more likely to attend the national or international schools.[9] It may be significant that there are many comments about student rebellions and high wash-out rates at the top level schools but none for the others. Perhaps this is an indication of the greater malleability of the intellectual who accepts, for one reason or another, the premise that "reason is stronger than emotion."

Party Assignments

The day-to-day business of the American Communist Party supposedly is "mobilizing the masses." Table 5 suggests, however, that this is the activity in which members least care to be personally and directly engaged. If, for example, the experience of our interviewees was representative, then at least a third of all issues of the *Daily Worker* are regularly "dumped" and the sales receipts paid into the party out of the pockets of the member responsible for selling the papers. Other data indicate that less than one-third of the party membership are regular readers of the *Worker*.[10]

[9] Where training involved the same content and techniques but for a longer period of time and with more prestige attached.

[10] Kempton cites statistics from party reports seized by the Pittsburgh police in that city, "Red Ink," *New York Post*, December 27,

More pertinently, Table 5 strongly suggests that communists do not like to be with non-communists. The question is, of course, more meaningful for intellectuals because they can cut themselves off from others when joining the party, whereas the trade unionist usually stays in his union and continues to deal with the same people. A few interview-excerpts may help to clarify the nature of the communist clannishness:

half a day free they'd look for another communist to spend it with."

"Sense of duty was very important. The world will fall apart if you don't do what you must do at that moment. You fear change of status while gone. People who went on summer vacations tried to go to places where they knew there would be other communists—avoid bourgeois—avoid need for self examination and too careful compari-

TABLE 5. *Most Disagreeable Tasks*

	FREQUENCY OF GROUPS			
TASK	Intellectual (N = 24)	Trade Union (N = 16)	Unclassified (N = 8)	Total (N = 50)
Selling the Daily Worker or distributing leaflets	7	4	3	14
Functioning alone on the outside; e.g., canvassing, recruiting	4	2	—	6
Trade union nonsense, decisions made in ignorance of conditions	—	6	—	6
Boring organizational tasks (e.g., collecting dues), dull meetings	4	2	—	6
Parades, demonstrations, police lines	1	—	2	3
Destroy innocents, attack friends	2	—	—	2
Censorship, handling false news	2	—	—	2
Tasks exposing self as CP member	1	1	—	2
Explaining line changes	—	1	1	2
Being away from the apparatus	—	—	2	2
None	1	—	1	2
Other (one response only)	2	—	2	4

"Most of the communists I knew seemed to be afraid of being alone. . . . Though I heard many say, 'Oh, how I wish I could get away for a week,' they did not. If they did go away they'd come back soon—got lonely and panicky almost. If they had

1950. It is also interesting to note that several of our interviewees emphasized that "the rank and file are just as likely to be uninformed communists as non-communists are likely to be uninformed citizens."

son with other types of people and styles of life. It also takes away the sense of importance to be with others. This is one of the great things the Communist Party gives you; you're important people."

"They have a lip-service attitude toward rest but when you're told to take a rest you have a mixed attitude—gratitude and fear; i.e. 'I must have done something wrong. They must want to get me out of here. Perhaps they're going to change my status.' "

"Physical demands were terribly, terribly hard. Even if you weren't invited you often felt you had to go to a meeting or your status would drop. Status in party very, very important."

Although the lowest rank communist is encouraged to feel superior to any non-communist, intra-party status is very flexible. It fits in very neatly with the attitude toward alertness for (or expectancy of) deviation, and the organizational demand for great energy-expenditure. In consequence, there evolves a pattern of "not being able to rest on one's laurels," "having to prove yourself over and over," etc. As one interviewee put it:

"Success reactions were always combined with caution. They always magnified failures and successes. Made an enormous fuss over your work but combined it with a threat not to get swell-headed. No matter how good you were you were not as good as the man higher up. No matter how well you thought you understood the standards for upgrading ('improvement of status') they'd always throw in something else about you and get you confused again. It was impossible to really figure out what made for ups and downs."

A status-insecure person may put forth great effort in such a setting, very much like the donkey pursuing the carrot held just out of reach. But a more fundamentally hostile and status-secure person may either (1) resent not being treated in accordance with his deeply confident expectations and leave the party, or (2) demand proper rewards, come to the attention of leadership, and perhaps be put in a new category altogether by being given power.

In general, however, the party's belief-system features an underlying emphasis on "attempting monumental deeds" and "dreaming great dreams." Too much success on a local or individual level, therefore, may be dangerous, if only in the

sense that it blinds one to the higher ends of the movement. Thus:

"All goals are impossibly high. If it looks as though you might achieve a quota it is raised in the middle of a campaign."

Half of the intellectuals in this study gave at least four evenings a week to party activities. Although feeling generally superior, the larger group of status-insecure respondents constantly engaged in a compulsive search for status security or proof—not only in the eyes of others, but in their own as well. As one respondent said:

"It's a challenge to one's endurance. 'How game are you?' It's a non-political competition—a game one plays with oneself—curiosity about how one can stand up under stress. Sure you're a pretty extraordinary person by being in the party, but just how extraordinary?"

The communist who is cut off from non-communists and is working hard for status is in no position to resist acceptance of the group values. Such values include, among others, militancy, firmness, and hatred for various enemies.

Party Hierarchy and the Role of Cynicism

The Communist Party is organized along hierarchical lines which place great emphasis on discipline and unquestioning obedience; each individual is expected to be submissive to those above him in rank and assertive to those below him. Since all members are encouraged to be anything but submissive outside the party, and even those of the lowest rank are encouraged to act in some leadership capacity in their neighborhoods, places of work, etc., the individual member participates in acts of both extreme conformance and rebellion. In a sense, the party thus offers the best of two worlds for those who are, or become, ambivalent conformers.

In such a setting the party is always looking (for purposes of promotion and development) for the rare people who can be completely trusted and yet have both ability and initiative—people who can fit into a hierarchical structure without damage to their political talents.[11] But to preserve the trustworthiness of such candidates for leadership, one must gently and gradually shift the basis of

People who would die for the party but had no illusions about it; i.e. they finally recognize the power aspect of the movement. It turns the original idealism into loyalty. . . ."

Idealism is not trusted. Trade unionists are more trusted either because they have "real" grievances (and intellectuals do not), or because they are more realistic (than intellectuals) in their recognition and appreciation of power. The breeding of cynicism seems to be the special proc-

TABLE 6. *Changes in Leaders as They Rise*

| | FREQUENCY BY GROUPS | | | |
CHANGES	Intellectual $(N = 17)$	Trade Union $(N = 12)$	Unclassified $(N = 6)$	Total $(N = 35)$
Arrogant, hard, superior	6	5	1	12
Cynical, less idealistic	6	1	1	8
Lose independence, fear deviation and superiors	2	3	1	6
Cold, dehumanized	2	—	2	4
Opportunistic, ambitious, prosperous, selfish	—	2	1	3
Less objective, lose pulse	2	1	—	3
No typical changes	2	1	—	3
Don't know	1	—	2	3
Other	—	1	3	4
Total Responses *	21	14	11	46

* Multiple responses tallied.

trustworthiness from idealism to something more realistic. As one interviewee put it:

"After awhile there is almost an effort to develop the kind of cynicism which will allow the leader to be willing to do almost anything. The combination of absolute loyalty and absolute cynicism is the final essence.

[11] Although some of the processes herein described are recognized and consciously encouraged by top leadership they are primarily processes which flow "automatically" as a consequence of party social structure.

ess whereby idealistic intellectuals are turned into "hard core" material. As Table 6 suggests, intellectuals are more likely than trade unionists to recognize and react strongly to "cynicism."

To develop cynicism the party gives power to the individual. The effect was described as follows by one respondent:

"The idealism you see in the rank-and-file makes you more cynical because you realize you created it. And you remember how you used to be idealistic."

"I became the 'doer' instead of 'receiver.' . . . I 'did things to other people.' I was taken into their confidence and learned to do to other people what had been done to me. I developed a 'knowing smile.' I learned to 'develop' people."

Thus, one develops contempt for the rank and file and is better able to adopt instrumental attitudes toward them (i.e., power breeds power). On the other hand, we must ask whether or not the intellectual would be willing to accept power. Would he not rather preserve a strictly intellectual role in preference to a political role in the party?

Several factors may press upon the intellectual in such a way that he may want to give up his intellectual role. First, almost all of the interviewees agreed that trade union and political organization duties had the most prestige:

> "The artists, writers, and front people had no prestige. Speaking and writing were only auxiliary. A person in my position as a (political) organizer would be apple-polished by the artists and intellectuals."

> "The intellectuals play a strange role. They enjoy a good deal of prestige on the one hand (e.g. on petitions the intellectual names are featured . . . as a matter of prestige toward the public . . . for show), but in the sphere of politics they are considered with contempt. This double-edged situation is absolutely characteristic. Therefore intellectuals never participate in making policy, are never on top committees."

In addition to contempt from above, the intellectual has to contend with the apathetic majority of the rank and file, a group which easily becomes suspicious:

> "These naive people, in a very primitive way, get to be guardians of the party line. Their politics consist of repeating and memorizing slogans. A wise-guy intellectual may get in trouble with these people because he may try to put a wrinkle on the line—and the naive people recognize that it is not said just as it was said in the *Daily Worker*."

There may be a real temptation to relinquish an intellectual role.

> "Politics is number one and covers everything. People who have other skills envy politicians—sometimes a good physicist becomes a bad politician—many have given up their own skills and careers to enjoy the prestige of having the preeminent one."

To become a "bad" politician for the sake of prestige may be something more characteristic of the least status-secure. To become a good politician, however, it is likely that greater status-security (and hostility) are required. These elements can more readily be fused with power in such a way that political-organizational talent is undamaged. For one reason or another, therefore, the intellectual is either pressured or required to give up his intellectuality in order to become a more prestigious or a more trusted member.[12]

To explain more fully why it is the fundamentally hostile intellectual who tends to become a politician and the fundamentally status-insecure intellectual who tends to leave the party (or become, for a while, a "bad" politician), we will have to devote more attention to the development of cynicism. In this connection we have already noted the effect of power; the origin and effect of guilt remain to be illustrated.

The Exploitation of Guilt

At one extreme the party consciously assigns certain tasks to those members to

[12] In the case of very important intellectuals the party will "coddle" the individual and exploit his prestige (e.g., Picasso).

whom the jobs are most repugnant. If a girl is to be expelled, for example, then her boy friend (party member) will be picked to testify against her. If he refuses this "test of faith," the party will be doubly cleansed by a double expulsion. If he does not refuse, however, his private sense of guilt is counted on to give him a greater need for a guilt-alleviating faith in the party's rightness. At the other extreme, and more pertinent to the problem of the intellectual, is the "test of faith" provided by history—the change of line:

> "For certain types of best intellectuals carrying out a decision with which you don't agree was the test of fire, the creator of cynicism."
> ". . . there is no doubt about the terrific impact of a big change of line. The first time is, of course, the most crucial one. It is a kind of political rape. Anyone who permits himself to be raped often enough cannot help but sink into a form of political prostitution."

It is important to emphasize that it is the individual and not the new "line" that is in question during the short but often chaotic changeover period:

> "Everyone knows that the line has been handed down from the top of the hierarchy outside anyone's control in the national party. No choice has been offered, or rather no choice in line. The only choice is whether to accept the new line and stay in the party or to reject it and get out of the party. Thus, curiously, the line is not in question; the individual is."

Such a test is most difficult emotionally for the "honest" intellectual. He will develop guilt if, in accepting the new line, he must at some point resort to:

> "Who am I to judge? Only the Cominform can see the whole picture. Stalin has always been right. I don't understand it, but I'm sure he'll be right again."

When these experiences are "successfully" weathered, there develops guilt, faith, cynicism, and a more direct and unrationalized appreciation of power. For intellectuals, furthermore, there is again a temptation to discard intellectuality because it is that part of the self-image that holds the greatest burden of guilt for "acceptance on faith." Some of our intellectuals realized that this would be the essence of their agreement with a new line and left the party:

> "Instead of getting explanations I got very unsatisfactory answers which boiled down to 'take it on faith.' This was not satisfactory."

As we have previously noted, however, few of our interviewees left at the time of a line change. They did apparently "take it on faith," felt the guilt, and could not tolerate the threat of becoming cynical. Cynicism is a process of adjusting more comfortably to self-contempt, but once the cynicism is admitted then the underlying self-contempt becomes fixed and relatively permanent. As Hoffer puts it:

> "As to cynicism. Its connection with self-contempt is fairly obvious. The remarkable thing is that we really do love our neighbor as ourselves; we do unto others as we do unto ourselves. Our attitude toward others is a reflection of our attitude toward ourselves. Self-contempt isolates a person; and cynicism serves to break down the isolation. By cynicism we bring down the whole world to our level, and we become again members of the human race. In the case of the communist, cynicism transmutes the feeling of isolation into one of apartness and exclusiveness. A guilty conscience tends to separate the communist from the masses and enhances his feeling of being one of the elite. His is a priestly

cynicism. The cynicism of a communist can almost always be traced back to some shameful performance. In Russia cynicism became pronounced with the terror, particularly after the Kronstadt massacre. Trotsky, Bukharin, and the other idealists were as brazenly cynical as Stalin, the narrow-minded realist. In the American communist the cynical view is quite conspicuous since the Hitler-Stalin pact." [13]

Hoffer's comments suggest not only that cynicism handles the problem of self-contempt, but also that it creates the need for separation from the masses—separation, for example, via political ("priestly") power.[14] Thus cynicism forces the "intellectual" towards abandoning that role and/or value on two counts: first, because he has betrayed it; and second, because he needs cynical power to hide his guilt.

The guilty intellectual meets cynicism face to face in the party—particularly after he has seemingly survived a change of line and can be drawn closer to the inner circle at the higher echelons, where cynicism flourishes:

"A leader is apt to take refuge in cynicism; a rank and filer in pure and simple faith. Moreover, a professional communist leader is apt to stay in the movement despite his cynicism; a rank-and-filer who gets cynical is apt to get out."

When the guilty intellectual meets cynicism he may be "shocked" or he may find that it "lent a certain charm" (the comment was made about Gerhardt Eisler), depending on his attraction to power. This is a critical point, but he may soon see, as one did, that:

"Cynicism is always exhibited privately. Indeed, it is sometimes overdone to prove that one is not an utter nincompoop. I even had the feeling that some people thought it smart to pretend to be cynical, when it seemed safe to do so, in order to seem more sophisticated politically than they were in reality. Therefore the most hardened sinner may be adept at putting up an irreproachable front in public. I knew a number of such characters who could criticize the communist movement to the satisfaction of the most rabid anti-communist. Yet no one outside of a tiny circle would have believed it possible. Before an audience they could throw themselves into an act of faith or discipline with such authority and fervor that only a most intimate friend could judge whether the party-man or the individual person was performing."

The hostile intellectual bent on destroying his sense of untalented (or no longer talented) identity may thrive in such an atmosphere. But this kind of double life with its undertones of self-contempt is no place for a status-insecure intellectual struggling to protect his sense of identity. Thus, the best intellectuals leave the party because their talents are being damaged: [15]

"Then again a writer can't be a true believer. When I was halfway through X (a novel) I knew it was a mistake. I knew I was handicapped as a writer by being a communist. I knew I couldn't be good at both."

"I went to the country that Sum-

[13] Hoffer, E. *Personal Letter*, San Francisco: December 9, 1951. In this connection see also Hoffer, E. *The True Believer*, New York: Harper and Brothers, 1951.

[14] That is, the cynic knows "the real truth" and thereby feels closer to those others (i.e. the leaders) who share the secret knowledge with him. In this connection see Wolff, K. H. (Ed.) *The Sociology of Georg Simmel*, Glencoe, Illinois: The Free Press, 1950, p. 365.

[15] That is, the intellectual tends to defect because two personal or private roles conflict. The trade unionist, in comparison, tends to defect because two public roles conflict.

mer and did some non-party type painting and began to realize what kind of painter I was. The Party expected me to carry on work that Summer but I ignored it."

". . . but the price I was paying was the abortion of my talent. . . . Finally the personal thing that made me break was the realization that I would kill something very previous in me if I stayed in the party."

A sense of identity and integrity, a personal sense of wholeness, seems to be basic for intellectuals. But the party says one must give up all other identities and become only a communist:

"We differed and he arranged for Piatnitzky to take me out to his summer home for a weekend. . . . Finally he asked, 'Are you a communist or a Negro?' "

"The first clash on which I got battered down was with the international representative at the Congress. English, American and Swiss representatives were against something and the international representative fumed,

'Are you students or are you communists?' "

Probably all of our interviewees had to face similar situations at one time or another.

Conclusion

We have seen that on the whole the Communist Party is well equipped to develop hostility and conformance in its members. Although it loses some members in the process, it has been able to develop leaders appropriate to its needs from among the ranks of both the proletariat and the intellectual bourgeois. It is suggested that the development process has great impact, and that personality change is frequently involved—particularly among the latter group. For those who defect, the change is of intolerably large dimensions. Those who remain have learned to live with the change, in large part as a result of the interplay between emotional needs and organizational pressures that have been outlined in this paper.

PART FIVE

Combination of Personality and Social Variables to Account for Empirical Regularities

IN PARTS III and IV we illustrated how variables at one conceptual level can be used to explain or predict the behavior of variables at another level. Now we turn to a number of items of research that employ a *combination* of personality and social-system variables to account for behavioral regularities. In the previous two Parts we asked one of two questions: How do social variables affect an individual's personality? How does an individual's personality affect his social environment? Now we ask: How do certain kinds of individuals *in* certain types of social situations behave?

As before, we begin with selections from experimental small-group research. Ray Canning and James Baker find that subjects scoring high on authoritarianism (personality variable) who are *also* under group pressure to conform (social variable) changed their behavior most markedly. William Smelser, employing a similar design, found that when personality structure (in particular, the variable of dominance-submission) and social role (in particular, the role of leader or fol-

lower) are congruent, the most effective performance in a task results.

In contrast to these more controlled studies, Erving Goffman's article presents numerous examples of the interplay between embarrassment (a personality variable) and social stiuations. Goffman interprets the expression of embarrassment as an adaptive response contingent both on the character of the social situation and the individual's sense of personality incongruity in that situation.

The remainder of the selections in Part Five deal with the interplay of personality and social variables in specific institutional contexts. The three contexts we have chosen are the school, occupational roles, and deviance. Jackson Toby's analysis of the causes of school maladjustment of lower-class children focuses on the incongruities and conflicts brought to the school by these children and the expectations of the teachers and school authorities. These discontinuities apparently persist and even accumulate throughout the school years.

Peter Blau, et al., develop a programmatic framework to guide research to ascertain the determinants of occupational choice. The authors' emphasize both socioeconomic determinants (both historical and contemporary) and the personality requirements of the potential role incumbent. The authors' framework encompasses both those personality variables emphasized by Guy Swanson (see his article in Part Four) and those social organizational variables stressed by Robert Merton (see his selection in Part Three). Victor Vroom investigates the interplay between personality variables (e.g., authoritarianism) and social variables (e.g., opportunity for participation in decision making) in influencing workers' job performance. Vroom's study resembles Smelser's in design and content,

but the former was conducted in a less controlled but perhaps more realistic social setting.

Two articles on deviance conclude Part Five. Jacqueline and Murray Straus set forth an interpretation of the differential suicide and homicide rates in Ceylon. Their rationale is that violence (whether directed inward or outward) is a product *both* of individual personality variables in a given stress situation *and* the availability of socially sanctioned behavioral alternatives. Bruno Bettelheim and Morris Janowitz' study of ethnic intolerance focuses *both* on the personalities of prejudiced individuals *and* on typical social experiences (such as upward mobility) of these individuals.

A · SMALL-GROUP RESEARCH AND ITS IMPLICATIONS

EFFECT OF THE GROUP ON AUTHORITARIAN AND NON-AUTHORITARIAN PERSONS

by Ray R. Canning and James M. Baker

A laboratory experiment was conducted to test the differential effects of group pressure upon authoritarian and non-authoritarian persons.[1] Autokinesis was used to test individuals' judgments when alone as compared to when in a group situation. Group pressure was exerted on one member by the other four of a five-man group who had been coached previously by the experimenter as to their responses. The experimental situation left the subject, the only naïve member, to face a conflict between his own judgment and the apparent judgment of all the others.

Hypotheses

First, based upon the findings of Moore, Asch, Sherif, and others, it was expected that most subjects would be affected markedly by group pressure. The degree and statistical significance of in-

[1] James M. Baker, "An Experimental Study of the Effect of Group Membership on Authoritarian and Non-authoritarian Personalities" (unpublished Master's thesis, Department of Sociology, Brigham Young University, August, 1957).

SOURCE: *American Journal of Sociology*, Vol. 64 (1959), pp. 579–581.

fluence were further concerns of the experiment.

Second, the authoritarian persons were expected to be affected to a greater degree by group pressure than the non-authoritarian. Adorno included "constant fear of not being like all others" and "inclined to submit blindly to power and authority" in his description of the authoritarian.

Allen found that Mormons were more authoritarian than certain other groups, as measured by scores on the Adorno scale. And between his two ideal types he noted the following differences based upon the Gough Adjective Check List:

The original hypothesis implied that differences in self-perception would fall along the lines of the authoritarian tending to accept his world and go along with it, whereas the non-authoritarian would be more inclined to see himself rebelling, questioning conventional values, and taking a more complicated and individualistic view of the world. Differences found are in general compatible with this hypothesis.[2]

[2] Mark K. Allen, "Personality and Cultural Factors Related to Religious Authoritarianism" (unpublished Ph.D. dissertation, De-

These tendencies of the authoritarian toward conventionality and greater need for conformity sustained the second hypotheses: that he would be influenced more by group pressure than would the non-authoritarian.

Third, on the basis of Asch's experiments [3] and the principle of summatory stimuli, it was expected that group pressure would mount with successive trials in the group tests.

Fourth, the experimenter assumed that group pressure would remain relatively effective in the second individual test following the group test. Sherif's discovery that subjects were influenced by other group members without being aware of it [4] indicates the possible internalization of group norms, a process which theoretically could account for a subconscious carry-over to the next set of individual judgments.

Method

Authoritarian—non-authoritarian personality scales were completed by 234 introductory sociology students, and subjects were then selected who were representative of each classification. The scale had been validated previously for Mormons by Allen,[5] utilizing items drawn

---

partment of Psychology, Stanford University, 1955), p. 80.

[3] Solomon Asch, "Opinions and Social Pressure," *Scientific American*, CXCIV (November, 1955), 31–35.

[4] Muzafer and Carolyn W. Sherif, *An Outline of Social Psychology* (rev. ed.; New York: Harper and Bros., 1956), pp. 251–257.

[5] Allen's scale of religious authoritarianism used the techniques and concepts underlying the Adorno scale but was made up of items related directly to Latter-day Saints, who comprised 97 per cent of Brigham Young University's student body in 1953–1954. He used five successive questionnaires, using an item analysis on each in order eventually to get those items which were the most dis-

from their religious beliefs. Therefore, actually, it measured religious authoritarianism. A good distribution of scores resulted. The fifty students at each extreme of the distribution were selected as representatives of the authoritarian and of the non-authoritarian. Twenty were selected randomly from each group to be used for testing group pressure.[6]

Each of the forty subjects was tested in three autokinetic tests—an initial individual test, a group test, and a second individual test. Each subject was given ten trials in each test. The distance from the subjects to the stimulus light was ten feet, and the time interval of illumination was five seconds.

In the first and third autokinetic tests, the subject's opinions were measured when he relied on his own judgment. In the second, the subject was subjected to group pressure; all others of the group had been coached to report greater distances than he expected. The change in scores, then, from the individual to the group test was used as an index of the group's influence upon him. After the group test was completed, he was tested again with autokinesis. His scores in this second individual test indicated whether he was still being affected by group pressure.

In the group test each member was instructed to respond by number. In this way a specific order of response was maintained, with the subject always responding last. The "judgments" of the coached members concerning how far the light moved were that it was a great distance, with a mean "estimate" of 36 inches. This

---

criminating. This scale was then validated by having mature judges select individuals of their acquaintance who fitted a verbal description of the authoritarian pattern and its opposite. When the persons selected were given the scale, the results were highly significant.

[6] No statistically significant differences in autokinetic perception were found either by sex or by age.

high figure was in contrast to the subject's mean score in the individual test: 4.2 inches. The coached members took care to vary their responses on each trial to allay suspicion.

Findings

All subjects experienced the autokinetic illusion. Changes between scores on the individual and on the group test showed conclusively that the majority of the subjects were influenced by group pressure, thus substantiating the first hypothesis. The mean scores of the subjects in the group test more than tripled those in the individual test, a difference significant beyond the .001 probability level.

Comparisons between subjects with authoritarian and those with non-authoritarian personalities validated the hypothesis that the authoritarian would be influenced to a greater degree by group pressure than the non-authoritarian. Both groups were affected markedly by group pressure. The mean scores of the non-authoritarian on the group test were more than double those on the individual test (11.2 and 5.5 inches). This difference was significant beyond the .001

level. But the mean scores of the authoritarian on the group test were more than five times greater than scores on the individual test (21.4 and 4.2 inches), a difference significant to the .0001 level.

However, the results of the group test did not clearly validate the hypothesis that group pressure would mount in successive trials. Subjects were influenced markedly by group pressure on their first trial, but the effect was relatively consistent throughout the remainder of the group tests. When the ten trials were all considered, a slight over-all increase toward the group norm could be seen. But there were obvious dips in the plotted line.

The last hypothesis was that the effect of group pressure would continue in the second individual test, although to a lesser degree than in the group test. Results show almost exactly what was expected: the mean scores were about halfway between the mean scores of the other two tests. Both types of personality tended to react similarly on the second individual test, the authoritarian again being influenced to a greater degree (14.9 inches for the authoritarian, 6.8 inches for the non-authoritarian) by group pressure.

DOMINANCE AS A FACTOR IN ACHIEVEMENT AND
PERCEPTION IN COOPERATIVE PROBLEM SOLVING INTERACTIONS

by William T. Smelser

The first part of this study relates different pairings of dominant and submissive males, interacting under various role assignments, with their joint achievement in a cooperative problem solving situation. The second part investigates the relationship of these different pairings

SOURCE: *Journal of Abnormal and Social Psychology*, Vol. 62 (1961), pp. 535–542.

to the perceived dominance of the self and the partner.

The thesis is advanced that different combinations of dominant and/or submissive individuals achieve more or less successfully according to the pair-combination as well as the conditions of assignment of dominant or submissive roles, and that it is possible to predict differential success among these permutations according to hypotheses derived from personality theory.

The hypotheses are derived from Sullivan's (1953) general assumption that a person's modes of relating to others are functional in that they enable him to maintain anxiety at a minimum. Interpersonal situations that permit, or encourage, the use of a salient interpersonal technique, such as dominance or submission, give rise to less anxiety than situations that do not. The experiencing of anxiety disrupts cognitive functioning and leads to a less effective performance in a task. Hence, there should be greater achievement when persons are permitted or encouraged to assume habitual modes of relating.

In spite of the explicitness and theoretical importance of this reciprocal aspect of interpersonal theory, few experimental studies have been concerned with it. Leary (1957), employing dominance as one of his central variables, posits a reciprocal theory of interaction. In Mann's (1959) review of the studies of the relation of personality and performance in small groups, he did not report any studies considering the relationship between interacting individuals differing in dominance and the influence of this relation upon either the nature of group achievement or mutual perception. Tuma (1955) found that dissimilarity in dominance between therapist and client, regardless of the direction of the difference, correlated highly with rated improvement in a counseling situation.

The following four hypotheses are based on a theoretical prediction of differences, among different pairings of male subjects under specified conditions of role assignment, in achievement in a cooperative task situation. Table 1 describes the seven different groupings and the interaction and the role assignments, when such assignments were made. The predicted rank orders of achievement of the groups involved in each of the four hypotheses are presented in Table 2.

Hypothesis 1 compares Groups A, B, and G. Following Sullivan (1953), the pairings in Group A perform the most productively, since each member of the pair has a salient interpersonal technique explicitly requested by the experimenter as well as "pulled for" by the behavior of the partner. The pairs of dominant and submissive subjects comprising Group B interact under somewhat less optimal conditions, since these pairs lack the congruent role assignments of the pairs in Group A. The pairs of dominant and submissive subjects in Group G interact with an assignment of roles contrary to their preferred modes, which arouses anxiety and disrupts achievement.

Hypothesis 2 compares Groups B, E, and F. Paired dominant subjects (Group E) do not interact under as optimal conditions as do the pairs in Group B, since each member of the paired dominant subjects interacts so as to induce submissive behavior in his partner, who is also a dominant subject. The paired subjects in Group E were predicted to perform more successfully than the paired submissive subjects in Group F, since dominant subjects are hypothesized to behave in the pursuit of satisfaction rather than security, and thus to be more at ease with each other and themselves than the paired submissive subjects. Sullivan (1953) considered the power motive as one of the pursuits of satisfaction, rather than security. Individuals lacking in dominance may have found it necessary to dissociate the expression and/or awareness of this motive.

Hypothesis 3 compares Groups C, D, E, and F. The prediction involves the differential achievement of two different pairings (two dominant subjects interacting and two submissive subjects interacting), each under two conditions (no role assignments and assignment of the dominant role to one subject and assignment of the submissive role to the partner). The predicted rank order of achievement, by groups, is C, D, E, and F, since it was hypothesized that pairings with role assignment perform more successfully than comparable pairings with no role assignment, and further, that the paired dominant subjects would perform more successfully than paired submissive subjects under comparable conditions. For a dominant subject to relinquish a dominant role should produce less anxiety than for Group A is predicted to be the most successful and Group G the least successful. Hypotheses 1 and 3 are independent, since their predictions do not involve any common groups. Hypothesis 2 has one group (Group B) in common with Hypothesis 1 and it has two groups in common with Hypothesis 3 (Groups E and F).

TABLE 1. *Pairings of Dominant and Submissive Subjects and Conditions of Role Assignments (10 pairs in each group)*

GROUP	DESCRIPTION OF INTERACTION	CODE
A	Dominant subject assigned dominant role; submissive subject assigned submissive role.	D:d–S:s
B	Dominant subject and a submissive subject interact with no role assignment.	D:x–S:x
C	One dominant subject assigned dominant role; other dominant subject assigned submissive role.	D:d–D:s
D	One submissive subject assigned dominant role; other submissive subject assigned submissive role.	S:d–S:s
E	Two dominant subjects interact with no role assignment.	D:x–D:x
F	Two submissive subjects interact with no role assignment.	S:x–S:x
G	Dominant subject assigned submissive role; submissive subject assigned dominant role.	D:s–S:d

a submissive subject to assume a dominant role. In Sullivan's (1953) terms, it is less disruptive to modify a mode of attaining satisfaction (dominant role) than it is to modify a security operation (submissive role).

TABLE 2. *Hypotheses of Rank Order of Achievement of Groups*

HYPOTH-ESIS	PREDICTED RANK ORDER OF ACHIEVEMENT
1	A > B > G
2	B > E > F
3	C > D > E > F
4	A > B > C > D > E > F > G

Hypothesis 4 is not independent of the other three hypotheses, but compares achievement among all seven groups. The predicted rank order corresponds to the alphabetical ordering of the groups, i.e.,

Method

The subjects were all male volunteers enrolled in either Military Science or Air Science at the University of California, Berkeley. Since enrollment in the university armed forces training program is compulsory, this group afforded a broad sampling of university undergraduate men. The total number of subjects who volunteered was 748. Participation in the experiment was credited as an excuse from one military drill period.

Before requesting volunteers, the students were administered a short form of Gough's California Psychological Inventory (CPI), which contained the Dominance (Do), Social Responsibility, and Self-Control scales (Gough, 1957). A vocabulary test (Thorndike and Gallup, 1944) was administered at the conclusion of the personality test. The subjects for the experiment were selected from the extremes of the distribution of the Do scores. The mean of this distribution was 28.5 (*SD*, 6.5) which is quite similar to Gough's (1957) standardization group mean of 28.5 (*SD*, 6.0). A subject scoring 34 or above was defined as dominant; a subject scoring 23 or below as submissive. The raw scores of 34 and 23 correspond to Gough's T scores of 110 and 92, respectively, on a scale with a mean of 100 and a standard deviation of 10.

EXPERIMENTAL SITUATION. The interaction of the paired subjects involved the joint operation of two model railroad trains. The apparatus was that employed by Ghiselli and Lodahl (1958). The main track was 6 feet in diameter, and had two bypass sidings by which the two trains could leave and enter the main track. The two subjects sat on high stools to operate their respective control panels, which were 3 feet high, on the same level with the tracks. The left half of each control panel contained switches that supplied power to different numbered sections of the track. The right half of each control panel contained several controls: direction and speed of the trains, switches to and from the sidings, and a master control switch. The subjects were thus able to control the speed, direction, and route of each train. Carelessness by either subject in operation of his switches could obstruct the efforts of the partner in operating his train.

PROCEDURE. Before the instructions for operation of the trains, the subjects were introduced, both as a matter of social convention, and also to determine whether the subjects were acquainted with each other. Subjects previously acquainted were not included in the results. Subjects from Military Science and Air Science were not mixed in the pairings. The instructions for operation of the two trains were given during the first 20

minutes. Both trains were operated by the experimenter at this time, and both control panels were equally employed for demonstration. The subjects were permitted to ask questions during the demonstration. They were allowed 3 minutes to discuss the operation of the trains before the first trial.

The role assignments, when given, were given just prior to the first trial. In the following example, "X" is assigned the dominant role and "Y" is assigned the submissive role.

Mr. X, your train will be the passenger train, and Mr. Y, your train will be the freight. Mr. X, you are the dispatcher and you will arrange and order the solutions to the problem, and Mr. Y, your task is to carry out, on your board, Mr. X's directions. Remember, Mr. X, you are to plan and organize the solutions, while both of you are to carry out the operations of the trains on your respective boards. Mr. Y, your function is to carry out as well as you can the directions of Mr. X. You are permitted to make suggestions, but the final decision rests with Mr. X. Do you have any questions?

TASK. At the start of the first trial, the passenger train was on one siding, pointed so as to move counterclockwise around the track. The freight train was on the main track, pointed so as to move clockwise around the track. The prescribed route for the passenger train was different from the route for the freight, so that the subjects frequently operated the switches to the sidings. Each subject was responsible for the operation of the assigned train. The subjects' task was to complete as many mutually complete trips as possible around the track in a 3-minute trial period. There were six 3-minute trials, with a 1-minute rest period between each trial. The trains were not run simultaneously. The subjects were free to communicate with each other during the entire procedure, but could not ask the experimenter for directions once the first trial had begun.

The achievement score for a given trial was the number of *mutually* complete trips around the track, e.g., if one subject made 8 trips and his partner made 5, the achievement score for that trial was

and verbal intelligence. No significant differences between any of the seven groups on any of these variables was found. The means and standard deviations of achievement scores for Groups A through G on Trials 1 through 6 and the sums of trials are presented in Table 3.

TABLE 3. *Means and Standard Deviations of Achievement for Trials 1 through 6 and Sums of Trials*

GROUP		1	2	3	4	5	6	SUMS
A	M	18.9	23.9	26.8	29.8	30.3	30.8	160.4
	SD	7.0	5.3	5.4	2.1	2.8	2.0	19.0
B	M	14.1	19.8	25.7	26.2	26.7	28.7	141.2
	SD	6.7	5.5	4.0	6.0	5.5	4.4	20.1
C	M	15.4	23.2	27.4	27.7	28.8	30.8	153.3
	SD	7.5	5.6	4.3	6.5	5.4	1.6	18.7
D	M	13.6	20.4	22.5	26.4	29.2	30.8	142.9
	SD	7.7	7.0	8.1	4.5	3.0	2.0	22.8
E	M	12.0	20.3	20.7	26.9	26.6	29.2	142.0
	SD	8.7	6.8	3.5	4.2	6.0	3.3	23.0
F	M	10.0	18.1	21.2	24.1	27.3	29.5	130.2
	SD	6.9	6.7	4.0	7.8	4.4	2.5	13.8
G	M	7.3	14.8	15.9	22.4	27.6	28.4	116.4
	SD	5.7	4.9	7.0	5.1	2.4	4.9	13.5

TRIALS (header spanning columns 1–6)

10. The maximum possible score for a given trial was 32. After the last trial, each subject checked Leary's (1957) Interpersonal Check List (ICL) twice: as he saw himself and as he saw his partner. This 128-item check list can be scored for dominance. The entire procedure lasted one hour.

Results

ACHIEVEMENT. Groups A through G were first compared on age, the Responsibility and Self-Control scales of the CPI,

Table 4 contains the results of testing Hypothesis 1. The analysis of variance employed was that recommended by Edwards (1950) when there are repeated measurements of the same subjects. Before any of the analyses of variance were performed, Bartlett's test of homogeneity was performed, which proved to be insignificant in all cases.

There is a highly significant difference in achievement between Groups A, B, and G. Inspection of Table 3 shows that Group A was more productive than Group B, which in turn was more productive than Group G. The significant mean square between trials indicates a marked increase in performance across trials for all three groups. The significant interaction of trials by groups reflects the initial higher achievement and greater rapid improvement in performance of Groups A and B over Group G. The analysis of variance confirms Hypothesis 1.

TABLE 4. *Analysis of Variance for Hypothesis 1*

SOURCE	df	MS	F
Between Groups A, B, G	2	811.02	13.91 ***
Between Trials 1 through 6	5	1,081.78	47.85 ***
Trials × Groups	10	56.56	2.50 **
Between subjects in same group	27	58.31	
Pooled subjects × Trials	135	22.61	
Total	179		

** $p = .01$.
*** $p = .001$.

The results of another simple analysis of variance to test Hypothesis 2 are presented in Table 5. The hypothesis was not confirmed, since the mean square between Groups B, E, and F was not significant, and the empirical ordering by achievement was E, B, then F, instead of B, E, then F as predicted. Thus paired

TABLE 5. *Analysis of Variance for Hypothesis 2*

SOURCE	df	MS	F
Between Groups B, E, F	2	72.47	1.04
Between Trials 1 through 6	5	1,175.57	41.40 ***
Trials × Groups	10	19.96	.70
Between subjects in same group	27	69.72	
Pooled subjects × Trials	135		
Total	179		

*** $p = .001$.

dominant subjects (Group E) outperformed paired dominant and submissive subjects (Group B), who in turn outperformed paired submissive subjects (Group F). The mean square between trials was again highly significant, a finding attributable to the increasing achievement with successive trials for all three groups.

A complex analysis of variance was performed to test Hypothesis 3, since the two variables of pairings and role assignments were each varied in two ways. The results are presented in Table 6. The empirical rank order of the four groups was C, D, E, then F, which corresponds to the predicted rank order. The mean squares between pairings and between role assignments were both significant. The results confirm Hypothesis 3. The mean squares between trials was again significant.

TABLE 6. *Analysis of Variance for Hypothesis 3*

SOURCE	df	MS	F
Between pairings (Groups C, D vs. E, F)	1	205.35	5.68 *
Between roles (Groups C, E vs. D, F)	1	240.00	6.50 *
Between trials 1 through 6	5	1,570.95	43.48 ***
Trials × Pairings	5	44.95	1.24
Trials × Roles	5	8.88	.25
Pairs × Roles	1	.81	.02
Pairs × Roles × Trials	5	3.66	.10
Within Groups	216	36.13	
Total	239		

* $p = .05$.
*** $p = .001$.

Hypothesis 4 predicted the rank order in achievement of all seven groups. The predicted rank order was alphabetical, A through G, while the empirical rank order was A, C, D, E, B, F, and G. The rank order correlation between predicted and empirical rank orders was .78, significant at the .05 level (Table P in Siegel,

1956). This empirical rank order is based on the sums of trials. The rank order correlations, on the other hand, between predicted and empirical rank order calculated separately for Trials 1 through 6 were: .96 ($p = .01$), .64, .61, .75 ($p = .05$), .39, and .55, respectively.

A frequency count of the subjects' spontaneous requests for the maximum possible score shows that 59 of the total N of 70 dominant subjects made such a request, while 12 of the total N of 70 submissive subjects made this request (chi square is 55.6, $p < .001$). Also, 15 additional dominant subjects operated the trains without a partner, as did 15 additional submissive subjects. An F test between the achievement of these two groups was significant at the .05 level, with the dominant subjects achieving more than the submissive subjects. In Mann's (1959) review of the relation of personality and performance in small groups, dominance is found to be positively related to the number of task contributions.

PERCEPTION. Since each subject checked the ICL as he perceived himself and as he perceived his partner, it was possible to determine the subjects' own definition of the situation in terms of dominance of self and partner. The ICL dominance scores are presented in Table 7.

The *intra*group differences in perceived dominance are considered first. The test employed was the Wilcoxon matched-pairs signed-ranks test (Siegel, 1956). Differences that attained statistical significance are presented in Table 8. Inspection of Table 7 shows that for every group which includes a dominant subject, the dominant subjects' self-check mean is always higher than the check of his partner mean. This difference attains statistical significance within Groups A and B. Thus in terms of a comparison of group means, the submissive subjects consistently perceived themselves as less dominant than they perceived their part-

ners and the dominant subjects as more dominant, regardless of the roles assigned and regardless of whether the partner was dominant subject or a submissive subject.

TABLE 7. *Interpersonal Check List Dominance Scale Means and Standard Deviations of Pair Combinations for Check of Self and Check of Partner* ($N = 10$ for each pair combination)

GROUP	PAIR COMBINA-TION	SELF M	SELF SD	PARTNER M	PARTNER SD
A	D:d	64.4	3.8	55.8	4.3
	S:s	49.6	9.6	61.2	6.8
B	D:x	62.7	2.9	60.1	6.7
	S:x	49.0	8.5	58.3	7.7
C	D:d	62.9	3.1	60.8	4.7
	D:s	61.7	5.3	61.5	5.9
D	S:d	53.1	8.2	54.3	8.5
	S:s	51.3	7.1	54.1	8.7
E	D:x_1	59.0	3.8	58.9	8.6
	D:x_2	62.6	3.7	57.7	3.8
F	S:x_1	49.8	9.9	57.4	5.9
	S:x_2	49.2	8.1	53.9	8.8
G	D:s	58.0	3.9	56.7	3.5
	S:d	52.1	6.9	57.5	7.0

In those groups where a dominant subject and a submissive subject interact (Groups A, B, and G), the dominant subjects' mean check of their partners was always higher than their partners' mean self-checks. This difference attains statistical significance in Group B. In Groups A, B, and G, the submissive subjects' mean self-check was consistently lower than the dominant subjects' mean self-check. This difference is statistically significant in Groups A and B.

Several *inter*group comparisons were made, employing, for the most part, the data as presented in Table 7. The standard deviations of the submissive subjects' self-checks are significantly greater than the standard deviations of the dominant subjects' self-checks $(p < .01)$, employing the Wilcoxon matched-pairs signed-ranks test (Siegel, 1956). Thus in their self-checks, dominant subjects are a more homogeneous group than are the submissive subjects. The standard deviations of the dominant subjects' self-checks are significantly greater $(p < .05)$ than the standard deviations of the dominant subjects' checks of their partners. Dominant subjects are less uniform in their perceptions of their partners than they are of themselves. This relationship is not true of the submissive subjects.

TABLE 8. *Statistically Significant Intragroup Differences in Interpersonal Check List Dominance ($N = 10$ for each pair combination)*

GROUP	PAIR COMBINATION WITH HIGHER DOMINANCE [a]	PAIR COMBINATION WITH LOWER DOMINANCE [a]	p
A	D:d (s)	S:s (s)	.006
B	D:x (s)	S:x (s)	.006
A	D:d (s)	D:d (p)	.006
E	D:x_1 (s)	D:x_1 (p)	.05
A	S:s (p)	S:s (s)	.01
B	S:x (p)	S:x (s)	.02
B	D:x (p)	S:x (s)	.01

[a] (s) denotes self-check; (p) denotes check of partner.

A comparison of the self-check of the dominant subjects interacting with submissive subjects under three different conditions of role assignment (Groups A, B, and G) shows that the dominant subjects assigned a dominant role (Group A) perceived themselves as more dominant than the dominant subjects assigned no role (Group B), who in turn perceived themselves as more dominant than the dominant subjects assigned a submissive role (Group G). These three groups are

significantly different $(p < .02)$, employing the Friedman two-way analysis of variance (Siegel, 1956). A similar (statistically insignificant) rank order holds for the submissive subjects' check of their respective dominant partners in Groups A, B, and G, i.e., the submissive subjects in Group A rated their own dominant partners as more dominant than did the submissive subjects in Group B rate their own partners. The submissive subjects in Group B in turn rated their dominant partners as more dominant than the submissive subjects in Group G rated their own dominant partners.

Discussion

The general pattern of the achievement of the seven groups tends to validate the hypotheses, both in statistical significance of the differences between groups and in the direction and ranking of the predicted differences. The failure of the results to support Hypothesis 2 is due largely to the unpredicted high achievement of Group E. Group C also achieved higher scores than predicted in Hypothesis 4. Both of these groups have paired dominant subjects. The greater achievement of these two groups is in part due to the higher aspiration level of the dominant subjects, as previously noted.

With the exception of Group G, the assignment of dominant and submissive roles to any of the pairings resulted in an increase in achievement. The greatest absolute increase in achievement as a result of assignment of roles was between the dominant subject with a submissive subject pairings (Group A compared with Group B). The assignment of roles to paired dominant subjects or paired submissive subjects resulted in virtually the same absolute increase in achievement, i.e., the difference between Group C and Group E is similar to the difference between Group D and Group F. The assignment of roles gave a structure within which the subjects were able to function more effectively than the comparable pairings without role assignment.

There was a rapid rise in achievement across trials for all groups, so that by Trial 6 all groups were performing at virtually the same level. This similarity of level of performance by Trial 6 is in part an artifact of the task, since the top possible score for a trial was 32. Group G made the greatest absolute gain from Trial 1 through Trial 6. However, this is due in part to the low initial performance on Trial 1. If there had been, e.g., only three trials instead of six, the differences in achievement would have been greater and in the same direction. The major differences in achievement between groups appeared in the initial trials. The effect of the relative dominance of the partners as well as the assignment of roles is greatest here.

The ICL results indicate that the subjects' definition of the situation in terms of dominance closely reflected both the selection of the subjects high and low in personal dominance as well as the assignment of dominant and submissive roles. The degree of dominance ascribed to the partner, relative to the subjects' own dominance, is a function of the subjects' personal dominance. These findings are in accord with those of Leary (1957) and Naboisek (1953). The degree of dominance ascribed to the self and the partner varied in the direction of the assigned role.

These relationships between the subject's own dominance and the degree of dominance he ascribes to others are in contrast to a study (Altrocchi, 1959) employing the same pool of subjects as the present study, where the dominant subjects did not ascribe less dominance to others than the submissive subjects. One critical difference between these studies is that Altrocchi's subjects observed movies of social objects before rating them, whereas the subjects in the present study

interacted before rating each other, thus both communicating as well as evoking cues (Bruner and Tagiuri, 1954) of dominance or submissiveness.

Both the dominant and submissive subjects attributed considerable dominance to their partners, regardless of the partner's personal dominance. This finding may be attributed in part to the cooperative nature of the task as well as the fact that dominance is an approved trait for males, so that attributing dominance to another is a way of indicating social desirability (Edwards, 1957).

Generalizations from the achievement and perceptual findings are restricted in that the subjects were males chosen from a rather restricted socioeconomic-educational stratum of society as well as from the extremes of the distribution of dominance. However, the task is representative (Brunswik, 1947) of many life experiences, where two individuals work together in the pursuit of some objectively mutual goal under circumstances requiring a good deal of communication and cooperation.

Summary

This study related different pairings of dominant and submissive males, who interacted under various role assignment conditions, to their joint achievement in a cooperative problem solving situation. Predictions of differential achievement were derived from the thesis that the productivity of a pair depends upon the degree to which conditions permit each member to utilize his habitual patterns of interpersonal behavior.

A personality inventory was administered to 748 male university undergraduates. Volunteer subjects scoring very high or very low on a dominance scale were selected for participation in the cooperative task situation. The task was the operation of two model railroad trains for a series of six 3-minute trials. All groups were homogeneous with respect to age, and score on social responsibility, self-control, and vocabulary tests.

Of four predictions concerning the relative achievement of the seven interaction groups, three were confirmed. The most productive group was composed of pairs in which the dominant subject was assigned the dominant role and the submissive partner the submissive role. The least productive group was composed of these pairings with the roles reversed. Paired dominant subjects were more successful than paired submissive subjects, and both of these pairings achieved more when assigned roles. All groups showed significant increases in performance across trials.

The degree of dominance attributed to others was a function of the subjects' personal dominance. Dominant subjects perceived their partners as less dominant than themselves and submissive subjects perceived their partners as more dominant than themselves. The degree of dominance ascribed to the self and the partner varied in the direction of the assigned role.

It was concluded that congruence of role and habitual pattern within the subject and complementarity of patterns as between subjects were major determining variables in cooperative achievement. Sullivan's (1953) personality theory was employed in theoretical consideration of these results.

REFERENCES

1. Altrocchi, J. C. Dominance as a factor in interpersonal choice and perception. *J. abnorm. soc. Psychol.,* 1959, 3, 303–308.

2. Bruner, J. S., and R. Tagiuri. The perception of people. In G. Lindzey (Ed.), *Handbook of social psychology.* Cambridge, Mass.: Addison-Wesley, 1954. Ch. 17.

3. Brunswik, E. *Systematic and representative design of psychological experiments, with results in physical and social perception.* Berkeley: University of California Press, 1947.

4. Edwards, A. L. *Experimental design in psychological research.* New York: Rinehart, 1950.

5. Edwards, A. L. Social desirability and probability of endorsement of items in the Interpersonal Check List. *J. abnorm. soc. Psychol.,* 1957, 55, 394–396.

6. Ghiselli, E., and T. M. Lodahl, Patterns of managerial traits and group effectiveness. *J. abnorm. soc. Psychol.,* 1958, 57, 61–66.

7. Gough, H. G. *Manual for the California Psychological Inventory.* Palo Alto, Calif.: Consulting Psychologists Press, 1957.

8. Leary, T. *Interpersonal diagnosis of personality.* New York: Ronald, 1957.

9. Mann, R. D. A review of the relationships between personality and performance in small groups. *Psychol. Bull.,* 1959, 56, 241–270.

10. Naboisek, H. Validation of a method for predicting role expectations in group therapy. Unpublished doctoral dissertation, University of California, 1953.

11. Siegel, S. *Nonparametric statistics for the behavioral sciences.* New York: McGraw-Hill, 1956.

12. Sullivan, H. S. *The interpersonal theory of psychiatry.* New York: Norton, 1953.

13. Thorndike, R. L., and G. H. Gallup. Verbal intelligence of the American adult. *J. genet. Psychol.,* 1944, 30, 75–85.

14. Tuma, A. H. An exploration of certain methodological and client-counselor personality characteristics as determinants of learning in the counseling of college students. Unpublished doctoral dissertation, University of Maryland, 1955.

B · FACE-TO-FACE INTERACTION

EMBARRASSMENT AND SOCIAL ORGANIZATION

by Erving Goffman

An individual may recognize extreme embarrassment in others and even in himself by the objective signs of emotional disturbance: blushing, fumbling, stuttering, an unusually low- or high-pitched voice, quavering speech or breaking of the voice, sweating, blanching, blinking, tremor of the hand, hesitating or vacillating movement, absent-mindedness, and malapropisms. As Mark Baldwin remarked about shyness, there may be "a lowering of the eyes, bowing of the head, putting of hands behind the back, nervous fingering of the clothing or twisting of the fingers together, and stammering, with some incoherence of idea as expressed in speech." [1] There are also symptoms of a subjective kind: constriction of the diaphragm, a feeling of wobbliness, consciousness of strained and unnatural gestures, a dazed sensation, dryness of the mouth, and tenseness of the muscles. In cases of mild discomfiture these visible and invisible flusterings occur but in less perceptible form.

In the popular view it is only natural to be at ease during interaction, embarrassment being a regrettable deviation from the normal state. The individual, in fact, might say he felt "natural" or "unnatural" in the situation, meaning that he felt comfortable in the interaction or embarrassed in it. He who frequently becomes embarrassed in the presence of others is regarded as suffering from a foolish unjustified sense of inferiority and in need of therapy. [2]

To utilize the flustering syndrome in analyzing embarrassment, the two kinds of circumstance in which it occurs must first be distinguished. First, the individual may become flustered while engaged in a task of no particular value to him in itself, except that his long-range interests require him to perform it with safety, competence, or dispatch, and he fears he is inadequate to the task. Discomfort will be felt *in* the situation but in a sense not *for* it; in fact, often the individual will not be able to cope with it just because he is so anxiously taken

[1] James Mark Baldwin, *Social and Ethical Interpretations in Mental Development* (London, 1902), p. 212.

SOURCE: *American Journal of Sociology*, Vol. 62 (1956–1957), pp. 264–271.

[2] A sophisticated version is the psychoanalytical view that uneasiness in social interaction is a result of impossible expectations of attention based on unresolved expectations regarding parental support. Presumably an object of therapy is to bring the individual to see his symptoms in their true psychodynamic light, on the assumption that thereafter perhaps he will not need them (see Paul Schilder, "The Social Neurosis," *Psycho-Analytical Review*, XXV [1938], 1–19; Gerhart Piers and Milton Singer, *Shame and Guilt: A Psychoanalytical and a Cultural Study* [Springfield, Ill.: Charles C. Thomas, 1953], esp. p. 26; Leo Rangell, "The Psychology of Poise," *International Journal of Psychoanalysis*, XXXV [1954], 313–332; Sandor Ferenczi "Embarrassed Hands," in *Further Contributions to the Theory and Technique of Psychoanalysis* [London: Hogarth Press, 1950], pp. 315–316).

up with the eventualities lying beyond it. Significantly, the individual may become "rattled" although no others are present.

This paper will not be concerned with these occasions of instrumental chagrin but rather with the kind that occurs in clear-cut relation to the real or imagined presence of others. Whatever else, embarrassment has to do with the figure the individual cuts before others felt to be there at the time.[3] The crucial concern is the impression one makes on others in the present—whatever the long-range or unconscious basis of this concern may be. This fluctuating configuration of those present is a most important reference group.

Vocabulary of Embarrassment

A social encounter is an occasion of face-to-face interaction, beginning when individuals recognize that they have moved into one another's immediate presence and ending by an appreciated withdrawal from mutual participation. Encounters differ markedly from one another in purpose, social function, kind and number of personnel, setting, etc., and, while only conversational encounters will be considered here, obviously there are those in which no word is spoken. And yet, in our Anglo-American society at least, there seems to be no social encounter which cannot become embarrassing to one or more of its participants, giving rise to what is sometimes called an incident or false note. By listening for this dissonance, the sociologist can generalize about the ways in which interaction can go awry and, by implication, the conditions necessary for interaction to be right. At the same time he is given good evidence that all encounters are

[3] The themes developed in this paper are extensions of those in the writer's "On Face-Work," *Psychiatry*, XVIII (1955), 213–231; "Alienation from Interaction," *Human Relations* (forthcoming); and *The Presentation of Self in Everyday Life* (University of Edinburgh, Social Sciences Research Centre, Monograph No. 2 [Edinburgh, 1956]).

members of a single natural class, amenable to a single framework of analysis.

By whom is the embarrassing incident caused? *To* whom is it embarrassing? *For* whom is this embarrassment felt? It is not always an individual for whose plight participants feel embarrassment; it may be for pairs of participants who are together having difficulties and even for an encounter as a whole. Further, if the individual for whom embarrassment is felt happens to be perceived as a responsible representative of some faction or subgroup (as is very often the case in three-or-more-person interaction), then the members of this faction are likely to feel embarrassed and to feel it for themselves. But, while a *gaffe* or *faux pas* can mean that a single individual is at one and the same time the cause of an incident, the one who feels embarrassed by it, and the one for whom he feels embarrassment, this is not, perhaps, the typical case, for in these matters ego boundaries seem especially weak. When an individual finds himself in a situation which ought to make him blush, others present usually will blush with and for him, though he may not have sufficient sense of shame or appreciation of the circumstances to blush on his own account.

The words "embarrassment," "discomfiture," and "uneasiness" are used here in a continuum of meanings. Some occasions of embarrassment seem to have an abrupt orgasmic character; a sudden introduction of the disturbing event is followed by an immediate peak in the experience of embarrassment and then by a slow return to the preceding ease, all phases being encompassed in the same encounter. A bad moment thus mars an otherwise euphoric situation.

At the other extreme we find that some occasions of embarrassment are sustained at the same level throughout the encounter, beginning when the interaction begins and lasting until the encounter is terminated. The participants speak of an uncomfortable or uneasy situation, not of an embarrassing incident. In such case, of course, the whole encounter becomes for one or more of the parties an incident that causes embarrassment. Abrupt embarrassment may often be intense, while sustained uneasiness is more commonly mild, involving barely apparent flusterings. An encounter which seems likely to occasion abrupt embarrassment may, because of this, cast a shadow of sustained uneasiness upon the participants, transforming the entire encounter into an incident itself.

In forming a picture of the embarrassed individual, one relies on imagery from mechanics: equilibrium or self-control can be lost, balance can be overthrown. No doubt the physical character of flustering in part evokes this imagery. In any case, a completely flustered individual is one who cannot for the time being mobilize his muscular and intellectual resources for the task at hand, although he would like to; he cannot volunteer a response to those around him that will allow them to sustain the conversation smoothly. He and his flustered actions block the line of activity the others have been pursuing. He is present with them, but he is not "in play." The others may be forced to stop and turn their attention to the impediment; the topic of conversation is neglected, and energies are directed to the task of re-establishing the flustered individual, of studiously ignoring him, or of withdrawing from his presence.

To conduct one's self comfortably in interaction and to be flustered are directly opposed. The more of one, the less, on the whole, of the others; hence through contrast each mode of behavior can throw light upon the characteristics of the other. Face-to-face interaction in *any* culture seems to require just those capacities that flustering seems guaranteed to destroy. Therefore, events which lead to embarrassment and the methods for avoiding and dispelling it may provide a cross-cultural framework of sociological analysis.

The pleasure or displeasure a social encounter affords an individual, and the affection or hostility he feels for the participants, can have more than one relation to his composure or lack of it. Compliments, acclaim, and sudden reward may throw the recipient into a state of joyful confusion, while a heated quarrel can be provoked and sustained, although throughout the individual feels composed and in full command of himself. More important, there is a kind of comfort which seems a formal property of the situation and which has to do with the coherence and decisiveness with which the individual assumes a well-integrated role and pursues momentary objectives having nothing to do with the content of the actions themselves. A feeling of discomfiture per se seems always to be unpleasant, but the circumstances that arouse it may have immediate pleasant consequences for the one who is discomfited.

In spite of this variable relation between displeasure and discomfiture, to appear flustered, in our society at least, is considered evidence of weakness, inferiority, low status, moral guilt, defeat, and other unenviable attributes. And, as previously suggested, flustering threatens the encounter itself by disrupting the smooth transmission and reception by which encounters are sustained. When discomfiture arises from any of these sources, understandably the flustered individual will make some effort to conceal his state from the others present. The fixed smile, the nervous hollow laugh, the busy hands, the downward glance that conceals the expression of the eyes, have become famous as signs of attempting to conceal embarrassment. As Lord Chesterfield puts it:

They are ashamed in company, and so disconcerted that they do not know what they do, and try a thousand tricks to keep themselves in countenance; which tricks afterwards grow habitual to them. Some put their fingers to their nose, others scratch their head, others twirl their hats; in short, every awkward, ill-bred body has his tricks.[4]

[4] *Letters of Lord Chesterfield to His Son* (Everyman's ed.; New York: E. P. Dutton and Co., 1929), p. 80.

These gestures provide the individual with screens to hide behind while he tries to bring his feelings back into tempo and himself back into play.

Given the individual's desire to conceal his embarrassment, given the setting and his skill at handling himself, he may seem poised according to some obvious signs yet prove to be embarrassed according to less apparent ones. Thus, while making a public speech, he may succeed in controlling his voice and give an impression of ease, yet those who sit beside him on the platform may see that his hands are shaking or that facial tics are giving the lie to his composed front.

Since the individual dislikes to feel or appear embarrassed, tactful persons will avoid placing him in this position. In addition, they will often pretend not to know that he has lost composure or has grounds for losing it. They may try to suppress signs of having recognized his state or hide them behind the same kind of covering gesture that he might employ. Thus they protect his face and his feelings and presumably make it easier for him to regain composure or at least hold on to what he still has. However, just as the flustered individual may fail to conceal his embarrassment, those who perceive his discomfort may fail in their attempt to hide their knowledge, whereupon they all will realize that his embarrassment has been seen and that the seeing of it was something to conceal. When this point is reached, ordinary involvement in the interaction may meet a painful end. In all this dance between the concealer and the concealed-from, embarrassment presents the same problem and is handled in the same ways as any other offense against propriety.

There seems to be a critical point at which the flustered individual gives up trying to conceal or play down his uneasiness: he collapses into tears or paroxysms of laughter, has a temper tantrum, flies into a blind rage, faints, dashes to the nearest exit, or becomes rigidly immobile as when in panic. After that it is very difficult for him to recover composure. He answers to a new set of rhythms, characteristic of deep emotional experience, and can hardly give even a faint impression that he is at one with the others in interaction. In short, he abdicates his role as someone who sustains encounters. The moment of crisis is of course socially determined: the individual's breaking point is that of the group to whose affective standards he adheres. On rare occasions all the participants in an encounter may pass this point and together fail to maintain even a semblance of ordinary interaction. The little social system they created in interaction collapses; they draw apart or hurriedly try to assume a new set of roles.

The terms "poise," "sang-froid," and "aplomb," referring to the capacity to maintain one's own composure, are to be distinguished from what is called "graciousness," "tact," or "social skill," namely, the capacity to avoid causing one's self or others embarrassment. Poise plays an important role in communication, for it guarantees that those present will not fail to play their parts in interaction but will continue as long as they are in one another's presence to receive and transmit disciplined communications. It is no wonder that trial by taunting is a test that every young person passes through until he develops a capacity to maintain composure.[5] Nor should it come as a surprise that many of our games and sports commemorate the themes of composure and embarrassment: in poker, a dubious claim may win money for the player who can present it calmly; in judo, the maintenance and loss of composure are specifically

[5] One interesting form in which this trial has been institutionalized in America, especially in lower-class Negro society, is "playing the dozens" (see John Dollard, "Dialectic of Insult," *American Imago*, I [1939], 3–25; R. F. B. Berdie, "Playing the Dozens," *Journal of Abnormal and Social Psychology*, XLII [1947], 120–121). On teasing in general see S. J. Sperling, "On the Psychodynamics of Teasing," *Journal of the American Psychoanalytical Association*, I (1953), 458–483.

fought over; in cricket, self-command or "style" is supposed to be kept up under tension.

The individual is likely to know that certain special situations always make him uncomfortable and that he has certain "faulty" relationships which always cause him uneasiness. His daily round of social encounters is largely determined, no doubt, by his major social obligations, but he goes a little out of his way to find situations that will not be embarrassing and to by-pass those that will. An individual who firmly believes that he has little poise, perhaps even exaggerating his failing, is shy and bashful; dreading all encounters, he seeks always to shorten them or avoid them altogether. The stutterer is a painful instance of this, showing us the price the individual may be willing to pay for his social life.[6]

Causes of Embarrassment

Embarrassment has to do with unfulfilled expectations but not of a statistical kind. Given their social identities and the setting, the participants will sense what sort of conduct *ought* to be maintained as the appropriate thing, however much they may despair of its actually occurring. An individual may firmly expect that certain others will make him ill at ease, and yet this knowledge may increase his discomfiture instead of lessening it. An entirely unexpected flash of social engineering may save a situation, all the more effectively for being unanticipated.

The expectations relevant to embarrassment are moral, then, but embarrassment does not arise from the breach of *any* moral expectation, for some infractions give rise to resolute moral indignation and no uneasiness at all. Rather we should look to those moral obligations which surround the individual in only one of his

[6] Cf. H. J. Heltman, "Psycho-social Phenomena of Stuttering and Their Etiological and Therapeutic Implications," *Journal of Social Psychology*, IX (1938), 79–96.

capacities, that of someone who carries on social encounters. The individual, of course, is obliged to remain composed, but this tells us that things are going well, not why. And things go well or badly because of what is perceived about the social identities of those present.

During interaction the individual is expected to possess certain attributes, capacities, and information which, taken together, fit together into a self that is at once coherently unified and appropriate for the occasion. Through the expressive implications of his stream of conduct, through mere participation itself, the individual effectively projects this acceptable self into the interaction, although he may not be aware of it, and the others may not be aware of having so interpreted his conduct. At the same time he must accept and honor the selves projected by the other participants. The elements of a social encounter, then, consist of effectively projected claims to an acceptable self and the confirmation of like claims on the part of the others. The contributions of all are oriented to these and built up on the basis of them.

When an event throws doubt upon or discredits these claims, then the encounter finds itself lodged in assumptions which no longer hold. The responses the parties have made ready are now out of place and must be choked back, and the interaction must be reconstructed. At such times the individual whose self has been threatened (the individual *for* whom embarrassment is felt) and the individual who threatened him may both feel ashamed of what together they have brought about, sharing this sentiment just when they have reason to feel apart. And this joint responsibility is only right. By the standards of the wider society, perhaps only the discredited individual ought to feel ashamed; but, by the standards of the little social system maintained through the interaction, the discreditor is just as guilty as the person he discredits—sometimes more so, for, if he has been posing as a tactful man, in destroying another's image he destroys his own.

But of course the trouble does not stop with the guilty pair or those who have identified themselves sympathetically with them. Having no settled and legitimate object to which to play out their own unity, the others find themselves unfixed and discomfited. This is why embarrassment seems to be contagious, spreading, once started, in ever widening circles of discomfiture.

There are many classic circumstances under which the self projected by an individual may be discredited, causing him shame and embarrassment over what he has or appears to have done to himself and to the interaction. To experience a sudden change in status, as by marriage or promotion, is to acquire a self that other individuals will not fully admit because of their lingering attachment to the old self. To ask for a job, a loan of money, or a hand in marriage is to project an image of self as worthy, under conditions where the one who can discredit the assumption may have good reason to do so. To affect the style of one's occupational or social betters is to make claims that may well be discredited by one's lack of familiarity with the role.

The physical structure of an encounter itself is usually accorded certain symbolic implications, sometimes leading a participant against his will to project claims about himself that are false and embarrassing. Physical closeness easily implies social closeness, as anyone knows who has happened upon an intimate gathering not meant for him or who has found it necessary to carry on fraternal "small talk" with someone too high or low or strange to ever be a brother. Similarly, if there is to be talk, someone must initiate it, feed it, and terminate it; and these acts may awkwardly suggest rankings and power which are out of line with the facts.

Various kinds of recurrent encounters in a given society may share the assumption that participants have attained certain moral, mental, and physiognomic standards. The person who falls short may everywhere find himself inadvertently trapped into making implicit identity claims which he cannot fulfil. Compromised in every encounter which he enters, he truly wears the leper's bell. The individual who most isolates himself from social contacts may then be the least insulated from the demands of society. And, if he only imagines that he possesses a disqualifying attribute, his judgment of himself may be in error, but in the light of it his withdrawal from contact is reasonable. In any case, in deciding whether an individual's grounds for shyness are real or imaginary, one should seek not for "justifiable" disqualifications but for the much larger range of characteristics which actually embarrass encounters.

In all these settings the same fundamental thing occurs: the expressive facts at hand threaten or discredit the assumptions a participant finds he has projected about his identity.[7] Thereafter those present find they can neither do without the assumptions nor base their own responses upon them. The inhabitable reality shrinks until everyone feels "small" or out of place.

A complication must be added. Often important everyday occasions of embarrassment arise when the self projected is somehow confronted with another self which, though valid in other contexts, cannot be here sustained in harmony with

[7] In addition to his other troubles, he has discredited his implicit claim to poise. He will feel he has cause, then, to become embarrassed over his embarrassment, even though no one present may have perceived the earlier stages of his discomfiture. But a qualification must be made. When an individual, receiving a compliment, blushes from modesty, he may lose his reputation for poise but confirm a more important one, that of being modest. Feeling that his chagrin is nothing to be ashamed of, his embarrassment will not lead him to be embarrassed. On the other hand, when embarrassment is clearly expected as a reasonable response, he who fails to become embarrassed may appear insensitive and thereupon become embarrassed because of this appearance.

the first. Embarrassment, then, leads us to the matter of "role segregation." Each individual has more than one role, but he is saved from role dilemma by "audience segregation," for, ordinarily, those before whom he plays out one of his roles will not be the individuals before whom he plays out another, allowing him to be a different person in each role without discrediting either.

In every social system, however, there are times and places where audience segregation regularly breaks down and where individuals confront one another with selves incompatible with the ones they extend to each other on other occasions. At such times, embarrassment, especially the mild kind, clearly shows itself to be located not in the individual but in the social system wherein he has his several selves.

Domain of Embarrassment

Having started with psychological considerations, we have come by stages to a structural sociological point of view. Precedent comes from social anthropologists and their analyses of joking and avoidance. One assumes that embarrassment is a normal part of normal social life, the individual becoming uneasy not because he is personally maladjusted but rather because he is not; presumably anyone with his combination of statuses would do likewise. In an empirical study of a particular social system, the first object would be to learn what categories of persons become embarrassed in what recurrent situations. And the second object would be to discover what would happen to the social system and the framework of obligations if embarrassment had not come to be systematically built into it.

An illustration may be taken from the social life of large social establishments —office buildings, schools, hospitals, etc. Here, in elevators, halls, and cafeterias, at newsstands, vending machines, snack counters, and entrances, all members are often formally on an equal if distant footing.[8] In Benoit-Smullyan's terms, situs, not status or locus, is expressed.[9] Cutting across these relationships of equality and distance is another set of relationships, arising in work teams whose members are ranked by such things as prestige and authority and yet drawn together by joint enterprise and personal knowledge of one another.

In many large establishments, staggered work hours, segregated cafeterias, and the like help to insure that those who are ranked and close in one set of relations will not have to find themselves in physically intimate situations where they are expected to maintain equality and distance. The democratic orientation of some of our newer establishments, however, tends to throw differently placed members of the same work team together at places such as the cafeteria, causing them uneasiness. There is no way for them to act that does not disturb one of the two basic sets of relations in which they stand to each other. These difficulties are especially likely to occur in elevators, for there individuals who are not quite on chatting terms must remain for a time too close together to ignore the opportunity for informal talk—a problem solved, of course, for some, by special executive elevators. Embarrassment, then, is built into the establishment ecologically.

Because of possessing multiple selves

[8] This equal and joint membership in a large organization is often celebrated annually at the office party and in amateur dramatic skits, this being accomplished by pointedly excluding outsiders and scrambling the rank of insiders.

[9] Émile Benoit-Smullyan, "Status, Status Types, and Status Interrelations," *American Sociological Review*, IX (1944), 151–161. In a certain way the claim of equal institutional membership is reinforced by the ruling in our society that males ought to show certain minor courtesies to females; all other principles, such as distinctions between racial groups and occupational categories, must be suppressed. The effect is to stress situs and equality.

the individual may find he is required both to be present and to not be present on certain occasions. Embarrassment ensues: the individual finds himself being torn apart, however gently. Corresponding to the oscillation of his conduct is the oscillation of his self.

Social Function of Embarrassment

When an individual's projected self is threatened during interaction, he may with poise suppress all signs of shame and embarrassment. No flusterings, or efforts to conceal having seen them, obtrude upon the smooth flow of the encounter; participants can proceed as if no incident has occurred.

When situations are saved, however, something important may be lost. By showing embarrassment when he can be neither of two people, the individual leaves open the possibility that in the future he may effectively be either.[10] His role in the current interaction may be sacrificed, and even the encounter itself, but he demonstrates that, while he cannot present a sustainable and coherent self on this occasion, he is at least disturbed by the fact and may prove worthy at another time. To this extent, embarrassment is not an irrational impulse breaking through socially prescribed behavior but part of this orderly behavior itself. Flusterings are an extreme example of that important class of acts which are usually quite spontaneous and yet no less required and obligatory than one self-consciously performed.

[10] A similar argument was presented by Samuel Johnson in his piece "Of Bashfulness," *The Rambler* (1751), No. 139: "It generally happens that assurance keeps an even pace with ability; and the fear of miscarriage, which hinders our first attempts, is gradually dissipated as our skill advances towards certainty of success. The bashfulness, therefore, which prevents disgrace, that short temporary shame which secures us from the danger of lasting reproach, cannot be properly counted among our misfortunes."

Behind a conflict in identity lies a more fundamental conflict, one of organizational principle, since the self, for many purposes, consists merely of the application of legitimate organizational principles to one's self. One builds one's identity out of claims which, if denied, give one the right to feel righteously indignant. Behind the apprentice's claims for a full share in the use of certain plant facilities there is the organizational principle: all members of the establishment are equal in certain ways qua members. Behind the specialist's demand for suitable financial recognition there is the principle that the type of work, not mere work, determines status. The fumblings of the apprentice and the specialist when they reach the Coca-Cola machine at the same time express an incompatibility of organizational principles.[11]

The principles of organization of any social system are likely to come in conflict at certain points. Instead of permitting the conflict to be expressed in an encounter, the individual places himself between the opposing principles. He sacrifices his identity for a moment, and sometimes the encounter, but the principles are preserved. He may be ground between opposing assumptions, thereby preventing direct friction between them, or he may be almost pulled apart, so that principles with little relation to one another may operate together. Social structure gains elasticity; the individual merely loses composure.

[11] At such moments "joshing" sometimes occurs. It is said to be a means of releasing the tension caused either by embarrassment or by whatever caused embarrassment. But in many cases this kind of banter is a way of saying that what occurs now is not serious or real. The exaggeration, the mock insult, the mock claims—all these reduce the seriousness of conflict by denying reality to the situation. And this, of course, in another way, is what embarrassment does. It is natural, then, to find embarrassment and joking together, for both help in denying the same reality.

C · EDUCATIONAL PERFORMANCE

ORIENTATION TO EDUCATION AS A FACTOR IN THE
SCHOOL MALADJUSTMENT OF LOWER-CLASS CHILDREN

by Jackson Toby

Even taking an extremely crude index of school achievement, that of grade placement, *for every age level* the average grade of middle-class urban children is higher than that of lower-class children. (See Tables 1, 2, and 3.) These differences can be observed at 7 and 8 years of age as well as at 17. Apparently whatever produces the difference starts operating to differentiate lower-class from middle-class children from the early grades. Another way of looking at class selectivity of the educational process is to observe the proportion of lower-class boys in high school a generation ago (Tables 4 and 5) or in college today.[1]

Why are middle-class children more successful in their studies? Why do lower-class children drop out at younger ages and complete fewer grades? One hypothesis is that school teachers are middle-class in their values, if not in their origins, and penalize those students who do *not* exhibit the middle-class traits of cleanliness, punctuality, and neatness or who *do* exhibit the lower-class traits of uninhibited sexuality and aggression.[2] Some social sci-

entists believe that lower-class children, even though they may have the intellectual potentialities for high levels of academic achievement, lose interest in school or never become interested because they resent the personal rejection of their teachers. Such rejection is, they say, motivated by the teachers' mistaken notion that lower-class children are deliberately defying them. Davis and Havighurst show that children are the prisoners of their experience and that lower-class children behave the way they do, not because of any initial desire to defy school authorities, but rather because of their lower-class childhood training.[3]

According to this hypothesis, teacher rejection makes the lower-class boy resentful and rebellious. His attitude is, "If you don't like me, I won't cooperate." Unfortunately for him, however, school achievement is related to later occupational advancement. Failure to cooperate with the teacher cuts off the lower-class boy from a business or professional career. Professor August Hollingshead describes what happens to lower-class boys from a small town in Illinois who withdraw from school to escape the psychic punishment meted out by the teachers and upper-class children.

The withdrawees' job skills are limited to what they have learned from

[1] Helen B. Goetsch, *Parental Income and College Opportunities* (New York: Teachers College, Columbia University, Contributions to Education, No. 795, 1940).

[2] W. L. Warner, R. J. Havighurst, and M. B. Loeb, *Who Shall Be Educated?* (New York: Harper and Brothers, 1944).

SOURCE: *Social Forces,* Vol. 35 (1957), pp. 259–266.

[3] Allison Davis and Robert J. Havighurst, *Father of the Man* (Boston: Houghton Mifflin, 1947).

contact with parents, relatives, friends, and through observations and personal experience, largely within the community; no withdrawee has any technical training for any type of job; furthermore, few have plans to acquire it in the future. . . . The boys have some acquaintance with working on farms, washing cars, loading and unloading grain, repairing cars, driving trucks, do-

ployer gives rise to a drift from job to job.[4]

The association between education, job levels, and prestige in the social structure is so high that the person with more education moves into the high-ranking job and the person with little education into the low-ranking job. Furthermore, and this is the crucial fact from the viewpoint of the person's

TABLE 1. *Median Years of School Completed by Native White Boys by Monthly Rental Value of Home and by Age in Cities of 250,000 Inhabitants or More, 1940*

	MONTHLY RENTAL VALUE OF HOME						
AGE	Under $10	$10–$14	$15–$19	$20–$29	$30–$49	$50–$74	$75 and over
7 years	1.3	1.5	1.6	1.7	1.7	1.7	1.7
8 years	2.1	2.4	2.4	2.5	2.6	2.6	2.7
9 years	2.8	3.2	3.3	3.4	3.5	3.7	3.7
10 years	3.6	4.0	4.2	4.4	4.5	4.6	4.7
11 years	4.4	4.9	5.1	5.3	5.5	5.6	5.6
12 years	5.4	5.7	6.0	6.2	6.5	6.6	6.7
13 years	6.0	6.7	7.1	7.2	7.5	7.7	7.8
14 years	7.2	7.8	7.9	8.2	8.5	8.7	8.8
15 years	8.3	8.5	8.8	9.2	9.4	9.6	9.8
16 years	8.6	9.3	9.6	9.8	10.3	10.5	10.6
17 years	9.4	9.9	10.2	10.7	10.7	11.3	11.5

SOURCE: Bureau of the Census, *Sixteenth Census of the United States (1940), Monograph on Population Education: Educational Attainment of Children by Rental Value of Home* (Washington: Government Printing Office, 1945), p. 3.

ing janitor work, clerking in stores, and odd jobs, but their lack of training, job skills, and experience combined with their youth and family backgrounds severely limit their job opportunities. These factors, along with need, force them to take whatever jobs they can find. . . . Menial tasks, long hours, low pay, and little consideration from the employer produces discontent and frustration, which motivate the young worker to seek another job, only to realize after a few days or weeks that the new job is like the old one. This desire for a more congenial job, better pay, shorter hours, and a better em-

relation to the social structure, each tends to remain in the job channel in which he starts as a young worker. This is especially true if he has less than a high school education; then he starts as an unskilled menial and has few opportunities in later years to change to skilled labor, business, or the professions. Therefore, his chances to be promoted up through the several levels of the job channel in which he functions are severely limited. As the years pass, his position in the economic system becomes fixed, and another gen-

[4] August B. Hollingshead, *Elmtown's Youth* (New York: John Wiley and Sons, 1949), p. 369.

eration has become stable in the class structure.[5]

In other words, Professor Warner and his colleagues point out that the American public school teacher is suspicious of lower-class children and unwilling to give them a chance. If they withdraw from school to escape the pressures, they must surrender their chance to realize the American dream: social mobility.

TABLE 2. *Distribution of Retarded and Nonretarded Pupils According to Occupational Status of Father (Sims' Scale) in the New York City Public Schools, 1931–1932*

FATHER'S OCCUPATIONAL STATUS	TOTAL	SLOW PROG-RESS	NOR-MAL PROG-RESS	RAPID PROG-RESS
Total	100.0	100.0	100.0	100.0
Professional	3.7	1.3	4.4	6.2
Clerical	19.8	11.2	19.4	31.9
Artisan	24.0	22.0	25.5	24.8
Skilled laborer	36.9	43.8	35.1	29.8
Unskilled laborer	15.6	21.7	15.6	7.3

Another hypothesis attributes the inferior performance of lower-class children at school *directly* to the economic disabilities of their families. John is a poor student because he lacks the nourishing food for sustained effort or because he is compelled to work after school instead of doing his homework; or he is a truant because he is ashamed to appear at school in ragged clothes or torn shoes. Like the rejecting teacher hypothesis, the economic disability hypothesis treats the child as essentially passive. According to both, he is victimized by a situation over which he has no control, in the one case by teachers who reject him, in the other by an economic system which does not allow him the opportunities to realize his ambitions.

But it is not at all clear that the average lower-class child has academic aspirations

[5] *Ibid.*, p. 388.

which are thwarted by his teachers or his economic circumstances. Studies of withdrawees from high school show that the majority leave school with no regrets; some volunteer the information that they hate school and are delighted to get through with it.[6] These data suggest that some lower-class children view the school as a burden, not an opportunity. Perhaps it is not only teacher prejudice and his parents' poverty that handicap the lower-class child at school. *He* brings certain attitudes and experiences to the school situation just as his teacher does.

Whereas the middle-class child learns a socially adaptive fear of receiving poor grades in school, of being aggressive toward the teacher, of fighting, of cursing, and of having early sex relations, the slum child learns to fear quite different social acts. His gang

TABLE 3. *Percentage Distribution of Pupils According to Father's Occupational Status and Pupils' Progress Status, 1931–1932*

FATHER'S OCCUPATIONAL STATUS	PUPILS' PROGRESS STATUS			
	Total	Slow	Nor-mal	Rapid
Professional	100.0	13.2	39.7	47.1
Clerical	100.0	21.3	32.7	46.0
Artisan	100.0	34.6	35.6	29.8
Skilled laborer	100.0	45.0	31.9	23.1
Unskilled laborer	100.0	53.0	33.6	13.4

SOURCE FOR TABLES 2 AND 3: Eugene A. Nifenecker, *Statistical Reference Data Relating to Problems of Overageness, Educational Retardation, Non-Promotion, 1900–1934* (New York: Board of Education, 1937), p. 233.

[6] Howard C. Seymour, The Characteristics of Pupils Who Leave School Early—A Comparative Study of Graduates with Those Who are Eliminated Before High School Graduation, unpublished Ph.D. dissertation, Harvard University, 1940; Harold J. Dillon, *Early School Leavers* (New York: National Child Labor Committee, 1949).

teaches him to fear being taken in by the teacher, of being a softie with her. To study homework seriously is literally a disgrace. Instead of boasting of

TABLE 4. *High School Attendance of the Children of Fathers Following Various Occupations, Seattle, St. Louis, Bridgeport, and Mount Vernon, 1919–1921*

PARENTAL OCCUPATION	NUMBER IN HIGH SCHOOL FOR EVERY 1,000 MEN 45 YEARS OF AGE OR OVER
Proprietors	341
Professional service	360
Managerial service	400
Commercial service	245
Building trades	145
Machine trades	169
Printing trades	220
Miscellaneous trades	103
Transportation service	157
Public service	173
Personal service	50
Miners, lumber workers, and fishermen	58
Common labor	17

good marks in school, one conceals them, if he ever receives any. The lower-class individual fears not to be thought a street-fighter; it is a suspicious and dangerous social trait. He fears not to curse. If he cannot claim early sex relations his virility is seriously questioned.[7]

Of course, not all lower-class children have a hostile orientation to the school. As a matter of fact, the dramatic contrast between the educational attainments of drafted enlisted men in the two World Wars show that the public schools are being used more and more; and some of this increase undoubtedly represents lower-class youths who eagerly take advantage

[7] Allison Davis, *Social Class Influences on Learning* (Cambridge, Massachusetts: Harvard University Press, 1949), p. 30.

of educational opportunities.[8] Still, many lower-class children do *not* utilize the educational path to social advancement.[9]

TABLE 5. *Percentage of Students in Each of Two High School Years From Each of the Occupational Groups, 1919–1921*

PARENTAL OCCUPATION	FRESHMAN CLASS	SENIOR CLASS
Proprietors	17.7	22.9
Professional service	7.7	12.5
Managerial service	15.4	19.1
Commercial service	8.6	11.1
Clerical service	5.9	5.9
Agricultural service	2.3	2.3
Artisan-proprietors	4.4	3.5
Building trades	8.8	5.3
Machine trades	8.3	4.6
Printing trades	1.0	0.8
Miscellaneous trades	4.8	2.3
Transportation service	6.2	3.6
Public service	1.7	1.1
Personal service	1.4	0.9
Miners, lumber workers, and fishermen	0.5	0.3
Common labor	1.8	0.6
Unknown	3.5	3.2

SOURCE FOR TABLES 4 AND 5: George S. Counts, *The Selective Character of American Secondary Education* (Chicago: University of Chicago Press, 1922), pp. 33, 37.

[8] 41 percent of the selectees of World War II were high school graduates or better, as contrasted with only 9 percent in World War I. Samuel A. Stouffer and others, *The American Soldier* (Princeton: Princeton University Press, 1949), I, 59. Compulsory school attendance laws may have something to do with this difference, but the average age of high school graduation is beyond the age of compulsory attendance in most states.

[9] The assumption here is that the goal of success is sufficiently widespread in the American ethos and the penalties for criminal deviance sufficiently great that the failure to utilize a legitimate channel of social mobility can usually be explained as due (1) to a failure on the part of the individual to *perceive* that channel as feasible for him

Apparently, one reason for this is a chronic dissatisfaction with school which begins early in their academic careers. Why should middle-class children "take to" school so much better?

To begin with, it should not be taken for granted that any child, whatever his socio-economic origin, will find school a pleasant experience from the very first grade. On the contrary, there is reason to believe that starting school is an unpleasant shock. The average child cannot help but perceive school as an invasion of his freedom, an obligation imposed on him by adults. Forced to come at set times, to restrain his conversation so that the teacher may instruct the class as a group, he may not see any relationship between what she asks him to learn and what he might be interested in doing. And in terms of maximizing his pleasure at the time, he is quite right. Except for kindergarten and ultra-progressive schools, the curriculum is a discipline imposed on the pupil rather than an extension and development of his own interests. This is not to condemn the school system. But it does point up the problematic nature of school adjustment.

Middle-class parents make it quite clear that school is nothing to be trifled with. They have probably graduated at least from high school, and their child is aware that they *expect* him to do the same or better. If he has difficulty with his studies, they are eager (and competent) to help him. And not only do his *parents* expect him to apply himself to his studies, so do

his *friends* and *their* parents. He is caught in a neighborhood pattern of academic achievement in much the same way some lower-class boys are caught in a neighborhood pattern of truancy and delinquency. This concern with education is insurance against the child's fall in social status. Middle-class parents convey to their children subtly or explicitly that they must make good in school if they want to go on being middle-class. This may be phrased in terms of preparation for a "suitable" occupation (an alternative to a stigmatized occupation such as manual labor), in terms of a correlation between a "comfortable" standard of living and educational level, or in terms of the honorific value of education for its own sake.

Middle-class parents constantly reinforce the authority and prestige of the teacher, encouraging the child to respect her and compete for her approval. The teacher makes a good parent-surrogate for him because his parents accept her in this role.[10] They urge him to value the gold stars she gives out and the privilege of being her monitor. But although the middle-class child's initial motivation to cooperate with the teacher may spring from his parents, motivation functionally autonomous of parental pressure usually develops to supplement it.[11] Part of this new motivation may be the intrinsic interest of the subject matter, or at least

and to define it as an opportunity, (2) to objective disabilities which cannot be overcome by effort, or (3) to his perception of other and better opportunities. We assume, therefore, that the lower-class subculture (uncongenial to social mobility) has its roots in a sour-grapes reaction. This does *not* mean that every lower-class boy yearns for higher socio-economic status at some time or other in his life. Some of them have been socialized into the sour-grapes tradition before having the experience on which they might personally conclude that the grapes are sour.

[10] Professor Green maintains that the middle-class boy is more closely supervised by his mother than the lower-class boy and that this "personality absorption" creates a dependence on adult authority much greater than that of the less well supervised lower-class boy. If this theory were accepted, we would thus find additional reason for the relative tractability and cooperativeness of the middle-class boy in school. Arnold W. Green, "The Middle Class Male Child and Neurosis," *American Sociological Review*, XI (1946), 31–41.

[11] See Gordon W. Allport, *Personality* (New York: Henry Holt and Company, 1937), pp. 191–206, for a discussion of functional autonomy.

some of it, once he has gotten well along in his course. *Learning* to read may be a disagreeable chore; but the time soon comes when interesting stories are made accessible by the development of reading skill. An even more important source of motivation favorable to school is the recognition he gets in the form of high marks. He learns that scholastic competition is somewhat analogous to the social and economic competition in which his parents participate. The object of scholastic competition is to win the approving attention of the teacher, to skip grades, and to remain always in the "bright" classes. (In grade school the "bright" and the "dull" classes take approximately the same work, but pupils and teachers have no difficulty in separating the high prestige groups. In high school, "commercial," "trade," and "general" courses have different curricula from the high prestige "college" course. Again, there is consensus among the students as well as the teachers that the non-college courses are for those who are not "college material.") [12]

Of course it is not competition alone that gives the middle-class child an emotional investment in continued scholastic effort; it is the *position* he achieves in that competition. Apparently his pre-school training prepares *him* much better for scholastic competition than his lower-class classmate.[13] His parents mingle with

[12] George S. Counts, *The Selective Character of American Secondary Education* (Chicago: University of Chicago Press, 1922), shows the middle-class orientation of the "college" course; see also R. E. Eckert and T. O. Marshall, *When Youth Leaves School* (New York: The Regents' Inquiry, McGraw-Hill, 1938), p. 67.

[13] Millie C. Almy, *Children's Experiences prior to First Grade and Success in Beginning Reading* (New York: Teachers College, Columbia University, Contributions to Education, No. 954, 1949); Dorris M. Lee, *The Importance of Reading for Achieving in Grades Four, Five, and Six* (New York: Teachers College, Columbia University, Contributions to Education, No. 556, 1933).

lawyers, accountants, businessmen, and others who in their day-to-day activities manipulate symbols. In the course of conversation these people use a sizeable vocabulary including many abstractions of high order. He unconsciously absorbs these concepts in an effort to understand his parents and their friends. He is stimulated in this endeavor by the rewards he receives from his parents when he shows verbal precociousness. These rewards are not necessarily material or conscious. The attention he receives as a result of a remark insightful beyond his years, the pride of his mother shows in repeating a bright response of his to her friends, these are rewards enough. This home background is valuable preparation for successful competition in school. For, after all, school subjects are designed to prepare for exactly the occupational level to which his parents are already oriented. Hence he soon *achieves* in school a higher than average status. (See Tables 1, 2, and 3.) To maintain this status intact (or improve it) becomes the incentive for further effort, which involves him deeper and deeper in the reward and punishment system of the school. Thus, *his success cumulates and generates the conditions for further success.*

A similar conclusion was reached after a study of the success and failure of children in certain nonacademic activities. Dr. Anderson concluded that success and practice mutually reinforce one another, producing remarkable differentiations in performance.

> . . . a child is furnished from early life with the opportunity to hammer nails. In the course of the next ten or fifteen years, the child has 100,000 opportunities to hammer nails, whereas a second child in the same period of time has only ten or fifteen opportunities to hammer nails. At the age of twenty, we may be tremendously impressed with the ease and accuracy with which the first child hammers nails and likewise

with the awkwardness and incapacity of the second child. We speak of the first child as an expert and the second child as a boob with respect to the nail hitting situation, and we may naively ascribe the ability of the first child to an inherited ability because its appearance is so inexplicable in comparison with the lack of ability of the second child.[14]

The most significant fact which comes out of these observations is the fact that if we take a particular child and record his relationship to the group, we find that in ninety-five percent of the situations with which he is presented in the play situation, he is the dominating or leading individual, whereas another child under the same conditions is found to be in the leading position only five percent of the time.

. . . the social reactions of these particular children . . . may be the product of hereditary factors, environmental factors, more rapid rate of development, or a large number of factors combined. The important fact for our discussion is that within a constant period one child is getting approximately twenty times as much specific practice in meeting social situations in a certain way as is a second child. Life is something like a game of billiards in which the better player gets more opportunity for practice and the poorer player less.[15]

For the average middle-class child, the effective forces in his life situation form a united front to urge upon him a favorable orientation to school. Of course, this may not be sufficient to produce good

[14] John E. Anderson, "The Genesis of Social Reactions in the Young Child," *The Unconscious: A Symposium*, ed. by E. S. Dummer (New York: Alfred A. Knopf, 1928), pp. 83–84.
[15] *Ibid.*, pp. 81–82.

school adjustment. He may not have the native intelligence to perform up to the norm. Or he may have idiosyncratic experiences that alienate him from scholastic competition. But, apparently, for the *average* middle-class child, this favorable orientation, combined with the intellectual abilities cultivated in his social milieu, results in satisfactory performance in the school situation.

The other side of the coin is the failure of some lower-class children to develop the kind of orientation which will enable them to overcome the initial frustration of school discipline.[16] To begin with, the parents of the lower-class child may not support the school as do middle-class parents. His parents probably do not have much education themselves, and, if not, they cannot very well make meaningful to him subjects that they do not themselves understand. Neither are they able to help him surmount academic stumbling blocks. Even more important, they lack the incentive to encourage him in and praise him for school accomplishment at that critical early period when he finds school new and strange and distasteful. Almost the same reasoning can be applied to the inculcation of a cooperative attitude toward school in the child as has been applied to an acceptant attitude toward toilet training. If the parents convey to the child their eagerness to have him adjust to irksome school discipline, he will probably accept it to please them and retain their love just as he learned to urinate and defecate at appropriate times and places. But toilet training and school adjustment training differ in an important particular. Parents *must* toilet train the child because permitting him to soil himself at will is a constant and immediate nuisance.

The consequences of a child's disinterest in school may also be unpleasant, both

[16] At this point we are abstracting from such situational considerations as teacher rejection, the economic resources of the family and native capacity. We are considering only the orientations of the boy himself.

for him and for his parents, but it is not immediate. In the short run, allowing him to neglect school may be the least troublesome course for his parents to take. If they are neutral or antagonistic toward school, a result (1) of the esoteric nature of the curriculum from the point of view of skills cultivated and appreciated in the lower-class milieu and (2) of their failure to see the relevance of education to occupational advancement into a higher socio-economic class, they do not *have* to give the kind of support to the school given by middle-class parents. There is no reason to assume that the value of education is self-evident. For those lower-class people who have lost hope in social mobility, the school is a symbol of a competition in which they do not believe they can succeed. If they themselves have given up, will they necessarily encourage their children to try to be better?

Moreover, coming as he does from a social stratum where verbal skills are not highly developed, the lower-class child finds school more difficult than does his middle-class contemporary. His father, a carpenter or a factory worker, manipulates concrete objects rather than symbols in his occupational role. In so far as he learns from his father, he is more likely to learn how to "fix things" than the importance of a large vocabulary.[17] This learning does not help him with his school work, for school tends to give a competitive advantage to those with verbal facility.

This disadvantage with respect to verbal skills may account for the poorer showing of lower-class children on standard intelligence tests.[18]

. . . the cultural bias of the standard tests of intelligence consists in their having fixed upon only those types of mental behavior in which the higher and middle socio-economic groups are superior. In those particular areas of behavior, the tests might conceivably be adequate measures of mental differences among individual children within the more privileged socio-economic groups. But they do not measure the comparative over-all mental behavior of the higher and lower socio-economic groups, because they do not use problems which are equally familiar and motivating to all such groups.[19]

In other words, middle-class children have an advantage because they are more familiar with the sort of problems that occur on the tests. This does not necessarily mean that the intelligence tests are invalid. It depends upon what the investigator thinks he is measuring. If he believes he is getting at "innate" ability, abstracted from cultural milieu and idiosyncratic learning, he is naive. An intelligence test is a valid measure of the native intellectual ability of an individual only under special circumstances, one of these being that the respondent's experience is similar to that of the group on which the test was standardized. Thus, a Navaho boy who scores 80 on the Stanford-Binet (Revised Form) may be unusually intelligent. Until a test is designed to tap the experiences of Navahos, there exists no reference point about which to assess superiority and inferiority.[20]

However, it is not only the *content* of the intelligence test that gives middle-class urban children a better chance at high scores. It is the *structure* of the test situation. Even if we could find items equally familiar or unfamiliar to everyone taking the test, differential interest in

[17] Of course this is a matter of degree. The lower-class boy acquires verbal skills but not on so high a level as the middle-class boy.

[18] Walter S. Neff, "Socio-economic Status and Intelligence: a Critical Survey," *Psychological Bulletin*, XXXV (1938), 727–757.

[19] Allison Davis, *op. cit.*, p. 48.

[20] Dorothy Leighton and Clyde Kluckhohn, *Children of the People* (Cambridge, Massachusetts: Harvard University Press, 1947), pp. 148–155.

solving abstract problems would work against the lower-class student.

> ... finding completely unfamiliar problems is not a possible choice, because such problems (namely, those involving some relationship between esoteric geometrical figures) do not arouse as great interest or as strong a desire to achieve a solution among low socio-economic groups as among high groups. The reason is clear: such an unrealistic problem can arouse the child's desire to achieve a solution only if the child has been trained to evaluate highly any and all success in tests. No matter how unreal and purposeless the problem may seem, the average child in a high socio-economic group will work hard to solve it, if his parents, his teacher, or other school officers expect him to try hard. The average slum child, however, will usually react negatively to any school test, and especially to a test whose problems have no relation to his experience.[21]

However justified the criticisms of the intelligence test as an instrument measuring native intellectual ability, it is highly predictive of academic accomplishment. A student with a high I.Q. score does better in his studies, on the average, than one with a low I.Q. score.[22] Hence the discrepancy between the scores of lower-class students and of middle-class students is an index of the former's disadvantage in the school situation.

One possible response of the lower-class child to his disadvantages in the school situation is to increase his efforts. But his initial orientation drives him in the opposite direction. He is more likely to respond to competitive failure by going on strike psychologically, neglecting

his homework, paying no attention in class, annoying the teacher. Uninterested in the curriculum, he learns as little as he can. Instead of a situation where the student and the teacher work toward a common goal, the development of the student's understanding of certain ranges of problems, he and his teacher are oriented antagonistically to one another. The teacher tries to stuff into his head as much of the curriculum as possible; he tries to absorb as little as is consistent with his own safety, in terms of sanctions mobilized by the school and his parents.

But school subjects are cumulative. Within a few years he is retarded in basic skills, such as reading, absolutely necessary for successful performance in the higher grades. Whether he is promoted along with his age-mates, "left back," or shunted into "slow" programs makes relatively little difference at this point. For whatever is done, he finds himself at the bottom of the school status hierarchy. He is considered "dumb" by the more successful students and by the teachers. This makes school still more uninteresting, if not unpleasant, and he neglects his work further. Eventually he realizes he can never catch up.

Without realizing what he was doing, he had cut himself off from the channels of social mobility. In those crucial early grades where the basis for school adjustment was being laid, he had not yet known that he wanted more out of life than his parents. Or, if he knew, he did not realize that school achievement and high occupational status are related. And he was not lucky enough to have parents who realized it for him and urged him on until he was old enough to identify with the school through choice. There is a certain irreversibility about school maladjustment. The student can hardly decide at 18 that he wants to become a lawyer if he is five years retarded in school. It is no longer possible for him to "catch up" and use school as a means to realize his ambitions. Sometimes lower-class men will rue their

[21] *Ibid.*, pp. 68–69.
[22] Eugene A. Nifenecker, *Statistical Reference Data Relating to Problems of Overageness, Educational Retardation, Non-Promotion, 1900–1934* (New York: Board of Education, 1937), p. 111.

failure to take advantage of the opportunities presented by the school. James
T. Farrell captured the flavor of this regret in the following passage from one of
his novels:

Walking on, seeing the lights of Ran-
dolph Street before him, he wondered
if they were college football players
[referring to the young men walking
in front of him]. That was what Studs
Lonigan might have been. Even if he
did admit it, he had been a damn good
quarterback. If he only hadn't been
such a chump, bumming from school
to hang around with skunky Weary
Reilley and Paulie Haggerty until he
was so far behind at high school that
it was no use going. It wouldn't have
been so hard to have studied and done
enough homework to get by, and then
he could have set the high school grid-
iron afire, gone to Notre Dame and
made himself a Notre Dame immortal,
maybe, alongside of George Gipp, the
Four Horsemen, Christie Flannagan
and Carideo. How many times in a
guy's life couldn't he kick his can
around the block for having played
chump.[23]

If, on the other hand, the social milieu
of the lower-class boy supported the school
and encouraged him to bend every effort
to keep up with his work, he would finish
high school whether he enjoyed it or not

[23] James T. Farrell, *Judgment Day* (New
York: Vanguard Press, 1935), p. 24.

—the way middle-class boys do. At graduation he might decide that he would
like to become a plumber. That is, he
might not crave middle-class status enough
to suffer the discipline of continued education. But if he were not content with a
lower-class status, if he wanted above all
things to "be somebody," the educational
route to high status would still be open.
He would still have a *choice;* he would
not be forced to accept a menial occupational role whether he liked it or not. As
it is, the crucial decision is made before
he is old enough to have a voice in it; it
is made by his parents, his neighbors, and
his friends.

To sum up, the middle-class child has
the following advantages in school compared with the lower-class child: (1) his
parents are probably better educated and
are therefore more capable of helping him
with his school work if this should be necessary; (2) his parents are more eager to
make his school work seem meaningful to
him by indicating, implicitly or explicitly,
the occupational applications of long division or history; (3) the verbal skills which
he acquires as part of child training on
the middle-class status level prepare him
for the type of training that goes on in
school and give him an initial (and cu-
mulating) advantage over the lower-class
child in the classroom learning situation;
and (4) the coordinated pressure of parents, friends, and neighbors reinforce his
motivation for scholastic success and increase the probability of good school adjustment.

D · OCCUPATIONAL CHOICE, PARTICIPATION, AND SOCIAL MOBILITY

OCCUPATIONAL CHOICE: A CONCEPTUAL FRAMEWORK

by *Peter M. Blau, John W. Gustad, Richard Jessor, Herbert S. Parnes, Richard C. Wilcock*

Why do people enter different occupations? The problem of explaining this can be approached from various perspectives. One may investigate, for example, the psychological characteristics of individuals and the processes of motivation that govern their vocational choices and, for this purpose, consider the social and economic structure as given conditions which merely impose limits within which these psychological processes operate. It is also possible to examine the ways in which changes in the wage structure and other economic factors channel the flow of the labor force into different occupations, in which case the psychological motives through which these socioeconomic forces become effective are usually treated as given. Still another approach would focus upon the stratified social structure, rather than upon either the psychological makeup of individuals or the organization of the economy, and would analyze the effects of parental social status upon the occupational opportunities of children. Each of these perspectives, by the very nature of the discipline from which it derives, excludes from consideration some important variables which may affect occupational choice and selection. For this reason, representatives from the three disciplines—psychology, economics, and sociology—have collaborated in the development of a more inclusive conceptual framework, which is presented in this paper.

Conceptual Scheme

It should be stressed that we are proposing a conceptual framework, not a theory of occupational choice and selection. A scientific theory must, in our opinion, be derived from systematic empirical research. To be sure, many empirical studies have been carried out in this area, and a variety of antecedents have been found to be associated with occupational position, such as intelligence,[1] interests,[2] and job-market conditions,[3] to

SOURCE: *Industrial and Labor Relations Review*, Vol. 9 (1956), pp. 531–543.

[1] Naomi Stewart, "A.G.C.T. Scores of Army Personnel Grouped by Occupation," *Occupations*, Vol. 26, 1947, pp. 5–41; Carroll D. Clark and Noel P. Gist, "Intelligence as a Factor in Occupational Choice," *American Sociological Review*, Vol. 3, 1938, pp. 683–694.

[2] Edward K. Strong, "Predictive Value of the Vocational Interest Test," *Journal of Educational Psychology*, Vol. 26, 1935, pp. 331–349.

[3] Donald E. Super and R. Wright, "From School to Work in the Depression Years," *School Review*, Vol. 49, 1940, pp. 123–130.

name but a few. The identification of isolated determinants, however, cannot explain occupational choice; indeed, it may be highly misleading. While it is true that Negroes are less likely to become surgeons than whites, this finding does not mean what it seems to imply (namely, that race determines the capacity to develop surgical skills). To understand this correlation, it is necessary to examine the intervening processes through which skin color affects occupational position, notably the patterns of discrimination in our society and their implications for personality development. In general, theory is concerned with the order among various determinants, that is, the interconnections between direct and more remote ones. The function of a conceptual scheme of occupational choice and selection is to call attention to different kinds of antecedent factors, the exact relationships between which have to be determined by empirical research before a systematic theory can be developed.[4]

Occupational choice is a developmental process that extends over many years, as several students of the subject have pointed out.[5] There is no single time at which young people decide upon one out of all possible careers, but there are many crossroads at which their lives take decisive turns which narrow the range of future alternatives and thus influence the ultimate choice of an occupation. Throughout, social experiences—interactions with other people—are an essential part of the individual's development. The occupational preferences that finally crystallize do not, however, directly determine oc-

cupational entry.[6] Whether they can be realized, or must be modified or even set aside, depends on the decisions of the selectors, that is, all persons whose actions affect the candidate's chances of obtaining a position at any stage of the selection process (which includes, for instance, acceptance in a teachers college as well as employment as a teacher). Of course, the candidate's qualifications and other characteristics influence the decisions of selectors, but so do other factors which are beyond his control and which may even be unknown to him, such as economic conditions and employment policies. Hence, the process of selection, as well as the process of choice, must be taken into account in order to explain why people end up in different occupations. Moreover, clarification of the selection process requires analysis of historical changes in the social and economic conditions of selection, just as study of the choice process involves analysis of personality developments.

The social structure—the more or less institutionalized patterns of activities, interactions, and ideas among various groups —has a dual significance for occupational choice. On the one hand, it influences the personality development of the choosers; on the other, it defines the socioeconomic conditions in which selection takes place. These two effects, however, do not occur simultaneously. At any choice point in

---

[4] For a discussion of the distinction between conceptual scheme and systematic theory, see Robert K. Merton, *Social Theory and Social Structure* (Glencoe: Free Press, 1949), pp. 83–96.

[5] See especially Eli Ginzberg, *et al.*, *Occupational Choice* (New York: Columbia University Press, 1951); and Donald E. Super, "A Theory of Vocational Development," *American Psychologist*, Vol. 8, 1953, pp. 185–190.

[6] Several studies have shown that occupational preferences are "unrealistic," that is, fewer students become professionals than had aspired to do so; for instance, Earl D. Sisson, "Vocational Choices of College Students," *School and Society*, Vol. 46, 1937, pp. 763–768. This disproportionate attractiveness of some occupations is, of course, the expected result of the fact that they offer much higher rewards than others. Occupational expectations, on the other hand, are much more realistic than aspirations; see, for example, E. S. Jones, "Relation of Ability to Preferred and Probable Occupation," *Educational Administration and Supervision*, Vol. 26, 1940, pp. 220–226.

their careers, the interests and skills in terms of which individuals make their decisions have been affected by the past social structure, whereas occupational opportunities and requirements for entry are determined by the present structure. The chart on this page. The left side suggests that the molding of biological potentialities by the differentiated social structure (Box 3) results in diverse characteristics of individuals (Box 2), some of which directly determine occupational choice

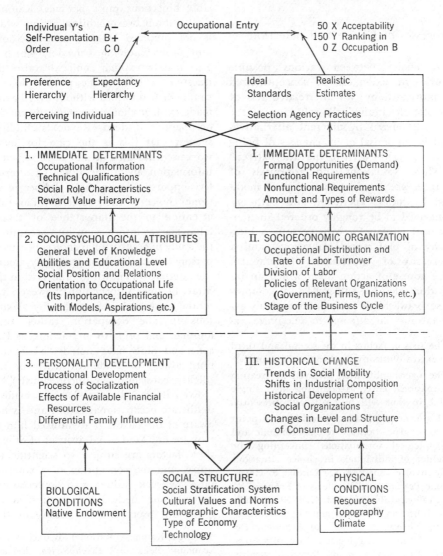

values that orient a person's efforts and aspirations may have developed in a period of prosperity, but he has to find a way to make a living in a depression.

This twofold effect of the social structure is schematically presented in the (Box 1). At the same time, as indicated on the right side, the social structure changes (Box III), resulting in a socioeconomic organization at any point in time (Box II), some aspects of which directly determine occupational selection

(Box I).[7] These two developments, separated only for analytical purposes, must be joined to explain entry into occupations. The explication of the schema may well start with the process of entry, presented at the top of the chart.[8]

Processes of Choice and Selection

A choice between various possible courses of action can be conceptualized as motivated by two interrelated sets of factors: the individual's valuation of the rewards offered by different alternatives and his appraisal of his chances of being able to realize each of the alternatives.[9]

These valuations and appraisals of chances are acquired through and modified by social experience, and both are conceived to be roughly ordered in hierarchical fashion for each person—a hierarchy of preferences (valuations) and a hierarchy of expectancies (appraisals). The course of action upon which an individual decides will reflect a compromise between his preferences and his expectations (an attempt to maximize ex-

[7] The lists of factors in the second and third boxes are illustrative rather than exhaustive.

[8] The oversimplification involved in treating occupational entry as occurring at a single point in time will be dealt with presently.

[9] This conceptualization constitutes a point of convergence between recent economic and psychological formulations concerning the conduct of individuals in choice situations that involve some risk. See Samuel P. Hayes, "Some Psychological Problems of Economics," *Psychological Bulletin,* Vol. 47, 1950, pp. 289–330; John von Neumann and Oskar Morgenstern, *Theory of Games and Economic Behavior* (Princeton: Princeton University Press, 1944); Kurt Lewin, *et al.,* "Level of Aspiration," in J. McV. Hunt, *Personality and the Behavior Disorders* (New York: Ronald Press, 1944); Julian B. Rotter, *Social Learning and Clinical Psychology* (New York: Prentice Hall, 1954); and Egon Brunswik, *The Conceptual Framework of Psychology* (Chicago: University of Chicago Press, 1952).

pected value). Thus, his actual choice will probably not be identical with his first preference if his expectation of reaching the preferred goal is very low.

Before applying this formulation to the study of occupational choice, some possible objections must be met. Katona's distinction between habitual action, which is not preceded by *deliberate* decisions, and problem-solving behavior, which is governed by explicit choices,[10] raises the question whether some people do not simply drift into jobs without ever having made explicit choices between alternative occupations. Indeed, Reynolds' findings suggest that this is the case for many workers, since they do not have sufficient information about the range of alternative opportunities to make deliberate rational choices in their careers.[11] This calls attention to the importance of taking labor market information into account in the study of occupational choice, because a person can obviously choose only among the alternatives known to him. Within the limits of their information, however, potential workers do take action by seeking jobs in one occupation rather than another, and prior to any action, as Parsons and Shils have noted, "a decision must always be made (explicitly or implicitly, consciously or unconsciously)."[12]

Even if an individual has not made a deliberate occupational choice and is not aware of the factors that induced him to look for one kind of job instead of others, these factors are subject to scientific inquiry, and the conception of a compromise between values and expectations suggests one method by which such inquiry can proceed. (The utility of this

[10] George Katona, "Rational Behavior and Economic Behavior," *Psychological Review,* Vol. 60, 1953, pp. 307–318.

[11] Lloyd G. Reynolds, *The Structure of Labor Markets* (New York: Harper and Brothers, 1951).

[12] Talcott Parsons and Edward A. Shils, eds., *Toward a General Theory of Action* (Cambridge: Harvard University Press, 1951), p. 89.

conception depends on the possibility of actually obtaining empirical data on the compromise process, a research problem which is discussed below.) To be sure, if it is a matter of *complete* indifference to a worker which of several occupations he enters, we cannot analyze the choice he made between them, but neither could he possibly have made such a choice. To the extent to which complete indifference prevails, it can only be the selection process (or fortuitous circumstances) which accounts for workers being in one occupation rather than another.

In sum, occupational choice is restricted by lack of knowledge about existing opportunities; it does not necessarily involve conscious deliberation and weighing of alternatives; and in the polar case of complete indifference, no choice between occupations does in fact take place. Variations in knowledge, in rationality, and in discrimination between alternatives constitute, therefore, the limiting conditions within which individuals choose occupations by arriving at a compromise between their preferences and expectancies. This compromise is continually modified up to the time of actual entry, since each experience in the labor market affects the individual's expectations, and recurrent experiences may also affect his preferences.

Let us examine, as a simplified illustration of this compromise process, a graduate of the Fashion Institute whose training as a designer included learning the various skills needed for making dresses. His first preference would be to become a fashion designer, but his expectation of getting a job in this most desirable occupation in the garment industry is so low that he does not even apply for one. The first occupational position for which he presents himself as a candidate is that of sample maker, which ranks lower on his preference hierarchy but where his expectation of success is somewhat greater. Unable to get such a position (A on top of the chart),

he tries to find work as a finisher, another skilled trade that may lead to a career as a designer. Since he obtains employment as a finisher (B), what position he would have looked for next (C) is irrelevant; indeed, this third alternative may not have crystallized in his own mind.

This account of why an individual chooses a given occupation must be supplemented by an explanation of why he is selected for it. Let us assume that the employment practices in the industry have the result, whether achieved by deliberate effort or inadvertently, that persons with certain characteristics, including considerable practical experience, have the greatest chance of being hired as finishers. Since only fifty candidates of this type present themselves for two hundred openings (X), employers also accept 150 applicants whom they consider not quite as suitable for the job, such as individuals with more than adequate training but without experience (Y). Having found a sufficient number of workers, employers are not forced to lower their requirements further and hire persons who are not properly trained (Z). There is probably a floor below which employers would not be willing to drop their requirements. The closer the qualifications of applicants approach this floor, the greater is the likelihood that employers will redefine the entry situation by increasing rewards in order to attract better qualified workers.

Occupational choice, then, can be conceptualized as a process involving a series of decisions to present oneself to employers or other selectors as a candidate for a number of more or less related occupations. Each decision is governed by the way in which the individual compromises his ideal preference and his actual expectations of being able to enter a given occupation, the latter being conditioned by previous rejections and other experiences. Occupational selection, on the other hand, consists of successive decisions of employers (or other selectors) about applicants for jobs. The decision concerning each candidate is guided by the employer's ideal standards and by his estimate of the chances that a better qualified candidate than the one under consideration will present himself in the near future. The process of occupational selection involves a regression from ideal standards (or an increase of rewards), the limits of which are defined by the occupational choices of potential workers. Correspondingly, the process of occupational choice involves a descent in a hierarchy of preferences (or the acquisition of new qualifications), which comes to an end, at least temporarily, by being selected for an occupation.

Determinants of Occupational Entry

Eight factors, four pertaining to occupations (Box I) and four characterizing individuals (Box 1), determine occupational entry. First, the demand for new members in an occupation is indicated by the number of vacancies that exist at any one time, which can be more easily ascertained, of course, for the employed than for the self-employed. The size of the occupational group, its tendency to expand, and its turnover rate will influence the demand for new members. The second factor, functional requirements, refers to the technical qualifications needed for optimum performance of occupational tasks. The third one, nonfunctional requirements, refers to those criteria affecting selection that are not relevant to actual performance, such as veteran status, good looks, or the "proper" religion. Fourth, rewards include not only income, prestige, and power, but also opportunities for advancement, congenial fellow workers, emotional gratifications, and indeed, all employment conditions that are defined as desirable.

Turning now from the attributes of

occupations to those of potential workers, a fifth factor that influences occupational entry is the information people have about an occupation—their knowledge about the requirements for entry, the rewards offered, and the opportunities for employment and advancement. Two characteristics of individuals are complementary to the two types of occupational requirements, namely, their technical skills to perform various occupational duties and their other social characteristics that influence hiring decisions, such as a Harvard accent or skin color.[13] Finally, people's value orientations determine the relative significance of different kinds of rewards and thus the attractive force exerted by them.[14]

To be sure, many other characteristics of individuals influence their careers—their level of knowledge, ability, and education, their social position and relationships, and their orientation toward occupational life, to cite only the most general ones (Box 2). It may be hypothesized, however, that the effects of all other factors can be traced through the immediate determinants of occupational entry. In other words, unless a social experience or attribute affects the information individuals have about occupations, their technical or social qualifications for entry, or their evaluation of occupations, it is not expected to influence their careers. Similarly, whereas many aspects of the socioeconomic organization (exemplified in Box II) must be examined to explain the four characteristics of occupations outlined in Box I, it is these four (plus the four directly relevant charac-

[13] Discrimination and nepotism illustrate how the relationship between nonfunctional requirements and role characteristics—being a Jew or a nephew, respectively—influences chances of entry.

[14] Indeed, these values determine which employment conditions constitute rewards; for instance, whether working in a group is more rewarding than working alone.

teristics of individuals) that directly account for occupational entry, according to the hypothesis advanced here.

Problems for Research

It is evident that the significance of such a conceptual scheme depends entirely on whether the empty categories it supplies can be "filled" through empirical research and, if so, whether theoretical propositions that explain occupational choice and selection can be derived from the data. The conceptual framework merely suggests the variables to be taken into account, but the crucial theoretical question concerning the relative influence of these various determinants of occupational entry cannot be answered by conceptual analysis but only on the basis of empirical research. The type of research needed for this purpose may be briefly illustrated.

As a starting point, one could select a town in which most of the labor force is employed by a few large companies. Interviews with a sample of high-school students would be designed to determine the four factors in Box 1; that is, the information they have about working conditions and opportunities in different occupations, their occupational skills and qualifications, their other social characteristics that may influence employment chances, and the value they place upon different kinds of rewards. Since reward is defined as any employment condition that contributes to satisfaction, an important function of the interview would be to identify the various conditions that constitute rewards for different individuals. Three of the four items called for in Box I could be obtained from personnel officers in the various companies: the number and types of vacancies to be filled, the qualifications required to fill each type, and the rewards offered by each position (including under rewards

again all working conditions that may contribute to satisfaction). The remaining factor, nonfunctional requirements, would be determined in a follow-up interview with the student respondents after they entered the labor market. By comparing applicants who were rejected with those who were accepted for a given position, it would be possible to discern the social characteristics that do, in fact, govern hiring practices, whether the selectors are aware of it or not. The occupational positions of the respondents, also ascertained in the follow-up survey, would constitute the criterion for constructing a theoretical model that makes it possible to predict occupational entry on the basis of a knowledge of the eight determinants. To validate this model, the predictions made with it in *other* studies *prior* to obtaining data on occupational entry would have to be confirmed by these data.[15]

The research outlined does not take into account the social and psychological processes through which the determinants affect occupational entry. An empirical investigation of the process of choice as here conceptualized would have to inquire, first, whether individuals actually rank occupations in a hierarchy of preferences and a hierarchy of expectancies, and, second, what the nature of these hierarchies is. One method for doing this is to administer questionnaires employing paired comparisons of occupations to young people prior to entry into the labor market. The instructions, which would be designed to control one of the two variables while measuring the other, might read, respectively: "If you had an oppor-

[15] To demonstrate that the model contains all immediate determinants of occupational entry, it would be necessary to show that the correlation between occupational position and any other antecedent factor (not included in the model) disappears if the variables included in the model are controlled.

tunity to get either of these two kinds of jobs, which one would you prefer?" and "Without considering which job you like better, which one of these two would you have the best chance of getting?" Respondents would be permitted to state that they are indifferent to the two alternatives.

Answers to such questions raise problems of validity as well as reliability. Repeating the same procedure after a month or so could furnish a check on its reliability, that is, on whether the answers are meaningful or sheer guesswork. Validation would consist of determining whether the data on preference and expectancies, properly weighted, make it possible to predict the occupational positions for which respondents later actually present themselves as candidates. If this is not possible, improved instruments for measuring preferences and expectancies might be devised. For example, short descriptions of different kinds of work could be substituted for occupational labels, which often have little meaning, particularly for less educated respondents. As a matter of fact, a comparative analysis of the rankings obtained by using occupational labels and different descriptive statements would itself help to clarify the character of preferences and expectancies.

Of course, not all people end up in the first occupation for which they present themselves. Many are not accepted; others quit or are fired after a brief trial period.[16] The individual's second choice,

however, is not likely to be governed by the same preferences and expectancies as his first one, since his experiences in the labor market, and possibly elsewhere, have probably given rise to changes in his expectations and even his preferences.

These socially induced changes in the two hierarchies constitute the core of the compromise process.[17] To study this process, repeated intensive interviews with entrants into the labor market would have to discern how modifications in occupational expectations and values are produced by various social experiences, such as inability to get a job, expulsion from professional or vocational school, being repelled by unanticipated aspects of the work, and many others. Also of interest would be an analysis of the contingency factors that influence the compromise process. For instance, what is the significance of differences in the tenacity with which an individual adheres to his first choice despite continuing inability to realize it? What difference does it make whether initial expectations are more or less realistic, as indicated by a comparison between an individual's expectations and the actual occupational chances of persons with his qualifications and social characteristics?

Inasmuch as the compromise process is conceived as an intervening variable between various determinants and occupational entry, its relationships to these antecedents raise a host of additional problems for research. What are, for example, the effects of differences in knowledge of employment and working conditions on preferences and expectancies? How does the importance his career assumes in the thinking of an individual influence the compromise process? What

---

[16] In any research on occupational choice, it has to be decided how long an individual must have remained in an occupation before he is considered to have entered it rather than merely to have tried it out or to have been tried out for it in the process of choice and selection. Various studies have shown that first jobs are not indicative of future careers. See, for example, Reynolds, *op. cit.*, pp. 113–114, 127–133; and Gladys L. Palmer, *Labor Mobility in Six Cities* (New York: Social Science Research Council, 1954), pp. 135–136.

[17] Super, *loc. cit.*, p. 187, emphasizes the importance of investigating the compromise process and criticizes Ginzberg, *et al.*, *op. cit.*, for failing to do so. We are here suggesting some conceptual tools with which the empirical investigation of the compromise process could be carried out.

differences are there between socioeconomic classes with respect to evaluation of various rewards, preferential ranking of occupations, and discrimination made in these rankings? Do members of the working class generally discriminate less in their occupational preferences, or do they make finer discriminations than middle-class people between different working-class occupations? What is the relative significance of income and education in producing these differences between socioeconomic classes? How is the process of occupational choice affected by other social characteristics, such as ethnic background, rural-urban residence, religious affiliation, and frequency of church attendance?

Empirical investigation of the processes of occupational selection is, perhaps, even more complicated than that of choice processes. At this point, a few illustrations to indicate the range of research problems in this area must suffice. How are selection practices changed in response to a shortage of skilled workers? Specifically, under what conditions does such a shortage result not in increased rewards, but in a reorganization of the production process that makes it possible to employ workers with lesser qualifications? (The answer to this question has far-reaching implications for economic theory as well as for social welfare.) If nonfunctional barriers to occupational entry (such as sex, age, or skin color) are withdrawn during a temporary labor shortage, what determines whether these nonfunctional requirements are reintroduced once the labor shortage subsides? Are the differences in nonfunctional requirements between occupations greater than those between employers within each occupation? (Only if analysis of variance gives an affirmative answer to this question is it permissible to speak of differences in nonfunctional requirements between occupations.)

Research might also test the hypothesis that the greater the rewards offered by an occupation, the more pronounced are the barriers to entry that are unrelated to technical qualifications. Cases of persisting shortages in essential occupations, such as nursing and teaching, could be investigated to determine the political and social factors that prevent the so-called law of supply and demand from increasing rewards sufficiently to overcome the shortages. The impact of bureaucratization on the selection process might be studied by comparing hiring procedures, say, for typists in the federal government, in a large private concern, and in a sample of small firms. Corresponding comparisons could be made to examine the influence of labor unions on occupational selection.

The Historical Dimension

We must now turn our attention to the developments that precede the period of occupational entry, to which only occasional references have been made so far. On the chart, the time dimension is presented as cut between the second and third boxes. The upper part indicates the social and psychological conditions of choice and selection; the lower part, the developments that produce these conditions. Thus, the family's position in the stratified social structure determines the financial resources available for preparing children for their careers. It is also reflected in the parents' value orientations, their child-rearing practices, the number of children, and the likelihood that the family is organized along authoritarian rather than egalitarian lines. These elements of family structure affect the process of socialization, in which biological potentialities are transformed into personality traits. Of course, the process of socialization is not confined to the home; associations with peers and teachers constitute other important socializing experiences for an individual, but these are not independent of the neighborhood in which his family lives, the attitudes toward people it has instilled in him, and the behavior patterns that it has cultivated and which encourage one kind of person instead of another to befriend him. With advancing specialization, the individual's educational development in school assumes increasing significance as a ladder for occupational mobility or as a barrier against it.[18] The internal conditions that govern occupational entry are the result of these different processes of personality development (Box 3), and the external conditions that govern entry have their roots in historical changes in the social structure (Box III).[19]

It is an oversimplification, however, to conceive of occupational choice and selection as occurring at one point in time, even if this is defined as a limited time interval rather than an instant, and even if the effects of earlier developments are taken into consideration. To think of the transition from graduation from medical school to the establishment of a medical practice as the time of occupational choice, and of entry into medical school as merely one of the factors that influenced it, is hardly realistic; but to treat

[18] The growing significance of specialized formal education first reduces the family's influence on careers but later enhances it again. At an early stage, it means that the school has become the substitute for parents as the provider of vocational skills. Once this is an accomplished fact, further specialization in the educational system has the consequence that educational decisions made before the child can act independently have crucial implications for his subsequent occupational life.

[19] Changes in the social structure also affect the course of personality development, as previously mentioned, and basic historical change, in turn, may well be contingent on the emergence of new personality patterns. See on this point Erich Fromm, *Escape from Freedom* (New York: Farrar and Rinehart, 1941).

entry into medical school as the point of choice is not a satisfactory procedure either, since not all students become physicians. A series of successive choice periods must be systematically analyzed to show how earlier decisions limit or extend the range of future choices.

This requires the repeated application of the conceptual scheme at crucial stages in the individual's development. Thus, choice of high-school curriculum could be investigated (see Box 1) by examining the information pupils have about each curriculum and its vocational significance, their grades, their role characteristics and relationships with other pupils and teachers in different programs, their value orientation toward education and occupational life, and the social experiences that gave rise to these characteristics, as well as the direct influence parents exerted on choice of curriculum. Of equal relevance would be (see Box I) an analysis of the existing opportunities for entering various high-school programs, the grades needed for acceptance, the other criteria that govern selection, the rewards offered by different programs (including parental resources or scholarships that permit a pupil to anticipate going to college), and the historical trends that produced these conditions in the educational system.[20] Once the curriculum has been decided upon, the consequent diverse experiences at high school become part of the developments of individuals that affect the immediate determinants of subsequent choices.

The study of the process of occupational entry itself often involves more than one application of the schema. An individual who is not accepted in the first occupation for which he presents

[20] For two studies of the significance of social class for the selection process in high school, see A. B. Hollingshead, *Elmtown's Youth* (New York: Wiley, 1949), and W. Lloyd Warner, *et al.*, *Who Shall Be Educated?* (New York: Harper and Brothers, 1944).

himself may have to retrace his steps before he can choose another, by reorienting his thinking or acquiring new skills. Hence, a new choice situation, influenced by the earlier rejection and the actions it stimulated, must be investigated the next time he presents himself as a candidate for an occupation. Indeed, there is no reason to discontinue the analysis with the first full-time job. The schema can be applied again to explain how shifts to new occupations result from the modifications of immediate determinants produced by the experiences during previous employment and the contemporaneous changes in social conditions.[21] The comparison of choice patterns at successive stages in the life history of individuals will indicate the way in which the relative significance of each determinant changes, and the contrast of patterns under varying socioeconomic conditions will suggest how such conditions affect the relative significance of the determinants. Technical qualifications, for example, may be of decisive importance at one stage or under certain conditions, but relatively unimportant at another stage or under different conditions.[22]

The study of historical trends in occupational selection also involves analysis of the processes through which the patterns of selection at an earlier period influence those at a later one. For example, interviews with high-school teachers and students could be designed to determine how differences in personality and conduct between natural science and social science instructors—differences which are expressions of earlier selection

processes—affect occupational selection in the next generation by attracting different types of youngsters to work in the two fields. Another project might be concerned with the effects that the contrasting social characteristics of the members of various occupations have upon the public image of these occupations and with the implications of differences in public image for occupational entry. A related question is that of the significance of upward mobility into an occupation for subsequent selection. If two professions are compared, one with many members who originated in lower socioeconomic strata and one with only few such members, is there any distinction between the criteria that govern the selection of future colleagues in the two groups? (A parallel problem is posed by the impact of upward mobility on occupational *choice,* which could be examined by contrasting the occupational choices of children whose fathers, although holding similar occupational positions now, had different socioeconomic origins.) As a final illustration of research in this area, a hypothesis may be suggested for investigation: the influence of parental social class on occupational selection is partly due to the fact that the common interests of individuals reared in the same social class affect their chances of being accepted in an occupational group.[23] Interviews with students in professional schools, repeated at successive stages in their training, could furnish data to test this hypothesis. Confirming evidence would consist of finding that there is a relationship between parental social class and failure to complete professional training, but that this relationship disappears if either degree of acceptance by fellow students or

[21] The experience can be "negative," such as the absence of expected promotions.

[22] In addition, variations in the relative significance of determinants exist among occupational groups. Thus, technical qualifications are not equally important for entry into all occupations, and discrimination against ethnic minorities is more prevalent in some than in others.

[23] On the relationship between occupational entry and having interests in common with the successful members of an occupation, see Edward K. Strong, *Vocational Interests of Men and Women* (Stanford: Stanford University Press, 1943).

extent of common interests with them is controlled.

Summary and Conclusion

The main points of this paper can be briefly outlined:

1. The conceptual scheme presented is not a substitute for a theory of occupational choice and selection, but merely a framework for systematic research which, in due course, will provide the material needed for constructing such a theory.

2. The social structure affects occupational choice in two analytically distinct respects, as the matrix of social experiences which channel the personality development of potential workers, and as the conditions of occupational opportunity which limit the realization of their choices.

3. Although four characteristics of individuals and four of occupations have been specified as determinants of occupational entry, the two crucial questions are: what developments in the lives of potential workers and in the history of the socioeconomic organization determine these characteristics, and what are the processes of choice and selection through which they affect occupational entry?

4. Occupational choice is conceived as a process of compromise between preferences for and expectations of being able to get into various occupations. This compromise is continually modified, since the experiences of individuals in the course of searching for suitable careers affect their expectations and often also their preferences.

5. Lest the complicated and extended developmental process that culminates in occupational choice be oversimplified, it is necessary to consider it as a series of interrelated decisions rather than as a single choice. The repeated application of the suggested framework for analysis at crucial turning points in the lives of individuals makes it possible to trace this development and to show how earlier decisions, by narrowing the range of future possibilities, influence the final choices of occupations.

6. The analysis of the processes by which individuals choose one occupation in preference to others must be complemented by an analysis of the processes by which some individuals, and not others, are selected for a certain occupation. To be sure, it is legitimate scientific procedure to treat the actions of selectors as given conditions in the investigation of occupational choice, and it is equally legitimate to treat the actions of choosers as given conditions in the investigation of occupational selection, but only the combination of both procedures makes it possible to explain why people end up in different occupations.

Although this article is concerned with the determinants of occupational entry, not its consequences, the distinction between the latter and the former breaks down once historical developments are taken into account, since the consequences of earlier occupational choices and selections become determinants of later ones. A labor shortage may result in changes in the wage structure or in technological reorganizations that permit the employment of less skilled workers—new conditions which help determine future occupational entry. When it becomes generally known that dissatisfaction with their career is less prevalent among the members of one occupation than of another, these psychological consequences of occupational entry become one of the rewards, the anticipation of which influences the occupational choices of the next generation. Whether a person experiences upward mobility or finds his aspirations frustrated in his career will also find expression in the orientation toward occupational life that he transmits to his children and thus in their occupational choices. At these points where consequences turn into determinants, the study of occupational choice and selection merges into the economic study of labor markets, the psychological study of personality adjustment, and the sociological study of social mobility.

SOME PERSONALITY DETERMINANTS OF THE EFFECTS OF PARTICIPATION

by Victor H. Vroom

Psychologists have long realized the importance of both environmental and personality variables in the explanation of behavior. Theorists have employed a variety of terms to describe the necessity of using both sets of concepts. Lewin (1951), for example, illustrates this dual focus in his statement that "behavior (B) is a function (F) of the person (P) and of his environment (E), $B = F (P, E)$" (p. 239).

There has, however, been a tendency for investigators in social psychology to concentrate on one or the other of these sets of variables in their explanation of social phenomena. Some emphasize personality, conceived as the relatively enduring psychological properties of an individual, as the locus of the basic causes of behavior, while others look to environmental variables such as group structure, communication, and role. Few have investigated environmental and personality determinants of behavior simultaneously.

The implications of this point of view for problems of leadership have been described by a number of writers (Gibb, 1954). The general conclusion is that leadership cannot be regarded as a unitary trait and must be evaluated in terms of a number of other variables including the attitudes, needs, and expectations of the followers. The most effective behavior in dealing with individuals with certain personality characteristics may be ineffective in dealing with persons differently predisposed.

SOURCE: *Journal of Abnormal and Social Psychology*, Vol. 59 (1959), pp. 322–327.

A similar point is made by those who argue for the adaptive nature of leadership. After reviewing research on the effectiveness of different methods of supervision in industry, Likert (1958) reaches the following conclusion:

> Supervision is, therefore, always an adaptive process. A leader, to be effective, must always adapt his behavior to fit the expectations, values, and interpersonal skills of those with whom he is interacting (p. 327).

The "authoritarian-democratic" continuum represents one aspect of leadership that has received much attention. In discussing studies dealing with this dimension Krech and Crutchfield (1948) suggest that its effects may vary from culture to culture:

> All the experimental evidence to be reported has been obtained by the study of so-called "authoritarian" and "democratic" leadership situations in our democratic culture. It is entirely possible that similar studies in other cultures might yield different results. The advantages for morale, the experiments find, seem to be with the democratically led group, but in an autocratic culture the reverse might possibly hold true (p. 423).

Despite frequent speculations that the superior effects of democratic leadership are specific to certain personality types or cultures, relatively little research has been done on this problem. The few studies which have been carried out (French, Israel, and Ås, in press; Sanford, 1950; Tannenbaum and Allport, 1956) have produced positive results. The task remains to determine the nature of the personality variables and their manner of interaction with democratic leadership.

The major purpose of the present study is to determine whether the effects of one aspect of the democratic leadership process—participation in decision-making—vary with the personality structure of the follower. Previous research has demonstrated that participation, or conceptually similar variables, has positive effects on the attitudes and performance of the participants. The general hypothesis of this study is that participation interacts with certain personality characteristics of the participant in determining both attitudes and performance.

The personality variables thought to be relevant in determining an individual's response in participation are (a) need for independence and (b) authoritarianism. Participation is hypothesized to have more positive effect on the attitudes and performance of persons with strong than weak independence needs and to have less positive effect on authoritarians than equalitarians. The relevance of need for independence in determining a person's reactions to participation was suggested by McGregor (1944), while Sanford (1950) has shown that authoritarians say they prefer more strongly directive kinds of leadership.

Participation, the independent variable in this study, has been used in a number of ways and has seldom been clearly defined. The present investigation employs the definition put forth by French, Israel, and Ås (in press): a process of joint decision-making by two or more parties in which the decisions have future effects on those making them. The amount of participation by any individual is the amount of influence he has on the decisions and plans agreed upon.

It is important to distinguish between psychological participation, or the amount of influence he perceives he has on decision-making and objective participation, or the amount of influence he actually does have on decision-making. If perception is veridical, the amount of psychological participation equals the amount of objective participation. Frequently, however, they differ as a result of the influence of processes such as the effects of needs on perception. Concern here is limited to psychological participation and, unless otherwise noted, the term "participation" is used to designate this variable.

Method

This study was carried out in a large company whose basic function is the delivery of small parcels and packages from department and other retail stores to private residents. The Ss were 108 first, second, and third line supervisors in the company's two largest plants.

Measures were obtained on each of the following variables:

1. Psychological participation. This index is derived by summing the responses of each supervisor to the following questions:

(a) In general, how much say or influence do you have on what goes on in your station? (b) Do you feel you can influence the decisions of your immediate superior regarding things about which you are concerned? (c) Does your immediate superior ask your opinion when a problem comes up which involves your work? (d) If you have a suggestion for improving the job or changing the setup in some way, how easy is it for you to get your ideas across to your immediate superior?

Each of these questions was answered by checking the most applicable alternative on a five-point scale. Scores ranging from 1, representing low participation, to 5, representing high participation, were assigned to each question and total scores obtained for each person by summing his scores for the four items.

The test-retest reliability of this index over a seven-month period is .61 for 91 supervisors. When 14 supervisors who changed either their position or their superior during this period were removed from this group, the reliability coefficient increased to .63. The correlation for the transferees is .44.

2. *Attitude toward the job.* The measure of attitude toward the job consists of the following items:

(a) How well do you like supervisory work? (b) How much of a chance does your job give you to do the things that you are best at? (c) How good is your immediate superior in dealing with people?

Each of the questions calls for the respondent to check the most appropriate answer on a five-point scale. Scores of 1 to 5 were assigned to each question and a total score obtained by adding over the three questions.

The test-retest reliability of this index over a seven-month period was computed for 91 supervisors and found to be .66. When 14 supervisors who had changed their superior or their position within the organization during this period were removed, the reliability coefficient was increased to .75. The reliability for the transferees was .06.

3. *Need for independence.* The measure of need for independence used in this study consists of 16 questionnaire items. Some of these items refer to the frequency with which the S regularly engages in independent behavior (e.g., "How often do you find that you can carry out other people's suggestions without changing them any?"), while others deal with the satisfaction that he gets from this behavior (e.g., "When you have a problem, how much do you like to think it through yourself without help from others?"). The items are adapted from a larger number

employed by Tannenbaum and Allport (1956). Each item required the S to check one of five alternatives.

No data were available concerning the reliability of this measure. However, the test-retest reliability over a seven-month period of a short form, made up of eight items selected on the basis of item analysis from the original items, was found to be .61 for 90 supervisors.

4. *Authoritarianism.* The degree of authoritarianism of the Ss [1] is measured by responses to 25 items from forms 40 and 45 of the F scale developed by Adorno, Frankel-Brunswick, Levinson, and Sanford (1950). In keeping with the rest of the questionnaire, Ss were asked to check their degree of agreement with each of the statements on a five-point scale, unlike the six-point scale usually used.

5. *Job performance.* Ratings of the job performance of 96 of the supervisors in the sample were completed by the immediate superior of the man being rated and reviewed by one other person who was acquainted with his work. These ratings consisted of two scores—over-all performance and summary appraisal. The over-all performance rating was obtained from a modification of the forced-choice merit rating technique. It consisted of ten sets of five statements, each describing some aspect of job behavior. The rater is asked to rank order the statements within each group in terms of the degree to which they describe accurately the man whose performance they are rating. The rankings on the ten sets of statements are scored to yield a single over-all performance score. The summary appraisal rating was of the graphic type. The rater is asked to check on a five-point scale his general evaluation of the degree to which the individual meets the demands of his job.

The hypothesis that participation has different effects on persons with different personality characteristics was tested in

[1] One S declined to complete the F scale, limiting the sample on this variable to 107 persons.

the following manner: The sample was divided into three approximately equal groups on the basis of their scores on each of the personality variables. Pearson product-moment correlation coefficients were then computed between participation and both attitude toward the job and job performance for the entire sample and for each of the subgroups.

Results

The findings presented first deal with the effects of participation in decision-making on the attitudes toward the job of persons with different personality characteristics. More positive relationships between participation and attitude toward the job are predicted for persons who received relatively high scores on the need for independence measure and low scores on the authoritarianism measure than for persons at the opposite ends of these two scales.

The data in Table 1 support this prediction. The correlation between the measure of participation and attitude toward the job is significantly positive, confirming past findings. Significant differences are found, however, between the magnitude of the correlations for the different personality groups. As predicted, the most positive relationships between psychological participation and attitude toward the job are found for persons high in need for independence and low in authoritarianism. Both correlations are significant at the .01 level of confidence. The least positive relationships are found for persons low in need for independence and high in authoritarianism. Neither of these correlations is significantly different from zero. The differences between correlations for high and low groups on both personality variables are statistically significant.

The data are interpreted as meaning that the attitudes toward the job of low authoritarian persons and of persons with high independence needs are favorably affected by opportunities to participate in making decisions in their jobs. On the other hand, the attitudes of highly authoritarian individuals and of individuals with low independence needs are relatively unaffected by this experience.

TABLE 1. *Relationship between Psychological Participation and Attitude Toward the Job for Persons with Different Personality Characteristics*

	NUMBER OF CASES	r
Total Group	108	.36 ***
1. High Need Independence	38	.55 ***
2. Moderate Need Independence	32	.31 **
3. Low Need Independence	38	.13
diff (1, 3) t = 2.04 [a]		
P = .02		
diff (1, 2) t = 1.20 [a]		
P = .12		
diff (2, 3) t = — [a]		
P = —		
4. High Authoritarian	34	.03
5. Moderate Authoritarian	34	.35 **
6. Low Authoritarian	39	.53 ***
diff (4, 6) t = 2.33 [a]		
P = .01		
diff (4, 5) t = 1.36 [a]		
P = .09		
diff (5, 6) t = — [a]		
P = —		

** $P < .05$.
*** $P < .01$.
[a] Indicates that the difference between correlations is in the predicted direction; t ratios over 1.00 are shown. Inasmuch as the direction of results has been specified in our hypotheses, one-tailed tests of significance have been performed.

The correspondence between the findings for need for independence and authoritarianism suggests the possibility that the measures of these two variables have a high negative relationship with one another. This possibility was tested by intercorrelating the two measures. The Pearson product-moment correlation coefficient between authoritarianism and need for independence is $-.11$ for 107 Ss. When age, occupational level, and education are partialled out from this relation-

TABLE 2. *Relationship between Psychological Participation and Ratings of Job Performance for Total Group and for Persons with Different Personality Characteristics*

| | | PEARSON r's BETWEEN PARTICIPATION AND SUPERVISORS' RATING ON: | |
	N	Over-all Perform- ance	Summary Appraisal
Total Group	96	.20 **	.20 **
1. High Need Independence	33	.33 **	.25 *
2. Moderate Need Independence	28	.19	.33 **
3. Low Need Independence	35	.06	−.01
diff (1, 3) $t =$		1.12 ᵃ	1.08 ᵃ
$P =$		.13	.14
diff (1, 2) $t =$		— ᵃ	— ᵃ
$P =$		—	—
diff (2, 3) $t =$		— ᵃ	1.30 ᵃ
$P =$		—	.10
4. High Authoritarian	30	−.08	−.06
5. Moderate Authoritarian	33	.28 *	.23 *
6. Low Authoritarian	32	.28 *	.27 *
diff (1, 3) $t =$		1.37 ᵃ	1.26 ᵃ
$P =$		.08	.10
diff (1, 2) $t =$		1.42 ᵃ	1.12 ᵃ
$P =$		.08	.13
diff (2, 3) $t =$		—	— ᵃ
$P =$		—	—

* $P < .10$.
** $P < .05$.
ᵃ In the predicted direction.

ship, the correlation is changed to .02, indicating that the two measures are independent.

Table 2 shows the intercorrelations between the measure of participation and the two measures of job performance for the entire sample and for the six subgroups. The significant correlations for the entire sample support previous findings that participating in making decisions in a job generally has positive effects on the job performance of the participant. In addition, some support is provided the hypothesis that the effects of participation on performance are a function of the need for independence and authoritarianism of the participant. Although none of the differences between correlations is significant, all of the high-low differences and most of the other differences are in the predicted directions.

The use of the correlational methods of field studies instead of the more precise techniques of laboratory experimentation increases the possibility that the results may be attributable to failure to control for relevant variables. The effects of the age, education, and occupational level of the Ss in the present sample were determined by partialling out these variables from the relationships between participation and the three dependent variables for the entire sample and for each of the six personality classifications. Table 3 shows the third-order partial correlation for each of these relationships.

A comparison of Table 3 with Tables 1 and 2 shows that partialling out the effects of background variables generally increases the magnitude of the differences between correlations and provides increased support for the hypothesis of interactions between participation and personality. All of the differences in correlations are in the predicted direction, and five of the six high-low differences are significant at the .05 level.

Discussion

The present study corroborates previous findings that participation in decision-making has positive effects on attitudes and job performance. It further demonstrates that the magnitude of these effects is a function of certain personality characteristics of the participants. Authoritarians and persons with weak independence needs are apparently unaffected by the opportunity to participate in making decisions. On the other hand, equalitarians and those who have strong independence

however, that the sample of supervisors used in this study is not representative of workers in general. It is possible that non-supervisory employees might be more authoritarian and have weaker independence needs which might lead, in the extreme, to negative consequences of participation.

TABLE 3. *Relationship between Psychological Participation and Attitude toward the Job and Ratings of Job Performance for Persons with Different Personality Characteristics with Age, Education, and Occupational Level Held Constant*

| | | PEARSON r's BETWEEN PARTICIPATION AND: | | |
		ATTITUDE TOWARD THE JOB	OVER-ALL PERFORMANCE	SUMMARY APPRAISAL
Total Group		.27 *** (108)	.21 ** (96)	.20 ** (96)
1. High Need Independence		.51 *** (38)	.51 *** (33)	.42 ** (33)
2. Moderate Need Independence		.25 * (32)	.18 (28)	.33 ** (28)
3. Low Need Independence		−.04 (38)	.04 (35)	.00 (35)
diff (1, 3)	$t =$	2.40 a	1.93 a	1.61
	$P <$	.01	.03	.05
diff (1, 2)	$t =$	1.15 a	1.31 a	— a
	$P =$	.12	.10	—
diff (2, 3)	$t =$	1.15 a	— a	1.26 a
	$P =$	.12	—	.10
4. High Authoritarian		.09 (34)	−.13 (30)	.14 (30)
5. Moderate Authoritarian		.35 ** (34)	.24 * (33)	.18 (33)
6. Low Authoritarian		.50 *** (39)	.33 ** (32)	.26 * (32)
diff (4, 6)	$t =$	1.77 a	1.68 a	— a
	$P =$	.04	.05	—
diff (4, 5)	$t =$	1.04 a	1.32 a	— a
	$P =$	.15	.09	—
diff (5, 6)	$t =$	— a	— a	— a
	$P =$	—	—	—

* $P < .10$.
** $P < .05$.
*** $P < .01$.
a Indicates that the difference between correlations is in the predicted direction.

needs develop more positive attitudes toward their job and greater motivation for effective performance through participation.

There is no evidence of any unfavorable effects of participation either on attitudes or on performance. It should be noted,

These results suggest the inadequacy of generalizations concerning the effects of participation. Studies that ignore the interaction of participation and personality yield relationships that are nothing more than average effects of participation for all the persons in the group. The statistic used to estimate the degree of relationship underestimates the effects of participation on some persons and overestimates the effects on others.

A word of caution should be injected here. The measure of participation used in this study was based on Ss' reports and conforms with what we have defined as psychological participation. Enough is known about distorting influences in complex perceptions of this sort to make it impossible to infer that our measure of psychological participation corresponds with objective participation. Since no data are available on objective participation, extension of the present findings to cover the latter variable will require further research.

The results suggest that an adequate theoretical explanation of the effects of participation in decision-making should include a consideration of the influence of personality variables that interact with participation. The present study also gives general support to a situational theory of leadership and indicates the possible values in simultaneous examination of environmental and personality variables.

Summary

The primary purpose of this study was to determine the effects of participation in decision-making on persons with different personality characteristics. It was hypothesized that equalitarians and individuals with strong independence needs would be more positively affected by the opportunity to participate in making decisions than authoritarians and persons with weaker independence needs.

The findings corroborated previous evidence that participation generally has positive effects on both attitudes and job performance. Hypotheses were also confirmed that the magnitude of these effects is a function of certain personality characteristics of the participant. Authoritarians and persons with weak independence needs are apparently unaffected by the opportunity to participate in making decisions. On the other hand, equalitarians and those who have strong independence needs develop more positive attitudes toward their jobs and increase in performance through participation.

This study suggests that an adequate theoretical explanation of the effects of participation in decision-making should include a consideration of the influence of personality variables. It also indicates the possible value of investigating the joint effects of leader and follower characteristics.

REFERENCES

1. Adorno, T., Else Frenkel-Brunswick, D. J. Levinson, and N. Sanford: The authoritarian personality. New York: Harper, 1950.
2. French, J. R. P., Jr., J. Israel, and D. Ås: An experiment on participation in a Norwegian factory. Hum. Relat., in press.
3. Gibb, C. A.: Leadership. In G. Lindzey (Ed.), Handbook of social psychology. Cambridge: Addison-Wesley, 1954. Pp. 877–920.
4. Krech, D., and R. S. Crutchfield: Theory and problems in social psychology. New York: McGraw-Hill, 1948.
5. Lewin, K.: Behavior and development as a function of the total situation. In D. Cartwright (Ed.), Field theory in social science. New York: Harper, 1951. Pp. 238–303.
6. Likert, R.: Effective supervision: An adaptive and relative process. Personnel Psychol., 1958, 11: 317–332.
7. McGregor, D.: Getting effective leadership in an industrial organization. J. consult. Psychol, 1944, 8, 55–63.
8. Sanford, F. H.: Authoritarianism and leadership. Philadelphia: Institute for Research in Human Relations, 1950.
9. Tannenbaum, A., and F. H. Allport: Personality structure and group structure: An interpretative study of their relationship through an event-structure hypothesis. J. abnorm. soc. Psychol., 1956, 53, 272–280.

E · DEVIANCE AND SOCIAL PROBLEMS

SUICIDE, HOMICIDE, AND SOCIAL STRUCTURE IN CEYLON

by Jacqueline H. Straus and Murray A. Straus

Newspaper reports, letters to the Ceylon equivalent of Dorothy Dix,[1] and the Thematic Apperception Test responses of University of Ceylon students [2] all give the impression that Ceylonese have a strong preoccupation with homicide and suicide. During May and June, 1951, there were no less than eight suicides and twenty-five homicides reported in the *Ceylon Daily News* and its Sunday edition. Suicide and homicide as solutions to thwarted love affairs were very common themes in the university students' T.A.T. interpretations. The carrying of knives of over a certain length has been prohibited in an attempt to curb the homicide rate, and a law to control the sale of acetic acid (widely used in the processing of rubber) is being considered in order to reduce the suicide rate.

The Ceylon suicide and homicide rates were compared with those of other countries, in order to test the conclusion that they are very high. Differential suicide and homicide rates among groups within the heterogeneous population of the is-

land are also of interest. In the course of the investigation certain theories were developed concerning the etiology of suicide, and, at the same time, facts are brought to light about subcultural variation within a national population. Whether or not Western theories will apply to an Eastern country has never been ascertained, and, in a sense, this study provides data to test their applicability to non-European cultures. Since few studies of suicide and homicide in the East are available, such a study should prove of more than local interest.

The basic data for this investigation are taken from the registrar-general's report for 1946.[3] The year 1946 was chosen because census data used in computing the rates are for that year, and there has been rapid population change since then.[4] The homicide and suicide statistics reported by the registrar-general and employed in this investigation represent part of a series reaching back to 1880. The registration system of Ceylon is unusually good in comparison with those of other Asian countries, and it is likely that the figures are directly comparable to similar statistics for Western nations, which, of course,

[1] The *Ceylon Observer* carried such a column during 1949 and 1950.

[2] From a study of personality patterns of University of Ceylon entrants by the junior author, to be reported in a forthcoming paper.

SOURCE: *American Journal of Sociology*, Vol. 58 (1953), pp. 461–469.

[3] G. L. D. Davidson, *Administration Report of the Registrar-General for 1946* (Colombo: Ceylon Government Press, 1948).

[4] Department of Census and Statistics, *Statistical Abstract of Ceylon, 1950* (Colombo: Ceylon Government Press, 1951).

includes all the usual deficiencies to which such figures are subject.[5]

The General Incidence of Homicide and Suicide

Contrary to the impression mentioned above—that suicide is very frequent—the actual rates, when calculated, were found to be 7.8 per hundred thousand for males and 3.7 per hundred thousand for females. These rates are lower than those prevailing in many Western countries (Table 1). The homicide rate, on the other hand, has lived up to the original impression, the rates being 9.7 per hundred thousand for males and 2.1 for females. Comparison of these rates with the Western countries, as shown in Table 1, indicates that the homicide rate for Ceylon is among the highest known.

In a number of ways, the pattern of homicide and suicide in Ceylon is in striking agreement with what is known about these phenomena in the West. For example, *suicide* rates are relatively low among rural Western peoples [6] and in Ceylon, too, which is predominantly rural. As for homicide, Sorokin and Zimmerman conclude that a large proportion of rural homicides either are the result of various animosities and grudges or occurred in intoxication during holidays and feasts. Unlike the urban homicides, they do not occur in connection with crimes against property, nor are they carefully thought out.[7] This description appears to apply

to Ceylon, for very few of the homicides reported in the newspapers are in connection with robberies, and many are committed in a moment of anger for apparently trivial causes. For example, on Sinhalese New Year's Day in 1952 seven murders were reported. Similarly, the Western phenomenon of greater frequency

TABLE 1. *Suicide and Homicide Rates per 100,000 for Ceylon and Selected Western Countries*

RATE PER 100,000
POPULATION

COUNTRY	Suicide	Homi-cide	YEAR
Ceylon *	5.9	6.1	1946
Czechoslovakia †	30.1		1930
Eire *	2.4	0.3	1947
England and Wales *	10.6	0.5	1947
Germany †	27.8		1930
Holland †	8.1		1930
New Zealand †	13.5	1.3	1930
North Ireland *	3.4	0.2	1947
Scotland †	10.2	0.6	1930
Sweden †	15.0		1930
Switzerland †	26.1		1930
United States ‡	11.5	6.3	1946

* From registrar-general's reports.
† Suicide figures from L. I. Dublin and B. Bunzel, *To Be or Not To Be* (New York: Smith and Haas, 1933). Homicide figures given in registrar-general's reports.
‡ *World Almanac, 1949* (New York: New York World Telegram, 1949).

of suicide among men than among women [8] is also shown in the Ceylon rates, which are more than two and one-half times as great for males as for females. As Table 2 shows, the suicide rate dropped steadily during the war. Thus trends in the frequency of suicide in Ceylon are apparently influenced by the

[5] See G. Simpson, "Methodological Problems in Determining the Aetiology of Suicide," *American Sociological Review*, XV (1950), 658–663.

[6] L. I. Dublin and B. Bunzel, *To Be or Not To Be: A Study of Suicide* (New York: Smith and Haas, 1933), Ch. vi; E. Durkheim, *Suicide* (Glencoe, Ill.: Free Press, 1951); P. Sorokin and C. C. Zimmerman, *Principles of Rural Urban Sociology* (New York: Henry Holt and Co., 1929), Ch. vii.

[7] Sorokin and Zimmerman, *op. cit.*, p. 398.

[8] Durkheim, *op. cit.*, p. 353; Dublin and Bunzel, *op. cit.*, Ch. iv.

same conditions as Durkheim and others found for Europe.[9] However, it should be pointed out that the wartime decline was not so steep as in the case of England, nor was the postwar rise so rapid. This may be due to the fact that the vast majority of the Ceylon population was relatively unaffected by the war, as compared with the British.

Other parallels between the findings for Ceylon and for Western countries are discussed in the succeeding sections. However, the superficial resemblance in certain aspects between the homicide and suicide rates of Ceylon and those of Western countries must not be allowed to obscure other differences which are perhaps of greater sociological significance. The culture of Ceylon—like that of the entire Indian subcontinent to which it is closely allied—has many features which differ markedly from those of the Western world. Because of these cultural differences, it might also be expected that the reasons for homicide would differ from those of the Western world. Caste, for example, is an important institution in the social structure of Ceylon. Since public discussion of caste is virtually taboo, it is difficult to tell how many of the homicides have their roots in this institution. However, during one three-month period there were at least two cases of homicides resulting from intercaste friction. According to traditional Kandyan Law, if a woman of high caste had intercourse with a low-caste man, it was permissible to kill the woman and thus remove the stain on the caste and family.[10] Such action was legal until forbidden by proclamation in 1821. It is noteworthy

[9] Durkheim, *op. cit.*, p. 205; Dublin and Bunzel, *op. cit.*, Ch. ix.

[10] Sir J. D'Oyly, *A Sketch of the Constitution of the Kandyan Kingdom* (Colombo: Ceylon Government Press, 1928), pp. 32 and 34; F. A. Haley, *A Treatise on the Laws and Customs of the Sinhalese Including the Portions Still Surviving under the Name Kandyan Law* (Colombo: Cave, 1923), p. 114.

TABLE 2. *Homicide and Suicide Rates per 100,000 Population, Ceylon, 1880–1950*

YEAR	HOMI-CIDE	SUI-CIDE	YEAR	HOMI-CIDE	SUI-CIDE
1880	0.6	2.3	1916	3.8	5.0
1881	1.6	2.7	1917	4.0	5.2
1882	1.0	3.4	1918	4.4	5.0
1883	1.4	2.6	1919	4.8	5.2
1884	1.8	3.0	1920	5.1	5.6
1885	1.9	3.3	1921	4.8	5.4
1886	1.8	3.0	1922	4.8	5.1
1887	2.4	3.3	1923	5.1	4.5
1888	1.8	4.4	1924	4.3	4.8
1889	1.7	3.1	1925	4.2	4.8
1890	2.3	2.9	1926	5.6	5.6
1891	1.5	2.8	1927	4.0	5.0
1892	1.8	3.6	1928	4.9	5.1
1893	3.1	3.2	1929	5.4	5.2
1894	3.0	2.9	1930	5.4	5.2
1895	3.3	2.5	1931	6.3	5.9
1896	3.7	3.1	1932	7.4	6.6
1897	4.1	4.0	1933	5.9	6.5
1898	3.5	4.1	1934	6.6	5.6
1899	3.5	2.9	1935	5.2	7.4
1900	3.5	3.7	1936	6.6	6.8
1901	3.8	4.1	1937	5.4	6.9
1902	3.7	4.0	1938	6.2	7.2
1903	3.6	4.2	1939	5.9	6.6
1904	4.1	4.4	1940	6.7	6.3
1905	3.9	3.6	1941	6.1	6.9
1906	4.8	4.2	1942	6.7	6.2
1907	4.4	5.4	1943	6.8	6.6
1908	4.6	6.2	1944	8.2	6.3
1909	4.1	5.0	1945	7.7	5.8
1910	4.5	5.2	1946	6.1	5.9
1911	4.5	5.2	1947	6.1	5.8
1912	5.0	5.0	1948	4.3	6.3
1913	4.6	5.5	1949	4.1	6.7
1914	4.9	4.9	1950	3.8	6.9
1915	7.8	4.7			

that today an important motive for homicide mentioned both in the press and in the responses to the T.A.T. pictures is unfaithfulness of a mate or lover. In these cases the killing of the mate or the rival is the traditionally acceptable solution, or, alternatively, one can commit suicide.

In the early nineteenth century, D'Oyly writes that "suicide is not infrequent amongst the Kandyans and is frequently committed under such circumstances, as show an extraordinary Contempt of Life, and at the same time a Desire of Revenge." [11] He mentions as provocations to suicide slander, inability to obtain satisfaction for a claim, damage to one's crops by another's cattle, or a thwarted love affair. There are instances of the first and especially of the last of these among the newspaper clippings collected. Other usual reasons for suicide include failing in an exam, losing a sum of money, or a painful illness. One of the most common reasons, or at least the reason of which one reads most frequently, is a thwarted love affair.[12] Although such cases existed earlier, the number of them has probably increased with the Westernization of the country and the introduction of the idea of romantic marriage—an idea which conflicts with two basic institutions in Ceylonese society, family and caste.

Religious suicides are probably nonexistent. Buddhism, the religion of the majority of the population, generally disapproves of suicide, and, although traditionally Hinduism, a minority religion, does permit suicide as a form of religious sacrifice,[13] suicide for any reason is illegal in Ceylon, and it is doubtful whether religious suicides have any significance today.

Part of the explanation for Ceylon's low suicide and high homicide rate may possibly be found in two aspects of the demographic structure of the Ceylon population: (1) The largest proportion of suicides in Western countries are committed by older people.[14] Since the age-sex pyramid for Ceylon is heavily weighted at the base with young people, there are proportionately fewer individuals in the Ceylon population of the age most prone to suicide. (2) There are social class differences in the frequency of suicide, the urban middle and upper classes having the higher rates.[15] The social class pyramid in Ceylon is broad-based. The vast majority of the population can be best described by the term "rural peasantry," and the population is especially deficient in an entrepreneurial middle class. Thus the most suicide-prone social strata are a much smaller proportion of the total population than is the case in Western countries.[16]

If this reasoning in respect to the role of demographic factors is correct, then it can help account for the general upward trend of the suicide rate in the last fifty years, since the proportion of aged and

[11] D'Oyly, op. cit., p. 37.

[12] According to the figures given in N. D. Gunasekara, "Some Observations on Suicide in Ceylon," *Journal of the Ceylon Branch of the British Medical Association*, XLVI (1951), 1–11, disappointed love figured in only 4 per cent of the 75 cases which he investigated (Appendix). It is noteworthy, however, that, in discussing etiology, "disappointed love" heads the list, and he describes it as "a very common cause of suicide in Ceylon."

[13] See the articles "Suicide (Hindu)" by A. B. Keith, and "Suicide (Buddhist)" by L. de la V. Poussin, in the *Encyclopaedia of Religion and Ethics* (New York: Charles Scribner's Sons, 1922), Vol. XIII; also D'Oyly, op. cit., and Haley, op. cit.

[14] Dublin and Bunzel, op. cit., p. 44.

[15] H. Alpert, "Suicides and Homicides," *American Sociological Review*, XV (1950), 673–674, Dublin and Bunzel, op. cit., Ch. viii.

[16] This does not mean that the aged and the upper-class groups necessarily have the high suicide rate that such groups have in Western countries. It is plausible to assume that old people in Ceylon do not often resort to suicide because they are adequately cared for by their relatives and occupy an honored position in the social structure. Thus what are believed to be the primary causes for the high suicide rate of the aged in the West are virtually nonexistent in Ceylon. Even if these two groups did have a high suicide rate, they constitute such a small proportion of the total population that the effect on the total rate would not be large.

of entrepreneurs and urban middle class are both slowly increasing.[17] Moreover, further increases can be expected as the demographic structure of Ceylon approaches that of Western countries, with the rapid reduction in mortality rates and the slow but inevitable growth of industry and urban population.

In contrast to the suicide rate, the homicide rate for Ceylon is high compared to Western countries, being 9.7 for males and 2.1 for females. The same factors pointed out in connection with the comparatively low suicide rate seem to be operating, but in reverse, e.g., (1) homicide rates have previously been found to be lowest for the urban middle and upper socio-economic strata, which constitute a very small proportion of the total population in Ceylon; (2) the young commit homicide far more frequently than do the old or middle-aged, and the age structure of the Ceylon population is youthful compared to Western countries. In England for example, 67 per cent of the 1947 homicides were of people under thirty, but only 33 per cent of the suicides were in this age group.[18] It is reasonable to suppose that, in addition to cultural differences, these two structural characteristics of the Ceylon population are important in accounting for the relatively high homicide rate.

Internal Differences

All previous investigators agree that suicide rates are much higher in urban than in rural areas. On the basis of the usual sociological explanations of rural-urban suicide differences, it is to be expected that these differences would be less pronounced in countries having the most

highly urbanized farm populations (e.g., the United States) as compared to those countries in which a peasant economy and way of life still hold sway. In Ceylon, especially, one would expect a pronounced rural-urban difference, since urban ways have had only superficial influence on the vast majority of village people.[19] The data presented in Table 3 bear out this expectation.

TABLE 3. *Suicide and Homicide Rate by Residence, Ceylon, 1946*

| | RATE PER 100,000 POPULATION | | PER CENT URBAN OF RURAL |
	Rural	Urban *	
Suicide	5.2	9.6	184.7
Homicide	5.1	12.4	243.2

* "Urban" refers to the following 43 areas which the census distinguishes as urban: 3 municipalities, 5 town-council areas, and 2 sanitary-board towns. The total population of all these areas is 1,025,600 and includes areas whose populations range from 362,000 (Colombo) to 2,100 (Kuliyapitiya).

In homicide, however, Ceylon differs from the West, in that the rate for homicide as well as for suicide is higher in urban than in rural areas: in most Western countries homicide has been found to be about equal for rural and urban populations.[20] Despite rural-urban differences, investigation revealed no correlation between the proportion of urban residents or the presence of a large city in a province and that province's suicide or homicide rate. This supports the interpretation given by Sorokin, Zimmerman, and Galpin to Wagner's study of suicide in European countries, i.e., that there are "cer-

[17] The suicide rate in Ceylon has been rising steadily since 1925 (Table 2).

[18] Registrar-General, *Statistical Review of England and Wales for the Year 1947* (London: His Majesty's Stationery Office, 1949).

[19] Cf. B. Ryan, "Socio-cultural Regions of Ceylon," *Rural Sociology*, XV (1950), 3–19; and "The Ceylon Village and the New Value System," *ibid.*, XVII (1952), 9–28.

[20] Sorokin and Zimmerman, *op. cit.*, p. 398.

tain great general causes [which] determine the frequency in city and country equally and exert a more powerful influence than the city and country factors." [21]

Ethnicity would appear to be one of these factors. The population of Ceylon is composed of ten ethnic groups, between each two of which are long-standing and deep-seated differences, in spite of many similarities. Although these groups are often referred to as "races," with one or two exceptions the differences between them are mainly cultural. This study will concern itself with nine of the ten ethnic groups for which data are available. The Veddas are excluded because of their small numbers and because of the unlikelihood of accurate statistics in their case. In addition, the Ceylon Moors, the Indian Moors, and Malays have been grouped under the term "Muslim." The term "others" refers mainly to the "Cochinese," "Malayalees," and "Telugus."

The Sinhalese form 69.4 per cent and are the largest segment of the population. Although they are found in all social strata, they are predominantly farmers. They are Buddhists and are considered to be good-natured and easygoing.

The Ceylon Tamils constitute 11.0 per cent of the population. They have lived in Ceylon for about as long as the Sinhalese. The majority of them farm in the dry Northern Province, although they also form a large part of the population of Colombo, where they are government employees, professionals, and clerks. They are Hindu and speak Tamil.[22] They are

considered to be industrious, hardworking, and thrifty.

TABLE 4. *Suicide and Homicide Rate by Ethnic Group, Ceylon, 1946*

| ETHNIC GROUP | RATE PER 100,000 POPULATION | |
	Suicide	Homicide
Total	5.9	6.1
Sinhalese	4.9	7.4
Ceylon Tamils	10.6	3.7
Indian Tamils	7.9	2.9
Muslims	2.1	2.5
Burghers and Eurasians	4.8	
Europeans	80.0	
Others	19.5	4.9

The Indian Tamils—11.7 per cent of the population—are recent migrants who came to Ceylon to work on the tea and rubber estates and consider India their home. Most of them live in Central, Uva, and Sabaragamuwa provinces—the south-central uplands. Their language and religion are the same as that of the Ceylon Tamils, but their socio-economic level is far lower.

The Muslims—6.6 per cent of the population—for the most part are not recent migrants and consider Ceylon their home. While the largest single concentration of them is in the Eastern Province, where

[21] P. A. Sorokin, C. C. Zimmerman, and C. J. Galpin, *Systematic Source Book in Rural Sociology* (Minneapolis: University of Minnesota Press, 1930), III, 398.

[22] Describing the religion of the Sinhalese and Tamils as Buddhism and Hinduism, respectively, is not strictly accurate. Approximately 7 per cent of the Sinhalese and 12.8 per cent of the Tamil population are Christian (calculated from Tables 111, 112, 115, and 116 of A. G. Ranasinha, *Census of Ceylon, 1946* [Colombo: Ceylon Government

Press, 1950], Vol. I, Part I: *General Report*). Unfortunately, homicide and suicide figures by religion are not available. Christianity in Ceylon is today as much an indigenous religion as is Buddhism or Hinduism. For some evidence of the importance of religion as a subcultural grouping in Ceylonese society see M. A. Straus, "Family Background and Occupational Choice of University Entrants as Clues to the Social Structure of Ceylon," *University of Ceylon Review*, IX (1951), 125–136 (reprint available on request); and "Subcultural Variation in Ceylonese Mental Ability: A Study in National Character," *Journal of Social Psychology*, 39 (1954), 129–141.

they are farmers, they are, for the most part, rural traders. Their language is also Tamil.

The Burghers—0.6 per cent of the population—while of Dutch or Portuguese descent, have intermarried to varying degrees with the Ceylonese and consider Ceylon their home. They are predominantly an urban middle-class group engaged in teaching, clerical work, business, and the professions.

The Europeans—0.08 per cent of the population—on the whole consider their stay in Ceylon as a temporary matter, even though they may frequently remain there for more than one generation. They rarely intermarry with the Ceylonese, and their children are usually sent "home" to school. They manage the tea and rubber estates, do professional work, and are engaged in the commerce of the island.

One of the most important relationships brought out by Table 4 is the fact that there are wide differences in the suicide rates for people of different ethnic subcultures. Durkheim, Cavan, Schmidt, et al. agree that one of the major factors in the differential incidence of suicide among people of varying religion, ethnic group, social class, or nationality is to be found in the degree of their "group solidarity," "anomie," or "psychosocial isolation." The data shown in Table 4 lend support to this view. It can be seen that the group with the weakest social ties among the Ceylon population—the Europeans—is the group with the highest suicide rate. This conclusion is strengthened by the fact that the suicide rate for Europeans in Ceylon is much higher than that for any of the European countries shown in Table 1 and many times higher than the rate for Great Britain, from which is drawn the majority of Ceylon's Europeans.

Among the Asian groups, the Ceylon and Indian Tamils have the highest suicide rates. Although there are important differences, it is significant that the two groups have a great deal in common.

They speak the same language; their religion is Hinduism; and they are members of the same caste system. The last two factors may be significant in explaining their relatively high suicide rates. Hinduism has a tradition of religious suicide which the other religions lack, and, in addition, the rigid caste system provides a setting for what Durkheim describes as "altruistic" suicide.

Another important relationship brought out by Table 4 is that those groups which have the *highest* suicide rates also have the *lowest* homicide rates, and vice versa. While such an inverse relation between the frequency of homicide and suicide has been previously reported in studies of European countries, and most recently for American cities and regions by Porterfield,[23] it is significant that the same sort of relationship should hold among peoples of an Asian culture.

TABLE 5. *Observed and Expected Suicide and Homicide Rates by Province Ceylon, 1946*

RATE PER 100,000
POPULATION

| | Suicide | | Homicide | |
PROVINCE	Obs.	Exp.	Obs.	Exp.
Western	5.7	5.3	8.6	6.6
Central	5.3	6.0	2.0	5.4
Southern	3.6	4.9	7.6	7.2
Northern	11.9	10.2	4.4	3.7
Eastern	6.5	6.4	3.6	3.6
Northwestern	6.1	5.1	7.6	6.9
North-Central	5.7	5.0	7.9	6.4
Uva	4.8	6.2	2.2	5.4
Sabaragamuwa	6.4	5.4	6.4	6.4

The homicide and suicide rates for each of the nine provinces of Ceylon reveal a

[23] Durkheim, op. cit., Book 3, Ch. ii; A. F. Porterfield, "Indices of Suicide and Homicide by States and Cities: Some Southern–Non-Southern Contrasts, with Implications for Research," *American Sociological Review,* XIV (1949), 481–490.

wide range. These differences probably represent the spatial concentration of the various ethnic groups rather than a regional difference per se. Table 5 shows that the Northern Province, which has the highest suicide rate, also has a population composed almost entirely (91.8 per cent) of Ceylon Tamils, the group with the highest suicide rate of all the indigenous groups in the population. At the other end, Southern Province, the province with the lowest suicide rate, has a population composed almost entirely (94.8 per cent) of Sinhalese, who have the lowest suicide rate in the total population.[24] Table 5 indicates even more conclusively the prominent place that the ethnic group plays in the suicide rate. A hypothetical or expected suicide and homicide rate is presented for each province, based on the assumption that ethnic group is the only factor affecting the frequency of homicide and suicide. The correlation between the observed and the expected rate is .90.

The homicide rates, too, are higher in those provinces where the proportion of Sinhalese is greater and lowest in those provinces where the proportion of Sinhalese is less than 60 per cent. The correlation between the observed and expected homicide rates is .69.

Conclusions

In so far as can be determined from the published statistics, the pattern of suicide and homicide in Ceylon is essentially similar in this Eastern culture to that found for Western countries. It is significant that, in spite of the wide difference in culture, there should be such a similarity.

From a broader theoretical viewpoint, the fact that an inverse relation between the frequencies of suicide and of homicide has been found for the Ceylon population, as well as for certain other populations previously investigated, is potentially of importance. This finding could be taken as support for the psychoanalytic view of suicide as an expression of a "death wish" which is turned upon one's self by identification with someone whom the individual desires to kill.[25] Although psychoanalytic writers have not formulated any such supposition, it is logical to expect that if, as they claim, suicide is a thwarted desire to kill, the incidence of suicide will be low among those groups in which homicide is frequent, since in such groups the desire to kill is not thwarted. The facts of this and other studies confirm this expectation.

Such an explanation has its attractions, as do also the sociological theories previously mentioned. However, a more adequate explanation can be formulated from a psycho-cultural point of view which is able to take into account all the known facts about suicide and homicide, such as cultural and sex differences, the frequent but not invariably inverse relation between the two rates, and also the fact that only a tiny proportion of the total population commits either homicide or suicide. At least three basic elements are necessary for such an explanation: (1) the individual personality, conceived as the resultant of both biological organism and culturally shared and personal-social experience; (2) tensions, frustrations, or conflicts which could be resolved by homicide or suicide and which vary in frequency and kind with the culture or subculture and the status and role occupied by the individual in that culture; and (3) the

[24] The fact that the Western Province suicide rate is not among the very lowest does not invalidate the argument, since it contains the city of Colombo and its suburbs. Though located in a Sinhalese part of Ceylon, recent internal migration has made Colombo 50 per cent Tamil (a high-suicide group). The presence in the province of such a large urban area as Colombo may raise the rate for the entire province.

[25] K. Meninger, *Man against Himself* (New York: Harcourt, Brace and Co., 1938).

solution which the society permits to such conflicts.

The first two of these factors have been treated extensively in previous work in the field. But the subject of alternatives permitted to members of various cultures has received little attention. One way to formulate the problem is through the concept developed by Embree of the "closeness" or "looseness" of a given social structure.[26] He describes Thailand as "a loosely structured social system," by which he means "a culture in which considerable variation of individual behavior is sanctioned." By contrast, closely woven social structures, such as Japan, emphasize close adherence to the behavioral norms.

In a closely structured society reciprocal rights and duties are stressed and strictly enforced. The identity of the individual merges with that of the group. This is the type of social structure in which altruistic suicide occurs. When the integration of the individual and the group is so close and intimate, suicide may occur for seemingly trivial causes. In Ceylon, two of the deepest and most widespread values are those centered around family and caste and those centering on academic success and the status symbols which it permits.[27] It is pertinent that there are numerous cases of suicide when parents have disapproved of love affairs and some also as the reaction to failure at examinations. In a familistic society, marriage to an individual of different status, and especially of different caste, raises the fearful possibility of family rejection. If the society is closely structured, virtually the

only alternative open to an individual who is unfortunate enough to become involved in such an affair is suicide. But in a loosely structured society having the same family values, the offending individual will in many cases eventually be re-accepted by the family group, and, even if not, interpersonal relations are not rigid enough for the individual to feel the need for suicide. This being the case, it is significant that, of the provincial rates shown in Table 4, the lowest is for Southern Province, which is almost entirely low-country Sinhalese. Along with Western Province, it has been subject to the longest and most intensive contact with Europeans. It is a center of political and caste protest and even in pre-European times was not so completely dominated by the stable but rigid feudal system which characterized the Kandyan highlands. In short, the low-country Sinhalese in Southern Province represent the most loosely structured section of Ceylonese society, and they have the lowest suicide rate.[28]

The culture of the Kandyan or highland Sinhalese is almost identical to that of the low country, with the important exception that conformity to the cultural norms is more rigidly expected. Kandyan society, then, is more closely structured than the low country, and it is noteworthy that the suicide rates for the Kandyan provinces are all higher than that for the Southern Province.

The most closely organized segment of Ceylonese society is the Tamils of Northern Province. The Ceylon Tamils are a Hindu people, and they share with their Indian neighbors a rigid caste system and an emphasis on strict conformity to traditional practices. The Ceylon Tamil does not share with his Sinhalese fellow-countrymen the easygoing ways for which the Sinhalese are noted. Indeed, he has a reputation for being frugal and hardwork-

[26] J. F. Embree, "Thailand—a Loosely Structured Social System," *American Anthropologist*, LII (1950), 181–193.

[27] Cf. B. Ryan, *Caste in the New Asia: The Sinhalese System* (New Brunswick: Rutgers University Press, 1953); M. A. Straus, "Mental Ability and Cultural Needs: A Psychocultural Interpretation of the Intelligence Test Performance of Ceylon University Entrants," *American Sociological Review*, XVI (1951), 372–375.

[28] The concept of "loose structure" as it applies to Ceylon is documented and developed more fully in a forthcoming paper.

ing—qualities of which few would accuse the Sinhalese.[29] This, then, is a relatively closely structured society, and it is significant that the suicide rate of the Northern Province is by far the highest in Ceylon.

In dealing with homicide, the concept of relative looseness or closeness of the social structure is also of aid. Probably all cultures prohibit homicide, but it is reasonable to expect that this prohibition will be more frequently violated in a loosely structured than in a closely structured society; for a loosely structured society is one "in which considerable variation of individual behavior is sanctioned." There is a tendency for this to be the case in Ceylon. Southern Province—a loosely woven society—has a high homicide rate. Its homicide rate is exceeded

by only one province (Western), and this province (except for the disturbing factor of the Colombo area population) is also of low-country Sinhalese. The three highland provinces of Central, Uva, and Sabaragamuwa all have lower homicide rates than Southern or Western Province. Finally, Northern Province—the relatively closely woven society—has a low homicide rate.

Reasoning from the characteristics of loosely as opposed to closely integrated social structures has led to the expectation that the *suicide* rate will vary *directly,* and the *homicide* rate *inversely,* with the degree to which a society is closely structured. The suicide and homicide rates for certain ethnic subcultures in Ceylon known to vary in their mode of integration have tended to confirm these expectations. These findings suggest that for Ceylon at least the way in which a society is integrated may provide an alternative to the "death-wish" theory in accounting for the baffling problem of the inverse relation of homicide and suicide rates.

[29] The historical evidence for this view is presented in R. Pieris, "Society and Ideology in Ceylon during a 'Time of Troubles,' 1795–1850," *University of Ceylon Review,* IX (1951), 171–185; see also T. L. Green, "Communal Stereotypes Held by Children in Ceylon" (paper being prepared for publication).

ETHNIC TOLERANCE: A FUNCTION
OF SOCIAL AND PERSONAL CONTROL

by Bruno Bettelheim and Morris Janowitz

In this study of ethnic intolerance [1] we attempt to throw light on the principles of group hostility in general and on ethnic hostility as a special subtype.

The four main hypotheses that the research sought to test were based on so-

[1] This paper summarizes parts of a study of the ethnic attitudes of Chicago veterans of World War II. The study will be published as *The Dynamics of Prejudice* by Harper and Brothers. It was made possible by a grant of the American Jewish Committee.

SOURCE: *American Journal of Sociology,* Vol. 55 (1949–1950), pp. 137–145.

ciological theory and dynamic psychology. They were: (1) hostility toward out-groups is a function of the hostile individual's feeling that he has suffered deprivations in the past; (2) such hostility toward out-groups is a function of the hostile individual's anxiety in anticipation of future tasks; (3) the individual blames out-groups for his failure at mastery and projects undesirable characteristics denied in himself upon members of the out-group because of inadequate personal and social controls which favor irrational discharge and evasion rather than rational action; (4) ethnic intolerance can be viewed in terms of the individual's position within the social structure either statically or dynamically. It was assumed that ethnic intolerance was related more to the individual's dynamic movement within the structure of society than to his position at a particular moment. No claim is made that these hypotheses are universally applicable, but they seemed useful in understanding hostility in modern industrialized communities.

A major premise of the study was that persons who believe they have undergone deprivations are disposed to ethnic intolerance. It seemed plausible to study ex-soldiers, since they had suffered deprivations in varying degrees and might be especially responsive to the appeal of intolerance. A random sample of one hundred and fifty male war veterans, all residents of Chicago, was studied. Former officers were eliminated from the study, since their experiences were at variance with those of enlisted men and since most of them came from social and economic backgrounds which differed from those of enlisted men. Hence the sample tended more adequately to represent the economic lower and lower-middle classes. Members of those major ethnic groups toward which hostility is projected were not included, that is, Negroes, Jews, Chinese, Japanese, and Mexicans.

The data were obtained through intensive interviews in which free associations were always encouraged. The interviewers were psychiatrically trained social workers, experienced in public opinion surveying. The wide range of personal data sought and the special problems of building rapport before gathering data on ethnic attitudes required long interviews which took from four to seven hours and in several cases were carried on in two sessions. The veterans were offered ample opportunity to express personal views on many issues and to recount their wartime experiences before ethnic minorities were mentioned.

On the basis of an exploratory study we found it necessary to distinguish four types of veterans with respect to their ethnic attitudes. For the sake of brevity, only the four types of anti-Semite are mentioned, but a parallel classification as regards anti-Negro attitudes was also developed. These four types of anti-Semite were designated as *intensely anti-Semitic, outspoken anti-Semitic, stereotyped anti-Semitic,* and *tolerant* toward Jews and were characterized as follows: (1) The *intensely anti-Semitic* veteran was spontaneously outspoken in expressing a preference for restrictive action against the Jews even before the subject was raised. (2) The *outspoken anti-Semitic* man revealed no spontaneous preference for restrictive action against the Jews. Instead, outspoken hostility toward the Jews emerged only toward the end of the interview when he was directly questioned. As in the case of the intensely anti-Semitic veteran, his thinking contained a wide range of unfavorable stereotypes. (3) The *stereotyped anti-Semitic* man expressed no preference for hostile or restrictive action against the Jews even when questioned directly. Instead, he merely expressed a variety of stereotyped notions about the Jews, including some which were not necessarily unfavorable from his point of view. (4) The *tolerant* veteran revealed no elaborately stereotyped beliefs about the Jews (among the statements of even the most tolerant veterans isolated stereotypes might from time to time be found). Moreover, not even when questioned directly did he advocate restrictive action against the Jews.

The interview situation was so constructed that the responses to questions would permit a clear discrimination between these four types of ethnic intolerance. The first portion of the interview was designed to offer the men an opportunity for spontaneous expression of hostility against minorities without bringing this subject to their attention. In a second portion, especially in connection with

Army experiences, ample opportunity was offered to display stereotyped thinking by asking, for example, who the "goldbrickers" or troublemakers had been. Only the last portion contained direct questions on ethnic minorities. There the stimuli "Negro" and "Jew" were introduced to determine which men were consistently tolerant. First it was asked what kinds of soldiers they made, next what the subject thought of social and economic association with them, and then

TABLE 1. *Distribution of Intolerance*

	ANTI-SEMITIC		ANTI-NEGRO	
	No.	Per Cent	No.	Per Cent
Tolerant	61	41	12	8
Stereotyped	42	28	40	27
Outspoken	41	27	74	49
Intense	6	4	24	16
Total	150	100	150	100

TABLE 2. *Correlates of Anti-Semitism*

TOTAL CASES	TOLERANT (61) (PER CENT)	STEREOTYPED (42) (PER CENT)	OUTSPOKEN AND INTENSE (47) (PER CENT)	TOTAL (150) (PER CENT)	NO.
Age:					
Under 28	44	27	29	100	94
29–36	34	30	36	100	56
Education:					
Did not complete high school	35	31	34	100	65
Completed high school	39	28	33	100	46
Some college or more	51	23	26	100	39
Religion: *					
Catholic	40	28	32	100	103
Protestant	48	25	27	100	33
No present religious denomination	33	33	33	100	12
Current salary:					
Up to $2,500	39	33	28	100	59
$2,500 to $3,000	39	24	37	100	43
$3,000 and over	43	18	39	100	28
Not applicable	45	35	20	100	20
Socioeconomic status:					
Top four groups	42	24	34	100	70
Semiskilled and unskilled	38	33	29	100	80

* Two cases of Greek Orthodox not included.

what his views were on possible changes in the current patterns of interethnic relations.[2] Table 1 shows the distribution of degrees of intolerance.

[2] The full methodological and statistical details of the procedure will be found in the forthcoming publication.

We tried to determine whether the men's social and economic history could account for their ethnic intolerance. Among the characteristics studied were age, education, religion, political affiliation, income, and social status. But the data indicate that—subject to certain limitations—these factors of themselves do not seem to account for differences in the degree or nature of intolerance.

Table 2, for example, shows that no statistically significant relation exists between income and socioeconomic status, on the one hand, and intensity of anti-Semitism, on the other.[3] The same was true for such other categories as education, age, and religious affiliation. Which newspaper, magazine, or radio program the men favored was also unrelated to the intensity of ethnic hostility. The pattern of anti-Negro distribution was similar.

Table 3 shows that ethnic hostility was most highly concentrated in the downwardly mobile group, while the pattern was *significantly* reversed for those who had risen in their social position. Those who had experienced no change presented a picture somewhat in the middle; the relationship between ethnic intolerance and social mobility (as defined in this study) was also present when educational level was held constant.

The group which was static showed the highest concentration of stereotyped opinions—that is, they were "middle-of-the-

TABLE 3. *Intolerance and Mobility*

	DOWNWARD MOBILITY		NO MOBILITY		UPWARD MOBILITY		TOTAL	
	No.	Per Cent	No.	Per Cent	No.	Per Cent	No.	Per Cent
Anti-Semitic:								
Tolerant	2	11	25	37	22	50	49	38
Stereotyped	3	17	26	38	8	18	37	28
Outspoken and								
intense	13	72	17	25	14	32	44	34
Anti-Negro:								
Tolerant and stereotyped	5	28	18	26	22	50	45	34
Outspoken	5	28	40	59	17	39	62	48
Intense	8	44	10	15	5	11	23	18
Total	18		68		44		130	

Social Mobility

The picture changes, however, if a static concept of social status is replaced by the dynamic concept of social mobility. It was possible to gather precise data on the social mobility of one hundred and thirty veterans. They were rated as having experienced downward mobility or upward mobility if they had moved at least one grade up or down on the Alba Edward's socioeconomic scale when compared with their previous civilian employment.

[3] Where a significant difference is reported, it is at least at the 0.01 confidence limit.

roaders" with regard to anti-Semitism. Over 70 per cent of the stereotyped anti-Semites were found in this middle category. This illuminates the relation between mobility and intolerance. On the other hand, the no-mobility group was most generally in the outspokenly anti-Negro category. This supplies another crude index of the limits of intolerance toward minority groups in a northern urban industrial community. In the case of the Jew the social norms were most likely to produce merely stereotyped thinking, while it was correspondingly "normal" to be outspoken on one's hostility toward the Negro.

In view of the association between upward social mobility and tolerance, the few cases (14) who displayed both upward mobility and were outspokenly anti-Semitic warrant special attention. The actual income gains associated with upward mobility reveal that the men who were both outspokenly anti-Semitic and upwardly mobile tended to be considerably more mobile than the others. This may be tentatively explained by the fact that sharp upward mobility is likely to be associated with marked aggressiveness in general. The data, particularly on those in the group downwardly mobile suggest

troduced between *actual* deprivations experienced and his *feelings* of deprivation. Whether the men reacted favorably to Army life primarily because they experienced relief from the insecurities of civilian life was also pertinent.

Army experiences which involved *objective* deprivations were found not related to differential degrees of ethnic intolerance (combat versus noncombat service, wounds, length of service, etc.). On the other hand, a clear association emerged between the display of *feelings* of deprivation and outspoken or intense anti-Semitic and anti-Negro attitudes.

TABLE 4. *Acceptance of Army*

	TOLERANT		STEREOTYPED		OUTSPOKEN AND INTENSE		TOTAL	
	No.	Per Cent	No.	Per Cent	No.	Per Cent	No.	Per Cent
Accepted Army life	44	81	21	64	6	17	71	50
Embittered toward Army life	6	11	7	21	20	56	33	35
Attached to or gratified by Army life	4	8	5	15	10	27	19	15
Total	54		33		36		123	

that to understand intolerance it is less important to concentrate on the social and economic background of the individual than to investigate the character of his social mobility.

Feeling of Deprivation

Whatever their social and economic life-histories had been, all the men interviewed had one common experience—the Army. Reactions to comparable wartime deprivations thus afforded a unique opportunity to examine the hypothesis that the individual who suffers deprivation tries to restore his integration and self-control by the expression of hostility, one form of which may be ethnic hostility. But here a sharp distinction must be in-

On the basis of a content analysis it was found that it was possible to make reliable decisions as to whether the veterans (1) accepted it in a matter-of-fact way, (2) were embittered about Army life, or (3) were attached to it or gratified by it. The overwhelming majority of those who were tolerant, regardless of the specific content of their wartime experiences, had an attitude of acceptance toward Army life, while the intolerant veteran presented a completely reversed picture (see Table 4). The latter were overwhelmingly embittered by Army life. In addition, those who declared themselves particularly attached to Army life displayed a high concentration of intolerance.

The judging of one's war experiences as depriving or not is a function of the individual's total personality and of the

adequacy of his adjustive mechanisms. The interview records of those who seemed gratified by Army life revealed that they were also the men who described themselves as economically and socially deprived before induction; they seem to have been poorly adjusted to civilian society and to have found gratification and release in the particular adventure and comradeship of Army life.

Controls for Tolerance

There seems little doubt that frustrating social experiences and the inability to integrate them account to a large degree for those aggressions which are vented in ethnic hostility. While our investigation could not ascertain which particular experiences accounted for the men's frustration, it permitted us to ascertain their readiness to submit in general to the existing controls by society. If, by and large, they accepted social institutions, it seems reasonable to assume that such acceptance implied a willingness to control their own aggressive tendencies for the sake of society. Or, oversimplifying complex emotional tendencies, one might say that those men who felt that society fulfilled its task in protecting them against unavoidable frustrations were also those who, in return, were willing to come to terms with society by controlling their aggressive tendencies as society demands. Hence, the hypothesis correlating the men's acceptance or rejection of society with their ethnic attitudes had to be tested. The Army is only one of many social institutions. The postulated association between intolerance and the rejection of social controls, which was central in terms of this study, had to be investigated for a number of other institutions as well.

Control, technically speaking, is the ability to store tension internally or to discharge it in socially constructive action rather than in unwarranted hostile action.

The predominant mechanisms of control which a person uses for dealing with inner tensions are among the most important elements characterizing his personality. Each of these mechanisms of control is more or less adequate for containing a particular type of aggression generated in the individual by anxiety. These controls or restraints remain adequate only if the level of tension does not become overpowering, thereby creating unmasterable anxiety. It will not suffice to investigate the association between control and tolerance in general; it is necessary to discriminate between tolerance as it relates to three types of control over hostile tendencies: (1) external or social control, (2) superego or conscience control, and (3) rational self-control or ego control.

Religion may serve as the prototype of an institution, the acceptance of, or submission to, which was found to be related to tolerance. Unquestioning acceptance of religious values indicates that the individual tends to rely on a type of control in which he is guided by traditional and nonrational external social forces. In contrast, control is exercised not by the minister or the priest but originates within the person, although such inner control may have come initially from their teachings. If the moral teachings of the church are accepted by the individual not through fear of damnation or of societal disapproval but because he considers them absolute standards of behavior independent of external threats of approval, then we say that the individual has "internalized" these moral precepts. They have become an internal control, but a control which is still only partially conscious and only partly rational. Such control is exercised over the individual by his "conscience," or, technically speaking, by his superego.

Markedly different from *external* control through outside institutions and from *super ego* control, which also depends for its effectiveness on props in the external world (such as parental images or institutionalized religion), is the rational control of irrational tendencies which forces them into consciousness and then deals with them along purely rational lines. The latter may be termed "ego control." In actuality, the three types of control are nearly always coexistent, and in each individual case control will depend in varying degrees on all three—external, superego, and ego control. In the men studied, wherever control was present it was overwhelmingly the result of a combination of external and superego control, with the first being dominant. Only few men were also motivated by ego control, and in even fewer was ego control dominant over superego or external control. Hence

Thus not only greater stability in societal status but the very existence of stable religious and political affiliations as well proved to be correlated with tolerance. These phenomena are indicative of the tolerant individual's relatively greater control over his instinctual tendencies, controls which are strong enough to prevent immediate discharge of tension in asocial action. Such delay in the discharge of tension permits its canalization into socially more acceptable outlets.

To explore more fully this relationship between tolerance and control, the responses to other symbols of societal authority which signify *external* control of the individual were also investigated. Two

TABLE 5. *Attitudes toward the Jew and toward Controlling Institutions*

ATTITUDE TOWARD CONTROLLING INSTITUTIONS	TOLERANT		STEREOTYPED		OUTSPOKEN AND INTENSE		TOTAL	
	No.	Per Cent	No.	Per Cent	No.	Per Cent	No.	Per Cent
Accept	41	67	20	48	11	23	72	48
Intermediate	15	25	17	40	13	28	45	30
Reject	5	8	5	12	23	49	33	22
Total	61		42		47		150	

a study of external, i.e., societal, control was the only one which promised to permit insight into the correlation between acceptance of, or submission to, social control and ethnic intolerance for this particular group.

The analysis of religious attitudes indicated that veterans who had stable religious convictions tended to be the more tolerant. When the political party system was viewed as another norm-setting institution, a similar relationship of at least partial acceptance or consensus with this basic institution was found to be associated with tolerance. Whether the veteran was Democratic or Republican was in no way indicative of his attitude toward minorities. But the veteran who rejected or condemned both parties ("they are both crooks") tended to be the most hostile toward minorities.

groups of institutions were analyzed separately. The first group, that of Army control through discipline and officers' authority, is discussed below. The second group was composed of significant representatives of civilian authority to which the men were relatively subject at the time of the interview.

Four institutions were singled out as being most relevant. They were: (1) the administration of veterans' affairs; (2) the political party system; (3) the federal government; and (4) the economic system, as defined by the subjects themselves.

The veterans' views of each of these institutions were quite complex and in some respects ambivalent. Nevertheless, it was possible to analyze attitudes toward them on a continuum of acceptance, rejection, or intermediate.

When acceptance or rejection of the

four representative institutions was compared with the degree of anti-Semitism (Table 5), it appeared that only an insignificant percentage of the tolerant men rejected them, while nearly half the outspoken and intense anti-Semites did so. This is in marked contrast, for example, to studies of certain types of college students, in whom radical rejection of authority is combined with liberalism toward minority groups.

Controls, it may be said, are not internalized by merely accepting society. On the contrary, general attitudes of accepting existing society and its institutions are the result of previous internalization

significantly more prone to claim they got along well than were the intolerant men.

In the case of the Negro (Table 6), societal controls exercise a restraining influence only on what would be classified as violent, as "intense," intolerance. Violence is generally disapproved of by the controlling institutions, while they approve, if not enforce, stereotyped and outspoken attitudes. The men who were strongly influenced by external controls were, in the majority, stereotyped and outspoken but not intense in their intolerance toward Negroes, as the present data show.

TABLE 6. *Attitudes toward the Negro and toward Controlling Institutions*

	TOLERANT		STEREOTYPED		OUTSPOKEN		INTENSE		TOTAL	
	No.	Per Cent	No.	Per Cent	No.	Per Cent	No.	Per Cent	No.	Per Cent
Acceptance	9	75	19	48	38	51	6	25	72	48
Intermediate	2	17	16	40	23	31	4	17	45	30
Rejection	1	8	5	12	13	18	14	58	33	22
Total	12		40		74		24		150	

of societal values as personally transmitted by parents, teachers, and peers. Hence the acceptance of individuals who are representatives of societal values should have been more closely related to internal control than the acceptance of discipline in general, which is more characteristic of external control. Attitudes toward officers seemed suitable gauges for the individual's attitudes toward control. Incidentally, most of the men evaluated their officers on the basis of personal quality, their moral authority, and not on the basis of their punitive power.

The tolerant veteran appeared able to maintain better relations with his officers; he was more willing to accept the authority and discipline of the Army as represented by them. In general, his attitude was reasonable. When queried as to how the fellows in their outfits got along with the officers, tolerant veterans were

The division between those who rejected and those who accepted external control came between outspoken and intense attitudes toward Negroes. To score "high" on the index of rejection for the four controlling institutions meant that an individual was likely to fall in the intensely anti-Negro category. Thus acceptance of external controls not only was inadequate in conditioning men to be tolerant of the Negroes but was not even enough to prevent them from holding outspoken views in that regard. It served only to restrain demands for violence.

Stereotyped Thinking

Precisely because most of the men in the sample based their restraint of aggressive tendencies on societal controls rather than on inner integration, some aggression remained uncontrolled. This the men needed to explain to themselves—and to others. For an explanation they fell back again on what society, or rather their associates, provided in the way of a justification for minority aggression. It has already been mentioned that most of the

TABLE 7. *Stereotypes Characterizing Jews*

STEREOTYPE	NO. OF VETERANS MENTIONING STEREOTYPES
They are clannish; they help one another	37
They have the money	26
They control everything (or have an urge to control everything); they are running the country	24
They use underhanded or sharp business methods	24
They do not work; they do not do manual labor	19

men voiced their ethnic attitudes in terms of stereotypes. The use of these stereotypes reveals a further influence—if not control —by society on ethnic attitudes and should therefore at least be mentioned.

One of the hypotheses of this study is that intolerance is a function of anxiety, frustration, and deprivation, while the intolerant person's accusations are ways to justify his aggression. While the rationalizations for this intolerance must permit a minimum of reality testing, they will also condition the ways in which hostile feelings are discharged.

All intolerant veterans avoided reality testing to some degree, and each of them made statements about minorities which showed that they neglected the individual's uniquely personal characteristics— in short, they used stereotypes. As was to be expected, those who were only moderately biased retained more ability to

test reality. They were more able to evaluate correctly the individuals whom they met, but they clung to stereotyped thinking about the rest of the discriminated group. In this way it remained possible to retain the stereotyped attitudes which permitted discharge of hostility despite actual experiences to the contrary. Such a limited amount of reality testing did not seem to be available to strongly biased individuals.

Because the intolerant person's rationalizations are closely, although not obviously, connected with his reasons for intolerance, he must take care to protect them. On the other hand, they also reveal the nature of the anxieties which underlie them.

An examination of the five most frequent Negro and five most frequent Jewish stereotypes reveals strikingly different results, each set of which presents a more

TABLE 8. *Stereotypes Characterizing Negroes*

STEREOTYPE	NO. OF VETERANS MENTIONING STEREOTYPES
They are sloppy, dirty, filthy	53
They depreciate property	33
They are taking over; they are forcing out the whites	25
They are lazy; they are slackers in work	22
They are ignorant; have low intelligence	18
They have low character; they are immoral and dishonest	18

or less integrated pattern (see Tables 7 and 8). The composite pattern of stereotypes about Jews does not stress personally "obnoxious" characteristics. In the main, they are represented in terms of a powerful, well-organized group which, by inference, threatens the subject.

On the other hand, the stereotypes about the Negro stress the individual, personally "offensive" characteristics of the Negro. As the stereotypes of the group characteristics of Jews implied a threat to the values and well-being of the intolerant white, so, too, those about the Negro were used to describe a conception of the Negro as a threat, particularly because the Negro was "forcing out the whites."

A comparison of the distribution of stereotypes applied to Jews and Negroes, as indicated by this enumeration, with those used by the National Socialists in Germany permits certain observations. In Germany the whole of the stereotypes, which in the United States were divided between Jews and Negroes, were applied to the Jews. Thus in the United States, where two or more ethnic minorities are available, a tendency emerges to separate the stereotypes into two sets and to assign each of them to one minority group. One of these two sets indicates feelings of being anxious because of one minority's (the Jews') assumed power of overwhelming control. The other set of stereotypes shows feelings of anxiety because of the second minority's (the Negroes') assumed ability to permit itself the enjoyment of primitive, socially unacceptable forms of gratification. Thus, of two minority groups which differ in physical characteristics, such as skin color, the minority showing greater physical difference is used for projecting anxieties associated with dirtiness and sex desires. Conversely, the minority whose physical characteristics are more similar to those of the majority become a symbol for anxieties concerning overpowering control. If we apply the frame of reference of dynamic psychology to these observations, then these stereotypes permit further emphasis on the relation between tolerance and control. The in-

dividual who has achieved an integration or an inner balance between superego demands and instinctual, asocial strivings does not need to externalize either of them in a vain effort to establish a control that he does not possess. The intolerant man who cannot control his superego demands or instinctual drives projects them upon ethnic minorities as if, by fighting them in this way or by at least discharging excessive tension, he seeks to regain control over unconscious tendencies.

Actual experiences later in life, once the personality has been formed, seem relatively incapable of breaking down this delusional mechanism. Questioning revealed, for example, that, although Army experience threw the men into new and varied contacts with Jews and frequently with Negroes, the stereotypes applied to the service of Jews and Negroes in the Army proved largely an extension of the conceptions of civilian life into Army experiences.

It seems reasonable to assume that, as long as anxiety and insecurity persist as a root of intolerance, the effort to dispel stereotypes by rational propaganda is at best a half-measure. On an individual level only greater personal integration combined with social and economic security seems to offer hope for better interethnic relations. Moreover, those who accept social controls are the more tolerant men, while they are also, relatively speaking, less tolerant of the Negro because Negro discrimination is more obviously condoned, both publicly and privately. This should lead, among other things, to additional efforts to change social practice in ways that will tangibly demonstrate that ethnic discrimination is contrary to the mores of society, a conviction which was very weak even among the more tolerant men.

PART SIX

Social Structures Geared
to Personality Rehabilitation

IN PARTS Three through Five we considered the empirical interaction among personality and social-system variables. In illustrating this interaction we chose a wide variety of social contexts—small groups, bureaucracies, electoral systems, communities, families, schools, and so on. In many of these contexts the major functional primacy of the role or organization is remote from the management of personality problems as such. The primary social objective of a business firm, for instance, is not to socialize its employees, or to provide them with therapy, but rather to produce goods and services for exchange in a market. Persons have to be motivated to assume a role in a business firm, to be sure; moreover, their motives (e.g., the desire for profit) sometimes spring from sources deep in the personality. Nevertheless, incumbency in roles in a business firm presupposes an individual with a reasonably well-developed and well-controlled personality. Whatever roles a firm has for managing personality tensions—e.g., personnel counsellor, official in charge of complaints—are clearly peripheral to the main business of the organization.

Many social roles and organizations, however, themselves specialize in dealing directly with personality motivations, problems, and tensions as such. In earlier sections we have included research items on familial and educational structures, both of which function primarily as agencies which shape the personalities of children. Other roles and organizations deal with the management of tensions in adult life. In marriage, for instance, it is expected that spouses will, in the normal course of events, be able to work through tensions that are generated but not expressed in more impersonal settings. Friendship groups also serve as an arena for blowing off steam (steam sometimes generated but not expressed in marriage). Other social contexts that are legitimate for expressing or vicariously gratifying personality needs are found in participant and spectator sports, drama, movies, television, radio, ceremonies, revelrous reunions, and so on. Participation in most of these social contexts is often assumed to be a normal part of adult life.

Certain of these personality-centered roles and organizations deal more exclusively with a special order of problems;

597

they focus on personalities that are judged socially to be imperfectly socialized, disturbed, diseased, or in need of rehabilitation. Sometimes this rehabilitation function is an auxiliary aspect of other kinds of roles—for instance, the roles between lawyer and client, teacher and student, friend and friend. In other cases the primary function of the role or organization is to rehabilitate personalities. Alcoholics Anonymous, for instance, has as its primary aim the control of one particular symptom that expresses a deep and chronic personality disturbance.

In Part Six we include a number of research items on roles and organizations that specialize in personality rehabilitation. We begin with psychotherapy. Because psychotherapy has historically been focused on the disturbed *individual,* the major emphasis in discussions and research has been at the psychodynamic level. Recently, however, interest has begun to focus on distinctively *social* aspects of the psychotherapeutic process. We include two articles on these social aspects. John Spiegel deals with the doctor-patient relationship as a role structure possessing characteristics above and beyond the personalities of the doctor and patient themselves. In his discussion Spiegel is hammering home a point voiced repeatedly in this volume: even in the most intimate interpersonal relations, social variables must be invoked to account for the behavior of the individuals involved. In the second selection, Nathan Ackerman stresses the importance of the family involvements of a patient in therapy. Ackerman bases his argument on the assumption that most psychological disturbances come to reflect themselves in symbiotic relations with the patient's family members, who also may be disturbed. Given this assumption, Ackerman explores the ways that psychotherapy can be administered to two or more family members simultaneously, or indeed to the family as a whole.

Until recent times the institutionalization of mentally disturbed people had very little to do with the rehabilitation of personalities. Mental disturbance historically has been interpreted as resulting from possession by evil forces, hereditary weakness, or organic disease. Hence the objective in institutionalizing the "insane" was to isolate them from the public and perhaps to punish them. In response to modern humanitarian social movements, however, the tone of the mental hospital has undergone gradual change during the past century or so. The focus has come to rest more and more on the patient's psychological problems. As a result of this trend, the mental hospital is now taking its place among those social organizations that are rehabilitative for personalities.

In the first of three selections on the mental hospital, we include the article by Doris Gilbert and Daniel Levinson, which explores the tensions between the traditional "custodial" attitudes about care of the mentally disturbed and the modern "humanistic" attitudes. The authors argue that individuals who work in mental hospitals vary along this dimension, and that this variation is closely related to the degree of "authoritarianism" in their personalities. Perhaps more important, Gilbert and Levinson suggest that custodial and humanistic ideologies lead to divergent hospital policies and these in turn influence the effectiveness of the hospital in dealing with the problems of its patients.

Two other research items concern the impact of the hospital's social organization on the patients' mental condition and behavior. In 1954 A. H. Stanton and M. S. Schwartz published *The Mental Hospital,* a pioneer study of a private mental hospital. A major conclusion of this study is that episodes of conflict and disagreement among hospital staff members (doctors, nurses, etc.) give rise to, sustain, and augment psychological disturbances among the patients. The Stanton-Schwartz study has stimulated much discussion, controversy, and subsequent research. As one example of this research we include the article by Anthony F. C. Wallace and Harold Rashkis, which challenges some of the Stanton-Schwartz conclusions.

Social work—another "rehabilitative" context—historically has been concerned with helping different kinds of problem families—those plagued by starvation, illness, unemployment, divorce and desertion, retarded children, and so on. Though social work is not always specifically geared to the personality problems of its clients, such problems inevitably arise in the administration of welfare. The importance of these problems is seen in the recent emergence of a specialty known as "psychiatric social work."

The social and psychological setting of the social worker and his client has scarcely been examined in the literature. In this volume we include two illustrations of the sorts of problems that may arise in the administration of social welfare. Sol Wiener Ginsburg, in the first selection, is concerned with the misunderstandings and misfirings that can arise because of the divergent cultural and ethnic backgrounds of the social worker and the client. In the second article, reminiscent of Ackerman's commentary on psychotherapy, Max Siporin argues that in social work it is indispensable to consider the family as a whole rather than the individual as the key unit in social casework.

To conclude this section on rehabilitative social arrangements, we include an article on the religious leader, whose "psychotherapeutic" functions are perhaps least well understood of all. Lloyd H. Rogler and August B. Hollingshead, basing their argument on a study of spiritualism in Puerto Rico, suggest that the religious leader offers a "solution" for the schizophrenic at two levels. At the personality level, the language and ideology of spiritualism organizes schizophrenic fantasies and behavior into some sort of whole. At the social level, spiritualism provides the schizophrenic with a publicly acceptable role that does not bear the stigma of psychiatric treatment.

A · PSYCHOTHERAPY

THE SOCIAL ROLES OF DOCTOR AND PATIENT
IN PSYCHOANALYSIS AND PSYCHOTHERAPY

by John P. Spiegel

The purpose of this paper is to discuss the possibility of clarifying some of the controversial aspects of psychoanalysis and psychotherapy as technical procedures by the use of a new set of concepts. It has often been observed that matters previously obscured by contending theories become somewhat clarified and easier to deal with when approached on the basis of new assumptions.

In recent years the question of the distinction between psychoanalysis and psychotherapy, in terms of their methods and goals, has received a great deal of attention. The discussion has had the effect of producing a great many different points of view without settling the fundamental difference in the two methods. Even among those who accept psychoanalytic theory and who are recognized analysts, there is some difference of opinion as to where psychotherapy leaves off and psychoanalysis begins. In the variety of theoretical and methodological issues that have been raised by the problem there have been two common and related themes: the fundamental importance of the doctor-patient relationship and the management of the transference.

It is with respect to the meaning of the doctor-patient relationship—especially as conceived in terms of transference—that I wish to apply the concepts of *transaction* and of *social role*. Transaction is a term introduced by Dewey and Bentley [1] to describe reciprocal, reverberating processes which occur in any system of action or behavior. In such a system, especially if it is in equilibrium, there occur two-way, phasic and cyclical exchanges which are largely self-regulating and self-correcting—that is, they keep the system going. A key example of transactional processes at the somatic level is the neural and hormonal exchanges which keep the body at a constant temperature. As a concept, transaction is in contrast to interaction—which describes behavior produced by the effect of one object upon another—and to self-action, which describes the isolated behavior of one object activated wholly by inner forces. A good example of interaction is the effect of one billiard ball upon another, where no systematic relations are maintained once the force is expended. A clock is an obvious example of self-action behavior.

How can we describe the relation between two or more human beings in the light of these concepts? It seems clear that if two people relate to each other at all, they become involved in a system of transaction characterized by mutually

SOURCE: *Psychiatry*, Vol. 17 (1954), pp. 369–376. Reprinted by special permission of The William Alanson White Psychiatric Foundation, Inc.

[1] John Dewey and A. F. Bentley, *Knowing and the Known;* Boston, Beacon Press, 1949. Bentley, "Kennetic Inquiry," *Science* (1950) 112:775.

regulative processes which we ordinarily term adaptation or adjustment. These processes are mediated by the exchange of information which is called communication. Thus if we want to describe the doctor-patient situation as systematically as possible, we will study the flow of communication—verbal and nonverbal—that occurs in the system of transactions as it becomes established by the incorporation of the doctor and the patient within it. If such a study is to be successful, we should be able to name and describe the mechanisms which disturb the equilibrium in the system as well as those which restore it. Furthermore, we should be able to assign responsibility for perturbations in the equilibrium of the system to either doctor or patient, as the case might be.

As the psychotherapeutic situation is ordinarily understood, the flow of communication refers to the statements and behavior of the patient and the 'interpretations' of the doctor. The therapist's 'interpretations,' as a general rule, refer to 'motivations' which govern the patient's statements and behavior, but which are hidden from his awareness. Among the most important of these unconscious motivations are the patient's attitudes and feelings toward the doctor, and this is what is understood by the term, transference. It is assumed that the patient's unconscious attitudes toward the doctor, insofar as they represent transference processes, are based upon experiences with significant figures in the past. They therefore constitute ways in which, without the knowledge of the patient, the past is distorting his current behavior and interfering with his ability to adjust to present reality.

According to this way of understanding the doctor-patient relationship, it is the transference which accounts, for the most part, for the perturbations in the equilibrium of the transactional system. Thus the concept of transference comes close to satisfying the demand for a mechanism to locate the disequilibrium in the communication system. There are two ways, however, in which it fails to qualify as an adequate concept for such a mechanism. On the one hand, it is a relatively abstract concept. Because of its high level of generalization, it provides no concrete way of specifying or distinguishing what is unconsciously transferred from what is appropriate and realistically oriented to the current situation. The therapist has to rely, for such distinctions, on his intuitive judgment and experience. On the other hand, it provides no way of describing the real nature of the therapist's involvement in the behavioral system. The picture of the therapist making perfectly neutral comments or interpretations of the meaning of the patient's productions leaves out all the nuances and richness of detail, the multiple choice of response, and the interplay of processes which actually occur in the doctor-patient relationship—whether it is psychoanalysis or psychotherapy. Such a picture is based on an interactional rather than a transactional model of the system of relations.

In my opinion, a more concrete way of getting at the intricacies of the communication process, still consistent with the general aspects of transference, is through the concept of social role. Since the term, role, and the expressions, role-playing and role-taking, always bring up a number of misunderstandings, it is necessary to make some definitions of these concepts. As used in social science, the terms have nothing to do with artificially adopting a role as an actor does in the theater. Rather, the concept of role is concerned with a description of behavior from the point of view of a social situation. All behavior is patterned in accordance with cultural standards to fit some part that the individual plays in a social situation, and these parts are called social roles.[2] Actually, it is impossible to de-

[2] Lionel J. Neiman and Joseph W. Hughes, "The Problem of the Concept of Role: A Resurvey of the Literature," *Social Forces* (1951) 30:141.

scribe behavior without referring it to the role played by the individual. Even in our clinical descriptions we are forced to refer to our patients in their roles as students, mothers, housewives, daughters, and so forth, in order to indicate what sort of behavior may be expected of them.

A role, however, is more than a descriptive term for the pattern of behavior which one may expect of an individual. Roles are governed both by motivational processes and by cultural value orientations, and it is important to keep these two aspects of role behavior distinctly separate. The distinction can be illustrated by an example. Let us contrast the patterning of roles in two doctor-patient situations. In the first situation the patient is an Eastern European Jew, and in the second he is an Englishman, but in all other respects the situation is the same. In the first situation the patient states his complaints with great drama, emphasizes his suffering with loud moans and groans, and considerably exaggerates the degree of disability. The doctor will most likely respond with tolerant sympathy and reassurance, telling the patient that he will take care of the difficulty and that his suffering will be relieved. In the second case the patient reports his complaint in an off-hand manner, and minimizes his suffering or treats it humorously. In this pattern, the doctor may very probably warn the patient that he must take better care of himself, but that if he follows orders and keeps his appointments, the situation will be cleared up.

These two completely dissimilar people, both playing the same role of patient, are both actuated by an identical motivation —to solicit the interest and care of the doctor. The motivation is inferred from the effort each participant makes to induce his prospective role partner to play the desired complementary or reciprocal role of doctor-interested-in-his-case. The variation in the way the roles are played can be accounted for by the difference in cultural value orientations. For the East-

ern European Jew, the dramatic and voluble exhibition of emotion, especially of suffering, has great value and can be counted on to elicit the interest of another person. For the Englishman, consideration for others and a calm attitude in the face of adversity have greater value than giving way to individual expressions of feeling. This contrast throws an interesting light on the way cultural values are built into the personality as a mechanism for the control of anxiety. The Jewish patient unconsciously fears that unless he presents a convincing picture of personal suffering, the doctor will not take his case seriously.[3] The Englishman fears that any undue show of feeling will make the doctor lose interest in his case.

A number of other important insights into role-playing as a system of communication can be gained from a consideration of this example. The chief homeostatic or regulative mechanism in the system is the complementarity of the roles.[4] Roles are culturally patterned to dovetail or integrate with each other by means of reciprocal actions, verbal communications, or symbolic gestures. A question calls forth an answer, and the answer maintains the equilibrium in the system. Not to answer a question introduces tension into the system as does any failure of complementarity. Thus the equilibrium state of the system is directly proportional to the degree of complementarity in the roles. For example, if in the situation just described the doctor refuses to pay attention to the complaints of the patient—that is, refuses to play the complementary role—the system is in danger of disintegrating, with the production of anger or anxiety in the participants. Another way of describing this is to say that the doctor *declines* the role *assigned* to him by the patient.

[3] Bruno Bettelheim, "The Dynamism of Anti-Semitism in Gentile and Jew," *J. Abnormal and Social Psychol.* (1947) 42:153–168.

[4] Talcott Parsons, *The Social System;* Glencoe, Ill., Free Press, 1951; see esp. pp. 36–45.

This phrasing calls attention to the highly significant fact that roles are consciously or unconsciously *assumed, assigned, accepted,* or *declined* in all human relationships. The to-and-fro play among these four transactions governs many aspects of the dynamics of the communication process.

Two other aspects of role relations remain to be considered before examining the doctor-patient relationship. One is the classification of roles into two general categories: *instrumental* and *expressive.* Instrumental roles are designed for solving problems, and emotion has little place in them. Expressive roles are patterned for the expression of feeling or emotion and are not concerned with getting anything done. The distinction is somewhat abstract since many roles have elements of both instrumental and expressive behavior, but the categories are nevertheless useful. For example, the role of patient is chiefly instrumental; he has to help the doctor solve the problem. But the Jewish patient just described may inject so much expressive behavior into the role that the doctor may be prevented from solving the problem. In psychotherapy and psychoanalysis, however, expressive behavior becomes a part of the instrumental problem to be solved.

The other aspect of role-playing concerns the interplay between *explicit* and *implicit* roles. If one focuses a high-power microscope—so to speak—on the processes inherent in role systems, it becomes plain that any two-person system is characterized by multiple, simultaneously enacted roles. Everyone wears many hats at the same time. For example, the Jewish patient we have discussed is wearing his patient hat, his Jewish hat, and his suffering hat. Under this array of millinery, he may also wear hidden hostile, affectionate, and anxious hats. It can be seen that this multiple, layered structuring of roles is arranged in an order of nearness and remoteness from the surface aspects of the social situation. The *explicit* roles are those that are closest to the surface and therefore closest to the observation and awareness of the participants. In addition, they are oriented to the most highly structured and therefore most stable aspects of the social situation. *Implicit* roles, on the other hand, are more remote from the sphere of awareness of the participants, and they are thus more subtle, complicated, and variable. Associated with their remote position in the role-structuring of human relations is the fact that the implicit roles are the seat of the chief emotional currents and dynamic trends in the social situation. It is the configuration of implicit roles assumed by a person that constitutes his "character." The life, the color, the vividness of any human situation is given by the interplay among explicit and implicit roles.

These structural relations can be brought into relief and applied to the basic distinction between psychoanalysis and psychotherapy if one studies the flow of explicit and implicit roles as they are delivered into the communication system established between doctor and patient. Let us dip into a clinical situation and take out a very small sample for study:

A 23-year-old, highly intelligent girl came for treatment with the problem of feeling generally frustrated and "lost" in her adjustment to life, and specifically unable to realize her ambition in her chosen career. She was constantly haunted by a deep and abiding sense of shame, on which account she was extremely shy and retiring in all her social relationships. She initiated the particular segment of the doctor-patient transaction that I wish to discuss by taking up the problem of her abilities and her career. She had a Ph.D. in mathematics but was unable to do much with it. Perhaps, she speculated, she had chosen the wrong field. Maybe she was more suited to the arts; she always found herself interested in aesthetic problems.

Up to this point I found myself, as the doctor, comfortably installed in my explicit instrumental role; the role assignment given me by the patient appeared to be concerned with her "problem." The system of roles was complementary and apparently well integrated. The next moment, however, the patient initiated a new role assignment. She asked me if I had seen a recent performance of "Don Juan in Hell" from *Man and Superman.* The question seemed a simple enough request for information regarding my playgoing habits. But since I did not know what role I was being invited to take, and because I suspected that behind whatever explicit role this might turn out to be there lurked a more important implicit one, I did not answer the question. The patient paused for a moment, and then, perceiving that I would not answer the question, she continued. She had already learned from previous transactions that I would decline implicit roles into which I was being inducted through a question, and although she still resented my "rudeness," as she usually described it, the behavioral system was by now no longer subjected to intense strain by my declining to play complementary roles in this fashion.

In continuing after the pause, the patient delivered a highly perceptive account of Shaw's intention in the Don Juan interlude, of the actors' interpretations, and of her reactions. The account was so long that I finally interrupted to ask if she knew why she wanted to tell all this. At the point of interruption I had become aware that my new role was an expressive one—to play the appreciative audience to her role as a gifted art and drama critic. I could have accepted this role and made it explicit by complimenting her, since she had certainly done a first-rate job. Or I could have modified my role slightly by discussing with her the points she had made. Either of these two responses would have maintained equilibrium in the system by re-establishing complementarity. But to do so would have meant passing up the opportunity

to get more information regarding the hidden, implicit role buried in this transaction and thus to learn more about her motivation for shifting out of her initial instrumental role in which she had started the interview.

Her response to my question was that she was just chattering because she felt like it, and that there was no particular reason for her talking about the play. Now in her response, especially in the tone of voice, I was aware that she had assumed yet another role; she had demoted herself, within her value system at any rate, from the brilliant art critic to the idle gossip and chatterer. But why should the patient choose this new, depreciated role? Such sharp jumps in explicit role-structuring are always indicators of intense unconscious affect connected with the implicit role, against the expression of which there is strong resistance. The key to the shift can be found if the therapist puts himself in the complementary role assigned. If she was now the gossip, it must have been I that thought her so. In other words, she must have interpreted my question as indicating I did not appreciate her talents and that I thought she was just chattering. In identifying with my assumed view of her, she was able to control her intense disappointment and thus to maintain the feeling of closeness to me which was being threatened.

To make this transaction explicit, I now told the patient that I thought she must be feeling disappointed because she had hoped to interest me in the quality of her grasp of aesthetics. To this description of what I assumed had taken place between us, the patient had an intense reaction. She immediately covered her face with her hands and declared herself to be horribly embarrassed. Her face felt hot and red, the whole room felt hot—so intense was her feeling of shame. She felt that I had reprimanded her, as if she were a child.

Although her description of herself in

the role of the child brought the buried implicit role somewhat nearer the surface, an exact definition of the role was still lacking. Because of the intensity of her reaction, I waited some moments until she became calmer. Then I speculated aloud that her expectation that I would accept the role of appreciator—of one who puts great emphasis on artistic achievements—must have been learned in some previous experience. In response she told me that her father was greatly interested in intellectual and artistic pursuits and could seldom make contact with anyone except at this level. When she was a child, dinner-table conversations used to consist of long orations by father on some intellectual topic—conversations which she was hardly ever allowed to enter, on the ground that she was not qualified.

As she spoke, the similarity of the role relations that she thought she had experienced with me to the role she felt she had occupied in relation to her father became clear to both of us. She felt that she had tried to master with me a situation which she had never mastered at home, had failed, and had then felt presumptuous, exposed, and ashamed—just as she had all her life. Thus the implicit role which guided her in talking to me about the play had finally become explicit and clear.

I would like, now, to review the significance of this clinical fragment for the distinction between psychoanalysis and psychotherapy from the point of view of role theory. In psychoanalysis, as I understand it, the intention of the technique is to help the patient to become aware of his own motivations and of the self-constriction, the narrowness of the ego, associated with the fear and guilt attached to his motivations. Since motivation can only be expressed in social behavior, the motivations with which treatment is concerned are built into social roles, which, because of the fear and guilt, are either repressed or given only very disguised expression as hidden implicit roles. As a technique, psychoanalysis is a system of behavior or communication wherein the explicit permissiveness and acceptance of all communications associated with the doctor's role encourages, through complementarity, the eruption of the buried implicit roles. This is the general process denoted by the concept of transference, which is signalled by the forcible intrusion of an implicit role into the explicit role system. The expression "the management of the transference" refers, then, to the roles assumed by the doctor with respect to the emerging implicit roles of the patient. If the procedure is a psychoanalytical one, the doctor will not play a complementary role to the emerging implicit role of the patient. It is this refusal on the part of the doctor which forces the role and its motivation explicitly into the consciousness of the patient. The reason for this is that a person is much more likely to become aware of his role, his motivation for it, and the feelings connected with it when the transactional system is at an optimum disequilibrium. No one is likely to give much thought to a role system that is running perfectly smoothly. In this connection, the opportunities for "interpretation" by the doctor represent an instrumental role in which he reviews what has happened in the transactions subsequent to his declining the complementary role. At the same time, he helps the patient define the role satisfactions that were sought for and thus sheds further light on the patient's motivation. Looked at from the point of view of this definition, the procedure in the clinical fragment just reported was that of psychoanalysis.

In my view, the role of the doctor, when the procedures are those of psychotherapy, is in some respects directly opposed to the process just described for psychoanalysis. Overlooking, for the moment, the factors which may structure the situation, the situation which calls for psychotherapy, as here defined, is one in which the communication system is potentially disturbed by disequilibria of great magnitude. The role balance of doctor and patient is continually threatened by the eruption of explicit roles which seem inappropriate to the purely instrumental role of the doctor. Because of the great disequilibrium, the doctor cannot refuse to play a role reciprocal to the dominant explicit role of the patient. Only through the re-establishment of complementarity can the disturbance be quieted or averted. But this takes place at the cost of suppressing the implicit roles, and therefore the specific complementary role must be chosen with great care so that it results in redefinition of the explicit roles.

This principle can best be illustrated in terms of concrete procedures by discussing a further development of the clinical fragment presented above. At the moment when the patient discovered that the role she had wanted to play with me was identical to the one she had wanted to play with her father, I had to make a procedural choice. On the one hand, there was the possibility of exploring further her motivation in wanting to play an intimate intellectual role with her father. I suspected then, and subsequent events proved, that her motivation was to be the sole possessor of her father's attention and to have a revengeful triumph over her mother. To have pursued this goal would have required a continuation of the analytical procedure. But at the moment such an exploration would have been doomed to failure because the explicit role situation was wholly dominated by the persistence of her sense of shame. She kept her face averted from me, and her whole attitude was one of shrinking away, as if she desired to be invisible. The shame of having revealed her intention to me and of having failed was reinforced by the memory of failures in the past. It was clear that some activity on my part was indicated in order to help her to master the overwhelming shame. But what role was to be chosen for this purpose? In this connection the expressions "ego support,"

"ego strengthening," "reassurance," and many others easily leap to mind. It is also precisely in relation to such maneuvers that our concepts are at their weakest.

The role I chose was related explicitly to the management of her shame. What she was expressing, it seemed to me, was her feeling that she had had little value in her father's eyes, and that she had just now made the discovery that she had very little in mine. I could have reassured her directly by denying this picture, by affirming my appreciation of her abilities in the area which she had just attempted. In other words, I could have redefined the explicit roles by letting her have an insight into my actual opinion of her intellectual performance. This is a perfectly feasible transaction in a psychotherapeutic procedure. The objection to it was that under the circumstances it would have appeared artificial, as if applied only to ease her pain. Instead of this, I pointed out that by placing me in her father's position, she neglected to explore the possibility of my seeing any values in her personality other than intellectual achievement. I tried to show her how her involvement with her father narrowed her view of herself and, reciprocally, the view that she could see others taking of her. In pursuing this line, my intention was to broaden the perspectives of her self-valuation. To accomplish this, I tentatively accepted the role of "appreciator," but I enlarged its range of application. In role-theory terms, I was working on the connection between her cultural values and the anxiety about values built into her personality by her unresolved relation with her father. As we discussed this area, her shame visibly decreased. The psychotherapeutic procedure restored the equilibrium in our relations with each other.

In my view, this procedure illustrates one of the principal contrasts in method and goal between psychotherapy and psychoanalysis. Whereas in the psychoanalytic procedure the explicit role assignment is refused by the doctor, in psychotherapy it is accepted but is redefined so that the patient is able to take a new view of himself and of others. This may be called reality interpretation, reassurance, or ego support, but the general principle is the same. It does not lead the patient to a discovery of his unconscious motivation nor to a clear realization of what his implicit role is, but it puts him on more secure ground so that the discovery is more easily made at a later time.

According to my experience and what I have been able to observe of the experience of others, both psychoanalytic and psychotherapeutic procedures may be indicated in the treatment of any patient. This is what makes it so difficult to draw hard and fast lines and what makes the discussions so confusing. Partly because of structural relations within the ego, and partly because of the socioeconomic situation of the patient and the amount of time he can give to the treatment, it is possible to engage in predominantly psychoanalytic transactions with some patients,

while with others psychotherapeutic procedures are what is principally required. In any event such quantitative distinctions are relative rather than absolute. If the concrete procedural distinction can be made exact, and if any treatment can be assumed to contain variable quantities of both procedures, then the choice of terms to apply to the over-all relation with any particular patient—that is, Is the patient "in psychoanalysis" or "in psychotherapy"?—becomes less controversial.

In conclusion, it should be said that this presentation of role theory overlooks many important technical and theoretical aspects of psychotherapeutic and psychoanalytic method. I do not know if it has anything to add to psychodynamic theory other than the possibility of greater precision in the examination of the details of the treatment process. But in view of the difficulties of assembling the vast array of data accumulated in the course of a patient's treatment and of relating the data to precise theory, this approach seems deserving of further exploration.

INTERPERSONAL DISTURBANCES IN THE FAMILY:
SOME UNSOLVED PROBLEMS IN PSYCHOTHERAPY

by Nathan W. Ackerman

If the specific tools of psychotherapy are to be extended reliably beyond the disturbed patient, into various group interactions, then the logical beginning is within the smallest social unit, the family. In this paper, I am concerned with the question: Is there a possible psychotherapeutic approach to the family as a family? At present, approaches to emotional disturbances of family life are made through the concomitant psychotherapy of several family members, sometimes with an at-

SOURCE: *Psychiatry*, Vol. 17 (1954), pp. 359–369. Reprinted by special permission of The William Alanson White Psychiatric Foundation, Inc.

tempt to integrate the several therapies in the interest of the mental health of the family as a whole. Certainly, concomitant psychotherapy of several family members —husband and wife, mother and child, for example—often results in some degree of improvement of family relationships, but such therapy is still one of individuals and not of family relationships or of the group. The effects of such psychotherapy on the family as a unit are in the main indirect rather than direct, nonspecific rather than specific. Even if every member of a family were given individual psychotherapy, this still would not constitute a psychotherapy of the family. Thus a systematic psychotherapeutic method for the family has yet to be evolved.

The historic province of the psychiatrist has been the individual personality and not the family. Problems of the family have traditionally been the province of the social worker and occasionally of the minister or the teacher. In recent years, the social scientist has become increasingly interested in the family as a subject for intensive investigation, but most of these studies have only broad ameliorative goals and no specific planned intervention for stated disturbances within the family. In psychiatrically oriented family agencies and child guidance clinics, one finds a broader concern with the family as a whole; but in the usual psychiatric clinic, the psychiatrist's interest tends to center on the most disturbed member of the group. Only to a limited degree is his effort ordinarily extended to encompass the problems of the family.

Historic Trends in the Handling of Family Problems

Some brief mention of the broad historical trends in the philosophy of therapy for disturbances in family relationships may serve to make more explicit the inherent problems. Over the years there has been an ebb and flow of a variety of therapeutic styles. This is to be expected, for such changing patterns of practice are a necessary expression of the natural evolution which accompanies the acquisition of new knowledge, and are also an inevitable effect of social and cultural change. But one may question the appropriateness of seizing upon new and untried methods, while casting overboard what has been laboriously learned in the past, or the wisdom of conforming slavishly and uncritically to prevailing psychotherapeutic styles. In some measure, such tendencies have hampered progress in the field.

In discussing the changes in philosophy

of therapy of family relationships, I am not attempting to present a balanced historical account, but only to trace certain trends which I have observed. A quarter of a century ago, the effort to correct disturbances in family relationships took mainly the form of social therapy rather than psychotherapy, and "therapists" attempted to meet disturbances in family relationships with social devices aimed at reorientation of attitudes and activities. Social agencies in the community emphasized a variety of social techniques for therapeutic intervention in the family, such as religious, social, and occupational guidance. In this form of help, mainly the conscious aspect of emotional experience was taken into account. Partly as a result of this, the eventual disillusionment as to the efficacy of these social techniques was abrupt and complete. Then came a new wave of tremendous emphasis on individual personality. Social agencies absorbed the philosophy of mental hygiene and entered a mad dash for an orientation to psychiatry and psychoanalysis.[1]

With the increasing emphasis on the emotional problems of the individual and on unconscious motivation, the study and treatment of the family environment became less popular. In some professional circles, the social approach to disturbances in family relations was brushed aside as "superficial"—which was, on the crest of this wave, the most damning indictment which could be made of a given therapeutic technique. Psychiatric casework came into being as a specialty with superior prestige value, and professional status and recognition came only to the social worker who achieved repute as a skilled casework therapist, relationship therapist, or psychotherapist. The influence of social and economic factors on the mental health of families was minimized, and the traditional social agency function

[1] For a fuller consideration of this problem see Albert Deutsch, *The Mentally Ill in America;* Garden City, N. Y., Country Life Press, 1937; pp. 318–323.

of mitigating the real threats to family welfare by such means as providing relief and employment services became regarded as routine, mechanical, and beneath the professional dignity of trained social workers. Home visits as a systematic social work technique for the study of family problems all but disappeared. Thus the external and the conscious conflicts were put to one side; the realistic situation of the family was minimized; concern with the tensions of interpersonal relations was subordinated to the primary concern with the individual psyche—with unconscious conflicts and irrational motivation; and families as families became virtually lost as objects of study.

During this phase, without doubt, a great deal was learned about people, but not without some cost. The understanding of the individual advanced somewhat out of context, in terms of the need for a parallel knowledge of the processes of social interaction. Social workers and psychiatrists seemed often to lose contact with social reality; they lacked clarity in distinguishing the real and unreal. They misapplied or used all too loosely such concepts as transference and resistance. There was a rushing concentration on the emotional life of the individual, to the extent that the social frame, within which the individual's reactions were to be judged, was lost sight of.

For the moment I am purposely overdrawing one side of the argument to make a point. Momentous advances have been made in the understanding of individual personality, but it should be obvious that the law of diminishing returns is now beginning to make itself felt. It appears that further significant additions to the knowledge of personality may be made if we now broaden our conceptual frame so as to examine the behavior of the individual, not in isolation, but rather in the context of comprehensive evaluation of the group structure of the family. Recently a wave of fashion has, in fact, asserted itself which once again emphasizes the relations of individual personality with family and wider society.

If we aspire to the goal of reducing to scientific terms the therapeutic approach to disturbances in family relations, it is necessary to adopt a critical, discriminating attitude toward changing psychotherapeutic fashions, to avoid stereotyping treatment methods, and to carefully test out what is specific and nonspecific, central or peripheral in these procedures. Equally essential is the building of a conceptual frame for a proper integration of techniques of social therapy and psychotherapy.

Experience with Family Pairs

In attempting to devise a psychotherapy of the family, it is important to look first at the present experience with the concomitant psychotherapy of several family members, usually family pairs. As I have already said, certainly the concomitant therapy of several individual members of a family often results in some degree of improvement of family relationships; but I believe that this is usually true to the extent that the therapists concerned take into consideration the disturbances of family relationships and integrate the several therapies. It is some of the unsolved problems of individual therapy for several family members which underline the need for a psychotherapeutic approach to the family as a whole.

Although psychiatrists have traditionally concerned themselves with the problems of the individual, they have long recognized that there is usually a second person in the family involved in the patient's pathology. Among psychiatrists, it is a truism that the person who accompanies a patient on his first visit to the psychiatrist's office is significantly involved in the patient's illness. A mother who accompanies a child, a husband who accompanies a wife, are obvious examples of this. Over and over again one finds such pairs of persons bound in neurotic love and neurotic competition. Pathological trends can be discerned in the interpersonal situation as well as in the individual personality make-up of each member of such a pair.[2] It is hopefully assumed that the therapeutic resolution of neurotic anxiety in one or both partners will mitigate the interpersonal disturbance. Sometimes it does; sometimes it does not; sometimes it succeeds in part only. Some of the reasons for this are clear. Neurotic anxiety, while a significant factor, is but one among many that determine the fate of a relationship. Other factors are the contingencies of external social influence, the compatibility of temperament, goals, interests, and values, the lines of identification between the two people, the reciprocity of emotional need, the quality of communication, and so on.

Furthermore, in the psychotherapeutic approach to neurotic anxiety, some therapists place the major focus on the internal economy of individual personality rather than on social relationships. While relationship experience is relived in psychotherapy, the primary point of reference tends to be the orientation to self rather than the social interaction per se. It is of course true that a person's orientation to self influences his orientation to others, and vice versa, but this is by no means a simple one-to-one correlation. The interplay of individual and group levels of experience is a complex phenomenon, the full scope of which cannot yet be clearly conceptualized. The extent to which a disturbance in a family relationship is alleviated by individual psychotherapy of one or both partners depends upon many factors: the nature of the pathology of this relationship; the secondary effects of ancillary relationships; the psychosocial condition of the family as a whole; the individual's adaptation to

this; and finally the nature of the pathology and psychotherapy of each partner in the relationship, and the extent to which the therapy of one partner is effectively coordinated with the therapy of the other.

The factors which determine disturbances in family relations certainly do not derive alone from the unconscious. Of specific relevance are the discrepancies between real and unreal attitudes, between real and unreal experience, between conscious and unconscious conflict, between the inner emotional orientation to self and the external orientation to other persons, between idealized goals and actual achievement. Success in psychotherapy for family relationships rests on the therapist's ability to place unconscious phenomena in correct context with regard to conscious experience and the prevailing interpersonal realities. In any case, whatever the vicissitudes of therapy of a neurotically involved family pair, this is not to be conceived as a therapy of the family per se.

The Failure of Individual Therapy to Improve Social Relationships

The social product of some forms of psychoanalytic therapy reflects certain limitations of individual therapy. Paradoxically, the patient as an individual may markedly improve, and yet in some respects his social relations may remain almost as bad as they ever were. Facetiously speaking, everything in the patient is cured except his human relations. Or, in the phrase of one analyst, "On completion of analysis, the patient is wiser, but sadder and lonelier."

It is by no means rare in the treatment of a family pair that as one member of the pair gets better, the other gets worse. In child guidance work, as the child improves, not infrequently the mother paradoxically worsens. Or, as the child responds to psychotherapy, the parental

[2] See N. W. Ackerman, "The Diagnosis of Neurotic Marital Interaction," *Social Case Work* (1954) 35:139–147.

conflict becomes drastically intensified. Similarly, in the treatment of marital problems, it is often the case that as one marital partner matures and becomes sexually more adequate, the other regresses; or one may respond to analytic therapy with an increased capacity for closeness, and the other may react with depression. This is impressively illustrated in those marital situations in which one partner markedly improves with therapy, but this very fact paradoxically hastens the relationship toward divorce. Apparently, in some circumstances, the increased strength or health of personality of one family member becomes a threat to another.

For example, a wife campaigns for her husband to enter psychotherapy for sexual impotence, threatening to leave him unless he is cured. The husband yields, is treated, and the symptom of impotence is quickly alleviated. The husband's therapist, pleased with his success, is shocked to discover that directly after the husband's potency was restored, his wife deserted him. This is paradoxical behavior, to be sure, but it can and does occur. Individual psychotherapy may help the individual, but under certain conditions it may fail to ameliorate the pathology of a family relationship. The tension of interpersonal conflict may remain largely unabated even though intrapsychic disturbance is measurably relieved. Somewhat in the same vein, I might quote the caustic comment of an unanalyzed wife of an analyst, who felt alienated from her husband's special sphere of interest. She quipped, "What we wives of analysts need is to form a union."

From such considerations as these, it does appear that our capacity for promoting mental health in social relationships lags behind our techniques for promoting health in the inner psychic life of the individual. One could multiply many times these examples of a dramatic, occasionally perverse shift in the delicate balance of interpersonal relations within the family, induced by therapeutic change in the be-havior of a single member. The emotional equilibrium of a family group may be seriously upset by poor timing of therapeutic intervention in two directions: by precipitously plunging several family members into psychotherapy at the same time; or by delaying too long in arranging for the psychotherapy of additional family members. In some instances where the family balance was quite tender, I have advised that only one member of the family at a time enter therapy, for if the involvement of members in psychotherapy is strategically staggered over a period of time, the danger of any critical upheaval of family life is somewhat mitigated. With precise knowledge of the existing tensions in family relationships and with appropriate timing, it is possible to facilitate therapy of individual members and also favorably influence the mental health of the family as a group; at the very least it is possible to avoid disorganization of the family equilibrium.

The Integration of Concomitant Therapies of Family Members

When each member of a neurotic family pair needs psychotherapy, the question arises as to whether they should be treated by the same or separate therapists. Naturally, the most efficient form of integration of the psychotherapies is that which can be achieved in the mind of a single therapist. Strong objections have been offered to such practice, however. The premise seems to be that two members of a family, interdependent but mutually distrustful and competitively destructive, would vie with each other for the therapist's favor, and that this rivalry would jeopardize therapeutic control. Therefore, the argument goes, provision for separate treatment is preferable. I think, however, that this argument overlooks the difficulty of integrating the two therapies, and the further problems which arise out of the failure to relate the psychotherapy of the neurotic pair to the total dynamics of family life. In providing for separate treatment, there should be no self-deception on the part of the therapist that the patients' suspiciousness will be disarmed by the mere fact of having separate therapists; nor should there be any self-deception that the tensions in the family relationships will take care of themselves. Definitive indications and contraindications for the treatment of a family pair by the same or separate therapists are badly needed.

When two members of a family pair are in conflict but are essentially loyal and genuinely motivated to improve the relationship, one would be wise to respect the substantial advantages of a single therapist for both persons. If basically each trusts the other, each one will in time build sufficient trust in the therapist and not be critically apprehensive of the misuse of his contacts with the other member of the pair.

It is true, on the other hand, that when two members of a family are locked in pathological conflict, with a deep layer of mutual mistrust and a strong propensity for destructive motivation, treatment by separate therapists may be preferable. I do believe, however, that such a plan is often initiated prematurely, without adequate clarification of the interpersonal level of disturbance, without sufficient emotional preparation of each partner, and without laying a foundation for effective collaboration between the two therapists at later stages. It has the effect, sometimes, of drawing the two family members apart rather than bringing them into closer relationship. Too often a pair of parents or a child and mother are plunged immediately into individual psychotherapy, before they have any chance to gain some understanding of the relationship conflict. In such cases it is useful for a single therapist to have a short series of interviews with both patients before dividing the therapy. This offers the advantage, for patients and therapist alike,

of beginning the therapy by obtaining a more accurate understanding of the meaning of the relationship conflict; clearing away misconceptions and unnecessary distortions; and getting a sharper definition of the dynamic relatedness of intrapersonality pathology to the disturbance in the relationship. I believe this often enables the separate psychotherapy of each partner to get started on the right foot, and it certainly provides a better basis for later collaboration between the two therapists—provided that their selection has been based in part on their ability to collaborate. It is then a question of careful judgment and timing as to when the members of such a family pair are emotionally ready for separate psychotherapy.

But as the principle of separate treatment is usually applied at present, it is most difficult to pursue the goal of integrating the two therapies. Occasionally such collaborative effort is successfully carried out. Frequently, in my experience, it fails. Theoretically, in a great many child and family guidance centers the integration of the effects of concomitant psychotherapy of several members of a family is supposed to be achieved through the application of the principle of the professional team. Such teams are usually drawn from the professions of psychiatry, social work, and psychology. The several therapists treating members of a single family are supposed to work within the framework of the team, collaborating with the other members. In some instances, unfortunately, allegiance to this principle turns out to be lip service, rather than effective integration.

In private psychiatric practice, effective collaboration between psychiatrists treating different members of the same family is also rare. It is interesting to observe the varying attitudes taken toward collaboration in such a situation. For instance, one of the psychiatrists may profess to the other a seemingly earnest desire for collaboration but fail to carry it out. Or he may curiously shy away from the whole question of collaboration. Some psychiatrists go so far as to openly declare that collaboration is intrinsically undesirable, that it jeopardizes the exclusiveness of their relationship with the patient, that it endangers the patient's privacy—all in all, that it menaces the psychiatrist's therapeutic control. Some psychoanalysts try to avoid involvement with other family members by refusing to interview them; while certainly they cannot avoid the impact of problems in family relationships, they tend to deal with these conflicted relationships *in absentia*. Thus, rightly or wrongly, the focus of the psychotherapy of each family member becomes sharply individual. The two therapeutic experiences tend to get dissociated, as each individual therapy goes its merry way. In such a setting the intrapsychic conflicts of each person may be ameliorated, but successful readaptation to the family relationships may nonetheless fail.

A specific difficulty which arises when two members of a family are in psychotherapy with separate therapists is that of dealing effectively with events which reflect a coincidence between reality and irrational projection. It is exactly in such situations that therapists differ in their evaluations and psychotherapeutic prescriptions. A few examples may illustrate this point:

When a child in therapy denies having emotional problems and insists, "It is my parents who are upset, not me," the child may be resisting therapy, to be sure; but the implied demand, *Do something about my parents,* is certainly not without justification.

The only son of a self-centered but highly successful attorney is in therapy because he is emotionally isolated and withdrawn, and repeatedly fails in his academic work even though he has a superior intelligence. He is weak and unassertive, but passively resists his father's ambitions for him. He does not feel like a person in his own right, but rather like a

piece of his father. He accuses his father of pursuing him constantly, and expresses the conviction that his father needs the psychiatrist more than he. He is partly right.

The mother of a disturbed child projects blame upon the father, the father turns it back on the mother. In effect, the mother says to her psychiatrist, *Why blame everything on me? My husband should be your patient*—an attitude which may be promptly chalked down by the psychiatrist as the mother's projection of guilt. So it is, but more often than not such an accusation carries with it an important core of truth as well.

A rather masculine woman, with a social work professional background, is married to a weak man, whom she belittles because he has "hips like a woman and suffers hysterical fits." They have an emotionally disturbed child. The woman denies personal problems, placing the main responsibility for the child's difficulty on the father's neurotic fears. She offers to collaborate with the therapist in treating her husband. This woman resists therapy for herself, to be sure, but there is a basis in fact for her insistence that her husband should receive therapy.

Should the other person concerned in each of these situations enter therapy with a different therapist, the areas of reality and the areas of irrational projection might continue to be obscure, for the two therapists might differ in their evaluations of the situation and in their prescriptions. The therapy of each patient might proceed without an opportunity for reality testing. Bela Mittleman [3] has drawn attention to this problem in an article on the simultaneous psychoanalytic therapy of husband and wife. In the procedure he describes, husband and wife were treated by the same psychoanalyst, thus violating the traditional psychoana-

[3] Bela Mittleman, "The Concurrent Analysis of Married Couples," *Psychoanalytic Quart.* (1948) 17:182–197.

lytic fashion of husband and wife being treated by different analysts. Mittleman points out the advantageous position of a single therapist for both marital partners in being able to discern accurately the irrational projections of each partner onto the other, and thus achieving a clear definition of the reality of the marital relationship. Using in each patient's therapy information derived from the therapy of the other can, of course, be done only with the full knowledge and consent of both. This is a therapeutic plan in which collaboration is truly achieved in the mind of a single therapist. Mittleman considers the specific gain in this arrangement to be the heightened opportunity for reality testing which can be used to effective advantage in the therapy of both partners. My own clinical experiences tend to confirm this point of view, as I shall try to illustrate by the following case:

A woman teacher, who was married to a gifted musician, was acutely depressed. They had one child who was suffering badly from the mother's disturbed mental state. In interview, the wife laid the blame for her depression at her husband's door. She complained bitterly that her husband, who had earlier been highly successful as a musician, now failed to earn an adequate living; she said that he didn't try hard enough, that he ought to pocket his artistic vanity and go out and get any work he could, no matter what, and that he owed this to his wife and child. In discussing her husband, she sounded vindictive almost to the point of violence. She confessed to refusing her husband sex satisfaction, and had calamitous fears of the imminent break-up of her marriage. When asked if she had directly expressed these feelings to her husband, she demurred, saying "No, it would hurt him too deeply, irrevocably." I suggested that we have a three-cornered interview, consisting of this woman, her husband, and myself, the psychiatrist. She resisted at first, fearing that this might

precipitate the destruction of her marriage. It did nothing of the kind; on the contrary, it cleared the air of unreal accusations and distorted projections, and, if anything, saved the marriage. The actual reality of the situation was that her husband was earnestly trying to get suitable employment; that his temporary failure was no doing of his own, but was the result of a critical turn in the economy of the music industry; and that he was deeply distressed by his wife's rejection of sex relations, but did not wish to force himself upon her. In this triangular discussion, the wife was stripped of the alibi for her depression. She was attaching her hostility and guilt to the wrong person and for the wrong reasons, since the real object of her hate was her mother. She could no longer falsely project on her husband the reason for her bitterness, and she recognized her irrational urge to exploit her husband's unfortunate professional situation for the purpose of humiliating him as a man and making him crawl before her eyes. She then admitted that her real fear was loss of sexual pleasure with the approaching menopause—a fear which had been profoundly strengthened in her by an earlier traumatic family experience in which her mother had been chiefly concerned. Further therapeutic contacts both with the wife alone and with the wife and her husband together relieved the depression and the marital crisis.

Child Guidance and Treatment of Parents in Terms of Family Role

In child guidance practice, the problems of treating the parents of disturbed children have not been solved. There have been many failures. We have not yet succeeded in formulating adequate criteria for the psychotherapy of parental role. In examining the causes of failure of treatment of mothers of disturbed children, several factors loom large: the complexity of the definition of mothering; the difficulty of relating the dynamics of individual personality to the mothering role; incomplete or incorrect diagnosis; vague and changing orientation to goals with resulting confusion of the therapeutic course; failure to properly integrate the treatment of child and mother; failure to understand the parental conflict and the fundamental interdependence of maternal and paternal functioning; and finally, the failure to relate the therapy of child and mother to a total psychosocial evaluation of the family as a unit.

This raises some pertinent questions: To what degree is the therapeutic goal for mothers related to maternal role and to what degree related to the mother's total personality? To what extent is the maternal role influenced by the paternal role and by the other significant relationships in the family? Should treatment of the mother in the child guidance program always be secondary to the primary goal of treatment of the child? Or should the therapy of the mother as a person be pursued beyond the point required by the needs of the child? By what criteria do we decide on a partial goal, such as achieving merely a reduction of emotional pressures and anxieties, a modification of conscious maternal attitudes, or a redirection of hostility away from the child? In contrast to this, under what conditions should we undertake the goal of basic character change in the mother?

My own observations of separate psychotherapy of child and mother [4] indicate that the extent to which the psychotherapies of child and mother are coordinated varies tremendously, and that the degree to which the therapy of the mother is child-oriented varies correspondingly.

[4] My remarks here are based to a large extent on a review which I have made of the results of the program of separate psychotherapy at the Child Guidance Institute of the Jewish Board of Guardians, as well as some of the recommendations I have made regarding this program.

From one child-parent unit to the next, there is little consistency. Some mothers talk, in their psychotherapeutic sessions, of their child and their child only. They seem obsessed with worry over the child and with the need to control and punish the child. Accordingly, they are motivated to exploit the social worker or therapist as the agent of their punitive attitude. They use their preoccupation with control of the child's behavior as a resistance to a real understanding of their maternal role and as an escape from confrontation with their personal responsibility for the child's disorder.

At the opposite pole there is a group of mothers who begin their psychotherapeutic experience with a concern with the child, but soon seem to forget the child altogether and become exclusively preoccupied with themselves. They exploit their therapeutic interviews for dealing with a variety of other personal problems, such as their marital difficulties and their own conflicts with their parents, but neglect the issues of their relatedness to the child. The child's behavior difficulties are dropped wholly in the lap of the child's therapist, with an attitude of *let the therapist worry*. Between these two extremes, there is every intermediate shade of maternal behavior. Both types of maternal attitude represent resistance to the therapy of disturbance in the maternal role. In the first instance, the mother looks accusingly at the child, but refuses to look at herself; in the second, she looks at herself but refuses to look at her child. In either case, in this program for separate treatment, effective access to the disturbance moving between child and mother is rendered more difficult. In all probability, these polar forms of resistance in mothers of disturbed children are influenced in part by the differences in orientation of different psychotherapists.

In such programs for separate treatment, the therapeutic orientation seems to move all too quickly to an exclusive preoccupation with the child as an individual and with the mother as an individual. It moves too quickly away from the level of real relationship experience to the level of unreal emotional experience and irrational unconscious conflicts. There is a conspicuous trend toward by-passing interpersonal levels of disturbance and plunging immediately into the intrapsychic conflicts of the individual patient. To be sure, the merits of separate treatment on a carefully selected individual case basis are well established. But I fail to see the logic of routine provisions for separate treatment in every family pair, nor can I make sense of the trend toward a quick by-passing of the interpersonal level of pathology in favor of too sharp and too early emphasis on structured intrapsychic conflict patterns. Therefore I think that more considered selection of cases for separate treatment, and also more careful timing of the arrangements for such therapy are needed. Certainly in some instances it is logical for a single therapist to treat both child and mother—that in fact it may be the treatment of choice—whereas in other instances the barrier of suspicion and mistrust between the respective members of the family pair may make provision for separate treatment a necessity. In some families it is appropriate for a single therapist to interview the family pair together in the beginning, to orient his early therapeutic efforts to an understanding of the interpersonal conflict and to help each member of the pair to see more clearly the coexistence of reality and projection, and then move gradually to a plan for separate treatment.

From all this, it is apparent that an appropriate frame of reference has not yet been designed, within which it is possible to integrate the therapy of an individual with the therapy of a family group. The treatment of a mother of a disturbed child is the treatment of a role, a highly specialized family function. It is not identical with the therapy of a whole woman, but rather of the personality of that woman integrated into a special social function, that of mothering. For a proper conceptual approach to this problem, it is necessary to recognize the interdependence and reciprocity of family roles, to devise criteria for accurate appraisal of the mental health functioning of family groups and dynamic formulae for interrelating individual personality and family role.

What is the challenge in terms of a therapy for the family as a group? What frame of reference must one design for such an effort? The family may be defined in diverse ways. Waller[5] describes it as a unity of interacting personalities, each with a history. This definition fails to convey the unique features of the family group: the union of male and female to produce offspring, and insure their survival. George Murdock[6] defines the family as follows: "The family is a social group characterized by common residence, economic cooperation and reproduction. It includes adults of both sexes, at least two of whom maintain a socially approved sexual relationship, and one or more children, own or adopted, of the sexually cohabiting adults. The vital functions of the family are sexual, economic, reproductive and educational."

The disturbances of family life are obviously disturbances both of the individual and the group. They must therefore be studied and treated at levels which interrelate the intra- and interpersonal processes, and the processes of the group as a whole. Logically viewed, a systematic therapy of the family would encompass techniques directed at the multiple interacting relationships, both within the family, and between family and outside community, and also techniques for psy-

[5] Willard Waller and Reuben Hill, *The Family: A Dynamic Interpretation;* New York, Dryden Press, 1951; p. 6.

[6] George P. Murdock, *Social Structure;* New York, Macmillan, 1949; p. 1.

chotherapy of individual family members. Within this frame of reference, the therapeutic approach to the family group per se would be primary and the psychotherapy of individual members secondary. In other words, the relation of individual psychotherapy to the therapy of the family would be the relation of the part to the whole. It is self-evident, however, that before we could make any substantial progress toward devising a therapy of the family, we would need to evolve definitive criteria for the psychosocial disorders of family life. We would need more exact understanding as to how the emotional forces moving between persons influence the psychic balance within the individual, and vice versa—in other words, a scientific definition of the dynamic interplay between intra- and extrapersonality factors. As we aspire to specificity in family therapy, we would hope, if possible, to reduce the definition of disturbance to a single formulation of the interaction patterns of the family, which encompasses within it the dynamics of intrapersonality processes. To achieve such formulation, it seems necessary to view the functioning of individual personality in the context of the dynamics of family role.[7]

The phenomena of family life are revealed at three interrelated levels: (1) the multiple interaction patterns between family members, beginning with the central relationship of man and wife; (2) the personal development of each family member; and (3) the interaction of the family unit with the outside community. And along with, and as a part of these three levels, one may view the dynamics of family life from the viewpoint of the emotional integration into the family group of each individual member, and the specific dynamic relations of individual personality structure to family role.

An effective therapeutic approach to interpersonal disturbances of the family

may be achieved through a series of logical steps as follows: (1) a psychosocial evaluation of the family group as a whole; (2) the application of appropriate techniques of social therapy; (3) a psychotherapeutic approach to significant family relationships; (4) individual psychotherapy for selected family members, oriented initially to the specific dynamic relations of family role to personality structure.

The psychosocial pattern of a given family is determined by the dynamic balance between intra- and extrafamilial processes. Tension and conflict within the family affect the external adaptation of the family to community; similarly, stress in the relations of family with community find an echo in the internal emotional processes of the family. The psychotherapeutic approach to significant family relationships and the individual psychotherapy of selected family members should be viewed in the context of the total psychosocial diagnosis of the family. This diagnostic evaluation should be made both in terms of current functioning of the family and its historical development. The therapy of interpersonal disturbances in the family is enhanced if we view the disturbed person both as an individual and as a member of an integrated family group.[8]

It is the assumption of this paper that the ultimate goals of psychiatry are the alleviation of problems in the social community. While at present the psychiatrist

---

[7] See N. W. Ackerman, " 'Social Role' and Total Personality," *Amer. J. Orthopsychiatry* (1951) 21:1–17.

[8] A study of family diagnosis is in process which attempts to correlate the emerging emotional disturbance of the young child with the total psychosocial structure of the family group. See the following: N. W. Ackerman and R. Sobel, "Family Diagnosis," *Amer. J. Orthopsychiatry* (1950) 20:744–752. Ackerman, "A Study of Family Diagnosis," *Amer. J. Orthopsychiatry* (forthcoming). Ackerman, "Child and Family Pathology: Problems of Correlation"; in *The Psychopathology of Childhood* (Proc. Annual Meeting Amer. Psycho-Pathological Assn., 1954) (forthcoming).

has no systematic tools for either the family group or the social community, it is my belief that the psychiatrist can take the first step towards the over-all goal by focusing more specifically on the mental health problems of the family, in addition to treating individual patients. The study of disturbed patients, with its emphasis on the emotional problems of the individual and on the unconscious, has yielded rich results in the last quarter of a century. But this emphasis on the individual has, to some extent, blinded psychiatry and related disciplines to the processes of social interaction. It is to this latter area, somewhat neglected by the psychiatrist, that this paper has been addressed.

B · THE MENTAL HOSPITAL

IDEOLOGY, PERSONALITY, AND INSTITUTIONAL POLICY
IN THE MENTAL HOSPITAL

by Doris C. Gilbert and Daniel J. Levinson

This inquiry concerns the ideologies of mental hospital members regarding the nature and causes of mental illness and regarding hospital aims and policies in treating the mentally ill. We are interested in the nature of these ideologies as well as their institutional and intrapersonal roots. Mental hospitals are going through a period of ideological ferment and organizational change. The newly emerging viewpoints involve much more than the application of new treatment techniques. What gives them their fundamental quality is their conception of the hospital as a community of citizens rather than a rigidly codified institutional mold, and their conception of the hospital members as persons rather than as mere objects and agents of treatment (2, 8, 9, 14). In this respect as in many others, the ongoing developments in the mental hospital parallel those in other "correctional" institutions such as schools and prisons, and in larger bureaucratic structures such as industry and government (10, 12, 15). Because of their wider relevance, research in the mental hospital can make use of, and contribute materially to, the main body of sociopsychological theory and knowledge.

SOURCE: *Journal of Abnormal and Social Psychology,* Vol. 53 (1956), pp. 263–271.

The primary aims of this study are the following:

1. To formulate the main characteristics of the old and the newly emerging viewpoints regarding mental illness, and to construct an ideology scale that will crudely measure the degree of an individual's preference for one or the other viewpoint.
2. To investigate the personality contexts within which these orientations most readily develop.
3. To investigate the relationships of individual ideology and personality to membership in particular types of hospital systems and occupational statuses.
4. To investigate the ways in which the hospital's over-all policy is related to the modal (most common) ideology and the modal personality of its members.

Custodialism and Humanism as Ideological Orientations in the Mental Hospital

We have found it most fruitful, in our attempts at ideological analysis, to begin by asking: What are the major "problems" or issues of institutional life for which some kind of adaptive rationale is needed? The mental hospital presents at least the following issues with which every individual member must deal. The *patient:* what is he like, how did he get that way, how much can he be helped and in what ways? *Patient-staff relations:* what should be the role of hospital personnel vis-à-vis the patient; how much interaction should there be, with what emotional qualities and therapeutic aims? *Staff-staff relations:* how should specific functions and responsibilities be distributed; how much communication and status distinction should there be? *General hospital practices:* what formal treatment methods are best; how should ward life be organized; in what ways should patients be encouraged, left alone, controlled, punished?

The traditional and the newly developing viewpoints offer two contrasting sets of answers to the above questions. Each is a mode of thought underlying institutional policy and individual adaptation. A brief, schematic formulation of each ideology is presented below. It is to be emphasized that these are prototypes, probably represented in pure form by few individuals or hospitals. The two types may be thought of as polar extremes of a continuum containing various intermediate positions. We assume that this continuum is *realistic,* in the sense that viewpoints and policies approximating the prototypes will commonly be found, and that the continuum is *significant,* in the sense that adherence to one rather than the other viewpoint will seriously affect the individual's or the hospital's mode of functioning.

We shall use the term "custodialism" to designate the traditional patterns. The model of the custodial orientations is the traditional prison and the "chronic" mental hospital which provide a highly controlled setting concerned mainly with the detention and safekeeping of its inmates. Patients are conceived of in stereotyped terms as categorically different from "normal" people, as totally irrational, insensitive to others, unpredictable, and dangerous. Mental illness is attributed primarily to poor heredity, organic lesion, and the like. In consequence, the staff cannot expect to understand the patients, to engage in meaningful relationships with them, nor in most cases to do them much good. Custodialism is saturated with pessimism, impersonality, and watchful mistrust. The custodial conception of the hospital is autocratic, involving as it does a rigid status hierarchy, a unilateral downward flow of power, and minimal communication within and across status lines.

The newer orientations will be termed "humanistic" (after Fromm (6)) in view of their concern with the individuality and the human needs of both patients and personnel. These orientations conceive of the hospital as a therapeutic community rather than a custodial institution. They emphasize interpersonal and intrapsychic sources of mental illness, often to the neglect of possible hereditary and somatic sources. They view patients in more psychological and less moralistic terms. They are optimistic, sometimes to an unrealistic degree, about the possibilities of patient recovery in a maximally therapeutic environment. They attempt in varying degrees to democratize the hospital, to maximize the therapeutic functions of nonmedical personnel, to increase patient self-determination individually and collectively, and to open up communication wherever possible. While the humanistic orientations have the above characteristics in common, and even more an opposition to custodialism, they still differ among themselves in important respects. For example, the concrete manifestations of humanism will differ, although the guiding spirit may be the same, in a large, architecturally horrendous, financially limited state hospital, as contrasted with a small, well-subsidized, private hospital that accepts only patients regarded as good therapeutic risks.

This inquiry makes no assumptions about the actual therapeutic effectiveness of the various approaches. Our primary

TABLE 1. *The Custodial Mental Illness Ideology (CMI) Scale*

ITEM	MEAN	DP
1. Only persons with considerable psychiatric training should be allowed to form close relationships with patients.	3.5	2.4
3. It is best to prevent the more disturbed patients from mixing with those who are less sick.	5.0	1.8
5. As soon as a person shows signs of mental disturbance he should be hospitalized.	3.3	4.2
*7. Mental illness is an illness like any other.	2.7	2.7
9. Close association with mentally ill people is liable to make even a normal person break down.	2.0	1.4
11. We can make some improvements, but by and large the conditions of mental hospital wards are about as good as they can be, considering the type of disturbed patient living there.	3.0	3.6
15. We should be sympathetic with mental patients, but we cannot expect to understand their odd behavior.	3.2	3.8
17. One of the main causes in mental illness is lack of moral strength.	2.8	3.2
*18. When a patient is discharged from a hospital, he can be expected to carry out his responsibilities as a citizen.	3.0	.5
19. Abnormal people are ruled by their emotions; normal people by their reason.	3.8	4.4
21. A mental patient is in no position to make decisions about even everyday living problems.	3.0	3.1
*23. Patients are often kept in the hospital long after they are well enough to get along in the community.	4.2	−.2
25. There is something about mentally ill people that makes it easy to tell them from normal people.	3.0	2.9
27. Few, if any, patients are capable of real friendliness.	2.2	1.7
31. There is hardly a mental patient who isn't liable to attack you unless you take extreme precautions.	2.5	3.0
33. Patients who fail to recover have only themselves to blame; in most cases they have just not tried hard enough.	1.8	1.5
37. "Once a schizophrenic, always a schizophrenic."	2.3	1.3
38. Patients need the same kind of control and discipline as an untrained child.	3.3	2.4
39. With few exceptions most patients haven't the ability to tell right from wrong.	2.4	2.3
40. In experimenting with new methods of ward treatment, hospitals must consider, first and foremost, the safety of patients and personnel.	5.3	2.3

* Items expressing a "humanistic" position; all others are "custodial."
Note: The item means and *DP*s are those obtained by a sample of 196 mental hospital personnel in Hospitals C, T, and H. Similar *DP*s have been obtained in other samples of personnel, patients, and visitors. Items are numbered as they appear in the questionnaire, which contained other scales and questions.

concern here is with the nature and the determinants of custodialism and humanism.

The Custodial Mental Illness Ideology Scale (CMI)

The initial, field exploration led to the formulation of the "custodialism-humanism" continuum, the polar extremes of which have been described above. The next step was to construct the Custodial Mental Illness Ideology Scale (CMI), an admittedly crude instrument that had two chief functions in the research: (a) To test the hypothesis that a set of seemingly disparate ideas do in fact "go together" to form a relatively coherent orientation in the individual. A derivative function is to determine whether viewpoints approximating our posited prototypes exist with some frequency within various hospital settings. (b) To provide a quantitative and at the same time meaningful measure that facilitates additional study of the nature of these ideas and their relation to other aspects of the individual and his milieu.

The CMI scale consists of 20 statements, broadly diversified to cover numerous facets of the ideological domain: the nature and causes of mental illness, conditions in the hospital, patient-staff relations, and the like. The items were derived from interviews, conversations, and observations of conferences and everyday hospital life. The scale is presented in Table 1. A more extensive description of the field work and derivation of the CMI scale can be found in Gilbert (7).

SCORING PROCEDURE. The subjects were instructed to indicate the degree of their agreement or disagreement with each item on a scale ranging from +3 (strong agreement) to −3 (strong disagreement). The responses were converted into scores by means of an a priori, 7-point scoring sheme. It was intended that a high score

represent strong adherence to "custodial" ideology as here conceived, and that a low score represent opposition to this viewpoint. Of the 20 scale items, 17 were regarded as custodial, 3 as humanistic. For the "custodial" items, seven points were given for the +3 response, one point for −3. For the "humanistic" items the scoring was reversed. For convenience in comparing scores from scales differing in length, we shall use the mean per item, multiplied by 10. The possible range is thus 10–70 points.

The CMI scale was initially developed on a sample of 335 staff members (aides, student nurses, nurses, and psychiatrists) in three Massachusetts mental hospitals: Hospital C, a large (1,800 bed) institution dealing largely with "chronic" patients; Hospital T, a Veterans Administration hospital of about the same size; and Hospital H, a small (120 bed) state institution providing short-term active treatment. The range for this sample was 15–52, the mean being 31.3 and the SD, 9.5. Comparative data for various subgroupings are presented below (Table 2). The reliability (split-half correlation, corrected by Spearman-Brown formula) was .85, and test-retest correlations on several small groups were of similar magnitude. Table 1 presents the means and discriminatory powers (DP) of the individual items.[1] The DPs of all items except numbers 18 and 23 reach the .05 level of statistical significance, and most of them are beyond the .01 level.

The above data indicate that the initial form of the CMI scale has adequate reliability and internal consistency, and they provide a basis for further improvement. They suggest, moreover, that a person's stand on any single issue represented in

[1] DP of an item reflects its ability to differentiate between extremely high scorers and extreme low scorers (the upper and lower 25 per cent) on the total scale. It is computed as the difference between the means of the high-scoring and the low-scoring groups.

TABLE 2. *CMI Mean, F Mean, and Index of Status-Custodialism*

HOSPITAL-STATUS UNIT	N	INDEX OF STATUS-CUSTO-DIALISM	CMI SCALE			F SCALE			$r\text{CMI}_\text{F}$
			Mean	Rank	SD	Mean	Rank	SD	
Attendants at hospital:									
C	29	12	38.0	12	10.2	46.1	12	13.0	.91
T	51	11	37.3	11	10.3	41.4	11	11.7	.82
H	46	10	32.1	8	9.7	32.5	9	13.0	.77
Student nurses at hospital:									
C	66	9	33.4	10	7.7	29.0	8	10.9	.44
T	38	8	33.3	9	6.8	28.9	7	8.9	.25
H	16	7	31.3	6	5.7	28.8	6	9.2	.99
Nurses at hospital:									
C	14	6	31.3	7	9.9	37.3	10	14.5	.90
T	18	5	22.4	2	5.2	26.7	5	8.7	.53
H	21	4	26.9	5	7.7	25.8	3	14.5	.73
Doctors at hospital:									
C	6	3	25.8	4	7.0	18.1	1	6.2	.75
T	4	2	21.6	1	4.8	26.6	4	12.8	.80
H	24	1	22.7	2	4.5	19.1	2	8.5	.50
Total status:									
Attendants	128	4	35.3	4	10.4	39.1	4	13.7	.82
Student nurses	120	3	33.1	3	7.3	28.9	3	10.2	.41
Nurses	53	2	26.5	2	8.3	27.9	2	12.8	.76
Doctors	34	1	23.1	1	5.3	19.7	1	9.1	.46
Total hospital:									
C	115	3	33.7	3	8.9	33.8	2	14.5	.67
T	111	2	32.9	2	10.2	34.2	3	12.4	.69
H	109	1	29.0	1	8.7	27.7	1	13.1	.76
Total sample	335		31.3		9.5	31.9		13.7	.71

the scale is part of a broader, fairly coherent (though seldom fully integrated) ideology that embraces numerous issues of hospital life.

Data were obtained on two "validation groups" to determine whether the CMI score adequately gauges an enduring ideological conviction. One group, containing 10 administrators at Hospital H who are known for their advocacy of humanistic policies, earned a CMI mean of 18.8, with an SD of 6.1. The second group comprised the professional staff at the Social Rehabilitation Unit, Belmont Hospital, England, (9) and would also be expected to have a low CMI mean. The obtained mean was 22.9, the SD, 6.7. These findings offer additional evidence of scale validity.[2]

[2] In a study to be published shortly, we have obtained correlations of .5 and .8 between the CMI scale and a measure of custodialism in role performance, in two samples of hospital aides. Since at least a moderate relation between ideology and action would be expected on theoretical grounds, evidence of such a relation has indirect validational relevance for the CMI scale (4).

Psychological Bases of Custodialism and Humanism

With the CMI scale developed, it was possible to test the hypothesis that *the custodial orientation is one facet of an authoritarian personality, the humanistic orientation a facet of an equalitarian personality*. Several lines of theory and observation led to this expectation. Custodialism is strongly autocratic in its conception of the hospital and ethnocentric in its conception of patients as an inferior and threatening outgroup entitled to few if any of the rights of "normal" people. Humanism, on the other hand, seeks a more democratic hospital structure and regards patients as individuals to be understood and treated rather than as an outgroup to be pitied or condemned. There is considerable evidence that autocratic viewpoints tend to exist within authoritarian personality structures (1, 5, 6). We accordingly predicted that the CMI scale would correlate significantly with the F scale (1), a relatively nonideological measure of authoritarianism, and with the Traditional Family Ideology (TFI) Scale (11), a measure of autocratic ideology regarding issues such as husband-wife and parent-child relations.[3]

The obtained interscale correlations are as follows: CMI and F correlate .67, .69, and .76 in Hospitals C, T, and H, respectively. The comparable correlations between CMI and TFI are .50, .56, and .77. The respective Ns in the three hospitals were 115, 111, and 109. The scale means and SDs are presented in Table 2. The findings lend support to the hypothesis that an individual's views regarding mental illness and the hospital are imbedded

[3] An abbreviated F scale of 8 items was used; it contained Items 9, 13, 18, 25, 26, 37, and 42 from Form 45, and Item 32 from Form 73 of the original F scale (1). The TFI measure contained Items 2, 3, 5, 6, 7, 9, 11, 12 of the short form presented by Levinson and Huffman (14, p. 268).

within a broader ideological and psychodynamic matrix.

It may be argued that the F scale is made of the same stuff as CMI, that it taps relatively superficial ideas or values rather than more central aspects of personality. If this be true, then the foregoing inferences concerning the psychodynamic bases of ideology are unjustified. It is certainly possible that a person may accept many of the ideas represented in the F scale without being an "authoritarian personality." However, we propose on both theoretical and empirical grounds that such persons are rather the exception than the rule. The F items taken as a whole do not comprise an organized body of doctrine. The obtained consistency of response to these items is, we believe, determined for the most part by an enduring pattern of intrapersonal dispositions. Empirical support for this view is given by Adorno, *et al.* (1) and others; for a critical summary, see Christie (3). Significant relationships between CMI scores and nonscale measures of authoritarianism have been obtained by Gilbert (7) and Pine (13). These studies utilized content analysis of interviews, TATs, open-ended questions, and the like in assessing authoritarianism. The F scale would seem to provide a relatively valid though by no means infallible estimate of personal authoritarianism.

Custodial ideology has important psychic functions for authoritarian hospital members. The idea that patient behavior is simply irrational and not understandable has great value in reducing inner strain and maintaining self-esteem for personnel who have difficulty at the outset in taking an intraceptive, psychological approach. Again, for the person who has a great defensive need to displace and project aggressive wishes concerning authority figures to those who can be regarded as immoral, custodial ideology has special equilibrium-maintaining value through its justification of punitive, suppressive measures.

Humanistic ideology has corresponding functions for its adherents. By supporting a critical attitude toward the established order, it permits many equalitarian individuals to express generalized anti-authority hostilities in an ego-syntonic form. The principle of "self-control through self-understanding," applied in the treatment of patients, often serves to maintain and consolidate the intellectualizing defenses of equalitarian personnel. In our view, then, both custodialism and humanism have important nonrational functions for their proponents.

Relationships among Ideology, Personality, and Hospital Policy

We have been concerned thus far with ideology as an aspect of personality. We have suggested that the individual's orientation to mental illness is an intrinsic part of his general approach to life problems and is related to deeper-lying personality dynamics. This, however, is only part of the story. Ideology is also an aspect of the social milieu; we must consider both the psychological and the social soil within which ideologies are formed and modified.

Various social factors operate to induce some degree of ideological uniformity among members of a given occupational status, as well as among members of a total hospital system. Many social scientists, including psychologists, argue or implicitly assume that ideological conformity is ordinarily achieved and that some sort of J curve or concentration of viewpoints approximating the institutional requirements will be found among members of a given institution. One serious limitation of this approach, in our view, is its neglect of the part played by personality. We would expect that the achievement of a policy-congruent modal ideology depends in part on the presence of a corresponding modal personality. Conversely, to the extent that there is variability in ideology-relevant personality characteristics, we would expect ideological variability among members of any system.

Our three domains of inquiry are ideology, personality, and system requirements. Within each domain we have measured individual or system differences along a given continuum: (a) The custodial-humanistic continuum of individual ideology, as measured by the CMI scale. (b) The authoritarian-equalitarian continuum of personality, as measured by the F scale, (c) The third continuum, custodialism-humanism in system requirements, which was assessed as follows. The sample contained 12 subsystems: four occupational statuses (aide, student nurse, nurse, and psychiatrist) in each of three hospitals. Our procedure was to rank the 12 systems in order from relatively most custodial to relatively most humanistic with regard to the demands and pressures each system placed on its members. We ranked the hospitals first, then the statuses, and then combined the two sets into one series of 12 ranks.

The hospitals were ranked in terms of their degree of change away from a predominantly custodial emphasis on protection and bodily care of patients. The large state hospital, C, was assessed as the most custodial in view of its structural emphasis on detention, protection, and custodial care of patients in a highly controlled setting. The pressures it exerted on personnel, and the kinds of experience it offered them, seemed most conducive of a custodial orientation. The large VA hospital, T, was considered intermediate or transitional in that it was in process of fairly rapid change away from custodialism. The third hospital, H, was the most humanistic of the three in its program of ward care, patient government, and general staff-patient relationships.

The four statuses were ranked in degree of custodialism on the basis of educational level and job requirements vis-à-vis the patient. In order from high to low in degree of custodialism, they fall as follows:

aide, student nurse, nurse, and psychiatrist.

The three hospitals and the four statuses were then combined into a series of 12 hospital-status units ranked according to degree of pressure toward custodialism. Since occupational status pressures operate over a longer period of time, and more selectively, than do hospital pressures, we made status a primary basis of stratification, and hospital secondary. That is, we assumed that statuses are relatively non-overlapping in degree of custodialism in their policy requirements and that hospitals make a difference only within a single status grouping. Accordingly the rank 12 was given to the most custodial status in the most custodial hospital, namely, the aide status at Hospital C; this is followed by the aide status at Hospital T, and at H; then come the student nurse statuses at C, T, and H; the nurse statuses at C, T, and H; and lastly the doctor statuses at Hospitals C, T, and H with ranks of 3, 2, and 1 respectively (see Table 2). Ideally a more intensive sociological analysis of the structure and policies of each status in each hospital should be carried out. However, the rankings used here seem adequate for our present purposes.

Having roughly assessed the degree of custodialism in the policy requirements of each hospital-status system, we can now investigate the degree to which these requirements are supported by the ideologies, and are congruent with the personalities, of the system members.

RELATIONS BETWEEN POLICY REQUIRE-MENTS AND IDEOLOGY. What is the relationship between the degree of custodialism in the policy requirements of a hospital-status system and the degree of custodialism in the modal ideology of its members? The relevant data are given in Table 2. We use the CMI mean as a measure of modal ideology, for in the distribution of CMI scores the mean, by and large, corresponds closely to the mode. The obtained rank-order correlation be-

tween degree of custodialism in policy requirements (status ranks) and in modal ideology (CMI mean) is .92. There is, in other words, relatively great congruence between policy demands and modal ideology. At the same time, the CMI means of the 12 status units do not correspond fully in absolute degree to the estimated degree of custodialism in their structural pressures. For example, the aide status at Hospital C was ranked most custodial both in policy requirements and in CMI mean; however, in an absolute sense, the policy requirements are highly custodial whereas the CMI mean is only moderate.

The above findings do not tell us how much ideological variability exists within each system. Data on variability are given in Table 2. It will be noted that the SDs of most of the 12 units approximate the SD for the total sample. Only in the doctor statuses is there anything approaching uniformity of opinion. Thus although *modal* ideology is fairly closely related to policy requirements, the findings on intrasystem variability suggest that an individual's ideology does not reflect in a simple way the demands of his occupational milieu.

In investigating the relationship between *individual* ideology and policy requirements, we consider system pressures as characteristics of the individual. Every individual in the sample of 335 was assigned an index figure representing the relative degree of custodialism in the policy requirements of his particular hospital-status unit. This index figure is simply the rank of the individual's status within the series of 12. For instance, each doctor at H, the least custodial status, is assigned an index figure of 1, and each aide at C is assigned an index of 12.

The obtained product-moment correlation [4] between CMI score and Index of

[4] The use of indices based on rank in a product-moment correlation involves the assumption of equal intervals between ranks. This constitutes a possible source of error, but probably not a great one.

Status-Custodialism is .47. This finding is evidence of a significant but moderate relationship between individual ideology and system pressures. If system pressures were the most weighty determinants of individual ideology, relative ideological homogeneity within statuses should follow, and thus a high correlation (of the order, .7 to .8) between an individual's CMI score and the degree of policy-custodialism of his work unit. However, the degree of uniformity within any system is not as great as a system-centered mode of thinking would require. An individual's ideology can be predicted with only fair accuracy on the basis of his occupational-hospital membership.

RELATIONS BETWEEN POLICY REQUIREMENTS AND PERSONALITY. If the individual's ideological orientation is thought to be simply and directly a result of pressures from his work milieu, relatively independent of his personality, one would not expect the degree of custodialism in system policy to be significantly related to the degree of authoritarianism in modal personality. Rather, the 12 units might be expected to show similar degrees of authoritarianism, as measured by the F-scale means.

In our view, however, some congruence is to be expected between the policy requirements of a system and the modal personality of its members. Such congruence would be facilitated through recruitment, selective turnover, and possible personality changes in the direction of congruence. We are supported in this hypothesis by the finding of congruence (the correlation of .92) between policy requirements and modal ideology in the 12 status units. We would expect a parallel correspondence between policy requirements and modal personality.

For the 12 status units, the obtained rank-order correlation between Index of Status-Custodialism and F mean is .90 (see Table 2). Thus, there is relatively great congruence between policy demands and modal personality. This congruence is as great as that between policy demands and modal ideology.

The obtained correspondence between modal personality (F) and system requirements is accompanied by appreciable variability on the F scale within most of the statuses (Table 2). The size of the variance on F tends to covary with that on CMI ($r = .61$). This leads us to consider the degree to which system membership and personality are related in the individual. We would expect that the correlation found above between status membership and individual CMI score (.47) will hold as well for index of status membership and F score. The findings bear out this prediction. The correlation between the individual's F score and the Index of Custodialism for his status membership is .46.

RELATIONS BETWEEN IDEOLOGY AND PERSONALITY. One of our fundamental postulates is that an individual's ideological orientation is intimately bound up with his deeper-lying personality characteristics. We therefore hypothesize, at the collective level, relative congruence between modal ideology and modal personality. The obtained rank-order correlation between CMI mean (our measure of modal ideology) and F mean (our measure of modal personality) for the 12 units is .81. Thus, the congruence between modal personality and social ideology in a system is relatively great. As noted earlier, the size of the variance on CMI is also associated with that on F.

With the individual hospital member as the focus of analysis, the CMI-F correlation for the total sample of 335 (regardless of specific status membership) is .71. We can now consider the relationship between ideology and personality when system membership is held constant. The F-CMI correlations for the single status groupings are presented in Table 2. They average .71, a value identical to the CMI-F correlations for the sample as a whole, and 11 of the 12 correlations are significant at the .05 level or better.

We thus have evidence that the differences in modal ideology among the 12 status units are closely related to differences in modal personality. When we find individual differences in ideology within a single status unit, these differences are closely related to differences in personality characteristics.

The theoretical formulations and results presented here concerning the mental hospital have their parallels in other social settings such as the school, the prison, industry, and the family. In all these institutions a small "administrative" elite has the power and responsibility to set goals and to control the destiny of a massive "membership." This larger population, whether children, patients, or prisoners, is a potential threat to society's values; various measures of education and social control are necessary. One of the major forms of conflict arising in these institutions is that between autocratic and democratic orientations. There is considerable evidence from both the present research and related studies that the autocratic-democratic ideological continuum is one aspect of a broader authoritarian-equalitarian personality continuum. Social ideologies have, to a considerable extent, a psychological basis in the personalities of their adherents. A socio-psychological approach provides, we believe, an important adjunct to historic-sociological approaches in the study of ideology.

Summary and Conclusions

This inquiry has taken as its starting point the distinction between "custodialism" and "humanism" in the mental hospital. These terms refer to two contrasting ideological orientations and to the corresponding forms of hospital policy. We have investigated ideology both as an individual and as a collective phenomenon—or, more accurately, we have used both individual and collective modes of analysis in the study of ideology. With regard to the individual, we have tried to assess ideology by means of a specially devised CMI (custodialism-humanism) scale, and to determine the relationships between ideology and other individual characteristics such as psychodynamics and membership in various groups. With regard to the collective unit (e.g., hospital or occupational status), we have tried to assess the degree of custodialism in its policy requirements and in the modal ideology of its personnel, as well as the degree of authoritarianism in the modal personality of its personnel, and to determine the relationships among these.

In the individual, preference for a custodialistic orientation is part of a broader pattern of personal authoritarianism. Correlations averaging about .70 were found between the Custodialism (CMI) scale and the scales measuring autocratic family ideology (TFI) and general authoritarianism (F). Although various hospital groupings differ significantly in mean CMI score, there are appreciable individual differences within most of the groupings studied. These ideological differences within single hospitals and occupations are quite closely related to differences in personality.

In the collective unit, we found relatively great congruence between prevailing policy, modal ideology, and modal personality. The hospital-status units having the most custodial policy requirements had as well the most custodial modal ideologies and the most authoritarian personalities. At the same time, it should be noted that the correspondence among policy, ideology, and personality is far from complete. Each of these aspects of collective life can vary to some extent independently of the others, and the phenomenon of incongruence is as important as that of congruence.

Although none of our groups can be regarded as ideologically homogeneous, some of them showed relatively small dispersion in CMI scores. These groups had a similar dispersion in F scores, and had low CMI and F means. Our data do not tell how the low diversity and the high ideology-personality congruence came about, but they point up the need for answers to at least the following questions. To what extent do relatively homogeneous systems maintain themselves by recruitment and selective maintenance of individuals whose personalities are receptive to the structurally required ideology? To what extent do systems change the personalities which initially are unreceptive to the prevailing policy? Under what conditions can a system induce most of its members to support the required ideology even when this ideology is personality-incongruent? Under what conditions can the "incongruent" members change the system to a personally more congenial form?

Systems characterized by relatively great ideological diversity were very common in our sample. Moreover, the ideological diversity went hand in hand with diversity in personality, the standard deviations on CMI correlating .61 with those on F. We incline to the belief that significant heterogeneity of opinion and of personality obtains in the majority of institutional settings within modern societies undergoing rapid technological and educational change.

REFERENCES

1. Adorno, T. W., Else Frenkel-Brunswic, D. J. Levinson, & R. N. Sanford: *The authoritarian personality.* New York: Harper, 1950.

2. Bettelheim, B.: *Love is not enough.* Glencoe, Ill.: Free Press, 1950.

3. Christie, R.: Authoritarianism re-examined. In R. Christie and Marie Jahoda (Eds.), *Studies in the scope and method of "The authoritarian personality,"* Glencoe, Ill.: Free Press, 1954.

4. Cronbach, L. J., and P. E. Meehl: Construct validity in psychological tests. *Psychol. Bull.,* 1955, 53, 281–302.

5. Dicks, H. V.: Personality traits and national socialist ideology. *Hum. Relat.,* 1950, 3, 111–154.

6. Fromm, E.: *Man for himself.* New York: Rinehart, 1947.

7. Gilbert, Doris C.: Ideologies concerning mental illness: A sociopsychological study of mental hospital personnel. Unpublished doctor's dissertation, Radcliffe Coll., 1954.

8. Greenblatt, M., R. York, and Esther L. Brown: *From custodial to therapeutic care in mental hospitals.* New York: Russell Sage Foundation, 1955.

9. Jones, M.: *The therapeutic community.* New York: Basic Books, 1953.

10. Leighton, A. H.: *The governing of men.* Princeton: Princeton University Press, 1944.

11. Levinson, D. J., and Phyllis E. Huffman: Traditional family ideology and its relation to personality. *J. Pers.,* 1955, 23, 251–273.

12. Mayo, E.: *Human problems of industrial civilization.* Cambridge, Mass.: Harvard University Press, 1933.

13. Pine, F.: Conceptions of the mentally ill and the self: A study of psychiatric aides. Unpublished doctor's dissertation, Harvard University, 1955.

14. Stanton, A., and M. Schwartz: *The mental hospital.* New York: Basic Books, 1954.

15. Tannenbaum, F.: *Crime and the community.* New York: Columbia University Press, 1951.

THE RELATION OF STAFF CONSENSUS TO
PATIENT DISTURBANCE ON MENTAL HOSPITAL WARDS

by Anthony F. C. Wallace and Harold A. Rashkis

In 1949 Stanton and Schwartz first published their hypothesis that episodes of disagreement among staff tend to precipitate and maintain episodes of increased pathological "excitement," "dissociation," "withdrawal," "incontinence," or otherwise disturbed behavior among hospitalized mental patients, and that resolution of the disagreement is regularly followed by reduction of such disturbances.[1] "Dissociation," for instance, is described as "a reflection of, and a mode of participation in, a social field which itself is seriously split. . . ."[2] Stanton and Schwartz expressed this hypothesis in several forms, however, leaving its parameters somewhat uncertain; they did not rigidly specify the kinds of disturbance, the types of patients, and the processes of agreement and disagreement to which the hypothesis might apply. More particularly, the patients they studied represent a rather limited group, composed predominantly of females, in a private hospital (who were diagnosed as chronic schizophrenic and who tended to be overactive rather than withdrawn). Furthermore, in their reports they seem to have used "excitement" and "dissociation" as overlapping terms for an indefinitely large number of behavior disturbances, including paranoid ideation, physical assaultiveness, euphoria, suicidal

pre-occupation, exaggerated dependency, and sleeplessness. Finally, their case materials do not entirely support their own hypothesis. They describe the processes of disagreement and agreement as typically involving a fairly heated dispute between two staff members or two staff factions concerning an individual patient. Such dispute, while productive of strong emotion in the participants, is supposedly "covert," "secret," "hidden"; and it is conceived to be resolved by "exposure" and "discussion." Examination of the cases reported, however, shows that disagreements were not necessarily "covert" (except possibly to the patient and to unconcerned members of the staff), and that their resolution was not regularly accompanied by "exposure." Moreover, discussion and accommodation of views among the disputants did not always occur. Two additional methods of resolution are described: removal of patient to another ward, and withdrawal to another assignment of one or both of the parties to the disagreement.

The very "weakness" of the hypothesis, however, constitutes its strength, since in its most abstract form the hypothesis is relevant to a large class of ward situations in state as well as private hospitals. It may also be viewed as a special form of the more general hypothesis that a pathogenic influence is exerted by any disorganized social field.[3] The staff con-

[1] A. H. Stanton and M. S. Schwartz, "Observations on Dissociation as Social Participation," *Psychiatry*, 12 (November, 1949), pp. 339–354. Cf. also Stanton and Schwartz, *The Mental Hospital*, New York: Basic Books, 1954.

[2] *The Mental Hospital*, p. 363.

SOURCE: *American Sociological Review*, Vol. 24 (1959), pp. 829–835.

[3] See, e.g., Robert E. L. Faris and H. Warren Dunham, *Mental Disorders in Urban Areas*, Chicago: University of Chicago Press, 1939; A. B. Hollingshead and F. C. Redlich, *Social Class and Mental Illness*, New York: Wiley, 1958.

sensus hypothesis has frequently been repeated by other students of the field and would seem now to occupy a fairly central position in social psychiatric theory. Nevertheless, in view of the importance of the hypothesis and the largely anecdotal nature of available evidence, further exploration and clarification seem to be desirable.

This study [4] undertakes to test a modified form of the staff consensus hypothesis. It was carried out with a total of 42 patients on two wards, male and female at the Eastern Pennsylvania Psychiatric Institute (in Philadelphia). Each ward contained a moderately disturbed, heterogeneous (chiefly diagnosed as psychotic) patient population. Staff members included psychiatrists, nurses, attendants, and occupational therapists.

Research Procedures

For the measurement of staff consensus, a schedule of ten statements was constructed. Each statement describes some aspect of the patient's personal behavior or hospital situation with which a respondent could agree or disagree by circling an appropriate letter:

1. This week he doesn't seem to understand what is said to him.
2. This patient truly is a very likeable person.
3. As he is now, you have to treat him firmly and let him know who's boss.

[4] We acknowledge with gratitude the collaboration of Arthur Adlerstein, James Framo, and Peter Lewinson in the development of the disturbance index and consensus measure and in the collection of data; the advice of James Casby in statistical matters and the definition of the consensus measure; the assistance of John Atkins, Josephine H. Dixon, and Martha Teghtsoonian in the definition of the consensus measure and in the tabulation and analysis of data; and the invaluable cooperation and indulgence of staff and patients at EPPI.

4. Most of the other patients seem to like him pretty well.
5. Treatment doesn't seem to have been helping him this week.
6. I think this patient likes me.
7. This patient probably won't be able to leave the hospital for several months at least.
8. He has been causing other members of the staff a lot of trouble this week.
9. He seems to get along well with the other patients.
10. This patient often has to be asked to do things.

These statements were selected from a 71-item pretest schedule. The two criteria of item selection were: the eliciting of a moderate diversity of response (agreement or disagreement with statement) on the pretest survey; and consensus of respondents and staff members that the item clearly appeared to be of major significance to the typical patient. Every Wednesday during a seven-week period in May and June, 1957, each regular staff member (psychiatrists, nurses, attendants, and occupational therapists, on all three shifts) privately filled out a schedule on each patient under his care. Some patients were rated throughout this period; others, owing to date of entry or discharge, for only part of it.

For the measurement of patient disturbance, weekly the nurses' notes on each patient were examined for the week ending on Wednesday. Using a procedure tested for reliability, clinical psychologists coded the comments on patient behavior on a mimeographed form, using the following categories:

1. Assaultive Behavior (against people)
   a. strikes others, attacks without provocation
   b. threatens assault verbally or by action
2. Assaultive Behavior (against self)
   a. self-injury, suicide attempt, accident

b. not defending self when physically attacked

3. Assaultive Behavior (against material objects)
   a. purposeful destructiveness
   b. accidental destructiveness
4. Bizarre Behavior
   a. posturing, grimacing
   b. tangential, irrelevant speech
   c. other (write in)
5. Compulsive Rituals
6. Cooperation Disturbances
   a. refuses to cooperate in any ward routine
   b. overcooperates, seeks work unnecessarily
7. Delusional Disturbances
   a. overt evidence of delusions
8. Demanding Behavior
   a. makes excessive demands, justified or not
   b. querulousness, whining, minor complaints
9. Eating Disturbances
   a. refusal to eat
   b. overeating
10. Feeling Disturbances
    a. panic, anxiety attack, extreme fear
    b. flat, apathetic, dull
    c. inappropriate affect
    d. "nervous," anxious, upset
11. Hallucination Disturbances
    a. overt evidence of hallucinations
12. Manners Disturbances
    a. unconcerned with social amenities
    b. overpolite, obsequious, ceremonious
13. Mood Disturbances
    a. elated, exhilarated
    b. notable depression
    c. sullen, resentful, seething
14. Motor Disturbances
    a. overactive, pacing, running, agitated
    b. immobile, catatonic
15. Noise Disturbances
    a. loud, boisterous, raucous, shouting
    b. mute, rarely talks
16. Paranoid Suspiciousness
    a. markedly paranoid behavior

17. Participation Disturbances
    a. refuses to go to OT or group activities
    b. likes group activity too much; too active
18. Privilege Behavior
    a. does not handle privileges responsibly; runs away from hospital, goes to restricted areas of hospital, etc.
    b. refuses privileges; does not want to leave protection of ward
19. Physical Complaints
    a. complains of headaches, stomach aches, etc.
    b. indifferent to bodily injury, illness
20. Responsivity Disturbances
    a. overdependent, clinging, helpless
    b. negativistic, resistant, very stubborn
21. Sex Disturbances (both homo- and heterosexual)
    a. masturbation, exhibitionism, seductiveness
    b. prudish, disapproving of sexual activities
22. Sleep Disturbances
    a. oversleeping
    b. insomnia; has trouble sleeping
23. Tidiness Disturbances
    a. sloppy dress; untidy in toilet habits
    b. overly fastidious in dress or toilet
24. Sociability Disturbances
    a. seclusive, withdrawn
    b. forces himself on people; a "pest"
25. Verbal Aggressive Disturbances
    a. argumentative, teasing, belligerent
    b. self-effacing, others pick on him as object of verbal attack; doesn't argue back
26. Miscellaneous (write in)

References to various types of disturbed behavior were then counted and summed, without weighting, for the week.[5] The

[5] We believed that a standardized weighting of some kinds of behavior as "more" disturbed than others would be inadvisable; only a weighting which reflected the significance of each instance of behavior in the

nurses' notes themselves were written by registered and practical nurses and by attendants, in conformance with standard operating procedure, which required the regular (thrice-daily, that is, at least once during each shift) and specific recording of both change and continuity in the patient's condition and behavior. The notes contain such entries as the following, selected at random from the record of a patient whose symptoms included psychosomatic asthma:

5/10/57   12–8   Slept about 7 hrs. Wheezing and coughing this A.M.—medication given—cooperative and ate well.

.... R.N.

8 to 4:30   Became somewhat upset when another patient raised his voice at a female attendant (and retired to his room). Overall attitude quite cheerful.

.... Att.

4–12   Pleasant and cheerful —attended show. No change in behavior.

.... R.N.

(This material was coded "10d" and "19a" on the disturbance chart, described above.)

Staff members were informed with deliberate vagueness that the purpose of the study was to learn more about how patients are perceived by staff; data were not available to any staff member (including

unique therapeutic history of each individual patient would be in order, and this was evidently impractical. For instance, the presence of "flat affect" early in treatment might represent a very serious emotional disturbance, in response to a crisis in therapy, while later it might represent the patient's chronic defense against the boredom of hospital life, a symptom of "hospitalism."

the administrator) during the collection phase. That the schedules were not filled at random, in collusion, or by stereotype is supported by the following facts: professional groups (for example, psychiatrists *versus* nurses *versus* attendants; day shift attendants *versus* night shift attendants; and so on) tended to differ systematically in modal attitudes; staff members in any one group nevertheless displayed considerable diversity of attitudes; and the profiles of attitudes by individual staff members toward given patients varied considerably over time.

Detailed review of the distributions on which the foregoing conclusions are based would go beyond the scope and purposes of this paper. However, an example may suffice to indicate the kind of information obtained as well as the method of analysis utilized. By way of background, it should be noted that each possible response to a question could be classified as indicating either a "negative" or a "positive" evaluation of the patient's state. The negative pattern was: 1A, 2D, 3A, 4D, 5A, 6D, 7A, 8A, 9D, and 10A. Accordingly, for every patient a form was compiled weekly with each negative evaluation represented as an X in the appropriate cell, as in Figure 1. This device yielded an accurate record of the responses and also made it possible to perceive on inspection gross differences in response patterns. One of the more obvious differences in group norms is illustrated by responses to question #3 as applied to male patients: "As he is now, you have to treat him firmly and let him know who's boss." The negative response to this was "agree." In 287 opportunities to respond the psychiatrists gave 174 negative responses, in 484 opportunities the nurses gave 213 negative responses, and in 628 opportunities the attendants gave only 117 negative responses. The chi-square for the relation between professional category and response is significant at far beyond the .01 level. Thus with respect to the same patients on the same days, the four psychiatrists as a group were clearly more prone to assert that the patient needed to be "treated firmly" and to be shown "who was boss" than were either the six nurses or the ten attendants.

One or more of three hypotheses may help to explain this situation. First, in view of the small number of raters, the personal predilections of individuals who were deviant from their professional group norms might have heavily biased the results in a direction away from the "true" group norms, despite the large number of individual observations. Second, differences in sex and ethnic affiliation rather than professional attitudes as such in large part could be responsible. Three of the four psychiatrists were white, including the two who produced most of the observations, and all were male; the six nurses were all white and female; nine of the ten attendants were Negro and all were male. Third, differing professional roles, with all that this implies in the way of education, training, career interest, conditions of self-esteem, and status anxiety, might constitute an important factor. Of course, all three circumstances may have contributed to the distribution of responses reported, as in the illustration given above.

But we must defer further discussion of this finding to another occasion.

A measure of consensus of staff (C) was calculated for each question on each patient for each week from the matrix of binary (agree-disagree) scores distributed over raters (numbering eight to fifteen), according to the following formula:

$$C = 1 - \frac{4t\,(N - t)}{N^2},$$

where t = maximum number of raters giving the same response (whether "agree" or "disagree'), and N = number of raters. Since t is variable between $N/2$ and N, C is variable between 1 (perfect consensus) and 0 (minimum possible consensus).[6] The consensus for each patient each week ($\overline{C}$) was taken as the mean consensus value over the ten questions:

$$\overline{C} = \frac{C}{10}.$$

An example of the computations is shown in Figure 1.

[6] The staff consensus formula was devised by John Atkins specifically for use with these data. It is based on the core term in the concept of standard deviation $[(x - \overline{x})^2/N]$. This core term transforms algebraically, in this application, and with the introduction

| | Respondents | | | | | | | | | | | |
	A	B	C	D	E	F	G	H	I	J	t	C
1								X			9	.64
2					X				X		8	.36
3	X	X			X		X	X	X		6	.04
4		X			X	X				X	6	.04
5	X		X			X	X	X	X	X	7	.16
6	X		X	X	X	X	X			X	7	.16
7	X	X	X	X	X		X		X		7	.16
8	X		X	X					X		6	.04
9		X				X				X	7	.16
10	X										9	.64

N = 10

2.40/10 = .24 = $\overline{C}$

Fig. 1. Sample of patient weekly consensus form.

The hypothesis being tested is that an increase of staff consensus concerning a patient during a given period is followed by a decrease of disturbance, and that a decrease of consensus is similarly followed by an increase of disturbance. Stanton and Schwartz do not make clear how large or how variable a time lag is implied by the concept of "followed" in their hypothesis. We assumed, however, that "simultaneous" changes of consensus and disturbance (that is, changes occurring during identically the same period of time) would not reflect such a cause-and-effect relationship as reliably as the case in which each measure of consensus change was paired with a measure of *subsequent* disturbance change. On the other hand, too great a time lag between pairs of measures would allow any effect to be diluted by other events. For these reasons we arranged the measures in such a fashion that their temporal fields overlapped, with the consensus field preceding the disturbance field. Changes in consensus are differences between attitudes expressed on one Wednesday and the next; the period of change is from Wednesday to Wednesday. But the disturbance score is not specific to a single day: it depends on the entire preceding week during which incidents have been accumulating; the "centers of gravity" of the disturbance scores are not the Wednesdays on which they were computed but the midpoints (Sundays) of the preceding weeks. Hence a change in disturbance scores in general refers not to the week between the Wednesdays on which they were computed but to the week between their "centers of gravity" (that is, between the preceding Sundays).

of constants to allow for variation in N and to bound the numerical range of the function by 0 and 1, into the expression given in the formula. A modified formula containing further correction for attenuation resulting from variability of number of raters was not used because on trial it yielded no significant differences in values of C and was more tedious to compute. It may be noted that the value of C is constant under the parameter t/N.

Findings

If the hypothesis is valid, then, an increase in consensus between the (n)th Wednesday and the $(n + 1)$th Wednesday should be reflected in a decrease of disturbance between the scores cumulated on the $(n + 1)$th Wednesday and on the $(n + 2)$th Wednesday; and a decrease of consensus from (n) to $(n + 1)$ should be associated with an increase of disturbance from $(n + 1)$ to $(n + 2)$. Accordingly, four-fold tables were constructed to display changes in consensus (n to $n + 1$) and disturbance ($n + 1$ to $n + 2$) for all male pairs, all female pairs, and all pairs combined. Each change was scored as "increase" or "decrease."

The data and the chi-squares are shown in Table 1. They fail to demonstrate any significant relation between direction of change in consensus and direction of change in disturbance, for male patients, for female patients, or for male and female patients together.

These negative findings suggest that if a relationship does exist between staff consensus and patient disturbance, it is either extremely weak or is dependent on qualifying conditions not made explicit in the hypothesis under test and therefore not measured in this situation. For instance, lack of consensus in some particular attitudinal area not represented in our questionnaire might possibly provoke disturbance. It may be noted, however, that the data display a tendency for events of increased consensus to outnumber events of decreased consensus, and for events of decreased disturbance to outnumber events of increased disturbance. In addition, over time the absolute values of consensus increase while the absolute values of disturbance decrease. There is a tendency, in other words, for a patient to become less disturbed, and for the staff to agree more about him, the longer he remains on the ward. While inadequately controlled observation of such circumstances could lead to the conclusion that increased

TABLE 1. *Relation of Direction of Change in Patient Disturbance from Week* $(n + 1)$ *to* $(n + 2)$ *to Direction of Change in Staff Consensus from Week* (n) *to* $(n + 1)$

		MALES ($N = 55$) * Consensus		FEMALES ($N = 70$) * Consensus		TOTAL ($N = 125$) * Consensus	
		+	−	+	−	+	−
DISTURBANCE	−	15	16	19	20	34	36
	+	16	8	17	14	33	22

$\chi^2 = 1.834$ .20 > p > .10 $\chi^2 = .259$ .70 > p > .50 $\chi^2 = 1.616$ .30 > p > .20

* N refers to number of pairs of change scores, not to number of patients.

consensus is responsible for reduced disturbance, our data suggest that this conclusion would be spurious.

Finally, it should be emphasized that this study does not consider the relationship of the *content* of staff attitudes to patient disturbance. Quite conceivably the presence of certain attitudes among staff members, with or without consensus, under appropriate conditions is highly disturbing to individual patients. Under such conditions, high consensus with regard to irritating attitudes could actually provoke more disturbance than low consensus, while high consensus with respect to non-irritating attitudes could stimulate less disturbance than low consensus. Thus a hypothesis based on this possibility would posit increase *or* decrease in disturbance with increase in consensus, and decrease *or* increase in disturbance with decrease in consensus. In this case, the determining factor would be the irritating or non-irritating content of the attitudes for the particular patient. Such a hypothesis would be compatible with our finding that change in consensus *per se* is unrelated to change in disturbance. It is not possible to say whether the data of Stanton and Schwartz might be successfully re-interpreted in the light of this second hypothesis, although these authors provide some anecdotal material suggesting that specific attitudes rather than disagreement, were in some cases the precipitants of disturbance.[7] In any event, development of concepts and procedures for testing the alternative hypothesis we have suggested is now underway in the context of a study of the relationship between therapeutic progress and attitudes toward "symptomatic" behavior.

[7] Thus, for instance, in *The Mental Hospital* (p. 363) we find the following passage: "In the course of a disagreement between Dr. Emron and Dr. Caff about 'how sick' Mr. Ossing was, Mr. Ossing began to develop plans for organizing a branch of the family business. At first Dr. Emron regarded this as 'reasonable' and Dr. Caff regarded it as 'grandiose.' Mr. Ossing's idea grew rapidly out of all possible proportion but disappeared in a few days when he was moved away from Dr. Caff." Here one can speculate that it was not the disagreement between Dr. Emron and Dr. Caff, but Dr. Caff's attitude (that Mr. Ossing's idea was "grandiose") that elicited the disturbance (the growth of the idea "out of all possible proportion").

C · SOCIAL WORK

THE IMPACT OF THE SOCIAL WORKER'S CULTURAL STRUCTURE ON SOCIAL THERAPY

by Sol Wiener Ginsburg

For a long time I have been interested in observing how quickly many technical words come to be used in everyday language, often a bit glibly and with an easy familiarity seldom based on real understanding of their meaning. We live in a time when that process is catalyzed by the existence of facilities for communication which spread ideas and words with almost frightening rapidity to vast numbers of people. Perhaps my favorite example of this phenomenon is the popular use of the word "neurotic," which no longer bears the slightest resemblance to its technical meaning—actually a very complicated concept and one not easy to define. Current usage appears to equate it with practically any undesirable (to the user) trait of character or personality and often makes it merely a more polite equivalent for some older derogatory term.

I am disquieted by the feeling that we are now bandying the words "culture" and "cultural" with the same too easy familiarity, seldom based on a clear recognition of just what we mean by the words and often without full awareness of the implications of culture theory for both the professions of social work and of psychoanalytic psychiatry. It is good to know that we have come so far—even though it is only part way down the road to be trav-

SOURCE: *Social Casework*, Vol. 32 (1951), pp. 319–325.

ersed—in the application of knowledge and concepts from anthropology and social psychology to our own fields. But I am deeply concerned about the possibility that we may substitute glibness for understanding or allow the pendulum too great a sweep away from our earlier emphasis on the unconscious factors that influence personality and behavior, which in turn were rooted in biology.

If I seem to use examples and points of emphasis from psychiatry and social work interchangeably, it is because I believe that in the particular context of this paper the basic problems are essentially the same for both. While the psychotherapist is less immediately concerned than the social worker with the need to influence the current reality situation of his patient, it is just as necessary for him to understand the cultural influences that have helped mold his patient's life, as well as his own, as it is for the social worker to understand these factors in his own and in his client's life.

In all discussions of the relation of culture theory to psychiatry and social work, the emphasis has been on the importance of the culture in influencing the personality and attitudes of the client or patient. The emphasis in this paper, however, is on examining the impact of cultural factors on the therapist's own attitudes. This emphasis demands recognition of the fact that the equation "worker-client" has, like all equations, two factors, equally important and equally consequential.

An instructive example to illustrate the very real "two-sidedness" of the therapeutic situation may be drawn from the history of psychoanalytic technique. There was a time when the most passive and non-interfering attitude on the part of the analyst was considered ideal. Parenthetically, I may add that a recent textbook [1] records, presumably in all seriousness, the debates supposedly devoted to the question of whether an analyst who slept throughout the therapeutic session might not be the theoretic ultimate in achieving this ideal. Fortunately, in many analytic circles, we are now aware that the concept of the analyst as merely a "mirror" is by no means ideal and, while recognizing the real and distinct limitations to the analyst's "interfering," we nevertheless acknowledge his need to be much more than a completely passive recipient of the patients' communications.

A social worker analysand, in discussing a marital problem, said, "I can't be a caseworker to my husband. I can't always be 'neutral'!" In her concept of the casework process, she had accepted "neutrality" as the ideal. I question very much whether such a goal is obtainable, or whether it would be at all "ideal" even if it were.

In this paper I shall use "culture" as defined by Gardner Murphy [2] to mean "the complex whole that includes knowledge, belief, art, morals, law, custom, and any other capabilities and habits acquired by man as a member of society." I think the very breadth and inclusiveness of the definition have distinct advantage for us in this discussion, which is not primarily concerned with the technical niceties of

anthropological or social psychological theory, but rather with the understanding of relatively simple human needs and forces.

The thesis of this discussion is that the personality that the social worker brings to his job is a complex resultant of many forces and that in the development of this personality, cultural factors have played a vital role; that his attitudes toward himself, his clients, and his job reflect his own life experiences, his values and goals, his expectancies and ambitions, and his image of himself as a person in a social setting; that these experiences will reflect not only the worker's racial, economic, and religious background and upbringing, but also his social class status and that of his family, his class allegiances and awareness and, especially in our country, practices and habits of thought and behavior which are native to the particular region in which he spent his formative years; that these attitudes and goals and needs may conflict with those of his clients who are also materially influenced by the impact of their own culture; that even when there is no conflict, the worker's own culturally influenced attitudes must inevitably play an important role in his understanding, handling, and treatment of the client's problems; and finally, that this interaction is not by any means always conscious and recognized but often, as with other human attitudes, may be active entirely at an unconscious level, disguised in rationalization, and rationalized in theoretical assumptions and technical procedures.

Influence of Cultural Forces on Vocational Service

Perhaps the very first place at which the social worker needs to understand and appreciate the impact of cultural forces is in an awareness of the importance of these factors in his choice of social work as a profession.

[1] Norman Alexander Cameron, *The Psychology of Behavior Disorders, A Biosocial Interpretation*, Houghton Mifflin, New York, 1947, p. 588.

[2] Gardner Murphy, *Personality, A Biosocial Approach to Origins and Structure*, Harper and Bros., New York, 1947, p. 983.

Relatively little is known of the factors that determine one's occupational choice. What has been written has largely reflected either the vocational guidance counselor's concern with understanding the problem in terms of interests and skills, the sociologist's and economist's concern with status and class considerations, the religionist's interest in work as a moral value and in one's occupation as contributing or not to such values, and the psychoanalyst's interpretation of one's occupational choice as determined by unconscious forces, largely in terms of occupation as providing partial instinctual gratification.

Just as in other aspects of the discussion of personality and culture there has been a tendency to magnify either the deep inner (unconscious) needs of the individual or the reality aspects of the culture—as though these were forces in opposition to one another and not, as is the fact, part of a continuum—so in the discussion of the forces influencing occupational choice, a similar dichotomy has often been postulated. It is especially pertinent to emphasize the fact that there is no useful line of cleavage between the inner and outer forces since much confusion in social work theory seems to stem from an overemphasis on one or another of these sets of influences; as though so-called dynamic (unconscious) factors could be arraigned against those stemming from the social reality situation.

One element in the choice of an occupation derives from the need to find in one's work the satisfaction of instinctual needs in a job that conforms to one's interests and goals and satisfies one's sense of values and purpose. Although, as far as I know, no accurate data have been compiled on the factors determining the choice of social work as a profession, it is fair to assume, I think, that such a choice must, most often, represent a need to help people in a profession that enjoys considerable prestige and allows one to exercise a degree of power over the lives of others.

Influence of Cultural Forces in Attitudes toward Clients

Such factors must clearly influence the worker's attitudes toward his clients. It may be fairly stated that consciously or otherwise we help people to be like ourselves. This is denied in the assumption (to my mind a false one) that we must bring to our work with people complete "objectivity," as though that stripped us of any need or desire to project our own values and needs and prevented any involvement in the client's life. This is also purported to be the goal of psychoanalytic therapy; I have pointed out elsewhere [3] that I believe it is an unobtainable one, and, further, that it is a goal that would not necessarily be desirable were it possible.

While such a goal may be undesirable in psychotherapy, I believe it would be even less desirable in social work therapy, which axiomatically is concerned with the attempt to help the client with his reality situation and, indeed, to help him modify it whenever that is wise or possible. To accept this does not require that the worker forfeit all his awareness and knowledge of dynamics, but rather that he make the fullest use of such knowledge in the understanding of the client's (and his own) reality situation.

Part of the need, common among social workers, to deny any involvement with the client (which, it seems to me, has now made such a useful concept as "empathy" almost a forbidden thing) stems from the worker's revulsion against an older stereotype almost universal in our culture, of the social worker as a kind lady bestowing her bounty on the poor; and also from an erroneous prestige which has come to be associated with dynamic therapy as

[3] Sol Wiener Ginsburg, "Values and the Psychiatrist," *American Journal of Orthopsychiatry*, Vol. XX, No. 3 (1950), p. 466.

opposed to what seems to be looked upon as the more humble desire and skill of "merely" helping people. The solution to the supposed dangers entailed in over-identifying with the client, which often must stem from the worker's own cultural background, will not be found in the effort to deny any identification whatsoever, and the failure to recognize that our technical knowledge, which is itself in good part a sort of self-awareness, is also conditioned and limited by the culture of the worker.

At a recent case presentation made jointly by a psychoanalyst and two social workers, the accusation was made (and it seemed definitely an "accusation") that they were too identified with the patient and hence overprotective and even "loving." The patient was a badly neglected, utterly deprived child, and it seemed to me that a perfectly adequate theoretical case could have been constructed for the techniques employed. But what interested me more was the need of several of those who participated in the discussion to find some *technical* justification for such feelings, some sanction for them in dynamic terms, as if just loving the child was somehow suspect.

Perhaps at this juncture we can find some useful illustrations for our thesis. A beginning social worker was asked to make a visit to the home of a Negro patient, particularly to talk with the patient's husband. Her report was full of admiration for their cleanliness, for the spotless appearance of the children, and especially for the courtesy of the husband. In our subsequent discussion of the visit it was apparent that the worker had undertaken the mission with much trepidation and that she was actually recording her own relief from anxiety when she found the type of conformity to which she was accustomed and none of the social and sexual deviations her stereotype of the Negro had led her to expect. She had so completely accepted the equation of the Negro with shiftlessness and irre-

sponsibility that she could not help recording her amazement at finding in these people the embodiment of many of her own middle-class virtues and values.

A clinic patient complained to me that, in discussing her child's problems, the social worker in the children's clinic made her feel very guilty about the fact that she began the toilet training of her youngster too early and was too harsh with him about his soiling. However correct the worker's theoretical formulations (and there is no question that my patient is too meticulous and overconcerned about her children's cleanliness), the worker had neglected, it seems to me, to take into account such important factors as these: Mrs. X, the mother of four small children, is the janitor of a lower class tenement, a much harassed and tired woman who works long hours to supplement her husband's marginal income. As she always reminds me, she "can't afford any fancy diaper service, and the quicker the kids are dry the better." This is a true and real factor in her attitude. In appraising it one must consider the mother's background in a strictly conventional, rigid farm family where she was one of six children, born within a year or so of each other, and her own training, which was most punitive. The social worker, recognizing properly the role of the mother's own training in the etiology of her obsessive traits, her querulous demands for cleanliness in her children, and so on, is naturally concerned for their development. "Reality," however, must include not only the mother's own sick attitudes, but also the harsh demands and the arduous task of earning a living, doing all one's own work, and coping with the manifold problems of child rearing.

Such middle-class mores affect the treatment situation in a variety of ways. A Negro social worker, in discussing a co-worker, commented to me on the keen ambition, in a middle-class sense, which this worker has, especially for the Negro clients; that she resents any attitude she thinks is too lenient and makes really excessive demands on these clients for compliance with middle-class white mores which they do not necessarily share. She has not only adopted what appears to be an over-compensatory attitude as a Negro, but projected it in typical middle-class mores. This is clear in such things as standards of housekeeping, job ambitions, and the overevaluation of what she believes ought to be the clients' educational expectations. Sensing this, the Negro clients seem to prefer white workers, finding them more relaxed and less demanding.

The other side of this situation is also pertinent. It may very well be that some of the white workers are less demanding of high standards of compliance and achievement in the Negro clients because of their (the workers') own culturally imposed estimate of the Negroes' capacities and potentialities.

A young psychiatrist was treating a Negro girl who had been referred to the clinic because the school authorities were especially concerned that she was wasting her quite exceptional artistic skills. In the course of treatment it developed that she worked long hours after school to earn enough money to buy supplies necessary for her painting. The psychiatrist seemed overcritical of this; he had interpreted this to her as evidence of her overambition and of a neurotic need for accomplishment. However, it was only later that his own attitudes became more clearly projected into the therapeutic situation: I had suggested that we try to find a studio of some sort where she could paint, since the only room then available to her was in her badly overcrowded home. When a room in the "Y" was suggested to her, she flatly refused, saying, "It's bad enough to be a charity case in the clinic; I don't want to get that treatment in the 'Y' too." The patient's neurotic handling of this opportunity is not our concern here; what I want to emphasize is the therapist's display of hostility at her refusal. Clearly he thought her "uppity" and ungrateful; just as clearly my discussion of this made plain his own culturally imposed concept of Negroes and his assumption that they should make peace with more menial jobs and not have such artistic ambitions.

Cohen and Witmer,[4] in their penetrating study of Russian Jewish clients' attitudes toward financial assistance, point out that "a caseworker judges whether the emotion which a client displays about a particular situation is excessive by comparing his behavior with the way in which most 'normal' people react to a similar situation. If a client reacts with what seems an excess of emotion, the caseworker concludes that the particular situation holds some special meaning for this client. . . . Such a judgment implies, however, that the caseworker knows how 'normal' people feel about given situations. If she is unfamiliar with the teachings and values and usual behavior of the cultural group to which the client belongs, she has little to guide her judgment and, *falling back on standards derived from her own culture* [my italics], may accept or reject cases inappropriately or proceed with treatment plans that are erroneous." The authors emphasize that a Jew's deeply rooted concept of charity as among the three highest virtues understandably determines his attitudes and behavior when he finds himself in a situation where he not only can no longer dispense charity to others but must ask for help. The worker called upon to estimate the needs of the client and his capacity to use help satisfactorily must understand the culturally rooted origins of such attitudes as well as his own (the worker's) toward accepting "charity." Thus, the study emphasizes the *diagnostic* criteria implied in establishing the fact that "the clients who are at least fairly well ad-

[4] Eva Cohen and Helen Witmer, "The Diagnostic Significance of Russian Jewish Clients' Attitudes toward Relief," *Smith College Studies in Social Work*, Vol. X, No. 4 (1940), p. 285.

justed adhere to the teachings and ideals of their culture, while those with marked emotional difficulties disregard or overemphasize their culture's ideals." [5]

Such an estimate of the attitudes of clients, here of great diagnostic import, reflects in a basic sense the worker's knowledge and skill and also his own culture and values. I do not mean to imply that a social worker can deal adequately only with clients who share his own cultural standards and needs. A thorough-going knowledge of the client's culture, gathered from direct observation, reading, and so on, can, of course, do much to give the worker the perspective necessary to interpret the client's conduct realistically.

A young psychiatrist, born and raised in a rural community in the deep South and educated in more or less rural settings, was treating a Jewish veteran under my supervision. He often reported serious quarrels between the veteran and his wife about the meals she prepared, but it took me quite a while to realize that he had entirely misunderstood the nature and meaning of the issue between the patient and his wife. The latter, raised in an extremely orthodox Jewish home, insisted on observing the ancient rituals and observances of Kashruth, the Jewish rules pertaining to the choice and preparation of foods. Her husband objected not only on the grounds of the additional expense imposed by such practices but also because he did not like certain foods that were permitted and missed others that were forbidden. The psychiatrist understandably failed to appreciate the cultural differences reflected by these quarrels; he thought of the issue in simple terms of food preferences and hence was interpreting, as "neurotic," behavior patterns deeply ingrained in the individual's cultural life. I do not mean to imply that there were no neurotic elements in the way the patient and his wife utilized these

differences; but a proper evaluation of the interplay between culturally influenced habits and neurotic needs requires a full understanding of both.

I recall my first experience with a Nisei (Japanese-American) patient. No patient of mine had ever been so unfailingly polite, so grateful, and yet so unrevealing. Her communications were, like her person, neat and meticulous; her attitude constantly one of deference. It was only when Dr. Charlotte Babcock, who has had extensive experience with the Japanese in Chicago, explained to me that the patient was merely living up to the usual Japanese value system that I could begin to understand her attitudes. For instance, the idea that one should never accept kindnesses that one cannot repay was inevitable in her value scheme and obviously affected our relationship and the treatment situation. Furthermore, as was to be expected, the transference situation was markedly affected by traditional Japanese attitudes toward the father. It was as necessary to understand the roots of such feelings in her culture as to appreciate the special dynamic significance they had for my patient.

Social workers as well as psychiatrists who work with adolescent children of European-born parents know how often much unhappiness is created in such homes by the clash between old world cultural values and those of the new world. The worker who shares none of these old world attitudes or the worker who has himself lived through a similar clash in his own adolescence can hardly be expected not to project at least in some measure his own attitude into such situations. The European-born parent often looks on the therapist as a biased special pleader for the youngster's point of view and as a threat to parental authority. It is obviously necessary for the worker to realize how much of his estimate of any such situation reflects his own upbringing in his own cultural setting.

So much of what I have been saying

[5] *Ibid.*, p. 314.

has been about the socially and economically deprived and about members of minority groups that I feel I must stop at this point to inject a word of caution. It is not only the destructive stereotype of the members of such groups that involves us in confusion; the well-meaning but condescending attitude that looks on all Europeans, or all Negroes, or all Jews, as stamped from a single piece is equally dangerous. Those therapists who share either of these biases will naturally fail to recognize the right of members of such groups to their own individuality and to the expression of their individual needs. Even among relatively prejudice-free people one finds an unconscious clinging to a stereotyped concept of an Italian or Englishman or Frenchman, and hence an inability to estimate a situation as the reflection of an individual need. I might add that a similar evil exists in many of the regional stereotypes in this country. Such attitudes must inevitably do violence to any treatment situation. It must always be remembered that a group has qualities of its own, that it is always more than a sum of its parts, and, most importantly, that each member of even the most homogeneous group differs from the others in some trait or characteristic.

It must not be thought, because of the emphasis of my examples, that I believe culture affects only the poor or the middle class. Since so much of social work deals inevitably with the economically poorer groups in the community, such a bias in my illustrations is, I take it, understandable. It is self-evident that culturally determined attitudes affect everyone in all stations and ways of life. I have, for instance, analyzed two social workers who are of the socially and economically privileged groups. Their own attitudes materially affected their relationships with clients and resulted in such overcompensatory, over-protective attitudes toward them as to influence their work seriously. In fact, in each instance it was

their awareness of this handicap that at least in part led them to seek help.

There are, of course, many other culturally determined attitudes in the therapist that could be discussed, some of them of the most basic significance. Thus, I have had no opportunity to discuss the role played by the sex of the therapist and the influence of the worker's own attitudes toward it. We live in a culture not yet by any means free of serious conflicts around one's role as male or female. Surely, such attitudes must, consciously or unconsciously, materially affect the worker's attitude toward the client. I recall vividly the attitude toward working women—especially married women—of a social worker I had in analysis. In her culture, for a woman to work was a stigma; for a woman to remain unmarried, a deeper one; but to be married and to work was unspeakable. Although she seemed intellectually free of any such notions, it was soon apparent how much they were reflected in her punitive estimate of the needs of her working-mother clients, especially those who worked not from necessity but because they enjoyed working, or worse still, because they wanted to earn money for comforts they would otherwise not have been able to afford.

I have tried to take examples, not from distant or ancient worlds, but from our own of here and now, to illustrate a few places where cultural forces influence social workers and their work with clients. As I see it, the social worker is privileged to work with people in distress in a troubled world. To work effectively he must bring to the task thorough understanding not only of the individual in need but of the community in which he lives. This is a grave and weighty responsibility, demanding an immense and wide-flung knowledge of the world and of one's self. Fortunately, it is as well a great opportunity to help people in trouble.

FAMILY-CENTERED CASEWORK IN A PSYCHIATRIC SETTING

by Max Siporin

Family-centered casework is a logical step in the development of social casework theory and practice. Moreover, it represents a new professional orientation whereby casework heritage and tradition are reaffirmed. This paper is concerned with several emerging concepts and principles of family-centered casework, as they are applied in a clinical psychiatric setting, illustrated by a report of a case. Several implications of this kind of practice are also discussed.

One of casework's distinguishing characteristics has been its concern with the welfare of the family. The social disorganization of modern living has been reflected in a higher incidence of family breakdown. An increasing number of family functions, including aspects of socialization, mutual aid, and social control of family members, have been allocated by society to social institutions outside the family, particularly to education, medicine, and social work. To meet the social needs created by these changes, social work, particularly casework, has traditionally focused its efforts on helping families in distress.

In its early developmental years, the approach made by social casework to family groups and to their social, economic, and cultural problems was chiefly a sociological one. Currently casework theory and practice reflect a return to some of the earlier insights and methods. Mary Richmond's remarks on work with "the family group as a whole" sound particularly fresh and modern as we rediscover them today. She stated, as one basic principle of social casework, that the family

SOURCE: *Social Casework*, Vol. 37 (1956), pp. 167–174.

is the unit of "social" diagnosis and treatment. Moreover, the caseworker influences, and is helped or hindered by, the client's family group, "many [of] whom he has never seen." [1] She observed that caseworkers see "several of the members of the family assembled in their own home environment, acting and reacting upon one another, each taking a share in the development of the client's story, each revealing in ways other than words social facts of real significance." [2]

Today there is increasing recognition that the mental hygiene and psychoanalytic movements led many social workers away from the concern with the family which had been emphasized by Mary Richmond toward an overconcern with individual psychopathology and intrapsychic problems. In spite of its overidentification with psychoanalysis and psychiatry, however, social casework found scope for its continued concern with families in distress. This is evident in the development of concepts of family diagnosis and treatment, particularly in the child guidance field. [3] Social workers also helped develop the movement in American psychiatry and psychoanalysis toward emphasizing interpersonal, familial, and socio-cultural factors, and toward including a consideration of these factors in the medical-social practice of the general hospital. As Gordon Hamilton has remarked,

[1] Mary E. Richmond, *Social Diagnosis*, Russell Sage Foundation, New York, 1917, p. 134.
[2] *Ibid.*, p. 137.
[3] Nathan W. Ackerman, M.D., and Raymond Sobel, M.D., "Family Diagnosis: An Approach to the Pre-School Child," *American Journal of Orthopsychiatry*, Vol. XX, No. 4 (1950), pp. 744–753.

"The social worker's primary contribution in the medical team is to accent the psychosocial, intra-familial component in study and treatment." [4]

The resulting process of cross-fertilization between psychiatry and social work led to a mutual concern with helping people achieve adequate ego functioning, improved interpersonal relationships, and reality adaptations. In recent years, there has also been a mutual and collaborative approach to treatment of psychosocial disorders and of mental illness, through treatment of the family.[5]

A natural consequence of this trend has been the emergence of "family-centered casework" and "family-oriented psychiatry." The concept of family-centered casework has been well defined by Frances Scherz as casework that is based on an understanding of the needs of the family as a unit, for the purpose of helping family members attain their best personal and social satisfactions, and to help improve the social functioning of the family group as a whole.[6] This is different from family-oriented psychiatry, which is psychiatric treatment directed toward helping the patient-family group, and which may utilize family-centered casework services.

The renewed interest in the family group, and in the individual as a member of the family group, reflects current social trends that value family and group membership, identification, and participation. Second, the need to deal with and treat the family group has been increasingly realized on a pragmatic basis, as we have become aware of the limitations of individual psychotherapy and of the desire of several members of a family to be given help. Third, recent developments in the social sciences, particularly in role theory, small group theory, and the analysis of disordered behavior as social deviation have made possible a conceptualization of theory and practice in the treatment of the family group. We are arriving at new insights and understandings about family structure, personality role structure, and cultural value-orientations, as well as about family role interactions, and the nuclear family as a social system.[7] Varied aspects of family dynamics as related to personality and family breakdown and illness are being explored.[8] The application of these new theoretical developments in psychiatric settings has led to novel and promising diagnostic and treatment methods. Treatment of the family group is now being achieved through treatment of individual members or through family group therapy.

In both family-centered casework and family-oriented psychiatry, the patient's illness and problems are evaluated in relation to the stress and strain in his family and socio-cultural situation, as well as to somatic and constitutional factors. We now see that the patient often is a member of a sick family group. In seeking help, or in being pushed by his family into treatment, the patient is seeking help not only for himself, but also for his family at this time of crisis. Similarly, signifi-

[4] Gordon Hamilton, *Theory and Practice of Social Case Work* (2d rev. ed.), Columbia University Press, New York, 1951, p. 298.

[5] M. Robert Gomberg and Frances T. Levinson, *Diagnosis and Process in Family Counseling*, Family Service Association of America, New York, 1951; Max Siporin, "Casework Treatment of Individuals with Marital Problems," *Journal of Psychiatric Social Work*, Vol. XXII, No. 1 (1952), pp. 25–30; Nathan W. Ackerman, M.D., "Interpersonal Disturbances in the Family," *Psychiatry*, Vol. XVII, No. 4 (1954), pp. 359–368.

[6] Frances H. Scherz, "What Is Family-Centered Casework?" *Social Casework*, Vol. XXXIV, No. 8 (1953), pp. 343–349.

[7] Talcott Parsons and Robert F. Bales, *Family—Socialization and Interaction Process*, The Free Press, Glencoe, Ill., 1955.

[8] Bertram H. Roberts and Jerome K. Myers, "Schizophrenia in the Youngest Male Child of the Lower Middle Class," *American Journal of Psychiatry*, Vol. CXII, No. 2 (1955), pp. 129–134.

cant relatives who accompany the patient to the hospital or clinic are asking for help for themselves as well as for the patient, that is, for the family group as a whole.

On the basis of our new insights the patient can be considered a deviant in the family (and social) group.[9] In his deviation he has failed to conform in some way to his family's norms, values, and expectations, and the family equilibrium has been disturbed. The patient, therefore, often becomes a scapegoat in the family's attempt to control him and to solve its problems.[10] This may take place even when other members of the family are as disturbed as or still sicker than the patient. In the process, the patient is often pushed out of the family or he withdraws from the family conflict as well as from society. Thus the family seems to want the patient "helped," "made well," "straightened out," "punished," or "put away." Often the patient, too, seems to want these things for himself or, in turn, he wants the family to be "straightened out."

In attempting to evaluate and treat the patient and his family, we use the concepts and methods of psychoanalytic ego psychology and personality theory. The patient's interpersonal relationships, his role behavior, and his attitudes and values in relation to his family, the therapist, and other hospital staff are the foci of diagnostic evaluation and of therapy.[11]

In addition, however, we place emphasis upon the pathogenic, family conflict situation—the level of behavior, adaptation, and pathology which is expressed in the social system of the family or the system of reciprocal family and social roles. Reciprocal family roles are the complementary behavior and relationship patterns normally expected of a family member by himself and by each of his family group.[12]

Family roles are a function of an individual's status or position in his family (father, mother, youngest girl, and so on). Although these roles are based on interrelated needs and aptitudes of the individual and of his family and on the social structure, they are also based on the family's cultural and ethnic value-orientations.[13] By examining the family roles and the patterns of interaction, we are better able to understand the needs and problems of the family. Stress and strain on the individual and his family group can often be understood as difficulty in meeting role expectations or as role conflict either within the individual or between family members. Important distortions and discrepancies about family role expectations and obligations may occur and the reciprocal role system of the family may thus be thrown out of balance.

We also find it helpful to understand the patient in terms of his role as a sick person, with the reciprocal expectations and obligations of such a role for him

---

[9] This aspect of deviation is discussed in: Talcott Parsons, *The Social System*, The Free Press, Glencoe, Ill., 1951; Edwin M. Lemert, *Social Pathology*, McGraw-Hill Book Company, New York, 1951.

[10] Robert F. Bales, "The Equilibrium Problem in Small Groups," *Small Groups*, A. Paul Hare, Edgar F. Borgatta, and Robert F. Bales (eds.), Knopf, New York, 1955, pp. 424–456.

[11] Edith Varon, "Localizing a Patient's Difficulties Through Systematic Study of His Interpersonal Relationships," *Journal of Psychiatric Social Work*, Vol. XX, No. 1 (1950), pp. 17–22.

[12] For a discussion of role theory see: Talcott Parsons, *op. cit.*; Nathan W. Ackerman, M.D., "The Diagnosis of Neurotic Marital Interaction," SOCIAL CASEWORK, Vol. XXXV, No. 4 (1954), pp. 139–147; John P. Spiegel, M.D., "The Social Roles of Doctor and Patient in Psychoanalysis and Psychotherapy," *Psychiatry*, Vol. XVII, No. 4 (1954), pp. 369–376.

[13] Florence Kluckhohn and John P. Spiegel, M.D., *Integration and Conflict in Family Behavior*, Group for the Advancement of Psychiatry, Topeka, Kansas, Report No. 27, 1954.

and his family.[14] Society expects an ill person to become temporarily dependent, to follow medical advice, to dislike being ill, and to try to get well. He is excused from social obligations, such as work or the disciplining of his children, and other family members are expected to take over some of these obligations while they remain sympathetic and supportive toward him. The above concepts are illustrated in the following account of Mr. Z and his family.

Early Phase of Z Case

The setting is a Veterans Administration general hospital, in which there is a treatment ward for neurological and psychiatric patients.

REFERRAL STATEMENT. Mr. Z was a 29-year-old, single veteran of World War II. He had been working as a factory stockroom laborer before being admitted to the hospital for evaluation of possible organic brain deterioration and of his overexcited, depressed, and somewhat confused behavior. The ward physician referred him to Social Service for a social study. When the social worker saw him to obtain his consent for contact with his family, he requested help with a number of problems, which he discussed in a very troubled way.

PRESENTING PROBLEMS. For about the past two years, Mr. Z had been becoming increasingly nervous, overexcited, easily upset, given to outbursts of tears and anger against his family. He complained about being involved in chronic quarrels between his parents and with his family. Many demands were being made on him by his mother, father, and younger sister, with whom he lived. Eight months previously his younger brother had married.

[14] Talcott Parsons and Renee Fox, "Illness, Therapy, and the Modern Urban American Family," *Journal of Social Issues*, Vol. VIII, No. 4 (1952), pp. 31–44.

Mr. Z was the only son remaining at home so he became even more a focus for the family conflict. He was giving all of his wages to his mother, then borrowing money from his father for his own expenses, with ensuing heated arguments. He blamed his father and sister for his being "mixed up and nervous." He wanted the worker to talk to his family and make them stop arguing and "making" him nervous. He also said that during recent years, he had withdrawn from his friends and from social activities; had not dated a girl in five years, and had some conflict about his lack of sexual outlets. He asked for help in getting permission to play his accordion in the hospital. He was dissatisfied with his job, complained that he was "picked on" by his co-workers and boss, was called "stupid," and was being kept from advancement. The slowness of his speech and comprehension made him appear to be mentally defective or retarded. He suffered from reading and speech difficulties; his thinking seemed fairly clear, but was characterized by overconcreteness and symbolization.

BACKGROUND INFORMATION. Mr. Z's father, age 64, was Italian-born. He had been ill, unemployed, and on relief for many years. He was currently working as an elevator operator, but was soon to be retired. He was concerned about the upkeep of the family home, which they owned, and about payments on a recently-bought freezer. He and the mother always quarreled about money. Their arguments were intensified when, after buying the freezer, he gave her only $10 a week for household and food expenses. He was critical of the patient's disobedience and his inability to manage money. He did not know that the patient had been giving his entire pay to the mother. He wept and expressed much feeling for Mr. Z when he was helped to recognize that Mr. Z was ill.

The mother was 53, American-born, of

Spanish and Italian parentage. She was extremely obese, overemotional, and had a history of epileptic seizures. She appeared to be of low intelligence. She had always had difficulty managing household finances. She blamed the teachers for Mr. Z's difficulties at school and she, as well as the father, seemed to minimize his mental retardation, while agreeing that he was "slow." She was worried lest Mr. Z get married or leave home since he was the only one she could depend on. She also wept a good deal when helped to see that Mr. Z was emotionally ill and that he needed much help.

Mr. Z was the second oldest of four living children. An older sister and a younger brother were married and living out of the home. They had withdrawn from the family. A younger sister, 27 years of age, lived at home. She suffered from epileptic seizures, appeared mentally retarded, and had never felt able to work. She expressed some distress about her own dependency on Mr. Z and about the many medical expenses she had incurred during the past two years, which he had paid. She seemed rather aggressive, like the mother. She expressed some willingness to explore ways of getting well enough to work.

Mr. Z's developmental history was largely negative, except that he had been born with deformed feet which, however, had developed normally. At the age of four he had had a severe sunstroke, to which the parents attributed his disabilities. He was a very obedient boy, but was "picked on" by the other children. He did poorly in school, and left at the age of 14 after completing the sixth grade. He was in the army for five months, was hospitalized for nervousness, but had had a dependency discharge. He had always been employed and had held his current job for four years. He earned more than the father. He was a devout person.

After discharge from the army, he had dated a number of girls but had been repeatedly rejected. He found himself being exploited by his neighborhood friends, who borrowed money from him without repaying it, so he withdrew and increasingly kept to his home and family. He spent much time in his room or watched television and quarreled with the family about which TV program to watch. About six weeks before admission to the hospital, he had stepped on a nail while at work, developed an infection, was treated at the company medical clinic, and became very dependent on the clinic staff. Because he seemed to need psychiatric treatment, he was referred to the Mental Health Center, where he was seen briefly and referred to the hospital.

The above history material was obtained from Mr. Z and from an interview in which the father, mother, and sister were seen together. At the end of the family interview, Mr. Z visited with his family and on greeting them he was embraced tearfully by his mother, was held tightly on the arm by his sister, while he glared angrily at his sad-looking father.

PSYCHOSOCIAL DIAGNOSIS. Mr. Z appeared to the caseworker to be of limited intelligence, to be very immature and overdependent, to feel picked on and deprived. He also seemed to have limited capacity for the paternal role thrust on him by his family, or for coping with the stressful family and job situations that he had helped provoke. He seemed most angry with his father, whose demands on him seemed excessive. Each member of the family seemed to be attempting to resolve his or her own personal problem, as well as the problem of this whole sick family, through Mr. Z. In keeping with their ethnic group characteristics, the family seemed overemotional and overclose, but were argumentative to a degree that indicated much disorganization. There was a strong push for upward social class mobility as evidenced by the way in which the parents expected Mr. Z to help them acquire a home of their own and such things as a freezer. The parents did not seem to see Mr. Z as emotionally ill or mentally defective.

In the staff case conference, the pooled findings of the staff study indicated a diagnosis of congenital chronic brain syndrome, with mental deficiency and a passive-aggressive personality.

Such a diagnostic evaluation as this frequently indicates that, to treat the patient effectively, his entire family group must be involved in treatment. In this sense the family is seen as a "sick" or a "problem" family, and the family becomes the patient.[15] Treatment of family members is no longer depreciated as "environmental manipulation" or regarded as "helping the family co-operate," but is considered therapeutically significant and is an integral part of a comprehensive treatment plan. The effect on other family members of treating the patient and the converse of this become important considerations in therapeutic planning. Treatment goals and methods are formulated for the entire family group and for the significant family members who are being seen directly. Not only is the patient helped to achieve ego integration and adaptation, but the family group also is helped to achieve its reintegration and reorganization. Treatment is directed toward the disturbed interaction patterns, the disequilibrium of reciprocal role relationships, and the defects in cohesiveness, solidarity, authority, affection, or communication in the family unit. The family group structure becomes available for use as a potent therapeutic influence.

Among the many therapeutic procedures avaliable for the caseworker to use in this kind of casework, several will be mentioned briefly. One technique involves the worker's teaching and encouraging the patient to improve his interpersonal skills, competence, and participation. An-

other consists in helping him to clarify his distorted perceptions and discrepancies in regard to family role expectations. The worker may also structure these expectations for the purpose of helping the patient and the family members to assume more mature and mutually gratifying family roles—for example, being a "good mother," or a "stronger husband," or an "adult son." A third procedure is to use the patient's role as a sick person to reorient the family's perceptions and attitudes—for example, by referring to the patient as "sick" or to the father as "having problems." A fourth technique is the caseworker's use of himself as a group leader in working with the family in a problem-solving process.

Treatment Techniques in the Z Case

The application of these techniques is illustrated in the treatment of Mr. Z and his family.

TREATMENT PLANS AND OBJECTIVES. The caseworker was given primary treatment responsibility for Mr. Z and his family. The initial objective was to help Mr. Z with situational problems. This counseling activity was to be correlated with the psychotherapeutic and other treatment programs for Mr. Z. The worker planned to encourage Mr. Z to take responsibility to improve the family situation. It was also tentatively suggested, on the basis of the psychological test findings, that an attempt be made to provide some instruction for Mr. Z in remedial reading and speech training, as well as vocational counseling and training in a trade, which Mr. Z seemed to want. The worker also suggested that casework help be given the family. This would involve helping the family members to understand Mr. Z's illness and limitations better, to expect less of him, and to try to resolve their personal problems without projec-

[15] Roy M. Whitman, M.D., and Imogene S. Young, "Psychiatric Social Work in a Brief Therapy Program in an Adult Outpatient Clinic," *Journal of Psychiatric Social Work,* Vol. XXIV, No. 4 (1955), pp. 210–214.

tion on him. It was planned to discuss directly with the father his retirement situation; to help the mother separate herself emotionally from Mr. Z and transfer her dependency focus to the father; to help the sister accept vocational counseling and training and also casework counseling from another agency. The family also needed help in accepting Mr. Z's resentment and the demands for independence which could be expected to result from treatment.

CASEWORK ACTIVITY WITH MR. Z. Mr. Z remained on the neuropsychiatric ward. Both a neurology resident and a psychiatrist maintained supportive relationships with him. Both of them focused on the extensive medical work-up which he had had and on his being used for medical school teaching purposes on two occasions. The physical findings were carefully discussed with the patient, and his feelings about them were handled by the psychiatrist as well as by the caseworker. Mr. Z was given occupational and manual arts therapy, at which he spent much of his time.

The caseworker had an office interview with Mr. Z on an average of once a week. He also was seen informally on the ward. The worker gave him much recognition for his achievement in having worked and maintained himself. His work in occupational therapy was given much approval. His self-concept of being "slow" and of being "picked on" was directly discussed with him and clarified so that he was helped to feel better about himself and his capacities. He was helped to look at his behavior and his responsibility in the family's quarrels, particularly at his own part in the family's use of him and his handling of the money problem. He was encouraged to take increasing responsibility for dealing with his family situation. He responded by declaring and demanding his independence of his family and by getting a more equitable agreement about his financial contribution to the home. He

was encouraged to feel free to date girls and to marry, to feel worthy to do so; he was also encouraged to participate in the social activities program of his church. He responded by getting romantically involved with a hospital volunteer and then by taking increasing part in the hospital social activities.

He clarified his job dissatisfaction and vocational plans. It developed that he thought he was being derided by his fellow employees because of his "slowness," and that he was being denied advancement for this reason. He wanted to learn a trade. However, he had a good earning capacity in his present job, and the psychological test findings showed severe limitations in visual-motor activities; these findings were corroborated by the occupational therapist. He was encouraged to return to work on his present job in order to earn needed money immediately, with the understanding that he could later apply for vocational rehabilitation. The worker talked by telephone with Mr. Z's job supervisor, to whom his condition was interpreted. Mr. Z was well thought of, even though he was used as a butt of jokes at times; the supervisor said that Mr. Z could have a promotion if his reading and speech could be improved. This information relieved Mr. Z and he was then advised about resources for obtaining remedial reading instruction and speech training.

CASEWORK ACTIVITY WITH THE FAMILY. The caseworker interviewed the father and helped him to recognize that Mr. Z had intellectual and emotional disabilities. The meaning to the father of his own retirement and of the cultural differences between father-son relationships in the old country and here was discussed. The father then seemed to understand Mr. Z's need for less control from him. He responded by having a long talk with Mr. Z and working out some of the difficulties about money.

At the time of Mr. Z's discharge, the

father, mother, and younger sister were interviewed again and an interpretation of his condition and needs was given. The mother was helped to recognize her own overdependence on Mr. Z and was encouraged to depend more on the father. The father, in trying to work out the money problem with the mother, had previously threatened to leave the family and to sell their house. He now thought he could manage his financial obligations with a little help from Mr. Z and he therefore felt better able to work out the financial and other problems with his wife. After much emotional outpouring and much recognition by the worker of their difficulties, the parents agreed that they would continue to try to work things out between themselves rather than through Mr. Z. It was suggested to the sister that she might be helped by vocational and casework counseling with the State Vocational Rehabilitation Division and this was interpreted to her and to the parents. The parents were also encouraged to talk with the social worker at the Mental Health Center to which the patient was being returned. The various recommendations worked out with Mr. Z were discussed with the family and they indicated their acceptance of these plans, as well as a more positive and mutual expression of support and help for him. The parting from the worker was an emotional one, with the father giving way to tears.

TERMINATION. Toward the end of his stay, Mr. Z was unwilling to leave the hospital. He showed good symptomatic improvement in his speech and thinking, expressed a positive mood and affect, seemed more hopeful about himself. He said he liked the hospital and the people in it very much and would rather stay on indefinitely. After threatening his family that he would leave home if they did not change, he decided to return home and to his job. Because Mr. Z needed continued supportive help and help also with his family situation, he was referred again to

the Mental Health Center. When he left the hospital, he expressed his pleasure at his improvement, his gratitude for the worker's help, and said that the worker had been "a good man for me."

FOLLOW-UP INFORMATION. Later reports from the Mental Health Center social worker and other sources revealed that Mr. Z continued to improve after leaving the hospital. He continued to visit the hospital in the evening several times a week and to participate in its social activities, until he became involved in his neighborhood church social group. Although there were periodic arguments in the home, these were much less severe and less frequent, and the family relationships continued to improve. He joined a public school class in remedial reading and speech, which he enjoyed. He continued on his job without complaint. The sister applied to the state vocational agency, and was accompanied by her father when she went for her first interview. After about two months, Mr. Z felt improved enough to tell the Mental Health Center social worker that he did not need any further help, and he terminated his contact there.

Conclusions

Family-centered casework, as carried on in a psychiatric setting, represents a particular type of casework competence and skill. The illustration that has been given highlights certain areas in this type of practice which require further development. Family-centered casework requires of the worker greater range in activity, greater flexibility in assuming various therapeutic roles, greater knowledge and skill in group as well as in individual treatment methods. Exploratory efforts in this type of casework lead us to emphasize the need for further knowledge and research. We need to know more about the family —about family dynamics, family structure, and family values and roles—particularly as related to psychosocial dysfunction and to psychiatric illness and hospitalization. We also need to undertake research in order to test, verify, extend, and make explicit the hypotheses, concepts, and principles which have been empirically formulated from clinical experience and insight.

The practice of family-centered casework also underlines our lack of workable problem classifications in casework and our professional problem in making classifications. There is increasing recognition that psychiatric classifications are inadequate and inappropriate to the problems and psychosocial disorders of the individual which casework attempts to treat. In addition, there is a further lack of adequate classification for types of families, for family conflict situations,[16] or for what Ackerman has termed "the psychosocial disorders of family life." [17] These classifications are needed so that family diagnosis and treatment can be more specific and so that family counseling and therapy can be related to specific therapeutic goals and methods.

In family-centered casework, group work and casework achieve a new measure of integration as complementary methods of help to individuals and to family groups. Casework-group work collaboration has previously been based on a separation of the individual from his family group. There has also been a rather sharp separation maintained between the two social work specialties. Yet caseworkers have often done a form of group work or group therapy in meeting with family groups, in group conferences and group interviews. Questions arise about whether such treatment of the family should be regarded as group leadership, group work, or group therapy; what relevant methods and skills from group work can be applied in this kind of casework; and how group workers can be used in family-centered treatment. These questions appear to present a fertile field for inquiry and investigation.

Family-centered casework in the psychiatric setting and family-oriented psychiatry constitute further developments of the psychiatric function of treating mental illness through treatment of the family. They are based on an expanded concept of mental illness—that there are "sick" or "problem" families as well as mentally ill individuals. The question of how to treat personality, behavior, or sociopathic disorders may seem to confound further the present confusion about psychiatric and social work function and about the division of responsibility between psychiatric and family service agencies. The present trends in family-oriented treatment, however, may help to clarify and differentiate between the problems appropriate for social work treatment and those appropriate for psychiatric practice. When these matters have been clarified, more effective patterns of collaboration can be established both in psychiatric settings and in family agencies.

Family-centered casework is an indication of the maturation of social work. Casework continues to help the individual achieve personality growth and interpersonal adaptation, but it also shows evidence of a movement toward rededication to the welfare of the family group and a renewed emphasis on family and social group values. It is a movement that is also expressed in our unified professional organization. We can look forward to further exploration and discovery in the development of family-centered casework, with further substantial contributions both to psychiatry and to social work.

[16] An attempt at this was made by James H. S. Bossard and E. S. Boll, *Family Situations*, University of Pennsylvania Press, Philadelphia, 1943.

[17] Nathan W. Ackerman, M.D., "Interpersonal Disturbances in the Family," *op. cit.*, p. 367.

D · RELIGIOUS ROLES

THE PUERTO RICAN SPIRITUALIST AS A PSYCHIATRIST

by Lloyd H. Rogler and August B. Hollingshead

In recent years social scientists have made a number of studies of interrelations between the social system and mental illness, some of which discuss the role the psychiatrist plays in society.[1] This paper focuses on the therapeutic role of a quasi-professional group only rarely thought of as being in the medical sphere—the spiritualists.[2]

Currently, we are doing research on mental illness in the lower classes of the San Juan metropolitan area of Puerto Rico. Early in our study we learned that persons afflicted with mental illness frequently come into contact with spiritualist mediums before, during, and after their visits to psychiatrists. Local psychiatrists are aware of these folk therapists. Likewise, spiritualist mediums have some understanding of the functions of psychiatrists. In some cases, a psychiatrist and a medium may share a patient: one psychiatrist, for example, told us that relatives brought a patient to him for a "special" purpose—they wanted him calmed so that he could be taken to a "genuine" therapist, a spiritualist medium! Psychiatric clinics in the San Juan area are known to have been used surreptitiously by local mediums to treat ambulatory patients. Furthermore, outpatients at one psychiatric clinic have been heard to refer to psychotherapy as *pases*. (*Pases* are the symbolic gestures performed by mediums for curative purposes; the term is rich in connotation.)

[1] Ivan Belknap, *Human Problems of a State Mental Hospital* (New York: McGraw-Hill Book Co., 1956), pp. 205–207; G. Morris Carstairs, *The Twice Born* (London: Hogarth Press, 1957); Elaine Cumming and John Cumming, *Closed Ranks* (Cambridge, Mass.: Harvard University Press, 1957), pp. 36–44; Joseph W. Eaton and Robert J. Weil, *Culture and Mental Disorders* (Glencoe, Ill.: Free Press, 1955); August B. Hollingshead and Frederick C. Redlich, *Social Class and Mental Illness* (New York: John Wiley and Sons, 1958), pp. 161–167, 353–355; Melvin L. Kohn and John A. Clausen, "Parental Authority Behavior and Schizophrenia," *American Journal of Orthopsychiatry*, XXVI (April, 1956), 297–313; Alexander H. Leighton, *My Name Is Legion* (New York: Basic Books, Inc., 1959); Alexander H. Leighton, John A. Clausen, and Robert N. Wilson, *Explorations in Social Psychiatry* (New York: Basic Books, Inc., 1957); Jerome K. Myers and Bertram H. Roberts, *Family and Class Dynamics in Mental Illness* (New York: John Wiley and Sons, 1959); Alfred H. Stanton and Morris S. Schwartz, *The Mental Hospital* (New York: Basic Books, Inc., 1954), pp. 143–144; Marion Radke Yarrow, Charlotte Green Schwartz, Harriet S. Murphy, and Leila Calhoun Deasy, "The Psychological Meaning of Mental Illness in the Family," *Journal of Social Issues*, XI (September, 1955), 12–24.

[2] Joseph Bram, "Spirits, Mediums, and Believers in Contemporary Puerto Rico," *Transactions of the New York Academy of Sciences*, 1957, pp. 340–347; also Morris Siegel, "A Puerto Rican Town" (unpublished manuscript).

SOURCE: *American Journal of Sociology*, Vol. 67 (1961–1962), pp. 17–22.

Our experiences have led us to the tentative conclusion that persons in the lower class rely upon spiritualist beliefs and practices as therapeutic outlets for mental illnesses. We hope to furnish here illustrative materials on the interrelations between the culture of the lower class and the identification and treatment of mental illnesses by nonmedical practioners. The materials are drawn from systematic interviews with mentally ill persons, ranging from mild neurotics to severe psychotics, with their spouses, and with a series of individuals diagnosed by qualified psychiatrists as having "no mental illness." In addition, we have interviewed spiritualist mediums and participated in many of their sessions in order to observe their patients acting and being reacted to in these settings.

Spiritualism is the belief that the visible world is surrounded by an invisible world populated by spirits. The latter are "good" or "bad." [3] Spirits have the power to penetrate the visible world and to attach themselves to human beings. They may manifest themselves as a reincarnation of some other person or thing. As metaphysical beings they are able to coerce and influence human affairs, often very dramatically. Persons may develop special faculties (facultades), "mystical antennas," which enable them to communicate with spirits. In this sense the person with facultades has gained a measure of control over the spirits. Consequently, an individual with facultades may influence human affairs by commanding the obedience or favor of the spirits.

The beliefs and practices of spiritualism are distributed throughout the society with, perhaps, a relatively pronounced tendency to concentrate in the lower classes. However, spiritualists and their followers in the upper classes are careful to distinguish their type of spiritualism from that of the lower classes. Upper-class spiritualists insist on the scientific and experimental character of their beliefs, arguing that lower-class spiritualism is irrational and superstitious.[4]

Spiritualism actively provides social meanings to its troubled participants. In the lower class, it is coterminous with social life, woven into the intimate trials, strife, and personal turmoil that enmesh the members of a socially and economically deprived stratum, where its function is to discharge the tensions and anxieties generated in other areas of social life. For example, when, as often happens in spiritualists' sessions, a married woman complains of the infidelity of her husband, the medium may call upon the spirit of her rival and assume her role. The medium indicates this change in her personality by gesticulating, changing the quality of her voice, and in general acting "como una mujer de la calle" (like a woman of the street), it being assumed that that is the kind of woman that would lure married men from their spouses. The troubled wife then attempts to convince the spirit that she should leave the husband alone and cease causing untold suffering. The effect of the dramatic exchange appears to be that the wife believes she has begun to cope with the problem.

"Crazy" (loco), "bad in the mind" (mal de la mente), and "weak in the brain" (debil del cerebro) are common expressions for mental illness in the vernacular of the persons studied. The words denote unusual and idiosyncratic behavior. One of our schizophrenic subjects said:

> A mentally ill person is one who has no control and can kill someone else. It is a person who is irrational, like an animal, one who does not use his mind. Such a person can do any horrible thing. They must be treated like children, otherwise they may fall upon you like a ray of lightning. Would I

[3] See Allan Kardec, El libro de los espíritus (Mexico City: Editorial Orion, 1951), pp. 147–180.

[4] The type of data required to determine the prevalence of spiritualism and its class distribution is unavailable.

marry such a person? Absolutely not. Why would I want to bring a piece of worthless furniture into my house? It would be best to put such a person in a hospital where she could die.

I am uncomfortable when I speak to [friends] about my illness. They may misinterpret what I say about my illness. They will laugh at me. They will not trust me. They will avoid me.

This man, and others, realize that the very act of going to a psychiatric clinic may be the first step in the assumption of this feared role, for the psychiatric clinic is known as a place where *locos* go.

The spiritualist, as believer and participant, takes the stigma from an afflicted person. The spiritualist may announce to the sick man, his family, and friends that the patient is endowed with special psychic faculties, a matter of prestige in this social class. Spiritualism is a form of folk psychiatry. It serves its believers without their suffering the stigma associated with psychiatric agencies.

Spiritualism claims competence in the interpretation and treatment of pathological symptoms. Does the individual report hallucinations? This clearly indicates to the believer in spiritualism that he is being visited by spirits who manifest themselves visually and audibly.[5] Does he have delusions? He is told that evil spirits are deceiving him about himself as well as others. His thoughts are being distorted by interfering bad spirits. Or, through the development of his psychic faculties, spirits have informed him of the true enemies in his environment. Is his talk incoherent, rambling, and cryptic? This indicates that he is undergoing a test, an experiment engineered by the spirits to see if he is of the right moral fiber. Does he wander aim-

lessly through the neighborhood? He is being pursued by ambulatory spirits, unmercifully tormenting him. To illustrate: a thirty-seven-year-old woman, subject, according to the psychiatric diagnosis, to "hysterical hyperkinetic seizures," stated:

Yes, I went to consult a spiritualist to see what the attacks meant. The medium told me that there was a young man who was in love with me. The mother-in-law of this young man bewitched me through an evil spirit. This evil spirit takes me over in a violent way.

Did I believe the medium? Of course I did. She described many events in my life that were true. When I would see the mother-in-law of this young man I would get an attack. This proves that she [the medium] was right.

The basis for the medium's claims of competence is the assumption that all individual problems are material, or spiritual, or a combination of both material and spiritual things. The latter may have little or nothing to do with the outstanding complaint; rather, it classifies the source of the problem. Consequently, if the etiology of the illness is traced to the invisible world, it is a spiritual problem and, as such, within the control of the medium. Material problems, in contrast, have their causes in the visible world of "hard" facts. These, consequently, fall within the competence of doctors, druggists, nurses, and other professionals.

Few behavioral or medical problems have a conspicuous "material cause," immediately apparent to the subject, to the medium, or to others; therefore, problems are classified invariably as spiritual by the medium. Thus, the spiritualist medium effects a rough division of labor, relegating to herself (mediums are usually women) therapeutic competence to deal with a vast range of problems, many of which are disorders of personality in the broad, non-technical sense of the term.

[5] Allan Kardec discusses the different ways in which the spirits may communicate and the corresponding *facultades* that spiritualists may have in *El libro de los mediums* (Mexico City: Editorial Orion, 1951), pp. 183–224.

The contacts between the medium and a patient takes place variously in, to mention two possibilities, a private consultation or a session involving, usually, from fifteen to twenty participants. These meetings are organized explicitly to serve the participants; social interaction, consequently, is channeled toward the solution of problems they bring.

The room in which the session is held may be decorated with portraits of Franklin D. Roosevelt, Mahatma Gandhi, and banners of "Charity and Humility." A sober-faced, almost life-sized figure of a cigar-store Indian with arms crossed, looking ominously to the ceiling, may be a part of the setting. The odor of burning incense may pervade the room. The head medium opens the session with a long prayer, frequently from one of Allan Kardec's works,[6] directs herself to the auxiliary mediums, and asks them to concentrate. Preparations are designed to develop the "correct" mood to welcome the spirits. As the session develops, the head medium may direct her attention to the participants' order of seating as they face the table where she and the auxiliary medium(s) are seated. The head medium then proceeds to probe, interpret, treat, and prescribe for the ills and maladies afflicting the individual. Prescriptions include a variety of herbs, ointments, medicated hot baths, massages with symbolic meaning, and prayers. The session generally requires intense participation by the members, which the medium frequently relieves by joking.

Participants who have developed psychic faculties show through their contortions, spasms, screeching, babbling, and deep breathing that they have been pos-

sessed: the behavior varies in accordance with the kind of spirit that has communicated with the one possessed.

The group meeting then is structured around four social roles: those of the head medium, the auxiliary medium(s), and participants with and those without faculties,[7] the four being arrayed according to the participants' alleged degree of influence over spirits. The roles are differentiated and co-ordinated by the charisma imputed to the incumbents: we have observed psychiatrically diagnosed schizophrenics effectively play each role.[8] Moreover, their performance was enthusiastically received by the others at the session.

Although we lack direct evidence bearing on the therapeutic effect on mental illness of participation in spiritualist sessions, we have abundant information describing the manner in which participation served to cope with specific problems. To illustrate: the wife of a paranoid schizophrenic described to us the disrupting effect her husband's incessant and pervasive suspicions were having on her. Were she to get up during the evening to take one of their children to the outside toilet, her husband would accuse her of conspiring to see a lover, waiting outside. Were she to leave the house to feed the chickens, a similar charge would be made. In short, she had to be within the radius

---

[6] For an official biography of Kardec see Henri Sausse, *Biografía de Allan Kardec* (Buenos Aires: Editorial Victor Hugo, 1952). This biography contains its own review (pp. 138–139), allegedly provided by Kardec's spirit, which spoke through one of the participants in a session attended by the author of the biography.

[7] This fourfold role structure has been derived from observations of problem-oriented sessions in small spiritualist groups; other spiritualist groupings may be different.

[8] Lee R. Steiner, who has made the same observations in New York City, says: "I've encountered psychopathic personalities with Jehovah complexes, at the lowest rung in both integrity and knowledge, who have effected emotional cures. It is my very definite impression that there is not very much correlation between validated knowledge and emotional cures. And I feel that this same condition obtains, at the moment, in professional therapy as well as in the occult" ("Why Do People Consult the Occult?" *The Humanist*, XIX [January–February, 1959], 27).

of her husband's vision or suffer accusations of unfaithfulness. As she says:

> Then I decided to take him to see a spiritualist medium since his suspicions had created an impossible situation. She [the medium] and the other people in the session advised him. He has not been suspicious since then. They explained to him that it was a test that he was undergoing since he was in the process of developing *facultades*. They told him that he should devote himself to charity and to the good and that he should concentrate on the development of his *facultades*. My husband is now a medium, and when he does not feel well he performs *pases* on himself in front of the mirror. He feels better afterward.

Another schizophrenic reports that, when he feels restless and fearful inside, dissatisfied with himself and others, and not wanting to see anyone, he turns to the spiritualist for help:

> I go to sessions because they make me feel good and rested inside. They bring me peace. I go to them because the medium is the maximum authority in knowing how to rid one of those evil spirits and demons that upset one inside.

Another with a severe psychotic illness reports:

> Before I go to a session I feel very unhappy. When I get to the group I talk to the medium and the others, and I feel good. When the others begin to talk about their problems I feel as if I am not alone. They [the group] make me feel sure of myself.

Such reports so often come from the mentally afflicted individuals in our study that we are led to the conclusion that attending group sessions serves, at least, to ease and alleviate personal stresses.

We do not have the research design to test the proposition that spiritualist sessions alter the personality of the mental patient in the direction of mental health. However, we believe that spiritualist sessions have a good many of the therapeutic advantages of group psychotherapy.[9] In addition to the presumed advantages of group psychotherapy as practiced in clinical settings, spiritualist sessions are coterminous with the values, beliefs, aspirations, and problems of the participants: no discontinuity in social contacts is required of participation. Little social distance separates the afflicted person from the medium, but, in contrast, visiting a psychiatrist involves bringing persons together who are separated by a vast social gulf. The others in the session are often neighbors, and so the spiritualist and her followers form a primary group where problems are discussed in a convivial setting, classified, interpreted, and rendered understandable within a belief system that is widely accepted even by those who profess not to believe in it.[10]

Persistent hallucinations to the believer in spiritualism are not symptoms of a deranged mind experiencing things unper-

[9] On the therapeutic advantages of group therapy see Marvin Opler, "Values in Group Psychotherapy," *International Journal of Social Psychiatry*, IV (Spring, 1959), 296.

[10] "If you ever talk to a Puerto Rican who says he doesn't believe in spirits, you know what that means? It means you haven't talked to him long enough"—statement attributed to a Puerto Rican in Dan Wakefield's *Island in the City* (Boston: Houghton Mifflin Co., 1959), p. 59. Though an exaggeration, it offers a very valuable hint to the interviewer. Often respondents will deny their belief in spiritualism when first questioned. However, once the interviewer has established a warm relationship with the respondent, the latter may not only admit his belief but may describe incidents that substantiate it dramatically. It is our impression that members of the upper class are more hesitant to admit to such beliefs than are lower-class individuals.

ceived by others—a definition which serves to isolate the sick. Rather, they demonstrate the development of psychic faculties that may eventually put the lucky person in more permanent contact with the invisible world. Thus, participation in a spiritualist group serves to structure, define, and render behavior institutionally meaningful that is otherwise perceived as aberrant.

Index of Authors

659